ISBN 978-0-266-90408-3
PIBN 10907385

REGISTER

OF ALL

OFFICERS AND AGENTS,

CIVIL, MILITARY, AND NAVAL,

IN

THE SERVICE OF THE UNITED STATES,

ON

THE THIRTIETH SEPTEMBER, 1845,

WITH

THE NAMES, FORCE, AND CONDITION OF ALL SHIPS AND VESSELS BELONGING TO THE UNITED STATES, AND WHEN AND WHERE BUILT;

TOGETHER WITH

THE NAMES AND COMPENSATION OF ALL PRINTERS IN ANY WAY EMPLOYED BY CONGRESS, OR ANY DEPARTMENT OR OFFICER OF THE GOVERNMENT.

PREPARED AT THE DEPARTMENT OF STATE,

In pursuance of Resolutions of Congress of April 27, 1816, and July 14, 1832.

WASHINGTON:

J. & G. S. GIDEON, PRINTERS.

1845.

RESOLUTION requiring the Secretary of State to compile and print, once in every two years, a register of all officers and agents, civil, military, and naval, in the service of the United States:

Resolved by the Senate and House of Representatives of the United States of America in Congress assembled, That, once in two years, a Register, containing correct lists of all the officers and agents, civil, military, and naval, in the service of the United States, made up to the last day of September of each year in which a new Congress is to assemble, be compiled and printed, under the direction of the Secretary for the Department of State. And, to enable him to form such Register, he, for his own Department, and the Heads of the other Departments, respectively, shall, in due time, cause such lists as aforesaid, of all officers and agents, in their respective Departments, including clerks, cadets, and midshipmen, to be made and lodged in the office of the Department of State. And the said lists shall exhibit the amount of compensation, pay, and emoluments, allowed to each officer, agent, clerk, cadet, and midshipman, the State or country in which he was born, and where employed.

2. *Resolved*, That the Secretary of the Navy subjoin to the list of the persons employed in his Department the names, force, and condition, of all the ships and vessels belonging to the United States, and when and where built.

3. *Resolved*, That five hundred copies of the said Register be printed; and that, on the first Monday in January, in each year when a new Congress shall be assembled, there be delivered to the President, the Vice President, each Head of a Department, each member of the Senate and House of Representatives of the United States, one copy of such Register; and to the Secretary of the Senate, and Clerk of the House of Representatives, each ten copies, for the use of the respective Houses; that twenty-five copies shall be deposited in the Library of the United States, at the Seat of Government, to be used like other books in that Library; and that the residue of the said copies be disposed of in such manner as Congress shall, from time to time, direct.

4. *Resolved*, That, for the information of the present Congress, such Register, as aforesaid, be prepared and distributed as aforesaid, on the first day of its next session.

APPROVED, *April* 27, 1816.

RESOLUTION respecting the Biennial Register.

Resolved by the Senate and House of Representatives of the United States of America in Congress assembled, That, in addition to the matter heretofore contained in the Biennial Register, published by direction of a joint resolution, passed on the 27th of April, one thousand eight hundred and sixteen, there shall be included a correct list in the next Register, of all printers of the laws of the United States, subsequent to the 30th of September, one thousand eight hundred and thirty one, to the 30th of September, one thousand eight hundred and thirty-three, with the compensation allowed to each; and of all printers within the period aforesaid, in any way employed by Congress, or by any Department or officer of the Government, with the compensation allowed to each, designating the Department or officer causing the printing to be executed; and that said Register shall contain a correct statement of all allowances made by the Postmaster General, within the period last aforesaid, to each contractor on contracts for carrying the mail, discriminating the sum paid as stipulated by the original contract, and the sum as additional allowance. And to enable the Secretary of State to comply with this resolution, the several Heads of Departments, and officers directing or incurring the expense, or making the allowance mentioned, shall cause the lists, and the matter thereby required to be added, to be lodged in the office of the Department of State, as is directed in other cases, by the resolution of April twenty-seventh, one thousand eight hundred and sixteen.

Resolved, That said Register shall contain a correct list of the Presidents, Cashiers, and Directors of the Bank of the United States and its branches, in office on the thirtieth of September, eighteen hundred and thirty-three; which list shall be transmitted by the President of said Bank to the Secretary of State, by the first Monday of October, one thousand eight hundred and thirty-three.

Resolved, That all Biennial Registers, under the said resolution of April twenty-seventh, one thousand eight hundred and sixteen, shall hereafter be compiled and published conformably to the principles therein and hereby established.

APPROVED, *July* 14, 1832.

INDEX.

INDEX.

REGISTER.

SEPTEMBER 30, 1845.

EXECUTIVE.

PRESIDENT OF THE UNITED STATES.

JAMES K. POLK,*

Of Tennessee.

$25,000 per annum.

VICE PRESIDENT OF THE UNITED STATES.

GEORGE M. DALLAS,†

Of Pennsylvania.

$5,000 per annum.

DEPARTMENT OF STATE.

Names and offices.	Where employed.	Where born.	Compensation.
			Dol. cts.
SECRETARY OF STATE.			
James Buchanan	Washington	Pennsylvania	6000 00
CHIEF CLERK.			
Nicholas P. Trist	do	Virginia	2000 00
DIPLOMATIC BUREAU.			
William S. Derrick	do	Pennsylvania	1600 00
William Hunter, jr	do	R. Island	1500 00
Francis Markoe, jr	do	Santa Cruz‡	1400 00
Alexander H. Derrick	do	Pennsylvania	900 00
CONSULAR BUREAU.			
Robert S. Chew	do	Virginia	1400 00
Samuel L. Gouverneur	do	N. York	1400 00

* Born in North Carolina. † Born in Pennsylvania.
‡ Of parents native citizens of Pennsylvania, transiently abroad.

DEPARTMENT OF STATE—*Clerks—Messengers, &c.*

Names and offices.	Where employed.	Where born.	Compensation.
			Dol. cts.
HOME BUREAU.			
George Hill	Washington	Connecticut	1400 00
Edwin W. Hutter	do	Pennsylvania	1400 00
Lund Washington, jr	do	Virginia	1400 00
Horatio Jones	do	Maryland	1000 00
William C. Zantzinger	do	Dist. Colum	800 00
TRANSLATOR AND LIBRARIAN.			
Robert Greenhow	do	Virginia	1600 00
DISBURSING AGENT.			
Edward Stubbs	do	Ireland	1450 00
EMPLOYED IN PACKING, FILING, ARRANGING, AND PRESERVING NEWSPAPERS, PRINTED DOCUMENTS, &c.			
William P. Faherty	do	Maryland	800 00
MESSENGERS.			
John Kavanaugh	do	Ireland	700 00
George Bartle	do	Dist. Colum	350 00
SUPERINTENDENT OF NORTHEAST EXECUTIVE BUILDING.			
Edward Stubbs	do	Ireland	250 00
WATCHMEN.			
George McDuell	do	do	365 00
Andrew R. Locke	do	Dist. Colum	365 00
George Bartle	do	do	365 00
DESPATCH AGENTS.			
Fernando Wood	New York		800 00
Nathaniel D. Hubbard	Boston		800 00

PATENT OFFICE—*Examiners—Draughtsman—Machinist—Clerks, &c.*

Names and offices.	Where employed.	Where born.	Compensation.
			Dol. cts.
PATENT OFFICE.			
COMMISSIONER.			
Edmund Burke	Washington	Vermont	3000 00
CHIEF CLERK.			
H. H. Sylvester	do	Massachusetts	1700 00
EXAMINERS.			
Charles G. Page	do	do	1500 00
W. P. N. Fitzgerald	do	Vermont	1500 00
ASSISTANT EXAMINERS.			
Henry Stone	do	England	1250 00
Thomas G. Clinton	do	Ireland	1250 00
DRAUGHTSMAN.			
Arthur L. McIntire	do	Dist. Colum	1200 00
ASSISTANT DRAUGHTSMAN.			
A. A. Von Schmidt	do	Germany	By piece.
MACHINIST.			
Hazard Knowles	do	Connecticut	1250 00
CLERKS.			
S. T. Shugert	do	Pennsylvania	1200 00
J. J. Roane	do	Virginia	1000 00
Lewis S. Fales	do	Maine	800 00
Thomas Johns	do	Maryland	10 cents per 100 words.
E. G. Smith	do	Connecticut	
E. McDonnell	do	Ireland	
MESSENGER.			
W. H. Ward	do	New York	700 00
LABORERS.			
Anthony Bowen	do	Maryland	360 00
Richard Brooks	do	do	360 00

DEPARTMENT OF STATE—*Ministers, Consuls, &c.*

Names and offices.	Where employed.	Where born.	Compensation.
			Dol. cts.
DAY WATCH.			
John Holohan	Washington	Ireland	365 00
NIGHT WATCH.			
Jackson Edmonson	do		300 00
Matthias W. White	do		300 00

Ministers, Consuls, and other Diplomatic and Commercial Agents of the United States in Foreign Countries.

BRITISH DOMINIONS.			
ENGLAND.			
Envoy Extraordinary and Minister Plenipotentiary.			
Louis McLane	London	Delaware	9000 00
Secretary of Legation.			
Gansevoort Melville	do	New York	2000 00
Thomas Aspinwall......Consul	do	Massachusetts	2000 00 & fees.
Albert Davy......do	Leeds	Pennsylvania	Fees
Robert Armstrong......do	Liverpool	Tennessee	do
Francis B. Ogden......do	Bristol	New Jersey	do
Robert W. Fox......do	Falmouth	England	do
Thomas W. Fox......do	Plymouth	do	do
Joseph R. Croskey......do	Cowes		do
SCOTLAND.			
Robert Grieve......do	Leith	Scotland	do
Stewart Steel......do	Dundee	Ireland	do
Joseph Cowdin......do	Glasgow		do
IRELAND.			
Thomas Wilson......do	Dublin		do
Thomas W. Gilpin......do	Belfast	Delaware	do
James McDowell......do	Londonderry	Virginia	do
John Murphy......do	Cork	United States	do
Michael Kennedy......do	Galway	Ireland	do

DEPARTMENT OF STATE—*Consuls, &c.*

Names and offices.	Where employed.	Where born.	Compensation.
			Dol. cts.
CHINA.			
Frederick T. Bush......Consul	Hong Kong......	New York ...	Fees...
EAST INDIES.			
Joseph Balestier..........do..	Singapore.......	United States..	..do...
James B. Higginson.......do..	Calcutta.........	Massachusetts	..do...
IN AND NEAR EUROPE AND AFRICA.			
Horatio Sprague...........do..	Gibraltar	.....do......	..do...
William W. Andrews.....do..	Island of Malta..	.....do......	..do...
Isaac Chase...............do..	Cape Town, Cape of Good Hope.	.....do......	..do...
William Carroll.....Com. agent	Island St. Helena.	....	..do...
NORTH AMERICA.			
Israel D. Andrews......Consul	St. John's, New Brunswick.....	N. Brunswick.	..do...
T. B. Livingston..........do..	Halifax..........	New York....	..do...
John J. Peavey...........do..	Pictou	Maine	..do...
SOUTH AMERICA.			
Moses Benjamin..........do..	Demerara, British Guiana........	....	..do...
WEST INDIES.			
Alexander J. Bergen.......do..	Bermuda.........	New York....	..do...
John F. Bacon.............do..	Nassau, New Providence	.....do......	..do...
John T. Pickett...........do..	Turk's Island....	Kentucky.....	..do...
Robert M. Harrison.......do..	Kingston, Jamaica	Virginia.......	..do...
William R. Hayes........do..	Barbadoes.......	Vermont......	..do...
Rich'd S. Higinbothom, Commercial agent............	St. Christopher's and Antigua...	....	..do...
AUSTRALIA, OR NEW HOLLAND.			
James H. Williams.....Consul	Sidney, New South Wales...	Massachusetts	..do...
VAN DIEMAN'S LAND.			
Elisha Hathaway, jr......do..	Hobart Town....	....	..do...

DEPARTMENT OF STATE—*Ministers, Consuls, &c.*

Names and offices.	Where employed.	Where born.	Compensation.
			Dol. cts.
RUSSIA.			
Envoy Extraordinary and Minister Plenipotentiary.			
Charles S. Todd	St. Petersburg	Kentucky	9000 00
Secretary of Legation.			
John R. Clay	do	Pennsylvania	2000 00
Abraham P. Gibson ... Consul	do	New York	Fees
Alexander Schwartz ... do	Riga		do
Edmund Brandt ... do	Archangel		do
John Ralli ... do	Odessa		do
FRENCH DOMINIONS.			
Envoy Extraordinary and Minister Plenipotentiary.			
William R. King	Paris	N. Carolina	9000 00
Secretary of Legation.			
J. L. Martin	do	do	2000 00
Robert Walsh ... Consul	do	Maryland	Fees
Thomas Hulme ... do	Sedan	Pennsylvania	do
Reuben G. Beasley ... do	Havre	Virginia	do
Essex R. Livingston ... do	Nantes	New York	do
Francis M. Auboyneau ... do	La Rochelle		do
John W. Grigsby ... do	Bordeaux	Virginia	do
Daniel C. Croxall ... do	Marseilles	New York	do
WEST INDIES.			
John W. Fisher ... do	Pointe-a-Pitre, Guadaloupe	New Jersey	do
Gabriel G. Fleurot ... do	St. Pierre, Martinique		do
FRENCH GUIANA.			
Joseph W. Fabens ... do	Cayenne	Massachusetts	do
AFRICA.			
Francis Lacrouts ... do	Algiers	France	do

DEPARTMENT OF STATE—*Ministers, Consuls, &c.*

Names and offices.	Where employed.	Where born.	Compensation.
			Dol. cts.
SPANISH DOMINIONS.			
Envoy Extraordinary and Minister Plenipotentiary.			
Washington Irving	Madrid	New York	9000 00
Secretary of Legation.			
Jasper H. Livingston	do	do	2000 00
Maximo de Aguirre.....Consul	Bilbao	Spain	Fees...
Alexander Burton.........do..	Cadiz	Pennsylvania	..do...
George Reed.........do..	Malaga	do	..do...
P. Pou.........do..	Barcelona	Spain	..do...
N. B. Boyle.........do..	Port Mahon, Minorca	Washington	..do...
CUBA.			
Robert B. Campbell.......do..	Havana	S. Carolina	..do...
Simeon M. Johnson.......do..	Matanzas	New York	..do...
Samuel McLean.........do..	Trinidad de Cuba.	Dist. Colum.	..do...
John W. Holding.........do..	St. Jago de Cuba.	Maryland	..do...
PUERTO RICO.			
James C. Gallaher.........do..	Ponce	Virginia	..do...
Henry G. Hubbard.........do..	St. John's	New York	..do...
Thomas B. Abrams.........do..	Mayaguez	Pennsylvania	..do...
William H. Tracy.........do..	Guayama	Connecticut	..do...
OTHER SPANISH ISLANDS.			
Joseph Cullen.........Consul..	Teneriffe, Canary	....	Fees...
Henry P. Sturgis.........do....	Manilla, Philipine	Massachusetts	..do...
PORTUGUESE DOMINIONS.			
Chargé d'Affaires.			
Abraham Rencher	Lisbon	N. Carolina	4500 00
William H. Vesey.......Consul..	do	Pennsylvania	Fees...
PORTUGUESE ISLANDS.			
Samuel Haight.........Consul..	Fayal, Azores	New York	..do...
John H. March.........do....	Funchal, Madeira	N. Hampshire	..do...

DEPARTMENT OF STATE—*Ministers, Consuls, &c.*

Name and offices.	Where employed.	Where born.	Compensation.
			Dol. cts.
Ferdinand Gardner....Consul..	St. Jago, Cape de Verd..........	....	Fees...
BELGIUM.			
Chargé d'Affaires.			
Thomas G. Clemson...........	Brussels..........	United States..	4500 00
Francis J. Grund......Consul..	Antwerp..........	Germany.....	Fees...
DOMINIONS OF THE NETHERLANDS.			
Chargé d'Affaires.			
Auguste Davezac.............	Hague..........	West Indies..	4500 00
Charles Nichols......Consul..	Amsterdam......	Connecticut...	Fees...
William S. Campbell....do....	Rotterdam........	New York....	..do...
William H. Freeman, Commercial Agent.............	Curaçao, West Indies..........	Pennsylvania..	..do...
Owen M. Roberts.....Consul..	Batavia, Island of Java..........	....	..do...
DANISH DOMINIONS.			
Chargé d'Affaires.			
William W. Irwin.............	Copenhagen	.......do.....	4500 00
Charles F. Ryan......Consul..	.......do........	....	Fees...
Edmund L. Rainals.....do....	Elsineur..........	....	..do...
David Rogers..........do....	Santa Cruz, West Indies..........	....	..do...
David Naar, Commercial Agent.	St. Thomas, West Indies..........	New Jersey...	..do...
SWEDEN AND NORWAY.			
Chargé d'Affaires.			
Henry W. Ellsworth..........	Stockholm........	Connecticut...	4500 00
Charles D. Arfwedson, Consul..	.......do.......	Sweden......	Fees...
C. A. Murray...........do....	Gothenburg......	Great Britain..	..do...
Helmich Janson........do....	Bergen..........	Norway.......	..do...
Jorgen Flood..........do....	Porsgrund.......	......do.....	..do...

DEPARTMENT OF STATE—*Ministers, Consuls, &c.*

Names and offices.	Where employed.	Where born.	Compensation.
			Dol. cts.
PRUSSIA.			
Envoy extraordinary and minister plenipotentiary.			
Henry Wheaton..............	Berlin...........	Rhode Island..	9000 00
Secretary of Legation.			
Theodore S. Fay..............	.......do.......	Massachusetts	2000 00
Frederick Schillow....Consul..	Stettin	Prussia........	Fees...
WESTPHALIA AND THE PRUSSIAN PROVINCES OF THE RHINE.			
Charles Hecker, Acting Consul.	Elberfeld.........	Germany......	..do...
AUSTRIA.			
Chargé d'Affaires.			
William H. Stiles.............	Vienna...........	United States..	4500 00
J. G. Schwarz.........Consul..	.......do........	....	Fees...
William A. Sparks......do....	Venice...........	South Carolina	..do...
George Moore*.........do....	Trieste...........	Great Britain..	..do...
SAXONY.			
George Mohr........Consul..	Dresden..........	Germany......	..do...
John G. Flugel..........do....	Leipsick	......do......	..do...
WURTEMBURG.			
Frederick List........Consul..	Stuttgard.........	....	..do...
HANOVER, GRAND DUCHY OF HESSE, AND GRAND DUCHY OF HESSE DARMSTADT.			
Charles Graebe......Consul...	Cassel	Germany......	..do...
BADEN.			
George F. Gerding.....Consul..	Manheim.........	......do......	..do...

* Recalled, but *acting* till another shall have been appointed.

DEPARTMENT OF STATE—*Ministers, Consuls, &c.*

Names and offices.	Where employed.	Where born.	Compensation.
			Dol. cts.
HANSEATIC OR FREE CITIES.			
John Cuthbert........Consul..	Hamburg	United States.	Fees...
William H. Robertson...do....	Bremen	......do......	..do...
Ernest Schwendler......do....	Frankfort on the Main	....	..do...
SWITZERLAND.			
George H. Goundie...Consul..	Basel	Pennsylvania.	..do...
SARDINIAN STATES.			
Chargé d'Affaires.			
Robert Wickliffe, jr...........	Turin............	Kentucky....	4500 00
C. E. Lester...........Consul..	Genoa	Connecticut....	Fees...
Victor A. Sasserno......do....	Nice............	Italy.........	..do...
TUSCANY.			
J. A. Binda............Consul..	Leghorn	Italy..........	..do...
J. Ombrosi.......Acting do....	Florence	......do......	..do...
PONTIFICAL STATES.			
Nicholas Brown.......Consul..	Rome	United States.	..do...
Henry J. Brent..........do....	Ravenna	Dist. Columbia	..do...
James E. Freeman......do....	Ancona	United States.	..do...
KINGDOM OF THE TWO SICILIES.			
Chargé d'Affaires.			
William H. Polk..............	Naples..........	Tennessee....	4500 00
Alexander Hammett...Consul..	.......do........	Maryland	Fees...
John M. Marston.......do....	Palermo.........	Massachusetts	..do...
Charles Sherwood.......do....	Messina..........	Connecticut....	..do...
TURKISH DOMINIONS.			
Minister resident.			
Dabney S. Carr...............	Constantinople...	Maryland	6000 00

DEPARTMENT OF STATE—*Ministers, Consuls, &c.*

Names and offices.	Where employed.	Where born.	Compensation.
			Dol. cts.
John P. Brown....Dragoman..	Constantinople...	United States..	2500 00
George A. Porter.....Consul..	.......do.......	......do......	Fees...
David W. Offley........do....	Smyrna..........	......do......	..do...
Jasper Chasseaud.......do....	Beirout, Damascus and Said...	France.......	500 00
EGYPT.			
Alexander Todd......Consul..	Alexandria......	Scotland......	Fees...
BARBARY STATES.			
Thomas N. Carr......Consul..	Tangier, Morocco	New York....	2000 00
Samuel D. Heap........do....	Tunis...........	Pennsylvania.	2000 00
Daniel S. Macauley.......do....	Tripoli..........	......do......	2000 00
DOMINIONS OF THE IMAUM OF MUSCAT.			
Syed Ben Calfaun.....Consul..	Muscat..........	Muscat.......	Fees...
Charles Ward..........do....	Zanzibar island...	Maine.........	..do...
CHINA.			
Alexander H. Everett, Commissioner....................	Canton..........	Massachusetts	5000 00
Peter Parker, Secretary and Chinese Interpreter............	.......do.......	United States.	2500 00
Paul S. Forbes.......Consul..	.......do.......	......do......	Fees...
A. Follen..............do....	Amoy...........	....	..do...
Robert L. McIntosh....do....	Fuchowfou......	United States..	..do...
SANDWICH ISLANDS.			
Anthony Ten Eyck, Commissioner.....................	Honolulu........	New York....	3000 00
Joel Turrill..........Consul..	Oaho............	Vermont.....	Fees...
SOCIETY ISLANDS.			
Azel P. Ladd........Consul..	Tahiti...........	N. Hampshire	..do...
NAVIGATOR'S ISLANDS.			
John C. Williams, Commercial Agent.....................	Apia............	....	..do...

DEPARTMENT OF STATE—*Ministers, Consuls, &c.*

Names and offices.	Where employed.	Where born.	Compensation.
			Dol. cts.
FEEJEE ISLANDS.			
John B. Williams, Commercial Agent	Bay of Islands, N. Zealand	Massachusetts	Fees
NEW ZEALAND.			
John B. Williams.....Consul	Bay of Islands	do	do
HAYTI OR SAN DOMINGO.			
Commercial Agents.			
Joseph C. Luther	Port au Prince	do	do
Richmond Loring	Aux Cayes	United States	do
George F. Usher	Cape Haytien	Rhode Island	do
TEXAS.			
Morgan L. Smith.....Consul	Velasco	New York	do
Thomas N. Herndon....do	Galveston	Virginia	do
Stewart Newell.........do	Sabine	United States	do
MEXICO.			
John Black..........Consul	City of Mexico	do	do
Manuel Alvarez........do	Santa Fé		do
Franklin Chase.........do	Tampico	Maine	do
J. P. Schatzell..........do	Matamoras		do
F. M. Dimond...........do	Vera Cruz and Alvarado	Rhode Island	do
Edward Porter..........do	Tabasco	Virginia	do
Eneas McFaul, jr.......do	Laguna, Carmen island	Ireland	do
Pedro de Rigil y Estrada.do	Merida and Sisal	Mexico	do
Thomas O. Larkin......do	Monterey	Massachusetts	do
John Parrott............do	Mazatlan	United States	do
José Maria Castanos....do	San Blas	Mexico	do
John A. Robinson......do	Guaymas	New York	do
CENTRAL AMERICA.			
Stephen H. Weems...Consul	Guatemala	Maryland	do
A. Follin...............do	Omoa and Truxillo	New York	do

DEPARTMENT OF STATE—*Ministers, Consuls, &c.*

Names and offices.	Where employed.	Where born.	Compensation.
			Dol. cts.
NEW GRANADA.			
Chargé d'Affaires.			
Benjamin A. Bidlack	Bogota	Pennsylvania	4500 00
Ramon L. Sanchez.... Consul	Cartagena	Florida	Fees...
Southy Grinalds........do	Santa Martha	Virginia	..do...
William Nelson........do	Panama	United States	..do...
VENEZUELA.			
Chargé d'Affaires.			
Benjamin G. Shields	Caraccas	S. Carolina	4500 00
Robert Hutton........Consul	Maracaibo	N. Foundland	Fees...
Wm. P. Chandler.......do	Puerto Cabello	Delaware	..do...
John P. Adams.........do	Laguayra	Massachusetts	..do...
ECUADOR.			
Seth Sweetzer........Consul	Guayaquil	....	..do...
BRAZIL.			
Envoy extraordinary and minister plenipotentiary.			
Henry A. Wise	Rio de Janeiro	Virginia	9000 00
Secretary of Legation.			
Robert M. Walsh	.......do.......	Pennsylvania	2000 00
Charles B. Allen......Consul	Maranham island	Massachusetts	Fees...
Charles J. Smith........do	Para	Rhode Island	..do...
George P. Manouvrier...do	Pernambuco	Bremen	..do...
Gorham Parks..........do	Rio de Janeiro	Maine	..do...
George Black...........do	Santos	New York	..do...
Lemuel Wells...........do	Saint Catherine's island	......do......	..do...
Alexander H. Tyler.....do	Bahia or St. Salvador	Maryland	..do...
URUGUAY OR CISPLATINE REPUBLIC.			
Robert M. Hamilton..Consul	Montevideo	....	..do...

DEPARTMENT OF STATE—*Ministers, Consuls, &c.*

Names and offices.	Where employed.	Where born.	Compensation.
			Dol. cts.
ARGENTINE CONFEDERATION OR BUENOS AYRES.			
Chargé d'Affaires.			
William Brent, jr	Buenos Ayres	Virginia	4500 00
James H. Tate....Consul	do	United States	Fees
Jefferson Adams....do	Rio Negro	do	do
CHILE.			
Chargé d'Affaires.			
William Crump	Sant Jago	Virginia	4500 00
Eben Ritchie Dorr....Consul	Valparaiso	United States	Fees
William Crosby....do	Talcahuano	do	do
Samuel F. Haviland....do	Coquimbo		do
PERU.			
Chargé d'Affaires.			
Albert G. Jewett	Lima	Maine	4500 00
Stanhope Prevost....Consul	do	United States	Fees
Alexander Ruden, jr....do	Paita		do
Agent on the coast of Africa, under act of Congress of 3d March, 1819.			
James W. Lugenbeel	Liberia	Maryland	1500 00

WAR DEPARTMENT.

List of all officers and agents in the service of the United States, under the supervision of the War Department, made up to the last day of September, 1845, conformable to resolutions of Congress of April 27, 1816, and July 14, 1832, under the direction of the Secretary for the Department of State, of July 8th, 1845.

Names and offices.	Where employed.	Where born.	Compensation.
			Dol. cts.
SECRETARY OF WAR.			
William L. Marcy	Washington	Massachusetts	6000 00
CHIEF CLERK.			
Daniel Parker	War Office	do	2000 00
CLERKS.			
Archibald Campbell	do	New York	1600 00
Hampton C. Williams	do	Georgia	1600 00
Nathan Rice	do	Massachusetts	1400 00
Charles Calvert	do	England	1400 00
John Holmes Offley	do	Virginia	1400 00
John Potts	do	Dist. Colum.	1000 00
John D. McPherson	do	do	1000 00
John P. Wolf	do	Pennsylvania	1000 00
MESSENGERS.			
Thomas Wallace	do	do	650 00
Francis Datcher	do	Maryland	400 00
William Joyce, Assistant	do	Dist. Colum.	$12p.m.
INDIAN DEPARTMENT.			
COMMISSIONER.			
T. Hartley Crawford	Washington	Pennsylvania	3000 00
CHIEF CLERK.			
Saml. Humes Porter	do	do	1600 00

WAR DEPARTMENT—*Indian Department.*

Names and offices.	Where employed.	Where born.	Compensation.
			Dol. cts.
CLERKS.			
Hezekiah Miller	Washington	Maryland	1600 00
Chas. E. Mix	do	Connecticut	1600 00
Saml. J. Potts	do	Virginia	1400 00
Townshend Waugh	do	do	1400 00
Timothy R. Cruttenden	do	Connecticut	1400 00
William Devereux	do	Ireland	1400 00
William B. Waugh	do	Dist. Colum	1200 00
Leroy H. Berryman	do	Virginia	1000 00
Saml. D. Leib	do	Pennsylvania	1000 00
Stanhope R. Munford	do	Virginia	1000 00
Nicholas Quackenbush	do	New York	1000 00
Sewell Brintnall	do	Massachusetts	1000 00
MESSENGERS.			
Charles Draine	do	Ireland	700 00
William A. Wilson	do	Maryland	500 00
Michigan Superintendency.			
W. A. Richmond, Ac. Su. & Ag't	Detroit, Mich		1500 00
And'w T. McReynolds, Sub-ag't	Saganaw Sub-ag'y		750 00
James Ord ... do	S't Ste. Marie do	Virginia	750 00
R. H. Graveraet ... Interpreter	Mackinac		300 00
M. Moran ... do	Detroit		300 00
Eustache Roussain ... do	S. Ste Marie S. A.		300 00
G. D. Gardner ... do	Saganaw ... do		300 00
Wisconsin Superintendency.			
Henry Dodge, Sup't ex officio	Wisconsin Ter		
Albert G. Ellis ... Sub-agent	GreenBay S. Ag'y		750 00
James P. Hays ... do	La Pointe ... do		750 00
William Franks ... Interpreter	Green Bay ... do		300 00
W. Warren ... do	La Pointe ... do		300 00
Iowa Superintendency.			
John Chambers, Sup't ex officio	Iowa Territory		
John Beach ... Agent	Sac and Fox Ag'y	Massachusetts	1500 00
Amos J. Bruce ... Agent	St. Peter's ... do	Virginia	1500 00
Jonathan E. Fletcher	Winnebago S. A.		750 00
Josiah Smart ... Interpreter	Sac and Fox Ag'y	Georgia	300 00
Philander Prescott ... do	St. Peter's ... do	New York	300 00
Simeon Leguire ... do	Winnebago S. A.		300 00

WAR DEPARTMENT—*Indian Department.*

Names and offices.	Where employed.	Where born.	Compensation.
			Dol. cts.
St. Louis Superintendency.			
Thos. H. Harvey, Superintend't	St. Louis........	Virginia......	1500 00
John Haverty, Clerk to do.....	......do.........	Ireland........	1200 00
Richard W. Cummins.....Agent	Ft. Leaven'h Ag'y	Pennsylvania..	1500 00
Jonathan L. Bean............do..	C'l Bluffs Agency	....	1500 00
Andrew Dripps.............do..	Up'r Missouri do.	......do......	1500 00
Richard S. Elliott.....Sub-agent	C. Bluffs Sub-ag'y	......do......	750 00
Joel Cruttenden.........do....	Osage......do...	Connecticut...	750 00
Alfred Vaughan.........do....	Osage river.do...	Virginia........	750 00
Richard Hewitt.........do....	Wyandot..do...	....	750 00
Armstrong McClintock..do....	Gt. Nemaha do...	....	750 00
John Rubité.........Interpreter	......do.........	....	300 00
J. B. Roy.............do....	......do.........	....	300 00
Clement Lessert.........do....	Ft. Leaven'h Ag'y	Canada.......	300 00
Henry Tiblow..........do....	......do.........	Missouri......	300 00
Joseph Swiss...........do....	Osage Sub-agency	Osage nation..	300 00
Gabriel P. Cerre........do....	U. Missouri Ag'y	Missouri......	300 00
Joel W. Barrow........do....	Osage river S. A'y	Indiana.......	300 00
Joseph La Framboise...do....	C. Bluffs Sub-ag'y	Illinois........	300 00
James W. Cleghorn.....do....	C'l Bluffs Agency	....	300 00
Lewis Sansoree.........do....	......do.........	....	300 00
Logan Fontenelle........do....	......do.........	....	300 00
Western Superintendency.			
Wm. Armstrong, Ac. Su. & Ag't	Choctaw Agency.	....	1500 00
John B. Luce, Clerk to same...	......do.........	....	1000 00
James McKissack.........Agent	Cherokee Agency	....	1500 00
James Logan.............do..	Creek Agency ...	....	1500 00
A. M. M. Upshaw........do..	Chickasaw Ag'y.	....	1500 00
James S. Raines......Sub-agent	Neosho Sub Ag'y	....	750 00
Marcellus Du Val........do....	Seminole...do...	....	750 00
Thomson McKinney, Interpreter	Choctaw Agency.	....	300 00
Abraham ....do....	Seminole Sub A'y	....	300 00
Gilbert.................do....	Neosho Sub Ag'y	....	150 00
James Vallier...........do....	......do.........	....	150 00
Louis Davis............do....	......do.........	....	150 00
Benjamin Love.........do....	Chickasaw Ag'y.	....	300 00
Independent.			
Joseph Sinclear.......Sub-agent	Miami Sub Ag'y.	....	750 00
Stephen Osborne.........do....	N. York Sub A'y	....	750 00
Elijah White............do....	Oregon Sub Ag'y.	....	750 00
George Hunt........Interpreter	Miami Sub Ag'y.	....	300 00
Maris B. Pierce.........do....	N. York Sub A'y	....	300 00

WAR DEPARTMENT—*Pension Office.*

Names and offices.	Where employed.	Where born.	Compensation.
			Dol. cts.
Miscellaneous.			
P. M. Butler and M. G. Lewis, Commissioners to negotiate treaty of peace with the Camanches and others	Indian country		per day. 8 00
Henry Dodge, Commissioner to treat with Oneidas of Green Bay	Green Bay Sub A.		8 00
Thomas H. Harvey, Commission to negotiate treaty with Chippewas, Ottawas, and Pottawatomies	Council Bluffs		8 00
George W. Clarke, Agent in the removal of the Choctaws	Mississippi		5 00
PENSION OFFICE.			
COMMISSIONER.			
James L. Edwards	Washington	Virginia	2500 00
CHIEF CLERK.			
George W. Crump	do	do	1600 00
CLERKS.			
John D. Wilson	do	Maryland	1400 00
Andrew Porter	do	Pennsylvania	1400 00
George C. Ames	do	Virginia	1400 00
French S. Evans	do	do	1200 00
W. Ogden Niles	do	Delaware	1200 00
William M. Steuart	do	Virginia	1000 00
Daniel Brown	do	New Jersey	1000 00
William Gordon	do	Maryland	1000 00
Thomas Lumpkin	do	Virginia	800 00
MESSENGERS.			
Charles Hibbs	do	England	500 00
John L. Anderson	do	Pennsylvania	500 00

WAR DEPARTMENT—*Pension Agents.*

Name and offices.	Where employed.	Where born.	Compensation.
			Dol. cts.
AGENTS FOR PAYING PENSIONS IN THE DIFFERENT STATES AND TERRITORIES.			
William Woodbury	Portland, Me.		None
Isaac Hill	Concord, N. H.		..do...
Richard Jenness	Portsmouth, N.H.		..do...
Paris Hill	Providence, R. I.	Massachusetts	..do...
Rawsel R. Keith	Montpelier, Vt.		..do...
Merritt Clark	Poultney, Vt.		..do...
Franklin Haven	Boston, Mass.	Massachusetts	..do...
Horace Goodwin, 2d	Hartford, Conn		..do...
John A. Stevens	N. Y. City, N. Y.		..do...
Thomas W. Olcott	Albany, N. Y.	New York	..do...
P. Dickinson	Trenton, N. J.	New Jersey	..do...
S. F. Smith	Philadelphia, Pa.		..do...
Thomas M. Howe	Pittsburgh, Pa.		..do...
Jacob Alrichs	Wilmington, Del.	Delaware	..do...
James Swan	Baltimore, Md.	Maryland	..do...
James Caskie	Richmond, Va.		..do...
A. Robinson, senior	......do......	Virginia	..do...
J. Steene Browne	Wheeling, Va.		..do...
John Huske	Fayetteville, N. C.	N. Carolina	..do...
John C. Cochran	Charleston, S. C.		..do...
Hugh W. Mercer	Savannah, Ga.	Virginia	..do...
G. W. Meriwether	Louisville, Ky.		..do...
Joel M. Smith	Nashville, Tenn.	N. Carolina	..do...
William K. Blair	Jonesboro', Tenn.	Tennessee	..do...
Thomas Martin	Pulaski, Tenn.	Virginia	..do...
William Lyon, jr	Knoxville, Tenn.		..do...
John W. Campbell	Jackson, Tenn.	Kentucky	..do...
James Hall	Cincinnati, Ohio		..do...
James Perrine	Mobile, Ala.		..do...
James H. Dearing	Tuscaloosa, Ala.		..do...
W. C. Anderson	St. Louis, Mo.	New Jersey	..do...
J. F. D. Lanier	Madison, Ind.	N. Carolina	..do...
Mason C. Fitch	New Albany, Ind.	Massachusetts	..do...
James F. Reed	Springfield, Ills.		..do...
E. P. Hastings	Detroit, Mich.	Connecticut	..do...
W. E. Woodruff	Little Rock, Ark.	New York	..do...
Pierce M. Butler	Fort Gibson, Ark.		..do...
Francis H. Flagg	Tallahassee, Flor.		..do...
A. M. Reed	Jacksonville, Flor.	Connecticut	..do...
George W. Jones, agent for Iowa Territory	Sinsinawa Mound, Wisconsin Ter.	Indiana	..do...
John P. Van Ness	Washington, D.C.	New York	..do...
Greenberry Dorsey	New Orleans, La.		..do...
Paraclete Potter	Milwaukie, Wis.		..do...
David C. Glenn	Jackson, Miss.		..do...

WAR DEPARTMENT—*Quartermaster's Department.*

Names and offices.	Where employed.	Where born.	Compensation.
			Dol. cts.
QUARTERMASTER'S DEPARTMENT.			
In Quartermaster General's Office.			
CHIEF CLERK.			
Wm. A. Gordon	Washington	Maryland	1600 00
CLERKS.			
James Goszler	do	Dist. Columbia	1200 00
L. A. Fleury	do	Pennsylvania	1000 00
Wm. L. Bailey	do	Virginia	1000 00
Tho. J. Abbott	do	do	1000 00
J. W. Jones	do	New York	1000 00
MESSENGER.			
Geo. Phelps	do	Maryland	500 00
In the Clothing Branch of the Quartermaster's Department.			
CHIEF CLERK.			
James Warren	Philadelphia	England	1550 00
CLERKS.			
Jno. Andrews	do	Maryland	1100 00
G. W. North	do	Pennsylvania	850 00
SUPERINTENDENT.			
W. C. Irwin	do	do	1100 00
CLERK TO MILITARY STOREKEEPER.			
G. R. Orme	do	do	800 00
INSPECTOR OF CLOTHING.			
N. Campbell	do	Ireland	800 00

WAR DEPARTMENT—*Quartermaster's Department.*

Names and offices.	Where employed.	Where born.	Compensation.
			Dol. cts.
INSPECTOR OF SADDLERY, BOOTS, &c.			
J. Grier, jr.	Philadelphia	Ireland	720 00
MESSENGER.			
Geo. Canning	do	do	540 00
In the Department at large.			
CLERKS.			
D. Stinson	New York	N. Hampshire	1200 00
J. P. Moore	Washington	England	1000 00
E. Burgevin	Fort Gibson		780 00
C. S. Fayssoux	Philadelphia	Pennsylvania	600 00
G. A. Gannett	Saint Louis, Mo.	Connecticut	600 00
S. M. Willard	Fort Towson	Vermont	600 00
Chas. R. Tyler	Fort Gibson, Ark.	Virginia	600 00
A. H. Adams	Detroit, Mich.		480 00
Geo. Sunderland	Baltimore		480 00
J. H. Sarber	Pittsburgh, Pa		300 00
J. W. Garnier	Corpus Christi, Texas		720 00
AGENTS OF THE QUARTERMASTER'S DEPARTMENT.			
E. Shaler	Ft. Howard, Mich.	Connecticut	600 00
Jno. Lane	Bangor, Me.		300 00
Jas. Maher	Albany, N. Y.		300 00
D. J. Odell	Fort Sullivan, Me.		258 00
WAGON AND FORAGE MASTERS.			
L. Hinkle	Fort Leavenworth Missouri	Pennsylvania	$40 per mo. and 3 rations per day, at 20 cents each.
J. Meek	Fort Scott, Mo.	Kentucky	
G. S. Wilkins	Fort Towson, Ark.	Pennsylvania	
Rufus Beach	Fort Adams, R. I.	New York	
J. C. Goolrick	Washington City	Virginia	
P. A. Carnes	St. Louis, Mo.	Maryland	
D. O. Neal, acting	Corpus Christi, Texas		45 p. m.
M. Sanno....do	Carlisle, Penn	Pennsylvania	40 p. m

WAR DEPARTMENT—*Engineer Department.*

Names and offices.	Where employed.	Where born.	Compensation.
			Dol. cts.
KEEPERS OF DISMANTLED WORKS.			
M. T. Perkins	Marblehead, Mass		$5 per month and 1 ration per day, at 15 cents.
Wm. Webb	Fairhaven, Mass.	Virginia	
Jona. Edwards	Salem, Mass	Massachusetts	
MASTERS OF TRANSPORTS.			
W. C. Templeton	Texas		200p.m.
B. Hussey			60.do.
J. Monta D'Oca	Florida		45.do.
ENGINEER DEPARTMENT.			
CHIEF CLERK.			
F. N. Barbarin	Engineer Bureau	New York	1200 00
CLERKS.			
James C. Wilson	do	Virginia	1150 00
James Eveleth	do	Maryland	1000 00
R. Cruikshank	do	Dist. Col	1000 00
Joseph H. Pawling	do	Pennsylvania	800 00
MESSENGER.			
O. B. Denham	do	Virginia	500 00
FORT KEEPER.			
John Corkrin	Fort Delaware	Not known	75 p. m.

The foregoing list exhibits the names of all persons, other than officers of the Corps of Engineers, permanently employed by the Department. Besides these, however, other persons are *temporarily* employed by Engineer Officers in charge of works, to act in subordinate capacities, who are not embraced in the resolutions.

WAR DEPARTMENT—*Topographical Engineers.*

Names and offices.	Where employed.	Where born.	Compensation.
			Dol. cts.
BUREAU OF TOPOGRAPHICAL ENGINEERS.			
CHIEF CLERK.			
			per ann.
George Thomson	Washington	Dist. Colum.	1400 00
CLERKS.			
Charles Tschiffely	do	Switzerland	1000 00
Joseph G. Bruff	do	Dist. Colum.	1000 00
John R. Dorsey	do	Maryland	1000 00
MESSENGER.			
James Lawrence	do	do	300 00
ASSISTANT MESSENGER AND LABORER.			
George Thompson	do	England	300 00
AGENTS.			
George Morton	Buffalo, N. Y.		1000 00
Jonathan Johnson	Ashtabula, Ohio		150 00
Daniel Remich	Kennebunk, Me.	N. Hampshire	200 00
F. Bradford	Portland, Maine	Maine	50 00
			per day.
N. B. Haswell	Burlington, Vt.	Vermont	3 00
J. W. Judson	Oswego, N. Y.		4 00
William H. Pettes	Genesee Riv., N.Y	Vermont	4 00
Calvin Britain	St. Joseph, Mich.		3 00
Charles L. Schlatter	Chicago, Illinois		3 00
			per mon.
Henry Smith	Monroe, Mich	New York	75 00
William Milford	Cleveland, Ohio	Ireland	75 00
Erwin A. Cowles	Black River, Ohio		10 00
Charles A. Fuller	Louisville, Ky		100 00
Franklin Saunders	do		100 00
H. S. Blair	do		75 00
William Gamble	Chicago, Illinois		40 00
H. A. Pratt	Portland, N. Y.		15 00
John R. Bowes	Michigan city, Ind.	Pennsylvania	75 00
George S. Patterson	Huron, Ohio		50 00
J. A. Potter	Fairport, Ohio		75 00
Henry Hubbard	Ashtabula, Ohio		50 00
Loriston Averill	Cattaraugus, N.Y.		15 00
T. B. W. Stockton	Cleveland, Ohio		100 00

WAR DEPARTMENT—*Ordnance Office.*

Names and offices.	Where employed.	Where born.	Compensation.
			Dol. cts.
J. L. Woodside	Racine, W. T	Dist. Colum	50 00
Joshua Barney	Dubuque, Iowa	Maryland	100 00
C. R. Alton	Southport, W. T		75 00
ORDNANCE OFFICE.			
CHIEF CLERK.			
George Bender	Washington	Massachusetts	1200 00
CLERKS.			
Morris Adler	do	Germany	1150 00
Samuel Rainey	do	Ireland	1000 00
William McDermott	do	do	1000 00
John W. Butler	do	Pennsylvania	1000 00
William C. Reddall	do	Virginia	1000 00
J. P. Keller	do	France	1000 00
N. W. Fales	do	Maine	800 00
MESSENGER.			
N. Mulliken	do	Maryland	500 00

WAR DEPARTMENT—*Ordnance Department.*

Names and offices.	Where employed.	Where born.	Compensation.
Department at Large.			
ATTENDING OFFICER AT FOUNDRIES.			
William Wade	At the several foundries employed to cast cannon for the Ordnance Department	New Jersey	Pay and emoluments of a major of Ordnance.
MASTER ARMORERS AT NATIONAL ARMORIES.			
Benjamin Moor	Harper's Ferry, Virginia	Massachusetts	$1200 and quarters.
J. Weatherhead, acting	Springfield, Massachusetts	do	do.
MINERAL LANDS.			
Galena District.			
SUPERINTENDENT.			
John Floyd	The Galena District embraces fifteen townships in the N. W. corner of Illinois; those in Wisconsin, from the Illinois line north to the Wisconsin river, and several on the opposite side of the Mississippi river in Iowa	Virginia	$1000, and 15 per cent. on collections.
ACTING SPECIAL AGENT.			
A. Sigourney Bender	do do	Massachusetts	$800.

WAR DEPARTMENT—*Ordnance Department.*

Names and offices.	Where employed.	Where born.	Compensation.
CLERK.			
—— ——	Galena District		$500.
Upper District on the Mississippi.			
SUPERINTENDENT.			
John C. McLemore	The Upper District embraces all the mineral lands on both sides of the Mississippi, from Prairie du Chien to the Falls of St. Anthony		1200.
Lake Superior.			
SUPERINTENDENT.			
John Stockton	Southern shore of Lake Superior	Kentucky	1500.
[illegible]TS TO SUPERINTENDENT.			
J. B. [illegible]ll	do. do.		1200.
A. B. Gray	do. do.	Virginia	do.
Shelden McKnight	do. do.		do.
D. R. McNair	do. do.		do.

SURVEYOR.				
S. V. Talcott	do.	do.	New York	do.
SUB-ASSISTANTS.				
W. A. Eliason	do.	do.		600.
F. S. K. Russell	do.	do.		do.
A. T. Hale	do.	do.		do.

WAR DEPARTMENT—*Subsistence and Pay Departments.*

Names and offices.	Where employed.	Where born.	Compensation.
			Dol. cts.
SUBSISTENCE DEPARTMENT.			
CHIEF CLERK.			
Richard Gott	Washington	Maryland	1600 00
CLERKS.			
W. J. Smith	do	Ireland	1200 00
Charles G. Wilcox	do	Pennsylvania	1000 00
Columbus Munroe	do	Dist. Colum.	1000 00
MESSENGER.			
Joseph Schwartz	do	Germany	500 00
Department at Large.			
CLERKS TO COMMISSARIES OF SUBSISTENCE.			
J. K. Casey	New York		800 00
John Lendrum	Baltimore		600 00
N. Dupuy	New Orleans		1000 00
George A. Gannett	St. Louis		500 00
PAY DEPARTMENT.			
CHIEF CLERK.			
Nathaniel Frye	Washington	Maine	1700 00
CLERKS.			
William D. Beall	do	R. Island	1400 00
Charles Whitman	do	Massachusetts	1150 00
Daniel W. Davis	do	Pennsylvania	1150 00
Edmund H. Brooke	do	Maryland	1000 00
MESSENGER.			
Jacob Brodbeck	do	Switzerland	700 00

WAR DEPARTMENT—*Paymasters' Clerks—Medical Department.*

Names and offices.	Where employed.	Where born.	Compensation.
			Dol. cts.
PAYMASTERS' CLERKS.			
George C. Watson	Detroit, Mich	Unknown	500 00
George Townsend	Boston, Mass	Massachusetts	500 00
Thomas Phenix, jr	In Texas	Unknown	500 00
John McKay	New York city	do	500 00
Albert J. Smith	Norfolk	do	500 00
Jacob B. Kirby	Brownsville, N. Y.	do	500 00
S. Carter	St. Louis, Mo	do	500 00
George Andrews	Charleston, S. C.	Dist. of Col	500 00
J. H. Cloud	Jefferson b'ks, Mo.	Tennessee	500 00
H. R. Teasdale	St. Augustine, Fl.	Unknown	500 00
George S. Seaton	N. Orleans, La	do	500 00
W. E. Helen	Fort Smith, Ark	do	500 00
L. Brooke	In Texas	Maryland	500 00
Timothy O. Maher	West Point, N. Y.	Unknown	500 00
A. P. Skinner*	City Washington.	Virginia	......
MEDICAL DEPARTMENT.			
Surgeon General's Office.			
CLERKS.			
Richmond Johnson	Washington	Maryland	1150 00
Andrew Balmain	do	Dist. of Col	1000 00
James P. Espy	do	Pennsylvania	2000 00
MESSENGER.			
James H. Collins	do	Dist. of Col	500 00
PRIVATE PHYSICIANS TEMPORARILY EMPLOYED IN THE MEDICAL DEPARTMENT OF THE ARMY.			
			per mo.
Augustus Viele	Watervliet arsenal New York		30 00
Lawrence Byrne	Pikesville arsenal, Maryland		15 00
Horatio Adams	Watertown arsen'l Massachusetts		30 00
Landon C. Rives	Newport barr'cks, Kentucky		20 00
Matt. Gayle	Mount Vernon arsenal, Alabama		40 00

* An enlisted man, double pay of a first sergeant, ($32 per month,) with the usual allowance.

WAR DEPARTMENT—*Army Head Quarters.*

Names and offices.	Where employed.	Where born.	Compensation. Dol. cts.
Cyrus Briggs	Kennebec arsenal, Maine		20 00
Samuel Boardman	Apalachicola arsenal, Florida		25 00
Th. M. Sweeny	Detroit arsenal, Michigan		18 75
A. N. McDowell	Pittsburg, Pa		25 00
Robert Murray	Ft. Gratiot, Mich.		35 00
Clement Remes	Fort Wood, La.		60 00
Thomas S. Hopkins	Fort Brooke, E. F.		100 00

ARMY HEAD QUARTERS, WASHINGTON.

Names and offices.	Where employed.	Where born.	Compensation. Dol. cts.
Citizens employed at the Head Quarters of the Army under existing laws.			
COMMANDING GENERAL'S OFFICE.			
CLERK.			
Edward Brewer	Washington	Maryland	1000 00
MESSENGER.			
Joseph Williamson	do	England	500 00
ADJUTANT GENERAL'S OFFICE.			
CLERKS.			
John M. Hepburn	Washington	Maryland	1200 00
James L. Addison	do	do	1150 00
John G. Law	do	England	1000 00
James H. Lowry	do	Dist. of Col.	1000 00
A. F. Wilcox	do	Connecticut	1000 00
T. M. Hanson	do	Dist of Col.	1000 00
L. R. Hamersley	do	Pennsylvania	800 00
MESSENGER.			
Charles Baker	do	Massachusetts	500 00

ARMY LIST—*Generals and Staff.*

Names.	Bank.	Where born.
GENERAL OFFICERS.		
Winfield Scott	Major General	Virginia
Edmund P. Gaines	Brig Gen., Maj. Gen. brevet	do
John E. Wool	Brigadier General	New York
GENERAL STAFF OFFICERS.		
ADJUTANT GENERAL'S DEPARTMENT.		
Roger Jones	Col. & Adj. Gen. Brig Gen. bvt.	Virginia
Samuel Cooper	Brevet Major & Ast. Adj. Gen.	New York
Lorenzo Thomas	do	Delaware
Edmund Schriver	Brevet Captain & Ast. Adj. Gen.	Pennsylvania
James H. Prentiss	do	Massachusetts
William W. S. Bliss	do	New York
William G. Freeman	do	Virginia
INSPECTOR GENERAL'S DEPARTMENT.		
George Croghan	Colonel and Inspector General	Kentucky
QUARTERMASTER'S DEPARTMENT.		
Thomas S. Jesup	Br. Gen. & Q. M. Gen. M.G. bvt.	Virginia
Henry Stanton	Col. & Asst. Qr. Mr. General	Vermont
Trueman Cross	do	Maryland
Henry Whiting	Lt. Col. & Dep. Qr. Mr. Gen	Massachusetts
Thomas F. Hunt	do	N. Carolina
Æneas Mackay	Major and Quartermaster	New York
Charles Thomas	do	Pennsylvania
Samuel McRee	do	N. Carolina
Daniel D. Tompkins	Capt. and Assist. Quartermaster	New York
Thomas Swords	do	do
George H. Crosman	do	Massachusetts
Samuel B. Dusenbery	do	N. Carolina
David H. Vinton	do	R. Island
Edmund B. Alexander	do	Kentucky
Frederick Searle	do	England
Osborne Cross	do	Maryland

ARMY LIST—*Subsistence and Medical Departments.*

Names.	Rank.	Where born.
S. P. Heintzelman	Capt. and Assist. Quartermaster	Pennsylvania
James R. Irwin	do	do
Michael M. Clarke	do	Virginia
Ebenezer S. Sibley	do	Michigan
Edwin B. Babbitt	do	Connecticut
Robert E. Clary	do	Massachusetts
Charles O. Collins	do	New York
Abner R. Hetzel	do	Pennsylvania
Edmund A. Ogden	do	New York
James M. Hill	do	Maine
W. S. Ketchum	do	Connecticut
A. C. Myers	do	S. Carolina
S. M. Plummer	do	Maine
W. M. D. McKissack	do	New Jersey
William Wall	do	Pennsylvania
Morris S. Miller	do	New York
SUBSISTENCE DEPARTMENT.		
George Gibson	Colonel and Brig. General bvt. Com. Gen. of Subsistence	Pennsylvania
Joseph P. Taylor	Lieut. Col. Ast. Com. Gen. Sub.	Kentucky
Thomas W. Lendrum	Major and Com. of Subsistence	Virginia
Richard B. Lee	do	do
John B. Grayson	Capt. and Com. of Subsistence	Kentucky
Amos B. Eaton	do	New York
John C. Casey	do	England
G. G. Waggaman	do	Virginia
MEDICAL DEPARTMENT.		
Thomas Lawson	Surgeon General	Virginia
Thomas G. Mower	Surgeon	Massachusetts
B. F. Harney	do	Delaware
W. V. Wheaton	do	New York
Lyman Foot	do	Connecticut
C. A. Finlay	do	Ohio
P. H. Craig	do	Pennsylvania
R. S. Satterlee	do	New York
S. G. J. De Camp	do	New Jersey
H. S. Hawkins	do	Maryland
Robert C. Wood	do	Rhode Island
H. A. Stinnecke	do	Pennsylvania
W. L. Wharton	do	Dist. of Col.

ARMY LIST—*Medical Department.*

Names.	Rank	Where born.
C. S. Tripler	Surgeon	New York
Henry L. Heiskell	do	Virginia
C. McDougall	do	Ohio
Barton Randall	do	Maryland
N. S. Jarvis	do	New York
A. N. McLaren	do	Scotland
G. F. Turner	do	Massachusetts
J. J. B. Wright	do	Pennsylvania
James H. Sargent	Assistant Surgeon	Massachusetts
Sylvester Day	do	Vermont
Joseph Eaton	do	Massachusetts
Joseph P. Russell	do	Vermont
Benjamin King	do	Maryland
Lawrence Sprague	do	Maine
Joel Martin	do	Virginia
John B. Porter	do	Connecticut
T. Henderson	do	Virginia
John B. Wells	do	Maryland
John M. Cuyler	do	Georgia
Madison Mills	do	New York
William Hammond	do	Maryland
Joseph H. Bailey	do	New York
Leonard C. McPhail	do	Maryland
Samuel P. Moore	do	South Carolina
A. F. Suter	do	Dist. Colum
C. M. Hitchcock	do	Maryland
B. M. Byrne	do	Ireland
E. H. Abadie	do	France
R. Southgate	do	Virginia
C. McCormick	do	Dist. Colum
C. H. Laub	do	do
Josiah Simpson	do	New Jersey
W. J. Sloan	do	Pennsylvania
W. S. King	do	do
James R. Conrad	do	Virginia
John Byrne	do	Maryland
D. C. De Leon	do	S. Carolina
Joseph Walker	do	Bermuda
J. W. Russell	do	New York
H. H. Steiner	do	Maryland
J. C. Glen	do	South Carolina
H. E. Cruttenden	do	Dist. Colum
James Simons	do	South Carolina
T. C. Madison	do	Virginia
A. W. Kennedy	do	Kentucky
W. H. Van Buren	do	Pennsylvania
J. K. Barnes	do	do
L. H. Holden	do	Rhode Island
J. S. Griffin	do	Virginia

ARMY LIST—*Pay Dept.—Corps of Eng.*

Names.	Rank.	Where born.
R. F. Simpson	Assistant Surgeon	Virginia
W. E. Fullwood	do	Georgia
C. E. Isaacs	do	New York
R. H. Coolidge	do	do
R. S. Holmes	do	Pennsylvania
William Levely	do	Maryland
A. S. Wetherspoon	do	New York
George Buish	do	South Carolina
C. C. Keeney	do	New York
PAY DEPARTMENT.		
Nathan Towson	Paymaster General	Maryland
Benjamin F. Larned	Paymaster	Massachusetts
Thomas J. Leslie	do	England
David S. Townsend	do	Massachusetts
Daniel Randall	do	Maryland
Charles H. Smith	do	Virginia
Timothy P. Andrews	do	Ireland
Edmund Kirby	do	Connecticut
Adam D. Stewart	do	Virginia
Christopher Andrews	do	Ireland
Benjamin Walker	do	Vermont
Eugene Van Ness	do	New York
St. Clair Denny	do	Pennsylvania
David Hunter	do	Dist. Colum
Lloyd J. Beall	do	Rhode Island
Roger S. Dix	do	N. Hampshire
CORPS OF ENGINEERS.		
Joseph G. Totten	Colonel	Connecticut
Sylvanus Thayer	Lieut. Colonel, Colonel brevet	Massachusetts
René E. De Russy	Lieutenant Colonel	New York
John L. Smith	Major	South Carolina
William H. Chase	do	Massachusetts
Richard Delafield	do	New York
Cornelius A. Ogden	do	New Jersey
Henry Brewerton	Captain	New York
George Dutton	do	Connecticut
Joseph K. F. Mansfield	do	do
Alexander H. Bowman	do	Pennsylvania
Robert E. Lee	do	Virginia
Alexander J. Swift	do	N. Carolina
Frederick A. Smith	do	Massachusetts

ARMY LIST—*Topo. Eng.*

Names.	Rank.	Where born.
Jonathan G. Barnard	Captain	Massachusetts
George W. Cullum	do	New York
William D. Fraser	do	do
John Sanders	do	Kentucky
Charles H. Bigelow	do	Massachusetts
George L. Welcker	First Lieutenant	Tennessee
James L. Mason	do	Rhode Island
Henry W. Benham	do	Connecticut
Danville Leadbetter	do	Maine
Montgomery C. Meigs	do	Georgia
Daniel P. Woodbury	do	N. Hampshire
William H. Wright	do	N. Carolina
P. G. T. Beauregard	do	Louisiana
James H. Trapier	do	South Carolina
Jeremiah M. Scarritt	do	N. Hampshire
Isaac J. Stevens	do	Massachusetts
Henry W. Halleck	do	New York
Jeremy F. Gilmer	Second Lieutenant	N. Carolina
Henry L. Smith	do	Maine
Zealous B. Tower	do	Massachusetts
Horatio G. Wright	do	Connecticut
Masillon Harrison	do	Maryland
Henry L. Eustis	do	Massachusetts
John Newton	do	Virginia
John D. Kurtz	do	Dist. of Col.
William S. Rosecrans	do	Ohio
Barton S. Alexander	do	Kentucky
Gustavus W. Smith	do	do
William H. C. Whiting	do	Mississippi
Edward B. Hunt	Brevet Second Lieutenant	New York
Louis Hébert	do	Louisiana
CORPS TOPOGRAPHICAL ENGINEERS.		
John J. Abert	Colonel	Maryland
James Kearney	Lieutenant Colonel	Ireland
Stephen H. Long	Major, Lieut. Col. brevet	N. Hampshire
Hartman Bache	Major	Pennsylvania
James D. Graham	do	Virginia
William Turnbull	do	Maryland
William H. Swift	Captain	Massachusetts
William G. Williams	do	South Carolina
Augustus Canfield	do	New Jersey
Campbell Graham	do	Virginia
George W. Hughes	do	New York
Thomas J. Cram	do	N. Hampshire
John McClellan	do	Pennsylvania

ARMY LIST—*Ord. Dept.*

Names.	Rank.	Where born.
John Mackay	Captain	Georgia
Howard Stansbury	do	New York
Thomas B. Linnard	do	Pennsylvania
Joseph E. Johnston	Fisrt Lieut., Capt. brevet	Virginia
Thomas J. Lee	First Lieutenant	Dist. of Col.
Andrew A. Humphreys	do	Pennsylvania
William H. Emory	do	Maryland
John N. Macomb	do	New York
James H. Simpson	do	New Jersey
Jacob E. Blake	do	Pennsylvania
Lorenzo Sitgreaves	do	do
William H. Warner	do	New York
Israel C. Woodruff	do	New Jersey
John W. Gunnison	Second Lieutenant	N. Hampshire
Eliakim P. Scammon	do	Maine
Charles N. Hagner	do	Dist. of Col.
William R. Palmer	do	New Jersey
John C. Fremont	Second Lieut., Capt. brevet	South Carolina
Joseph D. Webster	Second Lieutenant	N. Hampshire
George Thom	do	do
Amiel W. Whipple	do	Massachusetts
George Meade	do	Spain
Martin L. Smith	do	New York
John Pope	Brevet Second Lieut	Kentucky
James W. Abert	do	New Jersey
William B. Franklin	do	Pennsylvania
William F. Raynolds	do	Ohio
William G. Peck	do	Connecticut
William F. Smith	do	Vermont
Thomas J. Wood	do	Kentucky
ORDNANCE DEPARTMENT.		
George Bomford	Colonel	New York
George Talcott	Lieut. Colonel	Connecticut
Henry K. Craig	Major	Pennsylvania
Rufus L. Baker	do	Connecticut
James W. Ripley	do	do
John Symington	do	Mayland
William H. Bell	Captain	N. Carolina
Edward Harding	do	Maryland
Alfred Mordecai	do	N. Carolina
Benjamin Huger	do	South Carolina
James A. J. Bradford	do	Tennessee
George D. Ramsay	do	Virginia
William Maynadier	do	Maryland
William A. Thornton	do	New York

ARMY LIST—*Military Storekeepers.*

Names.	Rank.	Where born.
John Williamson	Captain	New Jersey
Robert H. K. Whiteley	....do	Maryland
George H. Talcott	First Lieutenant	New York
John F. Lee	First Lieut., Capt. brevet	Virginia
James M. Morgan	First Lieutenant	New York
Louis A. B. Walbach	....do	N. Hampshire
Peter V. Hagner	....do	Dist of Col
Robert A. Wainwright	....do	Massachusetts
Alexander B. Dyer	Second Lieutenant	Virginia
Alexander H. Dearborn	....do	New York
Franklin D. Callender	....do......1st Lieut. brevet	.....do
Thomas L. Ringgold	....do	Virginia
Charles P. Kingsbury	....do	New York
John McNutt	....do	Ohio
Josiah Gorgas	Brevet Second Lieut	Pennsylvania
Thomas J. Rodman	....do	Indiana
Theodore T. S. Laidley	....do	Virginia
James G. Benton	....do	N. Hampshire
George Deshon	....do	Connecticut
Thomas J. Brereton	....do	Dist. of Col
Thomas G. Rhett	....do	South Carolina
Charles P. Stone	....do	Massachusetts
MILITARY STORE-KEEPERS.		
Attached to purchasing branch of Quartermaster's Department.		
E. S. Fayssoux		South Carolina
Thomas Grosvenor King		New York
Attached to Ordnance Department.		
Sanders Lansing, jr		New York
Richard Parker		Virginia
Edward Ingersoll		Massachusetts
Richard B. Butler		Pennsylvania
Silas Halsey		Connecticut
Daniel Ragan		Virginia
David Butler		New York
John A. Webber		Massachusetts
James S. Abeel		Pennsylvania
James R. Hanham		England
William R. Shoemaker		Pennsylvania
Samuel J. Carr		South Carolina

ARMY LIST—*First Dragoons.*

Names.	Rank.	Where born.
John M. Galt		Virginia
Richard J. R. Bee		Georgia
Stevens T. Mason		Virginia
FIRST REGIMENT OF DRAGOONS.		
Stephen W. Kearny	Colonel	New Jersey
Richard B. Mason	Lieutenant Colonel	Virginia
Clifton Wharton	Major	Pennsylvania
Edwin V. Sumner	Captain	Massachusetts
Eustace Trenor	do	New York
Nathan Boone	do	Kentucky
Philip St. G. Cook	do	Virginia
Thomas Swords	do Asst: Quartermaster	New York
Benjamin D. Moore	do	Kentucky
James Allen	do	Ohio
John H. K. Burgwin	do	N. Carolina
Enoch Steen	do	Kentucky
William Eustis	do	Rhode Island
Lucius B. Northrop	First Lieutenant	South Carolina
Henry S. Turner	do Adjutant	Virginia
Abraham R. Johnston	do	Ohio
Philip R. Thompson	do	Georgia
William N. Grier	do	Pennsylvania
Thomas McCrate	do	Maine
Philip Kearney, jr	do	New York
Robert H. Chilton	do	Virginia
Daniel H. Rucker	do	New Jersey
Andrew J. Smith	do	Pennsylvania
James H. Carleton	do	Maine
Richard S. Ewell	Second Lieutenant	Virginia
John W. T. Gardiner	do	Maine
Leonidas Jenkins	do	New York
John Love	do	Virginia
Abraham Buford	do	Kentucky
Patrick Noble	do	South Carolina
Henry W. Stanton	do	New York
Thomas C. Hammond	do	Maryland
Rufus Ingalls	do	Maine
Cave J. Couts	do	Tennessee
Alfred Pleasonton	Brevet Second Lieutenant	Dist. Colum.
Bezaleel W. Armstrong	do	Ohio
John W. Davidson	do	Virginia
Newton C. Givens	do	Kentucky
Richard C. W. Radford	do	Virginia
Joseph McElvain	do	Indiana

ARMY LIST—*Second Dragoons—First Artillery.*

Names.	Rank.	Where born.
SECOND REGIMENT OF DRAGOONS.		
David E. Twiggs	Colonel	Georgia
William S. Harney	Lieut. Colonel, Col. brevet	Louisiana
Thomas T. Fauntleroy	Major	Virginia
Benjamin L. Beall	Captain, Major brevet	Dist. of Col.
William M. Fulton	Captain	Virginia
Marshall S. Howe	....do	Maine
George A. H. Blake	....do	Pennsylvania
Croghan Ker	....do	Lousiana
Seth B. Thornton	....do	Virginia
Charles A. May	....do	Dist. Col
Nathaniel W. Hunter	....do	Georgia
Lawrence P. Graham	....do	Virginia
William J. Hardee	....do	Georgia
Hamilton W. Merrill	First Lieutenant	New York
Owen P. Ransom	....do	Connecticut
Henry H. Sibley	....do.... Adjutant	Louisiana
Ripley A. Arnold	....do.... Captain brevet	Mississippi
Zebulon M. P. Inge	....do	Alabama
Washington J. Newton	....do	Dist. Colum
William H. Saunders	....do	Virginia
John H. Hill	....do	Pennsylvania
Albert Lowry	....do	....do
Fowler Hamilton	....do	New York
Oscar F. Winship	....do	....do
Reuben P. Campbell	Second Lieutenant	N. Carolina
William Steele	....do	New York
Daniel G. Rogers	....do	Pennsylvania
Philip W. McDonald	....do	....do
Patrick Calhoun	....do. Aid to Bt. Mj. G. Gaines	Dist. Colum
Elias K. Kane	....do	Illinois
George Stevens	....do	Vermont
Lewis Neill	....do	Virginia
Richard H. Anderson	....do	South Carolina
George T. Mason	....do	Virginia
Joseph H. Whittlesey	Brevet Second Lieutenant	New York
Augustus Cook	....do	Connecticut
John Y. Bicknell	....do	Tennessee
William T. Allen	....do	Virginia
James M. Hawes	....do	Kentucky
Delos B. Sacket	....do	New York
FIRST REGIMENT OF ARTILLERY.		
Ichabod B. Crane	Colonel	New Jersey

ARMY LIST—*First Artillery.*

Names.	Rank.	Where born.
Benjamin K. Pierce	Lieutenant Colonel	N. Hampshire.
Levi Whiting	Major	Massachusetts
Giles Porter	Captain	New York
David Van Ness	do	do
Justin Dimick	do Major brevet	Vermont
Daniel D. Tompkins	do Maj. bt., Ast. Q. M.	New York
Lucian B. Webster	do	Vermont
George Nauman	do	Pennsylvania
Francis Taylor	do	Virginia
James R. Irwin	do Asst. Quartermaster	Pennsylvania
John H. Winder	do	Maryland
Ebenezer S. Sibley	do Asst. Quartermaster	Ohio
Timothy Green	First Lieut., Captain brevet	Massachusetts
Miner Knowlton	do	Connecticut
James H. Prentiss	do Cpt. bt. & A. A. G.	Massachusetts
John B. Magruder	do	Virginia
Erastus A. Capron	do	Connecticut
George G. Waggaman	do Capt., Com. Sub.	Virginia
Martin J. Burke	do	New York
John S. Hatheway	do	do
James L. Donaldson	do	Maryland
William W. Mackall	do	Dist. of Col.
Israel Vogdes	do	Pennsylvania
Bennett H. Hill	do	Dist. Colum'a.
William H. French	do	Maryland
Joseph Hooker	do Adjutant	Massachusetts
William H. Fowler	do	Maryland
Isaac S. K. Reeves	do	S. Carolina
Henry C. Wayne	do	Georgia
Irvin McDowell	co A. D. C. to B. G. Wool	Ohio
Joseph A. Haskin	do	New York
Henry D. Grafton	do	Massachusetts
James B. Ricketts	Second Lieutenant	New York
William S. Smith	do	do
Samuel K. Dawson	do	Pennsylvania
James G. Martin	do	N. Carolina
Joseph F. Irons	do	Pennsylvania
Samuel Jones	do	Virginia
John M. Brannon	do	Dist. Colum'a.
Isaac Bowen	do	New York
Seth Williams	do	Maine
Abner Doubleday	do	New York
John H. Grelaud	Brevet 2d Lieutenant	Pennsylvania
James A. Hardie	do	New York
Daniel M. Frost	do	do
Asher R. Eddy	do	Rhode Island
Thomas J. Curd	do	Kentucky
Thomas B. J. Weld	do	Maine

ARMY LIST—*Second Artillery.*

Names.	Rank.	Where born.
SECOND REGIMENT OF ARTILLERY.		
James Bankhead	Colonel	Virginia
A. C. W. Fanning	Lieut. Col., Col. Brevet	Massachusetts
John Erwing	Major	do.
Gustavus S. Drane	Captain	Maryland
Charles S. Merchant	do	New York
Allen Lowd	do	Massachusetts
Samuel Mackenzie	do	N. Carolina
William C. De Hart	do	New York
Charles F. Smith	do	Pennsylvania
Michael M. Clark	do...Assist't Quarterm'r.	Virginia
John B. Grayson	do...Commis. of Subsist.	Kentucky
Henry Swartwout	do	New York
Edmund Schriver	do...Assist't Adj't Gen'l.	Pennsylvania
James Duncan	First Lieutenant	New York
Thomas P. Ridgely	do	Maryland
Horace Brooks	do	Massachusetts
Henry L. Kendrick	do	N. Hampshire.
Roland A. Luther	do	Pennsylvania
John F. Roland	do	do
Muscoe L. Shackelford	do	Virginia
Robert Allen	do	Ohio
Charles B. Daniels	do	N. Hampshire.
William W. Chapman	do	Massachusetts
Lewis G. Arnold	do	New Jersey
Francis Woodbridge	do	Vermont
Edward D. Townsend	do.....Adjutant	Massachusetts
Henry C. Pratt	do	do
John Sedgwick	do	Connecticut
William Armstrong	do	Indiana
Arnold Elzey	do	Maryland
William B. Blair	do	Virginia
William F. Barry	do	New York
William A. Nichols	do	Pennsylvania
Leslie Chase	Second Lieutenant	New York
Lucius H. Allen	do	do
Henry J. Hunt	do	Ohio
Augustus A. Gibson	do	Maine
Arthur B. Lansing	do	New York
William Hays	do	Virginia
Harvey A. Allen	do	N. Carolina
Samuel S. Anderson	do	Virginia
James Totten	do	Pennsylvania
David Gibson	do	Virginia
Isaac F. Quinby	Brevet 2d Lieutenant	New Jersey
John J. Peck	do	New York
Henry F. Clarke	do	Pennsylvania

ARMY LIST—*Third Artillery.*

Names.	Rank.	Where born.
Josiah H. Carlisle	Brevet 2d Lieutenant	Maine
George Edwards	do	England
Henry Coppée	do	Georgia
THIRD REGIMENT OF ARTILLERY.		
Walker K. Armistead	Colonel, Brig. General brevet	Virginia
William Gates	Lieutenant Colonel	Massachusetts
William L. McClintock	Major	do
Thomas Childs	Captain, Lieut. Colonel brevet	do
John R. Vinton	do	Rhode Island
Samuel Ringgold	do . . Major brevet	Maryland
David H. Vinton	do . . Ass't Quartermaster	Rhode Island
Martin Burke	do	Maryland
Richard D. A. Wade	do . . Major brevet	New York
Robert Anderson	do	Kentucky
Erasmus D. Keyes	do	Massachusetts
William Wall	do . . Ass't Quartermaster	Pennsylvania
John A. Thomas	do	N. Carolina
Morris S. Miller	First Lieut., Capt. bv't, A. Q. M.	New York
Thomas W. Sherman	do	Rhode Island
Christopher Q. Tompkins	do	Virginia
Braxton Bragg	do	N. Carolina
George Taylor	do . . Captain brevet	Georgia
Edward J. Steptoe	do	Virginia
Randolph Ridgely	do	Maryland
Francis O. Wyse	do	do
William H. Shover	do	Ohio
William A. Browne	do . . Adjutant	Connecticut
Henry S. Burton	do	New York
James L. Rankin	do	Pennsylvania
Henry B. Judd	do	Connecticut
Edward O. C. Ord	do	Dist. Colum
William Gilham	do	Indiana
William T. Sherman	do	Ohio
William H. Churchill	do	New York
Stewart Van Vliet	do	do
George H. Thomas	do	Virginia
Horace B. Field	do	New York
George W. Ayers	Second Lieutenant	New Jersey
Sewall L. Fremont	do	Vermont
Richard P. Hammond	do	Maryland
John F. Reynolds	do	Pennsylvania
Edward G. Beckwith	do	New York
Joseph Stewart	do	Kentucky
Richard W. Johnston	do	Virginia
Charles L. Kilburn	do	Pennsylvania

ARMY LIST—*Fourth Artillery.*

Names.	Rank.	Where born.
Hachaliah Brown	Second Lieutenant	New York
Lucien Loeser	do	Pennsylvania
Daniel H. Hill	Brevet 2d Lieutenant	S. Carolina
Roswell S. Ripley	do	Ohio
Samuel G. French	do	New Jersey
Francis J. Thomas	do	Virginia
Louis D. Welch	do	Connecticut
George P. Andrews	do	do
FOURTH REGIMENT OF ARTILLERY.		
John B. Walbach	Colonel	Germany
Matthew M. Payne	Lieutenant Colonel	Virginia
Francis S. Belton	Major	Maryland
John L. Gardner	Captain, Major brevet	Massachusetts
John Munroe	do do	Scotland
Patrick H. Galt	do	Virginia
John M. Washington	do	do
Harvey Brown	do Major brevet	New Jersey
Samuel Cooper	do Maj. bvt. and A. A. G.	New York
William W. Morris	do Major brevet	do
Samuel B. Dusenbery	do Ass't Quartermaster	N. Carolina
John B. Scott	do	Connecticut
William P. Bainbridge	do	Kentucky
Frederick Searle	First Lieut., Maj. bvt., A. Q. M.	England
Raphael C. Smead	do	N. Hampshire
Charles O. Collins	do Capt., Ass't Q. M.	New York
Franklin E. Hunt	do	New Jersey
Simon H. Drum	do	Pennsylvania
Samuel C. Ridgely	do	Maryland
Edward Deas	do	S. Carolina
John H. Miller	do Adjutant	Pennsylvania
Alexander E. Shiras	do	do
William G. Freeman	do Capt. brevet, A. A. G.	Virginia
Joseph Roberts	do	Delaware
John P. J. O'Brien	do	Pennsylvania
John W. Phelps	do	Vermont
Thomas L. Brent	do	Virginia
Thomas Williams	do Aid to Maj. G'l Scott	New York
Edmund Bradford	do	Pennsylvania
John C. Pemberton	do	do
Charles F. Wooster	do	New York
James R. Soley	do	Massachusetts
John P. McCown	do	Tennessee
Francis N. Clarke	Second Lieutenant	New York
George W. Getty	do	Dist. Colum.
Albion P. Howe	do	Maine

ARMY LIST—*First Infantry.*

Names.	Rank.	Where born.
Julius P. Garesché	Second Lieutenant	Cuba
Simon S. Fahnestock	....do	Pennsylvania
Robert S. Garnett	....do	Virginia
Mansfield Lovell	....do	Dist. Colum.
Calvin Benjamin	....do	New York
Henry M. Whiting	....do	Massachusetts
George W. Rains	....do	Alabama
John P. Johnstone	Brevet 2d Lieutenant	Virginia
Joseph J. Reynolds	....do	Kentucky
Samuel Gill	....do	.....do
Fitz-John Porter	....do	N. Hampshire.
Francis Collins	....do	New York
Joseph F. Farry	....do	Pennsylvania
FIRST REGIMENT OF INFANTRY.		
William Davenport	Colonel	Pennsylvania
Henry Wilson	Lientenant Colonel	.....do
Greenleaf Dearborn	Major	Massachusetts
William R. Jouett	Captain	Tennessee
John J. Abercrombie	....do..Major brevet	.....do
Albert S. Miller	....do	.....do
Electus Backus	....do	New York
Osborne Cross	....do..Ass't Quartermaster	Maryland
Joseph H. Lamotte	....do	N. Carolina
John R. B. Gardenier	....do	New York
Sidney Burbank	....do	Massachusetts
Seth Eastman	....do	Maine
Samuel M. Plummer	....do..Ass't Quartermaster	.....do
John M. Scott	First Lieutenant	Kentucky
John H. King	....do	Michigan
Robert S. Granger	....do	Ohio
Alexander W. Reynolds	....do	Virginia
Ferdinand S. Mumford	....do	New York
William E. Prince	....do	Massachusetts
George W. F. Wood	....do	Pennsylvania
Frederick H. Masten	....do	New York
Garrett Barry	....do	Maryland
George W. Wallace	....do	Pennsylvania
John C. Terrett	Second Lieutenant	Virginia
Benjamin H. Arthur	....do..Adjutant	New York
Theophilus d'Orémieulx	....do	France
James N. Caldwell	....do	Ohio
Stephen D. Carpenter	....do	Maine
Joseph B. Plummer	....do	Massachusetts
Schuyler Hamilton	....do	New York
Frederick J. Denman	....do	.....do

ARMY LIST—*Second Infantry.*

Names.	Rank.	Where born.
Cyrus Hall	Second Lieutenant	New York
Eugene E. McLean	....do	Dist. Colum.
Joseph H. Potter	Brevet 2d Lieutenant	N. Hampshire.
Henry R. Selden	....do	Vermont
George W. Hawkins	....do	N. Carolina
Rankin Dilworth	....do	Ohio
Abram B. Lincoln	....do	New York
David A. Russell	....do	.....do
SECOND REGIMENT OF INFANTRY.		
Hugh Brady	Colonel, Brig. Gen'l brevet	Pennsylvania
Bennet Riley	Lieut. Colonel, Colonel brevet	Maryland
Joseph Plympton	Major	Massachusetts
Ephraim K. Barnum	Captain	Vermont
Carlos A. Waite	....do	New York
Thompson Morris	....do	Ohio
Julius J. B. Kingsbury	....do	Connecticut
Joseph R. Smith	....do	New York
Hannibal Day	....do	Vermont
Samuel P. Heintzelman	....do..Ass't Quartermaster	Pennsylvania
Amos B. Eaton	....do..Commissary Subsist'e	New York
Silas Casey	....do	Rhode Island
Abner R. Hetzel	....do..Ass't Quartermaster	Pennsylvania
James W. Penrose	First Lieutenant	Missouri
Edwin R. Long	....do	N. Carolina
George W. Patten	....do	Rhode Island
Isaac R. D. Burnett	....do..Adjutant	Virginia
Henry W. Wessells	....do	Connecticut
James W. Anderson	....do..Captain brevet	Virginia
Marsena R. Patrick	....do	New York
William Alburtis	....do..Captain brevet	Virginia
Justus McKinstry	....do	New York
Christopher S. Lovell	....do	S. Carolina
Delozier Davidson	Second Lieutenant	Dist. Colum.
George C. Westcott	....do	New Jersey
Julius Hayden	....do	New York
Edward R. S. Canby	....do	Kentucky
John W. Martin	....do	Virginia
Bryent P. Tilden, jr	....do	Massachusetts
Nathaniel Lyon	....do	Connecticut
Alfred Sully	....do	Pennsylvania
Edward Murray	....do	Maryland
James W. Schureman	....do	New Jersey
Charles S. Hamilton	Brevet 2d Lieutenant	New York
Frederick Steele	....do	.....do
Simon B. Buckner	....do	Kentucky

ARMY LIST—*Third Infantry.*

Names.	Rank.	Where born.
John Trevitt	Brevet 2d Lieutenant	N. Hampshire.
Gordon Granger	....do	New York
THIRD REGIMENT OF INFANTRY.		
James B. Many	Colonel	Delaware
Ethan A. Hitchcock	Lieutenant Colonel	Vermont
William W. Lear	Major	Maryland
John B. Clarke	Captain	Kentucky
Lewis N. Morris	....do	New York
Henry Bainbridge	....do	.....do
John. W. Cotton	....do	Massachusetts
Edmund B. Alexander	....do..Ass't Quartermaster	Kentucky
Edwin B. Babbitt	....do.......do	Connecticut
Nathaniel C. Macrae	....do	Virginia
Jefferson Van Horne	....do	Pennsylvania
John C. Casey	....do..Commissary Subsist'e.	England
George P. Field	....do	New York
Joseph L. Coburn	First Lieutenant	Vermont
Philip N. Barbour	....do..Capt. bvt., Adjutant	Kentucky
William S. Henry	....do	New York
Joseph H. Eaton	....do	Massachusetts
Lewis S. Craig	....do	Virginia
James M. Smith	....do	.....do
William H. Gordon	....do	.....do
Daniel T. Chandler	....do	Dist. Colum.
Stephen D. Dobbins	....do	Pennsylvania
Bushrod R. Johnson	....do	Ohio
Oliver L. Shepherd	Second Lieutenant	New York
William B. Johns	....do	Dist. Colum.
Douglass S. Irwin	....do..1st Lieut. brevet	.....do
Thomas Jordan	....do	Virginia
Don Carlos Buell	....do	Ohio
Israel B. Richardson	....do	Vermont
William T. H. Brooks	....do	Ohio
Andrew W. Bowman	....do	Pennsylvania
George Sykes	....do	Maryland
Andrew J. Williamson	....do	Virginia
Charles E. Jarvis	Brevet 2d Lieutenant	Maine
John C. McFerran	....do	Kentucky
George C. McClelland	....do	Pennsylvania
Henry B. Schroeder	....do	Maryland
John J. C. Bibb	....do	Kentucky
John P. Hatch	....do	New York
Barnard E. Bee	....do	S. Carolina

ARMY LIST—*Fourth and Fifth Infantry.*

Names.	Rank.	Where born.
FOURTH REGIMENT OF INFANTRY.		
William Whistler	Colonel	Maryland
John Garland	Lieutenant Colonel	Virginia
Thomas Staniford	Major	Connecticut
George W. Allen	Captain, Major brevet	Massachusetts
John Page	....do	Maine
William M. Graham	....do..Major brevet	Virginia
Pitcairn Morrison	....do	New York
George A. McCall	....do	Pennsylvania
Lorenzo Thomas	....do..Major brevet, A. A. G.	Delaware
Gouverneur Morris	....do	New York
Robert C. Buchanan	....do	Maryland
Charles H. Larnard	....do	Rhode Island
Bradford R. Alden	....do	Pennsylvania
William W. S. Bliss	First Lieut., Capt., A. A. G.	New York
Benjamin Alvord	....do	Vermont
Abraham C. Myers	....do..Capt. bvt., Ass't Q. M.	S. Carolina
Henry L. Scott	....do..Aid to Maj. G'l Scott	N. Carolina
Henry Prince	....do	Maine
Charles Hoskins	....do..Adjutant	N. Carolina
Richard H. Graham	....do	Kentucky
John H. Gore	....do	Maryland
Richard E. Cochrane	....do	Delaware
Edward G. Elliott	....do	Dist. Colum.
Theodoric H. Porter	Second Lieutenant	.....do
Sidney Smith	....do	Virginia
Granville O. Haller	....do	Pennsylvania
Henry D. Wallen	....do	Georgia
Henderson Ridgely	....do	Maryland
Allen H. Norton	....do	Ohio
Jenks Beaman	....do	Vermont
Christopher R. Perry	....do	Rhode Island
Christopher C. Augur	....do	New York
Franklin Gardner	....do	.....do
Ulysses S. Grant	Brevet 2d Lieutenant	Ohio
Robert Hazlitt	....do	Pennsylvania
James S. Woods	....do	.....do
Alexander Hays	....do	.....do
John A. Richey	....do	Ohio
Patrick A. Farrelly	....do	Pennsylvania
FIFTH REGIMENT OF INFANTRY.		
George M. Brooke	Colonel, Brig'r Gen'l brevet	Virginia
James S. McIntosh	Lieutenant Colonel	Georgia

ARMY LIST—*Sixth Infantry.*

Names.	Rank.	Where born.
Waddy V. Cobbs	Major	Virginia
Martin Scott	Captain	Vermont
Anthony Drane	....do	Maryland
Moses E. Merrill	....do	Maine
Ephraim K. Smith	....do	Connecticut
Alexander S. Hooe	....do	Virginia
Isaac Lynde	....do	Vermont
Robert E. Clary	....do..Ass't Quartermaster	Massachusetts
James L. Thompson	....do	Tennessee
Caleb C. Sibley	....do	Massachusetts
William Chapman	....do	Maryland
Randolph B. Marcy	First Lieutenant	Massachusetts
Daniel Ruggles	....do	.....do
J. C. Reid	....do.Aid to Bvt. M. G. Gaines	New York
William M. D. McKissack	....do.Capt. A. Q. M	New Jersey
Joseph H. Whipple	....do	Massachusetts
William Root	....do	New York
Daniel H. McPhail	....do	Maryland
Carter L. Stevenson	....do	Virginia
Nathan B. Rossell	....do	New Jersey
John A. Whitall	....do	Dist. Colum.
George Deas	Second Lieutenant, Adjutant	Pennsylvania
Sterne H. Fowler	....do	Connecticut
Robert L. Brooke	....do	Pennsylvania
Spencer Norvell	....do	.....do
Paul D. Geisse	....do	.....do
John C. Robinson	....do	New York
Henry Whiting	....do	.....do
Pinkney Lugenbeel	....do	Ohio
Joseph L. Folsom	....do	N. Hampshire.
Mortimer Rosecrants	....do	New York
Edwin Howe	Brevet 2d Lieutenant	.....do
Joseph P. Smith	....do	N. Hampshire.
Henry Merrill	....do	Massachusetts
Edmund K. Smith	....do	Florida
Thomas G. Pitcher	....do	Indiana
William L. Crittenden	....do	Kentucky
SIXTH REGIMENT OF INFANTRY.		
Zachary Taylor	Colonel, Brig'r Gen'l brevet	Virginia
Gustavus Loomis	Lieutenant Colonel	Vermont
Benjamin L. E. Bonneville	Major	France
Thomas Noel	Captain, Major brevet	Maryland
George Andrews	....do......do	Dist. Colum.
George H. Crosman	....do..Ass't Quartermaster	Massachusetts
Joseph D. Searight	....do	Maryland

ARMY LIST—*Seventh Infantry.*

Names.	Rank.	Where born.
William Hoffman, jr.	Captain	New York.
Albemarle Cady	....do.	N. Hampshire.
Thomas L. Alexander	....do.	Virginia.
William S. Ketchum	....do. . Ass't Quartermaster.	Connecticut.
Samuel Woods	....do.	Indiana.
John B. S. Todd	....do.	Kentucky.
William H. T. Walker	First Lieutenant.	Georgia.
James Monroe, jr.	....do.	Virginia.
Charles S. Lovell	....do.	Massachusetts
Henry W. Wharton	....do.	Dist. Colum.
Langdon C. Easton	....do.	Missouri.
Edward Johnson	....do.	Kentucky.
Thomas Hendrickson	....do.	Pennsylvania.
James Belger	....do. . Adjutant.	New York.
Rensselaer W. Foote	....do.	....do.
Lewis A. Armistead	....do.	N. Carolina.
Edward H. Fitzgerald	Second Lieutenant.	Pennsylvania.
Leonidas Wetmore	....do.	New York.
John D. Bacon	....do.	Maine.
Richard B. Garnett	....do.	Virginia.
Franklin F. Flint	....do.	N. Hampshire.
Anderson D. Nelson	....do.	Kentucky.
Randolph F. Ernst	....do.	Illinois.
Ralph W. Kirkham	....do.	Massachusetts
George W. Lay	....do.	Virginia.
Charles T. Baker	....do.	Connecticut.
Frederick T. Dent	Brevet 2d Lieutenant.	Missouri.
Norman Elting	....do.	New York.
William T. Burwell	....do.	Virginia.
William Read	....do.	Delaware.
Winfield S. Hancock	....do.	Pennsylvania.
James N. Ward	....do.	Kentucky.
William Rhea	....do.	Virginia.
SEVENTH REGIMENT OF INFANTRY.		
Matthew Arbuckle	Colonel, Brig. Gen. brevet.	Virginia.
William Hoffman	Lieutenant Colonel.	New York.
Jacob Brown	Major.	Massachusetts
Edgar S. Hawkins	Captain	New York.
Francis Lee	....do.	Pennsylvania.
Dixon S. Miles	....do.	Maryland.
Washington Seawell	....do. . . Major brevet.	Virginia.
Gabriel J. Rains	....do. ......do.	N. Carolina.
Stephen W. Moore	....do.	S. Carolina.
Theophilus H. Holmes	....do.	N. Carolina.
Richard H. Ross	....do.	Maryland.

ARMY LIST—*Eighth Infantry.*

Names.	Rank.	Where born.
Daniel P. Whiting	Captain	New York
Richard C. Gatlin	....do	N. Carolina
Gabriel R. Paul	First Lieutenant	Missouri
Seneca G. Simmons	....do	Vermont
Forbes Britton	....do	Virginia
Alexander Montgomery	....do	Pennsylvania
Nevil Hopson	....do	Kentucky
Charles Hanson	....do	Dist. Colum.
John C. Henshaw	....do	New York
Henry Little	....do	Maryland
James R. Scott	....do	Pennsylvania
Charles H. Humber	....do	Massachusetts
Richard S. Smith	Second Lieutenant	Pennsylvania
Francis N. Page	....do	Virginia
Levi Gantt	....do	Dist. Colum.
Napoleon J. T. Dana	....do	Maryland
Lafayette McLaws	....do	Georgia
Samuel B. Hayman	....do	Pennsylvania
Earl Van Dorn	....do	Mississippi
John M. Jones	....do	Virginia
Thomas R. Quimby	....do	Maine
Edmunds B. Holloway	....do	Kentucky
William K. Van Bokkelen	Brevet Second Lieutenant	New York
Alfred Crozet	....do	....do
Erastus B. Strong	....do	Arkansas
James M. Henry	....do	Kentucky
Henry B. Clitz	....do	New York
William H. Wood	....do	Massachusetts
EIGHTH REGIMENT OF INFANTRY.		
William J. Worth	Colonel, Brig. Gen. brevet	New York
Newman S. Clarke	Lieutenant Colonel	Connecticut
William G. Belknap	Major, Lieut. Col. brevet	New York
Thomas P. Gwynne	Captain	Virginia
George Wright	....do..Major brevet	Vermont
Joseph S. Worth	....do	Massachusetts
William R. Montgomery	....do	New Jersey
Richard B. Screven	....do	S. Carolina
William O. Kello	....do	Virginia
Edmund A. Ogden	....do..Ass't Quartermaster	New York
James M. Hill	....do......do	N. Hampshire
Henry McKavett	....do	New York
James V. Bomford	....do	....do
Isaac V. D. Reeve	First Lieutenant	....do
Collinson R. Gates	....do	....do
Larkin Smith	....do........Adjutant	Virginia

ARMY LIST—*Eighth Infantry, Chaplains, &c.*

Names.	Rank.	Where born.
John T. Sprague	First Lieutenant, Capt. brevet	Massachusetts
George Lincoln	do	do
William C. Browne	do	Maryland
Augustus L. Sheppard	do	Dist. Colum.
Joseph Selden	do	Virginia
Arthur T. Lee	do	Pennsylvania
Calvin Hetzel	do	do
Robert P. Maclay	Second Lieutenant	do
John G. Burbank	do	Massachusetts
John Beardsley	do	New York
Charles F. Morris	do	do
John D. Clark	do	N. Carolina
Charles D. Jordan	do	Massachusetts
James Longstreet	do	S. Carolina
James O. Handy	do	Rhode Island
Jacob J. Booker	do	Indiana
Theodore L. Chadbourne	do	Maine
Lafayette B. Wood	Brevet Second Lieutenant	Virginia
Henry M. Judah	do	Maryland
Charles G. Merchant	do	N. Hampshire
George Wainwright	do	Massachusetts
James G. S. Snelling	do	
Thomas J. Montgomery	do	Maine

Names of persons employed to officiate as Chaplains and Schoolmasters, under the provisions of the 18th section of the act of July 5, 1838.

Names.	Posts where officiating.	Where born.
Charles Reighley	Fort Gratiot, Michigan	
W. H. Brockway	Fort Brady......do.	
E. G. Gear	Fort Snelling, Upper Miss	
Leander Ker	Fort Leavenworth, Missouri	
D. McManus	Fort Gibson, Arkansas Ter	
M. L. Chevers	Fort Monroe, Virginia	
G. C. McRoberts	Fort McHenry, Maryland	
John O'Brien	Fort Mackinac, Michigan	
J. D. Carder	Fort Hamilton, New York	
John McVickar	Fort Columbus....do	
Henry Axtell	Fort Brooke, Florida	
William Scull	Fort Washita, Arkansas Ter	
J. L. Elliott	Fort Atkinson, Iowa Ter	

ARMY LIST—*Military Academy—Cadets.*

MILITARY ACADEMY.

Names.	Posts where officiating.	Where born.
Dennis H. Mahan	Professor of Engineering	Virginia
William H. C. Bartlett	Professor of Natural and Experimental Philosophy	Missouri
Albert E. Church	Professor of Mathematics	Connecticut
Jacob W. Bailey	Professor of Chemistry, Mineralogy, and Geology	Massachusetts
Martin P. Parks	Chaplain, and Professor of Geography, History, and Ethics	N. Carolina
Claudius Berard	Teacher of French	France
Henry R. Agnel	do	do
Robert W. Weir	Teacher of Drawing	
H. R. Hershberger	Instructor of Riding	Pennsylvania

CADETS.

Names.	Where born.	Names.	Where born.
FIRST CLASS—60.		Henry A. Ehninger	N. Y.
		Orren Chapman	N. Y.
Charles S. Stewart	At sea	Hamilton L. Shields	Va.
Charles E. Blunt	N. H.	Charles C. Gilbert	Ohio
John G. Foster	N. H.	Alexander P. Rodgers	N. Y.
George B. McClellan	Penn.	John Adams	Tenn.
George H. Derby	Mass.	George Stoneman, jr.	N. Y.
Edmund L. F. Hardcastle	Md.	Samuel D. Sturgis	Penn.
Jesse L. Reno	Penn.	Richard H. Rush	England.
Francis T. Bryan	N. C.	James Oakes	Penn.
Edmund Hayes	Penn.	Dabney H. Maury	Va.
Darius N. Couch	N. Y.	William D. Smith	Georgia.
Thomas M. Whedbee	N. C.	Innis N. Palmer	N. Y.
William Dutton	Conn.	David R. Jones	S. C.
Albert Magilton	Penn.	Delancy F. Jones	N. Y.
Edward C. Boynton	Vt.	Parmenas T. Turnley	Tenn.
Henry B. Sears	Mass.	James Stewart	S. C.
Rufus J. Bacon	Maine	Oliver H. P. Taylor	R. I.
John A. Brown	Md.	Clermont L. Best	N. Y.
Clarendon J. L. Wilson	Va.	George H. Gordon	Mass.
Thomas F. Castor	Penn.	Frederick Myers	Conn.
Thomas J. Jackson	Va.	George F. Evans	Maine
Truman Seymour	Vt.	John D. Wilkins	Penn.
Colville J. Minor	D. C.	Thomas R. McConnell	Georgia.
Marcus D. L. Simpson	N. Y.	Joseph N. G. Whistler	Wis.

ARMY LIST—*Cadets.*

Names.	Where born.
Cadmus M. Wilcox	N. C.
William H. Tyler	Va.
Mathew R. Stevenson	N. Y.
Alfred Gibbs	N. Y.
Nelson H. Davis	Mass.
Edmund Russell	Penn.
William M. Gardner	Georgia.
Archibald B. Botts	Va.
George S. Humphreys	Conn.
Thomas Easley	Va.
Samuel B. Maxcy	Ky.
George E. Pickett	Va.
SECOND CLASS—40.	
John C. Symmes	Ky.
John Hamilton	At sea.
Julian McAllister	N. Y.
Daniel T. Van Buren	N. Y.
Joseph J. Woods	Ohio.
John H. Dickerson	Ohio.
Orlando B. Willcox	Mich.
Samuel Chaflin	Illinois.
George W. Hazzard	Del.
Daniel Beltzhoover	Penn.
George Patten	S. C.
Ambrose E. Burnside	Indiana.
Romeyn B. Ayres	N. Y.
Richard H. Long	Penn.
Otis H. Tillinghast, jr.	N. Y.
John S. Mason	Ohio.
Horatio G. Gibson	Md.
John Gibbon	Penn.
James B. Fry	Illinois.
Henry M. Black	Penn.
Henry B. Hendushott	Ohio.
Montgomery P. Harrison	Indiana.
Lewis C. Hunt	Wis.
Charles F. Griffin	Ohio.
Egbert L. Viele	N. Y.
William Burns, jr.	Ohio.
Thomas H. Neill	Penn.
Augustus H. Seward	N. Y.
John De Russy	N. Y.
Tredwell Moore	Ohio.
Peter W. L. Plympton	Mo.
Edward F. Abbott	Ohio.
A. Gailbrath Miller	Penn.
Washington P. Street	Ky.
John Bonnycastle	Va.
Edward D. Blake	S. C.
George C. Barber	N. J.
Henry Heth	Va.
Anson J. Cook	Mass.
Ambrose P. Hill, jr.	Va.
THIRD CLASS—56.	
William P. Trowbridge	Mich.
Andrew J. Donelson	Tenn.
Nathaniel Michler, jr.	Penn.
James Holmes	N. C.
Walter H. Stevens	N. Y.
James C. Duane	N. Y.
Enoch Q. Fellows	N. H.
Thos. F. M. McLean	Mo.
Robert S. Williamson	N. Y.
William E. Jones	Va.
Rufus A. Roys	N. H.
James M. Haynes	Tenn.
Joseph C. Clark, jr	Tenn.
Grier Tallmadge	N. Y.
Charles W. Green	R. I.
William G. Gill	N. J.
George H. Paige	N. H.
Truman K. Walbridge	N. Y.
Thomas S. Rhett	S. C.
William A. Slaughter	Ky.
Reuben H. Adams	N. Y.
Richard J. Dodge	N. C.
Edward B. Bryan	S. C.
John C. Tidball	Vt.
Benjamin D. Forsythe	Ky.
Robert M. Russell	Tenn.
John Buford, jr.	Ky.
Ferdinand Paine	Maine.
George A. Lucas	Md.
Thomas K. Jackson	S. C.
John Withers	Tenn.
James G. Hillis	Mich.
Charles H. Tyler	Va.
George H. Stewart, jr.	Md.
Thomas D. Johns	Penn.
Charles H. Ogle	Penn.
Hugh B. Ewing	Ohio.
Arthur Forstall	Lou.
Nathaniel H. McLean	Ohio.
William N. R. Beall	Ky.

ARMY LIST—*Cadets.*

Names.	Where born.	Names.	Where born.
Duff C. Green	D. C.	Thomas J. Haines	N. H.
James W. D. Lyon	Georgia.	Samuel B. Holabird	Conn.
William L. Graham	Va.	Edward M. Hudson	Conn.
N. George Evans	S. C.	Francis Ingraham	Penn.
William T. Mechling	Penn.	George P. Ibrie	Penn.
Archibald G. Williams	Ky.	Richard Johnson	Ky.
Charles H. Poole	Mass.	Joseph W. Jones	N. C.
George W. Horoland	R. I.	John Kellogg	Mass.
Jesse Valentine	N. C.	William H. Lewis	Ala.
John C. Booth	Georgia.	William H. Miller	Ohio.
William F. Tilghman	Md.	John C. Moore	Tenn.
Samuel Chunu	Tenn.	Daniel W. McClure	Indiana.
James Casedy	Penn.	Lucian V. B. Martin	Ala.
John M. Heckaddy	Ky.	Louis H. Marshall	Va.
William H. Hill	N. C.	Chauncey McKeever	Md.
Daniel Huston, jr.	Maine.	John G. Murphy	N. Y.
		Elisha G. Marshall	N. Y.
FOURTH CLASS—81.		James McIntosh	Florida.
		Joseph H. McArthur	Mo.
Charles B. Alvord	N. Y.	Joseph C. Morehead	Ky.
Francis H. Bates	Md.	William A. Nimmo	Tenn.
David C. Bolles	Ohio.	Lewis Nicholds	Ala.
Stephen V. Benet	Florida.	Edward R. Platt	Vt.
Charles C. Butler	N. Y.	Albanus S. Powell	Penn.
George Brown, jr.	N. Y.	John G. Parke	Penn.
Absalam Baird	Penn.	Benjamin C. H. Phenix	Md.
Robert N. Boyd	Penn.	Delavan D. Perkins	N. Y.
George G. Boyd	Ky.	Henry Probasco	Ohio.
Seth M. Barton	Va.	Beverly Robertson	Va.
Milton Cogswell	Indiana.	Hiram Russell	N. Y.
Henry M. Clark	Ky.	Samuel M. Reynolds	Va.
William M. Campbell	S. C.	James P. Roy	Va.
Darius P. Clark	N. Y.	John B. Richards	Maine.
William H. Chipman	Ala.	Samuel H. Sibley	Lou.
Alfred Cumming	Georgia.	Melancthon Smith	Ala.
John B. Davis	S. C.	Alden Sargent	Maine.
Johnson K. Duncan	Penn.	Edward D. Stockton	Ky.
Edward A. Dunlap	Maine.	Rufus Saxton, jr.	Mass.
Beekman Du Barry	N. J.	William Silvey	Ohio.
Horace F. De Lano	Conn.	John Tammany	Penn.
Thomas C. English	Penn.	Washington C. Teris	Penn.
David A. Fox, jr.	Conn.	Joseph L. Tidball	Penn.
Thomas B. Fuqua	Va.	James M. Turner	Ohio.
John W. Frazer	Tenn.	John G. Taylor	Ky.
Charles W. Field	Ky.	Thomas G. Williams	Va.
Edward A. Gallagher	Va.	Watson Worthington	Mass.
John R. Gaines	S. C.	Thornton A. Washington	Va.
Newel Graham	N. Y.	Thomas Wright	Georgia.
Quincy A. Gilmore	Ohio.	Charles A. Wickliffe, jr.	Ky.
William A. Hacker	Illinois.	John H. Wise	Va.

ARMY LIST—*Pay of the Army,*

Rank and Grade.	Pay per month.	Subsis'e. No. of rations per day.	Forage. No. of horses allowed.	Servants. No. of servants allowed.
Major General	$200 00	15	3	4
Aid-de-camp, in addition to pay, &c., of Lieutenant	24 00	–	1	
Brigadier General	104 00	12	3	3
Aid-de-camp to Brigadier, in addition to pay, &c., of Lieutenant*	20 00	–	1	
Adjutant General	90 00	6	3	2
Assistant Adjutant General, with the rank of Major	60 00	4	3	2
Assistant Adjutant General, with the rank of Captain	50 00	4	1	1
Inspector General	90 00	6	3	2
Quartermaster General	104 00	12	3	3
Assistant Quartermaster General	90 00	6	3	2
Deputy Quartermaster General	75 00	5	3	2
Quartermaster	60 00	4	3	2
Assistant Quartermaster	50 00	4	1	1
Paymaster General, $2,500 per annum.				
Paymaster	60 00	4	1	2
Commissary General of Subsistence	90 00	6	3	2
Ass't Commissary General of Subsist.	75 00	5	3	2
Commissary of Subsistence, with the rank of Major	60 00	4	3	2
Commissary of Subsistence, with the rank of Captain	50 00	4	1	1
Assistant Commissary of Subsistence, in addition to pay, &c., of Lieutenant*	20 00			
Surgeon General....$2,500 per annum.				
Surgeon of ten years' service	60 00	8	1	2
Surgeon, less than ten years' service	60 00	4	1	2
Assistant Surgeon of ten years' service	50 00	8	1	1
Assistant Surgeon of five years' service	50 00	4	1	1
Assistant Surgeon, less than five years' service	33 33⅓	4	1	1
Professor of Natural and Experimental Philosophy	75 00	5	1	2
Assistant Professor of Natural and Experimental Philosophy	50 00	4	1	1
Professor of Mathematics, and Com'dt Corps of Cadets, each	60 00	4	1	2
Assistant Professor of Mathematics	50 00	4	1	1
Professor of Engineering	60 00	4	1	2
Assistant Professor of Engineering, and Instructor of Practical Engineering, each	50 00	4	1	1

* Entitled to but three rations per day as Lieutenant.

ARMY LIST—*Pay of the Army.*

Rank and Grade.	Pay per month.	Subsis'e. No. of rations per day.	Forage. No. of horses allowed.	Servants. No. of servants allowed.
Professor of Chemistry, Mineralogy, and Geology	$60 00	4	1	2
Assistant Professor of Chemistry, Mineralogy, and Geology, and Assistant Professor of Ethics, each	50 00	4	1	1
Chaplain, and Professor of Ethics	60 00	4	1	2
Instructor of Artillery and Cavalry tactics	50 00	4	1	1
Teacher of French Language	50 00	4	1	1
Teacher of Drawing	50 00	4	1	1
Master of the Sword	46 66	2		
Military Storekeeper, Clothing Department ... $1,250 per annum.				
Storekeeper of Ordnance, at Arsenals of Construction ... $1,250 per annum.				
Storekeeper of Ordnance, $800 per ann.				
Chaplain, not to exceed	40 00	4		
Colonel of Engineers, Topographical Engineers, Ordnance, or Dragoons	90 00	6	3	2
Lieut. Colonel of Engineers, Topographical Eng's, Ordnance, or Dragoons	75 00	5	3	2
Major of...do...do...do...do	60 00	4	3	2
Captain of...do...do...do	50 00	4	1	1
Captain of Dragoons	50 00	4	2	1
Lieutenant (1st and 2d) of Engineers, Topographical Eng's, and Ordnance	33 33⅓	4	1	1
Lieutenant of Dragoons	33 33⅓	4	2	1
Adjutant of Dragoons, in addition to pay, &c., of Lieutenant*	10 00			
Sergeant Major of Dragoons	17 00			
Quartermaster Sergeant of Dragoons	17 00			
Chief Bugler of Dragoons	17 00			
First Sergeant of Dragoons	16 00			
Sergeant of Dragoons	13 00			
Corporal of Dragoons	10 00			
Bugler of Dragoons	9 00			
Farrier and Blacksmith of Dragoons	11 00			
Private of Dragoons	8 00			
Master Armorer, Master Carriage-maker, Master Blacksmith, of Ordnance	30 00			
Armorer of Ordnance	16 00			
Blacksmith of Ordnance	16 00			
Carriage-maker of Ordnance	16 00			
Artificer of Ordnance	13 00			
Laborer of Ordnance	9 00			
Hospital Steward, at a post of more than four companies, pay of Ordnance Sergeant	18 00			

* Entitled to but three rations per day as Lieutenant.

ARMY LIST—*Pay of the Army.*

Rank and Grade.	Pay per month.	Subsis'e. No. of rations per day.	Forage. No. of horses allowed.	Servants. No. of servants allowed.
Hospital Steward, pay of First Sergeant	$16 00			
Matron	6 00			
ARTILLERY AND INFANTRY.				
Colonel	75 00	6	3	2
Lieutenant Colonel	60 00	5	3	2
Major	50 00	4	3	2
Adjutant, in addition to pay, &c., of Lieutenant*	10 00	–	1	
Captain	40 00	4	–	1
First Lieutenant	30 00	4	–	1
Second Lieutenant	25 00	4	–	1
Cadet	24 00			
Sergeant Major	17 00			
Quartermaster Sergeant	17 00			
Principal Musician of Infantry	17 00			
First Sergeant	16 00			
Ordnance Sergeant, in addition to pay of Sergeant	5 00			
Sergeant	13 00			
Corporal	9 00			
Artificer of Artillery	11 00			
Musician	8 00			
Private	7 00			

*Entitled to but three rations per day as Lieutenant.

Commanding officer of a company is entitled to $10 per month additional pay, for responsibility of arms and clothing.

Officers' subsistence is commuted at twenty cents per ration; forage at $8 per month for each horse, actually owned and kept in service.

Officers are entitled to the pay of private solder, $2 50 per month clothing, and one ration per day for each private servant actually kept in service.

Double rations are allowed to the Major General commanding the army, to the officers commanding military geographical departments, and to the commandant of each permanent or fixed post garrisoned with troops, including the Superintendent of the Military Academy.

Officers below the rank of Brigadier are entitled to one additional ration for every five years they may have served as such.

NAVY DEPARTMENT.

Names and offices.	Where employed.	Where born.	Compensation.
			Dol. cts.
SECRETARY'S OFFICE.			
Secretary of the Navy.			
George Bancroft	Washington	Massachusetts	6000 00
John Appleton, Chief Clerk	do	do	2000 00
Charles Eames, Principal Corresponding Clerk	do	do	1500 00
L. B. Hardin, Registering Clerk	do	N. Carolina	1400 00
B. Homans, Warrant Clerk	do	France	1200 00
Jas. Callaghan, Assistant Corresponding Clerk	do	Pennsylvania	1200 00
Geo. S. Watkins, Assistant Corresponding Clerk	do	do	1200 00
C. W. Welsh, Additional Clerk	do	Massachusetts	1200 00
Henry L. Harvey.....do	do	New York	1200 00
Abel B. Upshur, Recording Clk	do	Virginia	1000 00
Albert G. Allen.......do	do	N. Hampshire	1000 00
John J. Berret.......do	do	Maryland	1000 00
W. Brenton Boggs, Miscellaneous Clerk	do	New Jersey	1000 00
Samuel Mickum, Messenger	do	Maryland	650 00
Lindsay Muse, Asst. Mess	do	Virginia	400 00
BUREAU OF NAVY YARDS AND DOCKS.			
Chief of Bureau.			
Lewis Warrington	do	do	3500 00
Wm. G. Ridgely, Chief Clerk	do	Maryland	1400 00
Stephen Gough........Clerk	do	do	1000 00
Wm. P. Moran.........do	do	Virginia	800 00
Geo. F. de la Roche, Draught'n	do	New York	1000 00
Charles Hunt......Messenger	do	Massachusetts	700 00
BUREAU OF ORDNANCE AND HYDROGRAPHY.			
Chief of Bureau.			
W. M. Crane	do	New Jersey	3500 00
Gustavus Harrison.....Clerk	do	Virginia	1200 00
Joseph P. McCorkle.....do	do	Pennsylvania	1000 00
Charles K. King........do	do	Virginia	1000 00

NAVY DEPARTMENT—*Clerks, Messengers, &c.*

Names and offices.	Where employed.	Where born.	Compensation.
			Dol. cts.
Geo. W. Kimberly.....Clerk..	Washington......	Ohio..........	1000 00
Conrad Schwarz..Draughtsman	....do...........	Germany.....	1000 00
John McArann......Messenger	....do...........	Ireland.......	700 00
BUREAU OF CONSTRUCTION, EQUIPMENT AND REPAIR.			
Chief of Bureau.			
Charles Morris.................	....do...........	Connecticut ..	3000 00
Philip C. Johnson, Chief Clerk..	....do...........	N. Hampshire	1400 00
Henry J. Wilde.........Clerk...	....do...........	Maine........	1200 00
Samuel A. Allen.........do....	....do...........	Massachusetts	1200 00
John H. Reiley..........do....	....do...........	Pennsylvania .	1000 00
Henry J. Drayton........do....	....do...........	.....do......	1000 00
James Selden............do....	....do...........	Dist. Colum..	1000 00
Lauriston Ward.........do....	....do...........	Maine	1000 00
Clement Humphreys..Draught'n	....do...........	Pennsylvania..	1000 00
Edward Chapman...............	....do...........	Maryland	600 00
Edmund Brook......Messenger	....do...........	Virginia......	700 00
BUREAU OF PROVISIONS AND CLOTHING.			
Chief of Bureau.			
W. Branford Shubrick..........	....do...........	S. Carolina...	3000 00
W. S. Parrott, Chief Clerk......	....do...........	Virginia......	1400 00
Thomas Fillebrown....Clerk..	....do...........	Maine........	1200 00
Joseph Pugh..............do....	....do...........	Pennsylvania..	1200 00
H. A. Goldsborough ....do....	....do...........	Dist. of Col...	800 00
Ignatius Lucas......Messenger	....do...........	Maryland	700 00
BUREAU OF MEDICINE AND SURGERY.			
Chief of Bureau.			
Thomas Harris..................	....do...........	Pennsylvania .	2500 00
Robert Woodworth, Assistant to Chief.....................	....do...........	New York....	1400 00
Moses Poor...............Clerk..	....do...........	N. Hampshire	1200 00
S. A. Elliot...............do....	....do...........	New York	800 00
Marsh B. Clark.....Messenger	....do...........	Pennsylvania..	700 00

NAVY LIST—*Captains.*

Names.	Where born.	Duty or Station.
CAPTAINS.		
James Barron	Virginia	Waiting orders.
Charles Stewart	Pennsylvania	Waiting orders.
Jacob Jones	Delaware	Port Captain, New York.
Charles Morris	Connecticut	Chief of Bureau of Construction, Equipment and Repairs.
Lewis Warrington	Virginia	Chief of Bureau of Yards and Docks.
William M. Crane	New Jersey	Chief of Bureau of Ordnance and Hydrography.
James Biddle	Pennsylvania	Commanding East India squadron.
Charles G. Ridgely	Maryland	Waiting orders.
John Downes	Massachusetts	Port Captain, Boston.
Jesse D. Elliott	Maryland	Commanding navy yard, Philad'a.
Stephen Cassin	Pennsylvania	Waiting orders.
James Renshaw	do.	Waiting orders.
Alex'r S. Wadsworth	Maine	Inspector of Ordnance.
George C. Read	Ireland	Waiting orders.
Henry E. Ballard	Maryland	Waiting orders.
John B. Nicolson	Virginia	Commanding navy yard, Boston.
Jesse Wilkinson	do.	Commanding navy yard, Norfolk.
T. Ap Catesby Jones	do.	Waiting orders.
Wm. Compton Bolton	England	Port Captain, Norfolk.
Wm. B. Shubrick	South Carolina	Chief of Bureau of Provisions and Clothing.
Charles W. Morgan	Virginia	Governor of Naval Asylum, Philad.
Lawrence Kearney	New Jersey	Waiting orders.
Foxhall A. Parker	Virginia	On leave.
Edward R. McCall	S. Carolina	Waiting orders.
Daniel Turner	New York	Comm'ng squadron, coast of Brazil.
David Conner	Pennsylvania	Commanding Home squadron.
William M. Hunter	do.	Waiting orders.
John D. Sloat	New York	Commanding Pacific squadron.
Matthew C. Perry	Rhode Island	Special service.
Charles W. Skinner	Pennsylvania	Commanding African squadron.
John Thomas Newton	Virginia	Waiting orders.
Joseph Smith	Massachusetts	Command'g Mediterranean squad'n.
Lawrence Rousseau	Louisiana	Commanding frigate Columbia.
George W. Storer	N. Hampshire	Command'g navy yard, Portsmouth.
Francis H. Gregory	Connecticut	Commanding frigate Raritan.
Philip F. Voorhees	New Jersey	Under suspension.
Benjamin Cooper	do.	Waiting orders.
David Geisinger	Maryland	Waiting orders.
Robert F. Stockton	New Jersey	Commanding frigate Congress.
Isaac McKeever	Pennsylvania	On leave.
John P. Zantzinger	do.	Waiting orders.
William D. Salter	New York	Waiting orders.
Charles S. McCauley	Pennsylvania	Waiting orders.
Thomas M. Newell	Georgia	Waiting orders.

NAVY LIST—*Commanders.*

Names.	Where born.	Duty or Station.
Elie A. F. Lavalette..	Virginia........	Waiting orders.
Thomas T. Webb......	.....do.......	Waiting orders.
John Percival.........	Massachusetts	Commanding frigate Constitution.
John H. Aulick.......	Virginia.......	Comm'ng navy yard, Washington.
William V. Taylor...	Rhode Island.	Waiting orders.
Bladen Dulany........	Virginia.......	Waiting orders.
Silas H. Stringham...	New York....	Comm't navy yard, New York.
Isaac Mayo...........	Maryland	Waiting orders.
William Mervine......	Pennsylvania .	Commanding sloop Cyane.
Thomas Crabb........	Maryland	Waiting orders.
Thomas Paine.........	Rhode Island..	Waiting orders.
James Armstrong.....	Kentucky	Waiting orders.
Joseph Smoot.........	Maryland	Waiting orders.
Samuel L. Breese......	New York....	Commanding frigate Cumberland.
Benjamin Page........	England.......	Waiting orders.
John Gwinn..........	Maryland	Commanding frigate Potomac.
Thomas W. Wyman.	Massachusetts	Commanding Columbus 74.
Andrew Fitzhugh....	Virginia.......	Commanding steamer Mississippi.
Wm. K. Latimer......	Maryland	Commandant Pensacola yard.
Hiram Paulding......	New York....	Commanding sloop Vincennes.
Uriah P. Levy........	Pennsylvania .	Waiting orders.
Charles Boarman.....	Maryland	Waiting orders.
French Forrest........	.....do.......	Waiting orders.
William Jamesson....	Virginia.......	Waiting orders.
COMMANDERS.		
Charles Gauntt.......	New Jersey...	Navy yard, Philadelphia.
William Ramsay.....	Virginia.......	Waiting orders.
H. Henry............	Maryland	Commanding sloop Plymouth.
Samuel W. Downing..	New Jersey...	On leave.
Henry W. Ogden	......do.....	Special duty.
Thomas A. Conover..	.....do.......	Commanding rendezvous, Philad'a.
John C. Long........	N. Hampshire	On leave.
John H. Graham.....	Vermont	Command'g rendezvous, New York.
James M. McIntosh..	Georgia.......	Inspector of Provisions at Norfolk.
Josiah Tattnall.......	......do.....	Waiting orders.
Hugh N. Page.......	Virginia......	Commanding sloop Levant.
William Inman......	New York....	Commanding steamer Michigan.
Stephen Champlin....	Rhode Island.	Waiting orders.
Joel Abbot...........	Massachusetts	Waiting orders.
Lewis E. Simonds....	......do.....	Commanding sloop Marion.
John M. Dale........	Pennsylvania .	Waiting orders.
Harrison H. Cocke...	Virginia......	Waiting orders.
Wm. J. McCluney....	Pennsylvania .	Commanding sloop John Adams.
John B. Montgomery.	New Jersey...	Commanding sloop Portsmouth.
Horace B. Sawyer....	Vermont......	Inspector of Provisions at George-town, D. C.
Cornelius K. Stribling.	South Carolina	Special duty.
Joshua R. Sands......	New York....	Commanding sloop Falmouth.

NAVY LIST—*Commanders.*

Names.	Where born.	Duty or Station.
John Jay Young......	New York....	Commanding rendezvous, Baltimore.
Charles H. Bell......	.....do......	Commanding sloop Yorktown.
Abraham Bigelow....	Massachusetts	Waiting orders.
Frederick Varnum....	.....do......	Commanding receiving vessel, Phila.
Joseph R. Jarvis.....	.....do......	Commanding brig Lawrence.
Thomas W. Freelon..	New York....	On leave.
Samuel W. Le Compte	Maryland	Waiting orders.
Charles T. Platt......	New York....	Waiting orders.
Wm. M. Armstrong..	Kentucky	Commanding rendezvous, Norfolk.
William F. Shields...	Georgia.......	Waiting orders.
Garrett J. Pendergrast	Kentucky.....	Commanding sloop Boston.
William C. Nicholson.	Maryland	Commanding rendezvous, Boston.
James B. Cooper.....	New Jersey ..	Waiting orders.
Ed. W. Carpender...	New York....	Navy yard, Norfolk.
John L. Saunders....	Virginia.......	Commanding sloop St. Mary's.
Joseph B. Hull.......	New York....	Commanding sloop Warren.
John Stone Paine.....	Maine	On leave.
Joseph Morehead	Maryland	Waiting orders.
Thomas Petigru......	South Carolina	Waiting orders.
John S. Chauncey....	New York....	Waiting orders.
Irvine Shubrick......	South Carolina	Commanding sloop Saratoga.
John Kelly..........	Pennsylvania .	Waiting orders.
Edmund Byrne.......	.....do......	Waiting orders.
William H. Gardner..	Maryland	Waiting orders.
David G. Farragut....	Tennessee....	Receiving ship, Norfolk.
Richard S. Pinckney..	South Carolina	Commanding station, Charleston.
Stephen B. Wilson...	New York....	Navy yard, Boston.
Edward C. Rutledge..	South Carolina	Waiting orders.
William S. Harris....	Kentucky	Waiting orders.
Thos. Aloysius Dornin	Ireland	Navy yard, Washington.
Robt. B. Cunningham	Virginia......	Commanding sloop Jamestown.
James Glynn........	Pennsylvania .	Waiting orders.
Joseph Myers........	N. Carolina...	Waiting orders.
William C. Wetmore.	New York.....	Waiting orders.
Thomas R. Gedney...	South Carolina	Coast survey.
John Bubier.........	Massachusetts	Waiting orders.
Victor M. Randolph..	Virginia.......	Waiting orders.
Jacob Crowninshield..	Massachusetts	Waiting orders.
Frederick Engle......	Pennsylvania .	Commanding steamer Princeton.
John Rudd...........	Rhode Island .	Inspector of Provisions at Norfolk.
Robert Ritchie.......	Pennsylvania .	Frigate Columbia.
William W. McKean.	.....do......	Waiting orders.
Franklin Buchanan...	Maryland	Sup't Naval School, Annapolis, Md.
Samuel Mercer.......	.....do......	Waiting orders.
Charles Lowndes.....	.....do......	Waiting orders.
L. M. Goldsborough..	Dist. Colum'a.	Waiting orders.
George N. Hollins....	Maryland	Navy yard, Pensacola.
Duncan N. Ingraham.	South Carolina	Commanding brig Somers.
John Marston........	Massachusetts	Waiting orders.

NAVY LIST—*Commanders.*

Names.	Where born.	Duty or Station.
Henry Bruce........	Maine	Commanding brig Truxtun.
Henry A. Adams......	Pennsylvania .	Steamer Mississippi.
James D. Knight......	South Carolina	Waiting orders.
Joseph Mattison.......	New Jersey...	Waiting orders.
William S. Walker...	N. Hampshire	Receiving ship at Boston.
Alex'r S. Mackenzie..	New York....	Waiting orders.
George F. Pearson...	N. Hampshire	Navy yard, Portsmouth.
James T. Gerry.......	Massachusetts	On leave.
John S. Nicholas.....	Virginia........	Com'g receiving ship at Baltimore.
Samuel F. Dupont....	New Jersey..	Frigate Congress.
William L. Hudson..	New York....	Navy yard, New York.
James P. Wilson.....	Maryland	Waiting orders.
George A. Magruder..	Virginia........	Ordnance duty.
John Pope...........	Massachusetts	Waiting orders.
Levin M. Powell......	Virginia........	Ordnance duty.
Charles Wilkes.......	New York....	Special duty.
Elisha Peck..........	Connecticut....	Waiting orders.
Thomas J. Manning..	New Jersey ..	Waiting orders.
William Pearson.....	.....do.......	Waiting orders.
William L. Howard..	.....do.......	Waiting orders.
William P. Piercy....	Pennsylvania .	Waiting orders.
Richard A. Jones.....	New York....	Waiting orders.
Thomas J. Leib......	Pennsylvania .	Waiting orders.
Thomas O. Selfridge..	Massachusetts	Columbus 74.
Henry Eagle..........	New York....	Waiting orders.
Andrew K. Long.....	Maryland	Waiting orders.
LIEUTENANTS.		
James P. Oellers......	Pennsylvania..	Navy yard, Philadelphia.
Charles E. Crowly....	South Carolina	Waiting orders.
Wm. A. C. Farragut..	Tennessee....	Waiting orders.
Frank Ellery.........	Rhode Island .	Waiting orders.
Arthur Lewis........	Virginia......	On furlough.
G. J. Van Brunt......	New Jersey ..	Waiting orders.
Henry Pinkney......	Maryland	Waiting orders.
William M. Glendy..	Virginia.......	Waiting orders.
John H. Little.......	Maryland	Waiting orders.
George P. Upshur....	Virginia.......	Rendezvous, Norfolk.
George S. Blake.......	Massachusetts	Coast Survey.
Zach. F. Johnston....	Maryland	Navy Yard, Washington.
William Green.......	Virginia......	Waiting orders.
Samuel Barron.......	.....do......	Ordnance duty.
Timothy G. Benham..	Connecticut....	Waiting orders.
Alex. G. Gordon.....	Dist. Colum..	Receiving ship at New York.
Albert G. Slaughter...	Virginia......	Bureau of Yards and Docks.
Oscar Bullus.........	Dist. Colum..	Rendezvous, New York.
Charles H. Jackson...	Georgia......	Waiting orders.

NAVY LIST—*Lieutenants.*

Names.	Where born.	Duty or station.
Andrew A. Harwood	Pennsylvania	Ordnance duty.
Theodorus Bailey	New York	Rendezvous, New York.
Hugh Y. Purviance	Maryland	Waiting orders.
George Adams	Delaware	Receiving ship at New York.
Cadwalader Ringgold	Maryland	Inspector of Provisions at Baltimore.
John Graham	Kentucky	Waiting orders.
Wm. F. Lynch	Virginia	Navy Yard, Pensacola.
Henry W. Morris	New York	Comm'ding store-ship Southampton.
Isaac S. Sterett	Maryland	Rendezvous, Baltimore.
Francis B. Ellison	New York	Comm'ding store-ship Lexington.
Edward B. Boutwell	Virginia	On furlough.
John E. Bispham	Pennsylvania	Navy Yard, Philadelphia.
Sidney Smith Lee	Virginia	Frigate Potomac.
Wm. C. Whittle	do.	Commanding steamer Col. Harney.
John H. Marshall	do.	Frigate Columbia.
Thompson D. Shaw	Pennsylvania	Rendezvous, Philadelphia.
Robert D. Thorburn	Virginia	Waiting orders.
Samuel Lockwood	Connecticut	Navy Yard, Portsmouth, N. H.
Lloyd B. Newell	Georgia	Waiting orders.
Hillary H. Rhodes	Dist. Colum.	Waiting orders.
William S. Ogden	New York	Waiting orders.
Frederick A. Neville	Virginia	Waiting orders.
Charles C. Turner	do.	Commanding store-ship Erie.
John Manning	N. Carolina	Waiting orders.
James L. Lardner	Pennsylvania	Waiting orders.
Robert G. Robb	Virginia	Commanding store-ship Relief.
Fitzallen Deas	New York	Waiting orders.
John Colhoun	Pennsylvania	Navy Yard, New York.
Charles W. Chauncey	New York	Sloop Falmouth.
Law. Pennington	Pennsylvania	Commanding brig Bainbridge.
Thomas T. Craven	Dist. of Col.	Waiting orders.
Andrew H. Foot	Connecticut	Frigate Cumberland.
William W. Hunter	Pennsylvania	Special duty.
Amasa Paine	Vermont	Frigate Constitution.
Nathaniel W. Duke	Kentucky	Waiting orders.
Edward G. Tilton	Delaware	Waiting orders.
James H. Ward	Connecticut	Naval school, Annapolis, Md.
Henry K. Hoff	Pennsylvania	Waiting orders.
Murray Mason	Dist. Colum.	Waiting orders.
Charles H. Davis	Massachusetts	Special duty.
Stephen Johnston	Indiana	Columbus 74.
Jonathan W. Swift	Massachusetts	Waiting orders.
Charles M. Armstrong	New York	Waiting orders.
Ebenezer Farrand	do.	Waiting orders.
Henry H. Bell	N. Carolina	Waiting orders.
Wm. Smith	Kentucky	Steamer Mississippi.
Charles H. McBlair	Maryland	Rendezvous, Baltimore.
James M. Watson	Virginia	Special duty.
John W. Livingston	New York	Frigate Congress.

NAVY LIST—*Lieutenants.*

Names.	Where born.	Duty or Station.
Junius J. Boyle	Maryland	Naval Storekeeper, Mahon.
Wm. E. Hunt	New Jersey	Commanding brig Porpoise.
Robert L. Browning	Kentucky	Waiting orders.
Jona. D. Ferris	New York	Waiting orders.
Archibald B. Fairfax	Virginia	Ordnance duty.
Neil M. Howison	do.	Commanding schooner Shark.
Peter Turner	Rhode Island	Brazil squadron.
John A. Davis	N. Carolina	Navy Yard, Norfolk.
Henry K. Thatcher	Maine	Receiving ship at Boston.
James H. Rowan	New York	Receiving ship at New York.
Samuel E. Munn	Maryland	Waiting orders.
Wm. H. Noland	Virginia	Waiting orders.
Wm. D. Porter	Louisiana	Waiting orders.
Wm. McBlair	Maryland	Waiting orders.
John S. Missroon	S. Carolina	Sloop Portsmouth.
James Noble	Kentucky	Frigate Cumberland.
Richard L. Page	Virginia	Rendezvous, Norfolk.
Frederick Chatard	Maryland	Commanding schooner Flirt.
Gabl. G. Williamson	Virginia	Frigate Columbia.
Benjamin J. Totten	West Indies	Waiting orders.
Harry Ingersoll	Pennsylvania	Sloop John Adams.
Charles G. Hunter	New Jersey	On leave, (in Europe.)
Arthur Sinclair	Virginia	Commanding schooner On-ka-hy-e.
Robert B. Hitchcock	Connecticut	Frigate Savannah.
C. H. A. H. Kennedy	Virginia	Sloop St. Mary's.
Thomas W. Brent	Dist. Colum.	Navy Yard, Pensacola.
Geo. M. Bache	Pennsylvania	Coast Survey.
Joseph Lanman	Connecticut	Ordnance duty.
John K. Mitchell	N. Carolina	Waiting orders.
Thomas Turner	Virginia	Rendezvous, Philadelphia.
Henry Moor	Maine	Navy Yard, New York.
Charles H. Poor	Massachusetts	Navy Yard, Washington.
Jas. Findlay Schenck	Ohio	Frigate Congress.
Lewis G. Keith	Virginia	Waiting orders.
Matthew F. Maury	do.	Supt. Hydrographical Office.
Timothy A. Hunt	Connecticut	On leave.
Sylvanus Wm. Godon	Pennsylvania	Sloop Boston.
James S. Palmer	New Jersey	Waiting orders.
William Radford	Virginia	Sloop Warren.
Samuel F. Hazard	Rhode Island	Waiting orders.
John M. Berrien	Georgia	Frigate Potomac.
George A. Prentiss	N. Hampshire	Waiting orders.
John C. Carter	Virginia	Steamer Mississippi.
George Hurst	Pennsylvania	Waiting orders.
Alfred Taylor	Virginia	Sloop Boston.
Samuel Phillips Lee	do.	Waiting orders.
John P. Gillis	Delaware	Waiting orders.
Simon B. Bissell	Vermont	Waiting orders.
Samuel Swartwout	New York	Sloop Vincennes.

NAVY LIST—*Lieutenants.*

Names.	Where born.	Duty or station.
John J. Glasson	New York	Store-ship Lexington.
Raphael Semmes, jr.	Maryland	Home squadron.
James F. Miller	N. Hampshire	Waiting orders.
James P. McKinstry	New York	Steamer Michigan.
Wm. A. Wurts	New Jersey	Frigate Potomac.
Henry A. Steele	Delaware	Sloop Yorktown.
John M. Gardner	Pennsylvania	Waiting orders.
Spencer C. Gist	Tennessee	Waiting orders.
Charles Heywood	Maine	Navy Yard, New York.
Oliver S. Glisson	Ohio	Sloop Saratoga.
John A. Dahlgren	Pennsylvania	Frigate Cumberland.
Stephen C. Rowan	Ireland	Sloop Cyane.
Edward R. Thomson	Pennsylvania	Home squadron.
James T. McDonough	Delaware	Waiting orders.
Guert Gansevoort	New York	Sloop John Adams.
Robert Handy	Rhode Island	Sloop Levant.
Henry Darcantel	Louisiana	Sloop Plymouth.
Burritt Shepard	Connecticut	Frigate Raritan.
Charles Green	do	Waiting orders.
E. Lloyd Handy	Maryland	Receiving vessel at Philadelphia.
Melancton Smith	New York	Steamer Col. Harney.
Francis Huger	S. Carolina	On leave, (sick.)
Wm. C. Chaplin	Pennsylvania	Frigate Constitution.
Cicero Price	Kentucky	Sloop Marion.
John R. Goldsborough	Dist. Colum.	Coast survey.
Charles S. Boggs	New Jersey	Waiting orders.
A. H. Kilty	Maryland	Waiting orders.
Wm. Chandler	Dist. Colum.	Sloop Jamestown.
John A. Russ	Maine	Sloop Falmouth.
Theodore P. Green	Vermont	Frigate Congress.
John R. Tucker	Dist. of Col.	On leave.
Richard W. Meade	Spain	On leave.
Thos. Jefferson Page	Virginia	Hydrographical Office.
George Minor	do	Frigate Savannah.
Percival Drayton	S. Carolina	Columbus 74.
Wm. P. Griffin	Virginia	Frigate Columbia.
Oliver Tod	Pennsylvania	Columbus 74.
Robert F. Pinkney	Maryland	Frigate Savannah.
Thomas R. Rootes	Virginia	Frigate Potomac.
Edward M. Yard	New Jersey	Receiving vessel, Philadelphia.
John T. McLaughlin	Maryland	Waiting orders.
James M. Gilliss	Dist. of Col.	Special duty.
Alexander Gibson	Virginia	Frigate Raritan.
William S. Young	Dist. Colum.	Inspector of Provisions at Phila.
William W. Bleecker	New York	Steam ship Princeton.
Joseph F. Green	Maine	Rendezvous, Boston.
Zachariah Holland	Maryland	On furlough.
John De Camp	New Jersey	Sloop Boston.
Bushrod W. Hunter	Dist. Colum.	Navy yard, Norfolk.

NAVY LIST—*Lieutenants*

Names.	Where born.	Duty or Station.
M. G. L. Claiborne...	Tennessee....	Waiting orders.
Charles W. Pickering.	N. Hampshire.	On leave.
Overton Carr........	Dist. Colum..	On leave, (in Europe.)
Luther Stoddard.....	New York....	Sloop Marion.
William M. Walker..	Maryland....	Waiting orders.
George R. Gray......	Delaware.....	Sloop Jamestown.
Robert E. Johnson...	N. Carolina...	Under suspension.
John A. Winslow....	....do.......	Waiting orders.
Benj. More Dove.....	Virginia......	On leave.
Bernard J. Moeller...	Pennsylvania..	Waiting orders.
Henry Walke........	Virginia......	On leave.
Thornton A. Jenkins..	....do.......	Special duty.
Joseph C. Walsh.....	Pennsylvania .	Brazil squadron.
John Rodgers........	Maryland....	Special duty.
John B. Marchand....	Pennsylvania..	On leave.
Wm. Rogers Taylor..	Rhode Island..	Sloop St. Mary's.
Henry J. Hartstene ..	S. Carolina...	On leave.
Benjamin F. Sands...	Maryland....	Hydrographical office.
Henry French.......	Massachusetts	Columbus 74.
William Leigh.......	Virginia......	On leave.
Samuel Larkin.......	N. Hampshire.	Navy yard, Portsmouth.
Henry S. Stellwagen..	Virginia......	Waiting orders.
Jas. L. Henderson....	....do.......	African squadron.
Daniel B. Ridgely....	Kentucky.....	Brig Lawrence.
John L. Ring........	S. Carolina...	Sloop Saratoga.
Robert Emmett Hooe.	Virginia......	Waiting orders.
William T. Muse....	N. Carolina...	On leave.
William H. Brown...	Maryland.....	Waiting orders.
Charles Steedman....	South Carolina	Sloop St. Mary's.
Wm. Lewis Herndon.	Virginia......	Hydrographical office.
John P. Parker......	N. Hampshire.	Waiting orders.
James Alden, jr......	Maine	Frigate Constitution.
Augustus L. Case....	New York....	On leave.
Roger Perry.........	Maryland....	Waiting orders.
Joseph W. Revere....	Massachusetts	Sloop Cyane.
Alex'r M. Pennock...	Virginia	Navy yard, Norfolk.
George F. Emmons...	Vermont.....	Sloop Boston.
Edward Middleton....	South Carolina	Waiting orders.
Montgomery Lewis...	Pennsylvania .	Steam ship Princeton.
George M. White....	Georgia......	Brig Somers.
Thomas T. Hunter...	Virginia......	Special duty.
Albert A. Holcomb...	New Jersey ..	Sloop John Adams.
Gustavus H. Scott....	Virginia......	On leave.
Richard Forrest......	Dist. Colum..	Sloop Portsmouth.
David McDougal.....	Ohio.........	Steamer Michigan.
Charles F. McIntosh.	Virginia......	Sloop Vincennes.
James W. Cooke.....	N. Carolina...	Frigate Constitution.
C. F. M. Spotswood..	Virginia......	Waiting orders.
Henry C. Flagg......	Connecticut...	On furlough.

NAVY LIST—*Lieutenants.*

Names.	Where born.	Duty or Station.
Daniel F. Dulany....	Virginia......	Waiting orders.
George L. Selden.....	.....do......	Sloop Cyane.
William H. Ball......	Dist. of Col...	Special duty.
Charles C. Barton....	Pennsylvania..	Sloop Marion.
John J. B. Walbach..	N. Hampshire	Sloop Jamestown.
Oliver H. Perry......	Rhode Island.	Navy yard, Boston.
Charles W. Morris...	Massachusetts	Sloop St. Mary's.
Joshua Humphreys ..	Pennsylvania .	On leave.
Richard Bache.......	.....do......	Special duty.
John B. Dale........	Massachusetts	Frigate Constitution.
Stephen Decatur......	New Jersey ..	On leave, (sick.)
William L. Maury...	Virginia......	Sloop Warren.
David D. Porter......	Pennsylvania .	Hydrographical office.
John J. Almy........	Rhode Island .	Hydrographical office.
Edward C. Bowers...	Connecticut...	Waiting orders.
Otway H. Berryman..	Virginia......	On furlough.
Thomas A. Budd.....	New York....	Special duty.
Andrew F. V. Gray..	West Indies..	Frigate Congress.
Edmund Jenkins.....	Maryland	Waiting orders.
T. Augustus M. Craven	N. Hampshire	On furlough.
Dominick Lynch.....	New York....	Sloop Plymouth.
Francis B. Renshaw..	Pennsylvania .	Brig Lawrence.
Horace N. Harrison..	Georgia.......	On leave.
James H. North......	South Carolina	Waiting orders.
Robert B. Pegram....	Virginia......	On leave.
Edward C. Ward....	New York....	Receiving ship at New York.
Richard C. Cogdell ...	S. Carolina...	African squadron.
Edwin J. De Haven..	Pennsylvania..	Brig Somers.
Charles Thomas......	Maryland	Waiting orders.
Richard L. Tilghman.	.....do......	Frigate Congress.
James H. Strong.....	New York....	Columbus 74.
J. Madison Frailey...	Maryland	On leave.
Carlisle P. Patterson..	Mississippi...	Coast survey.
Augustus S. Baldwin.	New Jersey ..	Waiting orders.
Edmund T. Shubrick.	New York....	Frigate Raritan.
William B. Whiting..	.....do.......	Hydrographical office.
Charles Hunter......	Rhode Island.	Sloop Saratoga.
Benjamin F. Shattuck.	N. Hampshire	Navy yard, Boston.
Thomas M. Brasher..	New York....	On leave.
George T. Sinclair....	Virginia......	Schooner On-ka-hy-e.
John Mooney........	Maine	Receiving ship at Boston.
Samuel R. Knox.....	Massachusetts	Sloop Plymouth.
Enoch G. Parrott.....	N. Hampshire	Frigate Congress.
James McCormick....	Ohio.........	Receiving ship at Norfolk.
Richard S. Trapier...	South Carolina	Frigate Savannah.
Richard Wainwright..	Massachusetts	Frigate Columbia.
George M. Totten....	New York....	Special duty.
William Ross Gardner	Georgia......	Sloop Falmouth.
William B. Renshaw..	New York....	Sloop Warren.

NAVY LIST—*Lieutenants.*

Names.	Where born.	Duty or Station.
Carter B. Poindexter..	Virginia........	Home squadron.
Henry T. Wingate.....	Maine.........	Waiting orders.
Alonzo B. Davis.......	Louisiana	Sloop Saratoga.
Richard L. Love.......	Virginia.......	Pensacola, (invalid.)
William Reynolds.....	Pennsylvania .	Frigate Cumberland.
Woodhull S. Schenck.	Ohio..........	Sloop Portsmouth.
James L. Parker.......	Pennsylvania.	Waiting orders.
Lewis C. Sartori.......	New Jersey ..	Mediterranean squadron.
Edmund Lanier.......	Virginia	Receiving ship at Baltimore,
John H. Sherburne...	N. Hampshire	Receiving ship at Boston.
Fabius Stanly.........	N. Carolina...	Steam ship Princeton.
Latham B. Avery....	Connecticut...	Waiting orders.
James B. Lewis.......	Virginia.......	Frigate Cumberland.
George W. Chapman.	Pennsylvania .	Navy yard, Philadelphia.
Wm. P. McArthur...	Missouri......	Coast survey.
William S. Drayton..	S. Carolina...	Frigate Columbia.
Simon F. Blunt.......	Virginia.......	Brig Truxtun.
Wm. Taylor Smith...	.....do.......	On leave.
William May.........	Dist. Colum'a.	Sloop Plymouth.
Henry H. Lewis......	Virginia.......	On leave.
Joseph P. Sanford....	.....do.......	Frigate Cumberland.
George W. Harrison .	West Indies ..	Sloop Cyane.
James F. Armstrong..	New Jersey ..	Sloop Vincennes.
Montgomery Hunt...	New York....	On leave.
Henry Eld, jr.........	Connecticut....	Special duty.
John Contee..........	Maryland	Receiving ship at Baltimore.
Joseph H. Adams....	Massachusetts	Sloop Levant.
William A. Parker...	N. Hampshire	Steamer Mississippi.
James D. Johnston...	Kentucky	Frigate Columbia.
John N. Maffit........	Ireland	Coast survey.
Washing'n Gwathmey	England.......	Home squadron.
Wm. Ronckendorff...	Pennsylvania .	Waiting orders.
William B. Beverley..	Virginia.......	Waiting orders.
John Hall...........	New York....	Coast survey.
Francis Lowry.......	Vermont.......	Sloop John Adams.
William E. Le Roy...	New York....	Brig Porpoise.
Maxwell Woodhull...	.....do.......	Frigate Raritan.
Strong B. Thompson .	Vermont.......	On leave.
Lafayette Maynard...	Virginia.......	Hydrographical office.
Roger N. Stembel....	Maryland	Coast survey.
George Colvocoressis.	Greece........	Schooner Shark.
Washington Reid.....	New York....	Waiting orders.
Francis S. Haggerty..	Pennsylvania .	Steamer Mississippi.
Thomas Brownell....	Rhode Island..	Sackett's Harbor.
Theo. B. Barrett......	Ohio..........	On furlough.
J. R. M. Mulany......	New York....	Coast survey.
James A. Doyle.......	Virginia.......	On leave.
Matthias C. Marin....	Florida........	Under suspension.
Thomas M. Mix......	New York....	Waiting orders.

NAVY LIST—*Surgeons.*

Names.	Where born	Duty or Station.
John Cassin Henry...	Pennsylvania..	On leave, (sick.)
William A. Wayne...	Georgia......	Frigate Savannah.
James S. Biddle......	Tennessee....	Frigate Potomac.
C. R. Perry Rogers...	New York....	Waiting orders.
James Withers Read..	S. Carolina...	On furlough.
Wash'n A. Bartlett...	Maine........	Sloop Portsmouth.
Francis Winslow.....	Massachusetts	Waiting orders.
James C. Williamson.	New Jersey...	Sloop Vincennes.
Gough W. Grant.....	N. Carolina...	Frigate Constitution.
Cornelius Vanalstine..	New York....	Waiting orders.
Albert G. Clary......	Massachusetts	On furlough.
Henry L. Chipman...	S. Carolina...	Sloop Marion.
George W. Doty.....	New York....	Coast survey.
SURGEONS.		
Jonathan Cowdery....	Massachusetts	Rendezvous, Norfolk.
Wm. P. C. Barton....	Pennsylvania .	Waiting orders.
Thomas Harris......	.....do......	Chief of Bureau Med. and Surgery.
William Turk.......	New York ...	Waiting orders.
John A. Kearney.....	Ireland.........	Navy yard, Philadelphia.
Bailey Washington...	Virginia........	Waiting orders.
William Swift.......	Massachusetts	Waiting orders.
Thomas B. Salter....	New Jersey ..	Rendezvous, Boston.
Peter Christie........	.....do......	Steamer Michigan.
Samuel Jackson......	New York....	Rendezvous, New York.
Thomas Williamson. .	Maryland	Hospital, Norfolk.
Benajah Ticknor......	Vermont.......	Fleet surgeon, East India squadron.
James Cornick.......	Virginia.......	Navy yard, Norfolk.
Charles Chase.......	Maine	Fleet surgeon, Pacific squadron.
David S. Edwards....	Connecticut...	Receiving ship at New York.
Isaac Hulse..........	New York....	Hospital, Pensacola.
John S. Wily........	Maryland	Waiting orders.
George Terrill.......	Virginia......	Navy yard, Pensacola.
John Haslett.........	S. Carolina...	Waiting orders.
Edmund L. Du Barry.	Pennsylvania .	Marine barracks, head-quarters.
Waters Smith........	New York....	Hospital, Chelsea.
Benjamin F. Bache...	Virginia.......	Naval asylum, Philadelphia.
Thomas Dillard......	.....do......	Waiting orders.
Stephen Rapalje......	New York....	Navy yard, New York.
James M. Greene....	Ireland.......	Fleet surgeon, Home squadron.
Benjamin R. Tinslar..	New York....	Navy yard, Boston.
George W. Codwise..	West Indies ..	Waiting orders.
Gustavus R. B. Horner	Virginia.......	Rendezvous, Philadelphia.
W. S. W. Ruschenberger..............	New Jersey...	Hospital, New York.
William Johnson.....	Delaware.....	Waiting orders.
Samuel Moseley......	Virginia......	Frigate Congress.
Robert J. Dodd......	Pennsylvania .	Waiting orders.

NAVY LIST—*Passed Assistant Surgeons.*

Names.	Where born.	Duty or Station.
Wm. Fairlie Patton..	Virginia.......	Fleet surgeon, African squadron.
John F. Brooke......	.....do.......	Receiving ship at Boston.
William Wheelan....	Pennsylvania .	Fleet surgeon, Mediterranean squad.
Samuel Barrington....	.....do......	Sloop John Adams.
Thomas L. Smith....	New Jersey ..	Waiting orders.
George Blacknall.....	N. Carolina...	On leave.
Horatio N. Glentworth	Pennsylvania .	Navy yard, Portsmouth.
Lewis B. Hunter.....	New Jersey ..	Sloop Cyane.
John C. Spencer	Ohio.........	Waiting orders.
George Clymer......	Pennsylvania .	Navy yard, Washington.
Isaac Brinckerhoff....	New York....	Sloop Marion.
Wm. Maxwell Wood	Maryland	Sloop Levant.
J. Vaughan Smith....	Pennsylvania .	On return from hospital, Port Mahon.
Jones W. Plummer...	.....do......	Waiting orders.
George B. McKnight.	New York....	Sloop Vincennes.
Solomon Sharp.......	Pennsylvania .	Waiting orders.
Daniel Egbert........	New Jersey ..	Receiving ship at Norfolk.
Amos G. Gambrill ...	Maryland	Steamer Mississippi.
W. A. W. Spottswood	Virginia......	Waiting orders.
Jonathan M. Foltz....	Pennsylvania .	Fleet surgeon, Brazil squadron.
Samuel C. Lawrason..	Dist. Colum..	On leave.
Edward Gilchrist.....	Massachusetts	Frigate Savannah.
John A. Lockwood...	Delaware.....	Naval school, Annapolis.
Daniel C. McLeod....	New York....	Frigate Constitution.
Lewis W. Minor.....	Virginia......	Waiting orders.
William J. Powell....	New York....	Sloop Warren.
J. Frederick Sickels ..	.....do......	Waiting orders.
N. C. Barrabino......	Pennsylvania .	Waiting orders.
Henry S. Rennolds...	Virginia......	Sick.
M. G. Delaney.......	Ireland.......	Sloop Saratoga.
Wm. F. McClenahan.	Virginia......	Sloop Plymouth.
Wm. L. Van Horn...	Pennsylvania .	Sloop Yorktown.
Daniel S. Green......	Virginia......	Waiting orders.
James C. Palmer.....	Maryland	Sloop St. Mary's.
Ninian Pinkney......	New Jersey...	Receiving ship and rendezvous, Balto.
Robert T. Barry......	Pennsylvania .	Sloop Boston.
Charles A. Hassler...	New York....	Sloop Falmouth.
PASSED ASSISTANT SURGEONS.		
John B. Elliott.......	New Jersey ..	On leave, (sick.)
David Harlan........	Maryland	Brig Somers.
Robert Woodworth...	New York....	Bureau of Medicine and Surgery.
J. Dickinson Miller...	.....do......	On leave.
John L. Fox.........	Massachusetts	Frigate Cumberland.
Charles F. B. Guillou.	Pennsylvania .	Columbus 74.
Augustus J. Bowie...	Maryland	Sloop Vincennes.
Joseph Beale........	Pennsylvania .	Hospital, New York.

NAVY LIST—*Asst. Surgeons.*

Names.	Where born.	Duty or Station.
S. Wilson Kellogg...	New York....	On leave.
John T. Mason......	Virginia.......	On leave.
Charles D. Maxwell..	Delaware......	Sloop Cyane.
Edward J. Rutter.....	Maryland	Coast survey.
John J. Abernethy....	Connecticut....	Store-ship Lexington.
J. Malcolm Smith.....	West Indies..	On leave, (sick.)
George Maulsby.....	Pennsylvania .	Brig Porpoise.
Charles J. Bates......	Massachusetts	Receiving ship at New York.
J. Winthrop Taylor..	New York....	Sloop John Adams.
James Monroe Minor.	Virginia......	Hospital, New York.
Silas Holmes........	Rhode Island..	Brig Truxtun.
J. Howard Smith.....	Pennsylvania .	On return from Hospital, Mahon.
Wm. B. Sinclair	Virginia......	Hospital, Norfolk.
James J. Brownlee....	Pennsylvania .	On leave, (sick.)
John S. Whittle......	Virginia......	Frigate Congress.
Stephen A. McCreery.	......do.......	Brig Lawrence.
James McClelland.....	Pennsylvania .	Brazil squadron.
J. O'Connor Barclay..	Louisiana	Frigate Columbia.
James B. Gould......	Connecticut....	Sloop Marion.
C. H. Wheelwright...	Massachusetts	Navy Yard, Pensacola.
William A. Nelson....	Virginia......	Steamer Col. Harney.
John H. Wright......	N. Hampshire.	Steam ship Princeton.
ASSISTANT SURGEONS.		
John S. Messersmith..	Pennsylvania .	On leave.
Wm. Grier..........	Ireland........	Schooner Shark.
E. H. Van Wyck	New York ...	Invalid.
Samuel R. Addison...	Maryland	Receiving ship at Boston.
Samuel Jackson......	Pennsylvania .	Frigate Cumberland.
Joshua Huntington...	Massachusetts	Waiting orders.
Augs. F. Lawyer.....	New York....	On leave.
Richard W. Jeffery....	Virginia......	On leave.
Thomas M. Potter....	Rhode Island .	Frigate Raritan.
Joseph Hopkinson....	Pennsylvania .	Sloop Plymouth.
John Thornley.......	Virginia......	Hospital, Pensacola.
Daniel L. Bryan	S. Carolina...	Columbus 74.
Andrew A. Henderson	Pennsylvania .	Store-ship Erie.
John Hastings.......	.....do......	Sloop Plymouth.
Richard T. Maxwell..	Delaware.....	Waiting orders.
Alex. Y. P. Garnett...	Virginia......	Frigate Columbia.
Morris B. Beck.......	.....do......	Schooner On-ka-hy-e.
J. Francis Tuckerman.	Massachusetts	Store-ship Southampton.
Oscar F. Baxter......	N. Carolina...	Schooner Flirt.
Lewis J. Williams....	Maryland	Sloop Yorktown.
Marius Duval........	.....do......	Frigate Constitution.
William S. Bishop....	Pennsylvania .	On leave.
Joseph Wilson, jr.....	....do.......	Frigate Savannah.
Charles Eversfield....	Maryland.....	Frigate Congress.

NAVY LIST—*Pursers.*

Names.	Where born.	Duty or Station.
Elisha K. Kane		Navy Yard, Philadelphia.
Edward Hudson	Pennsylvania	Sloop Warren.
Richard McSherry, jr.	Virginia	Frigate Constitution.
Ephraim J. Bee	New Jersey	Sloop Falmouth.
John L. Burtt	do	Frigate Potomac.
John T. Bartow	Georgia	Brazil Squadron.
James Hamilton	Scotland	On leave.
Charles H. Oakley	New York	Sloop Portsmouth.
Bernard Henry, jr	Spain	Sloop Saratoga.
Robert T. Maccoun	Pennsylvania	Sloop Jamestown.
William A. Harris	do	Sloop St. Mary's.
Robert E. Wall	Virginia	Columbus 74.
Washington Sherman	Pennsylvania	Steamer Mississippi.
PURSERS.		
Samuel Hambleton	Maryland	Navy yard, Philadelphia.
Francis A. Thornton	Virginia	Waiting orders.
Edward Fitzgerald	Pennsylvania	Receiving ship at Norfolk.
Samuel P. Todd	do	Waiting orders.
Joseph Wilson	Massachusetts	Waiting orders.
William Sinclair	do	Navy yard, New York.
John N. Todd	Pennsylvania	Waiting orders.
Joseph H. Terry	New York	Waiting orders.
Thomas Breese	Rhode Island	Inspector of Provisions at Boston.
John de Bree	New Jersey	Special duty.
Chas. Overing Handy	Rhode Island	On furlough.
John N. Hambleton	Maryland	Sloop Yorktown.
Garrett R. Barry	Pennsylvania	Sloop Boston.
D. McF. Thornton	Virginia	Settling accounts of the Brandywine.
Dudley Walker	Massachusetts	Frigate Columbia.
McKean Buchanan	Maryland	Waiting orders.
Henry Etting	do	Waiting orders.
Francis B. Stockton	New Jersey	Navy yard, Washington.
Francis G. McCauley	Pennsylvania	Frigate Potomac.
Nathaniel Wilson	Maine	Waiting orders.
Benjamin J. Cahoone	Rhode Island	Special duty.
Sterrett Ramsey	Pennsylvania	Navy yard, Pensacola.
Edward T. Dunn	Dist. Colum.	Columbus 74.
John A. Bates	Massachusetts	Waiting orders.
Andrew J. Watson	Virginia	Frigate Cumberland.
Wm. A. Bloodgood	New York	Steamer Michigan.
Daingerf'ld Fauntleroy	Virginia	Frigate Savannah.
T. Marston Taylor	New Jersey	Frigate Constitution.
Adolphus E. Watson	Massachusetts	Frigate Raritan.
Joseph Bryan	Georgia	Waiting orders.
Samuel Forrest	Dist. Colum.	Navy yard, Norfolk.
Robert Pettit	Pennsylvania	Waiting orders.
Richard R. Waldron	N. Hampshire	Receiving ship at Boston.

NAVY LIST—*Chaplains.*

Names.	Where born.	Duty or Station.
William Speiden	Dist. of Col.	Frigate Congress.
Horatio Bridge	Maine	Navy yard, Portsmouth.
George F. Sawyer	Vermont	Sloop John Adams.
Hugh W. Greene	N. Hampshire.	Navy yard, Boston.
Thomas B. Nalle	Virginia	Receiving ship at New York.
Christopher C. Rice	Ireland	On furlough.
Thomas P. McBlair	Maryland	Sloop Plymouth.
Edward Bissell	New York	Waiting orders.
John D. Gibson	Georgia	Store-ship Southampton.
John B. Rittenhouse	Dist of Col	Sloop Levant.
Edward Storer	Maine	Store-ship relief.
Rodman M. Price	New York	Sloop Cyane.
Andrew D. Crosby	Pennsylvania	Settling accounts of the Preble.
Lewis Warrington, jr.	Virginia	Steamer Mississippi.
George H. White	Pennsylvania	Brig Bainbridge.
H. Marshall Heiskell	do.	Sloop Falmouth.
William A. Christian	Virginia	Steam ship Princeton.
Littleton P. Waller	do.	Sloop St. Mary's.
James C. Douglass	Delaware	Settling accounts of the St. Louis.
Charles Murray	Ireland	Store-ship Erie.
Thomas R. Ware	Virginia	Sloop Warren.
John C. Spencer, jr.	New York	Sloop Marion.
George F. Cutter	Massachusetts	Brig Truxtun.
William H. Kennon	Virginia	Brig Lawrence.
James A. Semple	do.	Sloop Jamestown.
James H. Watmough	Pennsylvania	Sloop Portsmouth.
John O. Bradford	Delaware	Sloop Saratoga.
John Y. Mason, jr.	Virginia	Sloop Vincennes.
J. George Harris	Connecticut	Waiting orders.
John F. Steele	Pennsylvania	Brig Somers.
E. C. Doran	do.	Brig Dolphin.
CHAPLAINS.		
Addison Searle	N. Hampshire.	Navy Yard, Boston.
John W. Grier	Pennsylvania	Navy Yard, Philadelphia.
Charles S. Stewart	New Jersey	Receiving ship at New York.
William Ryland	Ireland	Navy Yard, Washington.
Timothy J. Harrison	Connecticut	Receiving ship at Norfolk.
Walter Colton	Vermont	Frigate Congress.
George Jones	Pennsylvania	Naval School, Annapolis.
Thomas R. Lambert	Maine	Waiting orders.
Peter G. Clark	Connecticut	Waiting orders.
Rodman Lewis	Massachusetts	Navy Yard, Pensacola.
Fitch W. Taylor	Connecticut	On furlough.
Charles Henry Alden	do	Waiting orders.
Mortimer R. Talbot	New York	Sloop Jamestown.
Moses B. Chase	N. Hampshire.	Receiving ship at Boston.
Chester Newell	Massachusetts	Frigate Cumberland.

NAVY DEPARTMENT—*Passed Midshipmen.*

Names.	Where born.	Duty or Station.
Theodore Bartow	New York	Waiting orders.
Joseph Stockbridge	Maine	Navy Yard, New York.
William McKenney	Maryland	Waiting orders.
Photius Kavasales	Greece	Waiting orders.
William G. Jackson	Pennsylvania	Waiting orders.
J. W. Newton	Connecticut	Columbus 74.
Nathaniel Frost	Maine	Frigate Potomac.
George W. Latham		Navy Yard, Norfolk.
PASSED MIDSHIPMEN.		
George Wells	Vermont	Waiting orders.
John S. Neville	Pennsylvania	On leave.
Peter U. Murphy	N. Carolina	Ordinary, Norfolk.
John B. Randolph	Virginia	Waiting orders.
Johnston B. Carter	N. Carolina	Frigate Savannah.
Samuel Pearce	Rhode Island	Invalid.
Henry P. Robertson	Tennessee	Waiting orders.
Isaac N. Brown	Kentucky	On leave.
R. Delancey Izard	Pennsylvania	On furlough, (in Europe.)
Napoleon Collins	.....do.....	Waiting orders.
John L. Worden	New York	Hydrographical office.
William L. Blanton	Kentucky	Mediterranean squadron.
Benjamin S. Gantt	Dist. of Col.	Store-ship Lexington.
Henry A. Wise	New York	On leave.
Callender St.G. Noland	Virginia	Waiting orders.
Edward C. Anderson	Georgia	Coast survey.
Reed Werden	Pennsylvania	Waiting orders.
William H. Macomb	Michigan	Rendezvous, New York.
Stephen D. Trenchard	New York	Coast survey.
Wilson R. McKinney	Tennessee	Brig Bainbridge.
Abram Harrell	Virginia	Waiting orders.
Samuel J. Shipley	Delaware	Waiting orders.
John J. Guthrie	N. Carolina	Schooner On-ka-hy-e.
Mayo C. Watkins	Virginia	On leave.
Melancton B. Woolsey	New York	Store-ship Lexington.
Joseph N. Barney	Maryland	Waiting orders.
Alexander Murray	Pennsylvania	On leave.
Louis McLane	Delaware	Sloop Levant.
Edward Donaldson	Maryland	Coast Survey.
S. Chase Barney	.....do.....	Waiting orders.
Ben. F. B. Hunter	Pennsylvania	Sloop Cyane.
George H. Preble	Maine	On leave.
Thomas B. Huger	South Carolina	On return from Mediterranean.
Robt. B. Riell	New York	On leave.
Matthew C. Perry	.....do.....	Waiting orders.
Chas. S. McDonough	Connecticut	On leave, (sick.)
Joshua D. Todd	Pennsylvania.	Sloop St. Mary's.
William M. Caldwell.	Massachusetts	Mediterranean squadron.

NAVY LIST—*Passed Midshipmen.*

Names.	Where born.	Duty or station.
Wilmer Shields	Louisiana	Hydrographical office
Charles E. Fleming	New Jersey	Brig Porpoise.
James S. Ridgely	Maryland	Receiving ship at Baltimore.
John Rutledge	S. Carolina	Sloop Warren.
John Q. Adams	Massachusetts	Rendezvous, Boston.
Charles Deas	South Carolina	Receiving ship at Baltimore.
Francis Alexander	Mississippi	Naval storekeeper, coast of Africa.
Wm. C. B. S. Porter	N. Hampshire	Sloop Marion.
Thomas M. Crossan	Pennsylvania	On leave.
Thomas H. Stevens	Connecticut	Naval storekeeper, Sandwich Islands.
Charles Sinkler	South Carolina	On furlough.
Catesby Ap. R. Jones	Virginia	On leave.
James L. Blair	Kentucky	On leave.
T. Harman Patterson	Louisiana	Coast survey.
Francis Key Murray	Maryland	Frigate Potomac.
Silas Bent	Missouri	Waiting orders.
John C. Howell	Pennsylvania	On leave.
Edward Higgins	Virginia	Store-ship Erie.
Wm. E. Boudinot	N. Carolina	On leave.
Van Renssel'r Morgan	Kentucky	Frigate Congress.
Madison Rush	England	Columbus 74.
Daniel Ammen	Ohio	Sloop Vincennes.
Henry Rolando	South Carolina	Store-ship Southampton.
Andrew Weir	Virginia	On leave.
John S. Taylor	do.	Frigate Columbia.
Isaac N. Morris	Ohio	Sloop Jamestown.
John Hogan Brown	Alabama	On leave.
Edward F. Beale	Dist. Colum.	Frigate Congress.
Edward T. Nichols	Georgia	Waiting orders.
Thos. L. Kinloch	South Carolina	On furlough.
John P. Decatur	New York	Waiting orders.
Edward Lloyd Winder	Maryland	Sloop John Adams.
John K. Duer	New York	Special duty.
Henry A. Clemson	New Jersey	Brig Truxtun.
Richard Allison	do.	Brig Lawrence.
Israel C. Wait	Virginia	Vincennes.
John Henry Parker	do.	Schooner Flirt.
William B. Muse	N. Carolina	Schooner Flirt.
George W. Rodgers	New York	Steamer Col. Harney.
Archibald McRae	N. Carolina	Sloop Boston.
Robert H. Wyman	N. Hampshire	On leave.
Edward A. Barnett	Pennsylvania	Naval storekeeper, Hong Kong.
Nathaniel C. Bryant	Maine	Sloop Plymouth.
George B. Balch	Tennessee	Store-ship Southampton.
Jona. M. Wainwright	New York	Columbus 74.
George W. Hamersley	do.	Store-ship Relief.
Foxall A. Parker	do.	Steamer Michigan.
Isaac G. Strain	Pennsylvania	Frigate Constitution.
Egbert Thompson	New York	Frigate Cumberland.

NAVY LIST—*Passed Midshipmen.*

Names.	Where born.	Duty or Station.
Robert Townsend....	New York...	Brig Porpoise.
Joel S. Kennard......	Alabama......	Hydrographical office.
John Wilkinson......	Virginia........	Sloop Portsmouth.
John Guest..........	Missouri.....	Frigate Congress.
Wm. H. Montgomery	New York....	Sloop Warren.
Donald McN. Fairfax.	Virginia.......	Columbus 74.
Robert H. Getty......	Dist. Colum..	Sloop Saratoga.
Isaac N. Briceland....	Pennsylvania..	Hydrographical office.
Henry Rodgers......	Dist. Colum..	Steamer Mississippi.
John M. B. Clitz......	New York....	Sloop Falmouth.
John Dorsey Read....	Delaware.....	Sloop Levant.
Courtlandt Benham...	Ohio.........	Sloop Plymouth.
Wm. F. De Jongh....	South Carolina	Frigate Savannah.
Wm. H. Thompson..	Virginia.......	Frigate Congress.
John F. Abbott......	Pennsylvania.	Waiting orders.
George H. Cooper....	New York....	Schooner Flirt.
Bayse N. Westcott...	New Jersey..	Brig Somers.
Wm. Winder Pollock.	New York....	Steamer Michigan.
J. Fenwick Stenson...	Maryland.....	Sloop Cyane.
Andrew Bryson......	New York....	Steamer Michigan.
John Downes, jr.....	Massachusetts	Frigate Cumberland.
Charles M. Morris...	South Carolina	Frigate Raritan.
Andrew J. Drake.....	New Jersey...	Columbus 74.
James M. Spotts.....	N. Carolina...	Store-ship Southampton.
James M. Duncan....	Ohio..........	Frigate Congress.
Lardner Gibbon......	Pennsylvania.	Sloop Boston.
Samuel Marcy.......	New York....	Naval school, instructor.
John P. Bankhead....	South Carolina	Coast survey.
James Foster........	Massachusetts	Coast survey.
George W. Clark....	Dist. Colum..	Mediterranean squadron.
George B. Bissell....	Connecticut....	Frigate Potomac.
J. W. A. Nicholson..	Massachusetts	Steamer Princeton.
Thomas G. Corbin...	Virginia......	Frigate Columbia.
Gustavus V. Fox.....	Massachusetts	On leave.
John Matthews, jr....	New York....	Frigate Potomac.
John C. Beaumont...	Pennsylvania.	Sloop Jamestown.
Charles H. B. Caldwell	Massachusetts	Schooner On-ka-hy-e.
Charles M. Fauntleroy	Virginia......	Brig Somers.
Wm. B. Fitzgerald...	Dist. of Col..	Hydrographical office.
Miles K. Warrington.	Virginia.......	Frigate Congress.
Henry K. Davenport.	Georgia......	Frigate Columbia
N. B. Harrison......	Virginia......	Store-ship Erie.
Edward F. Tattnall...	Georgia......	Store-ship Lexington.
Selim E. Woodworth.	New York....	Sloop Jamestown.
James H. Moore.....	.....do......	On leave.
Samuel Edwards.....	Pennsylvania..	Sloop Yorktown.
Thomas L. Dance....	Maryland.....	Frigate Potomac.
Charles W. Place....	N. Hampshire	Brig Lawrence.
Alphonse Barbot.....	Louisiana....	Waiting orders.

NAVY LIST—*Passed Midshipmen.*

Names.	Where born.	Duty or Station.
William H. Jamesson.	Virginia........	Schooner On-ka-hy-e.
Albert N. Smith......	Maine	Frigate Cumberland.
William H. Hudson..	New York....	Brig Bainbridge.
John C. Febiger......	Pennsylvania..	Frigate Potomac.
Dillaplaine R. Lambert	New Jersey...	Steamer Michigan.
Frederick W. Colby..	N. Hampshire.	Store-ship Lexington.
Henry S. Newcomb..	Rhode Island .	Sloop Yorktown.
John S. Maury......	N. Carolina...	Sloop Falmouth.
Pierce Crosby......	Pennsylvania..	Coast survey.
Richard T. Renshaw.	New Jersey ..	Steamer Col. Harney.
Charles W. Hays....	Alabama......	Store-ship Erie.
Johnston B. Creighton	Rhode Island..	Brig Truxtun.
Aaron K. Hughes....	New York. ..	Frigate Columbia.
Edmund R. Colhoun..	Pennsylvania..	On leave.
James D. Bulloch....	Georgia......	Store-ship Erie.
Charles H. Baldwin..	New York ...	Frigate Congress.
Robert W. Shufeldt...	.....do......	Coast survey.
Beverley Randolph...	Virginia.......	On leave.
Henry K. Stevens....	Connecticut...	Frigate Columbia.
Abner Read.........	Ohio.........	Brig Dolphin.
Alexander C. Rhind..	New York ...	Coast survey.
Richard M. Cuyler...	Georgia......	Coast survey.
Alexander J. Dallas..	Pennsylvania..	On leave.
George M. Ransom...	New York ...	Hydrographical office.
William F. Spicer....	.....do......	Brig Dolphin.
Edward C. Stiles.....	Pennsylvania..	Steam ship Princeton.
Wm. W. Roberts....	N. Carolina...	Steam ship Princeton.
Reginald Fairfax.....	Virginia.......	On leave.
Sommerville Nicholson	New York ...	Coast survey.
William A. Webb....	Virginia......	Store-ship Southampton.
John Stuart..........	Michigan.....	On leave.
Joseph S. Day.......	Vermont.....	On leave.
Maurice Simons......	South Carolina	Frigate Congress
James Wilcoxson....	New York ...	Sloop John Adams.
Wm. E. Hopkins....	Virginia......	Frigate Columbia.
Paul Shirley.........	Kentucky	Frigate Columbia.
Charles C. Simms....	Virginia.......	Sloop Marion.
Robert C. Rogers	Delaware.....	Coast survey.
Henry N. T. Arnold .	New York ...	Steamer Colonel Harney.
James M. Ladd.......	Maine	Coast Survey.
John R. Hynson......	Maryland	Sloop John Adams.
Tenant McLanahan...	Louisiana.....	Sloop Cyane.
Thomas Pattison.....	New York....	On leave.
Henry Ashton.......	Maryland	Waiting orders.
Wesley W. Bassett...	Connecticut....	Steam ship Princeton.
Julian Myers........	Georgia.......	Waiting orders.
James Higgins.......	New York....	Sloop Marion.
Julius S. Bohrer......	Dist. of Col...	Sloop Cyane.

NAVY LIST—*Midshipmen.*

Names.	Where born.	Duty or Station.
MIDSHIPMEN.		
Charles W. Aby	Virginia	Naval School.
Richmond Aulick	Connecticut	Naval School.
Wm. D. Austin	Massachusetts	Naval School.
James Armstrong	Virginia	Sloop Jamestown.
Albert Allmand	do	Sloop Cyane.
Alex. R. Abercrombie	Maryland	Sloop Levant.
Elijah T. Andrews	Massachusetts	Sloop Jamestown.
Lehman P. Ashmead	Pennsylvania	Frigate Columbia.
John Adams	Tennessee	Naval School.
Joseph M. Bradford	do	Naval School.
John W. Bennett	Maryland	Naval School.
Homer C. Blake	Connecticut	Naval School.
Frederick B. Brand	Louisiana	Naval School.
Edward Brinley, jr	New Jersey	Sloop Falmouth.
Edward Barrett	Louisiana	Sloop Falmouth.
Wm. King Bridge	Maine	Steamer Mississippi.
John R. Barker	Pennsylvania	Coast Survey.
H. G. D. Brown	South Carolina	Sloop Jamestown.
Allen T. Byrens	Ohio	On leave, (sick.)
Thomas W. Brodhead	N. Hampshire	Frigate Potomac.
John M. Brooke	Florida	Frigate Columbia.
Charles S. Bell	Dist. Colum.	Sloop Portsmouth.
Wash'n P. Buckner	Kentucky	Frigate Constitution.
Oscar C. Badger	Connecticut	Steamer Mississippi.
Joseph T. Bartlett	Maine	Sloop Marion.
Simeon S. Bassett	Dist. Colum'a.	Frigate Cumberland.
John T. Barraud	Virginia	Sloop John Adams.
George H. Bier	Maryland	Brig Bainbridge.
Josiah S. Byers	Kentucky	Frigate Congress.
Sylvanus J. Bliss	Massachusetts	Sloop Marion.
Charles C. Bayard	Delaware	Columbus 74.
H. A. Colborn	Ohio	Columbus 74.
Samuel P. Carter	Tennessee	Home squadron.
John Q. A. Crawford	Kentucky	Naval School.
Jonathan H. Carter	N. Carolina	Naval School.
Francis S. Conover	New York	Naval School.
William S. Cushman	N. Hampshire	Sloop Yorktown.
Greenleaf Cilley	Maine	Frigate Cumberland.
Cornelius Comegys	Pennsylvania	Frigate Constitution.
Edward T. Carmichael	Virginia	On leave.
Gideon D. Chenoweth	Kentucky	On leave, (sick.)
Horace N. Crabb	Pennsylvania	Sloop Cyane.
David Coleman	N. Carolina	Frigate Raritan.
David A. Chever	Massachusetts	Steamer Mississippi.
Joseph J. Cook	N. Carolina	Frigate Constitution.
Francis G. Clark, jr.	Massachusetts	Brig Somers.
Walter O. Crain	Louisiana	Sloop Warren.

NAVY LIST—*Midshipmen.*

Names.	Where born.	Duty or Station.
Robert R. Carter......	Virginia.......	Frigate Savannah.
Ralph Chandler......	New York....	Naval School.
Charles Dyer, jr......	Connecticut....	Naval School.
Wash'n F. Davidson .	Virginia.......	Frigate Constitution.
Garrit V. Denniston..	New York....	Frigate Potomac.
John L. Davis.......	Indiana.......	Frigate Potomac.
George M. Dibble....	New York....	Columbus 74.
William DeKoven....	Connecticut...	Naval School.
George B. Douglass ..	Tennessee....	Frigate Constitution.
Ebenezer D. Denny...	Pennsylvania .	Naval School.
Alex. M. de Bree	Virginia.......	Sloop Warren.
Joseph D. Danels	Maryland	Frigate Cumberland.
J. Chas. P. De Krafft.	Dist. of Col...	Frigate Raritan.
Joseph E. DeHaven ..	Pennsylvania .	Frigate Raritan.
Robert C. Duvall.....	N. Carolina...	Frigate Savannah.
Adrian Deslonde.....	Louisiana	Waiting orders.
Hunter Davidson.....	Dist. Colum ..	Sloop Portsmouth.
Francis G. Dallas	Massachusetts	Navy Yard, Pensacola.
Samuel B. Elliott.....	Pennsylvania..	Frigate Congress.
Earl English.........	New Jersey...	Naval School.
Thomas C. Eaton....	Maine	Sloop Marion.
J. Malachi Ford......	S. Carolina...	Sloop Saratoga.
Samuel R. Franklin...	Pennsylvania .	Sloop Levant.
Wm. H. Fauntleroy..	Virginia......	Brig Lawrence.
Joseph A. Forrest....	Maryland	Sloop Vincennes.
James L. Ferguson....	Massachusetts	Sloop Jamestown.
Joseph Fry..........	Florida.......	Sloop Boston.
Thos. S. Fillebrown..	Dist. Colum..	Steamer Mississippi.
Joseph L. Friend.....	Virginia......	Sloop Saratoga.
Francis Gregory......	New York....	Steamer Mississippi.
William Gibson.......	Maryland	Frigate Potomac.
William M. Gamble...	Pennsylvania .	Frigate Savannah.
Samuel P. Griffin.....	Georgia.......	Frigate Savannah.
Edward Gordon......	Virginia.......	Sloop Levant.
Edward C. Grafton...	Massachusetts	Sloop Portsmouth.
Charles K. Graham...	New York....	Columbus 74.
John Gale...........	Maryland	Sloop John Adams.
Charles Gray........	Delaware.....	Frigate Raritan.
Walter V. Gilliss.....	Dist. Colum..	Sloop St. Mary's.
Stanwix Gansevoort..	New York....	Sloop Warren.
Fred'k M. Humphrey	Connecticut...	On leave, (sick.)
Benj. L. T. Henderson	Kentucky	Brig Porpoise.
Reuben Harris.......	Ohio..........	Naval School.
John E. Hopson......	Kentucky.....	Frigate Constitution.
John P. Hall.........	Illinois.......	Naval School.
Wash'n Hammond...	Pennsylvania .	Naval School.
John E. Hart........	New York....	Frigate Constitution.
Alex. W. Habersham	.....do......	Frigate Raritan.
Daniel C. Hugunin...	.....do......	Sloop Portsmouth.

NAVY LIST—*Midshipmen.*

Names.	Where born.	Duty or Station.
Thomas C. Harris....	Pennsylvania.	Frigate Potomac.
Henry C. Hunter.....	Maine........	Frigate Raritan.
Frederick A. Hallett..	New York....	Waiting orders.
John J. Hanson......	Dist. Colum..	Sloop Saratoga.
Wm. W. Holmes....	Connecticut...	Frigate Raritan.
Wm. G. Hoffman....	Maryland	Sloop Plymouth.
Milton Haxtun......	New York....	Brig Bainbridge.
James Heron........	Virginia......	Sloop Portsmouth.
Charles F. Hopkins..	Georgia.......	Sloop Saratoga.
Philem'n H. Haywood	N. Carolina...	Schooner Shark.
George H. Hare......	Pennsylvania.	Frigate Columbia.
Gustavus Harrison....	Dist. Colum..	Frigate Raritan.
H. St. George Hunter	Virginia......	Frigate Potomac.
Edm'd Wilkes Henry	New York....	Columbus 74.
Charles C. Hunter....	Vermont.....	Naval School.
Th's Truxtun Houston	Pennsylvania.	Naval School.
John R. Hamilton....	Alabama......	Naval School.
William N. Jeffers, jr.	New York....	Naval School.
Alonzo C. Jackson....	.....do.......	Frigate Savannah.
Merriwether P. Jones.	Virginia......	Frigate Constitution.
James E. Jouett......	Kentucky	Sloop John Adams.
Elliott Johnston......	Maryland	Sloop Portsmouth.
Walter F. Jones......	Virginia......	Sloop St. Mary's.
Copeland P. Jones....	.....do.......	Brig Dolphin.
James L. Johnston....	.....do.......	Naval School.
John P. Jones.......	.....do.......	Naval School.
Andrew W. Johnson.	Dist. Colum..	Sloop Warren.
John H. Johnson.....	Maryland	Frigate Cumberland.
Frederick Kellogg....	New York....	Sloop Warren.
John Kell	Georgia.......	Schooner Shark.
Henry H. Key.......	Maryland	Sloop Saratoga.
George S. King......	Massachusetts	Brig Somers.
Lyman R. Law......	Connecticut....	Invalid.
Reigart B. Lowry.....	S. America...	Naval School.
Richard L. Law......	Indiana......	Brig Lawrence.
William W. Low.....	Massachusetts	Columbus 74.
Charles Latimer......	Dist. of Col...	Sloop Saratoga.
Theodoric Lee.......	Virginia......	Frigate Congress.
Leonard H. Lyne....	Kentucky	Frigate Raritan.
Robert F. R. Lewis...	Dist. of Col...	Sloop Cyane.
Stephen B. Luce.....	New York....	Columbus 74.
John Laurens.......	South Carolina	Naval School.
Jno. Devall Langhorne	Kentucky	Frigate Columbia.
Leonidas McDougall..	Ohio.........	Naval School.
Robert Milligan......	Pennsylvania.	Naval School.
Richard P. Mason....	Virginia......	Brazil Squadron.
Augustus McLaughlin	Maryland	Naval School.
James B. McCauley..	Pennsylvania.	Naval School.
John Madigan, jr.....	Maine........	Sloop Boston.

NAVY LIST—*Midshipmen.*

Names.	Where born.	Duty or Station.
Robert A. Marr	Virginia	Naval School.
Robert M. McArann	Pennsylvania	Sloop Falmouth.
John McL. Murphy	New York	Frigate Cumberland.
George E. Morgan	do	Frigate Savannah.
John V. McCollum	Illinois	On leave.
Robert D. Minor	Virginia	Sloop Warren.
Andrew F. Monroe	do	Waiting orders.
Jefferson McRoberts	Illinois	Sloop Warren.
Alex. J. Mitchell	Kentucky	Waiting orders.
Wm. H. Murdaugh	Virginia	Naval School.
Jefferson Maury	do	Sloop Plymouth.
Edw'd Y. McCauley	Pennsylvania	Frigate Cumberland.
Thomas J. Miller	Georgia	Frigate Savannah.
David P. McCorkle	Dist. Colum.	Steam ship Princeton.
Wm. Mitchell	do	Frigate Congress.
Wm. K. Mayo	Virginia	Sloop St. Mary's.
Charles P. McGary	Maryland	Sloop Plymouth.
John Howard March	New York	Frigate Raritan.
Chas. M. Mitchell	Connecticut	Naval School.
David A. McDermut	New York	Sloop Vincennes.
Samuel Magaw	Pennsylvania	Brig Porpoise.
William R. Mercer	Maryland	Waiting orders.
Allen McLane	Delaware	Naval School.
F. Buchanan McKean	Pennsylvania	Naval School.
William Nelson	Kentucky	Naval School.
Jefferson H. Nones	Pennsylvania	Naval School.
David Ochiltree	Florida	Naval School.
Arthur H. Otis	Massachusetts	Sloop John Adams.
Cyrus H. Oakly	New York	On leave.
Thomas S. Phelps	Maine	Sloop Boston.
John Julius Pringle	South Carolina	Naval School.
Henry O. Porter	Dist. Colum.	Naval School.
Leonard Paulding	New York	Sloop Boston.
Edward C. Pasteur	N. Carolina	Sloop Falmouth.
John Van Ness Philip	New York	Sloop Cyane.
Wingate Pilsbury	Maine	Steamer Mississippi.
Robert Patton	Virginia	Brig Truxtun.
Richd. J. D. Price	Maryland	Frigate Raritan.
Wm. L. Powell	Virginia	Naval School.
Dawson Phenix	Maryland	Unders orders for Pacific squadron.
Wm. H. Parker	New York	Frigate Potomac.
Seth Phelps	Ohio	Sloop Jamestown.
Joseph Parrish	Pennsylvania	Brazil squadron.
Step'n P. Quackenbush	New York	Naval School.
Walter Queen	Dist. Colum.	Naval School.
William Reily	do	Steam ship Princeton.
Thomas Roney	Maryland	Frigate Raritan.
Samuel B. Rathbone	New York	Waiting orders.
James Rochelle	Virginia	Sloop Falmouth.

NAVY LIST—*Midshipmen.*

Names.	Where born.	Duty or Station.
John H. Russell	Maryland	Sloop St. Mary's.
Francis A. Roe	New York	Sloop Yorktown.
Edward Renshaw	New Jersey	Brig Lawrence.
Edward Simpson	New York	Naval School.
Edward C. Stout	do	Naval School.
Robert Savage	N. Carolina	Naval School.
George A. Stevens	Massachusetts	Naval School.
Wm. Henry Smith	Virginia	Frigate Potomac.
T. Branford Shubrick	Delaware	Sloop Saratoga.
Robert Selden	Dist. of Col.	Sloop St. Mary's.
Robert W. Scott	Virginia	Sloop Saratoga.
John B. Stewart	N. Carolina	Columbus 74.
Byrd W. Stevenson	Virginia	Columbus 74.
William Sharp	do	Sloop Jamestown.
Stephen D. Spence	Maryland	Naval School.
James H. Somerville	do	Naval School.
Alex'r R. Simmons	Virginia	Sloop Vincennes.
Edmund Shepherd	do	Sloop Cyane.
Marshall J. Smith	do	Naval School.
Edward H. Scovell	Georgia	Sloop Levant.
Edward B. Stone	do	Naval School.
Watson Smith	Pennsylvania	Brig Porpoise.
Robert Stuart	New York	On leave.
Joseph B. Smith	Maine	Frigate Cumberland.
Edward A Selden	Vermont	Columbus 74.
George T. Simes	Maine	Sloop Portsmouth.
Alex'r A. Semmes	Dist. Colum	Sloop Vincennes.
Robert B. Storer	N. Hampshire	Frigate Potomac.
Joseph Seawell	Virginia	Frigate Congress.
Colville Terrett	do	Frigate Constitution.
William G. Temple	Vermont	Brig Lawrence.
James S Thornton	N. Hampshire	Sloop John Adams.
William R. Thomas	N. Carolina	Sloop Jamestown.
Wm. Talbot Truxtun	Pennsylvania	Brig Truxtun.
William P. Toler	S. America	Frigate Savannah.
James L. Tillotson	Vermont	Steamer Michigan.
John H. Tillotson	New York	Frigate Savannah.
John H. Upshur	Virginia	Sloop St. Mary's.
Elias Vander Horst	S. Carolina	Sloop Cyane.
William Van Wyck	Maryland	Steam ship Princeton.
Nich's H. Van Zandt	Dist. Colum	Columbus 74.
Samuel Wilcox	do	Naval School.
Peter Wager, jr.	Pennsylvania	Naval School.
Alexander F. Warley	South Carolina	Steamer Col. Harney.
John Walcutt	Ohio	Steamer Mississippi.
James Wiley	Pennsylvania	Steamer Mississippi.
Fred'k P. Wheelock	Virginia	Sloop Falmouth.
Charles Waddell	Pennsylvania	Frigate Potomac.
George P. Welsh	do	Naval School.

NAVY LIST—*Masters.*

Names.	Where born.	Duty or Station.
Clark H. Wells	Pennsylvania	Naval School.
William H. Wilcox	Connecticut	Pacific squadron.
William C. West	New York	Sloop Vincennes.
Nathaniel T. West	Massachusetts	Naval school.
John T. Walker	Michigan	Sloop Plymouth.
William D. Whiting	Massachusetts	Columbus 74.
John K. Wilson	Maryland	Store ship Relief.
John Wilkes, jr.	New York	Steamer Mississippi.
John G. Whitaker	do	Store ship Relief.
James I. Waddell	N. Carolina	Steamer Col. Harney.
Henry Willis	Maryland	Frigate Columbia.
Theodoric L. Walker	do	Columbus 74.
P. G. Watmough	Pennsylvania	Sloop Portsmouth.
Thos. B. Wainwright	Massachusetts	Frigate Cumberland.
Benjamin F. Wells	Dist. Colum.	Frigate Congress.
William H. Weaver	Virginia	Naval School.
Archibald H. Waring	South Carolina	Frigate Congress.
Wm. W. Wilkinson	Pennsylvania	Waiting orders.
Charles Woolley	Missouri	Sloop Levant.
Ellicott D. Wall	Ohio	Waiting orders.
Jonathan Young	do	Columbus 74.
George W. Young	New York	Sloop Levant.
Thomas Young	Virginia	Naval School.
James B. Yates	Pennsylvania	Sloop St. Mary's.
MASTERS.		
Salvadore Catalano	Sicily	Navy yard, Washington.
Augustus Ford	Rhode Island	Waiting orders.
Abram B. Bloodgood	New York	New York station.
Robert Knox	Massachusetts	Ordinary, Boston.
William Vaughan	Pennsylvania	Sackett's Harbor.
Marmaduke Dove	Maryland	Waiting orders.
John Clough	Massachusetts	Waiting orders.
Francis Mallaby	New York	Waiting orders.
James Ferguson	do	Naval storekeeper, Rio.
William Miller	Scotland	Navy Yard, Philadelphia.
Heury Worthington	Maryland	Waiting orders.
John Carlton	Massachusetts	Waiting orders.
Alex'r Cunningham	South Carolina	Waiting orders.
John Robinson	Massachusetts	Waiting orders.
John Quin	Pennsylvania	On furlough.
Nathaniel A. Prentiss	Massachusetts	Waiting orders.
Jacob Mull	Maryland	Navy Yard, Portsmouth.
Fred'k W. Moores	New York	Navy Yard, Boston.
H. A. F. Young	England	Navy Yard, Norfolk.
Robert H. Nichols	New York	Ordinary, New York.
John Freeman	Sweden	Navy Yard, Norfolk.
Thomas Goin	New York	Rendezvous, New York.

NAVY LIST—*Masters' Mates—Professors of Mathematics.*

Names.	Where born.	Duty or station.
Michael Clear	Virginia	Waiting orders.
George Marshall	Greece	Navy Yard, Norfolk.
Robert A. Cassin	Pennsylvania	Navy Yard, Philadelphia.
Charles V. Morris	New York	Navy Yard, Washington.
William Brady	do	Navy Yard, New York.
Samuel C. Reid	Connecticut	Receiving ship at New York.
Benjamin F. Coston	Pennsylvania	Navy Yard, Washington.
Robert Jones	Louisiana	Receiving ship at Philadelphia.
John Pearson	Virginia	Navy Yard, Pensacola.
MASTERS' MATES.		
William H. Morse		Waiting orders.
John W. Palmer	Connecticut	On leave.
Adam Young	Pennsylvania	Navy Yard, New York.
William H. Burns	New York	Navy Yard, Philadelphia.
Jonathan M. Ballard	Maine	Receiving ship at Boston.
James T. Power	Ireland	Frigate Raritan.
Richard P. Robinson	Pennsylvania	Frigate Columbia.
John W. W. Dyes	Virginia	Sloop Saratoga.
James H. Polley	New York	Sloop Boston.
Charles B. Oliver	Massachusetts	On leave.
Edmund F. Olmstead	New York	Receiving ship at Norfolk.
PROFESSORS OF MATHEMATICS.		
Edward C. Ward	England	Frigate Raritan.
Duncan Bradford	Massachusetts	Special duty.
Martin Roche	Ireland	Waiting orders.
John H. C. Coffin	Maine	Hydrographical office.
Joseph T. Huston	do	Special duty.
Thomas H. Perry	Massachusetts	Waiting orders.
A. G. Pendleton	Virginia	On furlough.
John Pierce, jr		Waiting orders.
Jarvis McDuffie		Frigate Columbia.
Mordecai Yarnall	Ohio	Columbus 74.
Julius Meiere	France	Waiting orders.
Wm. B. Benedict	New York	Receiving ship at New York.
Mark H. Beecher	Connecticut	Steamer Mississippi.
John Clar	Minorca	On leave.
Henry H. Lockwood	Delaware	Naval School, Annapolis.
William Flye	Maine	Sloop Jamestown.
William Chauvenett	Pennsylvania	Naval School, Annapolis.
J. Henshaw Belcher		Waiting orders.
Ethan Estabrook	N. Hampshire	Frigate Constitution.
James Major	Ireland	Frigate Potomac.
Jos. S. Hubbard	Connecticut	Hydrographical office.
Reuel Keith	Dist. Col	Hydrographical office.

NAVY LIST—*Teachers of Languages—Boatswains—Gunners.*

Names.	Where born	Duty or Station.
TEACHERS OF LANGUAGES.		
L. A. Bianchini	Genoa	Waiting orders.
T. Morel, jr.	France	Receiving ship at New York
W. W. Delacy	Virginia	Receiving ship at Norfolk.
BOATSWAINS.		
Edward Crocker	Virginia	Waiting orders.
John Morris	Massachusetts	Receiving ship at Boston.
Laurence Gallagher	Ireland	Ordinary, Boston.
Robert H. O'Neal	N. Carolina	Frigate Cumberland.
William Hart	Virginia	Waiting orders.
William Black	N. Hampshire	Navy Yard, Boston.
William Waters	New York	Navy Yard, Washington.
Joshua Bryant	Massachusetts	Steamer Mississippi.
V. R. Hall	New York	Columbus 74.
John Mills	Connecticut	Navy Yard, New York.
John Shannon	Massachusetts	Sloop Vincennes.
Wm. Whitehead	Virginia	Ordinary, Norfolk.
Thomas G. Bell	N. Carolina	On leave.
William Smith	Maine	Sloop Saratoga.
Charles Johnston	New York	Waiting orders.
Samuel Drew	Maine	On leave.
Joseph Lewis	Virginia	Sloop Yorktown.
John Munro	Massachusetts	Sloop John Adams.
Edward Cavendy	Belgium	Sloop Jamestown.
Robert Simpson	N. Carolina	Frigate Constitution.
Eleizer Foster	Connecticut	Navy Yard, Norfolk.
George Wilmuth	Maine	Frigate Savannah.
William Hoff	Massachusetts	Frigate Columbia.
John Dunderdale	Maryland	Sloop Levant.
John Featherson	New York	Sloop Plymouth.
Alfred Hingerty	Virginia	Sloop Falmouth.
Robert Dixon	England	Frigate Raritan.
Robert Whitaker	New York	Sloop Portsmouth.
Michael Hall	do.	Frigate Potomac.
George Williams	Florida	Sloop Marion.
GUNNERS.		
John Blight	New York	Navy Yard, Boston.
Asa Curtis	Massachusetts	Naval Asylum, Philadelphia.
William B. Brown	Germany	Frigate Columbia.
Alexander Stephenson	New York	Frigate Cumberland.
Charles Cobb	Maine	Frigate Congress.
Archibald S. Lewis	do.	Frigate Potomac.
Samuel G. City	Maryland	Navy Yard, Norfolk.

NAVY LIST—*Carpenters.*

Names.	Where born.	Duty or Station.
Thomas Robinson	Scotland	Columbus 74.
John Myrick	Rhode Island	Magazine, New York.
Gustavus Newman	Sweden	Frigate Raritan.
Adrian A. Peterson	Belgium	Ordinary, Boston.
Jos. W. Pennington	Maryland	On leave.
Daniel James	Massachusetts	Sloop John Adams.
James M. Cooper	New Jersey	Frigate Savannah.
William Burton	Pennsylvania	Sloop Marion.
Richard F. Dunn	England	Navy Yard, Portsmouth.
John Clapham	Maine	On leave.
William Craig	New Jersey	Steamer Michigan.
John Martin	Maryland	Steamer Mississippi.
Elisha Whitton	Massachusetts	Sloop Jamestown.
Washington Bright	Dist. Colum.	Navy Yard, Pensacola.
Benjamin Bunker	Massachusetts	On leave.
John G. Williamson	Pennsylvania	Sloop Saratoga.
John D. Benthall	South Carolina	On leave.
Thomas Dewey	New York	Sloop Plymouth.
George Sirian	Greece	Frigate Constitution.
William H. Myers	Pennsylvania	Navy Yard, Washington.
John Barr	do.	Receiving ship at Norfolk.
John Caulk	Maryland	Sloop Falmouth.
Samuel Allen	Massachusetts	Navy Yard, New York.
John Owins	Maryland	Sloop Warren.
Robert S. King	Dist. of Col.	Steamer Princeton.
S. M. Beckwith	Maine	Sloop Levant.
And'w A. Randall	Rhode Island	Sloop Portsmouth.
George J. Marshall	Dist. Colum.	Brig Lawrence.
David Rankin	Maryland	Brig Truxtun.
Thomas M. Crooker	Massachusetts	Sloop Yorktown.
William Arnold	New York	Sloop Vincennes.
Daniel Douglass	Maryland	Sloop Cyane.
Elijah Haskell	Massachusetts	Waiting orders.
John C. Ritter		St. Mary's.
CARPENTERS.		
John A. Dickason	Massachusetts	Ordinary, New York.
John Southwick	do.	Frigate Congress.
William E. Sheffield	Connecticut	Navy Yard, Pensacola.
Francis Sagee	Pennsylvania	Waiting orders.
Patrick Dee	Ireland	Navy Yard, Boston.
John Green	N. Hampshire	Sloop Levant.
Joseph Cox	Maine	Steamer Mississippi.
Henry P. Leslie	South Carolina	Navy Yard, Norfolk.
William M. Laighton	N. Hampshire	Frigate Raritan.
John Rainbow	Virginia	On duty connected with Nav. School.
John Cahill	Maryland	Sloop Jamestown.
Francis M. Cecil	Rhode Island	Frigate Savannah.

NAVY LIST—*Sailmakers.*

Names.	Where born.	Duty or Station.
Christopher Jordan	Massachusetts	Receiving ship at Boston.
Jonas Dibble	Connecticut	Columbus 74.
Amos Chick	N. Hampshire	Waiting orders.
William Knight	Maine	Sloop Warren.
John M. Webb	New York	Waiting orders.
James Meads	Maryland	Frigate Columbia.
Wm. D. Jenkins	Maine	Sloop Marion.
David Marple	Massachusetts	Navy Yard, New York.
James McDonnell	Maryland	Brig Truxtun.
Hugh Lindsay	Ireland	Sloop Yorktown.
William Lee	New York	On leave.
John O. Butler	Virginia	Sloop Saratoga.
Robert L. Sheffield	New York	Sloop Falmouth.
Edward W. Barnicoat	Massachusetts	Frigate Potomac.
George Wisner	Pr. Ed. Island	Sloop Portsmouth.
Charles Boardman	Massachusetts	Sloop John Adams.
Samuel J. Seely	New York	Frigate Cumberland.
James Magill	Maryland	Naval Asylum, Philadelphia.
Jesse C. Morrisen	Virginia	Sloop Plymouth.
Luther Manson	Maine	Waiting orders.
Henry G. Thomas	Virginia	Frigate Constitution.
Thomas Johnson	do.	Sloop St. Mary's.
Gerard Henderson		Sloop Vincennes.
M. M. Dodd	do.	Sloop Cyane.
SAILMAKERS.		
James R. Childs	Maryland	Waiting orders.
Nath'l B. Peed	Virginia	Receiving ship at New York.
William Ryan	New York	Frigate Savannah.
J. G. Gallagher	do.	Steamer Mississippi.
John Heckle	do.	Receiving ship at Boston.
Henry Bacon	Massachusetts	Sloop Plymouth.
Thomas J. Boyce	New York	Waiting orders.
Richard Van Voorhis	do.	Sloop John Adams.
Madison Wheeden	Maryland	Frigate Congress.
George Thomas		Sloop Falmouth.
James Ferguson	Pennsylvania	Waiting orders.
John Burdine	Dist. Colum.	Waiting orders.
Isaac Whitney	Massachusetts	Frigate Constitution.
Wm. H. Brayton	do.	Navy Yard, New York.
John Joins	Maryland	Sloop Warren.
Benj'n B. Burchsted	Massachusetts	Waiting orders.
Isaac D. Freeman	New Jersey	Sloop Marion.
William Bennet	Virginia	Sloop Levant.
Nicholas Buck	Pennsylvania	Navy Yard, Philadelphia.
John Peed	Virginia	Frigate Congress.
Robert C. Rodman		Columbus 74.
George T. Lozier	New York	Frigate Raritan.

NAVY LIST—*Marine Corps.*

Names.	Where born.	Duty or Station.
George Parker.......	Massachusetts	On leave.
Electius Middleton ...	Dist. of Col...	Sloop Saratoga.
James Frazer........	New York....	Frigate Potomac.
Charles Harvey.......	Ireland.......	On leave.
George D. Blackford..	New Jersey....	Frigate Columbia.
Theodore C. Herbert..	New York....	Sloop Vincennes.
David B. Park.......	Virginia.......	Sloop St. Mary's.
Thaddeus W. Kelly..	Pennsylvania..	Waiting orders.
Jacob Stevens........	.....do.......	Sloop Jamestown.
David Bruce.........	Massachusetts	Sloop Portsmouth.
Robert Hunter.......	New York....	Sloop Cyane.
Samuel Rhoades......	Massachusetts	Waiting orders.

MARINE CORPS.

Names.	Lineal rank.	Brevet rank.	Where born.	Duty or Station.
Col. Commandant.		*Brig. G'l Bvt.*		
Arch'd Henderson.	1 July, 1834	27 Jan., 1837	Va....	Head Q'rs Wash.
Lieut. Colonel.		*Lt. Cols. Bvt.*		
Samuel Miller.....	6 Oct., 1841	3 Mar., 1827	Mass..	Marine Barracks, Brooklyn, N. Y.
Majors.				
Samuel E. Watson	1 July, 1834	20 Mar., 1830	Va....	Marine Barracks,* Charlest'n, Mass.
Levi Twiggs......	15 Nov. 1840	*Captain brevet* 3 Mar., 1825	Ga....	Marine Barracks,* Philadelphia.
John Harris......	6 Oct., 1841	*Major brevet* 27 Jan., 1837.	Penn..	Marine Barracks,* Gosport, Va.
		Captains Brvt.		
Thos. A. Linton ..	12 Mar., 1834	18 April, 1827	Va...	Waiting orders.
Captains.				
James Edelin.....	1 July, 1834	.....do.....	Md...	Head Q'rs Wash.*
Parke G. Howle, *Adj't and Insp'r*..	.....do.....	.....do.....	Va....	Head Quarters.
William Dulany...	.....do.....	*Major brevet* 3 Mar., 1843	Va....	Mar. bar., Pens'la.*

* Commanding the Marine Barracks at those stations.

NAVY LIST—*Marine Corps.*

Names.	Lineal rank.	Brevet rank.	Where born.	Duty or Station.
Captains.		*Captains Brvt.*		
Thos. S. English..	1 July, 1834	11 Aug., 1829	Mass..	Marine Barracks, Brooklyn.
Geo. W. Walker, *Pay Master....*	....do.....	3 Mar., 1831	D. C..	Head Quarters.
Ward Marston ...	....do.....	30 Oct., 1831	Mass..	Frigate Savannah.
A. A. Nicholson, *Quartermaster.*	25 July, 1834	27 May, 1832	S. C...	Head Quarters.
Benj. Macomber...	18 Jan., 1838	2 April, 1833	R. I..	On leave.
Ab'm N. Brevoort.	6 Mar., 1838	26 Sept., 1833	N. Y.	Marine Barracks, Charlest'n, Mass.
Richard Douglass.	24 Feb., 1839	....	Penn..	Waiting orders.
Job G. Williams...	15 Nov., 1840	....	Mass..	Marine Barracks, Philadelphia.
Alvin Edson......	6 Oct., 1841	....	Vt....	Receiv'g ship Ohio.
Henry B. Tyler...	12 Mar., 1845	....	Va....	Columbus 74.

Names.	Lineal rank.	Where born.	Duty or Station.
First Lieutenants.			
Joseph L. C. Hardy...	13 June, 1830	N. Y..	Marine Barracks, Head Qrs.
George F. Lindsay, *Assistant Quartermaster..*	23 Sept. 1831	Va....	Philadelphia.
Landon N. Carter......	7 April, 1832	Va....	Sick.
John G. Reynolds......	17 May, 1833	N. J...	Rec'g ship North Carolina.
Francis C. Hall.........	1 July, 1834	Md...	Rec'g ship Pennsylvania.
George H. Terrett.......	......do......	Va....	Frigate Cumberland.
William E. Stark........	......do......	Va....	Norfolk, Va., Clothing Store.
Nathaniel S. Waldron .	25 July, 1835	N. H.	Columbus 74.
William Lang...........	13 June, 1836	N. Y.	Frigate Raritan.
Jacob Zeilin	12 Sept. 1836	Penn .	Frigate Congress.
D. D. Baker...........	30 Dec. 1837	Mass..	Waiting orders.
Archibald H. Gillespie.	18 Jan. 1838	N. Y..	Norfolk, Va., just returned in the Brandywine.
Benjamin E. Brooke....	7 Feb. 1839	Va....	Marine Barracks, Head Qrs.
Jabez C. Rich...........	24 Feb. 1839	Maine	Marine Barracks, Brooklyn.
Thomas T. Sloan.......	31 Oct. 1840	Ky...	Marine Barracks, Brooklyn.
Addison Garland.......	15 Nov. 1840	Va....	Marine Barracks, Philadel'a.
Frederick B. McNeil ..	15 April, 1841	Mass..	Sloop Jamestown.
Edward L. West.......	6 Oct. 1841	Md....	Marine Bar. Charlest'n, Mass.
Robert C. Caldwell.....	....	Ohio..	Marine Barracks, Pensacola.
William L. Young.....	12 Mar. 1845	N. C..	Sloop Plymouth.
Second Lieutenants.			
Josiah Watson.........	21 July, 1835	D. C..	Sloop Boston.

NAVY LIST—*Engineer Corps.*

Names.	Lineal rank.	Where born.	Duty or Station.
Henry B. Watson......	5 Oct. 1836	N. C..	Sloop Portsmouth
Thomas A. Brady......	3 Feb. 1837	N. J..	Frigate Potomac.
Isaac T. Doughty......	26 Sept. 1837	N. Y..	Marine Barracks, Brooklyn.
William A. F. Maddox	14 Oct. 1837	Md...	Sloop Cyane.
William B. Slack......	28 Jan. 1839	N. J..	Marine Bar., Gosport, Va.
John S. Devlin.........	21 Feb. 1839	Irel'nd	Sloop Saratoga.
Algernon S. Taylor....	.....do.....	Va....	Mahon, Mediterranean, on duty in Quarterm'rs dept..
Wm. L. Shuttleworth..	28 Feb. 1839	N. J..	Marine Barracks, Pensacola.
Robert D. Taylor.......	2 Mar. 1839	Va....	Marine Bar., Gosport, Va.
Joseph W. Curtis	4 May, 1840	N. H..	Frigate Constitution.
Robert Tansill.........	4 Nov. 1840	Va....	Under sentence court martial.
John C. Grayson.......	4 May, 1841	Ky...	Marine Barracks, Philadel'a.
Matthew R. Kintzing..	8 Sept. 1841	Penn .	Marine Barracks, Philadel'a.
John D. Simms.........	7 Oct. 1841	Va....	Sloop St. Mary's.
Henry W. Queen.......	14 Mar. 1842	Md...	Frigate Savannah.
Daniel J. Sutherland...	29 Mar. 1842	Penn .	Frigate Cumberland.
William W. Russell...	5 April, 1843	Md...	Aid to Gen. Henderson.
John C. Cash..........	14 Mar. 1845	......	Columbus 74.
George Adams........	19 Mar. 1845	Ky...	Marine Barracks, Pensacola.

ENGINEER CORPS.

Names.	Where born.	Duty or Station.
ENGINEER IN CHIEF.		
Charles H. Haswell..	New York....	Washington.
CHIEF ENGINEERS.		
John Faron, jr.........	Ireland........	Special duty.
Andrew Hebard........	Connecticut...	Steamer Michigan.
William Sewell, jr.....	New York....	Steamer Mississippi.
Wm. W. W. Wood..	N. Carolina...	Under orders to Pensacola navy yard.
Wm. P. Williamson..	Virginia......	Steamer Princeton.
Charles B. Moss......	.....do......	On furlough.
FIRST ASSISTANTS.		
Alexander Birkbeck, jr	New York....	Pittsburg, Pa.
*William Scott.......	.....do......	Steamer Michigan.
Henry Hunt..........	.....do......	Steamer Princeton.
Daniel B. Martin.....	New Jersey ..	Steamer Mississippi.

* Assistants not yet re-examined.

NAVY LIST—*Engineers—Navy Agents.*

Names.	Where born.	Duty or Station.
Hiram Sanford	New York	Under orders to Mississippi.
James Cochrane	do	Under orders to Princeton.
*Benj'n F. Isherwood	do	Navy Yard, Pensacola.
Livingston S. Bartholomew	do	Waiting orders.
SECOND ASSISTANTS.		
Joshua Follansbee	Dist. Colum'a	Steamer Mississippi.
John Alexander	Pennsylvania	Navy Yard, Norfolk.
*John K. Matthews	New York	Steamer Michigan.
*Gilbert Sherwood	do	Navy Yard, Pensacola.
James Atkinson	Ireland	On furlough.
Levi T. Spencer	New York	Waiting orders.
Albert S. Palmer	do	Under orders to Pensacola navy yard.
Jesse S. Rutherford	Pennsylvania	Steamer Princeton.
Samuel Archbold	Ireland	Steamer Col. Harney.
Naylor C. Davis	Maryland	Steamer Princeton.
Daniel Murphy	Ireland	Steamer Mississippi.
THIRD ASSISTANTS.		
John M. Middleton	Delaware	Steamer Engineer.
*John Gallagher	Europe	Steamer Michigan.
William F. Mercier	Pennsylvania	Waiting orders.
*Smith Thompson, jr.	New York	Waiting orders.
William Taggert	Pennsylvania	Steamer Princeton.
William Luce	New York	Under orders to Mississippi.
James W. King	Maryland	Under orders to Mississippi.
*Thomas Dickson	Virginia	Steamer Michigan.
Theodore Zeller	New York	Steamer Col. Harney.
Robert Danby	Delaware	Under orders to Col. Harney.
William H. Shock	Maryland	Under orders to Pensacola navy yard.
John Serro	Dist. Colum.	Waiting orders.
M. M. Thompson	New York	Under orders to Mississippi.
*Charles Coleman	Europe	Steamer Princeton.
Edward Faron	New York	Office of Engineer in Chief.
William E. Everett	do	Under orders to Pensacola navy yard.

*Assistants not yet re-examined.

NAVY LIST—*Navy Agents, &c.*

CIVIL BRANCH.

Names.	Where born.	Station or Residence.
NAVY AGENTS.		
Samuel Cushman	Maine	Portsmouth, N. H.
Isaac Hull Wright		Boston.
Prosper M. Wetmore	Connecticut	New York.
S. D. Patterson	Pennsylvania	Philadelphia.
Joseph White	Ireland	Baltimore.
William B. Scott	Maryland	Washington city.
George Loyall	Virginia	Norfolk.
Benjamin D. Heriot	N. Carolina	Charleston, S. C.
Octavus Cohen		Savannah.
Walker Anderson		Pensacola.
Jos. S. Watkins	Virginia	Memphis, Tennessee.
*Baring, Brothers & Co		London.
†Nathaniel Denby		Marseilles.
‡Wm. P. Furniss & Co		St. Thomas, W. I.
§Edw'd McCall & Co.		Lima.

Names.	Where born.	Station or Residence.	Salary.
NAVAL STOREKEEPERS.			
Daniel Pierce	Maine	Portsmouth, N. H	$1400
Seth J. Thomas	Massachusetts	Boston	1700
Tunis Craven	New Jersey	New York	1700
Robert Kennedy	Pennsylvania	Philadelphia	1250
James M. Selden	Virginia	Washington City	1700
Merit Jordan	Virginia	Norfolk	1700
Robert Joyner	N. Carolina	Pensacola	1700
Wm. R. Brown	Virginia	Memphis, Tennessee	1250
OFFICERS IN CHARGE OF NAVAL STORES FOR FOREIGN SQUADRONS.			
Junius J. Boyle, Lieut.	Maryland	Port Mahon	1500
Jas. Ferguson, Master.	New York	Rio de Janeiro	1500

*Paid one per cent. commission, and interest on advances, at the rate of five per cent.

†Paid four and three-fourths per cent. upon advances.

‡Paid a commission of two and one-half per cent. on purchases.

§Paid $4,000 per annum, and allowances for storage, wharfage, eartage, and other necessary expenses, upon receipt and delivery of supplies.

NAVY LIST—*Naval Constructors, &c.*

Names.	Where born.	Station or Residence.	Salary.
F. Alexander, P. Mid.	Mississippi....	Port Praya.................	$1500
Thos. H. Stevens.do..	Connecticut....	Sandwich Islands..........	1500
Edw'd A. Barnett.do..	Pennsylvania .	Hong Kong, East Indies....	1500
CHIEF NAVAL CONSTRUCTOR.			
Samuel Humphreys ..	Pennsylvania .	Washington City..........	3000
NAVAL CONSTRUCTORS.			
Samuel M. Pook......	Massachusetts	Charlestown, Mass.........	2300
Josiah Barker.......	Massachusetts	Portsmouth, N. H..........	2300
Samuel Hartt........	Massachusetts	On special duty............	2300
John Lenthall........	Dist. Colum..	Philadelphia................	2300
Foster Rhodes.......	New York....	Norfolk......................	2300
Francis Grice........	Virginia......	New York..................	2300
Charles D. Brodie....	Virginia......	Pensacola	1500
PRINCIPAL ENGINEER.*			
Charles W. Copeland.	Connecticut....	New York..................	2500
CIVIL ENGINEERS.†			
Wm. P. S. Sanger....	Massachusetts	New York..................	3000
W. J. McAlpine, Asst.	New York....	New York..................	2400
A. B. Warford.......	Pennsylvania .	Memphis	2500
T. L. O'Sullivan, Asst.	....	Memphis	1500
D. Morrison.........	....	Memphis	1000
Geo. O'Driscoll	Ireland.......	Pensacola..................	1700
AGENTS FOR THE PRESERVATION OF LIVE OAK TIMBER.			
A. G. Southall, Sup't..	Virginia	Washington, D. C..........	1200
John F. H. Claiborne.	Mississippi....	Louisiana, Miss., and Ala...	2000
John W. Rochelle....	Virginia.......	Middle Florida	2000
Andrew Henshaw....	....	Alabama...................	250
—— De la Roche.....	....	Grover's Island, Geo	None.

* Employed under direction of the Bureau of Construction, Equipment, and Repair.

† Employed under direction of the Bureau of Yards and Docks.

NAVY LIST—*Vessels of War.*

Names.	Where born.	Station or Residence.	Salary.
INSPECTORS OF HEMP.			
Lewis Saunders	Virginia	Kentucky	$1000
John Smith	Kentucky	Missouri	1000
PENSION AGENT.			
Isaac P. Davis		Boston	500
LITHOGRAPHER.*			
Curtis B. Graham		Washington, D. C	950

VESSELS OF WAR OF THE UNITED STATES NAVY.

Names.	Rate.	Where and when built.	Situation.
Ships of the Line.	Guns		
Pennsylvania	120	Philadelphia 1837	Receiving ship at Norfolk.
New Orleans	110	Sacket's Harbor 1814	On the stocks at Sacket's Harbor.
Franklin	74	Philadelphia 1815	In Ordinary at Boston.
Ohio	74	New York 1820	Receiving ship at Boston.
North Carolina	74	Philadelphia 1820	Receiving ship at New York.
Delaware	74	Gosport, Va 1820	In ordinary at Norfolk.
Alabama	74		On the stocks at Portsmouth, N. Hampshire.
Vermont	74		On the stocks at Boston.
Virginia	74		On the stocks at Boston.
New York	74		On the stocks at Norfolk.
Columbus	74	Washington 1819	Flag ship, East India squadron.
Razee.			
Independence	54	Boston 1814	In ordinary at Boston.
Frigates, 1st Class.			
Potomac	44	Washington 1821	Flag ship, Home squadron.
Brandywine	44	Washington 1825	In ordinary at Norfolk.
Columbia	44	Washington 1836	Under orders as flag ship of Brazil squadron.

* Employed under direction of the Bureau of Ordnance and Hydrography.

NAVY LIST—*Vessels of War.*

Names.	Rate.	When and where built.	Situation.
	Guns		
Congress	44	Portsmouth, N. H. 1841	Under orders as flag ship of Pacific squadron.
Cumberland	44	Boston 1842	Flag ship Mediterranean squadron.
Savannah	44	New York 1842	Flag ship Pacific squadron.
Raritan	44	Philadelphia 1843	Flag ship Brazil squadron.
Santee	44		On the stocks at Portsmouth, N. H.
Sabine	44		On the stocks at New York.
St. Lawrence	44		On the stocks at Norfolk.
United States	44	Philadelphia 1797	Repairing for sea at Boston.
Constitution	44	Boston 1797	Special service, East Indies.
Constellation	36	Baltimore 1797	In ordinary at Norfolk.
Macedonian	36	Captured 1812 Rebuilt 1836	In ordinary at New York.
Sloops of War.			
Saratoga	20	Portsmouth, N.H. 1842	Home squadron.
John Adams	20	Charls'n, S. C. 1799 Rebuilt 1820	Home squadron.
Boston	20	Boston 1825	Brazil squadron, ordered home.
Vincennes	20	New York 1826	East India squadron.
Warren	20	Boston 1826	Pacific, on her way home.
Falmouth	20	Boston 1827	Home squadron.
Fairfield	20	New York 1828	In ordinary, at Norfolk.
Vandalia	20	Philadelphia 1828	At Norfolk
St. Louis	20	Washington 1828	In ordinary at Norfolk.
Cyane	20	Boston 1837	Pacific squadron.
Levant	20	New York 1837	Pacific squadron.
Portsmouth	20	Portsmouth, N.H. 1843	Pacific squadron.
Plymouth	20	Boston 1843	Mediterranean squadron.
Albany	20	New York 1843	On the stocks at New York.
Germantown	20	Philadelphia 1843	On the stocks at Philadelphia.
St. Mary's	20	Washington 1844	Home squadron.
Jamestown	20	Norfolk 1844	Flag ship, African squadron.
Ontario	18	Baltimore 1813	Receiving ship at Baltimore.
Decatur	16	New York 1839	At Norfolk.
Preble	16	Portsmouth, N.H. 1839	In ordinary at New York.
Yorktown	16	Norfolk 1839	African squadron.
Marion	16	Boston 1839	African squadron.
Dale	16	Philadelphia 1839	Preparing for sea at New York.
Brigs.			
Dolphin	10	New York 1836	Preparing for sea at Norfolk.
Porpoise	10	Boston 1836	Home squadron.

NAVY LIST—*Vessels of War.*

Names.	Rate.	Where and when built.	Situation.
	Guns		
Somers........	10	New York........1842	Home squadron.
Truxtun......	10	Norfolk..........1842	African squadron.
Bainbridge	10	Boston...........1842	Brazil squadron.
Perry.........	10	Norfolk..........1843	In ordinary at Norfolk.
Lawrence	10	Baltimore........1843	Home squadron.
Boxer.........	10	Boston...........1831	In ordinary at Boston.
Schooners.			
Shark..........	10	Washington......1821	Pacific squadron.
Experiment....	....	Washington......1831	Receiving ship at Philadelphia.
Flirt...........	4	Transf'd fm. War Dept.	In packet service.
Wave..........	....	.....do......do.....	On coast survey.
Phenix........	....	.....do......do.....	In ordinary at Norfolk.
On-ka-hy-e.....	....	Purchased.......1843	In packet service.
Steamers.			
Mississippi	*10	Philadelphia......1841	Home squadron.
Fulton.........	4	New York.......1837	In ordinary at New York.
Union.........	*4	Norfolk..........1842	In ordinary at Washington.
Princeton	12	Philadelphia......1843	Home squadron
Michigan.......	†6	Erie..............1844	Lakes.
Water Witch..	3	Washington......1844	Prepar'g for sea at Philadelp'a.
Col. Harney...	2	Transf'd fm. War Dept.	Packet service.
Gen. Taylor...	....	.....do......do.....	Tender at Pensacola.
Engineer......	....	....	Tender at Norfolk.
(Not named)...	....	....	On stocks at Pittsburgh.
Store Ships and Brigs.			
Relief.........	6	Philadelphia......1836	Pacific squadron.
Erie...........	8	Baltimore........1813	Pacific squadron.
Lexington......	8	New York.......1825	Home squadron
Southampton ..	6	Norfolk..........1844	African squadron.

* Paixhan guns. † 2 Paixhan Guns.

NAVY LIST—*Pay, &c.*

RECAPITULATION.

Grade and number in service.	Pay per ann.	Rations.
CAPTAINS—68.		NOTE.—One ration per day, only, is allowed to all officers when attached to vessels for sea service.
Senior captain in service	$4500 00	
......Do.....on leave, &c	3500 00	
Captains of squadron	4000 00	
...Do...on other duty	3500 00	
...Do...off duty, &c	2500 00	
COMMANDERS—97.		
Commanders in sea service	2500 00	
.....Do.....at navy yards, or other duty	2100 00	
.....Do.....on leave, &c	1800 00	
LIEUTENANTS—326.		
Lieutenants commanding	1800 00	
....Do....on other duty	1500 00	
....Do....waiting orders	1200 00	
SURGEONS—69.		
Surgeons, first five years after date of commission	1000 00	
....Do........do.....at navy yards, &c	1250 00	
....Do........do.....in sea service	1333 33$\frac{1}{3}$	
....Do........do.....of the fleet	1500 00	
....Do...second five years	1200 00	
....Do........do.....at navy yards	1500 00	
....Do........do.....in sea service	1600 00	
....Da........do.....of the fleet	1800 00	
....Do...third five years	1400 00	
....Do........do.....at navy yards	1750 00	
....Do........do.....in sea service	1866 66$\frac{2}{3}$	
....Do........do.....of the fleet	2100 00	
....Do...fourth five years	1600 00	
....Do........do.....at navy yards	2000 00	
....Do........do.....in sea service	2133 33$\frac{1}{3}$	
....Do........do.....of the fleet	2400 00	
....Do...twenty years, and upwards	1800 00	
....Do........do.....at navy yards	2250 00	
....Do........do.....in sea service	2400 00	
....Do........do.....of the fleet	2700 00	
PASSED ASSISTANT SURGEONS—30.		
Passed assistant surgeons at sea	1200 00	

NAVY LIST—*Pay, &c.*

Grade and number in service.	Pay per ann.	Rations.
Passed assistant surgeons at navy yards, &c..........	$1150 00	NOTE.—One ration per day, only, is allowed to all officers when attached to vessels for sea service.
..Do..........do......waiting orders............	850 00	
ASSISTANT SURGEONS—37.		
Assistant surgeons at sea.........................	950 00	
...Do......do....at navy yards, &c...............	950 00	
...Do......do....waiting orders..................	650 00	
PURSERS—64.		
Pursers of ships of the line.......................	3500 00	
..Do...of frigates or razees......................	3000 00	
..Do...of sloops or steamers of the first class........	2000 00	
..Do...of brigs and schooners and steamers less than first class..........................	1500 00	
..Do...of navy yards, Boston, New York, Norfolk, and Pensacola.........................	2500 00	
..Do...of navy yards, Portsmouth, Philadelphia, and Washington.........................	2000 00	
..Do...of naval stations within the United States....	1500 00	
..Do...of receiving ships at Boston, New York, and Norfolk.............................	2500 00	
..Do...of other places...........................	1500 00	
..Do...on leave and waiting orders, the same pay as surgeons..........................	....	
CHAPLAINS—23.		
Chaplains in sea service..........................	1200 00	
...Do....on leave, &c............................	800 00	
PASSED MIDSHIPMEN—184.		
Passed midshipmen on duty.......................	750 00	
..Do......do.....waiting orders..................	600 00	
MIDSHIPMEN—267.		
Midshipmen in sea service.........................	400 00	
....Do.....on other duty.........................	350 00	
....Do.....on leave, &c..........................	300 00	
MASTERS—31.		
Master of a ship of the line at sea.................	1100 00	
..Do...on other duty............................	1000 00	
..Do...on leave, &c.............................	750 00	

NAVY LIST—*Pay, &c.*

Grade and number in service.	Pay per ann.	Rations.
MASTERS' MATES, (WARRANTED)—11.		
Masters' mates on duty	$450 00	NOTE.—One ration per day, only, is allowed to all officers attached to vessels for sea service.
......Do......on leave, &c.	300 00	
PROFESSORS OF MATHEMATICS—22.		
Professors of mathematics on duty	1200 00	
TEACHERS OF LANGUAGES—3.		
Teachers at naval schools	*480 00	
BOATSWAINS.—30. GUNNERS.—41. CARPENTERS.—36. SAILMAKERS.—34.		
Of a ship of the line, or in navy yards at Boston, New York, and Norfolk	800 00	
On other duty	700 00	
On leave, &c., first ten years	500 00	
....Do......after...do	600 00	
MARINE CORPS.	Pay per month.	Rations per day.
Colonel Commandant—1†	$75 00	12 And allow'es.
Lieutenant Colonel—1	60 00	5
Majors—4	50 00	4
Captains—13‡	40 00	4
First Lieutenants—20	30 00	4
Second Lieutenants—20	25 00	4
ENGINEER CORPS.	Pay per ann.	Rations.
Engineer in Chief—1	$3000 00	None.
Chief Engineers—6	....	One ration per day when on duty.
.....Do......on duty	1500 00	
.....Do......waiting orders	1200 00	
First Assistant Engineers—8	....	
....Do..........do....on duty	900 00	
....Do..........do....waiting orders	700 00	

* Teachers receive in addition two rations per day, at 20 cents each.

† As Brevet Brig. General, he receives the same pay as officers of that grade in the Army

‡ Three of these captains are in the Staff, as Paymaster, Quartermaster, and Adjutan and Inspector, and receive pay as Majors.

NAVY LIST—*Pay, &c.*

Grade and number in service.	Pay per ann.	Rations.
Second Assistant Engineers—11	....	One ration per day when on duty.
....Do..........do....on duty	$700 00	
....Do..........do....waiting orders	500 00	
Third Assistant Engineers—16	....	
....Do..........do....on duty	500 00	
....Do..........do....waiting orders	350 00	
CIVIL BRANCH.		
Navy Agents—11*	....	
Temporary Agents—4	....	
Naval Storekeepers—8†	....	
......Do.........(officers of the Navy)—5	1500 00	
Chief Naval Constructor—1	2000 00	
Naval Constructors—7†	....	
Principal Engineer—1	2500 00	
Civil Engineers—6†	....	
Agents for the preservation of live oak timber—5†	....	
Inspectors of Hemp—2	1000 00	
Pension Agent—1	500 00	
Lithographer—1	950 00	

LIST OF DEATHS IN THE NAVY,

Since the 30th of September, 1843, as ascertained at the Department.

Name and rank.	Date.	Place.
CAPTAINS.		
E. P. Kennedy	March 28, 1844	Norfolk, Virginia.
Alexander J. Dallas	June 3, 1844	Frigate Savannah, Callao Bay.
Beverly Kennon	Febr'y 28, 1844	Steamship Princeton, Potomac river.
E. R. Shubrick	March 12, 1844	Frigate Columbia, at sea.
A. S. Ten Eick	March 28, 1844	New Brunswick, New Jersey.
COMMANDERS.		
Jonat'n D. Williamson	April 10, 1844	Island of Cuba.
Wm. D. Newman	October 11, 1844	Drowned at Montevideo.

* Commissions not to exceed $2,000 per annum.
† The salaries of these are affixed opposite their respective names.

NAVY LIST—*Deceased Officers.*

Name and Rank.	Date.	Place.
LIEUTENANTS.		
George J. Wyche....	October 25, 1843	At Boston.
Alberto Griffith......	Dec'r 20, 1843	Kingston, Jamaica.
John F. Mercer......	Febr'y 10, 1844	New York.
Francis E. Baker.....	May 16, 1844	Valparaiso.
Francis E. Barry.....	August 19, 1844	St. Louis, Missouri.
James E. Brown......	Sept'r 3, 1844	Westmoreland Court House, Va.
Ferdinand Piper	October 28, 1844	Drowned in Pensacola Bay.
George M. Hooe.....	April 10, 1845	Sloop Vandalia, at sea.
James M. Lockert....	April 10, 1845	Sloop Vandalia, at sea.
B. S. B. Darlington...	Febr'y 28, 1845	Portsmouth, New Hampshire.
Stephen Dod.........	Sept'r 19, 1845	Newark, New Jersey.
SURGEONS.		
A. A. Adee..........	Febr'y 22, 1844	New York.
Lewis Wolfley.......	July 21, 1844	Port Praya, Cape de Verdes.
ASSISTANT SURGEONS.		
Robert B. Banister...	July 12, 1844	Petersburg, Virginia.
Wm. Pitt Canning...	April 7, 1845	Sloop Vandalia, at sea.
PURSERS.		
Grenville C. Cooper..	March 2, 1844	Washington city.
James H. Clark......	Sept'r 19, 1844	Brooklyn, New York.
Arthur W. Upshur...	Sept'r, 1844	At sea, on board sloop Falmouth.
Robert S. Moore......	April 3, 1845	Sloop Vandalia, at sea.
E. N. Cox...........		
CHAPLAIN.		
George W. Swan.....	Sept'r 22, 1844	At Philadelphia.
PASSED MIDSHIPMEN.		
Henry Cadwalader...	July, 1844	At Philadelphia.
Hambleton F. Porter .	August 10, 1844	Schooner Flirt, Charleston, S. C.
William A. Henry...	Dec'r 14, 1844	Porto Grande, St. Vincent's.
S. D. Lavellette......	Febr'y 14, 1845	Chester, Pennsylvania.
R. Poinsett Lovell....	May 7, 1845	Sloop Boston, Montevideo.
Wm. Reed Low......	August, 1845	Concord, New Hampshire.
MIDSHIPMEN.		
Jno. E. Prentiss......	Dec'r 31, 1843	Rio de Janeiro.
George W. Harrison .	June 6, 1844	Brig Perry, at Macao.

NAVY LIST—*Deceased Officers.*

Name and Rank.	Date.	Place.
Jesse M. Smith......	Dec'r 3, 1844	Porto Grand, St. Vincent's.
Timothy W. Fiske...	Febr'y 16, 1845	Philadelphia.
Lucius M. Mason....	January 7, 1845	At sea, on board Constitution.
MASTER.		
R. S. Tatem.........	January 3, 1844	Philadelphia.
PROFESSOR OF MATHEMATICS.		
Wm. S. Fox.........	May 31, 1844	Drowned in Pensacola Bay.
BOATSWAIN.		
John Smith..........	October 7, 1843	Brooklyn, New York.
GUNNERS.		
Thomas Ryley.......	——, 1845	
Lewis Parker........	August 31, 1845	Pensacola.
CARPENTERS.		
Loman Smith........	May 31, 1844	Norfolk.
John Overman........	March 19, 1845	Sloop Vandalia, Port au Prince.
Wm. Jordan.........	June 5, 1845	
SAILMAKERS.		
Wm. Ward	May 24, 1844	Baltimore.
Josiah Faxon........	June 30, 1844	Frigate United States, at Callao.
Samuel V. Hawkins..	July 27, 1844	Portsmouth, New Hampshire.
Benjamin Crow......	March 31, 1845	Sloop Vandalia, at sea.
MARINE CORPS.		
MAJOR.		
Wm. H. Treeman....	March 11, 1845	
FIRST LIEUTENANT.		
George W. Robbins..	March 1, 1845	

LIST OF RESIGNATIONS IN THE NAVY,

Since the 30th of September, 1843.

Name and Rank.	Date of acceptance.
LIEUTENANTS.	
James J. Forbes......	Nov. 3, 1844
Wm. A. Jones.......	May 13, 1845
PASSED ASSISTANT SURGEONS.	
Charles Wm. Tait....	Nov. 17, 1843
V. L. Godon........	Sept. 20, 1844
Alex'r J. Wedderburn	June 14, 1844
H. D. Taliaferro	Nov. 15, 1844
ASSISTANT SURGEONS.	
J. W. B. Greenhow..	Sept. 10, 1844
Alfred C. Holt	Nov. 18, 1844
PURSERS.	
John C. Holland.....	Nov. 29, 1844
Thomas E. Norris....	Aug. 29, 1845
Philo White.........	Sept. 15, 1845
CHAPLAINS.	
J. P. B. Wilmer......	July 23, 1844
N. C. Fletcher........	June 9, 1845
PASSED MIDSHIPMEN.	
A. Hubley Jenkins ...	Mar. 12, 1844
C. S. Throckmorton..	Aug. 4, 1845
MIDSHIPMEN.	
E. Randolph Neilson .	Oct. 11, 1843
George Edward West.	June 24, 1844
Lewis Beard.........	July 23, 1844
H. H. Harrison......	April 27, 1845
E. A. Hopkins.......	June 9, 1845 to take effect July 1st.
Peter Kemble........	June 24, 1845

Name and Rank.	Date of acceptance.
John P. McFarland...	July 2, 1845
Alfred Bailey........	July 7, 1845
C. F. Collins.........	Sept. 8, 1845
M. Duralde..........	Sept. 18, 1845
E. C. Genet	Sept. 22, 1845
PROFESSORS OF MATHEMATICS.	
Joel Grant...........	Oct. 2, 1843
James P. Espy.......	July 5, 1845
BOATSWAINS.	
John Hunter.........	Mar. 9, 1844
Wm. C. Burns.......	Mar. 10, 1844
GUNNERS.	
Thomas Lewis.......	Jan. 14, 1845
George Bell..........	Jan. 14, 1845
SAILMAKERS.	
Samuel B. Banister...	July 10, 1844
George S. Dow	Sept. 18, 1844
C. C. Bartling........	July 18, 1845
ENGINEERS.	
Thomas McDonough, 3d assistant.........	Nov. 14, 1844
George M. Copeland, 3d assistant........	Nov. 30, 1844
NAVY AGENTS.	
William Mackay, at Savannah	Oct. 10, 1844
Timothy W. Upham, at Portsmouth, N. H.	April 1, 1845
NAVAL STOREKEEPER.	
Charles W. Cutter ...	May 1, 1845

NAVY LIST—*Officers Dismissed.*

LIST OF DISMISSIONS FROM THE NAVY,

Since the 30th of September, 1843.

Name and Rank.	Date of dismission.	Name and Rank.	Date of dismission.
LIEUTENANTS.		PROFESSORS OF MATHEMATICS.	
Addison R. Taliaferro.	Oct. 10, 1843 (Cashiered.)	James Major.........	Oct. 27, 1843
John W. West.......	Nov. 21, 1844	Bartholm'w McGowan	April 12, 1845
Wm. Decatur Hurst..	April 12, 1845	GUNNER.	
PURSERS.		Henry Keeling.......	May 22, 1845
Wm. P. Zantzinger...	Jan. 17, 1844		
*Wm. Grant.........	....	ENGINEER IN CHIEF.	
CHAPLAINS.		Gilbert L. Thompson.	Oct. 3, 1845
†John Robb..........	....	ENGINEER.	
*John Grigg..........	....	Thomas Copeland, 1st assistant...........	July 30, 1845
PASSED MIDSHIPMEN.			
James W. Ripley	Nov. 18, 1844	NAVY AGENTS.	
Charles T. Crocker...	Nov. 18, 1844		
Robert A. Knapp.....	May 17, 1845 (Cashiered.)	Robert C. Wetmore, at New York.........	July 1, 1844
MIDSHIPMEN.		J. Vincent Browne, at Boston.............	April 1, 1845
		Samuel McClellan, at Baltimore.........	April 8, 1845
James L. S. Beckwith.	Sept. 23, 1844		
Albert G. Cook......	Nov. 21, 1844	*James H. Suydam, at New York.........	
Albert G. Enos.......	Dec. 10, 1844		
F. P. Baldwin.........	June 5, 1845	T. Hayes, at Philad'a.	Commission expired Mar. 15, 1845.
Edward Allen.........	Aug. 9, 1845		
John L. Nelson......	Aug. 19, 1845	J. Morton, at Pensacola	Commission expired April 29, 1845.

* Commissions expired March 3d, 1845, they having been rejected by the Senate.

† Commission expired June 17, 1844, with the session of Congress, he having been rejected by the Senate.

TREASURY DEPARTMENT.

Names and offices.	Where employed.	Where born.	Compensation. Dol. cts.
SECRETARY OF THE TREASURY.			
Robert J. Walker	Washington	Pennsylvania	6000 00
CHIEF CLERK.			
McClintock Young	do	Maryland	2000 00
CLERKS.			
James N. Barker	do	Pennsylvania	1800 00
S. M. McKean	do	do	1600 00
Charles Dummer	do	Maine	1600 00
Richard Ela	do	N. Hampshire	1600 00
Charles Abert	do	New Jersey	1600 00
Gilbert Rodman	do	Pennsylvania	1400 00
John N. Lovejoy, jr	do	Maryland	1400 00
John McGinniss, jr	do	Pennsylvania	1400 00
John F. Heartley	do	Maine	1400 00
Charles M. Ingersoll	do	do	1150 00
Charles Fisher	do	Germany	1150 00
William Gulager	do	Massachusetts	1000 00
Samuel Green	do	N. Hampshire	1000 00
William P. Mathews	do	Maryland	1000 00
George Harrington	do	Massachusetts	1000 00
S'l D. Baker, (*Statistical Bureau*)	do	Virginia	1500 00
MESSENGERS.			
Charles Pettit	do	Pennsylvania	700 00
James W. Shields	do	New York	650 00
SUPERINTENDENT OF THE SOUTH-EAST EXECUTIVE BUILDING.			
J. P. Pepper	do	Pennsylvania	500 00
WATCHMEN.			
Elijah Ourand	do	Maryland	365 00
William C. Goddard	do	do	365 00
Jo n C. Steuart	do	Dist. Colum.	365 00
Philip Hines	do	Maryland	365 00
J. W. Marlow	do	do	365 00
William Clark	do	Virginia	365 00
J. P. Hilton	do	Maryland	365 00
Charles W. Pettit	do	Dist. Colum.	365 00

TREASURY DEPARTMENT—*Comptrollers, Clerks, &c.*

Names and offices.	Where employed.	Where born.	Compensation.
			Dol. cts.
FIRST COMPTROLLER.			
James W. McCulloh	Washington	Maryland	3500 00
CHIEF CLERK.			
James Larned	do	Massachusetts	1700 00
CLERKS.			
Nicholas B. Van Zandt	do	Delaware	1400 00
William Anderson	do	Tennessee	1400 00
Thomas Feran	do	Pennsylvania	1400 00
J. Bartram North	do	do	1400 00
Augustine L. McCrea	do	New York	1400 00
William H. Wright	do	do	1400 00
Robert Cochran	do	N. Carolina	1400 00
Horatio N. Crabb	do	Pennsylvania	1400 00
Thomas F. Anderson	do	do	1150 00
William Miller	do	Virginia	1150 00
James R. McCorkle	do	Pennsylvania	1150 00
Lewis L. Taylor	do	Virginia	1150 00
Hilary Langtry	do	do	1150 00
John Y. Laub	do	Dist. of Col.	1000 00
Benjamin F. Rogers	do	New Jersey	1000 00
Hopeful Toler	do	Virginia	1000 00
George Johnson	do	Maryland	1000 00
J. Quinton Washington	do	Dist. of Col.	1000 00
MESSENGER.			
William J. McCulloh	do	Maryland	700 00
ASSISTANT MESSENGER.			
Philip Hines	do	do	700 00
SECOND COMPTROLLER.			
Albion K. Parris	do	Maine	3000 00
CHIEF CLERK.			
John M. Brodhead	do	N. Hampshire	1700 00

TREASURY DEPARTMENT—*Comptrollers, Clerks, &c.*

Names and offices.	Where employed.	Where born.	Compensation.
			Dol. cts.
CLERKS.			
James M. Cutts	Washington	Maine	1400 00
George D. Abbot	do	Dist. Colum.	1400 00
Joseph Manahan	do	N. Hampshire.	1150 00
Tobias Purrington	do	Maine	1150 00
William A. Evans	do	do	1150 00
Alfred Schucking	do	Prussia	1000 00
William Flinn	do	Pennsylvania	1000 00
Thomas J. Cathcart	do	Dist. of Col.	800 00
Martin M. Moor	do	Pennsylvania	800 00
MESSENGER.			
George C. Jackson	do	Virginia	700 00
FIRST AUDITOR.			
William Collins	do	do	3000 00
CHIEF CLERK.			
John Underwood	do	Pennsylvania	1700 00
CLERKS.			
James M. Torbert	do	Delaware	1400 00
Thomas L. Ragsdale	do	N. Carolina	1400 00
J. W. Bronaugh	do	Virginia	1150 00
M. H. Miller	do	Mississippi	1150 00
J. M. Ramsey	do	Pennsylvania	1150 00
D. W. Mahon	do	do	1150 00
J. Colegate	do	Maryland	1150 00
Alexander Mahon	do	Pennsylvania	1150 00
Joseph Ingle	do	do	1000 00
F. Doyle	do	Georgia	1000 00
John A. Hunnicutt	do	Virginia	1000 00
John Ferguson	do	Pennsylvania	1000 00
J. A. Brightwell	do	Maryland	800 00
MESSENGER.			
James W. Garner	do	Virginia	700 00
SECOND AUDITOR.			
John McCalla	Washington	Virginia	3000 00

TREASURY DEPARTMENT—*Auditors, Clerks, &c.*

Names and offices.	Where employed.	Where born.	Compensation.
			Dol. cts.
CHIEF CLERK.			
Josiah F. Polk	Washington	Maryland	1700 00
CLERKS.			
William Mechlin	do	Pennsylvania	1400 00
Wm. H. English	do	Indiana	1400 00
Peter Brady	do	Ireland	1150 00
O. S. Hall	do	Maryland	1150 00
D. E. Dunscombe	do	New York	1150 00
Theodore O'Hara	do	Kentucky	1150 00
Vinal Luce	do	Massachusetts	1150 00
Charles W. Forrest	do	Virginia	1150 00
Richard T. Queen	do	Maryland	1000 00
Theodore L. Moody	do	Maine	1000 00
Brooke Mackall	do	Maryland	1000 00
James W. Brown	do	N. Carolina	1000 00
Samuel Lewis	do	England	1000 00
Wm. S. Jackson	do	Virginia	1000 00
Eleazer Brown	do	New Jersey	800 00
MESSENGER.			
Francis A. Dunn	do	Pennsylvania	700 00
THIRD AUDITOR.			
Peter Hagner	do	Pennsylvania	3000 00
CHIEF CLERK.			
James Thompson	do	Maryland	1700 00
CLERKS.			
Charles Vinson	do	do	1400 00
Richard Burgess	do		1400 00
Bennet Clements	do	Maryland	1400 00
Henry K. Randall	do	do	1400 00
Samuel S. Rind	do	Dist. Colum.	1400 00
Charles S. Wallach	do	do	1400 00
Gideon Pierce	do	Maryland	1150 00
Levin Jones	do	do	1150 00
John Harry	do	do	1150 00
Anthony Hyde	do	do	1150 00
Silas H. Hill	do	N. Hampshire	1150 00
Daniel D. Davidson	do	Dist. Columbia	1150 00

TREASURY DEPARTMENT—*Auditors, Clerks, &c.*

Names and offices.	Where employed.	Where born.	Compensation.
			Dol. cts.
Walter H. S. Taylor	Washington	Maryland	1150 00
John R. Hagner	do	Dist. Columbia	1150 00
James M. Smith	do	Virginia	1150 00
Thomas R. Hampton	do	do	1150 00
Benjamin L. Bogan	do	do	1150 00
Erastus T. Montague	do	do	1150 00
Edward Smith	do	do	1000 00
Thomas C. Daniel	do	do	1000 00
Charles Abbot	do	Dist. Columbia	1000 00
John B. Kirkpatrick	do	New Jersey	1000 00
Samuel H. Janney	do	Dist. Columbia	1000 00
William Tyson	do	Maryland	1000 00
Alfred B. Thruston	do	Dist. Columbia	1000 00
Brook B. Williams	do	do	1000 00
Richard K. Watts	do	Maryland	800 00
Samuel Norment, jr	do	Virginia	800 00
James Minor	do	do	800 00
MESSENGER.			
Thomas Dove	do	Maryland	700 00
ASSISTANT MESSENGER.			
Richard Dove	do	Dist. Columbia	350 00
FOURTH AUDITOR.			
A. O. Dayton	do	New Jersey	3000 00
CHIEF CLERK.			
Thomas H. Gilliss	do	Maryland	1700 00
CLERKS.			
William Hunter	do	New Jersey	1400 00
J. B. Thomas	do	Maryland	1400 00
George M. Head	do	Kentucky	1200 00
A. H. Mechlin	do	Dist. Columbia	1150 00
Hobart Berrian	do	New York	1150 00
John B. Sullivan	do	Pennsylvania	1150 00
W. H. Topping	do	New York	1000 00
R. L. Mackall	do	Dist. Columbia	1000 00
John Etheridge	do	Massachusetts	1000 00
A. H. Evans	do	Virginia	1000 00
Henry Hill	do	do	1150 00

TREASURY DEPARTMENT—*Auditor, Treasurer, Clerks, &c.*

Names and offices.	Where employed.	Where born.	Compensation.
			Dol. cts.
H. G. O'Neale	Washington	Maryland	1000 00
Enos M. Morris	do	Pennsylvania	1000 00
Matthew McLeod	do	Ireland	1000 00
MESSENGER.			
John E. Holland	do	Maryland	700 00
FIFTH AUDITOR.			
Stephen Pleasonton	do	Delaware	3000 00
CHIEF CLERK.			
Thomas Mustin	do	Virginia	1700 00
CLERKS.			
John H. Houston	do	Pennsylvania	1400 00
James D. King	do	Dist. Colum.	1400 00
John Devlin	do	Ireland	1150 00
Arthur Campbell	do	Virginia	1150 00
Robert Ricketts	do	Maryland	1150 00
Alexander Spear	do	Pennsylvania	1150 00
Ashbell Steele	do	Connecticut	1000 00
George G. Cox	do	Dist. Colum.	1000 00
MESSENGER.			
Edward Holland	do	Maryland	700 00
TREASURER.			
William Selden	do	Virginia	3000 00
CHIEF CLERK.			
William B. Randolph	do	do	1700 00
CLERKS.			
Henry Jackson	do	Pennsylvania	1400 00
Jonathan Guest	do	do	1400 00
William D. Nutt	do	Dist. Colum.	1200 00
Hopkins Lightner	do	Pennsylvania	1200 00
William H. West	do	Maryland	1200 00

TREASURY DEPARTMENT—*Register, Clerks, &c.*

Names and offices.	Where employed.	Where born.	Compensation.
			Dol. cts.
Samuel M. Bootes	Washington	Dist. Colum.	1200 00
William S. Morgan	do	Virginia	1200 00
Andrew Smith	do	Scotland	1150 00
Henry Brooks	do	Virginia	1000 00
John G. Hedgman	do	do	1000 00
MESSENGER.			
James Moore	do	Ireland	700 00
REGISTER.			
R. H. Gillett	do	New York	3000 00
CHIEF CLERK.			
Michael Nourse	do	Virginia	1700 00
CLERKS.			
James McClery	do	Ireland	1400 00
John D. Barclay	do	Maryland	1400 00
John B. Blake	do	Virginia	1400 00
George H. Jones	do	do	1400 00
John W. Williams	do	do	1400 00
James G. Berret	do	Maryland	1200 00
Francis Lowndes	do	England	1150 00
James Laurie	do	Scotland	1150 00
Simeon Smith	do	New York	1150 00
John Nourse	do	Virginia	1000 00
Edgar Patterson	do	Dist. Colum.	1000 00
George W. Barry	do	Maryland	1000 00
Henry Brewer	do	Dist. Colum.	1000 00
Wm. B. Berryman	do	Virginia	1000 00
C. March	do	N. Hampshire.	1000 00
H. K. Laughlin	do	New York	1000 00
S. Yorke Atlee	do	Pennsylvania	1000 00
T. W. Ritter	do	New York	1000 00
Thomas Clairborne, jr	do	Tennessee	1000 00
W. N. Barker	do	Pennsylvania	800 00
O. P. Sutton	do	New York	800 00
Tully R. Wise	do	Virginia	800 00
MESSENGER.			
James C. Haviland	do	New York	700 00
ASSISTANT MESSENGER.			
Thomas Goddard	do	do	350 00

TREASURY DEPARTMENT—*Gen. Land Office.*

Names and offices.	Where employed.	Where born.	Compensation.
			Dol. cts.
COMMISSIONER OF THE GENERAL LAND OFFICE.			
James Shields	Washington	Ireland	3000 00
RECORDER.			
S. Laughlin	do	Virginia	2000 00
PRINCIPAL CLERK OF PUBLIC LANDS.			
John M. Moore	do	Pennsylvania	1800 00
PRINCIPAL CLERK OF PRIVATE LAND CLAIMS.			
Joseph S. Wilson	do	Dist. Colum.	1800 00
PRINCIPAL CLERK OF THE SURVEYS.			
John Wilson	do	do	1800 00
PRINCIPAL DRAUGHTSMAN.			
William T. Steiger	do	Maryland	1500 00
ASSISTANT DRAUGHTSMAN.			
Ephraim Gilman	do	N. Hampshire	1200 00
CLERKS.			
Charles S. Frailey	do	Maryland	1500 00
N. A. Randall	do	do	1400 00
Benjamin T. Reilly	do	Pennsylvania	1300 00
Edward Barnard	do	Massachusetts	1300 00
John Y. Bryant	do	Pennsylvania	1300 00
William D. Slade	do	Dist. Colum	1300 00
Benjamin Evans	do	Pennsylvania	1300 00
Isaac C. Smith	do	Connecticut	1300 00
George C. Whiting	do	Virginia	1300 00
William W. King	do	Maryland	1300 00
Edward A. Cabell	do	Virginia	1300 00
James H. Blake	do	Dist. Colum	1300 00
Albert Greenleaf	do	N. Hampshire	1300 00
Wm. V. H. Brown	do	Dist. Colum	1300 00
John L. Barnhill	do	do	1300 00

TREASURY DEPARTMENT—*Gen. Land Office.*

Names and offices.	Where employed.	Where born.	Compensation.
			Dol. cts.
John W. DeKrafft	Washington	Dist. Colum.	1300 00
Walter T. Brooke	do	Virginia	1200 00
William Henry	do	Pennsylvania	1200 00
Henry Hungerford	do	Virginia	1200 00
Moses Kelly	do	N. Hampshire	1200 00
Parker H. Sweet	do	Rhode Island	1200 00
William H. Deitz	do	Pennsylvania	1200 00
John H. Waggaman	do	Virginia	1200 00
William Nourse	do	Dist. Colum.	1200 00
John P. Wingerd	do	do	1200 00
Joseph H. Robins	do	Virginia	1200 00
Nathaniel P. Causin, jr.	do	Maryland	1200 00
John Hood	do	Pennsylvania	1200 00
Marinus Willett	do	New York	1200 00
William W. Curran	do	Maryland	1200 00
John Robb	do	do	1200 00
James L. Cathcart	do	Dist. Colum.	1200 00
F. A. Tschiffely	do	do	1100 00
Richard J. Morsell	do	do	1100 00
A. G. Seaman	do	Connecticut	1100 00
J. S. Cunningham	do	S. Carolina	1100 00
Merit L. Covall	do	New York	1100 00
William Wood	do	Massachusetts	1000 00
Owen H. Bestor	do	Dist. Colum.	1000 00
John N. Ashton	do	Virginia	1000 00
A. S. H. White	do	N. Hampshire	1000 00
Peter Wilson	do	Ohio	1000 00
John Todd	do	Pennsylvania	1000 00
William Clyde	do	New York	1000 00
Henry B. Foster	do	Pennsylvania	1000 00
William Darby	do	do	1000 00
John P. Frazer	do	do	1000 00
William M. Royce	do	New York	1000 00
De Witt Kent	do	Maryland	1000 00
William F. Wallace	do	Pennsylvania	1000 00
T. W. McCalla	do	Kentucky	1000 00
S. H. Laughlin	do	Tennessee	1000 00
William H. Minnix	do	Virginia	1000 00
Amos F. Patrick	do	New York	1000 00
Cornelius S. Whitney	do	do	1000 00
Alexander Bielaski	do	Poland	1000 00
MESSENGERS.			
Grafton Powell	do	Virginia	700 00
John McMahon	do	Ireland	700 00
ASSISTANT MESSENGERS.			
Samuel Walker	do	Pennsylvania	638 00
Isaac Goddard	do	Maryland	350 00

TREASURY DEPARTMENT—*Solicitor, Auditor, Clerks, &c.*

Names and offices.	Where employed.	Where born.	Compensation.
			Dol. cts.
PACKERS.			
Thomas H. Quincy	Washington	Massachusetts	450 00
Michael Hill	do	Virginia	450 00
SOLICITOR.			
Seth Barton	do	Maryland	3500 00
CHIEF CLERK.			
Benjamin F. Pleasants	do	Virginia	1150 00
LAW CLERK.			
Alexander B. Meek	do	S. Carolina	1500 00
CLERKS.			
Basil Warring	do	Maryland	1150 00
Joseph Warring	do	do	1150 00
Benjamin C. Ridgate	do	do	1150 00
Green H. Barton	do	Alabama	1150 00
William Clare	do	Ireland	1150 00
John W. Compton	do	Dist. Columbia	600 00
MESSENGER.			
John Phillips	do	Pennsylvania	500 00
AUDITOR OF THE TREASURY FOR THE POST OFFICE DEPARTMENT.			
Peter G. Washington	do	Dist. Columbia	3000 00
CHIEF CLERK.			
William J. Brown	do	Kentucky	2000 00
CLERKS.			
John Suter	do	Maryland	1600 00
William G. Eliot	do	Massachusetts	1600 00
David Saunders	do	Virginia	1600 00
Richard Dement	do	Maryland	1600 00
Nicholas Tastet	do	Spain	1400 00

TREASURY DEPARTMENT—*Clerks.*

Names and offices.	Where employed.	Where born.	Compensation.
			Dol. cts.
Samuel Fitzhugh	Washington	Maryland	1400 00
Josiah F. Caldwell	do	New Jersey	1400 00
William C. Lipscomb	do	Virginia	1400 00
John F. Boone	do	Maryland	1400 00
Thomas A. Scott	do	do	1400 00
John A. M. Duncanson	do	Dist. Columbia	1400 00
James Coolidge	do	Maryland	1400 00
John P. Wheeler	do	Dist. Columbia	1400 00
Elbridge Gerry Eastman	do	N. Hampshire	1400 00
Wm. J. Bronaugh	do	Virginia	1400 00
Henry Rogers	do	Delaware	1400 00
Joseph Reynolds	do	Pennsylvania	1200 00
Perrin Washington	do	Virginia	1200 00
Joseph Carter	do	do	1200 00
John Thaw	do	Dist. Columbia	1200 00
Giles Dyer	do	do	1200 00
Samuel A. Houston	do	Pennsylvania	1200 00
George Dale	do	Ireland	1200 00
Grafton D. Hanson	do	Maryland	1200 00
Lewis Welch	do	Pennsylvania	1200 00
Wm. S. Darrell	do	Virginia	1200 00
James M. Hanson	do	do	1200 00
James D. Seavey	do	Maine	1200 00
Joseph Quicksall	do	New Jersey	1200 00
Samuel McPherson	do	Virginia	1200 00
Isaac H. Robbins	do	Dist. Columbia	1200 00
George W. Mountz	do	do	1200 00
Charles Monroe	do	Massachusetts	1200 00
Joseph Harris	do	Maryland	1200 00
James H. Durham	do	New York	1200 00
Leonard J. Anderson	do	Dist. Columbia	1200 00
Samuel Harkness	do	do	1200 00
John C. Kennedy	do	Virginia	1200 00
Thomas P. Trott	do	Connecticut	1200 00
Nahum Stone	do	Massachusetts	1200 00
William D. Wallach	do	Dist. Colum.	1200 00
James B. Taggart	do	Pennsylvania	1200 00
James Caden	do	Ireland	1200 00
Samuel Dexter	do	Massachusetts	1000 00
Edwin W. Forteney	do	Dist. Colum.	1000 00
John W. Bronaugh	do	do	1000 00
John F. Sharretts	do	Pennsylvania	1000 00
John McKenney	do	Maryland	1000 00
Charles T. Pope	do	Maine	1000 00
John Voorhees	do	New Jersey	1000 00
Woodville Latham	do	Virginia	1000 00
John Douglass	do	do	1000 00
Samuel M. Edwards	do	do	1000 00
Francis Hume	do	do	1000 00

TREASURY DEPARTMENT—*Clerks, &c.*

Names and offices.	Where employed.	Where born.	Compensation.
			Dol. cts.
Alfred Russel	Washington	Tennessee	1000 00
James A. McLaughlin	do	Kentucky	1000 00
Austin H. Brown	do	Indiana	1000 00
John C. Mullay	do	Pennsylvania	1000 00
Stephen J. Dallas	do	Poland	1000 00
James R. McAllister	do	Missouri	1000 00
Thomas E. Browne	do	Ireland	1000 00
Wyndham Robertson, jr.	do	Virginia	1000 00
Washington C. Whitthorne	do	Tennessee	1000 00
Lucius H. Emmons	do	Vermont	1000 00
Joseph Wimsatt	do	Maryland	1000 00
Henry St. George Offutt	do	Virginia	1000 00
Asaph H. Parish	do	New York	1000 00
MESSENGER.			
Wm. W. Cox	do	Maryland	750 00
ASSISTANT MESSENGER.			
Richard White	do	do	350 00

CUSTOMS—*Maine.*

Names and offices.	Where employed.	Where born.	Time employed during the year ending Sept. 30, '45. Months	Days	Compensat'n for the time employed.
MAINE.					
Passamaquoddy.					
Bion Bradbury........Collector	Eastport	Maine	12	....	$500 & fees.
Micajah Hawks........Surveyor	do	Massachusetts	4	17	694 38
Lucius Bradbury, Inspector and acting Deputy Collector	do	Maine	......	365	1095 00
Robert Burns........Inspector	do	New Hampshire	......	353	1095 00
Humphry Pike........do	do	Massachusetts	......	365	1095 00
George W. Mowe........do	do	Maine	......	148	444 00
Joseph A. Coolidge........Temporary Inspector	do	do	......	365	828 00
John C. Talbot, jr., Inspector and acting Deputy Coll'r	Lubec	do	......	361	1083 00
James W. Lyman........Inspector	do	Vermont	......	268	804 00
William Pike, Inspector and acting Deputy Collector	Calais	Maine	......	362	1086 00
Isaac W. Tabor........do........do........do	Houlton	Vermont	......	365	1095 00
Mark Trafton........do........do........do	Fort Fairfield	Maine	......	365	1095 00
Columbus Cooper........Inspector	Robbinston	do	......	340	680 00
Edmund Snow........Weigher and Measurer	Eastport	New Hampshire	12	....	234 35
Thomas J. Sherman........do........do	Pembroke	Massachusetts	12	....	395 38
Machias.					
William Brown........Collector	Machias	Maine	4	26	301 00
James Moore........Inspector	On Revenue Boat	do	4	5	258 00
Mark D. Meuns........do	do	do	4	5	193 00

Ellery Turner	do	Cutler	do	4	5	87	84
Lewis Burnham	Deputy Collector and Inspector	Cherryfield	do	4	2	85	10
Frenchman's Bay.							
Henry S. Jones	Collector	Frenchman's Bay	Maine	12	....	591	43
Leonard F. E. Jarvis	Inspector	Ellsworth	do	12	....	800	00
Joseph A. Deane	do	Sullivan	Massachusetts	12	....	500	00
Leonard J. Thomas	do	Southwest Harbor	Maine	12	....	500	00
Ivory H. Foss	Inspector in charge of Revenue Boat	Frenchman's Bay	do	11	23	353	00
Benjamin Thomas	Inspector	Eden	do	......	27	54	00
Penobscot.							
Rowland H. Bridgham	Collector	....	....	......	....		
Frederic A. Hooke	Inspector	Castine	Maine	12	....	980	35
John Lee	do	Bucksport	do	3	20	336	00
James C. Madigan	Inspector	Fort Kent	do	3	28	345	00
George S. Vose, Deputy Collector and Occasional Insp.		Castine	do	5	9	485	88
Abel Moore	do ... do	Houlton Road	do	12	....	100	00
Belfast.							
Nathaniel M. Lowney	Collector	Belfast	Maine	5	4	1052	66
Ansel Lennan	Inspector	do	do	5	4	474	
Darius D. Pinkham	Occasional Inspector	do	New Hampshire	1	14	132	
Bradford S. Foster	Weigher, Guager, and Measurer	Belfast and other ports	Maine	......	....	15	
James Clark, Occ'l Insp., Weigher, Guager, and Meas.		Camden	do	1	14	132	
Jonathan R. Cole	Occasional Inspector	Searsport	New Hampshire	......	13	39	
Jonathan G. Dickerson	do ... do	Frankfort	do	5	2	468	
Lyman Wisweer, Occ'l Insp., Weigher, Guager, & Meas.		Frankfort & other ports	Maine	2	....	225	24
Cyrus Moore	Inspector	Bangor	do	5	4	474	
Herman Fisher	Weigher, Guager, and Measurer	Bangor and other ports	do	......	....	327	05

CUSTOMS—*Maine*—*Continued.*

Names and offices.	Where employed.	Where born.	Time employed during the year ending Sept. 30, '42. Months	Days	Compensat'n for the time employed.
Waldoboro'.					
Parker McCobb, jr.......Collector	Waldoboro'	Maine	4	25	$380 99
Henry D. McCobb, Deputy Collector, Inspector, Weigher, Guager, and Measurer	do	do			429
Edwin Rose......do......do......do	Thomaston	do			381
William R. Webb.do......do......do	Nobleboro'	do			240
Ebenezer Otis, Inspector, Weigher, Guager, and Measurer	St. George	do			118
John Merrill......do......do......do	East Thomaston	do			156
David Plummer...do......do......do	Bristol	do			117 25
Leander Morton, Occ'l Inspector, Guager, and Measurer	do	do			79 50
Robert Gay, Occ'l Insp., Weigher, Guager, and Measurer	Cushing & Friendship	do			24 00
Wiscasset.					
James Taylor.......Collector	Wiscasset	England	5	16	430 66
John Babson.......Deputy Collector and Inspector	do	Maine	5	16	465 00
William Trundy.......do	Wiscasset, and on board Rev. Boat	do	5	16	393 00
William Taylor.......do	Wiscasset & Edgecomb	do	5	16	270 00
Stevens Smith.......Deputy Collector and Inspector	Boothbay	Massachusetts	5	13	272 00
Westbrook Greenleaf, jr.......do	Westport	Maine	5	9	104 00
John Babson.......Weigher	Wiscasset	do	5	16	41 78
John Babson.......Measurer	do	do	5	16	275 95
John H. Converse.......Temporary Inspector	Newcastle	do	2	16	50 00

Bath.					
Amos Nourse.............Collector....	Bath...............	Massachusetts	......	....	877 96
Edward S. J. Nealley, Deputy Collector and Inspector....	......do...........	New Hampshire .	12	....	1095 00
James H. Nichols.............Inspector..	Bath, Topsham, h[illegible]d, &c ..	Maine..........	5	27	498 00
James H. Nichols...Weigher, Guager, and Measurer....	......do...........	......do.......	......	....	361 47
George W. Nichols......do.......do......do.......	Bath, Bowdoinham, &c.	......do.......	......	....	247 87
George W. Nichols.............Inspector....	......do...........	......do.......	5	16	453 00
Joseph C. Snow.............do.....	Bath, in Rev. Boat, and on Canada road	......do.......	5	27	531 00
Thomas Morse.............do.......	George and Phipsburg	......do.......	5	....	294 00
John Jordon.............do.......	Harpswell & Brunsw'k	......do.......	5	....	138 00
Bernard Esmond.............do.......	Gardiner and Pittston.	......do.......	5	....	147 00
Robert A. Cony.............do.......	Hallowel and Augusta.	......do.......	5	....	156 00
Charles Hasmer......Deputy Collector and Inspector..	Canada Road and Canada Line.....	New Hampshire .	5	....	313 50
Peter H. Green.............Occasional Measurer....	Bath...............	......do.......	......	....	121 50
Samuel Crowell.............do......do.......	......do...........	Maine..........	......	....	77 44
Portland.					
John Anderson, [illegible]r, Agent for the Marine H[illegible]al, and Superintendent of Light Houses............	Portland............	Maine..........	12	....	2450 59
Peter Merrill...........Deputy [illegible]or and Clerk....	......do...........	......do.......	12	....	900 00
Benjamin Kingsbury, jr......Surveyor and Inspector....	......do...........	Massachusetts....	12	....	844 80
Joshua Knight.............Inspector....	......do...........	Maine..........	12	....	1095 00
David Drinkwater.............do.......	......do...........	......do.......	12	....	1095 00
Nathaniel Shaw.............do.......	......do...........	......do.......	12	....	[illegible]095 00
William T. Smith.............do.......	......do...........	......do.......	12	....	1095 00
John K. Hooper.............do.......	......do...........	......do.......	12	....	1095 00
Ezra Carter, jr.............do.......	......do...........	......do.......	2	....	183 00

CUSTOMS—*Maine*—*Continued.*

Names and offices.	Where employed.	Where born.	Time employed during the year ending Sept. 30, '45. Months	Days	Compensat'n for the time employed.
Allen Drinkwater, Inspector	North Yarmouth	Maine	5	....	$262 00
Nathan Nutter, Occasional do	Portland	New Hampshire	12	....	180 00
John Williams, do do	do	Massachusetts	12	....	210 00
Joel Chandler, do do	do	Maine	12	....	195 00
Edward Hinds, do do	do	do	12	....	183 00
Alexander H. Putney, Guager, Weigher, and Measurer	do	New Hampshire	12	....	1390 00
Amos Nichols, do do do	do	Massachusetts	12	....	1390 00
Jonathan Smith, do do do	do	Maine	12	....	1390 00
John Williams, Appraiser	do	Massachusetts	12	....	103 00
Lemuel Gooding, do	do	Maine	12	....	103 00
Saco.					
Ichabod Jordan, Collector	Saco	Maine	6	17	204 78
Hiram Woods, Inspector	Outer Harbor	Massachusetts	2	15	225 00
Sylas I. Libby, do	Scarborough	Maine	......	4	12 00
Kennebunk.					
James Osborn, Collector	Kennebunk	Maine	6	....	52 59
Oliver Walker, Deputy Collector	do	do	12	....	
Oliver Walker, Inspector	do	do	12	....	500 00
Oliver Walker, Weigher, Guager, and Measurer		do	......	....	
William Bourn, Inspector	Wells	do	7	22	64 00
Christopher Littlefield, do	do	do	4	9	36 00
Aaron Maxwell, do	Ogunquit	do	7	22	8 00

Name	Office	Where employed	Where born	Months	Days	Pay
Joshua Hubbard	do	do	do	4	9	4 00
York.						
Joseph P. Junkins	Collector	York	Maine	8	15	250 00
Washington Junkins	Inspector	do	do	8	....	186 64
Samuel Adams	do	Cape Neddick	do	4	15	111 39
NEW HAMPSHIRE.						
Portsmouth.						
Augustus Jenkins, Collector, Superintendent of Light Houses, and Agent for Marine Hospital		Portsmouth	New Hampshire	12	....	468 44
Joseph M. Edmonds	Deputy Collector and Inspector	do	do	12	....	730 00
Sampson B. Lord	Inspector and Measurer	do	do		81	482 42
Kittredge Sheldon	do do	do	Mass.		81	482 42
Thomas F. Rowe	do do	do	New Hampshire		81	482 42
Eliphalet Currier	do do	do	do		81	482 42
John R. Hill	Inspector	do	do	12	....	300 00
Benjamin Weeks	do	do	do	12	....	360 00
Timothy Ham	do	[illegible]	do	12	....	200 00
George Morrell	Weigher and Guager	do	do		1	60
Gideon H. Rundlett	Occasional Inspector	do	do	12	....	730 00
Joseph Harrold, Occasional Inspector and Night Watch		Portsmouth	New Hampshire	15 days & 53 nights.	..	122 42
William Downes	do do do	do	do		..	122 42
William Laskey	do do do	do	Massachusetts		..	122 42
Joseph B. Adams	do do do	do	New Hampshire		..	122 42
Daniel Frisbee	Inspector and Boarding Officer	Kittery	Maine	12	....	500 00
Thomas B. Frost	do do do	New Castle	New Hampshire	12	....	500 00

CUSTOMS—*Vermont.*

Names and offices.	Where employed.	Where born.	Time employed during the year ending Sept. 30, '45. Months	Days	Compensat'n for the time employed.
James Frye.........Inspector and Deputy Collector...	Dover..............	New Hampshire .	12	....	$200 00
Warren Parsons..............Occasional Inspector....	Rye................	......do........	12	....	100 00
Uri Lamprey......................do.......do......	Hampton & Seabrook.	......do........	12	....	124 00
Ephraim Cross........................Inspector....	Lancaster and vicinity.	......do........	12	....	300 00
VERMONT.					
Archibald W. Hyde......................Collector....	Burlington	Vermont.........	12	....	1090 84
Danford M[illegible]tt.......Deputy Collector and [illegible]r....	Wind Mill Point.....	......do........	12	....	500 00
Zoroaster Fisk ....do......do..........do......	Alburgh	......do........	12	....	360 00
Isaac B. Bowdish ....Deputy [illegible]or and Inspector....	Swanton	......do........	12	....	360 00
Robert L. Paddock .....do......do...........do......	Highgate............	......do........	12	....	360 00
John J. Deavitt ....do......do...........do......	Franklin	New York	12	....	240 00
Jasper Rand ....do......do...........do......	Berkshire	Vermont	12	....	240 00
Sylvanus M. Parsons ...do......do...........do......	Richford	......do........	12	....	240 00
Frederick Fuller........do......do...........do......	[illegible]y	......do........	12	....	200 00
[illegible]es [illegible]y ......do......do...........do......	Derby	Massachusetts ...	12	....	360 00
William Ri[illegible]o.........do......do...........do......	Canaan	Vermont.........	12	....	240 00
[illegible]an B. Haswell, jr...do......do...........do......	Burlington	......do........	12	....	250 00
Nathaniel Parker.......do......do...........do......	Steam Boats.........	New Hampshire .	12	....	500 00
Richard P[illegible]wers..[illegible]o.Inspector and Master of Revenue Boat	[illegible]nd Mill Point.	New York	12	....	360 00
Alvah B. Stanton......do.........do...........do......	Alburgh	Vermont.........	12	....	500 00
Jeptha Bradley.......................Inspector....	St. Alban's.........	......do........	4	....	120 00
Charles S. Noyes.........................do......	Hyde Park...........	......do........	12	....	240 00

Almon H. Fuller	do.	Westfield	do.	12	....	160 00
George W. Hill	do.	Derby	New Hampshire	12	....	500 00
John Beckwith	do.	Sutton	Rhode Island	12	....	240 00
Harry Richardson	do.	Montpelier	New Hampshire	12	....	240 00
MASSACHUSETTS.						
Newburyport.						
William Nichols	Collector	Newburyport	M[illegible]s.	2	21	685 64
Nathaniel Jackson	Surveyor	do.	do.	12	....	520 38
Asahel H. Wildes	do.	Ipswich	do.	12	....	250 00
Enoch Fowler	Naval Officer	Newburyport	do.	2	21	98 44
Joseph B. Hervey,	Weigher, Meas'r, and Occasional Insp.	do.	do.	2	21	943 16
George Emery	Inspector	do.	do.	2	....	180 00
John M. Cooper	Inspector and Guagor	do.	do.	1	24	162 00
Thomas W. Burnham,	Inspector and Deputy Collector	do.	do.	2	21	246 00
Philip H. Hills	Weigher and Measurer	do.	do.	.....	....	
Daniel L. Wilcumb	Inspector	Ipswich	do.	.....	25	75 00
Anthony Knap	Occasional Inspector	Newburyport	do.	.....	10	30 00
Gloucester.						
Eli F. Stacy	Collector	Gloucester	Massachusetts	12	....	1459 58
John Woodbury	Surveyor	do.	do.	12	....	528 10
Gideon Lane	Weigher and Guager	do.	do.	12	....	557 95
David White	do. do.	do.	do.	6	....	230 48
Addison Winter	Inspector	do.	do.	12	....	1095 00
Moses Tarr	do.	do.	do.	5	3	459 00
Thomas O. Marshall	do.	Rochport	do.	12	....	300 00

CUSTOMS—*Massachusetts—Continued.*

Names and offices.	Where employed.	Where born.	Time employed during the year ending Sept. 30, '45. Months	Days	Compensat'n for the time employed.
Ezra Stanly .... Inspector	Manchester	Massachusetts	12	....	$150 00
Marblehead.					
Peter Dixcy .... Collector	Marblehead	do	1	13	63 70
Peter Dixcy, jr., Deputy Collector, Inspector, and Measurer	do	do	1	11	191 66
William Bartoll .... Inspector	do	do	1	....	30 42
William Rodgers .... do	do	do	1	....	30 42
Caleb M. Long ...... Deputy Collector and Inspector	Lynn	do	1	....	22 92
William Philips .... Inspector	do	do	1	....	4 58
Benjamin Wormstead .... Surveyor	Marblehead	do	12	....	Fees.
Salem and Beverly.					
James Miller .... [illegible]r	Salem	New Hampshire	12	....	2430 81
Ephraim F. Miller .... Deputy [illegible]r	do	do	12	....	1000 00
Zach. Buckmoup .... Clerk	do	Massachusetts	12	....	930 00
Abraham True .... Naval [illegible]r	do	New Hampshire	12	....	872 50
Nehemiah Brown .... Surveyor	do	Massachusetts	12	....	946 65
Perley Putnam .... Weigher and Guager	do	do	12	....	569 13
William Story .... do .... do	do	do	12	....	482 69
Thomas West .... do .... do	do	do	12	....	908 68
William [illegible]e .... Inspector	do	do	12	....	1095 00
Devereaux Dennis .... do	do	do	12	....	507 00
Joseph Noble .... do	do	do	12	....	585 00
Hardy Phippen .... do	do	do	12	....	555 00
Daniel Bray, jr. .... do	do	do	12	....	600 00

Abel Lawrence	do	do	do	12	....	606 00
William Webb	do	do	do	12	....	513 00
Henry Prince	do	do	do	4	....	177 00
Stephen Haraden	Temporary do	do	do	3	....	156 00
Stephen Burchmore	do do	do	do	12	....	426 00
Nathan Millett	do do	do	do	12	....	510 00
Stephen Burchmore	do Measurer	do	do	12	....	191 80
Daniel Foster	Surveyor	Beverly	do	12	....	176 00
Lawson Walker	Inspector	do	do	12	....	297 00
Daniel Foster	Temporary Measurer	do	do	12	....	154 80
Boston and Charlestown.						
Marcus Morton	Collector	Boston	Massachusetts	5	....	6400 00
Adams Bailey	Deputy Collector	do	do	12	....	1500 00
William A. Wellman	Deputy Collector	do	do	12	....	1500 00
Ephraim L. Frothingham	Cashier	do	do	12	....	1800 00
Henry D. Clary	Foreign Clearance Clerk	do	do	12	....	1407 23
William H. Montague	Debenture Clerk	do	do	12	....	1407 23
William English	Clerk of Correspondence	do	Ireland	9	18	1039 10
William Alline	Impost Clerk	do	Massachusetts	12	....	1257 30
Charles D. [illegible]oln	Foreign Entry Clerk	do	do	12	....	1250 00
N. M. Tucker	Bond and Statistical Clerk	do	Maine	12	....	1230 23
Samuel Andrews	Marine Clerk	do	Massachusetts	12	....	1182 23
John E. Billings	Assistant Impost Clerk	do	do	12	....	1064 23
Lewis E. [illegible]n	Bond Accountant	do	do	12	....	1000 00
Llewellyn P. Davis	Export Bookkeeper	do	Maine	9	18	807 06
William Williams,	Assistant Bond and Statistical Clerk	do	Massachusetts	4	....	328 83
George F. Emery	Impost Bookkeeper	do	Maine	4	....	326 52
George B. Wellman	Coastwise Clerk	do	Massachusetts	12	....	982 20
Henry A. S. D. Payne	Assistant Impost Clerk	do	do	12	....	912 00
Ephraim L. Frothingham, jr	Assistant Cashier	do	do	4	....	299 18

CUSTOMS—*Massachusetts*—*Continued.*

Names and offices.	Where employed.	Where born.	Time employed during the year ending Sept. 30, '45. Months	Days	Compensat'n for the time employed.
Robert S. Smith .... Assistant Coastwise Clerk	Boston	Connecticut	12	....	$886 48
Eli A. Yale .... Miscellaneous Clerk	do	do	12	....	912 50
Nathaniel Gale .... Arranger of Papers	do	New Hampshire	12	....	912 50
William Stocker .... Messenger	do	do	12	....	730 00
William Parmenter .... Naval Officer	do	Massachusetts	6	7	4538 90
R. McGay .... Deputy Naval Officer	do	Maine	12	....	1500 00
George H. Cutter .... Naval Officer's Clerk	do	Massachusetts	12	....	1000 00
D. Hyde .... do .... do	do	do	12	....	1000 00
[illegible] Locke .... do .... do	do	do	1	....	83 33
John McNeil .... Surveyor	do	New Hampshire	5	23	4092 54
Hugh Jameson .... Deputy Surveyor	do	do	12	....	1500 00
William W. Parker .... Surveyor's Clerk	do	do	5	7	501 20
James Baker .... Weigher and Guager	do	do	2	17	319 87
Lemuel M. Barker .... do .... do	do	Vermont	12	....	1500 00
E. F. Bunnell .... do .... do	do	Connecticut	12	....	1500 00
Chauncy Clark .... do .... do	do	Massachusetts	12	....	1500 00
Horatio N. Crane .... do .... do	do	do	2	17	319 87
F. R. Gourgas .... do .... do	do	do	4	....	500 00
Luther Hamilton .... do .... do	do	do	12	....	1500 00
Henry Mitchell .... do .... do	do	Connecticut	2	17	319 87
Ezra Mudge .... do .... do	do	Massachusetts	12	....	1284 00
Nathaniel Sweet .... do .... do	do	do	2	....	250 00
Samuel Walker .... do .... do	do		12	....	1500 00
Andrew H. Ward .... do .... do	do	Massachusetts	12	....	1500 00
Hammond Whitney .... do .... do	do	do	12	....	1500 00
Samuel C. Allen .... Measurer of Salt and Coal	do	do	4	....	500 00

Henry E. Baldwin	do ... do	do	New Hampshire	4	....	60 00
Naham Ball	do ... do	do	Massachusetts	12	....	60 00
Andrew Green	do ... do	do	do	12	....	60 00
[illegible] Hall	do ... do	do	do	12	....	60 00
[illegible] Snow	do ... do	do	do	2	15	32 50
Edward Palfrey	do ... do	do	do	12	....	60 00
George Dennet	do ... do	do	New Hampshire	8	10	42 00
Benjamin D. Baxter	Ins[illegible]r	do	Massachusetts	12	....	95 00
William S. Bartlett	do	do	do	4	....	63 00
Joseph H. Berrett	do	do	Maryland	1	....	90 00
Abner Child, jr.	do	do	Massachusetts	2	18	27 00
Samuel W. [illegible]r.	do	do	do	12	....	95 00
[illegible]	do	do	do	12	....	95 00
Ephraim M. [illegible]ingham	do	do	do	12	....	95 00
[illegible]s W. [illegible]s	do	do		12	....	95 00
Samuel O. Dearborn	do	do	New Hampshire	12	....	95 00
[illegible] Dickinson	do	do	Massachusetts	12	....	[illegible]
William B. Duggan	d[illegible]	D[illegible], Weymouth, and Quincy	do	12	....	400 00
Francis A. Durivage	do	Boston		12	....	95 00
George F. Emery	do	do	New Hampshire	12	....	95 00
Hiram Ferry	do	do	Massachusetts	4	....	63 00
Thomas W. Flagg	do	do	do	12	....	95 00
James G. Foster	d[illegible]	do	do	2	18	27 00
Thomas [illegible]n	do	do	do	12	....	95 00
[illegible] S. [illegible]n	do	do	New York	2	18	27 00
Samuel [illegible]s	do	do	[illegible]t.	3	29	83 00
Lewis [illegible]	do ... and marker	do	[illegible]etts	4	....	60 00
[illegible]s Kettell	do	do	[illegible]e	12	....	95 00
Perkins Kimball	do	do	New [illegible]e	12	....	95 00
George Kuhn	d[illegible] ... do	do	[illegible]ts	12	....	60 00
William A. Wellman	do ... of light-houses	do	do	12	....	60 00

CUSTOMS—*Massachusetts—Continued.*

Names and offices.		Where employed.	Where born.	Time employed during the year ending Sept. 30, '45.		Compensat'n for the time employed.
				Months	Days	
Abraham Lansing	Inspector	Boston	New York	4	....	$363 00
John C. Leach	do	do	Massachusetts	12	....	1095 00
William A. Lewis	do	do	do	12	....	1095 00
Samuel R. B. Lewis	do	do	do	2	18	237 00
John P. Lord	do	do	Maine	4	....	363 00
William P. Loring	do	do	Massachusetts	12	....	1095 00
Henry K. May	do	do	do	12	....	1095 00
Francis McKenna	do	do	Ireland	12	....	1095 00
Horatio C. Merriam	do	do	Massachusetts	4	....	363 00
John Muzzy	do	do	New Hampshire	12	....	1095 00
Merrill Pettingill	do	do	do	12	....	1095 00
Orlando M. Randall	do	do	Vermont	12	....	1095 00
Alfred A. Roberts	do	do	Massachusetts	12	....	1095 00
Henry W. Robinson	do	do	Virginia	12	....	1095 00
David Saville	do	do	Massachusetts	12	....	1095 00
John M. Sibley	do	do	do	12	....	1095 00
William R. Stacy	do	do	do	12	....	1095 00
James M. Storre	do	do	Massachusetts	4	....	363 00
Newton Talbot	do	do	do	12	....	1095 00
Rinaldo R. Taylor	do	do	do	2	18	237 00
David Thatcher	do	do	do	12	....	1095 00
Henry Thaxter	Deputy Collector and Inspector	Hingham	do	12	....	500 00
Sullivan Thayer	Inspector	Boston	do	2	18	237 00
David Townsend	do	do	do	12	....	1095 00
James P. Treadwell	do	do	do	12	....	1095 00
William P. Tuckerman	do	do	do	12	....	1095 00

Leander Warren	do.	do.	do.	12	....	95 00
Henry J. Turner	Deputy Collector and [illegible]	Cohasset	do.	12	....	90 00
Charles Walley, Keeper of Wine & Spirits Stores & [illegible]	[illegible]	Boston	do.	12	....	95 00
Benjamin Whipple	[illegible]	do.	do.	12	....	95 00
Stephen L. White	do.	do.	do.	4	....	83 00
Nathan Whitten	do.	do.	Maine	2	18	90
Joseph H. Wright	d.	do.	Massachusetts	12	....	95 00
Gideon W. Young	do.	do.	do.	12	....	95 00
William Alexander	Night Inspector	do.	do.	12	....	60 00
Joseph C. Bartlett	do.	do.	Maine	4	....	20 00
Seth W. Barton	do.	do.	Rhode Island	12	....	60 00
Jesse D. Bates	d.	do.	Massachusetts	4	....	20 00
George Blish	do.	do.	do.	4	....	20 00
Jonathan Burnham, jr.	do.	do.	do.	12	....	60 00
Joseph Buxton, jr.	do.	do.	do.	12	....	60 00
Shadrach Dickson	do.	do.	Maine	12	....	60 00
Frederick W. Hall	do.	do.	Massachusetts	12	....	60 00
Daniel D. Hartley	do.	do.	do.	12	....	60 00
Daniel B. Haynes	do.	do.	New Hampshire	12	....	600 00
Shadrach Keen	do.	do.	Massachusetts	12	....	60 00
Justus Lane	do.	do.	do.	4	....	20 00
Theodore C. Leeds	d.	do.	do.	12	....	60 00
Joseph Lovett	do.	do.	do.	12	....	600 00
Charles McLellan	do.	do.	Maine	12	....	60 00
William B. Moffatt	do.	do.	do.	12	....	6 00
Timothy R. Page	do.	do.	Massachusetts	12	....	60 00
George B. Proctor	do.	do.	do.	4	....	20 00
Edward H. Whyte	do.	do.	do.	12	....	60 00
John W. Worison	do.	do.	do.	12	....	60 00
C. J. F. Allen	Appraiser	do.	do.	12	....	1500 00
S. J. Bridge	do.	do.	do.	12	....	1500 00
Samuel Eveleth	Assistant Appraiser	do.	do.	12	....	20 00

CUSTOMS—*Massachusetts*—*Continued*.

Names and offices.	Where employed.	Where born.	Time employed during the year ending Sept. 30, '45. Months	Days	Compensat'n for the time employed.
George Gibson......Assistant Appraiser	Boston	Massachusetts	3	....	$300 00
William Hardwick......Appraiser's Clerk	d.	do	12	....	1000 00
C. Dana Lincoln......Square Yard Measurer	d.	do	1	....	66 66
Isaac How......do....do....do	do	do	12	....	800 00
F. A. Colburn......do....do....do	do	do	12	....	800 00
Thomas Morey ....Clerk and Square Yard Measurer	do	lo	12	....	800 00
Michael Riley, jr......Examiner of Invoices	do	do	1	....	66 66
J. T. Ripley......Clerk and Messenger	do	do	12	....	750 00
Lemuel S. Williams......Public Store Keeper	do	do	9	17	870 00
John C. Brown......Clerk in Public Store	do	d.	12	....	1095 00
Isaac N. Biddle......do......do	do	New Hampshire	12	....	600 00
Plymouth.					
William M. Jackson......Collector	Plymouth	M sitts	6	....	274 63
Jacob Jackson......Deputy Collector	do	do	5	15	504 00
Jacob Jackson......ector	do	do	5	15	
Barnabas H. Holmes......Mr	do	lo	5	15	121 06
Charles H. Thomas......Ir	Duxbury	do	12	....	800 00
Edwin Young......do	Scituate	do	4	22	235 72
Horace L. Collamore......d o	Kingston	do	4	15	120 33
William Sherman......do	Marshfield	do	4	19	61 54
Fall River.					
Phineas W. Leland......Collector	Fall River	do	4	13	1001 46

Jonathan Slade, Deputy Collector, Inspector, Measurer, Weigher, and Guager		do	do	3	28	375 00
Moses Lawton	Inspector, Weigher, and Measurer	do	New Jersey	3	17	384 00
Joseph Pitts	Inspector, Measurer, and Weigher	Taunton and Somerset	Massachusetts	3	13	424 00
Ephraim Atwood	Measurer and Weigher	do	do	3	16	375 00
Barnstable.						
Josiah ey	Collector	Barnstable	do	6	....	403 19
Freeman Hinckley	Inspector	do	do	1	27	171 00
Freeman Hinckley	Deputy Collector	do	do	6	Paid by Collec'r	
as Holmes	Inspector	do	do	1	21	153 00
m Nye	do	Sandwich	do	1	17	141 00
Silas J. e	Deputy Collector	th	do	5	10	111 80
Ephraim Taylor	do do	Chatham	do	6	....	125 00
Ephraim Taylor	Inspector	do	do	1	8	114 00
Thomas Newcomb	Deputy or	Wellfleet	do	6	....	125 00
as Newcomb	Inspector	do	do	....	22	66 00
Eb r S. Smith	Deputy or	Provincetown	do	6	....	125 00
Eben'r S. Smith	Inspector	do	do	....	26	78 00
New Bedford.						
Joseph T. Adams	Collector	New Bedford	do	12	....	2605 02
Joseph T. Adams	Superintend nt of Light House	do	do	12	....	91 20
Joseph T. Adams	Agent of Marine Hospital	do	do	12	....	1 19
James Fr man	Deputy or and Inspector	do	do	12	....	1095 00
James Tayler	Clerk	do	Rhode Island	12	....	500 00
d Silvester	Inspector	do	Maine	12	....	1095 00
John ler	Inspector, Weigher, and Measurer	do	Rhode Island	12	....	710 43
John Terry	Inspector	Fairhaven	Massachusetts	12	....	396 00
David Nye	Inspector and er	Wareham	do	12	....	923 56

CUSTOMS—*Rhode Island.*

Names and offices.	Where employed.	Where born.	Time employed during the year ending Sept. 30, '45. Months	Days.	Compensat'n for the time employed.
Noble E. Bates, Inspector	Sippican	Massachusetts	1	18	$18 00
Ansel Weeks, do	Mattepoisett	do	12	....	105 00
Isaac Cory, do	Westport	do	12	....	102 00
Humphrey Shearman, do	Dartmouth	do	11	....	115 00
Edgartown.					
Joseph T. Pease, Collector	Edgartown	do	....	14	9 51
Henry P. Worth, Deputy Collector and Inspector	Holmes' Hole	do	12	....	600 00
Jeremiah Pease, do do do	Edgartown	do	12	....	500 00
Richard Luce, do	Tarpaulin Cove	do	12	....	500 00
Nantucket.					
William R. Easton, Collector	Nantucket	Rhode Island	12	....	699 60
Andrew J. Morton, Inspector	do	Massachusetts	12	....	771 00
Andrew J. Morton, Weigher	do	do	....	13	77 75
Andrew J. Morton, Measurer	do	do	....	11	89 86
Jesse Parker, Boatman	do		12	....	144 00
Jesse Parker, Temporary Inspector	do		....	24	72 00

RHODE ISLAND.

Providence.

Hezekiah Willard	Collector	Providence	Massachusetts	5	15	393 96
John S. Harris	Deputy Collector and Measurer	do	Rhode Island	5	15	1500 00
Abraham Thurston	Clerk	do	do	5	15	275 27
Silas A. Comstock	Naval officer	do	do	....	18	24 54
Douglass F. Seamans	Surveyor	do	do	5	24	316 37
James Fisher	do	Pawtuxet	do	2	9	38 04
Franklin Cooley	Inspector	Providence	Connecticut	2	19	168 00
Peter W. Ferris	do	do	Vermont	4	8	201 00
David Parmenter	do	do	New Hampshire	4	21	219 00
Samuel Low	do	do	Rhode Island	4	14	210 00
Samuel Thurber	do	do	do	....	60	180 00
Edward S. Underwood	do	do	do	....	60	180 00
John B. Barton	do	do	do	....	59	177 00
Joseph A. Waite	do	do	do	....	56	168 00
John S. Eddey	do	do	do	....	55	165 00
Benjamin Arnold, jr	do	do	do	....	56	168 00
Joseph T. Sisson	do	Pawtucket	do	4	....	100 00
William Carder	do	do	do	1	15	55 03
James Thurber, jr	Guager	Providence	do	4	22	131 88
William T. Pearce	Weigher	do	do	1	25	15 96
Nicholas R. Arnold	Measurer	do	do	1	17	78 38
Charles E. Newell	do	do	do	....	7	85 89
Daniel V. Ross	Appraiser	do	do	....	....	15 00
Joseph Remington	do	do	do	....	....	5 00
Shubael H. Cady	do	do	do	....	....	10 00

Bristol and Warren.

William J. Miller	Collector	Bristol	do	1	....	33 30
Nathan Bardin	Surveyor	do	do	2	24	66 89

CUSTOMS—*Rhode Island.*

Names and offices.		Where employed.	Where born.	Time employed during the year ending Sept. 30, '45.		Compensat'n for the time employed.
				Months	Days	
Benjamin M. Bosworth	Surveyor	Warren	Rhode Island	....	17	$12 13
B[illegible]min B. Noyes	Deputy Collector	Bristol	do	12	....	
Benjamin B. Noyes	[illegible]or	do	do	12	....	547 50
H[illegible]still P. Dimond	do	do	do	12	....	547 50
Henry A. Manchester	do	do	do	....	....	
John [illegible]g, jr	do	do	do	....	....	
Martin Luther	do	Warren	do	23	....	27 00
John [illegible]ry	do	do	do	2	4	192 00
George A. Parker	do	do	do	....	....	
Philip A. Manchester	G[illegible]r	Bristol	do	1	15	194 16
J[illegible] K. Barney	do	Warren	do	....	....	
William [illegible]o	Measurer	Bristol	do	....	....	
John K. Barney	do	Warren	do	....	....	
William [illegible]o	Weigher	Bristol	do	....	....	
John K. Barney	do	Warren	do	....	....	
Newport.						
Edwin Wilbur	Collector and Superintendent	Newport	do	4	11	331 65
George C. Shaw	Naval Officer	do	do	7	....	252 79
William G. Hammond	Surveyor	do	do	12	....	428 00
Silas Weaver	do	East Greenwich	do	4	18	95 43
William Halloway	do	North Kingston	do	12	....	250 00
Asa Gray	do	Tiverton	do	6	....	100 00
Henry J. Hudson	Inspector	Newport	Rhode Island	....	182	546 00
George W. Ellery	Deputy Collector and do	do	do	....	183	549 00

Henry J. Hudson	do	do	do		182	546 00
Daniel Brown	do	do	do		45	135 00
William Rider	Occasional do	do	do		94	282 00
Edward Willis	do do	do	do		84	252 00
Jeremiah Bliss	do	do	do		48	144 00
Samuel Dunn	do	New Shoreham	do	12	....	400 00
John Hall	do	North Kingston	do		43½	130 50
18 Benjamin Baker	do	do	do		57	171 00
Gr Harrington	do	East Greenwich	do		25¾	77 25
Carr Harrington	Measurer	do	do		....	46 28
J. O. Burdick	do	Newport	do		....	54 73
David Mill	Guager	do	do		....	290 04
David Mill	Weigher	do	do		....	10 29
Samuel Hunter	Occasional Inspector	do	do	6	....	18 00

CONNECTICUT.

Middletown.

Philip Sage, Collector and Agent for Marine Hospital		Middletown	Connecticut	12	....	1173 33
Leverett Hubbard, Deputy Collector, Inspector, and Guager		do	do	12	....	679 12
Daniel Burrows, Surveyor and Keeper of Public Stores		do	do	12	....	402 00
Robert Williams	Weigher and Mr	do	Bermuda	12	....	90 74
Epaphras Clark	Inspector	do	Connecticut	8	....	267 00
Oliver P. Sage	do	do	do	4	....	231 00
Penfield B. Goodsell, Surveyor, Weigher, Guager, and Mr		Hartford	do	12	....	383 10
William Hayden	Inspector	do	do	12	....	498 00
William Willard, Surveyor, Weigher, Guager, and Meas'r		Saybrook	do	12	....	392 19
Horace Stillman, Inspector and Keeper of Revenue Boat		do	do	12	....	390 00
Bushnell Kirtland	Inspector	do	do	4	8	75 00

CUSTOMS—*Connecticut—Continued.*

Names and offices.	Where employed.	Where born.	Time employed during the year ending Sept. 30, '45. Months	Days	Compensat'n for the time employed.
Erastus Haskell....Inspector	Saybrook	New Hampshire	7	18	$207 00
William J. Clark....Temporary..do	do	Connecticut	......	4	12 00
New London.					
C[illegible]es F. Lester, Collector and Superintendent of Light Houses, and Agent for Marine Hospital fund	New London	Connecticut	12	....	1185 93
Perry Douglass....Surveyor and Inspector	do	do	12	....	333 31
Elijah Ames, Deputy Collector, Inspector, Guager, Weigher, &c	do	do	12	....	620 00
[illegible]es D. Lester....Clerk	do	do	9	....	75 00
H[illegible]y Douglass....Inspector	do	do	12	....	600 00
William Faulkner....do	Norwich	do	12	....	750 00
[illegible]am Manworing....do	East Lyme	do	12	....	94 00
James Treadway....do	Lyme	do	12	....	150 00
New Haven.					
Norris Wilcox....[illegible]r.	New Haven	Connecticut	6	....	1685 95
Charles A. Judson....Surveyor and Storekeeper	do	do	10	6	707 34
Walter Asborne....Insp[illegible]tor and Guager	do	do	3	28	854 24
William H. Jones, Inspector, Weigher, and Measurer	do	do	12	....	1046 84
John S. [illegible]ll....Inspector	do	do	12	....	600 00
Hezekiah Gorham....do	do	do	5	....	310 33
Alfred Bassett....do	do	do	5	....	371 00
William [illegible]rs....do	do	Germany	12	....	389 00

S. W. Wadsworth	Temporary ... do	do	Connecticut	....	9	27 00
John Colbourn	do ... do	do	do	....	7	21 00
George L. Dowa	do	Guilford and Madison	do	5	....	25 50
J. J. Bartholomew	do	Branford & Sachem's Head	do	5	....	28 50
Mark Bristol	do	Milford and Derby	do	5	....	16 67
Fairfield.						
Stephen Lounsbury	Collector	Fairfield	New York	4	26	739 04
E. A. Parrott	Inspector	Bridgeport	Connecticut	4	26	276 00
E. A. Parrott	Weigher	do	do	4	26	48 70
E. A. Parrott	Guager	do	do	4	26	36 36
E. A. Parrott	Mr	do	do	4	26	226 15
George W. Selleck	Inspector	Norwalk	do	4	26	144 00
James H. Hoyt	do	Stamford	do	4	26	102 00
James H. Hoyt	Mr	do	do	4	26	132 59
Stonington.						
Ezra Chesebro	Collector	Stonington	Connecticut	2	....	208 53
George Brown	Surveyor	Pawcatuck	Rhode Island	12	....	150 00
Luther Ripley	Inspector	Stonington	Connecticut	12	....	500 00
Elihu Spicer	do	Port of Mystic	do	4	....	100 00
Ephraim Williams, jr.	Weigher, Guager, and Measurer	Stonington	do	....	7	

CUSTOMS—*New York.*

Names and offices.		Where employed.	Where born.	Time employed during the year ending Sept. 30, '45. Months	Days	Compensat'n for the time employed.
NEW YORK.						
Champlain.						
William F. Haile	Collector	Plattsburgh	Vermont	12	....	$1050 71
Thomas Crook	Deputy and Inspector	Plattsburgh and on Steamboat	do	12	....	750 00
John H. Bromley	do do	Rouse's Point	New York	12	....	600 00
Ezra Stiles	do do	Fort Covington	Vermont	12	....	450 00
Robert Stetson	do do	Champlain	New York	12	....	500 00
Henry B. Smith	do do	Chateaugay	do	12	....	400 00
Washington [illegible]er	do do	Trout River	Massachusetts	12	....	400 00
Edward Springer	do do	[illegible]'s	Maine	12	....	400 00
Elias Bowker	do do	Hogansburgh	Vermont	12	....	400 00
Samuel T. Buel	Inspector	Rouse's Point	New York	12	....	500 00
Dean Delance	do	Whitehall	do	12	....	400 00
Samuel [illegible]	do	Plattsburgh	Ver mnt	12	....	250 00
Theodore Rodgers	do	Fort Covington and [illegible] River	New York	12	....	250 00
Oswegatchee.						
David C. Judson	Collector and Inspector	Ogdensburgh	Connecticut	12	....	1460 10
Matthew W. Tillotson	Deputy Collector and Inspector	do	Vermont	12	....	900 00
Horace Hurlbut	do do do	Morristown	Connecticut	12	....	708 00

Richard Edsall	do.......do.......do	Waddington	Pennsylvania	12	....	365 00
Lewis Lyon	do.......do.......do	Louisville	New Jersey	12	....	365 00
Lemuel Haskell	do.......do.......do	Massena	Massachusetts	......	7	7 00
Timothy Olmsted	Temporary Inspector	Ogdensburgh	New York	8	25	492 00
John G. McCormick	do.......do	Hammond	Pennsylvania	12	....	365 00
Cape Vincent.						
Peleg Burchard	Collector	Cape Vincent	Connecticut	12	....	1014 00
Heman Millard	Deputy Collector and Inspector	French Creek	New York	12	....	730 00
Azariah Walton	do.......do.......do	Alexandria Bay	New Hampshire	12	....	547 50
John L. Mansfield	Inspector	French Creek	New York	12	....	547 50
William H. Lawton	Deputy Collector and Inspector	Cape Vincent	do	12	....	547 50
Sacket's Harbor.						
Otis N. Cole	Collector	Sacket's Harbor	New York	4	10	254 37
Joshua Eaton	Deputy Collector	do	New Hampshire	3	8	200 00
[illegible]on Curtiss	Deputy Collector and Inspector	do	Massachusetts	3	....	184 00
Joseph D. Bealles	Inspector	Dexter	do	3	29	121 00
Eli E. Adams	do	Three Mile Bay	New York	3	14	106 00
Frederick Coffun	do	Chamnot Bay	New Hampshire	3	14	69 32
John Fay	do	Isthmus	New York	3	....	60 00
Emory Burnham	do	Grenadier Island	New Hampshire	3	....	60 00
Oswego.						
George H. McWhorter	Collector	Oswego	New Jersey	12	....	1015 84
John L. McWhorter	Deputy Collector	do	New York	12	....	750 00
John W. Turner	Inspector	do	do	12	....	730 00
David Harmon, jr.	do	do	do	12	....	730 00
Joseph Williams	Deputy Collector	Sodus	do	8	16	366 50

CUSTOMS—*New York—Continued.*

Names and offices.		Where employed.	Where born.	Time employed during the year ending Sept. 30, '45.		Compensat'n for the time employed.
				Months	Days	
Seth Turner	Inspector	Little Sodus	New York	9	....	$252 00
James A. McChesney	Deputy Collector	Port Ontario	do	12	....	416 62
Samuel Cook	do do	Sandy Creek	do	12	....	250 32
Harry Huntington	Inspector	Texas	do	12	....	365 00
Samuel Hall	do	Utica	New Hampshire	10	....	333 75
William J. Hovey	Occasional Aid	Oswego	New York	......	61	122 00
Niagara.						
Reuben H. Boughton	Collector	Lewiston	New York	4	....	451 79
Oliver Grace	Deputy Collector and Inspector	do	Ireland	12	....	900 00
John Porter	do do do	Youngstown	New York	12	....	730 00
George W. Simms	do do do	Niagara Falls	do	7	7	241 11
Alex. Butterfield	do do do	18 Mile Creek	do	12	....	200 00
Milton Randall	Inspector	Lewiston	do	12	....	730 00
Samuel Chubbuck	do	Youngstown	do	12	....	730 00
Timothy Paige	do	Lockport	do	12	....	730 00
Walter Durkee	Travelling Inspector	District of Niagara	do	12	....	730 00
Buffalo Creek.						
Henry W. Rogers	Collector	Buffalo	New York	5	....	816 04
Charles M. Hopkins	Deputy Collector	do	do	2	....	166 00
Robert H. Best	Deputy Inspector	do	Pennsylvania	12	....	1000 00
William J. Mack	do do	do	New York	4	11	268 00
Patrick Milton	do do	do	Ireland	4	19	213 13

Charles Norton	do. do	do	New York	12	....	607 00
Chipman P. Turner	Deputy Collector	Black Rock	do	4	9	262 00
Oscar F. Crary	do. do	Black Rock Dam	do	12	....	500 00
Nathaniel Root	do. do	Tonawanda	Connecticut	3	....	62 50
Henry P. Willcox	do. do	Silver Creek	do	3	....	125 00
Ernest Mullett	do. do	Dunkirk	Vermont	12	....	250 00
Hiram A. Pratt	do. do	Portland Harbor	New York	4	5	86 47
Sag Harbor.						
Abel Huntington	Collector	Sag Harbor	Connecticut	5	12	457 00
Noah Washburn	Inspector	do	do	12	....	123 00
Alexander Eddy	Deputy Collector	do	Rhode Island	8	18	
Joseph H. Skillman	Inspector	Greenport	New York	12	....	174 00
Joseph Crolins	Temporary Inspector	Sag Harbor	do	......	4	12 00
Sidney C. Hallock	do. do	do	do	......	2	6 00
Joseph [illegible]	[illegible]tor	do	do	3	....	21 00
Genesee.						
Lyman B. Langworthy	Collector	Rochester	New York	12	....	784 24
Charles Mortimer	Deputy Inspector	do	Virginia	3	6	196 00
John Smyles	do. do	Carthage Landing	Scotland	9	....	546 00
George B. Benjamin	do. do	Kelsey's Landing	[illegible]ut	12	....	730 00
Nicholas Read	do. do	Charlotte	Ireland	12	....	730 00
Charles G. Richards	do. do	Pultneyville	New York	8	28	540 00
New York city.						
Cornelius W. Lawrence	Collector	New York	New York	3	....	*6400 00
Cornelius S. Bogardus	Assistant do	do	do	12	....	2500 00

* Maximum fees and commissions limited by law per annum.

CUSTOMS—*New York—Continued*

Names and offices.		Where employed.	Where born.	Time employed during the year ending Sept. 30, '45.		Compensat'n for the time employed.
				Months	Days	
New York city—Continued.						
Giles P. Clinch	Deputy Collector	New York	New York	12	....	$1500 00
George Davis	do ..... do	do	do	12	....	1500 00
James T. Talman	do ..... do	do	do	12	....	1500 00
Henry A. Cargill	do ..... do	do	do	1	....	1 25
Thomas J. Gillilan	Clerk	do	do	12	....	1200 00
James L. Sawyer	do	do	Vermont	12	....	1000 00
Joseph E. Lawrence	do	do	New York	2	18	128 80
George A. Brown	Entry Clerk	do	do	11	26	989 07
William C. Gray	do	do	do	12	....	1000 00
Tobias V. Mumford	do	do	do	10	8	854 40
Elias D. Ogden	do	do	do	12	....	1000 00
Moses F. Odell	do	do	do	4	23	395 60
[illegible] C. Walden	do	do	do	12	....	1000 00
William C. Dayton	Order Clerk	do	do	12	....	1000 00
Theodore H. Jenkins	do	do	do	12	....	1000 00
Charles Monell	do	do	do	12	....	900 00
Peter S. Hoes	[illegible] do	do	do	5	8	458 79
George F. H. Young	do .. do	do	Pennsylvania	7	....	667 39
Marshall Bryan	do .. do	do	New York	12	....	700 00
James B. Stuart	do .. do	do	Massachusetts	7	4	382 69
Isaac Bluxome	Bond and Deposite do	do	England	12	....	1000 00
Charles J. Cannon	License and Enrolment do	do	New York	12	....	1000 00
John P. Haff	Assistant Enrolment do	do	do	12	....	666 48
John B. Satterthwaite	Clearance do	do	do	12	....	900 00

William H. Brown	Protection do	do	do	12	....	800	00
Fraley C. Mhr	Register do	do	Pennsylvania	12	....	700	00
Henry P. Randolph	Assistant do do	do	Virginia	8	....	398	33
George Taylor	Record of Arrivals do	do	England	10	....	667	39
Gamaliel B. Sawyer	Copying do	do	Vermont	10	11	604	89
Gre C. Waller	Messenger	do	do	12	....	500	00
James B. Kinslow	do	do	Ireland	8	....	333	00
John M. Catlin	Liquidating Clk	do	New York	12	....	1200	00
William G. Mcy	do do	do	do	10	....	817	39
ed G. Van Kleeck	do do	do	do	12	....	1000	00
Willis Patten	do do	do	Maine	12	....	1000	00
Hamilton Bruc o	do do	do	New York	12	....	900	00
William H. H. Prall	do do	do	New Jersey	12	....	800	00
Lewis P. Bayard	do do	New Yrk	New Jersey	12	....	700	00
Lynde Catlin	do do	do	New York	12	....	300	00
William J. McMaster	Export Clerk	do	do	12	....	1000	00
J hn Z. Hartt	do do	do	Nova Scotia	11	8	937	50
Edward A. Bibby	do do	do	New York	12	....	816	57
James H. Brady	do do	do	do	3	1	236	17
James P. Wright	do do	do	England	8	....	531	11
William H. Weincke	Messenger	do	Pennsylvania	8	....	239	00
Henry T. Kiersted	Cashier	do	Holland	3	....	625	00
William D. Robinson	Assistant do	do	New York	12	....	1500	00
Rph Bunner	Clerk	do	do	12	....	900	00
George W. Pleasants	do	do	Kentucky	12	....	800	00
Samuel G. Ogden, jr.	Auditor	do	New York	12	....	3000	00
John W. Hunter	Assistant do	d	do	11	19	1440	19
Ebenezer B. Billings	Book Keeper	do	Massachusetts	12	....	1200	00
Richard B. Cnolly	Statistical Clerk	do	Ireland	5	....	502	95
Mortimer Lnt	do do	do	New York	12	....	1000	00
Edin G. Livingston	do do	do	do	12	....	900	00
Edward L. Mrs	(Exports) do do	do	do	7	23	642	15

CUSTOMS—*New York—Continued.*

Names and offices.		Where employed.	Where born.	Time employed during the year ending Sept. 30, '45.		Compensat'n for the time employed.
				Months	Days	
New York city—Continued.						
James Purdy	Register of Entries Clerk	New York	New York	12	....	$850 00
Nathaniel Olcott	Debenture do	do	Connecticut	12	....	1012 50
Charles Price	Ab't of Drawbacks do	do	New York	4	23	316 48
Melancton S. Swartwout	Export and Bounty do	do	do	12	....	1000 00
John Y. Van Tuyl	Examining do	do	do	12	....	1000 00
William Frean	Accountant	do	Maryland	12	....	900 00
Daniel Sullivan	Impost Clerk	do	Ireland	12	....	1012 50
Arthur G. Powell	do do	do	New York	10	....	817 39
Edward H. Plume	do do	do	do	3	3	206 59
George Hammeken	Abstract do	do	Tunis	12	....	1000 00
Stephen P. Russell	do do	do	Pennsylvania	12	....	1000 00
Horatio N. Kilby	do do	do	New York	12	....	900 00
Peter G. Sharp, jr	do do	do	do	12	....	800 00
John J. Rowan	do do	do	do	2	....	132 61
[illegible]as G. Wait	Passenger Lists do	do	Vermont	12	....	800 00
Ogden P. Edwards	Copying do	do	New York	12	....	800 00
Peter V. Remsen	Square Yard do	do	do	11	14	953 80
Samuel Beman	do do	do	Maine	12	....	1000 00
[illegible]rt S. [illegible]by	do do	do	England	12	....	900 00
Henry Doane	do do	do	Massachusetts	12	....	900 00
James [illegible]loss	do do	do	Scotland	12	....	900 00
Archibald McVickar, jr	Square Yard Clerk	New York	New York	12	....	783 42
John Day	do do do	do	do	3	1	236 17
William H. Van Dalsem	do do do	do	do	4	....	265 93

William H. Botts	do...do...do	do	Virginia	12	....	600 00
David B. McNiel, jr.	Invoice Examiner	do	New York	12	....	1000 00
Alfred W. Upham	do.....do	do	Vermont	12	....	800 00
Enoch E. Camp	do.....do	do	New York	4	23	316 48
Edward Stephens	do.....do	do	Massachusetts	3	29	263 74
William M. Storms	do.....do	do	New York	4	25	320 88
Ingham Corryell	Keeper of Records	do	Pennsylvania	7	19	608 24
Samuel P. Goldson	do.....do	do	do	7	12	557 50
Francis McNerhany	do.....do	do	Ireland	3	16	176 37
Naval Office.						
Michael Hoffman	Naval Officer	do	New York	Limited by law	to	5000 00
Francis E. Spinner, Auditor and Deputy Naval Officer		do	do			1500 00
John Cockle	Deputy Naval Officer	do	New Jersey			1500 00
Leonard Lee	do...do...do	do	Vermont			1500 00
Jacob R. Pentz	Chief Clerk	do	New York			1200 00
Cornell S. Franklin	Entry Clerk	do	do			1050 00
Edward W. Telfair	do...do	do	do			1050 00
Charles B. Battelle	Cash Clerk	do	West Indies			1050 00
Wade Hough	[illegible]ting Clerk	do	New Hampshire			1050 00
Stephen Paret	Deb. and Exp. Clerk	do	New York			1050 00
Thomas Hays	Book Keeper	do	do			1050 00
Samson M. Isaacs	Refunding Clerk	do	Connecticut			1050 00
[illegible]ge W. [illegible]tz	Impost Clerk	do	New York			1050 00
William J. Tenney	Square Yard Clerk	do	Rhode Island			1050 00
[illegible] [illegible]er, jr	Assistant Cash Clerk	do	New York			950 00
William Lumby	Assistant Liquidating Clerk	do	do			950 00
Benjamin S. Hart	Book Keeper	do	do			950 00
[illegible]ah Ingraham	Assistant Impost Clerk	do	do			950 00
Peter F. Burroughs	Clearance Clerk	do	New Jersey			900 00
[illegible] [illegible]ge, jr	do.....do	do	New York			900 00

CUSTOMS—*New York—Continued.*

Names and offices.		Where employed.	Where born.	Time employed during the year ending Sept. 30, '45.		Compensat'n for the time employed.
				Months	Days	
New York city—Continued.						
John F. Doyle	Register of Entries Clerk	New York	New York			$900 00
John W. Buckland	Assistant Liquidating Clerk	do	England			900 00
Alexander Wells	do do do	do	New York			900 00
James G. Maclay	do do do	do	do			900 00
Tunis S. Barkeloo	do do do	do	do			900 00
Elias B. Dayton	Assistant Square Yard Clerk	do	New Jersey			900 00
Harvey Barmore	do do do do	do	New York			900 00
Daniel R. Hitchcock	Assistant Impost Clerk	do	do			900 00
Peter Fairchild	Endorsing Clerk	do	do			900 00
Barnabas Hallock	Clerk in charge of Papers	do	do			700 00
William Handley	Porter	do	Ireland			450 00
Surveyor's Office.						
Elijah F. Purdy	Surveyor and Inspector	do	New York	6		2400 00
Daniel D. Briggs	Deputy Surveyor	do	do	3	26	483 29
Joseph C. Potter	First Clerk	do	do	12		1200 00
Charles F. Lineback	Second Clerk	do	New Jersey	12		1200 00
Thomas M. Gahagan	Third Clerk	do	New York	12		1150 00
James H. Blasdell	Fourth Clerk	do	Maine	1		70 83
Hachaliah Purdy	Fifth Clerk	do	New York	12		700 00
Augustus Purdy	Clerk	do	do	1		45 83
Hiram Riddle	Porter and Messenger	do	do	12		600 00

Inspectors.

John H. Abe lo	Inspector	New York	New York	12	....	1095 00
Samuel Allen	do	do	Pennsylvania	12	....	1095 00
Alexander G. Anderson	do	do	New York	12	....	1095 00
Nathan T. Arnold	do	do	New Jersey	7	12	678 00
Herman Atwill	do	do	Massachusetts	12	....	1095 00
ahles W. Atwood	do	do	Conn at.	12	....	1095 00
William H. Baker	do	do	New York	1	5	105 00
Edwin Baldwin	do	do	do	12	....	1095 00
Charles S. Baldwin	do	do	New Jersey	12	....	1095 00
Samuel Barton	do	Staten Island	New York	12	....	1095 00
Ges Baxter	do	New York	do	3	13	315 00
William S. Bennett	do	do	do	12	....	1095 00
Gilbert M. Bogardus	do	Brooklyn	do	12	....	1095 00
John R. Bowne	do	New York	do	7	17	693 00
Loundes Brown	do	do	South Carolina	12	....	1095 00
William J. Brown	do	do	New York	7	17	693 00
enrH C. Boswell	do	do	New Jersey	3	4	288 00
Bernard R. Burling	do	do	New York	6	....	549 00
John T. Cairns	do	do	do	12	....	1095 00
hles Carter	do	do	Ireland	12	....	1095 00
Joseph F. Casserley	do	do	do	12	....	1095 00
Aan Chamberlin	do	do	New York	1	4	102 00
Henry Gns	do	d.	England	5	16	507 00
hles B. Ks	do	d.	New York	7	17	690 00
William L. Clark	do	do	do	7	17	693 00
Lewis P. Gr	do	do	New Jersey	12	....	1095 00
John J. Kte	do	do	New York	12	....	1095 00
Jaes Coad	do	do	Ireland	10	6	819 00
Gerhon Gn	do	do	New Yk	3	4	288 00
Jacob Kin	do	do	do	8	28	810 00

CUSTOMS—*New York—Continued.*

Names and offices.		Where employed.	Where born.	Time employed during the year ending Sept. 30, '45.		Compensat'n for the time employed.
				Months	Days	
New York city—Continued.						
John Colvill	Inspector	New York	New York	12	....	$1095 00
John V. Coon	do	do	New Jersey	12	....	1095 00
Warmuldus S. Cooper	do	do	do	7	17	693 00
Thomas A. Cooper	do	do	England	3	4	288 00
William Cornell	d	do	New York	1	4	105 00
John F. Davis	do	do	Connecticut	12	....	1095 00
Daniel Davis	do	do	New York	12	....	1095 00
Ira B. Davis	do	do	Massachusetts	7	17	693 00
Andrew B. Decker	do	Staten Island	New York	12	....	1095 00
Charles Delvecchio	do	New York	Italy	12	....	1095 00
Charles A. Denike	do	do	New York	12	....	1095 00
Denyse Denyse	do	do	New York	12	....	1095 00
William De Peyster	do	do	do	10	2	915 00
Moses E. Dewitt	do	do	do	5	10	489 00
Cornelius Dickenson	do	do	do	7	17	693 00
Jeremiah Dodge	do	do	do	1	5	108 00
Stephen M. Drew	do	do	do	12	....	1055 00
Tarleton B. Earl	do	do	Pennsylvania	12	....	1095 00
Alexander T. Eaton	do	do	New York	11	5	996 00
Edward Eccleston	do	do	Ireland	12	....	1095 00
James English	do	do	New York	12	....	1095 00
David Feeks	do	do	do	11	4	1014 00
Benjamin F. Ferris	do	do	do	7	17	693 00
Charles W. Fitch	do	do	New Jersey	5	21	522 00

John Fitch	do	do	do	1	5	105 00
William Francis	do	do	New York	7	17	693 00
Donald Fraser	do	Staten Island	do	12	....	1095 00
John Frazee	do	New York	New Jersey	12	....	1095 00
Nathaniel Freeman	do	do	Massachusetts	12	....	1095 00
Charles R. Friedricks	do	do	Germany	12	....	1083 00
Elisha Foot	do	do	Massachusetts	11	24	1071 00
Edward Gallagher	do	do	Delaware	7	17	693 00
Robert Gamble	do	do	New York	11	29	1089 00
Leonard Gansevoort	do	do	do	12	....	1095 00
David Gardiner	do	do	do	12	....	1095 00
Franklin Gilmore	do	do	New Hampshire	10	3	921 00
George G. Glasier	do	do	New York	7	17	693 00
William F. Godfrey	do	do	Connecticut	12	....	1095 00
Gustavus A. Goodrich	do	do	Vermont	12	....	[illegible] 00
William R. Gorham	do	do	New York	8	5	741 00
William H. P. Graham	do	do	Connecticut	12	....	1095 00
Abner Gleaf, jr	do	do	New Hampshire	9	16	867 00
Jaes Grogan	do	do	Ireland	8	5	741 00
William Gdey	do	do	Pennsylvania	....	19	57 00
Walter Heyer	do	do	New York	12	....	1095 00
John Hillyer	do	do	do	12	....	1095 00
Edward Hitchcock	do	do	do	12	....	1095 00
Peter Hogeboom	do	do	do	3	4	288 00
H ward Hge	do	do	do	7	5	657 00
Wm Honay	do	do	Maryland	1	5	105 00
Gge F. Hopkins	do	do	New York	12	....	1095 00
Jos pho Hopkins	do	do	New Hampshire	12	....	1095 00
John C. Houston	do	do	New York	12	....	[illegible]5 00
Thomas Howland	do	do	Massachusetts	3	29	363 00
Ge Hubbell	do	d	Connecticut	12	....	1095 00
John H. Hunt	do	d	New York	12	....	1035 00

CUSTOMS—*New York*—*Continued.*

Names and offices.		Where employed.	Where born.	Time employed during the year ending Sept. 30, '45.		Compensat'n for the time employed.
				Months	Days	
New York city—Continued.						
John E. Hunt	Inspector	New York	New York	12	....	$1095 00
Joseph Hunt	do	do	Ireland	12	....	1095 00
William H. Hyatt	do	do	New Jersey	12	....	1095 00
James E. Hyde	do	do	New York	12	....	1095 00
Thomas Jenkins	do	do	Massachusetts	12	....	1095 00
Charles P. Johnson	do	do	do	12	....	1095 00
Henry D. Johnson	do	do	New York	3	1	252 00
Andrew A. Jones	do	do	Holland	12	....	1095 00
Henry A. Jones	do	do	New York	3	10	306 00
Edgar Irving	do	do	do	12	....	1095 00
Oscar Irving	do	do	do	12	....	1095 00
William W. Kidder	do	do	Maine	7	9	669 00
[illegible]as Kirk	do	do	Ireland	1	6	108 00
Thomas H. [illegible]e	do	do	Pennsylvania	12	....	1095 00
[illegible]ce Langton	do	do	Ireland	7	17	693 00
Andrew [illegible]er	do	do	New York	12	....	1095 00
Horatio G. Lewis	do	do	do	12	....	1095 00
William Lewis	do	do	New Jersey	12	....	1095 00
Samuel Lloyd	do	do	Pennsylvania	12	....	1095 00
Richard A. Locke	do	do	New York	12	....	1095 00
Thomas H. Lyell	do	do	do	12	....	1095 00
Elam Lynds	do	do	Massachusetts	11	30	1092 00
Leroy McEvers	do	do	New York	12	....	1095 00
Henry McKinstry	do	do	do	12	....	1095 00

Dennis McMahon	do.	do.	Ireland	12	....	1095 00
John McMahon	do.	do.	do.	10	3	894 00
Hugh McNally	d.	do.	do.	3	4	288 00
James McNespic	do.	do.	do.	3	3	285 00
John Marston	do.	do.	New York	8	6	744 00
John Mersereau	do.	do.	do.	12	....	1095 00
Alexander Ming, jr.	do.	do.	do.	12	....	1095 00
Alexander Ming	do.	do.	do.	12	....	1095 00
George G. Mitchell	do.	do.	do.	12	....	1095 00
Michael Molloney	do.	do.	Ireland	12	....	1095 00
Joseph Moser	do.	do.	Connecticut	10	....	915 00
Thomas Murphy	d.	do.	New York	12	....	1092 00
Orville J. Nash	do.	do.	do.	1	5	105 00
Samuel Nichols, jr.	do.	do.	do.	3	1	279 00
c [illegible]ild Noble	do.	do.	do.	1	5	105 00
Daniel W. Norris	d.	do.	do.	3	4	288 00
James [illegible]ey	do.	do.	do.	12	....	1095 00
Francis Ogsbury	d.	do.	do.	12	....	1095 00
Ajah G. Palmer	do.	do.	do.	12	....	1095 00
Naphtali Phillips	do.	do.	do.	12	....	1025 00
Samuel A. Phillips	do.	do.	England	7	17	693 00
William V. Porter	do.	do.	New York	....	29	87 00
Henry Post	do.	do.	do.	12	....	1095 00
Abraham B. Purdy	do.	do.	do.	7	17	693 00
Henry Raymond	do.	do.	do.	12	....	1095 00
James Raymond	do.	do.	Connecticut	12	....	1095 00
James Reed	d.	do.	New York	12	....	1095 00
Cyrus Riell	do.	do.	do.	7	17	693 00
Robert S. Robertson	do.	do.	New Jersey	12	....	1095 00
John Rusk	do.	do.	Ireland	3	4	288 00
Squire H. Russ	do.	do.	New York	12	....	1025 00
William D. Scally	do.	do.	do.	12	....	1095 00

CUSTOMS—*New York—Continued.*

Names and offices.		Where employed.	Where born.	Time employed during the year ending Sept. 30, '45. Months	Days	Compensat'n for the time employed.
New York city—Continued.						
Jerome Scofield	Inspector	New York	New York	3	4	$288 00
John Sheilds	do	do	Ireland	10	3	921 00
John B. Sickles	do	do	New York	10	20	972 00
John Sickles	do	do	do	5	25	528 00
James Smyth	do	do	do	12	....	1086 00
Sylvester S. Southworth	do	do	Massachusetts	12	....	1095 00
George P. Stedman	do	do	do	12	....	1095 00
James R. Steers	do	do	England	12	....	1095 00
John H. Stuart	do	do	Massachusetts	12	....	1050 00
Edward Suffern	do	do	New York	7	5	657 00
Peter Tappan	do	do	do	12	....	1095 00
Henry A. Talman	do	do	do	1	4	102 00
William R. Taylor	do	do	Pennsylvania	12	....	1086 00
James [illegible]e.	do	do	New York	12	....	1095 00
[illegible]rd C. [illegible]ton	do	d.	do	12	....	1095 00
Griffin Tompkins	do	Staten Island	do	12	....	1095 00
Thomas Trenor	do	New York	Ireland	12	....	1095 00
Thomas Tucker	do	do	Massachusetts	12	....	1095 00
Richard Tyson	do	Staten Island	New York	3	8	300 00
Beekman M. Van Beuren	do	do	do	12	....	1095 00
John L. Van Boskerck	do	New York	New Jersey	12	....	1095 00
John Van Bussum	do	do	do	7	17	693 00
Lawrence L. Van Kleeck	do	do	New York	12	....	1095 00
William L. Van Zandt	do	do	do	3	4	288

John W. Vethake	do	do	New Jersey	12	....	1095 00
John S. Vosburgh	do	do	New York	7	9	769 00
Jacob M. Vreeland	do	do	New Jersey	12	....	1095 00
Daniel Ward	do	do	New York	1	5	105 00
Everadus W[illegible]r	do	do	do	12	....	1095 00
George Weir	do	do	Rhode Island	9	24	891 00
Job W[illegible]lt	do	do	New Jersey	5	17	510 00
John W. [illegible]r	do	do	New York	12	....	1095 00
Barnum Whipple	do	do	do	12	....	1095 00
Thomas Wiswall	do	do	do	1	19	54 00
Samuel M. Wolfe	do	do	Virginia	12	....	1095 00
Henry Wood	do	do	Pennsylvania	12	....	1095 00
Isaac N. Woolley	do	do	New York	3	4	288 00
James Wright	do	do	Massachusetts	1	2	96 00
Joseph A. Yard	do	do	New Jersey	3	4	288 00
Albert J. Zabriskie	do	do	do	8	12	762 00
Joseph Bailey ... at $2	do	do	New York	11	25	718 00
Smith Rider ... do	do	Long Island	do	12	....	730 00
Raynor R. Smith ... do	do	do	do	12	....	730 00

Night Inspectors.

John Angus	Night Inspector	New York	New Jersey	10	10	471 00
[illegible]e C. Barbarin	do. do.	do	New York	12	....	547 50
Winnebald Bissinger	do. do.	do	Germany	5	14	390 00
Daniel B. Boden	do. do.	do	New York	5	20	259 50
[illegible]el Boggs	do. do.	do	do	1	4	51 00
Isaac L. [illegible]r	do. do.	do	do	5	5	237 00
Joseph Clark	do. do.	d[illegible]	Connecticut	12	....	547 50
Joseph Cornell	do. do.	do	New York	12	....	547 50
Patrick Dalton	do. do.	do	Ireland	12	....	547 50
Henry C. Day	do. do.	do	New York	7	7	331 50

CUSTOMS—*New York—Continued.*

Names and offices.		Where employed.	Where born.	Time employed during the year ending Sept. 30, '45. Months	Days	Compensat'n for the time employed.
New York city—Continued.						
Moses G. De Pew	Night Inspector	New York	New York	7	5	$328 50
John McDonald	do. do.	do.	Ireland	1	4	52 50
Moran Dugan	do. do.	do.	New Hampshire	12	....	547 50
Leonard Dunkley	do. do.	do.	New York	12	....	547 50
James P. Fagan	do. do.	do.	do.	12	....	547 50
Patrick Finnegan	do. do.	do.	Ireland	12	....	547 50
Daniel Fisher	do. do.	do.	New York	1	4	51 00
Joseph P. Flynn	do. do.	do.	Ireland	1	5	52 50
William Freeland	do. do.	do.	New York	12	....	547 50
George W. Frey	do. do.	do.	Germany	12	....	547 50
Charles Gannon	do. do.	do.	Ireland	1	5	52 50
Charles Gallagher	do. do.	do.	Delaware	12	....	547 50
Ira C. Gardner	do. do.	do.	New Jersey	12	....	547 50
Mathias H. Gooderson	do. do.	do.	do.	12	....	547 50
David T. Gray	do. do.	do.	do.	12	....	547 50
Edward Green	do. do.	do.	New York	10	3	460 50
William Grehan	do. do.	do.	Ireland	7	25	346 50
James L. Henry	do. do.	do.	Pennsylvania	12	....	547 50
Philo T. Hoyt	do. do.	do.	New York	12	....	547 50
John S. Hyatt	do. do.	do.	do.	4	20	213 00
George W. Isaacs	do. do.	do.	Connecticut	12	....	547 50
Phillip Keeler	do. do.	do.	France	1	6	54 00
John Kelly	do. do.	do.	New York	12	....	547 50
William Kelly	do. do.	do.	Ireland	12	....	547 50

David H. Kelly	do	do	do	Massachusetts	4	20	213 00
John Ketchum	do	do	do	New York	12	....	547 50
Harman Lefferts	do	do	do	do	12	....	547 50
[illegible]us L. Lewis	do	do	do	do	12	....	547 50
[illegible]as [illegible]re	do	do	do	do	7	15	343 50
Hugh [illegible]re	do	do	do	Ireland	1	6	54 00
James McKeon	do	do	do	New York	8	29	319 50
Peter McLaughlin	do	do	do	Ireland	12	....	547 50
James McNalley	do	do	do	New York	12	....	547 50
Edward Mallaly	do	do	do	do	12	....	547 50
Abraham E. Miller	do	do	do	do	3	8	150 00
Charles A. Molan	do	do	do	do	12	....	547 50
Andrew Morrison	do	do	do	Ireland	1	5	52 50
Dennis Mullins	do	do	do	do	1	6	54 00
John Mullowney	do	do	do	do	8	19	391 50
[illegible]w [illegible]t	do	do	do	New York	12	....	547 50
Daniel C. Nichols	do	do	do	do	11	14	522 00
[illegible]e	do	do	do	do	12	....	547 50
William Phillips	do	do	do	Pennsylvania	12	....	547 50
Francis P[illegible]st[illegible]	d[illegible]	do	do	New York	12	....	547 50
David Pollock	do	do	do	Massachusetts	1	6	54 00
John Quinn	do	do	do	Ireland	7	10	336 00
[illegible]el Reed	d[illegible]	do	do	Connecticut	8	16	387 00
[illegible]ac W. Riker	do	do	do	New Hampshire	12	....	547 50
R[illegible]ard R[illegible]an	do	do	do	New York	12	....	547 50
[illegible]ab W. Schultz	do	do	do	do	12	....	547 50
Gilbert P. [illegible]od	do	do	do	do	7	12	339 00
Matthew H. Spittle	do	do	do	England	4	20	213 00
John Swartcope	do	do	do	New York	12	....	547 50
[illegible]llip Tabele	do	do	do	do	12	....	547 50
[illegible]dell Trenchard	do	do	do	do	12	....	547 50
Albro Vail	do	do	do	do	12	....	547 50

CUSTOMS—*New York—Continued.*

Names and offices.		Where employed.	Where born.	Time employed during the year ending Sept. 30, '45.		Compensat'n for the time employed.
				Months	Days	
New York city—Continued.						
Aaron Vanderbilt	Night Inspector	New York	New York	12	....	$547 50
Peter Vandervoort	do....do	do	New Jersey	7	12	339 00
Adrian Van Riper	do....do	do	do	10	6	464 50
Garrett Van Velsor	do....do	do	New York	12	....	547 50
James R. Waldron	do....do	do	do	7	....	321 00
William Wasson	do....do	do	Ireland	1	5	52 50
Frederick Watkins	do....do	do	New York	12	....	547 50
Thomas Wheelan	do....do	do	Ireland	12	....	547 50
William O. Webb	do....do	do	New York	4	20	213 00
Weighers.						
Joseph W. Bouck	Weigher	New York	New York	8	9	1500 00
James Campbell	do	do	Scotland	12	....	1500 00
William E. Cruger	do	do	New York	12	....	1500 00
Robert Dumont	do	do	do	12	....	1500 00
Thomas D. English	do	do	Pennsylvania	3	8	996 92
Nathan B. Graham	do	do	Vermont	12	....	1500 00
Parke Godwin	do	do	New Jersey	7	20	1500 00
Anson Herrick	do	do	Maine	12	....	1500 00
James Kelly	do	do	New York	12	....	1500 00
Lewis Loutrel	do	do	West Indies	12	....	1500 00
John J. Mumford	do	do	New York	12	....	1500 00
John Orser	do	do	do	12	....	1500 00

John W. Richardson	do	do	do	12	....	1500 00
An rew J. Smith	do	do	Kentucky	3	22	1099 76
John M. [illegible]	do	do	New York	7	17	1500 00
Calvin C. Waller	do	do	Vermont	12	....	1500 00
Ward B. Burnett	do	do	England	3	7	991 91
William Holdredge	do	do	Vermont	1	....	283 80
Thomas Herring	od	do	New York	1	....	283 80
Guagers.						
Henry C. Atwood	Guager	New York	Connecticut	5	....	1301 83
Thomas W. Donovan	do	do	Maryland	12	....	1500 00
Abraham T. Hillyer	do	do	New York	3	22	884 52
[illegible]as Morris	do	do	Pennsylvania	12	....	1500 00
[illegible]ry M. [illegible]s	do	do	Vermont	12	....	1500 00
Charles Radcliff	do	do	New York	12	....	1500 00
Joseph Rose, jr	do	do	do	7	17	1500 00
Ferd mnd L. Wilsey	do	do	do	12	....	1500 00
Measurers.						
John Alwaise	Measurer	New [illegible]k	New York	1	....	258 38
Barnabus Bates	d	do	England	12	....	1500 00
George E. Baldwin	do	do	New York	12	....	1260 28
Peter Crawford	do	do	do	8	....	928 54
Joseph Cunningham	do	do	New J[illegible]ey	12	....	1341 43
[illegible]am M. Eddy	do	do	New York	3	13	643 41
Joseph O. Hasbrouck	do	do	do	1	....	258 38
Stephen B. Hoffman	do	do	do	3	7	614 80
John F. Ropes	do	do	Massachusetts	12	....	1359 14
John J. B. Rowan	do	do	New York	1	....	258 38
Isaiah Rynders	do	do	do	3	10	622 91

CUSTOMS—*New York—Continued.*

Names and offices.		Where employed.	Where born.	Time employed during the year ending Sept. 30, '45.		Compensat'n for the time employed.
				Months	Days	
New York city—Continued.						
George Sharp	Measurer	New York	New York	12	....	$1428 55
Isaac B. Smith	do	do	do	7	17	920 89
Arthur H. Snowden	do	do	New Jersey	12	....	1351 33
Conrad Swackhamer	do	do	do	12	....	1489 62
George C. Thomas	do	do	do	12	....	1338 18
Markers.						
James B. Glover	Marker	New York	New York	12	....	1500 00
John D. Kellogg	do	do	Connecticut	1	4	528 60
David Martin	do	do	New Jersey	12	....	1500 00
George Van Ness	do	do	Vermont	12	....	1500 00
Appraisers' Stores.						
Vanbrugh Livingston	Appraiser	New York	New York	12	....	2000 00
George W. Pomeroy	do	do	Massachusetts	4	12	736 27
Samuel J. Willis	do	do	New York	4	12	736 27
John M. Jacquelin	Assistant do	do	France	4	12	552 20
John S. McKibbin	do	do	Ireland	12	....	1500 00
George F. Thompson	do	do	New Jersey	4	12	552 20
James Zeiss	do	do	New York	4	12	552 20
Robert Sarjeant	Clerk to Appraisers	do	do	12	....	1200 00
John A. Baush	do do	do	Pennsylvania	12	....	1000 00

Michael Burnham	do	d.	do	New York	1	13	116 84
Warren Carter	do	do	do	Virginia	12	....	1000 00
Elias Chatterton	do	do	do	New York	12	....	1000 00
George W. Coe	do	do	do	do	8	....	663 89
Henry B. Gay	do	do	do	Massachusetts	12	....	1000 00
Henry M. Graham	do	do	do	New York	12	....	1000 00
John R. S. Huggett	do	do	do	do	12	....	1000 00
William T. Prall	do	do	do	do	12	....	1000 00
Frederick A. Sterling	do	do	do	Connecticut	12	....	1000 00
Richard H. Teller	do	do	do	New York	9	....	750 00
William W. Thomas	do	do	do	New Jersey	12	....	336 11
John Townsend, jr	do	do	do	New York	3	....	250 00
Francis Vosburgh	do	do	do	do	12	....	1000 00
Edward Vincent	do	do	do	Virginia	3	....	250 00
William H. Walton	do	do	do	New Jersey	12	....	1000 00
William F. White	do	do	do	England	12	....	1000 00
George W. Bleecker	do	do	do	New York	11	11	945 65
Elam Bliss	do	do	do	Massachusetts	3	....	225 00
Jacob Foster	do	do	do	New York	12	....	900 00
Peter Duffy	do	do	do	Ireland	3	....	175 00
James W. McCulloh, jr	do	do	do	Maryland	12	....	725 00
Storekeepers' Clerks in Appraisers' Stores.							
Charles J. Chipp	Clerk to Storekeeper		do	New York	12	....	1000 00
Munson Gray	do	do	do	do	12	....	1000 00
Philip Livingston	do	do	do	do	10	18	877 96
Isaac Phillips	do	do	do	do	12	....	1000 00
David Strong	do	do	do	do	12	....	1000 00
General Storekeepers and Clerks.							
Sidney Wetmore	General Storekeeper		New York	Connecticut	12	....	1500 00

CUSTOMS—*New York—Continued—New Jersey.*

Names and offices.		Where employed.	Where born.	Time employed during the year ending Sept. 30, '45		Compensat'n for the time employed.
				Months	Days	
New York city—Continued.						
Edward Bleecker	Clerk to Storekeeper	New York	New York	12	....	$1000 00
Fitz Henry Fay	do do	do	do	12	....	1000 00
John C. Given	do do	do	do	12	....	1000 00
Nicholas C. Hunter	do do	do	Massachusetts	12	....	1000 00
Daniel Munroe	do do	do	Scotland	12	....	1000 00
George M. Wetmore	do do	do	Connecticut	12	....	1000 00
Titus Hutchinson, jr	Porter	do	Vermont	12	....	800 00
Keepers of Public Stores and Clerks.						
Henry Arcularius	Storekeeper	do	New York	11	....	915 76
Francis B. Fitch	do	d.	Connecticut	10	10	861 41
John P. Mumford	do	d.	New York	10	12	866 85
William Brown	Clerk to Storekeeper	do	Scotland	5	....	384 00
William W. Hooper	do do	do	New York	10	15	700 00
Paul B. Lloyd	do do	do	do	10	15	700 00
Addison P. Lyon	do do	do	do	10	....	667 39
Edward Patterson	do do	do	do	4	23	316 48
John H. Tyler	do do	do	Virginia	11	....	732 61
Charles Wood	do do	do	New York	6	21	446 67
Deputy Collectors, &c.—Albany, Troy, &c.						
Albert Gallup	Deputy Collector and Inspector	Albany	do	12	....	1095 00

William Seymour	do	do	do	12	....	1095 00
Darius Allen	do	Troy	Connecticut	8	....	804 00
Samuel Crawford	Measurer	Saugerties	New York	12	....	89 99
Martin Russell	Surveyor	Troy	do	8	21	181 25
Hiram Perry	do	Albany	do	12	....	150 00

NEW JERSEY.

Perth Amboy.

James A. Nichols	Collector	Perth Amboy	New York			305 38
W. T. Rogers	Deputy Collector	do	do			600 00
Andrew [illegible]w	Surveyor	New Brunswick	New Jersey			150 00
James L. Compton	Inspector	Perth Amboy	do			600 00
Edwin R. Hanks	do	South Amboy	New York			600 00
Theophilus M. Holcomb		New Brunswick	New Jersey			600 00
John A. Perrin		Princeton	do			600 00
James Green		Long Branch	do	$3 per	diem	
Samuel C. Dunham		Tom's River		when	emp.	105 00

Burlington.

Gershom Mott	Collector	Lamberton	New Jersey	12	....	186 20
John R. Slack	Deputy Collector	Mount Holly	do	12	....	25 75

Little Egg Harbor.

Samuel S. Douns	Collector	No return				
William S. Lippincott	Deputy Collector	do				
Samuel M. Oliphant	do Inspector	do				

CUSTOMS—*New Jersey—Continued—Pennsylvania.*

Names and offices.		Where employed.	Where born.	Time employed during the year ending Sept. 30, '45.		Compensat'n for the time employed.
				Months	Days	
Isaac Peckworth	Deputy Inspector	No m				
Nathan Crane	do....do	do				
James M. Douns	do....do	do				
Archelaus R. Pharo	do....do	do				
Elkanah W. Palmor	do....do	do				
Recompence Darby	do....do	do				
Stephen Willets, jr	do....do	do				
Nathaniel Cowperthwaite	Weigher	do				
Great Egg Harbor.						
Robt. B. Risley	Collector					
Samuel R. Risley	Inspector	Great Egg Harbor	New Jersey	2	15	$225 00
Bridgetown.						
Lorenzo F. Lee	Collector	Bridgetown	New Jersey	12		250 00
E. Stephens	Deputy Collector	Cape May	do	12		
Israel Stratton	Inspector	Port Elizabeth	Pennsylvania			
John S. Ware	do	Bridgetown	New Jersey			
Camden.						
Charles S. Garrett	Surveyor	Camden	New Jersey	12		250 00
Newark.						
Archer Gifford	Collector	Newark	New Jersey	12		250 00

Francis W. Brinley	Deputy Collector and Inspector	Do and the District	Rhode Island		101	202 00
Charles L. Gifford	Temp. Insp. and Measurer	Do do do	New Jersey		75	150 00
Thomas J. Foote	Temporary Inspector	Jersey City	do		92	184 00
John J. Plume	do do	Newark	do			
PENNSYLVANIA.						
Philadelphia.						
Henry Horn	Collector	Collector's Office	Pennsylvania	4	16	*2291 21
Charles Ehel	Deputy Collector	do	do	12		1500 00
Richard L. Howell	do	do	New Jersey	12		1500 00
Elias F. Vallette	Clerk	do	Maryland	12		1020 00
Abraham Martin	do	do	Pennsylvania	12		1000 00
Elias Ashmead	do	do	do	12		720 00
John McAdam	do	do	do	12		720 00
Robert Steele	do	do	do	12		720 00
John C. Pechin	do	do	do	12		660 00
John S. Cummings	do	do	Delaware	12		840 00
Leonard K. Bell	do	do	Pennsylvania	12		900 00
Thomas Latimer	do	do	do	12		660 00
Samuel Eckel	do	do	do	12		650 00
Augustus C. Salaignac	do	do	Port au Prince	3	21	186 26
Sheldon U. Hopkins	do	do	Pennsylvania	1	25	92 93
Joseph B. Howell	do	do	New Jersey	12		650 00
John D. Miles	do	do	Pennsylvania	5	9	356 04
Reuben Hanse	do	do	do	1	19	83 15

* Cannot exceed $6,000, act March 3, 1841.

CUSTOMS—*Pennsylvania—Continued.*

Names and offices.		Where employed.	Where born.	Time employed during the year ending Sept. 30, '45.		Compensat'n for the time employed.
				Months	Days	
Charles P. Hayes	Clerk	Collector's Office	Delaware	12	....	$660 00
John A. Dungan	do.	do.	Pennsylvania	1	12	78 91
George Lowry	Messenger	do	do.	12	....	511 00
John L. Friedlein	do.	do	do.	12	....	511 00
Thomas McGovern	Laborer	do	Ireland	10	....	250 00
Henry W[illegible]h.	Naval Officer	Naval office	Pennsylvania	4	16	*1909 34
John D. George	Deputy Naval [illegible]r	do.	do.	12	....	1500 00
Robert Heysham	Clerk	do	New Jersey	12	....	1000 00
Charles Ferguson	do.	do.	Missouri	12	....	720 00
Henry Hay	do.	do.	New Jersey	12	....	720 00
John Davis	Surveyor	Surveyor's Office	Pennsylvania	6	10	†2342 63
John W. Forney	Deputy Surveyor	do	do	6	9	800 00
David Marple	Clerk	do	do	6	10	459 83
Jacob R. Hibbs	Messenger	do	do	2	18	118 50
Charles F. Breuil	Appraiser	Appraiser's Office	do	12	....	1500 00
Benjamin E. [illegible]er	do.	do.	do.	4	13	556 32
[illegible]as Stewart	Assistant Appraiser	d.	Ireland	4	13	445 07
William [illegible]le	do.	do	Pennsylvania	4	....	398 91
Peter A. Grotjan	Clerk	do	Germany	3	....	200 00
Henry J. Horn	do	do	Pennsylvania	2	....	132 61
George Kern	Messenger	do	do	4	2	186 00
Hugh McClellan	Laborer	do	do	4	....	183 00
Peter Snyder	do.	do	do	4	....	183 00
Benjamin Mifflin	Weigher	Custom H'se & Whv's	do	4	....	498 62
Charles H. Fisher	Deputy Weigher	do	do	12	....	1200 00
William Bonsall	do.	Delaware Wharves	do	3	....	300 00

Benjamin F. Crispin	do	do	do	12	....	1000 00
George [illegible]r, jr	do	do	do	3	20	307 70
Phillip Hoffman	Foreman	do	Bavaria	12	....	540 00
William Buck	Lab rero	do	Pennsylvania	12	....	360 00
Benjamin F. Christy	do	do	do	4	....	120 00
Peter Dorsey	do	do	Ireland	3	26	117 00
John Lorrenge	do	do	Pennsylvania	3	25	115 00
George Staub	do	do	Strasburg, F.	3	12	107 00
John D. Wood	do	d.	Ireland	3	....	90 00
Alexander Diamond	Gauger	do	do	12	....	1070 71
[illegible]ington Hei[illegible]g	do	do	Pennsylvania	12	....	1070 71
Richard Bacon	Measurer of Salt, &c.	do	New Jersey	5	7	604 16
George Hergesheimer	do	do	Pennsylvania	2	12	305 70
Robert [illegible]h	do	do	Ireland	2	12	305 70
George Snyder	do	do	Pennsylvania	2	12	305 70
[illegible]as J. Donelson	Marker	do	Tennessee	4	....	498 62
Edmund C. Watmough	do	do	Pennsylvania	4	....	498 62
George Merrick	Laborer	do	do	3	17	138 00
David B. McGinley	Public Storekeeper	Public Stores	do	12	....	1095 00
Louis Thirion	Assistant Store Keeper	do	Louisiana	2	25	198 59
[illegible]lip Tear	Watchman	do	Pennsylvania	12	....	360 00
James R. [illegible]er	Inspector	Delaware Wharves	do	12	....	1095 00
Michael Barr	do	do	Ireland	8	3	558 00
George Clymer	do	do	Pennsylvania	12	....	1095 00
Enoch Carter	do	do	New York	4	....	366 00
William H. Coleman	do	do	Maryland	3	14	318 00
Miles N. Carpenter	do	do	Pennsylvania	2	14	225 00

*Cannot exceed $5,000, act March 3, 1841. †Cannot exceed $4,500, act March 3, 1841.

NOTE.—In the salaries of the clerks the amount of surplus distributed to them under the acts of Congress is not given, but forms a separate emolument to them.

CUSTOMS—*Pennsylvania*—*Continued.*

Names and offices.		Where employed.	Where born.	Time employed during the year ending Sept. 30, '45.		Compensat'n for the time employed.
				Months	Days	
Thomas D. Dougherty	Inspector	Delaware Wharves	Pennsylvania	12	....	$1095 00
Joseph Donaldson	do.	do.	do.	3	26	354 00
John Dallam	do.	do.	do.	3	4	288 00
Samuel Edwards	do.	Marcus Hook	do.	12	....	1095 00
Robert Ford	do.	Delaware Wharves	do.	12	....	1095 00
Henry J. F ugeray	do.	do.	do.	3	....	276 00
George Gideon	do.	do.	do.	3	11	309 00
James Hoy	do.	do.	Ireland	12	....	1095 00
Sandy Harris	do.	do.	North Carolina	12	....	1095 00
Francis S. Hubley	do.	do.	Pennsylvania	12	....	1095 00
John Heiss	do.	Bristol	do.	7	13	454 00
James H. Hutchison	do.	Delaware Wharves	do.	4	....	366 00
John Hill	do.	do.	do.	3	27	357 00
Alexander Henry	do.	do.	do.	3	17	327 00
Daniel M. Keim	do.	do.	do.	12	....	1095 00
Carey F. Kneass	do.	do.	do.	4	....	366 00
John J. Logue	do.	do.	do.	12	....	1095 00
Edward T. Lescure	do.	do.	do.	8	....	726 00
John Lane	do.	Schuylkill Wharves	Ireland	3	....	276 00
Barnard Maguire	do.	Delaware Wharves	do.	12	....	1095 00
Robinson R. Moore	do.	do.	Delaware	12	....	1095 00
Thomas Morris	do.	Richmond	Pennsylvania	6	5	564 00
Daniel K. Miller	do.	Delaware Wharves	do.	7	....	639 00
James McCully	do.	do.	do.	12	....	1095 00
Charles McKaraher	do.	do.	do.	4	....	366 00
John Napier	do.	do.	do.	2	22	249 00

Daniel Oldenbergh	do	do	do	3	....	276	00
J hnoPascal	do	do	France	4	....	366	00
Lvi Reynolds, jr	do	Chester	Maryland	8	13	765	00
Francis S. Shulze	do	Delaware Wharves	Pennsylvania	12	....	10	00
Samuel T. Shunk	do	do	do	6	27	630	00
Richard Simpson	do	Schuylkill Wharves	do	4	....	366	00
James R. Scott	do	Delaware Wharves	do	4	....	366	00
Ottinger G. Streper	do	do	do	4	....	366	00
Jeremiah [illegible]	do	do	Maryland	3	27	357	00
Joseph [illegible]r, jr	do	Lazaretto	Pennsylvania	8	....	726	00
Thomas McGittigan	Principal Night Inspector	Delaware Wharves	do	3	12	224	18
John H. Steck	do	do	do	6	24	453	34
W. W. Adl	Night Inspector	do	do	12	....	547	50
Ge Alexander	do	do	Portugal	12	....	547	50
Jab Albright	do	do	Pennsylvania	12	....	547	50
Rob rt F. Bower	do	do	do	12	....	547	50
John Boyle	do	do	Delaware	3	....	138	00
George T. Coffee	do	do	Pennsylvania	2	14	112	50
Ge Carpenter	do	Custom House Stores	do	3	....	138	00
Thomas Downing	do	Custom House	Ireland	3	....	138	00
Ines M. Davis	do	Schuylkill Wharves	Pennsy ia	2	14	112	50
Patrick Garrigan	do	do	Ireland	12	....	547	50
William Headman	do	Delaware Wharves	Pennsylvania	2	21	123	00
John Kiesley	do	do	do	3	....	138	00
John Kames	do	do	do	2	14	112	50
Daniel A. Kelly	do	do	do	2	7	102	00
James Lamb	do	do	Ireland	12	....	547	50
John Logan	do	do	Pennsylvania	2	7	102	00
James McCaraher	do	do	do	12	....	547	50
Luke McGlue	do	do	do	3	....	138	00
Henry McCormick	do	do	do	2	7	102	00
Samuel J. Pearson	do	do	do	12	....	547	50

CUSTOMS—*Pennsylvania—Continued.*

Names and offices.		Where employed.	Where born.	Time employed during the year ending Sept. 30, '45.		Compensat'n for the time employed.
				Months	Days	
John Potts	Night Inspector	Delaware Wharves	Pennsylvania	2	14	$112 50
Christian Read	do	do	do	12	....	547 50
John Scott	do	do	do	2	7	102 00
Anthony Tully	do	do	do	12	....	547 50
Henry Winterberg	do	do	Germany	12	....	547 50
George Warner	do	Custom House	Pennsylvania	2	7	102 00
Henry Ovenshine	Agent	Del. & Schuyl. Whv's	do	8	....	484 00
William R. Power	do	do	do	5	10	326 00
Patrick Sharp	do	do	Ireland	3	....	184 00
Benjamin Barger	do	do	Pennsylvania	2	....	91 50
Curtis Grubb	do	do	do	10	15	478 50
Hugh Harbeson	do	do	Ireland	1	20	75 00
John Steel	Sampler	Delaware Wharves	do	3	....	138 00
Presque Isle.						
Murray Whallon	Collector	Presque Isle	New York	2	22	89 59
Abner P. Durlin	Deputy Collector and Inspector	do	do	2	9	140 00
Pittsburgh.						
John B. Guthrie	Surveyor and Inspector	Pittsburgh	Pennsylvania	2	20	76 00

DELAWARE.

Henry Hicks	Coll r	Wilmington	Maryland	3	....	259 66
Jacob B. Vandever	Inspector	do	Delaware	11	24	1077 00
Wm. Booth	do	New Castle	do	12	....	1095 00
Daniel Cowgill	do	Port Penn	do	9	10	849 00
Edward Worrell	do	do	do	2	20	246 00
John Wood	do	Delaware City	do	9	10	388 70
Isaac Hunter	do	do	do	2	20	111 30
Henry F. Hall	do	Lewes	d.	2	17	106 00
Alfred P. Robinson	do	do	do	9	6	384 40
Jacob B. Vandever	Measurer	Wilmington	do	....	5	67 44
Jacob B. Vandever	Weigher	do	do	....	1	17 19

MARYLAND.

Baltimore.

Wm H. Marriott	[illegible]r	Baltimore	Maryland	10	7	*1540 86
John C. Van Wyck	Deputy [illegible]r	do	do	12	....	1500 00
James Hamilton	Clerk	do	Ireland	12	....	1200 00
William H. Van Wyck	do	do	Maryland	4	....	466 00
Henry R. Pratt	do	do	do	3	13	188 00
James Polk	Naval Officer	do	do	5	....	*1366 08
Benj min A. Vickers	Clerk	do	do	5	....	262 00
William Dickinson	Appraiser	do	do	12	....	1500 00

*Exclusive of what may be received under 7th section act July 21, 1840.

CUSTOMS—*Maryland*—*Continued.*

Names and offices.		Where employed.	Where born.	Time employed during the year ending Sept. 30, '45.		Compensat'n for the time employed.
				Months	Days	
Michael McBlair	App[illegible]r	Baltimore	Ireland	5	21	713 02
Alexander Young	Clerk	do	Mar[illegible]nd	12	....	1000 00
Philip R. J. Friese	Assistant [illegible]	do	Hanover, King. of	3	12	182 00
Daniel Shannon	Porter	do	Ireland	12	....	350 00
William H. [illegible]le, jr.	Surveyor	do	Maryland	6	....	**986 60
James P. Heath	Weigher	do	do	12	....	1249 18
Emanuel Stansbury	Gauger	do	do	7	1	537 05
Philip I[illegible]n	Measurer	do	England	11	27	1367 40
John Nants	Inspector	do	Maryland	12	....	1095 00
Richard Mackubin	do	do	do	12	....	1095 00
James Tilghman	do	do	do	12	....	1095 00
Robert [illegible]n	do	do	Ireland	12	....	1095 00
George W. Burke	do	do	Maryland	12	....	1095 00
Robert Aitken	do	do	do	12	....	1095 00
Marcus R. Hook	do	do	do	12	....	1095 00
[illegible]as Kendall	do	do	do	12	....	1095 00
Lloyd [illegible]as	do	do	do	12	....	1095 00
Floyd Waggaman	do	do	do	12	....	1095 00
John Patrick	do	do	do	12	....	1095 00
James C. Barry	do	do	Ireland	12	....	1095 00
Robert M. Welch	do	do	Maryland	4	26	*447 00
Samuel Harker	do	do	Delaware	4	26	*447 00
John R. Diggs	do	do	Maryland	4	26	*447 00
Hamlet Duval	do	do	do	4	26	*447 00
Michael McDonald	do	do	do	4	26	*447 00
Edward A. Slicer	do	do	do	4	26	*447 00

Beall Randall	do		do	do	4	17	*141 00
John E. Tble	do		do	do		19	*57 00
Hamilton Ring	do		do	do	4	....	*366 00
Barzillai Marriott	do		do	do		19	*57 00
William Krebs	Inspector and Storekeeper		do	do	4	27	*447 00
John Mortimer	Storekeeper		do	Ireland	12	....	600 00
Stephen C. Roozel	Dep. Insp. of the Revenue, or Marker		do	Dist. of Columbia	4	27	455 32
William V. J[illegible]s	Watchman or Night Inspector		do	Maryland	12	....	†456 25
Emanuel Weinman	do	do	do	Germany	9	....	†341 25
James D. Smith	do	do	do	Maryland	12	....	†456 25
Ormsby Webster	do	do	do	do	9	....	†341 25
William Durham	do	do	do	do	8	....	†302 50
John Wysham	do	do	do	do	8	....	†302 50
Daniel Cox	do	do	do	Delaware	5	....	†191 25
James C. Murray	do	do	do	Maryland	5	....	†191 25
Robert Moore	do	do	do	Ireland	4	29	†188 75
Patrick R. Fryer	do	do	do	do	4	29	†188 75
Thomas R. Scott	do	do	do	Pennsylvania	4	29	†188 75
William H. Gordon	do	do	do	Maryland	4	29	†188 75
James Myers	do	do	do	do	4	29	†188 75
John Smith	do	do	do	do	4	29	†188 75
Robert McElwee	do	do	do	do	4	29	†188 75
Stephen Wellslager	do	do	do	do	4	29	†188 75
Joseph Brockholtz	do	do	do	do	4	29	†188 75
David McDonald	do	do	do	Ireland	4	29	†188 75
Andrew Hannegan	do	do	do	Maryland	4	29	†188 75
Joseph J. Laty	do	do	do	France	4	18	†175 00
William Roche	do	do	do	Ireland	4	18	†175 00

**Exclusive of what may be received under 7th section act July 21, 1840.
*At $3 per diem. †At $1 25 per diem.

CUSTOMS—*Maryland—Continued—District of Columbia.*

Names and offices.		Where employed.	Where born.	Time employed during the year ending Sept. 30, '45. Months	Days	Compensat'n for the time employed.
Alexander McKinley	Watchman or Night Inspector	Baltimore	Ireland	4	....	†152 50
Simon Kemp	do	do	do	1	28	†72 50
William Shaw	Storekeeper	Lazaretto, near Balto.	Maryland	12	....	150 00
Annapolis.						
Richard Sands	Collector	Annapolis	Maryland	12	....	317 14
John Randall	Inspector	do	do	2	20	243 00
James H. Inglehart	do		do	9	11	852 00
George Calvert	do	Drum Point	do	8	4	125 29
Thomas W. Hoye	Surveyor	Nottingham	do	12	....	150 00
James W. Roach	do	St. Mary's	do	12	....	250 00
A. Thompson	Surveyor and Inspector	Lewellensburg	do	12	....	200 00
Oxford.						
Nicholas Willis	Collector	Oxford	Maryland	12	....	250 00
Vienna.						
B. H. Crockett	Collector	Vienna	Delaware	12	....	$200 & fees.
Charles Parker	Surveyor	Snow Hill	Maryland	3	15	250 00
Town Creek.						
James R. Thompson	Surveyor	No return				

DISTRICT OF COLUMBIA.

Georgetown.						
Robert White	Collector and Inspector	Georgetown	Virginia	12	....	1326 96
David Hedrick	Deputy do do	do	Maryland	12	....	800 00
David Hedrick	Weigher	do	do	12	....	196 41
David Hedrick	Measurer	do	do	12	....	56 32
James Towles	Deputy Collector and Inspector	Washington	Virginia	12	....	821 25
Edward Mattingly	do do do	do	Maryland	12	....	200 00
John Waters	Gauger	Georgetown	do	......	5	23 40
Alexandria.						
Edward Green, Collector, Agent of Marine Hospital, and Superintendent of Light Houses		Alexandria	England	5	12	460 66
Benjamin T. Fendall	Surveyor and Inspector	do	Maryland	12	....	509 27
Edward S. Hough	Deputy Collector and Inspector	do	Dist. of Columbia	4	29	456 00
Matthias Snyder, jr.	Inspector	do	do	12	....	1095 00
Richardson S. Douglas	do	do	do	4	29	456 00
George McClush	Gauger	do	do	12	....	4 68
Francis C. Triplett	Weigher	do	Virginia	8	28	9 51
Thomas Swann	Measurer	do	Maryland	4	29	725 80

†At $1 25 per diem.

CUSTOMS—*Virginia.*

Names and offices.	Where employed.	Where born.	Time employed during the year ending Sept. 30, '45.		Compensat'n for the time employed.
			Months	Days	
VIRGINIA.					
Tappahannock.					
John A. Parker.....Collector	Tappahannock	Virginia	12	....	$386 01
Robert S. Hipkins.....Deputy...do	do	do	12	....	300 00
[illegible]es W. Hipkins.....Inspector	do	do	12	....	300 00
John J. Underwood.....do	do	do	12	....	300 00
[illegible]er K. [illegible]ps.....Surveyor	Fredericksburg	do	12	....	311 92
[illegible]es W. Lawson.....do	Carter's [illegible]k	do	1	18	33 75
William [illegible]y.....do	Port Royal	do	12	....	276 50
A[illegible]ed P[illegible]er.....do	Urbanna	do	12	....	152 00
Robert B. [illegible]hant.....do	Dumfries	do	2	24	34 23
Richmond.					
Thomas Nelson.....Collector	Richmond	Virginia	12	....	fees&com's
William Nelson, Per[illegible]nt Inspector, Weigher and Mea[illegible]r, Deputy Collector, and Clerk	do	do	12	....	1095 00
William H. Lorton, Permanent Inspector, W[illegible]igher and [illegible]r, Deputy [illegible]r, and Clerk	do	do	12	....	1095 00
James A. [illegible]d, Permanent Inspector, Weigher, and Measurer	Bermuda Hundred	do	12	....	1095 00
John Lynch, Permanent Inspector, Weigher, and Meas.	Rockets	do	2	30	273 00

Petersburg.						
J. Travis Rosser	Collector	Petersburg	North Carolina	3	22	197 67
Charles Campbell	Clerk and Deputy Collector	do	Virginia	3	22	230 00
Joel Hammon	Permanent Inspector	do	do	12	....	1095 00
William P. Porter	Surveyor	City Point	do	12	....	400 00
William G. Birchett	Permanent Inspector	do	do	3	18	312 00
John H. Batte	Weigher, Guager, and Measurer	do	do	12	....	230 47
Dr. Nathaniel Harrison	Hospital Physician	do	do	12	....	631 41
Yeocomico.						
Gordon Forbes	Surveyor	No return				
Cherry Stone.						
Peter S. Bowdoin	Collector	Cherrystone	Virginia	12	....	200 00
Samuel C. White	Surveyor	Accomac Court House	do	4	6	87 22
William H. Williams	Temporary Inspector	Cherrystone	do	....	....	
East River.						
William Williams	Surveyor	East River	Virginia	12	....	200 00
Yorktown.						
William Nelson	Collector	Yorktown	Virginia	12	....	200 00
G. L. C. Salter	Deputy do	do	do	12	....	
Wheeling.						
Michael Edwards, jr	Surveyor	Wheeling	Pennsylvania	2	9	66 79

CUSTOMS—*Virginia—Continued—North Carolina.*

Names and offices.	Where employed.	Where born.	Time employed during the year ending Sept. 30, '45. Months	Days	Compensat'n for the time employed.
Norfolk and Portsmouth.					
Conrad Whittle........Coll[illegible]ctor	Norfolk	Virginia	12	....	$1497 19
Conrad W[illegible]e........Superintendent of Lights	Virginia	do	12	....	583 02
[illegible]ad Whittle........Agent Marine Hospital	Washington Point	do	12	....	22 27
Thomas Gatewood........Naval [illegible]fficer	Norfolk	do	12	....	789 14
George W. Camp........Naval Officer's Clerk	do	do	12	....	612 00
Dennis Dawley........Surveyor	do	do	12	....	510 82
Robert Butler........do	Smithfield	do	12	....	250 00
Robert H. W[illegible]b........do	Suffolk	do	12	....	250 00
Richard G. Banks........do	Hampton	do	12	....	250 00
William [illegible]all........Inspector	Norfolk	do	12	....	1095 00
S. L. [illegible]ot........do	do	do	12	....	1095 00
Horatio [illegible]e........do	do	do	11	26	1083 00
Richard Walke, Deputy Collector, Inspector, and Keeper of Public Stores	do	do	12	....	1095 00
Edward S. Gayle........Inspector	do	do	11	16	1053 00
J[illegible]shua James........Temporary....do	Princess Anne	do	....	23	69 00
Jacob Vickery........Weigher	Norfolk	Massachusetts	12	....	171 68
Jacob Vickery........Gauger	do	do	12	....	163 49
Cary Fentress........Measurer	do	Virginia	....	....	377 13
O. E. Edwards........Temporary....do	do	do	....	....	223 17

NORTH CAROLINA.

Camden.					
W. D. Pritchard.......Collector	Elizabeth City	....	3	26	fees&com's
Jas. Barker.......Inspector	do	Pennsylvania	.....	28	148 23
E. L. Stephens.......do	do	Maine	.....	28	148 23
G. A. Williams.......do	do	do	.....	28	148 23
Edenton.					
Rizop Rawls.......Collector	Edenton	Virginia	3	....	73 10
Duncan McDonald.......Inspector	do	North Carolina	.....	11	47 34
Plymouth.					
Joseph Ramsey, Collector, Agent for Marine Hospital, and Superintendent of Lights	Plymouth	North Carolina	12	....	509 35
George Nichols, Inspector, Gauger, Weigher, and Meas	do	do	1	....	273 45
Edmund Windley, Temporary Inspector, Gauger, Weigher, and Measurer	do	do	.....	4½	32 60
Marcus C. Ryon.......Surveyor	Windsor	do	12	....	150 00
Washington.					
Jas. K. Hatton.......Collector	Washington	North Carolina	4	3	251 80
William L. Lavender.......Deputy....do	do	do	12	....	250 00
M. W. Ellison.......Measurer, &c	do	do	12	....	215 01
Benj. M. Selby.......do	do	do	.....	1	14 04
J. C. Jennett.......Inspector, &c	do	do	12	....	92 40
Newbern.					
Thomas S. Singleton.......Collector	Newbern	North Carolina	12	....	488 45

CUSTOMS—*North Carolina—Continued—South Carolina.*

Names and offices.		Where employed.	Where born.	Time employed during the year ending Sept. 30, '45.		Compensat'n for the time employed.
				Months	Days	
William G. Singleton	Deputy Collector	Newbern	North Carolina	12	....	
William G. Singleton	Inspector	do	do	12	....	$250 00
William G. Singleton	Gauger	do	do	12	....	25 92
William G. Singleton	Weigher	do	do	12	....	4 29
William G. Singleton	Measurer	do	do	12	....	181 67
Ocracoke.						
Thomas J. Pasteur	Collector	District of Ocracoke	North Carolina	5	3	425 00
John S. Hunter	Inspector	do	Virginia	6	....	240 00
Beaufort.						
James E. Gibble	Collector	Beaufort	North Carolina	12	....	339 21
James E. Gibble	Superintendent of Lights	do	do	12	....	20 37
James E. Gibble	Agent for Marine Hospital	do	do	12	....	2 82
Elijah Whitehurst	Inspector	do	do	1	10	120 00
Elijah Whitehurst	Gauger	do	do	......	....	
Elijah Whitehurst	Weigher	do	do	......	....	
Elijah Whitehurst	Measurer	do	do	......	....	38 69
Wilmington.						
Murphey V. Jones	Collector	Wilmington	North Carolina	12	....	1125 04
James T. Miller	Naval Officer	do	do	......	3	
Joseph S. Murphy	Surveyor	do	do	12	....	806 76

James Burch	Inspector of Staves	do	do	6	....	300 00
Neill McLaurin	Permanent Inspector	do	Scotland	12	....	600 00
William I. Price	Inspector and Boarding Officer	Between Wilmington and sea	North Carolina	6	....	241 00
James T. Morris	Temporary Inspector	Wilmington	do	12	....	298 22
Alfred M. Laspeyre	do do	Smithville	do	9	4	218 35
Richard B. Burnett	do do	Wilmington	do	9	4	157 99
William B. Jones	Gauger and Weigher	do	do	6	....	45 24
SOUTH CAROLINA.						
Charleston.						
Wm. J. Grayson	Collector	Charleston	South Carolina	12	....	3500 00
Thos. D. Jervey	Deputy Collector	do	do	12	....	1000 00
Wm. T. McCready	do	do	do	12	....	1300 00
Robert Howard	Naval Officer	do	do	12	....	1754 83
H. M. Howard	Assistant do	do	do	12	....	626 00
Thos. H. Jervey	Surveyor	do	do	12	....	1672 20
Robert Wilson	Boarding Officer	do	Pennsylvania	12	....	1095 00
S. J. Wagner	Storekeeper	do	South Carolina	12	....	1095 00
Theo. Gaillard	Measurer Salt and Coal	do	do	12	....	1500 00
Isaac Cardosa	Weigher	do	do	12	....	1500 00
J. T. Elsworth	Gauger	do	do	12	....	555 70
Wm. Perrineau	Debenture Export Inspector	do	do	12	....	1095 00
Wm. J. Smith	Coastwise do	do	do	12	....	1095 00
Jno. B. White	do do	do	do	12	....	1095 00
Gershon Lazarus	Steamboat do	do	North Carolina	12	....	1095 00
Sam'l Champlain	Permanent do	do	Connecticut	12	....	1095 00
Thos. Steedman	do do	do	South Carolina	12	....	1095 00

CUSTOMS—*South Carolina—Continued—Georgia.*

Names and offices.		Where employed.	Where born.	Time employed during the year ending Sept. 30, '45. Months	Days	Compensat'n for the time employed.
Peter Ehney	Permanent Inspector	Charleston	South Carolina	12	....	$1095 00
C. Pinckney	do do	do	do	12	....	1095 00
W. A. Plane	do do	do	England	12	....	1095 00
Patrick Cantwell	do do	do	Ireland	12	....	1095 00
Edw'd Harvey	do do	do	do	12	....	1095 00
H. Sparnick	do do	do	Hanover	12	....	1095 00
A. B. [illegible]	Temporary do	do	South Carolina	12	....	717 00
E. S. Courtnay	do do	do	do	12	....	789 00
J. C. Jervey	do do	do	do	12	....	795 00
G. W. Wilkie	do do	do	do	12	....	813 00
J. Marshbourn	do do	do	do	12	....	768 00
John Bay	do do	do	do	7	....	528 00
William Elfe	do do	do	do	3	....	96 00
J. Stillman	do do	do	Connecticut	12	....	879 00
William Perry	do do	do	England	12	....	804 00
J. A. Miller	do do	do	South Carolina	12	....	883 00
Myer Jacobs	Night Watch	do	do	12	....	1095 00
Edger Stoney	do	do	do	12	....	1095 00
J. P. Waites	do	do	do	12	....	1095 00
Jhn Righton	do	do	do	12	....	1095 00
Georgetown.						
T. L. Shaw	Collector and Inspector	Georgetown	do	12	....	615 14
O. M. Roberts	Deputy Collector and Inspector	do	Maryland	3	....	31 25
J. C. Porter	do do do	do	South Carolina	9	....	93 75

Beaufort.						
B. R. Bythewood	Collector	Beaufort	do	12	....	250 00
B. R. Bythewood	Deputy Collector	do	do	....	....	
GEORGIA.						
Savannah.						
Wi llm B. Bulloch	Coll tor	Savannah	Georgia	5	5	457 13
John ewis	Deputy Coll otor	do	d o	4	24	481 33
Robert Mackey	Naval Officer	do	do	12	....	1031 15
Thomas S. Wayne	Surveyor	do	do	12	....	903 23
Charles Steph ns,o	Appraiser	do	do	12	....	1500 00
William Mackey	do	do	do	12	....	1500 00
Joseph George	Inspector	do	New York	4	24	438 00
John Cass	do	do	Ireland	4	24	438 00
Lewis F. Nicoll	do	do	New Jersey	4	24	438 00
Levi J. Myers	do	do	Georgia	4	24	438 00
Joseph Felt	do	do	Massachusetts	4	24	438 00
William Starr	do	do	Pennsylvania	12	....	1095 00
Abial Winn	do	do	Georgia	8	3	738 00
Isaac De Lyon	do	do	do	12	....	1095 00
William J. Moore	do	do	do	12	....	1095 00
Thomas Bourke	do	do	do	12	....	1095 00
John Postell	Storekeeper	do	South Carolina	12	....	800 00
Frederick A. Tupper	Weigher and Gauger	do	Maine	4	5	50 67
Hardwick.						
Benjamin Stiles	Surveyor	No return				

CUSTOMS—*Georgia—Continued—Alabama—Louisiana.*

Names and offices.		Where employed.	Where born.	Time employed during the year ending Sept. 30, '45.		Compensat'n for the time employed.
				Months	Days.	
Sunbury.						
William Maxwell	Surveyor	No return				
St. Mary's.						
Archibald Clark	Collector	St. Mary's	Georgia	12	....	$688 78
Armand Lefils	Surveyor	Darien	France	5	12	250 00
G. P. Cohen	Inspector	Jefferson	South Carolina	12	....	200 00
Woodford Mabry	do	Brunswick	Georgia	12	....	250 00
ALABAMA.						
Mobile.						
Collier H. Minge	Collector	Mobile	Virginia	12	....	3000 00
Charles J. Fox	Deputy Collector	do	do	12	....	1000 00
Walter Smith	Inspector and Gen. Clerk	do	New York	12	....	1500 00
[illegible]as J. Butler	Inspector and Impost Clerk	do	South Carolina	1	19	200 52
Emanuel [illegible]ez	Inspector	do	Alabama	9	25	894 00
John R. Elliot	do	do	Virginia	6	18	567 00
Henry O. Hall	Weigher and Measurer	do	do	12	....	1500 00
B. C. Gay	do	do	do	12	....	1500 00

John N. Mott	Assistant Appraiser and Gauger	do	New York	12	....	338 77
H. V. H. Voorhees	Assistant Appraiser	do	New Jersey	12	....	280 00
MISSISSIPPI.						
Pearl River.						
Willis H. Arnold	Collector	Shieldsborough	Virginia	12	....	316 33
Natchez.						
J. D. Elliot	Collector	Natchez	Vermont	......	....	500 00
Vicksburg.						
Edmund H. Taylor	Collector	Vicksburg	Tennessee	12	....	500 00
LOUISIANA.						
New Orleans.						
Elias Barrett	Collector	New Orleans	Ireland	12	....	6400 00
Alcée La Branche	Naval Officer	do	Louisiana	2	23	421 50
David Hayden	Surveyor	do	Connecticut	12	....	4500 00
David O. Hincks	Deputy Collector	do	Maryland	12	....	1500 00
Wm W. Hincks	do	do	do	12	....	1500 00
Louis Delétra	Deputy Naval Officer	do	France	12	....	1500 00
Bernard Mé	Clerk in Naval Office	do	Louisiana	12	....	730 00
Paul Soniat	do do	do	do	2	8	138 00
James Graham	Deputy Surveyor	do	Ireland	10	19	1326 79
Ernest Morphy	Appraiser	do	South Carolina	12	....	1500 00
John Duncan	do	do	Ireland	4	....	500 00

24

CUSTOMS—*Louisiana—Continued.*

Names and offices.		Where employed.	Where born.	Time employed during the year ending Sept. 30, '45. Months	Days	Compensat'n for the time employed.
Bennett Voorhies	Clerk in Appraiser's Office	New Orleans	Louisiana	12	....	$1200 00
Samuel Boyd	Weigher	do.	Connecticut	12	....	1500 00
Wm. S. Brown	Deputy Weigher	do.	Massachusetts	12	....	1200 00
Nicolas D. Rind	Gauger	do.	Dist. of Columbia	12	....	1500 00
John E. Queré	Deputy Gauger	do.	Louisiana	11	25	1180 64
Charles W. [illegible]	Measurer	do.	Ireland	12	....	1500 00
C. S. Hayden	Deputy Measurer	do.	[illegible]	8	6	753 00
William S. McCulloh	Assistant Marker	do.	Pennsylvania	9	14	948 25
Nicholas C. Snethen	Marker	do.	Maryland	12	....	1500 00
Dewitt Clinton Vandergriff	Deputy [illegible]	do.	Ohio	12	....	1095 00
Ephraim Whitehead	Registering Clerk	do.	England	12	....	1500 00
Louis H. Desforges	Assistant Clerk	do.	Louisiana	12	....	1200 00
Ebenezer Colfax	Impost Book Keeper	do.	Connecticut	12	....	1500 00
Pierre M. Ozanne	First Impost Clerk	do.	[illegible]	12	....	1200 00
Samuel M. Read	Second Impost Clerk	do.	Pennsylvania	12	....	1200 00
John Brainard	Third Impost Clerk	do.	[illegible]	11	....	1100 00
Felix B. Bernard	Commercial Abstract Clerk	do.	Louisiana	12	....	1200 00
Francis J. Jones	Debenture Clerk	do.	Maryland	12	....	1500 00
Adelard Blondeau	General Book Keeper	do.	Louisiana	12	....	1500 00
Edmund [illegible]	Cash Clerk	do.	do.	12	....	1500 00
Henry [illegible]	Assistant Clerk	do.	Dist. of Columbia	11	....	1100 00
Theodorick B. Skinner	Corresponding Clerk	do.	Maryland	12	....	1500 00
[illegible] Rouquette	Permit Clerk	do.	Louisiana	12	....	1000 00
[illegible] Hagan, jr.	do.	do.	Ireland	12	....	1000 00
John P. White	First Assistant Clerk	do.	Louisiana	12	....	962 50
John W. Wilson	Second Assistant Clerk	do.	Dist. Columbia	3	....	225 00

William H. Wilder	Store Keeper	do	South Carolina	12	....	1500 00
Felix Ducayet	Inspector and Deputy Store Keeper	do	Louisiana	12	....	1095 00
Richard Rust	Inspector	do	Vermont	12	....	1095 00
Valery Duplessis	do	do	Louisiana	12	....	1095 00
Pierre Gin	do	d.	Switzerland	12	....	1095 00
Edward Heath	do	do	Maine	12	....	1095 00
Paul E. Crozat	do	do	Louisiana	10	26	990 00
Richard T. Avis	do	do	Nova Scotia	12	....	1095 00
Michael Egan	do	do	Ireland	12	....	1095 00
Ge W. Reeder	do	do	Maryland	12	....	1095 00
Du Verney Farrar	do	do	South Carolina	12	....	1095 00
Cornelius Hurst	do	do	North Carolina	12	....	1095 00
Ge W. Heyl	do	do	Pennsylvania	12	....	1095 00
R. S. Upshur	do	do	Virginia	12	....	1095 00
Stanislas St. Cyr	do	do	St. Domingo	12	....	1095 00
Evariste Wtz	do	do	Louisiana	12	....	1095 00
William M. Carter	do	do	Ireland	12	....	1095 00
Harris G. Pearson	do	do	Pennsylvania	12	....	1095 00
Alfred B. Shelby	do	do	Tennessee	12	....	1095 00
Samuel W. Smith	do	do	Louisiana	12	....	1095 00
Peregrine Barnes	do	do	Maryland	12	....	1095 00
Augustine H. Gilland	do	do	Pennsylvania	12	....	1095 00
Augustin Rousseau	do	do	Louisiana	12	....	1095 00
Edward A. Harrison	do	do	Virginia	12	....	1095 00
Pliny Maspero	do	do	Louisiana	12	....	1095 00
John Wilcox	do	do	New York	12	....	1095 00
John C. Taylor	do	do	South Carolina	12	....	1095 00
John Juden	do	do	Maryland	12	....	1095 00
Jules Durrive	do	do	Louisiana	12	....	1095 00
William P. Berry	do	do	Maine	12	....	1095 00
Elias J. Jenkins	do	do	South Carolina	12	....	1095 00
James E. Waldo	do	do	New Hampshire	12	....	1095 00

CUSTOMS—*Louisiana*—*Continued.*

Names and offices.		Where employed.	Where born.	Time employed during the year ending Sept. 30, '45.		Compensat'n for the time employed.
				Months	Days	
David R. Godwin	Inspector	New Orleans	New Jersey	12	....	$1095 00
Benjamin Williams	do	do	Virginia	9	8	843 00
Alphonse M. Duperu	do	do	do	7	8	666 00
Joshua S. Harris	do	do	New Hampshire	6	21	612 00
J. J. Nicholson	do	do	North Carolina	6	14	591 00
Joseph Genois, jr	do	do	Louisiana	6	15	687 00
George V. Forbes	do	do	Massachusetts	6	10	579 00
Musgrove Evans	do	do	Pennsylvania	6	14	591 00
Thomas K. Handy	do	do	Ireland	6	....	549 00
Thomas A. Williams	do	do	Virginia	3	....	276 00
John Taylor	do	do	Ireland	12	....	1095 00
A. Lartigue	Boarding Inspector	Pointe a la Hache	Louisiana	7	6	660 00
George U. Bowditch	do ... do	South West Pass	Massachusetts	12	....	1095 00
W. W. Wiggins	do ... do	Balize	Pennsylvania	12	....	1095 00
Charles L. [illegible]	River Inspector	On the river between New Orleans and the Passes of the Mississippi riv.	Louisiana	12	....	1095 00
John Jones	do ... do		Massachusetts	11	25	1077 00
L. E. Collins	do ... do		Ireland	12	....	1095 00
Milton M. Thomas	do ... do		Louisiana	12	....	1095 00
Edward Segot	do ... do		France	12	....	1095 00
Oscar A. Kirkland	do ... do		Louisiana	12	....	1095 00
Aaron Fitzgerald	do ... do		New York	12	....	1095 00
Nicholas Sinnott	do ... do		Louisiana	12	....	1095 00
Charles G. Perrault	do ... do		do	11	....	1002 00
Peter W. Kennedy	do ... do		Maryland	2	24	255 00
Thomas J. Beck	do ... do		Virginia	4	19	423 00
James Pennoyer	Night Inspr	New Orleans	New York	12	....	1095 00

Henry Crane	do....do.	do	Ireland	12	....	1095 00
John Gillaspie	do....do.	do	do	12	....	1095 00
John Dolan	do....do.	do	do	12	....	1095 00
Francis Barnes	do....do.	do	do	12	....	1095 00
Cady	do....do.	do	Louisiana	12	....	1095 00
Andrew J. Fallen	do....do.	do	Ireland	12	....	1095 00
Robert F. Nugent	do....do.	do	do	12	....	1095 00
Pierre Suzeneau	do....do.	do	Louisiana	12	....	1095 00
William Silk	do....do.	do	Ireland	11	25	1077 00
John Dallman	do....do.	do	Pennsylvania	11	4	1014 00
Walter Hicky	do....do.	do	Ireland	4	15	414 00
J. P. Ross	do....do.	do	New York	6	13	588 00
Patrick leg	do....do.	do	Ireland	6	8	573 00
J. A. Noble	do....do.	do	Massachusetts	2	....	183 00
James Holbert	Custom House Watchman	do	Ireland	....	18	36 00
Jam so Anderson	do........do.	do	Norway	2	14	150 00
Charles B. Lenes	Surveyor	Bayou St. John	Louisiana	12	....	250 00
S. M. Page	do	Port Pontchartrain	New York	12	....	250 00
Matthew Diks	do	Madisonville	Not ascertained	12	....	250 00
Daniel lark	do	La Fayette	Massachusetts	12	....	250 00
J hno Bryce	Deputy Collector	Shreveport	Virginia	8	15	1069 86
William P. Reyburn	do	Natchitoches	Kentucky	8	29	1117 00
Teche.						
George Royster	Collector	Franklin	Virginia	12	....	500 00
Farnifold Green	....	Mouth Sabine River	North Carolina	4	20	420 00

CUSTOMS—*Tennessee—Kentucky—Ohio—Missouri.*

Names and offices.		Where employed.	Where born.	Time employed during the year ending Sept. 30, '45.		Compensat'n for the time employed.
				Months	Days	
TENNESSEE.						
Nashville.						
Joseph Litton	Surveyor	Nashville	Ireland	12	....	$415 00
KENTUCKY.						
Louisville.						
N. P. Porter	Surveyor and Inspector	District of Mississippi	Maryland	12	....	350 00
OHIO.						
Cuyahoga.						
Smith Inglehart	Collector	Cleveland	New York	4	20	229 90
George B. Tibbitts	Deputy Collector and Inspector	do	do	4	20	282 00
John S. Perry	Inspector	do	Ohio	4	20	231 33
Sylvester Remington	do	do	New York	4	....	198 36

Conrad Reed	do.	Black River	Pennsylvania	12	....	240 00
Jonathan Johnson	do.	Ashtabula	New York	12	....	240 00
Harry Stroud	do.	Fairport	do.	1	19	32 67
Gustavus A. Cozens	do.	Conneaut	do.	12	....	240 00
Miami.						
James H. Forsyth	Collector	Miami		No return.		
J. Utley	Deputy Collector	Perrysburg	New York	12	....	200 00
D. Chase	do. do.	Manhattan	Pennsylvania	12	....	200 04
D. Steele	do. do.	Toledo	New York	12	....	200 00
H. W. Horton	Inspector	Maumee City	Tennessee	12	....	200 00
Cincinnati.						
Patrick Collins	Surveyor and Inspector	Cincinnati	Ireland	4	9	800 00
Sandusky.						
Elias H. Haines	Collector	Sandusky	New Jersey	12	....	409 04
John G. Pool	Deputy Collector	do.	Pennsylvania	12	....	400 00
Barton Wilson	Inspector	Huron	New Jersey	12	....	300 00
Stanton H. Brown	do.	Port Clinton	New York	12	....	200 00
John R. Pease	do.	Lower Sandusky	Vermont	12	....	200 00
Charles P. Judson	do.	Vermillion	Connecticut	12	....	200 00
MISSOURI.						
St. Louis.						
Isaac A. Hedges	Surveyor and Inspector	St. Louis	New York	2	20	428 21

CUSTOMS—*Michigan*—*Florida*.

Names and offices.		Where employed.	Where born.	Time employed during the year ending Sept. 30, '45.		Compensat'n for the time employed.
				Months	Days	
MICHIGAN.						
Detroit.						
Charles G. Hammond	Collector	Detroit	Connecticut	4	....	$539 46
Sereno C. Hammond	Deputy Collector	do	New York	3	....	250 00
Calvin C. Jackson	do	do	do	12	....	540 00
Charles V. Selkrig	Inspector	do	do	12	....	480 00
Ebenezer B. Wales	do	do	do	1	....	40 00
Alexander H. Stowell	do	do	Vermont	9	....	210 00
Francis Cicott	do	do	Michigan	12	....	240 00
John V. Reuhle	do	do	Germany	9	....	180 00
James Hanmer	do	do	New York	9	....	180 00
John O'Callaghan	do	do	Ireland	12	....	240 00
Anthony O'Madden	do	do	do	3	....	60 00
William B. Hunt	do	Hamt rak	Michigan	3	....	60 00
George Moran	do	Grosse Point	do	12	....	240 00
John K. Smith	Deputy Collector	Algonac	New York	12	....	240 00
Andrew J. Bradford	Inspector	Mount Clemens	New Hampshire	12	....	235 00
James D. Brown	do	Newport	Michigan	3	....	60 00
Joseph Welley	do	St. Clair	New York	9	....	180 00
Andrew Mark	do	River St. Clair	Connecticut	12	....	240 00
Elisha B. Clark	do	Port Huron	Massachusetts	12	....	450 00
Sidney S. Campbell	do	Saginaw	Unknown	9	....	150 00
Francis B. Gilbert	do	Grand Haven	do	3	....	45 00

Jerome B. Fitzgerald	do	St. Joseph	Indiana	12	....	360 00
John White	do	Milwaukie, W. T	Ireland	3	....	60 00
William B. Snowhook	do	Chicago, Illinois	do	6	....	240 00
Edward Campau	do	Springwells	Michigan	9	....	180 00
Francis H. Cicott	do	River Rouge	do	12	....	360 00
Harry Saunders	do	Monguagon	Rhode Island	3	....	60 00
Hiram Blakeley	do	Gibraltar	New York	12	....	145 00
Robert Duff	do	Brest	do	9	....	90 00
John Mullholland	Deputy Collector	Monroe	do	9	....	180 00
John Paxton	do	do	Canada	3	....	60 00
William Ten Eyck	Inspector	River Rouge	Michigan	12	....	300 00
Michilimackinac.						
Samuel K. Haring	Collector	Michilimackinac	New York	12	....	835 84
John Agnew	Deputy Collector	Sault Ste. Marie	New Jersey	12	....	400 00
Bela Chapman	Inspector	Michilimackinac	New Hampshire	12	....	240 00
FLORIDA.						
St. Augustine.						
George Center	Collector	St. Augustine	Massachusetts	1	11	56 29
Peter Benet	Inspector	do	Florida	....	18	7 00
Douglas Dummett	Deputy Collector and Inspector	New Smyrna	England	1	2	74 00
Pensacola.						
Robert Mitchell	Collector	Pensacola	North Carolina	12	....	890 08
Robert A. Mitchell	Inspector	do	do	9	20	879 00

CUSTOMS—*Florida*—*Continued.*

Names and offices.		Where employed.	Where born.	Time employed during the year ending Sept. 30, '45.		Compensat'n for the time employed.
				Months	Days	
Alexander P. Pute	Inspector	Pensacola	Virginia	2	11	$216 00
St. John's.						
James Delle	Collector	Jacksonville	Georgia	12	....	500 00
Thomas O. Holmes	Inspector	do	Massachusetts	12	....	$2 per day.
Lawrence Ryan	do	St. John's Bar	Virginia	12	....	do
John A. Cavedo	do	Fernandina	Florida	12	....	300 00
Apalachicola.						
Samuel W. Spencer	Collector	Apalachicola	Maryland	3	....	125 00
Marshall P. Ellis	Deputy Collector	do	Massachusetts	12	....	1095 00
Baker W. Johnson	Temporary Inspector	do	Maryland	7	12	666 00
Daniel N. McLean	do do	do	Rhode Island	2	16	228 00
H. R. Taylor	do do	do	New York	......	23	69 00
D. N. McLean	Weigher, Gauger, and Measurer	do	Rhode Island	......	....	1040 03
St. Mark's.						
N. W. Walker	Inspector	St. Mark's	South Carolina	......	17	
Augustus Steele	do	Cedar Key	Ohio	12	....	1095 00
John Palmer	do	Tampa Bay	South Carolina	12	....	1095 00
Moses Scott, jr.	do	St. Mark's	New York	11	13	1038 00
A. P. W. Crane	do	do	do	......	16	48 00

Key West.

S. R. Mallory	Collector	Key West	Trinidad		13	75 82
Charles Howe	Deputy Collector and Inspector	do	Massachusetts	12		1095 00
S. R. Mallory	do	do	Trinidad	11	17	1056 00
Francis Wathington	Temporary do	do	New York		13	39 00
Alexander Patterson	Temporary Weigher	do	Connecticut			
Alexander Patterson	Temporary Appraisers, at $5 each per day while employed	do	do			
D. W. Whitehurst		do	South Carolina			
Ben. Sawyer		do	Connecticut			
William Russel	Inspector	Indian River		12		550 00

UNITED STATES REVENUE MARINE.

Corrected to 30th September, 1845.

Names.	Where Born.	Name of Vessel.	Compensation.
CAPTAINS.			
John A. Webster	Maryland	Jackson	$1200
Winslow Foster	Virginia	Woodbury	1200
Henry D. Hunter	Pennsylvania	Special duty	1200
William W. Polk	Maryland	Madison	1200
Andrew Mather	Connecticut	Ewing	1200
Robert Day	New York	Crawford	1200
Ezekiel Jones	Massachusetts	Sick	1200
Thomas C. Rudolph	Georgia	Van Buren	1200
Caleb Currier	N. Hampshire	Sick	1200
Green Walden	Maine	Morris	1200
Henry B. Nones	Virginia	Forward	1200
Josiah Sturgis	Massachusetts	Hamilton	1200
Henry Prince, jr	do.	Steamer Spencer	1200
John Whitcomb	Maine	Steamer Jefferson	1200
Lewis C. F. Fatio	Pennsylvania	Sick	1200
Michael Conner	do.	Erie	1200
Alexander V. Fraser	New York	Bureau, Washington	1200
William A. Howard	Maine	Special duty	1200
Richard Evans	Virginia	Special duty	1200
Daniel Dobbins	Pennsylvania	Taney	1200
FIRST LIEUTENANTS.			
Napoleon L. Coste	South Carolina	Van Buren	960
William R. Whitehead	Virginia	Waiting orders	960
Gay Moore	Maryland	Steamer Jefferson	960
Levi C. Harby	South Carolina	Crawford	960
John J. Nimmo	Virginia	Woodbury	960
Douglass Ottinger	Pennsylvania	Steamer Dallas	960
Charles Grover	do.	Steamer Legare	960
Thomas Sands	Maryland	Taney	960
Thomas Stoddard	Massachusetts	Alert	960
Francis Martin	New York	Steamer Spencer	960
Stephen Cornell	Rhode Island	Jackson	960
Joseph Noyes	Maine	Special duty	960
John McGowan	Pennsylvania	Forward	960
James H. Roach	Maine	Morris	960
George Clark	Virginia	Madison	960
John B. Fulton	do.	Ewing	960
John S. S. Chaddock	Maine	Waiting orders	960
Beverly Digges	Maryland	do.	960
Supply C. Foss	N. Hampshire	Revenue boat Castine	960

UNITED STATES REVENUE MARINE—*Lieutenants.*

Names.	Where born.	Name of vessel.	Compensation.
James J. Morrison	Georgia	Wolcott	$960
Caleb Prouty	Massachusetts	Hamilton	960
Horatio N. Tracy	Connecticut	Rev. boat Sacket's Har.	960
SECOND LIEUTENANTS.			
Stephen Thatcher	Connecticut	Sick	860
George Berryman	Pennsylvania	Erie	860
Arnold Burroughs	New Jersey	Morris	860
Osmond Peters	Virginia	Van Buren	860
Joseph Amazeen	N. Hampshire	Wolcott	860
William Norris	Rhode Island	Steamer Legare	860
John Faunce	Massachusetts	Forward	860
William B. McLean	New York	Woodbury	860
Herman H. Greene	N. Hampshire	Steamer Bibb	860
John L. Prouty	Massachusetts	Jackson	860
William Pease	do	Hamilton	860
Charles W. Bennett	Delaware	Steamer Jefferson	860
John L. Stull	Maryland	Alert	860
William M. Wilson	South Carolina	Rev. boat St. Mary's	860
Nicholas Austin	Rhode Island	Jackson	860
John G. Breshwood	Virginia	Steamer Spencer	860
John M. Jones	Maryland	Crawford	860
George Hayes, jr	Maine	Bureau, Washington	860
James H. Jones	Delaware	Madison	860
Robert K. Hudgins	Virginia	Taney	860
John T. Stoneall	New York	Ewing	860
THIRD LIEUTENANTS.			
John A. Webster, jr	Maryland	Steamer Legare	790
Josiah Murch	Delaware	Jackson	790
William H. Brown	Massachusetts	Morris	790
John Hendren	Virginia	Steamer Spencer	790
Richard S. Jones	do	Forward	790
Edmund C. Kennedy	do	Steamer Bibb	790
William R. Pearce	do	Madison	790
Winfield Scott Bell	do	Wolcott	790
Charles L. Collier	do	Steamer Jefferson	790
Henry J. Benson	Connecticut	Woodbury	790
Camillus Saunders	North Carolina	Hamilton	790
Bushrod W. Frobel	Virginia	Erie	790
Charles F. Wood	Dist. Columbia	Forward	790
Kirby S. Woodward	Connecticut	Alert	790
William Handy	Dist. Columbia	Van Buren	790
Benjamin J. Kellum	Virginia	Taney	790
Samuel Smith	Maryland	Ewing	790
Edward T. Hyatt	Pennsylvania	Steamer Legare	790
James D. Usher	Virginia	Woodbury	790

UNITED STATES REVENUE MARINE—*Engineers, &c.*

Names.	Where born.	Name of vessel.	Compensation.
William H. Albertson	Pennsylvania	Crawford	$790
CHIEF ENGINEERS.			
William W. Luke	New York	Steamer Bibb	960
Pearson H. Bonham	Pennsylvania	Steamer Jefferson	960
James Wright	Massachusetts	Steamer McLane	960
Jacob F. Wilson	Pennsylvania	Steamer Spencer	960
Charles French	Connecticut	Steamer Dallas	960
Jno. Dougherty	Maryland	Steamer Legare	960
LIST OF WARRANT OFFICERS.			
ASSISTANT ENGINEERS.			
J. Rush Hays	Indiana	Steamer Bibb	790
James Turnbull	Massachusetts	Steamer McLane	790
Robert N. Stewart	Pennsylvania	Steamer Jefferson	790
Henry L. Hoff	do	Steamer Spencer	790
Alexander Auchinleck	do	Steamer Dallas	790
Jno. A. Ruggles	Indiana	Steamer Legare	790

REVENUE BOATS COMMANDED BY REVENUE OFFICERS.

Veto	Castine	Castine	Maine
Active	Sacket's Harbor	Lake Ontario	New York
Ingham	St. Mary's	St. Mary's	Georgia

IRON REVENUE STEAMERS BUILDING.

McLane, at Boston	Walker, at Pittsburg
Dallas, at Buffalo	Polk, at Richmond

LIGHT HOUSES—*Maine*.

Light Houses.	Superintendents.*	Keepers.	Compensation.	Lights.	Lamps.
MAINE.					
Portland	John Anderson	Richard Lee	$350 00	1	15
Wood Island	do	Jonathan Perkins	350 00	1	10
Sequin	do	Moses M. Haskell	500 00	1	14
West Quoddy Head	do	William D. Small	410 00	1	10
Whitehead	do	William Perry, jr.	410 00	1	10
Petit Manan	do	Moses Thompson	350 00	1	13
Franklin Island	do	William Jameson	350 00	1	10
Pond Island	do	John F. Mereen	350 00	1	8
Baker's Island	do	William Gilley	350 00	1	10
Burnt Island	do	Jason Fuller	350 00	1	10
Cape Elizabeth	do	Hiram Staples	350 00	2	27
Goat Island	do	Oliver Freeman	350 00	1	7
Brown's Head	do	Howland Dyer	350 00	1	8
Owl's Head	do	William Masters	350 00	1	8
Dice's Head	do	William Hutchings, jr.	350 00	1	10
Negro Island	do	Obadiah Brown	350 00	1	8
Marshall's Point	do	John Alexander	350 00	1	7
Hendrick's Head	do	Joshua Berry	350 00	1	8
Moose Peak	do	Alexander Milliken	400 00	1	10
Martinicus Rock	do	Samuel S. Abbott	450 00	2	14
Bear Island	do	John G. Bowen	350 00	1	7
Libby Island	do	Isaac Stearns	350 00	1	10

* For compensation of superintendents, see note to "Recapitulation.

LIGHT HOUSES—*New Hampshire, Massachusetts, Vermont.*

Light Houses.	Superintendents.	Keepers.	Compensation.	Lights.	Lamps.
Fort Point	John Anderson	William Clewley	$350 00	1	8
Nash's Island	do.	John Wass	350 00	1	10
Eagle Island	do.	John Spear	350 00	1	10
Pemaquid Point	do.	Ephraim Tibbets	350 00	1	10
Mount Desert Rock	do.	Benjamin Ward, jr	600 00	1	10
Monhegan Island	do.	Francis Pierce	350 00	1	10
Saddleback Ledge	do.	Watson Hopkins	450 00	1	10
NEW HAMPSHIRE.					
Portsmouth	Augustus Jenkins	James E. Robinson	350 00	1	13
White Island	do.	Thomas B. Laighton	600 00	1	15
Boon Island	do.	John Kennard	600 00	1	12
Whale's Back	do.	J. Prentiss Locke	600 00	1	15
MASSACHUSETTS.					
Boston	Marcus Morton	Tobias Cook	400 00	1	14
Thatcher's Island	do.	Charles Wh ler	450 00	2	22
Baker's Island	do.	Ambrose Martin	400 00	2	25
Plumb Island	do.	Phinehas George	375 00	2	16
Cape Cod	do.	James Small	350 00	1	15
Plymouth	do.	Joseph Burgiss	400 00	2	16
Long Island Head	do.	Charles Beck	350 00	1	9
Ipswich	do.	Ebenezer Pulsifer	375 00	2	14
Long Point	do.	Charles Derby	350 00	1	10

Gloucester Point	do	Samuel Wonson	400 00	1	10
Ten Pound Island	do	Amos Story	350 00	1	6
Mayo's Beach	do	Joseph Holbrook jr	350 00	1	3
Scituate	do	Ebenezer Osborn	350 00	2	15
Billingsgate Island	do	Abijah Gill	400 00	1	8
Race Point	do	Elijah Dyer	350 00	1	10
Sandy Neck	do	Henry Baxter	400 00	1	6
Marblehead	do	Ezekiel Darling	400 00	1	10
Straitsmouth Island	do	John Davis	350 00	1	6
Nanset Beach	do	Benjamin H. A. Collins	425 00	3	18
Wigwam Point	do	George Day	350 00	1	6
Gayhead	Joseph T. Pease	Ellis Skiff	350 00	1	10
Cutterhunk	do	Fanny Chase	350 00	1	10
Cape Poge	do	Aaron Norton	350 00	1	11
Chatham	do	Simeon Nicherson	400 00	2	20
Point Gammon	do	John Peak	350 00	1	10
Holmes' Hole	do	James West	350 00	1	10
Tarpaulin Cove	do	John Hayden	350 00	1	10
Monomoy Point	do	Solomon Doane	400 00	1	8
Nobsque Point	do	Peter Daggett	350 00	1	10
Edgartown	do	Jeremiah Pease	350 00	1	9
Nantucket	William R. Easton	Aaron Folger	450 00	1	15
Nantucket Beacon	do	David Coffin (2d)	300 00	1	8
Nantucket Harbor	do	Caleb Cushman	300 00	1	3
Nantucket Cliff Beacons	do	Peleg Easton	300 00	2	15
Clark's Point	Joseph T. Adams	Henry M. Smith	350 00	1	10
Bird Island	do	John Clark	400 00	1	10
Dumpling Rock	do	Levi Smith	400 00	1	10
Ned's Point	do	George Braley	350 00	1	8
VERMONT.					
Juniper Island	Russell G. Hopkinson	Thomas Chambers	350 00	1	10

LIGHT HOUSES—*Rhode Island—Connecticut—New York.*

Light houses.	Superintendents.	Keepers.	Compensation.	Lights.	Lamps.
RHODE ISLAND.					
Block Island	Edwin Wilbur	Simeon Babcock	$400 00	2	14
Newport	do	Robert H. Weeden	350 00	1	15
Watch Hill	do	Gilbert Pendleton	350 00	1	10
Dutch Island	do	William P Babcock	350 00	1	8
Poplar Point	do	Samuel Thomas	350 00	1	8
Point Judith	do	William A. Weeden	350 00	1	10
Nayat Point	do	Daniel Wightman	350 00	1	6
Goat Island	do	Henry Oman	350 00	1	8
Warwick Neck	do	John W. Green	350 00	1	8
CONNECTICUT.					
New London	Charles F. Lester	Nathan Buddington	350 00	1	11
Faulkner's Island	do	Eli Kimberly	350 00	1	8
Lynde Point	do	Catharine F. Whittlesey	350 00	1	10
Stonington	do	Patty Potter	350 00	1	8
Morgan's Point	do	Eliza A. Daball	350 00	1	10
Five Mile Point	Norris Wilcox	Elihu Ives	350 00	1	8
Stratford Point	do	Samuel Budington	350 00	1	10
Fairweather Island	do	Stephen T. Moore	350 00	1	8
Norwalk Island	do	Lewis Whitlock	350 00	1	10
Great Captain's Island	do	James Bird	350 00	1	10
NEW YORK.					
Coxsackie	Cornelius W. Lawrence.	Wm. Rea	300 00	1	7

Stuyvesant	do	Christina Witbeck	350 00	1	4
Four Mile Point	do	Jer'h H. Winney	350 00	1	7
Saugerties	do	Abr'm E. C. Schoonmaker	350 00	1	4
Esopus Meadows	do	Geo. W. Murdagh	350 00	1	4
Rondout Creek	do	Johannes D. Hasbrouck	350 00	1	4
Stony Point	do	Thomas Ackerson	350 00	1	6
Robbins' Reef	do	Michael M. Marsac	600 00	1	15
Fort Tompkins	do	John Bird	350 00	1	11
Prince's Bay	do	Jacobus Hardenbergh	400 00	1	10
Sandy Hook, (N. J.)..*and 2 beacons	do	John V. Conover	650 00	3	18
		..(4 assistants)	600 00		13
Nk.....do	do				
do.....do	do	Jos. J. Thompson	1440 00	2	38 Fr. len's
Fine Island	do	Eliphalet Smith	500 00	1	14
Eaton's Neck	do	Benj'n Downing	350 00	1	13
Old Field Point	do	Elizabeth Smith	350 00	1	10
Sands' Point	do	Danl. H. Calkins	350 00	1	11
Throgg's Nk,	do	Wm. Bayles	350 00	1	11
Nk Point	Abel Huntington	Patrick T. Gould	350 00	1	18
Plumb Island	do	Henry Conklin	350 00	1	10
Gull Island	do	Chas. D. Manwaring	600 00	1	15
Cedar Island	do	Moses Bears	350 00	1	9
Fort Niagara	Lyman B. Langworthy	H. W. Phillips	350 00	1	9
Genesee	do	Peter Hillman	350 00	1	9
Sodus Bay..(10)....and beacon..(4)	do	Bennett C. Fitzhugh	350 08	1	14
Galloo Island	Otis N. Cole	John Pringle	400 00	1	15
Oswego	do	Orl'o Steele	400 00	1	13
Tibbitt's Point	do	Nelson B. Williams	350 00	1	9
Salmon Bay	do	Lewis Conant	350 00	1	8
Stony Point	do	Wiley G. Nickles	350 00	1	9
Horse Island	do	Samuel McNitt	350 00	1	8
Portland Harbor	Henry W. Rogers	Joshua Lane	350 00	1	nat. gas

LIGHT HOUSES—*New Jersey—Pennsylvania—Delaware—Maryland—Virginia.*

Light houses.	Superintendents.	Keepers.	Compensation.	Lights.	Lamps.
Silver Creek	Henry W. Rogers	Moses Fuller	$350 00	1	4
Dunkirk (11) and beacon (4)	do	Jno. J. Cassity	450 00	1	15
Buffalo	do	Alex. Ramsdell	350 00	1	8
Ogdensburgh	David C. Judson	Amos Wells	350 00	1	10
Cumberland Head	Wm. F. Haile	Samuel Emery	350 00	1	11
Split Rock	do	Elisha Royce	350 00	1	11
NEW JERSEY.					
Barnegat Shoals	Samuel S. Downs	Jer'h Spragg	350 00	1	11
PENNSYLVANIA.					
Presque Isle	Murray Whallon	Eli Webster	350 00	1	8
Presque Isle Beacon	do	Leonard Vaughn	300 00	1	4
DELAWARE.					
Cape Henlopen	Henry Hicks	Richard Beebe	400 00	1	18
Cape Henlopen Beacon	do	do	250 00	1	10
Cape May, (N. J.)	do	Ezekiel Stevens	400 00	1	15
Mispillion	do	Charles Hamm	400 00	1	8
Mahon's Ditch	do	Jno. Smith	450 00	1	10
Bombay Hook	do	Duncan Stuart	450 00	1	10
Christiana	do	Chas. B. F. Smith	350 00	1	gas.
Cohanzey Creek	do	Robert Richardson	350 00	1	10

Egg Island, (N. J.)	do	Henry Rogers	350 00	1	10
Reedy Island do (12)..and Breakwater (5)	do	John Cooper	400 00	1	17
MARYLAND.					
Bodkin Island	William H. Marriott	Rosannah Tatham	400 00	1	13
Lazaretto Point	do	Wm. Shaw	350 00	1	11
North Point	do	Elizabeth Riley	600 00	2	18
Sharp's Island	do	Samuel Harris	350 00	1	10
Cove Point	do	Walter Wyville	350 00	1	11
Poole's Island	do	Ezekiel Morrison	460 00	1	13
Thomas' Point	do	John Hebb	350 00	1	13
Turkey Point	do	Elizabeth Lusby	350 00	1	11
Concord Point	do	Thomas Courtney	350 00	1	9
Smith's Island	do	Matthias D. Wainwright	400 00	1	10
Point Look Out	do	Ann Davis	350 00	1	11
Clay Island	do	Jno. S. Evans	400 00	1	10
Little Watts' Island	do	Jas. W. Twiford	350 00	1	11
VIRGINIA.					
Cape Henry	Conway Whittle	Thos. Davis	500 00	1	18
Smith's Island	do	Thos. S. Brickhouse	400 00	1	15
Smith's Point	do	Jno. Pettit	500 00	1	15
Old Point Comfort	do	Henry C. Bell	400 00	1	11
New Point Comfort	do	Wm. R. Brownley	400 00	1	10
Back River	do	Wm. Jett	400 00	1	10
Assateague	do	John Hope	400 00	1	11
Piney Point	Edward Green	Charlotte Sutor	350 00	1	10

LIGHT HOUSES—*North Carolina—South Carolina—Georgia—Ohio—Louisiana.*

Light Houses.	Superintendents.	Keepers.	Compensation.	Lights.	Lamps.
NORTH CAROLINA.					
Bald Head	Murphy V. Jones	Bryan Morse	$400 00	1	18
Federal Point	do.	Jas. S. Newton	400 00	1	11
Cape Hatteras	James K. Hatton	Benjamin Fulcher	400 00	1	18
Pamptico Point	do.	Samuel Fulford	400 00	1	10
Cape Look Out	James E. Gibble	Wm. Fulford	400 00	1	16
Ocracoke	Thomas J. Pasteur	Anson Harker	400 00	1	15
SOUTH CAROLINA.					
Charleston	Wm. J. Grayson	St. Lo. Mellichamp	600 00	2	13
Racoon Key *and beacon	do.	Thaddeus C. Skrine	450 00	1	*15
Morris Island Beacons	do.	Jud. W. Amiel	450 00	2	4
North Island	Thos. L. Shaw	Sam'l N. Marsh	400 00	1	11
GEORGIA.					
Tybee (15) and beacon (8)	Wm. B. Bullock	Wm. T. Baker	533 33	2	23
Little Cumberland Island	Arch'd Clarke	David Thompson	400 00	1	15
Sapelo	do.	W. M. Thomas	400 00	1	15
St. Simon's Island	do.	L. McIntosh	400 00	1	9
Wolf Island Beacons	do.	Henry Cannon	400 00	2	12
OHIO.					
Cleveland (7) and beacon (4)	Smith Inglehard	Lewis Dibble	450 00	1	11

Grand River.............*and beacon	........do............	Thos. Greer..................	450 00	1	*11
Conneaut River Bed................	........do............	Ezra Dibble..................	350 00	1	6
Cunningham Harbor................	........do............	J. R. Cunningham........	350 00	1	3
Black River...........................	........do............	Thomas Brown............	350 00	1	8
Ashtabula..............................	........do............	Joel H. Thomas...........	350 00	1	7
Port Clinton...........................	Elias H. Haines........	Austin Smith...............	350 00	1	6
Huron River Beacon................	........do............	Alexander P. Chesley......	350 00	1	8
Cedar Point...........................	........do............	Leonard Beatty............	350 00	1	5
Turtle Island..........................	........do............	Gideon L. Kelsey......... ....1 assistant............	400 00 100 00	1	11
Sandusky.....*.......................	........do............	Chas. F. Drake............	350 00	1	11
LOUISIANA.					
Bayou St. John......................	Dennis Prieur........	Robt. Allen................. ....1 assistant............	500 00 300 00	1	9
Port Ponchartrain..................	........do............	S. H. Page..................	500 00	1	10
Pleasanton's Island................	........do............	Jas. J. White..............	600 00 360 00	1	10
South Point...........................	........do............	Robt. Johnson.............	600 00 360 00	1	14
Frank's Island.......................	........do............	Jonas Lory..................	600 00 360 00	1	30
Pass Manchac........................	........do............	Robt. Daniels..............	600 00 300 00	1	9
New Canal............................	........do............	Thos. Beattie..............	600 00 360 00	1	9
South West Pass....................	........do............	Sam'l Hill...................	600 00 360 00	1	29
Cat Island.............................	........do............	Redmond Cuevas.........	500 00 350 00	1	10
Tchefuncte River....................	........do............	Benjamin Thurston........	500 00	1	9

LIGHT HOUSES—*Alabama—Florida—Michigan.*

Light houses.	Superintendents.	Keepers.	Compensation.	Lights.	Lamps.
Pass Christian	Dennis Prieur	Miss C. A. Hiern	$500 00	1	8
Vermillion Bay	do	Amos C. Butcher	500 00 360 00	1	14
Point Defer	do	Daniel Tufts	600 00	1	15
ALABAMA.					
Round Island	Collier H. Minge	Hy. S. C. McRea	500 00	1	11
Choctaw Point	do	Carmelite Philibert	500 00	1	11
Sand Island	do	Sam'l Jackson	500 00	1	14
Mobile Point	do	Elijah F. Dinsmore	500 00	1	21
FLORIDA.					
St. Augustine	George Center	Jno. Andrew	400 00	1	10
Key West	Stephen R. Mallory	Barbara Mabrity	500 00	1	15
Sand Key	do	Jos. Appleby ....1 assistant	600 00 300 00	1	14
Dry Tortugas	do	John Thompson ....2 assistants	600 00 350 00	1	23
St. Mark's	Nath'l W. Walker	Needham Dudley	450 00	1	15
St. John's River	James Dell	Geo. C. Acosta	400 00	1	14
Amelia Island	do	Edmund Richardson	400 00	1	14
St. George's Island	Sam'l W. Spencer	David Adkins	500 00	1	13
Dog Island	do	Oliver Crawford	500 00	1	14
St. Joseph's Bay	do	Ephraim Andrews	500 00	1	15

Pensacola	Dillon Jordan	Mrs. M. Ingraham	550 00	1	10
IN MICHIGAN.					
Thunder Bay	Sam'l K. Haring	J. J. Malden	400 00	1	11
Bois Blanc	do.	Lyman Granger	400 00	1	9
Pottawatamie Island	do.	David E. Corbin	350 00	1	10
South Manitou Island	do.	Geo. Clarke	350 00	1	8
Presque Isle	do.	H. L. Woolsey	350 00	1	11
Fort Gratiot	Chas. G. Hammond	Wm. Wright	350 00	1	8
Otter Creek	do.	Lewis Bond	350 00	1	7
Windmill Point	do.	Lawrence Tremble	350 00	1	5
Gibraltar	do.	Alanson Parsons	350 00	1	9
Saginaw Bay	do.	Thos. Simpson	350 00	1	7
Grand River	John McReynolds	Nehemiah Merritt	350 00	1	6
Kalamazoo River	do.	Wm. Scoville	350 00	1	6
St. Joseph's River	do.	Abner P. Stinson	350 00	1	5
New Buffalo	do.	Elijah B. Pressy	350 00	1	4
Michigan City, (Indiana)	do.	Harriet C. Towner	350 00	1	4
Chicago, (Illinois)	do.	James Long	350 00	1	5
Root River, (W. T.)	do.	Amaziah Stebbins	350 00	1	9
Milwaukie ....do	do.	Eli Bates, jr.	350 00	1	7
Sheboygan ....do	do.	Stephen Woolverton	350 00	1	8
Manitouwoc...do	do.	Thos. A. H. Edwards	350 00	1	6

RECAPITULATION.

Districts.	*Superintendents.	Lights.	Keepers and assistants.	Salaries.	Lamps.
Maine	John Anderson	31	29	$11070 00	302
New Hampshire	Augustus Jenkins	4	4	2150 00	55
Massachusetts	Marcus Morton	28	20	7575 00	239
Do	Joseph T. Pease	11	10	3600 00	108
Do	Wm. R. Easton	5	4	1350 00	31
Do	Joseph T. Adams	4	4	1500 00	38
Vermont	Russell G. Hopkinson	1	1	350 00	10
Rhode Island	Edwin Wilbur	10	9	3200 00	87
Connecticut	Charles F. Lester	5	5	1750 00	47
Do	Norris Willcox	5	5	1750 00	46
New York	Cornel's W. Lawrence	20	17 4ast.	8340 00	200
Do	Abel Huntington	4	4	1650 00	52
Do	L. B. Langworthy	3	3	1050 00	32
Do	Otis N. Cole	6	6	2200 00	62
Do	Henry W. Rogers	4	4	1500 00	27
Do	David C. Judson	1	1	350 00	10
Do	William F. Haile	2	2	700 00	22
New Jersey	Samuel S. Downs	1	1	350 00	11
Pennsylvania	Murray Whallon	2	2	650 00	12
Delaware	Henry Hicks	10	10	3800 00	108
Maryland	William H. Marriott	14	13	5060 00	151
Virginia	Conway Whittle	7	7	3000 00	90
Do	Edward Green	1	1	350 00	10
North Carolina	Murphy V. Jones	2	2	800 00	29
Do	James K. Hatton	2	2	800 00	28
Do	James E. Gibble	1	1	400 00	16
Do	Thomas J. Pasteur	1	1	400 00	15
South Carolina	William J. Grayson	5	3	1500 00	32
Do	Thomas L. Shaw	1	1	400 00	11
Georgia	William B. Bullock	2	1	533 33	15 8 23
Do	Archibald Clarke	5	4	1600 00	51
Ohio	Smith Inglehart	6	6	2300 00	46
Do	Elias H. Haines	5	5 1ast.	1900 00	41
Louisiana	Dennis Prieur	13	13 9ast.	10310 00	176
Alabama	Collier H. Minge	4	4	2000 00	57

*Note.—Superintendents are allowed 2½ per cent. commission on the amount of their disbursements relative to Light Houses, &c., subject to a proviso in the civil appropriation bill of 3d March, 1845, limiting this allowance to such as receive over $2,000 per annum for other public services; and excepting the Inspector for the lakes, (J. McReynolds,) who has $1200 per annum salary without commission.

FLOATING LIGHTS.

Districts.	Superintendents.	Lights.	Keepers and assistants.	Salaries.	Lamps.
Florida.........	Stephen R. Mallory...	3	3 2ast.	$2350 00	52
......Do	George Center.........	1	1	400 00	10
......Do	James Dell...........	2	2	800 00	28
......Do	Samuel W. Spencer..	3	3	1500 00	42
......Do	Dillon Jordan........	1	1	550 00	10
......Do	Nathaniel W. Walker	1	1	450 00	15
Michigan.........	Samuel K. Haring...	5	5	1850 00	49
......Do	Charles G. Hammond	5	5	1750 00	36
......Do	John McReynolds ...	10	10	3500 00	60
J. McReynolds'	salary, as Insp., &c..	......	......	1200 00	
		257	236 16	$100588 33	2577

FLOATING LIGHTS.

Floating Lights.	*Superintendents.	Keepers.	Salary.
MASSACHUSETTS.			
Tuckanuck Shoal......	J. T. Pease........	David F. Chase....	$650 00
CONNECTICUT.			
Bartlett's Reef.........	C. F. Lester.......	Wm. H. Young ...	500 00
NEW YORK.			
Stratford Point	C. W. Lawrence...	Jno. Taylor........	700 00
Sandy Hook...........	......do...........	Thomas Moriarty..	700 00
DELAWARE.			
Five Fathom Bank.....	Henry Hicks......	Isaac P. Merritt...	700 00
Brandywine Shoal, No. 1	......do..........	Wm. Simpson.....	500 00
Upper Middle Sh'l, No. 2	......do..........	Geo. H. Geddes ...	500 00
MARYLAND.			
Hooper's Straits........	Wm. H. Marriott..	Henry Shenton	500 00
VIRGINIA.			
Crany Island..........	Conway Whittle...	Wm. Tee..........	450 00
Smith's Point	......do..........	Cyrus Sutton......	500 00

*See note to "Recapitulation" for pay of superintendents.

FLOATING LIGHTS—*Continued.*

Floating Lights.	Superintendents.	Keepers.	Salary.
Willoughby Spit	Conway Whittle	Jno. B. Sale	$500 00
Wolf Trap Shoals	do	Barzillia Kirwan	500 00
Windmill Point	do	Jno. G. Cox	500 00
Lower Cedar Point	Edward Green	Thos. Shorter	400 00
Upper Cedar Point	do	Thos. Lloyd	400 00
Bowler's Rock	Jno. A. Parker	Albert G. McCarty	400 00
NORTH CAROLINA.			
Roanoke Island	Wm. D. Pritchard	Joshua Harrison	500 00
Wade's Point	do	Jas. C. Scott	500 00
Long Shoal	Th. J. Pasteur	Wallace H. Styron	500 00
Royal Shoal	do	Bryan H. Rumley	500 00
Nine Feet Shoal	do	Valentine Robinson	500 00
Neuse River	do	Saml. Fulford	500 00
Brant Island	do	Otway Burns	500 00
Harbor Island	do	Thomas Robinson	500 00
Roanoke River	Jos. Ramsey	Lemuel Douglass	500 00
SOUTH CAROLINA.			
St. Helena Bar	Benj. R. Bythewood	Henry Harvey	500 00
GEORGIA.			
Tybee Channel	Wm. B. Bullock	Wm. Craig	700 00
FLORIDA.			
Carysfort Reef	St. R. Mallory	Joseph Ximenez	700 00
Key West	do	Henry Benners	700 00
MICHIGAN.			
Ocean (Mich'k Sts.)	Samuel K. Haring	Christian Barkenbill	500 00

RECAPITULATION.

States.	Superintendents.	Keepers.	Salary.
Massachusetts	J. T. Pease	1	$650 00
Connecticut	C. F. Lester	1	500 00
New York	C. W. Lawrence	2	1400 00
Delaware	Henry Hicks	3	1700 00
Maryland	W. H. Marriott	1	500 00
Virginia	C. Whittle	5	2450 00

REGISTERS, RECEIVERS, AND SURVEYORS.

States.	Superintendents.	Keepers.	Salary.
Virginia	E. Green	2	$800 00
......do	Jno. A. Parker	1	400 00
North Carolina	W. D. Pritchard	2	1000 00
......do	T. J. Pasteur	6	3000 00
......do	Jos. Ramsey	1	500 00
South Carolina	B. R. Bythewood	1	500 00
Georgia	W. B. Bullock	1	700 00
Florida	S. R. Mallory	2	1400 00
Michigan	S. K. Haring	1	500 00

REGISTERS, RECEIVERS, AND SURVEYORS.

Names and offices.	Where employed.	Where born.	Compensation.
REGISTERS.*			
Thomas J. Winship	Chillicothe . . Ohio	Virginia	Salary of Registers $500 per annum, and one per cent. commission on moneys entered at their offices respectively. Commission not to exceed $2,500 per annum.
Robert McKelly	U. Sandusky . do.	Pennsylvania	
John F. Read	Jeffersonville. . Ia.	Indiana	
John Myers	Vincennes . . . do.	Pennsylvania	
David V. Cully	Indianapolis . . do.	......do	
John W. Rush	Crawfordsville do.	Ohio	
William S. Edsall	Fort Wayne. . do.	New York	
John Gardner	Winamac . . . do.	North Carolina	
James C. Sloo	Shawneetown . Ill.	Kentucky	
Jacob Feaman	Kaskaskia . . . do.	Virginia	
Jacob Judy	Edwardsville . do.	Illinois	
Robert K. McLaughlin	Vandalia . . . . do.	Maryland	
Harman Alexander	Palestine . . . . do.	Kentucky	
James W. Barrett	Springfield . . . do.	Virginia	
William E. Russell	Danville . . . . do.	Connecticut	
William G. Flood	Quincy . . . . . do.	Virginia	
George Mixter	Dixon . . . . . . do.	Massachusetts	
William M. Jackson	Chicago . . . . . do.	New Jersey	
Thomas Watson	St. Louis . . . Mo.	Ireland	
William McNair	Fayette . . . . . do.		
Benjamin Davies	Palmyra . . . . do.	Dist. Columbia	
Franklin Cannon	Jackson . . . . . do.	North Carolina	
A. B. Morton	Clinton . . . . . do.	Kentucky	
James H. McBride	Springfield . . . do.	......do	
James H. Birch	Plattsburg . . . do.	Virginia	
James Magoffin	St. Stephen's. Ala.	Pennsylvania	

*Registers and Receivers are allowed for superintending public sales $5 per day during the continuance of such sales, which cannot exceed two weeks. (See note to "Receiver.")

REGISTERS—*Continued*—RECEIVERS.

Names and offices.	Where employed.	Where born.	Compensation.
Alanson Saltmarsh	Cahaba, Ala.	New York	Salary of Receivers $500 per annum, and one per cent. commission on moneys accounted for by them respectively. Commission not to exceed $2,500 per annum.
John J. Coleman	Huntsville, do.	Georgia	
Richard Whiting	Tuscaloosa, do.	Massachusetts	
Wade H. Greening	Sparta, do.	South Carolina	
Lewis B. McCarty	Demopolis, do.	Tennessee	
Duncan B. Graham	Montgomery, do.	North Carolina	
Hugh P. Caperton	Lebanon, do.	Tennessee	
Thomas W. Newman	Washington Miss.	Mississippi	
John S. Howze	Augusta, do.	South Carolina	
Benjamin R. Cowherd	Jackson, do.	Virginia	
Thomas B. Ives	Grenada, do.	North Carolina	
William Dowsing	Columbus, do.	Virginia	
Andrew J. Edmonson	Pontotoc, do. Chickasaw cession	Tennessee	
Peter Laidlaw	New Orleans, La.	Scotland	
Peter L. Hebrard	Opelousas, do.	Louisiana	
Daniel B. Richardson	Ouachita, do.	Virginia	
Richmond Dennis	Greensburg, do.	Louisiana	
William T. Walmsley	Natchitoches, do.	Maryland	
Robert A. Forsyth	Detroit, Mich.		
Abraham Edwards	Kalamazoo, do.	New Jersey	
John Bartow	Genesee, do.	New York	
Benjamin Sherman	Ionia, do.	do.	
Robert C. Newland	Batesville, Ark.	North Carolina	
William W. Stevenson	Little Rock, do.	South Carolina	
Benjamin P. Jett	Washington, do.	Virgina	
Ephraim D. Dickson	Fayetteville, do.	North Carolina	
Henry L. Biscoe	Helena, do.	Virginia	
John Bruton	Johnson C. H. do.	South Carolina	
Hiram Smith	Champagnole, do.	Mississippi	
Albert W. Parris	Min'l Pt., Wisc'n	Maine	
John S. Horner	Green Bay, do.	Virginia	
George H. Walker	Milwaukie, do.	do.	
Warner Lewis	Dubuque, Iowa	do.	
Bernhart Henn	Fairfield, do.	New York	
Thomas J. Hodson	Tallahassee, Fla.	Maryland	
William H. Simmons	St. Augustine, do.	South Carolina	
Samuel Russell	Newnansville, do.	North Carolina	
RECEIVERS.*			
John Hough	Chillicothe, Ohio	Ohio	
Christian Huber	U. Sandusky, do.	Pennsylvania	

* Receivers are also allowed, as a compensation for *expense labor* incurred in depositing the public moneys, for every mile travelled from their respective offices to the place of deposite and returning, computing the distance by the nearest route, if by land, at the rate of 12½ cents per mile; if by water,

RECEIVERS.

Names and offices.	Where employed.	Where born.	Compensation.
David G. Bright	Jeffersonville, Ia.	Pennsylvania	Salary of Receivers $500 per annum, and one per cent. commission on moneys accounted for by them respectively. Commission not to exceed $2,500 per annum.
Samuel Wise	Vincennes ... do.	Maryland	
Seton W. Norriss	Indianapolis .. do.	Virginia	
Philip E. Engle	Crawfordsville do.	.... do	
Isaac D. G. Nelson	Fort Wayne .. do.	New York	
Amzi L. Wheeler	Winamac .... do.	.... do	
Braxton Parrish	Shawneetown . Ill.	North Carolina.	
John A. Langlois	Kaskaskia ... do.	Illinois	
John G. Cameron	Edwardsville . do.	New York	
Henry Smith	Vandalia ..... do.	Ireland	
William Wilson	Palestine .... do.	Virginia	
Archer G. Herndon	Springfield ... do.	.... do	
Lunsford R. Noel	Danville ..... do.	.... do	
Samuel Leech	Quincy ...... do.	Kentucky	
John Dement	Dixon .... do.	Tennessee	
Thomas Dyer	Chicago ..... do.	Connecticut	
Edward Dobyns	St. Louis ... Mo.	Kentucky	
Alfred W. Morrison	Fayette ...... do.	....	
Parker Dudley	Palmyra ..... do.	Kentucky	
Aaron Snider	Jackson ...... do.	North Carolina.	
Daniel Ashby	Clinton ...... do.	Virginia	
Nicholas R. Smith	Springfield ... do.	.... do	
Bela M. Hughes	Plattsburg .... do.	Kentucky	
Elijah H. Gordy	St. Stephen's. Ala.	Alabama	
Matthew Gayle	Cahaba ...... do.	South Carolina.	
Samuel Cruse	Huntsville .... do.	Maryland	
Edward F. Comegys	Tuscaloosa ... do.	.... do	
Armstead D. Carey	Sparta .... do.	Virginia	
David E. Moore	Demopolis ... do.	.... do	
Nimrod E. Benson	Montgomery .. do.	South Carolina.	
John G. Winston	Lebanon ..... do.	Tennessee	
William N. Whitehurst	Washington Miss.	Mississippi	
Wyatt J. Draughn	Augusta ..... do.	South Carolina.	
David C. Glenn	Jackson ...... do.	North Carolina.	
George S. Gollady	Grenada ..... do.	Pennsylvania	
Edward B. Randolph	Columbus .... do.	Virginia	
John F. Wray	Pontotoc ..... do. Chickasaw cession	.... do	
Oliver B. Hill	New Orleans . La.	N. Hampshire	
Robert Benguerel	Opelousas .... do.	Louisiana	
Hardy Holmes	Ouachita ..... do.	North Carolina.	
George W. Womack	Greensburg ... do.	Louisiana	
John Tucker	Natchitoches . do.	Tennessee	

six cents per mile, and a per centage of one hundredth part of one per cent. on the amount deposited, for every ten miles of distance between the land office and place of deposite, by the nearest route, for *risk* incurred. (See note to "Registers of Land Offices.")

RECEIVERS—*Continued*—SURVEYORS.

Names and offices.	Where employed.	Where Born.	Compensation.
Jonathan Kearsley	Detroit ... Mich.	Pennsylvania	Salary of Receivers $500 per ann., and 1 per cent. commiss'n on moneys accounted for by them respectively. Com. not to exceed $2,500 per ann.
Mitchell Hinsdell	Kalamazoo ... do.	Vermont	
Charles C. Hascall	Genesee ... do.	Connecticut	
Frederick Hall	Ionia ... do.	Vermont	
D. J. Chapman	Batesville ... Ark.	Tennessee	
Gerrard N. Causin	Little Rock ... do.	Maryland	
Daniel T. Witler	Washington ... do.	Connecticut	
Matthew Leeper	Fayetteville ... do.	North Carolina	
George Jefferies	Helena ... do.	Virginia	
William Adams	Johnson C. H. do.	Tennessee	
Albert G. Rust	Champagnole . do.	Virginia	
John W. Argyle	Tallahassee .. Fla.	... do	
George W. Cole	St. Augustine . do.	... do	
John Parsons	Newnansville . do.	N. Hampshire	
Paschal Bequette	Min'l Pt. . Wis. T.	Missouri	
Alexander J. Irwin	Green Bay ... do.	Pennsylvania	
J. Albert Helfenstein	Milwaukie ... do.	... do	
Stephen Langworthy	Du Buque Iowa T.	Vermont	
Ver Planck Van Antwerp	Fairfield ... do.	New York	
SURVEYORS.			
(*Ohio, Indiana, and Michigan.*)			
Lucius Lyon ... Surv. Gen'l	Detroit, Mich.	Vermont	$2000 00
John Almy ... Chief Clerk	... do	Massachusetts	1500 00
Jas. T. Higbee .. Draughstman	... do	New Jersey	1100 00
George S. Frost ... do.	... do	New York	1000 00
Hiram Burnham ... Clerk	... do	Vermont	Paid by the 100 words.
Joseph E. Hyde ... do.	... do	New York	
George W. Thayer ... do.	... do	Vermont	
(*Illinois and Missouri.*)			
F. R. Conway ... Surv. Gen'l	St. Louis, Mo.	Tennessee	2000 00
Jenifer T. Sprigg . Chief Clerk	... do	Maryland	1000 00
Amasa R. Parker ... Clerk	... do	New York	900 00
Frederick Welcker Draughts'n	... do	Germany	Paid by the piece or 100 words.
George Gahan ... do.	... do	Ireland	
Fred'k Mosberger . do. & Clerk	... do	Switzerland	
John K. Rycklicki ... Clerk	... do	Poland	
Adolphe Renard ... do.	... do	Switzerland	
John Widgery ... do.	... do	Maine	
Thomas Rector ... do.	... do	Missouri	
(*Alabama.*)			
Jas. H. Weakley . . Surv. Gen'l	Florence, Ala.	Virginia	2000 00
Ferd'd Sannoner . . Draughts'n	... do	Italy	1000 00
Samuel D. Weakley ... Clerk	... do	Tennessee	1000 00

SURVEYORS—*Continued.*

Names and offices.	Where employed.	Where born.	Compensation.
(Louisiana.)			
Pierre T. Landry, Surv. Gen'l	Donaldson, La...	Louisiana	$2000 00
A. J. Powell.....Chief Clerk	......do.........	Mississippi	1500 00
J. A. L. R. Landry ....Clerk	......do.........	Louisiana	900 00
A. W. Warren..Draughtsman	......do.........	Massachusetts .	Paid by the piece.
J. B. F. Gaudet..........do.....	......do.........	Louisiana	1200 00
T. La Fayette Randall..Clerk	......do.........	....do..........	600 00
D. A. Watterston..Ass't Surv.	Greensburg Dist..	Dist. Columbia.	1000 00
R. W. Boyd ....P. Clerk	......do.........	Ireland.........	$5 p. day
	......[for the time actually employed.		
(Mississippi.)			
Chas. A. Bradford.Surv. Gen'l	Jackson, Miss...	Pennsylvania ..	2000 00
R. H. M. Bradford.Chief Cl'k	......do.........	....do..........	1200 00
(Arkansas.)			
William Pelham..Surv. Gen'l	Little Rock, Ark..	Kentucky	1500 00
J. Wilamowicz.........Clerk	......do.........	Poland.........	1000 00
James A. Johnson........do..	......do.........	Tennessee......	800 00
John B. Pelham.........do..	......do.........	Virginia	800 00
John Hutt..............do..	......do.........	....do..........	800 00
C. Langtree....Draughtsman	......do.........	Ireland.......	Paid by the plat.
D. F. Shall.............do..	......do.........	Tennessee ...	
V. Sevier..............Clerk	......do.........	....do..........	Paid by the piece.
J. H. Crease.............do..	......do.........	England........	Paid by the 100 words.
(Florida.)			
Robert Butler.....Surv. Gen'l	St. Augustine, Fla.	Pennsylvania ..	2000 00
Albert A. Nunes..Draughts'n	......do.........	Jamaica.........	1100 00
B. F. Whitner, jr......Clerk	......do.........	South Carolina.	1100 00
(Vacancy)...............do..	......do.........	....	800 00
(Iowa and Wisconsin.)			
Geo. W. Jones...Surv. Gen'l	Du Buque, Iowa..	Indiana	1500 00
Elisha Dwelle....Chief Clerk	......do.........	Massachusetts .	1200 00
James A. Reid........Clerk	......do.........	Michigan ...	Paid by the piece or 100 words.
Henry A. Wiltse.......do..	......do.........	New York..	
George L. Nightingale...do..	......do.........	England.....	
Patrick Quigley.........do..	......do.........	Ireland	
George Ord Karrick.....do..	......do.........	Pennsylvania	
RECORDER OF LAND TITLES IN MISSOURI.			
Loren Spencer..............	St. Louis.........	Vermont	500 00

UNITED STATES MINT.

Names and offices.	Where employed.	Where born.	Compensation.
Robert M. Patterson...Director	Philadelphia.....	Pennsylvania.	$3500 00
Isaac Roach.........Treasurer	......do.......	......do.....	2000 00
Franklin Peale....Chief Coiner	......do.......	......do.....	2000 00
Jacob R. Eckfeldt......Assayer	......do.......	......do.....	2000 00
Jonas R. McClintock, Melter and Refiner..................	......do.......	......do.....	2000 00
James B. Longacre...Engraver	......do.......	......do.....	2000 00
William E. Duboise, Ass. Ass'r	......do.......	......do.....	1300 00
Randal Hutchenson......Clerk	......do.......	......do.....	1100 00
Edw. Sprague, Cl'k Weigh-room	......do.......	......do.....	1200 00
Geo. W. Edelman..Bookkeeper	......do.......	......do.....	1100 00
Robt. Patterson, Director's Clerk	......do.......	......do.....	1000 00
BRANCH MINT AT NEW ORLEANS.			
Jos. M. Kennedy, Superintend't	New Orleans....	Louisiana	2500 00
William P. Hort.......Assayer	......do.......	......do.....	2000 00
Philos B. Tyler.........Coiner	......do.......	Massachusetts	2000 00
John L. Riddell, Melter and Refiner..................	......do.......	Louisiana	2000 00
F. W. Smythe...........Clerk	......do.......	......do.....	1200 00
Martin Kennedy.........Clerk	......do.......	......do.....	1200 00
BRANCH MINT AT DAHLONEGA, GEORGIA.			
Jas. F. Cooper..Superintendent	Dahlonega.......	Georgia.......	2000 00
Isaac L. Todd.........Assayer	......do.......	......do.....	1500 00
David H. Mason, Coiner, Melter, and Refiner..............	......do.......	......do.....	1500 00
William Grisham........Clerk	......do.......	......do.....	1000 00
BRANCH MINT AT CHARLOTTE, NORTH CAROLINA.			
G. W. Caldwell, Superintendent	Charlotte.......	......do.....	2000 00
John H. Gibbon.......Assayer	......do.......	Pennsylvania .	1500 00
J. R. Bolton...........Coiner	......do.......	......do.....	1500 00
William F. Strange......Clerk	......do.......	......do.....	1000 00

ATTORNEY GENERAL.—JUDICIARY—*Supreme Court, &c.*

Names and offices.	Where employed.	Where born.	Compensat'n.
OFFICE OF THE ATTORNEY GENERAL OF THE UNITED STATES.			
ATTORNEY GENERAL.			
John Y. Mason	Washington	Virginia	$4000 00
CLERK.			
John T. Reid	do	Scotland	1000 00
MESSENGER.			
Henry A. Klopfer	do	Maryland	500 00

JUDICIARY.

Names and offices.	Residence.	Where born.	Compensat'n.
SUPREME COURT OF THE U. S.			
Chief Justice.			
Roger B. Taney	Baltimore	Maryland	$5000 00
Associate Justices.			
John McLean	Cincinnati, Ohio	New Jersey	4500 00
James M. Wayne	Savannah, Geo.	Georgia	4500 00
John Catron	Nashville, Tenn	Virginia	4500 00
John McKinley	Louisville, Ky.	do	4500 00
Peter V. Daniel	Richmond, Va.	do	4500 00
Samuel Nelson	Cooperst'n, N.Y		4500 00
Levi Woodbury	Portsm'th, N.H	N. Hampshire	4500 00
(One vacancy.)			4500 00
William T. Carroll.....Clerk	Washington	Maryland	Fees, &c.
D. W. Middleton..Dep. Clerk	do	Dist. Columbia.	Fees.
Benj'n C. Howard..Reporter	Baltimore	Maryland	1300 00

JUDICIARY—*District Courts.*

Names and offices.	Residence.	Where born.	Compensat'n.
DISTRICT COURTS OF THE U. S.*			
Maine.			
Ashur Ware, Judge........	Portland.......	Massachusetts .	$1800 00
Augustine Haines, Attorney..	......do......	N. Hampshire.	200 & fees.
Virgil D. Parris, Marshal....	Paris..........	Maine	200 & fees.
New Hampshire.			
Mathew Harvey, Judge......	Hopkinton	N. Hampshire.	1000 00
Franklin Pierce, Attorney....	Concord.......	....	200 & fees.
Cyrus Barton, Marshal......	Hopkinton	N. Hampshire.	200 & fees.
Massachusetts.			
Peleg Sprague, Judge........	Boston........	Massachusetts .	2500 00
Robt. Rantoul, jr., Attorney..	......do......	......do......	200 & fees.
Isaac O. Barnes, Marshal....	......do......	N. Hampshire.	Fees.
Connecticut.			
Andrew T. Judson, Judge....	Canterbury....	Connecticut....	1500 00
Jonathan Stoddard, Attorney..	New Haven...	......do......	200 & fees.
Benning Mann, Marshal.....	Hartford......	N. Hampshire.	200 & fees.
Rhode Island.			
John Pitman, Judge.........	Providence	Rhode Island..	1500 00
Walter S. Burges, Attorney..	......do......	Massachusetts .	200 & fees.
Burrington Anthony, Marshal	......do......	Rhode Island..	200 & fees.
Vermont.			
Samuel Prentiss, Judge......	Montpelier	Connecticut.....	1200 00
Charles Linsley, Attorney...	Middlebury....	Vermont.......	200 & fees.
Jacob Kent, Marshal........	Well's River...	....	200 & fees.
Northern District of New York.			
Alfred Conkling, Judge......	Auburn.......	New York......	2000 00
William F. Allen, Attorney..	Oswego	......do......	200 & fees.
Jacob Gould, Marshal.......	Rochester	Massachusetts .	200 & fees.
Southern District of New York.			
Samuel R. Betts, Judge......	New York.....	New York.....	3500 00

* Including other courts in the District of Columbia.

JUDICIARY—*District Courts.*

Names and offices.	Residence.	Where born.	Compensat'n.
Benjamin F. Butler, Attorney.	New York		Fees.
Ely Moore, Marshal	do.	New Jersey	Fees.
New Jersey.			
Philemon Dickerson, Judge	Patterson	New York	$1500 00
James S. Green, Attorney	Princeton	Pennsylvania	200 & fees.
Samuel McClurg, Marshal	Trenton	do.	200 & fees.
Eastern Dist. of Pennsylvania.			
Archibald Randall, Judge	Philadelphia	Pennsylvania	2500 00
Thomas M. Pettit, Attorney	do.	do.	200 & fees.
Geo. M. Keim, Marshal	do.	Pennsylvania	Fees.
Western Dist. of Pennsylvania.			
Thomas Irwin, Judge	Pittsburg	Pennsylvania	1800 00
John L. Dawson, Attorney	Brownsville	do.	200 & fees.
Samuel Hays, Marshal	Pittsburg	Ireland	200 & fees.
Delaware.			
Willard Hall, Judge	Wilmington	Delaware	1500 00
William H. Rogers, Attorney	New Castle	do.	200 & fees.
Alexander Porter, Marshal	Wilmington	do.	200 & fees.
Maryland.			
Upton S. Heath, Judge	Baltimore	Maryland	2000 00
William L. Marshal, Attorney	do.	Kentucky	200 & fees.
Moreau Forrest, Marshal	do.	Virginia	Fees.
Eastern District of Virginia.			
James D. Hallyburton, Judge	New Kent C. H	do.	1800 00
Robert C. Nicholas, Attorney	Richmond	do.	200 & fees.
Edmund Christian, Marshal	do.	do.	200 & fees.
Western District of Virginia.			
Isaac S. Pennybacker, Judge	New Market	do.	1600 00
Moses C. Good, Attorney	Wheeling	Maryland	200 & fees.
James Points, Marshall	Staunton	Virginia	200 & fees.
North Carolina.			
H. Potter, Judge	Raleigh	do.	2000 00
Duncan K. McRae, Attorney	Fayetteville	North Carolina	200 & fees.
Wesley Jones, Marshal	Raleigh	do.	400 & fees.

JUDICIARY—*District Courts.*

Names and offices.	Residence.	Where born.	Compensat'n.
South Carolina.			
Robert B. Gilchrist, judge....	Charleston	South Carolina.	$2500 00
Edward McCrady, attorney.	......do......	......do......	200 & fees.
Thomas D. Condy, marshal...	......do......	......do......	Fees.
Georgia.			
J. C. Nicoll, judge..........	Savannah	Georgia........	2500 00
Henry R. Jackson, attorney..	......do......	......do......	200 & fees.
Henderson Willingham, marshal..................	......do......	......do......	200 & fees.
Northern District of Alabama.			
William Crawford, judge....	Mobile........	Virginia........	2500 00
Joseph A. S. Acklin, attorney	Huntsville.....	Alabama......	200 & fees.
Benjamin Patteson, marshal..	......do......	Virginia.......	200 & fees.
Southern District of Alabama.			
William Crawford, judge....	Mobile........	Virginia........	2500 00
Geo. J. S. Walker, attorney..	Cahaba........	Georgia........	200 & fees.
William Armistead, marshal..	Mobile........	Virginia........	200 & fees.
Northern District of Mississippi.			
Samuel J. Gholson, judge....	Athens........	Kentucky	2000 00
Oscar F. Bledsoe, attorney...	Columbus......	Tennessee	200 & fees.
And'w A. Kincannon, marshal	......do......	North Carolina.	200 & fees.
Southern District of Mississippi.			
Samuel J. Gholson, judge....	Athens........	Kentucky	2000 00
Richard M. Gaines, attorney.	Natchez........	......do......	200 & fees.
Thomas Fletcher, marshal ...	Jackson	Tennessee.......	200 & fees.
Louisiana.			
Theodore H. McCaleb, judge.	New Orleans...	Mississippi......	3000 00
Solomon W. Downs, attorney	......do......	Tennessee......	600 & fees.
William F. Wagner, marshal..	......do......	Louisiana	200 & fees.
Eastern District of Tennessee.			
Morgan W. Brown, judge...	Nashville......	Tennessee	1500
Thomas C. Lyon, attorney...	Knoxville	......do......	200 & fees.
Arthur R. Crozier, marshal...	......do......	......do......	200 & fees.

JUDICIARY—*District Courts.*

Names and offices.	Residence.	Where born.	Compensat'n.
Middle District of Tennessee.			
Morgan W. Brown, judge...	Nashville......	Tennessee.....	$1500 00
Thomas D. Mosely, attorney.	......do......	......do......	200 & fees.
Benj'n H. Sheppard, marshal.	......do......	North Carolina.	200 & fees.
Western District of Tennessee.			
Morgan W. Brown, judge...	Nashville.......	Tennessee.....	1500 00
Henry W. McCorry, attorney	Jackson	......do......	200 & fees.
Robert J. Chester, marshal...	......do......	Pennsylvania..	200 & fees.
Kentucky.			
Thomas B. Monroe, judge...	Frankfort......	Kentucky.....	1500 00
P. S. Loughborough, attorney	Louisville.....	......do......	200 & fees.
John Lane, marshal.........	Shelbyville	Pennsylvania ..	200 & fees.
Ohio.			
Humphrey H. Leavitt, judge.	Steubenville....	New Jersey....	1500 00
Thomas W. Bartley, attorney	Mansfield......	Ohio..........	200 & fees.
Daniel A. Robertson, marshal	Lancaster......	Pennsylvania ..	200 & fees.
Indiana.			
Elisha M. Huntington, judge.	Terre Haute...	New York.....	1500 00
Daniel Mace, attorney......	Lafayette......	Ohio..........	200 & fees.
Abel C. Pepper, marshal.....	Rising Sun	Virginia.......	200 & fees.
Illinois.			
Nathaniel Pope, judge.......	Kaskaskia.....	Kentucky.....	1500 00
David L. Gregg, attorney....	Chicago.......	New York.....	200 & fees.
Stinson H. Anderson, marshal	Mount Vernon.	Tennessee.....	200 & fees.
Missouri.			
Robert W. Wells, judge.....	Jefferson city ..	Virginia......	1500 00
Thomas T. Gantt, attorney ..	St. Louis......	Dist. Columbia.	200 & fees.
Robert C. Ewing, marshal ...	Richmond.....	Kentucky.....	200 & fees.
Arkansas.			
Benjamin Johnson, judge....	Little Rock....	Virginia.......	2000 00
Sam'l H. Hempstead, attorney	......do......	Connecticut....	200 & fees.
Elias Rector, marshal........	Van Buren	Arkansas......	200 & fees.

JUDICIARY—*District Courts.*

Names and offices.	Residence.	Where born.	Compensat'n.
Michigan.			
Ross Wilkins, judge	Detroit	Pennsylvania	$1500 00
John Norvell, attorney	do	Kentucky	200 & fees.
Levi S. Humphrey, marshal	do	Michigan	200 & fees.
Eastern District of Florida.			
Isaac H. Bronson, judge	St. Augustine	Connecticut	2300 00
Thomas Douglass, attorney	do	do	200 & fees.
John Beard, marshal	do	North Carolina	200 & fees.
Middle District of Florida.			
Samuel J. Douglass, judge	Tallahassee	Virginia	1800 00
Charles S. Sibley, attorney	do	New Jersey	200 & fees.
(Vacant,) marshal			200 & fees.
Western District of Florida.			
Dillon Jordan, jr., judge	Pensacola	North Carolina	1800 00
Chandler C. Yonge, attorney	Mariana	Florida	200 & fees.
(Vacant,) marshal			200 & fees.
Southern District of Florida.			
William Marvin, judge	Key West	Dist. Columbia	2300 00
Geo. W. Macrae, attorney	do		200 & fees.
Joseph B. Browne, marshal	do	Virginia	200 & fees.
Apalachicola District, in Florida.			
(Vacant,) judge			1800 00
(Vacant,) attorney			200 & fees.
(Vacant,) marshal			200 & fees.
Supreme Court of Wisconsin.			
Charles Dunn, chief justice	Elk Grove	Kentucky	1800 00
David Irvine, associate judge	Madison	Virginia	1800 00
Andrew G. Miller do	Milwaukie	Pennsylvania	1800 00
William P. Lynde, attorney	do	New York	250 & fees.
John S. Rockwell, marshal	do	do	250 & fees.
Supreme Court of Iowa.			
Charles Mason, chief justice	Burlington	do	1800 00
T. S. Wilson, associate judge	Du Buque	Ohio	1800 00
Joseph Williams do	Bloomington	Pennsylvania	1800 00

JUDICIARY—*District Courts.*

Names and offices.	Residence.	Where born.	Compensat'n.
Edward Johnston, attorney..	Fort Madison..	Pennsylvania..	200 & fees.
Gideon S. Bailey, marshal...	Bentonsport...	Kentucky.....	200 & fees.
District of Columbia.			
William Cranch, chief judge.	Washington...	Massachusetts.	*2700 00
James S. Morsel, assis'nt judge	Georgetown...	Maryland.....	2500 00
One vacancy....do...do..	....	....	2500 00
James Hoban, attorney......	Washington...	Dist. of Colum.	Fees.
Alexander Hunter, marshal..	......do......	Virginia.......	do
William Brent, clerk........	......do......	......do.......	do
Cassius F. Lee..do..........	Alexandria....	Dist. of Colum.	do
Orphans' Court of Washington county, D. C.			
Nathaniel P. Causin, judge..	Washington...	Maryland.....	1000 00
Ed. N. Roach, register of wills	......do......	......do......	Fees.
Orphans' Court of Alexandria county, D. C.			
Christopher Neale, judge.....	Alexandria....	Virginia.......	1000 00
Bernard Hooe, register of wills	......do......	......do......	Fees.
Criminal Court, D. C.			
James Dunlop, judge........	Georgetown...	Maryland.....	2000 00
Levy Court for Washington county, D. C.			
J. F. Cox..................	Washington...	Pennsylvania..	
Henry Naylor..............	......do......	Dist. of Colum.	
Joshua Peirce..............	Georgetown...	Maryland.....	
John Cox..................	......do......	Pennsylvania..	
Lewis Carbery..............	......do......	Maryland.....	
Robert White..............	......do......	......do......	

*Allowed $100 additional from the Patent fund.

JUDICIARY—*Justices of the Peace.*

JUSTICES OF THE PEACE IN THE DISTRICT OF COLUMBIA.

Names and residence.		Where born.	Compensat'n.
For Washington county.			
Addison, Henry	Georgetown		Fees.
Brady, Nathaniel	Washington	Maryland	do.
Beck, Jos. W.	do	do.	do.
Clark, John D.	do	Virginia.	do.
Callan, N. C., jr.	do	Dist. of Colum.	do.
Cox, J. F.	do	Pennsylvania	do.
Cox, John	Georgetown	do.	do.
Carbery, Lewis	do	Maryland	do.
Carbery, Thomas	Washington	do.	do.
Coote, Clement T.	do	England	do.
Crandell, James	do	Maryland	do.
Clements, Robt. H.	do	Virginia.	do.
Drury, Samuel	do	Maryland	do.
Donn, T. C.	do	do.	do.
Donoho, Thomas	do	do.	do.
Fearson, Jos. N.	Georgetown	Virginia.	do.
French, Benj. B.	Washington	N. Hampshire.	do.
Goddard, John H.	do	Rhode Island	do.
Holtzman, Thomas	Georgetown		do.
Hogmire, Conrad	do	Maryland	do.
Hampton, Thos. R.	Washington	Virginia.	do.
Howison, Henry	do	do.	do.
King, Samuel D.	do	Dist. of Colum.	do.
Kane, Theodore	do	New York	do.
Lawrenson, James	do	England	do.
Morsell, B. K	do	Maryland	do.
Mackall, B. F.	Georgetown	do.	do.
Marshall, James	Washington	Pennsylvania.	do.
Milburn, Benedict	do	Maryland	do.
Mattingly, Edward	do	do.	do.
Nourse, C. J.	do	New York	do.
Naylor, Henry	do	Dist. of Colum.	do.
Plater, Wm.	Georgetown	Maryland	do.
Peirce, Joshua	do	do.	do.
Reaver, Henry	do	Pennsylvania	do.
Stewart, Wm. W.	Washington	Dist. of Colum.	do.
Smith, A. T.	do		do.
Stull, John I.	Georgetown	Maryland	do.
Stettinius, Samuel	Washington	Dist. of Colum.	do.
Smallwood, E. W.	do	do.	do.
Smoot, Samuel	do	Maryland	do.
Smith, John L.	do	Dist. of Colum.	do.
Saunders, David	do	Virginia	do.
Thompson, Wm.	do	England	do.

JUDICIARY—*Justices of the Peace—Insolvent Commissioners.*

Names and residence.		Where born.	Compensat'n.
Van Zandt, N. B.	Washington	Delaware	Fees.
Walker, Z.	do	Maryland	do
Wiltberger, C. H.	do	Pennsylvania	do
Waters, Wm.	do	Maryland	do
Watts, Richard K.	do	do	do
Williams, H. C.	do	Georgia	do
White, Robert	Georgetown	Maryland	do
For Alexandria county.			
Ball, Horatio	Alexandria	Virginia	do
Brockett, Robert	do	do	do
Custis, Geo. W. P.	do	do	do
Eaches, Joseph	do	do	do
Fowle, Wm.	do	Massachusetts	do
Grubb, John	do	Maryland	do
Harris, Joseph	do	New Jersey	do
Hooe, Bernard	do	Virginia	do
Johnston, Reuben	do	Dist. of Colum.	do
McKnight, C.	do	Maryland	do
Mills, Wm. N.	do	Virginia	do
Snowden, Edgar	do	Dist. of Colum.	do
Scott, Charles	do	Maryland	do

INSOLVENT COMMISSIONERS OF THE UNITED STATES.*

Names and offices.		Names and offices.	
Dist. of Maine.	Allen Haines	Dist. of W. Pa.	Wm. G. Hawkins.
Do....Mass	Edward Crafts Andrew H. Ward	Do....Md.	T. Watkins Ligon Wm. L. Marshall
Do....N. H.	Jotham Lawrence	Do....D. C.	William Hebb
Do....Conn.	Robinson S. Kinman	Do....Ga.	Richard B. Cuyler Mordecai Myers
Do....N.Y.	Charles Taylor Elijah Yerks Samuel A. Crapo	Do....Ala.	Joseph Seawell
Do....N. J.	H. C. Boswell	Do....S. C.	Benjamin Elliott Martin Strobel James Hervey
Do....E.Pa.	Ed. D. Ingraham James M. Broom Sam'l H. Perkins	Do....Florida	Geo. Centre
		Do....Ky.	Alex'r R. Defew

*These Commissioners are paid out of the estates of insolvents claiming their services.

MISCELLANEOUS—*Governors of Territories, &c.*

MISCELLANEOUS.

Names and offices.	Residence.	Where born.	Compensat'n.
GOVERNORS OF TERRITORIES.			
Wisconsin.			
Henry Dodge	Madison	Indiana	$2500 00
Iowa.			
John Chambers	Burlington	New Jersey	2500 00
SECRETARIES OF TERRITORIES.			
Wisconsin.			
George K. Floyd	Madison	Virginia	1200 00
Iowa.			
Jesse Williams	Iowa City	Ohio	1200 00
COMMISSIONER			
Under the 6th article of Treaty of the United States with Great Britain, of 9th August, 1842.			
Albert Smith		Maine	3000 00
Edward Webster, clerk			1500 00
PUBLIC BUILDINGS.			
Wm. Noland, Commissioner.	Washington	Virginia	2000 00
POLICE OF THE CAPITOL.			
David M. Wilson, Principal	do.	Maryland	1450 00
James D. Waller, Assistant	do.	do.	1100 00
Thomas Scrivener, do.	do.	Dist. Columbia.	1100 00
Isaac H. Wailes, do.	do.	Maryland	1100 00
John L. Wirt, do.	do.	do.	1100 00
James Wilson, Watchman	do.	do.	547 00
Patr'k Heffernan, Lamplighter	do.	England	360 00

MISCELLANEOUS—*Secretary for signing Land Patents, &c.*

Names and offices.	Residence.	Where born.	Compensat'n.
C. Hoffman, Ass't Lamplighter	Washington ...	England.......	$216 00
James Maher, Princ'l Gardener	......do......	Ireland	1200 00
Patrick Bulger..............	......do......	......do......	730 00
Hannibal Graham............	......do......	Maryland	300 00
SECRETARY			
To the President for signing Land Patents.			
J. K. Walker	Washington ...	Tennessee	1500 00
KEEPERS			
Of Archives in Florida.			
Antonio Alvarez............	St. Augustine..	....	500 00
Joseph E. Caro.............	Pensacola	....	500 00
PENITENTIARY			
In the District of Columbia.			
Robert Coltman .....Warden	Washington....	Dist. Columbia.	1500 00
Geo. W. Phillips ...Inspector	......do......	Maryland	250 00
Richard Jones..........do..	Georgetown ...	......do......	250 00
William Minor.........do..	Alexandria Co.	Virginia.......	250 00
William Minor, jr., Secretary to Inspectors.......	......do......	......do......	200 00
Benj'n S. Bohrer...Physician	Georgetown ...	Dist. Columbia.	500 00
John B. Furgerson..Chaplain	Washington....	Maryland	250 00
William Wheatly......Clerk	......do......	......do......	1000 00
John A. Young..Ass't Keeper	......do......	Germany......	750 00
James Parsons.......do....	......do......	Dist. Columbia.	750 00
Geo. B. Smith.......do....	......do......	Virginia.......	750 00
Wilfred Van Reswick..Guard	......do......	Maryland	550 00
Michael Nash..........do..	......do......	Ireland........	550 00
Benjamin F. Dyer ......do..	......do......	Maryland	550 00
Richard Pierce..........do..	......do......	......do......	550 00
Charles Fraler...........do..	......do......	Pennsylvania ..	550 00
Thomas Sutton....Messenger	......do......	Dist. Columbia.	180 00

MISCELLANEOUS—*Library of Congress, &c.*

Names and offices.	Residence.	Where Born.	Compensat'n.
LIBRARY OF CONGRESS.			
John S. Meehan....Librarian	Washington....	New York.....	$1500 00
Edward B. Stelle, Asst..do..	......do.......	Dist. Columbia.	1150 00
Chas. H. W. Meehan...do..	......do......	Pennsylvania ..	1150 00
Robert Kearon....Messenger	......do......	Maryland	700 00
WASHINGTON CITY GUARD.			
J. H. Goddard, Captain......	Washington....	Rhode Island..	1000 00
Five others................	......do.......	....	35each p.m.
Ten others................	......do.......	....	30....do...
WEIGHTS AND MEASURES.			
Alexander D. Bache, Superintendent and Disbursing Agt.	....	....	1500 00
Jos. Saxton, Assistant and Foreman................	....	....	1800 00
COAST SURVEY.			
Alexander D. Bache, Superintendent............	....	....	Comp. $4500, exp's. $1500.
James Ferguson....Assistant	....	....	3500 00
Edmund Blunt..........do...	....	....	3500 00
C. M. Eakin...........do...	....	....	3500 00
W. M. Boyce...........do...	....	....	2000 00
F. H. Gerdes..........do...	....	....	2000 00
John Farley...........do...	....	....	2000 00
T. T. S. Hassler.......do...	....	....	1500 00
H. L. Whiting.........do...	....	....	1500 00
W. M. C. Fairfax......do...	....	....	1200 00
Theo. W. Werner.......do...	....	....	1000 00
T. B. Gluck...........do...	....	....	1000 00
T. C. Neilson.........do...	....	....	1000 00
Geo. D. Wise..........do...	....	....	1000 00
Richard D. Cutts......do...	....	....	1000 00
Charles O. Bouteller...do...	....	....	1000 00
Samuel Hein, Disburs'g Officer	....	....	1500 00

PRINTING—*Department of State.*

Names.	Nature of Printing.	Compensation.
From 1st	*October*, 1843, *to 30th September*, 1845.	
B. Chambers	Blank commissions, exequaturs, &c. &c., copper plate................	$163 80
J. & G. S. Gideon....	Laws 28th Congress, 1st sess., Biennial Register, blanks, &c.........	3921 09
Alexander & Barnard.	Sea letters	11 12
Wm. Greer	Laws 2d session 28th Congress.....	980 00
Wm. Q. Force	Blanks, circular, &c................	66 48
	Advertising.	
Th. Fisk............	Notice death of American citizen....	50
Anson Herrick.......	Notice deaths of American citizens .	3 50
Hale & Hallock......	Settlement with Chile	2 25
Miller & Mœller	Treaty with Wyandots...............	42 00
B. D. Foster & Co ...	Notice deaths of citizens..........	2 26
J. B. Jones..........	Proposals for print'g, &c., equa'rs, &c.	344 50
Spirit of the Times...	Notice death of citizen	1 25
D. N. White	....do....do....do.	1 00
Joseph Ristice	Proclamation calling extra session ..	5 00
Estate J.C.de St.Romes	Notice deaths of citizens, indemnity for slaves, &c..................	118 00
Gales & Seaton.......	Notice to publishers, proposals printing, &c.........................	22 12
Harris & Heart.......	Proposals for printing, &c..........	16 25
P. A. Sage	Exequaturs	10 00
J. E. Dow & Co.......	....do....proposals for printing, &c.	18 25
Ritchie & Heiss......	Relating to postage and publishers, proposals for printing and station'y	31 25
Caleb Foote	Death of American citizen.........	1 00

PUBLISHERS OF LAWS, 28th CONGRESS.

Names.	Sums allowed.	
	1st session.	2d session.
John B. Jones	$156 00	$130 00
Gales & Seaton..............................	156 00	130 00
Harris & Heart..............................	....	130 00
P. A. Sage	156 00	....
J. G. Klenck	....	130 00

PRINTING—*Patent Office—War Department.*

Names.	Nature of work done.	Compensation.
George Roberts	Advertising	$91 00
Herrick & Ropes	....do	3 00
Hale & Hallock	....do	13 23
A. S. Abel & Co	....do	77 45
Anson Herrick	....do	29 89
Peter Hay & Co	....do	15 00
William Faulkner	....do	2 00
Gales & Seaton	....do	105 18
John B. Jones	....do	107 25
Thomas Dunn English	....do	24 00
John H. Frick	....do	57 87
Severns & Magill	....do	74 05
Pierre Deverge	....do	12 00
Blair & Rives	....do	15 81
Harris & Heart	....do	50 00
J. E. Dow & Co	....do	61 62
J. M. Church	....do	52 12
Beals & Green	....do	51 63
E. & S. Croswell	....do	6 65
W. F. & T. Ritchie, jr.	....do	7 87
Pratt, Cloud & Bro	....do	38 68
Ritchie & Heiss	....do	44 00
Edmund Charles	....do	38 68
John H. Guinan	....do	41 62
Harney, Smith & Hughes	....do	42 59
J. & G. S. Gideon	Printing and binding	536 00
John M. Collem	Printing	37 50
Gales & Seaton	....do	13 12
John P. Stalling	....do	4 00
C. P. Sengstack	....do	63 98

PRINTERS—*War Department.*

Names.	Compensation.	By whom employed.
		Secretary of War.
John B. Jones	$174 00	Advertising
Alexander & Barnard	87 50	By contract under act of August 26, 1842
Jesse E. Dow & Co	21 25	Advertising
Gales & Seaton	30 31	....do
Ritchie & Heiss	28 00	....do
Pratt & Co	57 87½	Comm'r of Indian Affairs
A. Sage	58 00	..........do

PRINTING—*War Department.*

Names.	Compensation.	By whom employed.
L. H. Steck	62 12½	Comm'r of Indian Affairs
Herrick & Ropes	53 90½	do
William Simons	28 00	do
Severns & McGill	137 40	do
Salisbury, Manchester & Co	63 88	do
Peter Hay & Co	48 00	do
James A. Dunlap	40 00	do
G. Roberts	117 00	do
V. Scribe	43 00	do
J. M. Church	117 00	do
Isaac Hill & Son	13 50	do
Beals & Green	83 25	do
Alexander & Barnard	739 33	do
V. Ellis	38 50	do
John B. Jones	165 50	do
S. Penn	22 50	do
G. A. Newman	32 50	do
John H. Frick	32 00	do
William Faulkner	25 00	do
T. D. English	59 50	do
Thomas Todd	24 00	do
Philips & Smith	26 00	do
Miller & Mœller	49 00	do
Blair & Rives	40 10	Commiss'er of Pensions.
Gales & Seaton	14 00	do
J. B. Jones	30 00	do
Alexander & Barnard	845 75	do

Names.	Nature of work done.	Compensation.
QUARTERMASTER'S DEPARTMENT.		
Alexander & Barnard	Clothing estimates Quartermaster General's Office	$22 50
Do	Blank requisitions Quatermaster General's Office	5 00
Do	Blanks, Quartermaster General's Office	5 00
Do	Blank forms, Assistant Quartermaster's Office	14 00
Do	do do	8 00
Do	do do	8 00
Gibson & Hibbard	do do	15 00
J. B. Jones	do for Pay Department	60 00
C. Alexander	do do	17 50

PRINTING—*War Department.*

Names.	Nature of work done.	Compensation.
Alexander & Barnard	Final statement of soldiers' clothing accounts, Quartermaster General's Office	$60 00
C. Alexander	Certificates of muster of horses	2 00
T. Barnard	Blank forms, Assistant Quartermaster's Office	7 00
Do	do do	11 00
C. Alexander	2,000 copies military resources of the West	65 00
T. Barnard	2 check books, Assist. Quartermaster	16 00
Do	Blank forms do	7 00
Do	Final statements Qartermaster General's Office	86 25
ENGINEER DEPARTMENT.		
Alexander & Barnard	To furnish paper and print 7 reams of cadet class reports	36 00
Do	To furnish paper and print 1 ream of blank requisitions	7 00
Do	To furnish paper and print 1½ reams of regulations for admission of cadets to military academy	9 00
Do	To furnish paper and print ½ ream of cadet appointments	4 00
Do	To furnish paper and print ½ ream of extracts from regulations of the military academy	10 00
Theodore Barnard	To furnish paper and print 4 reams of cadet class reports	10 00
William Q. Force	To furnish paper and print 250 copies of "Papers on Practical Engineering"	61 20
TOPOGRAPHICAL ENGINEERS.		
Alexander & Barnard		177 00
John Windt		33 67
C. Alexander		64 00

PRINTING—*War Department.*

Names.	Nature of work.	Compensation.	Where employed.
ORDNANCE DEPARTMENT.			
Alexander & Barnard	Printing blanks	$63 50	Washington
Theodore Barnard	do	27 50	do
Blair & Rives	Advertising proposals	18 00	do
Gales & Seaton	do	26 00	do
J. B. Jones	do	40 50	do
Phillips & Smith	do	27 50	Pittsburgh, Pa
T. D. English	do	40 50	New York
A. S. Abell & Co	do	18 90	Baltimore
J. M. Church	do	40 50	Providence, R. I
S. Penn	do	10 00	St. Louis, Mo
A. Wright	do	40 50	Norwich, Conn

Names.	Compensation.	By whom employed.
SUBSISTENCE DEPARTMENT.		
Duhy, Graham & Williams	$150 00	Com. Gen'l Subsistence.
James A. Dunlap	75 00	do
W. W. Holden	21 00	do
J. R. Chandler	42 00	do
J. B. Marshall	82 50	do
Miller & Mœller	186 25	do
Morgan Bates	45 50	do
George Roberts	316 75	do
J. S. Abell & Co	205 06	do
Isaac Hill & Son	71 55	do
Alexander & Barnard	44 83	do
Peter Hay & Co	50 37	do
Bragg & Harmon	78 75	do
J. B. Jones	276 00	do
T. D. English	75 00	do
J. H. Steck	50 00	do
Severns & Magill	74 37	do
Salisbury, Manchester & Co	70 30	do
W. Faulkner	77 50	do
Keuster, Elwell & Co	36 00	do
J. M. Church	140 00	do
T. S. Luckett	76 00	do
V. Ellis	72 50	do
Phillips & Smith	22 50	do
Brough, Robinson & Martin	40 00	do
Dobbin, Murphy & Bose	24 50	do
C. McIntyre & Co	51 00	do
Flinn & Kaine	20 00	do

PRINTING—*War Department.*

Names.	Compensation.	By whom employed.
Brough & Robinson	$36 00	Com. Gen'l Subsistence.
Ritchie & Heiss	197 75	do
C. C. & G. H. Hazewell	25 00	do
John H. Guion	40 00	do
E. & S. Croswell	41 25	do
Bigler, Sargent & Bigler	40 00	do
Harney, Smith & Hughes	48 00	do
PAY DEPARTMENT.		
Alexander & Barnard	$26 00	
Theodore Barnard	13 50	

Names.	Nature of work done.	Compensation.
MEDICAL DEPARTMENT.		
Washington City.		
Alexander & Barnard	For printing and ruling 4 reams of returns for medical and hospital stores and 1 ream of requisitions for Medical and hospital stores for distribution to military posts	$60 00
Do	For printing and ruling 2,000 copies of meteorological register, form No. 3, and 700 copies of meteorological register, form No. 4, for distribution to military posts	152 50
Do	For printing quires circulars in relation to sulphate of quinine	4 00
Do	For printing 4 quires duplicate contingent vouchers	4 00
Do	For printing 200 circular letters of invitation to candidates for examination before Army Medical Board	5 00
Do	For printing 150 circulars in relation to salicine	4 00
New York.		
N. Y. Courier & Enquirer	For advertising meetings of medical board	2 00
Do	For advertising for hospital steward	2 00
New York Evening Post	For advert'g meeting of medical board	1 50
New York Comm'l Adv.	do do do	1 25

PRINTING—*War Department—Navy Department.*

Names.	Nature of work done.	Compensation.
New York American	For advert'g meeting of medical board.	$1 50
New York Journal Com.	......do........do........do.	2 00
Joseph H. Jennings	For printing 500 copies meteorological directions and 300 tables pasted on boards	235 38
H. Ludwig	For printing 1 ream invoices of medical and hospital stores	11 00
W. C. Bryant	For advert'g meeting of medical board.	1 13
Hale & Hallock	......do........do........do.	1 50
J. W. Webb	......do........do........do.	1 50
ADJUTANT GENERAL'S OFFICE.		
Alexander & Barnard	For printing army registers, regulations, orders, &c	$1003 36
Do	For printing muster and pay rolls, returns, &c., &c	1432 72

PRINTING—*Navy Department.*

Names.	Compensation.	Nature of work done.
Duhrey, Graham &Co.	$112 00	Advertising proposals
A. Shucking	72 87	......do......do
A. F. Cunningham	511 00	......do......do
J. B. Jones	1573 12	......do......do
J. R. Chandler	38 50	......do......do
Pratt, Cloud & Co.	925 47	......do......do
Carroll & Baker	5 00	......do......do
George Roberts	1255 09	......do......do
A. Herrick	315 49	......do......do
Phillips & Smith	216 00	......do......do
Gales & Seaton	393 49	......do......do
P. A. Sage	108 25	......do......do
Blair & Rives	303 25	......do......do
Peter Hay & Co	357 67	......do......do
John Heart	181 50	......do......do
A. S. Abell & Co.	761 73	......do......do
Osburn & Baldwin	58 60	......do......do
John A. Stuart	88 10	......do......do
Wm. R. Smith & Co.	97 04	......do......do
Beals & Greene	594 24	......do......do
Isaac Hill & Sons	108 65	......do......do

PRINTING—*Navy Department.*

Names.	Compensation.	Nature of work done.
John H. Steck	$126 00	Advertising proposals
Walter & Weber	56 00	do do
Collins & Brown	38 00	do do
Graham & Williams	169 00	do do
Wm. Faulkner	35 00	do do
John S. Cunningham	56 50	do do
Vespasian Ellis	42 00	do do
Charleston Mercury	51 00	do do
Thomas Ritchie & Sons	269 11	do do
Miller & Mœller	102 25	do do
Severns & Magill	642 89	do do
O. S. Dermott	34 00	do do
Thos. Dunn English	292 20	do do
T. Y. N. Beach	178 25	do do
Swain, Abell & Simmons	413 98	do do
Jasper Harding	4 25	do do
Herrick & Ropes	138 75	do do
George Hawes	424 89	do do
Haswell & Bushnell	72 00	do do
Salisbury, Manchester & Co	155 40	do do
S. Medary	43 50	do do
Chambers & Knapp	35 00	do do
Boggs & Harmon	19 50	do do
D. C. Wickliffe	33 00	do do
Hale & Hallock	349 86	do do
Wm. C. Bryant & Co.	368 61	do do
True Sun, N. Y	157 50	do do
J. G. Bennett	192 51	do do
F. Hall & Co	2 00	do do
Commerc'l Adv., N.Y.	214 91	do do
John McKinley	157 50	do do
Wm. Simons, jr	139 06	do do
G. M. Church	233 00	do do
Rufus Green, jr	30 00	do do
Case & Holden	115 54	do do
John H. Eastburn	27 00	do do
C. W. Brewster	73 00	do do
Moses Greenleaf	124 19	do do
Wm. E. Cunningham	880 00	do do
T. G. Boughton & Co.	148 38	do do
Journal of Commerce	65 28	do do
Daily Times	5 50	do do
Daily Emporium	5 00	do do
Daily Keystone	18 75	do do
Illinois State Register	50 00	do do
Baltimore American	154 87	do do
Jesse E. Dow & Co	24 75	do do

PRINTING—*Navy Department.*

Names.	Compensation.	Nature of work done.
Harris & Heart	$124 50	Advertising proposals
John Frick	167 37	......do......do
Eliphalet Currier	2 75	......do......do
A. S. Willington & Co.	2 80	......do......do
C. B. Foster & Co.	44 28	......do......do
Mifflin & Parry	161 86	......do......do
S. Penn	20 50	......do......do
Thos. L. Luckett	78 93	......do......do
Bigler & Co.	47 25	......do......do
Charles Alexander	3 50	......do......do
Public Ledger	5 17	......do......do
M. Ballentine & Co.	22 00	......do......do
John T. Birch	12 62	......do......do
R. Geddes	4 00	......do......do
Townshend & Brooks	40 13	......do......do
J. D. Beniss	2 00	......do......do
Daily Plebeian	6 00	......do......do
American Sentinel	21 87	......do......do
J. Henderson	28 19	......do......do
J. N. Cardoza & Co.	2 80	......do......do
C. C. Childs	154 50	......do......do
Kenston, Elwell & Co.	15 00	......do......do
E. Charles	11 75	......do......do
Courier & Enquirer	19 50	......do......do
Daily News	78 00	......do......do
Lambert & Lane	6 50	......do......do
J. Van Auder	2 95	......do......do
Morning News	79 00	......do......do
John Wentworth	14 25	......do......do
J. N. Throop	10 00	Printing commisions on parchment
Alexander & Barnard	412 30	..do..Navy Register
........do	188 62	..do..various blank forms
........do	1627 52	..do..for Medical Bureau
........do	81 50	..do..for Bureau of Con. & Equip't
........do	4129 12	..do..for Bureau of Prov. & Cloth'g
Joseph R. Chandler	1 62	..do..for Com. Hull's funeral
A. Herrick	21 00	..do..weekly returns
Beals & Green	2705 86	..do..blank forms
Gales & Seaton	54 00	..do..docum'ts for President's mess.
C. G. Childs	4 25	..do..notice to attend funerals
John McKinley	82 00	..do..sundry blank forms, &c.
John C. Clark	22 00	..do..blank books
J. W. Bell	80 00	..do..labels, &c.
J. Van Auder	5 70	..do..blanks

PRINTING—*Treasury Department.*

Names and nature of work.	Amounts.	By whom employed.
J & G. S. Gideon..........Printing	$667 95	Secretary's Office........
Peter Hay & Co..............do....	24 99	........do............
G. M. Church...............do....	55 00	........do............
Severns & Magill............do....	46 62	........do............
Jesse E. Dow & Co..........do....	62 25	........do............
Ritchie & Heiss.............do....	110 00	........do............
W. Q. Force................do....	1571 62	........do............
B. Chambers................do....	4 00	........do............
Graham & Williams..........do....	68 50	........do............
Blair & Rives...............do....	192 87	........do............
Gales & Seaton..............do....	173 97	........do............
Hale & Hallock..............do....	16 13	........do............
J. R. Goodsell..............do....	4 00	........do............
P. A. Sage..................do....	117 62	........do............
Beals & Green...............do....	19 50	........do............
Harris & Hart...............do....	128 50	........do............
G. Roberts..................do....	96 37	........do............
Miller & Co.................do....	14 00	........do............
A. Herrick..................do....	7 00	........do............
E. D. Foster................do....	3 00	........do............
Abell & Co..................do....	3 85	........do............
J. B. Jones.................do....	529 50	........do............
Herrick & Ropes.............do....	7 00	........do............
J. G. Klenck................do....	37 50	........do............
J. & G. S. Gideon...........do....	647 50	1st Comptroller's Office..
William Q. Force............do....	39 37	........do............
J. & G. S. Gideon...........do....	22 00	2d Comptroller's Office..
Alexander & Barnard........do....	2 50	........do............
William Q. Force............do....	3 00	........do............
J. C. McGuire, binding and..do....	228 35	........do............
J. & G. S. Gideon...........do....	37 62	1st Auditor's Office.....
W. Q. Force.................do....	40 50	........do............
J. C. McGuire, Binding and..do....	14 00	........do............
J. & G. S. Gideon...........do....	56 00	2d Auditor's Office......
......Do........Paper and.do....	14 00	3d Auditor's Office......
......Do...........do.....do....	12 00	........do............
W. Q. Force.........do.....do....	15 00	........do............
J. C. McGuire...............do....	10 50	........do............
......Do........Paper and.do....	11 00	........do............
J. & G. S. Gideon.....do.....do....	33 25	4th Auditor's Office.....
W. Q. Force..........do.....do....	54 66	........do............
J. & G. S. Gideon...........do....	19 50	5th Auditor's Office.....
Blair & Rives...............do....	33 50	........do............
Gales & Seaton..............do....	12 50	........do............
W. Q. Force.................do....	14 33	........do............
B. Chambers, Engraving and..do....	125 00	........do............
C. Alexander................do....	197 75	........do............
J. & G. S. Gideon...........do....	167 00	Treasurer's Office.......
W. Q. Force.................do....	90 80	........do............

PRINTING—*General Land Office.*

Names and nature of work.	Amounts.	By whom employed.
Blair & Rives, for work done in July, 1841..........................Printing	$46 50	Treasurer's Office........
Rawdon, Wright & Hatch, half of their accounts for engraving plates for drafts, &c..........................	300 00	........do............
J. & G. S. Gideon..Paper and Print'g	16 25	Solicitor's Office........
W. Q. Force........do.....do....	11 75	........do............
J. & G. S. Gideon....do.....do....	1457 87	Register's Office........
J. C. McGuire.......do.....do....	1455 00	........do............
W. Q. Force........do.....do....	282 00	........do............
J. & G. S. Gideon...........do....	631 50	Auditor of the Treasury for P. O. Department..
W. Q. Force...............do....	624 75	........do............
C. Alexander...............do....	383 00	........do............

PRINTERS—*General Land Office.*

To whom paid.	For what service.	Amount.
P. A. Sage................	Advertising land sales in German National Gazette..............	$657 25
George Roberts............	Adver. land sales in..Boston Times	371 12
J. H. Steck................	......do........National Enquirer	201 25
Herrick & Ropes...........	......do.......Aurora and Union	384 50
Anson Herrick.............	......do...............do.....	258 75
Peter Hay & Co............	......do.......American Sentinel	302 85
Thomas S. Allison.........	......do.....Somerset Messenger	120 25
Salisbury, Manchester & Co.	......do.......... Buffalo Gazette	374 10
John Heart................	......do......Spectator, W. City	657 25
P. B. Goodsell............	......do.........Patriot and Eagle	130 00
Miller & Mœller...........	......do... Old School Republican	656 87
John A. Stuart............	......do.....Charleston Mercury	1311 35
James G. Bennett..........	......do..........N. York Herald	311 00
Haswell & Bushnell........	......do.........Vermont Gazette	229 12
John M. Church............	......do......Providence Gazette	669 00
Severns & Magill..........	......do....Philadelphia Mercury	720 30
Y. S. Walter..............	......do....Delaware Republican	189 75
Pratt, Cloud & Brother....	......do....Baltimore Republican	271 25
Joseph A. Yard............	......do...Emp'm and True Am'n	190 62
William H. Bullock........	......do..........Daily Georgian	669 37
C. A. Bradford............	......do........Southern Tribune	130 00
S. Penn, jr...............	......do.......Missouri Reporter	88 00
Erastus Sheppard..........	......do....Rochester Eve'g Post	212 60
Phillips & Smith..........	......do..Pittsburg Morning Post	222 75
Hale & Hallock............	......do....Journal of Commerce	247 24

PRINTING—*General Land Office.*

To whom paid.	For what service.	Amount.
W. W. Wyman	Adv. land sales in Mad. City Express	$38 25
James Clark	......do..........Iowa Gazette	56 00
Alfred Thucking	......do.........German Gazette	6 50
T. A. S. Donippan	......do.......Miss. Free Trader	365 00
M. Y. Beach	......do...........N. York Sun	253 12
Vespasian Ellis	......do.....Old School Democrat	811 25
A. S. Abell & Co	......do...........Baltimore Sun	70 72
Rust & Besançon	......do.....Morning Herald N. O.	255 00
John B. Jones	......do..............Madisonian	2170 00
Hiram Cummins	......do...Emp'm State Democrat	192 37
David M. Keeler	......do......Wisconsin Standard	161 50
Walters & Wobert	......do........Ohio and Illinois	30 00
L. A. Wallenweber	......do...Philadelphia Democrat	63 25
S. Borland & Co	......do.........Arkansas Banner	66 50
A. V. Wood	......do..........Iowa Standard	2 00
John G. Klenck	......do........National Zeitung	236 00
W. F. & T. Ritchie	......do......Richmond Enquirer	52 50
William Faulkner	......do.........Norwich News	28 00
E. & S. Croswell	......do..........Albany Argus	66 99
Brough & Robinson	Adver. notice Surveyor Gen'ls Office	4 00
J. & G. S. Gideon	Printing blanks, &c., abstracts and circulars	517 72
William Q. Force	Printing reports, certificates, parchments, &c	484 08

PRINTERS—POST OFFICE DEPARTMENT.

Statement of payments made by the Post Office Department for advertising, and for printing and distributing blanks during the two years from 1st *July*, 1843, *to* 30*th June*, 1845.

Name and nature of the work.	Amount paid.	Name and nature of the work.	Amount paid.
John Heart....advertising	$522 02	Toler, Townley & Stratham	$7 50
Alfred Schuching........do	34 00	V. Ellis................do	57 25
Herrick & Ropes........do	18 00	John B. Jones..........do	5450 62
Pratt, Cloud & Bro.....do	7 56	Thos. G. Broughton & Son	7 50
A. H. Spilman..........do	4 00	B. Bossel, jr...........do	4 00
Duhy, Graham & Williams	8 75	P. Hay & Co...........do	21 86
W. C. Bettincourt......do	3 00	D. Frost...............do	3 00
Marsh & McKenney....do	3 00	Wm. Harper...........do	3 00
Edw'd D. Ellis.........do	12 00	L. Eichelberger........do	3 75
John H. Wartman.....do	3 00	J. S. F. Smith..........do	5 00
Bethune & Ellis........do	237 25	S. Rhea.................do	8 00
R. W. Claxton.........do	1 50	E. Graham.............do	13 75
S. S. Sibley............do	61 75	Wm. E. Jones..........do	3 75

PRINTING—*Post Office Department.*

Name and nature of the work.	Amount paid.		Name and nature of the work.	Amount paid.	
J. N. Cardozo..advertising	$7	88	J. W. Robinson..advertising	$5	25
Alexander & Barnard...do	27	90	J. A. Brown..........do	1	00
Miller & Brown........do	8	25	Graham & Williams....do	7	75
Sherman & Harron.....do	3	13	James M. Gould.......do	5	00
E. A. Ware...........do	7	50	Edmund Anthony......do	25	00
Severns & McGill......do	575	25	Munn & Brownson.....do	5	00
J. Mattingly...........do	2	50	Middleton & Ballentyne.do	7	75
J. R. Chandler.........do	2	50	R. Farnham...........do	117	00
Geo. Roberts..........do	28	75	Justice & Mills.........do	5	00
Wm. H. Bailey........do	130	00	J. C. St. Rome.........do	11	25
Wm. J. Price...........do	3	12	J. L. Graham...........do	146	87
M. F. Whittemore & Co.do	2	00	N. A. Foster..........do	386	75
J. H. Stick............do	578	50	Casper C. Childs.......do	1235	50
John Bailhache.........do	2	68	J. S. Knowlton........do	398	59
Harker & Johnson.....do	55	25	Wm. Faulkner.........do	225	75
A. O. Houghton.......do	139	75	Osborne & Baldwin.....do	223	73
John G. McLain.......do	425	75	Haswell & Bushnell....do	230	50
Gales & Seaton........do	23	06	J. T. Marston.........do	229	25
J. P. McGill............do	559	00	Geo. Roberts..........do	412	75
Brough, Robinson & Martin	419	25	J. Kinney & Co........do	1277	25
J. W. Gray.............do	416	00	Carroll & Baker........do	6	25
Hineline & Curts.......do	134	87	R. G. Stone...........do	1268	25
T. G. Broughton.......do	1	50	Wm. T. Johnson......do	358	62
Thos. Sterne...........do	12	75	Carleton & Harvey.....do	6	25
Miller & Mœller ....do	487	00	Beals & Green.........do	403	31
McCann & Camp......do	442	00	Jos. M. Church........do	90	90
Walters & Weber......do	34	75	McConnell & Curtis....do	1271	25
M. Y. Beach...........do	8	75	E. & S. Croswell.......do	1270	25
Collins & Brown.......do	3	25	I. Hill & Sons.........do	328	05
Thos. Ritchie & Son....do	10	00	C. G. Eastman.........do	230	00
H. Ferry..............do	4	50	Mifflin & Parry........do	1	87
J. E. Wharton.........do	3	00	J. F. Hubbard.........do	1269	25
B. D. Howard..........do	97	50	Wm. Thompson.......do	360	55
Salisbury, Winchester & Co	1285	91	James M. Rix.........do	6	50
Jos. A. Yard..........do	139	75	Wm. A. Davis.........do	4	50
J. Wentworth.........do	16	00	Holden & Sanborn.....do	5	88
Phillips & Smith.......do	523	00	P. M. Kent............do	5	00
Mason & Moody.......do	25	00	Brough & Robinson....do	1	50
P. A. Sage............do	22	00	Moses & Greenleaf.....do	224	00
J. M. Earle............do	2	25			
S. P. Collings.........do	2	50	Agg. am't for advertising.$	25279	73
Wm. Mitchell..........do	3	00			
Sam'l Perly............do	2	50			
Whiting, Dumas & Wright	2	50	John Heart, printing blanks	1412	20
Orris Nichols..........do	1	50	J. Campbell & Co. pap. for do	1267	36
S. Penn, jr............do	19	50	R. Farnham.....do....do	1143	40
J. B. Marshall.........do	2	50	W. Fischer.....do....do	21	25

PRINTING—*Congress—Supreme Court.*

Name and nature of the work.	Amount paid.	Name and nature of the work.	Amount paid.
S. Stettinius, trans. of paper	$60 57	Miller & Mœller, print'g, &c.	11110 86
E. L. Childs, in superint'g distribution of blanks...	50 00	C. B. Glascock.........do	57 00
R. B. Boyd, packing and sending out blanks......	390 00	Cyrus Barton..........do	191 03
Wm. Greer, printing blanks and furnishing paper....	2158 89	D. Agnew.............do	33 00
Severance & Dorr.......do	173 41	Allen & Lounsby.......do	64 25
E. Graham............do	5760 62	Paine & Clark.........do	372 98
Wm. Sheets & Co.......do	3055 97	M. Patton.............do	5 00
Swain, Abell & Simmons do	2122 26	C. C. Haddock.........do	8 00
Alexander & Barnard...do	257 95	Morton & Griswold.....do	63 00
I. Hill & Sons.........do	13250 28	S. Penn, jr............do	47 00
Beals & Green.........do	357 34	McKee & Ruth..........do	6 00
Houston & Mills.......do	2 00	James Graham..........do	133 32
		Agg. am't for blanks.....$	43574 94

PRINTERS—*Congress.*

Names.	Compensation.
SENATE.	
Gales & Seaton..	$123901 08
Blair & Rives...	1853 04
Thomas Allen..	5971 81

These sums include payments for binding. Of the amount paid to Messrs. Blair & Rives, $630 33 is for printing executed in 1841.

Names.	Nature of work done.	Compensat'n.
HOUSE OF REPRESENTATIVES.		
Gales & Seaton........	For printing, from 30th September, 1843, to 7th December, 1843.......	$9154 55
	For binding during same period.......	7254 75
Thomas Allen........	For binding—his account being for work done during the 26th Congress	842 50
Blair & Rives.........	For printing, from 7th December, 1843, to 30th September, 1845..........	165351 67
	For binding during same period......	4134 98

PRINTING—*Supreme Court.*

The clerk of the Supreme Court, under a rule of that court, has a contract with J. & G. S. Gideon to print the records, and Congress appropriates $3000 per annum for the same.

TWENTY-NINTH CONGRESS—*Senate.*

SENATORS.—*On the 30th of September*, 1845.

Names.	Where born.	Names.	Where born.
PRESIDENT OF THE SENATE.		PENNSYLVANIA.	
		Daniel Sturgeon....	Pennsylvania..
George M. Dallas..	....	Simon Cameron....	....
SENATORS.		DELAWARE.	
		Thomas Clayton...	Delaware.......
MAINE.		John M. Clayton...	....
John Fairfield......	Maine	MARYLAND.	
George Evans........	......do......		
		James A. Pearce...	....
NEW HAMPSHIRE.		Reverdy Johnson...	....
Charles G. Atherton	N. Hampshire.	VIRGINIA.	
(Vacancy.)			
		William S. Archer..	Virginia.......
VERMONT.		(Vacancy.)	
Samuel S. Phelps...	Connecticut.....	NORTH CAROLINA.	
William C. Upham.	Massachusetts.		
		Willie P. Mangum.	North Carolina.
MASSACHUSETTS.		W. H. Haywood, jr.	......do......
Daniel Webster....	N. Hampshire.	SOUTH CAROLINA.	
John Davis........	....		
		Daniel E. Huger...	South Carolina.
RHODE ISLAND.		George McDuffie...	Georgia.......
James F. Simmons.	Rhode Island..	GEORGIA.	
Albert C. Greene...	....		
		John McP. Berrien.	New Jersey ...
CONNECTICUT.		Walter T. Colquitt.	Virginia.......
J. W. Huntington..	Connecticut.....	ALABAMA.	
John M. Niles.....	....		
		Arthur P Bagby...	Virginia.......
NEW YORK.		Dixon H. Lewis...	....
		MISSISSIPPI.	
Daniel S. Dickinson.	....		
John A. Dix......	....	Jesse Speight......	....
		(Vacancy.)	
NEW JERSEY.		LOUISIANA.	
William L. Dayton.	New Jersey ...	Alexander Barrow..	Tennessee.....
Jacob W. Miller...	......do......	Henry Johnson....	....

CONGRESS—*Senate—House of Representatives.*

Names.	Where born.	Names.	Where born.
TENNESSEE.		MISSOURI.	
Spencer Jarnagin...	Tennessee.....	Thomas H. Benton.	North Carolina.
(Vacancy.)		David R. Atchison..	Kentucky.....
KENTUCKY.		ARKANSAS.	
James T. Morehead.	Kentucky.....	Ambrose H. Sevier.	Tennessee.....
John J. Crittenden..	......do......	Chester Ashley....	....
OHIO.		MICHIGAN.	
William Allen.....	North Carolina.	Wm. Woodbridge..	Connecticut.....
Thomas Corwin....	....	Lewis Cass........	....
INDIANA.		FLORIDA.	
Edw'd A. Hannegan	Ohio..........	David Levy.......	....
(Vacancy.)		J. D. Westcott, jr..	....
ILLINOIS.			
James Semple......	Kentucky.....		
Sidney Breese......	New York.....		

The compensation of Senators is $8 for each day's attendance, and $8 for every twenty miles of estimated distance from their places of residence to the seat of Government, at the commencement and end of every session.

HOUSE OF REPRESENTATIVES.

Names.	Residence.	Where born.
SPEAKER.		
John W. Davis..............	Carlisle..........	Pennsylvania......
MAINE.		
John F. Scammon.............	Saco.............	Maine.............
Robert P. Dunlap............	Brunswick........	......do..........
Luther Severance............	Augusta..........	Massachusetts.....
John D. McCrate.............	Wiscasset........	Maine.............
Cullen Sawtelle.............	Norridgewock.....	......do..........
Hannibal Hamlin.............	Hamden...........	......do..........
Hezekiah Williams...........	Castine..........	Vermont...........

CONGRESS—*House of Representatives.*

Names.	Residence.	Where born
NEW HAMPSHIRE.		
Moses Norris, jr	Pittsfield	New Hampshire
Mace Moulton	Manchester	do
James H. Johnson	Bath	do
(One vacancy.)		
MASSACHUSETTS.		
Robert C. Winthrop	Boston	Massachusetts
Daniel P. King	Danvers	do
Amos Abbott	Andover	do
Benjamin Thompson	Charlestown	do
Charles Hudson	Westminster	do
George Ashmun	Springfield	do
Julius Rockwell	Pittsfield	Connecticut
John Quincy Adams	Quincy	Massachusetts
(One vacancy.)		
Joseph Grinnell	New Bedford	do
RHODE ISLAND.		
Henry Y. Cranston	Newport	Rhode Island
Lemuel H. Arnold	Wakefield	Vermont
CONNECTICUT.		
James Dixon	Hartford	Connecticut
Samuel D. Hubbard	Middletown	do
John A. Rockwell	Norwich	do
Truman Smith	Litchfield	do
VERMONT.		
Solomon Foot	Rutland	Vermont
Jacob Collamer	Woodstock	New York
George P. Marsh	Burlington	Vermont
Paul Dillingham, jr	Waterbury	do
NEW YORK.		
John W. Lawrence	Flushing	New York
Henry J. Seaman	Richmond	do
William S. Miller	New York	Connecticut
William B. McClay	do	New York
Thos. M. Woodruff	do	do
Wm. W. Campbell	do	do
Joseph H. Anderson	White Plains	do
Wm. W. Woodworth	Hyde Park	Connecticut

CONGRESS—*House of Representatives.*

Names.	Residence.	Where born.
Archibald C. Niven	Monticello	New York
Samuel Gordon	Delhi	do
John F. Colin	Hillsdale	do
Richard P. Herrick	Greenbush	do
Bradford R. Wood	Albany	Connecticut
Erastus D. Culver	Greenwich	New York
Joseph Russell	Warrensburgh	do
Hugh White	Cohoes	do
Charles S. Benton	Mohawk	Maine
Preston King	Ogdensburgh	New York
Orville Hungerford	Watertown	Connecticut
Timothy Jenkins	Oneida Castle	Massachusetts
Charles Goodyear	Schoharie	New York
Stephen Strong	Owego	Connecticut
William J. Hough	Cazenovia	New York
Horace Wheaton	Pompey	do
George Rathbun	Auburn	do
Samuel S. Ellsworth	Penn Yan	Vermont
John DeMott	Lodi	New Jersey
Elias B. Holmes	Brockport	Vermont
Charles H. Carroll	Groveland Centre	Maryland
Martin Grover	Angelica	New York
Abner Lewis	Panama	Vermont
William A. Moseley	Buffalo	New York
Albert Smith	Batavia	do
Washington Hunt	Lockport	do
NEW JERSEY.		
James G. Hampton	Bridgeton	New Jersey
George Sykes	Springfield	do
John Runk	Kingwood	do
Joseph E. Edsall	Hamburg	Vermont
William Wright	Newark	New York
PENNSYLVANIA.		
Lewis C. Levin	Philadelphia	South Carolina
Joseph R. Ingersoll	do	Pennsylvania
John H. Campbell	do	do
Charles J. Ingersoll	do	do
Jacob S. Yost	Pottstown	do
Jacob Erdman	Coopersburgh	do
Abm. R. McIlvaine	Brandywine Manor	do
John Strohm	New Providence	do
John Ritter	Reading	do
Richard Brodhead	Easton	do
Owen D. Leib	Catawissa	do
David Wilmot	Towanda	do

CONGRESS—*House of Representatives.*

Names.	Residence.	Where born.
James Pollock	Milton	Pennsylvania
Alexander Ramsey	Harrisburgh	do
Moses McClean	Gettysburgh	do
James Black	Newport	do
John Blanchard	Bellfont	Vermont
Andrew Stewart	Uniontown	Pennsylvania
Henry D. Foster	Greensburgh	do
John H. Ewing	Washington	do
Cornelius Darragh	Pittsburgh	do
William S. Garvin	Mercer	do
James Thompson	Erie	do
Joseph Buffington	Kittaning	do
DELAWARE.		
John W. Houston	Georgetown	Delaware
MARYLAND.		
John G. Chapman	Port Tobacco	Maryland
Thomas Perry	Cumberland	do
Thomas W. Ligon	Ellicott's Mills	Virginia
William F. Giles	Baltimore	Maryland
Albert Constable	Perryville	do
Edward H. Long	Princess Ann	do
VIRGINIA.		
Archibald Atkinson	Smithfield, Isle of Wight	Virginia
Geo. C. Dromgoole	His post office, Summit, N. C.	do
Wm. M. Treadway	Dannville	do
Edmund W. Hubard	Curdsville	do
Shelton F. Leake	Charlottesville	do
James A. Seddon	Richmond	do
Thomas H. Bayly	Accomac C. H.	do
Robt. M. T. Hunter	Loyds	do
John S. Pendleton	Culpeper C. H	do
Henry Bedinger	Charlestown	do
William Taylor	Lexington	do
Aug. A. Chapman	Union	do
George W. Hopkins	Abingdon	do
Joseph Johnson	Bridgeport	New York
William G. Brown	Kingwood	Virginia

CONGRESS—*House of Representatives.*

Names.	Residence.	Where born.
NORTH CAROLINA.		
James Graham		
Daniel M. Barringer	Concord	North Carolina
David S. Reid	Reidsville	do
Alfred Dockery	Dockery Store	do
James C. Dobbin	Fayetteville	North Carolina
James J. McKay	Elizabethtown	do
John R. J. Daniel	Halifax	do
Henry S. Clarke	Washington	do
Asa Biggs	Williamston	do
SOUTH CAROLINA.		
James A. Black	CherokeeIronW'rks	South Carolina
Richard F. Simpson	Pendletonville	do
Jos. A. Woodward	Winsboro'	do
Alexander D. Sims	Darlington C. H.	Virginia
Armistead Burt	Willington	South Carolina
Isaac E. Holmes	Charleston	do
R. Barnwell Rhett	Ashepoo	do
GEORGIA.		
Thomas Butler King		
Seaborn Jones	Columbus	Georgia
(One vacancy.)		
Hugh A. Haralson	La Grange	Georgia
John H. Lumpkin	Rome	do
Howell Cobb	Athens	do
Alex. H. Stephens	Crawfordsville	do
Robert Toombs	Washington	do
KENTUCKY.		
Linn Boyd	New Design	Tennessee
John H. McHenry	Hartford	Kentucky
Henry Grider	Bowling Green	do
Joshua F. Bell	Danville	do
Bryan R. Young	Elizabethtown	do
John P. Martin	Prestonsburgh	Virginia
Wm. P. Thomasson	Louisville	Kentucky
Garrett Davis	Paris	do
Andrew Trumbo	Owengsville	do
John W. Tibbatts	Newport	do
TENNESSEE.		
Andrew Johnson	Greenville	North Carolina

CONGRESS—*House of Representatives.*

Names.	Residence.	Where born.
William M. Cocke	Rutledge	Tennessee
John H. Crozier	Knoxville	do
Alvan Cullom	Livingston	Kentucky
George W. Jones	Fayetteville	Virginia
Barclay Martin	Columbia	South Carolina
Meredith P. Gentry	Franklin	North Carolina
Joseph H. Peyton	Gallatin	Tennessee
Lucien B. Chase	Clarksville	Vermont
Fred. P. Stanton	Memphis	Dist. of Columbia
Milton Brown	Jackson	Ohio
OHIO.		
James J. Faran	Cincinnati	Ohio
Frs. A. Cunningham	Eaton	South Carolina
Robert C. Schenck	Dayton	Ohio
Joseph Vance	Urbana	Pennsylvania
William Sawyer	St. Mary's	Ohio
Henry St. John	Tiffin	New York
Joseph J. McDowell	Hillsborough	North Carolina
Allen G. Thurman	Chillicothe	Virginia
Augustus L. Perrill	Lithopolis	do
Columbus Delano	Mount Vernon	Vermont
Jacob Brinkerhoff	Mansfield	New York
Samuel F. Vinton	Gallipolis	Mississippi
Isaac Parish	Parish's Mills	Ohio
Alexander Harper	Zanesville	Ireland
Joseph Morris	Woodsfield	Pennsylvania
John D. Cummins	New Philadelphia	do
George Fries	Hanoverton	do
D. A. Starkweather	Canton	Connecticut
Daniel R. Tilden	Ravenna	do
Joshua R. Giddings	Jefferson	Pennsylvania
Joseph M. Root	Norwalk	New York
LOUISIANA.		
John Slidell	New Orleans	New York
B. G. Thibodaux	Thibodaux	Louisiana
John H. Harmanson	Simmsport Avoyells	Virginia
Isaac E. Morse	St. Martinsville	Louisiana
INDIANA.		
Robert Dale Owen	New Harmony	Scotland
Thomas J. Henley	New Washington	Indiana
Thomas Smith	Versailles	Pennsylvania
Caleb B. Smith	Connersville	Massachusetts
William W. Wick	Indianapolis	Pennsylvania

CONGRESS—*House of Representatiaes.*

Names.	Residence.	Where born.
John W. Davis	Carlisle	Pennsylvania
Ed. W. McGaughey	Greencastle	Indiana
John Pettit	Lafayette	New York
Charles W. Cathcart	La Porte	Island Madeira
Andrew Kennedy	Muncietown	Ohio
MISSISSIPPI.		
Stephen Adams	Aberdeen	South Carolina
Jefferson Davis	Warrenton	Kentucky
Robert W. Roberts	Hillsboro'	Delaware
Jacob Thompson	Oxford	North Carolina
ILLINOIS.		
Robert Smith	Upper Alton	New Hampshire
J. A. McClernand	Shawneetown	Illinois
Orlando B. Ficklin	Charleston	Kentucky
John Wentworth	Chicago	New Hampshire
Stephen A. Douglass	Quincy	Vermont
Joseph P. Hoge	Galena	Ohio
Edward D. Baker	Springfield	England
ALABAMA.		
Edward S. Dargin	Mobile	North Carolina
Henry W. Hilliard	Montgomery	do
William L. Yancey	Wetumpka	South Carolina
William W. Payne	Gainesville	Virginia
George S. Houston	Athens	Tennessee
Reuben Chapman	Blountsville	Virginia
Felix G. McConnell	Talladega	Tennessee
MISSOURI.		
James B. Bowlin	St. Louis	Virginia
James H. Relfe	Caledonia	do
Sterling Price	Keitsville	do
John S. Phelps	Springfield	Connecticut
Leonard H. Simms	do	North Carolina
ARKANSAS.		
Archibald Yell	Fayetteville	Tennessee
MICHIGAN.		
Robert McClelland	Monroe	Pennsylvania
John S. Chipman	Centreville	Vermont

CONGRESS—*House of Representatives—Officers of Senate.*

Names.	Residence.	Where born.
James B. Hunt	Pontiac	South America
FLORIDA.		
E. Carrington Cabell	Tallahassee C. H.	Virginia
Delegates from the Territories.		
WISCONSIN.		
Morgan L. Martin	Green Bay	New York
IOWA.		
Augustus C. Dodge	Burlington	Missouri

The compensation of each member of Congress is eight dollars per day during each session; and eight dollars for every twenty miles of actual travel in going to, and returning from, the place of the meeting of Congress.

OFFICERS OF THE SENATE AND HOUSE OF REPRESENTATIVES.

Names and Offices.	Where born.	Compensation.
OFFICERS AND AGENTS		per ann.
In the service of the Senate.		
Asbury Dickens.....Secretary	North Carolina.	$3000 00
Lewis H. Macben.....Principal Clerk	Maryland	1800 00
William Hickey.....Executive Clerk	do.	1500 00
Thomas W. Dickens....1st Legislative Clerk	England, Am. parentage.	1500 00
Wm. J. McDonald.....2d.....do.....do.	District Colum.	1500 00
John C. Fitzpatrick.....1st Engrossing Clerk	Virginia	1500 00
William Patton.....2d....do.....do.	Pennsylvania	1500 00
(Vacant).....Sergeant-at-Arms and Doorkeeper		1500 00
Robert Beale.....Assistant Doorkeeper	Virginia	1450 00
(Vacant).....Chaplain		500 00
John L. Clubb.....Messenger Secretary's Office	District Colum.	$3 00 per day.
Lewis Sanders...Asst. Mess'r Secretary's Office	Maryland	$2 00 per day.
Robert P. Anderson.....Messenger Senate	Pennsylvania	$3 00 per day.
Isaac Bassett.....do.....do.	District Colum.	do

CONGRESS—*Officers of the House of Representatives.*

Names and Offices.	Where born.	Compensation.
LIST OF OFFICERS AND AGENTS		
In the service of the House of Representatives on the 30th September, 1845.		
Benjamin B. French........Clerk of the House	N. Hampshire.	$3000 00
Daniel Gold..........Chief Clerk of the Office	New York.....	1800 00
Joseph F. Brown......................Clerk	Indiana	1500 00
Thomas D. Harris......................do.	Georgia.........	1500 00
Adam J. Glossbrenner..................do.	Maryland	1500 00
Darwin E. Stanton......................do.	Ohio............	1500 00
Mahlon H. Medary......................do.	Pennsylvania ..	1500 00
Daniel Buck............................do.	Vermont.......	1500 00
Royal P. Stow..........................do.	N. Hampshire.	1500 00
Randall McLaughlin....................do.	Pennsylvania ..	1500 00
Simon Brown...........Librarian to the House	Massachusetts .	1500 00
William S. Robertson. Messenger to Clerk's Office	Ohio..........	$2 50 per day.
J. Edmund Millard........do............do....	New York.....	do
Edmund F. French.........do............do....	N. Hampshire.	do
Newton Lane.................Sergeant-at-Arms	Kentucky.....	1500 00
Wm. T. Stewart, Messenger to Sergeant-at-Arms	Dist Colum....	$2 50 per day.
Jesse E. Dow.......................Doorkeeper	Connecticut....	1500 00
Horatio Webb.......Messenger to Doorkeeper	........do......	$2 50 per day.
Charles W. Stewart..............do............	Maryland	do
J. R. Queen.......................do............	Virginia.........	do
E. D. Gumaer......................do............	New York.....	do
Wm. McPeak.......................do............	Pennsylvania ..	do
A. Gillespie........................do............	New York.....	do
George McD. Burke..............do............	Dist. Colum...	do
John Raub..........................do............	Pennsylvania ..	do
Thos. McKay.......................Fireman	Dist. Colum...	do
J. T. Clements....................Laborer	Maryland	do
Geo. D. Spencer....................do.	......do......	do
John M. Johnson......Postmaster to the House	Virginia.......	1500 00
Peter Laphin.........Messenger to Postmaster	Dist. Colum...	$2 50 per day.

CHANGES IN POST OFFICES SINCE THE FOLLOWING LIST WAS PREPARED.

Lovington,	Illinois,	now in	Moultrie	county.
Rock Spring,	North Carolina,	do	Orange	do
New Castle,	Tennessee,	do	Hardeman	do
Germantown,	Indiana,	do	Marion	do
Jersey Prairie,	Illinois,	do	Cass	do
Draper's Valley,	Virginia,	do	Pulaski	do
Fulwood's Store,	North Carolina,	do	Mecklenburgh	do
High Shoals,	Georgia,	do	Morgan	do

POST OFFICE DEPARTMENT.

Names and offices.	Where employed.	Where born.	Compensation.
			Dol. cts.
POSTMASTER GENERAL.			
Cave Johnson	Washington	Tennessee	6000 00
ASSISTANT POSTMASTERS GENERAL.			
Selah R. Hobbie	do	New York	2500 00
William Medill	do	Delaware	2500 00
N. M. Miller	do	Virginia	2500 00
CHIEF CLERK.			
John Marron	do	Ireland	2000 00
PRINCIPAL CLERKS.			
William H. Dundas	do	Virginia	1600 00
E. L. Childs	do	Massachusetts	1600 00
Samuel B. Beach	do	Connecticut	1600 00
TOPOGRAPHER.			
Henry A. Burr	do	do	1600 00
CLERKS.			
James Snyder	do	Pennsylvania	1400 00
Jacob B. Moore	do	N. Hampshire	1400 00
Alexander N. Zevely	do	N. Carolina	1400 00
Nicholas Halter	do	Switzerland	1400 00
Robert A. Lacey	do	Virginia	1400 00
John Smith	do	Maryland	1400 00
John Hunter	do	Virginia	1400 00
John Ferguson	do	Ohio	1400 00
Nathaniel C. Towle	do	N. Hampshire	1400 00
D. D. T. Leech	do	New York	1400 00
Horatio King	do	Maine	1400 00
Joseph H. Wheat	do	Maryland	1400 00
James H. Marr	do	do	1400 00
James Laurenson	do	England	1200 00
George A. Bohrer	do	Dist. Colum.	1200 00
James Owner, jr.	do	Pennsylvania	1200 00
Henry Johnson	do	Maryland	1200 00
Chester A. Colt	do	Pennsylvania	1200 00
Robert B. Rust	do	Virginia	1200 00

GENERAL POST OFFICE—*Clerks, Messengers, &c.*

Names and offices.	Where employed.	Where born.	Compensation.
			Dol. cts.
William P. Young	Washington	N. Carolina	1200 00
William J. Darden	do	Virginia	1200 00
E. Hotchkiss	do	Connecticut	1200 00
E. H. Metcalf	do	New York	1200 00
D. Vass	do	Virginia	1200 00
Chauncey Smith	do	Vermont	1200 00
William Bell	do	Virginia	1200 00
W. V. Voorhies	do	Tennessee	1200 00
Cranstoun Laurie	do	Dist. Colum.	1200 00
James G. Sturgeon	do	Pennsylvania	1200 00
Thomas J. Williams	do	Dist. Colum.	1200 00
Robert J. Powell	do	N. Carolina	1200 00
Thomas B. Reily	do	Dist. Colum.	1200 00
George Lumpkin	do	Georgia	1000 00
Watkins Addison	do	Dist. Colum.	1000 00
Robert Wallace	do	Maryland	1000 00
George M. Kendall	do	Massachusetts	1000 00
Charles L. Weller	do	Ohio	1000 00
T. E. S. Russwurm	do	Tennessee	1000 00
Comfort S. Whittlesey	do	Ohio	1000 00
Jeremiah O'Brien	do	Massachusetts	1000 00
James H. Hamilton	do	New Jersey	1000 00
MESSENGER.			
William J. Sibley	do	Maryland	750 00
ASSISTANT MESSENGERS.			
Richard H. Gordon	do	Dist. Colum.	350 00
William E. Lightelle	do	do	350 00
Nathaniel Herbert	do	do	350 00
WATCHMEN.			
Eli Davis	do	Maryland	300 00
Allen B. Peddicord	do	do	300 00

POST OFFICES—*Maine*.

MAINE.

NOTE.—Compensation of Postmasters, and net proceeds of their offices, from July 1, 1844, to June 30, 1845.

Post Offices.	Counties.	Postmasters.	Compensation.	Net proceeds.
Abbot	Piscataquis	John How	$31 01	$52 27
Acton	York	Jonathan Brackett	9 23	15 33
Acton Corner	York	Horace Bodwell	18 55	33 39
Addison Point	Washington	William Nash, to 4th March	33 69	66 58
		William V. Bowen	17 74	34 71
Albany	Oxford	Jacob H. Lovejoy	24 78	39 93
Albion	Kennebeck	John Wellington	69 70	62 14
Alexander	Washington	Jesse Stephenson	13 64	22 17
Alfred	York	John Skeele, to 18th April	92 08	147 90
		Silas Derby	24 10	37 46
Alna	Lincoln	Stephen Coker, to 30th Nov	14 67	23 31
		Ward L. Lewis	22 27	36 87
Amherst	Hancock	John B. Foster	23 17	37 06
Amity	Aroostook	Columbus Dunn	3 53	8 13
Andover	Oxford	Lewis Crockett, to 6th May	52 71	50 30
		James F. Bragg, jr.	8 68	6 84
Anson	Somerset	Asher Moore, to 20th April	116 51	174 78
		Rodney Collins	27 36	36 16
Aroostook	Aroostook	David Dudley	33 06	66 18
Athens	Somerset	Samuel Jewett, to 28th Oct	24 90	38 81
		L. D. P. Palmer	50 02	81 02
Atkinson	Piscataquis	Elisha L. Hammond	36 64	63 80
Auburn	Cumberland	Enoch Littlefield	32 53	48 22
Augusta	Kennebeck	Asaph R. Nichols	986 21	2206 01
Aurora	Hancock	David Silsby	10 47	18 12
Avon	Franklin	Daniel Towle	8 43	16 82
Baileyville	Washington	Wm. Thornton, to 31st March	2 93	4 97
		John N. Farrar	89	1 50
Bangor	Penobscot	Charles K. Miller	988 59	5593 76
Bar Harbor	Hancock	Tobias Roberts	10 10	19 17
Baring	Washington	William A. Gould	31 66	55 92
Bath	Lincoln	Thomas Eaton	976 68	2136 86
Belfast	Waldo	Henry Colburne, to 30th May	455 52	872 76
		Wm. T. Colburne	34 19	72 80

POST OFFICES—*Maine.*

Post Offices.	Counties.	Postmasters.	Compensation.	Net proceeds.
Belgrade	Kennebeck	William Rogers	$15 54	$23 25
Belgrade Mills	Kennebeck	Robert T. Whitten	13 20	23 07
Belmont	Waldo	William Rust	11 06	19 44
Bethel	Oxford	Robert A. Chapman	65 96	108 78
Bingham	Somerset	William Rowell	43 34	74 63
Blacks	Waldo	Ananiah Dodge, jr., to 31st Dec	7 54	13 14
		Amasa F. C. Dodge	6 74	11 74
Blanchard	Piscataquis	Ruel K. Packard	13 17	20 14
Bloomfield	Somerset	Joseph Locke	67 29	136 09
Blue Hill	Hancock	B. W. Hinckley, to 24th May	117 03	194 46
		Frederick A. Holt	12 99	23 52
Bolster's Mills	Cumberland	Wyatt Turner	16 86	27 32
Boothbay	Lincoln	Marshall Smith	52 14	91 32
Bowdoin	Lincoln	Moses Starbird	14 36	27 75
Bowdoin Centre	Lincoln	David Y. Pierce, to 24th May	8 89	14 68
		Abner Coombs	1 06	1 71
Bowdoinham	Lincoln	Robert Butterfield	238 05	240 60
Bower Bank	Piscataquis	Edward Robinson	5 24	8 23
Bradford	Penobscot	Gorham Davis	43 09	69 26
Bremen	Lincoln	Waite W. Keene	16 21	30 81
Brewer	Penobscot	Edward H. Burr	96 05	169 52
Brewer Village	Penobscot	Rufus K. Cushing	47 13	80 65
Bridgeton	Cumberland	Renss'r Cram, to 10th May	77 55	131 85
		Samuel Andrews	12 54	22 01
Brighton	Somerset	Andrew Hall	13 80	25 26
Bristol	Lincoln	Arnold Blaney	79 67	138 32
Brooks	Waldo	Woodbury Davis, to 18th April	36 37	64 05
		John McArthur	7 33	15 11
Brooksville	Hancock	Joseph Walker	17 92	31 82
Brownfield	Oxford	Isaac Spring, to 27th August	8 48	15 67
		Richard Paine, to 13th Jan	16 17	27 99
		Jesse P. Sweat	27 09	43 02
Brown's Corner	Kennebeck	Josiah B. Wentworth	43 58	72 94
Brownsville	Piscataquis	Eleazer A. Jenks	42 04	68 19
Brunswick	Cumberland	T. S. McLellan	874 40	1507 54
Buckfield	Oxford	Samuel F. Brown, to 31st Dec	54 90	74 60
		Orville Bridgham	56 05	87 15
Bucksport	Hancock	Samuel Little	319 28	610 40
Burlington	Penobscot	Amzi Libbey	12 33	18 81
Burnham Village	Waldo	Dennis L. Millikin	21 30	32 91
Buxton	York	Amos Spafford	41 77	80 75

POST OFFICES—*Maine.*

Post Offices.	Counties.	Postmasters.	Compensation.	Net proceeds.
Buxton Centre...	York........	Jonathan C. Lewis.	$36 68	$53 70
Byron..........	Oxford......	Andrew Brown....	7 55	13 27
Calais	Washington..	William Goodwin, to 30th April.....	622 15	1711 29
		Japheth C. Washburn...........	109 44	322 25
Cambridge......	Somerset....	David Bailey.......	14 11	26 49
Camden.........	Waldo......	Hiram Bass, to 18th April...........	216 95	375 24
		Ephraim K. Smart..	39 78	79 18
Canaan.........	Somerset....	Henry C. Newhall.	57 28	100 76
Canton..........	Oxford......	James M. Holland..	28 47	47 49
Canton Mills.....	Oxford......	Andrew Barrows...	28 78	45 87
Cape Neddick ...	York........	Geo. M. Freeman..	26 95	46 92
Carmel..........	Penobscot....	Geo. W. Chamberlain, to 28th Feb..	23 87	45 14
		David Fuller.......	17 31	32 06
Carritunk.......	Somerset....	Joseph Spaulding, jr	6 05	10 71
Carthage........	Franklin	Lowell Mitchell....	9 93	16 19
Casco...........	Cumberland..	Levi Holden.......	17 79	31 48
Castine.........	Hancock....	Charles Rogers.....	275 38	492 53
Centre Lebanon..	York........	Nathan Lord......	15 50	26 09
Centre Lincolnv'le	Waldo......	Michael B. Gordon.	28 30	46 34
Centre Minot.... (Ch'd to "North Auburn.")	Cumberland..	Oliver Pollard......	30 77	51 12
Centre Montville.	Waldo......	Jonathan Bean.....	10 97	20 78
Centre Sidney....	Kennebeck ..	Elisha Clark.......	19 35	33 75
Charleston.......	Penobscot....	Duston Page.......	30 77	53 86
Charlotte........	Washington..	Ebenezer Fisher....	6 66	11 89
Chesterville......	Franklin	William Morgridge.	39 06	63 35
China...........	Kennebeck ..	Oliver W. Washburn	91 55	167 38
Clinton.........	Kennebeck ..	Charles Jewett.....	22 55	42 69
College Grant....	Aroostook...	Rufus Hamilton, (3 qrs.).........	35	76
Columbia........	Washington..	John A. Ruggles, to 13th June.......	91 88	116 38
		Josiah D. Pulsifer..	3 77	6 05
Concord	Somerset....	Jacob Savage......	10 61	16 97
Conway	Aroostook...	Maria McNamara..	11 47	24 13
Cooper.........	Washington..	Asaph Sawyer, (3 qrs.)............	7 10	13 68
Cooper's Mills...	Lincoln.....	James Gray.......	15 86	29 28
Corinna.........	Penobscot....	James Hawes......	21 80	37 98
Corinna Centre...	Penobscot....	Luther Harmon....	13 14	20 23
Corinth.........	Penobscot....	Elbridge H. Bragdon	26 40	48 95
Cornishville.....	York........	John Jameson......	48 56	78 80
Cornville........	Somerset....	Moses F. Judkins..	25 43	43 77

POST-OFFICES—*Maine*.

Post Offices.	Counties.	Postmasters.	Compensation.	Net proceeds.
Crawford	Washington	Joel F. Nason	$6 20	$9 02
Cumberland	Cumberland	Charles Poland	44 66	43 08
Cumberl'd Centre	Cumberland	Joel Prince, jr	31 13	57 64
Cushing	Lincoln	Darius Norton	19 76	40 24
Cutler	Washington	Mariner A. Wilder	34 50	70 73
Damariscotta mills	Lincoln	David Gorham, to 30th Sept	9 73	17 41
		Joseph Haines	47 17	76 68
Danville	Cumberland	Nath'l L. Ingersoll	17 05	32 01
Dead River	Somerset	Freeman Grover, to 31st Dec	5 08	8 52
		Jos. W. White	6 28	11 18
Deer Isle	Hancock	John P. Johnson	51 72	89 91
Denmark	Oxford	Samuel Gibson	33 83	59 78
Dennysville	Washington	John Kilby	60 35	99 38
Detroit	Somerset	Eb'r A. Boynton	20 64	31 98
Dexter	Penobscot	Augustus S. French	191 48	314 39
Dixfield	Oxford	Hiram A. White, to 29th Jan	50 82	80 39
		Isaac N. Stanley	24 51	45 59
Dixmont	Penobscot	Charles H. Adams	74 57	120 30
Dover	Piscataquis	Charles E. Kimball	76 63	126 46
Dresden	Lincoln	Thomas Johnson	59 77	101 56
Dresden Mills	Lincoln	Edward Kidder, to 1st May	31 50	54 89
		John Chism	4 61	7 55
Dunn's Corner	Kennebeck	Peter Dunn	6 45	8 71
Durham	Cumberland	William G. Hoyt	17 62	30 42
East Auburn	Cumberland	John C. Briggs	79	1 38
East Baldwin	Cumberland	William Wingate	33 72	55 20
East Bethel	Oxford	Timothy Carter, to 18th April	10 30	16 83
		Hiram Holt, 2d	1 56	3 62
East Brewer	Penobscot	Timothy George, to 16th June	27 68	46 86
		Luther N. Jones	1 29	2 19
East Burnham	Waldo	David O. Williams	4 45	6 78
East Corinth	Penobscot	Reuben Ball	57 80	89 86
East Dixfield	Oxford	Geo. R. Randall	25 40	43 73
East Dover	Piscataquis	Eli Towne	4 09	5 30
East Eddington	Penobscot	Wm. H. Y. Johnson	20 52	30 40
East Elliott	York	James Goodwin	12 51	24 44
East Harrington	Washington	Temple Coffin	18 45	19 77
East Hebron	Oxford	Jos. Hutchinson, jr	9 84	17 74
East Knox	Waldo	William Foster	14 30	23 31
East Limington	York	Henry Small	21 89	36 55
East Livermore	Oxford	Francis F. Haines	25 75	42 37

POST OFFICES—*Maine.*

Post Offices.	Counties.	Postmasters.	Compensation.	Net proceeds.
East Machias	Washington	Jno. C. Talbot	$187 33	$350 07
East Madison	Somerset	Nathaniel B. Chadbourn	20 56	32 37
East Monmouth	Kennebeck	Chs. S. Norris	19 03	32 33
East Mt. Vernon. (Dis. 3d June.)	Kennebeck	Silas B. Wing, to 30th September	1 26	2 47
		Stephen Gilman	3 56	6 01
East Newport	Penobscot	Stephen Spaulding	11 33	16 57
East Newportland	Somerset	Rodney G. Dennis	7 06	7 08
East New Sharon	Kennebeck	Jos. S. Kelley, to 22d April	6 11	10 86
		Elisha Small, jr.	80	1 59
East Orrington	Penobscot	Warren Ware, jr.	23 13	42 23
East Parsonfield	York	James W. Weeks	18 52	30 36
East Pittsfield	Somerset	James Willis	16 29	26 28
East Pittston	Kennebeck	Cyrus Rundlett	22 86	38 11
Eastport	Washington	Oliver Shead	488 13	1222 13
East Raymond	Cumberland	Wentwh. R. Lane	13 71	21 39
East Readfield	Kennebeck	Jos. A. Sanborn	17 74	27 66
East Rumford	Oxford	Alvan Bolster	12 09	15 57
East St. Albans	Somerset	Nathan Douglass, to 20th January	20 88	31 00
		Harris Garcelon	17 81	28 27
East Sangerville	Piscataquis	Benjamin Lane	21 47	32 83
East Standish	Cumberland	Benja'in Chadbourn	18 01	24 00
East Sumner	Oxford	Bethuel Cary	11 25	19 30
East Thomaston	Lincoln	John Spofford	441 44	902 21
East Trenton	Hancock	Henry Hodgkins	17 03	33 79
East Turner	Oxford	Ezekiel Martin	11 02	18 42
East Vassalboro'	Kennebeck	Jacob Butterfield, to 16th April	55 74	99 21
		Addison Stinchfield	17 02	29 67
East Wilton	Franklin	Josiah Perham, jr.	72 98	73 01
East Winthrop	Kennebeck	Horace Parlin	28 89	37 30
Eden	Hancock	Nichs. J. Thomas	30 57	63 82
Eddington	Penobscot	John Chadwick	28 74	44 78
Edgecomb	Lincoln	Samuel G. Wilson	21 32	39 22
Elliott	York	William Fogg	35 63	53 48
Elliottsville	Piscataquis	John F. Thombs	15 54	30 20
Ellsworth	Hancock	Henry S. Jones, to 8th February	176 67	342 18
		William Bennett	129 19	263 44
Embden	Somerset	Willard C. McFaden	8 01	15 12
Embden Centre	Somerset	Eli Littlefield	3 12	5 84
Emery's Mills	York	John Gowen, to 27th July	65	1 33
		John Hubbard	11 34	23 18
Enfield	Penobscot	John S. Patten	10 85	20 29
Etna	Penobscot	Anson E. Moseley	19 91	31 59

POST OFFICES—*Maine*.

Post Offices.	Counties.	Postmasters.	Compensation.	Net proceeds.
Exeter	Penobscot	John Shaw	$72 35	$120 41
Exeter Mills	Penobscot	David N. Buffum, from 1st January.	9 08	10 96
Fairfield	Somerset	Ebenezer Lawrence.	36 86	63 04
Fairfield Corners.	Somerset	Alben Emery	19 62	32 53
Falmouth	Cumberland	John E. Donnell	34 52	63 97
Farmington	Franklin	Chs. E. Johnson, to 2d June	268 87	267 07
		Samuel Belcher	22 99	21 94
Farmington Falls.	Franklin	Enoch C. Rolfe	45 18	80 95
Fayette	Kennebcek	Daniel Judkins	31 66	50 11
Fort Fairfield	Aroostook	Wm. H. Cary, jr. to 31st December	11 87	22 68
		John B. Trafton	11 77	18 00
Fort Kent	Aroostook	Stover Rines, to 30th September	26 53	58 04
		William A. Winder	102 69	208 83
Foxcroft	Piscataquis	Melvin Stevens	75 35	137 87
Frankfort	Waldo	Archibald Jones	217 31	429 24
Frankfort Mills	Waldo	Barnabas Atwood	70 63	134 18
Franklin	Hancock	David Springer, jr.	55 50	102 83
Freedom	Waldo	George Raulet	85 16	140 04
Freeman	Franklin	Thomas Allen	12 42	22 68
Freeport	Cumberland	Samuel Thing	286 96	291 48
Friendship	Lincoln	Cornelius Bradford.	19 93	32 22
Fryeburgh	Oxford	Asa Charles	202 82	188 29
Gardiner	Kennebeck	Thomas Gay	664 77	1380 33
Garland	Penobscot	Jos. Springall	53 68	86 58
Georgetown	Lincoln	Jacob Power	47 34	80 90
Gilead	Oxford	Thomas Peabody	15 91	21 53
Glenburn	Penobscot	Andrew Merrill	12 64	24 77
Goff's Corners	Cumberland	James Goff, jr	89 34	154 60
Goodwin's Mills	York	Benjamin Dudley	10 99	20 70
Goose River	Waldo	Silas Piper	95 00	107 51
Gorham	Cumberland	Stevens Smith	215 82	369 59
Gouldsboro'	Hancock	Oren Whitaker	19 23	37 75
Gray	Cumberland	Meshach Humphrey to 31st December.	49 25	79 62
		James O'Donnell	45 80	70 50
Great Works	Penobscot	Samuel Bullen	36 37	67 72
Greeley	Piscataquis	John Greeley	11 05	25 69
Greenbush	Penobscot	Henry Campbell	15 85	27 86
Greene	Kennebeck	Alfred Pierce	57 68	87 65
Greenville	Piscataquis	Charles W. Gower	28 76	53 07
Greenwood	Oxford	Joseph Stevens	8 45	16 14
Guilford	Piscataquis	Wm. W. Lucas, to 13th June	46 83	68 88
		Willard W. Harris	1 88	2 31

POST OFFICES—*Maine.*

Post Offices.	Counties.	Postmasters.	Compensation.	Net proceeds.
Hallowell	Kennebeck	Ichabod Nutter	$666 85	$1187 99
Hallowell ⋈ Rds	Kennebeck	Jabez Churchill	58 02	57 63
Hampden	Penobscot	Joshua P. Trask, to 23d February	161 94	151 37
		Jonathan R. Holt	98 05	88 59
Hancock	Hancock	Lemuel Crabtree, jr.	18 77	33 27
Harmony	Somerset	Amos Bartlett	31 41	50 72
Harrington	Washington	Geo. D. Dinsmore	22 01	21 84
Harrison	Cumberland	Francis Blake	65 80	118 24
Hartford	Oxford	Harvey Bartlett	21 27	34 74
Hartland	Somerset	James Fuller	9 59	17 67
Haynesville	Aroostook	Thomas F. Hall	28 32	55 02
Hebron	Oxford	Robert Carr	21 60	30 45
Hermon	Penobscot	Jno. H. Hinckley	26 15	39 96
Hill's Corners	Penobscot	Henry Hill	9 85	17 80
Hiram	Oxford	Alpheus Spring	38 96	64 31
Hodgdon	Aroostook	Rufus Wiggin	8 26	13 54
Hodgdon's Mills	Lincoln	Caleb Hodgdon	23 38	43 06
Hollis	York	Alexr. F. Chisholm	52 64	89 44
Hope	Waldo	Solomon Harwood	40 32	62 01
Houlton	Aroostook	Leonard Pierce	495 76	874 38
Howland	Penobscot	Elisha Ayer	17 70	32 06
Industry	Franklin	Ira Emery	18 45	36 10
Isle of Haut	Hancock	John Turner	8 02	14 86
Islesborough	Waldo	Andw. P. Gilkey, to 10th July	08	19
		Nelson Gilkey	26 01	45 22
Jackson	Waldo	Uriah Warren	33 71	56 77
Jackson Brook	Washington	Watson Dyer	1 22	2 54
Jay	Franklin	Silas Jones, jr.	49 32	44 51
Jefferson	Lincoln	Jessee Rowell, three quarters	23 80	41 41
Jonesboro'	Washington	Zachs. M. Hall	23 45	26 87
Keith's Mills	Franklin	Joseph Keith	16 58	27 37
Kendall's Mills	Somerset	Eben S. Page	43 07	78 21
Kennebunk	York	Abel M. Bryant	243 72	517 53
Kennebunk Depot	York	Abial Kelley, jr	19 15	35 78
Kennebunkport	York	Enoch Cousens	180 56	295 89
Kent's Hill	Kennebeck	Dudley Moody	56 03	101 10
Kezar Falls	York	Flanders Newbegin	18 66	31 81
Kilmarnock	Piscataquis	John Hichborn	12 49	20 38
Kingfield	Franklin	John B. Wellcome	24 89	41 11
Kingsbery	Piscataquis	Sanford Kingsbery	8 03	12 78
Kirkland	Penobscot	Luke Wilder	12 85	23 56
Kittery	York	Ephm. F. Shackford	29 44	52 32
Knox. Dis. 20th Decem.	Waldo	Benjamin Vose, to 30th September	3 11	4 39

POST OFFICES—*Maine.*

Post Offices.	Counties.	Postmasters.	Compensation.	Net proceeds.
Knox Centre	Waldo	Seth Webb, (1 qr.)	$2 21	$3 70
La Grange	Penobscot	Thomas H. Bates	19 30	35 91
Lebanon	York	Increase S. Kimball, to 1st June	28 61	46 91
		Alvah Parker	3 22	5 23
Lee	Penobscot	Joseph Mallet	33 54	58 86
Leeds	Kennebeck	Franklin B. Leonard	29 30	41 20
Letter B	Oxford	John J. Bragg	15 78	27 98
Levant	Penobscot	Tim'y P. Batchelder	99 72	155 04
Lewistown	Lincoln	Mark Lowell	83 83	158 95
Lexington	Somerset	Andrew Boardman, to 31st March	11 78	19 52
		Evander W. Leonard	3 63	6 23
Liberty	Waldo	David E. Longfellow	16 28	30 87
Lights' Corners	Waldo	Beckf'd C. Mathews	5 31	7 93
Limerick	York	Humphrey Pike	94 12	153 98
Limington	York	David Otis, to 30th Sept.	10 86	21 11
		Isaac L. Mitchell	41 42	75 77
Lincoln	Penobscot	Timothy Fuller, to 14th June	90 36	155 43
		James H. Bowlen	3 06	6 36
Lincoln Centre	Penobscot	Richmond Hayward	14 85	27 80
Lincolnville	Waldo	Albert Reed	69 25	64 37
Linneus	Aroostook	Isaiah Morrison	16 93	31 83
Lisbon	Lincoln	Joshua Gerrish	39 67	73 85
Litchfield	Kennebeck	Asa Batchelder	31 92	54 05
Litchfield Corners	Kennebeck	Wm. Robinson	37 76	65 87
Little River Village	Lincoln	Moses Tebbets	28 74	48 63
Livermore	Oxford	G. W. C. Washburn	51 95	93 28
Livermore Centre	Oxford	Abner More	5 88	7 40
Livermore Falls	Kennebeck	David Hale	39 23	67 23
Locke's Mills	Oxford	Samuel B. Locke	10 35	20 19
Lovell	Oxford	James Walker	52 37	55 09
Lowell	Penobscot	Joseph Stickney	9 82	15 57
Lubec	Washington	Jos. W. Sumner	195 02	388 55
Lyman	York	Jefferson Moulton, to 31st Dec.	4 05	6 63
		Chs. D. Moulton	4 71	7 76
Lyman Centre	York	Wm. Waterhouse, jr., to 31st Dec.	3 26	5 52
		Hiram Waterhouse	3 20	5 56
McLain's Mills	Waldo	Chester B. Sumner	45 87	74 76
Machias	Washington	David G. Wilson	309 69	541 68
Machiasport	Washington	Jonathan Marston, to 18th July	2 60	4 86
		Jonathan Marston, jr	64 06	116 79

POST OFFICES—*Maine.*

Post Offices.	Counties.	Postmasters.	Compensation.	Net proceeds.
Madison	Somerset	Calvin Fletcher	$39 87	$65 16
Madison Centre	Somerset	Joshua Blackwell	12 25	14 55
Mariaville	Hancock	Jeremiah Jordan	9 40	16 53
Marion	Washington	John G. Mayo, to		
(Dis. 2d Sept.)		22d Aug	52	1 10
Masardis	Aroostook	Alexr. Woodard	9 31	18 89
Mattawamkeag	Penobscot	Asa Smith	33 98	50 48
Maxfield	Penobscot	Prince Thomas	8 30	14 10
Mechanic's Falls	Cumberland	Saml. F. Waterman	22 52	36 11
Medybemps	Washington	Ezra Whitney	6 55	11 17
Mercer	Somerset	John P. Emerson	74 02	130 74
Mericoneag	Cumberland	Washing'n Garcelon	21 98	38 43
Mexico	Oxford	David K. Gleason	11 68	25 90
Milford	Penobscot	Peleg Hall	53 76	97 12
Milltown	Washington	Isaac S. Kelsey	124 86	209 02
Milo	Piscataquis	Russell Kittredge	41 02	73 79
Minot	Cumberland	Nath. P. Woodbury	62 18	103 18
Moluncus	Aroostook	John Rollins	7 66	16 80
Monmouth	Kennebeck	Augustin Blake	73 33	116 55
Monroe	Waldo	Jos. S. Clark, to		
		31st Dec	33 35	52 80
		Greenl'f C. Nealley,		
		to 31st March	23 01	36 73
		Timothy Mayo	21 72	32 64
Monson	Piscataquis	P. H. Rice, to 3d		
		March	45 69	74 08
		Alexr. G. Houston	22 06	34 44
Monticello	Aroostook	Joel Wellington	5 33	10 06
Montville	Waldo	Samuel Atkinson	31 96	57 71
Moose River	Somerset	Jacob Lowell	(No ret.)	
Mount Desert	Hancock	John Somes, jr	33 56	56 04
Mount Vernon	Kennebeck	John Philbrick, to		
		31st March	10 47	18 50
		Darius Robbins	3 33	6 83
Mount Vernon Village	Kennebeck	Wm. H. Hartwell,		
		7 mos	45 45	68 54
		Benj. H. Gilbreth,		
		from 3d June	4 09	3 86
Naples	Cumberland	James Sanborn, to		
		30th Sept	9 89	15 90
		Nath. M. Pike	33 80	57 76
Narraguagus	Washington	John L. Campbell	295 92	354 50
Newburgh	Penobscot	Jabez Knowlton	16 25	27 33
New Castle	Lincoln	Daniel Flye	285 32	551 68
Newfield	York	James Ayer, to 24th		
		Sept	5 13	9 49
		Mark Wood	27 93	43 88

POST OFFICES—*Maine.*

Post Offices.	Counties.	Postmasters.	Compensation.	Net proceeds.
New Gloucester..	Cumberland..	Elisha H. Moseley.	$64 13	$98 05
Newport.	Penobscot...	Parker C. Prescott.	63 75	129 95
New Portland ...	Somerset....	Ward Spooner, jr..	36 69	65 98
Newry	Oxford	Samuel Eames......	9 93	19 25
New Sharon.....	Franklin. ...	Joseph Bullen, to 5th March......	70 52	109 30
		Henry E. Dyer.....	31 58	53 37
New Vineyard...	Franklin	Isaac Daggett......	5 46	9 91
Noblesboro'.....	Lincoln	John A. Chapman..	24 24	44 99
Norridgewock ...	Somerset....	Mark S. Blunt.....	117 60	192 33
North Auburn... ("Late Centre Minot.")	Cumberland..	Stephen Packard...	(no ret.)	
North Bangor....	Penobscot...	Samuel L. Fish....	21 61	39 69
North Belgrade ..	Kennebeck ..	Thomas Eldred....	16 68	28 66
North Belmont...	Waldo......	Cotton Ward......	16 38	28 57
North Berwick...	York	Benajah Buffum....	63 05	133 65
North Bethel....	Oxford......	Eliphas C. Bean....	12 91	24 29
North Blue Hill..	Hancock....	Lewis H. Green....	10 42	17 20
North Boothbay..	Lincoln	Robert Spinney....	29 08	46 33
North Bridgeton..	Cumberland..	Jacob Hazen, jr., to 17th Feb'y......	23 84	43 20
		Caleb Stevens......	22 82	35 98
North Bucksport..	Hancock....	Nehemiah Cole....	30 63	61 10
North Castine....	Hancock....	Geo. H. Emerson..	24 59	39 58
North Dixmont..	Penobscot...	William Harris....	31 05	43 58
North Edgecombe	Lincoln	Woodbridge Clifford	39 94	70 05
North Ellsworth..	Hancock....	William Jellison....	17 68	22 88
North Fairfield...	Somerset....	Galen Soule.......	12 76	20 33
Northfield	Washington..	Sherburn Huse.....	2 79	5 58
North Frankfort..	Waldo......	Thomas Snow.....	15 78	28 23
North Freeman ..	Franklin	Step'n D. Wellcome	5 20	4 14
North Fryeburg..	Oxford......	Dan'l W. O'Brien..	21 45	35 29
North Hancock...	Hancock....	Sam'l N. McFarland	8 31	12 74
North Hermon...	Penobscot...	Lionel D. Phillips, from 1st Oct......	4 09	5 58
North Hollis.....	York	Abijah Usher......	7 70	11 67
N.Kennebunkport	York	Edmund Currier, jr.	6 18	11 32
North Leeds.....	Kennebeck...	Ruel Foss.........	9 31	17 34
North Lincoln ...	Penobscot...	Charles Merrill.....	20 17	34 09
North Livermore.	Oxford......	Reuel Washburn...	57 28	88 98
North Newburgh,	Penobscot...	Isaac S. Stackpole..	5 40	8 30
North Newport..	Penobscot. ..	John B. Ireland....	8 56	13 06
North Newportland.........	Somerset. ...	Wm. Bartlett......	17 65	29 72
North Norway...	Oxford......	Daniel Noble......	17 28	31 32
North Palermo...	Waldo	Sumner Carr	77 18	25 28
North Paris......	Oxford......	Wm. Russ, to 30th Sept..........	5 74	8 10
		Calvin F. Bonney..	14 29	23 68

POST OFFICES—*Maine.*

Post Offices.	Counties.	Postmasters.	Compensation.	Net proceeds.
North Parsonfield	York	Moses Sweat	$18 01	$25 33
North Penobscot	Hancock	Harry Lowell	12 93	18 94
Northport	Waldo	Jones Shaw	36 66	36 17
North Pownal	Cumberland	Gr'd P. Thompson	18 35	30 08
North Prospect	Waldo	Luther Mudgett	28 75	47 42
North Searsmont	Waldo	Geo. U. Barstow	28 47	44 78
North Turner	Oxford	Samuel B. Holt, to 31st March	19 99	36 19
		Jesse Drew	6 35	11 78
North Turner Bridge	Oxford	Church P. Leavitt	11 56	18 30
North Vassalboro'	Kennebeck	Henry Weeks	58 63	96 06
N'th Waldoboro'	Lincoln	Reuben Orff	10 21	13 95
North Whitefield	Lincoln	James Merrill	20 43	36 44
North Wilton	Franklin	Tim'y Woodward	3 29	5 56
North Windham	Cumberland	Edmund Boody	10 94	21 35
North Yarmouth	Cumberland	Jacob G. Loring	292 83	357 30
North Yarmouth Centre	Cumberland	Edw'd G. Buxton	47 90	84 22
Norway	Oxford	Geo. J. Ordway, to 4th June	111 13	164 84
		Asa Thayer, jr	6 05	11 46
Number Three	Aroostook	Spaulding Robinson	12 24	22 75
Oak Hill	Cumberland	John Libby, 3d	16 03	29 81
Ogunquit	York	George Littlefield	30 41	56 51
Olamon	Penobscot	Jos. G. Folsom	8 63	15 94
Oldtown	Penobscot	Ira Wadleigh	170 04	300 22
Orient	Aroostook	Abraham Longley	1 89	3 85
Orland	Hancock	Parker W. Perry	56 30	99 90
Orneville	Piscataquis	Ebenezer Ewer, to 14th May	12 34	24 96
		Abner Hoxie	1 43	96
Orono	Penobscot	Samuel Buffum	163 36	307 50
Orrington	Penobscot	Warren Nickerson	41 54	72 79
Otisfield	Cumberland	Levi Patch	35 29	58 35
Oxford	Oxford	Jairus S. Keith	45 93	79 40
Palermo	Waldo	Hiram Worthing	30 04	53 59
Palmyra	Somerset	Thomas Lancey	60 73	97 73
Paris	Oxford	Geo. W. Millett	86 67	146 23
Parker's Head	Lincoln	James L. Todd	37 59	66 86
Parkman	Piscataquis	John Pratt	42 53	62 86
Parsonfield	York	Rufus McIntire	35 72	58 21
Passadumkeag	Penobscot	James Sanders, jr., to 18th June	50 05	95 69
		Aaron Haynes	77	1 68
Patricktown	Lincoln	Eleazer Sherman	6 33	12 22

POST OFFICES.—*Maine.*

Post Offices.	Counties.	Postmasters.	Compensation.	Net proceeds.
Patten	Penobscot	Eph'm C. Fairfield, to 18th July	$2 01	$4 05
		John Gardiner	78 75	139 97
Pemaquid	Lincoln	John Fossett	37 38	69 08
Pembroke	Washington	Peter G. Farnsworth	90 17	161 12
Penobscot	Hancock	Wilson Carpenter	16 73	28 27
Perry	Washington	John F. Nutt	28 93	53 27
Peru	Oxford	William Walker	18 48	33 50
Philips	Franklin	Charles Church, jr., to 14th January	68 13	83 04
		Jos. A. Linscott	61 75	68 26
Phipsburg	Lincoln	Nath'l C. Reed	73 92	138 79
Pishon's Ferry	Kennebeck	John Totman	14 16	24 47
Pittsfield	Somerset	George Whitney	20 11	26 94
Pittston	Kennebeck	Alph. H. Clark	129 96	249 08
Plymouth	Penobscot	Dan'l Stone	39 71	58 85
Poland	Cumberland	William Cousins, to 15th June	47 95	83 87
		David Dunn	1 56	2 12
Porter	Oxford	Ebenezer Blazo, jr.	28 43	46 04
Portland	Cumberland	Sylvanus R. Lyman, to 15th April	1582 42	2030 70
		Na'n L. Woodbury	410 43	576 13
Pownal	Cumberland	Hosea Newell	34 34	58 50
Presque Isle	Aroostook	William Towle	45 76	76 80
Princeton	Washington	Putnam Rolf	1 91	3 88
Prospect	Waldo	Nathaniel Stowers	43 58	79 91
Prospect Harbor	Hancock	Asa Cole	18 76	30 75
Raymond	Cumberland	John Sawyer	20 15	31 86
Readfield	Kennebeck	John Lambert	103 41	177 61
Richmond	Lincoln	Jabez R. Blanchard, to 14th January	48 85	86 22
		Thos. J. Southard	46 73	86 87
Richmond Corner	Lincoln	James W. Grant	40 62	46 31
Ripley	Somerset	John Hale	14 06	25 04
Robinston	Washington	Josiah H. Vose, to 9th June	392 14	75 63
		Jas. M. Balkam	21 56	75
Rome	Kennebeck	Thomas Whittier, (3 qrs.)	7 70	16 01
Ross' Corners	York	Otis R. Ross	7 90	12 82
Rumford	Oxford	Otis C. Bolster	61 23	100 32
Sabatus	Lincoln	Jacob Hill	12 81	21 72
Saccarappa	Cumberland	David Hayes	192 22	343 39
Saco	York	Thos. W. Shannon	795 44	1767 46
Saint Albans	Somerset	Thomas Smith	53 12	89 60
Saint George	Lincoln	George Gilchrest	39 63	79 64

POST OFFICES—*Maine.*

Post Offices.	Counties.	Postmasters.	Compensation.	Net proceeds.
Salem	Franklin	John F. Russ	$11 98	$22 83
Sanford	York	John W. Bodwell	53 47	95 57
Sangerville	Piscataquis	Wm. O. Ayer, to 13th June	44 29	72 81
		Thomas Sanders	2 04	3 39
Scarboro'	Cumberland	John Donnell	25 44	34 98
Scotland	York	Sylvester McIntyre	11 18	16 32
Seal Cove	Hancock	Jacob Sawyer	12 88	23 83
Searsmont	Waldo	Sumner Pattee	54 84	89 90
Sebago	Cumberland	William Fitch, jr	17 73	31 15
Sebasticook	Kennebeck	Crosby Hinds	34 89	57 79
Sebec	Piscataquis	Wm. P. Lamson	64 49	105 89
Sedgwick	Hancock	Nath'l K. Sawyer	95 65	162 68
Sedgwick Bay	Hancock	Joseph Herrick	13 98	23 88
Shapleigh	York	Elisha Bodwell	20 69	36 74
Sheepscott Bridge	Lincoln	Daniel Carney	69 38	116 85
Shirley	Piscataquis	Isaac Phillips	6 12	11 89
Sidney	Kennebeck	William Tilley	58 97	92 12
Skowhegan	Somerset	Lewellyn Kidder, to 31st December	77 24	130 46
		Abner Kirby, to 31st March	34 86	66 99
		John A. King	37 38	64 39
Smithfield	Somerset	Sam. S. Greeley	14 28	27 95
Smyrna	Aroostook	Oliver H. Perry	21 67	39 29
Solon	Somerset	Asa Vickere, to 26th November	20 64	35 88
		W. M. E. Brown	36 81	60 81
South Albion	Kennebeck	Thomas Burrill	8 69	11 82
South Anson	Somerset	Arthur Dinsmore	9 33	12 27
South Atkinson	Piscataquis	Leonard Hathaway	11 62	19 58
South Berwick	York	Samuel Parks	314 53	666 57
South Bridgeton	Cumberland	Marshal Cram	17 71	29 40
South Chesterville	Kennebeck	Elisha Perry	14 10	21 28
South China	Kennebeck	Ambrose H. Abbot	31 87	58 93
South Deer Isle	Hancock	Richard Warren	17 45	28 49
South Dover	Piscataquis	Stephen Lambert	14 96	27 38
South Durham	Cumberland	John Collins	8 04	13 81
South Freedom	Waldo	John W. Smith	7 69	11 66
South Hartford	Oxford	Richard Hutchinson	5 44	10 03
South Jefferson	Lincoln	John Trask, 2d	8 38	12 16
South Leeds	Kennebeck	Salmon A. Wing	13 34	23 68
South Levant	Penobscot	Jos. R. Sawyer	16 31	26 19
South Lincoln	Penobscot	Jas. W. Thompson	8 83	15 99
South Moluncus	Aroostook	Henry K. Robinson, from 1st January	3 44	6 74
South Newburgh	Penobscot	Rufus Gilmore	16 38	24 03
South Newry	Oxford	Geo. G. Chapman, fr. 1st Oct. (2 qrs.)	4 66	9 44

POST OFFICES—*Maine.*

Post Offices.	Counties.	Postmasters.	Net proceeds.	Compensation.
South Norridgewock	Somerset	Henry Butler	$32 36	$52 75
South Orrington	Penobscot	Timothy Nye, jr	29 93	52 87
South Paris	Oxford	John Dennett	66 83	106 25
South Parsonfield	York	George Hilton	13 94	20 50
South St. George	Lincoln	Joseph Fish	27 78	59 18
South Sebec	Piscataquis	Caleb C. Wingate	9 37	18 13
South Solon	Somerset	Geo. W. Fargo	11 47	17 99
South Thomaston	Lincoln	Arch'd McKellar, jr. from 5th March	12 26	24 57
South Vassalboro'	Kennebeck	Pelatiah Pierce	21 13	34 75
South Vinalhaven	Waldo	Reuben Carver	11 57	20 51
South Waterford	Oxford	Sprout Hapgood	37 61	61 24
Southwest Bend	Cumberland	Wm. L. Harmon	32 20	58 95
Southwest Harbor	Hancock	Moses Hale, to 13th June	47 19	75 02
		James R. Freeman	77	1 21
South Windham	Cumberland	Albert Webb	65 29	98 42
South Windsor	Kennebeck	Asa Heath	22 96	37 35
Springfield	Penobscot	Biab H. Scribner	17 60	35 69
Spring Vale	York	John T. Paine	88 26	168 29
Standish	Cumberland	Jos. S. Thompson	82 53	124 28
Stark	Somerset	James Varnum	22 17	35 98
Stetson	Penobscot	Horace Shepley	40 23	69 00
Steuben	Washington	Samuel Moore	52 01	94 54
Stevens' Plains	Cumberland	Christopher C. Tobie	39 10	77 82
Stow	Oxford	Moses Abbott	16 28	24 66
Strong	Franklin	Philip M. Stubbs	45 78	70 95
Sullivan	Hancock	George Hinman	45 02	73 17
Sumner	Oxford	Abel W. Bisbee	12 88	24 06
Sunkhaze	Penobscot	Charles Bailey	12 73	20 60
Surry	Hancock	Edwd. S. Jarvis	42 23	73 89
Swan's Island	Hancock	John Adams, from 9th August	13 95	26 62
Swanville	Waldo	Solo'n Cunningham	17 42	31 05
Sweden	Oxford	Benjamin Nevers	22 82	36 01
Temple Mills	Franklin	Samuel Hilton, jr	28 30	52 24
The Forks	Somerset	Moses W. Burnham	53 23	101 50
Thomaston	Lincoln	John M. Gates, to 1st June	315 58	683 38
		Samuel Fuller	26 56	60 73
Thorndike	Waldo	Josiah Harman	28 78	42 34
Topsfield	Washington	Dan. Pineo	11 06	121 53
Topsham	Lincoln	John H. Thompson, to 4th December	129 83	126 62
		Nathaniel Walker	139 62	135 93
Troy	Waldo	Samuel Heald	34 51	51 42

POST OFFICES—*Maine.*

Post Offices.	Counties.	Postmasters.	Compensation.	Net proceeds.
Turner	Oxford	John Blake, to 9th December	$47 33	$71 67
		Hiram Clark	67 51	108 33
Umcolcus	Aroostook	Benj. H. Hews	2 67	5 22
Union	Lincoln	Ebenezer Alden	107 65	194 61
Unity	Waldo	Hiram Whitehouse	94 09	157 98
Upper Gloucester	Cumberland	Joseph Cross	33 11	53 50
Upper Stillwater	Penobscot	Sam'l F. Hersey	32 19	58 56
Upper Yarmouth	Cumberland	Jabez Cushman	6 58	11 95
Vassalboro'	Kennebeck	Thomas Frye	93 67	170 99
Vienna	Kennebeck	Levi Johnson, (3 qs.)	13 91	26 80
Vinalhaven	Hancock	John Kent	27 80	40 09
Waite	Washington	John Dudley	3 95	6 22
Waldo	Waldo	Henry Davidson	21 51	36 07
Waldoboro'	Lincoln	John Balch	198 96	404 96
Wales	Lincoln	Arthur Given	24 87	44 88
Warren	Lincoln	Seth B. Wetherbee	132 14	236 43
Washington	Lincoln	Robt. E. Rider	27 58	49 47
Waterboro'	York	Jeremiah Roberts, jr.	20 19	33 58
Waterboro' Centre	York	James M. Burbank	26 57	48 93
Waterford	Oxford	Edward Carlton	72 51	113 63
Waterville	Kennebeck	Samuel Appleton	434 37	846 68
Wayne	Kennebeck	Sumner C. Moulton	93 82	164 95
Webster	Lincoln	Philip M. Garcelon	23 38	41 34
Weeks' Mills	Kennebeck	Chs. A. Russ	16 61	25 38
Welchville	Oxford	Simeon Lane	19 11	35 98
Weld	Franklin	Sumner B. Walker	37 44	70 29
Wellington	Piscataquis	Gilman Weeks	6 63	12 02
Wells	York	Matthew Lindsey	59 37	113 01
Wells' Depot	York	Adoniram J. Eaton, from 9th Aug	15 49	27 48
Wesley	Washington	John Averill	11 43	16 51
West Argyle	Penobscot	Wm. J. Thomas, (3 qrs.)	4 57	9 17
West Baldwin	Cumberland	Enoch Sanborn	16 34	27 77
West Bethel	Oxford	Henry Ward	10 91	20 91
West Brookville	Hancock	David Wasson	12 81	18 32
West Buckfield	Oxford	Nathaniel Harlow	7 59	11 08
West Buxton	York	Samuel R. Lord	45 67	72 44
West Camden	Waldo	Stephen Barrows	14 16	23 61
West Charleston	Penobscot	Joseph Bridgham, jr	11 17	17 49
West Embden	Somerset	John Pierce, jr	3 25	5 74
West Enfield (Disc'd 15th Nov., Re-est'd 6th Dec.)	Penobscot	Theodore Taylor, to 4th Dec	3 02	3 12
		Theodore Taylor, from 1st Jan	2 73	2 22

POST OFFICES—*Maine.*

Post Offices.	Counties.	Postmasters.	Compensation.	Net proceeds.
West Falmouth..	Cumberland .	Ozias Merrill	$21 56	$39 26
West Gardiner...	Kennebeck ..	George W. French.	22 19	37 53
West Glenburn..	Penobscot....	Seth Staples.......	2 43	4 02
West Gloucester.	Cumberland .	William Proctor....	15 97	26 99
West Gorham ...	Cumberland .	Daniel B. Clement..	14 95	26 94
West Gouldsboro'	Hancock	Barney S. Hill.....	13 69	20 97
West Gr't Works	Penobscot....	Hiram Miller......	20 80	34 94
West Jefferson...	Lincoln	Leander Martin....	13 61	23 72
West Lebanon...	York	Samuel W. Jones ..	21 61	34 72
West Minot	Cumberland .	William Lowell....	29 89	48 05
West Newfield...	York	Samuel C. Adams..	40 69	73 83
West New Vineyard	Franklin	Solomon Luce	10 46	15 12
Weston..........	Aroostook...	Samuel Springer ...	14 96	24 84
West Parsonfield.	York	John Bailey.......	11 15	21 56
West Poland	Cumberland .	John Megquier.....	14 82	22 49
Westport	Lincoln	Samuel Tarbox....	17 09	29 94
West Prospect...	Waldo.......	Andrew Leach.....	206 61	282 05
West Ripley.....	Somerset	Samuel A. Todd ...	4 73	7 98
West Sidney.....	Kennebeck ..	David Robinson....	6 06	10 83
West's Mills.....	Franklin	Jesse Thing	14 91	24 88
West Sumner....	Oxford......	Whitney Cummings	17 38	28 31
West Trenton ...	Hancock	Alfred Hopkins....	24 33	46 98
West Waterville .	Kennebeck ..	Wm. H. Hatch....	41 62	66 08
Whitfield.........	Lincoln	Reuben Lewis	24 84	46 69
Whiting.........	Washington..	James Crane.......	15 76	26 52
Whitneyville.....	Washington..	John Knox, from 26th May.......	9 22	9 10
Williamsburg....	Piscataquis...	Moses Greenleaf ...	10 50	18 48
Wilson..........	Piscataquis...	H. G. O. Barrows..	9 69	17 02
Wilton	Franklin	Jno. H. Willard....	137 18	122 57
Windham........	Cumberland .	Henry Houghton ..	43 07	80 42
Windsor.........	Kennebeck ..	Alonzo Rogers.....	29 29	51 19
Winslow	Kennebeck ..	Frederick Paine....	52 72	80 31
Winslow Mills...	Hancock	Samuel Wheeler, 2d (3 qrs.).........	3 47	6 31
Winthrop	Kennebeck ..	Cyrus Bishop......	261 72	454 69
Wiscasset........	Lincoln	Asa F. Hall.......	381 26	754 70
Woodstock	Oxford......	David P. Hanoford.	17 93	29 44
Woolwich.......	Lincoln	David Hathorn.....	49 53	82 55
York	York	Charles O. Clark...	87 97	155 06

POST OFFICES—*New Hampshire.*

NEW HAMPSHIRE.

NOTE.—Compensation of Postmasters, and net proceeds of their offices, from June 1, 1844, to July 30, 1845.

Post Offices.	Counties.	Postmasters.	Compensation.	Net proceeds.
Acworth	Sullivan	Daniel J. Warner	$87 34	$145 93
Alexandria	Grafton	Horace Ballou	30 00	58 37
Allenstown	Merrimack	John Rand	21 58	37 02
Alstead	Cheshire	Whitney Breed	21 20	42 72
Alton	Belknap	Nathaniel Dorman	29 48	47 84
Amherst	Hillsborough	Aaron Lawrence	189 30	315 20
Amoskeag	Hillsborough	Darwin J. Daniels	81 36	146 93
Andover	Merrimack	Samuel Butterfield	56 90	102 98
Antrim	Hillsborough	James C. Breed	33 13	68 83
Atkinson	Rockingham	Moses Dow, 2d	42 18	67 39
Barnstead	Belknap	Samuel D. Nutter	16 52	30 17
Barrington	Strafford	Solomon Waldron	34 00	62 37
Bartlett	Coos	Jonathan Hall	5 67	10 36
Bartlett Centre	Coos	Cornelius Stilphin	7 32	10 95
Bath	Grafton	Wm. V. Hutchins	171 20	306 84
Bedford	Hillsborough	Isaac Riddle	56 93	98 02
Bennington	Hillsborough	Geo. A. Whittemore	41 20	78 18
Benton	Grafton	Ira Witcher, to 2d June	5 84	11 51
		Moses Witcher	0 45	0 92
Berlin	Coos	Daniel Davis	6 52	6 72
Bethlehem	Grafton	Edward O. Kenney	24 87	44 95
Boscawen	Merrimack	Worcester Webster	78 10	135 52
Bow	Merrimack	Willeby C. Hadley	9 92	16 78
Bradford	Merrimack	Levi Morrill	81 56	143 56
Brentwood	Rockingham	Ephraim Robinson	16 57	30 82
Bridgewater	Grafton	Ab'm P. Hoit	13 47	26 02
Bristol	Grafton	Oscar F. Fowler	114 76	207 19
Brookfield	Carroll	Daniel Wiggin	9 01	19 35
Brookline	Hillsborough	James N. Tucker, to 30th Sept	5 45	9 74
		Ithamar B. Sawtell	28 46	55 76
Campton	Grafton	Jno. P. Rogers	58 48	106 90
Canaan	Grafton	Jonathan Kittredge	94 76	179 35
Candia	Rockingham	Henry M. Eaton	56 15	90 97
Canterbury	Merrimack	Jos. M. Harper	38 46	74 51
Carroll	Coos	John Howe	5 00	9 28
Carroll House	Coos	Ethan A. Crawford	4 58	8 18
Centre Barnstead	Belknap	Jeremiah Elkins, to 7th June	13 69	21 37
		Daniel Bickford	1 06	2 24

POST OFFICES—*New Hampshire.*

Post Offices.	Counties.	Postmasters.	Compensation.	Net proceeds.
Centre Conway..	Carroll......	Chs. W. Emerson, to 3d June.......	$16 13	$23 56
		Elijah Farrington...	1 69	2 93
Centre Harbor...	Belknap.....	Silas S. Whitney...	39 22	70 58
Centre Ossipee...	Carroll......	Edward Grant, jr...	28 86	55 91
Centre Sandwich.	Carroll......	Jesse Ambrose.....	56 68	99 76
Centre Strafford..	Strafford	John B. Foss......	16 36	30 52
Charlestown.....	Sullivan	J. H. Hubbard, (3 qrs.)...........	219 91	212 00
		Matthew Tole, from 11th May.......	39 34	32 01
Chesnut Hill....	Strafford	John Hayes.......	11 45	17 78
Chester	Rockingham.	Thomas J. Melvin..	79 05	138 48
Chesterfield......	Cheshire	Warham R. Platts..	117 65	112 15
Chesterfield Fac'y	Cheshire	ela Chase, to 7th B January........	18 72	33 67
		Samuel Burt, jr	21 58	40 78
Chichester	Merrimack ..	Edward Langmaid .	18 28	37 66
Claremont	Sullivan.....	John J. Prentiss, to 12th June	446 85	694 85
		A. B. Williamson..	18 72	32 44
Colebrook.......	Coos	Frederick G. Messer	83 55	134 68
Columbia........	Coos	R. D. Atherton.....	19 37	31 56
Concord.........	Merrimack ..	Robert Davis, to 31st March...........	777 28	1485 58
		Joseph Robinson...	276 19	591 12
Contoocook Village...........	Merrimack ..	Franklin R. Fuller..	56 49	105 87
Conway..........	Carroll......	John Hill	98 25	80 54
Cornish..........	Sullivan	Israel Hall.........	55 43	54 18
Cornish Flat.....	Sullivan	John S. Blanchard..	75 05	131 64
Croydon	Sullivan......	William Dodge....	45 25	76 07
Croydon Flat....	Sullivan.....	Paul Jacobs, to 1st Sept............	3 69	7 36
		Paul J. Wheeler...	15 50	29 24
Dalton..........	Coos........	Nathan H. Wilder, to 31st March....	26 53	41 61
		Linus Blakeslee....	7 36	14 68
Danbury.........	Grafton......	Cummings Hubbard	25 03	48 62
Danville.........	Rockingham.	Jonathan Sanborn..	17 35	27 87
Deerfield	Rockingham.	Enoch F. Stevens, jr	35 32	60 45
Deering..........	Hillsborough	Jas. B. Ellsworth...	20 28	34 24
Derry...........	Rockingham.	Geo. W. Pinkerton, to 2d Nov.......	72 47	127 48
		Jos. A. Gregg......	111 76	205 71
Dorchester	Grafton......	Samuel P. Wright..	14 59	27 64
Dover...........	Strafford	Asa A. Tufts......	903 64	1763 68
Drewsville.......	Cheshire.....	F. G. Drew (3 qrs.)	20 39	38 14

POST OFFICES—*New Hampshire*.

Post Offices.	Counties.	Postmasters.	Compensation.	Net proceeds.
Dublin	Cheshire	Asa Heald	$43 44	$81 78
Dunbarton	Merrimack	Isaac Stearns	42 85	68 87
Durham	Strafford	George F. Frost	92 74	168 06
East Alton	Belknap	Oliver Gilman	8 19	12 60
East Chester	Rockingham	Robert Shirley, jr.	9 40	12 34
East Haverhill	Grafton	Nathaniel Kimball, from 26th Aug.	10 45	16 00
East Kingston	Rockingham	Wm. S. Bachelder	19 10	34 71
East Landaff	Grafton	Sargent Moody	6 30	11 14
East Lebanon	Grafton	Abel Low, jr.	28 29	46 36
East Lempster	Sullivan	Sam'l P. Cawlkins	15 15	29 07
East Lyman	Grafton	Jesse Bailey	29 13	49 00
East Moultonboro	Carroll	Edward Shaw	11 78	22 76
East Northwood	Rockingham	Joel B. Virgin	24 66	45 36
East Plainfield	Sullivan	Sylvanus Martin	11 16	17 52
East Sanbornton	Belknap	Chas. W. Sanborn	22 56	39 90
East Unity	Sullivan	Tappan Sanborn	3 77	7 26
East Washington	Sullivan	Edmund Davis	25 73	39 30
East Weare	Hillsborough	Eldridge A. Bailey, to 26th July	1 45	2 59
		John Johnson	16 35	30 76
East Westmorel'd	Cheshire	Foster Wight	35 98	42 79
East Wilton	Hillsborough	James M. Dane	25 07	50 44
Eaton	Carroll	Jos. R. Hunt	58 10	53 48
Effingham	Carroll	Isaac Lord, to 31st Dec'r	16 56	30 39
		Carr Leavitt	19 56	36 48
Enfield	Grafton	Nath'l W. Westgate to 23d Jan'y	59 03	58 99
		Thomas Merrill	38 88	72 29
Epping	Rockingham	Geo. W. Lawrence, to 31st May	70 27	132 45
		John W. Morrill	5 98	11 25
Epsom	Merrimack	Benj. L. Lock	38 20	72 61
Errol	Coos	James F. Bragg	6 27	12 02
Exeter	Rockingham	Jeremiah Dearborn	456 91	985 64
Farmington	Strafford	Hiram Barker	79 07	140 99
Fishersville	Merrimack	Luther G. Johnson	78 89	129 51
Fitz William	Cheshire	Jared D. Perkins	140 77	255 21
Francistown	Hillsborough	Joseph Willard	98 67	188 24
Franconia	Grafton	Philemon Putnam	46 43	76 17
Franklin	Merrimack	Caleb Merrill	168 39	323 63
Freedom	Carroll	William Cushing	26 58	50 82
Gilford	Belknap	Benjamin Boardman	216 18	410 13
Gilford Village	Belknap	Meshach Sanborn	17 14	31 39

POST OFFICES—*New Hampshire.*

Post Offices.	Counties.	Postmasters.	Compensation.	Net proceeds.
Gilmanton	Belknap	Thomas Adams, jr., to 30th May	$108 64	$210 02
		David B. Merrill	7 01	12 78
Gilmanton Iron Works	Belknap	Cyrus W. Paige	35 73	61 61
Gilsum	Cheshire	Ezra Webster	18 58	35 86
Goffstown	Hillsborough	Erastus Woodbury, to 8th Aug	8 09	13 95
		Alonzo F. Carr, to 26th May	57 17	102 07
		David M. Taggart	8 05	15 33
Gorham	Coos	John T. Peabody	5 38	6 57
Goshen	Sullivan	Wm. H. McCrillis	25 71	47 26
Grafton	Grafton	Eleazer Barney	37 78	75 36
Grantham	Sullivan	Seth C. Sargent, to 20th Jan'y	9 14	15 41
		Oliver B. Buswell	12 56	20 07
Great Falls	Strafford	Nathaniel Wells, to 28th June	382 40	844 19
		Joseph Dam	2 25	6 21
Greenfield	Hillsborough	W. H. Whittemore	31 66	51 98
Greenland	Rockingham	John G. Pickering, to 17th Aug	6 00	11 62
		Edward Holmes	50 58	89 32
Groton	Grafton	Gilman Heath	33 45	65 74
Hampstead	Rockingham	Henry Putnam	48 68	82 25
Hampton	Rockingham	Edmund Toppan	61 66	96 31
Hampton Falls	Rockingham	Elijah Valentine	55 75	92 94
Hancock	Hillsborough	John Whitcomb	112 92	199 19
Hanover	Grafton	Jonathan Freeman	554 19	950 84
Hanover Centre	Grafton	John Smith, 2d	16 19	27 51
Harrisville	Cheshire	Cyrus Harris	29 74	55 81
Harts' Location	Coos	N. T. P. Davis	1 60	3 36
Haverhill	Grafton	John S. Bryant, to 31st Dec	97 42	167 84
		Henry W. Reding	122 01	162 15
Hebron	Grafton	David Hazleton	35 50	65 65
Henniker	Merrimack	Robert B. Eaton	92 07	169 75
Hill	Grafton	Albert Blake	76 62	141 81
Hillsboro'	Hillsborough	L. M. Kimball	77 61	139 94
Hillsboro' Bridge	Hillsborough	Daniel Brown	47 51	82 55
Hillsboro' Centre	Hillsborough	Benjamin Priest	13 32	24 22
Hinsdale	Cheshire	Frederick Boyden	138 16	135 28
Holderness	Grafton	John H. Thompson	86 34	159 42
Holderness Centre	Grafton	Barnet Currier	6 76	13 50
Hollis	Hillsborough	Edward Emerson	95 44	164 05

POST OFFICES—*New Hampshire.*

Post Offices.	Counties.	Postmasters.	Compensation.	Net proceeds.
Hookset	Merrimack	Amos G. Gale	$84 52	$161 31
Hopkinton	Merrimack	Horace Chase	94 42	177 91
Hudson	Hillsborough	Elbridge Dow	20 31	35 99
Jackson	Coos	Noah S. Lucy	11 60	22 98
Jaffrey	Cheshire	William Lacy	111 52	188 12
Jefferson	Coos	Benj. H. Plaisted	14 31	28 29
Keene	Cheshire	Chs. L. Putnam, (3 qrs.)	339 86	771 65
		William Foster, fr. 22d May	45 75	101 08
Kensington	Rockingham	John T. Blake	26 56	41 66
Kilkenny	Coos	John L. Martin	1 40	2 88
Kingston	Rockingham	Luther D. Peaslee	58 63	94 86
Lake Village	Belknap	Brackett Palmer	53 26	97 39
Lancaster	Coos	Reuben L. Adams	281 39	292 60
Landaff	Grafton	Daniel Clark	21 37	33 42
Langdon	Sullivan	Royal Shumway	28 80	45 37
Lebanon	Grafton	Geo. S. Kendrick	289 22	288 89
Lee	Strafford	Thos. B. Hall	19 20	37 76
Leighton's Corners	Carroll	Jacob Leighton	5 96	11 80
Lempster	Sullivan	Amos Dodge	48 76	81 98
Lincoln	Grafton	Simon Tuttle	7 01	13 36
Lisbon	Grafton	James Allen, to 31st March	46 95	83 09
		Bela Young	17 63	33 68
Littleton	Grafton	Simeon B. Johnson	168 32	271 89
Londonderry	Rockingham	Arley Plummer	45 81	82 49
Loudon	Merrimack	Winthrop True	38 18	72 42
Loudon Centre	Merrimack	Ira Osgood	6 11	10 11
Loudon Ridge	Merrimack	Elkins Moore	18 49	31 75
Lower Bartlett	Coos	Dan'l E. Pendexter	19 87	32 79
Lower Gilmanton	Belknap	Charles G. Kelley	11 15	22 33
Lyman	Grafton	Darius Blodgett, jr.	25 59	48 97
Lyme	Grafton	Arthur Latham, jr.	195 97	179 40
Lyndeboro'	Hillsborough	Dan'l Woodward, jr.	29 69	55 86
Manchester	Hillsborough	Paul Cragin, jr	898 79	2453 28
Marlboro'	Cheshire	Silas Collister, to 20th May	47 57	91 18
		Elijah Boyden	4 63	8 62
Marlow	Cheshire	Russell Huntley	37 92	74 32
Mason	Hillsborough	Willis Johnson	31 75	60 73
Mason Village	Hillsborough	George Elliott	75 32	140 65
Melvin Village	Carroll	Wm. S. Hersey, to 15th Nov	3 83	8 45
		James French	8 46	14 51

POST OFFICES—*New Hampshire.*

Post Offices.	Counties.	Postmasters.	Compensation.	Net proceeds.
Meredith Centre..	Belknap	Lane Plumer......	$21 92	$37 86
Meredith Village.	Belknap	Daniel Smith......	81 65	150 64
Meriden.........	Sullivan	Levi Bryant, to 31st May...........	101 28	172 17
		Perley Fifield......	9 47	11 49
Merrimack.	Hillsborough	Samuel McConihe..	46 25	83 67
Middleton.......	Strafford	Aug. G. Orne......	14 79	28 13
Milan	Coos........	Lewis Hutchinson..	6 58	12 60
Milford	Hillsborough	Jonathan Bartlett...	123 49	236 92
Milton..........	Strafford	Samuel Nudd......	27 28	54 24
Milton Mills.....	Strafford	Brackett Merrill. to 30th Sep........	4 63	8 86
		James Berry.......	17 29	34 04
Moultonboro'....	Carroll......	Nathan Morse.....	27 92	52 03
Mount Vernon....	Hillsborough	Franklin O. Kittridge	53 23	93 91
Nashua.........	Hillsborough	David Philbrick....	799 89	1905 35
Nelson..........	Cheshire	Ruel Nims........	25 64	52 23
Nelson Factory..	Cheshire	Pembroke Fisher...	8 97	16 52
New Alstead....	Cheshire	Jas. F. Isham......	24 63	40 93
New Boston.....	Hillsborough	Waterman Burr....	85 74	155 47
Newbury........	Merrimack ..	Eli Dodge.........	12 19	17 57
New Durham....	Strafford	Jere. D. Evans.....	17 53	31 54
New Hampton...	Belknap	James Simpson....	173 78	325 81
Newington	Rockingham .	F. W. De Rochemont	12 38	20 49
New Ipswich....	Hillsborough	Charles Hastings, jr.	251 03	457 70
New London....	Merrimack ..	Benj. W. Seamans.	91 09	160 21
New Market.....	Rockingham .	David Murray, to 23d May........	230 63	438 83
		Geo. A. Bennett....	24 65	45 00
Newport.	Sullivan.....	Calvin Wilcox, to 25th May.......	201 48	313 54
		John B. Stowell....	14 44	26 25
Newtown	Rockingham .	M. F. Hayt........	21 01	33 64
North Barnstead.	Belknap.....	Sam'l Webster.....	15 38	26 61
North Branch....	Hillsborough	Hiram Griffin, to 22d May.........	20 45	37 52
		Wm. P. Little......	3 03	5 88
North Charlesto'n	Sullivan.....	Lewis Gilmore.....	41 84	40 87
North Chichester.	Merrimack ..	Henry Robey......	7 51	14 87
North Conway...	Carroll	Dan'l Eastman.....	33 47	58 30
North Dunbarton.	Merrimack ..	Peter C. Page......	6 50	13 39
North Enfield....	Grafton.	Alpheus Conant....	23 01	38 08
Northfield.	Merrimack ..	John Mooney......	14 52	28 12
North Hampton..	Rockingham .	John Hobbs.......	22 86	37 62
North Haverhill..	Grafton.	Willard Whitman..	57 23	112 87
North Littleton..	Grafton.	Sylvester P. Williams, (3 qrs.)...	8 54	15 83

POST OFFICES—*New Hampshire.*

Post Offices.	Counties.	Postmasters.	Compensation.	Net proceeds.
N'th Londonderry	Rockingham	David Flanders	$23 58	$38 04
North Lyman	Grafton	Albert Mason	13 21	20 43
North Marlow	Cheshire	Alden Huntley	6 97	11 96
North Salem	Rockingham	Ebr. G. Duston	13 67	19 56
North Sandwich	Carroll	Jacob F. Moulton	12 19	24 31
Northumberland	Coos	Henry Hall	28 50	55 12
North Wakefield	Carroll	Alva Bickford	13 05	27 07
North Wolfboro'	Carroll	Henry Veasey	14 40	29 50
Notch House	Coos	Thos. J. Crawford	5 36	8 74
Nottingham	Rockingham	Ebenezer Butler	14 16	26 37
Nottingham Turnpike	Rockingham	B. W. Crawford, to 31st Dec'r	1 91	3 87
		John Crawford	2 19	4 14
Orford	Grafton	Henry H. Howard	112 14	207 39
Orfordville	Grafton	Rufus C. Beal	47 91	87 51
Ossipee	Carroll	Luth'r D. Sawyer	34 98	65 32
Paper Mill Village	Cheshire	Thos. R. Prentiss	64 40	109 55
Pelham	Hillsborough	David Cutler	71 35	113 38
Pembroke	Merrimack	George Noyes	73 01	139 27
Peterboro'	Hillsborough	Samuel Gates	244 35	491 16
Piermont	Grafton	Isaiah E. Emerson	48 11	76 64
Pittsfield	Merrimack	John Berry	116 20	205 61
Plainfield	Sullivan	Asa D. Kingsbury	59 79	68 58
Plaistow	Rockingham	Levi B. Tucker	39 86	64 10
Plymouth	Grafton	Denison R. Burnham to 27th May	169 19	260 54
		Timothy Eastman	14 90	25 17
Poplin	Rockingham	Chs. W. Follett	12 43	19 60
Protsmouth	Rockingham	Samuel Gookin, to 26th April	1126 11	2791 63
		Nehemiah Moses	18 60	541 14
Randolph	Coos	Robt. P. Hodgdon, jr	4 11	4 87
Raymond	Rockingham	Joseph Blake	32 54	60 29
Richmond	Cheshire	Danford Tyler	37 05	73 21
Rindge	Cheshire	Chs. E. Plummer	86 34	147 47
Rochester	Strafford	Dominicus Hanson	175 43	322 01
Roxbury	Cheshire	Asa Lawrence	7 41	15 75
Rumney	Grafton	Abram Ward	62 08	111 50
Rye	Rockingham	J. T. Walker	33 60	60 71
Salem	Rockingham	Jno. C. Ewins	38 06	69 13
Salisbury	Merrimack	Moses Eastman	93 79	180 06
Sanbornton	Belknap	Jas. B. Abbott, to 6th June	57 03	111 58
		Bartlett Hill	3 36	6 33

POST OFFICES—*New Hampshire.*

Post Offices.	Counties.	Postmasters.	Compensation.	Net proceeds.
Sanbornton Bridge	Belknap	John Taylor	$89 78	$168 41
Sandown	Rockingham	Frederick Seavy	17 87	26 12
Sandwich	Carroll	Paul Wentworth	42 97	74 61
Seabrook	Rockingham	John Philbrick	26 25	46 83
Shaker Village	Merrimack	Orville Messer	37 68	72 00
Shelburn	Coos	George Green	15 19	26 94
South Alton	Belknap	John Lang	5 30	10 16
South Bradford	Merrimack	Geo. H. Hubbard	23 06	36 61
South Deerfield	Rockingham	Josiah Butler	22 86	45 35
South Hampton	Rockingham	Moses Eaton, jr	19 32	36 25
South Kingston	Rockingham	Gideon Webster	5 18	9 07
South Lyndeboro'	Hillsborongh	Joel H. Tarbell	12 08	17 90
South Merrimack	Hillsborough	Rhodolphus D. Bennett, from 29th Aug.	9 50	17 26
South Newmarket	Rockingham	John Choate	67 38	121 54
South Stoddard	Cheshire	James Wilson, jr	5 95	11 24
South Tamworth	Carroll	John T. D. Folsom, jr., from 21st Sept.	11 23	18 40
South Weare	Hillsborough	James Wallace	32 36	51 21
South Wolfboro'	Carroll	Solomon P. Horn	22 49	42 97
Springfield	Sullivan	Owa C. Howard	16 45	28 49
Stark	Coos	Abijah Potter, jr	1 73	3 29
Stewartstown	Coos	John Harriman	24 35	40 82
Stoddard	Cheshire	Wm. H. Ireland, to 21st May	39 81	81 82
		Ashley Jones	3 57	7 03
Strafford	Strafford	B. W. Jenness	14 01	31 45
Strafford Corner	Strafford	John O. Howard	11 82	21 56
Stratford	Coos	Elisha A. Barlow	14 28	30 83
Stratham	Rockingham	Zebulon Wiggin	41 87	70 45
Sugar Hill	Grafton	Artemas Wells	25 38	37 53
Sullivan	Cheshire	J. N. Wardwell	15 88	31 24
Suncook	Merrimack	Joseph Emery	44 45	78 39
Surry	Cheshire	John Johnson	23 19	26 24
Sutton	Merrimack	Nath'l A. Davis	67 26	101 06
Swanzey	Cheshire	Amos Bailey	73 24	129 03
Tamworth	Carroll	Enoch Remick	72 57	105 95
Temple	Hillsborough	George Whiting	26 46	48 25
Thornton	Grafton	Jos. E. Dow	25 44	52 68
Thornton's Ferry	Hillsborough	Caleb Jones, from 27th July	23 40	39 41
Troy	Cheshire	Brown Nurse	51 93	98 58
Tuftonboro'	Carroll	John Peavey	36 95	32 23
Union	Carroll	Andrew G. Hall, to 30th September	3 17	3 82
		Josa. G. Hall	10 64	13 94
Unity	Sullivan	Francis Chase	46 77	63 76

POST OFFICES—*New Hampshire.*

Post Offices.	Counties.	Postmasters.	Compensation.	Net proceeds.
Upper Gilmanton.	Belknap.....	John Evans, jr., to 2d June.........	$34 49	$50 77
		Ira Mooney	2 94	5 04
Upper Strafford..	Strafford....	Nath. E. Hanson...	2 63	5 54
Wadley's Falls...	Strafford	Gardner Towle	18 70	28 78
Wakefield.......	Carroll......	Samuel Yeaton.....	74 98	147 32
Walpole........	Cheshire	George Allen.......	386 40	468 04
Warner.........	Merrimack ..	Geo. A. Pillsbury ..	71 10	127 00
Warren.........	Grafton	David C. French....	35 48	66 43
Washington	Sullivan.....	C. G. Pressey......	56 98	96 24
Weare..........	Hillsborough	Hiram Simons.....	61 14	116 99
Wendell........	Sullivan.....	John Hopkins	11 11	19 58
Wentworth.......	Grafton	Thos. J. Whipple..	61 67	113 94
West Alton......	Belknap.....	John Flanders	6 11	11 89
West Boscawen..	Merrimack ..	F. H. Boyden	42 54	61 82
West Branch	Grafton......	Robert Smith......	9 04	18 41
West Chester....	Rockingham.	David Currier......	52 82	82 38
West Claremount.	Sullivan.....	John Tyler.........	33 86	33 35
West Deerfield...	Rockingham.	Tim. Batchelder, jr.	7 11	14 27
West Enfield.....	Grafton......	Denison Sargent, f'm 14th February...	1 67	2 69
West Lebanon...	Grafton......	Wm. R. Barron....	58 80	55 63
Westmoreland ...	Cheshire	Simeon Cobb, 2d...	75 05	134 53
West Northwood.	Rockingham.	Simon Vesey......	36 45	69 32
West Plymouth..	Grafton......	Jos. D. Osgood.....	29 49	53 93
Westport........	Cheshire	Sylvanus Bartlett...	21 56	41 52
West Rumney...	Grafton......	Kendall Osgood....	54 30	52 79
West Shelburn...	Coos.........	Jonathan Lary......	1 03	1 40
West Springfield.	Sullivan......	Levi Richardson....	28 14	44 78
W't Stewartstown	Coos........	Jeremiah Pickard...	9 14	15 60
West Thornton..	Grafton......	Jas. P. Tilton......	10 87	19 79
West Winchester.	Cheshire	Alvan W. Ball.....	56 51	101 16
West Windham..	Rockingham.	Daniel Blaisdell....	11 99	18 97
Whitefield.......	Coos........	Baker Dodge	56 56	90 11
Wilmot.........	Merrimack ..	Merrill Cross......	36 99	70 54
Wilton..........	Hillsborough	Timothy Parkhurst.	54 83	96 67
Winchester......	Cheshire	Calvin Burnap.....	169 86	303 24
Windham........	Rockingham.	Robert Bartley.....	55 34	100 41
Wolfboro'.......	Carroll......	Daniel Pickering...	61 57	114 95
Woodstock......	Grafton	Thomas Vincent, jr.	27 78	53 01

VERMONT.

NOTE.—Compensation of Postmasters, and net proceeds of their offices, from July 1, 1844, to June, 30, 1845.

Post Offices.	Counties.	Postmasters.	Compensation.	Net proceeds.
Addison	Addison	Gideon Seeger, to 6th Oct.	$12 18	$20 39
		Warren S. Brown	26 96	50 00
Albany	Orleans	Jonathan Fitz	31 42	55 27
Alburgh	Grand Isle	S. J. Davis	28 90	51 30
Alburgh Springs	Grand Isle	Elisha Reynolds	14 26	26 36
Andover	Windsor	John B. Manning	27 32	43 41
Arlington	Bennington	Cyrus B. Hills	78 74	133 88
Athens	Windham	Ethalstan Bayley	25 53	43 90
Avery's Gore	Franklin	Ebenezer Wellman	7 76	10 70
Bakersfield	Franklin	Chs. C. Stone	77 56	143 18
Barnard	Windsor	Jos. B. Danforth, jr.	76 95	137 44
Barnet	Caledonia	Henry Stevens	69 03	122 48
Barre	Washington	George S. Johnson, to 9th August	10 10	19 66
		James Hale	107 38	199 23
Barton	Orleans	Ellis Cobb, to 13th May	66 84	119 24
		S. S. Hemenway	9 24	15 05
Bartonsville	Windham	Chs. F. Barrett	57 31	55 60
Bellows Falls	Windham	John W. Moore	280 12	300 46
Bennington	Bennington	John C. Haswell, to 18th July	16 61	25 25
		Edward Rice	221 38	418 93
Benson	Rutland	E. H. Aiken, to 24th May	102 22	172 12
		John Kellogg, jr.	5 07	10 37
Berkshire	Franklin	Harrison S. Bowen	28 71	56 04
Berlin	Washington	Israel Dewey	26 01	50 77
Bethel	Windsor	Jacob Smith	179 17	264 48
Bloomfield	Essex	Selden Burbank, to 25th August	0 74	1 33
		Stephen A. Foss, to 12th June	5 54	9 13
		Martin French	0 37	0 53
Bolton	Chittenden	Joseph Smith	11 58	23 83
Boltonville (Disc. 15th April.)	Orange	Thomas Wason	7 55	13 08
Bradford	Orange	George Prichârd	213 71	345 18
Braintree	Orange	Jefferson P. Kidder	43 40	78 56

POST OFFICES—*Vermont.*

Post Offices.	Counties.	Postmasters.	Compensation.	Net proceeds.
Brandon	Rutland	Aaron J. Ketcham, to 23d May	$272 38	$561 54
		Edward Jackson	27 99	63 97
Brattleboro'	Windham	F. H. Fessenden	659 58	1081 88
Bridgewater	Windsor	Forest Henry, to 30th Sept	20 66	33 74
		Philander Smith	61 88	107 73
Bridport	Addison	Friend P. Fletcher	106 04	188 54
Bristol	Addison	Datus R. Gaige	62 26	122 41
Brookfield	Orange	Andrew W. Bigelow	91 16	140 72
Brookline	Windham	Joel Codding	12 76	23 56
Brownington	Orleans	Thomas C. Stewart	40 22	77 87
Brownsville	Windsor	Samuel Parker	70 41	109 72
Brunswick	Essex	David Hyde	5 45	10 88
Burke	Caledonia	Lucius Denison	46 86	87 73
Burlington	Chittenden	William Noble	1021 37	2395 21
Cabot	Caledonia	George W. Stone	64 95	121 70
Calais	Washington	Jonas Hall	25 40	46 11
Cambridge	Lamoille	Henry Stowell, to 14th May	58 69	106 77
		Wm. S. Meech	6 80	11 87
Cambridge Port	Windham	John S. Fullerton	37 74	62 90
Canaan	Essex	Alex'r M. Morrill	31 19	59 69
Castleton	Rutland	Chester Spencer, to 30th Sep	91 74	125 15
		Cullen Moulton	261 26	374 25
Cavendish	Windsor	Otis Robbins	130 49	143 33
Charlotte	Chittenden	Samuel H. Barnes	105 78	171 55
Chelsea	Orange	Jonathan Smith, jr.	192 84	366 57
Chester	Windsor	Joel Gould, (3 qrs)	233 68	236 75
Chimney Point	Addison	George B. Pease	18 56	32 46
Chipman's Point	Rutland	Walter Chipman	2 89	5 08
Chittenden	Rutland	Edward Fales	22 49	40 89
Clarendon	Rutland	Caleb B. Hall	50 89	54 60
Clarendon Springs	Rutland	Harry Hitchcock	32 63	51 07
Colchester	Chittenden	Cassius Phelps	33 07	45 76
Concord	Essex	John G. Darling	29 66	53 25
Corinth	Orange	Theodore Cook, to 17th June	57 27	94 70
		William Spencer	1 20	2 27
Corners	Windsor	Amasa Gay	29 88	55 13
Cornwall	Addison	Samuel Everts	89 81	157 95
Coventry	Orleans	Elijah Cleveland, to 8th March	41 00	67 92
		Holland Thrasher	17 74	21 51
Craftsbury	Orleans	Wm. E. Paddock	87 01	156 19
Cuttingsville	Rutland	David B. Jones	59 56	91 41

POST OFFICES—*Vermont.*

Post Offices.	Counties.	Postmasters.	Compensation.	Net proceeds.
Danby	Rutland	Aaron R. Vail	$86 20	$79 71
Danby 4 Corners	Rutland	Isaac M. Daniels	14 28	25 46
Danville	Caledonia	S. J. Y. Vail, to 18th May	245 49	221 21
		Jos. C. Fuller	31 91	28 76
Derby	Orleans	Nehemiah Colby	97 74	160 42
Derby Line	Orleans	Elbridge G. Johnson	245 47	205 14
Dorset	Bennington	James A. Hodge	85 08	146 45
Dover	Windham	Martin Perry	24 76	41 84
Dummerston	Windham	Luther Allyn	49 58	90 53
East Barnard	Windsor	Seymour Belknap, to 23d May	27 20	43 64
		Oliver Walcott	3 02	4 78
East Bennington	Bennington	Henry Robinson	139 67	249 17
East Berkshire	Franklin	William Clapp	47 58	70 17
East Bethel	Windsor	Oliver H. Brooks	49 44	84 97
East Brookfield	Orange	Marshall P. Davis	10 52	20 89
East Calais	Washington	Asa Alden	15 49	28 80
East Charleston	Orleans	Edward D. Goodwin	21 48	38 19
East Clarendon	Rutland	Ruel Parker	23 50	41 19
East Corinth	Orange	John Merrill	32 93	59 94
East Dorset	Bennington	Marcus B. Roberts	19 45	32 23
East Fairfield	Franklin	H. H. Beardsley	10 05	16 49
East Highgate	Franklin	Dan'l H. Farrington	11 86	18 58
East Middlebury	Addison	Levi Needham	35 55	58 95
East Montpelier	Washington	Apollos Metcalf	31 59	51 97
East Poultney	Rutland	James P. Harris	192 31	187 91
East Randolph	Orange	Alfred Hebard, to 19th April	57 25	98 86
		Harvey Curtis	11 40	20 14
East Roxbury	Washington	Samuel Ruggles	11 16	18 55
East Rupert	Bennington	Kinne Prescott	30 50	41 72
East Sheldon	Franklin	Phineas Kingsley	12 92	18 90
East Swanton	Franklin	Alonzo Green	12 51	19 70
Eden	Lamoille	Luther H. Brown	31 33	48 55
Elmore	Lamoille	Abel Camp	17 03	31 01
Enosburgh	Franklin	Thomas Fuller	44 72	70 40
Enosburgh Falls	Franklin	Samuel Kendall	11 46	19 72
Essex	Chittenden	Lorin Tyler	83 03	138 58
Factory Point	Bennington	Lyman Harrington, to 11th June	101 24	178 21
		C. A. Roberts	5 29	10 39
Fairfax	Franklin	Silas W. Brush	66 74	105 77
Fairfield	Franklin	Albert G. Soule	59 07	98 20
Fair Haven	Rutland	Azel Willard, jr.	90 12	117 77
Fairlee	Orange	Jerome B. Bailey	23 46	37 90

POST OFFICES—*Vermont.*

Post Offices.	Counties.	Postmasters.	Compensation.	Net proceeds.
Fayetteville	Windham	Franklin Sawyer, to 24th May	$58 60	$109 74
		Jacob Dunklee, jr.	5 66	9 52
Felchville	Windsor	Walton Brown	40 26	68 74
Fletcher	Franklin	Medad P. Blair	19 45	31 81
Franklin	Franklin	Rollin S. Tenny	44 66	76 23
Gaysville	Windsor	Merrick Gay	44 11	72 30
Georgia	Franklin	Albert Bliss	82 86	135 82
Glover	Orleans	Enoch B. Simonds	49 86	101 50
Grafton	Windham	Fabius Bancroft	96 33	162 21
Grand Isle	Grand Isle	John Williamson	37 94	61 05
Granville	Addison	Warren Hayden	17 75	29 16
Greenbush	Windsor	George White	16 44	30 80
Green River	Windham	Wm. G. Cutting, to 30th Sept	4 37	7 10
		Hiram S. Cutting	13 31	25 20
Greensboro'	Orleans	Loring F. Waterman	73 23	72 52
Groton	Caledonia	William Darling	28 93	52 29
Guild Hall	Essex	David E. Denison	37 27	68 00
Guilford	Windham	Daniel Jacobs	43 95	76 83
Guilford Centre	Windham	George A. Hunt	18 47	31 12
Halifax	Windham	Stephen Niles	26 74	50 76
Hammond's Mill	Windham	Peter Hammond	25 66	43 26
Hancock	Addison	Royal Flint	28 12	45 13
Hardwick	Caledonia	Lewis H. Delano	54 93	93 73
Hartford	Windsor	Justin C. Brooks	141 82	138 19
Hartland	Windsor	Curtis Cady, to 25th May	182 26	178 55
		Reuben Weld	17 71	17 55
Highgate	Franklin	Samuel W. Keyes, to 28th April	264 65	103 62
		Stephen S. Keyes	20 03	32 61
Highgate Spring	Franklin	Harvey N. Cole, (3 qrs.)	3 61	7 03
Hinesburg	Chittenden	Thomas W. Gibb	105 05	200 46
Holland	Orleans	Matthew P. Davis	13 84	22 17
Houghtonville	Windham	Thos. P. Houghton	6 41	10 05
Hubbardton	Rutland	Eb'r B. Dewey	37 20	68 03
Huntington	Chittenden	Orange Dyke	34 78	53 44
Hyde Park	Lamoille	Carlos S. Noyes	78 44	131 36
Ira	Rutland	Joseph Chapman	12 82	23 75
Irasburg	Orleans	T. P. Redfield	78 43	110 96
Jacksonville	Windham	David D. Wilcox, to 31st Dec	9 05	18 80
		Laban J. Childs	9 45	19 30

POST OFFICES—*Vermont.*

Post Offices.	Counties.	Postmasters.	Compensation.	Net proceeds.
Jamaica	Windham	Lyman Merrifield	$50 99	$84 54
Jay	Orleans	Lanson Sanborn	4 49	8 64
Jeffersonville	Lamoille	Nathaniel Read, jr.	41 90	70 90
Jericho	Chittenden	Silas C. Witherley	51 36	83 68
Jericho Centre	Chittenden	Simeon Bicknell	44 20	73 25
Johnson	Lamoille	Stoughton S. Pike	109 41	189 99
Land Grove	Bennington	Selah Warner	11 66	22 25
Leicester	Addison	Silas S. Johnson	28 99	55 83
Lemington	Essex	Abdiel Blodgett	4 08	9 07
Lincoln	Addison	Luther M. Kent	18 90	39 02
Londonderry	Windham	Peter Dudley, jr.	76 00	127 74
Lowell	Orleans	Amasa Paine	24 60	44 50
Lower Waterford	Caledonia	T. R. Fairbanks, to 30th Sept.	7 81	14 93
		Russell Armington	26 96	51 72
Ludlow	Windsor	Danl. Perry, to 31st Aug.	47 26	45 91
		John R. Smith, to 22d May	164 46	172 40
		Charles S. Mason	14 89	13 46
Lunenburgh	Essex	Seneca Sargent, to 27th July	2 35	5 51
		Nathl. W. French	44 71	88 31
Lyndon	Caledonia	Ephr'm Chamberlin	149 01	197 63
Lyndon Centre	Caledonia	John M. Hoyt	31 26	48 59
McIndoe's Falls	Caledonia	John McNab	40 90	63 14
Manchester	Bennington	Levi C. Orvis	158 90	273 75
Marlboro'	Windham	Jesse Cone	29 25	55 64
Marshfield	Washington	Samuel Ainsworth, to 30th Sept	4 61	9 41
		Jabez L. Carpenter	20 08	37 15
Mechanicsville	Rutland	Dan Peck	29 03	42 71
Mendon	Rutland	Edward Mussey	8 34	15 52
Middlebury	Addison	Charles Bowen	579 89	1187.89
Middlesex	Washington	Wm. C. Stowell, to 31st May	30 83	61 47
		Geo. T. Stowell	1 92	4 36
Middletown	Rutland	Orson Clark	69 19	118 37
Milton	Chittenden	George Ayres, to 11th Oct	25 90	44 18
		Hiram B. Smith	68 63	104 45
Monkton	Addison	Leavens C. Keeler	43 15	81 31
Montgomery	Franklin	Asa Wheeler	21 93	38 81
Montpelier	Washington	George W. Reed	702 15	1546 58
Moretown	Washington	Lester Kingsley	20 77	42 24
Morgan	Orleans	Samuel Bartlett	14 53	22 73
Morristown	Lamoille	William Stevens	52 63	45 50

POST OFFICES—*Vermont.*

Post Offices.	Counties.	Postmasters.	Compensation.	Net proceeds.
Morrisville	Lamoille	Daniel Gilbert	$55 78	$92 20
Mount Holly	Rutland	Geo. E. Bingham	49 21	77 95
Newark	Caledonia	Wm. G. Denison, to 21st Nov	3 03	6 28
		Hollis Bruce	4 50	9 35
Newbury	Orange	Prentiss Knight	189 36	379 20
New Haven	Addison	Anson Bird	59 64	107 12
New Haven Mills	Addison	Hiram Rider	17 67	31 79
Newport	Orleans	Phineas Page	18 88	33 64
North Bennington	Bennington	Wm. E. Hawks	101 00	172 39
North Danville	Caledonia	Wm. J. Stanton	28 74	54 42
North Dorset	Bennington	Lewis Curtis, (3 qrs)	6 54	12 08
		Daniel Curtis	1 66	3 61
North Fairfax	Franklin	John H. Richardson	13 73	20 34
North Ferrisburg	Chittenden	John W. Martin	85 15	148 02
Northfield	Washington	Elijah Smith	174 01	335 20
North Hartland	Windsor	William Griffin, to 30th Nov	10 00	12 35
		Jas. N. Willard, jr.	14 43	14 42
North Hero	Grand Isle	Asahel Allen	22 22	37 96
North Montpelier	Washington	Benjamin Southwick	19 44	33 73
North Springfield	Windsor	John White	56 28	92 29
North Troy	Orleans	Wm. C. Gilman	39 22	73 65
North Wardsboro'	Windham	Josiah G. Higgins	30 64	60 77
Norwich	Windsor	Harvey Burton, to 24th May	214 92	203 67
		Ira Davis	25 29	24 99
Orange	Orange	Orange Fifield	10 37	22 00
Orwell	Rutland	G. A. Austin, to 24th Sept	38 92	71 67
		Miner B. Catlin	114 67	251 12
Panton	Addison	Wareham Brown	12 28	25 89
Passumsic	Caledonia	Levi P. Parks	43 44	69 07
Pawlet	Rutland	Thos. J. Swallow	149 36	254 57
Peacham	Caledonia	Ephraim C. Brown	98 41	188 66
Perkinsville	Windsor	Joseph Kidder	79 09	132 01
Peru	Bennington	Oliver P. Simonds	21 00	40 87
Pittsfield	Rutland	Asa Gaines, to 31st Oct	12 31	24 32
		Benjamin F. Baker, to 22d June	27 96	49 10
		Asa Gaines	93	1 93
Pittsford	Rutland	Saml. D. Winslow	181 12	341 63
Plainfield	Washington	Nathaniel Bancroft	51 81	108 75
Plymouth	Windsor	Rowland P. Pollard	19 43	36 13

POST OFFICES—*Vermont.*

Post Offices.	Counties.	Postmasters.	Compensation.	Net proceeds.
Pomfret	Windsor	Crosby Miller, to 2d June	$27 00	$48 02
		Alon. L. Chamberlin	2 31	3 97
Post Mill Village	Orange	Thos. B. Brown	52 78	92 96
Pownal	Bennington	Jno. M. Potter	54 64	89 11
Proctorsville	Windsor	Elijah F. Parker	137 13	182 52
Putney	Windham	Peyton R. Chandler	176 41	290 34
Quechee Village	Windsor	Jacob Dimick	75 27	138 44
Randolph	Orange	Philander Perrin	129 62	215 32
Reading	Windsor	Hom. H. Hammond, to 23d May	22 80	41 05
		David Hammond	2 65	4 40
Readsboro' City	Bennington	Joel Ranney	16 53	21 27
Richford	Franklin	Alden Sears, to 30th Sept.	6 51	9 86
		Guy R. Butler	24 89	29 08
Richmond	Chittenden	Kilburn Whitcomb, to 31st Oct.	30 07	55 83
		John Delaware, jr.	97 04	96 31
Ripton	Addison	Daniel Chipman	15 74	28 46
Rochester	Windsor	Charles Morgan	115 04	183 81
Rockingham	Windham	Elias Olcott, jr.	70 93	68 38
Roxbury	Washington	John M. Spalding	13 13	26 36
Royalton	Windsor	Edward P. Nevins	138 67	226 44
Rupert	Bennington	David Sheldon	23 91	37 74
Rutland	Rutland	Moses Hawks, to 3d Dec.	200 93	263 96
		J. C. Dexter, to 14th Feb.	81 18	112 21
		Moses Hawks	144 57	236 32
Ryegate	Caledonia	George Cowles	40 23	71 34
Saint Albans	Franklin	Luther L. Dutcher	404 26	838 72
Saint George	Chittenden	Reuben Lockwood	5 10	8 79
Saint Johnsbury	Caledonia	Moses Kittredge	301 25	381 08
Saint Johnsbury Centre	Caledonia	Wm. P. Stoughton	72 06	100 65
St. Johnsbury East	Caledonia	David Goodall	61 59	104 68
Salisbury	Addison	Harvey Deming	61 71	125 43
Sandgate	Bennington	Joseph Tuttle	21 90	36 08
Sax's Mills	Franklin	Allen Barr	38 68	57 48
Saxton's River	Windham	Benjamin Frost	164 65	159 65
Searsburgh	Bennington	John Harris	10 43	18 99
Shaftsbury	Bennington	Norman R. Douglass	50 49	89 25
Sharon	Windsor	Chester Baxter, to 29th May	97 61	116 55
		Wooster Downer	4 83	9 89

POST OFFICES—*Vermont.*

Post Offices.	Counties.	Postmasters.	Compensation.	Net proceeds.
Sheffield	Caledonia	Joseph Ide	$20 02	$37 86
Shelburn	Chittenden	Geo. B. Isham	149 90	147 19
Sheldon	Franklin	Saml. B. Sheldon, to 14th Jan	35 41	60 13
		Alfred Keith	29 66	42 59
Sherburne	Rutland	Benjamin Maxham	15 55	30 48
Shoreham	Addison	Edm'd B. Hill	165 03	298 30
Shrewsbury	Rutland	Stephen Gleason	32 61	56 57
Simonsville	Windsor	Charles Sherwin	19 29	31 25
Snow's Store	Windsor	Philip T. Snow	32 07	47 71
South Barre	Washington	Alvan Carter	39 47	75 94
South Halifax	Windham	Jedediah Stark	3 17	6 76
South Hardwick	Caledonia	Alden E. Judevine	59 29	100 98
South Hero	Grand Isle	Orville G. Wheeler	42 89	63 09
South Newbury	Orange	Thos. J. Doe	20 42	40 45
South Pomfret	Windsor	Leml. S. Murdock	8 05	15 20
Suoth Reading	Windsor	Rufus Buck	27 96	44 25
South Shaftsbury	Bennington	Chas. E. Houghton	25 17	43 71
South Strafford	Orange	Harry Russ	66 56	109 83
South Walden	Caledonia	Leonard Farrington	28 58	45 52
South Wallingford	Rutland	John H. Vail	28 38	28 02
South Woodstock	Windsor	Oliver Bailey	61 35	89 61
Springfield	Windsor	George Washburn	305 48	334 01
Stamford	Bennington	Stephen C. Millard	18 16	31 71
Starksboro'	Addison	Elisha Ferguson	42 21	72 57
Stockbridge	Windsor	Justin Morgan, jr., to 24th May	25 80	41 39
		Azro B. Morgan	2 24	3 54
Stowe	Lamoille	Nathaniel Robinson	134 93	130 25
Strafford	Orange	Wm. H. Sanborn	70 92	125 57
Stratton	Windham	Freeman Wyman, from 16th Aug	7 24	15 83
Sudbury	Rutland	Chas. W. Horton	41 18	76 44
Sunderland	Bennington	Giles B. Bacon, to 16th Sept	3 04	7 27
		Gilbert Bradley	14 44	25 70
Sutton	Caledonia	John Beckwith	36 61	66 83
Swanton	Franklin	H. B. Farrar	86 98	150 04
Swanton Centre	Franklin	Erastus B. Rounds	14 64	25 03
Taftsville	Windsor	Dustin Bates	34 18	61 39
Thetford	Orange	Loved Garey	103 76	179 94
Tinmouth	Rutland	William Vaughan	20 47	39 87
Topsham	Orange	Isaac McNiece	29 37	57 34
Townshend	Windham	John Roberts	75 02	132 61
Troy	Orleans	Frederick Fuller	84 50	75 81
Troy Furnace	Orleans	Hubbard Hastings	12 06	20 38
Tunbridge	Orange	Francis Sturtevant	81 28	137 63
Tyson Furnace	Windsor	Joseph Martin	42 31	74 24

POST OFFICES—*Vermont.*

Post Offices.	Counties.	Postmasters.	Compensation.	Net proceeds.
Underhill	Chittenden	John H. Tower, to 2d November	$27 72	$46 42
		John H. Tower, jr.	49 50	91 01
Union Village	Orange	Merrill J. Walker	34 83	64 82
Vergennes	Addison	Wm. R. Bixby	367 84	796 44
Vernon	Windham	Marshall Whithed	31 82	70 58
Vershire	Orange	Horace T. Keyes	37 80	68 59
Vineyard	Grand Isle	Ira Hill, to 30th September	3 77	6 41
		Joseph S. Hill	13 28	21 45
Waitsfield	Washington	Jas. M. Richardson	86 88	139 78
Walden	Caledonia	Thos. W. Vincent	23 86	37 79
Wallingford	Rutland	John Ives	170 27	166 32
Wardsboro'	Windham	John Rice, jr.	22 33	44 54
Warren	Washington	Harvey D. Morgan	40 41	71 20
Washington	Orange	John Stone, to 30th September	8 93	15 09
		Benj. F. Dickinson	20 77	42 58
Waterbury	Washington	Ahira S. Richardson	172 79	266 57
Waterbury Centre	Washington	Jeremiah Clark	19 25	32 43
Waterford	Caledonia	Eph'm C. Parks	29 29	53 22
Waterville	Lamoille	Horace A. Fisk	46 93	88 84
Weathersfield	Windsor	Bailey Bartlett, jr.	97 01	93 57
Wells	Rutland	Levi Lewis	33 33	56 26
Wells River	Orange	Hiram Tracy, to 31st December	63 02	105 54
		Charles B. Leslie	56 73	100 68
West Alburgh	Grand Isle	Wm. L. Sowles	20 68	34 18
West Arlington	Bennington	Jonathan Baker, jr.	25 37	43 42
West Berkshire	Franklin	Jasper Rand	50 71	83 30
West Braintree	Orange	Joseph Spear	6 45	11 47
West Brattleboro'	Windham	Ros'ell Goodenough	82 13	78 36
West Charleston	Orleans	Samuel M. Cobb	22 62	45 83
West Derby	Orleans	Brigham Pike	17 19	28 80
W't Dummerston	Windham	Nelson W. Willard	14 92	29 35
West Enosburgh	Franklin	James M. Dean	28 18	43 38
West Fairlee	Orange	A'w B. Southworth	34 59	64 30
Westfield	Orleans	Henry Richardson	12 06	21 92
Westford	Chittenden	Stedman G. Meriam	69 14	115 30
West Halifax	Windham	Salmon Swan	18 96	32 32
West Hartford	Windsor	Wm. H. Steele, to 31st December	22 39	19 65
		Sam. G. Steele	27 61	26 31
West Haven	Rutland	Ran'm S. Armstrong	38 63	56 21
West Milton	Chittenden	Chauncey L. Drake	53 19	90 98
Westminster	Windham	Pliny Safford	101 05	104 07
Westminster West	Windham	Amos T. Ball	49 58	80 39

POST OFFICES—*Massachusetts.*

Post Offices.	Counties.	Postmasters.	Compensation.	Net proceeds.
Weston	Windsor	John Wilder	$81 21	$128 46
West Poultney	Rutland	James Richardson	277 01	301 34
West Randolph	Orange	Edward Hobart	81 59	138 85
West Rupert	Bennington	Enoch S. Sherman	9 76	20 77
West Rutland	Rutland	Lorenzo Sheldon	106 96	96 56
West Topsham	Orange	Moses Wallace	37 67	71 84
West Townshend	Windham	John Fessenden	37 29	71 28
Weybridge Lower Falls	Addison	Orange Brittell	35 01	60 41
Wheelock	Caledonia	Jefferson Cree	22 94	42 35
Whiting	Addison	Simon Taft	60 01	117 56
Whittingham	Windham	Nathan L. Butler	44 60	75 37
Williamstown	Orange	Rodolp's Ainsworth	90 57	160 32
Williamsville	Windham	Chs. W. Joy	58 42	89 62
Williston	Chittenden	Abm. V. Holley	169 22	161 99
Wilmington	Windham	Estes C. Sargent	115 29	191 40
Windham	Windham	William Harris, jr.	33 25	58 25
Windsor	Windsor	Walter R. Gilkey	376 27	470 77
Winhall	Bennington	Horace C. Dean	8 53	19 81
Wolcott	Lamoille	Isaac Pennock	45 59	83 07
Woodbury	Washington	Asa Preston, to 31st March	12 79	25 68
		Wm. McGregor	7 51	14 32
Woodford	Bennington	Roswell Day	8 09	17 14
Woodstock	Windsor	Chs. G. Eastman	581 73	863 85
Worcester	Washington	Samuel Andrews	24 52	47 73

MASSACHUSETTS.

NOTE.—Compensation of Postmasters, and net proceeds of their offices, from July 1, 1844, to June 30, 1845.

Post Offices.	Counties.	Postmasters.	Compensation.	Net proceeds.
Abington	Plymouth	Benjamin King	176 64	324 67
Acton	Middlesex	Eliah Grimes	81 69	145 08
Adams	Berkshire	George A. Lapham	177 39	298 67
Adamsville	Franklin	John Wilson	15 96	27 30
Agawam	Hampden	Lyman Whitman	37 07	71 27
Alford	Berkshire	Mark R. Vandeusen	29 24	47 06
Amesbury	Essex	David Nayson	247 85	535 50
Amherst	Hampshire	Samuel C. Carter, to 5th June	495 65	1020 92
		Seth Nims	26 33	59 95
Andover	Essex	Samuel Phillips	642 93	1473 45
Annisquam	Essex	William W. Chard	64 46	108 96

POST OFFICES—*Massachusetts*.

Post Offices.	Counties.	Postmasters.	Compensation.	Net proceeds.
Ashburnham	Worcester	Samuel Barrett	$176 07	$315 81
Ashby	Middlesex	Lloyd Hall	94 13	172 05
Ashfield	Franklin	Richard Cook	92 32	179 43
Ashleyville	Hampden	Edward Kneeland	45 73	52 13
Athol	Worcester	Wm. H. Williams	179 00	326 99
Attleboro'	Bristol	Lyman W. Dean	212 91	415 43
Auburn	Worcester	Elisha M. Knowles	53 64	105 72
Baldwinsville	Worcester	Joseph Davis, jr	76 54	131 51
Barnstable	Barnstable	Richard Ainsworth	216 26	198 77
Barre	Worcester	Charles Caldwell	347 12	702 69
Beckett	Berkshire	Alexander Clark	32 04	58 23
Bedford	Middlesex	Reuben Bacon	71 54	132 47
Belchertown	Hampshire	Joshua Longley, to 15th May	133 62	269 02
		Calvin Bridgeman	24 46	43 77
Bellevilleport	Essex	Joseph Jackman	25 78	52 92
Bellingham	Norfolk	Ellery Thayer	66 22	110 59
Berkley	Bristol	Jos. D. Hathaway	38 29	68 30
Berlin	Worcester	Haman Hunt, to 5th Nov	20 05	35 90
		Dexter B. Saunders	37 18	63 33
Bernardstown	Franklin	Henry W. Cushman	128 65	162 65
Beverly	Essex	Stephens Baker	227 13	489 28
Beverly Farms	Essex	Josiah Obear, from 1st Oct	10 62	13 75
Billerica	Middlesex	Marshall Preston	125 05	225 42
Blackstone	Worcester	John Cady	174 00	308 42
Blanford	Hampden	Orin Sage	66 97	111 66
Bolton	Worcester	Amos Parker	96 53	177 34
Boston	Suffolk	Nathaniel Green	502 20	86214 37
Boston Corner	Berkshire	Andrew Vandeusen, to 31st Dec'r	1 99	3 59
		Miranda Burch	1 37	2 71
Boxboro'	Middlesex	Joseph Blanchard	24 62	43 23
Boxford	Essex	William Lowe	42 47	65 93
Boylston	Worcester	Eli B. Lamson	44 04	80 59
Bradford	Essex	Nathan Fletcher	171 00	328 28
Braintree	Norfolk	Asa French, 3 qrs	82 39	176 52
		Oliver Perkins	23 13	49 98
Brewster	Barnstable	Jeremiah Mayo	75 60	139 58
Bridgewater	Plymouth	Mitchell Keith	326 18	650 43
Brighton	Middlesex	William Warren	206 03	463 02
Brimfield	Hampden	Otis Lane, jr., to 3d March	87 14	147 70
		Asa Lincoln	37 65	70 75
Brookfield	Worcester	Henry Reed	133 09	253 85
Brookline	Norfolk	Stephen S. C. Jones	174 04	331 42
Buckland	Franklin	Ebenezer Maynard	36 57	64 29

POST OFFICES—*Massachusetts.*

Post Offices.	Counties.	Postmasters.	Compensation.	Net proceeds.
Burlington	Middlesex	Silas Cutler	$28 39	$45 26
Byfield	Essex	Benjamin Coleman	29 10	63 20
Cabotville	Hampden	Amos W. Stockwell	711 16	1682 62
Cambridge	Middlesex	Thos. J. Whittemore	724 56	1880 02
Cambridgeport	Middlesex	Calvin Morse	345 87	846 22
Canton	Norfolk	Elihu Carpenter	205 61	437 93
Carlisle	Middlesex	James W. Wilkins	28 39	48 79
Carver	Plymouth	Eliab Ward	38 60	71 86
Centreville	Barnstable	Ferdinand G. Kelley	29 64	28 06
Charlemont	Franklin	Luther Bodman, jr.	127 23	207 11
Charlestown	Middlesex	William Sawyer	825 54	2406 87
Charlton	Worcester	Alex'r C. Thurston	67 82	122 65
Charlton Depot	Worcester	Harvlin Town	52 01	74 97
Chatham	Barnstable	Josiah Mayo	196 38	186 61
Chelmsford	Middlesex	Eli F. Webster	73 18	123 12
Chelsea	Suffolk	Benjamin Dodge	241 66	540 87
Cheshire	Berkshire	Russel C. Brown	59 22	111 26
Chester	Hampden	Thad's K. DeWolf	22 12	48 27
Chester Factories	Hampden	William Shepard	73 54	136 20
Chesterfield	Hampshire	Dyer Bancroft	65 06	120 96
Chickopee Falls	Hampden	David M. Bryant	260 24	582 33
Chilmark	Dukes	Tristram Allen, jr.	27 22	44 67
Clappville	Worcester	Abraham Firth, jr.	105 85	194 11
Cohasset	Norfolk	Zenas Stoddard	112 64	196 00
Cold Brook	Worcester	Freeman French	43 26	76 74
Colerain	Franklin	Samuel Coolidge, to 21st April	94 20	174 33
		Calvin W. Shattuck	18 61	35 81
Concord	Middlesex	John Stacy	323 06	630 79
Conway	Franklin	James S. Whitney	132 00	241 161
Cotuit Village	Barnstable	Rowland T. Crocker	48 44	70 46
Cummington	Hampshire	Francis Bates	95 69	174 16
Cumm'gton West Village	Hampshire	Elisha Mitchell	55 50	90 81
Curtisville	Berkshire	Albert F. Dickinson	91 82	165 86
Dalton	Berkshire	Franklin Weston	148 00	274 37
Dana	Worcester	James S. Brown	51 38	96 20
Danvers	Essex	Joseph Osgood	430 10	927 81
Dartmouth	Bristol	Abner R. Tucker	47 16	80 49
Dedham	Norfolk	Elisha Thayer	461 79	941 77
Deerfield	Franklin	Charles Williams	240 12	232 81
Dennis	Barnstable	N. Y. Hall	53 29	89 56
Dighton	Bristol	Charles Talbot	35 97	65 48
Dorchester	Norfolk	Joseph Marshall, to 15th Oct.	63 20	134 88
		Robert Vose	155 46	342 10
Douglass	Worcester	David Holman	56 21	50 98

POST OFFICES—*Massachusetts.*

Post Offices.	Counties.	Postmasters.	Compensation.	Net proceeds.
Dover	Norfolk	Ralph Sanger	$36 31	$63 78
Dracut	Middlesex	Oliver Morse	42 40	80 58
Dudley	Worcester	Elisha W. Williams	110 59	185 87
Dunstable	Middlesex	Josiah Cummings	50 31	81 04
Duxbury	Plymouth	Zenas Faunce	226 95	414 58
East Abington	Plymouth	Goddard Reed	126 87	238 57
East Bradford	Essex	George Savary	71 76	124 65
East Brewster	Barnstable	George W. Higgins	29 54	53 66
East Bridgewater	Plymouth	Hector O. A. Orr	172 24	306 15
East Brookfield	Worcester	Charles Flagg	76 78	133 03
East Cambridge	Middlesex	John W. Donalan, to 6th May	243 30	559 18
		Rufus Shattuck	46 40	112 05
East Dennis	Barnstable	Judah Paddock	50 98	91 97
East Douglass	Worcester	Turner Thayer	158 87	155 49
East Falmouth	Barnstable	John Robinson	50 01	84 21
East Foxboro'	Norfolk	Joseph Kingsbury	37 34	58 35
East Granville	Hampden	James Cooley	49 87	89 33
Eastham	Barnstable	George Seabury	35 47	58 67
East Hampton	Hampshire	Ebenezer Ferry	208 94	392 23
East Harwich	Barnstable	B. F. Eldridge	29 27	28 92
East Haverhill	Essex	Ebenezer Fullington, 3 qrs	16 86	31 62
		Eustis Chase	6 30	12 16
East Lexington	Middlesex	Amos Adams	54 27	92 23
E't Long Meadow	Hampden	William Lathrop	28 84	49 32
East Marshfield	Plymouth	John Tilden	24 24	43 17
East Medway	Norfolk	Geo. H. Holbrook	46 81	79 40
East Middleboro'	Plymouth	Nathaniel Eddy	36 63	64 89
Easton	Bristol	H. W. B. Wightman	125 91	261 69
East Orleans	Barnstable	Lewis Doane, jr	27 77	53 21
East Randolph	Norfolk	W. W. Linfield	50 73	110 29
East Salisbury	Essex	Cyrus Dearborn	21 86	33 98
East Sandwich	Barnstable	Joseph Hoxie, 3d	13 17	22 41
East Sharon	Norfolk	Jonathan Cobb	13 52	18 70
East Sheffield	Berkshire	Elijah S. Deming	28 81	54 70
East Stoughton	Norfolk	Isaac Blanchard	94 86	184 94
East Wareham	Plymouth	David Nye, to 22d April	31 30	56 93
		Nich's H. Sherman	7 82	14 65
East Weymouth	Norfolk	Albert Humphrey	62 98	118 07
East Whately	Franklin	David Stockbridge	28 23	26 76
Edgartown	Dukes	Silvanus L. Pease	206 09	350 52
Eel River	Plymouth	Nathan Whiting	36 39	67 50
Enfield	Hampshire	Oliver Bryant	173 45	306 97
Erving	Franklin	Fordyce Alexander	37 00	63 54
Essex	Essex	Enoch Low	86 07	126 95

POST OFFICES—*Massachusetts.*

Post Offices.	Counties.	Postmasters.	Compensation.	Net proceeds.
Fairhaven	Bristol	Charles Drew	$348 78	$711 16
Falley's X Roads	Hampden	Jabin B. Williams	71 70	115 99
Fall River	Bristol	Caleb B. Vickery	1213 17	3068 35
Falmouth	Barnstable	Frederick Davis	286 04	297 33
Farnumsville	Worcester	Levi Rawson	53 21	94 98
Feeding Hills	Hampden	Hinsdale Smith	41 25	72 07
Feltonsville	Middlesex	Geo. E. Manson	44 49	71 09
Fitchburg	Worcester	Nathaniel Wood	479 34	1016 79
Florida	Berkshire	Dennis Thayer	12 21	19 64
Forge Village	Middlesex	Luther Prescott	12 61	19 34
Foxborough	Norfolk	Wm. R. Hitchcock, to 12th Feb'y	116 04	202 13
		Warren Bird, to 10th June	72 54	129 40
		David Hersey	6 84	15 64
Framingham	Middlesex	Samuel Warren	227 25	436 34
Franklin	Norfolk	David P. Baker	110 61	191 59
Franklin City	Norfolk	Sam'l B. Scott	29 52	54 52
Freetown	Bristol	Guilford H. Hathaway, to 28th May	87 28	153 70
		Joshua Shove	7 32	12 17
Gardner	Worcester	Levi Heywood	78 08	130 16
Georgetown	Essex	Benjamin Little	231 85	461 96
Gill	Franklin	Josiah W. Canning	33 67	58 46
Gloucester	Essex	Gorham Parsons	298 88	615 59
Goshen	Hampshire	Hinckley Williams	28 59	52 92
Grafton	Worcester	Otis Adams	303 07	643 37
Granby	Hampshire	William Belcher	88 38	143 02
Great Barrington	Berkshire	Samuel Newman	374 96	712 83
Greenfield	Franklin	Richardson Hall, to 10th June	557 98	950 84
		David N. Carpenter	25 53	46 28
Greenwich	Hampshire	Thomas Smith	60 07	103 42
Greenwich Village	Hampshire	Ira Haskell	41 52	62 07
Groton	Middlesex	Caleb Butler	269 63	476 25
Hadley	Hampshire	Orlando Smith	145 22	273 18
Halifax	Plymouth	Henry Pope	58 99	100 91
Hamilton	Essex	George Appleton	41 29	59 63
Hancock	Berkshire	Calvin P. Lapham	38 17	65 15
Hanover	Plymouth	Samuel Eells, to 1st Nov'r	44 39	73 83
		Stephen Josselyn	73 06	126 90
Hanson	Plymouth	Jeremiah Soper	75 90	113 83
Hardwick	Worcester	Fredk. W. Delano	123 44	216 36
Hartsville	Berkshire	Henry L. Hill, to 31st Dec'r	17 60	29 07
		Artemas W. Dorman	17 00	25 72

POST OFFICES—*Massachusetts.*

Post Offices.	Counties.	Postmasters.	Compensation.	Net proceeds.
Harvard	Worcester	Jno. P. Whitcomb	$138 32	$222 81
Harwich	Barnstable	Obed Brooks	83 25	127 64
Hatfield	Hampshire	Alpheus Longley	169 85	179 49
Haverhill	Essex	Chs. B. Hall	687 01	1523 99
Hawley	Franklin	Calvin S. Longley	19 79	34 17
Haydenville	Hampshire	Josiah Hayden	95 44	176 08
Heath	Franklin	Winslow Buck	48 67	90 65
Hingham	Plymouth	Rufus W. Lincoln	230 36	481 51
Hinsdale	Berkshire	Monroe Emmons	147 22	267 73
Holden	Worcester	Charles Chaffin	199 00	348 34
Holland	Hampden	E. G. Fuller	26 37	42 45
Holliston	Middlesex	Sewall G. Burnap	228 59	420 39
Holmes' Hole	Dukes	George Dunham	144 78	221 28
Holyoke Place	Hampshire	Zadock Lyman	6 80	11 38
Hopkinton	Middlesex	Sam'l D. Davenport, to 1st Feb'y	98 59	184 64
		Silas Moore	72 51	135 62
Housatonic (Disc'd 7th Feb.)	Berkshire	Wells Laflin, (no return.)		
Hubbardston	Worcester	Abijah S. Clark	139 24	250 57
Hyannis	Barnstable	Abner W. Lovell	98 07	202 08
Hyannisport	Barnstable	Daniel Bassett	28 58	26 18
Ipswich	Essex	Stephen Coburn	321 56	545 51
Ireland	Hampden	Chester Crafts	154 17	169 83
Irvingsville	Franklin	Ansel. Lesure	29 50	56 71
Jamaica Plain	Norfolk	Robert Seaver	126 97	269 17
Kingston	Plymouth	R. B. Bradford, to 31st Aug	26 57	48 15
		Horace L. Collamore	173 22	306 61
Lancaster	Worcester	Jos. W. Huntington, to 6th Jan'y	141 40	312 47
		Nathaniel Rand	183 62	353 37
Lanesborough	Berkshire	Richard Whitney	153 88	261 09
Lee	Berkshire	Hubbard Bartlett	510 29	838 31
Leicester	Worcester	John Sargent	358 52	784 47
Lenox	Berkshire	Wm. P. Walker	232 65	500 30
Leominster	Worcester	Chs. H. Colburn	310 45	548 04
Leverett	Franklin	Francis Frary	40 73	62 56
Lexington	Middlesex	John Davis, (3 qrs.)	70 07	128 53
Leyden	Franklin	Abel Carpenter	34 51	60 78
Lincoln	Middlesex	Rufus Morse	42 37	75 62
Littleton	Middlesex	Benjamin Kimball	110 69	183 45
Locks' Village	Franklin	Eli Ames	6 13	12 12
Long Meadow	Hampden	William White	104 33	192 59
Long Plain	Bristol	Chs. F. Thatcher	26 80	45 77

POST OFFICES—*Massachusetts.*

Post Offices.	Counties.	Postmasters.	Compensation.	Net proceeds.
Lowell	Middlesex	Jacob Robbins	$1633 03	$8970 61
Ludlow	Hampden	Ephraim C. Jenks	141 21	241 73
Lunenburgh	Worcester	Otis Abercrombie	114 59	186 69
Lynn	Essex	Benjamin Mudge	771 49	2162 00
Lynnfield	Essex	John Andrews	46 35	77 60
Malden	Middlesex	Jas. C. Richardson	187 41	402 10
Manchaug	Worcester	Smith J. C. Bartlett	34 48	58 89
Manchester	Essex	William Dodge	143 02	282 58
Mansfield	Bristol	Wm. B. Bates	91 73	163 91
Marblehead	Essex	Samuel Homan	286 78	568 55
Marlboro'	Middlesex	John Cotting	106 60	206 49
Marshfield	Plymouth	Proctor Bourne	80 94	122 81
Marston's Mills	Barnstable	Nathaniel Hinkley	43 67	41 94
Mattapoisett	Plymouth	Wilson Barstow	185 24	311 69
Medfield	Norfolk	Charles Onion	82 94	165 23
Medford	Middlesex	Luther Angier	243 36	586 18
Medway	Norfolk	Clark Partridge	101 05	211 20
Mendon	Worcester	Henry A. Aldrich	95 25	152 09
Methuen	Essex	Ebenezer Sawyer, to 31st Dec'r	172 28	325 42
		Frederick George	164 61	311 39
Middleboro'	Plymouth	Allen Shaw	254 78	491 20
Middlefield	Hampshire	Solomon Root	65 47	113 89
Middlesex Village	Middlesex	Eben Adams	22 83	39 94
Middleton	Essex	Amos Batchelder	24 92	43 10
Milford	Worcester	Hiram Hunt	327 48	555 19
Millbury	Worcester	Asa H. Waters	368 44	804 49
Millington	Franklin	Charles Pierce	22 01	32 66
Mill River	Berkshire	Dan Adams	28 84	53 28
Millville	Worcester	George Staples, to 31st March	65 98	116 73
		Willard Wilson	27 21	43 54
Milton	Norfolk	George Thompson	281 00	634 75
Monroe	Franklin	Martin Ballou	5 96	11 04
Monson	Hampden	Wm. N. Packard	261 01	534 66
Montague	Franklin	Jonathan Hartwell	76 04	132 32
Montague Canal	Franklin	Benjamin Henry	19 43	37 68
Montgomery	Hampden	Oren Parks	14 01	24 42
Monument	Barnstable	Betsey C. Perry	41 07	80 66
Nantucket	Nantucket	Sam'l H. Jenks	837 24	2161 62
Natick	Middlesex	Nathaniel Clark	223 88	421 36
Needham	Norfolk	Israel Whitney	56 80	94 79
Neponset Village	Norfolk	Orin P. Bacon	57 21	104 09
New Bedford	Bristol	Simeon Bailey	1387 86	6145 92
New Boston	Berkshire	Sam'l C. Parsons	36 52	65 25
New Braintree	Worcester	Oramel Martin	92 29	164 24

POST OFFICES—*Massachusetts.*

Post Offices.	Counties.	Postmasters.	Compensation.	Net proceeds.
Newburyport....	Essex......	Benj. W. Hale.....	$1103 14	$3115 42
New England Village..........	Worcester...	Chandler M. Pratt..	151 09	264 69
New Marlborough	Berkshire...	Seth Norton, to 20th Dec'r...........	39 60	64 08
		Jabez Bozworth....	46 18	74 09
New Mills.......	Essex......	Henry A. Potter, fr. 1st Jan'y........	39 00	68 48
New Salem......	Franklin....	Alpheus Harding, jr.	35 26	65 13
Newton.........	Middlesex..	Jos. N. Bacon.....	140 58	270 79
Newton Centre...	Middlesex..	Asa R. Trowbridge.	113 39	221 36
Newton Lower Falls.........	Middlesex..	Amos Allen.......	124 95	235 15
Newton Upper Falls.........	Middlesex..	Jesse Winslow.....	235 97	447 56
North Adams....	Berkshire....	Wm. E. Brayton...	447 08	959 75
North Amherst..	Hampshire..	Horace Cutler......	60 28	105 91
Northampton....	Hampshire..	Amos H. Bullen...	967 94	1964 99
North Andover..	Essex......	James Stevens, 2d..	225 09	397 02
North Attleboro'.	Bristol......	Alfred Barrows, (3 qrs)...........	88 89	146 38
North Becket....	Berkshire....	David McElwain...	58 57	108 84
North Blanford...	Hampden...	Lyman Gibbs......	32 06	59 03
Northborough...	Worcester...	Henry R. Phelps, to 31st Dec'r.......	79 93	139 18
		Anson Rice........	77 40	142 80
Northbridge.....	Worcester...	Sylvanus Holbrook.	84 21	151 66
NorthBridgewater	Plymouth...	Ed. Southworth, jr.	252 31	465 43
North Brookfield.	Worcester...	John Hill.........	231 51	473 76
North Carver....	Plymouth...	William Barrows...	11 65	19 56
North Chatham..	Barnstable....	Josh'a Nickerson, jr.	47 13	47 08
North Chelmsford	Middlesex...	Benjamin Adams...	128 85	228 68
North Chester...	Hampden...	Thos. E. Stevens...	22 94	47 21
North Danvers....	Essex.......	Thomas Bowen....	215 09	478 76
North Dartmouth.	Bristol.......	John Cummings....	34 10	61 44
North Dighton...	Bristol.......	John Rose.........	52 76	98 79
North Eastham..	Barnstable....	Cushing Horton....	13 26	21 79
North Easton....	Bristol.......	Aug. O. Howard...	169 94	328 61
North Egremont.	Berkshire....	Ephraim Baldwin..	34 22	60 71
North Fairhaven.	Bristol.......	Cyrus E. Clark....	67 21	128 10
North Falmouth..	Barnstable....	Ebenezer Nye.....	40 21	38 62
Northfield.......	Franklin....	Dan'l L. Callender.	258 72	250 06
North Hadley...	Hampshire..	Dexter M. Leonard.	62 06	103 52
North Leverett...	Franklin....	E. M. Hatch.......	24 46	44 27
North Marshfield.	Plymouth...	Daniel Philips......	27 38	42 14
N'th Middleboro'.	Plymouth...	Morrill Robinson...	74 51	109 76
North New Salem	Franklin....	Wm. Whittemore..	32 76	54 94
North Oxford....	Worcester...	Abisha Larned.....	61 75	108 81
North Plympton.	Plymouth...	Zenas Cushman....	12 74	19 61

POST OFFICES—*Massachusetts.*

Post Offices.	Counties.	Postmasters.	Compensation.	Net proceeds.
North Reading...	Middlesex...	Edwin Foster......	$65 21	$107 12
North Rehoboth. (Late "Rehoboth.")	Bristol.......	Granville Stevens...	21 93	33 70
North Rochester.	Plymouth ...	Noah C. Perkins...	30 15	45 86
North Sandwich..	Barnstable....	Mason White......	21 20	37 17
North Scituate...	Plymouth ...	Shadrach B. Merritt.	24 50	38 18
North Spencer...	Worcester...	Jonas Wilson......	19 74	31 24
North Sudhury..	Middlesex...	John Sawyer......	27 78	47 20
North Sunderland	Franklin	Lewis Puffer.......	12 10	18 39
North Swansea..	Bristol.......	Mason Barney.....	23 33	39 40
North Tewksbury	Middlesex....	Henry A. Kittridge.	27 61	49 14
North Truro.....	Barnstable...	Edward Armstrong.	15 96	29 89
N'th West Bridgewater.........	Plymouth ...	Levi French.......	40 89	61 16
North Weymouth	Norfolk	James Torrey......	20 82	31 43
North Wrentham.	Norfolk	Ebenezer Blake	42 01	68 10
Norton..........	Bristol......	Laban M. Wheaton.	107 77	186 98
Norwich.........	Hampshire...	Whitman Knight...	17 25	36 15
Oakham	Worcester....	James Allen, to 1st March..........	38 21	67 44
		Dexter Hill........	21 02	34 95
Orange..........	Franklin	Hillel Baker.......	31 58	54 99
Orleans	Barnstable....	Sparrow Horton ...	117 53	100 75
Osterville........	Barnstable....	Josiah Scudder, jr..	70 38	69 33
Otis.............	Berkshire....	Lester Filley, to 30th September.......	23 30	35 61
		Sam'l Pickett......	73 60	114 74
Oxford..........	Worcester...	William Sigourney.	195 27	417 24
Palmer..........	Hampden ...	Theoph's H. Knight	67 84	125 23
Palmer Depot....	Hampden ...	Chester Strong, to 1st February.....	140 20	235 87
		John Bowles.......	80 66	166 44
Paxton..........	Worcester...	Silas D. Harrington.	97 31	175 75
Pelham	Hampshire...	Calvin D. Eaton....	20 08	38 16
Pembroke.......	Plymouth ...	Horace Collamore..	63 53	95 35
Pepperell.......	Middlesex....	John Loring.......	197 50	359 51
Peru...........	Berkshire....	Oliver Nash........	40 23	63 61
Petersham.......	Worcester...	Seth Hapgood.....	201 96	350 79
Philipston.......	Worcester...	Curtis Powers, to 13th February ...	58 60	91 10
		Edward Powers....	38 33	66 61
Pittsfield	Berkshire....	Jonathan Allen, to 13th June........	654 20	1702 36
		Phinehas Allen, jr..	20 03	53 37
Plainfield........	Hampshire...	Jacob Clark........	60 54	109 70
Plymouth.......	Plymouth ...	Ephraim Spooner...	518 90	1210 05

POST OFFICES—*Massachusetts.*

Post Offices.	Counties.	Postmasters.	Compensation.	Net proceeds.
Plympton	Plymouth	Isaac Wright	$43 13	$69 74
Pocassett	Barnstable	Howard Perry	50 67	99 12
Prescott	Hampshire	Stacey Linzie	33 00	54 03
Princeton	Worcester	Charles Russell	159 56	280 91
Provincetown	Barnstable	John L. Lathrop	185 35	353 14
Quincy	Norfolk	Daniel French	396 12	852 47
Randolph	Norfolk	Sam'l N. Howard	325 74	724 73
Reading	Middlesex	John Weston	185 69	360 67
Rehoboth	Bristol	John C. Marvel	78 63	135 33
Late "Rehoboth Village.")				
Richmond	Berkshire	Eleazer Williams	83 62	145 26
Rochester	Plymouth	Theophilus King	48 60	91 07
Rock Bottom	Middlesex	Franklin Rice	33 04	58 96
Rockport	Essex	Henry Clark, jr	231 01	399 68
Rockville	Norfolk	Timothy Walker	37 95	60 75
Rowe	Franklin	Sam'l H. Read	61 35	114 23
Rowley	Essex	Benj. H. Smith	72 56	136 67
Roxbury	Norfolk	Horace Bacon	586 50	1596 10
Royalston	Worcester	Ch's A. Bullock	95 88	168 12
Russell	Hampden	R. P. White	26 06	48 12
Rutland	Worcester	George Estabrook	92 39	162 47
Salem	Essex	Caleb Foote, to 31st August	256 70	700 42
		Benj. F. Browne	1303 17	3735 52
Salisbury	Essex	Seth Clark	43 03	84 04
Sandisfield	Berkshire	George Hull	87 96	130 11
Sandwich	Barnstable	Zenas R. Hinckley	209 13	395 09
Sangus	Essex	George Newhall	61 02	124 28
Savoy	Berkshire	Liberty Bowker	40 75	68 43
Saxonville	Middlesex	Charles Fiske	237 33	476 39
Scituate	Plymouth	John Beal	98 74	174 31
Scotland	Plymouth	George Chipman	21 84	34 45
Seekonk	Bristol	Church Gray, to 1st February	39 50	68 23
		William Ide	25 55	45 24
Sharon	Norfolk	Charles Johnson, to 30th September	19 55	31 63
		Elon Richards	72 16	116 78
Sheffield	Berkshire	Edw'd F. Ensign	169 15	291 94
Shelburne	Franklin	Walter Wells	45 59	71 05
Shelburne Falls	Franklin	Jarvis B. Bardwell	114 82	193 78
Sherburne	Middlesex	Oliver Everett	81 57	139 55
Shirley	Middlesex	James P. Whitney	47 75	74 67
Shirley Village	Middlesex	Israel Longley	72 30	133 78
Shrewsbury	Worcester	Wm. W. Pratt	94 56	182 88

POST OFFICES—*Massachusetts.*

Post Offices.	Counties.	Postmasters.	Compensation.	Net proceeds.
Shutesbury	Franklin	Henry Pierce	$41 75	$66 75
Sippican	Plymouth	Walton N. Ellis	92 68	159 95
Somerset	Bristol	Elisha Slade	61 83	117 86
Somerville	Middlesex	Stephen B. Sewall	76 03	164 44
South Abington	Plymouth	Wm. Bonney, jr	178 72	301 74
South Amherst	Hampshire	Waitstill Dickinson	43 22	68 21
Southampton	Hampshire	Owen S. Cowles	83 73	150 75
South Attleboro'	Bristol	Lemuel May	43 33	79 63
Southboro'	Worcester	Sullivan Fay	105 80	175 41
South Braintree	Norfolk	Jud'n Stoddard, f'm 30th June	6 23	12 58
Southbridge	Worcester	William Edwards	305 77	639 76
South Dartmouth	Bristol	William Potter, 2d	56 55	110 73
South Deerfield	Franklin	Howland Cowing	73 19	70 16
South Dennis	Barnstable	Eleazer Nickerson	52 36	98 85
South Egremont	Berkshire	N. K. Bills	82 10	143 63
S'th Framingham	Middlesex	Edw'd A. Clark	48 73	85 82
South Gardner	Worcester	Lewis H. Bradford	83 21	145 88
South Hadley	Hampshire	David Chandler	236 22	532 73
S'th Hadley Falls	Hampshire	Dan'l P. Gillett, to 14th May	109 42	230 16
		O. P. Ingraham	12 58	23 98
South Harwick	Barnstable	Jos. P. Nickerson	46 91	63 49
South Hawley	Franklin	Nelson Joy	6 67	12 51
South Hingham	Plymouth	Quincy Lane	46 52	69 98
South Lee	Berkshire	Thomas Hurlbut	85 63	159 89
South Mendon	Worcester	Elbridge G. Daniels	21 75	34 23
South Middleb'ro'	Plymouth	Cyrus Le Baron	13 87	25 80
South Milford	Worcester	Jesse E. Razee	28 50	43 39
South Natick	Middlesex	John Gilman, jr	62 24	111 66
South Orange	Franklin	John R. Whipple	72 41	135 34
South Orleans	Barnstable	Seth Sparrow, 3d	14 87	27 38
South Reading	Middlesex	Ch's H. Stearns	187 25	343 58
South Royalston	Worcester	Hiram W. Albee	68 71	121 64
South Sandisfield, (Dis. 13th M'ch.)	Berkshire	Philemon Sage, to 20th March	3 83	6 38
South Sandwich	Barnstable	Sol'n C. Howland	24 56	39 48
South Scituate	Plymouth	Eb'r F. Fogg	44 99	77 82
South Seekonk	Bristol	Nathan Munroe	6 97	12 39
South Shrewsbury	Worcester	Levi J. Hemenway	25 46	37 60
South Tyringham	Berkshire	Wilbur C. Langdon	52 12	84 72
South Walpole	Norfolk	Truman Clarke	55 64	99 82
South Wellfleet	Barnstable	Reuben Arey	21 95	39 41
South Westport	Bristol	Frederick Brownell	23 00	31 81
South Weymouth	Norfolk	Jacob Loud	164 70	300 69
Southwick	Hampden	Jos. M. Forward	79 91	152 72
South Wilbraham	Hampden	S. C. Spelman	42 72	71 82
S'th Williamstown	Berkshire	B.F. Mills, to 31st Dec	20 67	37 47
		Daniel C. Morey	21 62	39 96

POST OFFICES—*Massachusetts.*

Post Offices.	Counties.	Postmasters.	Net proceeds.	Compensation.
South Woburn...	Middlesex...	Humphrey B. Howe, to 30th Sept.....	$18 53	$37 70
		N. A. Richardson..	61 16	126 84
South Wrentham.	Norfolk.....	Benj. N. Shepard...	18 49	34 68
South Yarmouth.	Barnstable...	David K. Akin.....	68 91	129 32
Spencer.........	Worcester...	Eleazer B. Draper..	182 36	327 10
Springfield.......	Hampden...	Galen Ames, to 12th May............	1422 80	3772 69
		Harvey Chapin....	240 62	655 13
Sterling.........	Worcester...	Thomas H. Blood..	140 27	219 17
Stockbridge......	Berkshire....	Seymour Rockwell.	310 81	570 26
Stoneham.......	Middlesex...	Warren Sweetzer, to 5th May........	113 20	236 63
		George W. Dike...	23 82	44 93
Stoughton.......	Norfolk.....	Lemuel Gay.......	203 60	398 41
Stow...........	Middlesex...	Winthrop Robinson	70 08	121 47
Sturbridge.......	Worcester...	Alfred M. Merrick.	205 16	305 49
Sudbury.........	Middlesex...	Ephraim Stone.....	53 53	87 02
Sunderland......	Franklin....	William Delano....	67 62	109 96
Sutton..........	Worcester...	Gibbs Lilley.......	90 19	169 28
Swansea.........	Bristol.......	John Mason.......	68 29	105 45
Taunton.........	Bristol.......	Chs. R. Vickery...	889 04	2302 83
Templeton.......	Worcester...	John Boynton.....	194 60	371 39
Tewkesbury......	Middlesex...	Henry E. Preston..	38 08	68 37
Three Rivers....	Hampden...	Asa Shumway.....	80 55	151 65
Tolland.........	Hampden...	Roger Harrison....	33 67	49 25
Topsfield........	Essex........	Richard Philips, jr..	102 16	199 07
Townsend.......	Middlesex...	Thomas Farrar....	137 93	240 18
Townsend Harbor	Middlesex...	Charles Emery....	20 21	31 54
Truro...........	Barnstable...	Hincks Gross......	62 77	121 03
Tyngsboro'......	Middlesex...	Supply C. Wilson..	65 17	109 92
Tyringham......	Berkshire...	Samuel Fargo, jr...	42 32	69 85
Unionville.......	Middlesex...	William Jennison..	118 57	206 89
Upton...........	Worcester...	David B. Fisk.....	149 08	256 93
Uxbridge........	Worcester...	Sullivan Thayer....	260 14	439 53
Van Deusenville..	Berkshire...	Washington Adams.	156 49	270 94
Wales...........	Hampden...	James C. Royce...	47 43	87 72
Walpole.........	Norfolk......	Edmund W. Clap..	132 16	221 20
Walpole East....	Norfolk......	David Morse......	65 16	108 70
Waltham........	Middlesex...	Nathaniel Maynard, to 30th Nov.....	138 19	300 27
		John M. Peck.....	212 64	448 03
Ware...........	Hampshire..	Ansel Phelps, jr....	391 47	852 25
Wareham.......	Plymouth...	W. Bates, to 26th Ap'l	185 45	359 11
		David Nye........	33 37	71 41

POST OFFICES—*Massachusetts.*

Post Offices.	Counties.	Postmasters.	Compensation.	Net proceeds.
Warren	Worcester	Jos. F. Hitchcock	$265 00	$451 84
Warwick	Franklin	William Cobb	100 47	173 66
Washington	Berkshire	Wm. G. Ballantine.	17 62	32 51
Waterford	Worcester	Welcome Farnum	190 03	388 38
Watertown	Middlesex	Benjamin Dana	253 34	539 90
Wayland	Middlesex	Newell Heard	79 79	131 70
Webster	Worcester	Jonathan Day	203 31	415 90
Wellfleet	Barnstable	Giles Holbrook	70 38	120 66
Wendell	Franklin	Lucius Cooke	30 51	52 17
Wenham	Essex	A. J. Dodge	58 37	93 64
West Amesbury	Essex	Stephen Bayley	66 67	123 31
West Barnstable	Barnstable	Jabez Howland, jr	40 19	65 38
West Becket	Berkshire	Wm. S. Phillips, to 31st Dec	6 51	8 96
		Kendal Baird	6 91	8 56
Westboro'	Worcester	W. L. G. Hunt	223 57	410 96
West Boxford	Essex	Samuel W. Jenkins.	47 06	77 81
West Boylston	Worcester	Waldo Winter	160 23	281 21
West Brewster	Barnstable	Freeman Rider	31 32	50 10
West Bridgewater	Plymouth	John M. Reed	75 66	124 67
West Brookfield	Worcester	Allen Newell	183 84	362 45
West Cambridge	Middlesex	Edwin R. Prescott	191 20	355 55
West Dedham	Norfolk	Abner Ellis, to 31st March	57 39	99 62
		Theodore Gay, 2d	18 95	33 39
West Dennis	Barnstable	Luther Child	66 70	125 68
West Duxbury	Plymouth	George B. Standish.	19 16	30 40
West Falmouth	Barnstable	Stephen Dillingham.	37 09	36 36
Westfield	Hampden	Joseph Root, to 16th April	434 14	981 86
		Matthew Ives	104 87	234 15
Westford	Middlesex	Samuel Fletcher	105 93	179 01
West Foxborough	Norfolk	Henry Hobart	10 08	16 63
West Granville	Hampden	Vincent Holcombe	36 93	68 76
West Hampton	Hampshire	John A. Judd	50 45	89 87
West Harwick	Barnstable	Anthony Killey	82 15	155 88
West Medway	Norfolk	Daniel Wiley	97 19	160 41
West Millbury	Worcester	Clark Holman	82 41	141 84
Westminster	Worcester	Joseph Whitman	130 36	224 77
West Needham	Norfolk	William Flagg	46 27	71 52
West Newbury	Essex	John C. Carr	123 87	235 16
West Newton	Middlesex	John Mead	76 64	140 75
Weston	Middlesex	Abraham Hewes	78 75	134 44
West Pittsfield	Berkshire	Wm. T. Lane	35 01	65 80
Westport	Bristol	Stephen Howland	70 76	113 90
Westport Point	Bristol	Alexander H. Cory.	29 15	43 80
West Roxbury	Norfolk	Wm. S. Keith	104 05	203 57
West Sandwich	Barnstable	Chs. H. Burgess	36 11	60 36
West Scituate	Plymouth	Zattee Cushing	56 52	81 40

POST OFFICES—*Massachusetts.*

Post Offices.	Counties.	Postmasters.	Compensation.	Net proceeds.
West Springfield.	Hampden ...	Edw'd Southworth, to 14th May.....	$190 29	$186 48
		M. M. Tallmadge..	9 68	20 59
West Stockbridge	Berkshire....	Martin R. Kellogg..	187 48	367 12
West Stockbridge Centre	Berkshire....	Orlando Edwards....	14 87	24 36
West Sutton......	Worcester....	Reuben Waters, jr..	17 95	35 66
West Tisbury,...	Dukes......	Willard Luce.......	37 12	59 55
West Wareham..	Plymouth ...	Edw'd H. Sparrow, to 30th Oct......	8 59	14 64
		Darius Miller.......	17 48	29 82
West Worthingt'n	Hampshire ..	Russel Bartlett.....	20 61	37 99
West Wrentham.	Norfolk......	Otis Rawson.......	31 95	50 91
West Yarmouth..	Barnstable...	Elnathan Lewis....	29 99	60 20
Weymouth......	Norfolk	Fisher A. Kingsbury	219 89	382 96
Whately.........	Franklin	Samuel Lesure.....	97 37	96 15
Whitinsville......	Worcester....	Paul Whitin.......	159 22	283 69
Wilbraham......	Hampden ...	Clark B. Stebbins, to 31st March......	122 13	216 98
		Luther B. Bliss	41 70	73 40
Wilkinsonville....	Worcester....	Jonas Brown	94 95	164 11
Williamsburgh...	Hampshire...	Lewis Bodman.....	114 81	213 21
Williamstown....	Berkshire....	Isaac Latham......	267 38	563 03
Willimansett......	Hampden ...	Closson Pendleton..	20 58	35 22
Wilmington	Middlesex...	James Jaques......	50 35	92 19
Winchendon.....	Worcester...	Mark Whitcomb...	275 76	516 62
Windsor	Berkshire....	Charles Reed......	34 15	54 23
Woburn	Middlesex...	Bowen Buckman...	303 91	616 37
Wood's Hole....	Barnstable...	John C. Parker....	33 81	53 93
Woodville.......	Middlesex...	Albert Wood......	44 03	66 60
Worcester.......	Worcester...	Martin L. Fisher...	1710 47	5555 65
Worthington.....	Hampshire ..	William Ward.....	90 90	161 15
Wrentham	Norfolk	Curtis Stone.......	221 73	401 50
Yarmouth........	Barnstable...	James Mathews....	46 42	77 14
Yarmouthport....	Barnstable...	Edward Thacher...	137 52	122 31

RHODE ISLAND.

NOTE.—Compensation of Postmasters, and net proceeds of their offices, from July 1, 1844, to June 30, 1845.

Post Offices.	Counties.	Postmasters.	Compensation.	Net proceeds.
Barrington	Bristol	Enoch Remington..	$22 92	$36 62
Brand's Iron Works	Washington .	Silas Richmond	48 28	76 35

POST OFFICES—*Rhode Island.*

Post Offices.	Counties.	Postmasters.	Compensation.	Net proceeds.
Bristol	Bristol	Wm. B. Tilley, to 23d April	$446 86	$933 18
		Benjamin Hyatt	69 88	179 21
Burrillville	Providence	James Harris	74 86	120 57
Centreville	Kent	Moses Fifield	166 19	315 96
Charlestown	Washington	Jos. H. Cross	18 73	31 60
Chepachet	Providence	Horace Kimball	88 05	147 28
Commons	Newport	Henry T. Brown	75 24	110 36
Coventry	Kent	Russell Briggs	74 36	138 27
Cumberland Hill	Providence	Leonard Wakefield	80 05	132 26
East Greenwich	Kent	Jas. C. Green	205 33	396 41
Fiskeville	Providence	Nathan Young	69 05	121 66
Foster	Providence	James G. Cook	23 02	34 71
Fruit Hill	Providence	Stanton Belden	42 29	84 04
Greenville	Providence	Nich's S. Winsor, to 31st March	33 53	51 50
		Emor H. Smith	10 79	17 58
Hopkinton	Washington	Jesse Brown	55 10	97 04
Kingston	Washington	Powell Helme	123 35	193 70
Lime Rock	Providence	Benjamin Lindsey	56 37	98 14
Lippitt	Kent	Saml. R. Hopkins	72 75	127 92
Little Compton	Newport	Wm. A. Brown	50 85	83 98
Lonsdale	Providence	Preston H. Clark	117 92	215 33
Mount Vernon	Providence	Peleg Place	26 97	36 95
Natick	Kent	Wm. E. Van Riper	48 53	75 24
Newport	Newport	Asher Robbins, to 31st March	1195 16	3702 52
		Joseph Joslen	366 40	986 18
New Shoreham	Newport	Alfred Card	29 06	52 70
North Scituate	Providence	A. K. Brayton, to 31st Oct	34 61	53 86
		John A. Harris	73 29	115 96
Pawtucket	Providence	David Benedict, to 1st Dec	315 65	725 96
		Fred'k A. Sumner	417 24	996 27
Pawtuxet	Kent	Saml. W. Wightman	27 53	51 94
Peace Dale	Washington	E. D. Campbell, to 21st Dec	46 55	99 30
		Jon. H. Congdon	65 36	124 80

POST OFFICES—*Connecticut.*

Post Offices.	Counties.	Postmasters.	Compensation.	Net proceeds.
Perrysville	Washington	Thos. A. Haszard	$16 66	$23 47
Pine Hill	Washington	Thomas Philips, jr.	18 87	30 05
Portsmouth	Newport	Oliver D. Greene	83 22	142 44
Providence	Providence	Edwd. J. Mallett, to 31st March	1165 30	10631 31
		Welcome B. Sayles	407 55	3643 32
Rice City	Kent	James Burlingame	29 12	38 19
Shamrock Mills	Washington	Jirah M. Knowles	30 45	53 22
Slaterville	Providence	John Fellows	156 38	293 71
South Foster	Providence	Bennett L. Holden	8 93	15 37
South Scituate	Providence	Owen Batley	39 86	67 60
Tiverton	Newport	Samuel Seabury	40 73	63 09
Tiverton 4 Corners	Newport	Arnold Smith	27 11	43 03
Tower Hill	Washington	Benjamin Hull	7 88	13 00
Wakefield	Washington	Carden Hazard	75 98	123 84
Warren	Bristol	Samuel Randall, to 18th April	269 69	514 68
		Elis'a P. Phinney, 2d	60 66	127 27
Warwick	Kent	Benj. W. Vaughn	64 49	112 42
Westerly	Washington	Lyndon Taylor	350 13	666 79
West Greenwich	Kent	Pardon Hopkins	11 98	20 10
West Scituate	Providence	Joshua Williams	9 76	12 69
Wickford	Washington	Samuel Peirce	170 79	295 89
Woonsocket Falls	Providence	John Burnham	633 52	1258 87

CONNECTICUT.

NOTE.—Compensation of Postmasters, and net proceeds of their offices, from July 1, 1844, to June 30, 1845.

Post Offices.	Counties.	Postmasters.	Compensation.	Net proceeds.
Abington	Windham	Orrin Sumner	$47 33	$79 19
Andover	Tolland	Ransford Button	51 77	98 59
Ashford	Windham	Dyer Clark	65 98	127 20
Avon	Hartford	Francis Woodford, to 9th Dec	32 34	61 72
		Noble Towner	47 58	86 98
Bantam Falls	Litchfield	Leonard Kenney, to 22d Jan'y	24 33	35 31
		Murray Kenney	14 23	18 62

POST OFFICES—*Connecticut.*

Post Offices.	Counties.	Postmasters.	Compensation.	Net proceeds.
Barkhamsted.....	Litchfield....	George W. Merrill.	$18 79	$35 75
Berlin...........	Hartford..··	Edward Wilcox....	207 22	351 22
Bethany.........	New Haven..	Hezekiah Thomas..	14 23	28 17
Bethel...........	Fairfield.....	Hiram Weed......	164 81	323 69
Bethlehem........	Litchfield....	Homer Skidmore...	53 69	95 02
Bloomfield........	Hartford....	J. H. Hubbard, to 28th Nov........	28 20	51 80
		Watson Hubbard..	39 52	70 89
Bolton...........	Tolland......	Jabez L. White, to 30th Sept........	9 66	15 15
		Royal S. White....	30 36	43 19
Bozrah..........	New London	Stephen Fitch......	35 41	62 45
Bozrahville......	New London	Havelah Mowry, to 15th March......	18 80	36 31
		Sylv'r K. Andrews.	6 88	13 62
Branford........	New Haven..	Orin D. Squire.....	69 31	137 10
Bridgeport.......	Fairfield.....	Isaac Sherman, jr..	955 56	2615 92
Bridgewater	Litchfield....	Charles G. Sanford.	52 64	89 73
Bristol..........	Hartford....	George H. Mitchell.	359 31	822 73
Broad Brook.....	Hartford....	H. S. Kinsley, to 31st March......	23 35	40 89
		Bethuel Phelps.....	13 35	24 41
Brookfield.......	Fairfield.....	Henry Ruggles, to 18th Dec........	47 17	86 46
		David Burr........	70 22	122 71
Brooklyn........	Windham...	Byron Wheaton....	166 13	300 12
Buckland's Cor'rs	Hartford....	William Jones.....	35 34	73 84
Burlington.......	Hartford....	Frederick Bull, to 25th Jan'y.......	39 54	78 39
		Hiram Webster....	30 33	52 04
Canaan	Litchfield....	William Watson...	159 02	280 11
Canterbury......	Windham...	Richard Fenner, to 31st March......	65 55	132 56
		Samuel Burlingame.	18 85	38 11
Canton...........	Hartford....	Wm. H. Hawley...	44 52	59 74
Canton Centre...	Hartford....	Simeon Mills, to 1st Nov............	12 15	18 12
		Jere. H. Hallock...	17 70	26 25
Central Village...	Windham...	John J. Penrose....	57 26	105 21
Centre Groton...	New London	Henry Haley......	7 43	13 14
Chapinville......	Litchfield....	Horace Landon, to 26th Aug........	5 54	11 07
		Havillah Loop.....	22 59	42 90
Chaplin.........	Windham...	Walter Goodell....	48 31	65 45
Cheshire........	New Haven..	Elihu Yale, to 20th Jan'y..........	62 24	129 87
		Charles Shelton....	60 71	115 74

POST OFFICES—*Connecticut.*

Post Offices.	Counties.	Postmasters.	Compensation.	Net proceeds.
Chester	Middlesex	Gideon Parker, 2d	$128 52	$248 27
Chesterfield	New London	James Turner	15 45	30 15
Clinton	Middlesex	Achilles H. Elliott	86 40	178 90
Colchester	New London	Pomeroy Hall	203 04	367 87
Cold Spring	Fairfield	Edwin Botsford	20 71	35 79
Colebrook	Litchfield	Reuben Rockwell	97 92	155 28
Colebrook River	Litchfield	Daniel D. Wolf	34 90	61 93
Collinsville	Hartford	Samuel D. Marsh	184 46	302 60
Columbia	Tolland	Benjamin Hartson	59 44	108 57
Cornwall	Litchfield	John R. Harrison	33 54	55 44
Cornwall Bridge	Litchfield	Peter Bierce	94 56	154 72
Cornwall Hollow	Litchfield	Benjamin Sedgwick, from 29th Jan'y	7 92	14 30
Coventry	Tolland	Eleazer Pomeroy, jr.	55 70	109 01
Danbury	Fairfield	P. D. Crosby to 30th Sept	113 14	197 92
		Ira R. Wildman, fr. 29th Oct	327 58	658 30
Darien	Fairfield	Ira Scofield, to 30th Jan'y	55 51	102 50
		James H. Gorham	39 99	70 80
Deep River	Middlesex	Sedley Snow to 16th Dec'r	50 51	95 57
		Obadiah Spencer	72 88	128 23
Derby	New Haven	Robert Gates	312 28	717 87
Durham	Middlesex	Russel H. Shelley	107 14	209 43
Eastford	Windham	Joseph Dorsett, jr.	54 53	97 92
East Granby	Hartford	Charles T. Hillyer	51 59	95 62
East Haddam	Middlesex	F. W. Green, to 22d Aug	21 07	41 26
		Daniel B. Warner	147 45	276 55
East Hampton	Middlesex	David Buell	59 69	110 34
East Hartford	Hartford	Henry Phelps	100 34	209 62
East Haven	New Haven	Reuel Andrews	26 58	52 53
East Killingly	Windham	William Stone	40 77	68 74
East Lyme	New London	Francis B. Loomis	40 27	36 31
East Windsor	Hartford	James H. Charleton	120 34	238 85
Ellington	Tolland	John Hall	108 09	203 72
Ellsworth	Litchfield	Ichabod S. Everitt	17 20	28 38
Enfield	Hartford	Geer Terry	156 24	304 66
Essex	Middlesex	A. F. Whittemore	202 82	397 23
Exeter	New London	Elias L. Williams	7 47	12 09
Fairfield	Fairfield	Henry C. Smith, to 31st Dec	85 52	160 39
		Edmund Hobart	88 83	159 03

POST OFFICES—*Connecticut.*

Post Offices.	Counties.	Postmasters.	Compensation.	Net proceeds.
Fairhaven	New Haven	Lester Keep, to 17th Oct	$40 10	$82 95
		Horatio L. Scranton	110 57	215 09
Falls Village	Litchfield	John A. Ensign	117 25	229 10
Farmington	Hartford	George D. Cowles	268 91	488 88
Fishersville	Windham	Joel E. Fisher	49 38	82 24
Franklin	New London	James H. Hyde	34 53	67 91
Furnace Village	Litchfield	John G. Mitchell	72 63	131 17
Gales' Ferry	New London	Norman B. Brown	12 75	22 21
Gardner's Lake	New London	Eliphalet Beckwith	4 94	7 42
Gaylord's Bridge	Litchfield	Sylvanus Merwin	49 92	81 56
Gilead	Tolland	Harvey Hutchinson, to 22d Oct	9 08	14 28
		Bissell E. Post	16 36	22 30
Glastenbury	Hartford	Benjamin Taylor	105 19	188 39
Goshen	Litchfield	Myron Norton	128 57	249 09
Granby	Hartford	Daniel Hayes	51 91	100 56
Greenfield Hill	Fairfield	Ira Benedict	47 32	91 13
Greenwich	Fairfield	Samuel Close	167 01	313 34
Griswold	New London	Thomas T. Edmond to 14th Dec.	9 39	16 31
		Alex'r Stewart, jr.	6 78	13 65
Groton	New London	Elijah Bailey	42 45	82 09
Guilford	New Haven	A. B. Wildman, to 7th Feb'y	106 40	206 56
		George Hart, from 10th Feb'y	58 26	106 75
Haddam	Middlesex	Jonathan Arnold	66 92	137 06
Hadlyme	New London	Ely P. Wells	32 04	58 01
Hamburgh	New London	Sam'l M. Brockway	31 54	56 52
Hamden	New Haven	Leverett Hitchcock	94 38	182 77
Hampton	Windham	William Brown	85 95	141 04
Hartford	Hartford	Joseph Pratt	2000 00	8854 83
Hartland	Hartford	Calvin Banning	22 94	44 99
Harwinton	Litchfield	Julius Catlin, to 30th Sept	28 85	54 40
		Sheldon G. Catlin, to 13th May	60 73	112 32
		Freeman Kellogg	10 30	18 90
Hawleyville	Fairfield	Glover Hawley	16 97	27 33
Hebron	Tolland	Abner Hendee, to 26th Aug	18 26	23 64
		Orrin C. White, to 1st June	67 06	102 55
		Charles Post	4 86	9 45
Higganum	Middlesex	Harvey Child	58 77	113 84

POST OFFICES—*Connecticut.*

Post Offices.	Counties.	Postmasters.	Compensation.	Net proceeds.
Hitchcockville....	Litchfield....	Wm. H. Phelps, to 13th May.......	$90 74	$146 17
		John Phelps.......	13 78	22 18
Hope Valley......	Tolland......	David Chapman....	12 23	18 99
Howard's Valley.	Windham...	Septimeus Burnam.	22 22	32 33
Humphreysville..	New Haven..	John D. Smith.....	119 27	224 24
Huntington......	Fairfield.....	Ch'r N. Shelton....	28 73	57 95
Jewett City......	New London	Samuel Button.....	99 74	188 38
Kensington......	Hartford.....	Theron Hart, to 10th Sept............	18 98	31 77
		Samuel B. Cowles..	80 67	106 97
Kent............	Litchfield....	John H. St. John...	107 41	177 91
Ketch Mills......	Hartford.....	Sumner Shepard....	22 36	46 28
Killingly........	Windham...	Leavens Jenks.....	63 01	126 15
Killingworth.....	Middlesex....	Horace Redfield....	24 02	47 25
Lebanon	New London	Simeon Peckham...	97 62	162 25
Ledyard	New London	Erastus Gallup, to 25th Dec'r.......	7 93	13 68
		Christopher Newton	8 28	14 33
Leesville........	Middlesex....	Sol'n B. Wheelock..	12 57	23 73
Liberty Hill.....	New London	George S. Gay.....	36 96	54 96
Lime Rock......	Litchfield....	Milo Barnum, from 1st April........	6 44	11 06
Lisbon..........	New London	Hiram Tarbox.....	38 83	81 22
Litchfield........	Litchfield....	Geo. C. Woodruff..	489 34	693 37
Lyme...........	New London	Charles W. Wait, to 17th March......	191 04	185 62
		Jos. S. Brockway..	69 63	67 59
Madison	New Haven..	John Tibbals, to 22d Aug............	16 02	30 42
		Jonathan S. Wilcox	85 71	166 94
Manchester......	Hartford.....	H'y C. Woodbridge	122 83	243 75
Mansfield	Tolland......	Joseph Woodward.	122 54	196 41
Mansfield Centre.	Tolland......	Zalmon Storrs.....	89 45	144 73
Marlborough	Hartford.....	Asa Day..........	38 98	70 19
Meriden.........	New Haven..	Walter Booth......	491 21	1096 83
Middlebury......	New Haven..	Larmon Townsend..	42 49	75 04
Middle Haddam..	Middlesex...	Huntington Selden..	112 41	196 01
Middletown......	Middlesex...	Eli Wilcox, to 26th May...........	845 13	2292 59
		Allen May........	75 39	204 66
Milford	New Haven..	L. N. Beardsley, to 31st March......	139 00	176 14
		De Luzerne Hubbell	36 20	72 50
Mill Brook......	Litchfield....	Harvey W. Pinney.	14 53	20 56

POST OFFICES—*Connecticut.*

Post Offices.	Counties.	Postmasters.	Compensation.	Net proceeds.
Millington	Middlesex	Jos. P. Arnold	$28 95	$38 26
Mill Plain	Fairfield	Elias Birchard	11 56	20 02
Milton	Litchfield	Gerret P. Welch, to 29th April	27 58	42 34
		Alban Guild	7 21	10 16
Monroe	Fairfield	Cyrus H. Beardslee	39 43	77 79
Moodus	Middlesex	James C. Hyde, 3d June	54 45	94 75
		Ezra T. Jones	5 15	8 30
Moose Meadow	Tolland	Ira M. Bidwell, to 26th Oct	4 47	7 15
		Horace Bridwell, to 10th June	6 95	11 77
Moosop	Windham	John Dunlap	38 29	73 40
Mystic	New London	John Hyde, to 1st Nov	35 57	64 35
		Henry Harding	97 95	169 73
Mystic Bridge	New London	B. F. Palmer, to 6th Dec	58 73	105 22
		David Mallory	86 04	149 51
Naugatuck	New Haven	Enos Candee, to 31st Dec	86 78	186 55
		John A. Peck	87 36	193 60
New Boston	Windham	Chas. C. Wood	17 47	27 00
New Britain	Hartford	Henry Nash, to 23d Sept	74 47	181 77
		Marcellus Clark	313 50	604 45
New Canaan	Fairfield	T. S. Husted, to 10th Sept	40 45	71 57
		Charles Raymond	175 23	316 64
New Fairfield	Fairfield	Seelye Barnum	37 39	64 59
New Hartford	Litchfield	Tertius Wadsworth	125 69	246 18
New Hartford Centre	Litchfield	James F. Henderson	50 29	93 68
New Haven	New Haven	Henry Huggins, to 30th Sept	398 21	2434 89
		Edward A. Mitchell	1168 14	7423 69
Newington	Hartford	William Deming	41 79	75 03
New London	New London	James H. Turner	1152 32	2630 75
New Milford	Litchfield	Nathaniel Perry, to 20th January	144 95	254 26
		Sol. E. Bostwick	99 46	181 29
New Preston	Litchfield	Edw. P. Lyman	84 48	142 99
Newtown	Fairfield	Henry May	190 84	353 02
Noank	New London	William Latham, to 10th Dec	10 19	18 41
		Geo. W. Chipman	16 29	28 39
Norfield	Fairfield	David Platt	13 72	25 64

POST OFFICES—*Connecticut.*

Post Offices.	Counties.	Postmasters.	Compensation.	Net proceeds.
Norfolk	Litchfield	Jno. A. Shepherd, to 7th Jan	$104 58	$177 21
		Nathl. B. Stevens	82 42	148 86
North Ashford	Windham	Cyril Keyes	13 80	24 11
North Branford	New Haven	Timothy R. Palmer, to 31st May	14 63	27 88
		Wm. R. Reynolds	1 06	2 10
North Canton	Hartford	Oliver C. Adams	9 17	17 47
North Colebrook	Litchfield	James Marvin, from 21st March	6 16	9 11
Northfield	Litchfield	Dan Catlin	45 94	74 48
Northford	New Haven	Tim. Bartholomew	40 55	76 57
North Goshen	Litchfield	Nelson H. North	53 72	73 00
North Granby	Hartford	Abner Case	19 58	36 84
North Guilford	New Haven	Henry Fowler	12 90	22 99
North Haven	New Haven	Wm. S. Hall	57 47	80 85
North Kent (Dis. 25th Sept.)	Litchfield	Lemuel B. Bull, to 3d Aug	37	65
		John Smith, 2d, to 5th Oct	76	1 45
North Killingly	Windham	George Warren	10 53	16 64
North Lyme	New London	Erastus Stark	15 70	30 89
North Madison	New Haven	Sam. L. Blatchley	5 81	12 37
North Somers	Tolland	Amariah Kibbe	15 61	23 93
North Stamford	Fairfield	Abishai Weed	27 17	44 90
North Stonington	New London	Wm. B. Hull, to 2d May	50 92	90 31
		Thos. P. Wattles	8 56	14 03
Northville	Litchfield	Sheld. Buckingham, to 31st July	2 45	3 13
		HarveyBuckingham	17 23	26 90
North Windham	Windham	Ralph Lincoln	29 24	54 46
North Woodstock	Windham	Amasa Carpenter	80 21	138 20
Norwalk	Fairfield	Stephen Smith	464 54	1001 82
Norwich	New London	John H. Townsend	1185 66	3100 64
Norwichtown	New London	Henry B. Tracy	199 02	306 60
Oakland	Hartford	Jas. H. Porter, to 30th Sept	6 66	13 06
		Edw. M. Hudson, to 16th Jan	9 96	18 18
		Whiting Risley	10 92	21 26
Orange	New Haven	Philo N. Curtis, from 14th Aug	21 94	21 81
Oxford	New Haven	Harvey W. Upson, to 31st Dec	35 61	66 27
		Samuel Wire, from 1st April	13 66	25 29

POST OFFICES—*Connecticut.*

Post Offices.	Counties.	Postmasters.	Compensation.	Net proceeds.
Pendleton Hill...	New London	E. B. Pendleton, to 2d Sept.........	$3 42	$5 12
		Andrew Chapman..	14 74	19 99
Pequot.......... (Changed to 'Poquanoc Bridge')	New London	Jefferson Perkins, to 22d Jan.........	2 27	3 43
Plainfield.........	Windham...	Henry Sabin......	111 06	201 44
Plainville.........	Hartford	William Hitchcock.	100 78	180 80
Pleasant Valley..	Litchfield ...	Virgil Taylor, to 23d Nov........	10 02	18 43
		Cornwall Doolittle..	19 07	32 19
Plymouth.........	Litchfield ...	John C. Calhoun, to 30th Sept........	42 98	75 87
		Edwin Talmage:...	113 26	211 27
Plymouth Hollow	Litchfield ...	Seth Thomas, jr ...	148 76	253 76
Pomfret.........	Windham...	Benjamin Child....	97 12	177 65
Pomfret Landing.	Windham...	Benj. F. Durkee ...	25 04	47 73
Poquanoc Bridge. (Late 'Pequot.')	New London	Sandford Morgan, from 22d March .	2 59	3 71
Poquetanuck	New London	Asa L. Latham	30 94	62 29
Poquonock.......	Hartford	Cicero Phelps......	48 56	92 43
Portersville......	New London	Jedediah Randall, to 4th Nov........	21 73	41 73
		Peleg Denison	48 11	87 97
Portland	Middlesex ..	Charles H. Sage ...	171 11	342 94
Preston..........	New London	Henry Brown	40 46	74 68
Prospect........	New Haven.	Robert H. Platt....	36 91	58 69
Reading.........	Fairfield	Jared Olmstead	68 40	121 78
Reading Ridge...	Fairfield	Floyd Tucker	40 84	74 00
Ridgebury	Fairfield	Thomas St. John ..	11 72	21 19
Ridgefield	Fairfield	Chas. A. Hanford, to 30th Sept.....	42 87	75 50
		R. Jones, fr. 21st Oct	105 09	184 64
River Head	New London	Elisha Beckwith, 2d	35 44	35 29
Rockville	Tolland.....	Samuel P. Rose....	171 51	370 98
Rocky Hill......	Hartford....	Henry Whitmore ..	100 05	178 46
Round Hill......	Fairfield	Odle C. Knapp	26 21	41 99
Roxbury........	Litchfield ...	Myron Downs.....	53 64	98 76
Salem	New London	Oramel Whittlesey, to 30th Sept.....	10 67	18 17
		Joseph Hillard.....	38 14	64 44
Salisbury	Litchfield ...	Daniel S. Clapp....	125 63	242 64
Saybrook	Middlesex ..	Richard E. Pratt...	106 71	206 29
Scantick Village .	Hartford....	Hiram Watson. ...	19 70	39 71
Scitico..........	Hartford....	John King	29 32	48 91
Scotland	Windham...	William Davison...	50 18	80 36
Scott's Ridge	Fairfield	David Scott	6 53	10 18

POST OFFICES—Connecticut.

Post Offices.	Counties.	Postmasters.	Compensation.	Net proceeds.
Sharon	Litchfield	Judson St. John, to 9th May	$174 06	$281 36
		David R. Gould	14 74	29 82
Sherman	Fairfield	Frederick Edwards, to 17th June	35 41	61 55
		Revillo Fuller	1 43	2 59
Simsbury	Hartford	Jeffrey O. Phelps	73 16	146 18
Somers	Tolland	Erasm. E. Hamilton	90 69	169 47
South Britain	New Haven	Anson Bray	36 65	67 78
Southbury	New Haven	Chas. H. Hall	36 79	59 58
South Canaan	Litchfield	Chauncey Reed, jr. to 31st Dec	31 09	48 86
		Wm. M. Burrall	23 65	40 01
South Coventry	Tolland	Solomon Bidwell	129 22	240 07
South Farms	Litchfield	Wm. L. Smedley	77 07	73 85
Southford (Dis. 9th Aug.) (Re-est. 27th Sept.)	New Haven	Cyrus Hinman, to 17th Aug	1 73	3 58
		Enos Foot, from 1st Oct	7 69	12 58
South Glastenbury	Hartford	George Merrick, to 13th May	69 57	135 85
		Oliver Brainard	11 00	20 89
Southington	Hartford	Chester Whittlesey	255 04	465 27
South Kent	Litchfield	W. T. Hopson, to 23d Oct	4 60	7 36
		Nelson Morehouse	9 85	18 24
South Killingly	Windham	Cyrus Day	16 49	29 49
South Lyme	New London	Russell L. Chadwick	26 10	45 67
South Norwalk	Fairfield	Horace Taylor	91 51	157 49
South Port	Fairfield	Wm. Sherwood, jr.	179 39	317 78
Square Pond	Tolland	Ephraim Dimmick	8 67	15 19
Stafford	Tolland	Horatio M. Bolton	142 25	266 58
Stafford Springs	Tolland	David Parkess	65 46	127 98
Stamford	Fairfield	Sands Seely, to 14th Sept.	75 90	159 90
		Roswell Hoyt	315 40	643 82
Stanwich	Fairfield	Harvey Smith	44 79	69 58
Stepney	Fairfield	Levi Edwards	43 76	74 27
Sterling	Windham	William Fenner	46 60	80 93
Stonington	New London	Franklin Williams, to 5th Dec	219 77	369 76
		Benj. F. States	197 52	276 46
Straitsville	New Haven	Ozro Collins	21 27	39 03
Stratford	Fairfield	David Brooks	218 90	379 33
Suffield	Hartford	Geo. A. Loomis	329 15	477 49
Tariffville	Hartford	James W. Adams	156 71	317 49
Terrysville	Litchfield	Philo Lewis	120 00	214 04
Thompson	Windham	Jeremiah Olney	175 28	316 15

POST OFFICES—*Connecticut.*

Post Offices.	Counties.	Postmasters.	Compensation.	Net proceeds.
Thompsonville...	Hartford	Geo. C. Owen	$167 41	$371 61
Tolland	Tolland	Luther Eaton......	104 91	201 58
Torringford	Litchfield ...	Nathaniel Smith ...	35 67	64 97
Trumbull	Fairfield	Elihu Beach	14 81	20 89
Trumbull Long Hill	Fairfield	E. B. Middlebrook, to 31st Dec......	7 96	17 54
		Miles Beardsley, from 11th Jan....	17 35	27 81
Uncasville.......	New London	Chas. H. Wheeler, to 31st May.....	91 25	160 94
		Wm. G. Johnson ..	4 58	7 55
Union	Tolland	David L. Newell...	43 57	67 89
Unionville.......	Hartford	George Richards...	42 16	83 56
UpperMiddletown	Middlesex ..	Nathaniel Bushnell.	59 71	111 77
Vernon	Tolland	L. P. Tinker, to 30th Sept	21 31	38 25
		Edwin G. Brigham.	67 65	119 94
Voluntown.	Windham...	Kinney Gallup.....	30 06	52 07
Wallingford	New Haven.	Samuel H. Dutton, to 10th Feb......	98 05	201 80
		Lorenzo Lewis	75 08	150 04
Warehouse Point	Hartford	Henry Pease, jr....	123 86	250 51
Warren.........	Litchfield ...	Edm'd R. Swift....	71 37	120 97
Washington	Litchfield ...	D. B. Brinsmade, to 14th Feb........	63 88	105 14
		William Moody	33 55	61 51
Waterbury......	New Haven.	Elisha Leavenworth	491 69	1143 95
Waterford	New London	Henry Gardiner, 2d	89 56	89 57
Watertown......	Litchfield ...	Merrit Heminway..	119 26	233 53
West Brook.....	Middlesex ..	Amos T. Wilcox ..	55 46	105 14
West Chester ...	New London	Robbins Tracy	25 55	41 22
West Cornwall ..	Litchfield ...	George Wheaton, to 14th Aug	8 32	14 36
		Chalker Pratt, to 14th Sept	6 22	10 50
		George Wheaton ..	54 84	87 45
Westford	Windham...	Michael Richmond.	26 56	48 64
West Granby ...	Hartford	Justus D. Wilcox..	19 99	37 03
West Hartford ..	Hartford	Elihu Olmstead	62 67	121 46
West Hartland ..	Hartford	Thos. D. Bosworth.	13 42	27 22
West Killingly ..	Windham...	Silas Clapp........	151 39	260 01
Westminster	Windham...	Peter Spicer.......	21 61	37 85
Weston.........	Fairfield	Edward Hill.......	47 34	84 68
Westport	Fairfield	Geo. L. Cable	246 66	488 71

POST OFFICES—*New York.*

Post Offices.	Counties.	Postmasters.	Compensation.	Net proceeds.
West Stafford....	Tolland......	Philip Orcutt, to 18th Oct........	$6 45	$10 79
		Eleazer W. Bugbey.	14 03	23 70
West Suffield....	Hartford....	Charles Denison...	44 29	79 52
Westville.......	New Haven.	Jas. G. Hotchkiss..	78 97	165 06
West Woodstock	Windham...	John F. Williams..	46 40	81 80
Wethersfield....	Hartford....	Jesse Goodrich....	185 37	397 78
Wilkinson......	Windham...	Jno. O. Fox.......	55 87	97 11
Willimantic.....	Windham...	Lloyd E. Baldwin, to 19th May.....	142 91	254 97
		Joshua B. Lord....	13 42	30 10
Willington......	Tolland.....	Jonathan Weston..	87 09	140 13
Wilton.........	Fairfield....	Jos. P. Fitch......	114 52	190 08
Winchester......	Litchfield...	John Boyd, to 17th March..........	212 30	409 13
		Wm. S. Holabird..	89 67	179 65
WinchesterCentre	Litchfield...	Samuel Hurlbert...	72 86	120 78
Windham.......	Windham...	Jno. A. Perkins....	151 88	252 28
Windsor........	Hartford....	Samuel O. Loomis.	157 95	178 26
Windsor Locks..	Hartford....	Chas. H. Dexter...	117 48	142 59
Winthrop.......	Middlesex..	John Denison......	9 03	14 25
Wolcott........	New Haven.	William Welton...	32 79	54 29
Wolcottville.....	Litchfield...	O. B. Freeman, to 23d Jan.........	161 36	251 66
		Russel C. Abernethy	125 55	159 54
Woodbury......	Litchfield...	Andrew Root, to 14th Oct........	49 99	98 49
		Chas. H. Webb...	127 47	241 33
Woodstock......	Windham...	Edward E. Bowen.	69 46	132 43
Woodville.......	Litchfield...	FrederickChittenden	17 17	23 76
Zoar Bridge.....	New Haven.	Ezekiel Curtiss....	10 26	20 07

NEW YORK.

Note.—Compensation of Postmasters, and net proceeds of their offices, from July 1, 1844, to June 30, 1845.

Post Offices.	Counties.	Postmasters.	Compensation.	Net proceeds.
Accommodation-ville.........	Orange......	Isaiah J. Whitten..	$20 36	$28 74
Accord.........	Ulster.......	Ms. J. Schoonmaker	55 97	91 48
Acra...........	Greene......	Moses Olmstead, to 31st March......	19 21	30 54
		William Telfair, G.	5 24	8 93

POST OFFICES—*New York.*

Post Offices.	Counties.	Postmasters.	Compensation.	Net proceeds.
Adams	Jefferson	Mason Curtis	$307 69	$373 70
Adams' Basin	Monroe	Marcus Adams	54 90	91 88
Adams' Centre	Jefferson	Danforth Doty	73 70	72 89
Adamsville	Washington	Abner Harden, to 30th Sept	2 78	4 50
		Alonzo W. Pratt	9 67	17 08
Addison	Steuben	Wm. R. Smith	142 52	242 37
Adriance	Dutchess	Abm. B. Stockholm	17 22	29 57
Akron	Erie	Elisha M. Adams	77 95	135 33
Alabama	Genesee	John Crombie, to 7th Nov	21 25	36 78
		Amasa Johnson	29 41	57 54
Albany	Albany	James D. Wasson	2000 00	21445 60
Albion	Orleans	Henry J. Sickles	695 90	1658 09
Alden	Erie	Sam'l M. Butler	101 59	195 74
Alder Creek	Oneida	Stephen Rich, to 4th Feb	37 43	36 89
		Lorin Miller	19 14	26 42
Alexander	Genesee	Van Ren. Hawkins, to 30th Sept	56 87	91 56
		Warren Thompson	143 54	245 77
Alexandria	Jefferson	John W. Fuller, to 19th April	19 44	34 08
		Alex'r C. Hamblin	5 47	10 64
Alexandria Centre	Jefferson	Richard Holmes	7 87	12 64
Alfred	Allegany	Samuel Russell	80 63	125 99
Allen	Allegany	John W. Stewart	10 01	18 95
Allen Centre	Allegany	Chester Rotch	7 23	14 97
Allen's Hill	Ontario	Harvey Jewett	85 90	145 71
Alloway	Wayne	William McGown	46 42	86 47
Almond	Allegany	Ambrose Corey, to 31st Dec	47 35	78 07
		Asher C. Smith	44 44	74 24
Alps	Rensselaer	Thomas Ten Eyck	34 42	55 96
Alton	Wayne	Edm. W. Lawrence	41 76	71 28
Amagansett	Suffolk	Eleazer M. Conklin	19 73	27 69
Amber	Onondaga	Albert Niles	37 53	61 69
Amboy	Oswego	John P. Hosselkus	20 73	43 66
Amenia	Dutchess	Hiram Vail, to 16th Nov	38 70	73 67
		Elijah D. Freeman	71 93	138 34
Amenia Union	Dutchess	Amariah Hitchcock	39 83	76 45
Ames	Montgomery	Chs. G. Robinson	79 83	124 01
Amity	Orange	Jno. W. Thompson, (3 qrs.)	17 14	34 21
Amsterdam	Montgomery	Isaac Morris, (3 qrs.)	250 97	528 53
Anaquasscook	Washington	James Thompson	29 05	45 02
Ancram	Columbia	John Davis	16 05	28 59
Ancram L'd Mines	Columbia	Asa Hoag	14 87	25 09

POST OFFICES—*New York.*

Post Offices.	Counties.	Postmasters.	Compensation.	Net proceeds.
Andes	Delaware	Dan'l B. Shaver	$52 26	$99 56
Andover	Allegany	Robt. L. Brundage, to 4th March	24 64	44 32
		Morris S. Brundage	11 53	24 27
Angelica	Allegany	Ezra Starr	270 10	545 28
Angola	Erie	Caleb Taylor	5 38	10 59
Antwerp	Jefferson	Alanson Drake	105 97	199 10
Apalachin	Tioga	Ransom Steele	16 11	30 89
Appling	Jefferson	Susan Howard	18 27	17 93
Apulia	Onondaga	Elijah H. St. John, to 31st Dec	23 79	38 63
		Justus Chollar	23 41	40 20
Argosville	Schoharie	John Simmons, jr.	17 14	31 30
Argyle	Washington	Jno. C. Rouse, to 9th Dec	58 03	94 71
		Wm. H. Rouse	63 89	113 69
Arkport	Steuben	James Hurlbut	15 55	28 68
Arkville	Delaware	Noah Dimmick	17 94	30 62
Arkwright	Chautauque	Simeon Clinton	12 28	25 29
Arthursburgh	Dutchess	Dan'l D. Jones	21 49	36 98
Ashford	Cattaraugus	David B. Jewett	12 93	27 32
Astoria	Queens	Edwin Gaites	77 64	157 54
Athens	Greene	Eli Pierce, to 21st Sept	30 09	54 13
		James G. Foster	121 59	185 41
Athol	Warren	Jno. L. Gilpin	13 04	26 85
Attica	Wyoming	Alden S. Stevens	262 13	511 69
Attica Centre	Wyoming	William Tanner	13 01	24 18
Attlebury	Dutchess	Phineas K. Sackett	24 02	40 21
Auburn	Cayuga	Wm. C. Beardsley	1457 40	4007 39
Augusta	Oneida	Robt. J. Norris	148 85	235 41
Aurelius	Cayuga	Alanson Partelow	36 13	51 82
Auriesville	Montgomery	John C. Van Alstine	22 19	37 12
Aurora	Cayuga	Edward Dougherty, to 16th Aug	33 42	32 87
		John L. Cuyler	197 45	282 96
Ausable (Changed to "Upper Jay.")	Essex	Benjamin Wells, to 30th Sept	2 98	5 90
Ausable Forks	Essex	Chs. H. Jones, to 18th Dec	49 07	89 28
		James Rogers	51 73	87 47
Austerlitz	Columbia	Anson Brown	37 91	67 89
Ava	Oneida	Joshua Colman	14 31	24 70
Avoca	Steuben	Oliver Rice	85 59	80 25
Avon	Livingston	Isaac Wells	212 34	460 82
Axeville (Dis. 3d June.)	Cattaraugus	Samuel Cowley	5 13	8 14

POST OFFICES—*New York.*

Post Offices.	Counties.	Postmasters.	Compensation.	Net proceeds.
Babcock Hill	Oneida	John H. Champion, from 1st Jan.	$4 24	$3 80
Babylon	Suffolk	Timothy P. Carll	69 30	125 87
Bainbridge	Chenango	Dexter Newell	225 21	181 45
Bainbridge Centre	Chenango	Francis G. Loveland, to 31st May	12 09	22 84
		David Van Horne	1 72	2 97
Baiting Hollow	Suffolk	Micah Howell	13 50	20 03
Baldwin	Chemung	John Goodwin	10 33	34 32
Baldwinsville	Onondaga	E. A. Baldwin, to 26th Nov.	103 18	190 36
		Dan'l T. Jones	154 57	309 58
Ballston	Saratoga	Jas. W. Horton, to 31st Dec.	214 10	464 76
		George Thompson	227 32	481 52
Ballston Centre	Saratoga	David Boyd	50 50	89 93
Bangor	Franklin	Danforth Patterson	74 89	73 69
Barboursville	Delaware	Steph'n Van Schoyk	8 02	14 86
Barcelona	Chautauque	Isaac Shaw	63 95	127 69
Barkersville	Saratoga	John Barker, to 30th Sept.	4 29	7 43
		Ira J. Barker	10 77	15 21
Barnerville	Schoharie	Jacob Russell	19 66	26 62
Barre Centre	Orleans	Nathan Raymond	89 94	157 57
Barrington	Yates	William Hedges	19 98	42 08
Barrytown	Dutchess	Augustus Martin	62 50	120 60
Barryville	Sullivan	Calvin P. Fuller	29 97	52 70
Barton	Tioga	Washington Smith, to 31st March	47 93	35 74
		Samuel Mills	13 98	24 49
Batavia	Genesee	Frederick Follett	844 42	2023 37
Bath	Steuben	Levi C. Whiting	633 76	1023 36
Battenville	Washington	Aaron M. McLean	36 06	63 22
Beach Hill	Ulster	Sam'l N. Hendrix	5 65	10 51
Beaver Brook	Sullivan	Chs. S. Woodward	17 42	31 63
Beaver Kill	Sullivan	Samuel Waterbery	16 70	26 63
Bedford	West Chester	Nehemiah S. Bates	113 08	214 66
Beekman	Dutchess	James Peters	43 12	78 19
Beekmantown	Clinton	Benj. J. Simonds	28 97	55 38
Belfast	Allegany	Thos. P. Alexander	46 32	82 69
Belle Isle	Onondaga	Marvin Armstrong, to 11th Dec.	26 96	45 07
		George Kimberly	27 70	48 59
Belleville	Jefferson	Alcander Dickinson	111 62	189 80
Bellport	Suffolk	James G. Howell	39 39	71 70
Bemus Heights	Saratoga	Henry Lent	53 83	95 39
Bennet's Corners	Madison	Prescott McDoel	10 39	19 11
Bennett's Creek	Steuben	John Coston, from 17th Oct.	1 84	3 35

9*

POST OFFICES—*New York.*

Post Offices.	Counties.	Postmasters.	Compensation.	Net proceeds.
Bennington	Wyoming	Philo Durkee	$42 83	$81 66
Benson	Hamilton	Leonard Aniball	14 23	21 31
Benton	Yates	De Witt C. Gage, to 1st March	82 02	133 53
		Stephen Garrison	35 65	60 37
Benton Centre	Yates	Isaac N. Gage	75 12	119 83
Bergen	Genesee	Moses S. Gibson, to 24th Oct	26 48	45 96
		Austin Wilcox	78 58	111 76
Berkshire	Tioga	Nath'l F. Moore	68 16	99 69
Berlin	Rensselaer	Robt. A. Lottridge	64 46	106 38
Berne	Albany	Jacob Settle	66 42	95 71
Bethany	Genesee	Jonathan K. Barlow, to 6th Sept	11 99	22 51
		Carlos A. Huggins	62 74	104 87
Bethel	Sullivan	Chs. B. Roosa, to 31st Dec'r	23 99	39 72
		Eleazer Morgan, to 5th March	14 84	14 24
		Wm. McCullough	16 69	29 19
Bethlehem	Albany	Nathaniel Adams	21 71	39 46
Big Brook	Oneida	Chauncey Hayden	8 51	14 34
Big Flatts	Chemung	Lauren A. Tuttle	61 74	113 19
Big Hollow	Greene	Friend Holcomb	20 01	32 98
Big Stream Point	Yates	Lar'n G. Townsend	68 69	108 11
Binghampton	Broome	Tracy Robinson	927 37	1886 16
Birdsall	Allegany	Isaac G. Freeman	8 21	16 45
Black Brook	Clinton	Norman B. Foot	45 35	64 88
Black Creek	Allegany	Thomas Carpenter	31 83	58 28
Black River	Jefferson	Francis Butterfield	31 41	55 78
Black Rock	Erie	Morgan G. Lewis	176 20	356 58
Blauveltville	Rockland	Isaac M. Dederer	22 53	32 69
Bleeker	Fulton	Eph'm A. Campbell	8 64	18 54
Blenheim	Schoharie	Colba Reed	22 45	40 77
Bloomingburgh	Sullivan	Verdine E. Horton	111 90	188 24
Blooming Grove	Orange	Samuel B. Breed	84 48	137 86
Bloomville	Delaware	Stephen H. Keeler, (2 qrs.)	22 85	16 86
Bolivar	Allegany	Nelson Hoyt	23 97	42 14
Bolton	Warren	William Stewart, to 31st Dec	17 02	29 40
		Truman Lyman	21 02	35 67
Bombay	Franklin	Wilson Randall	33 99	32 95
Booneville	Oneida	Henry Graves	198 86	191 41
Borodino	Onondaga	John Baxter, to 30th September	18 25	32 66
		William Legg	51 41	93 71
Boston	Erie	William Andre	67 67	110 63
Bouckville	Madison	Moses Maynard	53 76	45 07

POST OFFICES—*New York.*

Post Offices.	Counties.	Postmasters.	Compensation.	Net proceeds.
Bovina	Delaware	Thos. McFarland, jr	$23 42	$38 29
Bovina Centre	Delaware	James Coulter, to 6th March	21 35	33 88
		Seymour C. Wilcox, from 13th March	12 13	19 63
Brainard's Bridge	Rensselear	Seth Hastings	39 52	69 76
Braman's Corners	Schenectady	Joseph Braman	25 51	36 83
Branchport	Yates	Spencer Booth	62 79	97 06
Breakabeen	Schoharie	Gideon D. Hilts	11 07	18 33
Brant	Erie	Simeon Brown	20 67	33 00
Brantingham	Lewis	David H. Higby	9 84	20 11
Brasher Falls	St. Lawrence	Calvin T. Hulburd	34 74	60 79
Brewerton	Onondaga	William Bailey	39 01	69 28
Bridgehampton	Suffolk	Alanson Topping	89 53	121 50
Bridgeport	Madison	Joel G. Downer	41 45	79 39
Bridgeville	Sullivan	Munson L. Bushnell	37 31	66 53
Bridgewater	Oneida	Delos De Wolf	132 56	144 52
Brighton	Monroe	William Perrin, to 28th April	45 56	93 16
		Benj. B. Blossom	10 23	19 26
Brimmersville	Steuben	John Brimmer	2 81	5 47
Bristol	Ontario	Elijah Jones	86 81	144 16
Bristol Centre	Ontario	Erastus H. Crow	49 11	80 70
Broadalbin	Fulton	Marcellus Weston	98 84	171 98
Brockett's Bridge	Fulton	Zephi Brockett	55 81	93 56
Brockport	Monroe	Joseph Greenleaf	369 14	802 11
Bronx	West Chester	Abijah G. Morgan	37 24	71 34
Brookfield	Madison	Andrew Babcock	79 53	136 17
Brooklyn	Kings	George Hall, to 25th May	1791 89	6039 57
		Henry C. Conklin	197 80	720 27
Brook's Grove	Livingston	Henry S. Jarvis	20 14	40 45
Brookville	Genesee	Lucius Farnham	15 46	23 79
Brown's Haven	Sullivan	Joseph Brown	2 86	5 70
Brownville	Jefferson	James K. Bates, to 17th April	297 12	406 55
		John K. Adams	78 56	105 97
Bruynswick	Ulster	Charles Bruyn, to 18th February	22 38	35 46
		C. T. Schoonmaker	6 66	11 17
Buck Bridge	St. Lawrence	Orren Buck	8 17	12 61
Buckram	Queens	James Cock	19 41	35 07
Bucktooth	Cattaraugus	John Boardman	2 26	4 21
Buel	Montgomery	Samuel C. Hamilton	45 87	75 04
Buffalo	Erie	Chs. C. Haddock, to 15th April	1582 41	10069 80
		Philip Dorsheimer	358 78	3344 91
Bullville	Orange	Wm. W. Wallace	64 71	105 57
Burdett	Tompkins	Daniel Jackson	101 54	180 17

POST OFFICES—*New York.*

Post Offices.	Counties.	Postmasters.	Compensation.	Net proceeds.
Burke (Late "West Chateaugay.")	Franklin	Hiram Miner, from 1st January	$8 44	$17 14
Burlingham	Sullivan	Hezekiah Clark, to 23d April	16 52	27 23
		Ammi Abbot	3 85	6 58
Burlington	Otsego	George S. Gorham	96 69	92 40
Burlington Flatts	Otsego	Alderman E. Arnold	64 54	104 39
Burnt Hills	Saratoga	Wm. H. Satterlee	45 68	77 13
Burr's Mills	Jefferson	Foster Lewis	18 74	32 32
Burton	Cattaraugus	Jedediah Lathrop	23 74	45 34
Burtonville	Montgomery	Judah Burton	21 84	32 57
Bushnell's Basin	Monroe	Isaac Hastings	45 11	83 16
Bushnellsville	Greene	Alvin Bushnell, from 3d July	8 73	15 80
Buskirk's Bridge	Washington	Andrew Houghton	93 42	150 00
Busti	Chautauque	Emery Davis, to 16th April	38 65	59 96
		Lyman C. Fargo	11 25	17 73
Butler	Wayne	Lester Watson	17 88	31 04
Butterfly	Oswego	John Parsons, to 30th Sept.	1 07	2 09
		Sterling Newell	3 57	5 97
Butternuts	Otsego	Chester Jarvis	166 65	303 88
Byersville	Livingston	Samuel Stoner, jr	18 46	35 15
Byrnville	Schoharie	Richard F. Noxon	17 02	26 19
Byron	Genesee	Cyrus Jenks	129 66	236 43
Cabin Hill	Delaware	Andrew Marshall	12 40	23 15
Cadyville	Clinton	Heman Cady	3 99	7 33
Cairo	Greene	Horatio L. Day	189 15	212 48
Caldwell	Warren	Charles Roberts	55 07	89 08
Caledonia	Livingston	Gad Blakeslee	222 53	402 88
Cambria	Niagara	Charles Molyneux	38 48	77 67
Cambridge	Washington	Oliver Cook	174 04	329 94
Camden	Oneida	Hiram J. Miner	172 98	331 19
Cameron	Steuben	Elias Mason, to 22d February	5 38	9 54
		Hiram Averill, from 26th Feb.	3 33	6 49
Camillus	Onondaga	G. N. Sherwood, to 22d Jan	99 51	124 91
		Henry C. Kimberly	77 02	100 85
Campbell's Creek	Steuben	Johnson Dunham	1 75	2 69
Campbelltown	Steuben	Samuel Besley	38 68	68 97
Campville	Tioga	Joshua Mersereau	14 47	16 94
Canaan	Columbia	Samuel Frisbee	45 40	66 97
Canaan Centre	Columbia	D. Parsons (3 qrs)	19 85	36 47

POST OFFICES—*New York.*

Post Offices.	Counties.	Postmasters.	Compensation.	Net proceeds.
Canaan 4 Corners.	Columbia	Wm. A. Lord, to 6th March.......	$50 91	$93 66
		Jos. H. Cornwell...	22 42	41 80
Canadice	Ontario	Zebina C. Andruss.	41 90	71 07
Canajoharie......	Montgomery.	George Caldwell ...	396 85	728 43
Canal...........	Onondaga ...	Leonard Mason....	82 38	155 85
Canandaigua......	Ontario	Jonas M. Wheeler.	1130 87	2651 87
Canastota........	Madison	Darwin E. Hurd, to 21st Feb	87 47	166 58
		William Palmer....	55 88	108 98
Candor..........	Tioga.......	Samuel Baragar....	102 12	113 56
Caneadea........	Allegany....	Alanson Burr, to 7th March..........	22 27	20 34
		Abel S. Nicholson..	16 17	21 87
Canfield's Corner.	Tioga	Norman Lounsberry	7 06	12 21
Canisteo........	Steuben	Nathaniel C. Taylor	31 90	47 20
Cannonsville....	Delaware....	Jos. S. Babcock.....	46 04	79 94
Canoga	Seneca......	William Hoskins, to 31st Dec	21 75	38 42
		Samuel McIntosh ..	24 07	41 27
Cantatoe	West Chester	A. F. Dickinson, to 3d May..........	3 45	5 28
		Stephen Lyon......	1 13	2 13
Canterbury......	Orange	Henry F. Chadeayne	125 88	250 91
Canton..........	St. Lawrence.	Darius Clark.......	382 41	483 10
Cape Vincent....	Jefferson	John Duvillard, to 19th April.......	279 63	86 32
		Otis P. Starkey.....	51 91	11 41
Cardiff	Onondaga....	John Spencer.......	44 30	76 83
Carlisle..........	Schoharie ...	Samuel P. Shibley, to 16th Nov	24 58	39 41
		Peter W. Ferris.....	40 55	70 34
Carlton	Orleans......	Robert M. Brown..	27 46	53 29
Carmel	Putnam	J. Crosby, to 24th Oct.	28 40	46 64
		Thomas W. Taylor.	54 46	103 50
Caroline.........	Tompkins...	Madison Rounsavell	29 24	38 92
Caroline Centre..	Tompkins...	Reuben Higgins....	10 31	18 68
Carroll..........	Chautauque..	James Hall........	44 39	69 89
Carthage.........	Jefferson	William Blodget ...	214 56	359 14
Cassadaga	Chautauque..	James Beebe.......	14 89	26 82
Cassville	Oneida	Barzilla Budlong...	44 96	82 41
Castile..........	Wyoming...	John B. Halsted....	165 33	257 46
Castleton........	Rensselaer...	I. V. Schermerhorn.	51 87	88 14
Catharine........	Chemung ...	Elijah S. Hinman ..	64 98	109 18
Cato............	Cayuga	Almond Daniels, to 30th Sept........	15 31	27 85
		George Humphries, to 6th May......	41 04	72 34
		Reuben P. Conger..	9 82	18 53

POST OFFICES—*New York.*

Post Offices.	Counties.	Postmasters.	Compensation.	Net proceeds.
Cato 4 Corners	Cayuga	Wm. S. Ingham	$131 86	$235 59
Catskill	Greene	Wm. W. Van Loan	741 87	1492 59
Cayuga	Cayuga	Edwin H. Whitney.	132 73	153 71
Cayuta	Chemung	Zalmon F. Chase, to 30th Sept.	1 17	2 09
		Jacob Swartwood	6 74	8 66
Cazenovia	Madison	Benj. T. Clark, to 10th Nov.	241 63	512 19
		Sylvanus H. Henry	368 28	838 56
Cedar Hill	Albany	James G. Wayne, to 14th June	25 82	45 76
		H. Y. Schoonmaker	1 14	1 89
Cedar Swamp	Queens	Peter Luyster	30 86	54 39
Cedarville	Herkimer	Sardis Brainerd	52 89	87 37
Central Bridge	Schoharie	Olaf H. Williams	19 20	32 30
Central Square	Oswego	Henry S. Conde	57 04	101 41
Centre Almond	Allegany	L. S. Rathbun	16 53	28 02
Centre Berlin	Rensselaer	Jeffrey W. Thomas.	7 79	11 85
Centre Cambridge	Washington	James H. Hall	33 89	53 65
Centrefield	Ontario	Russell B. Johnson.	39 22	59 83
Centre Gorham	Ontario	Chauncey Stone	7 10	12 36
Centre Independ'e	Allegany	Hercules Darling	8 31	13 70
Centre Lisle	Broome	Hiram McCall	33 17	50 32
Centreport	Suffolk	Shubael M. Nichols.	12 66	24 07
Centre Sherman	Chautauque	Jos. S. Bell	8 52	13 53
Centreville	Allegany	Orrin T. Maxson	79 64	83 45
Centre White Creek	Washington	Henry Rice	21 42	29 76
Chalmers	Niagara	Eliphalet Gillet	17 48	26 09
Champion	Jefferson	Simeon Ingraham	108 72	107 59
Champion South Roads	Jefferson	Converse J. Johnson	12 12	19 55
Champlain	Clinton	Lucas Doolittle	137 95	221 73
Chapelsburgh	Cattaraugus	Russel Chapel	10 58	19 45
Chapinville	Ontario	Rensselaer Gardner.	30 80	62 03
Charleston	Montgomery.	Thompson Burton	12 69	20 40
Charleston 4 Corners	Montgomery.	Isaac S. Frost	19 32	32 47
Charlotte	Monroe	Peter A. Smith, to 21st June	21 92	38 35
		David S. Holden	0 71	1 27
Charlotte Centre	Chautauque	John Chandler	14 43	23 49
Charlotteville	Schoharie	Edmund Northup	12 92	22 00
Charlton	Saratoga	John A. Sweetman.	113 36	184 75
Chateaugay	Franklin	Henry B. Smith	96 76	152 19
Chatham	Columbia	Seth Daley	55 64	99 49
Chatham Centre	Columbia	Reuben Sleight, to 31st December	12 37	24 07
		Wm. L. V'n Alstyne	15 58	31 17

POST OFFICES—*New York.*

Post Offices.	Counties.	Postmasters.	Compensation.	Net proceeds.
Chatham 4 Corn's	Columbia....	Solomon Crandell..	$120 61	$231 05
Chaumont........	Jefferson	Solon Massey......	40 70	73 16
Chazy..........	Clinton......	Albert G. Carver, to 12th September..	18 65	33 17
		Miles Stevenson....	77 85	141 18
Cheektowaga.....	Erie........	Fred'k B. Merrill...	11 16	20 93
Chemung........	Chemung.....	Jefferson B. Clark..	62 44	113 77
Chenango Forks.	Broom.......	John B. Rogers....	85 25	153 28
Cheningo........	Cortlandt....	Abijah T. Pierce ...	3 68	5 76
Cherry Creek....	Chautauque..	Charles A. Spencer.	22 99	44 26
Cherry Valley...	Otsego......	William McLean, to 31st May........	324 13	673 04
		Charles McLean ...	24 04	45 70
Cheshire........	Ontario......	Eb'r S. Nott, to 31st March..........	22 19	41 47
		Lewis Taft........	8 55	15 76
Chesnut Ridge...	Dutchess....	Edgar Vincent.....	10 75	20 29
Chester.........	Orange......	John D. Wood.....	107 21	206 65
Chestertown.....	Warren	James W. Tubbs, to 31st December...	67 89	61 84
		William Hotchkiss.	68 61	58 59
Chili...........	Monroe......	T.Purdy,to25thNov.	20 10	36 60
		Pierpont Chapman..	24 61	49 07
China..........	Wyoming...	Lorenzo D. Davis..	76 56	131 17
Chittenango.....	Madison.....	Samuel Fuller......	237 95	469 36
Churchville......	Monroe......	E. C. Dibble, to 4th February........	55 74	107 61
		Elisha P. Davis....	30 40	63 33
Cicero..........	Onondaga ...	Judson Gage........	80 42	146 34
Cincinnatus......	Cortlandt....	Barak Niles, to 21st November.......	29 38	41 98
		Oliver Kingman....	56 36	95 22
City...........	Dutchess....	Calvin Chamberlin..	24 93	34 89
Clarence........	Erie........	Otis R. Hopkins ...	118 06	200 22
Clarendon.......	Orleans......	Eldridge Farwell...	102 22	174 65
Clarkson........	Monroe......	Gustavus Clark....	222 61	465 99
Clarkson Centre..	Monroe......	Henry Kimball, fr'm 14th September ..	32 32	59 09
Clarkstown......	Rockland....	Jabez Wood.......	20 76	39 67
Clarksville......	Albany......	David McCullock ..	28 09	41 58
Claverack	Columbia....	Peter Z. Snyder, to 31st December...	48 25	85 09
		Step. M. Van Wyck	43 64	67 57
Clay...........	Onondaga ...	Wilburn Hale, to 11th February...	66 45	78 92
		James Little.......	39 49	107 78
Clayton........	Jefferson	Lynds Grennell, to 17th April.......	123 58	254 84
		Amos Ellis........	28 24	56 25

POST OFFICES—*New York.*

Post Offices.	Counties.	Postmasters.	Compensation.	Net proceeds.
Clear Creek	Chautauque	Mason Sheldon	$27 43	$47 52
Clermont	Columbia	Wm. H. Wilson	43 61	75 69
Cleveland	Oswego	Abner H. Allen	102 49	189 92
Clifton Park	Saratoga	Seth W. Higgins	59 73	102 52
Clinton	Oneida	Chauncey C. Cook	308 37	516 55
Clinton Hollow	Dutchess	Seneca Butts, to 31st March	17 33	29 20
		Russel B. Abby	4 84	8 32
Clintonville	Clinton	Jacob Tuckerman	203 97	400 83
Clockville	Madison	Stephen Chapman	51 42	93 25
Clove	Dutchess	And'w J. Skidmore, to 30th April	17 58	31 58
		Gilbert H. Cristy	3 03	6 13
Clovesville	Delaware	John Beadle	37 98	64 78
Clyde	Wayne	Jos. D. Stone	394 06	757 50
Clymer	Chautauque	Ira F. Gleason	48 77	89 95
Clymer Centre (Dis. 12th July.)	Chautauque	David Dales, to 26th July	58	1 22
Cobleskill	Schoharie	Abm. L. Lawyer	46 63	87 33
Cobleskill Centre	Schoharie	John Howe	21 59	31 76
Cochecton	Sullivan	Jas. C. Curtis	25 95	25 98
Coeymans	Albany	And'w Van Antwerp	92 64	166 39
CoeymansHollow	Albany	John B. Shear	26 01	40 76
Cohocton	Steuben	Paul C. Cook, to 31st December	57 37	55 31
		Dan'l H. Davis	53 20	49 95
Cohoes	Albany	Hezekiah Howe	297 34	648 21
Colchester	Delaware	Hezekiah Elwood	36 14	63 00
Cold Brook	Herkimer	Stephen Smith, 2d	22 35	35 12
Colden	Erie	Benjamin Maltby	31 87	54 22
Coldenham	Orange	Peter Sears, to 31st March	47 30	55 23
		Theron M. Belknap	11 21	20 26
Cold Spring	Putnam	Seymour Birdsall	332 87	534 96
Cold Sp'g Harbor	Suffolk	Divine Hewlett	46 63	91 15
Colesville	Broome	Timothy Ruggles, to 21st August	2 04	3 91
		Walker A. Cole	12 42	21 77
College Point	Queens	Libertus Van Bokkelen, to 1st Feb	48 44	105 23
		Charles Gill	43 90	95 94
Colliersville	Otsego	Jared Goodyear	11 36	18 32
Collins	Erie	John Sherman	92 44	154 31
Collins Centre	Erie	Nathaniel Frank	41 29	71 33
Collinsville	Lewis	Homer Collins	41 42	79 44
Colosse	Oswego	T. Webb, to 13th June	50 83	97 15
		Joseph Torrey	1 39	3 14
Columbia	Herkimer	Martin L. Springer, (3 qrs.)	7 35	14 38

POST OFFICES—*New York.*

Post Offices.	Counties.	Postmasters.	Compensation.	Net proceeds.
Columbus..........	Chenango ...	Hiram E. Storrs, to 18th January....	$35 05	$55 72
		Grant B. Palmer...	22 21	38 67
Commack.......	Suffolk......	James Walters.....	24 56	44 64
Comst'ks Landing	Washington..	Ch's W. Kellogg...	25 87	40 57
Concord Centre.. (Dis. 24th May.)	Erie..........	Amaziah Ashmun..	9 25	17 23
Conesus..........	Livingston...	Gardner Arnold....	52 45	87 80
Conesville.......	Schoharie ...	Abraham Richtmyer	32 36	55 10
Conewango........	Cattaraugus..	Thomas J. Wheeler	31 60	52 47
Conklin..........	Broom.......	Benj. T. Miller, to 4th February........	10 57	19 37
		Henry Squires.....	5 79	12 94
Conquest.........	Cayuga	L. B. Phinney.....	37 43	74 53
Constableville.....	Lewis	Seth Miller, to 26th January.........	54 52	107 73
		Horace Johnson....	40 10	77 56
Constantia........	Oswego	Henry C. Champlin	55 74	106 64
Cooksburgh	Albany......	David Hitchcock, to 23d November...	28 12	48 01
		Shadrach R. Potter.	37 84	62 75
Cooper's Plains..	Steuben......	Alvin Corbin, from 16th August.....	25 34	44 22
Cooperstown	Otsego......	Robert Davis......	762 24	1431 76
Coopersville......	Clinton......	Horace Hayford ...	18 37	28 43
Copake	Columbia....	Orville H. Wilcox..	27 04	44 52
Copenhagen	Lewis.......	Horace Davenport..	83 80	156 53
Coram...........	Suffolk......	Richard W. Smith.	9 58	17 04
Corbettsville.....	Broome......	Sewell B. Corbett..	14 16	26 73
Corfu............	Genesee.....	Robert Millar......	44 78	70 84
Corinth	Saratoga	Beriah P. Rogers...	26 47	46 56
Corning.........	Steuben......	Shubael B. Denton, to 31st December.	177 52	362 79
		John McBurney....	180 76	371 42
Cornwallville	Green........	Elias B. Austin	10 92	18 18
Cortlandt Town..	West Chester	James McCord.....	81 87	97 87
Cortlandt Village.	Cortlandt....	Andrew Dickson...	458 25	642 83
Cossville.........	Steuben......	Allen Butler, jr., from 19th February...	1 42	1 16
County Line......	Niagara......	Geo. A. Fenn......	12 10	20 73
Coventry.........	Chenango ...	William Church, 6⅔ mos	61 91	102 66
		E. A. Phillips, from 20th June........	3 40	5 90
Coventryville.....	Chenango ...	Epaphras G. Waters	23 35	40 54
Covert...........	Seneca.......	James R. Pratt.....	43 33	72 42
Coveville.........	Saratoga	William Wilcox...	19 07	29 80
Covington.......	Wyoming...	William Tompkins.	31 77	50 06
Cowlesville......	Wyoming...	Jonathan B. Bass...	51 09	89 70

POST OFFICES—*New York.*

Post Offices.	Counties.	Postmasters.	Compensation.	Net proceeds.
Coxsackie	Greene	Geo. N. Keith, to 31st December	$159 53	$303 19
		Justus A. Wright	182 26	296 73
Craigsville	Orange	Seely C. Roe	19 41	38 00
Crain's Corners	Herkimer	Rufus Crain, to 9th January	9 44	16 64
		Job Bronson	9 45	14 53
Cranberry Creek	Fulton	Wm. S. Ingraham	8 04	12 94
Cranesville	Montgomery	Jeremiah Groat	34 89	59 89
Crawford	Orange	Cornelius Slott	15 70	27 23
Croghan	Lewis	Joseph Haman	6 92	14 69
Cross River	West Chester	William Hunt	37 72	63 67
Crown Point	Essex	Ch's F. Hammond	114 18	203 97
Crum Elbow	Dutchess	Israel Marshall	8 07	13 16
Cuba	Allegany	Sam'l M. Russell	213 56	197 20
Cuddebackville	Orange	Peter Cuddeback	32 05	59 74
Cutchogue	Suffolk	Benjamin Case	41 33	63 86
Cuyler	Cortlandt	Wm. Blanchard, 2d	36 56	47 43
Cuylerville	Livingston	Newell L. Bowman, to 31st December	42 60	76 77
		Lyman Odell	44 67	86 86
Dale	Wyoming	Daniel Smith	15 47	27 90
Danby	Tompkins	Sherman Miller	39 93	77 39
Dansville	Livingston	Samuel Shannon	607 83	1134 39
Danube	Herkimer	John A. Holmes, to 31st December	7 52	13 10
		Sylvester All	8 58	14 97
Darien	Genesee	Thomas Riddle	80 92	130 85
Darien Centre	Genesee	Stephen King	42 57	71 43
Davenport	Delaware	John Sherman	100 60	95 73
Davenport Centre	Delaware	John Shue	26 29	25 83
Day	Saratoga	Joseph Rockwell	7 13	13 19
Dayanville	Lewis	Caleb Ufford	9 02	18 06
Dayton	Cattaraugus	Ralph Johnson	9 93	18 38
Dean's Corners	Saratoga	Gilbert Wright, jr	25 51	39 03
Deansville	Oneida	John Dean	58 95	110 01
Decatur	Otsego	Robert Tripp	18 11	25 56
De Friestville	Rensselaer	John E. Van Allen	6 80	14 16
De Kalb	St. Lawrence	Elias P. Townsley, to 11th October	12 45	20 78
		Albert Holt	37 85	68 59
Delavan	Cattaraugus	D'n E. Goodenough	11 87	17 51
Delhi	Delaware	Nathan Hathaway, to 10th January	256 79	418 13
		Jas. B. How	265 44	428 35
Delphi	Onondaga	Elisha Litchfield, to 8th May	58 65	97 41
		Ch's C. Slocum	9 40	15 60

POST OFFICES—*New York.*

Post Offices.	Counties.	Postmasters.	Compensation.	Net proceeds.
Delta	Oneida	Phineas F. Peck	$48 92	$78 96
Denmark	Lewis	Amos Buck	119 11	146 96
Depauville	Jefferson	Stephen Martin, to 8th May	54 29	100 90
		Luke E. Frame	9 12	15 76
De Peyster	St. Lawrence	Levi Fay	26 04	51 60
Deposit	Delaware	Simon Lusk	111 42	186 47
De Ruyter	Madison	Stephen G. Sears	177 36	319 73
Devereaux	Herkimer	Henry Devereaux	45 65	78 33
De Witt	Onondaga	Henry C. Goodell, to 10th December	30 36	55 25
		Jas. H. King	39 46	70 15
De Witt's Valley	Allegany	Thomas Van Scoter	31 27	52 82
De Wittville	Chautauque	John Russell	35 22	62 76
Dexter	Jefferson	John Eaton, to 17th January	44 54	76 11
		Oliver D. Freeman	34 36	60 09
Dickinson	Franklin	Milton Heath	14 51	21 21
Dix (Disc'd 17 Mar.)	Jefferson	Barnet V. Vaneps, to 31st Dec'r	1 44	3 40
Dix Hills	Suffolk	Gilbert Carll	3 89	6 59
Doanesburgh	Putnam	Benjamin Doane	18 61	29 40
Dobbs' Ferry	West Chester	E. W. Walgrove, to 31st March	65 34	116 84
		Anthony Storms	20 79	37 69
Dolsentown (Chan'd to "New Hampton.")	Orange	Thomas Sergeant, to 31st Oct.	3 87	6 06
Doty's Corner	Steuben	George G. Babcock	4 25	8 47
Dover	Dutchess	James Ketcham, to 25th April	40 20	78 51
		Josa. H. Rodgers	10 14	13 45
Dryden	Tompkins	Abraham Tanner	203 69	197 45
Duane	Franklin	James Duane	4 56	8 89
Duanesburgh	Schenectady	Clark C. Ager	70 49	126 27
Dundee	Yates	Edward Hoogland	145 10	264 01
Dunkirk	Chautauque	Lysander B. Brown	125 18	245 15
Dunnsville	Albany	Gurdon Barrows	12 74	21 21
Durham	Greene	Platt Adams	111 63	195 27
Durhamville	Oneida	Willett Stillman	104 80	204 68
Eagle	Allegany	Oliver Phelps	27 14	48 62
Eagle Harbor	Orleans	Willis P. Collins	66 39	117 69
Eagle Mills	Rensselaer	Cornelius H. Dubois	6 29	9 96
Earlville	Madison	Sidney B. Webb, to 21st Feb.	118 11	117 15
		David Ransom	60 91	58 91
East Avon	Livingston	Thomas Wiard	85 56	162 77
East Bergen	Genesee	George Davis	15 26	22 93

POST OFFICES—*New York.*

Post Offices.	Counties.	Postmasters.	Compensation.	Net proceeds.
East Berne	Albany	John J. Gallup	$12 85	$22 46
East Bethany	Genesee	Dan'l L. Worthington, to 23d Oct	16 30	24 98
		Wm. K. Blasdell	37 67	66 96
East Bloomfield	Ontario	Henry W. Hamlin, to 12th Dec	126 74	229 52
		Henry Munson	126 05	236 29
East Branch	Delaware	Charles Baxter	21 02	36 50
East Canisteo	Steuben	Jeremiah Baker	6 01	9 67
East Carlton	Orleans	Everett Gray	23 46	30 60
East Chester	West Chester	George Faile, to 22d April	64 27	115 42
		Fisher F. Valentine	14 87	25 74
East China	Wyoming	Eli Waterman	7 15	14 91
East Constable	Franklin	Sylvester Langdon	35 73	38 52
East Durham	Greene	Amos Cleaveland	53 10	84 80
East Evans	Erie	Robert S. Ingersoll	22 63	26 71
East Florence	Oneida	Charles B. Thomson	12 47	25 02
East Franklin	Delaware	Minor Treadwell, to 27th Jan	33 37	26 68
		Sylvester Rich, from 29th Jan	18 19	18 15
East Genoa	Cayuga	Heman Holden, to 31st Dec'r	11 69	18 90
		Alex'r Bothwell, fr. 13th Jan'y	8 60	14 37
East Glenville	Schenectady	Philip H. Dedrick	12 04	19 94
East Greenbush	Rensselaer	Henry Goodrich, to 23d April	28 51	37 37
		William Hulsapple	6 78	10 18
East Greene	Chenango	John Stoughton, jr	21 92	37 02
East Greenwich	Washington	Moses Robertson	21 30	35 25
East Groveland	Livingston	Elijah Hunt	37 22	61 71
East Guilford	Chenango	Griswold Wright	20 25	31 03
East Hamburgh	Erie	Zebulon Ferris	55 21	97 51
East Hamilton	Madison	Amaza D. Carrier	77 19	126 34
East Hampton	Suffolk	Thomas T. Parsons	95 04	161 59
East Hill	Allegany	William Robinson	3 89	5 66
East Homer	Cortlandt	Augustus Cushing	23 52	29 55
East Java	Wyoming	Obed R. Marston	32 07	59 47
East Kill	Greene	N. Wm. Beach	13 01	15 35
East Koy	Allegany	Isaac Quackenbush	6 79	11 68
East Lansing	Tompkins	John Ludlow	17 88	25 67
East Lexington	Greene	Cyrus W. Pratt, to 20th Nov	3 51	5 37
		West Chase	8 12	15 77
East Line	Saratoga	Robt. A. Ogden	18 27	30 51
East McDonough	Chenango	Benjamin Randall	6 42	9 37
East Nassau	Rensselaer	Jared Root	34 44	62 65

POST OFFICES—*New York.*

Post Offices.	Counties.	Postmasters.	Compensation.	Net proceeds.
East New York..	Kings........	Edwin M. Strong..	$23 09	$35 42
Easton..........	Washington..	Aaron Barker, to 7th Nov............	11 67	21 47
		Charles R. Mosher..	19 55	38 21
East Otto........	Cattaraugus..	Hezekiah Scovel...	26 56	48 37
East Painted Post	Steuben......	Thomas Noyes, to 9th Feb.........	10 73	21 05
		Alvah Rowley.....	8 42	15 28
East Palmyra....	Wayne	Jacob Sherman.....	34 39	59 55
East Pembroke...	Genesee.....	Reuben Willett....	87 43	145 40
East Pharsalia...	Chenango....	Henry Baker......	17 97	28 43
East Pierpont....	St. Lawrence	Joseph Dimick, jr..	15 77	30 85
East Pike.........	Allegany....	Asa Sartwell, (3 qs.)	17 11	18 29
East Rodman....	Jefferson....	Richard Dean......	28 11	42 69
East Salem......	Washington..	Daniel Hobart, to 20th Sep........	2 74	5 46
		Edward Law......	9 88	18 54
East Sand Lake..	Rensselaer...	Cyrus Amidon, to 31st March......	7 70	11 30
		Dexter C. Amidon..	2 86	5 21
East Schuyler....	Herkimer....	Patrick M. Smith...	35 09	56 46
East Solon.......	Cortlandt....	Ezra Rockwell.....	18 83	32 83
East Springfield..	Otsego.......	Seth H. Field......	90 02	90 06
East Spring Water	Livingston...	Wm. B. Peabody..	10 10	16 26
East Virgil......	Cortlandt....	William Gray.....	15 01	29 50
East Worcester..	Otsego.......	Edmon B. Bigelow..	23 21	30 27
Eaton...........	Madison	Alpheus Morse.....	249 66	242 61
Eatonville........	Herkimer....	Mason S. Van Slyke	23 14	37 86
Eden	Erie.........	Lyman Pratt.......	60 24	111 95
Edenville........	Orange......	Le Grand Mead....	12 64	24 37
Edgecomb's Cor's	Saratoga.....	Abijah Gilbert.....	9 50	14 83
Edinburgh.......	Saratoga	John F. Beecher....	36 96	69 78
Edmeston	Otsego.......	Silas Burleson	47 11	51 85
Edwards	St. Lawrence	Elanson Ray.......	29 67	49 77
Edwardsville.....	St. Lawrence	Henry I. Pohlman..	8 04	14 03
Egypt...........	Monroe......	Robert W. Henry..	34 43	63 95
Elba............	Genesee.....	Wm. C. Raymond, to 31st Dec......	71 85	127 23
		Jonas S. Billings...	69 31	126 05
Elbridge.........	Onondaga....	Allen Monroe, to 23d Sept............	60 43	59 53
		Alonzo Wood......	169 35	245 08
Eleysville	Erie.........	Samuel Eley.......	5 78	9 91
Elgin............	Cattaraugus..	William Little.....	11 24	22 32
Elizabethtown ...	Essex.......	Orlando Kellogg....	103 93	190 99
Elizaville........	Columbia....	Peter Robison......	12 60	18 81
Ellenburgh......	Clinton......	Jos. R. Emerson...	21 35	37 93
Ellenville........	Ulster	Ditmas Hardenbergh	159 08	286 18
Ellery...........	Chautauque..	David Brown......	13 11	24 67

POST OFFICES—*New York.*

Post Offices.	Counties.	Postmasters.	Compensation.	Net proceeds.
Ellicottsville	Cattaraugus	Israel Day	$211 32	$452 53
Ellington	Chautauque	John F. Farman	58 84	104 49
Ellisburgh	Jefferson	Jonathan R. Bates	81 64	140 77
Elmira	Chemung	Levi J. Cooley	795 54	2065 52
Enfield	Tompkins	Carlos C. Applegate, to 31st Dec.	24 78	46 31
		Purvis A. Williams	22 05	43 58
Ephratah	Fulton	Thos. R. Benedict	31 21	55 03
Erieville	Madison	Clinton H. Jennings	60 89	60 93
Erin	Chemung	Duncan J. Stewart	8 29	15 54
Erwin Centre	Steuben	Jas. G. Mersereau, to 31st Dec.	12 37	18 78
		Ansel C. Smith	9 27	15 65
Esopus	Ulster	Samuel Elmore	52 09	108 71
Esperance	Schoharie	Samuel O. Riggs, to 9th Oct.	23 91	41 31
		Wm. R. Davis	75 65	132 87
Essex	Essex	John Gould	162 74	129 48
Etna	Tompkins	Walker Marsh	78 45	77 71
Euclid	Onondaga	Nathan Soule	49 16	81 46
Evans	Erie	Alonzo D. Winslow	91 37	107 23
Evans' Mills	Jefferson	William Palmer, to 24th April	105 98	186 52
		Allen Nims	20 83	35 74
Exeter	Otsego	Cornelius Jones, to 30th Sept.	16 99	30 75
		Wm. P. Jones	46 83	80 07
Fabius	Onondaga	Orvin E. Castle, to 7th Dec.	58 63	92 30
		Enoch Ely	79 72	130 65
Factoryville	Tioga	Arthur Yates	118 75	209 29
Fairfield	Herkimer	Norman Butler, to 16th Nov.	39 34	55 77
		Alex'r H. Buel	52 62	80 25
Fairport	Chemung	Jacob Westlake, 2d, to 30th Sept.	34 96	65 16
		William Reynolds	101 38	194 24
Fairview	Cattaraugus	Clark Rice	12 73	20 88
Fairville	Wayne	Jos. E. Crandell	23 18	43 49
Fallsburgh	Sullivan	Edward Palen	65 60	112 54
Farmer	Seneca	Edwin Chester, to 24th April	121 87	205 27
		Jac. D. Wintersteen	26 82	45 79
Farmer's Mills	Putnam	Horace Townsend	8 07	14 20
Farmersville	Cattaraugus	Levi Peet	71 07	76 85
Farmingham	Orleans	Charles Lee	13 83	20 33
Farmington	Ontario	Elias H. Lapham	77 28	143 86
Farrell Place	Clinton	Andrew Farrell	6 89	12 00

POST OFFICES—*New York.*

Post Offices.	Counties.	Postmasters.	Compensation.	Net proceeds.
Fayette........	Seneca......	Geo. W. Bachman.	$36 45	$66 30
Fayetteville......	Onondaga ...	Hicks Worden.....	206 52	396 54
Federal Store....	Dutchess....	Asa Thompson, to 31st March......	11 71	20 30
		Henry Holbrook...	3 46	5 32
Felt's Mills......	Jefferson	Ransom R. Brown..	20 25	38 43
Fenner..........	Madison	Anthony Barrett...	20 71	35 72
Ferguson's Corn's	Yates.......	Walter S. Ferguson	18 06	29 46
Finchville	Orange......	Elbert Thorne.....	12 82	22 78
Fireplace.........	Suffolk......	Silas Homan.......	20 09	38 89
Fish Kill........	Dutchess....	Samuel Bowne, to 21st April.......	196 72	313 25
		Amazia D. Williams	39 51	76 63
Fish Kill Landing	Dutchess....	Joseph Cromwell...	353 45	829 97
Fish Kill Plains..	Dutchess.....	David Van Bramer.	19 35	38 50
Fish Lake.......	Delaware ...	Geo. E. Chase.....	(no ret.)	
Five Corners....	Cayuga.	Allen Palmer......	44 09	51 92
Flanders	Suffolk......	Jesse Hallock......	3 38	7 09
Flat Brook......	Columbia....	Wm. S. Woodworth	40 11	62 07
Flatbush	Kings	Mich'l Schoonmaker	95 22	183 56
Flat Creek.......	Montgomery.	Isaac Folinsbee....	11 50	19 99
Fleming.........	Cayuga	Wm. P. Thornton..	93 22	113 34
Flemingsville	Tioga.......	David Fleming.....	14 15	28 22
Flint Creek......	Ontario......	Eras. B. Woodworth	35 99	60 86
Florence	Oneida......	Dan'l G. Dorrance, to 24th Nov......	23 97	45 57
		Safford S. Delano..	41 25	82 51
Florida	Orange......	W. V. N. Armstrong	56 97	103 06
Floyd	Oneida......	Linus L. Moulton..	48 46	85 84
Flushing	Queens......	Francis Bloodgood.	396 51	911 09
Fluvanna	Chautauque..	Samuel Whittemore	22 30	37 87
Fonda..........	Montgomery.	Jno. B. Borst......	190 86	369 24
Forestburg......	Sullivan.....	Charles Penney, to 1st March.......	21 70	34 71
		Robert Atkins.....	9 76	15 17
Fort Ann........	Washington..	Ebenezer Broughton to 7th Jan.......	85 45	152 36
		George Clements...	78 59	147 33
Fort Covington..	Franklin	John Parker, to 31st Dec............	139 59	138 60
		Francis D. Flanders	129 53	126 84
Fort Edward.....	Washington..	John F. Gandall....	71 52	132 26
Fort Edwd. Centre	Washington..	Warren Sprague...	21 41	38 67
Fort Hamilton...	Kings	Jas. C. Church.....	167 33	347 23
Fort Hunter.....	Montgomery.	Peter Enders.......	12 03	22 02
Fort Miller......	Washington..	Ludovicus S. Viele.	58 19	98 17
Fort Plain.......	Montgomery.	Chester L. Sims...	332 36	741 11
Fortsville........	Saratoga	Truman Wilcox...	39 80	71 95

POST OFFICES—*New York.*

Post Offices.	Counties.	Postmasters.	Compensation.	Net proceeds.
Fosterdale	Sullivan	Jesse M. Foster, to 21st May	$40 97	$48 56
		Alexander Brown	4 30	8 84
Fosterville	Cayuga	Jonathan Foster	15 74	29 80
Fowler	St. Lawrence	Jabez Glazier	30 32	51 96
Fowlersville	Livingston	William Fraser	62 56	103 59
Frankfort	Herkimer	Wm. R. Stevens	157 73	269 79
Frankfort Hill	Herkimer	Elisha Wetmore, jr.	15 69	31 38
Franklin	Delaware	William Waters	252 39	249 93
Franklinton	Schoharie	Martines Mattice	20 37	32 69
Franklinville	Cattaraugus	Flavel Partridge, to 27th Feb	77 64	141 73
		David McCluer	42 28	73 90
Fredonia	Chautauque	Ebenezer A. Lester	439 05	875 01
Freedom	Cattaraugus	Enoch Howlet	21 83	40 85
Freedom Plains	Dutchess	Elias White	17 86	35 19
Freetown	Cortlandt	Rodney French	13 29	23 33
Freetown Corners	Cortlandt	William Mantanye	30 50	54 35
French Creek	Chautauque	Isaiah Golding	12 98	22 55
Frewsburgh	Chautauque	John Frew	29 14	50 04
Freysbush	Montgomery	Wm. G. Deifendorf	9 00	14 49
Friedland	Lewis	Joseph Virkler	(no ret.)	
Friendship	Allegany	Warren Wellman	101 37	176 26
Fullersville	St. Lawrence	Chs. G. Edgerton	11 75	22 56
Fulton	Oswego	M. L. Lee, to 7th Nov	169 40	259 31
		Hiram Bradwey	284 72	544 87
Fultonham	Schoharie	John Best, jr	24 07	41 67
Fultonville	Montgomery	William Shuler	161 89	318 71
Gaines	Orleans	Arba Chubb, to 10th Jan	71 09	124 53
		Wm. W. Ruggles	71 78	86 94
Gainesville	Wyoming	Nehemia Park, jr	75 93	125 08
Gales	Sullivan	Alson Lord	8 30	13 10
Galesville	Washington	James Watson, to 31st Dec	29 68	49 25
		Aman. B. Sherman	19 71	25 26
Gallatinville	Columbia	Jas. D. Niver	8 99	18 18
Gallupville	Schoharie	Ezra Gallup, jr	57 08	90 10
Galway	Saratoga	Ezekiel O. Smith	111 24	205 42
Gardnersville	Schoharie	Douw B. Gardner	41 12	60 37
Garoga	Fulton	Cha'y Hutchinson	39 99	71 36
Garrattsville	Otsego	Daniel Herrington	57 30	95 73
Gates	Monroe	Horace Lee	20 10	39 79
Gay Head	Greene	Orson Howard	11 97	19 32
Geddes	Onondaga	Ferris Hubbell	92 72	163 18
Genegantslet	Chenango	Alvin Gray	16 96	22 15
Genesee Valley	Allegany	Sam'l Van Campen	11 23	16 71

POST OFFICES—*New York.*

Post Offices.	Counties.	Postmasters.	Compensation.	Net proceeds.
Geneseo	Livingston	Dan'l H. Bissell	$476 06	$1008 99
Geneva	Ontario	James Rees	1608 32	4025 01
Genoa	Cayuga	Alfred Avery, to 25th Jan	35 38	59 83
		Elihu A. Lester	30 83	56 64
Georgetown	Madison	Epaph. Whitmore	40 51	71 19
German	Chenango	Horatio N. Drew	(no ret.)	
Germantown	Columbia	William Overbaugh	22 92	34 77
Germondville	Rensselaer	Jno. M. Mott	13 41	21 34
Gerry	Chautauque	Milo Camp	113 29	205 94
Ghent	Columbia	Martin Gilbert	54 04	108 42
Gibsonville	Livingston	Isaac Halstead	11 26	20 93
Gilbertsville	Otsego	Abijah Gilbert, to 22d Jan	127 37	115 30
		William D. Babcock	89 30	85 17
Gilboa	Schoharie	John Reed, to 31st Dec	58 34	102 29
		John S. Tuttle	63 45	113 21
Gilman	Hamilton	Elias P. Gilman	1 93	3 06
Girls' Flatts (Changed to "Halsey Valley."	Tioga	Israel S. Hoyt, to 30th Sept	3 72	6 87
Glasco	Ulster	Henry D. Martin	27 62	48 35
Glen	Montgomery	John Hanchett	41 15	61 40
Glen Cove	Queens	Wm. M. Weeks	72 74	141 79
Glenham	Dutchess	Thos. E. Scofield	92 09	189 96
Glenn's Falls	Warren	Henry Philo, to 16th May	353 38	761 55
		James Palmeter	33 71	83 89
Glenville	Schenectady	Wm. N. Angle, to 31st Dec	21 32	32 39
		Peter C. Conde	20 27	33 24
Glen Wild	Sullivan	Wm. M. Bowers	7 36	12 88
Gloversville	Fulton	Harvey Jones	90 56	175 02
Goff's Mills	Steuben	William Goff	8 17	13 51
Goldens Bridge	West Chester	Stephen Frost	1 28	2 97
Good Ground	Suffolk	Alvin Squires	7 72	14 48
Gorham	Ontario	David Halstead	112 31	186 97
Goshen	Orange	Fred'k A. Hoyt	394 88	665 15
Gouverneur	St. Lawrence	Edwin Dodge	191 59	332 95
Grafton	Rensselaer	David See, jr.	23 97	44 80
Grahamsville	Sullivan	Horace Eaton	26 48	48 48
Granger	Allegany	Henry White	11 37	21 64
Grangerville	Saratoga	Calvin J. Reed	13 92	25 27
Granville	Washington	Henry Weeks, to 16th Dec	126 69	140 28
		Isaac W. Thompson	148 01	162 34
Grassy Point	Rockland	Edward Strang	11 18	22 55

POST OFFICES—*New York.*

Post Offices.	Counties.	Postmasters.	Compensation.	Net proceeds.
Great Bend	Jefferson	Daniel Potter	$36 74	$62 94
Great Valley	Cattaraugus	Daniel Farrington	19 09	30 87
Greece	Monroe	Edward Walker	89 47	179 36
Greenboro'	Oswego	John H. Corey	2 09	4 40
Greenbush	Rensselaer	Willard Lawrence, to 1st June	128 14	246 59
		James Hallenbeck	10 02	19 22
Greene	Chenango	Frederick Juliand, to 31st Dec	129 05	245 24
		Charles Squires	132 25	270 31
Greenfield Centre	Saratoga	Chs. B. Wing	24 16	47 70
Greenport	Suffolk	John Clark	138 67	263 76
Green River	Columbia	Rodney Hill	26 34	43 67
Greenville	Greene	Alex'r N. Bentley, to 31st March	84 56	141 19
		William Conkling	28 03	47 02
Greenwich	Washington	Jonathan K. Horton, to 23d Jan	166 14	309 52
		Joseph Holmes	114 60	232 92
Greenwood	Steuben	Levi Davis	26 88	52 45
Greigsville	Livingston	Edward R. Dean	43 63	77 08
Griffin's Mills	Erie	Josiah Mitchell	52 04	97 08
Griswold's Mills	Washington	David A. Potter	13 61	20 59
Groton	Tompkins	Chauncey Trumbull, to 31st March	87 16	147 69
		Robert C. Reynolds	38 95	64 76
Grove	Allegany	Samuel C Jones	17 91	34 87
Groveland	Livingston	Charles Goheen	44 15	64 56
Groveland Centre	Livingston	Samuel L. Fuller	23 26	40 31
Guilderland	Albany	Russell Case	44 28	84 55
Guilderland Centre	Albany	Elijah Chesebro	32 48	53 01
Guilford	Chenango	John Clark	94 26	122 41
Guilford Centre	Chenango	Chs. D. Cobb, to 10th June	75 41	71 64
		Wm. H. Beardsley	1 96	1 88
Hadley	Saratoga	David Stewart	12 12	23 91
Haerlem	New York	John S. Kenyon	202 46	449 26
Hagaman's Mills	Montgomery	Francis M. Hagaman	36 73	62 69
Hague	Warren	Nathaniel Garfield	17 70	36 13
Half Moon	Saratoga	Reuben Stewart	39 30	65 03
Hall's Corners	Ontario	Edward Hall	31 31	52 85
Hall's Mills	Albany	George Benn	36 63	56 51
Hallsville	Montgomery	George F. Carey	4 01	6 22
Halsey Valley (Late "Girls Flatts.")	Tioga	Israel S. Hoyt, from 1st October	8 96	18 43
Hamburgh	Erie	Levi Lawrence	74 21	133 56
Hamburgh on the Lake	Erie	Ira B. Patrick	43 08	41 47

POST OFFICES—*New York.*

Post Offices.	Counties.	Postmasters.	Compensation.	Net proceeds.
Hamden	Delaware	Daniel Coleman, to 31st Dec	$33 10	$56 72
		Rich'd M. Goodrich	19 48	38 64
Hamilton	Madison	Asa F. Chapin	606 54	1065 88
Hammond	St. Lawrence.	Alvin A. Hine	72 86	122 35
Hammond's Mills	Steuben	Seth Hammond	6 60	11 94
Hampton	Washington	Lucius M. Purdy, to 31st Dec	19 31	34 61
		Samuel H. Beman	17 20	32 98
Hamptonburgh	Orange	James Strong	41 89	74 16
Hancock	Delaware	Marvin Wheeler	37 90	47 10
Hanford's Land'g	Monroe	Nathaniel Hall	11 00	21 28
Hannibal	Oswego	Thomas Skelton	104 56	181 26
Hanover	Chautauque	Benajah Tubbs	132 54	245 95
Harford	Cortlandt	Geo. K. Williams	40 05	67 43
Harlemville	Columbia	Eleazer Tracy	16 28	30 99
Harmony	Chautauque	Theron S. Bly	75 59	129 67
Harpersfield	Delaware	Johnson B. Bragg	45 02	73 33
Harpersville	Broome	Henry A. Olendorf.	66 16	115 09
Harrisburgh	Lewis	Elias Gallup	11 62	17 92
Harris' Hill	Erie	Nathaniel F. Porter.	21 80	38 97
Harrison	West Chester	Charles Miller, jr.	17 82	29 05
Hartford	Washington	Calvin L. Parker, to 4th Dec	47 75	44 39
		Job Reynolds	62 18	61 21
Hartland	Niagara	F. H. Kittredge	41 23	78 59
Hart's Village	Dutchess	Isaac Haight, jr.	75 50	142 21
Hartsville	Onondaga	Pardon Thompson	13 76	27 39
Hartwick	Otsego	Lyman Harrington.	100 30	177 52
Hartwick Semin'y	Otsego	Ebenezer Chaffee	49 19	47 86
Hartwood	Sullivan	Wm. J. Clowes	4 32	6 68
Haskenville	Steuben	Alanson S. Phillips.	7 34	10 49
Hastings	Oswego	Peter Devendorf	34 17	60 92
Havanna	Chemung	J. Walker, to 9th Dec	82 96	170 02
		James Pine	123 86	240 48
Haverstraw	Rockland	Isaac Sherwood, to 31st Dec	61 07	115 24
		Sylvester Clark, from 4th Feb	54 89	115 97
Haviland Hollow.	Putnam	Benjamin Haviland.	13 10	20 98
Hebron	Washington	Nathaniel Ingersoll, to 31st Dec	19 96	26 68
		John S. McFarland.	28 92	27 44
Hector	Tompkins	Richard Smith	29 59	48 75
Helena	St. Lawrence.	Benjamin Nevin	36 82	68 40
Hemlock Lake	Livingston	Elijah Stephens	46 60	79 62
Hempstead	Queens	L. D. Rushmore, to 26th Dec	63 91	125 40
		Stephen C. Snedeker	84 43	147 10

POST OFFICES—*New York.*

Post Offices.	Counties.	Postmasters.	Compensation.	Net proceeds.
Hempst'd Branch.	Queens	John S. Wood, 7½ months	$9 36	$18 36
Hempst'd Harbor. (Ch'd to 'Roslyn')	Queens	Wm. Hicks, (1 qr.)	9 27	17 01
Henderson	Jefferson	Edwin Burnham	123 53	196 07
Henrietta	Monroe	James H. McHazeltine, to 20th Jan.	52 36	101 30
		Elihu Kirby	52 00	83 64
Herkimer	Herkimer	Harvey Doolittle, to 12th Nov.	84 75	167 81
		John A. Rasback	148 93	294 22
Hermitage	Wyoming	Sidney Stowe	28 45	46 49
Hermon	St. Lawrence.	Rosalvo Healy	41 92	76 53
Heuvelton	St. Lawrence.	William Thurston	83 57	57 20
Hickory Corners.	Niagara	Daniel Pomroy	32 79	68 65
Higginsville	Oneida	George B. Fitch	16 71	29 16
High Falls	Ulster	Jacob H. Depuy	17 51	29 45
Highland Mills	Orange	Wm. Vail, jr. (3 qrs)	24 10	42 94
Hillsdale	Columbia	Isaac Foster, to 31st December	65 23	110 31
		Thaddeus Reed	78 12	134 75
Hindsburgh	Orleans	Jabez Allison	44 11	86 12
Hinmansville	Oswego	Nathaniel Coburn	50 54	59 21
Hinsdale	Cattaraugus	Paul Clark, to 31st March	71 03	68 02
		Elihu M. Wasson	24 81	23 57
Hizerville	Oneida	Adam Hizer	4 27	5 54
Hoag's Corner	Rensselaer	Wm. B. Hoag	16 46	23 85
Hobart	Delaware	John Griffin	113 03	192 05
Hobbieville	Allegany	A. A. Cammann	33 42	65 51
Hoffman's Ferry.	Schenectady	Albert T. Dunham	20 01	35 10
Hoffman's Gate	Columbia	John Martin, to 31st December	4 42	7 76
		George Hoffman	6 48	12 48
Hogansburgh	Franklin	Gurdon S. Mills	47 21	54 55
Holland	Erie	Philip D. Riley	44 32	74 23
Holland Patent	Oneida	P. C. J. DeAngelis, jr	115 79	206 20
Holley	Orleans	Hiram Frisbie	126 12	229 18
Homer	Cortlandt	George Cook, to 30th September	97 42	198 11
		William Brown	342 12	528 48
Honeoye	Ontario	Hiram Pitts	106 22	172 20
Honeoye Falls	Monroe	Horace Wheeler	157 29	315 48
Hoosick	Rensselaer	P. M. Armstrong	89 50	158 76
Hoosick Falls	Rensselaer	Seth Parsons	170 44	318 16
Hope	Hamilton	Wm. R. Van Arnam	4 44	8 00
Hope Centre	Hamilton	Thomas Blake	3 76	5 61
Hopewell	Ontario	Nathaniel Lewis	42 18	69 74
Hopkinton	St. Lawrence.	C. S. Crittenden	52 09	89 87

POST OFFICES—*New York.*

Post Offices.	Counties.	Postmasters.	Compensation.	Net proceeds.
Horicon	Warren	Howard Waters	$8 10	$12 40
Hornby	Steuben	Chs. D. Thomas, to 20th Feb	24 48	36 81
		Isaac P. Goodsell	17 33	28 46
Hornellsville	Steuben	John K. Hale, to 14th Dec	37 65	68 86
		Thos. J. Reynolds	55 89	97 50
Houseville	Lewis	Selden Goff, to 17th May	39 18	38 47
		S. M. Van Namee	7 11	7 13
Howard	Steuben	Charles Graves	66 81	117 18
Howlet Hill	Onondaga	John Case	25 33	42 78
Hudson	Columbia	Justus McKinstry, to 15th May	1068 52	2582 59
		Paul Dean Carrique	140 54	349 94
Huguenot	Orange	J. S. Van Inwegen	10 11	14 41
Hulburton	Orleans	Abijah Reed	43 71	71 92
Hull's Corners	Oswego	Burr Hull	15 56	29 90
Hull's Mills	Dutchess	Edward P. Barton	11 22	19 13
Hume	Allegany	C. G. Ingham, to 8th January	75 23	73 38
		Wm. N. Emerson	66 86	85 95
Hunter	Greene	Hiram Hatch	77 03	150 60
Hunter's Land	Schoharie	George W. Tippets	12 34	20 57
Huntington	Suffolk	Stephen C. Rogers	182 19	331 29
Hunt's Hollow	Allegany	Sanford Hunt	64 12	105 05
Hurley	Ulster	Hiram Patterson	17 75	30 12
Huron	Wayne	John F. Curtis	27 53	45 61
Hyde Park	Dutchess	David Johnson, to 31st March	269 06	363 23
		J. A. Stoutenburgh	74 32	95 74
Hyde Settlement	Broome	Franklin Hyde	9 66	16 97
Hyndsville	Schoharie	Peter Hynds	15 74	30 52
Ilion (Late "Remington.")	Herkimer	David D. Devoe, fr. 1st January to 31st May	39 05	70 80
		John V. Brown	6 76	11 11
Independence	Allegany	John P. Livermore	11 93	19 34
Indian River	Lewis	James Barrett	1 99	3 13
Ira	Cayuga	John Thompson, to 31st March	47 31	85 35
		Joseph Earl	15 29	27 36
Irondequoit	Monroe	Caleb K. Hobbie	10 40	20 74
Irving	Chautauque	Cephas R. Leland	146 53	173 87
Islip	Suffolk	Henry Brewster	67 39	107 07
Italy Hill	Yates	Elisha Doubleday	32 65	64 93
Italy Hollow	Yates	Lewis B. Graham	23 50	39 06
Ithaca	Tompkins	J. M. McCormick	972 56	2590 59

POST OFFICES—*New York.*

Post Offices.	Counties.	Postmasters.	Compensation.	Net proceeds.
Jackson	Washington	Francis McLean	$20 19	$34 43
Jacksonburgh	Herkimer	L. O. Gay, (3 qrs.).	9 98	14 69
Jackson Corners	Dutchess	Jacob J. Stall	8 00	11 13
Jacksonville	Tompkins	Abraham Chase, to 31st Dec	40 75	69 66
		Cyrus H. Howe	42 00	75 30
Jack's Reef	Onondaga	C. P. Richardson	14 92	31 37
Jamaica	Queens	John C. Smith	207 70	432 64
Jamesport	Suffolk	David Williamson	24 66	46 56
Jamestown	Chautauque	Joseph Kenyon, to 14th October	169 91	276 34
		Franklin H. Waite.	394 92	727 07
Jamesville	Onondaga	Geo. M. Richardson, to 30th Sept	30 87	51 26
		Isaac W. Brewster.	69 84	114 71
Jasper	Steuben	John G. Marlatt	32 19	49 32
Java	Wyoming	Joseph Currier	27 11	46 90
Java Village	Wyoming	Amory Barber	15 54	26 78
Jay	Essex	Geo. G. Tobey	43 09	75 98
Jefferson	Schoharie	Eli Boies	50 68	79 28
Jericho	Queens	Jacob Ellison, to 4th Jan	18 16	31 08
		Albert G. Carll	20 19	35 36
Jersey	Steuben	Edgar Munson	74 71	125 26
Jerusalem	Yates	Henry Larzelere	19 67	36 70
Jerusalem South	Queens	Samuel S. Jones	18 61	34 33
Johnsburgh	Warren	Clark Burdick	42 22	63 83
Johnsonsburgh	Wyoming	Geo. A. Johnson	25 80	45 12
Johnson's Creek	Niagara	Luke Woodworth	119 76	171 66
Johnstown	Fulton	Henry B. Mathews.	265 35	523 32
Johnsville	Dutchess	Thomas Burroughs.	4 32	9 94
Jonesville	Saratoga	David H. Bullard, to 20th May	72 62	109 69
		Hiram Higgins	3 49	8 08
Jordan	Onondaga	Wm. T. Graves	238 87	476 46
Joslin's Corners	Madison	Sinclair Tousey	17 84	30 36
Junction	Rennselaer	Isaac T. Grant	29 91	49 16
Junius	Seneca	Abram B. Slawson.	44 46	81 16
Keene	Essex	Wait J. Lewis	24 92	39 32
Keeney's Settlement	Cortlandt	Alvin Brown	10 70	19 47
Keeseville	Essex	Gorton T. Thomas, to 31st March	399 27	644 36
		Melch'r S. Hoffnagle	(No ret.)	
Kelloggsville	Cayuga	William Slade	83 53	142 31
Kendall	Orleans	Calvin Benedict, to 14th Feb.	63 25	103 21
		Walter R. Sanford	35 85	65 49

POST OFFICES—*New York.*

Post Offices.	Counties.	Postmasters.	Compensation.	Net proceeds.
Kennedysville	Steuben	George Wheeler, to 31st March	$16 75	$28 07
		Brigham Hanks	4 98	8 56
Kent	Putnam	Stillman Boyd	6 03	11 16
Ketcham'sCorn'rs	Saratoga	David Weston	29 07	44 38
Kill Buck	Cattaraugus	John Green	3 13	4 47
Kinderhook	Columbia	David Van Schaack, to 12th June	375 11	588 50
		Lawr'ce Van Buren	12 47	24 16
Kingsboro'	Fulton	Daniel Potter	97 65	156 61
King's Bridge	New York	John P. Dodge	14 45	31 43
Kingsbury	Washington	Thos. A. Sherwood	37 84	68 26
King's Ferry	Cayuga	Darius Adams, to 31st Dec	66 35	72 24
		Lewis Seymour	56 15	71 52
King's Settlement	Chenango	Geo. H. King	7 30	12 55
Kingston	Ulster	William Culley, to 12th June	672 13	1268 51
		Isaac Van Buren	30 77	66 66
Kinney's 4 Corn'rs	Oswego	James Martin, jr	18 55	33 70
Kirkland	Oneida	Jas. M. Kimball	50 47	96 74
Kirkville	Onondaga	Obadiah Hubbs	42 88	80 87
Kiskatom	Greene	Isaac C. Bloom	16 40	29 41
Knowersville	Albany	George Keenhotts	16 62	26 05
Knowlesville	Orleans	Chas. J. Hood	138 32	244 12
Knox	Albany	Prentice Williams, jr	46 51	75 85
Kortright	Delaware	Martin Keeler, jr	38 47	67 10
Kyserike	Ulster	Mathew Jansen	22 37	33 46
Kysorville	Livingston	Nicholas Kysor, to 31st Dec	8 15	16 59
		Esther Kysor	9 18	18 35
Lackawack	Ulster	Nathan S. Perkins, (3 qrs.)	5 86	11 88
Lafargeville	Jefferson	Chesterfield Person, to 31st March	45 48	80 19
		Loren Bushnell	17 87	31 64
La Fayette	Onondaga	Chauncey Williams, to 14th Dec	19 52	37 64
		Harvey G. Andrews, to 3d June	23 33	44 83
		Ira Green	3 12	5 56
La Grange	Wyoming	James W. Hallett	45 17	76 11
Lairdsville	Oneida	Eliab Joslin, to 31st March	30 62	53 93
		Pomroy Jones	7 92	14 76
Lake	Washington	Abra'm Mathews, jr	40 14	61 43
Lake Hill	Ulster	Jacob Cooper	10 72	17 04
Lake Ridge	Tompkins	John Moe	30 31	41 96

POST OFFICES—*New York.*

Post Offices.	Counties.	Postmasters.	Net proceeds.	Compensation.
Lakeville	Livingston	Erastus West	$86 12	$148 39
Lancaster	Erie	Wm. H. Grimes, to 30th Sept	40 31	64 54
		Elias Safford, jr	126 18	223 81
Lansingburgh	Rennselaer	Sidney D. Smith	511 35	1123 01
Lansingville	Tompkins	Avon L. Palmer	47 88	57 29
Larned's Corners	Ontario	Owen Munson, to 3d Sept	4 70	6 49
		Sylvanus C. Hersey	20 48	35 82
Lassellsville	Fulton	William Lassell, jr	15 86	28 44
Laurens	Otsego	Harvey Strong	91 59	170 71
Lawrenceville	St. Lawrence	Lucius Hubburd	59 02	105 59
Lawyersville	Schoharie	Thomas Lawyer	24 46	40 57
Lebanon	Madison	Wm. L. Sheldon	48 79	86 87
Ledyard	Cayuga	Alfred Avery	52 82	64 01
Lee	Oneida	Augustus S. Potter	28 77	50 17
Leeds	Greene	John H. Person	88 37	85 59
Leedsville	Dutchess	Joseph D. Hunt	19 49	34 67
Leesville	Schoharie	William Beekman, jr	37 17	72 04
Lenox	Madison	Abner Northrop	39 30	65 56
Leon	Cattaraugus	William Kendall	8 13	16 78
Leon Mills	Cattaraugus	Jabez Thompson, to 15th Feb	23 41	39 21
		Chas. D. Darling, from 22d Feb	12 07	21 12
Leonardsville	Madison	Dennis Hardin	38 04	63 56
Le Raysville	Jefferson	Ennis Mosher	29 22	54 67
Le Roy	Genesee	John H. Stanley, to 22d Oct	184 16	373 25
		Charles Danforth	327 91	748 97
Levanna	Cayuga	Seneca Boyce	82 24	99 19
Levant	Chautauque	Samuel B. Winsor	19 80	26 42
Lewis	Essex	Lewis Sherman	45 89	84 08
Lewisboro'	West Chester	Cyrus M. Ferris, to 17th Dec	3 54	4 96
		Amos S. Northrup	4 33	3 79
Lewiston	Niagara	Leonard Bement, to 12th April	750 50	37 41
		A'm V.E. Hotchkiss	160 73	...
Lexington	Greene	John Schermerhorn, to 31st May	48 71	83 45
		J. Van Valkenburgh	2 60	4 84
Lexingt'n Heights	Greene	Remas Merwin	30 29	50 80
Leyden	Lewis	Thomas Baker	113 22	112 96
Liberty	Sullivan	Gideon Wales, to 26th May	78 11	132 04
		Billings Grant	7 46	13 43
Libertyville	Ulster	Philip Dubois	15 21	24 12
Lima	Livingston	Israel Nicklisson	296 85	541 69

POST OFFICES—*New York.*

Post Offices.	Counties.	Postmasters.	Compensation.	Net proceeds.
Limerick	Jefferson	Ely Smith	$37 66	$62 86
Linden	Genesee	Alex'r G. Perry	28 83	47 63
Lindleytown	Steuben	Albert C. Morgan	27 48	47 54
Linklaen	Chenango	Samuel Plumb, to 31st Dec	14 91	23 25
		James K. Bowen	13 28	24 26
Lisbon	St. Lawrence	Simeon Dillingham, to 21st May	59 94	69 35
		Joel Houghton	(No ret.)	
Lisle	Broome	Artemas Howland	30 04	52 95
Litchfield	Herkimer	Thad. R. Harrison	34 56	63 36
Lithgow	Dutchess	Jacob Sisson	39 79	68 81
Little Britain	Orange	Lewis Davenport, to 31st March	15 60	26 16
		John Tremper	4 39	7 00
Little Falls	Herkimer	Martin Bettinger	682 61	1788 81
Little Genesee	Alleghany	Wm. P. Langworthy	17 48	26 80
Little Sodus	Cayuga	Seth Turner	14 60	23 92
Little Valley	Cattaraugus	Cyrus S. Shepard	40 33	74 85
Little York	Cortlandt	Gideon Curtiss	27 36	45 25
Liverpool	Onondaga	Caleb Hubbard	196 09	227 80
Livingston	Columbia	Henry Baker	62 88	107 60
Livingstonville	Schoharie	David L. Sternberg, to 31st Dec	19 93	33 43
		Francis Norwood, from 27th Feb	18 80	32 47
Livonia	Livingston	Ashman Bebe, jr., to 28th Feb	129 49	214 57
		Josiah Clark	54 58	96 47
Locke	Cayuga	William Titus	84 70	149 25
Lock Berlin	Wayne	Wm. A. Cornell	43 65	55 95
Lockport	Niagara	Hezek'h W. Scovell	1373 65	3550 72
Locust Tree	Niagara	Lewis B. Horton	6 77	12 29
Lodi	Seneca	John De Mott	162 19	304 48
Logan	Tompkins	Jabez S. Smith	18 96	27 96
Lorraine	Jefferson	Moses Brown	31 26	57 07
Louisville	St. Lawrence	Levi Miller	45 27	79 67
Low Hampton	Washington	Wm. S. Miller	17 76	30 18
Lowville	Lewis	Stephen Leonard, to 12th May	266 98	376 50
		John Benedict	37 75	47 63
Loyd	Ulster	Jas. D. Terwilliger	13 01	18 74
Ludlowville	Tompkins	Wm. Morehouse, to 1st March	97 91	130 34
		Philip French	57 08	68 93
Lumberland	Sullivan	James Eldred	15 59	28 79
Luzerne	Warren	Reuben Wells	42 73	65 55
Lyons	Wayne	Ez Price, to 31st Dec	302 07	535 76
		Charles Poucher	275 75	613 02

POST OFFICES—*New York.*

Post Offices.	Counties.	Postmasters.	Compensation.	Net proceeds.
Lyonsdale	Lewis	Dean S. Howard...	$11 59	$21 84
Lysander	Onondaga ...	Chauncey Betts, to 31st Dec	32 80	56 47
		Geo. A. Allen......	35 33	65 18
McConnellsville..	Oneida......	Jos. L. McConnell .	28 51	56 24
McDonough.....	Chenango ...	John F. Hill......	39 59	68 45
McGrawsville	Cortlandt ...	Harry McGraw ...	59 98	109 02
McLean	Tompkins...	Joel Cooper, to 24th Jan..............	77 34	76 08
		Harvey Holden....	52 48	50 94
Mabbettsville	Dutchess	Sam. R. Wood, to 19th November..	16 00	27 98
		James Mabbett	19 77	36 56
Macedon.........	Wayne	Henry Reed........	130 59	226 40
Macedon Centre..	Wayne	Ira Odell..........	36 51	66 48
Machias.........	Cattaraugus .	Lyman Twomley, to 31st December...	20 59	37 45
		Rufus L. Whitcher.	24 80	42 27
Macomb	St. Lawrence.	David Day, 2d.....	4 56	7 79
Madison	Madison	Isaac Curtis, 2d....	220 63	210 34
Madrid	St. Lawrence.	Caleb Pierce.......	83 78	161 74
Magnolia	Chautauque..	Richard Whitney, jr	11 46	17 83
Maine	Broome......	Ezekiel H. Clark...	36 43	62 78
Malden	Ulster.......	Austin Preston.....	109 09	130 32
Malden Bridge...	Columbia....	Lor'n V. Volkenburg	56 85	94 67
Malone	Franklin	Fred'k P. Allen, to 30th January	181 24	303 50
		Geo. S. Adams....	134 53	181 29
Malta..........	Saratoga	Peter Derby........	26 78	48 06
Maltaville	Saratoga	Warren Parks......	26 20	47 13
Mamaroneck	W'st Chester	John J. Marshall...	103 67	178 35
Manchester	Ontario......	Stephen A. Power..	142 12	241 74
Manchest'r Bridge	Dutchess	Adam Graham, jr., to 31st March....	10 54	17 87
		Elias P. Farington..	2 51	4 80
Manchest'r Centre	Ontario......	Harvey Harmon...	53 80	86 98
Mandana........	Onondaga ...	Alex'r H. Allen....	21 63	36 45
Manhasset	Queens	Robert H. Titus....	67 78	126 11
Manheim........	Herkimer....	Abel Timerman, to 5th May........	32 50	56 90
		Alfred Snell........	4 34	7 80
Manheim Centre.	Herkimer....	John Markell......	15 10	27 10
Manlius.........	Onondaga....	Jos. S. Rhoades, to 28th February...	196 38	382 03
		John Grinnell......	92 69	185 64
Manlius Centre..	Onondaga....	Jonas P. Haner, to 31st March......	26 14	48 89
		Charles Huntley....	7 92	15 72

POST OFFICES—*New York.*

Post Offices.	Counties.	Postmasters.	Compensation.	Net proceeds.
Mannsville	Jefferson	William West, to 22d April	$51 72	$76 40
		John W. Persons	18 42	17 63
Manorville	Suffolk	Jere. G. Wilbury, from 18th Feb	3 66	5 92
Mansfield	Cattaraugus	James Huggins	6 34	12 79
Maple Grove	Otsego	Zenas Washbon	16 14	15 95
Marathon	Cortlandt	Horace Hayward, to 8th November	10 74	35 57
		John M. Roe	34 11	60 24
Marbletown	Ulster	Cor's M. Van Buren	14 11	23 30
Marcellus	Onondaga	Sanford Dalliba	217 55	384 96
Marcellus Falls	Onondaga	Geo. P. Herring	32 59	53 33
Marcy	Oneida	Wm. M. Mayhew	17 29	34 41
Marengo	Wayne	Daniel Johnson	44 30	83 89
Mariaville	Schenectady	Daniel Nellis	15 82	26 86
Marietta	Onondaga	Alanson Hicks	11 81	23 55
Marion	Wayne	Elisha R. Wright, to 17th February	50 98	101 37
		Levi Clark	35 43	59 75
Marlboro'	Ulster	Miles J. Fletcher	102 95	101 13
Marshall	Oneida	Henry L. Hawley	37 43	59 70
Martinsburgh	Lewis	John W. Martin, to 12th May	240 80	252 98
		William King	37 41	45 59
Martin's Hill	Chemung	John R. Brown	8 03	13 38
Martville	Cayuga	Edw'd R. Snider, to 30th September	6 69	12 15
		John Reed	24 35	46 25
Maryland	Otsego	Frank. B. Carpenter	76 86	131 12
Masonville	Delaware	Daniel Orcutt, jr., to 31st December	28 09	47 07
		Festus P. Cleveland	23 23	39 93
Massena	St. Lawrence	Alex'r H. Andrews	84 64	160 85
Matildaville	St. Lawrence	Wm. R. Stark	18 42	34 68
Mattituck	Suffolk	James Shirley	35 86	52 31
Mayfield	Fulton	Collins Odell	42 93	70 20
Mayville	Chautauque	Russell Sackett	199 83	399 14
Mechanicsville	Saratoga	Cramer Vernam, to 4th March	74 33	138 53
		James D. Hart	45 44	86 64
Mecklinburgh	Tompkins	Calvin Treman, to 23d December	47 32	83 05
		Dan'l B. Wheeler	57 10	105 16
Medina	Orleans	Christopher Whaley	264 67	494 81
Mellenville	Columbia	Ebenezer F. Bartlett, to 31st December	31 49	31 50
		George Decker	30 53	39 96

POST OFFICES—*New York.*

Post Offices.	Counties.	Postmasters.	Compensation.	Net proceeds.
Mendon..........	Monroe.......	Ogilvie L. Sheldon, to 31st March....	$109 08	$200 43
		Levi Benedict......	32 64	57 62
Meredith........	Delaware....	Sam'l. A. Law, to 31st March......	35 74	65 33
		Amasa P. Mann...	13 28	17 93
Merrick..........	Queens.......	Carman Smith.....	7 72	12 38
Merrillsville	Franklin	John R. Merrill....	3 12	6 82
Mexico	Oswego......	Geo. S. Ferris......	216 20	382 93
Middleburgh.....	Schoharie ...	Freeman Stanton...	80 07	144 14
Middlebury......	Wyoming ...	Otis Perkins........	19 51	36 51
Middlefield......	Otsego......	Mortimer Gilbert...	59 16	101 67
Mid'field Centre..	Otsego.......	Henry Bowen, jr...	31 01	58 74
Middle Granville.	Washington..	Geo. N. Bates, to 21st November...	49 95	49 45
		Geo. W. Porter....	63 85	61 59
Middle Hope.....	Orange	John W. Fenton...	37 18	37 11
Middle Island....	Suffolk......	Benj. T. Hutchinson	23 20	41 80
Middleport.......	Niagara......	Thos. N. Lee, to 30th September..	48 73	84 14
		Francis L. Taylor..	160 60	235 32
Middlesex	Yates.......	David G. Underwood	31 46	58 71
Middletown	Delaware.....	Asa Grant, to 11th January........	25 32	41 76
		Warren Dimmick..	20 99	40 91
Middleville.......	Herkimer ...	Varnum S. Kinyon.	71 27	119 28
Milan	Dutchess.....	Stephen Thorn......	41 87	70 84
Milford	Otsego	Elijah Brown......	89 94	88 58
Milford Centre...	Otsego.......	Joseph Westcott....	47 49	44 58
Military Road ...	Jefferson	Thomas Robinson...	6 34	12 79
Millen's Bay.....	Jefferson	Hyland Millen, to 12th November..	7 23	12 67
		Jacob Jones.......	13 91	29 21
Miller's Place....	Suffolk.......	Thomas Helme.....	29 28	45 61
Millport.........	Chemung....	Benjamin Hackney, to 18th January..	60 24	105 96
		Albert F. Babcock..	72 86	122 73
Mill's Corners....	Fulton.......	Elisha Alvord......	6 45	10 22
Milltown........	Putnam......	Asa Raymond	24 89	35 62
Millville.........	Orleans......	Stephen C. Johnston	65 36	117 65
Milo............	Yates........	W. M. Himrod, to 31st December...	14 95	27 32
		George Van Orsdall	16 34	30 03
Milo Centre.....	Yates........	Amos Y. Carr.....	29 24	48 04
Milton..........	Ulster.......	William Soper.....	101 56	95 35
Milton Centre.... (Dis. 17th Mar.).	Saratoga	Jonathan Sprague, 3 qrs	2 37	3 47
Mina...........	Chautauque..	Isaac Relf.........	36 48	65 57
Minaville........	Montgomery.	David Cady.......	77 74	129 71

POST OFFICES—*New York.*

Post Offices.	Counties.	Postmasters.	Compensation.	Net proceeds.
Minden	Montgomery	Isaac P. Keller	$29 63	$49 09
Minerva	Essex	Anson West	23 36	40 66
Minisink	Orange	Orvil J. Brown	16 03	32 88
Mixville	Allegany	Benjamin F. Green, to 31st December.	11 36	19 09
		Luther Conch	10 10	19 10
Modena	Ulster	Johannes Alsdorf	51 40	74 24
Moffett's Store	Columbia	Hiram Bigelow	20 59	31 71
Mohawk	Herkimer	Lawrence L. Merry	207 66	365 23
Moira	Franklin	Clark Lawrence	41 74	74 83
Monroe	Orange	Gates W. McGarrah, 3 qrs	48 01	87 60
Monroe Works	Orange	John Coffey	40 09	75 69
Montezuma	Cayuga	Norman Hurd, to 31st December	104 56	99 49
		Sam'l W. Budlong	67 61	133 19
Montgomery	Orange	Jas. W. Sears	336 49	368 83
Monticello	Sullivan	George Bennett	193 52	268 62
Moores	Clinton	James Fitch	53 10	102 26
Moravia	Cayuga	Leonard O. Aikin	158 39	291 22
Moreau	Saratoga	Luthena Reynolds	23 35	43 49
Morehouseville	Hamilton	And. K. Morehouse	11 64	19 74
Moreland	Chemung	Green Bennitt	30 42	48 22
Moresville	Delaware	John T. More	38 73	67 06
Moriah	Essex	Hiram Everest	126 17	240 70
Moriches	Suffolk	James M. Fanning	57 57	97 50
Morley	St. Lawrence	Luther B. Witherbee	31 68	64 87
Morristown	St. Lawrence	Erastus W. White	143 15	200 28
Morrisville	Madison	John Farwell	190 07	356 24
Morseville	Schoharie	Daniel Morse, 3 qrs	1 58	3 10
Morton's Corners	Erie	Alanson P. Morton	9 87	17 30
Moscow	Livingston	Horatio Jones, 3d	143 12	257 74
Mott's Corners	Tompkins	William Mott, 2d	33 36	27 86
Mottville	Onondaga	Howard Delano	85 83	118 74
Mount Cambria	Niagara	John Hodge	3 44	5 45
Mount Hope	Orange	Augustus P. Thompson, to 20th Jan	44 43	47 29
		John W. Martin	25 96	45 32
Mount Morris	Livingston	Henry Swan	422 35	970 41
Mount Sinai	Suffolk	Charles Phillips	6 39	9 64
Mount Upton	Chenango	Willis Gregory	89 31	81 66
Mount Vision	Otsego	Harvey Keyes	15 51	26 99
M't Washington	Steuben	Obadiah Wheeler	8 81	12 84
Mud Creek	Steuben	Archibald H. Gates	46 16	37 46
Mumford	Monroe	D'n McNaughton	65 72	103 93
Murray	Orleans	Samuel W. Gibson	59 47	111 93
Nanticoke Springs	Broome	Henry Smith	3 76	7 83
Napanock	Ulster	Gabriel W. Ludlum	81 43	144 98

POST-OFFICES—*New York.*

Post Offices.	Counties.	Postmasters.	Compensation.	Net proceeds.
Naples	Ontario	Denison H. Cheesebro, to 31st Dec.	$91 89	$157 53
		John W. Hinckley	88 19	160 26
Napoli	Cattaraugus	Orris Marsh	49 14	83 00
Narrowsburgh	Sullivan	Rich'd W. Corwin	12 52	22 28
Nashville	Chautauque	Hiram F. Smith, to 31st March	29 79	51 00
		Theodore S. Moss	7 16	12 99
Nassau	Rensselaer	Chester Griswold	99 33	180 09
Natural Bridge	Jefferson	Chester Andrus, to 8th April	16 57	31 42
		Arche's C. Ellis	5 64	10 20
Navarino	Onondaga	And'w J. Cummings	20 16	32 90
Nelson	Madison	John Donaldson	50 31	78 67
Nettle Hill (Dis. 26th June.)	Chautauque	Walter Strong, 3 qrs	7 01	12 47
Neversink	Sullivan	Amos Y. Grant	27 23	45 42
New Albion	Cattaraugus	Solomon G. Wright	21 69	38 76
Newark	Wayne	Rich'd P. Williams, to 23d November	229 21	341 04
		Eliab T. Grant	329 55	548 77
Newark Valley	Tioga	Sawyer Byington, to 31st December	55 35	68 11
		Wm. S. Lincoln	45 62	79 35
New Baltimore	Greene	Henry B. Hall	61 46	104 19
New Berlin	Chenango	John T. White	328 27	371 53
New Berlin Centre	Chenango	Adoniram Green	10 38	16 59
New Britain	Columbia	Kenneth M. Davis	18 58	32 03
Newburgh	Orange	James Belknap	1196 26	2862 45
New Castle	West Chester	Moses W. Fish	20 95	35 57
New Concord	Columbia	Obadiah Palmer	55 35	93 96
New Fane	Niagara	Arthur Patterson	38 01	68 75
Newfield	Tompkins	Daniel L. Tracy	94 40	170 28
New Hackensack	Dutchess	George W. Jones	31 55	46 16
New Hamburgh	Dutchess	Walter Millard	104 77	194 34
New Hampton (Late "Dolsentown.")	Orange	Moses H. Phillips, from 1st Nov.	21 02	38 54
New Hartford	Oneida	Hiram Shays	341 89	655 18
New Haven	Oswego	Sam'l G. Merriam	83 46	141 57
New Hurley	Ulster	Isaac Fowler, to 14th Feb.	20 26	32 69
		Francis Deyo	10 10	17 25
Newkirk's Mills	Fulton	Garret A. Newkirk	8 21	15 76
New Lebanon	Columbia	Moses Y. Tilden	102 59	183 35
New Lebanon Centre	Columbia	Fred'k W. Everest, 8⅔ mo.	38 00	58 04
New Lebanon Springs	Columbia	John Bull, jr.	91 94	162 64
New Lisbon	Otsego	David M. Hard	37 54	71 85

POST OFFICES—*New York.*

Post Offices.	Counties.	Postmasters.	Compensation.	Net proceeds.
New London....	Oneida......	Thomas J. Rudd...	$99 49	$182 21
New Milford.....	Orange......	Thomas Gale......	8 98	17 41
New Ohio.......	Broome......	Edwin S. Holcomb.	6 32	9 48
New Paltz.......	Ulster.......	Wade H. Budd....	110 99	179 35
New Paltz Land'g	Ulster.......	Josiah C. Dubois...	77 08	106 56
Newport........	Herkimer....	Geo. B. Raymond...	176 84	322 43
New Road.......	Delaware....	Daniel Weed......	9 83	13 87
New Rochelle....	West Chester	James T. Eells, to 14th Dec........	151 54	292 28
		Jas. P. Huntington..	154 74	305 40
New Salem......	Albany......	David G. Seger.....	13 05	20 78
New Scotland....	Albany......	Edmund Raynsford.	24 93	47 97
Newstead	Erie	John S. Ball........	35 34	59 98
New Sweden....	Clinton......	James C. Fitzgerald, from 1st Oct......	15 25	29 37
Newton's Corners	Fulton......	John Newton......	8 00	16 34
Newtown	Queens......	Charles Cook......	55 66	114 12
New Utrecht.....	Kings.......	Wm. W. Cropsey..	28 85	57 37
New Vernon.....	Orange......	Gilbert Beebe......	23 74	39 32
New Village.....	Suffolk......	Wm. J. Gould......	7 33	12 75
Newville	Herkimer....	Abraham Snyder...	17 32	30 91
New Windsor...	Orange......	Francis M. Denniston, to 31st Dec..	15 94	30 89
		G. L. Sherwood....	17 46	34 83
New Woodstock.	Madison.....	Sam'l L. Hubbard..	125 51	122 24
New York.......	New York...	John L. Graham, to 21st May........	1649 24	260091 10
		Robert H. Morris..	(no ret.)	
New York Mills..	Oneida......	Seth Maltbie.......	208 17	416 17
Niagara Falls....	Niagara.....	Rich'd H. Woodruff	296 80	636 14
Nichols	Tioga.......	John C. Barstow...	68 52	118 29
Nicholsville......	St. Lawrence	Lyman Day.......	36 76	61 63
Niles............ (Late "Twelve	Cayuga...... Corners.")	Cornel's D. DeWitt, from 23d April...	2 62	5 54
Nineveh..........	Broome......	Hial Edgerton......	30 56	54 27
Norfolk.........	St. Lawrence	William Floyd, to 15th May........	55 38	106 97
		Henry P. Judson...	7 78	13 33
North Adams....	Jefferson.....	Albert Rice........	7 26	11 14
North Almond...	Allegany	James Ward.......	13 76	22 97
Northampton.....	Fulton.......	Clark S. Grinnell...	55 27	97 63
North Argyle....	Washington..	John Clark, to 9th Jan.............	17 64	32 38
		William Stevenson..	14 31	28 56
North Bay......	Oneida......	Robert Paddock....	19 75	41 85
North Bergen....	Genesee......	Daniel Hooper.....	36 50	68 81
North Blenheim..	Schoharie ...	William Fink......	36 28	62 49
North Bloomfield.	Ontario......	Adon'h H. Fairchild	31 88	55 07
North Boston....	Erie........	Ira Fuller.........	24 81	43 07

POST OFFICES—*New York.*

Post Offices.	Counties.	Postmasters.	Compensation.	Net proceeds.
North Brookfield.	Madison	Franklin Blanding..	$23 09	$36 82
North Castle......	West Chester	Samuel P. Smith....	54 83	93 20
North Chatham..	Columbia....	Henry Hill........	26 56	40 35
North Chemung..	Chemung....	Anthony Collson...	5 09	7 95
North Chili......	Monroe......	Robert Fulton......	94 89	143 21
North Clarence...	Erie.........	Orange Mansfield...	7 11	16 66
North Clymer....	Chautauque..	George Ross.......	4 21	6 69
North Cohocton..	Steuben......	Elijah Heartwell....	34 37	57 04
North East......	Dutchess....	Sam'l Robertson, to 12th Feb........	17 13	32 93
		William Winchell..	16 18	20 51
North East Centre	Dutchess....	Lyman Bassett, to 13th Feb........	20 68	34 25
		John G. Caulkins..	15 81	22 60
North Easton....	Washington..	William Cozzens...	46 51	77 15
North Gage......	Oneida......	Lucius L. Howe, to 19th Dec........	14 07	21 85
		Adolp's F. Rockwell	17 00	28 34
North Galway....	Saratoga	Eliphalet S. Hanford	21 69	45 78
North Granville..	Washington..	Jehiel Dayton......	154 66	150 29
North Greenwich.	Washington..	William Reid......	19 97	30 10
North Hampden.. (Disc'd 15th Aug.)	Delaware....	Sam'l W. Andrews.	(no ret.)	
N'th Harpersfield.	Delaware....	Homer W. Hamilton	7 07	13 66
North Hebron....	Washington..	Jonathan Allen.....	21 76	29 50
North Hector....	Tompkins...	Joel H. Kennan, to 25th Jan.........	14 94	28 01
		Theodore Squires...	14 10	24 56
North Hemstead.	Queens......	James H. Poole....	16 37	31 15
North Kortright..	Delaware....	Edmund Keeler....	11 13	21 26
North Lansing...	Tompkins...	Roswell Beardsley..	19 11	36 11
North Mendon...	Monroe.....	Benjamin Tripp....	7 80	15 26
North Middlesex.	Yates.......	Ambrose S. Thomas	7 94	11 97
North Norwich..	Chenango....	John Wight.......	63 48	61 90
N'th Perrysburgh	Cattaraugus..	Charles Blackney...	7 08	12 75
Northport........	Suffolk......	Samuel E. Bunce...	41 25	69 87
North Reading...	Steuben......	John T. Andrews..	14 23	22 58
North Ridgeway..	Orleans......	Elijah W. Hawkins	23 20	39 68
North Salem.....	West Chester	Jacob Hess........	32 11	54 99
North Sheldon....	Wyoming...	Elihu H. Persons...	5 60	10 37
North Shore.....	Richmond...	N. P. H. Barrett...	102 35	210 83
N'th Stephentown	Rensselaer...	Henry R. Cranston.	11 70	19 26
North Sterling....	Cayuga......	Wm. T. Churchill..	20 57	40 24
Northumberland..	Saratoga	Benajah Barker....	65 24	127 67
North Urbana....	Steuben.....	Rich'd L. Chapman.	23 53	36 83
Northville.......	Fulton.......	Jos. F. Spier.......	45 11	77 03
North Western...	Oneida......	Arnon Comstock...	2 84	5 55
N'th Wethersfield	Wyoming...	Edwin Gardner....	15 67	29 23
N'th White Creek	Washington..	Luther I. Howe....	83 74	145 21

POST OFFICES—*New York.*

Post Offices.	Counties.	Postmasters.	Compensation.	Net proceeds.
North Wilna	Jefferson	Stephen Lewis	$13 57	$22 82
Norton's Mills	Ontario	Zurial Brown	14 35	21 09
Norway	Herkimer	David Du Bois	75 26	123 64
Norwich	Chenango	Squire Smith	607 26	1040 31
Nunda Valley	Allegany	Utley Spencer	285 21	470 18
Nyack	Rockland	Charles Humphreys	51 25	105 92
Nyack Turnpike	Rockland	Wm. O. Blemis	13 03	21 58
Oakfield	Genesee	George March	141 92	249 68
Oak Hill	Greene	Amos Pierce	46 56	85 12
Oakland	Allegany	George Williams	26 66	50 22
Oak Orchard	Orleans	Mason Turner	56 62	95 36
Oak Point	St. Lawrence	James H. Consall	14 46	25 50
Oak's Corners	Ontario	Elias Cost	57 05	99 73
Oaksville	Otsego	Charles Childs	49 11	92 94
O'Connelville	Monroe	John D. Walsh	9 68	18 95
Ogdensburgh	St. Lawrence	Platt B. Fairchild	1024 90	2172 11
Ohio	Herkimer	Wm. Coppernoll	16 13	28 91
Olcott	Niagara	James D. Cooper	61 28	105 05
Olean	Cattaraugus	David Day, 3 qrs	99 89	114 22
Olive	Ulster	John J. Tappen	21 32	24 69
Olive Bridge	Ulster	Wm. J. Davis	10 14	17 40
Omar	Jefferson	Tim. R. Stackhouse	18 03	32 10
Oneida Castle	Oneida	Horatio Stevens, to 31st Dec	54 82	102 35
		Hurlb't G. Wetmore	55 05	108 67
Oneida Depot	Madison	Erasmus Stone	67 15	133 48
Oneida Lake	Madison	Calvin W. Hart	21 33	37 22
Oneonta	Otsego	Wm. S. Fritts	234 60	221 86
Onondaga	Onondaga	Charles D. Easton, to 31st Dec	49 08	85 95
		Henry P. Shove	48 11	88 99
Onondaga Hollow	Onondaga	Arthur Pattison	84 08	154 62
Ontario	Wayne	Joseph More	73 16	132 94
Oppenheim	Fulton	George W. Burr	46 23	81 59
Oran	Onondaga	Lorenzo D. Loomis, to 14th May	36 37	48 90
		Josiah Brintnall	6 27	7 94
Orange	Steuben	Alonzo Gaylard	46 48	78 74
Orange Port	Niagara	Solomon R. Hart	38 10	48 92
Orangeville	Wyoming	Jerry Merrell	40 07	69 86
Oregon	Chautauque	John West	15 89	23 75
Orient	Suffolk	Joseph Terry	44 45	73 83
Oriskany	Oneida	Daniel C. Balis	186 68	340 74
Oriskany Falls	Oneida	David Murray	111 19	196 60
Orleans	Ontario	Kendal King, to 28th Feb	43 24	73 61
		John L. Rice	19 13	35 82
Orwell	Oswego	Eli Strong	26 71	52 91

POST OFFICES—*New York.*

Post Offices.	Counties.	Postmasters.	Compensation.	Net proceeds.
Osborn Hollow..	Broome......	John Carrol	$10 33	$18 63
Osborn's Bridge..	Fulton.......	Seth Cook..........	12 91	19 67
Ossian........	Allegany....	Samuel Porter......	23 39	45 28
Oswegatchie......	Lewis.......	Reuben Tyler......	6 27	11 41
Oswego.........	Oswego......	James Cochran.....	1539 51	4053 61
Otego..........	Otsego.......	Ezra R. Brewer....	117 02	192 63
Otisco..........	Onondaga ...	Horatio Smith.....	81 55	131 71
Otisville.........	Orange......	Johnson King......	23 17	41 71
Otsdawa.........	Otsego.......	Luman S. Osborn ..	21 21	20 21
Otselic	Chenango....	Amaziah Parker....	23 47	35 13
Otto	Cattaraugus .	Sellick St. John....	56 93	101 41
Ovid...........	Seneca......	Andrew S. Purdy, to 17th Feb.........	227 95	446 66
		Chs. A. Gibbs.....	122 73	246 18
Ovid Centre.....	Seneca......	Barnet D. Tibbets..	19 11	33 83
Owasco	Cayuga.	Joel R. Gore.......	59 64	111 15
Owego..........	Tioga.......	Daniel Ely, to 4th Dec'r............	364 61	509 60
		Stephen B. Leonard.	426 47	584 07
Owenville	West Chester	Thomas R. Lee....	17 69	31 49
Oxbow	Jefferson	Rufus H. King....	57 20	97 27
Oxford.........	Chenango ...	Cyrus A. Bacon....	499 94	1033 72
Oxford Depot....	Orange.......	John H. Tuthill....	28 04	48 32
Oyster Bay......	Queens	James Colwell	54 39	109 42
Paines Hollow...	Herkimer ...	Andrew Piper, jr...	16 67	26 63
Painted Post.....	Steuben.	Wm. J. Gilbert, to 31st Dec.........	56 44	91 98
		Francis E. Erwin...	51 40	90 55
Palatine.........	Montgomery.	Cornelius Mabee...	38 56	64 62
Palatine Bridge..	Montgomery.	Livingston Spraker.	126 41	273 61
Palenville	Greene......	Charles H. Teal....	19 82	35 38
Palermo.........	Oswego	Ad'sn K. Beckwith.	38 47	65 80
Palestine........	Allegany....	David Fargo.......	7 52	13 62
Palmyra.........	Wayne	David D. Hoyt, to 1st Nov..........	211 18	390 01
		Jno. O. Vorse......	444 19	868 79
Pamelia 4 Corners	Jefferson	Chs. G. Harger....	30 77	57 01
Panama.........	Chautauque..	Reuben Davis......	100 28	173 54
Paradox	Essex........	Nehemiah Wheeler.	3 36	7 65
Paris	Oneida......	Geo. W. Head.....	113 73	120 92
Paris Furnace....	Oneida......	Eason Allen.......	63 93	126 45
Parish	Oswego	Ephraim E. Ford...	44 66	79 53
Parishville	St. Lawrence.	Erasmus D. Brooks, to 14th May.....	88 40	162 42
		Ger. F. Brownson..	11 35	20 97
Parksville	Sullivan.....	James F. Bush.....	11 71	21 63
Parma..........	Monroe......	William Goodell...	69 05	131 21
Parma Centre....	Monroe......	Chauncey A. Knox.	86 67	146 95

POST OFFICES—*New York.*

Post Offices.	Counties.	Postmasters.	Compensation.	Net proceeds.
Partridge Island..	Delaware ...	James Wheeler, 2d.	$4 38	$6 55
Patchin's Mills...	Steuben.....	Warren Patchin....	46 83	46 86
Patchogue.......	Suffolk......	James Ketcham....	76 54	165 63
Patten's Mills....	Washington .	James W. Harvey .	13 24	22 30
Patterson	Putnam......	Frederick Stone....	33 93	59 28
Pauling	Dutchess....	Archibald Sill......	30 47	49 63
Paulingville	Dutchess....	Archibald Campbell.	13 50	23 65
Pavilion.........	Genesee.....	Elisha Mosher, jr., to 30th Sept.....	21 69	37 68
		Wm. M. Sprague..	77 00	126 23
Pavillion Centre..	Genesee.....	Gilman Barnett....	28 96	46 99
Paynsville.......	Onondaga ...	Nelson C. Dunham.	21 81	40 67
Pecksville.......	Dutchess....	George Smith......	8 64	16 49
Peekskill........	West Chester	Ward B. Howard..	477 91	1046 47
Pekin...........	Niagara.....	Sparrow S. Sage ...	89 41	154 98
Peltonville.......	Steuben.....	John Gload........	14 86	24 74
Pembroke.......	Genesee.....	John S. Dodge.....	22 80	32 89
Pendleton.......	Niagara.....	Justus Dunn.......	32 76	55 59
Penfield.........	Monroe.....	Dan'l E. Lewis....	176 10	328 51
Pen Yan........	Yates.......	Darius A. Ogden...	711 68	1570 19
Peoria	Wyoming...	James Gordon.....	32 47	51 21
Pepacton........	Delaware....	Charles Knapp.....	13 95	16 84
Perch River......	Jefferson	Hugh Smith.......	30 37	51 76
Perrington.......	Monroe.....	Chs. H. Dickinson.	110 30	205 45
Perry...........	Wyoming...	Anson D. Smith....	401 67	555 38
Perry Centre....	Wyoming...	Jason Lathrop.....	101 86	112 40
Perrysburg......	Cattaraugus..	William Cooper....	25 02	47 31
Perry's Mills....	Clinton	Lucian Perry......	10 57	19 22
Perryville	Madison	Silas Judd.........	58 55	98 57
Persia...........	Cattaraugus..	John B. Wilbor....	173 92	284 09
Perth...........	Fulton......	Jacob Swobe......	21 21	40 03
Peru............	Clinton......	Franklin Elmore...	178 20	167 59
Peruville........	Tompkins...	William Baldwin, to 23d Jan........	13 20	22 15
		Silenus Brown.....	14 52	25 62
Peterboro'.......	Madison	Harvey Williams, to 1st Feb.........	132 53	265 36
		Isaac Van Vleck...	84 35	161 68
Petersburgh	Rensselaer...	Squire Allen.......	59 52	105 74
Petersburgh 4 Corners..........	Rensselaer...	Stephen Reynolds, jr	11 70	20 44
Pharsalia........	Chenango ...	Chs. P. Browning..	22 10	37 55
Phelps..........	Ontario......	William Hildreth, to 26th Nov........	215 11	284 07
		John Watson......	256 15	520 15
Philadelphia.....	Jefferson	William Strong....	63 23	123 83
Philipsburgh	Orange......	Eleazer T. Clark...	22 18	43 04
Philipsport......	Sullivan.....	Gabriel David......	17 44	32 88
Philipsville......	Allegany	Alvan E. Parker...	44 13	81 92

POST OFFICES—*New York.*

Post Offices.	Counties.	Postmasters.	Compensation.	Net proceeds.
Phœnix	Oswego	Jos'a M. Rice, to 25th Dec	$81 39	$80 14
		Joseph R. Brown	82 21	106 35
Piermont	Rockland	P. H. Taulman	100 65	191 81
Pierpont	St. Lawrence	And'w A. Crampton	24 57	46 49
Pierrepont Manor	Jefferson	Tho. E. Williamson	59 79	86 52
Piffardiana	Livingston	Duty S. Thompson	16 33	32 41
Pike	Allegany	Ira Barnes	233 59	215 67
Pillar Point	Jefferson	John L. Alger	18 68	28 97
Pine	Oneida	Eli Bridges	28 00	39 13
Pine Grove	Stuben	Daniel Forshee	13 03	24 26
Pine Hill	Ulster	Thomas Smith	13 06	25 78
Pine Plains	Dutchess	R. W. Bostwick	146 63	258 29
Pine's Bridge	West Chester	Jackson Hyatt	18 15	34 36
Pineville	Steuben	Dan'l B. Bryan	7 84	12 47
Piseco	Hamilton	Ezra Thompson, fr. 30th June to 31st March	1 19	2 80
Pitcairn	St. Lawrence	John Sloper	11 92	23 80
Pitcher	Chenango	Eben'r C. Lyons	44 74	70 26
Pitcher Springs	Chenango	Roswell K. Bourne	13 62	18 37
Pittsfield	Otsego	Ransom Spafard	15 58	12 45
Pittsford	Monroe	Alexander Voorhees	231 59	460 68
Pittstown	Rensselaer	Leonard Reed, to 17th May	53 28	104 13
		Norman Baker	5 79	11 54
Plainfield	Otsego	Luther Smith	15 44	26 62
Plainville	Onondaga	John Buck	31 62	56 87
Plattekill	Ulster	Charles Drake	30 03	53 38
Plattsburgh	Clinton	Levi Platt	742 02	1334 13
Pleasant Plains	Dutchess	Benj. J. Van Keuren	10 49	15 84
Pleasant Valley	Dutchess	Franklin Dudley	93 20	176 50
Pleasantville	West Chester	Abraham Bronwer	24 65	40 06
Plesis	Jefferson	Jason Clark	41 97	73 16
Plymouth	Chenango	Dyar Munroe	30 70	56 63
Poestenkill	Rensselaer	Harmin Vanderzee	11 82	18 79
Point Peninsula	Jefferson	Welcome Wilcox	12 74	26 10
Poland	Herkimer	Oliver Franklin	42 62	74 35
Poland Centre	Chautauque	Eliakim Crosby	27 80	48 12
Pompey	Onondaga	Wm. J. Curtis	145 68	217 26
Pompey Centre	Onondaga	Levi S. Holbrook	24 10	43 06
Pond Settlement	Steuben	Abraham Hoagland	10 70	15 91
Poolville	Madison	Nathan Eaton	42 91	73 70
Pope's Corners	Saratoga	Aug. H. Pearsall	20 75	29 69
Poplar Ridge	Cayuga	Asa Shourds, to 31st Dec	43 38	52 48
		William Sprague	36 78	69 24
Portageville	Allegany	Alvah S. Green	86 59	164 59

POST OFFICES—*New York.*

Post Offices.	Counties.	Postmasters.	Compensation.	Net proceeds.
Port Byron	Cayuga	Hiram D. Eldridge, to 30th May	$278 07	$442 30
		Denison Robinson	21 12	44 96
Port Chester	West Chester	Geo. W. Smith	182 06	363 72
Port Crane	Broome	Isaac Bishop	16 40	31 27
Porter's Corners	Saratoga	Isaac I. Yates	31 18	51 17
Port Gibson	Ontario	Asbrah Huntoon	72 77	131 53
Port Glasgow	Wayne	Manlius W. Gage	11 69	23 86
Port Henry	Essex	John E. McVine, to 6th May	94 96	177 27
		Lucian P. Cheney	13 58	23 25
Port Jackson	Montgomery	William M. Hill, to 6th Jan	29 94	57 06
		Jacob G. Snell	33 34	62 61
Port Jefferson	Suffolk	John R. Mather	26 19	46 64
Port Jervis	Orange	Chas. Hardenbergh	115 50	130 43
Port Kendall	Essex	Levi Higby	4 24	7 22
Port Kent	Essex	Jas. R. Dickinson, to 14th June	29 92	57 31
		Liberty R. Branch	0 93	1 74
Portland	Chautauque	John R. Coney	69 67	89 27
Port Ontario	Oswego	Lucius B. Cole	28 35	50 62
Portville	Cattaraugus	Henry Dusenbury	46 71	73 24
Post Creek	Chemung	Jos. C. Hulburt, to 30th Sept	1 20	2 20
		Chs. D. Defrance	2 66	4 14
Postville	Herkimer	J. Post, to 16th Nov.	4 48	7 25
		Owen Kelly	10 32	16 28
Potsdam	St. Lawrence	Justus Smith, to 14th May	308 84	613 50
		Wm. A. Dart	35 39	74 96
Potter	Yates	Peleg Thomas	48 02	82 05
Pottersville	Warren	Wm. C. Potter, to 31st March	29 69	28 50
		Joshua Collar	6 84	6 37
Poughkeepsie	Dutchess	J. Van Benthuysen	1595 12	4320 28
Poughquag	Dutchess	Dan'l F. Brill	29 86	50 82
Poundridge	West Chester	Wm. L. Smith, to 23d Jan	19 65	27 22
		Alsop H. Lockwood	19 60	29 98
Prattsburgh	Steuben	Sam'l A. Johnson	153 59	266 92
Pratt's Hollow	Madison	Orason Chamberlain	42 06	64 26
Prattsville	Greene	Fred'k A. Fenn	205 97	383 71
Preble	Cortlandt	Jabez B. Phelps, to 12th Nov	29 84	48 62
		Robert Gillespie	47 02	81 66
Preston	Chenango	Daniel Noyes	34 53	59 83
Princetown (Dis. 12th July.)	Schenectady	Henry Van Vranken	(no ret.)	

POST OFFICES—*New York.*

Post Offices.	Counties.	Postmasters.	Compensation.	Net proceeds.
Prospect	Oneida	John Thomas	$19 90	$43 02
Prospect Hill	Rensselaer	Justus H. Akin	15 24	29 12
Providence	Saratoga	Seabury Allen	19 56	40 98
Pultney	Steuben	Jared T. Benton	31 88	61 07
Pultneyville	Wayne	John Reynolds, to 7th Dec	21 00	34 99
		Bethel Todd	54 49	92 65
Pulver's Corners	Dutchess	Chs. M. Morgan	4 65	10 35
Punchkill	Schoharie	Jabez Holmes	11 88	20 85
Purdy Creek	Steuben	Chs. N. Hart	5 93	8 96
Purvis	Sullivan	Burrows Phillips	7 19	10 90
Putnam	Washington	Wm. G. Corbet	61 95	60 33
Putnam Valley	Putnam	Amos Tompkins	7 12	14 54
Quaker Hill	Dutchess	John Toffey	46 39	78 03
Quaker Springs	Saratoga	Eliakim H. Mosher	17 01	32 51
Quaker Street	Schenectady	Kirby Wilber	54 81	82 98
Queensbury	Warren	Hiram Barber, to 24th July	1 52	2 44
		Lemuel C. P. Seelye	27 87	44 40
Quogue	Suffolk	Josiah P. Howell	30 06	55 92
Rackett River	St. Lawrence	Peter Vilas	15 75	28 91
Ramapo	Rockland	George W. Suffern	63 71	124 21
Randolph	Cattaraugus	Chs. D. Foote	99 31	185 14
Ransomville	Niagara	Leverett A. Bristol	26 94	51 18
Rathboneville	Steuben	Ransom Rathbone	30 02	54 83
Raymertown	Rensselaer	Clark Baker	28 59	34 07
Raymondville	St. Lawrence	Giles J. Hall	18 78	31 26
Reading	Steuben	Hiram Chapman	30 77	47 84
Reading Centre	Steuben	Alonzo Simmons	34 16	44 84
Red Creek	Wayne	Wm. S. Crosby	93 63	180 54
Redfield	Oswego	Reuben Drake	19 29	35 30
Redford	Clinton	Noah H. Lund	16 86	25 12
Red Hook	Dutchess	Philip N. Bonesteel	124 33	186 74
Red Mills	Putnam	Wm. B. Hazleton, to 31st Dec	14 43	24 15
		Jonathan Whiting	15 61	29 46
Redwood	Jefferson	Ralph Symonds	46 24	92 66
Reed's Corners	Ontario	Mason Reed	33 11	53 74
Reidsville	Albany	Frederick Ward	14 40	24 38
Remington (Ch'd to "Ilion," 30th Dec.	Herkimer	D. D. Devoe, (2 qrs)	41 73	73 13
Remsen	Oneida	Andrew Billings	132 14	218 59
Rensselaerville	Albany	John S. Huyck, to 27th Nov	90 36	149 51
		Robert L. Mulford	131 39	223 69
Republican	Oneida	E. Hunt, to 30th Sept.	10 22	15 69
		Norman Maltby	34 51	56 54

POST OFFICES—*New York.*

Post Offices.	Counties.	Postmasters.	Compensation.	Net proceeds.
Reservation........	Erie........	Erwin H. Ewell.....	$7 65	$11 10
Rexford Flats....	Saratoga....	George T. Wright..	32 38	54 58
Reynales' Basin..	Niagara.....	Sherman McLean..	60 89	77 49
Reynoldsville.....	Tompkins...	Ira Reynolds, to 30th September.......	8 59	14 23
		Selah Sarles	21 05	37 01
Rhinebeck........	Dutchess....	Wm. B. Platt......	386 75	584 87
Riceville.........	Fulton......	James Berry.......	12 97	18 81
Richburgh........	Allegany.....	Valentine P. Carter, to 31st Dec......	7 62	12 65
		Asher W. Miner....	9 60	17 37
Richfield	Otsego.......	Jared C. Munson...	70 34	119 29
Richfield Springs.	Otsego.......	Aug. R. Elwood...	260 83	258 75
Richford	Tioga.......	Chauncey L. Rich..	57 40	62 96
Richland	Oswego.....	Daniel H. Fisk, to 31st Dec........	152 18	296 43
		Henry N. Wright..	155 23	306 55
Richmond........	Richmond...	John Johnson......	67 94	118 71
Richmond Mills.. (Late "West Richmond.")	Ontario......	Fred'k W. Patterson, from 22d Jan.	15 28	27 95
Richmond Valley.	Richmond ...	Henry Cole........	19 19	35 52
Richmondville ...	Schoharie ...	John W. Mumford.	35 50	60 98
Richville.........	St. Lawrence.	John C. Rich......	35 30	66 12
Ridge...........	Livingston...	George Chidsey....	24 83	36 11
Ridgebury.......	Orange......	John C. Owen, to 28th April.......	15 58	32 58
		Richard A. Elmer..	3 53	6 28
Ridgeville	Madison	Benjamin Rider, jr..	9 92	18 54
Ridgeway........	Orleans......	Harvey Francis....	116 61	163 94
Riga............	Monroe......	Loren Baldwin.....	66 18	130 08
Ripley	Chautauque..	Persis Bruce.......	115 04	131 18
Ripley Hill...... (Dis. 1st August.)	Chautauque..	Alfred Palmer......	(no ret.)	
River Road Forks	Livingston...	Wm. W. Deak....	12 46	21 45
River Side.......	Ulster........	Laird M. H. Butler.	18 64	35 85
Roberts' Corners.	Jefferson	Orrin Marvin, to 31st March...........	11 30	14 72
		Robert H. Roberts.	4 79	7 00
Rochester	Monroe......	Samuel G. Andrews	1348 45	13426 37
Rockaway........	Queens	David T. Jennings..	26 39	42 60
Rock City.......	Dutchess	Jas. A. Stoutenburg	23 59	38 78
Rockland........	Sullivan.....	Chester Darbee	13 01	21 97
Rockland Lake...	Rockland.....	Thomas J. Wilcox..	20 34	37 43
Rock Stream.....	Yates	Hiram A. Newcomb	37 75	63 38
Rockville........	Allegany.....	Henry H. Munson.	9 55	16 58
Rodman.........	Jefferson	Wm. H. Moffett...	86 33	141 97
Rome	Oneida	Jay Hatheway.....	880 05	1810 33
Romulus	Seneca.......	Ethan Watson.....	99 31	161 75

POST OFFICES—*New York.*

Post Offices.	Counties.	Postmasters.	Compensation.	Net proceeds.
Rondout	Ulster	Edgar R. Bevier, to 22d Oct	$136 37	$180 23
		Edmond Suydam	217 38	298 60
Roosevelt	Oswego	Alexander Ross	14 88	23 72
Root	Montgomery	John Bowdish	35 40	62 89
Rose	Wayne	Hiram Salsbury, to 13th Jan	37 37	73 36
		Eron N. Thomas	45 10	78 32
Roseboom	Otsego	Wm D. Oaks	11 13	18 92
Rosendale	Ulster	Jacob A. Snyder	74 05	136 09
Roslyn (Late 'Hempstead Harbor.")	Queens	William Hicks, from 1st October	25 89	47 01
Rossie	St. Lawrence	Zacheus Gates	48 43	86 91
Rossville	Richmond	Borut P. Winant	42 07	79 27
Rotterdam	Schenectady	John W. Conklin	16 88	25 39
Rouse's Point	Clinton	George Sullivan	102 17	204 84
Roxbury	Delaware	Edw'd J. Burhans	68 27	121 89
Royalton	Niagara	Edward M. Clark	69 14	123 59
Rush	Monroe	John B. Crosby	116 11	203 93
Rushford	Allegany	Orvill Boardman, to 31st Dec	114 12	108 78
		James McCall	116 16	114 81
Rushville	Ontario	Periander Vorce	189 29	342 72
Russell	St. Lawrence	Harvey Knox, to 31st March	24 85	45 87
		Rollin C. Jackson	10 41	17 76
Russia	Herkimer	Isaac Betticher	62 21	93 53
Rutland	Jefferson	Jeremiah J. Tuttle	69 73	67 19
Rye	West Chester	Noah Stiles, jr., to 11th December	46 92	83 15
		Daniel Strang	55 88	99 48
Sackett's Harbour	Jefferson	Edmund M. Luff, to 25th April	462 78	794 48
		DeWitt C. McGuin	81 68	192 96
Sageville (Late "Lake Pleasant.")	Hamilton	John C. Holmes, jr.	24 65	33 23
Sag Harbour	Suffolk	Peletiah Fordham, to 31st Dec	234 32	461 46
		Ezra L. H. Gardiner	271 77	450 61
St. Andrews	Orange	Lotan Kidd	26 50	47 16
St. Johnsville	Montgomery	Lewis Averill	83 92	154 32
Salem	Washington	Alex'r M. Proudfit	299 94	564 23
Salem Centre	West Chester	Samuel H. Smith	13 77	25 47
Salem ⋈ Roads	Chautauque	Samuel Hall	77 68	103 51
Salina	Onondaga	Isaac R. Quereau	364 47	518 31
Salisbury	Herkimer	Alden S. Gage, to 3d December	34 66	61 04
		Lorenzo Carryl	42 79	73 32

POST OFFICES—*New York*.

Post Offices.	Counties.	Postmasters.	Compensation.	Net proceeds.
Salisbury Centre	Herkimer	Hiram Hadley	$52 95	$92 04
Salisbury Mills	Orange	Reuben Van Alen	66 59	121 71
Salmon Creek	Wayne	Wm. I. Filkins, to 31st Dec	7 61	14 04
		David Poucher	7 48	11 67
Salmon River	Oswego	Alonzo R. Angell	27 64	50 37
Salt Point	Dutchess	R. D. C. Vanderburgh, to 20th Sept.	8 58	14 17
		William Wilde	29 80	49 93
Salt Springville	Otsego	Stephen Bigelow	18 54	33 38
Salubria	Chemung	Edward Quin, to 1st November	50 13	86 92
		Alvah Nash	77 31	139 05
Sammonsville	Fulton	Noah Fitch	16 23	24 79
Sand Bank	Oswego	Sam'l A. Comstock	18 68	38 53
Sandburgh	Sullivan	Sturges Andrews	18 26	31 46
Sand Lake	Rensselaer	Calvin Sliter	155 32	171 08
Sandusky	Cattaraugus	Eber Holmes	25 27	42 38
Sandy Creek	Oswego	Amos B. Titus	91 12	159 52
Sandy Hill	Washington	James Wright	272 86	440 83
Sanford (Discontinued.)	Broome	John Luscomb, to 30th Nov	4 97	10 04
Sanford's Corners	Jefferson	Jacob R. Howard	15 52	24 06
Sangerfield	Oneida	Daniel North	69 33	68 32
Saranac	Clinton	Andrew Hull	22 30	40 77
Saratoga Springs	Saratoga	Thomas J. Marvin	1044 83	2798 62
Sardinia	Erie	Joseph Candee	53 95	89 90
Saugerties	Ulster	Edm'd J. McCarthy	485 82	863 64
Sauquoit	Oneida	Fred'k S. Savage, to 12th Oct	36 47	67 77
		Aaron B. Bligh	93 80	180 57
Savannah	Wayne	Henry W. Wood, to 31st March	7 17	15 22
		Chs. H. Torry	1 98	3 95
Sayville	Suffolk	Daniel Howell	20 26	32 99
Schagticoke	Rensselaer	Chs. J. Wilber	232 73	456 41
Schenectady	Schenectady	James M. Bouck	1072 23	2924 68
Schodack Centre	Rensselaer	Jno. H. Vanderburg, to 17th Aug	4 18	6 28
		Joseph Woodworth	29 41	50 62
Schodack Landing	Rensselaer	John S. Clapp, to 16th May	48 53	85 19
		Edgar Botsford	7 76	5 67
Schoharie	Schoharie	Almerin Gallup	225 73	262 47
Schroon Lake	Essex	Gay W. Lee, to 20th July	3 66	7 19
		Thomas Leland	61 27	109 66
Schroon River	Essex	Robert D. Lindsay	28 45	58 57
Schultzsville	Dutchess	Daniel H. Schultzs	32 57	48 93

POST OFFICES—*New York.*

Post Offices.	Counties.	Postmasters.	Compensation.	Net proceeds.
Schuyler's Falls..	Clinton......	Martin Bullis......	$37 49	$59 57
Schuyler's Lake..	Otsego......	J. P. Sill..........	45 99	75 36
Schuylersville.....	Saratoga.....	James P. Cramer...	148 89	265 32
Scienceville	Greene......	Albert Tuttle	29 61	55 80
Scio............	Allegany.....	Davis Browning....	15 83	29 84
Scipio	Cayuga	John E. Beardsley..	44 93	88 26
Scipioville.......	Cayuga	George L. Watkins.	67 81	80 12
Sconondoa	Oneida......	Samuel S. Breese ..	10 68	22 82
Scotchtown......	Orange......	John Crans........	28 14	50 01
Scotland	Rockland ...	Peter D. Talman...	8 28	14 00
Scott	Cortlandt ...	Horace S. Babcock.	99 40	159 41
Scottsburgh	Livingston ..	William Scott	43 32	68 35
Scottsville	Monroe......	Ira Carpenter......	185 93	355 65
Scriba	Oswego......	James Church.....	47 95	78 50
Searsburgh	Tompkins...	David F. Sears	22 74	41 36
Seely Creek	Chemung ...	Wm. R. Sheppard, to 30th Jan......	8 14	15 70
		Simeon R. Jones, 2d	6 93	13 05
Seelysburgh	Cattaraugus .	Lewis P. Thorp....	8 88	16 04
Sempronius	Cayuga	Abel Heald	42 18	71 64
Seneca Castle....	Ontario	Thomas Ottley.....	48 93	87 97
Seneca Falls......	Seneca......	Isaac Fuller, to 31st May..........	577 06	1110 55
		Josiah T. Miller....	36 01	93 76
Sennet	Cayuga	Holman Fisher	88 88	149 76
Setauket	Suffolk	John R. Satterly ...	48 26	74 50
Shandaken	Ulster	Benj. H. O'Neil, to 23d March	20 14	41 43
		Isaac Whispell.....	9 51	18 26
Shannon	Steuben	Thomas Begole	8 99	12 52
Sharon..........	Schoharie ...	Reuben Moak	28 38	56 43
Sharon Centre ...	Schoharie ...	Jacob Hiller.......	36 98	74 37
Shavertown	Delaware	Alfred Shaver	7 21	13 21
Shawangunk	Ulster	Geo. G. Graham, to 31st Dec........	22 33	39 31
		Matthew F. Deyo..	23 13	41 70
Shawnee........	Niagara......	Timothy Shaw	21 82	40 75
Shawsville	Broome	Joseph Bostwick, from 11th Dec...	90	1 33
Shelby..........	Orleans	James Gilson......	63 51	124 63
Shelby Basin	Orleans	Christopher Servoss.	21 73	40 15
Sheldon.........	Wyoming....	Warren S. Rogers .	52 79	102 85
Shenandoah	Dutchess.....	Wright J. Horton .	3 76	7 37
Sherburne.......	Chenango ...	Wm. C. White, to 23d Jan	214 43	249 95
		Edmund Shaw.....	152 99	181 11
Sheridan........	Chautauque..	Edmund Mead.....	81 48	100 22
Sherman........	Chautauque .	Elijah Miller	52 76	89 43
Sherwood'sCorn'r	Cayuga	Allan Thomas	68 40	88 71

POST OFFICES—*New York.*

Post Offices.	Counties.	Postmasters.	Compensation.	Net proceeds.
Shingle Creek....	St. Lawrence	Alexander Wight..	$14 79	$24 01
Shokan.........	Ulster......	Thomas Hill......	20 80	20 80
Short Tract......	Allegany....	Joseph Platt.......	19 22	35 72
Shrub Oak......	West Chester	Lewis Purdy......	19 26	28 42
Shushan........	Washington.	Mathew H. Stevens.	27 85	47 15
Sidney.........	Delaware....	Robert S. Hughston	19 85	19 02
Sidney Centre...	Delaware....	Robert Fitzgerald,		
		to 31st Dec......	4 29	6 39
		Chas. S. Hyatt....	3 55	6 10
Sidney Plains....	Delaware....	Milton Johnston....	58 04	56 48
Siloam..........	Madison.....	Urial P. Strong....	18 36	31 96
Silver Creek.....	Chautauque.	Clark S. Swift.....	218 83	304 97
Silver Lake......	Wyoming....	Jeremiah Fuller....	17 71	26 27
Sing Sing.......	West Chester	George E. Stanton.	416 24	889 64
Skaneateles......	Onondaga...	Joel Thayer.......	568 09	1115 85
Slate Hill.......	Orange......	Ezra Mills........	16 03	27 76
Slaterville.......	Tompkins...	James Heath......	50 84	50 90
Sloanville.......	Schoharie...	Garret L. Schuyler.	46 00	75 08
Smithsboro'.....	Tioga.......	Benjamin Brooks..	60 49	54 96
Smith's Mills....	Chautauque.	Rodney B. Smith..	18 82	30 46
Smithtown......	Suffolk......	Jesse Mills........	120 10	201 20
Smithville.......	Jefferson....	George Babbitt....	90 94	148 60
Smithville Flats..	Chenango...	Horace S. Read....	52 27	105 17
Smoky Hollow..	Columbia...	Jacob Holsapple, to		
		31st March......	27 14	43 03
		Jonas Miller.......	8 89	13 13
Smyrna.........	Chenango...	Milo Sutliff........	111 57	201 62
Sociality........	Cattaraugus.	Nelson Hillebert...	7 12	13 91
Sodus..........	Wayne.....	Jonathan Warner, to		
		2d Dec..........	67 46	56 07
		Al'zo M. Winchester	100 98	90 50
Sodus Centre....	Wayne.....	Othniel Taylor.....	14 46	26 04
Sodus Point.....	Wayne.....	William Wickham.	31 38	50 36
Solon..........	Cortlandt...	Harlow L. Emerson	25 92	43 59
Somers........	West Chester	Frederick J. Coffin,		
		to 29th May.....	74 20	148 88
		Hachaliah B. Green	8 87	16 87
Somerset.......	Niagara.....	James Mathews...	95 98	176 69
Somerville......	St. Lawrence	Solomon Pratt.....	24 50	44 71
South Amenia....	Dutchess....	Charles Reed, to		
		31st Dec.........	17 68	27 65
		Warren Parsons...	17 84	32 43
Southampton....	Suffolk......	Abigail Foster.....	82 38	148 75
South Argyle....	Washington.	William Congdon..	32 77	57 86
South Avon.....	Livingston..	Charles T. Isham..	31 20	55 52
South Bainbridge.	Chenango...	Merlin Jackson....	56 74	95 07
South Barre.....	Orleans.....	David Ketcham....	26 67	48 77
South Branch....	A gan....	Rowland T. Green.	19 98	29 98
South Bristol....	Ontario.....	Allen Brown.......	21 15	37 85

POST OFFICES—*New York.*

Post Offices.	Counties.	Postmasters.	Compensation.	Net proceeds.
South Butler	Wayne	Oliver P. Palmer...	$46 18	$85 84
South Byron	Genesee	Erastus Cash......	65 94	91 91
South Cairo	Greene	Zerah Ferry.......	27 58	37 51
South Cameron ..	Steuben	Peter Chase, to 15th Feb	17 93	28 62
		John Cherry	10 65	17 80
South Canton....	St. Lawrence	Alvan Ames.......	19 04	37 18
South Chili......	Monroe.....	William Pixley	49 86	90 06
South Columbia..	Herkimer	Jos. L. Hatch	19 60	33 99
South Corinth ...	Saratoga	Bosworth Martin ..	21 25	39 51
South Cortlandt..	Cortlandt....	Darius Sanders	14 61	26 99
South Danby	Tompkins....	Aaron Bennett.....	18 57	34 58
South Dansville ..	Steuben	Aaron W. Beach...	41 86	72 26
South Dickinson .	Franklin ...	Eldred Baker......	2 01	3 52
South Dover.....	Dutchess....	Shandanett Preston.	53 72	97 20
South Durham....	Greene	Peter P. Grant.....	16 90	33 10
South East......	Putnam	Orrin B. Crane, to 3d March	41 31	74 98
		Ebenezer Foster....	17 67	29 53
South Easton	Washington.	Thomas D. Beadle .	31 76	58 72
South Edmeston .	Otsego	Daniel H. Spurr ...	29 28	46 71
South Edwards ..	St. Lawrence	John C. Haile	13 88	23 67
South Franklin ..	Delaware	Ira Parish.........	6 58	9 22
South Granville..	Washington.	Samuel Woodard, to 14th Feb........	18 68	25 34
		Horace Smith......	11 67	14 29
South Hammond.	St. Lawrence	Henry King.......	10 25	19 84
South Hartford ..	Washington.	Jacob Allen	42 22	35 16
South Hill	Steuben	Chaun'y P. Hubbard	6 58	7 87
South Kortright..	Delaware	John S. Andrews ..	33 20	41 39
South Lansing ...	Tompkins...	Daniel D. Minier...	37 53	35 04
South Livonia ...	Livingston ..	Orrin Hastings	50 46	79 34
South Lodi......	Seneca......	John Ingersoll	6 56	9 15
South Marcellus .	Onondaga....	Caleb N. Potter....	8 29	13 99
South Middletown	Orange......	Lewis Vail, to 31st Dec	225 38	211 14
		William Hoyt	173 09	302 70
South New Berlin	Chenango ...	Alva Babcock	59 56	82 59
Southold	Suffolk......	Salter S. Horton ...	61 17	102 36
South Onondaga .	Onondaga ...	Titus J. Fenn......	24 66	46 25
South Otselic	Chenango ...	James Clark, to 31st Dec............	13 91	24 62
		Norman Ford	11 91	22 59
South Owego	Tioga.......	Caleb Lamb.......	4 50	8 33
South Oxford	Chenango ...	Ebenezer Park.....	8 44	16 22
South Oyster Bay	Queens	Timothy Carman ..	31 24	59 75
Southport.......	Chemung ...	Raymond T. Jones.	39 54	78 42
South Pultney ...	Steuben	Lebbeus Drew.....	6 19	10 19
South Richland ..	Oswego......	Stephen Tinker	22 71	38 37

POST OFFICES—*New York.*

Post Offices.	Counties.	Postmasters.	Compensation.	Net proceeds.
South Royalton	Niagara	Sidney B. Bratt	$5 91	$10 99
South Rutland	Jefferson	Simeon Oaks	33 83	57 88
South Salem	West Chester	Gould Hawley	48 08	73 98
South Schodack	Rensselaer	Jos. S. Hare	18 29	30 52
South Sodus	Wayne	Erastus Rogers	42 58	71 48
So'th Stephentown	Rensselaer	Claudius Moffitt	9 79	16 09
South Trenton	Oneida	Ebenezer Thomas	43 97	84 13
South Valley	Otsego	Daniel W. Rice	18 43	32 03
South Venice	Cayuga	Wm. S. Tupper	19 11	33 34
Southville	St. Lawrence	Sprague Livingston	11 03	19 63
South Wales	Erie	David S. Warner	38 96	64 02
South Westerloo	Albany	Thomas Saxton	49 38	79 17
Southwick	Ulster	Isaac Van Vaulkenburgh, to 31st Dec	5 23	8 71
		Gilbert Lefevre	5 87	10 92
South Windsor	Broome	Nathan P. Waller, to 30th Sept	2 30	2 62
		William Purdie	6 35	10 05
South Worcester	Otsego	John B. Strain	17 18	32 77
Spafford	Onondaga	John Collins	42 47	76 49
Spafford Hollow	Onondaga	Wm. O. Farrell	9 40	14 02
Sparta	Livingston	Henry Havens, to 17th Feb	19 11	33 80
		John Culbertson	11 49	21 12
Speedsville	Tompkins	Leroy W. Kingman	45 16	75 48
Spencer	Tioga	Henry Miller	71 10	118 17
Spencerport	Monroe	Charles Church	129 38	221 46
Spencertown	Columbia	Abm. P. Holdridge, to 30th Sept	21 06	37 65
		Chs. B. Dutcher	57 29	104 28
Speonk	Suffolk	Oliver Tuthill	17 61	26 07
Split Rock	Essex	James S. Whallon	18 72	31 91
Spraker's Basin	Montgomery	John L. Bevens	36 64	77 28
Springfield	Otsego	Wm. L. Bigelow	139 82	135 29
Spring Mills	Allegany	William Cobb	16 10	19 98
Springville	Erie	Elisha Mack	157 22	306 89
Spring Water	Livingston	Alva Southworth	84 53	144 84
Sprout Creek	Dutchess	Stephen Thorn	10 39	15 58
Staatsburg	Dutchess	James Russell	18 76	26 10
Stafford	Genesee	Samuel March	121 52	186 78
Stamford	Delaware	Charles Griffin	74 95	105 43
Stanfordville	Dutchess	Wm. H. Stewart	73 91	139 13
Starkey	Yates	Benjamin Tuthill	38 01	60 79
Starkville	Herkimer	John R. Hall	30 73	54 58
State Bridge	Madison	George T. Kirkland	24 01	42 49
Stephentown	Rensselaer	Nathan Howard	52 97	97 87
Sterling	Cayuga	Nathaniel Vilas	61 92	116 21
Sterlingville	Jefferson	James Sterling	33 43	58 26
Steuben	Oneida	Merit Brooks	30 82	60 43

POST OFFICES—*New York.*

Post Offices.	Counties.	Postmasters.	Compensation.	Net proceeds.
Stillwater........	Saratoga	Ashbel Palmer.....	$118 40	$216 66
Stockbridge......	Madison	Henry T. Sumner..	113 42	196 48
Stockholm........	St. Lawrence	Benjamin Holmes, to 18th June.....	37 95	68 11
		Dorus Pettibone....	1 21	2 40
Stockport........	Columbia ...	Philip Von Volkenburgh, to 31st Dec.	82 18	148 95
		Thomas Sedgwick..	83 64	159 60
Stockton........	Chautauque..	Philip Lazell.......	45 20	84 94
Stokes...........	Oneida......	George Hovey, to 31st Dec........	33 17	53 98
		Henry E. Gregory.	26 66	50 19
Stone Arabia.....	Montgomery.	Bernard Getman....	19 86	32 23
Stone Church....	Genesee.....	Martin C. Ward...	31 72	50 22
Stone Mills......	Jefferson.....	Wilson H. Harger..	28 58	54 63
Stone Ridge......	Ulster.......	John H. Wigton, to 26th Nov........	19 99	29 77
		John Lounsbery...	37 11	56 61
Stony Brook......	Suffolk......	James N. Gould....	42 59	72 97
Stony Creek.....	Warren......	Charles Kathan, jr..	6 97	11 42
Stormville.......	Dutchess....	Jacob Tompkins...	27 52	49 86
Stow's Square....	Lewis.......	Charles Davenport..	22 04	34 86
Stratton's Fall....	Delaware....	Ezra W. Stratton, to 30th Sept........	4 79	7 39
		Lewis Stratton, jr..	26 67	38 97
Strykersville.....	Wyoming...	Hez'h B. Rounds...	44 43	68 18
Stuyvesant.......	Columbia....	John S. Vosburgh, to 30th May.....	65 20	118 66
		Alexander Bidwell..	4 78	8 42
Stuyvesant Falls..	Columbia....	Edwin M. Coventry	53 50	93 26
Success.........	Suffolk......	John Luce.........	8 18	10 93
Suffolk..........	Suffolk......	George Halsey.....	85 86	147 20
Sugar Hill.......	Steuben.....	Archibald Scobey..	6 41	10 95
Sugar Loaf......	Orange......	Edgar Wells.......	22 07	41 60
Sullivan.........	Madison	Ebenezer Haseltine.	50 76	88 16
Summer Hill.....	Cayuga......	Ralph Barber, to 21st Dec............	32 01	53 50
		Hiram Baker......	34 37	60 47
Summit.........	Schoharie ...	Isaac W. Baird.....	27 32	43 10
Susquehannah ...	Broome......	William Doolittle...	19 31	23 94
Sweden..........	Monroe......	Ralph A. Gillett, to 18th April.......	53 44	97 38
		Samuel M. Olden...	13 86	25 37
Syracuse........	Onondaga ...	Henry Raynor.....	1953 87	5551 75
Taberg..........	Oneida......	R. Hyde, to 7th Nov.	42 41	62 62
		Julius C. Thorne...	53 84	99 06
Taghkanick	Columbia....	Cornelius Whitbeck, from 11th Oct....	4 74	9 62

POST OFFICES—*New York.*

Post Offices.	Counties.	Postmasters.	Compensation.	Net proceeds.
Tannersville	Greene	Egbert Vosburgh, to 4th Feb	$18 54	$32 40
		Samuel P. Perkins	11 94	22 32
Tappantown	Rockland	Morris Bartow, to 23d Sept	1 86	3 53
		Thos. B. Blauvelt, to 18th Jan	4 94	8 67
		Wm. Devoe, from 22d Jan	7 61	11 94
Tarrytown	West Chester	Jacob Odell	232 98	414 59
Ten Mile Spring	Cattaraugus	Ab'm M. Casler	7 53	13 56
Texas	Oswego	Hiram Parker	12 02	23 68
The Corner	Ulster	Ab'm D. Ladew	11 06	18 88
The Glen	Warren	Christian Whitaker, from 21st Dec'r	6 44	10 04
The Purchase	West Chester	James T. Carpenter	23 40	43 78
Theresa	Jefferson	John D. Davison	66 56	121 90
The Square	Cayuga	Peter Van Keuren	22 48	29 76
Thompsonville	Sullivan	Jonathan Stratton	8 40	16 44
Three Mile Bay	Jefferson	Seth P. E. Powers, to 21st Dec	34 37	60 24
		Henry Cline	43 62	75 49
Throopsville	Cayuga	Ludlow Williams	59 68	109 70
Ticonderoga	Essex	George R. Andrews	191 79	367 41
Tioga	Tioga	John Y. Smith	3 91	6 61
Tioga Centre	Tioga	William Ransom	31 55	30 69
Tivoli	Dutchess	James Outwater	205 38	222 20
Tobehanna	Steuben	Abel Kendall	18 54	30 61
Tomhannock	Rensselaer	James Mosher	47 92	85 19
Tompkinsville	Richmond	Edward Thompson	144 57	308 38
Tonawanda	Erie	Jacob Kibler	93 84	170 27
Towlesville	Steuben	Richard Towle	12 14	19 28
Towners	Putnam	James Towner	26 83	43 80
Town Line	Erie	Henry Clark	26 37	43 01
Townsend	Chemung	Samuel C. Swim	9 92	16 47
Townsendville	Seneca	John McLallen, jr	37 94	59 18
Trenton	Oneida	John Billings	134 13	203 73
Trenton Falls	Oneida	David W. Bacon	28 10	51 01
Triangle	Broome	Edward G. Kinney, to 3d March	20 63	36 02
		Wesley Jackson	12 95	24 13
Tripes' Hill	Montgomery	Fisher Putman	44 39	74 15
Troupsburgh	Steuben	Charles Card	17 68	23 35
Troy	Rensselaer	George R. Davis	980 20	10055 38
Trumansburgh	Tompkins	Lyman Strobridge	228 55	440 27
Truxton	Cortlandt	Alanson Coats	196 57	221 83
Tully	Onondaga	Henry F. King	77 75	123 91
Tully Valley	Onondaga	Job T. Irish	12 24	21 84

POST OFFICES—*New York.*

Post Offices.	Counties.	Postmasters.	Compensation.	Net proceeds.
TunungwantMills	Cattaraugus..	Ferdin'd E. Perkins, to 30th Sept.....	$0 61	$1 38
		Ira Rice...........	2 98	5 75
Turin...........	Lewis........	Orrin Woolworth...	169 99	157 90
Turners.........	Orange.......	Elmore Earl.......	17 66	33 64
Tuscarora........	Livingston...	Elias G. Kinne.....	33 34	58 05
Tuthill..........	Ulster........	Jos. O. Hasbrouck..	29 34	47 74
Twelve Corners.. (Ch'd to "Niles.")	Cayuga......	Roswell Johnson, to 9th April........	6 66	12 07
Tyler...........	Onondaga....	Wheeler Truesdale.	31 75	50 59
Tyre............	Seneca.......	Jason Smith.......	35 79	66 72
Tyrone	Steuben	Stephen H. Arnold.	97 97	171 27
Ulsterville.......	Ulster.......	Selah Otis.........	34 29	52 67
Unadilla.........	Otsego.......	George H. Noble...	242 09	217 19
Unadilla Centre..	Otsego.......	Ebenezer Gregory..	19 79	35 76
Unadilla Forks...	Otsego.......	Henry H. Babcock.	50 82	88 25
Union...........	Broome......	Eph'm Robbins, jr..	124 08	133 02
Union Corners...	Livingston...	Ruth Youngs......	24 85	44 30
Union Ellery	Chautauque..	Odin Benedict......	31 56	56 92
Union Falls......	Clinton......	Henry Frizill, to 30th Sept........	3 53	7 70
		Philip Neher.......	7 28	14 39
Union Mills......	Fulton	William Clarke....	44 77	57 67
Union Settlement.	Oswego......	Silas Penoyer......	7 03	9 82
Union Society....	Greene.......	Albert Parsons.....	9 27	15 72
Union Springs...	Cayuga......	Fred'k P. Cone....	260 60	319 97
Union Square....	Oswego......	Avery Skinner......	32 40	59 14
Union Village....	Broome......	Cyrus Salisbury....	21 79	34 09
Unionville.......	Orange.......	Joseph Chandler...	23 37	46 61
Upper Aquebogue	Suffolk......	Bartlett Griffing, jr..	17 80	28 87
Upper Jay....... (Late "Ausable.")	Essex........	Benj'n Wells, from 1st Oct..........	7 43	14 99
Upper Lisle......	Broome......	George Wheeler....	27 15	45 65
Upper Red Hook.	Dutchess....	John V. A. Lyle, to 27th Jan........	29 90	52 47
		Henry Benner, jr., to 31st March....	8 10	17 59
		Gottlob Haas......	12 93	21 67
Urbana..........	Steuben.....	Arunah M. Adsit, to 10th Jan.........	66 99	126 21
		Martin H. Rose....	77 72	143 77
Utica	Oneida......	Augustine G. Dauby	1328 54	8551 90
Uxbridge........	Montgomery.	J. P. Yates........	4 21	6 25
Vails' Mills......	Fulton	Bradf'd T. Simmons	22 35	32 64
Valatie..........	Columbia....	John H. Corning...	167 68	309 29
Vallonia Springs.	Broome.....	Lucian Stowell.....	4 49	7 49

POST OFFICES—New York.

Post Offices.	Counties.	Postmasters.	Compensation.	Net proceeds.
Van Buren	Onondaga	Asahel K. Clark, to 6th May	$20 12	$38 28
		Hezekiah R. Dow	3 86	7 07
Van Buren Centre	Onondaga	Jonathan Skinner	21 51	31 32
Van Buren Harb'r	Chautauque	Heman S. Stearns	13 91	28 20
Van Burenville	Orange	Isaac B. Everett	7 68	13 90
Vandermark	Allegany	Alexander Black	3 56	6 86
Van Ettenville	Chemung	Dan'l C. Van Etten	21 14	39 71
Vanhornesville	Herkimer	Daniel Van Horne	47 07	82 08
Varick	Seneca	John Y. Gambee	18 07	34 76
Varna	Tompkins	William Scutt, 2d	52 32	52 17
Varysburgh	Wyoming	Charles Wilder	32 58	55 89
Venice	Cayuga	Ezra W. Bateman	41 20	73 05
Verbank	Dutchess	John G. Greene	20 73	39 99
Vermillion	Oswega	Seneca V. Bryant	10 42	14 59
Vermont	Chautauque	Sidney E. Palmer	29 10	44 28
Vernal	Wyoming	Orrin Collins	10 35	20 12
Vernon	Oneida	J. Whipple Jenkins	218 33	440 61
Vernon Centre	Oneida	Nath'l S. Wright, to 25th Feb	48 19	84 69
		Jay Pettibone	25 74	44 84
Verona	Oneida	Geo. T. Peckham	109 07	195 92
Verplank	West Chester	Wm. Bleakley, jr	33 87	64 42
Versailles	Cattaraugus	Alex'r H. Barker	41 12	73 87
Vesper	Onondaga	Charles Tallman	20 32	35 01
Vestal	Broome	Daniel Foster	24 28	41 56
Veteran	Chemung	Wm. Van Duzer	12 20	22 30
Victor	Ontario	William C. Dryer	282 35	331 84
Victory	Cayuga	De Witt C. Miller	100 88	179 48
Vienna	Oneida	Lyman Bridges, to 10th Oct	10 19	19 27
		Amos S. Fassett	30 16	52 46
Villanova	Chautauque	Villeray Balcom	29 66	59 29
Virgil	Cortlandt	John Chamberlain	54 72	105 37
Vischer's Ferry	Saratoga	William Shepherd	35 39	59 82
Vista	West Chester	Wm. M. Crissey	11 85	20 18
Volney	Oswego	Samuel Griswold	56 79	95 54
Volusia	Chautauque	John Howard	5 47	10 06
Waddington	St. Lawrence	Henry W. Pratt, to 21st May	160 68	298 04
		Francis Fenton	18 57	39 91
Wadham's Mills	Essex	Jos. R. Delano	32 55	58 92
Wading River	Suffolk	Sylvester Miller	15 99	25 28
Walden	Orange	James Kidd, to 10th May	69 08	136 16
		Marcus K. Hill	12 83	26 16
Waldensville	Schoharie	Hiram Walden	6 46	10 13
Wales	Erie	James Wood	55 67	101 07

15*

POST OFFICES—*New York.*

Post Offices.	Counties.	Postmasters.	Compensation.	Net proceeds.
Wales Centre	Erie	Mort'r W. Stevens.	$23 56	$40 29
Walesville	Oneida	Nathan Foster, from 1st April	98	1 93
Walton	Delaware	Amos N. Wheeler	94 69	157 58
Walworth	Wayne	Theron G. Yeomans	98 42	191 55
Wampsville	Madison	Thos. T. Loomis	123 23	214 03
Wappinger's C'k.	Dutchess	E. D. Sweet, to 23d November	47 83	94 59
		Joseph Blackburn	74 90	155 11
Warren	Herkimer	William Kinne	104 71	97 24
Warrensburgh	Warren	Stephen Griffin, 2d.	138 72	135 34
Warsaw	Wyoming	Wm. K. Crooks	360 99	539 37
Warwick	Orange	Milton McEwen	119 71	196 30
Washington	Dutchess	Stephen Haight, to 3d December	29 92	50 71
		Ephraim Pray	44 85	88 21
Wash'ton Hollow	Dutchess	Josa. S. Simmons	35 81	75 83
Waterboro'	Chautauque	Zebina H. Wheeler.	11 92	13 53
Waterburgh	Tompkins	Lewis W. Owen	29 02	40 93
Waterford	Saratoga	Jas. I. Scott	397 23	796 50
Waterloo	Seneca	Franklin Gage	632 70	1301 63
Waterport	Orleans	Harmon Goodrich, from 17th March.	4 89	6 27
Watertown	Jefferson	John F. Hutchinson	1037 24	2370 76
Watervale	Onondaga	Ira Curtiss	24 90	39 61
Water Valley	Erie	Sterling Mallory	34 67	58 23
Waterville	Oneida	Ch's C. Bacon, to 30th November	142 63	191 15
		Miller Babbott	185 87	240 38
Waterv'e Corners	Erie	Abner Willson	3 02	5 88
Watervliet	Albany	Edward Learned, jr.	588 72	1337 69
Watervliet Centre.	Albany	Lewis Morris, to 17th January	17 73	33 81
		Peter B. Noxon	15 86	29 06
Watson	Lewis	Nelson J. Beach	14 58	27 28
Wawarsing	Ulster	Calvin Hoornbeck	53 11	94 88
Wayne	Steuben	John B. Mitchell, jr., to 31st December.	31 80	57 57
		Joseph Evland	33 63	62 52
Webster	Monroe	Oliver Reynolds	92 93	168 97
Weedsport	Cayuga	Orlando Gallt, to 19th December	156 27	168 97
		Dexter E. Havens	118 33	229 19
Wellington	Onondaga	Joel B. Bennett	30 96	49 90
Wells	Hamilton	Wm. R. Weld	11 19	21 74
Wellsburgh	Chemung	Abner Wells	11 95	12 69
Wells' Corner	Orange	John L. Knap, 3 qrs	18 03	29 48
Wellsville	Allegany	George B. Jones	36 41	65 08
West Addison	Steuben	Rowland Saunders	16 53	29 97

POST OFFICES—*New York.*

Post Offices.	Counties.	Postmasters.	Compensation.	Net proceeds.
West Almond..	Allegany.....	Rowland Carrington	$22 86	$39 76
West Bergen....	Genesee.....	Jas. D. Doolittle....	20 46	33 85
West Bloomfield.	Ontario......	Enoch A. Hall.....	207 52	351 21
West Branch....	Oneida.......	Richard Dopp......	18 64	30 85
West Brookville.	Sullivan.....	Abrah'm Westbrook	7 49	14 83
West Burlington.	Otsego......	Truman Moss, to 6th January.........	21 94	20 94
		Curtis Hemingway.	21 85	29 62
West Butler.....	Wayne	Smith Barnum.....	13 31	23 83
West Camden...	Oneida......	Manning Barnes, to 31st January......	6 82	14 12
		A. W. Barnes......	5 79	10 52
West Camp.....	Ulster........	Henry Dederick....	29 03	51 63
West Candor....	Tioga........	Ira Woodford......	9 13	15 82
West Carlton....	Orleans.......	George Kuck......	41 59	69 36
West Catlin.....	Chemung....	Gardner Crum, to 28th January,....	9 66	20 27
		Ralph Shephard....	14 26	20 83
West Cayuta....	Chemung....	Le Roy Wood.....	10 81	19 87
West Charlton...	Saratoga	Finley McMartin...	38 81	66 09
West Chateaugay (Changed to "Burke.")	Franklin	Hiram Miner, to 31st December........	7 80	14 40
West Chazy.....	Clinton.......	Ira P. Chamberlain.	37 22	59 06
West Chester...	West Chester	Sidney B. Bowne...	208 94	382 11
West Clarksville.	Allegany.....	Martin Butts, to 31st March..........	4 71	7 47
		Anson Congdon....	2 24	4 30
West Conesus..	Livingston...	Elnathan P. Foster.	8 35	14 08
West Constable..	Franklin	Dan'l P. Brigham, to 30th November..	17 47	25 30
		Charles Johnson...	31 87	31 89
West Davenport.	Delaware....	Cornelius Miller....	20 60	20 48
West Day.......	Saratoga	Zophar I. De Long.	9 74	19 50
West Dresden...	Yates........	William Holden....	65 07	120 12
West Dryden....	Tompkins...	John S. Barber.....	22 19	35 81
West Edmeston..	Otsego......	Eph. Chamberlain, jr	47 52	71 63
Westerlo.......	Albany......	Jeremiah Green....	64 20	105 08
Westernville.....	Oneida.......	Milton Brayton	114 97	210 42
West Exeter....	Otsego......	W. C. Chamberlain.	17 31	29 06
West Farmington.	Ontario......	Perez Hathaway...	23 07	38 12
West Farms.....	West Chester	Alexander Smith...	201 05	404 51
West Fayette....	Seneca.......	Samuel Gambie....	31 15	55 65
Westfield.......	Chautauque..	Orvis Nichols......	324 53	567 03
Westford.......	Otsego......	George Skinner....	52 88	86 71
West Gaines....	Orleans......	Isaac V. Saunders..	35 78	50 58
W't Galway Ch'h	Fulton.......	James Hayes, jr....	66 21	114 27
West Genesee...	Allegany.....	William Ennis.....	5 37	8 56
West Greece....	Monroe......	Lyman Granger....	24 96	46 16
West Greenfield..	Saratoga	Howell Gardner....	43 57	75 13

POST OFFICES—*New York.*

Post Offices.	Counties.	Postmasters.	Compensation.	Net proceeds.
West Groton....	Tompkins....	Cicero Phelps......	$24 66	$45 25
West Harpersfield	Delaware....	Roswell Hotchkiss.	14 71	25 44
West Hebron....	Washington..	Wm. J. Bockes.....	40 21	75 40
West Hempstead.	Rockland....	George Concklin...	7 09	11 13
West Henrietta..	Monroe.....	Chauncey Chapman	58 73	99 12
West Hills......	Suffolk.......	Aaron Oakley......	17 16	24 44
West Hinsdale...	Cattaraugus..	Wm. S. Pitcher....	6 56	12 00
West Hurley....	Ulster........	Humphrey Jewell..	5 24	7 99
West Kill......	Greene......	Corydon Bushnell..	30 60	51 45
West Lexington.	Greene......	Conger Avery, to 13th July........	11	26
		James Peck........	5 13	11 07
West Leyden....	Lewis........	Rich'son T. Hough.	26 08	46 91
West Linklean...	Chenango ...	Sam'l S. Lord......	13 17	23 71
West Lowville...	Lewis........	Amasa Dodge, jr...	9 32	18 14
W't Martinsburgh	Lewis........	Jervis Salmon......	35 19	62 52
West Meredith..	Delaware....	Martin Leet.......	37 71	36 86
West Milton....	Saratoga	Aaron Freeman....	42 78	77 44
West Monroe....	Oswego	Henry J. Jewell....	15 13	25 02
Westmoreland...	Oneida	Abm. H. Halleck...	141 46	254 98
West Niles......	Cayuga	Samuel Chandler...	14 37	26 32
West Oneonta ...	Otsego......	Samuel Derby.....	11 56	19 16
West Pennfield... (Chan'd to "West Webster.")	Monroe......	Benj. S. Whitehead, to 30th September	7 37	12 48
West Perth......	Fulton......	William Rob......	4 30	5 84
West Plattsburgh.	Clinton......	Nathan A. Vaughan	13 12	22 39
West Point......	Orange......	Claudius Berard....	957 15	2219 71
Westport........	Essex.......	Charles B. Hatch...	114 39	193 42
West Richmond. (Chan'd to "Richmond Mills.")	Ontario......	Silas Reed, to 22d January..........	22 20	40 63
West Rush......	Monroe......	Darwin E. Goodnow	39 78	70 53
West Sand Lake.	Rensselaer ..	Adam Cipperley....	58 16	91 44
West Schuyler...	Herkimer ...	Warren D. Cain, to 31st December...	19 60	35 56
		Horace H. Knapp..	13 79	28 09
West Somers....	West Chester	Ebenezer Frost.....	14 02	24 08
W't Stephentown.	Rensselaer ..	Daniel Allen.......	13 19	23 17
West Stockholm.	St. Lawrence.	Auletus M. Sanford.	30 02	61 07
West Taghkanic.	Columbia....	Hiram Lapham.....	12 13	22 76
West Town......	Orange......	Henry C. Halsey..	37 64	62 74
W't Troupsburgh	Steuben......	Charles Bishop, jr., to 31st December.	6 01	11 01
		Matthias Marlatt...	7 38	12 18
West Vienna.....	Oneida.......	Silas Jewell........	15 28	27 69
Westville........	Otsego.......	John A. Oliver.....	12 49	21 24
West Walworth.	Wayne	Wm. D. Wylie....	24 53	41 27
West Webster... (Late "West Pennfield.")	Monroe......	Benj. S. Whitehead, from 1st October..	22 09	39 08
Wt Williamstown	Oswego	Samuel Freeman....	7 12	12 39

POST OFFICES—*New York.*

Post Offices.	Counties.	Postmasters.	Compensation.	Net proceeds.
West Windsor...	Broome......	Charles Rose......	$18 08	$30 33
West Winfield..	Herkimer ...	David R. Carrier...	123 38	120 96
Wethersfield.....	Wyoming...	Horace Gibbs, to 30th September..	3 96	6 44
		John N. Smith, from 8th October......	14 50	25 39
WethersfieldSp'gs	Wyoming...	Eli Rood..........	28 73	49 33
Wheatland......	Monroe......	Clark Hall.........	50 24	102 97
Wheeler........	Steuben......	Ephraim Aulls.....	31 29	52 64
White Creek....	Washington..	Stephen Barker.....	39 26	75 97
White Hall......	Washington..	Wm. H. Kirtland, to 21st October.....	268 50	366 91
		Atherton Hall......	501 42	943 64
White Lake.....	Sullivan.....	John Morrison, to 15th February...	22 63	34 57
		Simeon M. Jordon..	14 49	25 59
White Plains....	West Chester	William Horton, 2d, to 31st December.	132 02	277 22
		Elijah Guion.......	129 54	286 18
Whiteside's Cor's	Saratoga	John Whiteside, f'm 10th July.........	7 32	13 05
White's Store....	Chenango ...	George Curtis......	11 09	20 04
Whitestown	Oneida	Morris M. Berry, to 31st May.........	308 28	675 82
		Whiting Smith.....	19 21	48 11
Whitesville......	Allegany.....	Micajah J. N. Haskins, to 8th Oct...	9 89	20 18
		Dugald C. White...	23 71	46 20
Whitlocksville...	West Chester	Wright M. Beyea..	17 17	33 26
Whitney's Point.	Broome......	John D. Smith.....	48 90	83 50
Whitney's Valley	Allegany.....	Joseph Leonard....	20 68	33 70
Willet..........	Cortlandt....	John S. Dyer......	18 12	30 54
Williamsburgh...	Kings........	Chauncey L. Cooke	233 82	536 60
Williamson......	Wayne	Wm. J. Stoutenburg	78 85	139 30
Williamstown ...	Oswego	Jacob Cromwell....	65 22	108 97
Williamsville	Erie........	Joseph Hutchinson.	131 76	239 95
Willink	Erie........	Erastus Wallis.....	194 25	365 29
Willsboro'.......	Essex.......	Levi Higby, jr.....	42 92	81 60
Willseyville......	Tioga.......	Jacob Willsey.....	16 23	17 21
Wilmington	Essex.......	Harvey Carter.....	18 85	37 32
Wilmut.........	Herkimer ...	Gardiner Hinckley.	6 71	11 09
Wilna	Jefferson	Henry Reis........	25 00	51 05
Wilson's........	Niagara	Luther Wilson.....	80 04	137 26
Wilton..........	Saratoga	Lyndes Emerson...	34 88	63 71
Windfall	Onondaga ...	David Preston.....	13 09	18 76
Windham.......	Greene......	Nathaniel Ormsbee.	23 03	41 54
Windham Centre.	Greene......	Jon'n M. Matthews.	124 35	200 34
Windsor........	Broome......	Benj. H. Russell...	114 44	193 51
Winfield	Herkimer ...	Benjamin Carver...	77 81	74 19

POST OFFICES—*New Jersey.*

Post Offices.	Counties.	Postmasters.	Compensation.	Net proceeds.
Wolcott	Wayne	John C. Watkins, to 10th April	$127 53	$224 90
		Geo. H. Arne	37 85	68 93
Woodbourne	Sullivan	Jno. W. Buckmaster	31 82	55 11
Woodhall	Steuben	Alfred Smith, to 31st December	16 70	29 96
		Hamilton Marlatt	16 75	29 78
Woodstock	Ulster	Wm. H. De Forest	24 74	44 32
Woodville	Jefferson	Augustus V. Wood	32 75	55 62
Woodwardsville	Essex	Amasa Willis	3 72	5 97
Worcester	Otsego	Sam'l S. Burnside	51 49	92 96
Wormley's	Steuben	Jacob Robbins	16 37	30 34
Wrightsburgh	St. Lawrence	Ralph Chamberlin	3 30	6 36
Wright's Corners	Niagara	Solomon C. Wright	44 74	88 95
Wurtsboro'	Sullivan	Wm. B. Hammond, to 20th May	59 27	108 37
		Isaac J. Rundle	7 22	11 48
Wynantskille	Rensselaer	Henry Frazee	31 97	38 47
Wyoming	Wyoming	Wm. B. Collar	134 38	235 62
Yaphank	Suffolk	Robert H. Gerard, from 24th Feb	5 43	10 10
Yates	Orleans	Peter Saxe	158 50	269 26
Yatesville	Yates	Baxter Hobart	18 85	26 03
Yonkers	West Chester	John Bashford	163 86	317 70
York	Livingston	Neil Stewart, to 15th May	144 38	269 78
		David McDonald	18 68	33 21
Yorkshire	Cattaraugus	Lewis Marsh	51 99	91 10
Yorktown	West Chester	Jas. H. Purdy	42 82	72 21
Youngstown	Niagara	Harry W. Phillips, to 15th February	158 79	256 72
		John Ladd	112 36	180 51
Zoar	Erie	Jehiel Hill	5 82	10 43

NEW JERSEY.

NOTE.—Compensation of Postmasters, and net proceeds of their offices, from July 1, 1844, to June 30, 1845.

Post Offices.	Counties.	Postmasters.	Compensation.	Net proceeds.
Absecombe	Atlantic	Jonathan Pitney	$16 15	$28 71
Allamuchy	Warren	I. Harris, to 30th Sept	9 44	17 00

POST OFFICES—*New Jersey*.

Post Offices.	Counties.	Postmasters.	Compensation.	Net proceeds.
Allentown	Monmouth	Andrew W. Tillman	$22 15	$40 85
		William Imlay, to 31st Dec.	50 52	76 42
		A. Alex'r Howell	50 50	78 69
Allowaystown	Salem	Samuel Craig	51 81	82 69
Anderson	Warren	John G. Johnston	27 72	45 70
Andover	Sussex	Richard W. Iliff	20 99	33 66
Aquackanock	Passaic	Richard Morrell	39 93	83 32
Arneytown	Burlington	John Darby	18 40	30 47
Asbury	Warren	Edwin T. Disosway	48 15	72 50
Augusta	Sussex	Wm. H. Roe	20 24	30 57
Baptistown	Hunterdon	And. B. Rittenhouse, to 5th May	14 55	23 90
		Albertus K. Wagner	1 99	2 93
Bargaintown	Atlantic	Mark Lake	16 47	27 54
Barnegat	Monmouth	Wm. D. Oliphant	13 91	27 77
Barnsboro'	Gloucester	And. H. Weatherby from 29th Jan.	93	1 70
Baskenridge	Somerset	Elias H. Dayton	40 11	70 85
Bass River Hotel	Burlington	Isaiah Adams, to 31st March	12 57	20 36
		Recompence Darby	4 04	8 08
Beatyestown	Warren	James Fisher	6 23	11 41
Beekman's Mills	Somerset	Charles Corle	11 47	17 68
Beemerville	Sussex	Gable. L. Dunning	21 65	39 99
Belleville	Essex	John C. Lloyd	202 50	435 73
Belvidere	Warren	Henry D. Swayze, to 30th Nov.	87 23	177 08
		John R. Hamilton	130 60	269 41
Bergen	Hudson	John Tise	39 12	83 41
Berkshire Valley	Morris	John Hardy	22 72	46 15
Bethlehem	Hunterdon	Edwin N. Ball, from 3d July	17 91	32 38
Bevans	Sussex	James C. Bevans	6 32	9 59
Blackwoodtown (Late "Good Intent.")	Camden	Geo. E. Braddock, from 5th Feb.	12 88	24 43
Blairstown	Warren	John J. Blair, to 3d Feb'y	15 60	24 76
		John Drishbaugh, to 20th Feb'y.	1 13	1 97
		John J. Blair	9 96	17 63
Blawenburgh	Somerset	Cornelius S. Stryker	26 35	41 47
Bloomfield	Essex	Benjamin Church	114 09	222 01
Bloomsbury	Warren	William Allshouse	42 28	70 82
Bordentown	Burlington	Thomas T. Bleyler, (1 qr.)	74 54	159 16
		Edward Robbins, fr. 14th April	54 64	121 34

POST OFFICES—*New Jersey.*

Post Offices.	Counties.	Postmasters.	Compensation.	Net proceeds.
Bound Brook....	Somerset.....	John H. Voorhees..	$85 77	$160 32
Branchville.......	Sussex......	William Lewis.....	64 25	83 37
Bridgeport.......	Gloucester....	John Sweeten......	8 59	15 02
Bridgeton	Cumberland .	Jer. H. Lupton, to 19th Jan........	123 31	249 29
		Dan'l B. Thompson	97 82	195 04
Bridgeville........	Warren.....	George Titman.....	8 37	17 33
Burlington.......	Burlington...	Budd Sterling......	630 33	1326 19
Caldwell	Essex........	Jonathan Provost...	54 22	101 44
Camden.........	Camden......	James Elwell......	266 11	637 03
Camptown	Essex.......	Matthias W. Ross..	65 93	126 08
Canton...........	Salem	George Githens....	9 17	15 51
Cape Island......	Cape May...	Jonas Miller.......	183 46	202 86
Cape May.......	Cape May...	John M. Hand.....	45 32	90 55
Carpenter's Landing	Gloucester....	Charles Clark......	21 10	34 81
Cedar Creek.....	Monmouth...	William Aumack...	13 05	25 44
Cedarville.........	Cumberland .	Rich'd D. Bateman.	38 07	66 40
Centreton	Salem	Thomas Whitaker, from 26th July to 16th Oct.........	2 55	4 59
		Lorenzo Lawrence .	7 52	13 53
Centreville.......	Hunterdon ..	Runkle Rea........	17 30	24 49
Chatham........	Morris......	Paul Day, to 19th Feb'y..........	25 07	46 70
		Wm. R. McDougall	15 08	28 80
Chester	Morris......	David S. De Camp.	54 56	102 33
Chew's Landing..	Camden.....	Joshua Sickler.....	8 21	17 04
Cinnaminson	Burlington...	Abraham Lippincott	23 20	36 90
Clarksboro'.......	Gloucester...	Samuel Sailor......	19 11	38 02
Clarksburgh.....	Monmouth. .	Addi Mount, to 10th May.............	7 07	12 56
		Charles Allen......	0 77	1 54
Clarkville.........	Hunterdon ..	Wm. A. A. Hunt..	7 37	14 54
Clinton...........	Hunterdon ..	Adam Stiger.......	85 86	152 64
Clove............	Sussex......	John B. Decker....	2 99	4 96
Clover Hill......	Hunterdon ..	George W. Nevius.	9 42	21 92
Cold Spring.....	Cape May...	Ezekiel Stevens....	31 46	28 54
Colt's Neck......	Monmouth...	Tunis Statesir......	14 54	26 37
Columbia	Warren......	Jno. J. Vankirk....	21 23	31 50
Columbus.......	Burlington...	Jno. W. Wright...	50 96	92 81
Coursenville.....	Sussex......	Henry J. Coursen..	2 85	6 34
Cranberry.......	Middlesex....	Frs. H. Holmes....	54 83	99 32
Cross Keys......	Camden.....	Joseph Nicholson..	14 61	29 39
Crosswicks......	Burlington...	Robert Vanderbeck.	58 96	95 31
Danville	Warren.....	Daniel Van Buskirk	21 60	39 91
Davison.........	Warren.....	John Davison......	7 64	13 71

POST OFFICES—*New Jersey.*

Post Offices.	Counties.	Postmasters.	Compensation.	Net proceeds.
Deckertown	Sussex	Jonathan Whitaker	$95 60	$163 68
Deerfield Street	Cumberland	George Benson	25 37	47 11
Dennis Creek	Cape May	Jacob Souder	52 82	100 52
Dividing Creek	Cumberland	John McIntosh, to 31st March	12 26	16 58
		Samuel Sloan	3 08	4 99
Dover	Morris	Jacob Lossey	85 44	167 68
Drakestown	Morris	Jesse M. Sharp	12 29	18 11
East Creek	Cape May	John Wilson	10 23	18 93
Eatontown	Monmouth	John P. Lewis	46 99	85 81
Elizabethport	Essex	Josiah Q. Stearns	46 95	91 78
Elizabethtown	Essex	Thos. B. C. Dayton	545 32	1039 53
Elmer	Salem	John Johnson	8 77	12 40
English Neighborhood	Bergen	Wm. H. Tracy	17 18	36 18
Englishtown	Monmouth	Moses S. McChesney	29 46	51 50
Evesham	Burlington	Samuel Swain	35 36	72 15
Fairton	Cumberland	Dan'l L. Burt	21 53	36 55
Finesville	Warren	Osmyn Lewis, from 8th Mar. to 8th June	1 95	3 01
Fishing Creek	Cape May	Leonard Cummings	8 58	16 97
Flaggtown	Somerset	Nicholas Williamson	15 68	28 51
Flanders	Morris	Rhece Nicholas	18 13	34 03
Flatbrookville	Sussex	Jacob Smith	5 51	10 19
Flemington	Hunterdon	Geo. W. Risler	183 31	286 26
Forked River	Monmouth	Dan'l P. Pierson	6 67	13 89
Franklin Furnace	Sussex	Wm. L. Ames, (3 qrs.)	34 13	54 76
Franklinville	Gloucester	John R. Graham, to 30th Sept	1 88	3 07
		John McClintock	6 87	11 56
Fredon	Sussex	Isaac V. Courson	11 16	20 52
Freehold	Monmouth	William Lloyd, jr.	218 26	386 88
Frenchtown	Hunterdon	Lewis F. Laroche	11 65	21 61
German Valley	Morris	Jacob M. Hager	41 79	73 43
Glassboro'	Gloucester	Woodward Warrick	59 70	93 77
Glou'ster Furnace	Atlantic	John Richards	5 06	9 95
Good Intent (Ch'd to "Blackwoodtown," Camden Co.)	Gloucester	John L. Cooper, to 5th Feb'y	22 53	39 51
Goshen	Cape May	James Mcguire	14 87	26 53
Gratitude	Sussex	John Hunt, jr.	11 92	24 23
Greenville	Sussex	Isaac Shiner	8 12	14 28
Greenwich	Cumberland	Francis Bacon, to 31st March	27 70	41 80
		Seeley Shute	8 58	13 25

POST OFFICES—*New Jersey.*

Post Offices.	Counties.	Postmasters.	Compensation.	Net proceeds.
Griggstown	Somerset	Abraham Veghte	$15 74	$25 64
Hackensack	Bergen	David D. Demarest.	96 35	189 25
Hackettstown	Warren	Robert Rusling, to 17th Aug.	9 94	15 53
		Jesse Smith	88 19	144 21
Haddonfield	Camden	Enoch Clements	78 66	154 23
Hainesville. (Late "Sandyston.")	Sussex	John A. Westbrook, from 1st Jan'y to 15th Feb'y.	3 39	3 41
		Isaiah V. Shay	9 24	9 26
Hamburgh	Sussex	Robt. A. Linn	79 31	137 58
Hamilton Square.	Mercer	William Tindall, fr. 7th Sept	4 47	7 52
Hammonton.	Atlantic.	William Coffin, to 19th Nov	5 85	9 44
		Edw'd W. Coffin	9 91	17 64
Hancock's Bridge	Salem	Dalymore Harris	7 31	13 64
Hanover	Morris.	William McFarlan.	33 22	67 13
Hanover Neck	Morris.	James Ely	18 46	39 23
Harlingen	Somerset	W. R. S. Williamson	25 66	43 14
Harmony	Warren	Henry Teel	30 28	54 10
Harmony Vale	Sussex	Andrew Linn	3 06	5 34
Harrisonville	Gloucester	Sam. H. Weatherby	28 79	33 54
Hightstown	Mercer	Israel C. Purdy	90 61	155 89
Hoboken	Hudson	Calvin Mulford	63 34	132 88
Holmdel	Monmouth	Robert W. Cook	35 55	59 83
Hope	Warren	Peter W. Blair	66 92	107 97
Hopewell	Mercer	Jon. V. Blackwell, to 31st March	15 44	22 59
		Jacob S. Weart	6 93	10 35
Howell Works	Monmouth	James P. Smith	13 75	26 93
Imlaystown	Monmouth	Sid'y C. Woodward	31 13	49 52
Jackson's Mills. (Dis. 4th June.)	Monmouth	Benjamin Mathews.	(no ret.)	
Jacksonville	Burlington	Samuel Fort	14 39	20 01
Jersey City	Hudson	David Smith	728 00	1890 32
Jobstown	Burlington	Benjamin Kemble	15 35	21 37
Johnsonburgh	Warren	Isaac Dennis, to 6th Feb	22 53	33 31
		Isaac J. Durling	11 77	21 98
Juliustown	Burlington	Samuel Smith	10 36	16 28
Keyport	Monmouth	Henry H. Seabrook	42 02	74 59
Kingston	Middlesex	Aaron S. Longstreet	44 28	87 03
Kingwood	Hunterdon	Francis Tomlinson	18 74	31 21
Klinesville	Hunterdon	Henry M. Kline	2 56	4 10

POST OFFICES—*New Jersey.*

Post Offices.	Counties.	Postmasters.	Compensation.	Net proceeds.
Knowlton	Warren	Thomas Fisher	$3 76	$7 85
La Fayette	Sussex	Alexander Boyles	47 74	89 44
Lambertsville	Hunterdon	John Lilly	153 43	276 51
Lawrenceville	Mercer	Charles Van Cleve	115 07	232 60
Lebanon	Hunterdon	Samuel Clark, to 13th Feb.	20 05	34 81
		Garret Servis	13 48	25 33
Leeds' Point	Atlantic	Japheth Leeds	15 57	27 61
Leedsville	Monmouth	Samuel T. Holmes	30 13	57 85
Leesburgh	Cumberland	James Ward	14 88	25 78
Lesser ⋈ Roads	Somerset	Cornel's W. Schomp	16 36	29 74
Liberty Corner	Somerset	Nicholas C. Jobs	18 04	32 06
Libertyville	Sussex	Ezra W. Overton	28 17	43 28
Little Falls	Passaic	Chs. T. Van Winkle	28 99	62 86
Little York	Hunterdon	Geo. V. Alpaugh	22 11	35 51
Livingston	Essex	David Morehouse	12 86	23 92
Lockwood	Sussex	Alexander McKain	9 37	14 09
Long-a-Coming	Camden	Jacob Leach, (3 qrs.)	22 91	43 02
Long Branch	Monmouth	Henry Howland	71 89	137 68
Long Hill	Morris	George H. Ludlow	12 39	24 65
Madison	Morris	Geo. T. Sayre	140 50	308 64
Malaga	Gloucester	John G. Rosenbaum	19 89	38 35
Manahawkin	Monmouth	Saml. M. Oliphant	20 85	42 15
Manalapan	Monmouth	Elias C. Clayton	23 75	35 67
Manasquam	Monmouth	Sidney Goble, to 1st June	8 49	17 34
		Abraham Osborn	83	1 82
Manchester	Monmouth	Peter D. Knieskern	19 41	33 78
Mansfield	Warren	John Kearns	116 15	214 32
Marksboro'	Warren	James Blair, (3 qrs.)	9 95	13 95
Martinsville	Somerset	Samuel K. Martin	6 86	12 74
Mauricetown	Cumberland	Joseph Butcher	17 95	27 84
Maxville	Sussex	Aaron H. Kelsey	5 79	12 49
May's Landing	Atlantic	Jonathan Gifford, (3 qrs.)	51 63	104 82
Mead's Basin	Passaic	Nathaniel Wilson	12 97	21 99
Medford	Burlington	John C. Egbert	82 59	166 25
Mendham	Morris	John J. Ballentine	115 42	210 34
Metedeconk	Monmouth	Benj. H. Fielder	5 57	12 31
Metuchen	Middlesex	Robert R. Freeman	40 00	80 65
Middletown	Monmouth	Wm. W. Murray	79 06	130 50
Middletown Point	Monmouth	William Little	78 96	155 61
Milford	Hunterdon	Thos. Vansyckel, to 31st Dec.	14 39	23 34
		Daniel Vansyckel	12 65	20 46
Millington	Somerset	Abraham Dunn	14 08	24 04
Millstone	Somerset	Wm. D. McKissack	30 60	58 04

POST OFFICES—*New Jersey.*

Post Offices.	Counties.	Postmasters.	Compensation.	Net proceeds.
Millville	Cumberland	Jeremiah Stratton	$89 63	$159 89
Milton	Morris	Squire Lum	17 65	30 73
Monroe	Sussex	William Ingles, jr.	3 31	6 14
Montague	Sussex	James Stoll	44 59	52 33
Montville	Morris	Silas Cooke	13 81	28 95
Moorestown	Burlington	William Collins	100 39	191 47
Morristown	Morris	Joseph J. Roy	460 87	1077 88
Mount Holly	Burlington	William Bowers, to 31st Dec.	136 89	301 92
		George Haywood, from 31st Jan.	123 15	267 36
Mount Pleasant	Hunterdon	Samuel C. Eckel	29 35	46 58
Mullico Hill	Gloucester	Jos. A. Chatham	37 60	62 96
Newark	Essex	John J. Plume	1658 73	8101 85
New Brunswick	Middlesex	John Simpson	959 08	2035 92
New Durham	Hudson	Henry Ackerson, from 1st April	1 01	2 12
New Egypt	Monmouth	George F. Fort, to 31st Dec.	36 51	53 22
		Abigail Wallin	39 04	60 35
Newfoundland	Morris	Peter P. Brown, to 18th Feb.	24 66	37 43
		John P. Brown	12 75	23 34
New Germantown	Hunterdon	Peter R. Fisher	49 24	87 97
New Hampton	Hunterdon	David Park, to 9th April	29 66	47 20
		Lewis H. Martenis	7 88	12 47
New Market	Middlesex	Israel R. Coriell	31 74	59 69
Newport	Cumberland	William Watson, to 14th May	10 06	15 56
		Peter Cambloss, jr.	98	1 52
New Prospect	Bergen	Elijah Rosencrantz	27 58	45 01
New Providence	Essex	Benj. T. Harris, to 3d Feb.	21 40	38 22
		John Wood	15 48	26 69
Newtown	Sussex	Edward C. Moore	242 52	485 95
New Vernon	Morris	Simeon Lindsley	10 36	17 40
New Village	Warren	Jacob Melick	29 56	53 40
North Branch	Somerset	James Q. Beekman	33 63	62 92
Old Bridge	Middlesex	Andrew J. Disbrow	16 78	30 12
Orange	Essex	Lewis C. Lighthipe	167 08	341 52
Oxford Furnace	Warren	Geo. W. Scranton	19 58	39 24
Parsippany	Morris	Andrew B. Cobb, to 6th Dec.	36 20	67 83
		Cyrus H. Righter	50 31	97 66
Paskack	Bergen	James Schoonmaker	7 70	10 99

POST OFFICES—*New Jersey.*

Post Offices.	Counties.	Postmasters.	Compensation.	Net proceeds.
Patterson	Passaic	Wm. D. Quinn	$958 83	$2722 87
Paulsborough	Gloucester	Jacob Price	10 83	18 88
Peapack	Somerset	Wm. A. Vandorn	16 60	30 87
Pedricktown	Salem	Shadrack Pedrick, to 31st Jan.	7 21	12 18
" "		Jacob S. Pedrick, from 3d Feb.	6 00	10 52
Pemberton	Burlington	Austin R. Haines	77 66	129 99
Pennington	Mercer	Henry P. Welling	105 95	178 81
Penn's Grove	Salem	David Smith	11 56	18 84
Pennsville	Salem	John V. Hill	(No ret.)	
Perrineville	Monmouth	John W. Davison	6 34	11 22
Perryville	Hunterdon	Cornelius Carhart	18 72	29 86
Perth Amboy	Middlesex	Benj. F. Arnold (Includes $2 95 comp., $6 90 n. pro. for 'South Amboy.')	253 28	560 89
Pine Brook	Morris	Benjamin Crane	7 67	16 19
Pitt's Grove	Salem	Judah Foster	46 52	76 17
Pittstown	Hunterdon	Leonard N. Boeman	10 08	16 08
Plainfield	Essex	John W. Craig	200 90	388 45
Pleasant Grove	Morris	Hulet Smith, (3 qrs)	8 79	14 36
Pleasant Mills	Atlantic	John Westcoat	30 51	65 60
Pluckemin	Somerset	Jacob Losey	32 91	61 95
Point Pleasant	Monmouth	Abraham S. Osburn	5 51	12 57
Pompton	Morris	James Jackson	74 06	151 43
Port Elizabeth	Cumberland	Francis Lee	67 30	125 35
Port Republic	Atlantic	John Endicott	17 24	35 95
Potter's Creek	Monmouth	Samuel R. Bunnell	5 26	9 25
Pottersville	Hunterdon	Sering Potter	9 81	15 90
Powerville	Morris	Jno. Righter, (5 mo.)	3 75	7 66
Prallsville	Hunterdon	Wm. L. Hoppock	16 33	23 38
Princeton	Mercer	Abraham J. Berry, to 17th Sept.	168 79	404 73
" "		Wm. R. Murphy	631 94	1618 58
Pyramus	Bergen	Cornelius D. Taylor	26 33	43 01
Quakertown	Hunterdon	Geo. W. Waterhouse	29 35	50 44
Rahway	Middlesex	Josephus Shann	434 71	814 94
Ramsaysburgh	Warren	James Ramsay	7 25	11 29
Rancocas	Burlington	Samuel Stokes, jr	38 50	63 46
Readington	Hunterdon	Herman Hageman	27 25	39 24
Recklesstown	Burlington	James Pearce	13 26	22 16
Red Bank	Monmouth	John R. Conover	38 61	73 83
Ringoes	Hunterdon	Nicholas O. Lowe, to 31st March	28 68	47 83
		Joseph Boss	8 90	15 50
Roadstown	Cumberland	Philip Fithian	36 16	52 07

POST OFFICES—*New Jersey.*

Post Offices.	Counties.	Postmasters.	Compensation.	Net proceeds.
Rockaway	Morris	John D. Jackson	$103 42	$213 41
Rocky Hill	Somerset	Thomas J. Skillman	27 92	44 82
Salem	Salem	Solomon H. Merritt	361 15	725 53
Sandyston (Ch'd to 'Haines-ville.')	Sussex	John A. Westbrook, to 31st Dec	18 10	18 13
Schooly's Mount'n	Morris	William Dellicker	74 25	142 36
Scotch Plains	Essex	Vincent L. Frazee	37 04	69 86
Sculltown	Salem	Alfred Simpkins, to 30th Sept	7 03	10 49
		Elias Jester	17 44	26 84
Serepta	Warren	Peter Winter	5 38	11 45
Sergeantsville	Hunterdon	Samuel R. Smith, to 31st March	13 40	25 04
		Jeremiah Smith	4 32	7 85
Sharptown	Salem	Job Ridgway	37 90	59 26
Shiloh	Cumberland	Isaac D. Titsworth	31 29	48 15
Shrewsbury	Monmouth	Harry Finch	50 01	92 28
Sidney	Hunterdon	David Phillips	16 55	26 81
Six Mile Run	Middlesex	Wm. M. Baker	34 99	64 12
Smith's Landing	Atlantic	Pardon Ryon	10 50	18 18
Somer's Point	Atlantic	Edmund Somers	32 18	66 70
Somerville	Somerset	William G. Steel	212 59	446 51
Sooy's Inn	Burlington	Wm. H. Sooy	24 44	50 89
South Amboy	Middlesex	John Fine, to 31st Dec	10 63	21 07
		Joseph Brown, to 22d March	6 19	12 47
South Orange	Essex	John D. Freeman	23 52	46 44
South River	Middlesex	Stephen Smith, jr	23 32	46 88
Sparta	Sussex	Elias Beach	54 57	102 62
Spottswood	Middlesex	Daniel Snowhill	48 30	101 04
Springfield	Essex	Abner Stiles	94 64	175 05
Squankum	Monmouth	Joseph Goodenough	8 58	17 29
Stanhope	Sussex	Charles Lewis, to 30th Sept	28 21	52 14
		Andrew A. Smalley	89 09	168 69
Stewartsville	Warren	John Fulmer, jr	40 62	68 36
Still Valley	Warren	Thomas Hunt	29 57	44 04
Still Water	Sussex	Nathan A. Shaffer, (3 qrs.)	14 29	28 47
Stockholm	Sussex	John M. Ford	24 09	43 67
Suck-a-Sunny	Morris	William Patterson	59 92	103 43
Summit	Essex	William Littell	9 41	19 73
Sweedsboro'	Gloucester	Chas. P. Shivers	55 06	99 14
Tinton Falls	Monmouth	Pears'n Hendrickson	14 49	23 82

POST OFFICES—*New Jersey.*

Post Offices.	Counties.	Postmasters.	Compensation.	Net proceeds.
Titusville	Hunterdon	Isaac S. Nevius, to 31st Dec	$7 54	$10 22
		Joshua Primmer	7 60	12 05
Tom's River	Monmouth	Wm. J. James	32 74	61 87
Townsbury	Warren	Archibald Stinson	6 23	12 60
Trenton	Mercer	Joseph Justice	1149 53	2960 71
Tuckahoe	Cape May	Martin Madden	65 32	140 41
Tuckerton	Burlington	Ebenezer Tucker	53 07	85 64
Turkey	Monmouth	John Hall	9 94	20 64
Tuttle's Corner	Sussex	Benjamin Tuttle, from 1st Oct	5 10	6 23
Union	Essex	Stephen H. Crane	13 43	25 17
Vansyckel's	Hunterdon	Aaron Vansyckel	8 66	12 32
Vernon	Sussex	William Brown	17 26	36 19
Vincentown	Burlington	Theodore Bodine	37 31	75 49
Walnut Grove	Morris	Silas C. Clark	14 08	25 21
Walnut Valley	Warren	Elias Jones	6 37	13 33
Waterford Works	Camden	Joseph C. Porter	34 77	72 08
West Bloomfield	Essex	Calvin S. Baldwin	78 26	152 52
Westfield	Essex	Wm. H. Pierson	50 01	95 39
West Milford	Passaic	Geo. E. Ackerson, to 30th Sept	3 83	5 92
		Thom. McMickens, to 31st Dec	3 00	5 07
		David D. Meeker	8 47	14 18
Weston	Somerset	Isaac R. Cornell	27 43	39 21
Westville	Gloucester	Wm. S. Doughton	18 83	33 36
White House	Hunterdon	Peter E. Voorhees	28 49	53 53
Winslow	Camden	Andrew K. Hay	66 29	111 72
Wiretown	Monmouth	William Birdsall	8 50	15 56
Woodbridge	Middlesex	Isaac Smith	107 98	184 62
Woodbury	Gloucester	John Cade	82 27	170 81
Woodstown	Salem	Jos. L. Risley	92 22	151 20
Woodsville	Mercer	John Hill	13 06	24 38
Wrightstown	Burlington	James Beck	19 76	31 60
Yardville	Mercer	Moses R. Quigley, to 31st Dec	5 84	10 43
		Robt. C. Hutchinson	10 05	17 96

POST OFFICES—*Pennsylvania.*

PENNSYLVANIA.

NOTE.—Compensation of Postmasters, and net proceeds of their offices, from July 1, 1844, to June, 30, 1845.

Post Offices.	Counties.	Postmasters.	Compensation.	Net proceeds.
Aaronsburgh	Centre	Oliver P. Duncan	$71 11	$110 96
Abbottstown	Adams	George Ickes, to 21st May	50 58	83 20
		Nicholas Carns	5 86	8 89
Abington	Montgomery	Moor Stevens	38 53	75 94
Abington Centre	Luzerne	William C. Green	65 43	103 59
Adamsburgh	Westmorel'd	Samuel Miller	52 27	51 35
Adamstown	Lancaster	Henry Flickinger	29 02	50 36
Adamsville	Crawford	Thomas Kilpatrick	17 97	31 14
Addison	Somerset	William Roddy	131 48	127 10
Agnews' Mills	Venango	James F. Agnew	27 82	35 37
Alba	Bradford	Oliver P. Wilson	15 55	25 41
Alexandria	Huntingdon	John Gemmill	161 70	238 14
Alleghany	Alleghany	William Karns	650 17	1444 45
Alleghany Bridge	McKean	Nathan Dennis	6 99	13 49
Allen	Cumberland	Daniel Krysher	59 80	90 17
Allensville	Mifflin	Adam Sigler, jr., to 23d May	43 11	73 37
		John C. Everhart	5 01	9 04
Allentown	Lehigh	Augustus L. Ruke, to 30th Sept	96 91	194 02
		Robert E. Wright	385 09	690 01
Alterton	Cumberland	David Alter	9 40	13 68
Alum Bank	Bedford	Thomas Vickroy	9 72	16 69
Alvira	Lycoming	Levi M. Wise, to 31st March	2 78	4 20
		John Foresman	1 31	2 03
Amity	Washington	Zachariah Sharp	35 88	57 28
Anandale (Disc'd 12th Oct.)	Butler	George Marks, to 30th Sept	91	1 47
Andalusia	Bucks	Samuel French, to 31st March	42 42	70 39
		Jesse Duffield	10 37	17 03
Andersonburgh	Perry	John Zimmerman	18 42	31 93
Andesville	Perry	David Kochendorfer	16 70	25 48
Andrews' Bridge	Lancaster	Benjamin Kent	17 38	26 93
Annville	Lebanon	Jacob Henning	110 06	202 92
Antestown	Huntingdon	John Bell	29 46	49 44
Antrim	Alleghany	Robert Ross	11 43	19 12
Apollo	Armstrong	John T. Smith	41 24	70 00
Apple Grove	York	Henry M. Webb	4 81	7 59
Aqueduct	Westmorel'd	James McCune	14 40	26 95
Arendtsville	Adams	Jacob Keckler	16 23	28 40

POST OFFICES—*Pennsylvania*.

Post Offices.	Counties.	Postmasters.	Compensation.	Net proceeds.
Armagh	Indiana	James Johnston	$118 24	$116 60
Ashland	Wayne	Isaac Doughty	3 71	5 19
Asylum	Bradford	O. D. Chamberlain	13 64	19 56
Athens	Bradford	Orrin D. Satterlee, to 31st Dec'r	100 20	174 62
		Consider S. Parke	99 85	178 51
Atkinsons' Mills	Mifflin	Charles Caughling	19 08	16 46
Attleboro'	Bucks	James Flowers	62 59	118 36
Auburn 4 Corners	Susquehan'h	Chester Adams	9 25	18 76
Avondale	Chester	Joseph Thompson	47 94	86 64
Baileyville	Centre	Samuel H. Stover	42 93	78 35
Bainbridge	Lancaster	Jacob B. Hamilton	64 84	109 99
Bakerstown	Alleghany	William Duncan	50 58	87 55
Bald Mount	Luzerne	Henry Litts	9 82	15 94
Baldwin	Butler	Robert Patton	18 50	36 58
Barbour's Mills	Lycoming	John Barbour	2 35	3 41
Bareville	Lancaster	Reuben Weidler	(No ret.)	
Barnhart's Mill	Butler	William Forquer	7 21	13 94
Barren Hill	Montgomery	John Dager	23 29	43 15
Bart	Lancaster	James M. Quigg	48 94	82 86
Bartonsville	Monroe	Henry Kintz	10 78	16 46
Bath	Northampton	Daniel Seigfried	69 42	115 31
Baumstown	Berks	Samuel Heckler	43 64	71 18
Bavington	Washington	John McBride, jr	24 53	38 34
Beach Grove	Luzerne	Nathan Beach	24 27	26 08
Beach Haven	Luzerne	Dan'l G. Driesbach, to 12th May	6 85	12 81
		James Campbell	1 45	2 67
Beale's Mills	Juniata	Jesse Beale	3 87	7 71
Beallsville	Washington	George C. Seaton, to 30th Sept	20 30	36 40
		Christian J. Parker	59 81	106 63
Bear Gap	Northumb'nd	Jacob Leisenring	10 43	17 25
Bearmont	Schuylkill	Edwin Ames, fr. 19th Jan. to 31st Mar.	1 07	2 43
Beartown	Lancaster	Andrew S. Weiler	17 07	26 91
Beaumont	Luzerne	Chas. L. Terwelliger	11 50	21 85
Beaver	Beaver	James Lyon	330 23	661 97
Beaver Meadows	Carbon	Wm. H. Wilson, to 11th Dec	52 19	100 09
		Abraham Cool	55 76	118 52
Beavertown	Union	M. Specht, to 31 May	29 44	61 49
		Simon Frank	2 62	5 61
Beaver Valley	Columbia	Christian Shuman	4 64	6 02
Bedford	Bedford	James Reamer	456 99	768 35
Belfast	Northampton	John J. Rogers, to 31st March	12 88	23 98
		Charles Steckel	3 96	7 23

POST OFFICES—*Pennsylvania.*

Post Offices.	Counties.	Postmasters.	Compensation.	Net proceeds.
Bellefonte	Centre	William Grafius, to 31st March	$334 48	$657 90
		Ellen H. Grafius	96 13	213 09
Belle Vernon	Fayette	Solomon Speers	33 66	63 47
Belleville	Mifflin	Daniel Overholser	73 93	127 10
Belvidere	Chester	Thos. C. McLoud, to 29th July (Est.)	3 40	7 94
		Mary E. Boyer	43 33	81 07
Bentleyville	Washington	Mark Mitchell, jr.	34 07	56 24
Benton	Columbia	Daniel Hartman	20 38	29 23
Benvenue	Dauphin	Rebecca H. Duncan	137 80	131 12
Berlin	Somerset	John H. Smith, to 1st Feb'y	52 27	94 80
		Daniel Heffley	45 00	82 39
Bermudian	Adams	Malon Griest, to 31st March	11 46	17 83
		David Newcomer	3 85	6 27
Bernville	Berks	William Runkle	49 56	74 50
Berrysburgh	Dauphin	John Deibler	50 05	78 69
Berwick	Columbia	C. B. Bowman, to 21st May	145 52	269 82
		Stephen Mansfield	21 25	35 31
Bethany	Wayne	Ira Vadakin, to 14th Nov	36 37	35 78
		Eph'm W. Hamlin	39 72	56 80
Bethel	Berks	Frederick Harner	39 76	54 57
Bethlehem	Northampton	Jacob Kummer, to 31st March	243 72	505 69
		Charles C. Tombler	92 09	189 90
Big Bend	Venango	John Craig	8 95	14 80
Big Equinunk	Wayne	Alex. Calder, (3 qs.)	5 48	9 53
Bingham	Potter	Joel L. Raymond	11 79	15 83
Birmingham	Huntingdon	David Cree	107 02	188 41
Black Hawk	Beaver	Alfred Lyon	9 52	16 82
Black Hole	Lycoming	John Fleming	12 60	21 47
Black Horse	Chester	Timothy Paxson	19 36	35 31
Blacklegs	Indiana	Andrew R. Sloan	16 65	24 91
Blairsville	Indiana	Daniel H. Barr	364 84	516 27
Blakeley	Luzerne	Levi Lillibridge	20 48	38 44
Blaney	Bradford	Nath'l N. Gamble	7 13	12 46
Bloody Run	Bedford	David A. T. Black	101 02	95 84
Bloomfield	Crawford	Andrew Bloomfield	13 40	24 70
Blooming Valley	Crawford	James A. Heard	14 79	25 75
Bloomsburgh	Columbia	John R. Moyer	197 75	353 40
Blossburgh	Tioga	Henry H. Welsh	81 01	163 03
Blue Ball	Lancaster	Henry Yundt	43 06	76 25
Blue Bell	Montgomery	Benjamin Hill, to 31st Dec	11 82	21 00
		Charles Gerhart	14 50	25 89

POST OFFICES—*Pennsylvania.*

Post Offices.	Counties.	Postmasters.	Compensation.	Net proceeds.
Blythe	Schuylkill	John W. Fetherolf, to 30th Sept.	$3 53	$5 29
		Jacob H. Lutz	12 31	20 89
Boalsburgh	Centre	Charles Rainey, to 31st Dec.	49 39	84 70
		George Jack	61 99	105 73
Bondville	Columbia	William Dale	8 38	11 87
Bowman's Creek	Wyoming	Abraham Frear	12 41	16 77
Bowmansville	Lancaster	Samuel Bowman	20 37	27 61
Boyerstown	Berks	Daniel B. Boyer	28 38	51 72
Brady's Bend	Armstrong	William H. Davis, from 13th March	32 90	62 62
Braintrem	Wyoming	John S. Lum	6 92	13 49
Brandywine Manor	Chester	James Lockart	65 77	109 60
Breakneck	Butler	John C. Marshall, to 31st Dec'r	9 92	14 08
		Francis Hamilton	12 03	20 22
Breinigsville	Lehigh	Peter Breinig	14 72	24 89
Brickerville	Lancaster	Jacob Miller	29 05	48 74
Bridesburgh	Philadelphia	Lewis F. Emery	73 24	158 43
Bridgewater	Bucks	William Goforth	28 06	49 41
Brier Creek	Columbia	John Conner, to 31st March	6 25	13 24
		John Klechner	1 93	4 11
Brighton	Beaver	Archibald Robertson	66 06	120 13
Bristol	Bucks	Gilbert Tomlinson, to 8th March	263 29	437 26
		William Kinsey	83 88	179 73
Broad Mountain	Schuylkill	Jacob Lindenmuth	17 67	31 89
Broad Top	Huntingdon	Jesse Cook	5 89	10 38
Brockwayville	Jefferson	Asaph M. Clarke	3 79	6 41
Brookfield	Tioga	A. H. Bacon, to 30th Sept.	1 68	2 52
		George W. Bacon	4 37	7 30
Brooklyn	Susquehan'h	Sally Bagley	47 04	82 82
Brookville	Jefferson	Samuel H. Lucas, to 8th Dec.	61 23	79 85
		Dan'l Smith, to 16th May	75 33	73 22
		Barton T. Hastings	25 64	17 74
Brower	Berks	Richard H. Jones	9 09	13 07
Brownington (Disc'd 21st Nov.)	Butler	John Sill	(No ret.)	
Brownsburgh	Bucks	Stacy Brown	12 76	24 84
Brown's Mills	Mifflin	Wm. B. Norris	88 32	137 72
Brownsville	Fayette	William Sloan, to 10th June	423 38	959 15
		Henry J. Rigden	30 61	64 89

POST OFFICES—*Pennsylvania.*

Post Offices.	Counties.	Postmasters.	Compensation.	Net proceeds.
Browntown	Bradford	Austin Stalford	$13 58	$19 46
Brumfieldville	Berks	John Breidenbach	7 91	13 49
Brush Valley	Indiana	Thomas Stewart	10 56	19 78
Buchanan	Alleghany	James Barr	60 38	123 53
Buck	Lancaster	George T. Clark, to 31st March	44 00	73 14
		Elisha S. Baily	13 23	22 29
Buckhorn	Columbia	Marshal G. Shoemaker, (3 qrs.)	6 42	12 75
Buckingham	Bucks	Joseph Morehead	25 91	54 66
Bucksville	Bucks	John Malone	15 22	27 92
Buffalo	Washington	Abraham Wotring	26 17	37 67
Buffalo X Roads	Union	James McCreight	27 80	52 56
Buffalo Run	Centre	Paulser Sellers	11 82	23 02
Bulger	Washington	Wm. H. H. Shields	6 72	11 26
Bunker Hill	Bucks	Joseph Walp	8 89	15 01
Burdsfield	Bedford	John W. Potts	16 52	28 41
Burgettstown	Washington	Jesse Spencer	41 04	64 51
Burlington	Bradford	Lorenzo D. Taylor	31 74	47 71
Burnside	Clearfield	George Atcheson	13 49	26 83
Burnt Cabins	Bedford	Nathaniel Kelly	16 97	33 52
Bushkill	Pike	Henry Peters	21 63	33 73
Bustleton	Philadelphia	Enoch C. Edwards	75 07	146 36
Butler	Butler	Wm. B. Lemmon, to 22d May	255 97	508 13
		David A. Agnew	24 00	48 71
Butztown	Northampton	Aaron W. Radley	14 38	21 87
Byberry	Philadelphia	Cyrus Peirce	54 24	85 51
Cains	Lancaster	Robert Baldwin	31 31	51 80
Caledonia	Elk	Hezekiah Warner	25 68	46 99
Callensburgh	Armstrong	Henry Alexander	32 82	52 51
Cambra	Luzerne	Henry Bittenbender	39 12	58 30
Campbelltown	Lebanon	John Wolfersberger	21 03	37 35
Camptown	Bradford	William Camp, to 21st June	14 22	19 78
		Edwin Hurlbut	0 17	0 41
Canaan	Wayne	John Jessup	22 86	26 19
Canal	Venango	Jos. A. Gilliland	11 29	20 42
Candor	Washington	Chauncey Weeks	20 72	34 37
Cannonsburgh	Washington	Jno. E. Black, to 10th Jan'y	144 66	308 71
		John Dickson	157 91	316 42
Canton	Bradford	Seneca Kendall, (3 qrs)	41 88	69 21
Carbondale	Luzerne	F. M. Crane, to 5th Sept	84 76	160 71
		Henry P. Ensign	362 89	715 72
Carlisle	Cumberland	Wm. M. Porter	1115 48	2511 24

POST OFFICES—*Pennsylvania.*

Post Offices.	Counties.	Postmasters.	Compensation.	Net proceeds.
Carlisle Springs..	Cumberland.	John Walt........	$2 25	$4 06
Carmichaels.....	Greene......	Jno. A. Patterson...	61 94	109 93
Caroline Furnace. (Dis. 31st Jany.)	Perry.......	John Allison, (3 qs.)	2 29	3 92
Carrick.........	Franklin....	John H. Dunn.....	11 96	18 53
Carversville......	Bucks.......	Wm. R. Evans....	11 58	20 51
Carverton.......	Luzerne.....	Jabez Carver, from 1st Jan'y........	0 64	1 00
Cashtown........	Adams......	Abraham Scott.....	27 98	42 61
Cassville........	Huntingdon.	Robert Speer.......	37 05	68 76
Castle Fin.......	York.......	John Finley, to 31st Dec'r..........	6 51	11 08
		Samuel McCalla....	14 98	26 19
Catawissa.......	Columbia....	Christian A. Brobst, to 13th Dec'r.....	118 36	97 04
		Paul R. Baldy.....	123 61	113 83
Catawissa Forge.	Columbia....	Sam'l B. Diemer, to 31st Dec'r.......	3 23	5 42
		Isaiah Shuman.....	2 93	4 40
Catawissa Valley.	Schuylkill...	Jacob Rapp........	8 20	14 93
Cedar Spring.... (Ch'd to "White Hill.")	Cumberland.	George Heck, to 30th Sept............	1 98	2 99
Central.........	Columbia....	Peter Hess........	3 83	4 54
Centre..........	Perry.......	Jas. L. McNeal....	25 10	32 71
Centre Bridge.... (Late "Centre Hill.")	Bucks.......	John D. Balderston, from 1st June....	0 98	1 44
Centre Hill...... (Ch'd to "Centre Bridge.")	Bucks.......	Smith Jones, to 31st May...........	15 39	26 54
Centre Line......	Centre......	William Coply, to 31st Dec'r.......	5 00	8 70
		J. S. Hewson, (1 qr.)	2 12	3 45
Centre Moreland.	Wyoming...	Chester Brown....	10 83	17 83
Centre Square...	Montgomery.	Jacob P. Reiff......	(no ret.)	
Centretown......	Mercer......	Hugh Beard......	9 86	13 99
Centreville......	Crawford....	Joel Bement.......	27 36	42 20
Cerestown.......	McKean....	John King........	40 28	65 30
Chadd's Ford....	Delaware....	Isaac Watkins.....	34 92	61 24
Chambersburgh..	Franklin....	David D. Durborau.	851 57	1822 45
Chanceford......	York.......	Joseph Tosh.......	17 64	34 79
Chapman........	Union.......	Jacob Bastress.....	14 35	24 82
Charleston.......	Tioga.......	Cyrus Dartt.......	8 73	17 06
Chase's Mills....	Luzerne.....	Joseph Chase......	1 40	3 03
Chatham........	Chester.....	Geo. W. Lefever...	38 84	64 19
Chatham Valley..	Tioga.......	Henry Eaton......	3 10	5 76
Chenango.......	Beaver......	James Warnock....	9 26	17 51
Cherry..........	Lycoming...	Isaiah Bartley......	30 81	48 28
Cherry Ridge....	Wayne.....	Eben H. Clark.....	12 34	20 64
Cherry Tree.....	Venango....	Samuel Irwin......	8 43	15 90
Cherryville......	Northampton	Robert Wentz.....	45 84	76 26

POST OFFICES—*Pennsylvania.*

Post Offices.	Counties.	Postmasters.	Compensation.	Net proceeds.
Chesnut Grove	Lycoming	Z. I. Britain	$2 15	$3 47
Chesnut Hill	Philadelphia	Jacob Stallman, to 25th April	31 15	60 78
		Jos. L. Carver	6 62	11 91
Chesnut Level	Lancaster	John Pusey	59 10	99 34
Chess Springs	Cambria	Andrew McGuire	8 54	13 48
Chest	Clearfield	James McGhee	7 72	16 35
Chester	Delaware	Charlotte Doyle	295 30	582 14
Chester Springs	Chester	Samuel Holman, to 24th May	43 23	81 20
		George Lingen	4 07	7 55
Chesterville (Ch'd to "Colesburgh.")	Potter	John C. Cavanaugh	8 21	14 17
Chillisquaque	Northumb'nd	Jesse Broomall	10 69	20 06
Chippewa	Beaver	Robert Dunlap	9 52	13 75
Choconut	Susquehan'h	Lewis Chamberlin	10 35	19 12
Churchtown	Lancaster	Edw'd S. Davies, to 22d Oct	27 16	47 29
		Edw'd D. White	70 70	124 72
Clarion	Clarion	John Lyon, to 8th Nov	77 27	74 02
		Seth Clover	155 18	149 12
Clark	Mercer	Joseph McClure	53 03	96 98
Clark's Ferry (Ch'd to "Petersburgh.")	Perry	Robert Clark, to 14th Feb'y	65 01	132 16
Clarksville	Greene	John Booze	25 08	43 71
Claussville	Lehigh	Joseph Slough	5 18	10 58
Claysville	Washington	James Shannon	92 30	165 09
Clearfield	Clearfield	Wm. L. Moore	121 04	239 47
Clearfield Bridge	Clearfield	Jas. C. Barrett, from 19th Dec'r	2 24	4 34
Clermontville	McKean	Ransom Beckwith	5 01	9 60
Clifton	Luzerne	Joseph Wragg	11 10	18 42
Clinton	Allegany	James Wilson, to 31st March	32 51	52 71
		John Pollock	9 65	16 45
Clinton Furnace	Clarion	Ralph Clapp	21 92	33 68
Clintonville	Venango	Robert Cross	21 51	36 80
Coatsville	Chester	Henry G. Thomas, to 26th April	179 14	372 99
		Enoch S. McCauhey	27 66	65 49
Cocalico	Lancaster	Benjamin Flickinger	11 65	16 10
Cochransville	Chester	Thomas A. Janney, to 31st Dec'r	29 23	52 25
		John A. Morrison	29 09	50 90
Codorus	York	Jenkins Carothers, to 31st March	7 37	11 59
		George Snodgrass	2 85	5 73
Coffee Run	Huntingdon	James Entrekin, jr.	13 58	25 41

POST OFFICES—*Pennsylvania.*

Post Offices.	Counties.	Postmasters.	Compensation.	Net proceeds.
Colebrook Dale..	Berks.......	Chs. K. Shultz.....	$25 95	$37 60
Colerain.........	Lancaster ...	Manasseh Blackburn to 31st March.....	15 15	24 53
		J. W. Hendrickson.	5 24	8 95
Colerain Forge...	Huntingdon .	David Stewart	35 22	65 41
Colesburgh. ...... (Late "Chester ville.")	Potter.......	Alanson Andrews..	(no ret.)	
Cole's Creek.....	Columbia....	Benjamin Cole.....	5 17	7 40
Collinsville	Huntingdon .	Michael Hileman, to 31st March......	11 29	19 31
		Rt. H. McCormick.	4 84	8 23
Collomsville	Lycoming...	Jesse Bower.......	12 83	20 40
Columbia........	Lancaster ...	Guilford G. Claiborn	568 04	1408 83
Columbia XRoads	Bradford	William Gernert ...	13 27	20 70
Columbus.......	Warren.....	Robert Campbell...	75 01	126 18
Commettsburgh..	Washington..	Alexander Blair, to 31st March......	5 26	6 31
		John Robb........	3 80	5 65
Concord	Franklin	James Wilson.....	38 01	69 22
Concordville.....	Delaware.....	George Rusk......	39 59	60 07
Conestoga........	Lancaster ...	Benjamin Urban...	28 56	44 23
Conneautville.....	Crawford....	William Powers....	95 52	163 74
Connellsville, ...	Fayette	Joseph Herbert....	153 86	267 53
Conshohocken....	Montgomery.	George L. Bates....	54 50	110 93
Conyngham	Luzerne	Moses S. Brundage, to 12th Jan'y....	22 90	42 37
		Henry Sybert.....	30 05	45 48
Cook	Erie	Gibson I. Stranahan	12 92	23 21
Cook's Run	Clinton......	John Baird........	2 58	4 16
Cookstown.......	Fayette	Abram Banks......	87 05	142 14
Coolbaughs.......	Monroe......	Ms. W. Coolbaugh.	9 66	15 63
Cool Spring......	Jefferson	James Gray, to 30th Sept..........	2 54	4 40
		John Scott.........	8 28	12 58
Coopersburgh....	Lehigh......	Milton Cooper.....	43 65	83 24
Cooperstown	Venango.....	Robert Mason.....	22 46	42 45
Coopersville	Lancaster ...	John Cain.........	17 90	26 80
Cornplanter......	Venango.....	William Young.....	7 90	13 26
Cornwall........	Lebanon	Wm. C. Bradley...	23 49	43 00
Corsica..........	Jefferson	Jno. I. Y. Thompson	15 96	13 61
Corydon	McKean	John L. Gibbs.....	14 39	24 24
Cosgrave Hall...	Union.......	Henry Cosgrave...	5 77	8 41
Cottage .... (Dis. 19th June.)	Huntingdon .	Miles Lewis.......	4 47	7 05
Coultersville......	Butler......	Henry C. Linn.....	11 72	18 18
Covington	Tioga	Ephm. B. Gerould, to 31st March....	60 47	100 63
		Edwin Dyer.......	17 99	31 42

POST OFFICES—*Pennsylvania.*

Post Offices.	Counties.	Postmasters.	Compensation.	Net proceeds.
Cowdersport	Potter........	William McDougall, to 31st March....	$70 60	$103 05
		Chs. B. Colter.....	19 15	31 24
Craig's Meadows.	Monroe.......	John Lander.......	5 78	9 58
Cranberry.......	Venango.....	James Allison......	11 96	16 78
Cranesville.......	Lehigh......	Samuel Colver.....	21 96	38 10
Crawford's Mills.	Westmorel'd.	James Fitzgerald...	14 75	21 32
Crooked Creek...	Tioga........	Ezra Potter........	6 57	13 40
Crooked Hill....	Montgomery.	Rufus B. Longaker.	16 17	27 77
Cross Cr'k Village	Washington..	Benj. F. Murray, to 24th Jan'y........	30 39	45 11
		Cornelius Simmons.	22 09	33 97
Cross Cut.......	Beaver......	David Bower......	22 61	37 61
Crossingville	Crawford....	E. W. Chamberlain, to 31st March....	13 93	24 38
		Vincent Phelps.....	4 89	8 64
Cross Roads.....	York	John Logan.......	20 87	32 52
Culbertson's.....	Mercer......	John W. Sheakley.	73 54	70 19
Cumberland Val'y	Bedford......	Jno. R. Anderson..	11 53	15 93
Cummings......	Lycoming...	Dan'l E. Callahan..	13 81	27 82
Curllsville.......	Clarion......	Lindsay C. Pritner.	25 53	41 39
Curwinsville.....	Clearfield....	Benj. Hartshorn, to 17th Oct.........	22 98	21 27
		Anthony Kratzer...	55 54	80 83
Cussawago.......	Crawford....	David Thickstun...	17 60	36 25
Custards	Crawford....	Richard Custard....	19 92	27 63
Daggetts' Mills... (Cha'd to "Spencerville.")	Tioga........	Richmond Jones....	22 35	40 42
Dale............	Berks.......	David Schall.......	17 85	30 87
Daleville	Luzerne.....	William Dale......	14 63	23 60
Dallas..........	Luzerne.....	Almon Goss.......	9 67	15 59
Dalmatia........	Northumb'nd	George Brosius.....	18 38	32 71
Damascus.......	Wayne......	Walter S. Vail.....	67 98	65 49
Danboro'........	Bucks.......	Isaac G. Thomas...	16 13	30 72
Danville.........	Columbia....	Alexander Best....	654 12	1268 62
Darby	Delaware....	Garrett Pearson....	108 37	210 58
Darlingsville.....	Pike........	Daniel Decker......	11 10	23 85
Darlington.......	Beaver......	John McClymonds.	116 60	114 83
Dauphin	Dauphin	Henry C. Sponsler, to 8th January...	99 14	99 75
		James Corbett......	74 57	132 37
Davidson........	Lycoming...	John Hiddleston...	7 65	11 09
Davidsville......	Somerset.....	Peter Levy.......	20 28	34 14
Davisville	Bucks.......	Alfred T. Duffield..	32 71	56 90
Day's Landing...	York	George H. Wolf...	14 80	26 47
Deer Creek......	Mercer......	William R. Cooper.	5 58	9 36
Deerfield......... (Dis. 6th Dec.)	Warren......	Thomas McGee, 1 qr	5 98	11 60

POST OFFICES—*Pennsylvania.*

Post Offices.	Counties.	Postmasters.	Compensation.	Net proceeds.
Delaware	Pike	Albert G. Brodhead	$6 58	$12 95
Delaware Grove	Mercer	James T. Black	13 20	27 58
Dempseytown	Venango	Peter Dempsey	6 02	12 37
Derry	Columbia	Jacob Strouse	14 90	25 22
Dickinson	Cumberland	John Mehaffie	35 80	66 71
Dillsburgh	York	G. L. Shearer, to 11th June	63 13	99 78
		Jacob B. Hurst	4 54	7 38
Dill's Ferry	Northampton	Michael Weller	18 23	31 71
Dilworthtown	Chester	Abm. B. Darlington	12 37	16 82
Dimock	Susquehan'h	John Baker	28 85	52 35
Dimocksville	Susquehan'h	Shubael Dimock	10 04	16 71
Dingman's Ferry	Pike	Martin W. Dingman	28 33	47 90
Doe Run	Chester	Robert Fairlamb	41 95	74 85
Dolington	Bucks	Wilson J. Carver	14 78	27 83
Donegal	Westmorel'd	Clement Hubbs, to 10th April	56 09	55 26
		John Cover	17 92	16 68
Douglassville	Berks	Michael Ludwig	63 71	108 01
Dover	York	Engle'rt Melchinger	20 22	39 23
Downingtown	Chester	Thos. Hutchinson	170 15	305 90
Doylestown	Bucks	Lester Rich, to 5th December	87 02	178 10
		Geo. T. Harvey	117 04	239 26
Dry Run	Franklin	James Ferguson	27 52	49 25
Dublin (Dis. 3d June.)	Bucks	Newton Rowland, to 4th June	4 31	9 13
Duncansville	Huntington	Samuel Confer	126 29	130 85
Dundaff	Susquehan'h	Jos. B. Slocum, to 1st March	112 86	125 36
		Arthur Smith	39 42	64 42
Dunningsville	Washington	William Dunning, to 31st March	32 52	50 19
		Matthew Wilson	9 42	15 51
Dunnsburgh	Clinton	Robert C. Miller, to 4th September	5 42	10 27
		Michael Spangler	26 61	50 89
Durlach	Lancaster	Harrison Elser	26 06	43 24
Dutotsburgh	Monroe	Luke Brodhead, to 31st March	8 82	14 95
		Luke W. Brodhead	3 97	7 33
Eagle Factory	Susquehan'h	William Young	4 56	7 00
Eagleville	Centre	John Brickley	33 00	61 46
Earlville	Berks	George Kline, jr	13 85	23 97
East Barre	Huntingdon	Wm. M. Murray	17 70	32 52
East Berlin	Adams	Emanuel Khune, to 9th December	26 55	38 32
		William Wolf	33 77	49 62

POST OFFICES—*Pennsylvania.*

Post Offices.	Counties.	Postmasters.	Compensation.	Net proceeds.
East Bethlehem	Washington	Isaiah Linton, to 30th September	$21 57	$36 39
		James G. Hart	63 74	106 86
East Bloomfield	Crawford	Jesse A. Blakeslee	19 44	32 21
Eastbrook	Mercer	T. H. Harrah	17 19	28 22
East Freedom	Bedford	Robert Todd	35 27	63 92
East Hanover	Lebanon	Michael Weise	31 67	60 08
East Hempfield	Lancaster	Andrew Holtsworth	46 66	75 59
East Herrick	Bradford	Jere. C. Barnes	7 15	10 69
East Liberty	Fayette	John McBurney	13 83	21 36
East Nantmeal	Chester	James Leighton	25 62	43 88
Easton	Northampton	Abraham Coryell	1216 91	2986 49
East Penn	Carbon	Charles Dinkey	16 48	24 38
East Smithfield	Bradford	Charles R. Hamilton	55 58	110 58
East Sterling	Wayne	William Bortree	9 77	17 80
East Sugar Loaf	Luzerne	Abraham Drum	21 20	30 21
East Waterford	Juniata	Enoch L. Anderson	14 32	25 29
Eaton	Wyoming	Elijah Lee, to 31st December	4 97	8 72
		David D. Dewitt	5 69	9 40
Ebensburgh	Cambria	Rees J. Lloyd	271 17	288 57
Economy	Beaver	Romelius L. Baker	63 40	98 62
Eden (Dis. 4th Oct'r.)	Clarion	John G. Mendenhall, to 19th October	2 70	4 08
Edgemont	Delaware	Hiram Green	17 87	31 13
Edinboro'	Erie	Abel Whitney	68 74	111 02
Edinburgh	Mercer	Arney Biddle	16 69	29 23
Edsallville	Bradford	Earl P. Wood	6 20	9 68
Eldersville	Washington	Hugh Patterson	30 62	47 67
Elderton	Armstrong	John Ralston	28 62	52 72
Eldred	Wayne	James Smith	3 77	4 62
Eldredville	Lycoming	Edw'd A. Eldred	9 42	16 54
Elimsport	Lycoming	Robert T. McCormick, 3 qrs	12 78	21 74
Elizabeth	Allegany	Samuel Walker	139 10	240 68
Elizabethtown	Lancaster	John Lynch, to 23d May	121 80	229 76
		Samuel Redsecker	12 37	22 78
Elizabethville	Dauphin	John J. Bowman	23 81	39 13
Elk Creek	Erie	Luke H. Cutler, to 7th May	53 04	88 47
		Newton Lownsbery	9 09	15 51
Elk Lake	Susquehan'h	Charles J. Lathrop	5 80	9 29
Elkland	Tioga	Joel Parkhurst, to 23d June	34 62	56 62
		Henry Sherwood	(no ret.)	
Elk Lick	Somerset	Gabriel Miller	25 33	47 95
Ellerslie	Susquehan'h	Anne F. Milligan	11 49	20 04
Elliottsburgh	Perry	James Kacy	13 07	17 89

POST OFFICES—*Pennsylvania.*

Post Offices.	Counties.	Postmasters.	Compensation.	Net proceeds.
Ellisburgh	Potter	Harry Ellis	(no ret.)	
Elysburgh	Northumb'nd	Hart'an H. Knoebel	$19 75	$19 61
Emaus	Lehigh	John I. Giering	12 48	25 61
Embreeville	Chester	S. B. Worth	24 80	42 41
Emlenton	Venango	John Keating	7 83	11 91
Ennisville	Huntingdon	John W. Myton, 3 qrs	24 83	43 22
Enon Valley	Beaver	George Robinson	47 13	62 53
Enterprise	Lancaster	Jesse K. Cooper	67 07	102 67
Ephratah	Lancaster	John Gross	93 06	146 46
Erie	Erie	Andrew Scott	1284 25	166 86
Erwinna	Bucks	Wm. S. Hunt	30 95	62 88
Espy	Columbia	Regina Worman	26 58	45 93
Espyville	Crawford	Russell Marshall	27 60	39 04
Etna (Dis. 18th Jan'y.)	Alleghany	Robert Hannah	(no ret.)	
Etters	York	Henry Etter	9 34	8 77
Evansburgh	Crawford	Robert Scott	55 11	96 74
Exeter	Luzerne	John Oliver	18 85	32 98
Experiment Mills	Monroe	James Bell, jr	16 16	26 18
Factoryville	Wyoming	John Wilson	16 31	28 30
Fair Dale	Susquehan'h	Daniel Hoff	5 49	10 10
Fairfield	Adams	John McCleary	57 97	99 62
Fairmount Sp'ngs	Luzerne	Solomon Taylor	3 82	6 65
Fairview	Erie	Walter W. Warner, to 24th May	99 40	140 34
		John Clemens	11 16	11 01
Fallowfield	Washington	Mark Mitchell	6 71	12 06
Falls	Wyoming	Abel C. Hartley, to 15th February	9 40	17 95
		Moses B. Phillips	6 68	12 08
Falls of Schuylkill	Philadelphia	Robert Evans	48 85	95 34
Fallston	Beaver	Alfred G. McCreary	193 86	369 52
Falmouth	Lancaster	Geo. H. Horning	6 49	12 02
Fannettsburgh	Franklin	William Uttz, to 31st May	47 91	72 85
		John Kyle	4 86	6 80
Farmers	York	Henry Boose	12 24	20 91
Farmers' Valley	McKean	Timothy R. Robbins	7 27	14 94
Farmington	Fayette	John J. Hare	29 97	29 60
Farrandsville	Clinton	Jonas Spering	14 40	27 30
Fawn Grove	York	Richard Webb	26 59	35 75
Fayette	Alleghany	John Stephenson	30 81	53 47
Fayette Springs	Fayette	Benj. W. Earl	(no ret.)	
Fayetteville	Franklin	Joseph Boggs	107 56	166 70
Fetherolfsville	Berks	Abraham Long	18 39	18 11
Finleyville	Washington	Levi Finley	53 75	88 17
Fishing Creek	Columbia	James N. Jones	3 16	5 27

POST OFFICES—*Pennsylvania.*

Post Offices.	Counties.	Postmasters.	Compensation.	Net proceeds.
Flatwoods	Fayette	John Townsend	$6 56	$9 53
Fleetville	Luzerne	Roland Richards	9 26	13 86
Fleming	Centre	Sam'l A. Lucas	2 77	5 03
Flicksville	Northampton	John Flick	12 97	21 60
Florence	Washington	Peter Livingston, to 31st May	77 23	134 53
		J. P. M. Buchanan	9 34	11 07
Fogelsville	Lehigh	Solomon Fogel	41 12	47 38
Forest	Butler	Silas Ferry, from 3d Jan'y	1 65	3 14
Forest Lake	Susquehan'h	Abner Griffis	10 92	17 71
Forkston	Wyoming	Richard Adams	14 87	22 29
Fort Littleton	Bedford	James Kelly	19 72	33 57
Foundryville	Columbia	S. F. Headley	6 12	12 19
Fountain Dale	Adams	Joseph Baugher, to 14th May	12 37	21 02
		Reuben Stem	1 74	2 85
Fountain Green	Chester	Amor Carter	17 82	28 80
Fountain Spring	Schuylkill	George Seitzinger	12 31	22 48
Fox Chase	Philadelphia	Amos Snyder	21 73	45 32
Franconia	Montgomery	George Bilger	4 28	8 88
Frankford	Philadelphia	John Deal	286 49	663 97
Frankfort Springs	Beaver	Wm. H. Frazer	49 45	77 71
Franklin	Venango	John H. Shannon	262 59	264 34
Franklin Dale	Bradford	Gilbert Gay	13 03	23 14
Franklintown	York	Henry Ritter	11 13	15 85
Frankstown	Huntingdon	David Durlinger	58 43	58 47
Frantz's Mill (Disc. 14th June.)	Armstrong	James Mitchell, jr	8 45	12 67
Frazer	Chester	Andrew Bear	55 08	96 68
Frederick	Montgomery	Jona. Nyce, (3 qrs.)	4 23	6 67
Fredericksburgh	Lebanon	Christian Long	29 37	48 66
Fredericktown	Washington	Israel Dalbey	19 05	31 38
Freeburgh	Union	Fred'k C. Moyer, to 3d April	13 35	23 10
		William Boyer	2 43	4 71
Freedensburgh	Schuylkill	John Snyder	14 70	25 99
Freedom	Beaver	Henry Bryan	90 56	154 26
Freemansburgh	Northampton	Edward Freeman	31 42	57 02
Freeport	Armstrong	Jacob Alter	141 19	242 06
French Creek	Mercer	John McCracken	2 57	4 46
French's Mills	Bradford	Wm. P. Wylie	11 43	15 67
Frenchville	Clearfield	Francois Coudriet	12 53	22 81
Friedensville	Lehigh	Aug. L. Halbach	15 74	27 29
Friendsville	Susquehan'h	Joseph Hyde, to 11th Nov	19 38	39 29
		Charles L. Brown	42 23	83 52
Fruit Hill	Clearfield	Fred'k W. Schoening, fr. 22d Aug	4 95	8 41

POST OFFICES—*Pennsylvania.*

Post Offices.	Counties.	Postmasters.	Compensation.	Net proceeds.
Fulton	Westmorel'd.	Thomas Copeland	$11 86	$20 15
Gambles	Alleghany	James Lindsay	10 96	20 11
Gap	Lancaster	Hawthorn Freeland, to 20th Feb'y	77 05	129 69
		Andrew C. Buyers	44 25	79 07
Garrettsville	Lycoming	Enos Garrett, from Nov	89	1 94
Gebharts	Somerset	John Knabel, to 1st May	26 71	44 86
		Wm. Aughenburgh	5 87	10 58
Geiger's Mills	Berks	Isaac Geiger	18 86	31 17
Georgetown	Beaver	Salah Pruden	11 86	20 32
Germantown	Philadelphia	Geo. H. Wilson	305 13	763 18
Gettysburgh	Adams	Hez. Van Orsdel, to 12th June	495 44	819 21
		C. N. Berluchy	25 66	49 64
Gibbon's Tavern	Delaware	John W. Ogden	19 95	38 88
Gibson	Susquehan'h	Nathan E. Kennedy	45 55	76 91
Gilchristville	Dauphin	Robert Gilchrist	7 57	11 38
Ginger Hill	Washington	Joseph Hamilton	19 00	30 45
Girard	Erie	Hiram Drury	203 97	194 89
Glade Mills	Butler	Thos. McLaughlin	32 38	53 72
Glade Run	Armstrong	John Borland	17 19	26 75
Glen Connell (Disc. 23d Oct.)	Cambria	Michael Clabaugh	(No ret.)	
Glen Hope	Clearfield	Samuel D. Rhule	17 94	33 21
Glen Rock	York	William Herbst	21 15	30 81
Good Intent	Washington	Robert Chase	14 94	24 20
Goshen	Lancaster	Reuben Cook (3 qs.)	35 92	47 19
Goshenville	Chester	Edmund Hood	12 78	23 08
Grahamville	York	Robert Graham	7 64	10 56
Grampian Hills	Clearfield	Joseph Boone	6 01	10 42
Granville	Bradford	Sylvester Taylor	10 83	15 85
Gratz	Dauphin	Daniel Lehr	44 15	71 33
Gray's Valley	Tioga	Marcus Strange	7 14	9 54
Graysville	Huntingdon	John D. Bell	18 50	32 88
Great Bend	Susquehan'h	Joseph Du Bois	59 73	86 01
Greenbrier	Northumb'd	Daniel Holshue	23 63	29 90
Green Castle	Franklin	David Watson	260 53	433 97
Greene	Lancaster	Fleming McSparran	33 06	55 27
Greenfield	Erie	Ebenezer Eaton	21 25	38 09
Greenland (Disc. 18th July.)	Lancaster	Benjamin Huber	(no ret.)	
Greensboro'	Greene	John Jones	48 71	83 00
Greensburgh	Westmorel'd.	Simon Drum	251 64	404 46
Green Tree	Alleghany	Moses Dunlavy	(No ret.)	
Green Village	Franklin	William Blankney	37 18	62 34
Greenville	Luzerne	Moses P. Berry	6 61	13 53

POST OFFICES—*Pennsylvania.*

Post Offices.	Counties.	Postmasters.	Compensation.	Net proceeds.
Greenwood	Columbia	Joseph Heacock	$8 07	$14 18
Grimville	Berks	Daniel B. Grim	10 49	14 43
Gulf Mills	Montgomery	Perry M. Hunter	40 39	66 86
Gum Tree	Chester	Joseph Hughes	37 95	57 55
Guthriesville	Chester	Alexander Rigg	46 87	79 60
Guy's Mills	Crawford	Wm. G. Coburn	19 19	34 73
Gwynned	Montgomery	Chas. F. Jenkins	18 34	30 28
Half Moon	Centre	John Griffin, jr.	44 09	77 15
Halifax	Dauphin	Henry Shammo, to 13th Feb'y	61 38	84 59
		Anthony W. Lomis	45 80	45 05
Hamburgh	Berks	William Feather	116 95	205 58
Hamlinton	Wayne	Butler Hamlin	55 42	84 90
Hamorton	Chester	Abraham Hamor	36 59	61 01
Hampton	Adams	Charles Blish, to 18th April	18 10	25 58
		Chr'u Cashman, jr.	4 29	7 11
Hanover	York	Theresa C. Myers	145 74	260 87
Harbour Creek	Erie	John Dodge, to 30th Sept.	12 25	11 86
		Solomon McCumber	39 79	47 41
Harewood	Susquehan'h.	William Main	4 96	9 26
Harford	Susquehan'h.	Saxa Seymour	58 67	97 89
Harlensburgh	Mercer	Ch. A. Miltenberger	38 30	66 41
Harleysville	Montgomery	Sam'l H. Cassell	4 33	8 21
Harmonsburgh	Crawford	John B. Rice	57 78	98 51
Harrisburgh	Dauphin	James Peacock	2000 00	19158 63
Harrison City	Westmorel'd.	Peter Highbarger	5 49	8 65
Harrison Valley	Potter	Thomas Colvin	7 85	12 63
Harrisonville	Bedford	Rowland Austin	62 20	56 71
Harrisville	Butler	Wm. P. Brown, to 17th Jan'y	23 38	31 83
		Samuel Kerr, jr.	24 09	39 58
Hartleton	Union	Robt. V. Glover, to 16th Oct.	13 98	27 65
		Daniel Long	46 80	92 82
Hart's X Roads	Crawford	Martin Martzall	40 61	65 09
Hartsville	Bucks	John Engart	73 33	139 53
Harveys	Greene	Wm. S. Harvey	11 50	18 69
Harvey's 5 Points	Westmorel'd.	Joseph Harvey	14 85	15 85
Hat	Lancaster	Esaias Kinzer	11 42	15 82
Hatboro'	Montgomery	Gilbert Hay	35 03	61 21
Havensville	Bradford	David C. Haven	2 90	4 83
Haverford	Delaware	William Bittle	25 45	44 74
Hazleton	Luzerne	Lewis Davenport, to 25th May	65 29	130 50
		William A. Tubbs	5 96	10 37
Heckla	Centre	John Zimmerman	37 37	49 11

POST OFFICES—*Pennsylvania.*

Post Offices.	Counties.	Postmasters.	Compensation.	Net proceeds.
Hecktown........	Northampton	Jacob Schweetzer...	$23 25	$39 61
Heidlersburgh....	Adams......	Leonard Delap.....	18 18	30 40
Hellam..........	York.......	John H. Hershey..	12 16	22 86
Hellen..........	Elk........	Daniel Oyster......	6 01	8 59
Hellertown......	Northampton	Peter Shaffer, to 31st March...........	39 74	68 42
		Wilson Shaffer......	11 94	21 29
Hempfield.......	Lancaster ...	William Myers....	23 67	39 21
Henderson......	Mercer......	Jonathan Henderson	19 39	28 27
Hereford........	Berks.......	Joel Y. Schelly.....	14 38	21 50
Hermitage.......	Mercer	John Hoagland.....	7 91	14 31
Herrick.........	Bradford....	Daniel Durand.....	1 53	2 63
Herriottsville	Alleghany...	John McEwen.....	40 57	65 80
Hetricks	York	Henry Stick.......	26 64	38 85
Hickory	Washington..	Sam'l M. Griffith, to 31st March......	40 70	64 25
		David Hughes......	14 32	22 46
Hickorytown....	Montgomery.	John Hart.........	10 33	21 99
Highland........	Bradford.....	John McCord......	4 12	8 22
High Spire......	Dauphin	Jacob Nisley.......	26 01	48 93
Hillegass........	Montgomery.	Abraham Croll.....	12 73	15 96
Hillsboro'.......	Washington..	Jos. W. Alexander, to 31st March....	43 78	76 69
		Geo. R. McKanna..	15 95	27 88
Hills Grove......	Lycoming...	John J. Sadler......	14 24	19 49
Hill's View......	Westmorel'd.	James Wiley......	11 23	17 66
Hillsville........	Mercer......	John Book, jr......	12 62	20 42
Hill Top........	Wayne	Erastus Skeels......	7 97	14 60
Hilltown........	Bucks.......	Jos. Rosenberger...	8 38	17 16
Hinkletown	Lancaster ...	John Wickel......	46 28	71 69
Hogestown......	Cumberland..	John Clendenin, jr..	74 86	133 89
Holland.........	Venango.....	Austin Merrick....	24 20	42 63
Hollidaysburgh ..	Huntingdon .	James Coffey......	707 52	1503 71
Holmesburgh....	Philadelphia.	Jacob Waterman, to 2d Dec..........	61 12	115 22
		Walter M. Hibbs...	77 43	150 04
Home...........	Indiana	Robert Cannon.....	15 65	25 78
Honesdale.......	Wayne	Thos. H. R. Tracy.	443 01	893 35
Honey Brook....	Chester	David M. Anderson.	62 00	106 69
Hookestown.....	Beaver......	Sam'l McLaughlin..	47 85	79 25
Hopewell	Bedford	Alexander Davis...	25 51	45 05
Hopewell Cotton Works........	Chester	Samuel J. Dickey ..	35 45	61 83
Hornbeck's	Pike........	Jacob Hornbeck ...	5 39	9 85
Hornbrook......	Bradford	Daniel Brink	5 81	10 11
Horse Shoe	Washington.	Felix Boyle, (3 qrs.)	4 49	6 37
Horsham	Montgomery.	Absalom Michener.	26 35	47 53
Houston	Alleghany...	James Hallstead ...	29 82	36 86
Howard	Centre	Jacob V. Thomas..	50 34	87 68

POST OFFICES—*Pennsylvania.*

Post Offices.	Counties.	Postmasters.	Compensation.	Net proceeds.
Howellville	Delaware	Ellis Smedley	$11 62	$19 44
Hughesville	Lycoming	Gershom Biddle	35 65	66 31
Hulmesville	Bucks	Richard Hulme	25 19	49 10
Hummelstown	Dauphin	George Fox	112 95	194 15
Hunterstown	Adams	Hugh King	21 09	31 25
Huntingdon	Huntingdon	David Snare, to 12th April	336 06	674 98
		Francis B. Wallace	63 10	154 10
Huntsville	Luzerne	Truman Atherton	8 06	11 39
Hyde Park	Luzerne	Joseph Griffin	79 03	161 30
Ickesburgh	Perry	Samuel Rice	30 17	46 73
Independence	Washington	Richard Carter	52 35	81 14
Indiana	Indiana	William Moorhead	177 41	339 58
Industry	Beaver	Jacob Ross	12 38	19 72
Intercourse	Lancaster	Moses Eaby	47 81	70 51
Irish Ripple	Beaver	Samuel S. Jackson	25 11	39 00
Irvine	Warren	Wm. A. Irvine	21 34	39 63
Ivy Mills	Delaware	Thos. V. Fairlamb	33 79	63 67
Jackson	Susquehan'ah	Nathaniel Hill, to 30th Sept	5 78	9 98
		James D. Hill	22 25	34 22
Jackson X Roads	Erie	Humphrey A. Hills, to 30th May	49 77	80 59
		Orsamus M. Clark	4 95	9 01
Jackson Hall	Franklin	John Wunderlich	22 80	33 51
Jackson Valley	Susquehan'ah	Charles Campbell	2 38	4 06
Jacksonville	Lehigh	Jacob Oswald	20 26	29 59
Jacobsburgh	Northampton	Thomas Gold	9 78	16 77
Jacob's Creek	Fayette	Solomon Keister	22 31	38 84
James' Creek	Huntingdon	John B. Given	11 50	19 15
Jamestown	Mercer	William Gibson	15 51	30 93
Jefferson	Greene	William Hiller, to 29th May	42 40	81 87
		John Walters	3 43	7 78
Jefferson Furnace	Clarion	Samuel F. Plumer	24 90	36 35
Jeffersonville	Montgomery	Edward L. Bean, (3 qrs.)	15 85	27 87
Jenkintown	Montgomery	William Coltman	39 57	72 71
Jennersville	Chester	Emmor Chandler	22 55	38 85
Jersey Shore	Lycoming	Jos. B. Torbett	296 03	370 58
Jerseytown	Columbia	Levi Bisel	30 78	46 75
Joanna Furnace	Berks	Ann H. Richards	17 74	26 90
Johnstown	Cambria	George W. Kern	287 98	563 70
Jonestown	Lebanon	John Bickel, jr	63 05	118 45
Juliann Furnace	Centre	John Adams	6 61	10 24
Juniata	Perry	Peter Toomey	12 97	20 11

POST OFFICES—*Pennsylvania.*

Post Offices.	Counties.	Postmasters.	Compensation.	Net proceeds.
Karthaus	Clearfield	J. F. W. Schnars	$18 95	$31 17
Kemblesville	Chester	George Kemble	13 76	22 75
Kendall	Beaver	Robert Patton	9 87	14 50
Kendall Creek	McKean	Jno. F. Melvin	40 63	70 94
Kennett's Square	Chester	Levi W. Hoopes	104 37	174 85
Kensington	Philadelphia	Jos. W. Hall	663 12	2012 85
Kent	Indiana	John P. Lafferty	16 52	28 35
Kentuckyville	Susquehan'ah	Stephen P. Chandler	5 47	8 50
Kepner's	Schuylkill	Samuel R. Kepner	5 51	7 85
Kern's Mills	Lehigh	Thomas Kern, to 31st March	8 25	14 61
		Owen Kern	2 33	4 15
Kersey's	Elk	John Green	17 20	36 03
Kimberton	Chester	George Moses	52 34	91 96
King of Prussia	Montgomery	James Miller	21 49	36 59
Kingsessing	Philadelphia	Isaac Leech	21 30	45 08
Kingsley's	Crawford	Ransom Kingsley	22 03	35 47
Kingston	Luzerne	Oliver Helme, to 15th Feb.	56 25	104 36
		Thomas Myers	40 77	70 67
Kingsville	Clarion	William King, jr.	9 88	13 83
Kinzer's	Lancaster	Henry Kinzer	77 28	126 70
Kinzua	Warren	Edward Evans	18 16	30 21
Kirby	Greene	Samuel L. Kirby	15 58	29 18
Kirk's Mills	Lancaster	John Kirk, jr.	20 95	34 59
Kishacoquillas	Mifflin	Jesse A. Cunningham	19 52	34 87
Kiskiminitas	Armstrong	Wm. H. Richardson	17 95	30 01
Kittaning	Armstrong	Benjamin Oswald, to 31st May	187 87	354 44
		Isaac Scott	16 13	31 76
Klecknersville	Northampton	Daniel Kleckner	20 29	26 11
Klinesville	Clarion	Peter A. Kline	14 06	22 25
Knoxville	Tioga	Aaron Alba	29 78	50 47
Kreidersville	Northampton	George Weber, jr.	50 12	80 32
Kulpsville	Montgomery	John Baker	6 75	11 53
Kutztown	Berks	Joseph Heist	113 08	188 44
Laceyville	Wyoming	Thomas S. Parker, to 6th June	39 88	55 17
		Tilston D. Spring	2 90	4 69
Lackawanna	Luzerne	Erastus Smith	13 83	23 52
Lackawaxen	Pike	John Westfall	14 70	19 71
La Fayette	McKean	Joseph Brush	1 92	3 24
La Grange	Wyoming	Joseph Marcy	5 34	7 22
Lahaska	Bucks	Thomas Betts	25 94	43 66
Lairdsville	Lycoming	Chas. W. Funston	6 29	11 59
Lamar	Clinton	William Develing	18 54	30 24
Lampeter	Lancaster	M. Barr, to 31st Mar.	27 81	43 14
		John H. Harman	7 94	11 76

POST OFFICES—*Pennsylvania.*

Post Offices.	Counties.	Postmasters.	Compensation.	Net proceeds.
Lancaster	Lancaster	Mary Dickson	$1337 39	$3659 47
Landisburgh	Perry	Jesse Hipple	87 86	142 79
Landisville	Lancaster	John C. Landis	24 75	36 25
Lanesboro'	Susquehan'ah	Benjamin Comfort	29 95	49 88
Laughlintown	Westmorel'd.	James Moore, jr.	35 66	35 71
Laurel	Cambria	Samuel Davis	3 03	4 44
Laurel Hill	Somerset	Edmund Kiernan	50 57	50 61
Lausanne	Carbon	Samuel Wolf	10 69	15 23
Lavansville	Somerset	David Lavan	21 74	44 77
Lawrenceburgh	Armstrong	Fullerton Parker, to 31st March	23 67	32 10
		Wm. D. Robinson	9 66	15 40
Lawrenceville	Tioga	Chs. H. L. Ford, to 31st Dec.	47 86	87 37
		James Ford	55 12	96 69
Lawsville Centre	Susquehan'ah	Reuben Ives	13 63	18 92
Leacock	Lancaster	Frederick Swope, to 11th Feb.	57 98	91 51
		Jacob Holl	37 41	58 63
Leatherwood	Clarion	James Laughlin	23 49	34 99
Lebanon	Lebanon	Catharine Karch	297 03	638 05
Leechburgh	Armstrong	John L. Leech	36 82	73 08
Leesburgh (Late 'New Lodge.')	Mercer	Chs. G. McFarlane, (1 qr.)	3 22	2 66
Lee's X Roads	Cumberland	John W. Clever, (3 qrs.)	14 69	24 94
Lehigh Gap	Carbon	Thomas Craig, jr.	56 70	100 11
Lehighton	Carbon	Peter Bowman	66 08	104 08
Lehman	Luzerne	Francis Major	4 90	9 08
Leipersville	Delaware	John H. Hill	55 14	105 39
Lenox	Susquehan'ah	Chs. W. Conrad, to 31st March	10 76	7 20
		Danl. H. Wade	3 67	4 99
Le Raysville	Bradford	Denison Johnson	102 99	113 80
Le Roy	Bradford	Martin Holcomb	17 33	28 88
Level Corner (Ch. to 'Linden.')	Lycoming	Paul Brewer, to 31st Dec.	11 05	19 72
Leverington	Philadelphia	John Omensetter	25 04	50 07
Lewisberry	York	Jacob Frankeberger	42 62	71 07
Lewisburgh	Union	William Murray	330 26	684 51
Lewistown	Mifflin	Wm. P. Elliott, to 15th May	527 45	1066 47
		Moses Montgomery	59 19	146 80
Lewisville	Indiana	Robert R. Adams, to 31st March	6 17	8 76
		John C. Armor	1 95	3 31
Liberty	Tioga	Jonathan Sebring	42 30	74 35
Library	Alleghany	John Moore	30 01	42 60

POST OFFICES—*Pennsylvania.*

Post Offices.	Counties.	Postmasters.	Compensation.	Net proceeds.
Light Street	Columbia	Henry B. Fairman, to 7th Nov.	$11 33	$16 02
		Matthew McDowell.	15 55	25 71
Ligonier	Westmorel'd.	John Hargnett	135 48	132 22
Lima	Delaware	Walker Y. Hoopes.	19 92	29 22
Limerick	Montgomery.	Deiter Bucher	17 42	29 13
Lime Ridge	Columbia	C. R. Andre, to 28th Nov.	7 92	14 21
		Sam. W. Thompson, (4 mo.)	6 39	11 26
Limestone	Clarion	John P. McGinity.	18 30	35 94
Linden (Late 'Level Corner.')	Lycoming	Paul Brewer, from 1st Jan.	10 15	18 49
Lindly's Mills	Washington	Joseph Miller	11 55	17 48
Line Lexington	Bucks	Garrett C. Wack	27 17	43 78
Line Mills	Crawford	Amos Line	36 42	62 75
Line Mountain	Northumb'nd	Joseph G. Renn	18 66	23 79
Linglestown	Dauphin	Thomas Barnett	24 44	47 55
Lionville	Chester	Joel Hawley	24 01	46 50
Lisburn	Cumberland	William Loyd	21 18	37 51
Litchfield	Bradford	Daniel Bush	8 94	14 86
Litiz	Lancaster	Fredk. A. Zitzman.	132 34	269 14
Little Marsh	Tioga	Redding Macomber.	4 10	7 12
Little Meadows	Susquehan'ah	Jonathan Barney	10 53	18 71
Little Pine Creek.	Lycoming	John M. English, from 18th Nov.	2 68	5 23
Littlestown	Adams	John A. Davis, to 2d April	64 20	100 85
		Joseph Dysert	16 53	25 58
Livermore	Westmorel'd.	John Gallagher	10 25	18 01
Liverpool	Perry	James Jackman	136 04	148 16
Loag	Chester	Rudolph Huzzard	12 12	22 50
Lobachsville	Berks	David Lobach	17 24	24 13
Lock Haven	Clinton	Geo. W. Parsons, to 1st May	168 28	357 68
		John Moorhead	33 85	62 49
Lockport	Erie	George C. Cranston.	55 45	93 82
Locust Dale	Westmorel'd.	Harrison P. Laird	3 79	5 49
Locust Hill	Washington	Robert Shaw	10 33	15 93
Logan Mills	Clinton	Robert Kleckner	3 69	6 32
Logan's Ferry	Alleghany	Hugh Logan	12 69	18 25
Loganville	York	John Beck	7 90	12 24
London Grove	Chester	David Walton	20 89	37 76
Long Swamp	Berks	Horatio Trexler	20 63	35 35
Loretto	Cambria	Peter Christy	46 29	81 71
Lottsville	Warren	Daniel Lott	34 65	54 81
London	Franklin	William Minich	83 80	92 69
Lower Bern	Berks	Peter L. Kershner	21 04	29 24

POST OFFICES—*Pennsylvania.*

Post Offices.	Counties.	Postmasters.	Compensation.	Net proceeds.
Lower Chanceford	York	Jas. L. M. Call	$31 78	$54 92
Lo'er Mahantango	Schuylkill	Aaron Mattis	13 98	24 47
Lower Merion	Montgomery	Hamilton Egbert	36 05	68 18
Lower Saucon	Northampton	Jacob Kinchline	12 28	13 79
Low Hill	Lehigh	Peter Lentz	8 18	13 32
Loysburgh	Bedford	John H. Keyser	49 39	91 82
Lucinda Furnace	Clarion	Sam'l M. Reynolds	11 56	22 01
Lumberville	Bucks	Albert Livezey	33 87	57 83
Luthersburgh	Clearfield	David Irvin	38 98	38 42
Lymansville	Potter	Cephas Nelson, to 31st Dec	1 60	3 43
		Charles Lyman	2 53	4 92
Lynn	Susquehan'ah	Thomas Cassedy	20 80	32 65
Lynnville	Lehigh	John Seiberling	18 07	23 57
McAlisterville	Juniata	Hugh Wilson	28 48	50 24
McCandless	Butler	John M. McCandless	2 84	4 82
McClellandtown	Fayette	Alexander Black, to 16th June	16 44	25 62
		James M. Allebaugh	1 34	2 65
McConnelsburgh	Bedford	John W. Bohn, to 5th Jan	91 32	119 70
		John C. Fetter	66 76	120 42
McCoysville	Juniata	Jos. S. Laird	12 48	20 61
McCulloch's Mills	Juniata	Samuel McCulloch	10 73	19 71
McEwensville	Northumb'rld	Charles Kelchner, to 20th Jan	34 02	62 33
		Jacob Hill	32 04	56 07
McKean	Erie	Martin Pinney	31 31	57 92
McKeansburgh	Schuylkill	Joshua Boyer	15 01	26 69
McKean's Old Stand	Westmorel'd	Oliver P. Fulton	12 40	19 86
McKees Half Falls	Union	Samuel Young, to 31st March	31 58	31 61
		Philip Hilbish	13 23	8 37
McKeesport	Alleghany	Hugh Rowland	74 41	135 39
McSherrystown	Adams	Henry Herring	30 69	60 24
McVeytown	Mifflin	Jno. C. Montgomery, to 10th June	194 56	187 96
		Geo. W. Brehman	7 35	16 58
McWilliamstown	Chester	Thomas T. Strode, to 31st March	22 78	38 63
		Joshua B. Broome	10 59	16 09
Macungy	Lehigh	John Shiffert, to 31st Dec	12 38	20 77
		Aaron Erdman	14 31	28 85
Madison	Westmorel'd	John McAyeal	15 96	33 48
Mahanoy	Northumbr'd	William Deppen	41 45	57 95
Mahoning	Indiana	John Ewing	13 57	25 16

POST OFFICES—*Pennsylvania.*

Post Offices.	Counties.	Postmasters.	Compensation.	Net proceeds.
Maiden Creek..	Berks.	Owen H. Wily	$41 80	$71 99
Mainesburgh	Tioga.	John Maine	16 17	28 60
Manayunk	Philadelphia..	George W. Davis..	247 51	554 58
Manchester	York	George Beck, jr., to 6th June	20 77	37 08
		John Drayer	(no ret.)	
Manheim	Lancaster	Samuel Ensminger..	107 12	167 03
Mannington (Disc. 18th Jan.)	Susquehan'ah	Jireh Bryan, (3 qrs.)	45	89
Manor	Lancaster	George W. Gibbs	61 26	109 39
Manor Hill	Huntington..	Benjamin Hartman.	29 29	51 79
Mansfield	Tioga	P. Dowd, to 22d May	35 81	61 82
		Benjamin M. Bailey	4 16	7 49
Marchand	Indiana	J. Kelly, to 14th Aug.	96	1 41
		Alexander Hamilton	5 36	7 30
Marcus Hook	Delaware	William S. Walker, to 22d May	73 06	130 53
		John Mustin	6 64	13 84
Margaretta Furn'e	York	Edmund Connellee..	46 57	92 06
Marietta	Lancaster	Jacob Glatz	181 42	360 97
Marion	Franklin	John Clugston	21 15	33 71
Marsh	Chester	Waters Dewees	27 32	47 42
Marshallton	Chester	George Martin	63 68	105 26
Martha Furnace	Centre	John Curtin	8 59	16 86
Marticksville	Lancaster	Henry Stock	34 61	50 87
Martinsburgh	Bedford	Theophilus Snyder..	110 08	208 12
Martin's Creek	Northampton	Wm. McIlhanney..	39 39	67 26
Masontown	Fayette	Elisha Langhead	39 95	68 69
Mauch Chunk	Carbon	Alexander Stedman.	438 72	716 84
Maytown	Lancaster	Wm. S. Campbell, to 10th Dec	25 89	41 27
		Peter Albright	33 45	54 82
Mead Corners	Crawford	Stillman Dewey	5 01	8 80
Meadville	Crawford	Joseph C. Hays, to 5th Oct	154 03	313 70
		Charles L. Rowand.	392 85	757 16
Mechanicsburgh	Cumberland	George F. Cain, to 20th Dec	64 61	115 06
		Jacob Dorsheimer..	88 36	157 82
Mechanicsville	Bucks	Peter Lester	2 86	6 66
Mehoopany	Wyoming	William H. Barnes.	30 80	50 24
Menallen	Adams	Jesse Houck	10 62	15 78
Mercer	Mercer	Thomas S. Cunningham, to 31st Dec..	175 63	238 31
		John McGill, from 25th Jan	159 76	225 30
Mercersburgh	Franklin	Thomas P. Bard, to 28th Jan	247 90	433 00
		Daniel Shaffer	169 33	348 04

POST OFFICES—*Pennsylvania.*

Post Offices.	Counties.	Postmasters.	Compensation.	Net proceeds.
Merrittstown	Fayette	George Brown	$36 70	$54 87
Mexico	Juniata	James Thompson	54 48	105 07
Meyer's Mills	Somerset	Peter Meyer	25 25	46 83
Meyerstown	Lebanon	Cyrus G. Stoever	113 11	206 93
Middleburgh	Union	John Smith, to 31st May	27 92	53 03
		Jacob Wittenmeyer	(No ret.)	
Middle Creek	Union	Andrew Ulsh	6 87	12 14
Middleport	Schuylkill	John Mertz	28 60	61 03
Middletown	Dauphin	John Hicks, to 31st Dec	136 62	286 17
		Edward S. Kendig	157 14	298 53
Mifflinburgh	Union	John Stitzer, jr., to 31st Dec	60 73	109 62
		Jacob Lashells	60 04	116 14
Mifflintown	Juniata	Mary W. Abraham	173 73	273 53
Mifflinville	Columbia	Elisha B. Brown	36 42	55 33
Milan	Bradford	Guy Tracy	10 82	14 78
Milesburgh	Centre	Chs. G. Ryman, to 4th Oct	40 23	37 84
		Isaac Buffington	82 36	115 63
Milestown	Philadelphia	Bennett Medary	42 71	81 50
Milford	Pike	John T. Cross, to 26th May	169 87	146 86
		James S. Wallace	17 52	15 66
Millardsville	Susquehan'ah	Edwin R. Grow	9 43	11 13
Mill Creek	Huntingdon	Leonard G. Kessler	34 46	68 59
Millersburgh	Dauphin	Adam Light, to 31st Jan	33 41	55 87
		Jacob Seal	20 88	39 06
Millerstown	Perry	William Robison, to 10th July	3 32	3 17
		William H. Leas	122 48	132 14
Millersville	Lancaster	Henry Funk	35 62	64 03
Mill Hall	Clinton	George W. Myers	57 08	105 71
Millheim	Centre	William H. Roush	86 04	99 45
Millport	Potter	Jos. C. Allen, (3 qrs)	4 46	7 87
Millsboro'	Washington	Nimrod Grabile, to 31st March	20 22	31 94
		Thomas J. Dalbey	6 62	10 26
Millville	Columbia	James Masters	14 54	24 98
Milton	Northumbr'ld	Leonard Stoughton, to 2d Dec	127 30	253 90
		William C. Wilson	173 29	366 88
Minersville	Schuylkill	John Provost, to 31st Dec	126 18	275 07
		Michael Weaver	142 03	314 21
Mitchell's Mills	Indiana	John Clarke	18 98	35 85
Mohrsville	Berks	John H. Mohr	47 58	97 35

POST OFFICES—*Pennsylvania.*

Post Offices.	Counties.	Postmasters.	Compensation.	Net proceeds.
Molltown	Berks	John Housnet	$7 20	$14 15
Monongahela City	Washington	Wm. S. Mellinger	146 76	271 65
Monroe	Bucks	John H. Johnson	96 67	189 87
Monroeton	Bradford	Gordon F. Mason	63 92	103 39
Montgomery's Ferry	Perry	Wm. Montgomery, to 5th June	12 22	19 83
		John Deckard	1 20	1 88
Montgomeryville	Montgomery	Mathias Young	38 08	69 24
Montours	Alleghany	John McCluskey	6 42	10 27
Montrose	Susquehan'ah	Rasselas Searle	404 88	498 20
Montures ville	Lycoming	Wm. Tomlinson	79 36	136 47
Moon	Alleghany	Joseph Cooper, to 31st May	16 10	26 27
		John Stevenson	(No ret.)	
Mooresburgh	Columbia	Hugh McWilliams	17 12	31 20
Moravia (Dis. 14th June.)	Beaver	Isaac N. Hoops, (3 qrs.)	4 08	6 37
Mordansville	Columbia	Frederick Miller	2 49	5 06
Moreland	Lycoming	Wm. Chamberlin	7 03	9 65
Morgantown	Berks	David Morgan, to 13th June	51 89	79 53
		Milton Rutherford	2 78	4 49
Morris	Tioga	William Babb	5 50	8 88
Morris Dale	Clearfield	James Allport	(No ret.)	
Morrisville	Bucks	Andrew Crozer	122 80	211 00
Mount Airy	Berks	Herman Umstead	17 21	27 18
Mount Alto	Franklin	John Kuhn	52 79	102 80
Mount Bethel	Northampton	Jesse Reichard, to 31st Dec.	22 36	35 06
		Aaron Hess	23 08	37 04
Mount Hope	Lancaster	A. Bates Grubb	12 29	23 48
Mount Jackson	Beaver	Cyrus Clark	72 87	114 95
Mount Joy	Lancaster	Jas. W. Hendrickson, to 18th Nov.	72 56	128 63
		James Laird	134 58	243 41
Mount Morris	Greene	Oliver Evans	23 52	43 05
Mount Pleasant	Westmorel'd.	Joseph Lippincott, to 24th April	195 92	146 56
		John Lloyd	39 14	35 96
Mt. Pleasant Mills	Union	Philip Schnee	6 15	10 59
Mount Pocono	Monroe	Peter Merwine, jr.	13 97	19 24
Mount Republic	Wayne	Alva W. Norton, (3 qrs.)	6 57	10 75
Mount Rock	Cumberland	Henry H. Grove	23 93	38 87
Mount Union	Huntingdon	James Morgan, to 31st March	16 52	30 58
		John Sharer	6 51	12 91
Mount Vernon	Chester	John D. Ross	18 57	25 36

POST OFFICES—*Pennsylvania*.

Post Offices.	Counties.	Postmasters.	Compensation.	Net proceeds.
Mount Zion	Lebanon	Daniel Light	$9 08	$12 62
Muddy C'k Forks	York	John Manifold	18 39	25 00
Muhlenburgh	Luzerne	Lawrence Hess, to 31st Dec	5 65	8 82
		George Muchler, fm. 24th April	1 45	1 79
Multicaulisville	Perry	Sam'l O. Keson, jr., to 31st March	9 74	14 44
		William Hipple	3 24	4 20
Muncy	Lycoming	John P. Schuyler, to 31st Dec	106 67	215 29
		William Michael	117 13	232 64
Munntown	Washington	Samuel Hamilton, (3 qrs)	6 63	9 12
Munster	Cambria	John Thomas	14 90	28 02
Murdocksville	Washington	Joseph McClarn	8 77	13 28
Murrinsville	Butler	Andrew J. Higgins	13 92	23 05
Murrysville	Westmorel'd	James Irwin, to 12th Feb'y	19 76	25 05
		Simon Hugus	13 03	24 34
Naglesville	Monroe	Ferdinand Dutot, fr. 13th May	0 09	0 22
Nanticoke	Luzerne	Silas Alexander	56 87	91 61
Nazareth	Northampton	Christian R. Hoeber	154 53	270 99
Neffsville	Lancaster	Jacob Minnich	21 44	38 42
Nelson	Tioga	Joseph M. White	21 13	37 77
Nescopeck	Luzerne	Rich'd M. Brundage to 10th May	13 03	23 42
		Joel C. Lance, from 15th May	1 35	2 32
Nesquehoning	Carbon	Wm. W. Blakslee	31 14	61 10
Nether Providence	Delaware	Peter Worrall	35 64	71 79
New Albany	Bradford	Wells Wilcox	25 35	47 64
New Alexandria	Westmorel'd	Wm. R. Speer	123 71	122 09
New Bedford	Mercer	Henry Hoagland	39 74	57 73
New Berlin	Union	Philip Franck	137 56	271 75
Newberry	Lycoming	Mary A. Cummings	43 88	70 56
Newberrytown	York	Thos. Wickersham, to 8th April	12 42	18 03
		Jesse C. Hays	4 77	7 10
New Bethlehem	Clarion	Thomas McKelvey	11 59	16 32
New Bloomfield	Perry	Robert R. Guthrie, to 31st Dec'r	57 25	110 46
		Sam'l G. Morrison, (1 qr.)	34 95	64 72
New Bridgeville	York	Joseph Kelley	8 00	13 10
New Britain	Bucks	Elias Shelley	1 65	3 90
New Buffalo	Perry	William Jackson	34 31	28 79

POST OFFICES—*Pennsylvania.*

Post Offices.	Counties.	Postmasters.	Compensation.	Net proceeds.
Newburgh	Cumberland	Jno. F. Eisenhower	$45 94	$71 05
Newcastle	Mercer	David Shafer	242 18	491 58
New Chester	Adams	Nich. Taughenbaugh	13 31	20 23
New Columbia	Union	Hy. R. Waggoner	27 34	46 58
New Cumberland	Cumberland	Henry Breneman, to 31st Dec'r	45 03	74 28
		Jas. K. Boak	47 86	83 53
New Derry	Westmorel'd.	Adam Beamer	41 57	66 29
New Garden	Chester	Jacob Taylor	39 65	61 53
New Geneva	Fayette	Daniel Hermany	59 19	93 41
New Germantown	Perry	William Hays, to 31st March	19 79	35 75
		Wm. A. Morrison	5 46	9 60
New Hanover	Montgomery	Fred'k Brendlinger	16 09	24 05
New Holland	Lancaster	Henry Roland, to 3d June	79 97	150 29
		Hamilton Ayars	10 87	12 31
New Hope	Bucks	Jos. D. Murray	192 61	356 58
New Jerusalem	Berks	Anthony Lefever	10 22	19 46
New Lodge (Ch'd to "Leesburgh.")	Mercer	Lewis Frankenburger, 3 qrs	9 71	11 76
New London X Roads	Chester	S. A. Cunningham	136 95	135 40
Newman's Mills	Indiana	Peter Newman	29 66	50 36
New Milford	Susquehan'h	John Badger, to 16th June	96 58	149 76
		Wm. C. Ward	3 64	6 74
New Oxford	Adams	Mary Melsheimer	46 03	75 95
Newport	Perry	Stuart Law	87 04	136 86
Newportville	Bucks	Thomas Baker, to 31st March	10 52	19 84
		John G. Hibbs	5 47	8 69
New Providence	Lancaster	John Peoples	36 41	57 92
New Richmond	Crawford	Samuel Cannon	8 41	15 18
Newry	Huntingdon	Robert McNamara	33 47	60 56
New Salem	Fayette	Perry C. Bolsinger	12 79	22 43
New Stanton	Westmorel'd	John Zuck	9 68	18 19
Newtown	Bucks	Rudolph C. Nagel	111 16	191 08
Newt'n Hamilton	Mifflin	James North, to 23d Jan'y	26 93	49 27
		John Purcell	26 92	48 57
Newtown Square	Delaware	Walter W. Green	22 46	43 53
New Tripoli	Lehigh	Samuel Camp	17 61	24 05
Newville	Cumberland	John Moore	206 99	379 67
New Wilmington	Mercer	Wm. D. Clark	53 88	103 95
Nicetown (Dis. 23d Aug.)	Philadelphia	Joseph Boucher, to 26th Aug	1 67	3 26
Nicholson	Wyoming	Nathan Bacon	15 48	25 25
Nippenose	Lycoming	John I. Sanderson	24 21	42 53

POST OFFICES—*Pennsylvania.*

Post Offices.	Counties.	Postmasters.	Compensation.	Net proceeds.
Nittany	Centre	John Martin	$40 62	$74 82
Noblestown	Alleghany	George S. Head	52 50	79 26
Norristown	Montgomery	Philip Hahn	406 37	948 74
Norritonville	Montgomery	Leonard Metz	4 15	6 25
North Bend	Venango	L. T. Reno, (3 qrs.)	5 48	10 11
North East	Erie	Truman Tuttle, to 25th May	220 87	299 63
		William Griffith	18 93	18 46
North Flat	Wyoming	Sam'l T. Sturdevant	2 81	4 63
North Liberty	Mercer	Robert Shaw	47 51	56 51
North Moreland	Wyoming	Asa Keeler	16 47	32 36
North Orwell	Bradford	John W. Alger	3 65	6 42
North Sewickly (Ch'd to "Wertembargh.")	Beaver	Nathaniel Hazen	22 41	39 38
North Smithfield	Bradford	Ira C. Bullock	9 06	15 76
North Star	Alleghany	William Johnston	8 29	14 46
Northumberland	Northumb'd	Daniel Weimer, to 8th Dec	217 95	132 61
		John W. Miles	317 65	165 59
Northville	Erie	Harcourt Morey, to 31st March	33 46	33 51
		Sidney Hills	6 77	12 43
North Washingt'n	Westmorel'd	John S. Alexander	24 12	39 42
North Whitehall	Lehigh	Stephen Balliet	35 95	68 59
Norwich	McKean	Geo. W. Burdick	5 41	10 02
Numidia	Columbia	Elijah Price	45 17	45 21
Oak Grove Furnace	Perry	Frederick Boger	17 89	30 16
Oak Hill	Lancaster	Jonathan Hamilton	36 88	57 07
Oakland	Armstrong	George Nulph	6 18	10 72
Oakland Mills	Juniata	Lucian Wilson	22 37	39 19
Ohioville	Beaver	Benoni Dawson	8 76	15 24
Oil Creek	Crawford	John Robison	51 22	83 73
Old Fort	Centre	Alexander McCoy	52 21	52 23
Old Hickory	Bradford	Alfred Forgerson, to 31st Dec'r	3 54	6 02
		Edward A. Ayers, from 17th March	3 92	5 98
Oley	Berks	Henry Dengler	16 07	30 90
Orange	Luzerne	Elihu Rogers	3 26	5 10
Orangeville	Columbia	Emanuel Lazarus	40 70	69 90
Orbisonia	Huntingdon	Thos. E. Orbison	30 36	59 55
Orrstown	Franklin	James B. Orr	35 70	60 67
Orwell	Bradford	Henry Gibbs	48 41	52 50
Orwigsburgh	Schuylkill	William Frailey	249 14	455 13
Ottsville	Bucks	Jonas Laubenstine, to 31st March	6 15	11 66
		Henry Cutwaltz	2 16	3 74

POST OFFICES—*Pennsylvania.*

Post Offices.	Counties.	Postmasters.	Compensation.	Net proceeds.
Oxford	Chester	Thos. S. Dickey	$91 00	$150 72
Palmyra	Lebanon	Peter Rodearmel	53 89	94 74
Panpack Eddy	Wayne	Wm. C. Conkling	10 83	14 26
Paoli	Chester	Sarah Davis	77 77	157 34
Papertown	Cumberland	Michael M. Ege	41 30	46 88
Paradise	Lancaster	Adam K. Witmer	154 50	252 24
Paradise Furnace	Huntingdon	Percival P. Dewees	8 15	15 64
Paris	Washington	Levi Shipley	39 31	67 64
Parkersville	Chester	Carpenter Webb	12 94	18 50
Parkesburgh	Chester	Joseph Stott	71 47	149 29
Parkison	Beaver	Thomas Parkison	9 72	16 04
Parrysville	Carbon	James Anthony	12 99	14 66
Patterson's Mills	Washington	James Patterson	19 45	30 04
Paxinos	Northumb'd	Henry Wasser	36 51	36 96
Peach Bottom	York	James McConkey	45 66	83 64
Pealers	Columbia	Daniel Pealer	2 95	5 32
Penningtonville	Chester	Thomas Pennington	77 20	137 89
Penn Line	Crawford	Jabez Holcomb	24 80	47 67
Penn Run	Indiana	Samuel Wiggins	6 20	11 25
Penn's Creek	Union	John A. Wolfley (Includes $1 98 com. $3 48 net pro. for Middleburg.)	6 89	13 29
Penn's Grove	Delaware	Samuel Riddle	112 94	204 62
Penn's Valley	Centre	John Housel, 3 qrs.	18 42	33 06
Pennsville (Dis. 31st Jan.)	Bucks	James Gaine, 2 qrs.	2 46	4 02
Perrine	Mercer	Enoch Perrine	19 45	34 27
Perry	Venango	Robt. J. Neill	14 65	19 27
Perryopolis	Fayette	William McCray	36 70	59 87
Perrysville	Alleghany	Alex'r McElwain	20 38	37 44
Petersboro' (Dis. 4th Sept.)	Tioga	John Rushmore	(no ret.)	
Petersburgh (Late "Clark's Ferry.")	Perry	Thomas Black, from 14th Feb'y	57 90	112 53
Petersville	Northampton	Jonas Snyder, to 30th Oct	6 86	9 39
		Samuel Seem	15 49	23 04
Philadelphia	Philadelphia	James Hoyt, jr., to 11th May	1725 27	120770 83
		George F. Lehman	274 73	19428 15
Philipsburg	Centre	John G. Runk	93 38	175 56
Phipps' Mills	Venango	John Phipps	7 22	13 14
Phœnixville	Chester	Major McVeagh	172 14	354 66
Pickering	Chester	Robert Hughes	20 73	30 17
Pike	Bradford	Edward Crandal	14 74	23 83
Pike Mills	Potter	Owen B. Goodman	13 67	24 12
Pike Run	Washington	William Morgan	46 59	79 60

POST OFFICES—*Pennsylvania.*

Post Offices.	Counties.	Postmasters.	Compensation.	Net proceeds.
Pike Township	Berks	Jacob Gabel	$20 49	$27 03
Pine Creek	Tioga	Hezekiah Stowell	14 84	25 35
Pine Grove	Schuylkill	John Kitzmiller	147 10	249 24
Pine Grove Mills	Centre	Sam'l E. Shultz	51 31	95 57
Pine Street	Elk	Wm. M. Mason	2 51	4 23
Pine Valley	Warren	Lyman Calkins	6 03	7 99
Pineville	Bucks	Jesse P. Carver	32 11	55 46
Pinksville	Armstrong	James Pinks	39 64	58 67
Piny	Armstrong	Thomas Magee	21 87	34 27
Piquea	Lancaster	Amos S. Henderson	47 45	80 70
Pittsburgh	Alleghany	Robert M. Riddle	2001 00	23962 98
Pittsfield	Warren	James L. Acocks	18 62	26 45
Pitts' Mills	Armstrong	John Jack	(no ret.)	
Pittston Ferry	Luzerne	Anson Curtis, 3 qrs.	41 49	66 42
Plainsville	Luzerne	Samuel Saylor	13 77	21 36
Pleasant Grove	Lancaster	Jeremiah B. Haynes	22 06	35 57
Pleasant Mount	Wayne	Thomas H. Brown	146 20	135 76
Pleasant Unity	Westmorel'd	John Latta	35 67	61 11
Pleasant Valley	Bucks	Lewis Ott	6 17	12 96
Pleasantville	Montgomery	Fred'k W. Hoover	5 98	9 86
Plumer	Venango	Henry McCalmont	10 01	15 34
Plumstead	Bucks	John L. Delp	13 70	27 61
Plymouth	Luzerne	Carleton L. Farnum, to 17th January	61 91	59 64
		Samuel Davenport, jr	40 22	55 26
Point Pleasant	Bucks	George W. Closson	17 46	32 11
Poke Run	Westmorel'd	John Craig, jr	7 08	12 68
Portage	Cambria	Bernard McColgan	26 55	46 38
Port Alleghany	McKean	Solomon H. Barrett	7 60	13 09
Port Carbon	Schuylkill	Henry Shissler	235 78	525 34
Port Clinton	Schuylkill	Samuel Boyer	76 26	136 81
Porterfield	Venango	Charles Shippen	19 43	27 52
Porter Ridge	Susquehan'h	Pliny Birchard, to 25th April	2 59	4 70
		Robert Griffis	62	1 24
Portersville	Butler	James Hall, to 31st March	39 79	64 35
		John Hall	11 62	19 00
Port Richmond	Philadelphia	Isaac Tustin	87 14	190 24
Port Royal	Juniata	Alex'r Magonagle	35 74	63 56
Potter's Mills	Centre	James Potter	117 43	198 32
Pottstown	Montgomery	Tobias Sellers	213 82	384 72
Pottsville	Schuylkill	John T. Werner, to 4th September	180 29	702 82
		Michael Cochran	874 37	2672 04
Preston	Wayne	Daniel Underwood	8 81	13 78
Pricetown	Berks	Charles Levan	9 59	18 64
Priceville	Wayne	Matthias Morgridge	10 82	14 58

POST OFFICES—*Pennsylvania.*

Post Offices.	Counties.	Postmasters.	Compensation.	Net proceeds.
Prompton	Wayne	Henry Dart, to 31st March	$57 59	$57 37
		Edwin Foote	12 29	20 57
Prospect	Butler	Matthew W. Spear	36 17	58 07
Prospect Hill	Jefferson	Tilton Reynolds	11 92	18 00
Providence	Luzerne	Jacob R. Bloom, to 31st March	53 22	92 96
		John P. Harding, fr. 25th June	1 13	2 52
Pughtown	Chester	Wm. H. Brown	31 79	49 88
Pulaski	Mercer	Hugh Bell	69 31	105 99
Punxutawney	Jefferson	John R. Rees	88 86	147 54
Purdyville	Wayne	Reuben R. Purdy	3 85	5 94
Putneyville	Armstrong	David Putney, from 14th September	9 15	11 29
Quakertown	Bucks	Jos. R. Lancaster	41 85	74 21
Quincey	Franklin	James McKinley	52 60	92 17
Rainsburgh	Bedford	J. L. McLaughlin	14 05	27 68
Ralston	Lycoming	Peter Thompson	25 93	31 46
Raubsville	Northampton	Luther Calvin	30 50	55 71
Rawlinsville	Lancaster	John Rawlins	20 56	28 19
Ray's Hill	Bedford	John Nycum	53 05	53 10
Reading	Berks	Charles Troxell, to 31st March	753 50	2038 09
		John R. Wright	(no ret.)	
Reamstown	Lancaster	Henry S. Shirk	64 96	104 55
Rebersburgh	Centre	John R. Burkert	30 31	52 16
Red Bank	Clarion	R. M. McFarland	26 86	46 01
Red Ba'k Furnace	Armstrong	Alexander Reynolds	16 41	33 65
Reidsburgh	Clarion	Jesse D. Porter, to 31st March	7 60	9 44
		Wm. F. Keever	2 69	3 61
Reinholdsville	Lancaster	John K. Schewer	15 39	21 89
Rice's Landing	Greene	Joseph Sedgwick	9 43	12 82
Richboro'	Bucks	Mahlon Miller	19 01	38 16
Richfield	Juniata	John Wallis	15 25	29 11
Rich Hill (Dis. 12 Aug. '45.)	Butler	David Garvin	4 00	7 68
Richlandtown	Bucks	Chris'n A. Snyder	7 35	12 95
Richmond	Northampton	John Simonton, to 15th June	12 78	24 31
		Philip Gross	3 58	6 53
Ridgebury	Bradford	John Burt	14 57	26 20
Ridgeway	Elk	Erasmus Morey, to 19th May	30 75	55 51
		Caleb Dill	3 03	6 40
Rileysville	Wayne	Francis Blair	9 85	16 25

POST OFFICES—*Pennsylvania.*

Post Offices.	Counties.	Postmasters.	Compensation.	Net proceeds.
Rising Sun	Philadelphia	Joseph Keyser, to 17th September	$7 22	$8 02
		John Purcil	28 98	51 58
Rittersville	Lehigh	Charles Ritter	9 50	15 28
Road Hall	Lycoming	William Sedam	12 97	25 69
Robeson	Berks	Henry B. Seidel	4 07	6 88
Rock Dale	Crawford	Amasa B. Ross	53 88	87 41
Rock Hill	Bucks	Jacob Worman	10 10	19 92
Rockland	Venango	John S. McKean	40 09	65 52
Rockport	Carbon	Robert Butler	10 95	20 94
Rockville	Chester	Samuel McClees	39 69	66 99
Rocky Spring	Franklin	Robt. E. Tolbert	7 31	12 41
Rodrocksville	Berks	Jonas Rodrock	17 29	32 24
Rohrersburgh	Berks	Valentine Brobst	43 47	58 31
Rohrsburg	Columbia	John Rees	19 26	28 20
Rome	Bradford	Wm. E. Maynard	40 44	43 57
Roseburgh	Perry	Edward Miller	8 23	14 28
Roseland	Cambria	Benjamin Byers	2 62	4 75
Ross Common (Dis. 9th May.)	Chester	Washington Ross, 3 qrs	6 51	10 88
Ross' Mills	Armstrong	George Ross	(no ret.)	
Rossville	York	Tempest T. Gardner	25 59	44 40
Rostraver	Westmorel'd.	Morgan W. Eckley.	21 23	34 12
Roulette	Potter	Burrel Lyman	3 78	7 24
Roxbury	Franklin	Samuel Staily	29 99	52 15
Royer's Ford	Montgomery.	David Gow	17 80	31 55
Rummerfield Cr'k	Bradford	Albert Newell	22 49	35 62
Rural Valley	Armstrong	Robert A. Robinson	28 21	48 81
Rush	Susquehan'h.	Almon Pickett	8 50	15 39
Rushville	Susquehan'h.	Henry I. Champion	18 05	33 56
Russell Hill	Wyoming	Wilber Russell	12 00	19 14
Russellville	Chester	Charles Wallace	41 88	65 61
Russelsburgh	Warren	Robert Russel	56 39	111 99
Rutland	Tioga	William Rose, jr	17 33	25 74
Ryerson's Station	Greene	Jonathan H. Vanata	19 97	34 78
Sadsburyville	Chester	David T. Ash, to 31st December	25 35	43 67
		Joseph Wiley	20 57	37 89
Saegerstown	Crawford	Jeremiah Hecker	40 72	74 24
Saegersville	Lehigh	Peter Miller, jr	16 56	28 01
Safe Harbor	Lancaster	John Herr	35 26	56 42
Saint Clair	Bedford	Fred'k D. Beegle	32 40	55 74
Saint Marys	Chester	Jacob Dampman	21 96	33 19
Saint Thomas	Franklin	Henry Smith	125 09	123 21
Salem	Mercer	William Leech	7 51	11 79
Salem ⋈ Roads	Westmorel'd.	John Hugus	42 85	48 36
Salfordville	Montgomery.	Sam'l K. Smith	10 32	19 72
Salona	Clinton	Abm. H. Best	73 74	125 15

POST OFFICES—*Pennsylvania.*

Post Offices.	Counties.	Postmasters.	Compensation.	Net proceeds.
Salt Lick........	Fayette	Samuel Scrichfield..	$5 26	$9 39
Saltsburgh.......	Indiana	Nelson B. Loughry.	114 78	206 11
Sandy Creek....	Mercer......	Elkannah Holloway	22 54	31 61
Sarah...........	Bedford......	Peter Shoenberger..	43 11	78 52
Saucon Valley...	Lehigh.......	Charles Wiltman...	19 94	36 93
Saxenburgh	Butler.......	Joseph Sheely......	31 53	55 69
Saylorsburgh	Monroe......	J.Mackis,to 7th May	28 03	41 75
		Lynford Troch.....	4 82	7 34
Schellsburgh.....	Bedford.....	Maria Schell.......	107 63	198 29
Schoeneck.......	Lancaster ...	Andrew Wissler, to 31st March......	11 48	17 27
		James Kirling......	4 05	6 33
Schuylkill	Chester	Isaac Price.........	52 44	83 61
Schuylkill Bend..	Berks.......	Jonas Shalter......	14 93	28 46
Schuylkill Haven.	Schuylkill....	Edward Huntzinger.	290 99	615 11
Schwenck's Store.	Montgomery.	Jacob Schwenck...	9 39	16 68
Scott..........	Wayne	H. D. Williams....	6 01	9 35
Scottsville	Wyoming....	John Fassett.......	5 89	10 12
Second Fork.....	Elk.........	Jacob Coleman.....	3 07	7 04
Seiberlingville....	Lehigh......	Joshua Seiberling, to 15th May.......	6 54	9 55
		Amos B. Frederici..	37	88
Seigfried's Ferry.	Northampton	Daniel Levan......	5 44	6 48
Selin's Grove....	Union.......	Anthony Keenstler.	207 91	408 76
Seller's Tavern...	Bucks.......	Henry Troxel......	10 64	21 80
Service..........	Luzerne.....	David Reed........	5 41	8 45
Setzler's Store....	Chester	Frederick Setzler...	24 06	42 90
Seventy Six.....	Beaver......	Daniel McCallister..	8 62	13 57
Seven Valleys...	York	John E. Zeigler....	8 01	15 74
Sewickly Bottom.	Alleghany...	David Shields......	90 17	164 94
Shade Gap......	Huntingdon .	Alex'r C. Blair.....	24 04	46 29
Shaefferstown....	Lebanon	Wm. M. Weigley...	53 45	83 63
Shafers.........	Monroe.....	Daniel Brown......	19 51	32 33
Shamokin........	Northumb'ld.	Samuel John.......	14 88	25 09
Shamokin Dam...	Union.......	George Keen.......	12 53	23 66
Shannonville.....	Montgomery.	John J. Dettro......	19 39	30 10
Sharon..........	Mercer......	Conrad G. Carver, to 19th May	63 47	114 77
		John E. Hull......	11 76	17 11
Sharon Centre....	Potter.......	Isaac W. Jones....	5 90	11 12
Sharpsburgh......	Alleghany....	Thomas Gardiner ..	106 10	105 36
Shartlesville......	Berks........	Solomon Albright ..	19 01	28 13
Shaver's Creek...	Huntingdon .	Joseph M. Stevens .	51 98	94 24
Shawnee.........	Monroe.....	Jos. V. Wilson	3 62	6 05
Shaw's Meadows.	Monroe.....	P. Kemerer, (3 qrs.)	5 31	8 34
Sheffield.........	Warren.....	Geo. H. Head	10 43	17 56
Shelocta.........	Indiana	Samuel McCartney, to 31st Dec.......	8 64	13 74
		Robert McChesney.	8 72	12 76

POST OFFICES—*Pennsylvania.*

Post Offices.	Counties.	Postmasters.	Compensation.	Net proceeds.
Shepherdstown...	Cumberland.	David Sheffer......	$58 10	$89 48
Sherers ✕ Roads..	Westmorel'd	Hy. K. McKallip..	12 50	19 26
Sheshequin......	Bradford....	Joseph Kingsbury..	24 91	38 79
Shickshinny......	Luzerne.....	William Hoyt, to 11th June.......	24 66	41 37
		Lot Search, jr......	1 72	3 20
Shippen.........	McKean....	Lemuel Lucore.....	4 60	8 30
Shippensburgh...	Cumberland.	Jonathan Peal, to 31st Dec............	241 20	256 32
		Levi K. Donavin, fr. 28th Jan.........	165 74	262 01
Shippensville....	Clarion......	Adam Black, to 22d Jan.............	56 62	56 08
		Henry Sloan.......	60 66	73 68
Shiremantown...	Cumberland.	Joseph Best, jr., to 31st Dec.........	32 02	56 58
		William Mateer....	35 09	61 03
Shirleysburgh....	Huntingdon.	Benjamin Leas.....	69 79	121 44
Shrewsbury.....	York.......	William McAbee..	57 15	96 06
Sidonsburgh.....	York.......	James Kerr, to 30th Sept............	3 05	4 44
		George Burns......	11 61	17 01
Silver Lake......	Susquehanna.	Edward W. Rose..	19 29	42 68
Simpson's Store..	Washington..	Jonathan Simpson..	8 97	12 55
Sinking Spring...	Berks........	Aaron Mull........	35 70	67 53
Sinking Valley Mills.........	Huntingdon.	Robert Stewart, jr..	33 70	51 73
Sinnamahoning..	Lycoming...	William Floyd, jr..	13 75	21 85
Skinner's Eddy..	Wyoming...	Charles Sturdevant, to 7th June......	37 23	64 68
		Henry W. Neigh..	2 77	5 18
Skippack.........	Montgomery	Jacob G. Sorver....	11 27	22 98
Slate Lick.......	Armstrong...	George F. Keener...	26 68	44 60
Slate Ridge......	York.......	Samuel Parke......	5 35	9 85
Slippery Rock....	Butler.......	George Christley...	77 60	76 36
Sloyersville......	Luzerne......	Jacob Sloyer.......	6 94	9 89
Smicksburg......	Indiana......	Joseph Robinson...	21 73	37 30
Smithfield........	Fayette.....	John Brownfield...	68 98	116 78
Smithport........	McKean....	Philetus Ford......	79 98	124 20
Smith's Ferry....	Beaver......	Samuel Smith......	15 66	22 30
Smith's Mills....	Clearfield.....	Jonathan Boynton, to 31st December.	5 11	7 25
		Isaac Wilson......	5 43	9 42
Smithville........	Lancaster...	John C. Smith......	7 86	11 80
Snow Shoe.......	Centre.......	James McMasters, from 12th Feb. '45	1 15	1 20
Snydersville......	Monroe......	Peter Snyder.......	21 59	35 51
Snydertown......	Northumb'ld.	Joseph Hoover.....	no ret'rn.	
Somerfield.......	Somerset....	J. S. Hagans, (1 qr.)	13 41	11 61

POST OFFICES—*Pennsylvania.*

Post Offices.	Counties.	Postmasters.	Compensation.	Net proceeds.
Somerset	Somerset	Gillian Lint, to 31st March	$148 52	$222 46
		Wm. P. Aukeny	70 49	73 78
Somerton	Philadelphia	Geo. W. Comly	28 56	43 85
Sorrel Horse	Montgomery	Isaiah Nitterauer	17 72	27 32
South Charleston	Tioga	Solomon Waterman	10 45	16 67
South Creek	Bradford	David R. Moore	12 19	21 30
South Hill	Bradford	William Warfield	4 49	6 68
South Shenango	Crawford	David Marshall	8 91	18 81
South Sterling	Wayne	Charles W. Gilpin	6 06	11 21
South Warren	Bradford	Benj'n Buffington	14 18	24 19
South Whitehall	Lehigh	Jeremiah Troxell	10 32	19 98
Sparta	Washington	Stephen L. Blackly	16 95	26 34
Speersville	Bedford	Thomas Speer	12 99	23 27
Spencerville (Late "Daggett's Mills.")	Tioga	John P. Brees	no ret'rn.	
Spinnerstown	Bucks	Edwin D. Spinner	6 09	12 91
Spread Eagle	Delaware	Mordecai Worrell, to 11th July	1 58	3 23
		Mifflin Lewis	54 34	80 50
Spring	Crawford	John A. Smiley	53 22	89 44
Spring Creek	Warren	George F. Eldred, to 31st March	11 61	18 91
		Warren Leonard	5 24	9 42
Springfield	Bradford	Hiram W. Root	29 45	47 89
Springfield ⋈ Rd's	Erie	William Doty	107 44	140 32
Springfield Furnace	Huntingdon	Samuel Royer	25 74	46 96
Spring Forge	York	Abraham Bletcher	16 82	25 96
Spring Garden	Philadelphia	John Tierney, to 31st December	48 06	108 56
		John Murray	52 43	118 39
Spring Grove	Lancaster	Joseph Elliot	19 53	28 21
Spring Hill Furnace	Fayette	John K. Duncan	17 54	27 13
Spring House	Montgomery	Isaiah Lukens	21 54	34 52
Spring Mills	Centre	David Duncan	60 05	101 82
Springtown	Bucks	Chas. H. Witte, to 31st March	3 93	8 15
		Francis L. Badder	2 18	4 90
Springville	Susquehanna	Spencer Hickox	38 13	69 71
Spruce Grove	Monroe	John M. Meyers	7 96	10 92
Spruce Hill	Juniata	Joseph Kelly	16 38	23 98
Stahlers	Lehigh	Henry Dillinger	4 90	9 28
Standing Stone	Bradford	Simon Stevens	23 36	38 52
Stanhope	Monroe	John S. Diettrick	4 66	6 58
Starucca	Wayne	Thomas Carr	13 83	22 68
State Line (Dis. 13th Feb.)	Franklin	Jacob Felmlee, to 14th Feb.	8 39	14 32

POST OFFICES—*Pennsylvania.*

Post Offices.	Counties.	Postmasters.	Compensation.	Net proceeds.
Steeleville	Chester	Thomas Wood	$8 89	$14 39
Sterling	Wayne	Phineas Howe	18 73	30 41
Sterlingville	Wyoming	F. W. Hunt, to 12th Dec	9 62	17 04
		Philip Hull	13 06	24 21
Sterrett's Gap	Cumberland	John Lauck	11 24	19 00
Stevensville	Bradford	Cyrus Stevens	5 62	8 65
Stewartstown	York	Anthony Stewart	19 82	29 78
Stockertown	Northampton	Peter Wotring, from 9th Jan	1 67	1 89
Stockport	Wayne	Paul S. Preston	22 66	27 82
Stoddartsville	Monroe	John Stoddart	48 44	94 78
Stone Church	Northampton	Thos. W. Knouss, to 14th May	24 17	39 88
		George Baker	3 62	5 36
Stonerstown	Bedford	Sam'l D. Buchanan, to 11th Dec	4 31	7 04
		Joseph Crissman	5 59	10 01
Stouchburgh	Berks	M. S. Thirwechter	77 86	121 05
Stoughstown	Cumberland	John Stough, jr	32 63	47 55
Stouts	Northampton	Isaac Stout	4 75	6 41
Stoyestown	Somerset	Geo. A. Clarke	147 78	143 57
Strasburgh	Lancaster	John McCallister	118 29	220 06
Strattonville	Clarion	Philip Clover	97 43	99 98
Strawbridge	York	Jno. Strawbridge, jr.	8 70	14 28
Strawntown	Bucks	Nich's Roudenbush	8 39	17 06
Street's Run	Alleghany	Adam Heuthorn	16 20	29 93
Strickersville	Chester	John C. Powley	25 42	39 29
Strode's Mills	Mifflin	Amor Strode	35 10	35 14
Strongstown	Indiana	William Loughry	16 94	33 24
Stroudsburgh	Monroe	Samuel Stokes	126 73	256 19
Sugar Creek	Crawford	John Smith	33 40	55 92
Sugar Grove	Warren	George W. Buel	72 61	118 50
Sugar Lake	Crawford	James Brawley	3 55	8 37
Sugartown	Chester	Garrett Pratt	10 49	21 37
Sugar Valley	Clinton	Geo. A. Achenback	20 73	36 79
Sullivan	Tioga	U. D. Welch, 3 qrs.	7 50	12 82
Summer Hill	Cambria	George Murray	14 45	26 16
Summersville	Jefferson	Ira Baldwin	23 76	23 80
Summit	Cambria	Peter Dougherty	110 14	150 54
Summit Hill	Carbon	George H. Davis	109 77	184 64
Sumneytown	Montgomery	George Shaid	30 05	49 23
Sunbury	Northumb'ld	Rachael B. Packer	281 11	350 27
Sunville	Venango	James Hayes	7 50	13 74
Surgeon's Hall	Alleghany	Joseph Curry	10 43	17 61
Susquehanna	Dauphin	Margaret Halbach	15 05	27 06
Sweden	Potter	Samuel Taggart	10 01	4 87
Sylvan	Franklin	John Zimmerman	14 21	22 82
Sylvania	Bradford	John H. Furman	19 02	27 90

POST OFFICES—*Pennsylvania.*

Post Offices.	Counties.	Postmasters.	Compensation.	Net proceeds.
Tafton	Pike	Thomas V. Taft	$37 10	$60 51
Tamaqua	Schuylkill	John N. Speece	106 30	208 07
Taneyville	Lycoming	John Little	7 26	8 16
Tannersville	Monroe	Charles G. Nebe, to 27th January	18 29	36 73
		David Edinger	11 22	20 76
Tarentum	Alleghany	Wm. J. McCleary	67 18	101 07
Taylor's Stand	Crawford	Silas Taylor	5 30	8 57
Taylorstown	Washington	Isaac Hodgens	40 66	63 14
Taylorsville	Bucks	Mahlon K. Taylor	28 28	58 57
Ten Mile	Washington	John Cary	17 41	22 97
Terrytown	Bradford	Geo. F. Horton	17 82	28 05
Thompson	Susquehanna	Jonas Blandin	9 98	13 76
Thompsontown	Juniata	Eras. D. Crawford	97 62	94 35
Thomsonville	Washington	James Moore	12 69	20 78
Thornbury	Chester	David H. Taylor	8 29	12 27
Thornton	Delaware	A. W. Ingram, 3 qrs.	1 48	2 86
Three Springs	Huntingdon	Moses Greenland	15 10	26 55
Tidioute	Warren	Levi Brigham	28 37	49 58
Tinker Run	Westmorel'd	Jacob Spencer	80 02	79 43
Tioga	Tioga	Alvah C. Bush, to 30th Sept	20 81	35 12
		Edwin C. Goodrich	66 99	125 20
Tionesta	Venango	John A. Dale	40 59	60 48
Towanda	Bradford	Sidney S. Bailey, to 17th Feb	231 73	347 15
		Alvah S. Chamberlin	148 26	218 16
Town Hill	Luzerne	George Bowman	27 17	47 95
Trappe	Montgomery	Valentine B. Reiff, to 31st March	57 99	100 85
		James F. Rambo	15 79	24 56
Treibleville	Monroe	Peter Treible	3 27	3 84
Trexlertown	Lehigh	Benneville Yoder	18 62	36 42
Trout Run	Lycoming	Charles Drum, to 31st Dec'r	16 32	24 64
		Robert Allen	14 71	24 52
Troy	Bradford	Volney M. Long, to 31st Dec'r	80 14	131 23
		Francis Smith	80 28	137 40
Trucksville	Luzerne	Jacob Rice	9 63	15 34
Trumbaursville	Bucks	Charles Dubbs	3 45	7 62
Tullytown	Bucks	John Cheston	42 12	56 04
Tunkhannock	Wyoming	Peter M. Osterhout, to 18th Jan'y	82 10	141 27
		William Bolton	66 29	118 24
Tunnel	Indiana	Wm. McQuiston	8 43	13 02
Turbotville	Northumb'd	William Levan, to 31st Dec'r	24 89	37 33
		William Stitzel	22 92	35 56

POST OFFICES—*Pennsylvania.*

Post Offices.	Counties.	Postmasters.	Compensation.	Net proceeds.
Turkey Foot	Somerset	John K. McMillen	$14 22	$25 58
Turns	Monroe	John Turn	1 95	2 39
Turtle Creek	Alleghany	Henry Chalfant	65 02	63 23
Tuscarora Valley	Juniata	James Milliken	53 14	96 63
Two Taverns	Adams	Victor Hass	10 64	17 89
Tyler	Luzerne	Joel Rogers	24 39	39 30
Tyler's Port	Montgomery	Joseph Beerer	3 85	6 68
Ulster	Bradford	Hermon Van Vleck	25 69	49 71
Ulysses	Potter	Daniel Olmsted	17 62	29 76
Union Furnace	Huntingdon	Sam'l P. Wallace	20 89	36 41
Union Iron Works	Berks	George Reagan	8 25	13 29
Union Mills	Erie	Fred'k W. Miles, to 31st March	28 44	49 53
		Robt. Smiley, from 1st June	2 15	3 56
Union Square	Montgomery	Thomas J. White	1 47	2 59
Uniontown	Fayette	Daniel Smith, to 8th May	459 19	977 78
		Armstrong Hadden	92 17	201 38
Unionville	Chester	Charles Buffington	90 05	162 68
Unity	Crawford	Wm. W. Bowerman	4 10	7 29
Unityville	Lycoming	Philip Young	2 79	4 18
Up'r Black's Eddy	Bucks	John Holahan	53 70	95 41
Upper Dublin	Montgomery	Isaac Thomas	19 78	37 60
Upper Hanover	Montgomery	Joseph Gerhard	20 68	31 17
Up'r Mahantango	Schuylkill	Charles Maurer	14 46	20 10
Up'r Middletown	Fayette	William Conden	10 42	17 08
Up'r Strasburgh	Franklin	John Grove, to 31st Dec'r	16 62	28 04
		William Gilmor	16 39	28 45
Upsonville	Susquehan'h	Titus L. Merriam	10 81	16 00
Upton	Franklin	George Cook	42 20	65 16
Utica	Venango	Brice Gilmore	20 73	34 55
Uwchland	Chester	Chas. M. Griffith	21 50	35 58
Valley	Mifflin	Wm. Thompson	66 31	125 24
Valley Forge	Chester	Elias Knaner, to 31st March	13 83	26 15
		John Widdicombe	4 13	7 86
Van Buren	Washington	Adam Wier, jr	18 51	33 21
Venice	Washington	Robert Riddell	20 98	30 91
Village Green	Delaware	Abraham Haldeman	21 84	37 60
Vincent	Chester	Penrose Wily	11 43	20 02
Vineyard Mills	Huntingdon	Sam'l H. Bell	12 38	24 37
Virginsville	Berks	Stephen Dreibelbis	1 48	3 01
Wagontown	Chester	Joseph Hughes	29 08	55 43
Walker	Centre	James McCullough	29 63	54 76

POST OFFICES—*Pennsylvania.*

Post Offices.	Counties.	Postmasters.	Compensation.	Net proceeds.
Walker's Mills	Alleghany	Isaac Walker, jr.	$4 35	$8 44
Walkerville	Lycoming	Thomas Brown	2 70	4 31
Wallace	Chester	George Stiteler	4 08	8 61
Wallsville	Luzerne	James T. Gorman	7 98	11 69
Walnut	Juniata	Joshua Beale	24 99	39 72
Warren	Warren	John A. Hall	228 81	437 89
Warrenham	Bradford	Alexander Dewing	30 09	30 14
Warrensville	Lycoming	John Curren, to 31st March	5 00	9 52
		Jona. O. Crawford	2 78	5 64
Warren Tavern	Chester	Abraham P. Temple	52 49	96 60
Warrington	Bucks	Benj. Hough, jr.	11 83	20 98
Warrior Run	Northumb'd.	J. Laycock, (3 qrs.)	5 37	8 68
Warrior's Mark	Huntingdon	S. W. Stonebraker, to 19th May	65 84	123 88
		George Orlady	10 16	18 78
Warsaw	Jefferson	David McCormick	8 10	15 04
Washington	Washington	Robert Colmery, to 31st March	419 01	1043 95
		Jonathan D. Leet	151 92	357 29
Washingtonville	Columbia	Neal McCay	79 04	128 04
Waterford	Erie	J. L. Cook, to 1st Nov.	74 40	87 05
		Timothy Judson	126 98	221 11
Waterloo'	Juniata	James M. Graham, to 31st Dec'r.	7 45	12 52
		Mary Graham	7 31	12 60
Water Street	Huntingdon	H'y B. Mytinger	103 62	130 32
Watsontown	Northumb'd	David Watson	16 93	30 66
Watterson's Ferry	Clarion	John Wilkins	9 98	18 65
Wattsburgh	Erie	Lyman Robinson	78 81	125 96
Waymart	Wayne	Thomas Clark	55 30	64 18
Wayne	Erie	James D. Smith	27 09	41 88
Waynesboro'	Franklin	John W. Stoner	239 63	395 09
Waynesburgh	Greene	Jesse Inghram, to 20th Feb'y	143 08	229 06
		John T. Hook	75 32	141 82
Weaversville	Northampton	Samuel Weaver	53 13	80 41
Wellersburgh	Somerset	Philip Dom, to 17th June	33 94	58 02
		Francis M. Deems	1 03	1 73
Wellsboro'	Tioga	William Bache	219 43	411 86
Welsh Run	Franklin	Thomas Bowles	30 64	50 96
Wertembargh (Late "North Sewickly.")	Beaver	Robert Mehard	(no ret.)	
Wesleyville	Erie	Christian Hull	72 40	72 45
West Alexander	Washington	James Stephenson	220 34	260 03
West Auburn	Susquehan'h	Ebenezer P. Morley, from 9th Sept.	67	1 60

POST OFFICES—*Pennsylvania.*

Post Offices.	Counties.	Postmasters.	Compensation.	Net proceeds.
West Barre	Huntingdon	Isaac Neff	$29 14	$56 67
West Beaver Dam	Erie	Patrick S. Weeks	7 95	16 12
West Burlington	Bradford	William Mitchell	19 48	31 04
West Chester	Chester	John McGinley	508 67	1083 63
West Elizabeth	Alleghany	Erastus Percival	23 17	39 89
West Fairfield	Westmorel'd.	John Kirker	23 95	37 63
Westfield	Tioga	Francis Strong	16 48	29 62
West Finley	Washington	Joshua Ackley	7 68	12 69
West Greenville	Mercer	Moses Varney	215 66	359 17
West Grove	Chester	Thos. W. Taylor	22 79	37 13
West Hanover	Dauphin	Jane S. Vanderslice.	44 26	80 05
West Haverford	Delaware	Thomas L. Priest	92 09	161 34
West Middlesex	Mercer	Robert B. Young	24 84	42 07
West Middletown	Washington	John Smiley, to 31st March	75 55	125 91
		Thos. B. Stemmons.	26 74	43 90
West Mill Creek	Erie	Andrew Nicholson	14 18	23 51
West Newton	Westmorel'd.	William Brookins	101 21	160 45
West Penn	Schuylkill	Moritz Forreider	18 19	29 43
West Philadelphia	Philadelphia	William Simpson	121 67	267 05
West Springfield	Erie	Gilbert Hurd	44 84	38 18
Wexford	Alleghany	Martin Byrne	15 54	29 60
Wharton	Potter	John Earll, jr	1 23	2 49
White Deer	Lycoming	Hugh Donley	14 84	29 52
White Deer Mills.	Union	James Calwell	6 86	11 60
White Hall	Columbia	John F. Derr	16 91	27 91
White Hallville	Bucks	William Stevens	2 57	5 13
White Haven	Luzerne	Edward Lockwood	51 92	92 92
White Hill	Cumberland	Thomas Craighead, jr., from 15th Oct.	4 80	8 50
White House	Cumberland	Andrew G. Miller	24 35	45 69
Whiteley	Greene	Jonathan Morris	7 77	14 68
White Marsh	Montgomery.	Jacob W. Haines	48 00	77 33
Whitestown	Butler	John A. Fletcher	16 15	21 27
Wiconisco	Dauphin	Henry Sheafer	10 45	19 53
Wilkesbarre	Luzerne	Jos. P. LeClere, to 10th May	738 10	1513 85
		Eleazer B. Collings	109 79	266 19
Wilkins	Alleghany	William Gore	107 10	105 62
Wilkinsburgh	Alleghany	Abraham Stoner, to 28th Feb'y	56 56	55 95
		Abram Horbach, jr., (1 qr.)	15 52	9 91
Williamsburgh	Huntingdon	Philip Rees, to 2d April	122 08	207 99
		Alex'r W. Kenny	32 68	63 14
Williamsport	Lycoming	Jos. S. Titus	388 57	899 40
Williamsville	Elk	Alonzo J. Wilcox	7 90	15 35
Willow Grove	Montgomery.	Henry Morris	18 14	36 21

POST OFFICES—*Pennsylvania.*

Post Offices.	Counties.	Postmasters.	Compensation.	Net proceeds.
Willow Street....	Lancaster ...	John H. Longnecker	$16 85	$23 71
Wilmore........	Cambria	Anthony Long.....	16 15	27 77
Wilsonville......	Adams......	George Wilson.....	35 20	55 90
Wind Gap......	Northampton	John Weaver......	21 51	33 87
Windham.......	Bradford.....	William Russell....	9 46	13 60
Windsor.........	York	Jas. L. Gemmill, to 12th Sept........	1 62	2 30
		Daniel Overdorff, jr., (6⅔ mo.)........	6 83	9 68
Wisenburgh.....	Lehigh......	G. S. Eisenhart, jr..	5 46	9 32
Wolf Creek...... (Dis. 16th Oct.)	Mercer......	William Fleming...	(no ret.)	
Wolf Run........	Lycoming...	Jacob Haines......	8 98	17 42
Womelsdorf......	Berks........	Sam'l Ermentrout..	183 14	300 93
Woodbury......	Bedford.....	D. S. Longenecker..	43 64	75 14
Woodcock.......	Crawford....	Samuel Knerr......	45 60	78 46
Woodcock Valley	Huntingdon..	Jas. Campbell, jr...	17 82	29 03
Worcester.......	Montgomery.	Charles Hendricks..	10 15	14 98
Worthington.....	Armstrong ..	Jos. M. Jordan.....	41 50	71 76
Wrightstown....	Bucks.......	Wm. McDowell....	14 42	26 85
Wrightsville.....	York	Wm. S. Cochran, to 6th March.......	78 05	137 92
		John Kerr.........	36 00	67 25
Wyalusing.......	Bradford.....	John Taylor.......	22 40	36 36
Wyoming.......	Luzerne.....	A. M. Jeffords, to 31st Dec'r.........	35 85	62 91
		Wm. Swetland.....	35 27	59 11
Wysox..........	Bradford.....	Darwin E. Martin..	66 79	63 08
Yardleyville......	Bucks.......	Geo. M. Bannister..	57 66	115 95
Yellow Spring....	Huntingdon..	James M. Kinkead..	79 10	65 22
Yocumtown	York	Henry Brubacker..	13 03	24 09
York	York	George Upp, jr., to 7th May.........	624 92	1624 37
		David Small.......	119 13	282 43
York Haven.....	York	Christian Fenzel....	9 76	18 11
York Sulphur Springs	Adams......	Anna Godfrey.....	91 27	168 96
Youngstown.....	Westmorel'd.	Judah Case.........	106 34	143 11
Youngsville......	Warren.....	F. W. Brigham....	50 20	81 49
Young Womanstown.........	Clinton......	Edward H. Ritchy..	7 46	15 12
Zeisersville....... (Dis. 24th Aug.)	Luzerne.....	John N. Zeiser.....	(No ret.)	
Zelienople.......	Butler.......	H. Muntz, to 22d Jan.	64 09	107 20
		Chas. S. Passavant, to 2d June.......	49 78	84 74
		Francis Wallace....	9 29	15 53

POST OFFICES—*Delaware.*

DELAWARE.

NOTE.—Compensation of Postmasters, and net proceeds of their offices, from July 1, 1844, to June 30, 1845.

Post Offices.	Counties.	Postmasters.	Compensation.	Net proceeds.
Black Bird	New Castle	Bassett Ferguson	$26 10	$47 30
Bridgeville	Sussex	Isaac J. Jenkins	22 59	38 82
Camden	Kent	Thomas Simpson	151 42	149 40
Cannon's Ferry	Sussex	Bayard Dawson	20 04	38 21
Canterbury	Kent	James W. Shaw	27 00	23 11
Cantwell's Bridge	New Castle	John Whitby, to 31st Dec.	49 95	84 45
		Charles Beasten, to 31st March	25 35	46 12
		Josiah Ridgway	23 77	44 81
Cedar Creek	Sussex	James Ward	8 13	12 28
Centreville	New Castle	James Delaplain	15 62	27 63
Christiana	New Castle	Howard Ogle	61 19	106 83
Concord	Sussex	Samuel J. Jefferson	22 42	37 12
Cooch's Bridge	New Castle	William Cooch	12 97	24 57
Dagsboro'	Sussex	Jos. S. Barnard, to 31st March	28 00	51 02
		Lemuel Littleton	9 19	16 27
Delaware City	New Castle	Geo. G. Cleaver	74 38	133 83
Dover	Kent	James Cowgill	431 50	653 61
Drawbridge	Sussex	John P. Paynter	22 74	38 79
Frederica	Kent	John E. Price	118 90	117 66
Georgetown	Sussex	Charles Tunnell	133 49	240 41
Glasgow	New Castle	Robert Cann	23 24	32 87
Hall's Store	Sussex	Wm. S. Hall	13 00	25 56
Horsey's X Roads	Sussex	Nathaniel Horsey	8 63	13 59
Laurel	Sussex	Benjamin Hitch	70 33	128 41
Leipsic	Kent	Thomas P. Hazel	16 61	27 70
Lewes	Sussex	P. B. Norman, to 15th Feb.	75 54	105 56
		Henry Wolfe	43 19	64 89
Loveville	New Castle	Thomas Love	18 45	30 27
McDonough	New Castle	Gassaway Watkins	16 75	28 26
Marshy Hope Bridge	Kent	Nicholas O. Smith	2 82	4 54
Middleford	Sussex	Nutter Cannon, jr.	10 46	18 33

POST OFFICES—*Delaware.*

Post Offices.	Counties.	Postmasters.	Compensation.	Net proceeds.
Middletown	New Castle	Henry D. Hoffecker.	$99 94	$166 57
Milford	Kent	Wm. N. W. Dorsey	273 14	283 13
Millsboro'	Sussex	John H. Benson, to 14th Oct.	9 53	19 38
		George Tunnell	30 18	58 24
Milton	Sussex	John Ponder	59 79	105 80
Newark	New Castle	James L. Miles	296 22	614 17
New Castle	New Castle	Hetty Ritchie	331 48	721 11
Newport	New Castle	Michael Kinch	51 92	97 55
Pleasant Hill	New Castle	Isaiah B. Eastburn, to 31st March	7 44	11 96
		Alban Buckingham.	2 64	4 43
Port Penn	New Castle	Joseph Cleaver	53 03	91 33
Red Lion	New Castle	William Silver	42 19	62 00
Saint George's	New Castle	James N. Sutton	80 09	135 08
Seaford	Sussex	Jeremiah McNeilly.	52 90	87 28
Smyrna	Kent	David Lockwood	309 48	628 50
Sowardtown	Kent	David Robinson, to 30th Sept	95	1 82
		Nathan P. Green, from 1st Jan	1 56	3 05
Staunton	New Castle	Aquilla Nebeker	68 68	115 57
Summit Bridge	New Castle	Manlove Jester	35 29	56 13
Talleyville	New Castle	John Talley	11 01	14 20
Tunnell's Store	Sussex	Ebe Watter, jr	8 60	16 29
Vernon	Kent	Henry C. Rawlings, to 31st Dec	7 35	10 65
		Robert E. Graham .	6 80	11 49
Whiteleysburgh	Kent	Jonathan N. Sipple, to 31st Dec	5 00	8 67
		Henry C. Rawlings.	6 03	11 08
Williamsville	Kent	John R. Whitby	4 41	5 52
Willow Grove	Kent	Ambrose Broadaway	6 06	10 82
Wilmington	New Castle	William R. Sellars	1673 37	4764 48

POST OFFICES—*Maryland.*

MARYLAND.

NOTE.—Compensation of Postmasters, and net proceeds of their offices, from July 1, 1844, to June 30, 1845.

Post Offices.	Counties.	Postmasters.	Compensation.	Net proceeds.
Abingdon	Harford	William Allen, to 17th Sept	$20 19	$34 73
		B. M. Billingslea	72 88	124 44
Accident	Allegany	John R. Brooke, fr. 1st January	6 84	13 56
Allen's Fresh	Charles	Richard Johnson	37 37	43 52
Annapolis	Ann Arundel.	George McNeir, to 8th December	388 15	907 23
		Martin F. Revell	1102 12	3094 88
Annapl's Junction	Ann Arundel.	Alexander Sumwalt, from 15th Sept	7 52	12 57
Aquasco	Prince Geo's.	John W. Thomas	42 16	73 21
Bachman's Mills	Carroll	David Bachman	7 46	12 47
Bakersville	Washington	Elias Baker	23 77	45 79
Baltimore	Baltimore	Thomas Finley, to 17th April	1593 40	67168 98
		James M. Buchanan	403 10	17514 68
Barnesville	Montgomery.	Wm. D. Poole	23 80	39 65
Barren Creek Springs	Somerset	Samuel Bratton	18 35	27 72
Barry	Frederick	John Hymes	45 90	82 60
Beantown	Charles	Edward D. Boone, from 19th Sept	9 03	14 94
Beaver Creek	Washington	Larkin S. Cook	18 03	30 17
Bel-Air	Harford	James A. Fulton	150 17	261 97
Beltsville	Prince Geo's.	John T. Holtzman	54 09	94 11
Benedict	Charles	John D. Bowling	15 80	27 73
Berlin	Worcester	Isaac Covington, to 11th March	115 27	198 10
		Cyrus L. Williams.	42 50	79 11
Big Mills	Dorchester	Thomas J. Saxton, to 30th Sept	1 72	2 59
		Francis Higgins	5 16	7 80
Black Horse	Harford	John Young	14 79	21 29
Bladensburgh	Prince Geo's.	John W. Scott, to 16th April	151 68	265 39
		Daniel Barron	42 02	76 08
Blue Ball	Cecil	John L. Biles	11 45	18 17
Boonsboro'	Washington	Septimus Stephens, to 5th June	268 37	525 74
		Edward Davis	17 67	35 21
Brandywine	Prince Geo's.	Leonard H. Early	11 44	17 46

POST OFFICES—*Maryland.*

Post Offices.	Counties.	Postmasters.	Compensation.	Net proceeds.
Brick Meeting House	Cecil	Ellis G. Chandlee	$93 82	$89 56
Bridgeport	Frederick	Grafton Grimes	4 41	6 43
Bridgetown	Caroline	John M. Cannan	3 88	7 32
Bristol	Ann Arundel.	Wm. H. Owens	45 48	65 58
Broad Creek	Queen Ann	Pere Granger	62 38	96 73
Brooklandville	Baltimore	John R. Gwynn, to 31st Dec	13 50	23 67
		Samuel Comly, jr.	15 34	29 92
Brookville	Montgomery.	Thomas McCormick	71 22	107 61
Brotherton	Ann Arundel.	Thomas Crown	12 21	22 62
Brownsville	Washington	John Brown, jr.	10 14	16 97
Bruceville	Carroll	George Mearing	8 94	14 14
Bryantown	Charles	Wm. N. Bean, to 4th February	44 25	77 52
		George T. Richards.	23 12	43 14
Buckeystown	Frederick	Grafton Duvall	65 06	103 14
Buckingham	Baltimore	Federal Eareckson	16 20	22 67
Bullocktown	Queen Ann	Benjamin Wallace	11 79	18 67
Burkittsville	Frederick	Adam Custard	48 02	75 02
Burrsville	Caroline	Wm. W. Medford	6 33	10 96
Cambridge	Dorchester	Edw'd A. Marshall.	295 51	476 81
Catonsville	Baltimore	John K. Smith	35 84	64 62
Cavetown	Washington	Wm. C. Webb	22 53	31 97
Cecilton	Cecil	Wm. H. Pearce	115 73	201 12
Centreville	Queen Ann	Chs. A. Gibson, to 31st March	153 39	275 34
		Thos. F. Larrimore.	47 72	86 28
Chaptico	St. Mary's	Wm. H. Garner	86 53	161 23
Charlestown	Cecil	John N. Black	26 88	41 42
Charlotte Hall	St. Mary's	Thomas C. Reeves	58 33	107 12
Chesapeake City.	Cecil	John L. Clayton	63 58	111 05
Chestertown	Kent	Elijah Dailey	321 82	583 41
Chewsville	Washington	Aaron Bachtell, to 31st Dec	8 33	12 41
		Jacob S. Bachtell	12 11	20 52
Church Creek	Dorchester	Amos Bowdle	29 56	45 80
Church Hill	Queen Ann	R. E. C. Downes, jr	64 30	96 67
Churchville	Harford	Robert N. Hanna, to 14th October	27 61	48 16
		Sylvester Macatee	44 19	77 21
Clarksburgh	Montgomery.	George W. Mobley.	50 30	87 90
Clarksville	Ann Arundel.	Wilson McBee	29 49	48 77
Clear Spring	Washington	William Cushwa	217 02	405 53
Colesville	Montgomery.	William Voldenear.	23 46	37 13
Cooksville	Ann Arundel.	William Cushen	24 29	44 98
Cottage	Montgomery.	John W. Carroll	10 34	15 10
Creagerstown	Frederick	Sam'l C. Stambaugh	30 39	51 76

POST OFFICES—*Maryland.*

Post Offices.	Counties.	Postmasters.	Compensation.	Net proceeds.
Cub Hill	Baltimore	Levi B. Finley	$5 92	$7 76
Cumberland	Alleghany	William Lynn	1065 08	3055 44
Damascus	Montgomery	John Burditt	(no ret.)	
Darlington	Harford	Benjamin Silver, jr., to 30th Dec.	38 61	64 42
		John Jewett, jr.	42 15	72 34
Darnestown	Montgomery	Leon'd W. Candler	42 78	69 48
Davidsonville	Ann Arundel	Nicholas D. Duvall	100 01	173 40
Dawsons	Alleghany	Thos. W. Dawson	5 40	10 27
Dawsonville	Montgomery	Thos. B. Dawson	15 24	22 78
Deer Creek Works (Dis. 19th June.)	Harford	Joshua Husband, fr. 19th June, 1844	3 97	7 75
Denton	Caroline	Chs. R. Nicholson, to 31st March	61 67	118 69
		John H. Emerson	21 00	43 12
Derickson's Roads	Worcester	James M. Fooks	6 08	10 78
Double Pipe Creek	Carroll	George Landers	10 52	17 21
Dublin	Harford	T. J. McCausland	16 70	27 30
Dunkirk	Calvert	Charles H. Johnson	23 37	35 33
East Newmarket	Dorchester	Thomas Higgins	47 38	66 15
Easton	Talbot	Eliza Hussey	351 80	767 51
Elk Ridge Land'g	Ann Arundel	Levin R. Mills, to 31st March	81 22	151 67
		J. L. Chabot	29 79	49 92
Elkton	Cecil	Adam Whann	341 03	727 07
Ellicott's Mills	Ann Arundel	John Butler	454 95	996 04
Emmitsburgh	Frederick	Joachim Elder	394 96	856 64
Fair Hill	Cecil	E. T. Mitchell	29 29	45 03
Federalsburgh	Dorchester	Wm. S. Goslin	20 55	36 17
Finksburgh	Carroll	William Horner	21 10	38 15
Flint Stone	Alleghany	John Piper, jr., to 23d January	19 35	30 31
		Jeremiah Berry	9 71	18 05
Fork MeetingH'se	Baltimore	Elijah Carman	39 11	67 27
Forktown	Somerset	John Gunby	13 25	23 40
Franklin	Baltimore	Ann Eliza Sigler, to 24th May	16 25	31 83
		Joseph Feelemeyer	(no ret.)	
Franklinville (Ch'd to "Jerusalem Mills.")	Baltimore	James Mahool, to 6th December	33 87	58 13
Frederick	Frederick	John Rigney	964 67	2591 95
Freedom	Carroll	Warren L. Little	12 31	22 21
Friendship	Ann Arundel	Robert S. D. Jones	88 56	138 96
Frostburgh	Alleghany	Thomas Blair	191 45	188 16
Funkstown	Washington	Samuel Bender	84 78	169 01

POST OFFICES—*Maryland.*

Post Offices.	Counties.	Postmasters.	Compensation.	Net proceeds.
Gallant Green....	Charles	J. Corcoran, 3 qrs..	$6 20	$10 91
Georget'n ⋈ Roads	Kent........	James T. Dunbar...	144 06	163 53
Golden...........	Baltimore	Peter F. Cockey.....	80 15	147 02
Golden Hill......	Dorchester ..	Philip H. Graham..	(no ret.)	
		Goodmun Gootee, fr. 6th November ...	14 18	24 29
Good Luck.......	Prince Geo's.	Wm. T. Duvall, to 31st December...	46 04	82 73
		Wm. T. Brown....	42 79	78 33
Goshen Mills....	Montgomery.	James H. Crawford.	10 31	15 88
Govanstown......	Baltimore	Robert Ramsey.....	21 99	43 64
Graceham........	Frederick.....	Jacob Gernand, to 30th November ..	9 61	16 25
		Simon Meredith.....	16 95	27 45
Great Mills.......	St. Mary's ..	Henry N. Kirk.....	94 25	151 64
Greenfield Mills..	Frederick....	Meredith Davis....	34 09	49 18
Greensboro'......	Caroline.....	Chs. N. Tilden.....	56 38	100 90
Grey Rock........	Harford......	Joseph Ross........	9 07	14 88
Hagerstown......	Washington..	Fdk. Humrichouse .	895 47	2282 67
Hall's ⋈ Roads..	Harford.....	T. Hanway, 3 qrs..	21 21	38 38
Hempstead........	Carroll.......	Joseph Ebaugh, to 2d December.....	15 49	25 74
		Adam L. Hoover...	19 09	34 66
Hancock.........	Washington..	Louisa G. Beall, to 30th Sept........	65 31	124 86
		Denton Oliver, 2 qrs.	126 00	237 81
Harrisonville	Baltimore ...	William Cook	29 87	47 90
Havre De Grace..	Harford.....	Stephen J. Magraw.	351 74	766 56
Head of Sassafras	Kent	Charles T. Lusby...	39 03	68 87
Hereford..........	Baltimore ...	N. R. Merriman ...	37 94	66 94
Hickory Tavern..	Harford......	John Wann, to 31st December........	6 62	11 82
		Alex'r J. Rider, from 5th February	11 20	19 67
Hicksburgh.......	Dorchester ..	William J. Vane...	13 86	16 45
Hillsboro'.........	Caroline.....	William Connolly..	20 48	36 26
Hood's Mills	Carroll......	Wm. T. R. Saffell, to 31st Dec......	3 29	6 25
		Thomas Barnes....	3 08	5 44
Horse Head......	Prince Geo's.	Robert Thompson..	12 05	17 19
Hoysburgh.......	Alleghany...	Thomas P. Swann..	18 30	29 79
Huntingtown	Calvert	Alexander Harris ..	26 16	35 12
Hyattstown.......	Montgomery.	Levi T. Hyatt.....	25 59	44 77
Ijamsville........	Frederick....	James Ijams.......	19 59	32 17
Ilchester Mills ...	Ann Arundel.	George Ellicott.....	26 01	52 87
Jarrettsville......	Harford.....	William L. Morse..	29 49	53 86

POST OFFICES—*Maryland*.

Post Offices.	Counties.	Postmasters.	Compensation.	Net proceeds.
Jefferson	Frederick	Daniel H. Thomas	$95 62	$161 68
Jennon's Run	Alleghany	Geo. W. McCulloh	299 77	736 29
Jerusalem Mills (Late Franklinv'e,	Harford Balt. Co.)	John C. Walsh, from 7th December	30 88	57 51
Johnsville	Frederick	John Kinzer, jr	21 68	34 81
Ladiesburgh	Frederick	Samuel Birely	10 16	15 59
Lappon's ⋈ Roads	Washington	Martin Emmert	9 85	19 29
Laurel Factory	Prince Geo's	Thomas C. Miller	155 15	287 40
Leitersburgh	Washington	David M. Good	100 74	169 19
Leonardtown	St. Mary's	John A. Clarke, to 31st March	124 59	228 77
		John Walton	12 92	27 65
Libertytown	Frederick	Ephraim Albaugh, to 31st Dec	31 43	54 84
		Joseph Taney	33 92	56 58
Lisbon	Ann Arundel	Elias Mantle	28 13	52 61
Little Crossings	Alleghany	James Burton	120 82	117 51
Little Gunpowder	Baltimore	Walter T. Allender	56 33	97 42
Lonaconing	Alleghany	Robert Graham	104 36	218 87
Long Green Academy	Baltimore	Davis Powell	7 01	12 07
Long Marsh	Queen Ann	John S. Price, from 4th Sept	11 94	18 82
Long Old Fields	Prince Geo'es	Elisha Perry	33 46	50 22
Lower Marlbro'	Calvert	James Humphreys	24 67	40 84
McKinstry's Mills	Carroll	Samuel McKinstry	25 09	34 45
Magnolia	Harford	James Reardan	15 24	21 45
Manchester	Carroll	Charles Miller	64 75	101 94
Marley	Ann Arundel	Thomas Robinson	9 30	11 37
Marriottsville	Ann Arundel	Beale Whalen	44 39	76 00
Maryland Line	Baltimore	Lysias Smith, to 17th May	26 14	39 77
		Charles Duer	3 25	5 17
Matthews' Store	Ann Arundel	James B. Matthews	25 78	40 62
Mechanicstown	Frederick	Leonard Picking, to 16th Nov	20 74	30 31
		Reuben Osler	31 44	49 56
Michaelsville	Harford	Jacob J. Michael	15 92	21 36
Middlebrook Mills	Montgomery	James G. House	23 50	45 09
Middleburgh	Carroll	John Clabaugh	13 29	22 21
Middletown	Frederick	Henry Herring	180 09	324 42
Millersville	Ann Arundel	George Miller	55 06	85 72
Millington	Kent	Edward H. Boyer, to 31st Dec	39 47	38 66
		Nicholas Vansant	55 05	55 05
Mill Mont	Calvert	George Calvert	10 11	22 58
Milton Hill	Charles	Notley T. Dutton	58 15	101 11

POST OFFICES—*Maryland.*

Post Offices.	Counties.	Postmasters.	Compensation.	Net proceeds.
Monrovia	Frederick	Jacob Cronise	$11 46	$20 82
Mount Pleasant	Frederick	John W. Ogborn	28 11	42 59
Nanjemoy	Charles	John J. Harvey	62 36	98 71
Newark	Worcester	Thomas H. Collins	13 00	22 92
New London	Frederick	George W. Webb	12 28	18 62
New Market	Frederick	Hamilton Stier, to 1st May	71 13	120 23
		Wm. P. Anderson	13 30	23 12
Newport	Charles	John M. Latimer, to 29th May	28 00	53 01
		John R. Turner	2 23	4 60
Newtown	Worcester	John S. Stevenson	42 78	82 69
New Windsor	Carroll	Jonas Ecker	42 19	66 21
North East	Cecil	Richard L. Thomas	104 62	188 57
Nottingham	Prince Geo'es	W. B. C. Worthington	69 46	120 85
Oakville	St. Mary's	John Parsons	6 13	8 26
Oldtown	Alleghany	Lionel M. Jameson	28 85	48 35
Orleans	Alleghany	James McAdams, to 30th Sept	10 41	21 82
		John G. Dabelstein, to 31st Mar	14 57	27 16
		William Lambright	7 09	12 50
Owing's Mills	Baltimore	James C. Conn	42 79	71 18
Owing's Run	Carroll	Thomas J. Carter, 3 qrs	6 29	10 53
Owingsville	Ann Arundel	Basil Owings, 1 qr	2 56	3 43
Palmer's Tavern	Prince Geo'es	Thomas Grimes	23 94	41 50
Park Head	Washington	John Moffett, to 30th Sept	4 71	8 90
		George Dickerhoof, 2 qrs	8 29	15 32
Parkton	Baltimore	Samuel Crockett	12 25	17 28
Partnership	Charles	William Simmons	9 75	15 26
Patuxent Forge (Dis. 27th July.)	Ann Arundel	Levi Gantt, to 31st July	82	1 31
Perrymansville	Harford	John W. Cannon	76 29	123 62
Perryville	Cecil	Joseph Cochran	62 65	123 55
Petersville	Frederick	Thomas Winter	83 76	152 96
Pikesville	Baltimore	Joseph Mettam	94 95	202 65
Piney Creek	Carroll	Lewis Peters	10 01	15 19
Piscataway	Prince Geo'es	John H. Monroe, to 22d Feb	96 68	164 42
		James H. Griffin	48 13	80 53
Pleasant Hill	Charles	John Spalding	34 46	60 27
Point of Rocks	Frederick	John Hann	43 66	77 33

POST OFFICES—*Maryland.*

Post Offices.	Counties.	Postmasters.	Compensation.	Net proceeds.
Pomonkey	Charles	Fs. L. Rogerson, to 3d Feb	$16 97	$29 00
		James Harris	18 52	29 08
Poolesville	Montgomery	Frederick S. Poole	83 52	148 90
Poplar Springs	Ann Arundel	Allen Dorsey	12 79	23 96
Port Deposit	Cecil	Allen Anderson	409 30	580 09
Porters	Carroll	Henry Carter	5 91	8 52
Port Republic	Calvert	John Kershaw	23 27	39 00
Port Tobacco	Charles	John J. Hanson, to 31st Dec	124 61	234 45
		George W. Barnes, 1 qr	61 90	117 51
PrinceFred'ktown	Calvert	John H. Basford	60 88	117 92
Princess Ann	Somerset	Wm. W. Johnston, to 18th Oct	82 61	130 29
		James C. Hyland	142 85	282 47
Principio	Cecil	Henry S. Stites	44 83	43 06
Quantico	Somerset	Beacham G. Hull	17 18	29 36
Queen Ann	Prince Geo'es	James R. Davis	131 59	235 05
Queenstown	Queen Ann	Chs. H. Mansfield, to 26th Nov	23 42	38 39
		John F. McFeely	32 51	54 60
Rehoboth	Somerset	Levin Tyler	28 01	50 52
Reistertown	Baltimore	Samuel Harryman	76 35	129 20
Ridge	St. Mary's	Jos. B. Smith, to 31st Dec	15 21	26 77
		Jas. L. Langley, jr.	14 22	28 83
Ridgeville	Carroll	Gustavus Dorsey, to 22d Aug	4 51	7 19
		Caleb Douty	28 41	49 62
Rising Sun	Cecil	Edwin Haines	68 47	114 09
Roach's Store (Dis. 16th Nov.)	Somerset	Thomas Miles	(No ret.)	
Robinson's Store	Harford	Samuel Martin	7 07	8 39
Rock Hall	Kent	Joseph Harris	51 17	76 78
Rock Run	Harford	J. C. Parker, to 30th Sept	14 87	25 34
		Robert H. Archer	40 57	71 22
Rock Springs	Cecil	Benjamin Gibson	18 73	28 75
Rockville	Montgomery	Nathan Holland, to 31st March	148 94	290 39
		H. F. Viers	44 56	80 79
Rohrersville	Washington	Frederick D. Rohrer	21 27	32 57
Rossville	Baltimore	Garrett Altvater, to 30th Sept	4 71	10 00
		William Slater	11 33	24 62
Rowlandsville	Cecil	Samuel Rowland	41 61	79 45

POST OFFICES—*Maryland.*

Post Offices.	Counties.	Postmasters.	Compensation.	Net proceeds.
Royal Oak......	Talbot......	Richard Benson....	$36 64	$54 79
Sabillisville......	Frederick....	John W. Coon, to 31st Aug........	3 30	4 79
		Wm. Arnsparger....	12 48	20 97
St. Clements' Bay	St. Mary's...	Richard Colton......	40 61	70 23
Saint Inigoes.....	St. Mary's....	Henry W. Beal.....	29 24	49 54
Saint James......	Baltimore....	Levi Curtis........	6 31	10 18
Saint Leonards...	Calvert......	Robert L. Clark....	29 55	48 75
Saint Martins....	Worcester...	Lemuel Showell....	10 29	18 69
Saint Michaels...	Talbot......	John B. Jefferson, to 24th Oct.........	34 30	50 56
		Leonidas Dodson....	77 68	114 24
Salisbury........	Somerset.....	M. L. H. Maddox..	94 32	190 78
Sam's Creek.....	Frederick....	Daniel Engel.......	32 56	49 36
Sandy Hill......	Worcester...	John W. Jones....	12 09	21 64
Sandy Spring....	Montgomery.	Edward Stabler....	58 37	92 45
Sang Run.......	Alleghany....	Elijah Friend.......	14 33	25 69
Savage..........	Ann Arundel.	Benjamin Williams.	80 89	137 51
Selbysport......	Alleghany....	David Hoffman.....	29 93	52 87
		(For "Friendsville")	36	55
Sharpsburgh.....	Washington.	Hilliard F. Hebb...	122 81	249 32
Shiwan..........	Baltimore....	John Tracey.......	22 67	34 45
Smithsburgh.....	Washington.	Henry Lydy.......	58 12	101 83
Snow Hill.......	Worcester....	Levin Townsend, to 24th Sept.........	38 32	60 95
		Richard T. Waters.	179 87	163 67
Sudlersville......	Queen Ann...	Richard S. Rolph, to 18th Dec.........	31 64	40 73
		Jos. E. Roberts....	22 71	41 06
Sunderland......	Calvert......	Richard Sunderland.	25 20	40 45
Sykesville.......	Carroll......	John E. Garrett....	41 78	68 83
Taneytown......	Carroll......	Hugh Shaw, jr.....	91 81	145 36
Tobacco Stick...	Dorchester...	William Hopkins..	11 62	18 37
Towsontown	Baltimore....	Benjamin N. Payne.	36 75	67 00
Tracy's Landing.	Ann Arundel.	John C. Weems, 3 qrs.............	32 65	40 91
Trappe..........	Talbot.......	John B. Leckie....	76 98	129 34
Triadelphia......	Montgomery.	Thomas Lansdale..	47 10	79 37
Union Bridge....	Carroll......	Moses Shaw.......	24 59	40 10
Union Meeting House.......	Baltimore....	John Michael......	32 16	62 59
Union Mills.....	Carroll......	William Shriver....	11 03	16 79
Uniontown......	Carroll......	John Hyder.......	67 78	106 72
Unionville.......	Frederick....	Nath'l H. Owings, to 31st Dec......	21 82	30 66
		Benjamin Lindsay..	20 22	31 29

POST OFFICES—*Maryland.*

Post Offices.	Counties.	Postmasters.	Compensation.	Net proceeds.
Unity	Montgomery	William Price	$17 81	$33 36
Upperco	Baltimore	Thomas Upperco	12 24	17 30
Upper Hunting Creek	Caroline	Richard Willis	15 98	27 34
Upper Marlboro'	Prince Geo'es	Polydore E. Scott	287 42	585 89
Urbana	Frederick	Henry Dronenburgh	47 40	95 22
Utica Mills	Frederick	John Todd	42 33	70 90
Vienna	Dorchester	William T. Vickers	41 67	66 73
Wakefield	Carroll	Abraham Cassell	11 70	16 12
Walkersville	Frederick	William Rinehart	34 77	56 81
Warfieldburgh	Carroll	Burgess Nelson, jr.	6 85	10 28
Warren	Baltimore	Alexander Sims, to 30th Sept.	9 70	15 82
		John Thompson	24 21	40 43
Warwick	Cecil	John B. Morton	27 26	48 37
Weisesburg	Baltimore	Pleasant Hunter	13 21	22 17
Wenfield	Carroll	Aquilla Pickett	8 46	10 76
Westerman's mills	Baltimore	David Peden	16 35	29 48
Westernport	Alleghany	George B. Murphy	16 80	24 84
Westminster	Carroll	Joshua Yingling	201 91	349 00
West River	Ann Arundel	John H. Hopkins	141 42	261 86
Weverton	Washington	Caspar W. Wever	36 17	71 02
Whaleysville	Worcester	Peter Whaley	8 77	14 83
White Haven	Somerset	Marcellus Jones	18 76	34 18
Wickliffe	Montgomery	William Trucks	8 08	11 06
Williamsport	Washington	John J. Sterrett, to 11th April	146 48	335 76
		William Steffey	57 40	113 73
Wolfsville	Frederick	Jacob Wolf	20 07	24 72
Woodbine	Carroll	Wm. G. Shipley, to 31st Dec.	5 08	10 16
		Gustavus W. Shaffer	3 96	8 33
Woodsboro'	Frederick	George W. Shank	36 90	55 91
Woodstock	Ann Arundel	Peter Gorman	(No ret.)	
		Ezekiel Dorsey, from 10th Dec.	23 32	41 62
Wye Mills	Talbot	Thomas Hopkins	55 52	98 73
Yough Glades	Alleghany	Isaac McCarty	18 45	33 99

POST OFFICES—*District of Columbia*—*Virginia.*

DISTRICT OF COLUMBIA.

NOTE.—Compensation of Postmasters, and net proceeds of their offices, from July 1, 1844, to June 30, 1845.

Post Offices.	Counties.	Postmasters.	Compensation.	Net proceeds.
Alexandria	Alexandria	Daniel Bryan	$1799 02	$5160 99
Georgetown	Washington	Henry W. Tilley	1524 43	4200 88
Washington City	Washington	William Jones, to 31st March	1500 00	7193 39
		Charles K. Gardner	500 00	2618 47

VIRGINIA.

NOTE.—Compensation of Postmasters, and net proceeds of their offices, from July 1, 1844, to June 30, 1845.

Post Offices.	Counties.	Postmasters.	Compensation.	Net proceeds.
Abingdon	Washington	James K. Gibson	$1065 34	$225 36
Accomack C. H.	Accomack	John Segar	131 43	219 02
Accoman	Accomack	Charles Tatham	18 11	32 16
Aldie	Loudon	Edwin A. Stover	100 47	187 36
Alum Springs	Rockbridge	James Campbell	13 25	27 57
Amacetta	Wayne	Tyree B. Black	5 08	8 96
Ambler's Mills	Louisa	Tarlton B. Hines	8 26	13 08
Amelia C. H.	Amelia	William Eggleston	40 34	61 59
Amherst C. H.	Amherst	John H. Roberts	139 47	243 13
Amissville	Rappahan'k	James R. Nelson	27 91	51 78
Amsterdam	Botetourt	Isaac Hanes	24 32	43 73
Anandale	Fairfax	William Garges	17 81	25 41
Andrews	Spottsylvania	Samuel Andrews	12 57	20 15
Anthony's Creek	Greenbrier	William Rodgers	11 29	17 60
Aquia	Stafford	Wm. F. Chapman	(No ret.)	
(Changed to "Garrisonville.")				
Arbuckle	Mason	Matthew T. Alexander, to 31st Dec.	6 95	13 12
		And. B. Alexander	7 37	14 33
Arcola	Loudon	Matthew P. Lee	31 39	57 12
Arnoldsburg	Kanawha	Chs. D. Arnold	3 58	5 60
Arnoldton	Campbell	Benj. W. Porter	16 23	22 53
Aspen Grove	Pittsylvania	James A. Luck	6 59	11 01
Aspenwall	Charlotte	Claiborne Barksdale	21 15	37 22
Athens	Caroline	Rufus C. Hackett, to 31st December	11 79	21 31
		Henry B. Hackett	8 59	14 76

POST OFFICES—*Virginia.*

Post Offices.	Counties.	Postmasters.	Compensation.	Net proceeds.
Auburn........	Fauquier.....	Stephen McCormick	$7 02	$13 13
Austinville........	Wythe......	Andrew F. Gregory.	25 19	46 37
Avent's ⋈ Roads.	Greenville....	Thomas Avent, jr., 3 qrs...........	13 92	24 82
Ayletts.........	King William	Brooking Samuel, to 30th September..	29 84	48 98
		Wm. T. Samuel....	87 96	152 35
Back C'k Valley.	Frederick....	John O. Lockhart..	17 50	26 17
Bacon Castle......	Surry.......	Willis Thompson..	26 10	26 13
Baileysburg......	Surry.......	James Harriss.....	18 11	31 24
Balcony Falls....	Rockbridge..	Samuel Darst......	10 14	17 27
Ballardsville......	Logan......	Blackburn E. Barrett	13 33	21 94
Ballsville.........	Powhatan....	Wm. C. Netherland	35 61	74 05
Baptist Valley...	Tazewell.....	Hugh S. Bailey, fm. 3d March.......	74	1 03
Barber's ⋈ Roads	Isle of Wight	Thos. M. Dashiell..	14 89	19 87
Barboursville......	Orange.......	William Douglass..	44 73	83 48
Barhamsville......	New Kent...	Thos. N. Timberlake	24 74	44 78
Barker's Settlem't	Randolph....	Solomon Yeager....	7 40	12 19
Barksdale........	Halifax......	John A. McCraw...	26 68	46 34
Barnett's Mills...	Fauquier....	Henry A. Embry...	6 47	10 99
Barry's Bridge...	Lunenberg...	Samuel Jefferson...	11 44	18 67
Barter Brook....	Augusta.....	Hugh G. Guthrie, to 31st December...	6 16	10 67
		Thomas W. Shelton	7 13	11 42
Bath C. H........	Bath.........	John S. Crawford..	117 24	223 14
Beaver Dam......	Goochland...	Tarlt'n W. Pleasants	20 61	33 97
Beaver D'm Depot	Hanover.....	Lancelot Philips....	57 04	110 84
Beckley.........	Fayette......	Thos. P. Fleeson....	5 17	8 76
Beddington......	Berkley......	And. W. McCleary.	24 71	44 26
Beeler's Station..	Marshall....	John Wilson, sr....	17 00	30 69
Belle Haven......	Accomack...	John T. Elliott, 3 qrs	18 48	34 28
Belleville.........	Wood........	George V. Lewis...	11 31	20 74
Bellona Arsenal..	Chesterfield...	Moses McArthur...	5 83	10 57
Bell Point........	Giles.........	James Adair, from 1st January.......	41	51
Bell's Valley......	Rockbridge..	Wm H. Bell........	14 80	22 98
Belmont.........	Loudon......	John M. Wilson...	67 10	146 40
Bent Creek.......	Buckingham.	Wilson Hix.......	32 93	58 65
Bentivoglio......	Albemarle...	Brook B. Walker..	69 24	96 22
Bentleyville.......	Halifax......	Robert Gayle......	11 93	22 05
Berger's Store....	Pittsylvania..	Geo. T. Berger.....	24 18	42 92
Berkley Springs..	Morgan.......	Charles Green......	90 69	178 71
Berlin...........	Southampton	Peyton H. Bilbro, to 31st December....	14 78	28 63
		Albert T. Villins...	16 12	29 91
Berryville........	Clarke.......	Jos. M. Nicklin, 3 qrs	185 12	340 58
Bethany.........	Brooke.......	Alexander Campbell	133 69	292 86

POST OFFICES—*Virginia.*

Post Offices.	Counties.	Postmasters.	Compensation.	Net proceeds.
Beverly	Randolph	David Blackman	$62 14	$99 29
Bickley's Mills	Russel	John Bickley	11 76	17 43
Big Lick	Roanoke	Thos. W. Micou	131 19	250 20
Bilton (Dis. 27th Nov.)	Logan	John Lawson	(no ret.)	
Blackface	Nottoway	John G. Powell	11 47	18 77
Black Rock	Rappahan'k	Chs. W. Yates	8 02	12 81
Blacks & Whites	Nottoway	John M. Vaughan	65 04	110 65
Blacksburgh	Montgomery	Thomas R. Evans	75 86	133 19
Blacksville	Monongalia	Eagon B. Tygard	20 43	32 54
Black Walnut	Halifax	R'n D. Fourqurean	50 68	92 08
Bloomfield	Loudon	William H. Gill	21 22	35 87
Bloomsburgh	Halifax	Alexander Watkins	34 63	62 72
Blue Ridge	Botetourt	Nath'l H. Claiborne	18 74	32 14
Blue Spring	Smyth	Andrew Lessly, jr.	5 94	10 10
Blue Stone	Tazewell	William Witten, to 31st March	8 36	14 36
		Chs. F. Tiffany	2 40	4 68
BlueSulphur Sp'gs	Greenbrier	Edwin M. Brown	61 40	109 67
Bolington	Loudon	Daniel Boland	11 49	17 66
Boone's Mill	Franklin	John A. Smith	10 07	21 27
Boothsville	Marion	John J. Stewart	13 45	25 16
Booton's Tan Y'd	Madison	Henry Tisinger	6 68	12 85
Boston	Culpeper	Charles Smith	7 19	12 15
Botetourt Springs	Roanoke	Thomas H. Barnes, 3 qrs	15 52	28 64
Bowers	Southampton	William Lankford	10 17	17 46
Bowlers (Changed to "Centre Cross.")	Essex	Edward M. Ware, to 1st March	18 65	36 36
(Name restored, 13th March.)		Robert H. Dillard, from 21st March	8 76	16 97
Bowlesville	Fluvanna	Nathan H. Payne	17 78	27 90
Bowling Green	Caroline	Seth Saunders, to 11th June	143 81	264 97
		James H. Wright	6 34	13 95
Bowman's Mills	Rockingham	Samuel Bowman	16 61	25 49
Boyd's Tavern	Albemarle	Geo. C. Omohundro	15 09	28 80
Boydton	Mecklenb'gh	Philip Rainey	367 64	433 45
Boykin's Depot	Southampton	Edward Beaton	23 18	44 39
Brandonville	Preston	Jas. H. O'Donovan	37 28	60 37
Braxton C. H.	Braxton	Morgan Dyer	41 47	59 84
Brentsville	Prince Wil'm	Mordecai B. Sinclair	87 90	153 20
Brickland	Lunenburg	Wm. J. Neblett	21 11	40 98
Bridgeport	Harrison	John Carpenter	30 98	19 47
Bridgewater	Rockingham	John Dinkel, jr.	51 43	79 14
Bridle Creek	Grayson	John K. Ballard	3 62	5 31
Bristersburg	Fauquier	Simon T. Taylor, 3 qrs	7 00	11 67
Broadford	Smyth	John Roberts	22 56	33 83

POST OFFICES—*Virginia*.

Post Offices.	Counties.	Postmasters.	Compensation.	Net proceeds.
Brock's Gap	Rockingham	Jeremiah Fifer, to 30th September	$3 90	$6 77
		Jacob Cootes	11 38	16 89
Brooklyn	Halifax	John C. Eldridge	26 98	48 08
Brookneal	Campbell	Reuben H. Garrett	40 45	76 39
Brooksville	Albemarle	William Gamble	30 56	52 41
Brownsburgh	Rockbridge	Andrew Patterson	69 14	116 86
Brown's Cove	Albemarle	Wm. W. Brown	13 35	20 37
Brucetown	Frederick	William Timberlake	65 08	109 61
Bruington	King&Queen	Thomas Walker	16 90	26 54
Brydie's Store	Lunenburg	Irby Hudson	7 93	15 96
Buchannon	Lewis	Henry F. Westfall	34 62	37 26
Buckingham C.H	Buckingham	Robert Shaw	217 45	379 75
Buckland	Prince Wil'm	Edw'd N. Robinson	48 40	89 40
Buffalo	Mason	Richard Childs, to 31st December	15 97	29 38
		Jesse Timms	20 64	37 53
Buffalo Ford	Wythe	Geo. W. Gleaves	3 17	6 06
Buffalo Forge	Rockbridge	William Weaver	9 06	15 47
Buffalo Gap	Augusta	John Pryde	5 41	10 11
Bufords	Bedford	Jacks'n W. Franklin	20 96	31 00
Bull Creek	Wood	Wm. McKinney	17 97	32 87
Bull Pasture	Bath	Thomas Graham	5 77	9 96
Bull Run	Franklin	John W. Powell	9 77	19 74
Bulltown	Braxton	Benj. W. Byrne	8 08	13 33
Bunker Hill	Bedford	Frazier O. Stratton	9 38	12 48
Burgess' Store	Northumb'nd	Benedict Burgess	24 14	31 30
Burke's Garden	Tazewell	Shadrach Heninger	25 19	46 08
Burkesville	Prince Edw'd	Wm. F. Burke	49 13	45 21
Burnersville	Barbour	Morgan H. Burner	8 28	17 04
Burnt Ordinary	James City	Beverly Slater	35 96	63 08
Burnt Quarter	Dinwiddie	Jos. W. Roper, to 17th March	4 23	6 87
		Page H. Vaden	1 59	2 69
Burtonsville	Greene	Benjamin Burton	12 40	19 30
Burwell's Bay	Isle of Wight	Arthur B. Stott	23 29	33 05
Bush's Mills	Lewis	Michael G. Bush	5 05	8 60
Cabell C. H.	Cabell	Wm. C. Miller	71 94	129 54
Cabin Point	Surry	Amos Sledge, jr.	69 91	125 23
Cacaponville	Hampshire	Nathaniel Scrogin	30 02	50 87
Ca Ira	Cumberland	Henry Scruggs	42 93	83 02
Callaghan's	Allegany	Wm. Y. Callaghan	9 98	18 04
Calland's	Pittsylvania	Wm. A. Dickenson	49 14	82 53
Callaway's Mills	Franklin	Moses C. Greer, fm. 18th February	1 25	2 02
Campbell C. H	Campbell	German Jordan	50 65	80 46
Capeville	Northampton	John A. Simkins	19 56	33 95
Capon Bridge	Hampshire	Darius Pugh	30 76	48 87

POST OFFICES—*Virginia.*

Post Offices.	Counties.	Postmasters.	Compensation.	Net proceeds.
Capon Springs...	Hampshire...	William Herin.....	$4 24	$8 83
Carlton's Store...	King&Queen	Younger P. Watkins	24 12	46 02
Carrsville........	Isle of Wight	Edward Rawls......	18 73	30 98
Carter's Bridge...	Albemarle...	Walker Timberlake	17 43	32 83
Cartersville......	Cumberland .	Francis B. Deane...	148 45	251 86
Cary Street.......	Essex.......	Zebulon M.P. Carter	(no ret.)	
Cascade..........	Pittsylvania..	Wm. A. Tinsley...	43 14	82 46
Castle Craig......	Campbell.....	Henry Hazlewood .	14 57	25 41
Cedar Creek......	Frederick.....	Philip Swann......	14 10	18 98
Cedar Grove Mills	Rockbridge..	Robt. B. Anderson.	42 03	69 87
Cedar Point	Page.......	Edward W. Wood.	7 65	13 80
Cedarville	Washington..	Pleasant Smith.....	75 22	149 56
Central Point....	Caroline.....	Henry B. Gouldman	13 58	18 41
Centre Cross.....	Essex.......	Wm. L. Brook, fr.		
(Late "Bowlers.")		5th to 21st March.	1 75	3 09
(Ch'd to "Bowlers	," 13th Mar.)			
Centreville.......	Fairfax	Enoch Grigsby.....	63 96	109 39
Chalk Level......	Pittsylvania..	William Pannill, jr.	40 95	65 68
Chambers' Mills.	Buckingham.	Samuel Ayres......	15 24	24 12
Chamblissburg...	Bedford.....	Stephen C. Hurt...	20 70	32 18
Chancellorsville...	Spottsylvania	Jacob E. Appler, to		
		31st March......	16 99	24 16
		James P. Chartters.	6 65	8 80
Chantilly.........	Fairfax	Thomas Ayre......	17 81	36 01
Chapmanville....	Logan.......	Lorenzo D. Hill...	4 76	9 29
Charlemont.......	Bedford......	Edmund Logwood..	24 94	44 30
Charles City C.H.	Charles City.	George B. Major...	111 22	193 14
Charlestown.....	Jefferson	Humphrey Keys...	584 50	1292 51
Charlotte C. H...	Charlotte....	John Morton......	296 81	381 04
Charlottesville ...	Albemarle. ..	Twyman Wayt....	795 86	1887 10
Chatham Hill....	Smyth.......	John F. Locke, to		
		31st Dec'r.......	5 04	8 80
		Legrand Sexton....	7 75	10 74
Cherry Stone....	Northampton	William Boudine...	(no ret.)	
Chesnut Grove...	Pittsylvania..	Wm. H. Payne....	23 39	38 81
Chesterfield C. H.	Chesterfield...	Jeremiah Hobbs, jr.	16 42	27 89
Chickahominy...	Hanover	William Chiles.....	8 07	15 39
Chilesburgh	Caroline.....	James Gatewood...	16 38	26 42
Christiansburg...	Montgomery.	John Gardner......	131 31	216 03
Christiansville....	Mecklenb'gh.	Rich'd C. Puryear..	39 46	63 70
Chuckatuck	Nansemond..	John D. Day......	57 17	102 57
Church Hill.....	Halifax.....	Robt. S. Carter....	22 11	38 36
Circleville	Loudon......	Thomas Brown....	15 53	24 34
City Point.......	PrinceGeorge	George E. Moody..	82 77	168 64
Clarksburgh.....	Harrison....	HamiltonG.Johnson	325 57	474 93
Clarksville.......	Mecklenb'gh.	Edw'd A. Holloway	264 28	602 27
Claysville	Hampshire...	William Brace.....	18 80	14 83
Clear Branch....	Washington..	Levi L. Waterman.	5 11	8 11
Clendenin	Kanawha....	George Osborne....	7 52	13 60

POST OFFICES—*Virginia.*

Post Offices.	Counties.	Postmasters.	Compensation.	Net proceeds.
Clift Mills	Fauquier	John H. Gaskins	$16 14	$25 59
Clifton Forge	Alleghany	Corbin M. Reynolds	39 27	63 02
Clintonville	Greenbrier	Alex'r S. Skaggs	22 73	37 20
Cloverdale	Botetourt	Hiram Martin	19 18	36 46
Cloverdale Hotel	Bath	Abm. S. Rhodes	10 94	21 68
Clover Hill	Appomatox	John Raine	40 27	33 00
Coal Hill	Goochland	Wm. A. Deitrick	11 62	19 47
Coal Mines	Chesterfield	Wm. Robinson, jr.	58 37	111 95
Coal Riv. Marshes	Fayette	Daniel Shumate, jr.	6 40	10 64
Coalsmouth	Kanawha	John Capehart	66 03	122 24
Cœlebs	Pittsylvania	Wm. H. Dupuy	4 65	8 90
Cold Stream	Hampshire	Nathaniel Offutt	8 61	15 22
Collierstown	Rockbridge	Henry McCorkle	22 29	41 17
Collins' Settlement	Lewis	Elijah Arnold	6 50	6 78
Columbia	Fluvanna	Joseph Hodgson	96 10	182 03
Columbia Furnace	Shenandoah	Jos. S. Machir	17 65	27 97
Columbia Grove	Lunenburg	Wm. M. Bagley	19 73	30 53
Colvin's Tavern	Culpeper	John R. Colvin	17 62	16 74
Coman's Well	Sussex	Wm. D. Taylor	28 52	47 85
Concord	Campbell	Raleigh Chilton	27 53	42 37
Concord Academy	Caroline	James D. Coleman	42 86	86 90
Conrad's Store	Rockingham	Henry Conrad	33 02	51 74
Coopers	Franklin	Robert H. Early, to 4th March	4 96	7 55
		Elizabeth J. Woods, from 10th March	2 68	4 79
Core's Mills	Tyler	And'w S. Core, 2 qs.	2 92	5 06
Covesville	Albemarle	John T. Hamner	22 37	35 30
Covington	Alleghany	Robert Skein	62 76	107 94
Crab Bottom	Pendleton	Andrew Seybert	20 47	35 47
Crab Run	Pendleton	Felix H. Hull	10 34	18 81
Crafton	Pittsylvania	George Craft	3 59	7 41
Craig's Creek	Botetourt	Alexander Hannah	11 39	17 27
Creed's Bridge	Princes Ann	Jesse B. Whitehurst from 1st Jan'y	1 16	1 55
Crichton's Store	Brunswick	James Crichton	3 63	8 52
Criglersville	Madison	Manuel C. Strickler	12 93	18 67
Cross Keys	Rockingham	Rodham Kemper	11 89	18 99
Cross Roads	Bedford	Elias James	16 11	29 80
Cub Creek	Charlotte	Jas. S. Buster	27 19	44 68
Cuckooville	Louisa	Jeremiah C. Harris	17 03	27 31
Culpeper C. H.	Culpeper	Henry Hill, jr.	296 10	318 37
Cumberland C. H.	Cumberland	Peter B. Foster	105 63	161 44
Curdsville	Buckingham	Albert Baldwin	66 74	112 84
Dabney's Mill	Louisa	Jno. O. Harris, jr.	5 19	8 82
Dallas (Late "West Union.")	Marshall	John B. Seaton, fr. 22d May	1 48	2 99

POST OFFICES—*Virginia.*

Post Offices.	Counties.	Postmasters.	Compensation.	Net proceeds.
Danielsville.	Spottsylvania	Wm. S. Brent, to 31st Dec'r	$7 37	$11 36
		Wm. A. Stephens	6 06	4 47
Dan River	Patrick	Gabriel D. Hanley	4 38	7 08
Danville	Pittsylvania	Thompson Coleman	418 41	700 46
Darkesville	Berkley	John Wysong	28 96	55 47
Darvills	Dinwiddie	Wm. B. Thompson	37 25	65 55
Davis' Mills	Bedford	Pleasant Preston	16 20	28 19
Davis' Store	Bedford	Richard Davis	19 01	26 92
Dayton	Rockingham	Michael B. Cline, to 31st Dec'r	8 66	17 10
		John Niswander	11 85	22 26
Deatonsville	Amelia	Owen H. Tucker	17 55	28 38
Deep Creek	Norfolk	Harrison E. Weston	60 83	98 68
Deerfield	Augusta	James S. Guy	44 32	41 64
De Kalb	Lewis	Alex'r J. Pickens	14 80	22 26
Dennisville	Amelia	John W. Foster	14 39	26 76
Dentonsville	Hanover	Allen Denton	15 95	26 29
Diamond Grove	Brunswick	William Raney	55 44	106 69
Diana Mills	Buckingham	Clement R. Fontaine	29 34	51 26
Dickensonville	Russell	Isaac B. Fugate, jr.	7 41	9 11
Dickinsons	Franklin	Joseph Dickinson	21 65	39 12
Dickinson's Store	Bedford	Wm. Dickinson, jr.	5 00	7 23
Dillon's Run	Hampshire	Jesse Lupton, jr.	4 35	6 48
Dinwiddie C. H.	Dinwiddie	John B. Chambers, to 31st Dec.	22 93	40 36
		Thomas Jones	23 99	42 47
Dixville	Henry	James Lamkins	12 17	14 30
Doe Hill	Pendleton	Jared Armstrong	15 43	23 80
Double Bridge	Lunenburg	Wm. W. Yarbrough	5 47	9 78
Dover Mills	Goochland	Lucien M. Watkins	21 81	44 28
Dranesville	Fairfax	Ira Gunnell	37 23	67 44
Draper's Valley	Wythe	Harvey Shepherd	36 15	54 48
Drapersville	Mecklenb'gh.	Lewis Williams	15 51	24 74
Drewrysville	Southampton	John Drewry	39 08	69 08
Dryburgh	Halifax	Sam'l B. Walden	6 12	8 88
Duffields	Jefferson	Alfred Duffield	47 42	90 69
Dumfries	Prince Wm.	Wm. D. Dowell	48 94	58 39
Duncan	Wood	Parkinson Reed	11 74	20 04
Dunnsville	Essex	Wm. C. Hughes. to 31st Dec'r	14 28	25 26
		Orville Jeffries	14 55	27 34
Dupree's Old Store	Charlotte	Thos. J. Morriss	11 64	20 03
Durrettsville	Richmond	Isaac O. Butler	10 09	18 09
East River	Mercer	Reuben Garretson	2 56	4 20
Eastville	Northampton	Leo. B. Nottingham	185 62	339 36
Edenburg	Shenandoah	Richard Miller	63 48	60 10
Edmunds	Brunswick	Nich's S. Edmunds	16 74	29 66

POST OFFICES—*Virginia.*

Post Offices.	Counties.	Postmasters.	Compensation.	Net proceeds.
Egypt	Monroe	Andrew Gwinn	$4 93	$9 32
Elamsville	Patrick	Wm. A. Hannah, to 31st Dec'r	2 41	3 64
		James C. Moir	3 59	5 91
Eldorado	Culpeper	Perry J. Eggborn	9 40	15 26
Eldridge	Buckingham	John H. Lesueur	14 20	24 61
Elk Creek	Grayson	Philander McCarter	10 60	18 53
Elk Furnace	Nelson	Alex'r N. Montgomery, to 31st Dec'r.	16 92	26 45
		Alfred W. Flippin	19 28	33 79
Elk Garden	Russell	John W. Lampkin	8 90	14 89
Elk Hill	Amelia	Wm. A. Mileston	49 78	85 80
Elk Run	Fauquier	William Shumate	2 73	5 03
Ellisville	Louisa	Littleton W. Sneed	18 61	29 88
Emaus	Bedford	Alexander Kasey, fr. 26th Feb'y	1 52	2 55
Enfield	King William	John H. Burch	34 34	58 42
Estillville	Scott	Isaac A. Gray	72 00	112 31
Etna	Hanover	Lucius H. Minor	45 87	79 44
Evansville	Preston	Stephen B. Wheeler, to 16th Oct	9 79	16 68
		Julius C. Kemble	22 39	37 46
Everettsville	Albemarle	David H. Wood, to 15th Nov	40 13	67 74
		Benj. H. Magruder, to 31st March	58 14	54 86
		James Fitz	39 62	35 62
Faber's Mills	Nelson	Henry G. Roberts	32 93	55 95
Fabius	Hardy	Abner Bean	4 65	8 09
Fairfax C. H.	Fairfax	Robert Allison	185 98	333 56
Fairfield	Rockbridge	James W. McClung	28 74	48 49
Fairmont	Marion	Ebenezer Newcomb	80 31	147 87
Fairview	Brooke	John C. McCown	43 67	68 24
Falling Bridge	Campbell	William Cock	15 09	23 66
Falling Spring	Greenbrier	Hiram Scott	10 17	19 13
Falling Waters	Berkley	James Ardinger	13 09	24 78
Falmouth	Stafford	Murray Forbes	172 21	346 22
Fancy Hill	Rockbridge	John P. Welch	60 64	81 71
Farley	Culpeper	Alexander Bell	23 83	43 56
Farmer's Grove	Southampton	Chs. F. Urquhart	23 20	41 90
Farmville	Prince Edw'd	Jas. M. McNutt	437 65	990 46
Farnham	Richmond	Christ'r D. Ficklin	35 59	63 42
Farrowsville	Fauquier	Benj. T. Bradford	63 78	112 91
Fayetteville	Fayette	Alfred Beckley	27 10	46 04
Fearnsville	Isle of Wight	Henry H. Womble	4 89	8 65
Fife's	Goochland	Jane Poore	39 59	71 58
Fincastle	Botetourt	Charles Aunspaugh	283 77	567 23
Finney Mills	Amelia	Benjamin Bridgforth	14 67	22 85

POST OFFICES—*Virginia.*

Post Offices.	Counties.	Postmasters.	Compensation.	Net proceeds.
Fish Creek...... (Dis. 26th June.)	Marshall. ...	John Bell	(No ret.)	
Fishersborough ..	Franklin	Daniel Wray......	$3 72	$6 38
Fishersville......	Augusta	Saml. B. Brown....	40 31	63 88
Flat Lick .... (Late 'Pattonsville.') (Ch. to Pattonsville, 3d Jun.)	Scott	David M. Kinney..	(No ret.)	
Flat Rock.......	Powhatan ...	John D. Sublett....	16 68	27 14
Flatwoods.......	Braxton.....	Elijah Squires	4 73	9 55
Fleetwood Acad'y	King&Queen	Oliver White......	26 97	44 91
Flint Hill	Rappahan'ck.	Thos. J. Massie....	49 95	82 38
Floyd C. H.....	Floyd	Jacob Douthat.....	72 17	112 04
Fluke's.........	Botetourt	Henry J. Stevens ..	16 13	29 72
Fork Inn........	Dinwiddie...	Winston Sutherland	16 93	29 28
Forksville	Mecklenb'gh.	Philip Pennington..	5 76	10 99
Fortsmouth	Warren.....	John G. Buck	2 49	3 91
Foxville	Fauquier	Chs. P. Chilton....	12 72	18 06
Frankford.......	Greenbrier ..	Andr'w D. Johnston	22 90	38 54
Frankfort	Hampshire ..	Charles Keller.....	27 17	45 20
Franklin	Pendleton ...	William Hammen..	84 63	116 16
Franklin Depot ..	Southampton	John B. Jenkins ...	18 03	31 68
Franktown	Northampton	Thomas B. Fisher, (3 qrs.).........	30 19	55 83
Fredericksburgh .	Spottsylvania	Reuben T. Thom ..	1299 62	3752 89
Fredrickshall ...	Louisa......	Wm. J. Pendleton .	44 94	66 83
Freeman's Creek.	Lewis	Vincent Alexander, (2 qrs.)........	11	29
Freeshade	Middlesex ...	Moses J. M. Walker	9 20	12 23
French Creek....	Lewis	Wm. S. Sumner....	10 18	16 91
Frenchton.......	Lewis	Saml. T. Tolbert...	8 25	11 69
Friend's Grove ..	Charlotte....	Walker Pettus.....	7 04	11 81
Front Royal.....	Warren.....	Samuel Reel.......	146 87	213 37
Gainesboro'	Frederick ...	Hiram Murphey...	19 56	33 68
Gaines' X Roads.	Culpeper....	John Deatherage...	27 74	45 06
Gap Mills	Monroe......	Andrew Summers..	13 75	27 37
Garland's	Albemarle...	Nathaniel Garland .	41 19	75 04
Garrisonville	Stafford	Wm. Bayly, (3 qrs)	13 54	22 64
Garysville.......	Prince George	Thos. S. Gary.....	25 74	53 04
Gauley Bridge....	Fayette	James H. Miller ...	39 41	71 50
Genito	Powhatan ...	Hiram W. Wall...	34 82	65 27
German Settlement	Preston	Wm. H. Grimes...	22 21	39 23
Germanton.......	Fauquier....	James McLearen...	19 73	33 92
Gerrardstown....	Berkley	John W. Stewart ..	36 98	63 70
Gholsonville	Brunswick ..	Drury W. Moore..	15 18	27 63
Gilboa..........	Louisa......	Jos. W. Pendleton .	12 77	19 74
Giles C. H......	Giles	J. M. Cunningham .	82 38	133 74
Ginseng	Logan	Mitch. Cook, (2 qrs)	1 27	1 98
Glade Hill.......	Franklin	Thomas Pinckard..	28 21	52 37

POST OFFICES—*Virginia.*

Post Offices.	Counties.	Postmasters.	Compensation.	Net proceeds.
Glade Spring	Washington	Nickerson Snead, to 31st Dec.	$34 03	$59 82
		J. K. Cunningham	33 31	63 29
Glady Creek	Randolph	Jesse Phillips	12 84	20 54
Glenn's	Gloucester	Matthew Glenn	4 11	5 89
Gloucester C. H.	Gloucester	Thos. B. Taliaferro	214 61	431 89
Goblintown	Patrick	John P. Carter	7 20	9 50
Golansville	Caroline	Benj. F. Dickinson	17 40	31 86
Goochland C. H.	Goochland	John Thompson, jr.	63 10	103 85
Goodall's	Hanover	Robert M. Carver	22 29	37 02
Goodwynsville	Dinwiddie	Wm. H. Hawkins	30 30	49 25
Gordonsville	Orange	Richard Caldwell	77 30	137 18
Granville	Monongalia	Marmaduke Dent	21 88	32 48
Grape Island	Tyler	Daniel Bailey	6 30	11 59
Grassland	Harrison	Andrew D. Coplin, (3 qrs.)	3 14	5 24
Grave Creek	Marshall	Benjamin Cockayne	129 89	223 94
Gravel Hill	Buckingham	Beverly A. Brown	25 70	46 43
Gravel Spring	Frederick	Henry Richards	10 03	19 14
Graves Mill	Madison	Thos. J. Allen	1 89	4 46
Grayson C. H.	Grayson	James P. Waugh	52 33	91 65
Grayson Sulphur Springs	Grayson	Robert C. Johnson	11 25	20 56
Greasy Creek	Floyd	Peter Slusher	2 87	5 65
Great Bridge	Norfolk	Iverson N. Hall	13 44	19 05
Green Bank	Pocahontas	John Wooddell	6 48	13 09
Green Bottom	Cabell	James Martin	7 53	13 80
Greenfield	Nelson	Samuel M. Page	21 84	37 65
Green Hill	Campbell	John Pannill	26 31	45 24
Green Level	Southampton	Alfred J. Brittle, from 29th Aug.	3 10	5 59
Green Valley	Bath	Wm. H. Allen	12 53	17 57
Green Vall'y Depot	Hampshire	Thomas Bryan	55 25	96 13
Greenville	Augusta	Benj. F. Graham	73 37	129 26
Griffinsburgh	Culpeper	John Conner	12 53	24 50
Groveton	Prince Wm.	Wm. H. Dogan	39 12	65 85
Guilford	Accomack	John A. Bundick, to 31st March	8 73	14 65
		Sylvester J. Marshall	2 19	3 67
Guiney's	Caroline	Wm. Timberlake	59 40	115 24
Gum Spring	Louisa	Micajah Parrish	23 53	38 36
Guyandotte	Cabell	Joseph Gardner	82 96	104 71
Hague	Westmorel'd	Wm. D. Nelson	46 77	71 86
Hale's Ford	Franklin	Smithson H. Holland	12 67	23 12
Haleysburgh	Lunenburg	Henry A. Fowlkes	11 78	22 13
Half-way House	York	Edward S. Amory, to 31st Dec.	11 81	15 41

POST OFFICES—*Virginia.*

Post Offices.	Counties.	Postmasters.	Compensation.	Net proceeds.
		James Jenings, to 1st May...........	$9 34	$11 01
		John T. Crockett..	(No ret.)	
Halifax C. H.....	Halifax.....	Jas. S. Easley.....	355 42	664 41
Hallsboro'.......	Powhatan ...	Aust. Spears, (3 qrs)	26 91	44 19
Hallsville .... (Dis. 21st Sept.)	Amelia	Geo. E. Rowlett ...	(No ret.)	
Halltown	Jefferson....	John Yates........	31 26	53 17
Hambaugh's	Warren......	Wm. Boyd........	10 27	18 32
Hamilton	Loudon	Wash. Vandevanter	50 04	85 01
Hampstead......	King George.	John E. Baker.....	83 81	157 95
Hampton	Elizab'th City	Wm. Massenburg..	213 62	354 57
Hanging Rock...	Hampshire ..	Mary C. Blue......	16 99	28 18
Hanover C. H...	Hanover.....	John R. Winston, to 31st Dec........	32 16	54 55
		Octavus M. Winston	31 80	55 49
Hansonville	Russell	James M. Hanson .	7 20	7 58
Hardin's Tavern .	Albemarle ...	John Wood, jr.....	127 29	144 08
Hargrove's Tav'rn	Nansemond..	James Hargrove ...	23 18	34 36
Harmony.......	Halifax.....	Jos. J. Lawson	19 74	38 10
Harper's Ferry..	Jefferson	Jas. A. Fitzsimmons, to 22d Jan.......	247 05	540 58
		John G. Wilson ...	164 17	380 04
Harris	Louisa......	Thomas Harris....	27 33	44 33
Harrisonburgh...	Rockingham.	Jos. H. Shue......	391 94	510 00
Harrisville	Brunswick ..	Chas. R. King.....	17 58	33 50
Hartwood.......	Stafford.....	William Irvine	24 26	44 30
Harvey's Store ..	Charlotte....	Thomas Harvey ...	17 71	24 91
Hat Creek	Campbell ...	Robert Armistead ..	15 06	22 86
Hawkinsville	Sussex	Benj. E. Hawkins..	10 24	16 26
Hawsbury	Rappahan'ck.	Andrew R. Barbee.	2 54	4 88
Haymarket......	Prince Wm..	Richard Graham, to 31st Dec........	18 13	32 52
		Garret Hulfish.....	18 79	30 58
Hazard Forge ...	Hardy......	Solomon Michael ..	13 97	27 11
Head Waters....	Pendleton ...	John D. Erwin	2 21	3 73
Heathsville......	Northumb'nd	Wm. D. Bell......	102 04	165 49
Hedgesville	Berkley.....	Peter H. Cookus...	127 75	245 84
Hendrick's Store.	Bedford.....	John Board	13 82	24 83
Hereford's	Mason.......	John M. Hanly....	16 30	31 59
Hermitage	Augusta	Jacob Keiser	10 65	15 21
Hevener's Store..	Pendleton ...	Jacob Hevener, jr..	12 05	22 72
Hickory Fork ...	Gloucester ..	Wm. H. Rowe	48 95	91 97
Hickory Ground.	Norfolk.....	Josiah Wilson.....	14 99	23 26
Hicksford.......	Greenville...	Jos. H. Cooper	305 92	319 10
Highview.......	Frederick ...	James Garvin......	13 34	19 46
Hill Grove	Pittsylvania .	R. A. Weatherford.	5 26	8 65
Hillsboro'	Loudon	Bernard Hough....	74 79	137 50
Hillsville........	Carroll......	William C. Long...	60 90	90 19

POST OFFICES—*Virginia.*

Post Offices.	Counties.	Postmasters.	Compensation.	Net proceeds.
Holliday's Cove	Brooke	William Brown	$70 19	$81 32
Holston	Washington	Abram Linder	5 16	8 70
Holston Springs	Scott	John E. Hutson	73	1 42
Honeyville	Page	John R. Bumgarner	21 69	32 46
Hope Mills	Page	Jos. W. Almond	13 64	19 33
Horntown	Accomack	John P. Laylor	36 54	46 65
Horse Pasture	Henry	Peter W. Watkins	31 30	48 78
Horton's Valley	Russell	Mesheck White	3 38	7 54
Hot Springs	Bath	Thomas Goode	54 42	115 60
Houston (C'd to 'Lodore.')	Amelia	Wm. H. Hillsman, from 14th Oct. to 31st Dec	6 15	12 04
Howardsville	Albemarle	Wm. A. Turner, to 31st Dec	29 07	59 55
		Benjamin S. Fortune	27 87	55 98
Howellsville	Warren	Charles B. Rust	4 76	8 42
Hoysville	Loudon	Sam'l Stoutsenberger	18 46	28 57
Hughesville	Loudon	John H. Hughes	19 22	33 99
Huntersville	Pocahontas	George E. Craig	30 84	49 59
Hunting Creek	Accomack	John R. Drummond	8 02	12 97
Huttonsville	Randolph	Jonathan Hutton	10 99	18 87
Hyco	Halifax	Wm. P. Tucker	18 28	35 29
Hydraulic Mills	Albemarle	Nathaniel Burney	13 36	22 06
Ice's Ferry	Monongalia	Evan T. Ellicott	42 55	76 55
Independent Hill	Pr. William	Basil Cole	9 64	14 77
Indian Creek	Monroe	Riley B. Cook	6 16	10 58
Ingles' Ferry	Pulaski	Thomas Ingles	10 49	18 67
Ives' Store	Princess Ann	William Ives, to 30th Sept	2 27	3 10
		Edwin W. Ives	6 61	9 20
Jackson	Louisa	Patrick H. Jackson, to 31st Dec	8 46	13 73
		Elisha Jackson	7 91	11 19
Jackson C. H.	Jackson	Robert Lowther	60 64	94 35
Jackson's Ferry	Wythe	John Sanders	20 87	36 20
Jacksonville	Wood	Alfred Beauchamp	17 42	33 78
Jake's Run	Monongalia	Richard D. Tennant	2 09	3 14
Jamaica	Middlesex	R. H. W. Godwin	23 37	44 48
Jamestown	Pr. Edward	William White	17 91	33 52
Janelew (Late "McWhorter's Mills.")	Lewis	Stephen P. Jackson, from 1st April	2 90	5 56
Jarratts	Sussex	Nicholas Jarratt	54 67	54 70
Jefferson	Powhatan	John C. Stratton	47 71	96 45
Jeffersonton	Culpeper	Thomas Luckett	56 20	60 17
Jeffress' Store	Nottoway	John L. Bruce	36 83	67 37
Jennings's Gap	Augusta	James A. Frazier	16 79	26 12
Jennings's Ordinary	Nottoway	Thacker Ellington	62 59	61 45

POST OFFICES—*Virginia.*

Post Offices.	Counties.	Postmasters.	Compensation.	Net proceeds.
Jerusalem	Southampton	Thomas Maget	$85 53	$162 34
Jetersville	Amelia	Royal B. Smithey	23 10	40 27
Johnson's Springs	Goochland	Wm. S. Crouch	10 50	15 33
Johnsontown	Northampton	Wm. J. Leatherbury	21 37	20 47
Jonesboro'	Brunswick	Robert B. Jones	10 65	17 93
Jonesville	Lee	F. S. Miles, 3 qrs	88 41	140 10
Junction	Hanover	W. Williamson, 3 qs.	24 38	48 55
Kanawha C. H.	Kanawha	James A. Lewis	522 24	535 04
Kanawha Saline	Kanawha	Thomas J. Buster	185 42	338 34
Kasey's	Bedford	James O. Hensley	8 66	11 78
Kempsville	Princess Ann	James O. Galbraith	26 71	36 44
Kennedy's	Brunswick	Isham H. Trotter	32 37	52 02
Kerneysville	Jefferson	Francis Dunnington	50 63	89 72
Kerr's Creek	Rockbridge	John C. Laird	12 38	17 96
Keysville	Charlotte	John D. Priddy	8 20	15 54
Kilmarnock	Lancaster	Addison Hall	43 89	69 23
K'g & Queen C.H.	K'g & Queen	Alexander Dudley	19 27	35 98
K'g George C. H.	King George	William Colton	114 86	192 30
K'g William C. H.	K'g William	Wm. N. Gregory	46 94	80 74
Kingwood	Preston	James H. Carroll	65 25	103 80
Kinsale	Westmorel'd.	Robert S. Bailey	27 43	45 30
Knob Fork (Dis. 26th June.)	Tyler	Daniel Anderson	no return	
Lafayette	Montgomery	James Heslep to 31st Dec.	32 18	28 28
		Andrew J. Deyerle.	30 75	29 96
Lancaster C. H.	Lancaster	George R. Waddey.	42 50	75 48
Lanesville	K'g William.	Thomas Starke	15 24	26 36
Langhorne's Tav.	Cumberland	Wm. R. Coupland.	43 58	43 63
Laurel	Washington.	David Rambo	2 51	5 57
Laurel Grove	Pittsylvania	Banister Anderson	27 65	49 98
Laurel Hill	Lunenburg	Littleberry Tunstill.	13 23	19 91
Lawrenceville	Brunswick	Robert Kirkland	142 91	267 75
Leading Creek	Lewis	Henry W. Sleeth	3 98	5 24
Leadsville	Randolph	William M. Phares.	4 03	5 89
Leatherwood's Store	Henry	Benjamin F. Gravely, to 22d Nov.	15 23	16 68
		Benjamin F. Dyer.	17 38	27 39
Lebanon	Russell	T. C. M. Alderson.	89 95	131 99
Leed's Manor	Fauquier	John S. Payne	50 73	95 27
Leesburgh	Loudon	Ramey G. Saunders	361 84	840 70
Leesville	Campbell	Carolus G. Terry	47 81	81 76
Leetown	Jefferson	John Sharff	38 59	77 00
Len's Creek	Kanawha	Chas. Morris, 1 qr	1 72	2 60
Leon	Madison	Nathaniel Tatum	13 29	23 63
Level Green	Giles	John S. Easley	7 82	14 88

POST OFFICES—*Virginia.*

Post Offices.	Counties.	Postmasters.	Compensation.	Net proceeds.
Lewisburgh	Greenbrier	Shannon Butt	$406 27	$606 81
Lewisport	Harrison	J. S. Davis, 3 qrs	17 67	27 89
(Chan'd to "West Union.")				
Lewis' Store	Spottsylvania	Frederick Frazer	20 07	34 38
Lewisville	Brunswick	Eaton J Mosely	8 39	14 56
Lexington	Rockbridge	Archibald Graham	641 22	1235 67
Liberty	Bedford	Reuben Parker	252 14	458 33
Liberty Hall	Washington	Joseph Snodgrass	2 26	3 78
Liberty Mills	Orange	David Howard	39 48	64 44
Linnville Creek	Rockingham	John Chrisman	24 38	40 22
Lisbon	Bedford	Samuel Williams	28 63	48 79
Little Level	Pocahontas	Josiah Beard	4 75	8 16
Little Plymouth	K'g & Queen	William B. Bird	24 25	41 92
Little River	Floyd	Thomas Franklin	3 49	5 30
Littleton	Sussex	William Kirby, to 31st December	18 88	31 01
		Howell A. Adkins	17 41	29 81
Litwalton	Lancaster	Wm. L. G. Mitchell	22 80	41 37
Lloyd's	Essex	Bevin D. Pitts	89 96	152 52
Lock Lomond	Goochland	Jos. K. Weiseger	39 77	34 80
Locust Creek	Louisa	William Bagby	28 35	51 41
Locust Dale	Madison	Reuben Garnett, jr.	42 97	59 86
Locust Grove	Orange	James L. Robinson	17 62	31 78
Locust Lane	Fayette	Geo. H. Patrick	10 07	18 11
Locust Level	Halifax	James J. Irby	8 80	17 67
Locust Mount	Accomack	Wm. B. Smith	20 30	34 87
Locustville	Accomack	Thomas P. Copes	7 23	12 33
Lodore (Late "Houston")	Amelia	Wm. H. Hillsman, from 1st January	22 50	35 62
Logan C. H.	Logan	Anthony Lawson, jr.	20 38	32 76
Lombardy Grove	Mecklenburg	Charles Baskerville	71 72	131 15
London Bridge	Princess Ann	Bennet Land	30 91	38 20
Long Branch	Wayne	Asa Booten, 2 qrs	47	74
Long Creek	Louisa	Wm. G. T. Nelson	4 26	6 85
Long Glade	Augusta	Jacob Crist	25 30	37 39
Long Level	Cabell	John Morris	10 34	19 44
Long Meadow	Page	Ambrose C. Booton	6 62	10 60
Longwood	Albemarle	James Michie, jr	28 49	47 05
Lorentz' Store	Lewis	Geo. W. Lorentz	8 41	14 59
Loretto	Essex	John Saunders	96 53	175 54
Lost Creek	Harrison	Abel Bond, to 15th May	6 98	8 62
		Eli Vanhorn	no return	
Lost River	Hardy	Samuel Harper	9 68	19 39
Lottsburgh	Northumb'ld.	Lucius S. Winstead	7 41	10 57
Louisa C. H.	Louisa	Wm. Stout, 3 qrs	137 79	300 49
		Alex. F. Butler	no return	
Louisville	Westmorel'd.	William Edwards	9 90	15 94
Love's Mills	Washington	Leonidas Love	7 15	12 99

POST OFFICES—*Virginia.*

Post Offices.	Counties.	Postmasters.	Compensation.	Net proceeds.
Lovettsville	Loudon	Jonathan Wenner	$49 74	$82 60
Lovingston	Nelson	John H. Loving	176 52	265 07
Lumberport	Harrison	James Y. Horner	15 16	21 33
Lunenburg C. H.	Lunenburg	John H. Smith, jr.	66 39	120 32
Luney's Creek	Hardy	Gabriel T. Barbee	70 34	112 34
Luray	Page	Gabriel Jordan	192 28	196 57
Lyell's Store	Richmond	Daniel Atwell	9 87	14 96
Lynchburgh	Campbell	Lillburn H. Trigg	1805 13	4803 51
McFarland's	Lunenburg	Enos H. Barnes	47 09	72 90
McGaheysville	Rockingham	David Irick	33 36	54 14
McWhorter's Mills (C'd to 'Janelew.')	Lewis	Blackwell Jackson, to 30th September	3 40	2 41
		Stephen P. Jackson, to 31st March	7 77	12 33
Macon	Powhatan	John Spears	40 74	75 03
Madison C. H.	Madison	Francis H. Hill	103 84	180 13
Maiden Spring	Tazewell	Rees T. Bowen	13 91	20 77
Manchester	Chesterfield	Zachariah Hall, to 30th Sept	20 43	42 33
		Arch. B. Bott	45 51	96 29
Mangohick	K'g William	David Rider	21 21	32 15
Mannboro'	Amelia	J. Harris, (includes part of quarter for "Namozine.")	34 17	55 31
Mansfield	Louisa	Wm. D. Mansfield	18 78	32 33
Marble Hill	Prince Edw'd	James H. Dupuy	16 87	28 83
Marion	Smyth	Jeremiah Rogers	98 34	141 65
Marksville	Page	Paschal Graves	9 38	15 54
Marl Spring	Sussex	German B. Gill	9 43	13 24
Martinsburgh	Berkley	John H. Likens	398 80	855 38
Martinsville	Henry	James M. Smith	88 79	132 05
Marysville	Campbell	John H. Swinney	34 23	55 69
Massanutten	Page	John R. Burner	6 22	11 04
Matthews C. H.	Matthews	Elijah Barnum	112 80	191 80
Matthewsville	Pocahontas	And'w G. Mathews	6 03	10 58
Mayfield	Isle of Wight	Wilson Holleman	14 65	23 97
Mayo	Halifax	Robert E. Owen	6 95	10 49
Mayoning	Patrick	George C. Dodson	7 40	9 33
Maysville	Greenbrier	Samuel Riffe	9 08	15 76
Meadow Dale	Bath	James Slaven	6 85	10 45
Meadville	Halifax	Jeremiah White	39 27	70 78
Meat House Fork	Doddridge	Amaziah Bee	24	28
Mechanicsburgh	Giles	Wm. H. Howe	13 18	21 95
Mechanicsville	Louisa	Colum. R. Boulware	14 82	25 27
Melville Mills	Rappahann'k	Richard Coppage	4 29	8 09
Melon	Harrison	John N. Hall	4 02	7 33
Menasses Gap	Warren	John Latham	6 61	11 57

POST OFFICES—*Virginia.*

Post Offices.	Counties.	Postmasters.	Compensation.	Net proceeds.
Merrimans Shop..	Prince Edw'd	Eldridge B. Land, to 31st Dec'r........	$5 90	$7 72
		Nicholas Pamplin..	7 01	11 16
Merry Point......	Lancaster ...	Eppa N. Dunaway..	12 59	11 99
Messongo	Accomack...	Thos. A. Northam..	1 98	4 22
Middlebourne....	Tyler.......	William Swan.....	53 86	89 85
Middlebrook	Augusta.....	Barnhard Lowman.	90 67	157 15
Middleburgh......	Loudon......	Edwin C. Brown...	230 70	404 68
Middle Mountain.	Botetourt....	William Scott......	5 97	7 87
Middletown	Frederick....	Jacob S. Danner....	100 84	76 16
Middleway.......	Jefferson	John H. Smith.....	89 25	159 73
Midland	Charlotte....	Jas. B. M. Osborne.	17 45	27 45
Midway Inn.....	Prince Edw'd	John F. Rice.......	8 87	13 97
Milford	Warren	Christian Forrer....	12 96	21 23
Milboro' Spring..	Bath	John Dickinson	24 82	34 89
Mill Creek.......	Berkley	John Grove, to 24th Aug............	5 71	10 13
		John T. Swartz, to 31st March......	22 27	40 48
		Benj. R. Boyd, from 23d May........	5 40	9 21
Miller's Tavern..	Essex........	Thos. N. Clarke....	56 32	97 68
Millford Mills....	Prince Wm..	Wm. J. Weir......	16 26	23 66
Millington	Albemarle ...	Richard I. Duke, to 31st Dec'r.......	9 89	15 32
		Thomas Ballard....	11 42	15 71
Mill Point.......	Pocahontas..	James Smith	15 40	25 54
Millview	Fauquier....	Jno. M. Fant, 3 qrs.	17 49	27 36
Millville.........	King George.	William A. Jones..	29 59	51 76
Millwood........	Clarke.......	Robert H. Little....	190 73	365 71
Mint Spring	Augusta......	Alexander Gardner.	4 38	8 14
Mitchells Store...	Goochland...	Obadiah T. Mitchell	19 69	32 89
Modesttown.......	Accomack ...	Wm. B. Jacobs, to 30th Sept..........	8 38	16 58
		Samuel S. Russell ..	32 17	61 62
Montague	Essex.......	Charles G. Layton..	25 36	50 35
Montpelier	Hanover	Henry Leadbetter..	26 01	46 90
Moorefield.......	Hardy	Mort'er W. Gamble	242 67	425 73
Moore's Store....	Shenandoah ..	Charles S. Wunder.	19 10	26 37
Moreman's River.	Albemarle...	George B. Brown...	13 00	22 07
Morgansburgh...	Fauquier....	Charles Morgan, to 31st Dec'r.......	3 90	5 92
		Wm. J. Wheatley..	6 97	11 55
Morgantown.....	Monongalia..	Nicholas B. Madera	233 81	450 17
Morganville......	Nottoway....	Austin L. Wills....	38 20	65 42
Morris' Hill	Alleghany...	James P. Shumate..	7 23	14 57
Morrisville	Fauquier....	Benj. W. Allen....	12 72	21 06
Mossingford.....	Charlotte	Isaac Overbey......	15 82	28 61
Mountain Cove ..	Fayette	Clem't Vaughn, 3 qs.	15 46	27 88

POST OFFICES—*Virginia.*

Post Offices.	Counties.	Postmasters.	Compensation.	Net proceeds.
Mountain Grove..	Bath........	Sam'l V. Gatewood.	$4 42	$7 76
Mount Airy	Pittsylvania..	William A. Corbin.	18 59	32 59
Mount Athos	Campbell....	Jas. Sutphin, f'm 6th Nov. to 31st Mar.	1 07	2 03
Mount Clinton....	Rockingham.	Ptolemy Brightwell.	17 94	26 72
Mount Crawford.	Rockingham.	Pleasant A. Clark ..	70 53	104 36
Mount Gilead....	Loudon......	Isaac Eaton........	16 02	28 76
Mount Horeb....	Nelson......	Wm. C. Roberts...	21 13	38 92
Mount Israel.....	Albemarle...	Samuel O. Moon...	21 03	35 67
Mount Jackson...	Shenandoah..	Daniel Gray, to 21st Feb'y..........	83 53	50 99
		James McCann....	38 53	37 18
Mount Juliet.....	Kanawha....	James S. Turner....	27 06	48 53
Mount Laurel....	Halifax......	Clem't M. Adkisson	39 52	66 92
Mount Level.....	Dinwiddie...	Nath'l P. Newbill..	10 69	21 21
Mount Linneus..	Marion	Joseph Morgan....	13 05	22 12
Mount Meridian..	Augusta......	James Craig........	30 93	51 46
Mount Pleasant..	Spottsylvania	Oscar L. Chewning.	31 18	47 25
Mount Salem	Kanawha....	R'd C. Chandler, jr.	2 04	3 98
Mount Sidney....	Augusta.....	Jacob C. Roler......	85 40	150 30
Mount Solon.....	Augusta.....	Heury Blakemore..	40 93	68 14
Mountville.......	Loudon......	John Lumm.......	11 82	20 77
Mount Vinco	Buckingham.	John C. Fritz, from 30th Nov........	10 95	18 34
Mount Zion......	Campbell....	Charles W. King, to 31st March......	5 49	8 24
		E. B. Wood.......	1 38	2 06
Mouth of Poca...	Kanawha....	Alex'r Simenton....	13 31	24 87
Mouth of Wilson.	Grayson	Ephraim Gentrey...	13 57	25 75
Muddy Creek....	Preston	Jacob Guseman....	5 18	8 12
Murraysville.....	Jackson.....	John Roberts.......	9 93	16 92
Murrill's Shop....	Nelson......	William Murrill....	8 93	16 65
Namozine....... (Dis. 4th Oct.)	Amelia......	Ag. M. Woodward, to 1st Aug.......	1 13	2 11
Natural Bridge...	Rockbridge..	Joel Lackland......	58 47	100 78
Neersville	Loudon......	Franklin Wigginton, to 30th Sept......	3 71	6 68
		Thos. W. Shriver, to 30th May........	9 74	17 50
		Fayette J. Conrad..	93	2 17
Negro Foot......	Hanover	Charles Vest.......	13 96	24 04
New Baltimore...	Fauquier....	F. W. S. Grayson..	42 22	82 26
Newbern........	Pulaski	John H. Vermillion.	154 43	261 40
New Canton.....	Buckingham.	Nathaniel Anderson.	49 81	93 22
New Castle......	Botetourt....	Jacob Hamman....	22 98	35 62
New Church.....	Accomack...	Jas. P. Selby, jr....	11 65	18 57
New Glasgow....	Amherst	Valerius McGinnis..	64 59	115 82
New Hope......	Augusta.....	James M. Stout....	40 10	63 82

POST OFFICES—*Virginia.*

Post Offices.	Counties.	Postmasters.	Compensation.	Net proceeds.
New Kent C. H.	New Kent	Harman Chandler	$92 51	$159 02
New London	Campbell	Henry Stevens	89 25	141 83
New Market	Shenandoah	Solomon Henkel	230 68	212 84
New Martinsville	Tyler	James McClure	39 67	71 52
Newport	Giles	Robert Payne	9 32	18 28
New Salem	Harrison	Jona. F. Randolph	9 98	14 94
Newsom's Depot	Southampton	John M. Neal	56 22	64 98
New Store	Buckingham	Monroe W. Jones	51 42	87 65
Newtown	King & Queen	Sam'l S. Gresham	52 82	77 70
Newtown Stephensburg	Frederick	John Allemong	94 91	158 74
Newville	Sussex	Wm. H. Marable	19 10	30 32
Nicholas C. H.	Nicholas	Ferguson Malcom	26 72	51 23
Nickell's Mills	Monroe	Jas. M. Nickell	13 92	24 64
Nickelsville	Scott	Robert Whitley, fr. 1st Oct	2 19	4 88
Ninneveh	Warren	William Cook, jr., to 30th Sept	4 55	7 92
		Giles C. Hamill	12 88	21 22
Noland's Ferry	Loudon	John Matthews	14 49	22 44
Norfolk	Norfolk	Alexander Galt	1960 14	11226 31
North End	Matthews	Wm. A. Spence, jr.	33 04	57 05
North Garden	Albemarle	John A. Brown	20 21	31 71
North River Mt'g House	Hampshire	William Horsman	10 35	13 50
North River Mills	Hampshire	John B. Miller	23 08	36 91
North West River Bridge	Norfolk	Wilson Corprew	13 65	21 17
Nortonsville	Albemarle	William G. Dunn	10 52	19 48
Nottoway C. H.	Nottoway	Timothy Wortham	120 31	100 66
Oak Flat	Pendleton	William Dyer	13 68	21 85
Oak Forest	Cumberland	Zachariah Talley	33 35	56 21
Oak Grove	Westmorel'd	George M. Carter	88 02	166 73
Oak Hill	Fauquier	Thomas Phillips	54 63	95 12
Oakland	Morgan	Basil E. Shockey	8 92	15 27
Oak Level	Henry	Columbus King, to 31st March	4 13	6 61
		Constantine Martin	2 68	3 46
Oakley	Mecklenb'gh	Anderson C. Morton to 31st Dec'r	20 16	33 48
		Wm. B. Easley	18 53	31 87
Oakville	Buckingham	Jonathan Christian	27 19	46 05
Oatlands	Loudon	John B. Grayson	10 25	20 06
Occoquan	Prince Wm.	Joseph Janney	59 77	110 06
Office Tavern	Amelia	John Wingo	27 54	50 27
Old Church	Hanover	James D. Ellett	102 28	187 87
Old Point Comfort	Elizab'th City	Robert Archer	451 40	1018 57
Onancock	Accomack	Stephen Hopkins	53 80	80 22

POST OFFICES—*Virginia.*

Post Offices.	Counties.	Postmasters.	Compensation.	Net proceeds.
Oral Oak	Lunenburg	Robert H. Allen	$11 00	$11 67
Orange C. H	Orange	David Hume	241 66	452 43
Orange Springs	Orange	John P. Coleman	17 87	33 48
Orlean	Fauquier	Amos Payne	18 52	29 44
Osborn's Ford	Scott	Wm. Richmond	7 55	12 90
Otter Bridge	Bedford	Wm. L. Bell	47 00	69 02
Otter Dale	Chesterfield	Abijah Cheatham, jr	(No ret.)	
Ottobine	Rockingham	Francis M. Ervine	8 91	13 08
Pack's Ferry	Monroe	G. C. Landcraft	2 75	4 90
Painesville	Amelia	Bernard Seay	25 24	47 15
Paint Creek	Kanawha	L. H. Brannon	19 99	33 02
Palatine Hill	Marion	William Haymond	27 52	46 73
Palestine	Greenbrier	John Alderson	6 96	11 14
Palmer's Springs	Mecklenb'gh	John M. Wright	33 76	61 02
Palmyra	Fluvanna	Robert E. Nelson	69 30	126 95
Panther's Gap	Rockbridge	Jas. McD. Moffett, 3 qrs	5 64	11 64
Parham's Store	Sussex	George S. Parham	17 70	30 05
Paris	Fauquier	Isaac Settle	87 12	166 84
Parkersburgh	Wood	George W. Saunders	312 76	640 65
Parnassus	Augusta	John R. Syrcle	20 13	25 72
Partlows	Spottsylvania	Thomas D. Smith	9 82	17 11
Patrick C. H	Patrick	Alexander A. Moir	61 19	95 76
Patterson's Depot	Hampshire	James L. Randolph	18 46	29 13
Pattonsburgh	Botetourt	Thomas Crews	169 64	345 20
Pattonsville	Scott	Colbert C. Fugate	2 80	4 79
(Changed to "Flat Lick.")				
(Late 'Flat Lick.')				
Peach Bottom	Grayson	Granville H. Cox, from 1st Oct	0 76	1 74
Pedlar's Mills	Amherst	Richard J. Pryor	43 38	63 37
Peel Tree	Harrison	Jesse W. Arnold	4 17	6 08
Pemberton	Goochland	Benajah B. Ayres, to 31st March	65 21	103 15
		John B. Pemberton	18 10	37 74
Pembroke	Giles	John Lybrook, to 12th May	5 63	9 26
		George R. Lybrook	1 04	1 81
Pendleton (Dis. 17th Feb.)	Scott	Ivy N. Pendleton	10 48	18 10
Pennsboro'	Ritchie	James Martin	13 30	23 63
Penn's Store	Patrick	Peter Penn	36 38	63 37
Percivals	Brunswick	W. Y. Mallory, 3 qrs.	5 68	8 79
Petersburgh	Dinwiddie	John Minge	1746 65	8520 66
Peterstown	Monroe	James M. Byrnside	21 40	38 11
Peytonsburgh	Pittsylvania	Chs. S. Lacy	20 66	35 88
Phillippa	Barbour	Isaac H. Strickler	44 14	79 80
Philomont	Loudon	Jos. P. Megrath	25 93	44 29

POST OFFICES—*Virginia.*

Post Offices.	Counties.	Postmasters.	Compensation.	Net proceeds.
Physic Spring....	Buckingham.	Benjamin A. Ford..	$20 30	$37 33
Pigeon Run......	Campbell.....	Achilles Herndon ..	20 65	30 81
Pine Grove......	Tyler	Stacy Stephens.....	3 81	6 24
Pittsylvania C. H.	Pittsylvania..	Ichabod T. Watson.	127 33	230 60
Plain View......	King & Queen	John M. Albright ..	12 48	21 03
Pleasant Flat.....	Mason	O. H. P. Vanmatre, to 30th Sept	2 36	3 85
		Joseph Yeager.....	4 90	7 46
Pleasant Gap	Pittsylvania..	Thomas W. Walton	9 23	12 64
Pleasant Grove...	Lunenburg ..	Alfred H. Hurt....	21 67	38 85
Pleasant Hill.....	Smyth........	Wm. W. Williams.	24 53	17 98
Pleasant Valley...	Fairfax	Elijah Hutchison...	17 05	31 30
Pocotaligo.......	Kanawha....	Edward R. Fife....	4 41	10 00
Poindexter's Store	Louisa	Wm. W. McGeehee, to 30th Sept	7 32	13 75
		Samuel P. Hackett .	20 50	36 79
Point Pleasant ...	Mason	Samuel G. Shaw...	120 66	203 34
Poplar Hill......	Giles........	Thomas G. Shannon	1 90	4 02
Poplar Mount....	Greenville....	John Cole.........	19 69	34 26
Port Conway....	King George.	Wm. S. Payne.....	36 40	65 98
Port Republic....	Rockingham.	James O'Brian.....	50 00	83 92
Port Royal......	Caroline......	William Gray......	127 68	246 38
Portsmouth......	Norfolk	John Hodges......	823 21	2086 11
Pottiesville	Louisa......	Charles Pottie......	16 66	29 20
Potts' Creek.. ...	Alleghany....	Thomas Rosser....	2 59	5 94
Powells Mountain	Lee..........	James S. Mehafey..	5 34	9 95
Powell's Tavern..	Goochland...	J. W. Powell......	14 58	29 67
Powelton	Brunswick ..	Wm. C. Cabiness..	22 57	39 73
Pribble's Mills...	Wood	John Foster	9 63	17 60
Prillimans........	Franklin	Jacob Prilliman....	9 49	16 44
Prince Edw'd C.H.	Prince Edw'd	Thomas J. Spencer.	214 57	398 04
Prince Geo. C. H.	Prince Geor'e	Robert H. Batte....	21 26	36 43
Princess Ann C.H.	Princess Ann	Wilson H. C. Lovitt	29 72	40 13
Princeton.........	Mercer.......	Benjamin Hall.....	34 85	41 24
Proctor's Creek..	Chesterfield...	Patrick A. Chalkley	25 32	33 51
Prospect.........	Prince Edw'd	Robert V. Davis ...	8 79	15 25
Prospect Hill....	Fairfax	Wm. W. Ball, to 7th December....	19 12	33 33
		Lewis D. Means...	28 65	54 10
Providence	Halifax......	Louisa McAdams..	22 61	41 23
Pruntytown	Harrison....	Abraham Smith....	76 45	149 42
Pryor's Vale.....	Amherst	Thomas M. Pryor..	7 19	8 51
Pungoteague.....	Accomack...	Wm. A. Kellam....	28 81	46 08
Purcel's Store....	Loudon......	James H. Purcel...	72 38	132 56
Quillinsville	Scott	Henry W. Ewing..	4 19	5 36
Raccoon Ford....	Culpeper.....	Philip P. Nalle.....	52 32	86 59
Raine's Tavern...	Cumberland .	Hugh Raine.......	58 32	54 76

POST OFFICES—*Virginia.*

Post Offices.	Counties.	Postmasters.	Compensation.	Net proceeds.
Rapidan........	Madison	Wm. N. Rose	$30 14	$48 07
Rappahannock Academy......	Caroline	Wm. A. Buckner...	22 21	37 86
Ravenswood......	Jackson......	Arch'd A. Quarrier.	32 26	48 73
Rebecca Furnace.	Botetourt	David I. Wilson...	20 37	42 06
Rector's ✕ Roads	Fauquier.....	Elijah M. Anderson, to 31st Dec......	11 99	22 61
		Joseph A. Taylor ..	14 66	26 15
Rectortown......	Fauquier.....	James H. Rector...	39 07	66 95
Red Banks	Shenandoah .	Lawrence Pitman, jr	17 14	24 72
Red Bluff........	Wythe.......	Abner Thompson ..	6 70	8 74
Red House......	Charlotte....	Wm. E. Lewis, to 10th Nov........	10 86	14 29
		C. Maloney, 4⅔ mo.	7 19	11 59
Red House Shoals	Mason	James A. Payne....	19 02	33 59
Red Oak Grove ..	Charlotte....	Albert G. Jeffress ..	25 18	44 74
Red Sulpher Spri's	Monroe......	Wm. Adair, jr......	61 34	119 11
Reed Island......	Pulaski	James Calfee, to 30th September........	1 56	2 19
		Wm. Tipton, 2 qrs.	2 69	3 48
Reedy Spring....	Campbell	Thomas M. Bass...	10 73	15 79
Rehoboth	Lunenburg ..	William Keeton....	17 91	33 70
Republican Grove	Halifax.......	Peter Barksdale....	28 53	51 26
Retreat...........	Franklin	S. S. P. Thompson.	17 72	25 99
Rexburgh	Essex........	Leroy W. Dobyns, to 11th Sept	7 70	12 96
		Henry M. Dobyns .	28 93	51 86
Rhea's Store..... (Ch'd to "Three	Washington.. Springs.")	Wm. R. Rhea, to 25th Feb........	5 95	9 16
Rice's Store......	Westmorel'd.	Steptoe T. Rice, to 12th Feb........	14 34	23 28
		Philip T. Chandler.	9 26	16 32
Richardsville......	Culpeper.....	Chs. C. Bailey.....	21 89	40 33
Richland	Tazewell.....	James Q. Kindrick.	8 68	16 26
Richmond........	Henrico	Bernard Peyton, to 22d March	1261 98	22021 34
		Thomas B. Bigger..	423 40	8594 59
Ridgeville	Hampshire...	Henry Trout.......	48 44	46 69
Ridgeway .... (Late 'Rough Cr'k	Charlotte.... Church.')	Andrew Bailey, jr., from 1st Dec.....	4 95	7 94
Ripleys	Tyler	John J. Ingle......	9 72	21 16
Ritchieville.......	Dinwiddie...	William Clark, jr...	13 59	18 01
Rivesville	Marion.......	Elisha Snodgrass...	8 70	13 14
Rixeyville.......	Culpeper.....	William Rixey.....	18 32	19 90
Roanoke Bridge..	Charlotte....	Jacob Morton......	42 69	58 06
Roaring Run.....	Botetourt	Wm. Borden, 2 qrs.	7 88	14 08
Robertson's Store.	Pittsylvania..	Thomp'n Robertson	10 91	11 78
Rock Castle	Patrick......	William Ayres.....	6 46	11 03
Rockland Mills...	Augusta.....	John Roller	7 50	11 20

POST OFFICES—*Virginia.*

Post Offices.	Counties.	Postmasters.	Compensation.	Net proceeds.
Rocky Mount	Franklin	Thomas S. Greer	$88 39	$149 95
Rodophil	Amelia	John W. Miner	10 67	15 64
Romine's Mills	Harrison	Jacob M. Eib, to 10th Feb	4 36	8 04
		J. H. Shuttleworth	2 48	4 62
Romney	Hampshire	E. M. Armstrong	301 66	333 61
Rose Grove	Buckingham	Wm. H. Still	9 93	16 34
Rose Hill	Lee	John Fulkerson	17 64	34 54
Roseland	Nelson	H. W. Heath, 3 qrs.	7 40	13 48
Rose Mills	Amherst	James McDonald	34 28	57 95
Rough Creek Ch. (Ch'd to "Ridgeway.")	Charlotte	A. Bailey, jr., 1 qr.	3 94	5 72
Ruckersville	Greene	Elisha J. Williams	18 65	30 34
Ruckmanville	Bath	John H. Ruckman	12 53	20 16
Rural Retreat	Wythe	John B. Straw	29 88	29 39
Ruther Glen	Caroline	John Chandler	32 46	56 21
Rye Cove (Late Stock Crk.)	Scott	Thomas Carter	(no ret.)	
Rye Valley	Smyth	Rufus K. Williams	12 59	8 41
St. James' Church	Bedford	Benjamin Gardiner	12 70	20 20
St. Tammany	Mecklenb'gh.	Armistead G. Boyd	17 76	32 55
Salem	Roanoke	Wm. C. Williams	223 14	215 82
Salem Fauquier	Fauquier	Andrew Barbee	60 34	113 07
Saline Rock (Dis. 23d Oct.)	Ritchie	Henry I. Jackson	(no ret.)	
Salt Sulphur Spr's	Monroe	Alexander Erskine	34 64	71 06
Saltville	Washington	John Ramage, to 1st March	20 96	37 31
		Thomas Findlay	13 68	27 98
Sandidges	Amherst	Samuel G. Cash	24 42	39 76
Sandy	Jackson	Thomas Mairs	3 24	5 27
Sandy Bottom	Middlesex	R. H. Crittenden	13 40	25 47
Sandy Level	Pittsylvania	G. W. Young, 1 qr.	0 52	0 63
Sandy River	Pittsylvania	John C. Royall	10 70	17 26
Sandy River Ch'h	Prince Edw'd	Booker Foster	25 17	40 21
Sapling Grove	Washington	James King	30 73	30 75
Savage Grant	Wayne	John McCormick	4 99	10 55
Schumla	Wood	Bazil Williamson	7 07	14 38
Scottsburgh	Halifax	John H. Garrett	9 27	15 84
Scott's Ferry	Albemarle	Edwin H. Jordan, to 30th Sept	42 94	77 71
		Peter C. Hogg	134 99	270 57
Scott's Run (Dis. 26th July.)	Monongalia	Peter A. Layton	(no ret.)	
Scottsville	Powhatan	Thaddeus H. Ivy	109 20	203 94
Sea View	Northampton	Luther Nottingham	11 89	16 78
Second Creek	Greenbrier	John Burdett	6 14	12 95
Seven Islands	Fluvanna	Joseph Pace	10 98	20 04

POST OFFICES—*Virginia*.

Post Offices.	Counties.	Postmasters.	Compensation.	Net proceeds.
Seven Mile Ford	Smyth	Wm. W. Hanson	$23 56	$45 79
Sewell Mountain	Fayette	George Dickson	8 57	16 88
Shacklefords	King & Queen	Robert B. Smith	28 09	46 92
Shady Grove	Franklin	Robert G. Mays	16 31	28 40
Shannon Hill	Goochland	Owen C. Morris	12 08	20 83
Sharon	Wythe	Thomas Shannon	7 15	10 82
Sheetz' Mills	Hampshire	Frederick Sheetz	10 27	14 27
Shenandoah Iron Works	Page	Henry Forrer	15 43	30 87
Shepherdstown	Jefferson	John K. White	304 41	620 94
Sherrard's Store	Hampshire	Robert B. Sherrard	27 26	49 12
Shiloh	King George	Philip P. Johnston	6 87	11 21
Shinnston	Harrison	James W. Janes	20 38	32 38
Simpsons	Floyd	John Gray	9 93	16 33
Sinclair's Bottom	Smyth	Levi Bishop	2 67	4 27
Sinking Creek	Botetourt	James R. Trenor	9 38	16 94
Sissonville	Kanawha	John R. Dawson	4 34	10 11
Sistersville	Tyler	Joshua Russell	53 99	107 09
Skinquarter	Chesterfield	Richard Goode	20 15	35 01
Slate Mills	Culpeper	John W. Miller	11 44	21 57
Smithfield	Isle of Wight	Shemuel Godwin, to 8th December	93 00	153 05
		Wm. H. Jordan	112 41	191 68
Smithsville	Powhatan	Wm. L. Smith	35 74	62 78
Smoky Ordinary	Brunswick	Wm. J. Mallory	19 30	35 65
Snicker's Ferry	Clarke	Mahlon Bleakley	35 91	64 37
Snickersville	Loudon	William Bradfield	70 24	116 08
Snoddy's (Dis. 26th June.)	Buckingham	Robt. W. Snoddy, 2 qrs	2 67	4 20
Snow Creek	Franklin	Gresham Choice	20 79	36 00
Solus	Ritchie	Spencer T. Bukey	38 48	68 80
Somerton	Nansemond	Jas. E. Smith	25 25	40 60
Somerville	Fauquier	Wm. A. Thompson	20 06	29 29
South Anna	Louisa	David B. Bullock	7 43	8 82
South Hill	Mecklenburg	Samuel Stone	11 96	17 14
South Quay	Southampton	Arthur E. Hall	16 66	24 62
Sparta	Caroline	Robt. S. Broaddus	28 95	47 96
Spartapolis	Rockingham	Richard Pickering	62 60	71 88
Speedwell	Wythe	William Ward	12 87	19 49
Sperryville	Rappahan'ck	Thomas Hill, jr., to 31st December	16 75	23 96
		Marcus Cooper	14 72	22 95
Spottedville	Stafford	Edward W. Latham	8 31	14 10
Spottsylvania C.H	Spottsylvania	James M. Nalle	48 38	82 75
Sprout Spring	Campbell	David A. Plunkett	44 75	63 35
Spring Creek	Greenbrier	Wm. L. Brown, to 1st September	87	1 58
		Sam'l J. Varner	4 00	6 80
Springfield	Hampshire	Wm. P. Stump	54 45	94 81

POST OFFICES—*Virginia.*

Post Offices.	Counties.	Postmasters.	Compensation.	Net proceeds.
Spring Garden...	Pittsylvania..	Jos. E. Anderson...	$12 75	$20 34
Spring Hill......	Chesterfield..	Stephen Wilkinson.	22 13	38 63
Spring Vale......	Fairfax	Joshua Loomis....	5 49	10 66
Stafford C. H....	Stafford......	Eustace Conway, to 30th September..	20 96	35 31
		Henry R. Conway.	42 94	59 56
Stanardsville.....	Orange.......	Geo. W. Price......	60 77	108 59
Stapleton.........	Amherst	Willis H. Plunkett, to 31st December.	10 42	18 66
		David Staples......	7 65	8 02
Staunton.........	Augusta.....	Norborne C. Brooks	672 94	1599 89
Steele's Tavern..	Augusta......	John Steele, jr......	41 02	73 16
Stevensburgh.....	Culpeper.....	James M. Griffin, to 31st December...	26 72	44 98
		Richard T. Nalle....	27 28	47 83
Stevensville......	King&Queen	John Bagley........	56 34	80 61
Steward's Creek.	Lewis.......	Peregrine Hays.....	6 29	6 08
Stewart's Draft...	Augusta.....	John P. Wilson....	7 16	10 81
Stillwell.........	Wood.......	Samuel Emrick.....	3 06	6 80
Stock Creek..... (Chan'd to "Rye Cove.")	Scott........	Wm. B. Neil.......	4 75	8 45
Stoner's Store....	Roanoke	Samuel Stoner, to 31st December...	14 90	29 92
		Wm. S. Minor......	14 59	28 90
Stone Wall Mills.	Buckingham.	Ambrose Plunkett..	13 51	22 80
Stony C'k Warehouse.........	Sussex	Alexander Albridge.	31 97	55 60
Stony Hill........	Richmond...	Stephen D. Purcell, to 31st March....	9 28	13 57
		William Carter.....	3 07	4 27
Stony Mount....	Brunswick...	George Stone.......	49 54	48 02
Stony Point.....	Albemarle....	Gideon F. Carver..	31 32	53 65
Stony Point Mills	Cumberland .	John R. Palmore...	57 52	108 33
Strasburgh	Shenandoah .	Philip A. Machir...	145 47	140 04
Sturgeonville.....	Brunswick...	Sabat Griffin........	19 47	32 27
Sublett's Tavern.	Powhatan	William Sublett.....	51 15	80 72
Suffolk...........	Nansemond..	Arthur Smith, to 24th May.............	249 98	436 67
		Kedar Hill..........	27 10	55 53
Sugar Tree......	Pittsylvania..	Walter Fitzgerald..	14 44	28 30
Summit Point....	Jefferson	Warner A. Thomson	37 83	67 74
Surry C. H.......	Surry........	Thomas Ruffin, to 12th July.........	2 57	4 21
		Jos. S. Judkins....	73 56	125 88
Sussex C. H.....	Sussex	Junius L. Dillard...	35 49	64 18
Sweet Springs....	Monroe......	Calvin S. Campbell.	70 32	149 94
Sydnorsville......	Franklin	Samuel Fishburn...	6 37	11 55
Tackett's Mills...	Stafford......	Jefferson Spindle....	17 06	30 05

POST OFFICES—*Virginia.*

Post Offices.	Counties.	Postmasters.	Compensation.	Net proceeds.
Tanner's Store...	Mecklenbu'h.	Evans Tanner......	$12 02	$20 82
Tappahannock...	Essex	Geo. H. Dobyns...	135 49	209 35
Taylor's Store...	Franklin	T. C. S. Ferguson..	16 17	28 76
Taylorsville	Hanover	Wm. D. Taylor....	70 13	121 83
Tazewell C. H...	Tazewell.....	Addison A. Spotts..	100 39	171 12
Teaze's Valley...	Kanawha....	Samuel Handley...	10 36	19 74
Temperance ..... (Dis. May, 1844.)	Amherst	Thomas Goodwin..	(no ret.)	
Templeton.......	Prince George	Wm. E. Proctor...	14 00	19 31
The Meadows...	Bedford......	Elijah C. Cundiff...	31 15	39 73
Theological Sem'y	Fairfax	William Sparrow...	145 87	301 96
The Plains......	Fauquier.....	James W. Foster...	34 80	60 53
Thompson's ✕ Roads	Louisa.......	Lancelot Minor, jr..	29 72	51 07
Thompsonville...	Culpeper....	Marcus Cooper, to 30th September...	4 50	8 40
		French L. Cooper..	14 18	24 54
Thornburgh......	Spottsylvania	Henry Carpenter...	21 25	37 09
Thorn Hill......	Orange.......	Jno. M. Goodwin..	9 22	13 93
Thoroughfare....	Prince Wil'm	William Roach.....	18 23	31 83
Three Fork......	Marion	John Parrill.......	11 79	22 09
Three Springs... (Late "Rhea's Store.")	Washington..	Wm. R. Rhea, from 4th March.......	2 01	3 78
Timber Ridge....	Rockbridge..	John A. Kinnear...	12 04	20 51
Timberville......	Rockingham.	Naason Bare.......	20 10	33 01
Tobacco Row....	Amherst	Thomas Barbour...	9 42	14 25
Todds	Spottsylvania	Charles Todd......	9 84	17 07
Tolersville.......	Louisa......	Robt. T. Gooch....	24 58	45 46
Tomahawk Spr'g.	Berkley	John Stewart......	8 82	13 70
Tom's Brook....	Shenandoah .	Chs. C. Maurer....	30 98	24 43
Traveller's Repose	Pocahontas..	Jacob G. Slaven....	5 05	6 01
Taylorsville	Henry.......	Sam'l H. Taylor....	27 75	52 84
Trevillian's Depot	Louisa......	Chs. G. Trevillian..	48 45	87 11
Triadelphia......	Ohio........	James Reed........	67 09	116 65
Turkey Cove....	Lee	William Richmond.	12 94	18 28
Turner's Store...	Caroline	Robt. M. Wright...	13 79	22 36
Two Mile Branch	Smyth.......	Nelson Hopkins...	3 37	5 73
Twyman's Store.	Spottsylvania	Jas. B. Peake......	32 42	51 40
Tye River Mills..	Nelson......	Nelson C. Clarkson, 3 qrs............	27 30	50 05
Tye River Warehouse........	Nelson......	Samuel Read.......	90 74	180 23
Union..........	Monroe......	James A. Shanklin,	132 55	237 29
Union Grove.....	Prince George	Wyley Daniel.....	3 46	5 97
Union Hall......	Franklin	Philemon Smith....	19 54	33 33
Union Level.....	Mecklenbu'h.	Wm. D. Ligon, fm. 1st January.......	8 52	15 04
Union Mills......	Fluvanna....	Claudius Tompkins.	38 79	70 80

POST OFFICES—*Virginia.*

Post Offices.	Counties.	Postmasters.	Compensation.	Net proceeds.
Union Village....	Northumb'd.	John H. Elmore....	$11 19	$19 39
Unison	Loudon......	Robert H. Kercheval, to 1st June...	19 97	36 84
		Henry St. G. Rust..	1 55	2 78
University of Va.	Albemarle...	Wm. Wertenbaker.	413 34	747 99
Upper Tract.....	Pendleton...	Adam Coil.........	8 29	13 22
Upperville.......	Fauquier....	Wm. A. Stephenson	203 90	403 88
Urbanna.........	Middlesex...	Alfred Healy......	70 49	138 39
Valley Mills.....	Augusta.....	Wm. W. Taylor....	(no ret.)	
Variety Mills....	Nelson......	Charles B. Hill.....	30 79	55 67
Vaucluse........	Wood.......	Alex'r H. Creel....	11 95	24 31
Verdierville......	Orange......	Henry Hatch......	40 82	68 70
Verdon..........	Hanover	John T. Anderson..	21 88	33 11
Vicksville.......	Southampton.	Jesse B. Vick......	7 53	11 53
Virginia Mills....	Buckingham.	John S. Nicholas...	24 73	43 97
Wades..........	Bedford.....	Alexander Wade...	14 32	23 47
Wagram.........	Accomack...	Thomas W. Hargis.	15 34	29 42
Walker's Church.	Appomattox.	Wm. D. Mathews..	44 79	80 75
Walkerton......	King&Queen	Jos. T. Henley, to 31st Dec.........	16 46	28 80
		Benj'n H. Turner...	16 42	27 97
Walling's Creek..	Lee.........	Jacob V. Fulkerson.	10 26	14 63
Walnut Branch..	Fauquier....	Samuel Catlett......	21 71	34 31
Walnut Grove...	Kanawha....	Lyle Millan........	19 59	31 53
Walnut Hill.....	Lee.........	Hugh Houston.....	7 27	14 08
Walton.........	Kanawha....	John Sinnett.......	1 81	2 96
Wardensville....	Hardy.......	Jesse O. Switzer....	27 74	41 15
Ward's Bridge...	Pittsylvania..	Hilton D. Walker..	18 52	25 23
Warminster.....	Nelson......	James Vigres......	33 26	60 71
Warren.........	Albemarle....	Austin M. Appling..	58 17	118 13
Warren Ferry... (Disc. 23d Oct.)	Buckingham.	John H. Tapscott, to 30th Sept......	0 65	1 46
Warrenton......	Fauquier....	Alex'r H. Spillman.	416 27	894 14
Warrenton Sp'ngs	Fauquier....	William McNish...	55 14	110 92
Warsaw........	Richmond....	Geo. W. Goldsby..	90 68	149 00
Warwick C. H..	Warwick....	Thos. R. Dunn, jr..	15 56	19 85
Washington.....	Rappahan'ck.	Frs. S. Browning...	108 22	181 13
Waterford.......	Loudon.....	Henry T. Gover...	89 83	148 09
Watkinsville.....	Goochland...	Edwin C. Fleming..	15 82	29 41
Wattsboro'......	Lunenburg...	Gill W. Watts.....	11 22	16 49
Waugh's Ferry..	Bedford.....	George L. Shrader..	33 19	55 90
Waylandsburgh..	Culpeper.....	Simeon B. Wayland	20 93	36 80
Wayne C. H....	Wayne......	Talton W. Everette.	12 39	19 97
Waynesboro'....	Augusta.....	Abraham Lynn....	133 42	221 64
Webb's Mills....	Ritchie......	John Webb.........	4 57	8 48
Wellsburgh......	Brooke......	Thomas McCarty..	311 32	394 46
Westernford.....	Randolph....	William Ewin.....	11 69	19 15

POST OFFICES—*Virginia.*

Post Offices.	Counties.	Postmasters.	Compensation.	Net proceeds.
West Liberty....	Ohio.........	John Steel.........	$73 49	$131 89
West Milford....	Harrison.....	William H. Patton.	12 47	23 00
Westmorel'd C.H.	Westmorel'd.	William H. Benson.	79 89	124 25
Weston........	Lewis........	Richard P. Camden.	102 47	187 79
West Union......	Doddridge...	Taliaferro K. Knight	6 35	11 08
West Union...... (Ch'd to "Dallas")	Marshall....	John Dickey.......	11 76	22 59
Wheatland.......	Loudon.......	John B. Dutton....	20 53	34 25
Wheatley.......	Fauquier....	Garland T. Wheatley	16 52	30 73
Wheeling........	Ohio.........	David Agnew......	1997 36	604 05
White Chimneys.	Caroline......	Mickelburro' Young	20 69	30 84
White Day.......	Monongalia..	James D. Watson..	16 47	26 87
White Gate......	Giles.........	Wilson Bane......	4 58	7 73
White Hall......	Frederick....	John Pugh.........	17 84	31 59
White House....	Mecklenb'rgh	Littlebury Overbey.	33 87	62 78
White Plains....	Brunswick....	James Woolsey....	31 27	57 19
White Post......	Clarke........	Hiram P. Evans...	88 85	140 34
White Stone.....	Lancaster....	Mordecai Lawson, 2 qrs.............	6 36	11 06
		George S. Lee.....	no ret'rn,	
White Sulphur Springs........	Greenbrier...	Alfred Plumb......	282 45	507 84
Whittle's Mills..	Mecklenb'rgh	Conway D. Whittle	35 63	56 74
Wicomico Church	Northumbr'ld	Charles L. Brown..	21 23	29 21
Wilderness.......	Spottsylvania	Richard T. Spotswood, 3 qrs......	15 87	31 25
Wilkinson's Shop	Chesterfield..	William Wilkinson.	13 42	23 19
Wilkinsonville...	Chesterfield..	H. W. Robertson..	19 12	32 46
Williamsburgh...	James City..	William Edloe.....	373 07	853 61
Williamsport....	Hardy........	Lionel F. Branson..	19 77	34 29
Williamsville....	Bath.........	Robert McClintie...	5 72	9 46
Wilmington......	Fluvanna.....	R. Omohundro, jr..	38 40	66 03
Wilsonville......	Bath..........	William Wilson ...	6 44	12 08
Winchester......	Frederick....	John Wall.........	1125 86	2739 85
Winnsville.......	Fluvanna....	Joseph Woolling, to 30th Sept........	17 18	31 32
		Philip I. Winn.....	45 53	79 42
Woodlands...... (Disc. 27th July.)	Marshall....	John J. Fullerton, to 6th August......	1 40	2 46
(Re-est'd 19 Dec.)		Chs. S. Whitaker, from 1st Jan.....	4 19	8 01
Woodlawn........	Accomack...	Thomas J. Rayfield.	14 32	26 33
Wood's ✕ Roads.	Gloucester...	Thomas Tuton.....	10 29	14 60
Woodstock......	Shenandoah..	James Allen.......	229 44	210 51
Woodville.......	Rappahan'ck.	Joseph Reid.......	77 95	127 99
Wright's Mills...	Jackson.....	David Woodruff ...	11 10	20 22
Wylliesburgh....	Charlotte....	Hillery M. L. Goode	31 97	59 99
Wyoming.......	Dinwiddie...	Joel Manlove......	35 07	56 17
Wytheville......	Wythe.......	John W. Truslow..	310 65	412 54

POST OFFICES—*North Carolina.*

Post Offices.	Counties.	Postmasters.	Compensation.	Net proceeds.
Yancey's Mills...	Albemarle...	John H. Cocke....	$48 55	$93 90
Yatesville........	Lunenburg..	John M. Yates.....	23 95	35 55
Yellow Branch...	Campbell....	Francis M. Adams.	21 66	28 54
Yellow Spring....	Hampshire..	Abraham Secrest...	3 42	5 16
Yocum Station...	Lee..........	Wm. C. A. Wynn.	2 02	3 25
Yorktown........	York........	Nathaniel Taylor...	54 93	99 91
Zanesville........ (Ch'd to "Mount Vinco.")	Buckingham.	Watson B. Cobbs, to 30th Sept.....	3 29	6 03

NORTH CAROLINA.

NOTE.—Compensation of Postmasters, and net proceeds of their offices, from July 1, 1844, to June 30, 1845.

Post Offices.	Counties.	Postmasters.	Compensation.	Net proceeds.
Abbott's Creek...	Davidson.....	Austin Raper, to 30th Sept...........	$3 43	$5 52
		William Raper.....	9 57	15 94
Abram's Plains..	Granville....	Sam'l S. Downey...	8 81	14 23
Airy Grove......	Lenoir........	Walter Dunn, jr....	11 40	18 78
Alarka...........	Macon.......	Wm. F. McKee....	1 20	1 60
Albemarle........	Stanly.......	Dan'l Freeman, 1 qr.	3 40	6 63
Albertson's......	Duplin.......	Alexander Grady ..	6 43	11 49
Albrights.........	Orange........	D. A. Montgomery.	6 05	11 06
Alexandriana.....	Mecklenb'gh.	Jas. McK. Alexander	10 16	16 41
Alfordsville......	Robeson.....	Warren Alford, to 30 Sept..........	5 53	10 49
		Sion Alford........	12 21	22 01
Allemance........	Guilford.....	Eli Smith..........	14 74	21 73
Anderson's Store.	Caswell......	Quintin Anderson..	10 57	19 07
Argyle...........	Cumberland.	Patrick Munroe....	1 46	2 28
Ashboro'.........	Randolph....	Jos. A. Worth.....	100 35	88 07
Ashland..........	Bertie........	Augustus Holley...	18 05	33 64
Ashville..........	Buncombe...	Montraville Patton..	803 79	0 00
Asylum.......... (Dis. 26th June.)	Granville....	Chas. Barker, 3 qrs.	3 42	4 18
Averysboro'.....	Cumberland.	Neill S. Stewart....	35 21	44 80
Ayersville........	Stokes.......	James Ayers.......	8 46	16 56
Bainbridge.......	Jones........	Robert Dickson....	(No ret.)	
Bakersville.......	Yancey	David D. Baker....	2 72	5 87
Bald Creek......	Yancey	Sam'l L. Wilson...	2 49	4 45
Ballard's Bridge..	Chowan.....	Allen Small........	19 12	35 01

POST OFFICES—*North Carolina.*

Post Offices.	Counties.	Postmasters.	Compensation.	Net proceeds.
Bath	Beaufort	Joseph Bonner	$32 48	$60 27
Battleboro'	Edgecombe	Jno. F. Bellamy	26 71	45 52
Bear Branch	Duplin	John Carr	21 27	31 85
Beattie's Ford	Catawba	Hugh C. Hamilton, to 1st Feb'y	36 74	59 41
		John H. Wheeler	19 01	32 76
Beaufort	Carteret	Wm. C. Bell	206 07	393 16
Beaver Dam	Union	Stephen Hasty	8 61	16 53
Belew's Creek	Stokes	George Brookes	10 36	19 99
Belford	Nash	Gray Sills	22 45	42 98
Berea	Granville	John Sherman	7 22	11 59
Bethania	Stokes	Israel G. Lash	23 41	31 46
Bethany Church	Iredell	Wm. A. Dunlap	19 25	29 08
Bethel	Hertford	Abner Harrell	18 23	34 08
Beverly	Anson	William Mendenhall	14 27	22 70
Big Creek	Stokes	Thos. H. Gregg	5 12	10 48
Big Falls (Lt. "Scottsville.")	Orange	Benjamin Hurdle	(No ret.)	
Big Swamp	Columbus	Moore Lennon	2 62	4 30
Birchettsville	Cleveland	Drury Birchett	4 25	6 94
Black Creek	Wayne	Bunyan Barnes	22 61	38 94
Black Riv. Chapel	New Hanover	John M. Corbett	15 09	26 72
Blackwell	Caswell	Henry Cobb	10 47	18 97
Blakely	Stokes	William Withers	6 46	11 64
Blue Wing	Person	Warren Amis, to 30th Sept	2 93	4 56
		James Amis	5 89	8 95
Bogles	Iredell	Robert L. Bogle, 3 qrs	1 51	3 57
Boilston	Henderson	Thos. R. Murray, fr. 30th Aug	1 51	2 17
Boon Hill (Dis. 4th Oct.)	Johnson	Jesse Holt, to 28th Aug	1 03	1 54
Bostick's Mills	Richmond	Tristram Bostick	15 51	28 41
Bost's Mills	Cabarras	Simon Bost	5 38	9 16
Botanic Hill	Nash	John Q. A. Drake, 3 qrs	5 59	9 80
Bowers' Store	Ashe	Allen Gentry	6 12	10 15
Boyle's Store	Stokes	William Boyles, to 27th July	1 11	2 26
		John W. Bitting	20 17	39 32
Brier Creek	Wilkes	James Martin, 3 qrs.	3 52	6 37
Brindletown	Burke	John M. Carson	24 68	49 22
Brinkleyville	Halifax	Sidney Weller	34 21	56 80
Britton's Store	Bertie	Stephen McDaniel	36 21	75 54
Brookville	Granville	Sam'l H. Cannaday.	12 36	19 61
Brower's Mills	Randolph	Nicholas Brower	14 57	26 80
Brown's Store	Caswell	Stephen Neal	52 56	69 68
Brownsville	Granville	Frederick M. Clack.	10 98	12 55

POST OFFICES—*North Carolina.*

Post Offices.	Counties.	Postmasters.	Compensation.	Net proceeds.
Brummells	Davidson	Hiram W. Brummell	$8 72	$16 63
Buck Shoals	Rutherford	Wyatt Gault	7 78	12 43
Buffalo	Cleveland	John Roberts	2 91	4 83
Buffalo Hill	Orange	Wm. J. Roberts	4 73	9 12
Bullocks	Granville	Lewis M. Jiggitts	12 87	25 14
Burnsville	Yancey	Bacchus I. Smith, to 9th Nov'r	9 09	16 07
		Lorenzo D. Poteet	19 65	34 20
Butler's Mills	Montgomery	Wm. McCallum	4 26	7 40
Caledonia	Moore	Francis Munroe	5 56	10 45
Camden	Camden	Sam'l D. Lamb	32 35	51 31
Camp Call	Cleveland	Wm. W. Green	1 79	3 29
Cane Creek	Chatham	William Lindley	5 13	9 07
Carthage	Moore	Cornelius H. Dowd	48 39	91 97
Casher's Valley	Macon	Jonathan Zachary	4 22	9 14
Catawba Creek	Lincoln	And'w B. Cox	9 18	13 20
Catawba Springs	Catawba	Thomas Hampton	5 12	8 86
Catawba View	Caldwell	Abner Payne	2 57	1 72
Cathey's Creek	Henderson	James Hamblen	5 96	7 88
Cedar Grove	Orange	Joseph Allison	9 61	14 91
Cedar Hill	Anson	David C. Lilly	40 99	69 67
Centre	Guilford	Andrew C. Murrow	11 48	21 10
Centreville	Moore	Neil McLeod	0 93	1 14
Chalk Level	Cumberland	And'w H. Dewar	6 21	10 93
Chapel Hill	Orange	James B. McDade	362 88	595 59
Charlotte	Mecklenb'gh.	Henry B. Williams, to 31st Dec'r	234 68	239 28
		Jos. W. Hampton, to 31st March	86 50	160 40
		Amzi McGinn	92 63	189 64
Cheoah Valley	Cherokee	H. P. King, 3 qrs	0 76	0 58
Chimney Rock	Rutherford	John W. Harris	5 81	9 62
China Grove	Rowan	Chs. L. Partee, to 30th Sept	2 65	4 25
		John D. Scheck	14 86	14 86
Chisholm's Store (Dis. 30th July.)	Montgomery	Peter D. Swaim	(No ret.)	
Church's Store	Wilkes	Alfred Forester, to 1st Dec'r	1 09	2 05
		John H. Vannoy	2 33	4 89
Clapps	Guilford	Abraham Clapp	12 17	19 32
Clark's Mills	Moore	Daniel McKenzie	3 36	5 07
Claytonville	Henderson	Leander S. Gash	10 52	13 83
Clear Creek	Mecklenb'gh.	Mat. A. Barnhardt	8 63	13 12
Clemmonsville	Davidson	Evander McIver	27 18	46 49
Clinton	Sampson	Josiah Johnson	235 66	233 25
Clover Garden	Orange	John Morrow	13 00	23 61
Coburn's Store	Mecklenb'gh.	Josiah H. Stewart	11 22	14 13

POST OFFICES—*North Carolina.*

Post Offices.	Counties.	Postmasters.	Compensation.	Net proceeds.
Coinjock	Currituck	Eugene Morton	$3 12	$5 25
Colerain	Bertie	Josiah Holley	26 07	51 35
Colesville	Stokes	John L. Cole	8 03	13 04
Collettsville	Caldwell	Chas. Collett, 3 qrs.	3 34	6 33
Columbia	Tyrrell	Henry H. Davenport to 30th Sept	17 24	35 01
		Abner Alexander	46 79	94 86
Columbian Inn	Stokes	De Witt C. Stone	6 65	11 42
Concord	Cabarras	Thos. S. Henderson	131 20	221 84
Contentnia	Pitt	Richard H. Adams	7 13	9 76
Cool Spring	Washington	Hardy Hardison	78 76	153 65
Copenhagen	Caldwell	Joseph Corpening	2 72	4 36
Cottage Home	Lincoln	Robt. H. Morrison	15 12	26 63
Cotton Grove	Davidson	James Wiseman	20 18	37 46
Councill's Store	Ashe	Jordan Councill	4 88	8 06
County Line	Davie	Amos B. Sanford, to 31st March	9 15	18 06
		Wilfred Turner	3 28	6 78
Covington	Richmond	Thomas Garrete	8 01	13 81
Cowan's Ford	Mecklenb'gh.	Rich'd F. Blythe	3 02	4 02
Cowansville	Rowan	Thos. C. Graham	11 31	19 40
Cowper Hill	Robeson	Jennet McNair	10 20	16 92
Cox's Store	Sampson	Moses Cox	28 39	48 84
Crab Tree	Haywood	Samuel Ferguson, fr. 1st Oct	2 21	3 30
Crain's Creek	Moore	Jacob Matthews	9 54	16 54
Crooked Creek	Stokes	John S. Patterson	4 89	8 21
Crowder's Creek	Lincoln	Lawson Wilson	10 15	15 99
Cunning'm's Store	Person	Alex. Cunningham	22 49	37 07
Currituck C. H.	Currituck	Jos'a W. Baxter	34 70	54 80
Davidson College	Mecklenb'gh.	John B. Davies	72 22	130 09
Davidson River	Henderson	Samuel Hefner	3 27	5 37
Davis' Spring	Robeson	John C. Davis	10 15	15 23
Deal's Mill	Caldwell	William Deal	2 70	4 69
Deep River	Guilford	Andrew Lindsay, to 31st Dec'r	5 05	11 48
		Eliz. Lindsay 1 qr.	2 65	4 69
Deep Well	Iredell	Hugh M. Gray	8 71	16 17
Diamond Hill	Anson	William Perry	7 48	14 07
Dillonsville (Dis. 30th July.)	Union	Jno. A. McCall	(No ret.)	
Dockery's Store	Richmond	John W. Ingram, to 31st Dec'r	4 49	8 12
		Oliver H. Dockery	5 36	8 63
Doweltown	Surry	Theoph's C. Hauser	9 80	17 22
Drowning Creek	Burke	Philip Warlick	4 32	7 45
Dry Ponds	Lincoln	Hail M. Munday	1 31	2 51
Dudley	Wayne	John W. S. West	49 03	96 21

POST OFFICES—*North Carolina.*

Post Offices.	Counties.	Postmasters.	Compensation.	Net proceeds.
Dumas' Store....	Richmond...	Isham A. Dumas...	$17 56	$27 62
Duncan's Creek..	Cleveland ...	James McFarland..	3 12	5 25
Durant's Neck...	Perquimans..	Geo. W. Reed.....	35 17	57 11
Dutchville......	Granville....	Alfred M. Veazey..	11 01	21 47
Eagle Falls......	Rockingham.	Franklin Harris....	16 13	25 04
Eagle Rock	Wake	Thomas R. Debnam	18 91	31 00
Early Grove.....	Lincoln	Adam Miller	11 00	20 82
Edenton	Chowan	Theodorick J. Bland	522 07	966 11
Edneyville	Henderson ..	James M. Edney ..	8 75	14 15
Elder Branch....	Wilkes	Wm. W. Wheatley	1 15	2 21
Elizabeth City...	Pasquotank .	Malachi Russell....	393 15	936 07
Elizabethtown ...	Bladen......	John McKeithen...	(No ret.)	
		Jas. J. McRee, from 1st Oct.........	81 60	171 11
Elk X Roads	Ashe	Buckner Tatum....	2 90	5 80
Elkville.........	Caldwell	Catlett Jones	7 55	10 80
Emerson's Tan Yard	Chatham....	Geo. W. Goldston .	8 47	13 96
Enfield..........	Halifax	L. H. B. Whitaker.	172 68	165 48
Enoe Mills	Orange	Thos. W. Holden, to 30th Sept.....	1 75	2 59
		John F. Lyon	6 90	13 11
Equality	Mecklenb'gh.	Benjamin Brown...	2 25	3 93
Erasmus........	Lincoln	Isom Ford	4 92	6 89
Erwinsville......	Cleveland ...	Charles Ellis	3 39	7 61
Exchange.......	Warren.....	Thos. P. Paschall ..	31 58	47 11
Fair Bluff.......	Columbus ...	Alva Smith........	11 23	19 55
Fair Grove......	Davidson....	Nathan Kendall....	12 63	23 90
Fairview	Buncombe ..	James Brevard	7 09	13 99
Faison's Depot ..	Duplin......	Elias Faison, to 31st Dec.............	13 88	25 87
		Henry Broadhurst .	17 63	34 51
Falkland........	Pitt	James L. Cobb	50 36	90 99
Falls	Lincoln	John Falls	7 16	13 07
Fallstown.......	Iredell......	John Young.......	5 90	9 60
Fancy Hill......	Iredell	James Mears.......	4 72	6 40
Farmington	Davie	Geo. W. Johnson..	23 84	39 23
Faucett's Store...	Orange......	Chesley F. Faucett, to 30th Sept.....	2 33	3 28
		George Hurdle	6 64	11 75
Fayetteville	Cumberland .	John McRae	1098 15	2684 33
Fentriss........	Guilford	Frederick Fentriss .	3 81	6 19
Fish Dam	Wake	Mark A. Tate	11 20	19 59
Fisher's.........	Lincoln	Henry Fisher	84	73
Flat Rock.......	Henderson..	George Summey, to 31st Dec........	36 80	77 88
		Peter Stradley......	15 72	32 18

POST OFFICES—*North Carolina.*

Post Offices.	Counties.	Postmasters.	Compensation.	Net proceeds.
Flemington	Wake	John Hayes, jr.	$7 45	$14 37
Flint Hill	Cabarras	Ibzan Cannon	4 70	7 39
Flint Rock	Lincoln	Jonathan R. Moser.	4 71	6 27
Forbush	Surry	Vestal Hutchens	4 70	8 76
Forestville	Wake	James S. Purify	119 55	153 89
Forks of Pigeon	Haywood	William Cathey	10 07	16 16
Forney's	Lincoln	Andrew Carpenter	6 11	9 52
Fort Defiance	Caldwell	Thomas Lenoir	15 43	30 27
Fort Hembree	Cherokee	Francis McGee, (3 qrs.)	9 97	13 94
Franklin	Macon	Jesse R. Siler	85 05	147 22
Franklintown	Franklin	Thomas W. Short, to 31st Dec.	40 21	72 05
		Wm. F. Hilliard	42 29	82 46
Franklinville	Randolph	Alex. S. Horney	46 46	35 26
French Broad	Buncombe	James M. Alexander	16 11	14 51
French Mills	Onslow	Jos. M. French	13 73	19 19
Friendship	Guilford	Alex. H. Lindsay	13 09	25 57
Fullwood's Store	Union	Robert Grier	6 19	10 98
Fulton	Davie	Joseph Hanes	8 45	14 73
Gaddeysville	Robeson	James Gaddey	2 80	5 03
Gardner's Bridge	Martin	Maurice S. Moore	13 63	28 44
Garner's Ford	Cleveland	Henry Schenck	8 81	16 09
Garysburgh	Northampton	Roderick B. Gary	48 07	55 43
Gaston	Northampton	Samuel W. Pugh	93 68	105 40
Gatesville	Gates	Thomas. A. Jordan.	52 44	103 55
Germanton	Stokes	Harmon Miller	54 19	90 88
Gilopolis	Robeson	John Gilchrist	23 97	41 15
Globe	Caldwell	Job Moore	2 26	5 13
Golden Valley	Rutherford	Williamson Fortune	8 59	15 04
Gold Hill	Rowan	Robt. E. Rives, to 30th Sept.	7 97	12 44
		David W. Honeycutt	25 89	46 57
Gold Region	Moore	Bethuel Coffin	5 31	11 60
Goldsborough	Wayne	John Pike	160 66	144 49
Gordonton	Person	Richard E. Gordon.	7 94	16 55
Graham's Forge	Lincoln	Chas. C. Graham	4 50	6 00
Grassy Creek	Yancey	Tilmon Blalock	5 07	9 75
Gravelly Hill	Bladen	John D. Beatty	34 33	56 76
Graves	Caswell	Henry Sawyer, to 14th June	3 39	5 58
		Banister Fitzgerald.	08	13
Green Plains	Northampton	Willie D. Moore	5 94	9 93
Greensboro'	Guilford	Isaac J. M. Lindsay	514 96	850 32
Greenville	Pitt	Jno. Brown, (printer)	109 21	211 63
Grogansville	Rockingham	John P. Grogan	6 83	11 70
Grove	Chatham	Bennett Lasater	11 04	21 35
Grove Hill	Warren	Wm. M. Powell	32 64	55 12

POST OFFICES—*North Carolina.*

Post Offices.	Counties.	Postmasters.	Compensation.	Net proceeds.
Gulph	Chatham	John Haughton	$9 74	$14 69
Gum Swamp	Columbus	John Mears	3 22	5 94
Hackney's X R'ds	Chatham	John Hackney	13 14	21 00
Hadley's Mills	Chatham	Jacob Hadley	5 47	9 09
Hadnot's	Carteret	Elijah S. Bell	3 11	4 15
Halifax	Halifax	Fredk. S. Marshall	367 10	531 23
Hallsville	Duplin	John W. Hall	23 37	37 64
Hamilton	Martin	Joseph Waldo	31 77	66 49
Hammond's Store	Anson	Allen Tye, to 31st Dec.	2 11	4 28
		Walter F. Burns	1 94	4 32
Hamptonville	Surry	Josiah Cowles	31 98	49 52
Harrell's Store	New Hanover	James Harrell	13 46	23 17
Harrington	Cumberland	John McLeod	6 06	9 97
Harrisburgh	Mecklenb'gh.	Chas. B. McGinnes.	11 34	20 78
Harrisville	Montgomery	Nelson Harris	5 01	9 08
Hartshorn	Orange	Henry Fogleman	4 76	6 85
Hawfield's	Orange	Samuel N. Tate	4 25	4 40
Haw River	Orange	George Foust	29 03	53 48
Haystack	Surry	James B. Tucker, (2 qrs.)	2 03	4 39
Haywood	Chatham	Joseph Utley	25 04	44 51
Healing Springs	Davidson	William Harris	4 26	6 03
Heathsville	Halifax	Beverly B. Daniel	14 63	25 09
Hemphill's Store	Mecklenb'gh.	Richard Peoples	20 89	33 36
Henderson	Granville	Geo. I. Reavis	205 68	306 35
Hendersonville	Henderson	Henry T. Farmer	71 58	148 84
Hertford	Perquimans	Malachi S. Berry	199 36	198 50
Hickory Grove	Mecklenb'gh.	Andrew Springs	8 71	14 58
Hickory Mountain	Chatham	Saml. H. Crutchfield	3 78	6 68
High Rock	Rockingham	Sampson L. Cryer	23 74	49 89
Hightower's	Caswell	William Hightower.	9 52	19 46
Hilliardston	Nash	Kelly Rawls	52 78	87 55
Hillsboro'	Orange	Thomas Clancy, to 31st March	339 21	513 74
		James M. Palmer	101 81	159 94
Hill's Bridge	Halifax	Peyton P. Hervey	19 99	36 51
Hillsdale	Guilford	Jno. S. N. Davis	7 79	13 78
Hill's Store	Randolph	Saml. Hill, 3 qrs.	7 08	12 59
Hokesville	Lincoln	Wm. J. Abernathy.	8 52	18 95
Holly Spring	Wake	Young Booker, 3 qrs.	4 08	9 59
Holt's Store	Orange	Edwin M. Holt	11 94	20 27
Hookerstown	Greene	Jesse W. Moore	40 05	70 35
Hopewell	Mecklenb'gh.	Marshall R. McCoy	12 08	13 32
Hotel	Bertie	John H. Grimes	61 96	109 75
Houstonville	Iredell	Placebo Houston	7 01	13 71
Hoylesville	Lincoln	Andrew Hoyle	8 56	17 38
Hunt's Store	Guilford	Nathan Hunt, jr.	33 05	47 72

POST OFFICES—*North Carolina.*

Post Offices.	Counties.	Postmasters.	Compensation.	Net proceeds.
Huntsville	Surry	Henry P. Poindexter, to 8th Oct.	$7 27	$13 02
		Jos. A. Bitting	19 08	35 75
Indian Town	Currituck	Gideon C. Marchant	15 03	24 06
Island Ford	Rutherford	Wm. D. Harris	7 76	12 35
Ivy	Yancey	Daniel Carter	6 82	12 85
Jackson	Northampton	Eldridge D. N. Clary	92 36	174 10
Jackson Hill	Davidson	Allen Newsom	8 34	16 76
James' X Roads	Iredell	Alex. C. McIntosh	17 08	23 74
Jamestown	Guilford	David Lindsay	57 53	105 50
Jamesville	Cherokee	Benjamin Mann, to 31st Dec.	7 41	15 32
		James Whitaker	7 86	16 48
Jefferson	Ashe	Roderick Murchison	50 55	86 47
Jenkins' Store	Union	George Little	5 96	13 21
Jericho	Wayne	Jas. J. Davis	8 12	12 58
Jersey Settlement	Davidson	Ira Fitzgerald	5 59	10 38
Johnson's Mills	Pitt	Lewis B. Pugh	6 36	8 59
Johnsonville	Cumberland	John W. Cameron	5 39	3 76
Jonesville	Surry	Nathan D. Hunt	20 72	41 33
Junto	Orange	Danl. W. Kerr	6 25	11 08
Kelvin Grove	Wake	Jas. B. Alford	3 15	5 55
Kenansville	Duplin	John I. Kelly	64 21	129 37
Kendall's Store	Stanly	Geo. W. Russell	9 56	19 09
Kernersville	Stokes	Philip Kerner	17 75	31 58
Killian's Mills	Lincoln	Absalom Brown	2 96	5 31
King's Mountain	Lincoln	H. A. Lowrance	5 34	8 70
Kingston	Lenoir	John C. Washington	129 58	259 43
Kirkland	Cabarras	Robert Kirkpatrick	12 21	18 76
Knap of Reeds	Granville	Carter Waller	6 85	11 27
La Grange	Randolph	De Witt C. Johnson	16 78	25 59
Lake Landing	Hyde	Thomas R. Gibbs	25 09	46 06
Lanesboro'	Anson	William Allen	8 10	15 93
Lane's Creek	Union	Th. L. Marsh, 3 qs.	4 95	10 58
Lapland	Buncombe	Jos. M. Rice	14 68	29 52
Laurel Hill	Richmond	Mat'w W. McNair	60 99	67 84
Laurel Springs	Ashe	Nathan Weaver, to 31st Dec.	64	1 16
		John Reves	1 43	2 81
Lawrenceville	Montgomery	Th. Williams, 3 qrs.	22 97	39 81
Lawson's Store	Rockingham	Robert W Lawson	18 29	32 75
Leaksville	Rockingham	Jones W. Burton	77 10	142 06
Leasburgh	Caswell	Jos. S. Thompson	62 98	88 53
Leechville	Beaufort	Geo. F. Satchwell	13 72	22 63
Leesville	Robeson	John W. Powell	18 71	36 32

POST OFFICES—*North Carolina.*

Post Offices.	Counties.	Postmasters.	Compensation.	Net proceeds.
Lenoir	Caldwell	James Harper	$40 66	$76 88
Lexington	Davidson	Mary Rounsaville	249 59	232 76
Liberty Hill	Iredell	Abner Feimster	10 96	19 54
Lilesville	Anson	Nelson P. Liles	36 91	65 28
Limestone	Buncombe	Jacob R. Shuford	35 43	65 20
Limestone Well	Stokes	Wm. F. Stockton	3 25	7 46
Lincolnton	Lincoln	Chas. C. Henderson	338 85	368 39
Lindley's Store	Orange	John Newlin	13 28	20 12
Linville River	Burke	Jos. L. McGimsey	4 90	8 67
Lipscombs (Dis. 26th June.)	Orange	William Lipscomb	1 78	1 92
Lisburn	Sampson	Benjamin Bronson, to 17th June	11 19	18 60
		Gustavus S. Bronson	no ret.	
Little River	Caldwell	Benj. W. Newland	3 63	6 01
Little Rockfish	Cumberland	Daniel G. Patterson	18 51	32 43
Littleton	Halifax	James M. Newsom	86 43	79 24
Little Yadkin	Stokes	John H. Bitting	12 82	21 09
Locust Grove (Dis. 26th Sept.)	McDowell	William Murphy, to 30th Sept	1 17	2 01
Logan's Store	Rutherford	Benj. W. Andrews	7 89	13 24
Long Creek	New Hanover	Samuel H. Bell	24 86	38 73
L'g Creek Shoals	Lincoln	Geo. W. McAllister	no ret.	
		John Webster, from 20th Jan'y	4 30	8 70
Long's Mills	Randolph	John Long	7 06	11 68
Long Street	Moore	John Sheppard	6 33	12 75
Louisburgh	Franklin	William Arendell	256 57	508 15
Lovelady	Caldwell	Israel P. Connelly	1 28	2 10
Lowrance's Mill	Lincoln	Jos. M. Lowrance	5 50	9 40
Lumberton	Robeson	John N. Dorre	50 65	100 26
Lynesville	Granville	John Hargrove, to 20th Nov	7 91	11 84
		Geo. B. Morgan, fr. 1st Jan'y	11 56	18 43
McCallum's Store (Late "Marion.")	Montgomery	Edward McCallum, from 1st Oct	8 31	13 44
McDaniels	Orange	Henry Cook	4 82	6 37
Macedonia	Montgomery	Malcom Lamonds	1 64	2 47
Macon Depot	Warren	Benj'n I. Egerton	30 94	60 19
Madison	Rockingham	Andrew G. Causey, to 12th Aug	9 91	18 01
		Wm. M. Ellington	71 67	129 01
Margaretsville	Northampton	John Ramsay	27 57	55 38
Marion (Ch'd to "McCallum's Store.")	Montgomery	Edw'd McCallum, to 30th Sept	2 36	3 99
Marion (Late "Pleasant Garden.")	McDowell	S. Bulow Erwin, to 31st Dec'r	17 25	26 32
		Jason C. Whitson	17 88	32 57

POST OFFICES—*North Carolina.*

Post Offices.	Counties.	Postmasters.	Compensation.	Net proceeds.
Market Place....	Onslow	John Shackelford, to 31st Dec'r........	$2 07	$3 49
		Dan'l A. Humphrey	3 58	6 15
Marley's Mills...	Randolph....	Thomas Marley....	16 49	27 74
Martha's Viney'rd	Chatham....	William Cross.....	5 16	9 21
Martindale	Mecklenb'gh.	James W. Martin..	7 24	12 34
Martinsville	Northampton	James Martin, 2 qrs.	41	95
Mason Hall......	Orange......	Geo. A. Mebane ...	39 86	36 68
Maxwell's Store..	Mecklenb'gh.	David Maxwell....	9 37	14 74
Meltonsville	Anson......	Hugh A. Crawford.	14 47	28 50
Merry Hill......	Bertie.......	Jos. W. Williford..	44 62	80 94
Middle Swamp... (Dis. 21st Aug.)	Gates.......	Willis F. Riddick..	no ret.	
Middletown......	Hyde.......	Wm. F. Higson....	41 06	79 04
Midway.........	Davidson....	Jos. H. Siceluff....	11 08	20 01
Military Grove...	McDowell...	William H. Neal...	4 94	7 30
Mill Creek......	Person......	James H. Street....	9 33	15 19
Milledgeville.....	Montgomery.	Wm. E. Burage....	5 59	11 75
Mill Grove......	Cabarras....	Charles W. Harris..	18 29	28 81
Mill Hill........	Cabarras....	Jacob Stirewalt, jr..	9 57	18 20
Mill River......	Henderson ..	Wm. T. Johnson ..	15 06	19 72
Milton..........	Caswell.....	Nath'l J. Palmer....	293 89	337 99
Milton Park...... (Dis. 23d Oct.)	Craven......	Noah Miller.......	no ret.	
Minersville......	McDowell...	Wm. F. McKesson.	16 18	32 03
Mintonsville.....	Gates.......	John Riddick......	10 22	18 02
Miranda........	Rowan......	James McLaughlin.	19 00	20 57
Mockville	Davie	Thomas McNeely..	119 08	221 48
Moffitt's Mills....	Randolph ...	Thomas C. Moffitt..	14 94	24 11
Monroe.........	Union.......	Th. D. Winchester.	14 40	27 54
Monroeton	Rockingham.	Ira D. Reed.......	5 96	12 40
Montford's Cove..	Rutherford ..	James Ledbetter....	5 30	10 34
Montpelier	Richmond...	John Gilchrist......	25 10	28 39
Mooresboro'.....	Cleveland ...	John W. Logan....	4 03	7 58
Moores Creek....	NewHanover	Chas. B. McAlester.	4 50	8 38
Mooresville......	Orange......	James Moore......	7 06	13 45
Moretz' Mill.....	Ashe.......	John Moretz.......	1 98	3 33
Morgantown.....	Burke.......	Robert C. Pearson..	149 10	255 88
Moringsville.....	Chatham....	Alfred Moring......	8 36	15 99
Morrison's Tan Yard..........	Mecklenb'gh.	Richard King......	4 04	6 60
Morven	Anson......	Chas. C. McCaskill.	22 87	42 40
Moseley Hall....	Lenoir......	Thomas Waters....	35 60	65 73
Mountain Creek..	Catawba....	John W. Gabriel...	13 02	27 18
Mount Airy......	Surry.......	Dan'l M. McGee...	79 99	94 40
Mount Comfort..	Cabarras....	Chs. A. Misenhimer	17 24	27 79
Mount Gilead....	Montgomery.	Samuel Scarbrough.	15 00	27 67
Mount Lebanon..	Davidson....	Joseph Spence.....	2 32	5 03
Mount Mourne...	Iredell......	Rufus Reid........	40 19	63 54

POST OFFICES—*North Carolina.*

Post Offices.	Counties.	Postmasters.	Compensation.	Net proceeds.
Mount Pisgah	Iredell	John N. Bennett	$6 07	$9 40
Mount Seer	Mecklenb'gh.	Augustus Alexander	7 05	11 00
Mount Tirzah	Person	Alonzo R. Moore	9 80	15 30
Mount Ulla	Rowan	James Cowan	19 63	36 41
Mount Vernon	Rowan	Jacob Krider	20 46	36 03
Mount Willing	Orange	Hugh Kirkpatrick	2 62	3 60
Mud Creek	Henderson	Henry E. Lain, 3 qs.	5 08	11 10
Muddy Fork	Cleveland	William Oates	2 92	4 72
Mud Lick	Chatham	James Woody	6 42	12 08
Mulberry	Wilkes	John M. Van Hoy	44	1 07
Mull Grove	Lincoln	Jacob Mull	2 35	4 93
Murchison's Mills	Cumberland	Alex'r Murchison, 3 qrs	8 32	14 49
Murfreesboro'	Hertford	Sam'l I. Wheeler	164 07	320 96
Murphey	Cherokee	Johnston W. King	45 01	84 01
Nahunta	Wayne	John Hooks	33 57	69 25
Nashville	Nash	Chas. M. Johnson, to 6th June	54 34	107 92
		Wm. H. Terrell	3 65	8 21
Neuse	Wake	Richard S. Pullen, from 15th Feb.	3 97	6 21
Newbern	Craven	William G. Bryan	840 43	2155 26
Newby's Bridge	Perquimans	Henry White	17 34	33 10
New Castle	Wilkes	James C. Hunt	5 80	12 46
New Garden	Guilford	Lambert Moore, to 31st Dec'r	22 22	21 85
		John Russell	23 03	22 89
New Gilead	Moore	Hugh McDonald	1 76	2 85
New Hope	Iredell	James McHargue	2 93	5 72
New Lebanon	Pasquotank	Peter W. Hinton	16 88	28 04
New Light	Wake	Peleg S. Rogers	7 19	12 85
New Market	Randolph	Joseph Newlin	10 40	17 63
New Salem	Randolph	William Clark	15 89	29 94
Newton	Catawba	George J. Wilkie	20 97	40 23
North Cove	McDowell	James M. Young	7 69	11 98
North Fork	Ashe	David Worth, jr.	4 32	10 04
Northington	Cumberland	Alex'r McDougald, to 28th Jan'y	3 14	5 43
		John L. Bethea	4 28	8 16
Norwood	Stanly	George I. Allen	30 30	59 41
Oak Forest	Iredell	Ninian F. Steele	7 31	13 37
Oak Grove	Edgecombe	Isaac Scarboro'	1 88	4 42
Oak Hill	Granville	William H. Webb	30 88	51 50
Oak Ridge	Guilford	Edw'd W. Ogburn, to 1st Nov.	77	1 61
		Jesse Benbow	10 52	20 25

POST OFFICES—*North Carolina.*

Post Offices.	Counties.	Postmasters.	Compensation.	Net proceeds.
Oakville	Union	William Houston, to 1st Dec.	$5 38	$8 37
		John P. Houston	6 03	11 39
Oconâ Lufty	Haywood	John Mingus, 2 qrs.	42	74
Ocracoke	Carteret	Wm. H. Howard	14 68	26 08
Old Fort	McDowell	Robert Burgin	11 51	18 44
Old Town	Stokes	John Butner	10 95	20 15
Onslow C. H.	Onslow	Theod. J. Hughes	50 69	94 53
Orrville	Mecklenb'gh.	John Orr	6 58	9 52
Owensville	Sampson	Calton Hall	19 42	34 20
Oxford	Granville	James C. Cooper	307 06	388 22
Pactolus	Pitt	Churchill Perkins	20 61	35 98
Palmyra	Halifax	John L. Hyman	24 56	48 52
Panther Creek	Surry	Nich's L. Williams	8 00	11 32
Parson's Mills	Guilford	James Parsons	11 47	18 53
Patterson's Store	Orange	George Patterson	6 24	10 71
Peach Tree	Cherokee	John Sudderth	3 00	4 86
Pedlar's Hill	Chatham	Wm A. Rives	6 93	10 09
Perkinsville	Burke	Rich'd V. Michaux, from 13th July	2 66	5 16
Persimmon Creek	Cherokee	Benjamin Stiles	1 90	3 08
Philadelphus	Robeson	Archibald Smith	9 38	15 21
Piedmont	Cleveland	James W. Cabaniss	3 69	5 46
Pigeon River	Haywood	Greene Moore	7 61	12 12
Pinckney	Rutherford	Geo. M. Reid	6 30	9 59
Pioneer Mills	Cabarras	Robert H. Morrison	21 17	40 15
Pitch Landing	Hertford	Jos. I. Scull	25 06	41 53
Pittsboro'	Chatham	Henry A. London	281 21	310 89
Pleasant Garden (Ch. to "Marion."	McDowell	George M. Carson	no ret.	
Pleasant Grove	Orange	Gabriel B. Lea	15 59	26 77
Pleasant Hill	Northampton	Samuel H. Daniel	42 17	42 22
Pleasant Plains	Cumberland	John Shaw	no ret.	
Pleasantville	Rockingham	William A. Joyce	5 25	12 01
Plymouth	Washington	Wm. A. Hardison	331 07	468 68
Pocket	Moore	Daniel M. McIntosh	12 36	22 35
Point Pleasant	Person	J. W. Hamlet, 3 qrs.	3 38	5 80
Pollocksville	Jones	Roscoe Barrus	37 83	66 63
Poplar Branch	Currituck	Lancelot Poyner	9 33	15 57
Poplar Grove	Iredell	Peter Little	7 15	11 98
Poplar Hill	Anson	James Gordon	8 45	12 58
Porter's Swamp	Columbus	Lott Williamson	2 59	3 63
Portsmouth	Carteret	Abner N. Dixon	24 57	44 08
Potecasi	Northampton	Jordan Beale	8 02	12 35
Powell's Point	Currituck	Joshua Harrison	8 37	12 77
Powelton	Richmond	Pleasant M. Powell	11 62	16 26
Prattsburg	Orange	William N. Pratt	11 32	21 55
Prospect Hall	Bladen	Bartram Robeson	26 09	46 92

POST OFFICES—*North Carolina.*

Post Offices.	Counties.	Postmasters.	Compensation.	Net proceeds.
Prospect Hill	Caswell	Franklin L. Warren	$10 70	$21 05
Prosperity	Moore	Daniel McNeill	6 08	10 90
Providence	Mecklenbu'h.	William Rea	11 69	19 04
Pungo	Beaufort	Richard Respess	17 30	31 94
Quallatown	Haywood	Samuel P. Sherrill	3 31	6 21
Queensdale	Robeson	Daniel McLeod	8 01	11 69
Raleigh	Wake	Thomas G. Scott, to 19th April	707 83	2402 38
		William White	305 27	485 94
Ramsboro'	Guilford	Noah M. Climer	24 39	48 30
Ranaleburgh	Mecklenbu'h.	Arthur R. Erwin	11 54	11 54
Randallsville	Robeson	Adam Currie	41 74	57 06
Ransom's Bridge	Nash	John A. Burt	26 57	42 91
Rawlingsburgh	Rockingham	Robt. P. Williamson, to 30th Sept	3 59	6 46
		George S. Dejarnatte	13 03	24 60
Red House	Caswell	James W. Jeffreys	18 00	20 69
Red Mountain	Orange	Abner Parker	13 73	13 56
Red Plains	Surry	Tyre Glenn	7 52	10 38
Red Shoals	Stokes	James Davis	8 70	13 68
Reidsville	Rockingham	Reuben Reid	36 12	50 10
Richardson's Cr'k	Union	Nathaniel Bivens	3 38	5 58
Rich Fork	Davidson	Wm. L. Kenneday	4 01	8 15
Richlands	Onslow	An'w H. Richardson	19 53	38 33
Rich Square	Northampton	M. W. Smallwood	17 86	36 76
Ridge Spring	Pitt	Charles Rounter, jr., 3 qrs	1 08	2 48
Ridgeway	Warren	Thomas T. Twitty	102 77	116 48
Roanoke	Martin	Thomas Jones	39 35	67 44
Robeson	Brunswick	Wm. B. Robeson	40 35	79 57
Rock Creek	Orange	Robert N. Albright	2 29	4 29
Rockford	Surry	John R. Burrows	47 98	83 12
Rockingham	Richmond	Dan'l P. McDonald	117 36	222 55
Rockville	Rowan	David Fraley	9 50	12 26
Rocky Mount	Edgecombe	Malachi Weston, to 1st Aug	11 32	11 06
		Thomas Williford, to 1st Nov	24 35	45 37
		Malachi Weston	100 68	96 66
Rogers' Store	Wake	Robert N. Jeffrey	8 46	14 91
Rolesville	Wake	Edward A. Janney, to 12th June	31 85	55 22
		John M. Fleming	1 66	3 21
Rollins' Store	Moore	Thomas Rollins	11 92	20 06
Roseneath	Halifax	Moses Smith	16 70	29 57
Rossville	Cherokee	Felix Axly, 2 qrs	2 43	3 83
Round Hill	Orange	Doctor C. Parrish	8 11	14 80

POST OFFICES—*North Carolina.*

Post Offices.	Counties.	Postmasters.	Compensation.	Net proceeds.
Roxboro'	Person	Allen T. Fitts	$44 92	$92 02
Rozell's Ferry	Mecklenbu'g.	R'd A. Rozell, 1 qr.	87	1 17
Ruffin's Mills	Orange	James A. Craig	15 97	29 76
Rutherfordton	Rutherford	William H. Miller	154 78	263 59
Saint John	Hertford	Willie B. Carter, to 6th Dec'r.	90	1 64
		James C. Wright	3 23	6 55
Saint Lawrence	Chatham	Daniel Hackney, to 30th Sept.	8 20	8 21
		James G. Marsh	25 27	25 30
Saint Paul's	Robeson	William Davis	12 07	21 07
Salem	Stokes	Emanuel Shober	307 85	594 07
Salem Church	Randolph	Frederick Garner	7 63	12 95
Salisbury	Rowan	Benjamin Julian	413 36	641 86
Sandy Creek	Randolph	George Brower	4 16	7 12
Sandy Grove	Chatham	James Whitehead	9 10	17 81
Sandy Mush	Buncombe	John H. Robeson	4 17	6 91
Sandy Plains	Rutherford	Robert McFarland	4 95	8 58
Sandy Run	Cleveland	Elijah A. Byars, 3 qrs.	2 08	3 25
Sarecta	Duplin	John Oliver, to 30th Sept.	1 92	3 59
		Robert J. Pearsall	7 08	10 67
Scotland Neck	Halifax	John Edmondson	87 29	156 90
Scott's Creek	Haywood	Allen Fisher	15 34	24 67
Scottsville	Orange	John Scott	8 93	14 47
(Changed to "Big Falls.")				
Scull Camp	Surry	Albert A. Oglesby	3 54	7 15
Shallotte	Brunswick	William Brantley	13 22	25 40
Sharon	Mecklenbu'h.	Silas Alexander	4 85	6 54
Shaw's Mills	Guilford	Finley Shaw	4 19	7 51
Shelby	Cleveland	Ansel J. Hardin	42 60	82 71
Sherrill's Ford	Lincoln	Jepthah Sherrill	6 94	11 09
Shiloah	Camden	Charles Taylor	7 77	12 87
Siegel's Store	Lincoln	Daniel Siegel	3 30	4 79
Sill's Creek	New Hanov'r	Alexander Lamont, from 21st Nov.	11 28	16 62
Siloam	Surry	Micajah Reeves	6 66	11 43
Simmons' Tan Y'd	Montgomery	Lockey Simmons	5 80	12 22
Slade's Creek	Hyde	Charles B. Russell, from 1st Oct.	8 01	16 86
Sleepy Creek	Wayne	James Herring	11 83	20 04
Smithfield	Johnson	Henry H. Hobbs	164 27	286 56
Smithville	Brunswick	Robert J. Potts	210 56	426 35
Snead's Ferry (Dis. 7th June.)	Onslow	Jarvis Marble, to 31st Dec'r.	6 25	9 07
		John B. Pollock	4 27	6 10
Sneadsboro'	Anson	John Grady, jr	4 64	8 70

POST OFFICES—*North Carolina.*

Post Offices.	Counties.	Postmasters.	Compensation.	Net proceeds.
Snow Camp......	Orange	John Stafford......	$14 07	$22 20
Snow Creek......	Iredell......	Shadrach Claywell.	15 35	28 45
Snow Hill.......	Greene......	Charles H. Harper.	37 63	61 49
Solemn Grove.....	Moore......	Archibald Buchan..	6 48	11 62
South Mills......	Camden......	Samuel J. Proctor..	36 01	66 49
South Point......	Lincoln	Winchester Pegram	7 41	12 11
Sparta..........	Edgecomb....	Joab P. Pitt.......	59 48	120 88
Speight's Bridge..	Greene......	William A. Darden.	10 17	16 62
Spencer.........	Davidson....	Richardson Finch, to		
		18th Nov........	1 02	2 21
		Seth Ward........	3 93	8 48
Spring Creek....	Buncombe...	William Plemmons.	no ret.	
Spring Grove....	Iredell......	William Hargrave..	18 36	30 49
Spring Vale......	Sampson....	Edward Vail, from		
		1st March.......	9 05	7 54
Stagville.........	Orange......	Paul C. Cameron, 3		
		qrs.............	4 66	7 71
Stanhope........	Nash	Richard H. Dozier,		
		to 30th Sept......	2 41	4 33
		Robert G. Terrell...	12 88	26 85
Stantonsburgh....	Edgecomb...	Robert S. Adams...	50 73	95 31
Statesville........	Iredell	William Morrison..	115 17	188 08
Staunton........	Granville.....	Blair Burwell.......	31 87	42 55
Steele Creek......	Mecklenbu'h.	William H. Neel, to		
		31st March......	2 90	5 06
		Alexander G. Neel.	1 90	3 01
Stewartstown.....	Richmond...	Daniel McIntosh...	9 36	12 07
Stewartsville.....	Richmond...	Daniel McNeill....	22 47	32 84
Stocksville	Buncombe....	Rob't V. Blackstock	5 96	10 51
Stone Bay.......	Onslow	Harvey Cox.......	no ret.	
		Jos. Ennett, jr., from		
		1st Jan. to 1st Mar.	55	79
		Green Canaday	61	98
Stony Creek.....	Caswell......	Hosea McNeill.....	9 25	16 07
Stony Point......	Iredell	Thomas S. Boyd...	6 89	10 85
Stony Ridge.....	Surry.......	Wm. W. Wolff....	5 59	11 13
Stowesville.......	Lincoln......	Edwin B. Stowe....	12 06	19 74
Strabane	Lenoir......	Thomas Rouse.....	19 51	34 95
Strickland's Depot	Duplin......	William A. Gwyer.	27 65	51 73
Stump Sound....	Onslow......	M. L. F. Redd, to		
		31st Dec........	1 34	2 04
		Thomas Ennett....	2 14	3 14
Sugar Grove.....	Ashe	John Mast.........	8 97	19 37
Sulphur Springs..	Buncombe...	Reuben Deaver.....	20 72	30 83
Summerfield......	Guilford.....	Robert C. Lindsay.	19 74	35 41
Summit.........	Northampton	Wm. H. Wesson ..	34 15	44 41
Sunbury	Gates.......	Costen Jordan.....	42 96	68 17
Sunflower.......	Union.......	Wm. H. Robison..	2 28	3 91
Swangstown.....	Cleveland ...	James Roberts.....	8 16	14 32

POST OFFICES—*North Carolina.*

Post Offices.	Counties.	Postmasters.	Compensation.	Net proceeds.
Swannano	Buncombe ...	Geo. C. Alexander.	$7 97	$14 29
Swan Quarter.....	Hyde.........	Thos. F. Credle.....	11 21	20 65
Swansboro'.......	Onslow.......	Wm. P. Ferrand....	20 93	41 61
Sweet Home......	Union........	Wm. C. Steele, 3 qrs	3 07	4 82
Swift C'k Bridge.	Craven.......	Thos. J. B. Schenck, to 30th September	6 03	8 91
		Sam'l R. Street.....	14 35	25 69
Sycamore Alley..	Halifax	James Moore.......	5 25	6 92
Tabor Church...	Iredell.........	Aaron D. Gage.....	6 37	12 19
Tally Ho........	Granville.....	Jefferson Horner...	12 45	20 85
Tarboro'.........	Edgecomb....	James M. Redmond.	280 18	593 19
Taylor's Bridge..	Sampson......	David Murphy, to 30th September..	4 47	8 14
		John Robinson......	19 44	35 84
Teachey's.......	Duplin........	Mary Teachey......	13 56	23 39
Tennessee River..	Macon........	Polaskia Howard...	4 33	8 08
Thompson's Store	Guilford......	Jesse Thompson ...	5 16	9 44
Tilmont..........	Surry.........	Andrew J. Folger..	8 59	9 35
Tindalsville...... (Dis. 4th Feb'y.)	Anson........	John L. Wall......	no ret.	
Tom's Creek......	Surry.........	Squire D. Gordon..	6 20	11 18
Topsail Sound...	New Hanov'r	John Howard......	5 31	7 44
Tossnot Depot...	Edgecomb...	James D. Barnes...	32 30	55 00
Tranquility.......	Granville.....	Nath'l E. Cannaday.	4 69	6 78
Trap Hill........	Wilkes.......	Charles Harris.....	5 85	10 74
Trenton..........	Jones.........	John Askew........ ($1 65 comp., $2 38 netpro. for "Tuckahoe.")	55 76	89 88
Trice's Store.....	Orange.......	William Trice.....	1 94	3 69
Trollinger's Bd'ge	Orange.......	Benjamin Trollinger, 3 qrs...........	4 21	7 45
Troublesome.....	Rockingham.	David Scott........	15 61	27 71
Troy's Store.....	Randolph....	John B. Troy......	8 15	16 21
Tryon...........	Rutherford ..	Enoch G. Foster...	5 63	9 15
Tuckahoe........ (Dis. 2d Sept'r.)	Jones	Owen B. Cox, to 31st December........	3 48	5 07
Tuckasaga.......	Mecklenbu'h.	Wm. H. McLeary.	6 88	11 35
Tull's Creek.....	Currituck....	Dan'l L. Dozier....	no ret.	
Turkey Cove.....	McDowell...	James H. Greenlee.	1 87	2 46
Turkey Creek...	Buncombe...	John Reynolds.....	5 20	8 45
Tyro	Davidson....	Jos. H. Thompson.	2 80	4 93
Unity	Cabarras.....	Thomas Douglass..	1 89	2 52
Van Hook's Store	Person.......	Augustine Van Hook	7 51	14 16
Vesuvius Furnace	Lincoln	John D. Graham...	9 74	16 09
Vicksville.......	Nash	Josiah Vick, 3 qrs..	9 27	16 41

POST OFFICES—*North Carolina.*

Post Offices.	Counties.	Postmasters.	Compensation.	Net proceeds.
Vienna	Stokes	Pleasant Hunt	$4 32	$7 34
Wadesboro'	Anson	Sam'l W. Neal	246 71	445 69
Wakefield	Wake	Augustus J. Foster	13 21	23 57
Walkersville	Union	James R. Wilson, to 31st December	3 63	6 07
		Hugh Wilson	3 26	5 45
Walnut Cove	Stokes	Wm. A. Lash	5 57	10 60
Walnut Lane	Surry	Samuel Johnson	6 99	13 59
Warlick's Store	Catawba	Peter Warlick	1 56	2 12
Warm Springs	Buncombe	John E. Patton	37 52	63 58
Warrenton	Warren	Robt. N. Verell	348 29	679 18
Warsaw	Duplin	Owen L. Fillyaw	47 92	91 80
Washington	Beaufort	Wm. O'Cain	745 77	1558 16
Washington Dep't (Dis. 6th July.)	New Hanov'r	Charles S. Gariss	no ret.	
Wataga	Ashe	Philip Shull	61	1 36
Waterloo	Granville	Wm. O. Gregory	10 64	16 43
Watson's Bridge	Moore	William Watson	17 49	30 33
Waynesboro'	Wayne	Richard Washington	75 07	150 85
Waynesville	Haywood	Eli B. Herrin	38 29	70 97
Webb's Ford	Rutherford	John Harrill	5 23	9 27
Welch's Mills	Cabarrass	Jos. M. Welch	10 68	18 63
Weldon	Halifax	John Campbell	133 15	126 76
Wentworth	Rockingham	James Johnson	42 49	63 59
West Brook	Bladen	John A. Robeson	52 89	58 81
Western Prong	Bladen	Daniel Shipman, to 30th September	1 99	2 91
		Shadrach Wooten, from 18th May	98	1 33
Westland	Halifax	James H. Walker	40 50	79 35
Westminster	Guilford	Wm. S. Beard	17 47	23 90
West Point	Orange	John W. Hancock	7 22	10 37
White Cross	Orange	John H. Crutchfield	8 50	14 01
White Hall	Mecklenbu'h	Samuel Cox	29 21	46 35
White Marsh	Columbus	Frederick Sasser	3 64	4 60
White Oak	Rutherford	Robt. G. Twitty	27 54	48 58
White Plains	Cleveland	Joseph Herndon	4 45	8 71
White's Store	Anson	Philip Gathings	12 02	18 98
Whitesville	Columbus	Stephen Inman	36 31	63 03
Wickliffe (Dis. 14th Sept.)	Richmond	James Williams, to 30th September	1 33	2 85
Wilfong's Mills (Dis. 16th May.)	Catawba	John Wilfong	8 27	12 86
Wilkesboro'	Wilkes	John T. Finley	129 84	155 12
Williamsboro'	Granville	Moses Neal	83 07	146 88
Williamsburgh	Iredell	Rich'd H. Parks	8 87	13 88
Williamston	Martin	William Watts	151 67	299 48
Williamsville	Person	Edmund D. Bolton	14 61	21 35

POST OFFICES—*South Carolina.*

Post Offices.	Counties.	Postmasters.	Compensation.	Net proceeds.
Willow Grove...	Lincoln	Electious Connor...	$3 49	$5 81
Wilmington	New Hanov'r	Wm. C. Bettencourt	1902 96	6011 65
Wilton	Granville....	Edw'd H. Carter...	5 43	10 81
Wind Hill.......	Montgomery.	Eli Harris, to 30th September........	54	1 27
		Peter D. Swaim....	5 33	11 52
Windsor.........	Bertie.......	Thomas Turner....	230 17	427 25
Winton.........	Hertford	John A. Anderson..	47 92	84 44
Wittenberg's.....	Caldwell	Daniel Wittenberg..	1 90	3 54
Wolfsville.......	Union	James N. Houston.	12 82	19 39
Woodlawn.......	Lincoln	F. L. Hoffman.....	29 05	51 30
Woodsdale.......	Person......	John Rogers.......	12 62	23 11
Woodville	Perquimans .	Matthew O. Jordan.	83 51	96 80
Woodworth's	Granville....	John Read.........	33 02	59 82
Yadkin	Davidson....	Jeremiah Barringer.	2 62	4 10
Yanceyville	Caswell......	Abner Miles.......	191 63	219 48
Young's ⋈ Roads	Granville....	Marcus D. Royster.	10 65	18 53
Zion...........	Iredell.......	John Howard......	2 20	4 59

SOUTH CAROLINA.

NOTE.—Compensation of Postmasters, and net proceeds of their offices, from July 1, 1844, to June 30, 1845.

Post Offices.	Districts.	Postmasters.	Compensation.	Net proceeds.
Abbeville C. H...	Abbeville.....	John McLaren, jr..	$325 02	$367 89
Adams' Run.....	Colleton......	Alfred P. Walter...	74 52	126 25
Aiken..........	Barnwell.....	Thos. R. Roberts...	273 35	401 82
Albion..........	Fairfield.....	John Adger........	24 29	41 93
Allen's Bridge...	Marion	Wyatt Fuller.......	20 32	39 13
Anderson C. H..	Anderson....	Edmund Webb....	171 79	318 43
Andersonville....	Pendleton ...	James Harrison....	22 58	31 96
Ashapoo Ferry..	Colleton	John Clark, from 16th Jan'y.......	27 92	48 83
Bachelor's Retreat	Pickens	Eben'r P. Verner...	15 32	27 67
Barnwell C. H...	Barnwell.....	John I. Ryan......	219 19	461 80
Barrowdale...... (Ch'd to "Ridgewood.")	Fairfield.....	Mitchell Peden, to 1st Aug.........	2 91	4 59
		Geo. R. Hunter, to 30th Sept........	3 70	7 31
Baton Rouge.....	Chester	James Darby......	11 97	19 74
Beach Branch....	Beaufort.....	William Forrester..	16 74	32 85

POST OFFICES—*South Carolina.*

Post Offices.	Districts.	Postmasters.	Compensation.	Net proceeds.
Beaufort	Beaufort	Benj. R. Bythewood	$510 86	$1066 18
Beaver Dam	Union	Chs. R. Slyder, to 30th Sep	5 31	8 75
		John C. Jeter	13 39	16 77
Beckamsville	Chester	William Anderson	13 22	21 83
Bel Air	Lancaster	David Hagins	21 22	34 04
Bell's Store	Fairfield	Charles Bell	15 32	24 18
Belmont	Newberry	Andrew McConnel	19 35	35 02
Bennettsville	Marlborough	John McCollum	240 60	488 79
Bethel	York	John B. Hunter	24 28	30 46
Bishopville	Sumter	John W. Stuckey	49 48	101 39
Bivingsvill	Spartanburgh	John Bomar, jr	20 37	33 43
Black Oak	Charleston	Henry Ravenel	74 84	127 81
Blackstocks	Chester	J. F. De Bardeleben	19 40	33 00
Blackville	Barnwell	Jacob Meetze	74 85	134 09
Blairsville	York	Allen Crosby, 3 qrs.	9 06	18 75
Blue House	Colleton	Francis H. Zahler	99 69	95 67
Bluffton	Beaufort	George Allen	87 14	174 08
Bogansville	Union	Caswell Bogan	10 37	20 87
Bordeaux	Abbeville	Jos. L. Bouchillon	12 81	22 49
Bounty Land	Pickens	Elijah Gillison	2 68	5 17
Bradford Springs	Sumter	Alfred D. Hinds, to* 30th Sept.	5 36	10 53
		(*See "Providence")		
		Wm. J. Reynolds, from 21st Feb'y	5 12	8 30
Bradleyville	Sumter	Mathew E. Muldrow	35 02	60 48
Branchville	Orangeburgh	Philip Chartrand	41 28	80 01
Brattonsville	York	Robt. McC. Bratton	29 12	45 81
Brewerton	Laurens	Wyly Murff	9 97	18 22
Brewington	Sumter	Wm. T. Brogdon	5 47	8 05
Brightsville	Marlborough	Jno. W. Stubbs	14 13	24 47
Britton's Neck	Marion	Geo. W. Woodbery, 3 qrs.	7 50	10 71
Browns	Fairfield	Edward Andrews	21 00	31 51
Brownsville	Marlborough	Simeon Emanuel	28 91	42 99
Broxton's Bridge	Colleton	Joseph Teasdale, fr. 7th April	1 76	2 66
Brushy Creek	Anderson	Wm. D. Sitton	5 19	8 12
Buck Creek	Spartanburgh	William Green	(No ret.)	
Buck Head	Fairfield	Edward Means	47 51	75 56
Buckhead Causey	Colleton	Reuben Stephens	32 73	49 56
Bucksville	Horry	Henry Buck	33 33	63 35
Bufords Bridge	Barnwell	Jas. J. Thurston, to 31st March	27 70	57 28
		Joseph Brabham	9 38	19 96
Cairo	Edgefield	Charles Freeman	8 71	16 22
Calhoun	Anderson	Benj. F. Mauldin	14 38	27 15

POST OFFICES—*South Carolina.*

Post Offices.	Districts.	Postmasters.	Compensation.	Net proceeds.
Calhoun's Mills..	Abbeville.....	Philip Le Roy.....	$89 12	$84 71
Cambridge......	Abbeville.....	Zach. W. Carwile..	32 35	56 84
Camden.........	Kershaw.....	John N. Gamewell.	810 93	1579 34
Campbell's Bridge	Marion	John Campbell.....	5 32	8 56
Cannon's Store...	Spartanburgh	Aaron Cannon.....	11 01	18 24
Carmel Hill......	Chester	John W. Estes.....	12 81	26 26
Cashville.........	Spartanburgh	S. L. Westmoreland	9 92	18 95
Cataba..........	Chester	Jacob W. Stinson, to 31st Dec'r.......	3 59	6 09
		Tillman Ingram....	2 03	3 90
Catfish..........	Marion	Wm. H. Moody....	9 50	16 29
Catourah........	Greenville....	J. Harvey Cleveland	1 50	3 16
Cedar Creek.....	Richland.....	Timothy Center....	15 79	23 92
Cedar Grove.....	Union......	James Hay........	6 58	10 35
Cedar Shoal.....	Chester	James A. H. Gaston	16 30	25 87
Cedar Springs....	Spartanburgh	Isaac Neighbours...	6 17	11 95
Centreville.......	Laurens.....	Abner Jones.......	4 61	10 04
Charleston.......	Charleston...	Alfred Huger......	2000 00	46594 35
Cheohee.........	Pickens......	Alexander Smith...	4 39	6 32
Cheraw..........	Chesterfield..	Brown Bryan......	698 34	1385 71
Cherokee Heights	Abbeville....	William Speer.....	6 43	11 32
Cherokee Iron Works........	York	Reuben Swann.....	24 85	48 16
Chesnut Grove...	Chester	John Poag........	17 01	29 78
Chester C. H....	Chester	Hiram C. Brawley.	283 27	578 08
Chesterfield C. H.	Chesterfield..	John C. Evans.....	44 85	74 19
China Grove.....	Williamsb'gh	James Snow.......	22 70	36 31
Christians....... (Dis. 8th Aug.)	Edgefield....	David Payne, to 30th Sept...........	1 10	1 73
Church Hill.....	Abbeville.....	Alex'r F. Wimbish.	29 99	59 34
Claremont.......	Pickens......	Thos. W. Harbin..	2 84	4 63
Clio............	Marlborough	Colin McRae......	35 02	63 22
Coates' Tavern...	York	Andrew Skillinglaw.	11 59	22 34
Cokesbury......	Abbeville.....	Sam'l A. Hodges...	174 38	207 27
Cold Spring	Edgefield....	John M. Clark.....	16 03	25 60
Colemans XRoads	Edgefield....	Ira Cromley.......	26 01	44 94
Colliers	Edgefield....	Sam'l C. Scott.....	21 58	33 20
Collins' X Roads.	Colleton.....	Benj. H. Barfield...	50 99	50 21
Columbia........	Richland.....	A. H. Gladden.....	1475 38	5919 66
Conwayborough .	Horry.......	James Potter......	37 37	72 38
Cookham........	Fairfield.....	Josiah Hinnant....	19 93	37 85
Coopersville......	Union.......	Robert Arnold.....	11 73	21 00
Coosawhatchie...	Beaufort.....	Philip I. Bessellen, from 1st Jan'y...	31 18	65 89
Craytonsville	Anderson....	J. W. Featherston..	9 58	14 00
Cripple Creek....	Greenville...	James Harrison, to 31st March......	4 99	8 33
		John H. Harrison..	1 86	4 03
Crosbyville......	Chester......	Coleman Crosby...	19 53	36 13

29*

POST OFFICES—*South Carolina.*

Post Offices.	Districts.	Postmasters.	Compensation.	Net proceeds.
Cross Anchor....	Spartanburgh	Wm. I. Whitmire..	$48 95	$40 76
Cross Hill.......	Laurens......	William Carter.....	22 11	41 40
Cross Keys......	Union........	Jesse Whitmire....	37 40	72 90
Crowsville.......	Spartanburgh	James M. Lanham.	21 95	31 90
Cureton's Store..	Lancaster ...	Thos. K. Cureton..	17 03	28 27
Dacusville.......	Pickens......	James Robinson....	5 97	11 68
Damascus........	Spartanburgh	Hazzael Hicks.....	12 65	10 04
Darlington C. H.	Darlington...	Sam'l A. Woods...	429 97	652 18
Davis' Ferry..... (Ch'd to "Waltons Ford." Ga.)	Pickens......	Hervey Davis, 2 qrs.	1 74	3 57
Davis' Mills.....	Barnwell.....	Needham Davis....	4 79	8 56
Deadfall.........	Abbeville.....	John Cochran......	16 41	20 89
Double Branches.	Anderson....	William McElmoyle	14 40	29 27
Douthet.........	Anderson....	William Orr.......	3 93	7 46
Draytonsville.....	Union........	Robt. C. M. Alexander, to 31st March	9 18	19 28
		Wm. D. Alexander.	4 82	9 69
Dry Creek	Lancaster ...	Starling G. Twitty..	10 64	20 09
Duck Branch	Barnwell.....	James M. Loper, to 31st Dec'r.......	16 13	31 79
		B. G. Branford.....	15 10	29 88
Due West Corner	Abbeville.....	Robt. C. Sharp, jr..	87 83	153 10
Duncansville.....	Barnwell. ...	Jacob H. O'Cain...	12 28	22 21
Dunlapville......	Laurens......	John Godfrey, to 31st Dec'r.......	6 51	10 93
		Sam'l M. Fairbain..	5 44	9 17
Duntonsville.....	Edgefield....	Hollis Dunton, to 27th Feb'y......	12 98	22 59
		Wiley B. Griffin...	6 00	10 30
Earlesville.......	Spartanburgh	Oliver P. Earle.....	9 29	15 51
Ebenezerville	York	Edward Avery, to 1st Dec..........	10 45	18 87
		Alex'r F. Fewell...	15 96	29 50
Eden	Laurens......	William Mahaffey..	5 30	9 36
Edgefield C. H...	Edgefield....	Marshall Frazier...	449 10	740 00
Effingham.......	Darlington...	Moses E. Lawrence	28 69	52 59
Elton...........	Edgefield....	Joseph Adams.....	18 90	30 18
Enoree..........	Spartanburgh	Nich's V. Van Patten	6 80	11 48
Equality	Anderson....	Simeon Smith......	4 39	7 32
Erwinton........	Barnwell.....	James D. Erwin....	24 71	43 14
Fairplay	Pickens......	Jacob R. Cox......	9 71	18 58
Fairview.........	Greenville...	Robert Peden......	9 96	17 71
Feasterville......	Fairfield.....	Jacob J. N. Feaster.	16 68	30 40
Fishdam	Union........	John T. Hill.......	20 19	37 95
Flat Rock........	Kershaw....	Wm. B. Fletcher...	12 26	24 69
Flintville........	Marion	Robert B. Exum...	16 02	18 17

POST OFFICES—*South Carolina.*

Post Offices.	Districts.	Postmasters.	Compensation.	Net proceeds.
Floyd's Mills	Horry	James Floyd	$1 01	$2 12
Fort Mill	York	Wm. E. White	12 33	19 67
Fountain Inn	Greenville	Wm. McNeely	18 09	32 65
Four Mile Branch	Barnwell	David M. Dunbar	34 14	56 53
Fraziersville	Abbeville	Sam'l B. McClinton, to 30th Sept	13 89	13 47
		William Cooke, to 31st Dec'r	19 28	18 70
		John Ruff	42 91	41 92
Friendship	Sumter	Jos. H. Stukes	74 46	98 06
Fruit Hill	Edgefield	John C. Allen	9 19	16 61
Fulton	Sumter	Edward Broughton	99 52	191 55
Gadsden	Richland	William Shiver	130 65	246 15
Gentsville	Abbeville	George Mattison	12 57	23 27
Georgetown	Georgetown	William McNulty	871 09	2236 09
Germanville	Edgefield	Robert A. Price	13 75	22 60
Gilder	Greenville	Wm. L. M. Austin	5 88	10 04
Gillisonville	Beaufort	Marcus Furth	133 00	260 61
Gladden's Grove	Fairfield	D. McCullough, jr.	29 77	52 02
Glenn Springs	Spartanburgh	Robert A. Cates	46 96	83 69
Glymphville	Newberry	John Glymph	29 79	52 48
Golden Grove	Greenville	Charles Garrison	12 20	22 42
Gold Springs	Anderson	David Spearman	6 87	13 74
Gold Mine	Chesterfield	Stephen D. Miller	23 26	44 52
Goshen Hill	Union	Wm. W. Glenn	26 33	47 98
Gowdeysville	Union	Benj. F. Dawkins	13 29	22 94
Gowensville	Greenville	Benjamin Wilkinson	14 37	25 48
Graham's Turn Out	Barnwell	Henry B. Rice	58 73	68 84
Grahamville	Beaufort	F. J. Eikerenkoetter	243 53	354 27
Grannie's Quarter	Kershaw	James Love	2 98	5 21
Grassy Pond	Spartanburgh	Bryant Bonner	3 73	5 69
Greenville	Greenville	Susan W. Thruston, 3 qrs	348 37	780 43
Greenwood	Laurens	Thos. A. Brownlee	9 46	19 87
Gully	Darlington	Spencer Harrell	11 14	22 87
Green Branch	Darlington	Burrell Segars	9 87	22 87
Guthriesville	York	Fs. A. Erwin	13 24	24 48
Halfway Swamp	Edgefield	Levi M. Churchill	7 23	12 33
Halsellville	Chester	Wm. Boyd, to 7th March	15 90	33 07
		Francis H. Land	5 79	11 63
Hamburgh	Edgefield	Caleb H. Lindsey	682 82	1485 09
Hancockville	Union	Elijah Dawkins	19 81	36 23
Hanging Rock	Kershaw	John U. Ingram, to 31st Dec	4 07	6 32
		James M. Ingram	4 27	7 22

POST OFFICES—*South Carolina.*

Post Offices.	Districts.	Postmasters.	Compensation.	Net proceeds.
Harlleesville	Marion	John A. McRae	$30 15	$60 92
Harmony	York	Joseph McCosh	3 97	5 65
Harper's Ferry	Abbeville	Lindsey Harper	7 42	14 35
Hartsville	Darlington	Joseph Norwood	8 51	14 70
Haynesville	York	Jos. W. McCorkle	13 26	16 28
Hazlewood	Chester	David Moffet	26 14	45 22
Hickory Grove	York	James McKinney	4 27	8 75
Hickory Head	Lancaster	John Pate	9 93	19 03
Hickory Hill	Beaufort	B. McBride	8 50	14 04
Higgins' Ferry	Edgefield	Elijah P. Abney	15 52	21 98
Highland Grove	Greenville	Lewis H. Dickey	6 15	7 86
Highway	Greenville	Absalom H. Harris, from 22d Feb	0 79	1 01
Hollands	Laurens	Joel T. Foster	15 16	25 51
Hollow Creek	Lexington	Uriah Crout	12 03	21 87
Hopewell	York	Samuel Wright	5 02	8 18
Horse Shoe	Pickens	Edward Hughes	4 44	8 32
Huntington	Laurens	Wm. D. Byrd	18 17	35 87
Huntsville	Laurens	David Martin	28 20	56 11
Hurricane	Spartanburgh	John T. Kirley	17 96	31 28
Indian Fields	Colleton	Thomas J. Sistrunk	14 05	27 21
Indian Town	Williamsb'gh	Robert Dick	33 37	56 67
Jacksonboro'	Colleton	John Walkington	no return	
Jacksonham	Lancaster	Thomas W. Huey, to 31st Dec	15 09	23 67
		Israel P. Davis	15 92	25 39
Jackson's Creek	Fairfield	Archibald McVea	14 26	23 87
Jacksonville	Sumter	Edward B. Davis	20 12	38 51
Jeffrey's Creek	Marion	Jos. S. Cunningham	75 34	75 35
Johnsonville	Williamsb'gh	John J. Gerard	15 89	20 54
Jonesville	Union	John Eison	19 52	37 53
Jordan's Mills	Orangeburgh	John Jordan	20 11	36 68
King Creek	Barnwell	David M. Laffitte	20 87	37 12
Kingstree	Williamsb'gh	Carter T. Baughan	76 69	153 52
Kirksey's ⋈ R'ds.	Edgefield	George J. Sheppard	15 84	26 11
Lake Swamp	Horry	Gilbert L. Johnson	10 74	14 31
Lancaster C. H.	Lancaster	Jos. B. Klingle	163 15	314 15
Landsford	Chester	Hyder A. Davie	30 13	56 74
Laurens C. H.	Laurens	Edward Anderson	254 78	273 37
Lawtonville	Beaufort	Edward H. Peebles	19 01	40 33
Lebanon	Abbeville	Nathaniel Moore	32 63	32 67
Leesville	Lexington	James E. Lee	37 42	73 17
Lewisville	Chester	James B. Magill	33 23	55 09
Lexington C. H.	Lexington	Reuben Harman	135 66	130 34
Liberty Hall	Newberry	James Bonds	18 46	29 86

POST OFFICES—*South Carolina.*

Post Offices.	Districts.	Postmasters.	Compensation.	Net proceeds.
Liberty Hill.....	Kershaw.....	Wyat Patterson....	$33 90	$69 51
Lickville.........	Greenville....	Sam'l Moore, 3 qrs.	2 96	5 17
Limestone Springs	Spartanburgh	David D. Rosa, to 31st Dec.........	18 50	33 06
		Abiel Foster.......	20 42	34 40
Line Creek.......	Laurens.....	Mason N. Gambrell	8 49	16 97
Little River......	Horry......	Joseph Vaught.....	20 79	32 42
Lodi.............	Abbeville....	Dabney P. Calhoun.	25 34	43 38
Lodi Bar.........	Sumter......	Wm. H. Brunson, from 21st Nov...	7 40	7 31
Longmire's Store.	Edgefield....	Robert Anderson...	45 27	88 39
Long Street......	Lancaster ...	James Perry.......	10 51	15 27
Lotts	Edgefield....	John Lott.........	26 48	44 63
LowerThree Runs	Barnwell	William Provost....	28 36	52 95
Lowndesville	Abbeville....	Samuel Lindsay....	60 04	118 74
Lynches Creek...	Marion......	John Gasque.......	no return	
		Henry Davis, from 11th Nov........	2 70	4 40
		For "Flintville"...	0 31	0 59
Lynches Lake ...	Williamsb'gh	Aaron F. Graham...	4 72	9 39
Lynchwood......	Kershaw	Sam'l P. Murchison, 1 qr...........	1 55	2 36
McBridesville....	Union.......	Stephen Kirby.....	12 10	20 97
McMeekins.......	Fairfield.....	Thomas McMeekin.	24 65	48 37
Manchester......	Sumter......	Alexander Campbell	31 34	58 28
Mapleton........	Abbeville....	Samuel C. Edmonds	14 10	29 51
Marion C. H	Marion	Robert J. Gregg....	143 70	300 30
Mar's Bluff......	Darlington...	Wm. H. Cannon...	85 02	146 92
Martin's Creek...	Pickens......	Thomas Dawson...	5 23	8 45
Maybinton.......	Newberry ...	John M. Allen.....	56 34	98 09
Mechanicsville....	Sumter	John Harrell.......	34 28	57 11
Meek's Hill	York	Eli Meek..........	7 23	11 21
Merrittsville.....	Greenville....	John W. Hodges...	6 29	12 53
Midway.........	Barnwell.....	Peter Carson.......	52 46	106 61
Milford	Greenville....	James Nolen.......	14 99	25 47
Mill Grove......	Sumter......	William McCutchen	7 58	13 41
Millville.........	Spartanburgh	Patrick Hoy.......	12 69	19 98
Milton..........	Laurens.....	John D. Williams..	20 14	34 13
Moffettsville	Anderson....	William Sherard...	29 47	53 51
Monk's Corner...	Charleston...	Daniel Sheppard ...	20 03	31 48
Monticello.......	Fairfield	Joseph Gladney, to 31st Dec.........	20 02	39 16
		John McCrorey....	22 31	44 30
Mountain Shoals.	Spartanburgh	James Nesbitt......	18 73	31 58
Mountain View..	Abbeville.....	James H. Baskin...	10 25	17 92
Mount Bethel....	Newberry ...	James P. Caldwell..	15 89	29 18
Mount Clio......	Sumter	Stephen La Coste ..	29 17	40 69
Mount Croghan..	Chesterfield .	Henry J. King.....	11 99	16 50

POST OFFICES—*South Carolina.*

Post Offices.	Districts.	Postmasters.	Compensation.	Net proceeds.
Mount Elon	Darlington	James G. Kelly, to 1st March	$7 84	$13 61
		Jesse W. Moore	4 09	8 00
Mount Gallagher	Laurens	John McClintock	15 19	29 96
Mount Hill	Abbeville	Enoch Barmore	28 18	48 15
Mount Joy	Union	Isaac J. Foster	3 07	5 38
Mount Lebanon	Spartanburgh	John Cunningham	3 51	5 75
Mount Olivet	Fairfield	Elijah Gayden	7 64	13 38
Mount Tabor	Union	James A. Stevenson	15 48	24 72
Mountville	Laurens	Alsey Fuller	11 20	19 13
Mount Willing	Edgefield	Jacob B. Smith, to 30th Sept.	5 96	10 15
		Benj. Lehmaier	15 73	28 86
Mount Zion	Spartanburgh	John Chapman, jr.	14 16	19 41
Murray's Ferry	Williamsb'gh	James M. Staggers	11 36	20 75
Mush Creek	Greenville	Oliver Barrett	9 60	14 39
Nation Ford	York	Archibald Whyte	12 24	16 72
Neal's Creek	Union	David T. Sims	6 94	11 14
Neely's Creek (Dis. 26th June.)	York	John Roddey	7 83	12 58
Nero (Dis. 19th Dec.)	York	Henry L. Killian, to 31st Dec	1 27	2 19
Newberry C. H.	Newberry	Thomas Johns	302 14	687 96
New Hope	Spartanburgh	James A. Miller	21 18	34 36
New Market	Abbeville	Milton W. Coleman	45 17	83 40
New Prospect	Spartanburgh	Oliver Clark	2 10	3 33
North Creek	Laurens	Thomas J. Pyles, from 29th July	6 83	8 34
Oak Grove	Union	Robert Lusk	5 71	11 89
Oakland	Edgefield	William Dozier, fr. 24th Aug. to 20th February	8 59	13 73
		John Huiet	4 23	5 48
Oakville	Lexington	Jesse Coogler	13 26	21 59
Oconee Station	Pickens	James A. Doyle	1 49	3 05
Orangeburgh C.H.	Orangeburgh	Sanders Glover	253 32	475 49
Orleans	Greenville	John H. Goodwin	5 77	9 28
Pagesville	Newberry	Abel Conner	31 94	27 27
Park's	Edgefield	Richard Parks	18 73	35 25
Parnassus	Marlborough	William Bristow	18 30	24 49
Pedensville	Chester	Cornelius Caldwell	12 49	22 92
Pendleton	Anderson	John B. Sitton	281 56	604 14
Perry's X Roads	Edgefield	Bennett Perry, 1 qr.	67	1 58
Phœnix	Edgefield	Wright N. Moore	28 48	47 66
Pickens C. H.	Pickens	Pleasant Alexander	50 88	75 41
Pickensville	Pickens	Wash. E. Holcombe	43 70	37 28

POST OFFICES—*South Carolina.*

Post Offices.	Districts.	Postmasters.	Compensation.	Net proceeds.
Pinckneyville....	Union	Jas. H. Alexander, 3 qrs............	$23 84	$32 89
Pineville	Charleston ..	Wm. R. Treadwell.	121 73	212 87
Pipe Creek	Beaufort	Alexr. W. Daley...	41 06	72 53
Plain	Greenville...	Silas Gilbert, to 7th Nov............	5 83	9 81
		Peter Simpson	7 46	14 38
Pleasant Grove ..	Spartanburgh	Jesse Foster.......	7 76	15 90
Pleasant Hill	Lancaster ...	Simon Beckham ...	22 94	43 85
Pleasant Valley..	Lancaster ...	Geo. D. Beckham..	15 39	23 96
Pleasant View ...	Darlington ..	Jesse Keith	9 32	18 73
Plinny..........	Greenville ...	Thos. P. Brockman.	7 36	12 95
Plowden's Mills .	Sumter	Thos. E. Dickey...	23 92	40 50
Pocotaligo.......	Beaufort	Jos. W. Davis, to 31st Dec.........	108 14	108 15
		G. W. Lawton......	118 12	126 58
Pomaria	Newberry...	William Summer ..	21 86	38 68
Poolsville	Spartanburgh	Samuel N. Evins...	9 65	18 40
Poplar Grove....	Newberry...	Geo. W. Glenn	7 78	13 97
Poplar Spring ...	Fairfield	Nich's G. Gibson ..	17 13	32 33
Poverty Hill.....	Edgefield....	John Mosely, to 31st Dec.............	4 27	6 80
		David Bunch......	4 37	7 31
Privateer	Sumter	William Nettles....	33 23	65 49
Providence......	Sumter	Wm. H. Bowen ... (Includes for 'Bradford Springs,' $3 62 comp., $7 54 n. pro.)	42 96	88 93
Pumpkintown ...	Pickens	Matthew Keith	6 60	12 62
Queensboro'.....	Anderson ...	Halbert Acker.	5 15	10 55
Raiborn's Creek .	Laurens	John S. James, to 31st March......	6 82	12 32
		John B. Pitts.......	1 83	3 56
Rantowles.......	Colleton	Law'ce J. Messervy	8 09	13 71
Red Bank.......	Colleton	George Raysor	23 47	40 66
Red Bluff	Marion	Allison H. Brown, 3 qrs............	5 26	9 98
Red Hill	Kershaw	James R. Dye.....	19 75	33 29
Rehoboth........	Edgefield....	Batte Howard	8 46	14 32
Rice Hope ...... (Dis. 16th May.)	Charleston ..	Theod. C. Tharin..	(No ret.)	
Richardsonville ..	Edgefield....	Jas. M. Richardson.	17 31	30 26
Ridge	Edgefield....	Elijah Watson.....	28 48	59 15
Ridgeville	Colleton	James Pressly	(No ret.)	
Ridgewood ...... (Late "Barrowdale.')	Fairfield	Geo. R. Hunter, fr'm 1st Oct..........	23 03	35 74
Roadville	Charleston ..	Thomas Bradwell ..	29 91	51 81

POST OFFICES—*South Carolina.*

Post Offices.	Districts.	Postmasters.	Compensation.	Net proceeds.
Robertsville	Beaufort	Benjamin Jaudon	$150 65	$282 94
Rock Mills	Anderson	David Humphreys	16 29	19 63
Rockville	Lexington	John Whites	7 17	12 32
Rocky Creek	Chester	James English	10 53	18 20
Rocky Mount	Fairfield	James Barkley	13 50	23 90
Rogersville	Anderson	Martin H. Smith	14 80	27 74
Russel Place	Kershaw	Wm. S. Stinson	14 52	21 92
St. Matthew's	Orangeburgh	David Stack	210 18	418 47
Salem	Sumter	Mid'n D. McIntosh	20 15	32 69
Salubrity	Pickens	Allen Fuller	11 24	20 12
Saluda	Greenville	Jas. C. Rowland	3 30	5 27
Sandersville	Chester	James Sanders	6 85	14 69
Sandover	Abbeville	Williams Truwit	7 32	13 83
Sandton	Kershaw	D. Geo. Fletcher	19 84	39 07
Sandy Run	Lexington	William Assman	34 97	60 02
Saxly	Greenville	Edmund Miller	1 17	2 16
Scuffletown	Laurens	Fleming Moseley	20 88	38 08
Shady Grove	Union	Jesse Briggs	9 87	19 41
Shop Spring	Newberry	Cary McClure	15 70	28 39
Silver Glade	Anderson	William Anderson	10 03	19 28
Silverton	Barnwell	Jas. J. Meyer	67 71	122 92
Simpson's Mill	Laurens	Jno. W. Simpson	8 43	14 01
Slabtown	Anderson	James McKinney	8 22	15 06
Sleepy Creek	Edgefield	James Dorn	14 63	28 66
Smith's Ford	York	John Smith	5 23	11 63
Smithville	Abbeville	William Smith	22 74	30 73
Snow Creek	Pickens	John A. Moore, 1 qr.	35	62
Society Hill	Darlington	Thomas Coker	254 90	498 70
Spartanb'rgh C.H.	Spartanburgh	Geo. W. H. Legg	197 81	374 34
Speedwell	Barnwell	A. Killingsworth, jr.	18 45	33 06
Spring Grove	Laurens	Jno. P. Watts, 3 qrs.	10 94	19 76
Spring Hill	York	Saml. W. Ruddock	8 31	15 51
Spring Rock	York	Alexander Crawford	21 41	32 53
Stantonville	Anderson	Jas. W. Lewis	6 74	13 37
Stateburgh	Sumter	Benjamin Hood	187 28	384 58
Steele's	Anderson	William Steele	13 21	26 68
Sterling Grove	Greenville	Henry Sherman	8 50	14 77
Stonesville	Greenville	Mat. E. Cunningham	6 73	10 97
Stony Point	Abbeville	James Bailey	55 05	54 22
Storeville	Anderson	Matthew Thomson	24 34	37 72
Summerville	Charleston	John R. Stall, to 31st Dec.	22 18	44 71
		Francis L. Phelps	27 65	49 30
Sumterville	Sumter	Henry Haynsworth	286 71	598 55
Temple of Health	Abbeville	John Cunningham	39 39	51 76
Terrysville	Abbeville	Jas. A. Norwood	14 82	24 73
Thompson's	Fairfield	Charles Thompson	19 89	36 06

POST OFFICES—*South Carolina.*

Post Offices.	Districts.	Postmasters.	Compensation.	Net proceeds.
Tiller's Ferry....	Kershaw....	James Tiller.......	$9 18	$18 26
Tituroy.........	Greenville...	Silas Benson......	2 12	2 97
Tomsville........	Chester.....	William McCreight.	6 90	9 87
Torbit's Store....	Chester.....	Thomas Torbit....	16 59	27 08
Townville.......	Anderson...	Samuel Brown.....	9 48	19 30
Traveller's Rest..	Greenville...	Henry E. Lynch...	9 08	13 10
Tullyton.........	Greenville...	Micajah Berry.....	7 42	13 86
Tumbling Shoals.	Laurens....	Joseph Sullivan....	22 06	43 62
Twelve Mile....	Pickens.....	Jas. H. Ambler....	5 14	11 21
Tylersville......	Laurens....	Saml. I. Craig.....	14 45	18 61
Unionville.......	Union......	Benj. H. Bradley..	214 91	448 41
Vance's Ferry...	Orangeburgh.	William Avinger...	59 49	105 41
Varennes........	Anderson...	Jesse W. Norris...	11 50	16 48
Walnut Grove...	Spartanburgh	Andrew B. Moore..	6 09	9 15
Walterboro'.....	Colleton....	John A. Fraysse....	207 58	386 12
Warrenton......	Abbeville...	J. Huey, to 31st Mar.	24 71	37 02
		Andrew Gillespie..	6 75	13 27
Waterloo.......	Laurens.....	Mat. J. K. Bowen..	65 48	77 32
Wellsville.......	Newberry...	Robert S. Phinney.	(No ret.)	
		Geo. F. Wells, 1 qr.	4 88	7 57
West Union.....	Pickens.....	Joseph Grisham....	17 92	20 95
Whetstone......	Pickens.....	Samuel Mosley....	3 04	5 52
Whippy Swamp..	Beaufort....	J. M. Terry, fr. 11th Aug. to 31st Dec..	3 91	7 03
White Plains.... (Dis. 30th July.)	Anderson...	West A. Williams, to 30th Sept.....	63	1 35
Wideman's......	Abbeville...	John Harris.......	18 44	33 20
Wilkinsville.....	Union......	Wm. M. Wilkins..	10 10	17 82
Willington......	Abbeville....	Saml. W. Boag....	38 54	55 48
Williston.......	Barnwell....	Willison B. Beazley	32 97	62 42
Willow Grove...	Sumter.....	Bartlett Sanders....	25 20	41 65
Wilson's Creek..	Abbeville...	John Speer........	7 64	13 31
Winnsboro'.....	Fairfield....	John McMaster....	337 21	765 62
Winter Seat.....	Edgefield....	Wade S. Cothran..	44 10	80 11
Wolf Creek.....	Pickens.....	John Hunter, to 31st Dec.............	5 76	10 25
		John O. Hendricks.	5 91	10 66
Woodlawn......	Edgefield....	John Middleton....	19 13	31 64
Woodruff's.....	Spartanburgh	Harr'n P. Woodruff, to 31st Dec......	15 62	22 51
		And'w B. Woodruff	13 45	22 31
Woodville.......	Abbeville....	Geo. W. Curtiss...	97 16	93 00
Yonguesville....	Fairfield....	John L. Yongue...	24 08	44 23
Yorkville........	York.......	Samuel Melton....	636 11	71 66
Young's Store...	Laurens.....	John N. Young....	20 23	35 81

GEORGIA.

NOTE.—Compensation of Postmasters, and net proceeds of their offices, from July 1, 1844, to June 30, 1845.

Post Offices.	Counties.	Postmasters.	Compensation.	Net proceeds.
Acworth	Cobb	Smith Lemon, from		
(Late "Anderson	ville.")	11th August	$21 96	$35 70
Adairsville	Cherokee	David Morrow	35 34	76 31
Adams	Irwin	James Brown	5 30	10 72
Alapaha	Lowndes	James S. Harris	12 13	20 84
Albany	Baker	Stephen T. Mallory	341 41	521 59
Allatoona	Cass	Wm. M. Puckett,		
		to 31st March	14 85	28 70
		Jefferson Clark	5 31	10 95
Allensville	Forsyth	Beverly Allen	6 35	10 25
Alpine	Chattooga	Henry Jackson	17 18	34 77
Amandaville	Elbert	Benjamin Winn	5 85	9 61
Americus	Sumter	Hawkins H. Nunn,		
		to 31st December	99 18	180 55
		William Mims	95 51	210 58
Andersonville	Cobb	Smith Lemon, to		
(Changed to "Ac	worth.")	11th August	2 10	3 84
Aonia	Wilkes	Wm. R. Foote	13 59	19 93
Appling	Columbia	Charles Rall, to 31st		
		March	62 31	104 93
		U. L. Leonard	21 93	37 28
Aquilla	Franklin	Samuel Knox	8 49	14 83
Argo	Hall	Philip M. Byrd	8 33	12 79
Armenia	Scriven	Edward Jones	16 82	30 99
Athens	Clark	(Maj.) William L.		
		Mitchell, to 31st Dec	422 50	1133 37
		Wm. L. Mitchell,		
		(attorney at law.)	416 71	1126 91
Attapulgus	Decatur	Emery Lasseter	32 06	55 41
Auburn	Gwinnet	James Peden	6 30	11 70
Augusta	Richmond	Edm'd B. Glascock	1962 23	9298 95
Auraria	Lumpkin	Allen E. Matthews	40 26	80 49
Bainbridge	Decatur	John P. Dickinson	155 12	320 34
Bairdstown	Oglethorpe	Hiram L. French, 1		
(Late "Woodvil	le.")	qr	10 65	19 31
Ball Ground	Cherokee	John F. Jones, to		
		31st December	2 25	4 47
		William Peeples	2 62	4 69
Bark Camp	Burke	James A. Murphree,		
(Ch'd to Midville.)		to 31st January	16 71	30 04
Barnesville	Pike	Sam'l S. Kendrick	95 64	142 58
Barrettsville	Lumpkin	Chapel A. Barrett	14 17	27 28

POST OFFICES—*Georgia.*

Post Offices.	Counties.	Postmasters.	Compensation.	Net proceeds.
Bascobel	Jackson	Milton Matthews	$11 25	$17 96
Bateman's Store	Houston	Cloburn Bateman	10 24	19 72
Batesville	Habersham	Joshua Sutton	4 63	9 81
Belair	Richmond	Robert Stoodley	47 95	46 88
Belleview	Talbot	Jas. M. Davis	85 77	65 86
Berzelia	Columbia	H. D. Leitner	43 55	75 55
Bethel	Glynn	Wm. D. Jenkins	50 18	94 00
Bexar	Coweta	Henry J. Bailey	8 05	14 94
Birdsville	Burke	Henry P. Jones	22 98	37 91
Black Creek	Scriven	Moses N. McCall	15 58	28 24
Blairsville	Union	Jas. J. Logan, 3 qrs.	21 06	41 23
Blakely	Early	James Hays	134 98	282 53
Blountsville	Jones	Francis Tufts	28 54	53 32
Bluff Spring	Talbot	Wm. B. Marshall, 3 qrs.	18 12	16 68
Boltonville	Cobb	Jas. A. Collins	12 35	16 44
Bowersville	Franklin	Job Bowers	5 22	10 94
Bowling Green	Oglethorpe	Nathan Hunter, to 11th January	13 55	20 73
		Ferdinand Phinizy, from 17th Jan.	10 81	15 15
Boxville	Montgomery	Wm. D. Wall	8 17	12 19
Brinsonville	Burke	Robert H. Gray	39 40	82 38
Brookline	Madison	Isaac Simmons	14 53	28 42
Brooksville	Randolph	Peyton D. Hill	26 54	53 20
Brunswick	Glynn	Alexander Scranton	65 77	133 30
Buck Creek	Scriven	Geo. H. Maner	13 57	25 23
Buck Eye	Laurens	James Bush	50 70	92 87
Buck Head	Morgan	Willis J. Rhymes	19 34	31 83
Busbayville	Houston	Daniel Gunn	55 88	54 58
Bushville	Franklin	Thos. S. Sisson	15 59	29 84
Cains	Gwinnet	Adam Pool	4 69	8 65
Cairo	Decatur	Jas. J. Lester	19 72	36 57
Calhoun	Lumpkin	Jas. W. Robinson, to 30th Sept.	2 01	3 68
		John W. Keith	6 35	10 94
Camak	Warren	William K. Heath, to 19th February	18 73	18 77
		Bell Thompson	13 19	13 21
Campbellton	Campbell	Thos. J. Foster	56 58	106 40
Cane Point	Troup	John C. Traylor, to 6th February	9 04	11 83
		Wm. E. Marcus	14 29	26 83
Canton	Cherokee	Geo. S. Hoyl	148 89	131 68
Carlisle (Dis. 22d Jan'y.)	Troup	Hillard O'Neal, to 4th February	19 18	31 57
Carnesville	Franklin	Henry Freeman	64 61	125 43
Carrollton	Carroll	Terence McGuire	45 61	83 75

POST OFFICES—*Georgia.*

Post Offices.	Counties.	Postmasters.	Compensation.	Net proceeds.
Carsonville........	Talbot......	Wm. A. Skellie.....	$26 46	$46 66
Cassville........	Cass........	George S. Black, to 15th January.....	224 13	230 00
		Rob't H. Patton....	96 45	190 49
Cave Spring......	Floyd	Carter W. Sparks..	43 68	83 80
Cedar Branch....	Campbell.....	Grant Roberts......	11 43	16 92
Cedar Creek......	Dooly........	William Slade, jr...	no ret.	
Cedartown......	Paulding	Dan'l H. Witcher..	47 46	94 04
Centre..........	Talbot......	Jos. M. Roberts....	32 03	53 13
Centre Village...	Camden.....	Domingo C. Acosta.	29 84	56 13
Centreville.......	Wilkes......	Luke Turner.......	18 65	32 57
Chattoogaville ...	Chattooga ...	R't W. Glenn, 3 qrs	9 81	19 56
Chenuba........	Lee..........	Wm. J. Parker....	14 22	25 33
Cherokee........	Cass	William Milner....	26 40	52 67
Chesnut Flat.....	Walker	Jno. W. Williams..	3 24	5 88
Chesnut Hill.....	Hall	Benj. F. Porter.....	12 60	22 96
Chester	Gwinnet.....	Wm. L. Born.......	6 02	10 61
Choice's Store ...	Gwinnet.....	William Crowell, to 13th March......	6 76	13 95
		Geo. B. Hudson...	4 79	9 71
Clarksville.......	Habersham..	Alex'r Erwin......	213 71	329 05
Clayton.........	Rabun......	And'w M. Norris..	19 36	31 58
Clinton	Jones.......	Charles Hutchings.	215 73	481 98
Clopton's Mills..	Putnam......	Pleasant J. Mullins.	19 35	37 89
Coal Mountain...	Forsyth	George Kellogg....	11 10	22 70
Cochran's ⋈ R'ds	Harris.......	Hiram B. Watson..	11 70	20 13
Cohuttah Springs.	Murray	James Edmondson.	4 48	7 03
Cold Water......	Elbert.......	Barnabas Barron....	5 61	10 60
Columbus........	Muscogee ...	G. W. E. Bedell...	2000 00	3804 75
Concord.........	Baker........	William Pierce....	13 33	25 85
Connaseena......	Cass.........	Andrew F. Woolley, fr. 9th Dec. 6⅔ mo	11 47	20 61
Cook's Law Office	Elbert.......	Jas. M. Palmer....	25 82	47 24
Cool Spring......	Wilkinson...	John W. Allen, to 31st March......	26 45	53 39
		Willis Allen.......	10 35	18 54
Coosawattee.....	Murray......	James McEntire....	22 77	38 85
Copeland's......	Telfair	Hugh McIntyre...	8 69	16 43
Corinth..........	Heard	Zadock T. Timmons	84 16	154 39
Cotton Hill......	Randolph ...	Lemmon Dunn, 3 qrs	7 94	15 48
Cotton River....	Henry.......	Philip T. Coker....	8 42	14 49
County Line.....	Campbell	James Hutcheson..	15 52	29 86
Courtesy........	Floyd	Wiley G. Parks....	11 21	20 68
Covington.......	Newton	Wm. P. Anderson.	341 87	727 53
Cracker's Neck..	Greene......	Geo. W. Slaughter, 3 qrs............	27 49	45 88
Crawfords....... (Dis. 4th Oct'r.)	Decatur	Hardy G. Crawford, to 24th November	6 37	11 78
Crawfordsville....	Taliaferro ...	Dan'l A. Williams.	168 23	168 26

POST OFFICES—*Georgia.*

Post Offices.	Counties.	Postmasters.	Compensation.	Net proceeds.
Cross Keys........	De Kalb	Jas. W. Reeve.....	$11 70	$22 01
Cross Plains......	Murray	Benj. C. Morse....	26 78	50 47
Cross Roads......	Cobb	Pinkney H. Randall	6 43	9 80
Crossville	Lumpkin.....	Walter R. Webster.	12 23	20 54
Culbreaths........	Columbia....	James Culbreath...	19 94	32 99
Culloden..........	Monroe	Arthur Ginn........	129 70	248 81
Cumming	Forsyth.....	C. B. Wellborn, to 31st December...	39 74	75 10
Cunningham's Store	Jackson.....	Wiley B. Hutchins.	44 81	74 93
		Jos. T. Cunningham, 3 qrs............	10 39	20 39
Currahee Mount'n	Habersham..	John Shed.........	9 50	15 12
Cuthbert.........	Randolph ...	James Buchanan...	201 83	398 67
Cut Off..........	Walton	Hope H. Camp....	12 51	21 21
Dahlonega........	Lumpkin....	Arch'd G. Wimpy.	234 36	505 60
Danburgh.........	Wilkes	Samuel Danforth...	34 70	65 29
Danielsville......	Madison	Walton H. Griffith.	53 10	103 40
Danville.........	Sumter......	Wm. J. Ronaldson.	38 64	73 45
Darbys	Columbia....	James R. Cook....	21 62	38 03
Darien...........	McIntosh....	Jas. F. S. Heald, to 13th February...	313 45	692 74
		Charles O'Neal....	182 46	441 98
Davisboro'......	Washington..	Wm. P. Hardwick.	50 42	99 75
Daviston.........	Talbot......	Jos. B. Swann.....	38 50	75 05
Dawson..........	Habersham..	Isaac A. Gibbs.....	3 18	6 27
Decatur..........	De Kalb....	John Glen.........	219 09	456 35
Devereaux's Store	Hancock	Sam'l M. Devereaux	14 61	27 63
Dirt Town.......	Chattooga...	Wil'n M. Shropshire	15 53	28 64
Dogwood	Walker	Jas. M. McSpadden	19 79	35 10
Double Branches.	Lincoln	Jno. C. Cunningham	22 19	39 01
Double Bridges ..	Upson......	Jas. W. Townsend, from March......	2 63	4 83
Double Cabins...	Henry......	Shatten C. Mitchell.	12 08	22 36
Double Wells....	Warren.....	Jethro Darden......	30 37	60 73
Drayton.........	Dooly	Thomas H. Key, to 31st March......	20 45	43 92
		William C. Greer ..	7 64	16 83
Dublin..........	Laurens.....	Francis Thomas....	126 91	228 71
Duncanville......	Thomas.....	Jackson J. Marsh ..	41 27	80 19
Eagle Grove......	Elbert.......	William Bowers ...	5 61	12 24
Eatonton........	Putnam.....	Sidney C. Prudden.	385 55	859 20
Ebenezer........	Morgan.....	John Durdin.......	11 43	19 10
Eden	Effingham...	Horace Powers, 3 qs.	13 83	27 38
Elberton	Elbert.......	Zachariah Smith ...	115 92	219 97
Ellejay..........	Gilmer......	James G. Gudger...	37 24	70 39
Ellerslie	Harris	Arch'd C. Tritt, to 31st Dec........	42 99	55 72

POST OFFICES—*Georgia.*

Post Offices.	Counties.	Postmasters.	Compensation.	Net proceeds.
		F. G. McElhaney	$52 87	$50 82
Emmitt	Wilkinson	Thomas McIntyre	15 37	33 11
Enon Grove	Heard	Wm. Bevis, 3 qrs	8 67	14 33
Erin	Merriwether	Josiah Pyron	20 57	38 23
Etowa Valley	Cass	John S. Rowland	20 81	39 93
Eubanks	Columbia	Samuel Crump	16 96	29 73
Eutaw	Randolph	John Ferguson, from 10th Sept	2 94	4 43
Fairplay	Morgan	Alexander Awtry	18 36	35 81
Fairview	Franklin	Jas. Attaway, from 24th Oct	1 63	2 67
Farmers	Meriwether	Milton Clayton	25 73	38 81
Farmington	Clark	Jesse C. Paulett, to 31st Dec	10 66	18 86
		William Fielding	6 85	12 81
Fayetteville	Fayette	Almond Stratton, to 31st Dec	61 93	110 52
		William N. Hill	68 26	114 86
Fenn's Bridge	Jefferson	Kinchen Womble	31 23	57 81
Flat Rock	Henry	Ira O. McDaniel	15 28	26 22
Flat Shoals	Meriwether	Wm. D. Alexander	23 70	46 81
Florence	Stewart	William Stafford	131 03	269 73
Florentia	Chattooga	Francis C. Taylor	8 67	15 08
Forsyth	Monroe	Oliver Morse	399 89	765 90
Fort Gaines	Early	William Mount	190 41	370 65
Fort Valley	Houston	Chas. H. Everett	95 59	192 16
Francisville	Crawford	Alex'r M. K. Swift	26 23	48 52
Franklin	Heard	John B. Ghent	76 35	138 83
Frank'n Academy	Upson	Elijah Smead	45 40	91 60
Frederica	Glynn	James F. Gould	64 48	132 85
Friendship	Sumter	Joseph Gilpin	32 86	61 35
Fryer's Ponds	Burke	James R. Moore, fr. 10th Aug	11 06	19 48
Gainesville	Hall	Minor W. Brown	205 30	394 04
Georgetown	Randolph	Green B. Lewis	53 96	124 73
Gillions	Baker	Charles W. Roby	41 57	84 61
Gillsville	Hall	Josiah H. Gill	10 29	21 21
Glades X Roads	Putnam	Thos. K. Slaughter	9 83	13 35
Glenalta	Marion	Wm. W. Shipp	21 10	36 94
Gold Hill	Meriwether	John T. Carter	21 21	36 37
Golgotha	Cobb	Cargill Drake	4 10	7 07
Good Hope	Walton	James Richardson	11 54	20 40
Goose Pond	Oglethorpe	Sol'n Jennings, jr	18 03	27 83
Gordon	Wilkinson	David Solomon	33 05	57 05
Goshen	Lincoln	John A. Simmons	16 89	30 77
Grangersville	Macon	James Gilbert	5 96	12 06
Green Hill	Stewart	John P. Grimes	17 33	30 70

POST OFFICES—*Georgia.*

Post Offices.	Counties.	Postmasters.	Compensation.	Net proceeds.
Greensboro'	Greene	William L. Strain	$419 36	$652 60
Greenville	Meriwether	Perry G. Singlefield	378 66	547 01
Griffin	Pike	James A. Beeks	386 49	589 58
Grooverville	Thomas	Jos'a S. Groover	27 16	48 80
Grove Hill (Dis. 21st Aug.)	Madison	Ira Freeman, 1 qr.	1 36	3 19
Grove Level	Franklin	William Mintz	6 16	9 56
Gullettsville	Monroe	Thomas M. Speer	22 25	35 19
Halcyon Dale	Scriven	Cuyler W. Young, to 31st Dec.	13 44	26 32
		Benj'n W. Lawton	22 53	24 70
Halloca	Muscogee	Joshua R. McCook	19 31	34 17
Hamburg	Macon	Thomas H. Morgan	29 31	49 94
Hamilton	Harris	Arch'd H. Scott	193 05	363 83
Hammock Grove	Crawford	John L. Woodward	15 85	27 04
Hannahatchee	Stewart	John Fleming, to 31st March	14 15	25 91
		John L. Porter	4 76	9 01
Hardins' Mills	Floyd	William Hardin	6 84	10 80
Hard Money (Dis. 23d Oct.)	Stewart	James B. Boyer, 1 qr.	2 57	4 44
Harmony Grove	Jackson	James W. Shankle	16 44	28 74
Harnageville	Cherokee	Samuel Tate	7 65	15 38
Harrisonville (Dis. 2d Sept.)	Elbert	F. Cunningham, to 18th Sept	66	1 34
Hartford	Forsyth	Jesse Ponder	8 85	8 92
Hawkinsville	Pulaski	Dar's R. Mathewson	229 37	502 24
Haynesville	Houston	Alfred S. Gillett	84 40	160 16
Hebron	Washington	Seaborn W. Buck	31 17	51 57
Henderson	Houston	James A. Stubbs	32 37	61 03
Hermitage	Floyd	Joseph Watters	12 13	23 11
Hickory Flat	Cherokee	George Gunby	25 83	48 64
Hickory Grove	Crawford	Allen G Simmons	27 74	48 76
Hickory Level	Carroll	James Baskin	5 85	10 85
High Falls	Lumpkin	John Spriggs	6 19	12 43
High Shoals	Walton	Eph. S. Hopping	21 12	37 29
High Tower	Forsyth	Roland Osborne	37 37	72 45
Hillsboro'	Jasper	Winston Gordon	52 05	92 21
Hinesville	Liberty	William Harrison	53 28	96 82
Holcomb	Burke	Oliver P. Cowart	35 49	65 84
Hollidaysville (Late 'Pinderton.")	Dooly	Abner Holliday, fr. 25th Dec	3 87	8 08
Hollingsworth	Habersham	Edwin M. Wynn	9 75	18 46
Holly Creek	Murray	Absalom Bishop	7 67	14 04
Holmesville	Appling	John Graham	12 86	27 39
Hootensville	Upson	Moses D. Johnston	25 49	46 87
Hopewell	Crawford	James A. Miller	30 01	46 95
Horse Head	Macon	Thomas S. Rives	12 89	21 08

POST OFFICES—*Georgia.*

Post Offices.	Counties.	Postmasters.	Compensation.	Net proceeds.
House Creek	Irwin	Jeremiah Mathews	$25 53	$46 52
Houston	Heard	Const'e L. Thomas	41 84	69 13
Huntsville	Paulding	Jacob B. Parlier	9 75	19 24
Indian Springs	Butts	Charles F. Newton	69 79	145 28
Iron Works	Cass	Moses Stroup	36 81	72 33
Irwin's X Roads	Washington	John L. Irwin	23 37	32 94
Irwinsville	Irwin	Joel W. Hand	(No ret.)	
Irwinton	Wilkinson	George A. Whipple	82 35	170 71
Islandtown	Chattooga	John T. Storey	8 06	14 37
Ivy Log	Union	Rich'd W. Roberts	3 57	4 98
Jackson	Butts	John McCord	122 19	242 76
Jacksonboro'	Scriven	Simeon Buford, to 30th Sept	14 54	22 18
		Green D. Sharpe	40 31	70 94
Jacksonville	Telfair	Christopher McRae	50 51	97 05
Jefferson	Jackson	James B. Nabers	77 48	158 96
Jeffersonton	Camden	George Lang	124 73	227 70
Johnson's Store	Coweta	John H. Johnson	29 12	59 17
Johnstonville	Monroe	Thomas Johnston	4 83	5 56
Jonesborough	Fayette	Elijah P. Allen, to 31st March	18 75	35 63
		Samuel G. Pegg	12 85	20 87
Kellogg's Store	Jackson	Jacob Braselton	4 17	8 39
Kidron	Coweta	King W. Perry	23 01	40 40
King's Gap	Harris	Wm. L. Culbreath	12 51	24 25
Kingston	Wilkinson	William O. Beall, to 30th Sept	5 83	11 68
		Leroy Fleetwood	23 27	46 31
Knoxville	Crawford	Francis H. Murdock	128 23	246 62
La Fayette	Walker	Benj'n F. Hawkins, to 10th June	110 70	203 86
		Richard M. Aycock	6 34	10 70
La Grange	Troup	Wm. C. D. Cook	528 78	871 59
Langsbury	Camden	Isaac Lang	44 74	86 90
Lanier	Macon	John A. Law, 2 qs.	29 79	58 90
Lannahassee	Stewart	Abraham Prim	38 68	68 83
Larksville	Jones	Hinton Duncan, fr. 1st Oct	3 08	5 10
Latimer's Store	De Kalb	Chas. Latimer, 3 qs.	17 79	34 60
Laurel Hill	Carroll	H. P. Mabry	6 01	11 20
Lauren's Hill	Laurens	David Harvard	18 72	36 86
Lawrenceville	Gwinnet	John Mills	163 65	282 45
Leakesville	Newton	Elbert H. Gay, 3 qs.	11 91	20 09
Lebanon	Cobb	Archibald Howell	138 76	269 41
Lexington	Oglethorpe	Wm. H. Deupree	274 05	530 02

POST OFFICES—*Georgia.*

Post Offices.	Counties.	Postmasters.	Compensation.	Net proceeds.
Liberty Hill	Pike	Michael D. Gaar, to 31st March	$6 64	$9 02
		T. S. M. Bloodworth	4 08	7 97
Lincolnton	Lincoln	Benjamin Bentley	83 04	143 58
Lineville	Bibb	H. T. Mann, 3 qrs.	11 94	15 02
Lisbon (Ch'd to Petersburg.)	Lincoln	Marsh S. Anthony, to 10th Dec.	15 33	27 65
Location	Coweta	John P. Miller	19 11	30 60
Locust Grove	Henry	William Kimball	12 52	22 78
Lodi	Coweta	James Hunt	7 71	15 47
Lofton's Store	Butts	John Lofton	17 25	33 56
Lombardy	Columbia	Jacob Printup, to 31st Dec.	19 27	19 28
		Thomas Roland	16 28	16 31
Long Cane	Troup	Iddo Ellis, to 18th January	23 37	41 89
		Irwin Wilkerson	15 68	32 97
Long's Bridge	Hancock	James Ray	14 42	29 14
Loudsville	Habersham	Francis Logan	5 51	12 11
Louisville	Jefferson	Ebenezer Bothwell, to 28th Jan.	90 55	168 95
		John M. Hayles	73 74	138 82
Lucksville	Hall	Francis Luck	9 08	15 48
Lumber City	Telfair	John Steele	13 74	26 29
Lumpkin	Stewart	Hollis Boynton	291 57	610 14
Luthersville	Meriwether	Wm. H. Wright, to 31st March	5 05	8 96
		Wash'n P. Parker	1 42	2 78
McDonough	Henry	David Knott	184 65	321 89
Mackville	Franklin	John H. McIntire	3 42	7 08
Macon	Bibb	Keeland Tyner	2000 00	7507 18
Madison	Morgan	Fielding W. Arnold	517 92	939 97
Madison Springs	Madison	Daniel Morrison	15 56	34 93
Mallorysville	Wilkes	Addison A. Bell	33 93	59 73
Marietta	Cobb	Wm. G. Robinson, to 30th Sept.	107 65	181 09
		Daniel Collins	271 79	419 25
Marion	Twiggs	Elijah E. Crocker, to 16th Feb.	77 87	142 75
		Wm. J. Stephens	51 42	105 01
Marlborough	Morgan	Bennet Robertson, 3 qrs	5 29	8 76
Marshallsville	Macon	Miles K. Harman, to 30th Sept.	8 39	14 50
		Silas W. Curtis	25 61	38 58
Marthasville	De Kalb	Frederick C. Arms, to 17th June	29 22	31 05
		George W. Collier	1 16	2 71

POST OFFICES—*Georgia.*

Post Offices.	Counties.	Postmasters.	Compensation.	Net proceeds.
Martin's Store...	Macon......	Arch'd W. Martin..	$14 36	$27 05
Mayfield........	Warren.....	William Harris....	57 07	67 12
Maysville	Stewart.....	James Jones, from 17th July to 27th April..........	3 03	5 93
Mechanicsville....	Jasper......	Henry Burdett.....	14 44	24 08
Medicinal Springs	Walker......	Zacha'h H. Gordon.	9 82	19 45
Middle River.....	Franklin....	William Jackson...	3 67	6 06
Midville........ (Late Bark Camp)	Burke.......	John T. Neely, from 1st Feb..........	6 63	10 28
		James Griffin.......	12 75	23 82
Milledgeville.....	Baldwin.....	Ezra Daggett......	1228 75	3683 91
Mill Grove.......	Cobb.......	Samuel Burdine....	3 30	6 05
Mill Haven.......	Scriven......	Thomas F. Lovett..	16 47	29 75
Mill Stone.......	Oglethorpe...	John D. Pass......	19 12	33 29
Millville.........	Cherokee....	Henry H. Waters, $5\frac{1}{3}$ months.......	2 55	5 86
Millwood........ (Dis. 30th July.)	Dooly.......	James Boatright....	no return	
Minerva.........	Houston	Daniel Bradwell, 2 qrs............	9 33	10 97
		James W. Belvin...	no return	
Missionary Stat'n	Floyd.......	Wm. S. Quin, to 31st Dec........	16 98	15 93
		Hugh Quin.........	14 52	13 19
Mobley Pond....	Scriven......	Thomas R. Smelie, from 29th Aug...	39 05	55 02
Monroe.........	Walton	Leroy Pattillo......	196 32	372 95
Montevideo......	Elbert.......	W. W. Dooly, 1 qr.	3 87	7 06
		Barna J. Dooly, from 1st Jan..........	7 28	13 39
Monticello.......	Jasper.......	Samuel A. Flournoy	250 48	537 93
Montpelier	Monroe	Sam'l H. Fay, 3 qrs.	87 69	175 55
Mount Pleasant.. (Dis. 16th May.)	Newton.....	John E. Parke, 3 qrs.	16 92	32 56
Mount Vernon...	Montgomery.	Christopher McRae.	15 80	30 70
Mountville.......	Troup.......	J. T. McLaughlin..	61 16	67 33
Mount Yonah....	Habersham...	Ezekiel McCravey..	36 83	67 27
Mount Zion	Hancock.....	Jos. J. Reeves.....	66 84	119 27
Mulberry........	Jackson......	Delmas R. Lyle....	11 96	24 40
Mulberry Grove..	Harris.......	James W. Pitts....	42 43	71 68
Nacoochee.......	Habersham...	Chs. L. Williams..	23 82	47 55
Naples.......... (Dis. 16th July.)	Gwinnet.....	H. W. Inzer, 1 qr..	0 24	0 36
New Babylon....	Paulding....	James Hall, to 30th September.......	0 25	0 51
		Francis Little......	2 50	4 81
Newborn.........	Newton.....	John W. Pitts.....	19 58	27 45

POST OFFICES—*Georgia.*

Post Offices.	Counties.	Postmasters.	Compensation.	Net proceeds.
New Bridge	Lumpkin	James Gowdy	$42 59	$41 14
New Echota	Cass	Henry C. Phelps, to 19th Feb	20 61	38 50
		Stephen Mays	14 18	28 26
Newnan	Coweta	Thomas W. Bolton	246 96	286 50
Newton	Baker	Mahlon Bedell	36 49	34 69
Oak Hill	Newton	Shelby Downs	43 34	73 50
Oak Lawn	Baker	George D. Royston	4 72	9 85
Oceola	Lee	George C. Ticknor	18 75	28 77
Ocmulgeville	Telfair	Nathaniel Ashley	7 09	13 85
Oconee	Washington	Robert P. Gayard	20 42	40 75
Old Church	Burke	Jos. A. Shewmake	17 29	29 08
Old Court House (Dis. 27th July.)	Bryan	James M. Butler, to 6th August	3 24	5 92
Olive Grove	Decatur	Wm. M. Owens	25 25	48 27
Orange	Cherokee	Joshua Burtz	18 79	37 01
Orrsville	Gwinnet	Wm. C. Orr	10 30	18 61
Oxford	Newton	Wm. H. Mell	194 13	393 91
Pachitta	Early	John Rogers	15 71	29 70
Palmyra	Lee	Joseph White	89 68	119 60
Panthersville	De Kalb	Hugh M. Boyd	14 37	26 19
Parker's Store	Franklin	John D. Parker	6 07	12 45
Park's Bridge	Morgan	James McKinzie	18 87	34 30
Penfield	Greene	William Richards	194 16	370 48
Perry	Houston	Bryant Batton	238 83	313 61
Perry's Mills	Tatnal	Nicholas Smith	26 64	43 90
Petawla	Randolph	Wm. C. Hill	27 88	46 44
Petersburgh (Ch'd to 'Lisbon')	Elbert	Archibald N. Sayer, to 25th July	2 15	4 08
(Late 'Lisbon.')		Archibald Stokes, from 10th Dec	19 32	34 06
Piedmont	Harris	Stephen Pace	4 98	9 33
Pinckneyville	Gwinnet	Thomas A. Pittman	16 27	27 51
Pindertown (Ch'd to "Hollidaysville.")	Dooly	John A. Graham, 1 qr	2 39	4 27
Pine Hill	Talbot	John W. G. Smith, to 31st March	7 22	11 80
		Buckner Bass	3 43	5 42
Pine Log	Cass	Edward Barrett	32 87	63 00
Pineville	Marion	Daniel M. Hall, to 30th Sept	15 71	28 02
		Cary S. Cox	45 11	79 93
Pistol Creek	Wilkes	Reuben Carter	6 69	12 33
Pittmans (Dis. 2d Sept.)	Monroe	Hilman Pittman	no return	
Pittsburgh (Dis. 26th July.)	Henry	Columbus W. Smith	no return	

POST OFFICES—*Georgia.*

Post Offices.	Counties.	Postmasters.	Compensation.	Net proceeds.
Plains of Dura	Sumter	John Coker	$15 06	$27 64
Planters	Jasper	Daniel McDowell, 3 qrs	1 18	2 28
Pleasant Hill	Talbot	John T. Howard	69 15	67 20
Pleasant Valley	Murray	Chilion Packard	6 25	13 00
Poindexter	Marion	James N. Harris	3 94	7 14
Polk	Union	John Butt	5 99	8 48
Pondtown	Sumter	Wm. G. Womack, to 30th Sept	14 96	28 91
		Walter T. Davenport	40 32	80 10
Poolesville	De Kalb	James Caldwell	12 72	20 43
Powder Springs	Cobb	Wiley J. Kiser	31 77	60 19
Powelton	Hancock	James Bell	58 31	97 61
Prattsburgh	Talbot	James M. Harvey	28 38	49 61
Prattville	Monroe	William Spicer	49 51	82 51
(Late "Stallings' Store.")				
Prince Edward	Gilmer	Samuel B. West	5 46	10 92
Public Square	Greene	Elisha S. Hunter	21 42	38 21
Quito	Talbot	Wm. M. Latimer, from 1st Oct	8 79	14 86
Raines' Store	Twiggs	Ellis Long	97 13	184 68
Raytown	Taliaferro	Aaron W. Grier	54 83	52 59
Red Clay	Murray	James H. Huff	12 50	20 40
Red Hill	Murray	George Fagala	13 29	21 80
Red Oak	Columbia	Wm. C. Parks	34 21	54 26
Reedy Creek	Jefferson	Moses Thompson	5 43	10 09
Reform	Effingham	Phares N. Elkins	12 88	26 82
Rehoboth	Wilkes	George W. Booker	14 62	24 01
Rehobothville	Morgan	John B. Hawkins	9 09	15 21
Reidsville	Tatnal	John A. Rogers	19 39	40 73
Republican	Columbia	John Adkins	8 00	13 15
Riceboro'	Liberty	Geo. W. Dunham	128 96	264 62
Richland	Stewart	Josiah W. Jossey	28 84	55 74
Richmond Fact'ry	Richmond	Daniel Hack	29 78	60 36
Rivertown	Campbell	Moses M. Smith	5 32	10 20
Rock Bridge	Gwinnet	Thomas Maguire	18 89	36 84
Rock Dale	Newton	John Burke 3 qrs	29 84	58 66
		Blake Bartlett, from 12th May	3 88	8 73
Rock Mills	Hancock	William Shivers	11 87	20 81
Rock Spring	Walker	James R. Jones	4 82	8 89
Rockville	Putnam	Riley Batchelor	19 73	31 66
Rocky Mount	Meriwether	Wm. T. Loftin	15 53	32 79
Rome	Floyd	Samuel Stewart, to 14th Feb	172 85	186 40
		Andrew Patterson	88 11	119 04
Rossville	Walker	Thos. G. McFarland	12 92	21 61

POST OFFICES—*Georgia.*

Post Offices.	Counties.	Postmasters.	Compensation.	Net proceeds.
Rotherwood	Carroll	James H. Rodgers	$16 64	$33 37
Ruckersville	Elbert	Chs. N. B. Carter	44 71	87 63
Russellville	Monroe	Bryant Parker	24 70	37 46
Ryals	Montgomery	Joseph Ryal	11 04	19 07
St. Clair (Dis. 2d July.)	Burke	George Gough, to 12th July	1 53	2 37
St. Mary's	Camden	Alfred Doolittle, 3 qrs	226 82	479 70
Salem	Clark	Samuel Fielding	35 65	67 27
Saliquoy	Cass	John G. B. Adams	9 00	17 75
Salmonville	Oglethorpe	Lewis S. Salmons, to 31st Dec	10 96	18 36
		Milledge S. Durham	14 14	22 61
Sandersville	Washington	Haywood Brookins	141 28	281 72
Sandtown	Campbell	John H. Coryell	36 27	64 09
Sandy Creek	Oglethorpe	Emanuel Zuber, 1 qr.	2 03	3 93
Sandy Ridge	Henry	Philip Wolf	18 92	35 36
Sardis	Burke	William Sapp	17 41	31 33
Savannah	Chatham	George Schley	1825 51	19409 05
Scarborough	Scriven	Enos H. Scarborough	15 48	30 37
Scull Shoals	Greene	Thos. N. Poullain	63 48	104 99
Searsville	Stewart	David C. Sears	16 22	25 76
Shady Dale	Jasper	Geo. L. Willy	48 41	84 77
Shady Grove	Union	Jesse Osborn	8 46	17 25
Sharpe's Store	Lowndes	Hamilton W. Sharpe	43 65	82 86
Sheffield	Newton	Allen Summers	14 20	27 86
Shell Creek	Muscogee	James McGuire	46 20	87 78
Shoals of Ogechee	Hancock	Thomas Cheely	18 42	31 35
Snow Hill	Walker	James Gordon, to 31st March	10 68	20 46
		James Hunt	4 51	7 32
Social Circle	Walton	Absalom B. Ross	108 21	213 65
Social Hill	Cherokee	Russell Jones	9 09	14 77
South Newport	McIntosh	Moses C. Heald	45 25	83 66
Sparta	Hancock	Jas. H. Burnet	494 76	757 52
Springfield	Effingham	John Charlton	70 54	133 18
Spring Place	Murray	John S. Beall	67 25	120 34
Stallings' Store (Ch'd to "Prattville.")	Monroe	Curtis G. Gray	(No ret.)	
Stanfordville	Putnam	Joshua Driskell	37 52	70 40
Starkville	Lee	Wm. G. Macon	73 51	110 41
Starrsville	Newton	Geo. W. Leak	15 64	26 61
State Line	Floyd	Edmund Southerlin, to 31st March	6 66	14 23
		Christian Reinhardt	4 94	9 87
State Rights	Oglethorpe	Moses Wright	29 33	52 00
Statesboro'	Bullock	Hardy B. Hodges	26 17	55 60
Stephens	Cobb	Israel Causey	5 12	8 72

POST OFFICES—*Georgia.*

Post Offices.	Counties.	Postmasters.	Compensation.	Net proceeds.
Stone Mountain..	De Kalb.....	Andrew Johnson...	$13 20	$25 07
Stony Point......	Wilkes.......	John L. Paschal....	28 37	53 52
Sugar Valley	Murray.......	Elias King.........	3 24	6 79
Summerfield......	Stewart......	Chs. N. Simpson...	31 05	60 36
Summerville.......	Chattooga...	Thos. T. Hopkins, to 31st Dec'r......	51 05	90 39
		Benjamin Branner..	43 36	84 55
Sumpterville......	Lee.........	Addison E. Harris..	21 30	40 79
Surrency's.......	Tatnal.......	Elijah E. Stafford ..	13 98	16 53
Suwane.........	Gwinnet	James Brown......	7 04	11 11
Swainsboro'......	Emanuel.....	Neil McLeod......	12 49	24 53
Sweet Water....	Gwinnet	Hiram R. Williams.	7 35	13 35
Sylvan Grove....	Jefferson.....	John R. Lowe......	21 19	36 33
Tacoah	Gilmer.......	Benjamin Chastain.	6 56	12 02
Talbotton	Talbot......	Wm. W. McNeil, to 3d June.......	360 52	605 16
		Jas. Y. Gardner....	26 39	46 89
Talking Rock.....	Gilmer.......	Joseph McCrary...	3 80	8 61
Tallapoosa.......	Carroll.......	John Robinson, 3 qs.	10 40	22 37
Tarversville......	Twiggs	John W. Myrick...	60 90	123 68
Tazewell.........	Marion	Churner B. Strange.	84 86	160 82
Teloga Springs...	Chattooga...	William McConnell.	14 45	29 38
Temperance	Telfair.......	Griffin Mizell......	7 73	13 08
Tennille..........	Washington..	Sam'l O. Franklin..	36 21	55 86
Texas	Meriwether...	James P. Perdue...	13 04	19 76
Thomaston.......	Upson......	Wm. D. Woodson, to 31st March....	229 26	269 61
		John W. W. Drake	79 64	102 45
Thomasville......	Thomas......	Jas. W. Smith......	241 06	473 43
Thompson	Columbia....	Michael L. Thomas	48 93	48 32
Tranquilla........	Jones........	Joseph Day........	19 36	31 81
Traveller's Rest..	Dooly........	Abel Holton.......	59 41	113 34
Trenton..........	Dade	Elijah J. George, 3 qs.	22 76	42 29
Troupville.......	Lowndes....	William Smith.....	94 21	163 80
Tuckaseeking.... (Dis. 23d Oct.)	Effingham...	Jas. W. Morgan...	(No ret.)	
Tucker's Cabin..	Henry.......	Isaiah Hollingsworth	17 74	33 63
Tyrone	Wilkes.......	Jas. T. Hackney...	17 34	16 40
Union...........	Crawford....	Theod'k W. Montfort, to 30th Sept.	4 44	8 79
		Henry Bradford....	13 72	26 56
Union Point.....	Greene.......	Pleasant H. Jones..	43 21	50 34
Unionville.......	Monroe......	Thos. S. M. Bloodworth, to 31st Dec.	13 85	22 11
		Wm. G. Ham......	15 65	21 72
Upatoie	Muscogee ...	Thos. H. Kendall..	43 42	75 22
Utoy............	De Kalb.....	Daniel Stone......	12 20	18 63

POST OFFICES—*Georgia.*

Post Offices.	Counties.	Postmasters.	Compensation.	Net proceeds.
Vann's Valley...	Floyd........	Madison Montgomery, to 21st Feb'y.	$4 67	$7 74
		John Boyle, jr. 1 qr.	0 55	0 91
Van Wert.......	Paulding	Henry Kingsberry.	49 76	101 89
Vernon	Troup........	James McDonough.	13 63	26 43
Vienna..........	Dooly.........	Jos. B. Clapp......	46 66	83 59
Villa Rica.......	Carroll.......	Ez'l S. Candler, 3 qs.	73 31	145 72
Villanow.........	Walker.	Constantine Wood..	3 45	6 52
Wallace..........	Jones.........	Augustus B. Sharpe	12 91	22 29
Walnut Hill......	Franklin	John M. Neal.........	12 98	23 77
Walthourville.....	Liberty	Edwin H. Bacon....	56 21	109 34
Walton's Ford... (Late "Davis Ferry," S. Car.)	Habersham..	Devereaux Jarrett, from 28th Oct....	5 77	9 96
Waresboro'.......	Ware.........	Thomas Hilliard...	21 74	40 15
Warm Springs...	Meriwether...	Robt. Bonner, 3 qrs.	44 83	92 59
Warrenton,......	Warren.......	John H. Roberts...	259 26	339 41
Warsaw	Forsyth......	Hiram H. Rosseau, to 31st March....	23 98	46 26
		Clark Howell.......	6 43	11 95
Warthen's Store.	Washington..	Richard Warthen..	28 18	46 70
Washington.......	Wilkes........	Jos. W. Robinson..	417 83	697 39
Watkinsville,.....	Clark.........	Thomas Simonton..	133 91	251 11
Watsons...........	Coweta	Thos. F. Wells....	13 77	21 78
Wauhatchee......	Dade	Anthony Tittle......	2 30	4 65
Waverly Hall...	Harris........	George Osborn......	53 07	59 98
Waynesboro'....	Burke.........	Thos. H. Blount 3 qs.	251 28	284 79
Waynesville.....	Wayne	Sylvester Mumford.	48 41	80 42
Webbs...........	Newton......	John Webb.........	22 04	39 06
Wellborn's Mills.	Houston	Carlton Wellborn..	21 86	40 04
West Point......	Troup	John M. Harrington	65 11	124 37
White House....	Henry........	Jno. T. Bentley....	8 82	17 02
White Oak......	Columbia....	Benjamin Young...	27 13	49 88
White Plains....	Greene.......	John Bonner.......	38 17	69 97
White Sulphur Spring	Meriwether...	Hope T. Hodnett, to 27th Feb'y......	28 71	56 65
		Charles B. Zuber...	14 52	26 86
Whites	Elbert	Wm. A. Stone......	4 79	7 57
Whitesville......	Harris.......	Wm. M. Cochran..	99 16	175 56
Willow Grove...	Coweta	Lewis Watkins, 3 qs.	9 73	18 36
Wilna.............	Houston	Henry Wood......	31 28	56 89
Windsor.........	Walton	Wm. H. Mayn....	15 40	25 62
Woodberry......	Meriwether...	Wm. T. Jenkins...	(No ret.)	
Woodhouse	Meriwether...	Jno. A. Crawford..	27 64	27 68
Woods' Station..	Walker	John Woods.......	5 16	10 01
Woodstock......	Cherokee....	Wm. M. McAfee..	13 18	25 50
Woodville....... (Ch'd to "Bairdsville.")	Greene......	Nathan Hobbs, 3 qs.	24 90	48 27

POST OFFICES—*Alabama.*

Post Offices.	Counties.	Postmasters.	Compensation.	Net proceeds.
Wrightsboro'....	Columbia....	Hy. W. Massingale	$75 88	$118 87
York..........	Fayette.....	Geo. P. Parker.....	13 17	25 13
Zachry's Store...	Newton.....	Jas. B. Zachry.....	7 12	15 98
Zebulon.........	Pike........	Wm. S. Griffin......	155 12	288 05

ALABAMA.

NOTE.—Compensation of Postmasters, and net proceeds of their offices, from July 1, 1844, to June 30, 1845.

Post Offices.	Counties.	Postmasters.	Compensation.	Net proceeds.
Abbeville.......	Henry.......	Robert Kennedy...	$72 97	$137 60
Aberfoil.........	Macon......	Thos. L. McGowan	43 03	87 34
Air Mount......	Clark........	John Hope........	9 77	19 34
Alexandria......	Benton......	James M. Litten...	89 81	164 66
Allenton........	Wilcox......	James Robinson...	117 30	213 46
Andalusia.......	Covington...	Chs. G. Lynch.....	14 03	26 66
Annawaika......	De Kalb....	Ellison Cook......	3 01	6 17
Arbacoochee.....	Randolph...	John Gooden, to 30th Sept.........	11 95	23 23
		Samuel Wells.....	28 32	53 84
Argus..........	Montgomery.	Robert I. Staggers, 3 qrs............	18 94	37 40
Asbury.........	Fayette.....	John Hamby......	8 14	19 05
Ashville.........	St. Clair.....	James Rogan......	48 27	96 72
Athens.........	Limestone...	Thomas Bass......	419 09	650 92
Auburn.........	Macon......	Geo. B. Nuckolls..	108 98	207 38
Aurora.........	Marshall....	Wm. G. Jordan....	3 44	6 33
Bainbridge......	Macon......	Ayres S. Turpin...	26 10	48 56
Barge's.........	Butler.......	John Barge.......	22 08	43 09
Barnes' X Roads.	Dale........	Colmon Barnes....	3 03	6 94
Barryton........	Washington.	Saml. S. Houston..	35 82	68 93
Beaver Dam..... (Dis. 30th July.)	Randolph...	Wm. McKnight...	(no ret.)	
Beech Grove.... (Dis. 24th May.)	Marshall....	Ben. Hickman, 2 qrs.	1 46	2 46
Bellefonte.......	Jackson.....	Isaac Wildbahn, to 12th June........	124 33	225 41
		Willia'n R. W. Cobb	7 30	7 46
Belleville........	Conecuh....	Henry A. Arnold, to 31st Dec.........	25 96	48 36
		Nathl. B. Arnold..	25 41	48 53

POST OFFICES—*Alabama.*

Post Offices.	Counties.	Postmasters.	Compensation.	Net proceeds.
Bell's Landing...	Monroe.....	James M. Burgess, to 31st Dec......	$27 65	$55 58
		Wm. W. Hunt....	26 94	55 64
Belmont	Sumter	Arnold A. Powell..	61 37	124 22
Benevola........	Pickens	Bartley Upchurch..	29 58	48 99
Bennettsville.....	St. Clair	George Holloway..	11 94	13 78
Benton	Lowndes....	Roswell W. Hill, 2 qrs............	115 27	126 42
Berlin	Sumter	John C. McGrew, 2 qrs............	16 61	33 28
Berrien	Sumter	Jas. F. Reid, from 23d July........	7 30	13 30
Bethel	Wilcox	Silas C. Dumas. ...	15 37	24 19
Bexar	Marion	John Brown, from 1st Jan...........	1 79	3 95
Big Rock........	Sumter	Wm. A. Camfield, 3 qrs............	29 11	50 69
Big Spring	Marshall....	Thos. J. Smith	3 17	6 66
Black's Bluff	Wilcox	Jas. A. Tait........	31 80	69 23
Bladon's Springs. (Late "Warrior Bridge.")	Washington.	Jos. A. Huber, from 1st Oct..........	9 52	18 23
Blakely	Baldwin	Isaiah Randall	44 07	74 88
Blount Spring ...	Blount......	Jones C. Lucy.....	51 89	110 97
Blountsville	Blount......	Thomas Shearer ...	74 55	63 22
Blue Eye........	Benton	Henry Carter	6 12	10 09
Blue Lick.......	Franklin	Joseph Wofford....	3 73	7 03
Bluffport........	Sumter	James Duren......	30 23	64 93
Boligee	Greene	William Kennedy..	61 34	111 71
Bolivar	Jackson.....	Geo. F. Overdeer...	47 47	87 76
Bonner's Mills...	Pickens	Jno. C. Bonner, from 1st Oct..........	7 03	11 07
Boston......... (Dis. 26th July.)	Marengo....	John P. Burwell ...	no return	
Bragg's	Lowndes....	Thomas Hobby....	28 14	53 35
Branchville......	St. Clair	Andrew Venable ...	7 32	16 17
Brewersville	Sumter	Geo. W. Brewer, to 30th Sept.........	3 72	6 04
		William Dowsing..	9 28	14 18
Brickville	Lawrence ...	William Wallis	28 83	54 77
Bridgeville	Dale........	Bartley M. Tucker.	14 08	30 51
Broken Arrow...	St. Clair	Francis B. Walker.	4 19	7 47
Brooklyn	Conecuh	Julius G. Robinson.	27 06	54 25
Brooksville	Blount......	Calv. W. Bryan, 1 qr.	4 02	7 93
Brownsville	Talladega ...	Duncan Brown	16 79	30 84
Buck Creek	Tuskaloosa..	William Archibald .	6 08	13 53
Burnsville	Dallas	Warren B. Andrews	48 49	98 58
Burnt Corn......	Monroe	Isaac Betts	74 60	121 61
Buzzard Roost...	Franklin	William Dickson ..	127 62	196 25

POST OFFICES—*Alabama.*

Post Offices.	Counties.	Postmasters.	Compensation.	Net proceeds.
Cabahatchee	Macon	Jere. S. Walker, to 31st March	$49 99	$95 07
		William B. Harding	15 84	29 41
Cahaba	Dallas	Jno. R. Hood	386 06	781 62
Cambridge	Dallas	Claud's M. Cochran	46 28	80 28
Camden	Wilcox	John P. Fairly, to 30th Sept	38 67	84 75
		John A. Jackson	116 68	245 09
Camp Spring	Lawrence	Wm. A. Milam	5 85	11 23
Cane Creek (Dis. 22d Jan.)	Benton	Richard W. Moore	no return	
Canton	Wilcox	Ephraim Pharr	67 16	119 82
Carlowsville	Dallas	Bern'd A. Reynolds, from 13th March	13 84	25 74
Carrollton	Pickens	Andrew M. Windle	195 47	268 59
Carter's Hill	Montgomery	John S. Carter	60 70	106 65
Carthage	Tuskaloosa	Jas. M. Harvey	57 53	57 55
Cauleysville	Covington	James Parker	4 50	10 11
Cedar Bluff	Cherokee	James V. Hogg	76 12	133 40
Cedar Grove	Jefferson	Clayton Thompson	8 81	16 06
Cedar Plains	Morgan	Joseph Herring	17 33	32 13
Centre	Cherokee	Pat. J. Chisolm, 1 qr.	2 33	2 19
Centreport	Dallas	Wm. S. La Tourette, fr. 25th Dec., 3 mo.	7 15	12 74
Centreville	Bibb	Morgan Howard (Includes $3 26 comp., $7 63 n. pro. for "Maplesville.")	194 03	192 73
Chambers C. H.	Chambers	John A. Frazier	296 90	607 87
Charlottesville	Franklin	Kelly Stegall, 3 qrs.	3 13	6 34
Cherry Grove	Lauderdale	Charles McClusky, to 31st Dec.	6 88	6 90
		James Ham	6 25	8 56
Chesnut Creek	Autauga	Allen Ray, to 31st March	7 64	16 47
		Wm. H. Johnson	2 91	6 27
Chesnut Hill	Perry	Anderson B. Davis	8 10	12 62
China Grove	Pike	Christo'r Tompkins	62 80	116 62
Chinnibee	Talladega	Greensville W. Penn	6 82	9 63
Chulafinnee	Randolph	Charles Rodahan	2 35	4 56
Church Hill	Lowndes	Jno. T. Bickley, 1 qr.	16 97	28 60
(Dis. 26th Sept.) (Re-est. 15th Nov.)		Archer B. Howard, from 30th Nov.	35 91	63 63
Claiborne	Monroe	Jno. N. McClure	218 76	409 69
Clarksville	Clark	John A. Coate	5 47	10 90
Clay Bank	Dale	Jno. B. Heidle	26 40	39 98
Claysville	Marshall	Jno. W. Jones	26 17	47 86
Clayton	Barbour	Benj. F. Petty	109 88	222 36
Clinton	Greene	John H. Copp	215 96	242 90

POST OFFICES—*Alabama.*

Post Offices.	Counties.	Postmasters.	Compensation.	Net proceeds.
Cobb's Store	Madison	Bryant Cobb	$10 69	$19 93
Cochran's Mills	Pickens	Saml. G. Cochran	14 02	26 88
Coffeeville	Clark	John W. Figures	70 81	135 06
Collirene	Lowndes	Claudius G. Rives	31 72	53 55
Columbia	Henry	Saml. L. Solomon	36 67	74 95
Columbiana	Shelby	Samuel Brasher	55 03	118 14
Coosada (Dis. 26th July)	Autauga	John S. Goree, from 1st Ap. to 24th Aug.	2 42	3 53
Corn Grove	Benton	Sevier Elston	21 54	39 43
Cotton Valley	Macon	Frederick Phillips, from 8th Nov.	7 32	13 91
Cottonville	Marshall	David Ricketts	15 93	23 91
County Line	Tallapoosa	Nath. S. Catching, to 31st March.	9 06	14 46
		Lewis H. Fargason.	2 65	4 73
Court Hill	Randolph	Thos. F. Lundie	12 58	24 06
Courtland	Lawrence	John C. Murphey, to 2d Feb.	157 64	333 70
		James C. Watkins	125 52	259 40
Cove Creek	Benton	Wm. P. Reid	5 25	12 23
Cowikee	Barbour	Wm. M. Bethune	10 46	20 59
Crawford	Russell	Eli C. Joiner	101 73	209 44
Cropwell	St. Clair	John Collins	6 33	12 31
Cross Keys	Macon	Richard Stratford	47 35	85 09
Cuba	Jackson	Randolph Ivy	3 30	5 98
Culstia Creek	Cherokee	John Doherty, to 30th Sept.	1 65	3 01
		Alvin N. Moore	5 01	10 39
Cusseta	Chambers	James Oates	112 17	188 70
Dadeville	Tallapoosa	Wm. C. Grisham	107 19	198 54
Daniel's Prairie	Greene	Young L. West	25 28	41 45
Dayton	Marengo	John C. Dansby	158 70	311 41
Decatur	Morgan	James A. Patterson.	248 35	541 65
Delight	Marion	John Barber	no return	
Demopolis	Marengo	Rowan A. Smith, to 29th Nov.	131 79	336 10
		Benajah P. Whitlow	179 53	427 34
Detroit	Marion	James Davison, 3 qrs	10 74	19 37
Diamond Rock	Franklin	Eli Selman	4 92	10 26
Dodsonville	Jackson	Jacob Gross	4 95	9 35
Double Springs	Cherokee	Gabriel Hughes	13 41	27 38
Dover	Russell	Goodman Franklin.	31 16	64 24
Dudleyville	Tallapoosa	Moses S. Buckelew.	87 98	166 91
Eastville	Randolph	Geo. H. Cosper, to 31st March.	5 65	11 57
		James G. Cosper	1 99	4 01
Eldridge	Walker	Eldridge Mallard	9 99	20 20

POST OFFICES—*Alabama.*

Post Offices.	Counties.	Postmasters.	Compensation.	Net proceeds.
Elyton	Jefferson	Thompson Camp	$109 29	$88 86
Enon	Macon	Granville White	69 99	136 26
Erie	Greene	Jas. A. Tallman	73 07	135 90
Eufaula	Barbour	Jacob Smith	568 72	1349 10
Eutaw	Greene	Thomas T. Chiles	434 38	958 91
Evergreen	Conecuh	Edwin Fay, to 31st Dec.	31 94	60 23
		David Davidson	29 50	55 58
Fairfield	Pickens	Richard B. Faircloth	77 57	158 94
Farmersville	Lowndes	Edmund Fowler, to 30th Sept.	9 78	19 47
		Richm'd S. Fletcher	20 16	37 77
Faun's Dale	Marengo	Richard H. Adams	37 55	69 27
Fayette C. H.	Fayette	Azor Vanhoose	51 19	101 86
Fayetteville	Talladega	Augustus W. Blount	36 75	75 37
Fife	Talladega	Thos. J. Caver	49 84	93 06
Flora	Shelby	James Meredith	2 69	6 32
Florence	Lauderdale	Joshua D. Coffee	619 69	1416 16
Forkland	Greene	William'n A. Glover	71 98	133 99
Fort Barbour	Barbour	William Beauchamp	30 65	55 23
Fort Decatur	Macon	Chesley D. Strange	10 08	18 11
Fort Henderson	Macon	James Delbridge	22 80	44 69
Fort Mitchell	Russell	Enoch Johnson	31 26	60 41
Fort Montpelier	Baldwin	Wm. H. Slaughter, from 24th Feb.	2 08	3 17
Fosters	Tuskaloosa	John L. S. Foster	43 72	81 21
Franklin	Henry	Richard C. Spann	32 59	62 44
Fredonia	Chambers	Jno. A. Hurst	65 33	125 09
Fullersville	Barbour	John Hickman, 1 qr	5 24	8 34
Gainer's Store	Pike	Jeremiah Darby	20 34	40 22
Gainesville	Sumter	Rob't G. McMahon	460 23	995 40
Gap	Walker	William Reid	4 89	8 97
Gaston	Sumter	Geo. H. Sheldon	122 09	222 88
Gaylesville	Cherokee	John Wilkinson, 3 qrs	20 47	39 90
Geneva	Coffee	Henry A. Yonge	39 29	81 85
Gilbertsboro'	Limestone	Isaac Edmundson	26 15	50 70
Girard	Russell	James T. Elliott, to 20th November	50 43	95 12
		James S. Moore	95 61	137 47
Glennville	Barbour	Virgil Bobo	151 99	299 24
Gold Hill	Chambers	William Costly, to 31st December	3 47	7 08
		Joseph Rogers	4 68	8 80
Goldville	Tallapoosa	Wm. C. Murdock	46 65	89 43
Goshen	Cherokee	Thos. R. Williams, to 31st December	5 02	9 11
		And'w N. Baird	6 62	13 11

POST OFFICES—*Alabama.*

Post Offices.	Counties.	Postmasters.	Compensation.	Net proceeds.
Gosport	Clark	Samuel Forwood	$39 36	$68 28
Gravelly Springs	Lauderdale	Ross Houston, jr	12 85	24 10
Greens	Jefferson	Benjamin Tarrant, 3 qrs	1 94	3 89
Greensboro'	Greene	John Street	830 83	1750 49
Greenville	Butler	Jas. L. Dunklin	254 35	283 30
Grove Hill	Clark	Isham Kimbell	62 02	130 72
Gunter's Landing	Marshall	Wm. H. Wiggs	23 46	43 18
Hallawoka	Chambers	Wm. H. H. Griffin	15 58	31 43
Hamburgh	Perry	William Spencer	87 71	87 74
Hamilton	Autauga	James Sharp	17 88	29 81
Harpersville	Shelby	Hudson W. Nelson	46 87	91 21
Harrell's ✕ Roads	Dallas	Hardiman J. Harrell, 2 qrs	4 74	7 41
		Whitmil F. Harrell	no ret.	
Hatchers	Talladega	Malcom Munroe, fr. 5th October	1 52	2 70
Havanna	Greene	Thos. H. Hampton	140 17	140 23
Hayneville	Lowndes	Jos. P. Dickson, to 30th September	68 65	157 69
		Ebenezer Marvin	263 71	559 44
Hazle Green	Madison	Wm. C. McDavid, to 31st March	28 02	54 49
		Ch's L. McGehee	7 94	16 04
Hickory Grove	Montgomery	William Moncrief	40 51	75 89
Hickory Level	Talladega	Lewis Pyles	20 15	37 50
Hillabee	Talladega	Archibald Munroe, to 1st October	1 09	1 90
Hilliam's Store	Marshall	Alfred D. Sotherland	1 57	3 66
Hillsborough	Lawrence	Robert Elliott	24 87	50 28
Hinton's Grove	Greene	Wm. W. Paschal	21 05	39 93
Hobbie	Greene	Sam'l D. Reid, from 15th October	8 48	14 82
Holly Grove	Walker	Lucius C. Miller, fr. 1st January	1 35	2 38
Honey Cut	Baldwin	Edw'd P. Brown	no ret.	
Honey Town	Dale	Levi Dowling	13 62	20 43
Hope	Pickens	John A. Boyd, to 31st December	84 50	84 52
		Thos. B. Gardner	89 01	87 74
Hopewell	Greene	Robert Craig	6 76	12 59
Horse Shoe Bend	Tallapoosa	James W. Boley	11 24	21 10
Houston's Store	Morgan	Joseph Hampton	19 89	35 21
Huntsville	Madison	George Cox, to 28th February	1178 05	1088 50
		Dan'l B. Turner	445 15	715 78
Indian Ridge	Clark	Sidney M. Finch, fr. 1st October	4 47	6 08

POST OFFICES—*Alabama.*

Post Offices.	Counties.	Postmasters.	Compensation.	Net proceeds.
Intercourse	Sumter	Isham Daniel	$26 29	$47 76
Isney	Washington	Jehu Everitt	10 97	19 27
Jackson	Clark	Peter Dubose	36 94	70 00
Jackson's Station (Dis. 6th Sept'r.)	De Kalb	Jas L. Skillman	no ret.	
Jacksonville	Benton	George Hoke	235 93	465 72
Jasper	Walker	Jesse D. Beauchamp, to 30th September	11 54	23 03
		Moses Camak	21 50	37 79
Jena	Tuskaloosa	Jacob Holland	10 34	19 05
Jones' Bluff	Sumter	Sam'l O. Scruggs	62 89	113 39
Jonesboro'	Jefferson	Sam'l A. Tarrant	45 67	83 53
Kelly's Creek	St. Clair	Geo. M. Duke	3 29	5 84
Kelly's Springs	Talladega	William Curry	45 30	80 57
Kemp's Creek (Dis. 22d Jan'y.)	Benton	Newman Pounds	no ret.	
Kimulga	Shelby	Louis S. Tulane, 3 qrs	6 77	12 55
Kings	Barbour	James Searcy, to 7th August	97	1 34
		James Wood	14 67	28 09
Kingston	Autauga	John J. G. Johnson	43 57	88 98
Kinlock	Lawrence	Charles Barker	14 51	25 74
Kirkville	Lowndes	James McFarland	31 93	55 00
Knoxville	Greene	Mathew Knox	33 73	57 78
Lacy's Springs	Morgan	Thos. H. Lacy	8 64	8 66
Ladiga	Benton	Chattin D. Scroggin	no ret.	
		William Young, fr. 11th November	7 66	15 09
La Grange	Franklin	James Kennerly	148 51	300 88
Lamar	Randolph	Francis M. Peryman	4 15	5 96
Langston	Jackson	Langston Coffee	6 64	14 33
Larkin's Fork	Jackson	Warn'g P. Robertson	10 56	20 07
Larkinsville	Jackson	David Larkin	14 92	27 72
Laurel Hill	Marengo	William Dossey	2 42	4 23
Lebanon	De Kalb	John G. Winston, jr	49 49	88 58
Leesburgh	Cherokee	Ch's P. Henslee	12 34	26 17
Leighton	Lawrence	William Leigh	120 91	226 54
Lexington	Lauderdale	E. B. Westmoreland	20 86	42 29
Liberty Hill	Dallas	Andrew C. Jackson	92 89	171 67
Linden	Marengo	Jas. N. Hill	172 78	363 52
Line Creek	Montgomery	Jas. M. Goodwin	24 73	43 90
Livingston	Sumter	Rob't F. Houston	493 45	1124 10
Lockland	Macon	Jos. N. Knox	20 67	39 92
Louisville	Barbour	Daniel McKenzie	47 88	98 57
Lower Peach Tree	Wilcox	John W. McCaskey	30 68	50 79

POST OFFICES—*Alabama.*

Post Offices.	Counties.	Postmasters.	Compensation.	Net proceeds.
Loweville	Madison	John Edwards	$64 68	$126 36
Lowndesboro'	Lowndes	Jas. K. Whitman, to 27th May	120 14	241 00
		Archibald Douglass	34 65	48 19
McKinley	Marengo	Elias W. King	37 33	67 50
McMaths	Tuskaloosa	Elisha McMath	26 77	49 38
Macon	Marengo	John Patterson	160 79	305 31
Madison ⋈ Roads	Madison	R. E. Brister	33 11	59 70
Manningham	Butler	Rob't S. Ware, to 31st December	11 35	21 69
		Joseph McGhee	12 20	23 39
Mantua	Pickens	John Storey, from 16th September	8 92	13 71
Maplesville	Bibb	Sam'l H. Cox, 2 qrs (See "Centreville.")	21 14	35 99
Mardisville	Talladega	Stephen Smith	88 38	163 67
Maria Forge (Late "Mountain Spring.")	Talladega	Sam'l S. Riddle, fr. 1st Oct., 2 qrs	7 91	15 97
Marion (Late "Perry C. H.)	Perry	Henry F. Godden	(no ret.)	
Marmion	Lauderdale	Geo. M. Ingram	31 23	54 72
Mars	Bibb	Robert Oldham	17 08	30 15
Martin's Stand (Chan'd to "Summit.")	Blount	Isaac Whorton, 3 qrs	8 93	18 30
Masonville	Lauderdale	John Harrison	20 56	27 73
Meltonsville	Marshall	Kinney C. Carter, 2 qrs	1 31	2 73
Memphis	Pickens	Ibrey J. Kidd	35 25	66 97
Meridianville	Madison	John Kirkland	67 51	130 84
Midway	Barbour	Sam'l Feagin	40 37	75 78
Millport	Fayette	Newton N. Barmore, to 30th Sept	3 59	6 47
		Jas. G. Breuton	8 42	14 75
Milton	Autauga	Wm. H. Bryant	33 46	60 78
Missouri	Pike	Malcom Blue	22 87	42 31
Mobile	Mobile	Jno. W. Townsend	2000 00	23808 25
Monroeville	Monroe	John W. Foster	58 93	131 27
Montevallo	Shelby	Hiram Butler	108 89	205 40
Montgomery	Montgomery	Neill Blue	1921 48	5478 38
Monticello	Pike	Henry Joyce	48 04	89 12
Montpelier	Marengo	Benjamin Du Bose	54 31	54 37
Moore's ⋈ Roads	Macon	Amos Moore	18 46	28 78
Mooresville	Limestone	John H. Hundley, to 31st March	58 62	118 66
		Rob't B. Peebles	23 49	49 30
Morgan Springs	Morgan	Peyton T. Manning	19 83	32 80
Moscow	Marion	Wm. E. Trotter	23 29	42 23
Motts	Clark	Stephen Hearon	30 52	54 73

POST OFFICES—*Alabama.*

Post Offices.	Counties.	Postmasters.	Compensation.	Net proceeds
Moulton	Lawrence	Crockett McDonald.	$154 18	$300 10
Mountain Spring. (Changed to "Maria Forge.")	Talladega	John Long, to 30th Sept.	2 27	4 20
Mount Hickory	Chambers	Thomas Smith	45 93	85 69
Mount Hill	Morgan	Samuel Haslett	6 66	8 64
Mount Hope	Lawrence	Wm. W. Downs	42 65	78 83
Mount Jefferson	Chambers	Henry J. M. Kennon	46 72	84 57
Mount Meigs	Montgomery	Jas. D. Freeny	151 28	230 61
Mount Moriah	Wilcox	Silas M. Wootan	22 15	35 28
Mount Niles	St. Clair	Wm. H. Shotwell	7 21	13 57
Mount Pinson	Jefferson	Zachariah Hagood.	5 85	10 99
Mount Pleasant	Monroe	Josiah Q. Guild	88 62	170 04
Mount Sterling (Dis. 13th Dec.)	Washington	Sanford E. Catterlin	40 03	80 70
Mount Vernon	Mobile	James M. Morgan	71 63	135 60
Mount Willing	Lowndes	A. M. Simmons	59 43	104 92
Mount Zion	De Kalb	James F. Mays	6 00	13 73
Mulberry	Autauga	William H. Boyd	55 04	117 17
Nanafalia	Marengo	Robert D. Marshall.	92 42	90 85
Nathansville	Conecuh	John L. Sansom	10 79	17 77
Newbern	Greene	Alfred Sexton, 3 qrs.	59 62	103 43
Newburgh	Franklin	Jas. R. Page, 3 qrs.	5 90	11 45
New Hope	Madison	George Russell	14 21	27 65
New Lexington	Tuskaloosa	F. W. Woodward	45 43	94 18
New Market	Madison	James F. Skirlock	63 21	127 08
New Prospect	Greene	Benjamin Travis	33 77	61 82
Newton	Dale	Darling Pitman	12 78	26 49
New Wakefield	Washington	James B. Slade	36 44	36 47
Nixburgh	Coosa	Henry Lee	48 43	76 83
Norrisville	Wilcox	Benj. Dulaney, 3 qs.	5 77	10 87
North Bend	De Kalb	John R. Smedley	3 65	5 41
Northport	Tuskaloosa	Lewis Etheridge	110 26	222 88
Oak Bowery	Chambers	Ninian W. Kidd	82 05	166 95
Oakfusky	Randolph	Archibald Sawyer	24 32	46 62
Oak Grove	Montgomery	Charles Kennon	10 16	20 23
Oakville	Lawrence	Thomas Q. Martin.	33 44	60 87
Oceola	Cherokee	James Bradford	5 26	10 21
Old Wash'n C. H.	Washington	Peter Myer	27 77	51 73
Oleander	Marshall	George W. Hale	17 93	32 87
Olney	Pickens	Alex'r M. Hanks, from 16th Sept.	14 76	22 13
Opellikan	Russell	Amos L. Mizell	22 97	39 32
Oselicha	Chambers	Thos. H. Lightfoot.	8 73	13 97
Oswichee	Russell	Sam'l W. Milward.	65 53	112 20
Payneville	Sumter	Ambrose W. Jones.	33 49	68 42
Pea River	Barbour	Harrison F. Bizzell.	9 48	18 58

POST OFFICES—*Alabama.*

Post Offices.	Counties.	Postmasters.	Compensation.	Net proceeds.
Penola	Sumter	Green W. Grant, fr. 28th Aug	$12 50	$21 10
Perry C. H. (Ch. to 'Marion.')	Perry	Henry F. Godden	742 32	1469 55
Perryville	Perry	Exum B. Melton	58 63	123 27
Pickens' Mills	Marengo	James Pickens	16 12	34 83
Pickensville	Pickens	Matthew Lyon	209 47	460 12
Pikeville	Marion	John D. Terrell, jr.	39 13	70 07
Pinckneyville	Tallapoosa	Thos. W. Hatton	12 53	25 39
Pine Grove	Macon	David B. Simpson	9 43	17 85
Pine Hill	Wilcox	George Sheldon	27 44	52 65
Pineville	Marengo	George W. Barney	24 84	52 43
Pint Lala	Montgomery	John Bonham	41 44	56 94
Plantersville	Perry	Thos. S. Driskell	34 31	63 36
Pleasant Grove	Pickens	John W. King	21 76	42 94
Pleasant Hill	Dallas	Green Underwood	113 69	199 48
Pleasant Plains	Marengo	Bowen Seabrook	33 46	67 10
Pleasant Ridge	Greene	Warner H. Lewis, 3 qrs	15 38	28 79
Pleasant Site	Franklin	Andrew George	7 54	15 00
Pleasant Valley	Washington	Robt. F. Hazard	5 25	10 32
Portland	Dallas	Alexander Hall	82 27	154 12
Prairie Bluff	Wilcox	Henry S. Atwood	76 57	154 54
Prairie Hill	Lowndes	William Gordon	19 15	34 14
Preston (Dis. 20th Dec.)	Sumter	Allen M'cDonald	no ret.	
Prospect Ridge	Pike	Isaac N. Hall	19 46	34 17
Providence	Pickens	William C. Henry	25 14	42 84
Randolph	Bibb	Kenneth Morrison	no ret.	
(Disc'd 22d Oct.)		Jared Cole	no ret.	
(Re-es. 7th June.)				
Rawlingsville	De Kalb	Jesse G. Beeson	9 92	20 14
Red Hill	Marshall	Caleb W. Rogers	13 07	26 38
Reform	Pickens	James B. Gladney	92 87	92 89
Richmond	Dallas	Wm. G. McKinnie	141 16	293 63
Ridgeville	Butler	John B. Lewis	13 86	26 53
Roanoke	Randolph	W. M. McClendon	22 02	41 94
Rockford	Coosa	Wm. W. Davison	80 23	149 90
Rockville	Jefferson	And'w S. Hamilton, to 31st Dec	1 67	2 56
		Wm. H. Wood, 1 qr.	69	1 12
Rocky Spring	Jackson	Wm. J. Price	5 35	10 47
Rogersville	Lauderdale	Robert Shane	55 96	108 81
Romulus	Tuskaloosa	John Sanders	2 49	5 29
Russellville	Franklin	Noble R. Ladd	209 89	194 36
St. Stephen's	Washington	James Magoffin	39 63	81 36
Salem	Russell	Henry M. Crowder	51 79	101 01

POST OFFICES—*Alabama.*

Post Offices.	Counties.	Postmasters.	Compensation.	Net proceeds.
Sand Fort	Russell	Robert Allen, to 30th Sept	$13 74	$24 84
		Bluford Colvin, 2 qs.	17 25	31 12
Sandy Ridge	Lowndes	William Payne, to 30th Sept	10 67	19 45
		Andrew J. Perry	24 01	45 74
Sauta	Jackson	James Smith	9 32	18 25
Saw Mill	Dale	John Ard, to 31st Dec'r	8 36	17 59
		Jacob K. Hutto	5 37	11 36
Scottsville	Bibb	Jus. Houghton, 2 qrs.	18 67	36 32
		David Scott	25 79	53 08
Scroggins' Mills	Dale	Edmund Black, 3 qs.	6 10	13 12
Selma	Dallas	John M. Strong	457 30	954 29
Sepulga	Conecuh	Andrew E. Jackson.	23 44	39 84
Sharon	Chambers	Thomas Shannon	29 35	49 89
Sharpesville	Montgomery.	Nath'l. W. Bush	11 39	22 24
Sheffield, (Dis. 2d Jan.)	Fayette	Henry P. Leonard, to 30th Sept	3 13	4 92
Shelby Springs	Shelby	Edward McNair	3 66	7 39
Shiloh	Marengo	Thomas Hosea	44 75	89 53
Shoal Ford	Limestone	Hez. B. Cartwright.	141 23	139 90
Silver Run	Talladega	Philip Archer	13 59	19 38
Sipsey Turnpike	Tuskaloosa	William C. Tierce	no ret.	
Snow Hill	Wilcox	James S. Benson	24 97	49 43
Society Hill	Macon	James Torbert	66 51	112 57
Soceopatoy	Coosa	William Winslett, to 30th Sept	10 81	20 31
		James L. Burgess	34 48	65 84
Somerville	Morgan	Christopher Welch.	145 49	238 34
Souchahatchee	Macon	Jacob Rape	21 92	37 06
South Canebrake.	Perry	Peter Vannorden	26 38	53 54
Sparta	Conecuh	Austin J. Robertson	84 36	160 36
Springfield	Greene	Lewis A. Ragsdale.	61 46	109 21
Spring Garden	Cherokee	James Montgomery.	19 91	41 56
Spring Hill	Marengo	Rush Tuller	89 17	180 14
Springville	St. Clair	Jos. H. Meanes	11 67	21 73
Starlington	Butler	Albert Butler	9 43	16 60
Stockton	Baldwin	Ward Taylor	60 54	105 84
Stroud's Creek	Chambers	John Terry, 3 qrs.	3 47	5 19
Suggsville	Clark	Samuel Coale	70 78	135 86
Summit	Blount	Isaac Whorton	no ret.	
(Late "Martin's Stand.")		Ab'm W. Arnold	3 81	7 19
Sumterville	Sumter	George Rix	161 30	286 05
Sylacauga	Talladega	A. M. Graham, to 31st Dec'r	39 53	74 09
		Geo. W. Johnson	26 35	52 32
Talladega	Talladega	James G. L. Huey	333 71	685 37

POST OFFICES—*Alabama.*

Post Offices.	Counties.	Postmasters.	Compensation.	Net proceeds.
Tallassee	Tallapoosa	Eli B. Scurlock	$31 07	$60 92
Tensaw	Baldwin	Z. P. Scott, to 31st Dec'r	25 32	48 13
		Alexander B. Conch, to 1st June	21 95	42 23
		Charles Daniels	3 93	8 41
Terrapin Creek	Cherokee	John Snider	7 38	13 93
Thorn Hill	Walker	George D. Cleere	9 62	14 40
Tiara	Montgomery	Zepheniah John	9 88	15 63
Toll Gate	Marion	Charles Thomas	16 79	38 53
Top Level	Dallas	Thompson M. Jackson, 1 qr	2 03	3 05
Trenton	Jackson	Thomas M. King	7 31	15 24
Triana	Madison	Edmund Toney	76 02	140 78
Troy	Pike	Thomas M. Harris	67 05	137 74
Truss	Jefferson	Thomas K. Truss	9 89	19 01
Turkeytown	Cherokee	James A. Patterson	19 09	36 94
Turnbull	Monroe	Thomas M. Riley	59 21	111 56
Turnpike (Dis. 31st Jan.)	Coosa	Thomas C. Dunlap, 2 qrs	11 19	22 12
Tuscahoma	Washington	David M. Dunlap, to 30th Sept	2 22	3 99
		C. N. Wilcox	4 95	9 56
Tuscumbia	Franklin	Jonas J. Bell	1758 56	
Tuskaloosa	Tuskaloosa	Wm. D. Marrast	1477 98	4137 81
Tuskegee	Macon	John B. Bilbro	538 20	1137 70
Uchee	Russell	Wilkins Smith	55 07	101 16
Union	Greene	William Miller	35 28	60 37
Union Springs	Macon	Wm. H. Waugh	138 33	257 90
Uniontown	Perry	Alex. J. Sanderson	263 88	493 41
Uphaupee	Macon	Chas. F. Gleaton, to 31st Dec'r	17 47	32 93
		John W. Pon	13 94	26 35
Valley Creek	Dallas	James V. Pettibone	118 57	238 52
Valley Head	De Kalb	George C. White	7 22	13 79
Valverdi	Macon	Albert G. Wray, 3 qrs	18 12	27 66
Van Buren	De Kalb	Simpson C. Newman	26 47	52 82
Vernon	Autauga	Lewis Simpson, to 5th June	97 59	176 96
		Robert W. Simpson	5 62	12 33
Vienna	Pickens	Reuben Weaver	60 80	121 27
Village Springs	Blount	Thomas H. Camp	16 15	31 65
Warrenton	Marshall	Montg'y Gilbreath	101 45	95 24
Warrior Bridge (Ch'd to "Bladon's Springs.")	Washington	Jos. A. Huber, to 30th Sept	4 20	8 39

POST OFFICES—*Florida.*

Post Offices.	Counties.	Postmasters.	Compensation.	Net proceeds.
Warsaw .... (Lt. "Jamest'n.")	Sumter........	Bennett B. Bell, to 20th July........	$11 13	$20 86
		Lewis Houston....	143 71	267 56
Washington......	Autauga.....	Seth V. Roberts, to 31st March......	89 65	188 48
		Casimere Krout....	30 31	63 78
Waterloo........	Lauderdale ..	James Humphrey..	27 07	57 42
Weedowee......	Randolph....	Ira P. Culbreath....	51 57	92 09
Weehadkee......	Randolph....	Fred'k W. Chandler	12 76	23 41
Weewokaville ...	Talladega ...	Adam Riser........	73 03	128 12
Wetumpka......	Coosa.......	Leander Bryan.....	664 24	1691 45
White Hall......	Marengo.....	Wiley Fort........	19 70	37 64
White Plains....	Benton......	Arthur T. Crozier, to 6th Sept.......	10 68	17 71
		Elijah Teague......	41 83	72 47
Whitesburgh....	Madison	Joel R. Love.......	44 81	42 91
White Water....	Pike........	Dan'l H. Horn, 2 qs.	0 18	0 44
Wickliffe........	Chambers....	Charles Simpson...	22 56	38 91
Williams' X Roads (Ch. to 'Yantley')	Sumter......	William Anderson, 2 qrs............	19 60	35 82
Wilsonville......	Shelby.......	James O'Hara.....	15 18	28 73
Womacks.......	Wilcox	David N. Sanders..	9 52	17 91
Woodardville....	Marengo.....	James H. Saint	15 86	30 49
Woodlawn.....	Dallas.......	Wheeler Randall...	12 99	22 67
Woodsboro'.....	Shelby......	William Woodruff.	13 03	23 39
Wood Shop.....	Dale........	Jno. J. Andrews ...	9 54	17 95
Woodville.......	Jackson.....	Migginson Loving..	16 17	31 21
Yantley......... (Late "Williams' X Roads.")	Sumter.......	William Anderson..	18 89	35 49
Yorkville........	Pickens......	Alexander Brownlee	31 74	68 07
Young's X Roads	Lauderdale..	Thos. K. Young....	12 11	24 29
Youngsville......	Tallapoosa ..	Reuben G. Young..	57 80	99 05

FLORIDA.

NOTE.—Compensation of Postmasters, and net proceeds of their offices, from July 1, 1844, to June 30, 1845.

Post Offices.	Counties.	Postmasters.	Compensation.	Net proceeds.
Alligator	Columbia ...	Asa A. Stewart, to 25th Oct........	$17 30	$34 40
		Washington M. Ives	38 57	64 60
Almirante	Walton	Dan'l A. Wilkinson	14 10	22 12
Apalachicola.....	Franklin	Geo. F. Baltzell....	1002 37	2852 39

POST OFFICES—*Florida.*

Post Offices.	Counties.	Postmasters.	Compensation.	Net proceeds.
Aucilla	Jefferson	Ayles B. Shehee	$37 27	$73 79
Augusta	Benton	Albert Clark, from 28th Feb'y	2 97	5 40
Benton	Hamilton	Allen G. Johnson	6 62	10 74
Blount's Ferry	Columbia	William Cone	No ret.	
		James L. King, from 13th May	1 13	2 26
Blountstown (Dis. 23d Oct.)	Calhoun	Shadrach Sutton, fr. 1st Oct., '43, to 1st Oct., '44	0 96	2 25
Camp Izard	Marion	John Bates, from 10th March	0 01	0 02
Casonville	Columbia	Joseph Dowling	No ret.	
Cedar Key	Leon	Augustus Steele, fr. 21st June	0 31	0 75
Chattahoochee	Gadsden	John B. Lewis, to 31st March	45 77	81 71
		Duncan Baker	20 16	25 60
Cherry Lake	Madison	Lucius Church, 2 qs.	6 57	12 58
China Hill	Gadsden	Zabud Fletcher	17 63	32 97
Chocochattee	Benton	Isaac Garrason, from 26th Feb'y	6 83	7 77
Columbus	Columbia	I. Wm. C. Loud	61 20	130 70
Ellisville	Columbia	Giles U. Ellis	12 90	22 31
Emathla	Marion	Jas. N. Badger	No ret.	
Enterprize	Orange	Wm. B. Fail	No ret.	
Fort Dade	Benton	Wm. S. Spencer, fr. 19th March	1 38	0 86
Fort Hamilton	Madison	Sam'l J. Perry	2 77	4 15
Fort Harlee	Alachua	Wyatt C. Allen	No ret.	
Fort King	Marion	John G. Reardon	45 55	79 84
Garey's Ferry	Duval	Amazia Coy	52 82	88 52
Gum Swamp	Madison	Robt. H. Shaffer, fr. 1st Jan'y	5 48	7 25
Holmes' Valley	Washington	William Miller	16 40	29 88
Homasassa	Benton	William Cooley, fr. 1st Feb'y	2 38	3 31
Iola (Dis. 6th Sept.)	Calhoun	John S. Hunter, 1 qr	1 34	2 94
Jacksonville	Duval	John M. Pons	353 63	675 81
Jasper	Hamilton	Perry G. Wall	29 41	46 64

POST OFFICES—*Florida.*

Post Offices.	Counties.	Postmasters.	Compensation.	Net proceeds.
Key West	Monroe	L. W. Smith, to 30th Sept	$53 63	$106 13
		Walter C. Maloney	229 07	516 98
Lipona	Jefferson	Octavius H. Gadsden	10 12	18 32
Little River	Columbia	Geo. E. McClellan, to 18th June	22 87	36 69
		Hugh A. Corley	1 03	1 98
Madison	Madison	John Westcott, 3 qs.	72 46	133 51
Mandarin	Duval	Calvin Read	35 53	64 09
Mannington	Leon	Reuben Manning	10 31	17 63
Mariana	Jackson	Wash'n Chapman	314 05	434 33
Marion	Jefferson	James C. Johnston	62 12	115 42
Micanopy	Alachua	Augustus E. Noyes	39 49	80 19
Miccosukee	Leon	George E. Dennis	53 30	99 56
Milton	Santa Rosa	Lawrence N. Amos	76 87	159 22
Mineral Springs	Columbia	Thos. D. Dexter	34 14	65 03
Monticello	Jefferson	Darius Williams	196 03	362 16
Newnansville	Alachua	Thos. I. Prevatt	154 58	308 02
Newport	Leon	Amos M. Alexander	98 17	199 36
New Smyrna		John Sheldon	No ret.	
Oaky Hill	Jackson	Robert Potter	3 80	7 50
Ochesee	Jackson	Isaac Jackson, to 31st Dec'r	5 45	10 76
		Lenn Griffin	8 41	16 75
Okahumka	Marion	James Caruthers, fr. 19th Feb'y	1 17	1 50
Pensacola	Escambia	Hanson Kelly	873 65	2342 19
Picolata	St. Johns	George Colee	73 77	81 03
Pilatka	St. Johns	James B. Cole	24 73	41 22
Piney Grove	Nassau	Henry F. Parmenter	No ret.	
Quincy	Gadsden	John T. Seegar	402 92	698 27
St. Augustine	St. Johns	Peter C. Zylstra	716 41	1459 14
St. Johns Bluff	Duval	Jno R. Mitchell, fr. 9th Sept., 8¾ mos.	7 68	9 36
St. Joseph	Calhoun	Jas. P. Penn, to 15th Feb'y	17 93	38 62
		Nehemiah Hayden	7 07	14 78
St. Marks	Wakulla	Francis B. Whiting	54 71	112 15
Scurlock's Spring	Jackson	Britton Barkley	39 08	67 45
Shell Point	Wakulla	Henry H. Walker	5 86	10 67
Spring Grove	Alachua	Isaac Garrason	No ret.	
Sugar Valley	Murray	Elias King	No ret.	

POST OFFICES—*Mississippi.*

Post Offices.	Counties.	Postmasters.	Compensation.	Net proceeds.
Tallahassee......	Leon.........	Miles Nash.........	$870 82	$2543 19
Talofa..........	Madison......	Jno. S. Broome.....	28 26	46 18
Tampa..........	Hillsborough	Manuel Olivella.....	105 33	225 15
Uchee Anna.....	Walton.......	James McLean.......	39 80	68 93
Wacahootie......	Marion........	Cotton Rawls, to 28th Feb'y.......	13 37	28 07
		George Helvenston.	6 53	12 87
White Springs....	Hamilton......	Wm. M. Reed......	7 77	7 40
Woodland........	Hamilton.....	Robt. B. Clayton....	14 95	25 17
Woodstock Mills.	Nassau.......	Edwin R. Alberti, fr. 10th Sept.........	42 28	84 72

MISSISSIPPI.

NOTE.—Compensation of Postmasters, and net proceeds of their offices, from July 1, 1844, to June 30, 1845.

Post Offices.	Counties.	Postmasters.	Compensation.	Net proceeds.
Abberville.......	La Fayette..	John B. Davis, 3 qrs.	$11 11	$19 51
Aberdeen.........	Monroe......	David Clarke......	581 68	1344 31
Adamsville......	Panola.......	James M. Adams...	25 26	50 43
Alamutcha.......	Lauderdale...	Daniel Cameron....	37 24	77 05
Athens..........	Monroe......	William Hill.......	64 12	120 48
		For Quincy, $1 39 comp., $3 26 net pr.		
Auburn.........	Hinds......	John M. Murchison	39 70	74 05
Augusta.........	Perry.......	H. H. McComb....	20 24	39 60
Bachelor's Bend.. (Late "Egg's	Washington.. Point.")	Isaac B. Beall, from 16th Feb.........	25 74	49 38
Bay Springs.....	Tishemingo .	Robert Lowry.....	5 65	9 09
Beatie's Bluff....	Madison	Henry Amsden, jr.	30 83	55 79
Belle Fontaine ...	Choctaw	Thomas J. Greer...	55 71	122 54
Belmont.........	Panola......	Henry Laird.......	182 90	375 70
Benton..........	Yazoo.......	Malatha A. Jenkins, 3 qrs..........	254 75	613 14
Biloxi..........	Harrison	Charles Bellman, to 31st March.......	26 05	47 87
		Isaac B. Currie.....	10 06	20 08
Black Hawk.....	Carroll......	William Gillespie, to 28th April.......	100 57	128 00
		James E. Farmer...	23 87	42 34
Black Oak.......	Tallahatchie.	Jos. A Young......	14 08	26 59

POST OFFICES—*Mississippi.*

Post Offices.	Counties.	Postmasters.	Compensation.	Net proceeds.
Black's Store	Tippah	Andrew L. Gatlin	$12 28	$25 11
Black Water	Kemper	Aug. E. McInnis, to 31st Dec	18 17	36 19
		Leroy Brewer	16 14	24 69
Bolands	Itawamba	William Boland	31 96	62 67
Bolivar	Bolivar	Chris. J. Field, 11 months	12 41	25 08
Bolton's Depot	Hinds	C. A. Walton, from 11th Feb	6 96	13 83
Border Spring	Lowndes	Wm. M. Payne	32 64	42 95
Bovina	Warren	David F. Cowan	60 39	100 61
Brandon	Rankin	Alex'r McDonnell	217 62	440 44
Brook Haven	Lawrence	Samuel Jayne	39 08	63 80
Brooklyn	Noxubee	John T. Ball	66 04	119 87
Brownsville	Hinds	C. A. Lanier	107 81	217 55
Buckhorn	Winston	Wiley W. Coleman, from 24th Dec	4 64	8 04
Burlingham	Panola	J. S. Kennedy, 1 qr.	2 96	6 01
Burtons	Tishemingo	Elijah Blythe	7 36	13 81
Burtonton	Copiah	Jacob K. Hill	28 12	52 62
Caledonia	Lowndes	Wm. G. Wright	25 87	44 74
California	Yalla Busha	John G. Brody	8 65	17 68
Camden	Madison	Anthaires Purviance	110 53	209 08
Canton	Madison	James Priestly, to 6th March	455 56	884 13
		William Priestly	219 59	436 78
Carlile's Mills	Perry	Jehu Carlile	9 02	16 18
Carrollsville	Tishemingo	Richard B. Clayton	53 43	100 47
Carrollton	Carroll	William Sanders, to 31st March	211 31	496 91
		Wm. M. Young	70 10	170 65
Cartersville	Tishemingo	John C. Carter	43 92	86 45
Carthage	Leake	U. R. Bobbitt, to 31st March	34 44	74 29
		Sewall Brown	15 28	31 68
Cayuga	Hinds	George W. Belcher	55 87	99 01
Centenary College	Rankin	James H. Belt	106 58	224 57
Centre Plain	Pike	Peter A. Quinn, from 1st Jan	4 28	7 51
Centreville	Amite	Robert Germany	73 76	146 49
Charleston	Tallahatchie	Edwin E. Armstrong	90 70	173 75
Chickasawhay	Clark	Wm. J. Houze	5 34	11 29
China Grove	Pike	Wm. B. Ligon	39 50	69 03
Choctaw Agency	Oktibbeha	Gustavus A. Batte	92 40	180 60
Chulahoma	Marshall	Samuel A. Wallace	158 52	295 25
Church Hill	Jefferson	Wm. C. Donoho	88 60	145 79
Claiborne	Jasper	Oliver C. Rhodes	13 83	20 49
Clairbornesville	Yazoo	Samuel Dilly	20 68	38 78

POST OFFICES—*Mississippi*.

Post Offices.	Counties.	Postmasters.	Compensation.	Net proceeds.
Clinton	Hinds	Seneca Pratt	$431 44	$934 37
Coffadeliah	Neshoba	Wm. F. Allen	11 59	22 42
Coffeeville	Yalla Busha	Chs. A. Davis	282 09	582 85
Colbert	Lowndes	James M. Capshaw	137 04	255 78
Cold Spring	Wilkinson	Meredith Meador	39 03	65 81
Columbia	Marion	Abram Bloom	52 68	109 92
Columbus	Lowndes	David P. Blair	1282 61	2982 28
Commerce	Tunica	Charles May	21 76	46 23
Como	De Soto	George Alexander, from 13th Aug	17 95	32 69
Cooksville	Noxubee	Fred'k D. Bulluck, from 17th July to 31st March	28 39	55 92
		Felix H. Walker	8 26	16 78
Cornersville	La Fayette	Benjamin F. Ruff, to 31st Dec	9 50	20 09
		James M. McCain	9 43	20 90
Cotton Gin Port	Monroe	Johnson Bickerstaff	126 89	241 76
Cotton Plant	Tippah	Andrew Jones	14 85	27 74
Cotton Ridge	Itawamba	Edmund Gannaway	16 24	29 17
County Line	Scott	Thomas M. Pettey	12 57	22 80
Cripple Deer	Tishemingo	Christopher Kays, from 16th July	6 37	8 43
Cross Roads	Jackson	William Holland	4 62	6 63
Cuddyhunk	Yalla Busha	Wm. H. Lovejoy	15 44	26 98
Cypress Creek	La Fayette	Lewis T. Wynn, to 13th April	29 48	55 85
		Benj. F. Withers	8 07	16 14
Daileys ✕ Roads	Lowndes	John A. Dailey	60 80	127 03
Daleville	Lauderdale	L. B. Moore	49 39	96 89
Danville	Tishemingo	T. Brewster; 1 qr	0 72	1 69
Decatur	Newton	Jonathan D. Finch, to 26th August	12 78	21 31
		Wm. W. Drinkwater	46 54	83 62
Deer Brook	Noxubee	Alex'r B. Stevens	59 03	115 69
De Kalb	Kemper	Archibald C. Adams	129 11	259 26
Delta	Coahoma	John C. Hayes	74 18	151 76
Double Springs	Oktibbeha	Asa Reed	7 91	15 54
Dry Creek	Covington	Joseph McAfee	27 37	45 77
Dumas	Tippah	Jackson D. Dumas, from 22d Feb	4 83	7 81
Eastport	Tishemingo	John Buttrill	54 35	91 74
Edinburg	Leake	Johnson M. Hooper	21 27	39 17
Edwards' Depot	Hinds	Theodore Jungherr	84 02	162 92
Egg's Point (Ch'd to Bachelor's Bend.)	Washington	Theodorick J. James, to 7th Feb	47 53	103 61
(Re-est'd 3d Mar.)		Theodorick J. James, from April 1	15 04	33 73

POST OFFICES—*Mississippi.*

Post Offices.	Counties.	Postmasters.	Compensation.	Net proceeds.
Electra	Monroe	Wm. D. Nabors	$16 19	$26 58
Ellistown	Pontotoc	Aaron W. Moore, from 24th July	7 72	15 05
Ellisville	Jones	John H. Powell	14 65	25 89
Elm Grove	De Soto	William Graham	27 80	47 88
Eutaw	De Soto	Moses M. White	45 15	81 55
Fairview	Pontotoc	George W. Henry	35 50	66 26
Farmington	Tishemingo	Benjamin Bruton	45 16	93 20
Fayette	Jefferson	John B. Carpenter	243 96	412 27
Fayette Hill	Simpson	Jeremiah Baugh, fr. 4th Dec	1 22	2 07
Fearn's Springs	Winston	Hugh McQuien	26 58	48 76
Fordsville	Marion	W. M. Rankin, 3 qrs	8 36	15 59
Fort Adams	Wilkinson	Seth Kline	84 50	155 19
Franklin	Holmes	William Coleman	213 99	210 29
Fulton	Itawamba	John Thomason	160 97	308 79
Gainesville	Hancock	Chs. A. Folsom	41 86	91 87
Gallatin	Copiah	Benjamin King	216 85	275 70
Garlandville	Jasper	Benj'n F. Reynolds, to 31st March	17 62	32 96
		James M. Williams	20 23	35 78
Georgetown	Copiah	Benj. H. Catching	32 15	58 65
Gholson	Noxubee	Wiley T. Seitzler	54 53	103 86
Grand Gulph	Claiborne	James Francis	318 21	665 61
Graysport	Yalla Busha	Wm. C. Bryarly	49 10	89 61
Greensborough	Choctaw	Daniel M. Johnson	162 93	280 72
Greenwood	Carroll	Wm. N. Miller	70 13	143 81
Grenada	Yalla Busha	James Sims	536 67	949 58
Grub Springs	Monroe	Benjamin T. Rees	8 37	12 55
Habolochitto	Hancock	Leonard Kimball	15 43	28 40
Hamburg	Franklin	John Barrett	57 17	62 75
Hamilton	Monroe	Griffin Roberts	25 32	44 75
Hammet	Issaquena	S. W. Wills	no return	
Hatchy Turnpike	Tippah	James Box	no return	
Herbert	Neshoba	William Herbert, to 31st Dec	38 56	84 35
		William Turner	18 38	39 07
Hernando	De Soto	Jos. R. Ferguson, to 25th Jan	169 52	349 84
		Jos. O. Lusher	124 76	271 22
Hickory Flat	Tippah	Joseph Marmon	26 47	49 22
Hickory Grove	Oktibbeha	James King	27 82	41 35
Hillsboro'	Scott	Alfred Eastland	103 75	194 65
Holly Springs	Marshall	Wm. E. Williams, to 22d Jan	382 88	1021 88
		Robert S. Greer	373 26	848 49

POST OFFICES—*Mississippi.*

Post Offices.	Counties.	Postmasters.	Compensation.	Net proceeds.
Holmesville	Pike	Linus H. Bridges	$123 33	$242 63
Hopahka	Leake	Jas. Lucky, to 19th August	5 28	10 72
		Robert J. Hall	46 13	55 46
Houston	Chickasaw	James Laughridge, to 1st Feb	89 56	184 31
		Jos. Lancaster, from 1st April	47 04	93 55
Hudsonville	Marshall	James H. Cowan	65 61	129 39
Hurricane Creek	Clark	Benj'n F. Willis	8 36	14 52
Jacinto	Tishemingo	Chrisley D. Key	129 88	164 28
Jackson	Hinds	Howell Hobbs	1382 58	3627 90
Jackson C. H.	Jackson	Samuel Davis	8 44	17 95
Jaynesville	Covington	Joshua R. White, jr.	15 60	28 42
Johnson	Warren	Benj'n F. Johnson	8 44	18 01
Kellertown	Wilkinson	Wade H. Gaulden	25 08	46 15
Kilmichael	Choctaw	Henry P. Barnes, to 2d May	17 89	36 54
		John Flowers	4 28	8 20
Kingston	Adams	Hiram Fowler, to 30th Sept	12 34	26 82
		Ammi P. Sweetser	35 27	64 62
Kosciusko	Attala	Silas H. Clark	219 76	422 96
Lamar	Marshall	Jas. H. Potts, to 4th March	98 56	190 86
		Tim'ns L. Treadwell	52 19	94 79
Lane's Landing	Issaquena	J. A. Lane	no return	
Leakesville	Greene	Danl. F. McInnes, 3 qrs	5 76	11 61
Lexington	Holmes	William Boyle	327 05	745 10
Liberty	Amite	Alexan'r McKowen	222 11	414 75
Lincoln	Yazoo	Martin Anding, to 30th Sept	12 02	22 65
		Franklin Davis	36 39	69 88
Linden	Copiah	Jacob B. Reid	26 94	52 33
Line Store	Hinds	Henry Mims	128 84	128 90
Livingston	Madison	Figures Lowe	93 35	191 54
Lockhart's Store	Holmes	Memucan Horton	26 51	53 45
Locust Hill	Adams	Stephen Kennedy	24 51	37 71
Louisville	Winston	James Phagan	304 19	417 80
McArson's Stand	De Soto	Wm. McArson, 3 qrs	32 45	62 44
McCall's Creek	Franklin	Thos. A. Magee, to 6th Nov	7 81	16 15
		Ahab K. Oncal	13 20	25 35
McLeod's	Greene	Norman McLeod	4 13	6 61

POST OFFICES—*Mississippi.*

Post Offices.	Counties.	Postmasters.	Compensation.	Net proceeds.
McManus	Greene	John McInnis	$3 75	$6 66
Macon	Noxubee	Sam. K. McIlhenny, to 14th April	235 96	539 36
		Isaac D. Wellborn	67 14	149 30
Madisonville	Madison	Jas. R. Russell	46 82	85 58
Malcolm	Jefferson	Malcolm Gilchrist	29 49	40 79
Marion	Lauderdale	Lewis Smith, to 14th Oct.	46 16	81 92
		Jas. M. Pigott	109 62	202 68
Mashulaville	Noxubee	John M. Cade	38 50	67 74
Meadville	Franklin	Wm. M. Ducker, to 29th July	3 80	8 60
		Stephen L. Guice	75 22	123 95
Meridian Springs	Hinds	Norvel R. Granberry	36 99	75 26
Middleton	Carroll	A. S. S. Newton	194 36	367 38
Midway	Madison	Saml. H. Lancaster	26 96	54 37
Mill Dale	Warren	Wm. L. Allen	47 30	89 61
Milton	La Fayette	William Sullivant	22 12	42 60
Miltonville	Wayne	Wm. G. Horne	18 07	30 57
Mingo Houma	Lauderdale	Henry Forbes	60 33	118 32
Mississippi City	Hancock	Wm. A. Champlin	46 66	90 35
Montgomery	Madison	A. V. Montgomery	10 86	18 81
Monticello	Lawrence	Don'n F. N. Turner	168 47	350 92
Mount Carmel	Covington	Alex'r H. Hall	22 41	44 68
Mount Olympus	Madison	Francis G. Greene	25 75	46 58
Mount Pleasant	Wilkinson	Dan. McGahey, 3 qrs	9 27	13 70
Nashville	Lowndes	Jno. A. B. Nash, to 31st Dec	15 82	31 23
		N. N. Nash	20 21	40 00
Natchez	Adams	Woodson Wren	1357 55	4596 62
New Albany	Pontotoc	Ira M. Camp	56 09	115 10
Newtown	Hinds	Lewis B. Hemphill	44 31	64 25
North Mount Pleasant	Marshall	Eli McNabb	109 54	225 23
Oakachickama	Yalla Busha	Wm. B. Wilbourn	63 20	119 04
Oak Grove	Chickasaw	Martin Murphree	22 10	43 68
Oakland	Yalla Busha	John B. Ashe	86 44	170 52
Oakland College	Claiborne	John Chamberlain	70 24	131 33
Oak Ridge	Marshall	Joab Maxey	35 08	66 16
Oaktibbeha	Kemper	Wm. A. Davis	8 56	16 55
Ofahoma	Madison	Washington Ford, to 3d Sept.	5 06	10 14
		Benj. T. Watkins	21 83	31 18
Orangeburgh	Marion	Stephen H. Wilks, to 13th Aug.	74	1 54
		William Barnes	6 39	13 25
Oxford	La Fayette	James E. Sheegog	321 84	638 96

POST OFFICES—*Mississippi.*

Post Offices.	Counties.	Postmasters.	Compensation.	Net proceeds.
Palestine.	Adams.	Richard K. Becktel.	$25 88	$45 77
Panola.	Panola.	Jas. C. Armstrong.	147 54	297 48
Parkerville	Noxubee.	Jos. W. Park, 1 qr.	83	1 63
Pascagoula	Jackson.	Lorenzo Post.	79 81	164 24
Pass Christian.	Harrison.	Finley B. Hiern, to 20th Nov.	57 68	129 21
		Sarah A. Hiern.	19 86	35 17
Paulding.	Jasper.	Simeon R. Adams.	137 88	235 71
Pearlington.	Hancock.	Elisha Benjamin, to 12th Feb.	17 75	34 53
		Geo. W. Robinson.	8 69	18 37
Philadelphia.	Neshoba.	Isaac Enloe.	73 53	140 24
Pigeon Roost.	Choctaw.	Seth C. Platner.	6 30	12 28
Pikeville.	Chickasaw.	Iredell P. Vaughan.	34 87	69 53
Pinkneyville.	Wilkinson.	Samuel Robinson.	74 49	138 23
Pine Bluff.	Copiah.	Stephen Tillman.	21 62	43 29
Planters.	Attala.	Alanson Nash.	12 73	27 10
Pleasant Mount.	Panola.	Elijah Wilbourn.	17 86	33 12
Pleasant Ridge.	Itawamba.	Andrew McClalen.	5 95	11 44
Pleasant Springs.	Kemper.	Le Roy B. Gaston.	11 11	22 35
Plymouth.	Lowndes.	John Billington, to 3d Feb.	17 55	25 74
		James Swearingen.	4 83	9 63
Pontotoc.	Pontotoc.	Wm. W. Leland, to 31st Dec.	199 44	442 64
		Jno. M. McPherson	215 29	491 48
Port Gibson.	Claiborne.	Richard Parkinson.	435 10	1058 95
Prairie.	Tishemingo.	John B. Smith.	4 68	8 70
Prairie Hill.	Lowndes.	Abram Belton.	31 37	59 78
Prairie Mount.	Chickasaw.	Littleberry Gilliam, from 2d Sept.	21 66	42 42
Prairie Point.	Noxubee.	Wm. H. Smith.	58 27	102 01
Preston.	Yalla Busha.	James N. Harper.	52 84	93 49
Princeton.	Washington.	Thos. J. Likens.	134 84	280 68
Quincy. (Dis. 16th May.)	Monroe.	Thos. C. Greenwood, to 31st Dec. (See "Athens.")	7 76	13 91
Quitman.	Clark.	Wm. H. P. Pool, to 20th May.	51 37	94 00
		Wm. A. White.	9 10	18 53
Ragdale's Stand.	La Fayette.	Jason C. Wilson.	42 01	69 84
Raleigh.	Smith.	James Lowry.	58 64	114 39
Raymond.	Hinds.	D. Peyton Harrison, to 24th Jan.	219 46	450 52
		Lucas D. Isom, 1 qr.	47 42	121 39
Red Land.	Pontotoc.	Thos. H. Williams.	25 38	48 90
Reid's Store.	Copiah.	Jesse P. Hargrave.	27 52	53 70

POST OFFICES—*Mississippi.*

Post Offices.	Counties.	Postmasters.	Compensation.	Net proceeds.
Rice's X Roads..	Panola......	Robert Clanton	$52 29	$111 07
Riceville	Hancock.....	Wm. G. Wheat ...	12 07	24 47
Richland.........	Holmes......	Levi Hurlbutt	100 55	212 38
Rienzi	Tishemingo .	Chs. W. Williams .	30 86	58 54
Ripley...........	Tippah	Simon R. Spight ...	252 66	497 63
Robinia..........	Panola......	William Rupe, from 29th July	8 44	17 07
Rocky Ford......	Pontotoc	Willis Jones.......	11 37	24 22
Rocky Mount ...	Kemper.....	Jno. H. Oden......	7 08	15 64
Rocky Spring ...	Claiborne ...	Galen Norton......	69 42	123 26
Rodney..........	Jefferson	Andrew B. Logan..	233 79	564 74
Rose Hill	Amite	Henry Hunt......	17 50	30 83
Salem	Tippah	Thomas Toombes..	188 23	367 32
Sandy Hill.......	Scott	Jno. S. Ludlow, fr'm 26th July........	5 77	12 72
Santee...........	Covington...	Elias Redman	6 10	9 49
Sarepta	La Fayette..	Moses Church.....	38 49	71 61
Satartia	Yazoo	Henry Douglas. ...	96 99	172 52
Selsartown ...... (Dis. 24th Oct.)	Adams......	Joseph Mix.	no return	
Senatobia	De Soto.....	Nathl. L. Harris...	69 28	140 67
Sharon..........	Madison	Matthew C. Cayce .	166 23	315 45
Shieldsboro'.....	Hancock....	John B. Tonline ...	34 30	66 96
Shongalo........	Carroll	Charles Kopperl ...	108 15	218 08
Silver Creek.....	Issaquena ...	Albert G. Bennett, from 4th May ...	1 62	3 79
Smith's Mills....	Carroll......	Thos. M. Smith ...	18 78	36 22
Snowsville	Choctaw	David Boyd.......	33 48	66 04
Spring Cottage...	Marion	James Ford	10 93	21 95
Springfield	Madison	J. T. Hollingsworth	6 16	12 82
Spring Hill......	Tippah	Homer Rainey	24 21	45 68
Spring Ridge	Hinds	John Raney.......	24 35	47 39
Starkville.......	Oktibbeha...	James Bell	183 73	347 90
Stewart's	Choctaw	Sidney S. Elkin....	25 97	50 77
Tacaluche	Marshall....	Erasmus F. Potts ..	10 53	19 20
Tallabincla	Pontotoc	Leroy H. Allen....	16 52	32 76
Tchula..........	Holmes.	David D. Bell......	81 51	163 45
Thomastown	Leake	John M. Yates.....	26 08	53 64
Toler's	Amite.......	James M. Gallent ..	20 45	34 29
Troy	Yalla Busha .	Geo. W. Tapp	56 00	104 71
Tuscahoma.	Tallahatchie .	Th. R. Girault, 1 qr.	3 02	5 30
Union	Newton.....	Jno. A. Thompson.	no return	
Union Church ...	Jefferson	Archibald Smith ...	35 22	63 71
Utica	Hinds	Geo. W. Mimms...	80 77	143 96

POST OFFICES—*Louisiana.*

Post Offices.	Counties.	Postmasters.	Compensation.	Net proceeds.
Van Buren	Itawamba	Jesse B. Hunter, to 31st Dec.	$14 91	$27 12
		Winf'ld S.C. Walker	21 17	37 41
Vernal	Greene	Jno. D. Thomson	8 11	12 47
Vernon	Madison	John M. Robb, to 31st March	88 92	171 72
		Robt. C. Cowan	28 45	56 26
Vicksburgh	Warren	Nich's D. Coleman	1042 80	3386 89
Victoria	Bolivar	Thos. J. Jackman	23 32	45 16
Waholock	Kemper	Matthias D. Conklin	114 49	210 53
Walnut Peak	Tishemingo	James Benham	3 05	5 02
Warrenton	Warren	Jno. W. Buck	143 94	283 96
Washington	Adams	Ezra T. Leggett	202 31	188 95
Waterford	Marshall	Saml. M. Allen	52 16	105 71
Waverly	Lowndes	John M. Hughes	54 41	112 96
Westville	Simpson	Jas. B. Mendenhall	63 39	122 16
Wheeling	Holmes	Cor's S. Whitcomb	37 74	71 68
Whitesville	Wilkinson	David L. Phares	74 13	105 79
Williamsburgh	Covington	Josh. Burkhalter, jr., to 31st Dec.	16 45	28 53
		Thos. P. Holloway	15 59	27 85
Willow Spring	Claiborne	Thos. J. Turpin	25 34	41 87
Winchester	Wayne	John E. Wright	32 25	53 57
Woodville	Wilkinson	John B. Therrel	587 25	1217 37
Wyatt	La Fayette	Geo. A. Taylor	62 33	124 74
Yazoo City	Yazoo	Richard E. Keys	358 72	878 61
Yellow Creek	Tishemingo	Jos. D. Phillips	5 51	7 95
Yocony	Itawamba	John Wylie	10 30	19 73

LOUISIANA.

NOTE.—Compensation of Postmasters, and net proceeds of their offices, from July 1, 1844, to June 30, 1845.

Post Offices.	Parishes.	Postmasters.	Compensation.	Net proceeds.
Adaies	Natchitoches	Stephen McLean	$4 92	$7 57
Alexandria	Rapides	Lewis Zim	423 10	936 35
Allen's Settlement	Claiborne	John Murrell	10 37	19 00
Ashton	Carroll	Peter O. Flynn, fr. 6th Dec'r.	3 21	7 18
Assumption	Assumption	Pierre F. Helluin	129 48	249 36
Atchafalaya	Point Coupee	Jno. T. Brooks, 3 qs.	2 37	5 31

POST OFFICES—*Louisiana.*

Post Offices.	Parishes.	Postmasters.	Compensation.	Net proceeds.
Ballew's Ferry..	St. Landry..	John Lyons, jr.....	$13 52	$29 29
Baton Rouge....	E. Bat. Rouge	Hugh T. Waddill..	755 80	1727 06
Bayou Chicot....	St. Landry..	William Akinhead..	62 96	108 15
Bayou Goula....	Iberville.....	Charles Fay, to 21st Jan'y...........	130 45	129 69
		Charles Leblanc....	98 93	98 25
Bayou Rouge....	Avoyelles...	Alanson G. Pearce..	30 19	63 42
Bedford.........	Assumption .	Philip L. Cox......	10 44	22 85
Bellevue Landing.	Tensas......	Wm. T. S. Compton, from 1st Jan'y...	8 64	11 60
Big Creek.......	Rapides.....	Thomas Hooper, 3 qrs.............	1 55	3 66
Big Woods.......	Calcasieu....	Hardy Coward, to 15th Aug........	4 07	7 65
		Needham Coward..	19 33	39 57
Black Lake......	Claiborne....	Allen Harris.......	21 19	39 72
Boeuff Prairie....	Franklin....	Abram B. Seay....	22 72	49 11
Bonnet Carre....	St. John Bapt.	Adolph Guyol	136 01	233 42
Bordeaux	Avoyelles...	Robt. H. Cochran..	5 83	9 91
Borodino........	Avoyelles ...	Ambroise Lacour, to 31st Dec'r.......	11 33	14 65
		Joseph Rebouche...	7 70	13 52
Brean's Bridge....	St. Martins..	Edmund Bulliard...	20 40	38 42
Bringiers........	St. James....	Joseph Landry, to 26th June	278 41	313 59
		Lauzin Poirier.....	4 44	8 92
Brown's Ferry... (Dis. 24th May.)	Catahoula....	Coleman Brown....	No ret.	
Bruly Landing...	W. Bt. Rouge	Elie Le Jeune, from 16th Sept.........	36 23	84 57
Burshley Creek..	Catahoula....	Moses Wiggins....	No ret.	
Caldwells........	Wachita	Thos. B. Rutland..	17 01	33 26
Campti..........	Natchitoches.	John Marcalle, to 30th Sept.........	2 84	6 30
Carrollton.......	Jefferson	James Gilbert, from 16th Dec........	15 35	32 96
Centreville.......	St. Marys...	Charles Nettleton...	103 77	101 93
Charenton.......	St. Marys...	Demary Nicholas, to 30th Sept........	1 04	2 45
		Jules Gaillard......	7 85	17 06
Cheneyville......	Rapides.....	Geo. C. Smith.....	89 67	165 29
Chesterfield......	Madison	Jos. W. Williams, from 18th Oct....	9 05	18 74
Chickama Bend..	Madison	John Seaton, from 13th Dec'r to 31st March.........	0 81	1 20
Clinton..........	East Feliciana	Bythell Haynes....	278 12	579 89
Cloutiersville....	Natchitoches.	Chs. F. Benoist....	25 81	55 44

POST OFFICES—*Louisiana.*

Post Offices.	Parishes.	Postmasters.	Compensation.	Net proceeds.
Columbia........	Caldwell....	Nathan L. Chaffin, 3 qrs..........	$52 23	$103 83
Colvins........	Union........	Jeptha Colvin, to 31st Dec'r.......	9 70	21 86
		Zephaniah B. Davis.	10 60	22 99
Copenhagen......	Caldwell....	Jacob Bollenhagen..	22 67	50 13
Cotile..........	Rapides.....	Robt. M. Henderson	56 53	94 05
Coushattie Chute.	Natchitoches.	George Hammett, from 13th June to 30th Sept........	2 38	4 12
		Jas. K. Belden, 2 qs.	4 45	9 55
Covington........	St. Tammany	Philip Kellar.......	153 97	309 88
Darlington.......	St. Helena...	Wm. S. Townsend.	24 64	46 10
Donaldsonville...	Ascension....	Andrew Gingry....	631 39	1011 74
Dotys.......... (Dis. 24th May.)	Catahoula....	Silas Lillard.......	No ret.	
Fairview........	Concordia...	Jesse Guice, from 1st October........	12 87	21 92
Farmersville.....	Union........	Enoch B. Whitson.	158 48	322 20
Flat Lick........	Claiborne....	Stephen Butler.....	23 09	45 87
Fontania........ (Dis. 23d Oct.)	E. Bat. Rouge	Jas. A. Ronaldson..	No ret.	
Fort Jessup......	Sabine......	Henry J. Lamb, to 9th Feb'y.......	259 77	624 09
		Nathan Darling....	173 42	415 05
Fort Pike.......	Orleans......	Francis Lee........	67 64	125 88
Franklin........	St. Marys...	Timothy J. Walker.	445 07	794 73
Franklinton......	Washington..	Benj. A. Beason, to 31st Dec'r.......	11 49	22 96
		Presly German.....	11 51	22 91
Grand Cane......	De Soto.....	Thos. D. Hailes....	66 84	130 42
Grand Coteau.....	St. Landry..	Auguste Lambre...	88 58	175 58
Greensburgh......	St. Helena...	Isaac H. Wright...	42 24	81 11
Greenwood.......	Caddo.......	Jas. K. Bayliss, fr. 6th Aug..........	179 05	390 96
Hard Times.....	Tensas......	J. Y. Hollingsworth	60 85	104 76
Harrisonburgh...	Catahoula....	Stephen T. Clark...	110 45	207 76
Holmesville......	Avoyelles...	Charles Kibbe.....	67 59	96 55
Houma........	Terre Bonne.	Jno. T. Rockwood..	179 88	351 67
Hurricane.......	Franklin....	Ralph Price, from 31st Oct.........	4 82	9 67
Iberville.........	Iberville.....	Maxile Le Blanc...	97 02	112 67
Jackson.........	East Feliciana	Sanford Perry......	193 69	410 63

POST OFFICES—*Louisiana.*

Post Offices.	Parishes.	Postmasters.	Compensation.	Net proceeds.
Jeaneretts	St. Marys	Clet Provost, 3 qrs	$34 22	$44 67
Keatchie	De Soto	Wm. A. Thorpe, fr. 25th July	11 39	21 53
Kirk's Ferry	Catahoula	David G. Pickens, from 10th Dec	7 03	12 95
La Fayette	Jefferson	Thomas Cook	146 46	316 31
Lake Providence	Carroll	J. C. Hollingsworth, to 10th Oct	70 72	147 34
		Hercules Hillman	203 04	464 53
Laurel Hill	W. Feliciana	Alexander Wilson	84 19	158 98
Lobdell's Store	W. Bt. Rouge	Stephen Winter, to 30th Sept	35 51	67 75
		Hiram Noyes, to 31st March	68 18	122 84
		Henry R. Graham	34 18	64 62
Lowe's Ferry	Natchitoches	Jno. A. McLanahan	19 11	43 92
Madisonville	St. Tammany	Ed. Lehmanowsky	47 83	76 45
Manchac	E. Bat. Rouge	Francis Roberts	88 22	88 26
Mandeville (Dis. 16th May.)	St. Tammany	Ant'e P. Lanaux, jr.	No ret.	
Manny	Sabine	Wm. L. Rogers, to to 30th Sept	3 20	6 36
		Chichester Chaplin, to 31st March	4 44	8 69
		William Taylor	5 29	4 24
Mansfield	De Soto	Jacob D. Wemple, from 28th Feb'y to 19th June	2 89	5 44
		War'n J. Massingall	0 46	1 03
Mansura	Avoyelles	Nelson Durand	32 88	57 99
Marburyville	St. Tammany	Eli Headen, 2 qrs	1 36	2 88
Marksville	Avoyelles	Thos. B. Tiller	74 23	128 15
Milliken's Bend	Madison	Hector H. McLean	123 39	256 22
Minden	Claiborne	John Baker	149 13	324 18
Monroe	Wachita	Jno. B. Filhiol	234 13	461 01
Mount Lebanon	Claiborne	Tandy A. Key	53 79	101 15
Natchitoches	Natchitoches	Chas. A. Bullard	507 31	1176 93
Negreet	Natchitoches	Robt. D. Wright	14 95	30 60
New Carthage	Madison	Wm. G. Frazier	56 11	98 00
New Iberia	St. Martins	John De Valcourt	133 76	274 84
New Orleans	Orleans	Alex'r G. Penn	2000 00	93950 78
New River	Ascension	Shubael Tillotson	217 69	211 33
Oak Grove	Washington	Isaac A. Myles	15 20	22 47
Oakly	Franklin	S. G. Cloud, fr. 1st Oct.	13 27	25 74

POST OFFICES—*Louisiana.*

Post Offices.	Parishes.	Postmasters.	Compensation.	Net proceeds.
Opelousas.......	St. Landry..	Guy H. Bell, 3 qrs..	$233 22	$454 07
Overton.........	Claiborne....	Wm. C. Copes.....	19 65	34 36
Paincourtville....	Assumption .	Elisse E. Malhiot..	51 57	104 16
Pattersonville.....	St. Marys...	Jno. A. Dwight....	268 66	310 64
Pecan Grove.....	Carroll.......	Geo. R. Newman...	55 42	119 04
Perry's Bridge...	La Fayette..	Robert Perry......	57 46	112 92
Pine Grove.......	St. Tammany	Thos. C. Terry....	10 79	23 34
Plaquemine......	Iberville......	Archibald Black....	368 32	490 83
Plaquemine Brulee	St. Landry..	Jesse B. Clark.....	6 15	11 45
Point Coupee....	Point Coupee	Victor Mourain....	218 88	383 77
Point Pleasant...	Wachita.....	John Temple......	54 29	112 32
Port Hudson	East Feliciana	Wallace Badger, to 31st March......	35 86	78 38
	....	James Hudson.....	19 82	38 18
Quay...........	Claiborne....	Jabez Sanders......	20 08	41 61
Red River Landing	Point Coupee	Francis Routh, from 13th to 30th Sept.	0 50	0 71
Richland Hill....	East Feliciana	Angus McCarstle, to 31st Dec'r.......	11 72	21 07
	....	James Keogh, from 24th May.......	0 44	0 87
Richmond.......	Madison	Nath'l C. Dorteh, to 31st March.......	70 19	142 83
	....	Geo. H. Morgan...	27 07	52 00
Russelville.......	Claiborne....	Thos. H. Jones....	19 32	37 98
Saint Charles.... (Dis. 16th May.) (Re-est. 10 J'y '45)	St. Charles..	Francois Chaix, from 28th Aug't to 31st Dec'r..........	13 46	22 62
		Onesime Touzanne, to 19th June.....	14 27	23 42
Saint Francisville.	W. Feliciana.	David Austen......	471 99	953 66
Saint Helena.....	St. Helena...	Blass Spiller.......	6 37	8 81
Saint Josephs.... (Late "Tensas.")	Tensas.......	Jas. W. Davenport, from 27th Aug...	26 01	44 77
Saint Martinsville.	St. Martins..	Valsin A. Fournet..	185 79	412 66
Shady Grove....	Washington..	Thomas Pearson...	No ret.	
Shreveport.......	Caddo.......	William Thatcher..	210 34	491 62
Sibila...........	Washington..	Robt. F. Sibley....	9 85	18 16
Simms' Port.....	Avoyelles ...	Ignatius Kirk......	32 78	60 06
Springfield.......	Livingston ..	Wm. Westmoreland 2 qrs............	25 42	49 39
Spring Ridge....	Caddo.......	Dan Bozeman......	34 21	56 69
Stony Point.....	E. Bat. Rouge	Michael Watson...	36 48	63 03
Summer Grove...	Caddo.......	Richard A. Catliffe, to 30th Sept.....	8 63	16 85
		Robt. V. Marye....	23 43	46 07

POST OFFICES—*Arkansas.*

Post Offices.	Parishes.	Postmasters.	Compensation.	Net proceeds.
Sweet Water ..... (Dis. 16th May.)	St. Tammany	William Marbury, 2 qrs.............	$0 76	$1 28
Tensas........... (Ch'd to "St. Josephs.")	Tenas.........	J. W. Davenport....	No ret.	
Terre Aux Boeuffs (Dis. 12th Sept.)	St. Bernard..	Vincente Nunez, to 30th Sept.........	1 82	4 07
The Village.......	Point Coupee	Jacob Fisher........	69 06	124 91
Thibodaux.......	La Fourche..	Jona. C. White.....	310 25	619 10
Trinity..........	Catahoula ...	Wm. H. Turnley..	71 41	128 20
Tylersville.......	Caddo.......	Ballard F. Eppes....	16 48	27 41
Vermillionville...	La Fayette..	James M. Moore...	125 71	252 46
Vidalia..........	Concordia...	Thos. B. Thorpe, 3 qrs.............	56 64	116 76
Ville Platte......	St. Landry..	Marcelin Garand...	18 95	31 11
Washington.......	St. Landry..	Nathan Gilbert......	74 18	121 93
Waterloo.........	Point Coupee	Jas. M. Bayley, to 31st March......	45 60	80 88
		William Clemans...	15 67	27 27
Waterproof......	Tensas......	Joseph Gorton, to 7th March.......	44 20	66 19
		Wm. F. Lynch.....	24 52	47 80
Williamsport.....	Point Coupee	Angus McPhaul, fr. 1st Oct..........	14 07	28 45
Woodland........	EastFeliciana	Stephen Tildon, to 7th May........	8 86	13 48
		Albert W. Poole...	3 51	4 86
Young's Point...	Madison......	Alfred M. Young, 3 qrs.............	27 86	54 18

ARKANSAS.

NOTE.—Compensation of Postmasters, and net proceeds of their offices, from July 1, 1844, to June 30, 1845.

Post Offices.	Counties.	Postmasters.	Compensation.	Net proceeds.
Aikins' Store	Montgomery.	Edward Aikin, 1 qr.	$0 07	$0 18
Antoin..........	Clark.......	John Speer........	21 45	38 84
Arkadelphia......	Clark.......	James S. Ward....	85 24	174 75
Arkansas Post...	Arkansas....	Richmond Peeler...	84 58	146 66
Athens..........	Izard	Benj'n H. Johnson, to 14th Jan'y....	10 29	15 73
		Asa McFettch	5 52	10 09

POST OFFICES—*Arkansas.*

Post Offices.	Counties.	Postmasters.	Compensation.	Net proceeds.
Barifield's Point..	Mississippi..	William L. Ward..	$8 03	$16 90
Bartholomew	Chicot......	Reese Bowden.....	26 28	58 46
Batesville........	Independence	Robert Williams...	260 83	451 75
Beatie's Prairie...	Benton.......	John A. P. Carr....	44 61	90 71
Benton..........	Saline	A. R. Hockersmith.	78 18	145 29
Bentonville......	Benton	Sam'l B. McClain..	63 58	128 44
Big Creek.......	Philips	Bailey Kendall.....	6 67	13 74
Blue's Point.....	Crittenden...	G. W. Underhill, 1 qr	1 03	1 84
Bolivar.........	Poinsett.....	Lewis H. Sutfin....	21 29	42 58
Boonsboro'......	Washington..	Samuel Newton....	65 76	125 03
Boonville........	Scott........	George Gill........	7 54	16 18
Boston .... (Dis. 23d Oct.)	Franklin	Mekings M. Knight	no ret.	
Bostonville......	Washington..	Tandy K. Kidd....	2 64	5 53
Cache River..... (Dis. 16th May.)	Jackson.....	Josiah McCall, 8⅓ months..........	1 35	2 34
Caddo Narrows..	Clark.......	Eli J. White.......	3 37	5 75
Caldwelton......	Saline.......	L. Milner, fr. 12th Oct	69	1 63
Camden.........	Washita	Thos. R. Murrell...	177 85	377 77
Carrollton.......	Carroll......	H. S. Laferty, to 27th Feb'y.......	33 03	61 68
		Jona. A. Hicks, 1 qr.	10 52	19 22
Cherokee Agency	Washington..	P. M. Butler.......	no ret.	
Cherry Grove....	Scott........	Daniel W. James...	6 43	11 28
Chikalah.........	Yell	Burk Johnson.....	25 53	51 06
Choctaw Agency.	Choctaw Nation.......	John B. Luce......	79 47	150 65
Clarendon.......	Monroe......	William Harvick...	13 79	26 22
Clark's Mills	Hempstead..	William Clark, to 30th Sept.........	5 01	9 89
		Edward C. Foulkes, from 14th Dec....	6 05	11 16
Clarksville.......	Johnson.....	Thomas Powers....	153 42	143 01
Clinton..........	Van Buren ..	David Maddux.....	21 45	44 64
Collegeville...... (Dis. 16th May.)	Saline.......	Shadrack B. Owen, to 31st Dec'r.....	7 26	11 68
		Andrew M. Dodd, to 23d April	4 19	5 86
Columbia.......	Chicot.......	Joshua M. Craig...	244 79	540 07
Columbus	Hempstead..	Wm. S. Johnson...	42 93	74 56
Conway......... (Dis. 2d July.)	LaFayette...	James S. Conway..	27 75	52 60
Cove Creek......	Washington..	John Morrow, 1 qr.	09	22
Creek Agency ...	Creek Nation	Wm. N. Anderson, to 1st Aug.......	2 49	5 83
		Geo. W. Baldwin, to 31st March....	13 61	22 79
		William Whitfield..	7 32	14 18

POST OFFICES—*Arkansas.*

Post Offices.	Counties.	Postmasters.	Compensation.	Net proceeds.
Crittenden	Clark	Adam Stroud	$12 18	$22 36
Crooked Creek	Carroll	William Beller	22 63	46 75
Cross Hollows	Benton	Eph'm D. Dickson, 2 qrs.	53	1 23
Crowleys	Greene	George B. Croft	10 71	12 20
Cypress Bend. (Dis. 20th July.)	Chicot	William Johnson, to 30th Sept.	3 03	6 49
Danville	Yell	Thomas W. Pound	28 40	51 70
Dardanelle	Pope	Jos. H. Brearly	15 04	29 66
De Bastrop	Chicot	Thomas F. Farrell	16 95	33 90
Delaware Hill	Greene	Adino McKnett	2 89	6 81
Dover	Pope	Matthew T. Logan, 3 qrs.	22 65	42 59
Dwight	Pope	Robert Davidson	17 87	33 50
Eagletown	Choctaw Nation	Amzi Robinson	17 64	30 51
Elizabeth	Jackson	William H. Morris, to 30th Sept.	17 63	35 50
		Noadiah Marsh	47 58	93 99
Elm Grove	Crittenden	Henry T. Hulbert	no ret.	
Evansville	Washington	Lewis Evans	47 58	79 00
Fairplay	Hot Springs	Sam'l W. Reyburn, 3 qrs.	5 37	9 73
Farm Hill	Poinsett	Wm. G. Arledge	2 13	4 11
Fayetteville	Washington	Isaac Strain	239 85	381 98
Fort Gibson	Cherokee Nation	Marcellus Duval	220 43	441 76
Fort Smith	Crawford	John Rogers	331 06	728 80
Fort Towson	Sevier	George C. Gooding	378 09	852 73
Fort Washita	Choctaw Nation	Samuel C. Humes, from 16th Dec'r	126 38	289 80
Fosters	Washita	Amos Wakefield, to 30th Nov.	31 70	61 66
		Edw'd T. Broughton	29 29	58 32
Fourche Dumas	Randolph	James G. Russell	12 71	22 68
Fulton	Hempstead	John S. Johnson	61 66	120 47
Gainesville	Greene	John M. Mitchell	16 22	34 43
Gally Creek	Pope	Kirkbride Potts	4 75	10 21
Grand Lake	Chicot	Thomas Lathrop	59 35	117 11
Grand Prairie	Pulaski	John Percefull, 1 qr.	52	1 24
Graves	Hempstead	Philip T. Graves	no ret.	
Greenock	Crittenden	Wm. D. Ferguson	14 60	27 31
Hadad	Pulaski	John Henderson	3 02	4 80

POST OFFICES—*Arkansas.*

Post Offices.	Counties.	Postmasters.	Compensation.	Net proceeds.
Harold..........	Montgomery.	Gibs'n K. Robinson, 1 qr..............	$0 19	$0 21
Helena..........	Philips......	John B. Ford......	273 81	582 51
Hix's Ferry......	Randolph ...	Erasmus D. Pitman.	15 13	33 52
Horse Head......	Johnson......	John Swagerty.....	17 67	31 59
Hot Springs.....	Hot Springs.	John C. Hale......	61 99	135 82
Hubbards........ (Dis. 21st Nov.)	Benton	James W. Cowan, 1 qr.............	07	18
Huntsville.......	Madison	Henry S. Wilson ..	37 61	79 06
Hurricane........	Conway......	Stephen D. Lewis..	5 80	9 25
Izard C. H....... (Ch'd to "North Fork.")	Izard	Jacob Wolf, to 30th Sept..............	4 17	7 29
Jackson..........	Lawrence ...	Andrew Hammond.	116 72	12 12
Jasper...........	Newton......	John M. Ross......	7 09	15 01
Johnston........ (Dis. 1st Aug.) (Re-es. 2d Sept.)	Marion......	William Sanders...	no ret.	
		Nathan Clements, fr. 21st Oct.........	2 69	5 16
Kenyon..........	Jackson......	Thomas Myers	3 89	7 15
Kidron..........	Cherokee Nation........	Jacob Hitchcock ...	33 89	49 74
Kinderhook......	Van Buren..	John O. Young, 1 qr.	1 22	2 86
		Luke Grimes, 1 qr..	1 41	3 16
King's River.....	Carroll......	Jesse Seitz.........	5 60	12 37
LaFayette C. H..	LaFayette...	Richard F. Sullivan, to 19th Dec'r.....	27 09	54 50
		Francis E. Whitfield	31 97	61 17
Languelle	St. Francis ..	Arch. G. McDaniel.	16 86	31 24
Lawrenceville....	Monroe......	Robert S. Bell......	23 37	47 46
Lebanon........	Searcy......	John M. Hensley ..	12 63	25 68
Lewisburgh......	Conway.....	Harr'n H. Higgins, to 4th Jan'y......	56 01	54 81
		Henry Hamilton...	41 94	83 16
Lick Creek......	Philips......	William Williams..	11 35	18 24
Lindsey's Prairie. (Dis. 16th May.)	Benton......	And'w Agnew, 2 qs.	2 77	4 93
Little Rock......	Pulaski	Barnet Williams ...	813 05	2128 90
McLean's Bottom	Franklin	Lorenzo C. Quin...	no ret.	
Magnolia........	Union........	Thos. R. Williams.	46 26	108 89
Marion..........	Crittenden...	Samuel T. Gilbert..	31 59	58 97
Mayhew.........	Choctaw Nation........	Ch. F. Stewart, 1 qr.	2 36	3 97
Middletown......	Van Buren ..	Wash'n B. Sillivan.	3 78	5 89
Mill Bayou......	Mississippi...	Elliott H. Fletcher..	no ret.	
Morrison's Bluff..	Johnson.....	Lorenzo N. Clark..	24 23	42 48

POST OFFICES—*Arkansas.*

Post Offices.	Counties.	Postmasters.	Compensation.	Net proceeds.
Mount Ida	Montgomery	G. Whittington	$7 01	$13 44
Mount Moriah	Hempstead	Wm. A. Nations	2 71	5 00
Mount Vernon	St. Francis	John M. Parrott, to 24th Dec'r	13 64	25 38
		John McCoy	17 30	34 63
Napoleon	Desha	Cyrus L. Kline, to 31st March	77 80	162 09
		Arthur Hays	32 95	68 12
Natural Dam	Crawford	Washington Duval	8 51	15 88
New Gascony	Jefferson	Stanislaus Dardenne	10 22	17 87
Niccottoo	Arkansas	Nathaniel Owen	15 07	30 11
Norristown	Pope	Samuel Norris	33 09	65 51
North Fork (Late "Izard C. H.")	Izard	Jacob Wolf, from 1st Oct	7 14	8 80
Oak Bluffs	Greene	James M. Cooper	4 42	10 38
Oak Grove	Crawford	Jas. B. McPherson	1 20	1 42
Oakland	St. Francis	Freeman E. Patrick	9 16	18 81
Oakland Grove	Pulaski	John Wassell	16 62	29 82
Oceola	Mississippi	William Bard	24 29	50 05
Old Town	Philips	Wm. B. Pool, 3 qrs	8 84	16 57
Owensville	Saline	Wm. H. Wolfe	4 15	8 43
Ozark	Franklin	Samuel Evans, to 30th Sept	6 74	14 73
		John D. Steele	33 66	69 19
Paraclifta	Sevier	John Robinson	41 69	84 02
Park Hill	Cherokee Nation	George M. Murrell	91 83	174 22
Parks	Scott	Wiley Tomlinson, 3 qrs	9 99	20 50
Pecan Point	Mississippi	Richard L. Simpson	5 65	10 97
Penultima	Crawford	James W. Bates	7 17	10 27
Perryville	Perry	John L. Houston	11 86	22 59
Pilot Hill	Fulton	Isaac King, from 1st Jan'y	3 06	6 00
Pine Bluff	Jefferson	James Scull, jr., to 31st March	85 10	169 20
		Hewes Scull	33 41	62 80
Pine Woods	Sevier	Allen T. Pettus	21 43	39 83
Piney	Johnson	George W. Patrick	8 45	13 81
Pittsburgh	Johnson	Seth J. Howell	22 53	26 82
Pleasant Hill	Franklin	David D. Williams	14 34	22 18
Pleasant Island	Independence	Alfred Bevins, to 31st March	6 45	13 30
		Edwin R. McGuire	2 67	5 58
Pleasant Plains	Independence	Fleming Pate, 3 qrs	1 68	2 46
Plum Bayou	Jefferson	Antoine Barraque	9 85	16 81

POST OFFICES—*Arkansas*.

Post Offices.	Counties.	Postmasters.	Compensation.	Net proceeds.
Pocahontas	Randolph	Wash'n R. Hunter	$27 39	$50 02
Point Prairie	Franklin	Elijah S. Moffet, to 31st Dec	8 47	16 64
		Charles S. Moffett	9 21	18 52
Powhatan	Lawrence	John S. Ficklin	6 14	9 72
Raymond	Clark	James M. Trigg	13 85	27 79
Reed's Creek	Lawrence	Geo. W. Wilkerson	11 38	21 75
Richland	Jefferson	Nath'l H. Fish	38 01	72 38
Richland Creek	Washington	Robert Buchanan	5 26	11 03
Richwood's	Izard	John Jacobs, to 30th Sept	4 03	8 91
		Francis M. Copeland	9 63	15 75
Rock Point	Independence	Richard Counts	2 65	5 52
Rockport	Hot Springs	Lorenzo Gibson	46 34	93 83
Rolling Prairie (Dis. 23d Oct.)	Marion	W. H. Baumgartner	no ret.	
Saint Francis	St. Francis	Archibald S. May	50 11	99 62
Saint Paul	Madison	John C. Sumner	8 06	15 14
Saline	Sevier	Cokely P. Williams	7 96	16 80
Scotia	Pope	Laban C. Howell, to 31st Dec'r	5 21	9 75
		Jesse May	6 04	11 12
Searcy	White	John W. Bond	24 86	52 50
Shoal Mountain (Dis. 23d Oct.)	Franklin	Joseph M. Clem	no ret.	
Smithville	Lawrence	Booker Bennett	33 27	56 40
South Fork	Izard	Enos C. Hunter	14 05	26 72
Spencer Academy	Choctaw Nation	William Wilson	19 56	33 11
Spring Hill	Hempstead	T. H. W. Maddux	106 08	211 37
Sweet Home (Dis. 27th Nov.)	Washington	James C. Pittman, to 31st Dec'r	4 82	8 84
(Re-es. 10th Jan.)		James C. Pittman, from Feb'y	2 17	4 20
Sylva	Washington	Chas. I. Severs	15 22	22 95
Ultima Thule	Sevier	Jos. W. McKean	8 73	17 09
Union C. H.	Union	Albert Rust	172 13	403 42
Van Buren	Crawford	John Drennon, to 30th Sept	61 96	140 08
		J. W. Washbourne	220 44	476 08
Walnut Camp	St. Francis	Charles Neely	15 15	34 00
Walnut Hill	LaFayette	Fleetwood Herndon	13 85	29 15
Warren	Bradley	John T. Cabeen, to 24th Jan'y	41 12	84 60
		Cyrus G. M. Prime	30 28	62 83

POST OFFICES—*Tennessee.*

Post Offices.	Counties.	Postmasters.	Compensation.	Net proceeds.
Washington	Hempstead	Robert L. Phillips	$303 25	$356 58
Wellington	Desha	Geo. B. Watson, jr.	10 26	22 45
Wheelock	Choctaw Nation	Henry K. Copeland	no ret.	
White River	Desha	Geo. A. Worthen, to 31st March	58 70	119 52
		John A. Harvick	17 30	35 73
Whittington	Hot Springs	William G. Chase	5 73	9 78
Wiley's Cove	Searcy	Benjamin Hull	3 71	7 26
Winfield	Scott	E. H. Featherston, to 31st Dec'r	3 96	8 21
		John Baxter	2 93	5 83
Yellville	Marion	Thos. F. Austin, to 31st March	22 14	29 32
		William Barrett	7 24	11 67
Zebulon	Pike	Jesse Jenkins, to 19th Dec.	14 77	27 29
		David S. Dickson	14 88	26 66

TENNESSEE.

NOTE.—Compensation of Postmasters, and net proceeds of their offices, from July 1, 1844, to June 30, 1845.

Post Offices.	Counties.	Postmasters.	Compensation.	Net proceeds.
Abbott's Mills	Rutherford	Granville S. Pierce	$8 00	$14 32
Academia (Dis. 19th Dec'r.)	Knox	John Westerfield, to 31st December	4 25	7 41
Adamsville	McNairy	Gilbert Combs, 3 qrs	10 81	19 60
Albany	Henry	John Dillahunty	12 07	17 86
Alexandria	De Kalb	Jacob Fite	41 61	75 93
Allen's Station	Hawkins	Absalom P. McCarty, 3 qrs	7 07	10 81
Asbury	Montgomery	Ch's H. Brame, fr. 1st June	11 22	19 39
Ashland (Dis. 26th June.)	Wayne	Ephr'm M. Dickson	no ret.	
Ashport	Lauderdale	Eras's S. Campbell, to 30th September	2 69	4 43
		Rob't C. Campbell	4 90	6 99
Ashwood	Maury	Isham Malone	68 00	122 03
Athens	McMinn	Geo. W. Mayo	274 88	493 02

POST OFFICES—*Tennessee.*

Post Offices.	Counties.	Postmasters.	Compensation.	Net proceeds.
Audubon	Hardeman	Wm. H. Rose, to 30th September	$3 59	$5 39
		John Rose	6 67	10 78
Bagdad	Smith	James Young	24 67	45 63
Bale's Branch	Greene	Joseph Rodgers	3 73	6 96
Ball Play (Dis. 3d June.)	Monroe	Squire S. Glenn	1 43	2 44
Barnardsville	Roane	Abington H. Leslie	5 38	10 67
Barren	Williamson	George Harris, to 30th September	98	1 74
		Jas. A. Cunningham	3 30	6 26
Barren Hill	Henry	James Walker	9 66	11 53
Barren Plain	Robertson	Isaac Mason, to 1st February	6 55	10 13
		Granberry B. Mason	3 10	5 51
Barton's Creek	Dickson	Belfield N. Carter	4 42	9 63
Bath Springs	Perry	Joel C. Hancock	13 52	25 66
Batson (Dis. 24th Jan'y.)	Humphreys	Spencer T. Hunt	no ret.	
Battle Creek	Marion	Geo. W. Rice	7 18	13 01
Bean's Station	Grainger	Thomas Whiteside	49 07	49 12
Beardstown	Perry	Robert Crudup	8 86	15 42
Beaver Dam Forks	Tipton	Irvine R. Sherrod	26 62	46 23
Beaver D. Springs	Hickman	Jesse Hart	1 29	3 06
Beaver Ridge	Knox	Jesse F. Foster	3 93	7 20
Beech Grove	Bedford	Wm. S. Watterson	52 55	87 59
Beech River	Perry	Amon M. Yarbro, 1 qr	97	1 79
Belfast	Marshall	Robert Williams	26 61	45 52
Belleville	Roane	Joseph Kimbrough	13 50	23 89
Belmont	Fayette	Felix R. David	75 18	136 61
Belvidere	Sumner	Thos. J. Franklin, 3 qrs	2 09	4 46
Benton	Marshall	Levi Cochran	7 85	11 27
Bentonville	Polk	Wm. B. Reynolds	44 09	76 11
Berlin	Marshall	Samuel Ewing	21 22	38 80
Bethesda	Williamson	Jas. G. Henderson	29 99	53 70
Bigbyville	Maury	Norflet R. Holden	45 22	76 82
Big Spring	Wilson	R. J. Evans	38 90	67 68
Birch Pond	Fayette	Rob't D. Guerrant	55 90	115 88
Blain's ⋈ Roads	Grainger	Richard Luttrell, to 31st December	16 39	25 43
		Thomas B. Reed	11 53	16 87
Blair's Ferry	Roane	James Johnston	20 22	37 56
Blooming Grove	Montgomery	Henry Neblett	16 77	35 81
Blountsville	Sullivan	Samuel Rhea	207 15	185 29
Blue Spring	Stewart	Richard Bagwell	8 75	17 26
Bodenham	Giles	Orv. W. McKissack	12 99	23 19

POST OFFICES—*Tennessee.*

Post Offices.	Counties.	Postmasters.	Compensation.	Net proceeds.
Boiling Spring...	Fentress	Alexander Gill.....	$0 62	$1 52
Bolivar..........	Hardeman ..	Hugh Harkins.....	318 04	673 27
Bon Air Springs.	White........	Jno. B. Rodgers....	19 57	19 04
Bon Aqua........	Hickman....	Wm. L. Weems...	7 92	16 47
Boon's Creek....	Washington..	Martin Kitzmiller..	14 18	16 92
Boon's Hill......	Lincoln	John H. Keith, to 31st December...	13 32	21 78
		John Wood.......	10 95	19 65
Botanick Garden.	Perry........	Rob't L. Gainuss..	3 30	5 98
Boyd's Creek....	Sevier	John Brabson......	7 08	10 35
Boydsville	Weakly......	Rufus P. Dodds...	42 55	54 10
Bradshaw	Giles	Arch'd S. Young, 2 qrs...........	3 14	5 51
Bradyville.......	Cannon	David Patton.......	15 14	29 11
Brownsport	Perry........	Samuel Vanleer, 1 qr	5 99	9 79
Brownsville	Haywood ...	Ch's P. Taliaferro..	309 71	662 64
Broyle's Store....	Hardin	Thos. J. Johnson...	3 77	5 77
Buffalo	Perry........	Hugh A. Catron...	7 78	15 07
Buffalo Hide.... (Ch'd to "Spring House.")	Grainger....	Geo. W. Moyers, to 31st December...	7 00	6 19
Bull Run.........	Grainger....	Calvin Huddleston.	7 66	16 81
Butler's Landing.	Jackson......	William Hawkins..	3 70	6 46
Cade's Cove......	Blount	Green Hill, from 1st January..........	62	1 12
Cainsville	Wilson	Wm. T. Harris.....	30 02	57 48
Cairo	Sumner	Sam'l K. Henderson	18 17	31 39
Caledonia	Henry	Wm. C. Rodgers..	28 28	58 97
Calhoun	McMinn	John D. Chattin....	28 70	47 31
Camden..........	Benton......	Anderson Lashlee, to 31st March...	52 19	90 33
		Wm. P. Morris.....	19 76	37 46
Campbell's Stati'n	Knox	James Keyes.......	43 37	52 61
Campbellsville ...	Giles........	Warner R. Harwood	29 89	52 68
Camp Creek......	Greene	Sam'l E. Snapp....	3 47	7 00
Canasauga	Polk.........	John Kennedy......	9 07	15 81
Cane Creek.......	Lincoln	Jos. H. Greer......	12 37	22 52
Caney Spring.....	Marshall.....	Ab'm F. Lillard, to 31st December...	7 21	14 24
		Aaron C. Wilson...	8 53	17 76
Carolina..........	Haywood ...	John Powell.......	18 08	28 65
Carrollville.......	Wayne.......	Rob't A. McCully..	40 35	83 16
Carter's Creek....	Williamson ..	Joseph Burnett.....	2 61	4 82
Carter's Station..	Greene.......	Elliott Jones.......	3 06	6 25
Carthage.........	Smith........	Sam'l T. Coker....	234 28	220 24
Caruth's ⋈ Roads	McMinn	Joseph Hamilton...	5 27	9 47
Castalian Springs.	Sumner	William I. Dixon, to 30th Sept......	14 65	27 28
		Jas. M. Clindining.	40 42	69 18

POST OFFICES—*Tennesseee.*

Post Offices.	Counties.	Postmasters.	Compensation.	Net proceeds.
Cave Hill (Dis. 16th May.)	Greene	Joseph Horton, to 30th May	$9 05	$15 04
Cedar Creek	Greene	William Girdner	10 76	20 28
Cedar Grove	Wilson	Archer Clay	32 52	56 77
Celina	Jackson	Robert Hemphill	18 38	32 96
Centreville	Hickman	Jas. D. Easley	65 97	117 86
Chalk Level	Benton	Rob't H. Hawthorn, 1 qr.	10	25
Chamberland	McNairy	Geo. W. Pratt	3 54	8 06
Chandler's Mill (Dis. 9th May.)	Robertson	William Chandler	1 89	3 34
Chapel Hill	Marshall	John H. Robinson	35 10	62 75
Charleston	Bradley	Wm. D. Dillon, to 1st March	18 60	34 35
		William Brittain	9 95	20 14
Charlotte	Dickson	Thomas Palmer	103 82	193 16
Chattanooga	Hamilton	John P. Long	234 48	215 26
Cheeksville	Marion	Robert Raines	10 40	18 44
Cherry Corner (Changed to "Conyersville.")	Henry	Simco A. G. Noel	13 40	24 29
Cherry Flat	Rutherford	Thomas Robertson	10 42	18 27
Cherryville	Haywood	Calvin W. Cherry	23 49	48 53
Chesnut Bluffs	Dyer	Robert Johnson	5 61	12 26
Chesnut Grove	Davidson	Martin Ussery	14 91	28 86
Chesterville	Gibson	Benj. P. Tyson	4 70	9 59
Chilhowe	Blount	Samuel Ghormly	7 24	10 95
China Grove	Gibson	Hiram Partee	9 91	15 84
Chota	Monroe	Arthur H. Henley	3 28	5 00
Christmasville	Carroll	J. Anderson Robinson, to 31st Dec.	11 74	23 33
		Peyton S. Parrish	11 56	20 78
Chucky Bend	Jefferson	Alex'r S. Landrum	14 46	24 97
Church Grove	Knox	John Mynatt	8 24	15 39
Citico	Monroe	H. McD. McElrath	3 41	4 18
Civil Order	Marshall	James Williams	6 57	11 97
Clarksville	Montgomery	John D. Bradley	821 57	1489 27
Clear Creek (Dis. 16th May.)	Morgan	Dan'l S. Lavender	no. ret.	
Clearmont	Cannon	Samuel Edmondson	9 40	14 47
Cleaveland	Bradley	Wm. H. White	125 20	227 04
Clinch Dale	Hawkins	Richard Mitchell	4 38	9 07
Clinton	Anderson	John Whitson	31 27	48 36
Clinton College	Smith	John Stevens	11 28	22 51
Clover Bottom	Sullivan	Geo. M. Bachman	1 96	3 17
Clover Hill	Blount	John Gault	9 38	14 53
Cloyd's Creek	Blount	Eli Richey	4 29	7 42
Coker Creek	Monroe	Geo. C. Harris	4 68	7 46
Colleton	Fayette	Leander Black	18 61	35 46

POST OFFICES—*Tennessee.*

Post Offices.	Counties.	Postmasters.	Compensation.	Net proceeds.
Colliersville	Shelby	Hamilton Bussey, 1 qr	$9 30	$18 42
		Sam'l T. Bufford, fr. 1st January	30 74	57 99
Columbia	Maury	Hillary Langtry	854 11	2135 65
Columbus	Polk	Alfred W. Buford	11 89	19 63
Comb's Store	Hardin	Thomas Comb, to 30th September	1 26	2 42
		Rich'd W. Crump	5 35	12 17
Commerce	Wilson	James B. Taylor, to 31st March	13 99	24 05
		John H. Foust	3 29	4 92
Concordia	Fayette	Littleberry Mullins	28 29	52 94
Convenient	Smith	Benj. J. Vaden	6 99	11 05
Conyersville (Late "Cherry Corner.")	Henry	Simco A. G. Noell	no ret.	
Coop's Creek	Marion	William Rankin	14 65	25 17
Copan	Haywood	Hugh S. King, to 31st December	4 98	9 11
		Thomas Traylor	5 12	9 21
Cornersville	Giles	Wm. L. McClelland	107 58	190 86
Cotton Grove	Madison	Jas. W. Glass	21 11	38 37
Covington	Tipton	Isaac R. Bledsoe	167 21	308 05
Crainsville	Hardeman	Robert Ward	7 08	14 46
Cripple Creek (Dis. 3d Feb.)	Rutherford	Christopher Batey, to 21st February	70	1 38
Cross Keys	Roane	Samuel Johnson	3 91	7 12
Cross Plains	Robertson	William Eatherley, to 31st March	34 15	76 51
		William Villines	16 72	25 72
Crucifer	Henderson	Jos. H. Gardner	6 97	14 66
Culloden	Bradley	C. C. P. Turner	2 50	4 41
Cumberland Gap	Claiborne	John M. Beaty, to 4th Nov	61 85	
		Brittain Poteet	115 91	
Cumberland Iron Works	Stewart	Samuel Stacker	64 18	112 47
Cyruston	Lincoln	Wm. H. Moores	7 71	12 68
Dallas	Hamilton	Albert W. Beddo	5 53	10 01
Dancyville	Haywood	Zachariah Payne	61 42	115 69
Dandridge	Jefferson	Wm. D. Fain	157 43	153 22
Danielsville	Dickson	James Daniel	7 30	13 30
Decatur	Meigs	Aaron King	25 42	47 33
Delphi	Marion	Thomas Pankey	7 28	12 09
Denmark	Madison	Charles Hickox	195 43	344 06
Dixon's Springs	Smith	Wm. S. Alexander	65 18	126 16
Double Springs	Jackson	Robert L. Lindsay	8 11	16 71
Dover	Stewart	Aaron Goodrich	61 73	122 43

POST OFFICES—*Tennessee.*

Post Offices.	Counties.	Postmasters.	Compensation.	Net proceeds.
Dresden	Weakly	Wm. W. Gleeson	$211 50	$418 93
Dry Hill	Lauderdale	Henry T. Blythe	8 54	13 12
Dugger's Ferry	Carter	John Berry	5 24	9 35
Dukedom	Weakly	Duke A. Beadles, 3 qrs	27 15	27 16
Durhamville	Lauderdale	Ivy Chandler	68 83	128 79
Dyersburgh	Dyer	Lewis Nolen, to 31st March; and from 17th April to 30th June	78 81	155 28
Eagle Creek	Benton	Wm. Hubbs, 3 qrs.	4 36	7 35
Eagleville	Williamson	Chesley Williams	25 71	49 07
Eaton	Gibson	Wm. J. Jennings	20 62	41 36
Eden's Ridge	Sullivan	John Shaver	18 27	28 97
Egypt	Fayette	Wm. C. Graves	20 92	35 60
Elizabethton	Carter	Wm. R. Rhea	100 95	175 00
Elk Ridge	Giles	John C. Walker	6 24	11 41
Elkton	Giles	Louis Hunnicutt	91 98	166 23
Ellejoy	Blount	Andrew Bogle	10 97	19 25
Elm Hill	Rutherford	John M. Williams	16 41	27 75
Estanaula	Haywood	Joab Wilson	9 85	15 49
Eve Mill	Monroe	Jesse Butler	4 69	8 55
Facility	McMinn	James H. Reagan	12 78	21 07
Fairfield	Bedford	John S. Davis	16 81	31 11
Fair Garden	Sevier	John Walker	5 81	11 31
Fall Branch	Washington	Jos. B. Gilman	16 01	30 71
Falling Water	White	Shadrach Price	6 93	12 42
Farmington	Marshall	Benj. C. Brantley, to 31st Dec	25 61	37 00
		Ephraim Hunter	24 69	41 60
Fayette Corner	Fayette	Noah Daman	12 24	24 47
Fayetteville	Lincoln	Ansleum T. Nicks	302 11	605 18
Fincastle	Campbell	James J. Mars	8 12	16 04
Flat Greek	Bedford	Thos. Newsom, 1 qr.	4 35	8 49
		James T. Snody, fr. 7th March	5 12	9 02
Flemings	Weakly	Robert R. Gilbert	6 81	14 65
Flynn's Lick	Jackson	Absalom Johnson	5 64	10 31
Fort Blount	Jackson	Andrew McClellin	3 96	6 32
Fort Pickering	Shelby	S. D. Nelson, 2 qrs.	7 39	13 05
Foster's X Roads	Bledsoe	William Foster	4 41	6 10
Fosterville	Rutherford	Thomas Edwards	53 65	104 88
Fountain Head	Sumner	O. P. Butler, 3 qrs.	7 02	14 39
Fountain Spring	Warren	James G. Hall	7 98	18 67
Four Mile Branch	Monroe	Miles Cunningham	14 82	25 45
Franklin	Williamson	James P. Maury	470 78	996 64
Franklin College	Davidson	T. Fanning, fr. 1st Jan	21 03	35 75

POST OFFICES—*Tennessee.*

Post Offices.	Counties.	Postmasters.	Compensation.	Net proceeds.
Fredonia	Montgomery	Sanford Wilson	$16 60	$30 69
Friendship	Dyer	Alfred T. Fielder	4 39	8 54
Fulton	Lauderdale	Wm. W. Lea, to 31st Dec	2 72	5 80
		Everett K. Dodge	3 56	5 30
Gainesboro'	Jackson	Nath'l G. Jackson	38 08	66 68
Gallatin	Sumner	Thomas G. Moss	404 87	977 22
Gap Creek	Knox	Jeremiah Johnson	3 98	5 97
Gardnersville	Weakly	John A. Gardner	8 48	15 76
Gas Factory	Lincoln	Thomas W. Hayes	5 54	9 04
Germantown	Shelby	Sam'l W. Ledbetter	172 44	319 03
Gill's Store	Lincoln	W. W. Gill, 2 qrs	5 64	10 21
Good Spring	Williamson	Collin McDaniel	12 66	23 84
Gordonsville	Smith	John Gordon	15 69	25 40
Grantsboro'	Campbell	James H. Grant	6 04	10 33
Granville	Jackson	John Hughes	31 71	56 90
Grape Spring (Dis. 24th May.)	Hamilton	Evan Parker, 1 qr	0 67	1 59
Grassy Cove	Bledsoe	Weathers'n S. Greer	5 81	9 36
Gravel Hill	McNairy	David Reding	1 91	3 58
Green Bottom	Shelby	Thomas Harwell, to 31st March	34 32	52 23
		Thomas H. Miller	13 33	13 02
Greenfield	Sullivan	Geo. W. Greenway	4 37	7 17
Green Hill	Wilson	Wm. W. Masterson	50 54	55 58
Greenville	Greene	Wm. M. Lowry	277 69	435 00
Grove Mount	Dyer	Richard Henderson	8 25	14 54
Gustavus	Greene	James G. Guthrie	14 43	28 31
Hamburg	Hardin	W. G. Campbell	28 30	58 92
Hampshire	Lewis	John W. Kilpatrick, to 31st March	13 23	21 82
		James T. Moore	5 39	8 83
Hanna	Sumner	James N. Malone	14 27	24 97
Hardiman's ⋈ Roads	Williamson	Jonathan Bostick, to 31st March	42 71	77 11
		Thos B. Claiborne	14 33	26 24
Harmony	Weakly	Edmund P. Latham	7 04	13 94
Harpeth	Williamson	Wm. S. Webb	17 11	23 62
Harrican	Humphreys	Samuel Epperson	3 68	5 74
Harrison	Hamilton	Sam'l A. McKenzie	40 49	73 42
Hartsville	Sumner	Francis Duffy	115 54	220 65
Haynes	Grainger	Joseph Yadon	7 58	13 76
Henderson	Lincoln	Rob't S. Woodward, to 21st Feb	0 90	
		Peter G. McMullen, 1 qr	2 51	4 27

POST OFFICES—*Tennessee.*

Post Offices.	Counties.	Postmasters.	Compensation.	Net proceeds.
Henderson's Mill	Greene	Robert Henderson	$22 19	$37 24
Hendersonville	Sumner	Priestly Bradford	69 85	137 94
Henry	Lawrence	Ezekiel Voss	no return	
Henry's ⋈ Roads	Sevier	Elisha Cates	8 37	13 25
Hickory Creek	Warren	Jonathan Wooton	28 24	50 25
Hico	Carroll	Leonidas J. McNeill	19 40	35 29
Highland	Jackson	John S. Cornwall, to 31st March	15 38	23 78
		Wm. W. Goodall	3 06	5 55
Hilham	Overton	Ormel Fisk	5 98	12 38
Hillsboro'	Coffee	Arch'd J. Price	67 23	65 97
Hill's Valley	Williamson	Robert A. Hill	5 48	7 09
Hiltons	Sullivan	Benj. L. Yoakley	18 42	17 46
Horse Creek	Greene	John J. Broyles	9 19	11 77
Houston	Wayne	Wm. Hawk, 3 qrs	2 37	4 95
Huddleston's ⋈ Roads	Wilson	Daniel Richmond	13 19	23 61
Huntingdon	Carroll	Thos. A. Hawkins	272 67	254 30
Hurt's ⋈ Roads	Maury	Robert A. Glenn	21 69	42 95
Ida (Dis. 19th Dec'r.)	Tipton	Wm. G. Black, to 31st Dec	10 01	13 65
Independence	Henderson	Kinsey S. Harrison	no return	
Indian Creek	Giles	L. A. Westmoreland	11 71	21 78
Irvine's Store	Weakly	Samuel Irvine	16 80	29 95
Isom's Store	Maury	Griffith Cathey	10 11	18 04
Jacksboro'	Campbell	Thomas Weir	37 83	69 02
Jack's Creek	Henderson	A. C. McCorkle	60 99	110 18
Jackson	Madison	John Tomlin	475 66	1190 46
Jamestown	Fentress	Rob't H. McIlvaine, to 31st Dec	11 54	13 61
		Clark G. Crozier	12 32	15 31
Jasper	Marion	Jos. P. Kelly	62 82	121 28
Jefferson	Rutherford	John Jones	48 29	90 89
Johnsons	Montgomery	Len. H. Johnson	29 80	51 63
Jonesboro'	Washington	John P. Chester	328 51	378 35
Kelly's Ferry	Meigs	James Blakely	5 55	9 62
Kincannon's Ferry	Meigs	Andrew Kincannon	2 75	4 84
Kingsport	Sullivan	John Lynn	144 88	254 16
Kingston	Roane	Henry J. Welcher, to 9th May	150 45	118 99
		Thomas A. Brown	21 12	20 09
Knoxville	Knox	James W. Campbell, to 3d Feb	335 31	759 22
		Samuel W. Bell	252 23	577 63
Lafayette	Macon	Hugh B. Flippin	29 11	51 64

POST OFFICES—*Tennessee.*

Post Offices.	Counties.	Postmasters.	Compensation.	Net proceeds.
Lagado	Wilson	Turner Vaughan	$15 50	$29 42
La Grange	Fayette	Patrick Gorman	301 01	617 96
Lancaster	Smith	T. C. Marchbanks	9 78	19 57
Landan (Dis. 21st March)	Haywood	Lewis H. Johnson, 3 qrs	3 69	6 48
Lanefield	Haywood	James S. Smith	17 99	34 36
Las Casses	Rutherford	Robert W. Martin, from 1st Oct	2 50	4 04
Laurel Creek	Fayette	Ashly D. Stainback	11 48	18 99
Laurel Gap	Greene	Allen Williams	5 57	10 51
Lawrenceburg	Lawrence	Stephanes Busby, to 9th May	145 70	138 88
		Roberson D. Parish	30 85	30 07
Leadvale	Jefferson	George S. Eckel	6 72	11 86
Lebanon	Wilson	Isaac Golladay	419 44	672 87
Leesburgh	Washington	Isaac McPherson	42 65	74 47
Lee Valley	Hawkins	John Mitchell	5 91	9 16
Leiper's Fork	Williamson	Geo. A. Conn	10 03	16 16
Lenoir's	Roane	Wm. B. Lenoir	16 14	25 72
Lewisburgh	Marshall	John Hatchett	81 05	152 53
Lexington	Henderson	Jno. A. M. Jeffreys	99 35	201 74
Liberty	De Kalb	Leonard Lamberson	38 15	64 41
Lick Creek	Hickman	John T. Primm	6 44	9 90
Limestone	Hamilton	Jonathan Wood	19 31	39 13
Little Chucky	Greene	Anthony Rankin	7 15	10 85
Livingston	Overton	Wm. G. Roberts, to 3d March	39 21	77 50
		Patrick Pool	24 16	47 04
Lockport	Wilson	William Pettway	6 51	12 96
Locust Grove	Weakly	Nath. K. Jones	5 86	13 17
Locust Mount	Washington	Thos. C. McAdams	2 92	4 48
Locust Shade	Overton	James McMillin	6 35	11 17
Longmire	Washington	Charles Longmire	7 23	11 69
Long Savannah	Hamilton	John Anderson	4 56	9 04
Long View	Morgan	G. F. Vickery	4 69	9 82
Look Out Valley	Hamilton	Elisha Parker, to 30th Sept	1 70	2 83
		Isaac C. Rowden	2 70	4 08
Lost Creek	Campbell	Elijah Hill	6 30	12 39
Louisville	Blount	H. Talbot Cox	32 84	55 29
Lowes	Robertson	William Shaw, to 21st Feb	23 91	44 91
		John B. Fiser	11 61	21 07
Lowryville	Hardin	Alfred H. Kindel	6 28	12 36
Loy's X Roads	Anderson	Lewis Miller	8 58	12 32
Lynchburgh	Lincoln	Benj. H. Berry	44 31	91 25
Lynnville	Giles	Frank. T. McLaurine	90 37	86 68
Lyon's Store	Hawkins	William Lyons	25 85	42 61

POST OFFICES—*Tennessee.*

Post Offices.	Counties.	Postmasters.	Compensation.	Net proceeds.
McAlister's XR'ds	Montgomery.	Wm. M. Stewart ..	$25 09	$48 92
McLeansville	Jackson.....	Alexander Keith ...	3 55	6 24
McLemoresville..	Carroll......	Anderson H. Smith.	69 32	132 88
McMinnville	Warren.....	Wm. L. S. Dearing.	229 14	425 00
McMurry's Store.	Maury......	Joseph McMurry ..	8 17	13 36
Macedonia	Carroll......	John W. Smith, to 31st Dec........	15 42	15 45
		Geo. H. Prince	13 59	12 73
Macon..........	Fayette	Thomas McIver ...	137 40	253 69
Madisonville.....	Monroe......	Guilford Cannon...	123 17	201 89
Manchester......	Coffee	Harwood Morgan. .	36 02	63 79
Mansker's Creek.	Davidson.. ..	Enoch P. Connell ..	24 31	45 11
Mantua..........	McMinn.....	Wm. B. Porter	7 85	15 39
Marshall's Ferry.	Grainger.....	James Shields	14 79	25 36
Martin's Creek ..	Carroll......	Jacob Martin......	9 39	15 08
Marysville	Blount......	Saml. T. Bicknell ..	114 54	205 56
Mason Hall	Obion.......	John Garrison.....	3 72	6 37
Mason's Grove ..	Madison	Ezekiel B. Mason..	23 06	39 15
Matamora.......	Hardeman ..	J. M. Rodgers, 2 qrs.	3 36	6 13
Meadorville ..... (Dis. 4th Nov.)	Macon......	Reason Barrow, to 1st Nov.........	2 81	5 12
Mecklenburgh...	Knox........	Jas. G. M. Ramsey.	9 60	16 53
Medon..........	Madison	Peter J. Swink	41 00	78 54
Meesville	Roane......	George Gordon	7 98	16 66
Meigsville.......	Jackson.....	Amos Kirkpatrick .	3 76	7 79
Memphis	Shelby......	Mar's B. Winchester	2000 00	5498 96
Middleburgh	Hardeman ..	John A. Jarratt....	117 98	129 66
Midway.........	Monroe.....	Jesse Cunningham .	3 41	5 60
Mifflin..........	Henderson ..	Richard S. Bradford	34 64	63 30
Milburnton......	Greene......	William Milburn ..	1 64	2 90
Mill Bend.......	Hawkins....	Absalom L. Burum.	93	1 36
Milledgeville.....	White......	Jose C. Dew	14 57	23 15
Millersburgh	Rutherford ..	Burrell G. White ..	26 16	24 06
Millville........	Lincoln	Jas. R. Chilcoate, to 31st Dec.........	4 84	9 40
		Benjamin Butler, fr. 19th March	4 54	7 87
Milton..........	Rutherford ..	Godfrey S. Newsom	31 13	55 47
Minor's Nursery. (Late "Graysville," Ky.)	Montgomery.	John C. Andrews, from 23d July ...	47 35	46 78
Mitchellsville	Robertson...	Wm. M. C. Barr ..	17 94	29 86
Monroe.........	Overton.....	Wm. P. Lacy	15 78	29 84
Montezuma	McNairy	Josiah R. Wamble .	21 39	42 47
Montgomery	Sumner.....	Jef. T. Montgomery	13 41	21 21
Montvale Springs.	Blount......	Dan. D. Fonte, 3 qrs.	1 48	3 52
Moore's X Roads.	Hardeman ..	John Smalley......	65 84	125 13
Moore's Iron W'ks	Johnson	Rufus Moore......	4 51	6 46
Mooresville	Marshall....	Bryan W. Nowlin .	31 47	50 40

POST OFFICES—*Tennessee.*

Post Offices.	Counties.	Postmasters.	Compensation.	Net proceeds.
Morgan C. H.	Morgan, ...	Saml. T. Cox, to 31st Dec.	$13 86	$23 60
		Fred. B. Guenther .	13 69	27 80
Morgan's Creek .	Perry.......	John Walker	10 41	21 87
Morgantown......	Blount	Edmund Wayman .	17 56	28 27
Morning Sun	Shelby.......	Chs. J. Nelson.....	61 90	104 05
Morrison's X R'ds	Warren......	Henry R. Etter....	16 42	28 31
Morristown	Jefferson. ...	John M. Coffin, to 31st March	21 74	20 84
		John B. Jackson. ..	6 77	6 58
Morse Creek	McNairy. ...	John A. McAlpin ..	3 41	7 16
Moscow	Fayette	Wm. H. Martin ...	41 58	83 40
Mossy Creek.....	Jefferson, ...	George Branner....	28 82	22 59
Mount Airy	Bledsoe	Levan'r W. S. Pope	4 52	9 70
Mount Carmel... (Late "Sparks.")	Wilson	Thomas E. Spain, from 7th Nov.....	7 48	12 07
Mount Comfort..	Fayette	John Graham.......	30 32	51 56
Mount Henry	Montgomery.	Henry Williams ...	13 99	20 85
Mount Holyoke .	Henry.	James Cowan	14 06	22 25
Mount Pinson	Madison	Geo. A. Connally ..	no return	
Mount Pleasant..	Maury.	Henry A. Miller...	175 15	308 10
Mount Reserve ..	Bedford.	Abr'm Myers, 2 qrs.	7 54	16 62
Mount Vernon....	Monroe......	Newton J. Spilman.	9 29	17 77
Mount View	Davidson. ...	Candor McFadden..	38 61	49 97
Mount Vista...... (Dis. 14th June.)	Henry.	John Cooney.......	14 54	26 85
Mouth of Sandy .	Henry.	J. T. Edmonds, 3 qrs	11 96	20 16
Mulberry	Lincoln	Paul Ingle.........	38 48	58 94
Mulberry Gap. ..	Claiborne	John Farmer......	6 15	10 09
Mulloy's.........	Robertson....	Smith Hughlett	18 20	32 56
Murfreesboro'...	Rutherford. .	Green.T. Henderson	518 07	1057 53
Nashville.	Davidson.....	Robert Armstrong, to 31st March ...	1500 00	7271 93
		Leon'd P. Cheatham	500 00	2453 13
New Canton......	Hawkins. ...	William Alexander, to 15th Jan......	13 14	21 79
		Wm. H. Duffield ..	7 79	15 56
New Castle	Fayette	James D. Hubbard.	105 09	100 66
Newmansville ...	Greene.	Jesse Ellis	2 70	4 64
New Market	Jefferson	William Brazleton .	79 59	149 47
Newport.	Cocke........	Wm. C. Roadman .	101 04	82 84
New Providcnee .	Montgomery.	Nace F. Trice	39 48	75 02
Noah's Fork ..... (Dis. 26th June.)	Coffee	John Patton.	3 11	5 56
Nolensville......	Williamson .	John Nolen	55 60	90 65
Nonconner.......	Fayette.	John Shaw........	50 50	97 88
Norris' Creek....	Lincoln.	Taz. W. Ledbetter .	7 73	12 38
Nubbin Ridge....	Hardeman ..	Woodson Vaden...	14 65	26 74

POST OFFICES—*Tennessee.*

Post Offices.	Counties.	Postmasters.	Compensation.	Net proceeds.
Oak Grove	Jefferson	John C. Turnley	$6 15	$6 18
Oak Hill	Overton	Eras. L. Gardenhire	13 72	28 95
Oakland	Fayette	Edward W. Tatum	59 29	109 49
Oakley	Overton	Haley Jackson	1 18	1 93
Ocoa	Polk	James Sloan	no return	
Old Town	Claiborne	Wm. R. Gibson	6 83	15 15
Olive (Dis. 24th Aug.)	McMinn	James Orten, to 30th Sept.	50	76
Oliver's	Anderson	John H. Kington	5 93	10 69
Olympus	Overton	William Chilton	3 00	4 74
Onecho	Montgomery	Jas. H. Williams	9 82	15 53
Onward	Stewart	Wm. G. Wynns	15 88	24 62
Orme's Store	Bledsoe	Wm. M. Orme, from 5th to 30th June	9	16
Owen Hill	Williamson	Richard C. Owen	18 10	27 94
Palestine	Hickman	Jas. H. Plummer	11 23	20 00
Pall Mall	Fentress	Berry Gatewood	10 30	19 96
Palmyra	Montgomery	Wm. P. Laird	12 04	21 15
Panther Springs	Jefferson	Wm. F. Daniel	27 66	22 65
Paperville	Sullivan	George Burkhart	23 74	39 86
Paradise	Macon	James Miller	4 35	8 24
Paris	Henry	Thos. K. Porter	419 79	702 83
Parrottsville	Cocke	Robert S. Roadman	14 54	26 01
Pekin	Jackson	Wm. R. Vance	18 23	32 73
Pelham	Grundy	Geo. W. Vaughn, to 31st March	26 34	45 41
		Wm. L. Vaughn	8 79	16 63
Perryville	Perry	Henry Wright	76 59	127 16
Petersburgh	Lincoln	John H. Stone	32 89	61 48
Peytonsville	Williamson	John G. Boyd	19 49	32 41
Philadelphia	Monroe	John Stanfield, to 31st Dec.	27 92	43 82
		Wm. S. Geers	25 50	45 88
Pigeon Creek	Greene	John McBride	3 36	6 24
Pikeville	Bledsoe	James A. Tulloss	60 96	117 99
Pinckney	Williamson	Mark M. Andrews	10 09	13 43
Piney River	Dickson	Abram C. Hogins	4 08	6 21
Pleasant Exch'ge	Henderson	Jas. E. Weathers	7 32	13 18
Pleasant Grove	Maury	Jonathan S. Hunt	29 76	52 99
Pleasant Hill	Davidson	Matthew P. Walker	16 79	34 57
Pleasant Shade	Smith	Geo. W. Herod, to 30th Sept.	2 61	3 98
		Jason R. Sloan	7 86	13 51
Pleasant Valley	Wayne	Henry Greeson	5 43	12 26
Pleasantville	Hickman	William B. Cooke, to 31st March	6 35	11 14
		Levin Watson	2 04	4 28
Pond Creek	Monroe	Thomas Vernon	7 58	13 61

POST OFFICES—*Tennessee.*

Post Offices.	Counties.	Postmasters.	Compensation.	Net proceeds.
Poplar Creek....	Roane......	Thomas Gallagher..	$3 92	$7 06
Poplar Grove.... (Dis. 16th May.)	Gibson......	Robert H. Goodloe, 3 qrs............	4 02	5 68
Portersville......	Tipton......	Alex'r L. McCain..	82 71	125 48
Port Royal......	Montgomery.	Abram C. Gaines...	50 51	87 39
Post Oak Springs.	Roane......	Moores S. Millican.	13 93	21 00
Prestonville......	Rhea.......	Ran'm P. Bowerman	8 99	16 12
Prospect	Giles.......	T. A. Westmoreland	28 04	43 88
Pulaski..........	Giles........	Edward W. Rose..	410 97	725 77
Purdy	McNairy ...	Geo. H. Burtwell..	113 59	234 89
Quincy	Gibson......	Sam'l J. Wilkins...	15 91	31 34
Rail Road Plains.	White......	Geo. W. Miller....	9 68	6 17
Raleigh	Shelby......	Thomas L. Smith..	221 77	221 33
Randolph........	Tipton......	George H. Evans, to 18th Jan'y.......	97 96	173 26
		Charles Sullivan....	62 94	128 12
Rankin's Creek..	Bledsoe.....	Samuel Rankin.....	1 20	1 53
Readyville.......	Rutherford..	Charles Ready.....	25 24	42 22
Red Bridge......	Hawkins....	Cleon Moore......	26 73	40 34
Red Hill	Grainger....	Alfred Noell.......	4 36	8 33
Red Mound......	Henderson ..	Addison Pyles, to 31st May........	35 83	67 89
		Cyrus Simmonds...	2 47	5 79
Red River.......	Robertson...	James Gunn.......	9 85	14 69
Reedy Creek.....	Sullivan.....	David Shaver......	3 64	6 24
Rhea Town......	Greene......	Jos. H. Earnest....	47 43	80 60
Richland	Giles	Samuel S. Smith ...	8 41	14 08
Richmond	Bedford.....	Jas. H. Curtiss, jr..	14 72	27 58
Rich Valley......	Bedford.....	Jordan C. Holt	10 84	22 15
Riggs' X Roads..	Williamson..	Gideon Riggs......	26 46	48 20
Ripley	Lauderdale...	James A. Lackey...	75 92	128 98
Rives	Wilson......	William T. Coles..	11 36	22 59
Roberson's X R'ds	Bledsoe.....	Isaac Roberson.....	7 36	12 56
Robertson's Store. (Dis. 6th Feb.)	Lincoln.....	Wm. B. Robinson, 1 qr.............	4 35	7 50
Robertsville.....	Anderson....	Douglas A. Peck, 3 qrs.............	7 12	12 74
Rock Creek...... (Dis. 20th Dec.)	Franklin....	Grant T. Hamilton, 3 qrs...........	2 40	3 90
Rock Island	Warren.....	John B. Rogers....	15 79	27 02
Rockville........	Monroe.....	John M. Croskey..	5 25	10 50
Rocky Mount....	Sullivan.....	Michael Massengill.	4 37	7 31
Rocky Spring....	Grainger....	Ethelred Williams..	32 90	38 00
Rogersville......	Hawkins....	Richard G. Fain....	230 20	377 15
Rome...........	Smith.......	John H. Bates......	60 81	116 79
Romeo..........	Greene......	George Kenny.....	1 60	3 78
Rose Creek......	McNairy....	Dempsey Moore ...	17 05	31 74

POST OFFICES—*Tennessee.*

Post Offices.	Counties.	Postmasters.	Compensation.	Net proceeds.
Ross	Anderson	James Ross	$6 54	$13 19
Rowesville	Bedford	Archibald M. Holt, to 31st March	23 63	45 71
		Williamson Haggard	10 07	17 64
Rural Hill	Wilson	Reuben M. Wood	32 14	62 66
Russellville	Jefferson	Chas. P. Nenney, to 21st Feb'y	62 94	57 15
		Franklin W. Taylor	32 83	27 10
Rutherford	Dyer	H'y F. Rutherford	11 53	22 94
Rutledge	Grainger	William Norton	65 08	58 48
Sail Creek	Hamilton	Th. Coulter, 3 qrs	1 98	3 77
Sailor's Rest	Montgomery	Geo. W. Jordan	35 75	66 27
Salem	Franklin	John R. Patrick	102 04	97 80
Salt Lick Creek	Macon	Samuel Jones	2 21	4 09
Sandy Bridge	Carroll	Aaron Green	8 87	17 21
Sandy Hill	Henry	Sol'n M. Atchison, to 31st Dec'r	7 26	12 50
		Jesse C. Cooper	8 78	14 50
Sandy Spring	Fayette	John F. Robertson	19 06	36 32
Saunders	Macon	Rylie Teel	2 24	4 91
Savannah	Hardin	James Irwin	115 88	222 17
Schoolfield's Store	Bledsoe	Jas. L. Schoolfield	13 45	25 18
Scotia	Lawrence	Geo. H. Nixon, from 28th Feb'y	50	89
Sevier C. H.	Sevier	Jona. M. Hammer	60 08	99 75
Shady Grove	Gibson	Jas. H. Driggers, to 31st Dec'r	16 62	30 76
		Charles O'Neill	14 90	29 51
Shannonville (Dis. 4th Nov.)	Perry	Washington West, to 31st Dec'r	2 58	5 73
Shelby Corner	Shelby	John W. Holt	20 76	33 88
Shelbyville	Bedford	Thomas Davis	353 02	788 48
Shiloh	Gibson	William Price	24 96	47 07
Shoal Spring	Giles	Elisha Waldrop, fr. 1st Aug	1 21	2 23
Silver Creek	Maury	Benony Gresham	3 64	6 87
Sinking Creek	Bedford	Thomas Coffey	10 48	16 26
Smiths	McMinn	Jackson Smith	5 54	8 27
Smith's X Roads	Rhea	Wm. Smith, jr	15 03	23 69
Smith's Fork	Hardin	Robert P. Bailey, to 24th Aug	1 17	2 19
		David Cooke	4 93	9 93
Smithville	De Kalb	Har'n O. T. Heald	45 87	95 37
Snoddyville	Jefferson	Cary Snoddy	19 89	32 58
Snow Creek	Maury	Hugh Forgey	23 47	41 09
Soddy	Hamilton	William Clift	7 24	12 22
Somerville	Fayette	Wm. D. Wilkerson, to 9th Jan'y	267 42	597 48

POST OFFICES—*Tennessee.*

Post Offices.	Counties.	Postmasters.	Compensation.	Net proceeds.
		Malcom W. Nelson	$270 22	$629 34
Sorby	Wayne	Abraham Montague	5 67	12 50
South Carroll	Carroll	Aug'n H. Carter	22 51	44 32
South Fork	Madison	Wm. A. Murchison, 2 qrs	5 63	11 23
South Gibson	Gibson	Wm. P. Williams	19 62	36 96
South Harpeth	Davidson	Thos. J. Allison	7 88	14 00
Sparks (Changed to "Mt. Carmel.")	Wilson	Nathan Sparks, to 5th Nov	4 04	7 10
Sparta	White	Jabez G. Mitchell	272 10	265 38
Speedwell	Claiborne	William Rogers	4 72	8 95
Spencer	Van Buren	John Stewart	19 44	32 92
Spring Creek	Madison	A. L. Wood, to 30th Sept	16 95	32 53
"		Jesse Gray	56 67	103 22
Springfield	Robertson	John W. Ferguson, to 20th Dec	66 05	114 52
		George C. Conrad	66 84	122 24
Spring Hill	Maury	Radford Satterfield, to 31st March	125 15	223 64
		Austin W. Potter	39 40	71 84
Spring House (Late "Buffalo Hide.")	Grainger	Chesley Jarnagin, from 1st Jan'y	5 68	7 60
Spring Place	Marshall	Robert Johnston	11 21	17 13
Springtown	Polk	William Morgan	91	1 48
Standing Rock	Stewart	Henry S. Palmer	5 65	11 37
Statesville	Wilson	Hardy S. Sypert, 3 qrs	24 46	44 87
Stewartsboro'	Rutherford	Silas Tucker	64 66	112 21
Stewart's Ferry	Davidson	William Stewart, to 21st Oct	1 28	3 00
		Benjamin Hurt	3 39	6 49
Strawberry Plains	Jefferson	Jas. A. Thornton, jr.	25 55	41 10
Sugar Creek	Giles	Robt. W. Appleton	5 18	11 38
Sulphur Springs	Rhea	James W. Vernon	12 70	24 75
Sweet Water	Monroe	Josiah K. Johnston	7 72	14 00
Sycamore	Claiborne	Jacob Shultz	8 31	15 32
Taylorsville	Johnson	Greene Moore	46 62	44 74
Tazewell	Claiborne	Hugh Graham	116 68	186 67
Tellico Plains	Monroe	Wm. P. H. McDermott, to 31st Dec	13 19	23 65
		Mort'r F. Johnson	12 32	20 59
Ten Mile Stand	Meigs	John McCallon	15 52	23 65
Tennessee Iron Works	Montgomery	Robert Baxter	7 45	15 19
Thomasville (Dis. 3d Feb'y.)	Washington	Elijah Embree, to 13th Feb'y	16 39	22 16
Thorn Hill	Grainger	C. W. Latham	8 63	16 06

POST OFFICES—*Tennessee.*

Post Offices.	Counties.	Postmasters.	Compensation.	Net proceeds.
Three Forks	Wilson	Nicholas Smith	$16 99	$26 02
Tippecanoe	Henderson	Thos. A. Noell, to 31st Dec'r	3 34	6 39
		Wm. W. Gordon	3 11	5 88
Tobacco Port	Stewart	Allen J. Shemwell	17 35	35 48
Totten's Wells	Obion	Benjamin Totten	32 87	55 93
Toulon	Haywood	Ebenezer G. Young	22 80	41 68
Tranby (Dis. 17th Mar.)	Stewart	Jas. Wilson, 2 qrs.	59	1 00
Trenton	Gibson	Nelson J. Hess	254 71	526 19
Troy	Obion	George Sheeks	no ret.	
Trundle's X R'ds.	Sevier	Dan'l L. Trundle	7 31	8 61
Tuckahoe	Jefferson	James A. Caldwell	8 10	14 79
Tuckaleechee cove	Blount	George Freshour	3 69	6 83
Turner's Hill	Overton	John Sevier	13 49	27 75
Turnersville	Robertson	Robert H. Alley	26 72	43 25
Tyree Spring	Sumner	John M. Curle	20 56	40 32
Unionville	Bedford	Green L. Poplin	47 58	85 17
Unitia	Blount	James Jones	11 78	21 04
Van Buren	Hardeman	Milton W. Pruitt, to 31st Dec'r	20 56	38 09
		Boling Branch	12 45	22 95
Van Hill	Hawkins	John Ball	1 34	2 44
Vernon	Hickman	Robert Shegog, to 30th Sept.	6 66	12 53
		Howell Huddleston	14 57	27 40
Versailles	Rutherford	M. L. Covington	13 78	15 22
Walden's Creek	Sevier	James Cumming	7 48	10 12
Walnut Hill	Bradley	Amos Potts	5 86	6 79
Warrensburgh	Greene	Allen Baker	20 26	36 65
Washington	Rhea	Robt. N. Gillespie	37 47	65 66
Wash'n College	Washington	Adam A. Broyles	58 45	108 05
Waterford	Gibson	Richard Harvey	11 87	22 33
Waverly	Humphreys	Zach's Drummonds	80 60	147 38
Waynesboro'	Wayne	Thomas M. East	57 33	94 16
Wesley	Haywood	Thomas Simmons	53 78	107 98
Westbrook	McMinn	Jonathan Thomas	1 35	2 04
West Fork	Overton	Jesse Roberts	5 36	10 14
West Point	Lawrence	Chas. I. Herrin	8 51	18 45
Wheeling	Giles	Matthew Davenport	7 25	10 49
WhiteCreek Sp'gs	Davidson	Henry R. Slatter	5 13	10 32
White Hall	Fayette	Leonard S. Langley	37 13	64 45
White Oak	Humphreys	Wesley Young	12 50	20 96
White Plains	Jackson	Stephen D. Burton	26 84	47 66
White's Store	Sullivan	Thomas White	3 96	6 26
White Top	Sullivan	Geo. P. Rutledge	8 23	12 22

POST OFFICES—*Kentucky.*

Post Offices.	Counties.	Postmasters.	Compensation.	Net proceeds.
Whiteville	Hardeman	Thos. B. Norment	$95 88	$177 32
Whitleyville	Jackson	Tandy K. Witcher	6 38	12 69
Williamsport	Maury	Powhatan Gordon	57 99	104 91
Williams' Store	Hardeman	John M. Richardson	17 18	31 49
Williamsville	Dickson	William Hill	3 14	6 78
Willow Grove	Sumner	William Stovall	7 44	13 14
Wilsons	Anderson	John Wilson	6 53	12 04
Winchester	Franklin	William Estill	383 59	522 50
Winches'r Springs	Franklin	William Burt	12 07	26 51
Winston	Weakly	David Winston	6 53	9 62
Wirt College	Sumner	Thos. M. Patterson	26 38	48 89
Witcher's X R'ds.	Smith	Gilbert Gibbs	4 14	7 34
Wolf River	Fayette	Amos David	11 61	21 90
Wolverton	McMinn	Ransom J. Moore	3 89	8 77
Woodbourne	Knox	Henry Graves, to 31st Dec'r	7 95	13 55
		Carrick W. Crozier	8 95	13 40
Woodbury	Cannon	Henry D. McBroom to 4th March	40 36	78 57
		William Bates	21 79	41 47
Woods' Ferry	Greene	John G. Farnsworth	8 99	12 69
Woods' Hill	Roane	Wm. L. Foute	9 33	10 55
Wright's X Roads	Fentress	Joshua Wright	1 35	2 81
Yellow Creek Furnace	Montgomery	Henry McFall	14 09	27 73
Yellow Springs	Claiborne	James Ritchie, from 17th Aug.	2 31	4 36
Yellow Store	Hawkins	Cornelius C. Miller	12 64	26 96
Yorkville	Gibson	Wm. H. H. Miller	36 13	69 22
Young's Tan Yard	Washington	Henry Young, 3 qs.	1 48	1 47

KENTUCKY.

NOTE.—Compensation of Postmasters, and net proceeds of their offices, from July 1, 1844, to June 30, 1845.

Post Offices.	Counties.	Postmasters.	Compensation.	Net proceeds.
Aaron's Run	Montgomery	Jas. R. Wilson	$12 17	$21 00
Adairville	Logan	Wm. K. Bowling, to 31st March	54 89	95 82
		R'd M. Shackelford	16 21	29 73
Adams' Mills	Pulaski	Alexander Adams	4 84	7 90
Albany	Clinton	Edward Long	42 46	73 93
Alexandria	Campbell	John J. Thomas	38 28	69 60

POST OFFICES—*Kentucky.*

Post Offices.	Counties.	Postmasters.	Compensation.	Net proceeds.
Allensville	Todd	Edw'd L. Anderson	$39 18	$69 08
Amanda	Greenup	William L. Pogue	46 49	91 58
Ashland (Dis. 26th Sept.)	Union	Nath'l J. Floyd, to 30th September	27	64
Ash Run	Pendleton	Geo. I. Hitch	5 14	8 35
Athens	Fayette	John Donley, to 19th August	7 71	14 38
		John E. Parker	55 98	106 20
Augusta	Bracken	Thomas Ingles	180 30	338 03
Aurora	Marshall	Gab'l P. Bagwell	3 56	7 74
Bainbridge	Christian	Wm. H. Bugg	26 16	23 18
Ballardsville	Oldham	Willi'm Shackelford, to 30th Sept	10 20	14 79
		John Swain	18 68	32 90
Barboursville	Knox	Benj. H. Ohler	72 82	143 76
Bardstown	Nelson	Wm. M. Powell	490 31	912 01
Barnett's Creek (Dis. 26th June.)	Ohio	William Field	5 46	8 42
Barry	Campbell	Hiram Klette	5 20	9 76
Bayard	Shelby	Jas. H. Drane	22 47	32 12
Bedford	Trimble	Silas Gatewood	74 71	138 66
Beech Park (Dis. 29th Nov.)	Gallatin	John O. Hamilton, to 6th December	3 78	5 26
Beech Woods (Dis. 17th Mar.)	Washington	Thomas Leachman	no ret.	
Begley's	Perry	Hiram Begley, from 1st January	11	16
Bellegrade (Dis. 10 July, '45.)	Callaway	Nathan Butler	3 93	6 94
Benton	Marshall	John H. Beardin, to 31st December	13 82	25 59
		Justus Shinn, from 8th February	11 06	23 83
Berry's Ferry	Livingston	Uriah G. Berry	11 83	19 46
Berry's Lick	Butler	Benjamin Porter	10 63	19 14
Bethel	Bath	G. North, to 21st Nov	5 69	7 97
		Thos. A. Matthews	15 64	28 31
Big Clifty	Grayson	Jas. M. Caldwell	94	1 91
Big Eagle	Scott	John Lindsy	16 52	28 79
Big Spring	Breckenridge	Ch'r W. Board	54 01	102 70
Blaine	Lawrence	Neri F. Sweetnam, from 15th Nov	70	1 59
Blandville	Ballard	John H. Stovall	60 19	122 83
Bloomfield	Nelson	Wm. R. Finley	130 95	216 81
Blue Spring Grove	Barren	Catharine R. Hord	27 24	29 29
Bolts	Lawrence	Alfred Bolt	1 15	1 77
Boonsboro' (Dis. 16th May.)	Madison	Samuel Halley	no ret.	

POST OFFICES—*Kentucky.*

Post Offices.	Counties.	Postmasters.	Compensation.	Net proceeds.
Boon's Knob	Jessamine	Philip Keatly	$10 36	$18 83
Bordley	Union	Wm. S. Ross	4 04	7 08
Boston	Nelson	John S. Hubbard	14 11	25 34
Bowling Green	Warren	Ch's D. Morehead	596 63	1175 47
Bradfordsville	Marion	Wm. F. Scanland	32 21	55 20
Brandenburgh	Mead	Josiah E. Haynes	114 78	223 11
Brashersville	Perry	Rob't S. Brashers	1 32	2 61
Breathitt (Chan'd to "Jackson.")	Breathitt	Wm. L. Griffing, to 31st December	10 47	22 82
Breedings	Adair	James Breeding	8 18	16 40
Bremen	Muhlenburgh	Peter Shaver	13 31	23 16
Bremo	Graves	John Woods	6 90	10 46
Bridgeport	Franklin	Fielding C. Whip, to 31st December	17 26	31 12
		Michael Robb	13 30	27 15
Broadwell	Harrison	Thos. R. Rankin	28 39	38 18
Brookville	Bracken	Jos. C. Linn, to 31st December	10 14	19 58
		John N. Furber	13 72	24 72
Brownsboro'	Oldham	Milburn Glore	46 86	84 03
Brownsville	Edmonson	Jas. W. Rogers, to 10th March	13 24	21 52
		Jas. R. Dabbs	6 09	11 61
Brush Creek	Greene	Obadiah F. Mackoy, to 21st November	4 79	8 76
		Alex. W. Allen, 1 qr	2 10	85
Brushy Fork	Breckenridge	Ch's B. Alexander	24 22	32 78
Bryantsville (Late "Burnt Tavern.")	Garrard	Geo. W. Mathews, 1 qr	11 05	20 58
Buckeye	Garrard	Jas. H. Letcher, jr., from 31st August	9 67	14 38
Burkesville	Cumberland	Jesse Ewing	102 71	207 28
Burlington	Boone	Nath'l E. Hawes, to 6th February	56 19	96 10
		Robert Sandford	34 75	62 96
Burnt Tavern (Ch'd to "Bryantsville.")	Garrard	Geo. W. Mathews, to 31st March	33 43	62 47
Cabin Creek	Lewis	William Norwood	7 06	12 45
Cadiz	Trigg	Robert Baker	230 80	231 88
Cairo	Henderson	David J. Hancock, to 30th September	8 47	15 14
		Simon L. Drewry	23 90	41 90
Camden	Shelby	James McDavitt, to 30th September	3 66	6 88
		George McDavitt	9 35	16 25
Campbellsburg	Henry	Wm. T. Voiers	30 28	58 71
Campbellsville	Greene	Thompson Sherrill	105 16	105 18
Camp Creek	Livingston	Job Truitt	5 47	8 61

POST OFFICES—*Kentucky.*

Post Offices.	Counties.	Postmasters.	Compensation.	Net proceeds.
Cane Spring	Bullitt	Sexton R. Samuels, from 1st Sept	$3 47	$5 16
Caneyville	Grayson	Jacob Miller	5 09	8 73
Canton	Trigg	Thos. N. Ingram	49 65	99 66
Carlisle	Nicholas	Joel Howard	132 15	228 82
Carlow	Hopkins	Thos. C. Buck	7 85	14 12
Carpenter's Mill	Allen	Henry S. Mitchell	8 67	17 80
Carrollton	Carroll	Aug'tus W. Gaines, to 30th Sept	24 04	47 76
		George W. Lee	96 52	150 11
Carter's Store	Nicholas	John Carter, 2 qrs	8 12	15 52
Carthage	Campbell	John C. Tarvin	4 20	7 36
Caseyville	Union	Benj. W. Johnston	58 25	116 19
Catlettsburgh	Greenup	Jas. W. Allison	35 24	49 08
Cedar Creek	Owen	John S. Hampton	14 97	27 50
Centre	Barren	Wm. O. Newman	13 71	25 98
Centreburgh	Oldham	Benj'n A. Asher, 3 qrs	1 24	2 61
Centre Point	Monroe	Harvey Kays	17 94	32 89
Centreville	Bourbon	John M. Taylor, to 31st March	29 92	48 17
		John Quire, from 3d March	14 09	25 07
Chaplin	Nelson	Thos. K. Marshall	18 73	36 16
Chesnut Grove	Shelby	Caleb Guthrie	17 93	32 09
Chilesburg	Fayette	Richard Chiles	48 02	91 26
Christiansburgh	Shelby	John Davis	62 35	117 57
Clarksburgh	Lewis	Larkin J. Proctor	19 54	40 69
Clay Lick	Owen	Jos. W. Rowlett, fr. 25th December	1 94	3 04
Claysville	Harrison	John Whitehead	16 21	29 94
Clay Village	Shelby	Isaac N. Guthrie, to 16th June	60 74	112 89
		Tyler Baird	2 55	4 55
Clear Fork	Whitley	William Snyder	3 22	6 87
Clear Point	Hart	J. R. G. Burks	14 94	16 74
Clinton	Hickman	Charles Hubbard	68 24	121 58
Clintonville	Bourbon	Ch's F. Scruggs	38 99	70 88
Clio	Wayne	Walter Emerson	10 05	22 52
Clover Dale	Barren	Henry V. Tobey	4 08	8 34
Cloverport	Breckenridge	George La Heist	78 82	138 20
Colbyville	Clark	Colby H. Taylor	78 42	148 48
Cold Spring	Campbell	Joel H. S. De Courcy	11 13	19 24
Colemansville	Harrison	Wm. M. Chambers	35 31	63 63
Columbia	Adair	Williamson Pittman	147 78	256 73
Columbus	Hickman	William Cook	64 64	91 10
Concord	Lewis	Samuel Stevenson	28 62	51 47
Corn Creek	Trimble	Jesse Connell	14 25	30 96
Corneliusville	Boone	Benjamin Mitchell	15 77	26 77

POST OFFICES—*Kentucky.*

Post Offices.	Counties.	Postmasters.	Compensation.	Net proceeds.
Covington	Kenton	Hamilton Martin	$383 25	$905 11
Crab Orchard	Lincoln	Archibald Shanks	102 26	110 15
Creelsburgh	Russell	John S. Page	14 25	27 28
Crittenden	Grant	Rich'd H. Homer	40 48	84 85
Cumberland Ford	Knox	James Renfro	13 19	26 90
Curreys	Jefferson	Edward Currey	8 91	16 95
Cynthiana	Harrison	Jere. V. Bassett	293 48	524 29
Cypress	Union	Hosea A. Pierson	9 45	16 29
Danville	Boyle	Am'a F. Greenwood	593 38	1486 58
Daysville	Todd	Benj. T. Perkins, to 31st Dec	2 78	5 69
		Geo. H. Day	4 87	9 45
Dover	Mason	Fred'k D. Hill	79 74	137 79
Downingsville (Dis. 14th Aug.)	Grant	Lawson Hopper	no ret.	
Drennons	Henry	Willet R. Owen, fr. 2d December	9 71	13 47
Dripping Spring	Edmonson	James M. Anderson	39 42	39 47
Dry Creek	Kenton	John G. Ellis	22 19	40 93
Dublin	Graves	Hayden E. Brown	5 08	11 14
Eddyville	Caldwell	Jas. N. Gracey	123 66	255 24
Edmonton	Barren	Bennet O. Neale	22 00	44 69
Elizabethtown	Hardin	Elisha S. Brown	246 25	477 27
Elizaville	Fleming	Garrett Chord	55 75	102 14
Elk Horn (Discontinued.)	Franklin	Wm. G. Harvie, to 15th November	2 34	4 19
Elkton	Todd	Thos. A. Anderson	214 62	412 46
Empire Ir'n W'ks (Late "Stacker Iron Works.")	Trigg	Thos. T. Watson	no ret.	
Etna	Greene	Fielding Hawks, to 31st Dec	2 85	6 34
		John Victor	2 04	4 02
Fair Dealing	Marshall	James Holloway, to 31st March	5 27	10 78
		Rob't A. Wade	1 82	3 69
Fairfield	Nelson	Thos. H. Milligan	22 22	35 31
Falls of Blaine	Lawrence	Geo. W. Hutchison	1 73	3 12
Falmouth	Pendleton	Geo. C. Lightfoot	53 57	99 13
Fancy Farm	Graves	John Peebles	11 28	22 30
Farmington	Graves	Thos. B. Hendley	11 59	22 10
Far View	Warren	Robert W. Lucas, 3 qrs	6 80	10 34
Feliciana	Graves	Wm. W. Alexander	45 76	43 02
Fish Point	Rock Castle	Thos. W. Pope, 2 qrs	68	1 32
Fisksburgh	Kenton	Augustus B. Regnier	8 41	17 03

POST OFFICES—*Kentucky.*

Post Offices.	Counties.	Postmasters.	Compensation.	Net proceeds.
Flag Spring.	Campbell	Edward Morin	$10 58	$14 74
Flat Rock	Bourbon	Wm. P. Payne, to 31st Jan'y	40 46	71 86
		Thos. J. Garrett	35 41	63 18
Flemingsburgh	Fleming	James Alexander	265 44	496 28
Flint Island	Mead	Jno. H. Staples, 3 qs.	15 12	28 89
Florence	Boone	Joshua Rouse, to 1st May	43 42	81 90
		Ezra K. Fish	11 28	17 91
Flower Creek	Pendleton	Heber Shomaker	11 19	18 92
Floydsburgh	Oldham	Jas. F. Wilson, 3 qs.	25 61	39 99
Forest Retreat	Nicholas	Sam'l L. Brunker	26 69	25 26
Fountain P'r Mills	Hart	Henry P Bosley, 3 qrs	8 36	15 10
Francisville. (Dis. 26th June.)	Boone	John H. Crawford	13 33	25 03
Frankfort	Franklin	William Hardin	1085 35	2799 23
Franklin	Simpson	Jas. C. Finley	157 20	286 69
Fredericktown	Washington	William Hogan	20 62	37 17
Fredonia	Caldwell	Henry Leigh	37 16	57 59
Fruit Hill	Christian	James Allder	6 31	13 17
Garnettsville	Mead	John C. Lawson	36 59	70 08
Garrettsburgh	Christian	Garrit M. Quarles	45 12	84 61
George's Creek	Lawrence	Reuben Burgess	3 09	6 15
Georgetown	Scott	William McDaniel	609 88	1297 82
Germantown	Mason	James Savage	61 82	111 11
Ghent	Carroll	James P. Cox	64 04	117 82
Gill's Mills	Bath	Marcus Gill	9 76	20 35
Glasgow	Barren	James P. Bates	352 37	448 75
Grant's Lick	Campbell	Ginnethon Hopkins, from 6th Aug	3 44	5 07
Grape Vine	Perry	Henry C. Duff, 3 qs.	0 53	1 29
Grass Hills	Carroll	Lewis Sanders	25 12	50 30
Grassy Creek	Pendleton	Thos. J. Thrasher	7 14	9 45
Grayson	Carter	Benj. F. Crawford	34 99	60 38
Grayson Springs	Grayson	Luther J. Talbott	2 70	5 63
Graysville (Ch'd to "Minor's Nursery'Te.)	Todd	John Ware, to 22d July	2 61	2 62
Great Crossings	Scott	Pres. H. Campbell	26 49	52 32
Greens	Grayson	Jefferson Jennings	9 54	16 14
Greensburgh	Greene	Robert Marshall	283 70	472 09
Greenup C. H.	Greenup	Chs. M. Wilson	95 06	182 82
Greenville	Muhlenburgh	James Weir	99 57	190 51
Griffiths	Nicholas	Wm. A. Griffith	17 53	21 72
Grissam's Cotton Gin	Christian	John W. Grissam	5 72	8 95
Gum Grove	Union	John Dyer, from 31st August	1 38	2 07

POST OFFICES—*Kentucky*.

Post Offices.	Counties.	Postmasters.	Compensation.	Net proceeds.
Hadensville	Todd	Benj. K. Tully	$29 79	$53 68
Hague	Logan	Jno. W. Smith	8 79	16 87
Hamburg (Dis. 14th Feb.)	Muhlenburgh	Henry Myers	No ret.	
Hardinsburgh	Breckenridge	Williamson Cox	118 45	226 96
Hardinsville	Shelby	Wm. N. Robb, to 31st Dec'r	6 23	11 53
		Richard Pemberton	5 12	10 24
Harlan C. H.	Harlan	Francis Hamblin, to 12th Aug	1 12	2 40
		Mastin G. Jones	15 21	20 83
Harmon's Ferry	Livingston	Samuel Harmon, fr. 7th Sept	0 58	1 38
Harmony Land'g.	Oldham	William Duerson, jr.	52 98	92 27
Harrisonville	Shelby	Wm. E. Cook, to 16th Aug	2 52	3 52
		Rich'd C. Terrell	8 92	16 07
Harrodsburgh	Mercer	Geo. T. Whitney, to 18th Jan'y	331 07	586 43
		Walter Wheatly	298 53	528 76
Hartford	Ohio	Richard L. Walker	104 30	193 33
Haskinsville	Greene	Robert Haskins	20 12	39 08
Havilandsville	Harrison	Robt. S. Haviland	19 39	30 32
Hawesville	Hancock	Geo. W. Williams, to 31st Dec'r	45 45	87 85
		Washington Carlton	45 88	91 65
Haydons	Owen	Jas. Wilson, 3 qrs.	1 97	2 72
Haynesville	Ohio	John Haynes	12 02	21 92
Hazle Green	Morgan	William Trimble	14 13	25 48
Hazlewood	Ballard	Oscar Turner, from 7th Sept	2 90	5 76
Head of Paint	Morgan	William Brown	2 00	3 95
Hebbardsville	Henderson	Geo. M. Priest	19 28	27 90
Helena	Mason	Sam'l W. Wood	22 72	36 95
Henderson	Henderson	Philo H. Hillyer	510 36	804 15
Hendrensville	Henry	John M. Watson	10 32	21 04
Hickman (Lt. Mill's Point.)	Hickman	Chs. F. Hanna, fr. 1st Jan'y	98 18	190 37
Hickory Flat	Simpson	Samuel Hatfield	6 11	11 24
High Grove	Nelson	Jno. C. Dillehay	21 23	31 46
Hillsboro'	Fleming	Henry Pickrel	27 78	50 41
Hodgensville	La Rue	Darwin J. Sparrow	52 68	103 26
Holt's Creek	Bracken	Peter Demoss	7 21	13 65
Hopkinsville	Christian	Harrison Ashford, to 6th June	593 81	1279 47
		Thos. H. Baker	38 66	88 90
Horseshoe Bottom	Russell	Wm. M. Green	2 36	4 64
Howell's Springs	Hardin	W. Neff, to 31st Dec.	4 94	8 90
		Jas. H. Pendleton	2 68	4 73

POST OFFICES—*Kentucky.*

Post Offices.	Counties.	Postmasters.	Compensation.	Net proceeds.
Hudsonville	Breckenridge.	Ralph E. Cox	$7 44	$15 02
Humphrey's Cr'k	Ballard	Caleb Terrell	6 56	13 29
Hustonville	Lincoln	Simon Vanarsdale	68 62	123 26
Independence	Kenton	W. H. H. Plummer	27 16	47 16
Irvine	Estill	Elijah Herndon	57 57	90 09
Jackson (Late 'Breathitt.')	Breathitt	Wm. L. Griffing, fr. 1st Jan'y	13 08	25 27
Jamestown	Russell	Jos. T. Rowe	42 84	87 78
Jeffersontown	Jefferson	Sam'l F. Miller	91 36	155 85
Jellico	Whitley	Solomon Stephens, jr	3 14	7 39
Jesse's Store	Shelby	Warner B. Jesse	9 08	15 07
Joe's Lick	Madison	Robert Cox	20 47	34 32
Keene	Jessamine	Chs. H. Spilman	34 29	61 25
Kentontown	Harrison	Duncan Harding	17 05	26 50
Keysburgh	Logan	Robt. C. Foster	46 40	80 96
Kiddville [illegible]	Clark	Stephen Adams, to 30th Sept	3 99	6 79
		Vivian Daniel	14 47	22 77
Kinniconick (Dis. 10th Jan'y.)	Lewis	George Truitt, to 31st Dec'r	4 54	6 93
(Re-est. 21st Feb.)		Thos. H. C. Bruce, from 6th March	1 89	3 61
Knottsville	Daviess	Thos. C. Aud	16 16	25 76
La Fayette	Christian	Francis B. White	75 81	144 89
La Grange	Oldham	Abraham Kightley	76 24	138 28
Lancaster	Garrard	Arabia J. Brown	194 87	348 29
Landing	Boone	Benj. E. Garnett	17 94	33 91
Lanesville	Floyd	Jas. S. Layne	5 28	9 85
Lawrenceburgh	Anderson	Thomas Davison	191 80	305 39
Lawson	Greenup	Thomas Lawson	3 28	5 59
Leander	Graves	Jos'a R. Wilcox	2 02	4 29
Lebanon	Marion	Green Forrest	305 55	456 99
Leesburgh	Harrison	Bushrod T. Boswell	64 82	117 65
Leesville	Hart	Silas Lee	9 09	19 15
Letcher	Harlan	Chs. J. Callaway	1 15	2 75
Lewis	Barren	John Lewis, to 30th September	4 39	9 79
		Jno. T. Rogers, 1 qr.	2 33	5 12
Lewisburgh	Muhlenburgh	Edmund Finch	14 24	29 25
Lewisport	Hancock	Wm. B. Schoolfield.	15 86	32 09
Lexington	Fayette	Joseph Ficklin	1238 01	7568 84
Liberty	Casey	James Belden	29 70	56 37
Lick Creek (Dis. 16th May.)	Clinton	Robt. A. Dabney, 3 qrs	2 72	3 75
Licking	Fleming	Wash'n McIntire, fr. 11th Jan'y	2 77	3 93

POST OFFICES—*Kentucky.*

Post Offices.	Counties.	Postmasters.	Compensation.	Net proceeds.
Licking Station	Morgan	Benj. F. Gardner	$7 57	$15 02
Lindleys	Ohio	Jno. A. Taylor	3 73	6 04
Lindsay's Mill	Trigg	Sackfield S. Lindsey, to 31st March	4 12	7 61
		Lunsford Lindsay	2 50	4 66
Litchfield	Grayson	Evan Rogers	46 21	79 44
Little Flat	Bath	Thomas Hawkins, fr. 31st Aug	4 81	7 50
Livermore	Ohio	Andrew J. Rowan	5 56	9 95
Lock No. 1	Carroll	Alex'r. H. Lothrop, from 28th Feb	0 76	1 29
Lockport	Henry	Henry Moore, from 10th Dec	3 97	8 54
Locust Forrest	Butler	John P. Carson	12 41	19 36
Locust Grove	Callaway	Abraham Thompson	5 42	10 56
Locust Mills	Bracken	Wm. A. Pepper	6 54	11 48
Logan	Carter	Jas. W. Riely	4 69	10 17
London	Laurel	Abraham Hunter	56 19	63 52
Long Falls Creek	Daviess	Jas. P. Moseley	16 04	31 66
Long Lick	Scott	Lewis C. Suggett	12 00	17 72
Long Run	Jefferson	David O. Conn	25 39	47 39
Longwood	Union	Albert G. Long	2 58	4 00
Loretto	Marion	Wm. D. Lancaster	17 68	34 13
Louisa	Lawrence	Wm. T. Nicholls	50 37	94 07
Louisville	Jefferson	Littleb'y H. Mosby	2000 00	18569 78
Lovelaceville	Ballard	Andrew Lovelace, jr.	20 10	36 84
Lower Blue Lick	Nicholas	Lewis P. Holladay	82 18	79 60
Lynn Camp	Knox	James Word	5 44	12 34
McNarys	Muhlenburgh	Hugh W. McNary	6 04	10 93
Mackville	Washington	John M. Smith	39 43	72 78
Madisonville	Hopkins	John G. Morton	159 47	308 43
Mammoth Cave	Edmonson	Archibald Miller	9 87	19 06
Manchester	Clay	Leander Miller	52 97	83 44
Marion	Scott	Hartwell E. Boswell	14 51	24 97
Marrow Bone	Cumberland	Walter J. Pace	27 65	48 01
Martha Mills	Fleming	John T. Walker	26 31	50 51
Martinsburgh	Monroe	John Mulkey	no return	
Martinsville	Warren	Hugh W. Johnston	5 94	8 97
Masonville	Daviess	Samuel Haynes, 10⅔ months	9 53	16 22
Mayfield	Graves	L. B. Holifield	70 26	137 48
May's Lick	Mason	Edw'd H. Herndon	205 87	207 49
Maysville	Mason	James W. Coburn	1827 64	672 37
Merry Oaks	Barren	Elias B. McFadin	10 73	19 91
Mershon's ⋈ R'ds	Laurel	Samuel Wilson	9 82	17 47
Middleburgh	Casey	Jesse Coffee	4 52	8 22
Middletown	Jefferson	David Lukenbill	79 80	149 34
Midway	Woodford	Ephraim E. Cooper	187 56	384 95

POST OFFICES—*Kentucky.*

Post Offices.	Counties.	Postmasters.	Compensation.	Net proceeds.
Millburn	Ballard	Andrew J. Warden	$35 01	$34 25
Milledgeville	Lincoln	Jos. S. McCormach	10 00	15 41
Millersburg	Bourbon	James Bassett	273 42	280 75
Miller's Mill	Christian	Jos. S. Dickinson, 1 qr.	3 87	6 45
		Josiah Carneal, from 1st Jan.	6 34	10 26
Millerstown	Grayson	Adam Keyser	15 58	26 92
Millersville	Adair	A. A. Strange, jr.	no return	
Mills' Point (Ch'd to "Hickman.")	Hickman	Chs. F. Hanna, to 31st Dec.	100 46	217 64
Mill Springs	Wayne	Henry W. Tuttle	9 86	21 34
Milton	Trimble	Albert M. King	55 88	75 80
Minerva	Mason	Wm. P. Thomas	58 82	111 25
Monroe	Hart	Joshua Brents	11 65	11 04
Monticello	Wayne	Henry R. Laufley	146 96	139 34
Moorefield	Nicholas	Dunlap Howe	37 93	71 05
Moreland	Bourbon	James W. Wright	38 16	75 75
Morganfield	Union	Jos. W. Cromwell, to 30th Sept	61 42	57 83
		John H. McCormick	179 30	168 76
Morgantown	Butler	Thomas D. Carson, to 31st Dec.	22 95	38 97
		Barrett J. Burke	22 43	40 46
Mortonsville	Woodford	Wm. M. Morris	42 17	78 77
Moscow	Hickman	Jos. M. Dudley	38 63	74 37
Motier	Pendleton	John Mains	6 03	10 90
Mount Carmel	Fleming	Gilbert Adams	56 75	104 03
Mount Eden	Spencer	David E. Harcourt	15 78	31 63
Mount Freedom	Jessamine	David P. Sutton, fr. 26th June	11 61	18 97
Mount Gilead	Mason	Joseph Wallingford, 2 qrs	6 34	12 63
Mount Hope	Henry	Christopher Peake	11 07	20 81
Mount Sterling	Montgomery	R. P. B. Caldwell	348 23	741 96
Mount Vernon	Rock Castle	Joseph Reynolds	79 69	161 25
Mount Washing'n	Bullitt	John Q. A. Hall	60 00	120 44
Mount Zion	Union	Jonat'n J. Williams	16 86	16 90
Mulberry Grove	Hopkins	Beckley Jackson	14 76	26 53
Munfordsville	Hart	John T. S. Brown	124 59	118 58
Murphysville	Mason	Joseph How	16 29	26 28
Murray	Callaway	Charles Curd	69 23	135 63
Narrowsville (Dis. 21st April)	Daviess	Wesley M. Little, to 22d Dec.	1 12	1 43
		Jesse B. Moseley, to 16th May	0 87	1 38
Neatsville	Adair	Samuel C. Caldwell	9 93	21 48
Nebo	Hopkins	Alfred Townes	5 64	10 04

POST OFFICES—*Kentucky.*

Post Offices.	Counties.	Postmasters.	Compensation.	Net proceeds.
Newberry	Wayne	John H. Phillips	$4 11	$8 72
Newburgh	Jefferson	John W. Smyser	11 27	18 97
New Castle	Henry	Jesse Bassett	194 45	347 44
New Concord	Callaway	Wm. B. Lawson, to 31st March	27 19	46 16
		Cyrus Owen	8 00	15 51
New Design	Christian	Ambrose E. Jones	37 33	40 47
New Haven	Nelson	Joseph Brown	30 18	55 30
New Hope	Nelson	Lawrence J. Berry	4 87	5 83
New Liberty	Owen	James O'Hara	127 12	218 70
New Market	Marion	William McAfee	7 97	11 82
Newport	Campbell	F. T. Helm, 3 qrs	131 55	267 79
Newtown	Scott	Jos. W. Kean	38 63	65 15
Nicholasville	Jessamine	David P. Watson	313 61	478 61
Nolen	Hardin	Josiah Mosher, to 19th Feb	14 89	28 46
		John A. Raine	9 03	17 59
North Fork	Mason	Isaac Lewis	64 64	116 71
North Middlet'n	Bourbon	Nathan G. Darnall	101 69	175 98
Oak Forest	Wayne	Stephen Scott	7 75	13 92
Oak Grove	Christian	Samuel Gordon	94 55	166 81
Oak Hill	Hardin	Jefferson Brownfield	4 53	8 16
Old Town	Greenup	Samuel Osenton	7 47	13 76
Olive Hill	Carter	James W. Scott	6 66	12 89
Olympian Springs	Bath	Harrison Gill	4 13	8 79
Owensboro'	Daviess	Jesse P. Bristow	308 90	650 91
Owenton	Owen	H. B. Vallandingham	69 55	120 80
Owingsville	Bath	James W. Thomas	118 80	220 84
Owsley C. H	Owsley	Francis Hamblen	7 69	13 89
Oxford	Crittenden	James M. Smith	32 37	59 84
Paces	Barren	Sanford R. Pace	17 48	30 87
Paducah	McCracken	Francis A. Harrison	343 58	584 28
Paint Lick	Garrard	James H. Spilman	46 76	85 62
Paintsville	Johnson	Jesse Wheeler	19 08	35 84
Paris	Bourbon	Otho Hughes	611 21	1364 14
Peeled Oak	Bath	Thomas Ficklin	6 57	12 82
Pembroke	Christian	Wm. H. Clark, to 31st Dec	7 13	12 50
		Robert C. Jameson	5 61	9 73
Perry C. H	Perry	Robert H. Godsey	10 86	7 43
Perryville	Mercer	John A. Burton	140 14	134 28
Petersburg	Boone	Chs. O. Alden	39 30	66 03
Peters' Creek	Barren	William Ellis	9 81	20 08
Piatt's Landing	Boone	Maltby Smith	14 44	28 67
Piketon	Pike	John Dils, jr	19 14	28 37
Planter's Hall	Breckenridge	James Moorman	5 04	6 03
Pleasant Grove	Ohio	Francis Sullinger	6 17	10 78

POST OFFICES—*Kentucky.*

Post Offices.	Counties.	Postmasters.	Compensation.	Net proceeds.
Pleasant Ridge	Bracken	O. T. McClenahan	$4 82	$9 39
Pleasureville	Henry	Henry K. Lucas	63 83	115 81
Poor Fork	Harlan	James J. Lewis, fr. 16th April	0 03	0 07
Poplar Flat	Lewis	Thomas Henderson	19 30	28 15
Poplar Grove	Owen	William Garvey	9 58	16 92
Poplar Plains	Fleming	Elias B. Pearce	54 60	102 48
Portland	Jefferson	Paul Villier	39 35	78 85
Port Royal	Henry	Richard Johnston, to 31st Dec	12 12	25 47
		Orlando Lane	14 60	29 02
Powersville	Bracken	James W. Morford	10 09	16 81
Prestonburgh	Floyd	Chs. W. Friend	44 38	80 77
Prestonville	Carroll	George W. Pullam, jr., from 15th Jan.	0 31	0 60
Prewitt's Knob	Barren	Elisha Dickey	28 29	28 15
Princeton	Caldwell	Alex'r H. Dudley	237 22	422 80
Proctor (Dis. 16th May)	Estill	Nathan Jacobs, 3 qrs.	9 40	19 29
Providence	Hopkins	Wiley B. Stations	36 43	69 73
Racoon	Laurel	Jesse Moore, 3 qrs	0 34	0 42
Raywick	Marion	John S. Ray	17 67	25 62
Red River Iron Works	Estill	Wm G. Jackson	30 42	51 60
Richland	Henderson	John H. Priest	4 24	8 34
Richmond	Madison	Jas. M. Shackelford, to 15th May	377 60	819 07
		Robert E. Kelly	47 97	110 84
Rochester	Butler	Wm. S. McDowell	7 29	15 80
Rock Creek	Lewis	Willis Bagby	9 84	19 58
Rockholds	Whitley	T. Rockhold, 3 qrs.	3 45	7 84
Rock Spring	Hickman	Council B. Coor	6 59	10 34
Rocky Ford	Casey	Henry H. Reynierson, from 1st Oct.	0 95	1 32
Rocky Hill	Barren	Franklin Settle	21 68	36 80
Rolling Fork	Nelson	Ogden W. Stiles	2 86	5 36
Rome	Knox	Ambrose Arthur	4 75	7 43
Ruddle's Mills	Bourbon	Isaac Johnson	36 32	68 87
Rumsey	Muhlenburgh	Wm. T. Short	46 56	87 12
Russellville	Logan	Bazil Wood, jr.	336 58	702 56
Salem	Livingston	Aquilla P. Greer	41 31	79 26
Salina	Jefferson	Wm. Q. Johnson	18 02	29 49
Salonia	Greene	Edward A. Parsons	25 99	47 86
Salvisa	Mercer	Wm. H. McAfee	77 78	145 22
Scottsville	Allen	Wm. F. Evans	97 63	189 34
Seventy Six	Clinton	Chs. D. Semple	5 71	12 92
Sexton's Creek	Clay	Henry Clark	3 61	7 47

POST OFFICES—*Kentucky.*

Post Offices.	Counties.	Postmasters.	Compensation.	Net proceeds.
Shannon	Mason	John M. Reed	$23 62	$39 74
Sharpsburg	Bath	Jonat'n L. Camplin	141 95	262 30
Shawnee Run	Mercer	John R. Bryant	36 00	64 50
Sheaffer's Mill	Ohio	A. Sheaffer, 1 qr	1 32	2 70
		Benj'n R. Briggs, fr. 1st Jan.	2 18	4 43
Shelbyville	Shelby	John Lane, to 30th September	140 95	311 94
		Harry Ellingwood, 2 qrs	275 77	616 12
Shepherdsville	Bullitt	Abm. Field, 3 qrs	80 28	156 39
Sherburne Mills	Fleming	Jno. Andrews, 3 qrs.	31 93	55 70
Silver Creek	Madison	Alexander Miller	20 68	36 75
Simpsonville	Shelby	Orlando C. Mershon	82 65	153 25
Six Mile	Union	Isaac Jones	0 91	1 67
Skegg's Creek	Barren	Wm. A. Norvell	4 56	8 34
Slate	Bath	Isaac Trumbo, to 28th Feb.	15 98	31 49
		Samuel F. Gault	7 76	16 61
Smithland	Livingston	John A. Martin	272 10	596 11
Smith's Grove	Warren	William Wright	14 25	27 04
Smith's Mills	Henderson	Horace S. Anderson	19 24	33 36
Somerset	Pulaski	Edward Kelly	126 15	244 14
South Fork	Owsley	Ab'h B. Gilbert, 1 qr.	03	09
South Union	Logan	David Smith	58 59	114 74
Southville	Shelby	Jesse Veech	11 64	20 91
Springfield	Washington	John C. Moffitt	198 39	407 34
Springville	Greenup	James H. Savage, to 31st December	4 87	9 58
		William Dupuy, jr.	7 98	16 66
Stacker Iron Wk's	Trigg	Thomas T. Watson	24 35	48 63
(Ch'd to Empire Iron Works.)				
Stamping Ground	Scott	Jesse S. Sinclair, to 31st March	34 41	68 69
		Richard J. Wisdom	11 73	22 78
Stanford	Lincoln	Josephus Campbell, to 2d June	225 78	185 18
		Clifton G. Rice	15 25	12 45
State Line (Dis. 26th Aug.)	Allen	James W. Foster, to 30th September	14	29
Stephensburgh	Hardin	Richard Porter, to 31st Dec.	8 97	16 77
		Wm. M. Howsley	8 71	16 82
Stephensport	Breckenridge	Chas. N. S. Taylor	20 17	37 70
Strongville	Breathitt	Ed'd Strong, 2 qrs.	1 29	1 28
Summersville	Greene	Fielding Chelf	18 30	33 36
Sylvan Dale (Dis. 24th Jan.)	Carter	Chas H. Stewart	no return	

POST OFFICES—*Kentucky*.

Post Offices.	Counties.	Postmasters.	Compensation.	Net proceeds.
Tar Springs	Breckenridge.	N. Faulconer, 1 qr.	$0 98	$2 02
Taylorsville	Spencer	M.B.Shelburne, 1 qr.	23 20	42 32
Terre Salis	Clay	Gust'us B. Quarrier	5 84	11 77
The Exchange (Dis. 16th May.)	McCracken	Kirby Jones	no return	
Three Forks	Barren	William Bell	20 40	23 42
Three Springs	Hart	Allen W. Durham	17 25	16 73
Tompkinsville	Monroe	Jos. P. Taylor	83 45	151 70
Trenton	Todd	Jas. L. Lawson	89 12	162 56
Triplett	Fleming	John R. Powers	9 24	15 37
Turman's Ferry	Lawrence	Geo. R. Burgess	4 35	9 39
Tygert's Creek	Greenup	Roger W. Waring	8 99	15 07
Union	Boone	Morris Lassing	19 18	30 03
Uniontown	Union	Nicholas Gwynn	30 92	65 40
Unity	Muhlenburgh	John S. Eaves, 1 qr.	21	37
Upper Tygart	Carter	John Thompson	5 24	8 63
Vanceburgh	Lewis	William Sutherland.	21 51	43 99
Verona	Boone	Jesse Gregory	12 19	23 97
Versailles	Woodford	Robert Kinkead	439 27	930 72
Viney Fork	Madison	D. S. Goodloe, 2 qrs.	2 23	5 23
Wadesboro'	Callaway	William Brown, to 31st March	27 50	47 59
		Wm. W. Williams.	8 47	13 51
Walkers	Livingston	Robert A. Walker	15 55	29 52
Wallonia	Trigg	James R. Hayes, f'm 27th Feb	4 74	9 47
Walnut Flat (Dis. 27th Nov.) (Re-est. 21st Feb.)	Lincoln	C. C. P. Joyce, to 14th Aug	1 78	3 36
		Jno. W. Dawes, to 15th Nov	3 43	6 05
		Jas. W. Farris, from 28th March	4 83	4 73
Walnut Grove	Caldwell	Wm. D. Miller	1 16	2 19
Walnut Ridge	Boone	Benj. W. Grant	8 25	16 95
Walnut Valley	Madison	Jonathan Nelson	7 00	12 69
Walton	Boone	O. H. P. Ingram, 3 quarters	33 99	63 58
Warrenton	Warren	William Brown	4 50	8 30
Warsaw	Gallatin	Jefferson Peak	138 88	290 17
Washington	Mason	Jacob P. Downing	245 43	379 18
Waynesburgh	Lincoln	W. F. Camden, 3 qrs.	2 84	6 53
Welborn's	Todd	William Welborn, from 20 Jan	13	14
Wesley	Hickman	Otho Hardin	6 99	7 17
West Liberty	Morgan	A. W. Turner, to 31st Dec	10 29	19 93

POST OFFICES—*Ohio.*

Post Offices.	Counties.	Postmasters.	Compensation.	Net proceeds.
		Edward E. Duke....	$12 94	$24 85
West Point......	Hardin......	Coleman Lewis.....	71 80	129 20
Westport........	Oldham......	George Armstrong..	57 02	109 70
White Hall......	Madison.....	Joel E. Fox.......	8 88	17 46
White House.....	Lewis.......	Joseph Linley......	10 69	19 39
Whitesburgh.....	Letcher.....	William B. Stamper, $8\frac{2}{3}$ months........	1 62	3 87
White Sulphur...	Scott.......	Daniel Vanderslice..	39 73	47 38
Whitley C. H....	Whitley.....	Squire Gatliff, to 15th Feb............	10 42	21 45
		Randolph C. Noe....	8 82	16 21
Wickliffe's Forge	Bath........	Joshua Ewing.......	no return	
Williams........	Christian....	John T. Brashear..	10 54	16 05
Williamsburgh...	Mason.......	Wm. O. Phillips...	33 47	56 91
Williamstown....	Grant.......	Seth Dowd.........	91 53	147 18
Willisburgh.....	Washington.	William W. Phelps, from 9th Jan.....	43	87
		John Yocum........	78	1 67
Willow Grove....	Crittenden....	Jas. W. Wilson.....	5 63	9 75
Wilmington......	McCracken..	Chiles Terrell......	3 88	8 00
Wilson's........	Ohio........	Simeon Wilson.....	8 16	14 22
Wilson's Creek...	Graves......	James Lamm.......	11 38	18 56
Wilsonville......	Spencer......	John M. Reid......	18 48	32 47
Winchester......	Clark.......	William Flanagan..	400 24	826 21
Woodbine	Whitley.....	James Wells.......	63	1 05
Woodburn.......	Warren......	Jonathan L. Samson	5 89	9 40
Woodsonville....	Hart........	Sinclair Garvin, to 31st March.......	21 44	38 42
		Spottswood Pemberton............	5 67	11 67
Worthington.....	Muhlenburgh	William Kincheloe.	9 74	16 70
Yarnallton	Fayette......	Isaac N. Yarnall....	12 70	26 76
Yellow Creek....	Knox........	John P. Bruce.....	5 50	11 56
Yelvington	Daviess......	James Martin......	43 00	54 81

OHIO.

NOTE.—Compensation of Postmasters, and net proceeds of their offices, from July 1, 1844, to June 30, 1845.

Post Offices.	Counties.	Postmasters.	Compensation.	Net proceeds.
Abbeyville......	Medina......	Charles Castle, to 30th Sept.........	$4 09	$6 45
		Asa Brownell......	10 48	17 14

POST OFFICES—*Ohio.*

Post Offices.	Counties.	Postmasters.	Compensation.	Net proceeds.
Aberdeen	Brown	Eli Davidson	$92 43	$116 26
Achor	Columbiana	Jacob Young	16 80	22 36
Adams	Seneca	Ebenezer Smith	19 80	41 05
Adams' Mills	Muskingum	Edward Adams	39 13	68 97
Adamsville	Muskingum	Jared Cone, jr	57 55	98 86
Adario	Richland	Henry Barnes, 1 qr.	1 00	1 41
Addison	Gallia	Augustus S. Guthrie	2 98	5 02
Adelphi	Ross	G. Will, to 23d Ap'l	57 37	96 56
		Samuel Haninger	10 67	18 24
Akron	Summit	Harvey H. Johnson	648 64	1559 36
Albany	Tuscarawas	Benj. D. Duhamell	1 47	2 96
Albion	Wayne	Robert Buchanan	20 98	38 21
Alexander	Athens	William Patterson	8 14	13 54
Alexandersville	Montgomery	Moses Smith, to 22d Jan.	27 21	48 65
		Danl. E. Hoff	28 57	51 58
Alexandria	Licking	Henry V. Owen	88 47	152 16
Alfred	Meigs	Peter Hoffman	12 00	21 87
Allen's	Miami	Joseph Merrit	14 61	22 79
Allensburgh	Highland	Oliver C. Collins	2 18	3 89
Allensville	Jackson	William Brady	9 74	19 06
Alton	Franklin	David P. Cole, to 1st March	7 12	12 87
		Edw. M. Shanks	5 44	5 02
Alum Creek	Delaware	Wm. P. Smith	25 86	42 10
Amanda	Fairfield	David Halderman	49 69	83 01
Amboy	Ashtabula	Jacob S. Flagler, to 23d Jan.	15 85	22 90
		Dioclesian Williams	12 89	17 05
Amelia	Clermont	Wm. D. Sutton	53 87	78 64
Amesville	Athens	Hiram Cable	37 14	70 41
Amherst	Lorain	Eliphalet Redington	52 77	51 31
Amsterdam	Jefferson	David Johnston, to 31st March	15 20	27 15
		Robert Leslie	4 98	8 87
Anderson's Store	Morgan	Samuel Reiner	18 50	31 25
Andover	Ashtabula	Ansel Russell	84 79	139 27
Andrew's	Richland	Benj. P. Truax	23 19	42 94
Annapolis	Jefferson	William Vantz	42 34	62 01
Antioch	Monroe	Elihu Morris	18 20	31 20
Antrim	Guernsey	James Stevenson	35 96	65 80
Antwerp	Paulding	Horatio N. Curtis	13 17	24 89
Apple Creek	Wayne	John L. Cheyney	53 75	76 90
Appleton	Licking	Gideon Long	18 09	31 03
Archer	Harrison	Abner Hixson	6 32	11 85
Arcole	Lake	Chs. F. Swan	56 47	95 10
Armstrong's Mills	Belmont	Alexan'r Armstrong	25 45	34 22
Arnheim. (Dis. 2 July.)	Brown	Jacob S. Campbell	5 98	9 44

POST OFFICES—*Ohio.*

Post Offices.	Counties.	Postmasters.	Compensation.	Net proceeds.
Arrowsmith's.	Defiance	Abraham Bercaw	$4 81	$8 56
Asbury	Perry	George Kishler	14 05	19 33
Asherry	Hancock	Joseph Twining	2 01	4 42
Ashland	Richland	Hulbert Luther	244 85	475 02
Ashtabula	Ashtabula	Nehemiah Hubbard	326 68	513 43
Astoria	Butler	Andrew D. Rodgers,		
(Dis. 25th Sept.)		to 30th Sept.	1 33	2 14
Athens	Athens	John Perkins	319 99	602 62
Attica	Seneca	William Moore, to		
		24th Nov.	27 63	45 44
		William McManigal	38 46	70 13
Atwater	Portage	Caleb Atwater	49 85	85 30
Auburn	Geauga	Hervey Harrington.	63 55	81 12
Auglaize	Van Wert	John McCollam	5 11	10 42
Augusta	Carroll	William Clinton	13 74	24 92
Aurora	Portage	Wm. R. Henry	99 65	156 50
Austinburgh	Ashtabula	Lewis B. Austin	118 11	190 11
Avon	Lorain	Wm. S. Hopkins	61 98	113 55
Bainbridge	Ross	Mather Gilfillan	143 60	132 70
Baker's	Champaign	Harvey Talbot	10 74	20 14
Baltimore	Fairfield	Tennis Cox	108 79	180 90
Bangor	Richland	Riley Whitten	7 82	12 01
Bantam	Clermont	Benjamin Ely	34 92	56 61
Bare's	Monroe	Jacob Bare	26 06	40 92
Barlow	Washington	Lyman Loflin	38 02	66 39
Barnes'	Richland	Wm. S. Paul	15 24	23 66
Barnesville	Belmont	Benjamin Mackall	178 67	302 40
Barry	Cuyahoga	Elbridge Smith	23 35	48 03
Barryville	Stark	Martin Hoover	15 31	29 73
Bartlett	Washington	Solomon King	32 32	53 27
Batavia	Clermont	George Medary	113 57	191 94
Batesville	Guernsey	Benjamin Davenport	48 45	81 22
Bath	Summit	Lewis F. Laine	45 76	79 76
Baxter's	Muskingum	Samuel Baxter	9 15	13 87
Bazetta	Trumbull	Lewis Abel, to 3d		
		June	22 65	43 39
		Ezra Marvin	2 89	5 36
Beallsville	Monroe	Citizen Beall, to 3d		
		May	49 77	88 38
		Thomas Cummings.	3 67	8 31
Beamsville	Darke	Philip Hartzell	14 35	26 08
Beaver	Pike	Geo. W. Reynolds,		
		to 30th May	17 60	23 90
		Michael Gall	1 21	2 42
Beaver Creek	Henry	John Sowers, 3 qrs.	85	1 51
Bedford	Cuyahoga	Wm. B. Hillman	120 66	214 78
Beechy Mire	Preble	John McCaughan	10 59	18 72
Beeson's Store	Highland	Geo. H. Baker	12 12	23 84

POST OFFICES—*Ohio.*

Post Offices.	Counties.	Postmasters.	Compensation.	Net proceeds.
Belfast	Clermont	John Simpkins	$9 94	$14 33
Bell Air	Belmont	John Archer	29 97	46 12
Bellbrook	Greene	Robt. E. Patterson	63 72	103 66
Bellefontaine	Logan	John B. Miller	228 57	416 81
Belle Point	Delaware	Job Liget	13 90	29 64
Belle Vernon	Wyandott	Jacob Curlis	3 53	6 79
Belleville	Richland	Elijah Clark	160 30	156 72
Bellevue	Huron	John Gross, 31st March	200 78	258 49
		Lowell Chandler	76 21	87 97
Belmont	Belmont	J. Dew Wright	95 08	160 43
Belpre	Washington	Josiah Henderson	23 86	40 51
Bennington	Delaware	Geo. N. Clark	47 82	90 12
Benton	Holmes	John Stiffler	16 98	34 30
Benton Ridge	Hancock	Michael Fishel	6 60	13 52
Bentonville	Adams	Asahel D. Keet	24 17	30 39
Berea	Cuyahoga	Henry O. Sheldon	29 61	55 95
Berkshire	Delaware	Jas. P. Crawford	30 56	51 15
Berlin	Holmes	Geo. W. Chapman	58 42	101 30
Berlin Centre	Trumbull	W. Kirk, to 25th Jan	13 00	20 14
		Isaac Cronk	13 55	20 71
Berlinville	Erie	Burrel Keeler	122 16	138 77
Berne	Monroe	Moses C. Morton	18 95	32 51
Bethany	Butler	Peter Williamson	36 23	56 96
Bethel	Clermont	Thos. J. Morris	82 00	143 93
Bettsville	Seneca	Rufus Norton	8 14	15 35
Beverly	Washington	John Keyhoe	91 19	163 20
Bevis' Tavern	Hamilton	Jesse Bevis	11 35	26 53
Big Island	Marion	Alson Norton	9 27	18 60
Big Prairie	Wayne	John P. Steward	44 25	42 65
Birmingham	Erie	Washingt'n E. Cook	125 95	145 13
Bissell's	Geauga	Justus Bissell	42 28	72 25
Blachlysville	Wayne	Henry Swart	18 99	32 74
Black River	Lorain	Danl. T. Baldwin	47 17	75 83
Black Swamp	Sandusky	Henry Reiling	10 35	15 85
Bladensburgh	Knox	John Wheeler, to 26th June	23 85	41 35
		Thomas Axtell	71	1 32
Blanchard Bridge	Hancock	Aquilla Gilbert	7 68	11 41
Blanchester	Clinton	James R. Darby, to 7th March	13 30	20 68
		Saml. Baldwin	6 40	10 23
Blendon	Franklin	Isaac Griswold	19 16	37 02
Bloom (Dis. 12th July.)	Seneca	John Stroh, to 30th Sept	42	85
Bloomfield	Knox	Samuel Whitney	21 22	30 45
Bloomingburgh	Fayette	Wm. R. Southward, to 19th June	72 27	121 55
		Azro C. Putnam	1 17	2 75

POST OFFICES—*Ohio.*

Post Offices.	Counties.	Postmasters.	Compensation.	Net proceeds.
Bloomingdale	Jefferson	Basil Carter	$52 30	$84 85
Bloomingville	Erie	Saml. B. Carpender	20 51	36 97
Bloomville	Seneca	Thomas Treat	30 62	49 04
Blue Ball	Butler	Robert McChesney, from 26th Aug	18 41	32 50
Blue Creek	Adams	Isaac N. Williams, from 1st Oct	2 54	3 84
Blue Rock	Muskingum	James Finley	44 29	74 19
Boardman	Trumbull	Arthur Patrick	49 24	45 90
Bolen's Mills	Athens	Jacob Lentner	4 45	8 52
Bolivar	Tuscarawas	Martin S. Tinker	74 07	139 87
Bonn	Washington	John K. Norton	11 31	18 90
Boston	Summit	Arthur Latham	29 09	49 60
Bourneville	Ross	William Fuller	52 20	85 10
Bowling Green	Wood	Lee Moore	37 57	58 63
Bowshersville	Wyandott	Wm. H. Hunt	7 10	13 57
Boyd's	Columbiana	James Boyd	4 11	7 12
Braceville	Trumbull	Auren Stow	34 56	62 06
Bradford	Scioto	Roswell Craine	4 54	8 14
Brandywine Mills	Summit	George Wallace	9 78	16 20
Bremen	Fairfield	Hylas Stiles, to 13th June	24 81	45 06
		Jesse G. Beery	1 29	2 43
Bricksville	Cuyahoga	Chauncey L. Young	54 37	94 70
Bridge Creek	Geauga	George Wilber	12 73	21 75
Bridgeport	Belmont	James A. Gray	82 32	141 41
Bridgeville	Muskingum	Samuel Weaver, to 16th Sept	6 10	11 66
		Henry Croll	24 95	43 25
Brighton	Lorain	Dan Clark	13 38	24 61
Brimfield	Portage	Edward Parsons	50 52	76 23
Brinton	Champaign	Leicester Ware	25 43	46 95
Bristol	Morgan	Elijah Stevens	14 03	27 16
Bristolville	Trumbull	Jacob Hammond	33 68	46 52
Broken Sword	Crawford	William Wingart	9 21	19 09
Bronson	Huron	John Lyon	23 92	45 25
Brookfield	Trumbull	Alex'r A. Adams	35 93	63 73
Brooklyn	Cuyahoga	Francis Fuller	70 74	93 03
Brownhelm	Lorain	James S. Brown	44 39	69 48
Brown's Grove	Hamilton	Mahlon Brown	8 19	13 92
Brown's Mills	Washington	Hiram Gard	14 62	25 62
Brown's Store	Warren	Samuel Brown	11 39	16 38
Brownsville	Licking	Moses Brotherlin, to 4th March	60 42	110 37
		John F. Bane	31 07	58 80
Brunersburgh	Defiance	Brice Hilton	21 95	35 68
Brunswick	Medina	Abner Martin	137 78	233 23
Bryan	Williams	William Yates	49 32	89 44
Buckeye	Putnam	Calvin T. Pomeroy	24 57	44 03

POST OFFICES—*Ohio.*

Post Offices.	Counties.	Postmasters.	Compensation.	Net proceeds.
Bucks	Columbia	Caleb Hawley	$35 26	$35 33
Bucyrus	Crawford	James McCracken, to 19th May	291 65	530 97
		Alex'r P. Widman	26 33	61 15
Buffalo	Guernsey	Peter D. Robins	20 80	26 97
Buford	Highland	John Hogsett	18 79	35 46
Bundysburgh	Geauga	Robert G. Porter	8 75	14 45
Burbank	Wayne	David S. Bryant	10 45	17 24
Burlingham	Meigs	John S. Clark	3 56	6 46
Burlington	Lawrence	Camillus Hall	65 61	111 11
Burton	Geauga	James Peffers	69 25	123 05
Butlersville	Warren	Isaac Leming	35 78	56 23
Byesville	Guernsey	Luther Burt	9 97	16 01
Byington	Pike	Isaac Holton	4 13	7 82
Cadiz	Harrison	John Beall	295 10	428 07
Cadwallader	Tuscarawas	Joshua Corey	31 85	65 21
Calais	Monroe	Crispin Oglebay	10 79	19 34
Calcutta	Columbiana	Josiah Thompson	71 94	80 65
Caledonia	Marion	Henry Bretz, to 30th September	8 07	12 67
		Greenville P. Cherry	32 01	56 67
Calvary	Athens	Sylvanus Howe	4 84	8 50
Cambridge	Guernsey	W.Smith,to13thMay	231 78	452 95
		Robert Burns	33 41	73 51
Camden	Preble	Chs. C. Walker	127 53	219 47
Campbell	Lawrence	John Campbell	29 88	51 19
Campbellsport	Portage	R. B. Campbell	40 93	62 32
Canaan	Wayne	Daniel Emerson	17 57	29 90
Canaanville	Athens	N. O. Warren	4 27	8 56
Canal Dover	Tuscarawas	Solomon Sala	208 36	440 85
Canal Fulton	Stark	Calvin P. Cobb	191 01	266 42
Canal Winchester	Fairfield	James B. Evans	73 53	121 88
Canfield	Trumbull	John R. Church	146 36	136 54
Cannonsburgh	Hancock	Jos. A. Leslie	11 65	22 67
Cannon's Mill	Columbiana	Henry Ewing	9 95	9 98
Canton	Stark	Ernest M. Krakan	460 42	971 83
Captina	Belmont	Michael Dorsey	10 25	17 86
Cardington	Marion	Thos. C. Thomson	38 36	66 34
Carey's Academy	Hamilton	Zebulon Strong	32 24	61 35
Carrollton	Carroll	Thomas Wilson, to 21st Jan	83 65	146 06
		Henry A. Stidger	74 91	130 50
Carthage	Hamilton	William D. Ludlow	93 18	105 92
Carysville	Champaign	Samuel Bowersock	17 03	33 59
Cass	Hancock	Daniel Fairchild	10 83	19 88
Castalia	Erie	Daniel P. Russell, to 31st March	52 67	88 82
		Wm. C. Baker	14 27	28 10

POST OFFICES—*Ohio.*

Post Offices.	Counties.	Postmasters.	Compensation.	Net proceeds.
Catawba	Clark	Samuel Conway	$16 44	$30 38
Cedar Valley	Wayne	Thos. G. Boydston	7 63	12 07
Cedarville	Greene	John Paris	84 92	83 94
Celina	Mercer	Samuel Ruckman	15 49	33 75
Central College	Franklin	Austin Stebbins	29 42	51 00
Centre	Delaware	Moses Decker	12 56	23 54
Centre Belpre	Washington	George N. Gilbert	30 06	53 38
Centreburgh	Knox	Harvey Jones	28 19	50 35
CentreFarmington	Trumbull	Harvey W. Collar	22 30	34 52
Centreville	Montgomery	Enos Doolittle	77 36	141 58
Chagrin Falls	Cuyahoga	Royal Dewey	155 82	263 71
Challensville	Hamilton	Wm. H. Scudder	19 37	18 68
Chambersburgh	Montgomery	Tilman W. Slick	20 84	36 83
Chandlersville	Muskingum	Nathaniel Chapman	86 41	136 08
Chaneyville	Morgan	William Harry, to 22d April	5 90	8 12
		Ortus N. Chaney	1 01	1 44
Chardon	Geauga	Barton F Avery	188 51	287 31
Charlestown	Portage	Julius Remington, to 24th August	7 92	12 75
		Luther L. Brown	49 36	79 60
Charloe	Paulding	Hugh R. Porter	30 87	59 90
Chatfield	Crawford	Richard Frisbie	27 04	45 59
Chatham	Licking	Samuel Myers	21 50	39 07
Chatham Centre	Medina	William Jurden	18 80	33 08
Chauncey	Athens	Chs. R. Smith, to 31st March	31 70	57 13
		Robert Sharp	5 04	7 42
Cherokee	Logan	James Langhead	48 34	88 92
Cherry Fork	Adams	James Ramsay	17 80	26 87
Cherry Valley	Ashtabula	Lockwood Lobdell	34 30	49 47
Cheshire	Gallia	Samuel H. Gates	15 77	16 44
Chester	Meigs	Oren Branch, to 14th February	42 97	60 40
		Josiah Branch	25 38	37 17
Chester ⋈ Roads	Geauga	Jas. E. Stephenson	84 37	144 18
Chesterfield	Lucas	Alfred C. Hough	25 39	48 20
Chester Hill	Athens	George G. King	28 78	51 27
Chesterville	Knox	Thomas Peterson	no return	
		Pascal B. Ayers, fr. 4th Sept	52 56	93 38
Cheviot	Hamilton	Josiah Bateman, to 31st March	70 30	69 94
		Thomas Wills	22 57	21 98
Chickasaw	Mercer	Samuel W. Ripley, to 31st March	15 93	29 60
		T. J. Young	5 26	9 21
Chili	Coshocton	John Winklepleck	30 87	47 69
Chilicothe	Ross	John R. Anderson	1455 02	3278 18

POST OFFICES—*Ohio.*

Post Offices.	Counties.	Postmasters.	Compensation.	Net proceeds.
Chilo	Clermont	John O. Prather, to 31st Dec	$7 91	$14 02
		Jesse Healy	8 74	17 29
Chippewa	Wayne	William Forster	76 25	135 04
Christiansburgh	Champaign	Andrew Wilson, jr.	47 38	87 58
Church Hill	Trumbull	Robert H. Walker	16 48	22 10
Cincinnati	Hamilton	Wm. H. H. Taylor	2004 50	42727 97
Circle (Dis. 14th Mar.)	Knox	William Blair, jr., to 31st March	5 26	8 42
Circle Green	Jefferson	Peter Barger, 1 mo.	0 10	0 10
Circleville	Pickaway	Wm. B. Brown	754 46	1838 75
Claridon	Geauga	Cotton Kellogg	39 14	65 30
Clarks	Coshocton	William Tidball	11 51	20 06
Clarksburgh	Ross	George Smith	31 42	56 05
Clarksfield	Huron	Smith Starr	96 06	155 74
Clark's Mills	Lawrence	Hammond Howe	6 11	11 07
Clarkson	Columbiana	Richard Stock	27 19	48 35
Clarksville	Clinton	Joseph Wysong	76 83	137 27
Claysville	Guernsey	Walter Bell	51 88	87 57
Clayton	Montgomery	Warren Estabrook	41 59	72 87
Clear Creek	Fairfield	Charles Sager	7 34	7 38
Cleveland	Cuyahoga	Benjamin Andrews, to 30th April	1415 18	8575 60
		Timothy P. Spencer	219 39	2149 69
Cleves	Hamilton	Jos. M. Runyan	73 86	122 25
Clifton	Greene	John Anderson	74 07	125 71
Clinton	Summit	Solomon Sorrick	56 40	108 59
Clinton House	Clinton	Charles Cline, to 31st March	5 48	7 07
		Robert Williams	1 70	2 81
Clyde	Mercer	John Partner	1 87	4 06
Coal Run	Washington	Benjamin Wilson	22 85	35 67
Cobb's Corners	Portage	Samuel Cobb	5 56	8 40
Coberly's	Union	Eben'r W. Crary	8 11	13 70
Cochran's	Putnam	William Cochran, jr.	3 50	7 07
Cochranton	Marion	Samuel L. Gray	9 81	21 78
Coe Ridge	Cuyahoga	Asher M. Coe	9 24	16 05
Cortsville	Trumbull	John Shields, to 30th September	4 21	7 15
		Andrew McFarlin, to 31st March	7 55	11 84
		James Milligan	3 32	5 39
Colerain	Belmont	Joshua Maule	46 91	84 84
Cole's Mills	Delaware	Jos. C. Cole	5 62	9 17
College Corner	Butler	James McCaw	54 69	92 55
Collinsville	Butler	Andrew P. Young	29 17	45 19
Columbia	Hamilton	Abraham Knicely	14 61	25 51
Columbiana	Columbiana	John Young	62 22	101 87
Columbus	Franklin	John G. Miller	1977 82	6464 50

POST OFFICES—*Ohio.*

Post Offices.	Counties.	Postmasters.	Compensation.	Net proceeds.
Concord	Lake	Zenas Wilson	$49 62	$88 31
Concordia	Darke	John S. Purviance	8 27	12 49
Congress	Wayne	Royce Summerton	87 10	140 16
Conneaut	Ashtabula	Ashbel Dart, to 31st December	172 04	202 34
		Samuel P. Fenton	160 89	203 44
Constitution	Washington	Ephraim Cutler	12 05	20 22
Convenience	Fayette	John De Witt	13 12	23 58
Cooke's Corners	Erie	Elihu Parker	4 41	5 69
Coolville (Late "Hocking City.")	Athens	John Pratt, from 1st January	24 54	40 58
Cope's Mills	Jefferson	Martin Adams, from 1st October	2 26	3 55
Copley	Summit	Heman Oviatt	58 98	89 12
Copopa	Lorain	John Weeden	25 92	46 59
Cork	Ashtabula	G. H. Secheverell	4 94	7 94
Cornersburgh	Trumbull	Thos. Harrison, jr.	11 30	15 02
Corsica	Richland	Urban G. Baker	20 11	31 61
Cortsville (Ch'd to 'Selma.')	Clark	Jos. C. Starry, to 30th September	12 84	19 44
Coshocton	Coshocton	Wm. K. Johnson, to 31st Dec	86 08	154 77
		Ch's H. Johnston	96 10	161 57
Courtwright (Ch'd to "Green Castle.")	Fairfield	Samuel Weiser	9 19	14 72
Covington	Miami	John Ross, to 21st May	85 84	131 26
		Jacob Widener	8 62	15 06
Cranesville	Paulding	Ephraim Burwell	7 88	12 30
Crawford	Wyandott	Asa Bixsby, to 30th September	3 25	6 22
		George Ames	15 85	30 25
Croghan	Putnam	Dan'l L. Goble	9 72	19 28
Crossanville	Perry	John Hays, jr., to 1st December	5 89	8 14
		Moses Fry, from 1st January	7 05	10 44
Cross Roads	Madison	David Williamson	30 91	56 91
Croton	Licking	William Winslow	49 52	83 39
Croxton	Jefferson	Benoni Wilkinson	21 81	35 98
Cuba	Clinton	William Davidson	14 76	29 46
Cumberland	Guernsey	William Abel	90 73	152 26
Cuminsville	Hamilton	Ephraim Knowlton	22 23	37 14
Cunningham	Putnam	Henry Miller	5 71	9 67
Cuyahoga Falls	Summit	Charles Babcock, to 17th May	401 45	930 68
		Oliver B. Beebe	56 08	125 56
Cynthiana	Pike	Elihu Hyatt	23 38	42 16

POST OFFICES—*Ohio.*

Post Offices.	Counties.	Postmasters.	Compensation.	Net proceeds.
Dalton	Wayne	Richard Cahill	$95 88	$177 23
Damascoville	Columbiana	Jas. B. Bruff	45 35	75 04
Damascus	Henry	John Burlin	31 71	60 05
Danville	Knox	Geo. H. Davidson	36 66	63 93
Darby Creek	Madison	Isaac Bigelow	48 03	75 58
Darby Plains	Union	Squire Deland	5 41	8 21
Darbyville	Pickaway	George Ambrose	35 42	57 76
Darlings	Knox	Orange Hollister	3 18	5 39
Darrtown	Butler	John McMechan	42 51	70 71
Dawkins' Mills	Jackson	James Elliott	10 01	19 05
Dayton	Montgomery	Thomas Blair, to 31st March	1008 13	2351 16
		Jos. W. McCorkle, from 19th April	216 26	639 25
Deardorff's Mills	Tuscarawas	William Goldrick	16 72	30 49
Deavertown	Morgan	Benjamin Graham	39 81	70 64
Decatur	Brown	Silas Thomas	38 82	72 02
Deep Cut	Mercer	Samuel Dellinger	13 84	22 37
Deerfield	Portage	Mason Gibbs	67 53	108 12
Deerfield Village	Warren	Wm. B. Lytle	10 43	20 77
Deersville	Harrison	Robert Pittis, jr	56 42	99 78
Defiance	Defiance	Orlando Evans, to 4th March	92 89	163 23
		Sam'l S. Case	46 22	85 03
De Kalb	Richland	David Anderson	37 68	62 38
Delaware	Delaware	Ezra Griswold	382 30	766 76
Delta	Lucas	Allen White	15 16	25 56
Democracy	Knox	John Gordon	68 79	68 05
Demos	Belmont	Alex'r S. Hoffman	18 81	27 97
Denman's Salt Works	Athens	Samuel Denman	18 71	27 34
Denmark	Ashtabula	Eben Williams	4 63	9 34
Dille's Bottom	Belmont	Benjamin Lockwood	20 89	36 33
Dinsmore	Shelby	Jacob Wiford	4 85	9 41
Dodsonville	Highland	George Shafer	6 19	10 29
Donnells	Allen	William Donnell	2 70	4 82
Donnelsville	Clark	John S. Morehouse	27 24	44 45
Dover	Cuyahoga	Marius Moore	44 53	78 79
Downington	Meigs	George Downing	8 75	15 21
Downingsville	Logan	Frederick Jasinsky	no ret.	
Dresden	Muskingum	Benjamin Adams, to 24th May	150 42	316 01
		Lawrence Bailey	20 02	41 82
Dry Ridge	Hamilton	Enoch W. Carson	19 11	29 91
Dublin	Franklin	John Eberly	52 18	97 86
Dudley	Hardin	Porteus Wheeler	24 65	28 96
Duff's Forks	Fayette	Wm. A. Phelps	21 69	38 45
Dukes	Putnam	Jesse Hall	5 44	9 63
Dumontville	Fairfield	Henry Alspaugh	12 43	22 49

POST OFFICES—*Ohio*.

Post Offices.	Counties.	Postmasters.	Compensation.	Net proceeds.
Dunbarton	Adams	H. J. Jackson, to 19th October	$15 69	$15 70
		Geo. W. Sample	32 60	38 72
Duncan's Falls	Muskingum	Henry S. Beeson	73 25	121 74
Dunganon	Columbiana	Hiram Gaver	8 09	12 94
Dunlap	Hamilton	Charles Richards	18 87	29 78
Eagle	Hancock	John W. Williams	16 16	27 96
Eagle Creek	Williams	Robert Ogle	9 55	19 37
Eagleville	Ashtabula	Myron Whiting	37 16	66 99
East Claridon	Geauga	William Depew	36 78	58 05
East Euclid	Cuyahoga	Austin H. Avery	46 10	45 24
East Fairfield	Columbiana	Jesse Williams	68 64	117 02
East Greenville	Stark	Abraham Johnson	22 16	40 23
East Lebanon	Wayne	John Freese	31 34	52 92
East Liberty	Logan	David W. Harrington, to 31st Mar.	33 10	57 79
		Thos. F. McAden	13 66	27 07
East Liverpool	Columbiana	John S. Blakeley, 3 qrs	53 25	103 05
East Monroe	Highland	David P. Dowell	17 37	29 42
East Palestine	Columbiana	Robert Chamberlain	10 67	22 13
Eastport	Tuscarawas	Richard Lyons	14 86	28 56
East Rochester	Columbiana	Thos. K. Armstrong	10 81	19 72
East Townsend	Huron	Hiram Boardman	9 15	15 71
East Union	Wayne	Rodney Carr	39 08	62 40
Eaton	Preble	John V. Campbell	210 83	394 47
Eckmansville	Adams	Amos Gulick	15 29	26 32
Eden	Trumbull	William Packard	6 50	13 86
Edinburgh	Portage	Joab Goddard	69 00	87 41
Edwardsville	Warren	Lewis Sever	11 28	18 78
Elizabethtown	Hamilton	Charles Mills	29 43	51 51
Elkton	Columbiana	Daniel Ikirt	11 80	20 58
Elliottsville	Jefferson	John C. Elliott	14 11	22 25
Ellsworth	Trumbull	Joseph Coit	105 45	101 45
Elmira	Lucas	Sam'l B. Darby	19 26	40 26
Elyria	Lorain	Geo. M. Chapman	454 99	721 99
Enoch	Monroe	John Wickham	3 44	7 82
Enon	Clark	John W. Wallace	91 26	89 80
Essex	Lucas	Smith Geer	3 32	5 85
Etna	Licking	Rollin C. Hard	63 76	111 55
Etna Furnace	Lawrence	Jos. W. Dempsey	11 78	22 54
Euclid	Cuyahoga	Sargent Currier	122 29	118 16
Euphemia (Late "Lewisburgh.")	Preble	Nelson Hilling	no ret.	
Evansport	Defiance	Everet W. Fuller	33 42	63 39
Fairfield	Greene	Morlin B. Hill	151 94	146 67

POST OFFICES—*Ohio.*

Post Offices.	Counties.	Postmasters.	Compensation.	Net proceeds.
Fairhaven	Preble	Reuben E. Hills, to 1st May	$39 13	$68 64
		Hiram D. Evans	7 17	14 34
Fairport	Lake	Dexter Knights	64 03	74 56
Fairview	Guernsey	Lemon Ryan	164 08	159 52
Fallsburgh	Licking	George Gardner	4 67	8 67
Farmer	Defiance	Oney Rice, jr.	12 28	20 96
Farmersville	Montgomery	Oliver Dalrymple	27 33	46 73
Farmington	Trumbull	Epaphroditus Fuller	30 51	52 96
Fayetteville	Brown	Wm. B. Thompson, to 30th January	25 45	49 31
		John Ballard	24 51	49 89
Fearing	Washington	Thos. F. Stanley	12 03	18 34
Federalton	Athens	Peter Beebee	7 10	12 99
Feesburgh	Brown	Hervey McKibben	16 18	29 15
Felicity	Clermont	Robert Chalfant, to 30th September	29 18	50 08
		Flavius J. Phillips	78 26	140 38
Fincastle	Brown	Adams Morrow	8 24	15 41
Finley	Hancock	Squire Carlin	175 80	307 74
Fitchville	Huron	Union White	74 49	118 70
Flag Spring	Gallia	Jas. S. Eakins	4 40	6 85
Fletcher	Miami	Isaac Dukemineer	40 11	70 30
Florence	Huron	Eli S. Barnum	149 20	168 04
Florida	Henry	Geo. W. Patterson	23 50	41 72
Flushing	Belmont	David Purviance	71 97	115 77
Fort Amanda	Allen	James Crozier	no ret.	
Fort Jefferson	Darke	Hezekiah Veits	10 50	17 58
Fort Jennings	Putnam	H. J. Boehmer	9 73	21 41
Fort Recovery	Darke	William McDaniel	21 61	45 62
Fort Seneca	Seneca	Lorenzo Abbott	23 64	42 89
Four Corners	Huron	Israel Cooke	37 83	37 43
Fowler	Trumbull	Moses R. Porter	51 35	78 75
Fowler's Mills	Geauga	Milo Fowler	20 46	33 35
Franconia	Putnam	Silas McClish	4 54	7 91
Frankfort	Ross	William Irwin	107 93	183 15
Franklin	Warren	James McEwen	164 08	313 83
Franklin Furnace	Scioto	Jas. S. Folsom, to 31st December	19 69	35 72
		John F. Gould	23 72	41 01
Franklin Mills	Portage	Dan'l P. Rhodes	147 18	209 94
Franklin Square	Columbiana	Nancy Shaler, to 30th September	5 05	9 75
		Jacob Whealen	12 07	22 41
Frazeysburgh	Muskingum	Richard Griffee	22 93	40 83
Frease's Store	Stark	Jacob Frease	29 57	52 10
Frederick	Trumbull	John Shoemaker, to 23d July	1 51	1 52
		Charles Winter	20 82	20 85

POST OFFICES—*Ohio.*

Post Offices.	Counties.	Postmasters.	Compensation.	Net proceeds.
Fredericksburgh	Wayne	David Griffith	$108 43	$192 47
Fredericktown	Knox	Abner Ayers	208 72	208 79
Fredonia	Licking	Jacob S. Duden	44 97	76 11
Freedom	Portage	Orsamus L. Drake	53 66	98 96
Freeport	Harrison	Israel A. Holliday	49 81	87 61
French Grant	Scioto	John Dutiel	24 88	43 73
Fulton	Hamilton	Josiah Streeter	111 82	159 28
Fultonham	Muskingum	Daniel Horn	78 36	105 07
Furnace	Erie	Lewis Wells	24 06	36 63
Galena	Delaware	William Hance	63 19	104 59
Galion	Richland	Solomon P. Nave	56 04	91 47
Gallatin	Allen	Chs. C. Marshall	6 53	14 40
Gallipolis	Gallia	Benajah Curtis	399 92	521 66
Gambier	Knox	Marcus T. C. Wing	214 34	391 87
Ganges	Richland	James N. Ayres	51 11	95 89
Gardner	Morgan	Jonathan D. Gibbs	no return	
Garrettsville	Portage	Sam'l H. Peffers	77 02	133 83
Gates' Mills	Cuyahoga	Parker Boynton, to 1st Nov	6 10	10 16
		John Lander, from 8th Nov	10 44	19 91
Geneva	Ashtabula	Eliphalet Mills, to 18th Sept	11 90	20 44
		Noah Smith	68 13	115 28
Genoa	Delaware	Marcus Curtiss	11 25	16 26
Georgesville	Franklin	Thomas Reynolds	8 14	15 41
Georgetown	Brown	James Allen	167 44	293 35
German	Darke	John M. Harter	10 92	19 77
Germano	Harrison	Josiah Crawford	40 36	67 50
Germantown	Montgomery	Jno. P. Achey, to 2d June	148 40	215 32
		Jacob Eminger	7 80	17 54
Gettysburgh	Preble	George Watt	9 12	12 95
Gilboa	Putnam	John E. Creighton	31 54	53 63
Gilead	Wood	Harvey Burritt	28 11	46 26
Gillespieville	Ross	John W. Williamson	39 26	64 78
Girard	Trumbull	Elmedorus Crandon	31 67	31 66
Glasgow	Columbiana	John McBean, to 30th Sept	1 52	2 67
		Wm. B. Orr	6 31	11 03
Glens (Dis. 4th April.)	Monroe	John D. Glenn, 3 qs.	0 73	1 76
Gnadenhutten	Tuscarawas	Edward Peter	24 90	45 03
Gordonville (Ch'd to "Marathon.")	Brown	Samp'n Newbrough	5 32	11 07
Gorham	Lucas	Erastus Cottrell	11 94	23 67
Goshen	Clermont	Moses Frybarger	73 04	109 78
Grafton	Lorain	David Ashley	42 28	71 19

POST OFFICES—*Ohio.*

Post Offices.	Counties.	Postmasters.	Compensation.	Net proceeds.
Graham's Station	Meigs	Peter M. Petrel	$37 34	$69 87
Grand Prairie	Marion	John C. Fitzhugh	14 88	26 71
Grand View	Washington	Sardin Y. Collins	29 45	59 35
Granger	Medina	Henry Tiffany, to 30th Sept.	8 02	13 11
		Daniel Burt	32 07	53 59
Granville	Licking	Anthony P. Prichard to 26th May	448 43	802 71
		Darwin Humphreys	27 69	67 05
Gratiot	Licking	William Sims	50 85	95 21
Gratis	Preble	David Beaver	79 06	136 15
Graysville	Monroe	C. L. Dungan	10 35	21 16
Great Bend	Meigs	Simeon F. Seely	12 24	20 64
Green Castle (Late "Courtwright.")	Fairfield	Samuel Weiser	no return	
Green Creek	Sandusky	Darwin E. Harkness	55 13	70 10
Greene	Harrison	Wm. B. Delany	52 43	92 27
Greenfield	Highland	Josiah Bell, to 1st May	202 36	341 48
		William Barnett	36 21	61 58
Greenford	Columbiana	David Weikart	29 15	49 19
Green Hill	Columbiana	Granville S. Bentley	8 43	14 11
Greensburgh	Trumbull	Geo. P. Curtis	38 08	62 77
Green Spring	Seneca	Robert Smith	28 07	48 97
Greene's Store	Lawrence	Elisha B. Greene, jr.	23 35	41 00
Greentown	Stark	Michael Wise	33 06	61 74
Greenville	Darke	Nich's Mark, 3 qrs.	111 26	169 37
Greenwich	Huron	Rufus Sheldon	19 86	37 33
Groton	Huron	John P. Deyo	16 12	27 25
Guilford	Medina	Milton Stiles, 2d	95 76	170 65
Gustavus	Trumbull	George Hezlep	130 54	207 96
Guysville	Athens	Guy Barrows	26 10	43 07
Hagerstown	Preble	Jacob F. Miller	7 87	12 24
Hall's Valley	Morgan	Mills Hall	6 26	10 00
Hallsville	Ross	Ephraim Dresbach	20 86	30 43
Hamersville	Brown	Wm. K. Flick	17 43	35 71
Hamilton	Butler	James B. Thomas	441 03	938 21
Hampden	Geauga	Thomas Brown	36 38	74 98
Hanging Rock	Lawrence	James Rodgers	120 19	228 46
Hanover	Licking	Chester Wells	27 38	52 26
Hanoverton	Columbiana	George Fries	77 44	126 83
Hansleys X Roads	Perry	John Hansley	3 74	6 16
Hardin	Shelby	Wilson V. Cowan	30 16	53 29
Harlem	Delaware	James Budd	11 41	21 15
Harlem Spring	Carroll	Robert Craven	24 83	42 82
Harmar	Washington	James Whitney	77 33	135 78
Harpersfield	Ashtabula	Oscar F. Gibbs	43 24	75 10
Harrietsville	Monroe	William Erskine	no return	

POST OFFICES—*Ohio.*

Post Offices.	Counties.	Postmasters.	Compensation.	Net proceeds.
Harrisburgh	Franklin	Heinrich Müller	$24 85	$42 58
Harrison	Hamilton	John Ashby	85 14	148 23
Harrisonville	Meigs	Alfred Dunlap	7 70	14 91
Harrisville	Harrison	Robt. R. Kennedy	64 56	113 28
Hartford	Trumbull	Elam Jones, to 4th November	36 11	58 26
		Garry C. Reed	60 91	101 82
Hartland	Huron	Daniel Miner	11 09	19 98
Hart's Grove	Ashtabula	William Jarvis	20 36	31 30
Hartsville	Stark	John Houghton	11 99	20 36
Harveysburgh	Warren	Robert E. Lafetra, to 25th July	4 73	6 54
		Budd Scroggy	67 22	100 58
Haskellville	Lawrence	James Haskell	17 04	29 37
Hastings	Richland	Joseph Hastings	11 43	19 09
Hastingsville	Columbiana	James B. Hull	4 37	6 51
Hayesville	Richland	John H. Cox	100 85	180 59
Hebbardsville	Athens	Peter Morse, to 13th June	21 46	33 26
		Samuel Earhart	0 79	1 51
Hebron	Licking	John W. Smith	130 99	219 63
Hendrysburgh	Belmont	Benjamin Eaton	53 77	55 65
Henrietta	Lorain	Edward Durand	60 66	60 70
Hickory	Carroll	Jacob Gladden	6 61	11 94
Hicksville	Defiance	Alfred P. Edgerton	19 73	27 18
Higginsport	Brown	Noah L. Robberts	37 42	78 00
Highland	Highland	Gustavus F. Stevens	48 54	82 89
Hildreths	Knox	Horace C. Lockwood	22 22	38 20
Hill Grove	Darke	Thomas Barnes, to 7th Feb	11 16	21 14
		Ralph A. Cooper	8 33	16 43
Hillhouse	Lake	Moses C. Wilcox	14 25	23 68
Hillsboro'	Highland	Jacob Kirby, to 18th April	209 84	447 60
		Daniel Browning	60 36	124 83
Hinckley	Medina	James Morrell	52 35	87 19
Hiram	Portage	Thos. F. Young	17 14	28 02
Hiramsburgh	Morgan	Asa Burlingame	15 89	25 55
Hocking City (Ch'd to "Coolville.")	Athens	John Pratt, 2 qrs	20 76	36 22
Hockingport	Athens	Ferdinand Paulk	18 30	31 36
Hog Creek	Allen	Michael Leatherman	4 91	10 32
Holmesville	Holmes	John Hutchinson	32 35	50 66
Homer	Licking	Buckman Chaflin	no return	
		Chs. M. Condict, fr. 18th Oct	62 33	106 15
Homerville	Medina	Henry P. Camp, fr. 7th Dec	2 94	6 09

POST OFFICES—*Ohio.*

Post Offices.	Counties.	Postmasters.	Compensation.	Net proceeds.
Hope	Franklin	Noble Landon, to 14th June	$27 33	$49 36
		Cyrus M. Humphrey	0 89	1 96
Hopewell	Muskingum	Joseph Richey	36 69	68 67
Hopkinsville	Warren	John Hopkins	54 86	90 09
Hoskinsville	Morgan	Erastus Hoskins	11 11	18 50
Houston	Shelby	Jos. L. Taylor	33 21	57 84
Howell	Logan	Alexander Young	4 32	8 36
Hubbard	Trumbull	Samuel Hine, to 14th May	32 94	53 30
		John Cramer	3 72	5 96
Hudson	Summit	Wm. M. Beebe, to 14th May	275 15	480 86
		John B. Whedon	41 07	80 06
Humphrey's Villa	Holmes	Meshach Cooper	11 12	19 29
Huntersville	Hardin	Thomas Hitchcock	8 40	17 01
Huntington	Lorain	Thos. H. Case	48 90	78 30
Huntsburgh	Geauga	Warren Loomis	47 36	73 60
Huron	Erie	Tower Jackson, to 30th Sept	59 13	58 25
		Alex'r P. Chesley	210 24	212 56
Hyattsville	Miami	Jos. P. Max, to 30th Sept	7 33	13 39
		Thomas Cutler	18 86	38 17
Iberia	Marion	Joshua M. Davis	41 16	72 33
Independence	Cuyahoga	Wm. H. Knapp, to 1st Nov	5 03	9 71
		Nathan Stafford, fr. 15th Nov	10 73	18 72
Inland	Summit	Isaac Hunsberger	25 25	43 97
Inverness	Columbiana	John E. Welsh	10 52	16 49
Iron Furnace	Scioto	John Clingman	35 39	61 55
Irville	Muskingum	Jno. W. Grier	31 64	56 20
Island Creek	Jefferson	James Scott	10 21	17 04
Ithaca	Darke	John Millett	23 21	31 35
Ives	Huron	Willard H. Pond, 2 qrs	1 85	2 93
		Joseph Crossett, 1 qr.	1 03	1 57
Jackson	Jackson	Martin Owens	101 38	192 86
Jacksonboro'	Butler	John H. Thomas	35 76	55 77
Jacksontown (Dis. 18th Jan'y.)	Licking	Jas. M. Layton, to 27th Jan'y	35 13	38 21
(Re-est. 31st Jan.)		John Zollinger	21 46	41 67
Jacksonville	Darke	James C. Wood, to 31st May	25 26	45 22
		Calvin D. Searle	3 61	6 71
Jacobsburgh	Belmont	Archim. Scatterday	30 70	48 84

POST OFFICES—Ohio.

Post Offices.	Counties.	Postmasters.	Compensation.	Net proceeds.
Jamestown	Greene	Matthias Winans	$65 78	$123 03
Jasper	Pike	Laughlin Currie	22 93	42 67
Jefferson	Ashtabula	Stephen McIntyre	155 76	165 78
Jeffersonville	Fayette	Ezekiel H. Crow	32 95	61 21
Jelloway	Knox	James Pearce	22 11	22 16
Jeromesville	Wayne	Jas. W. Boyd	92 43	158 43
Jersey	Licking	Jas. B. Condict	46 37	72 34
Johnsonville	Trumbull	John W. Jackson	46 08	73 14
Johnstown	Licking	Levi H. Duke	85 52	146 29
Johnsville	Montgomery	Wm. Clingenpeel, to 26th April	21 50	38 34
		William Zigler	5 05	8 80
Jolly	Washington	Frederick Semon	22 83	36 39
Jonesville	Monroe	Daniel Clark	2 25	4 05
Junction	Paulding	Henry Mercellus	29 65	56 80
Junior	Scioto	Peter Powell, 2 qrs.	1 18	1 42
Kalida	Putnam	G. Skinner, to 7th Feb	51 23	77 84
		Milton M. Gillett, to 30th May	19 46	32 03
		Winchton Risley	4 53	7 69
Keene	Coshocton	Robert Farwell, to 30th Sept	14 65	27 81
		James Wilson	48 88	88 44
Keiths	Morgan	George Baker	no ret.	
Kelley's Mills	Lawrence	Wm. H. Kelley	7 13	14 20
Kelloggsville	Ashtabula	Lemuel Moffitt	75 25	125 84
Kendall	Logan	Wm. McFarland	3 80	5 74
Kenton	Hardin	John P. Gordon	144 74	255 13
Kilgore	Carroll	David Hosteman	8 13	13 20
Killbourn	Delaware	Coton M. Thrall	20 92	35 36
Kilbuck	Holmes	David Martin, to 30th Sept.	3 26	7 00
		James B. Woods	11 78	23 41
Kimbolton	Guernsey	Jesse Smith	29 88	55 80
Kingston	Ross	Reed Armstrong, to 31st March	152 20	148 76
		John A. Hays	41 72	40 38
Kingsville	Ashtabula	Geo. G. Gillett	146 98	192 90
Kinsmans	Trumbull	John Kinsman	101 08	163 28
Kirkersville	Licking	Isaac Jennings, to 6th May	69 25	133 35
		Benjamin Gibbony	10 56	21 77
Kirtland	Lake	Nathan Daggett, to 31st Dec.	44 82	82 85
		Lyman Cowdery	46 62	87 25
Knox	Knox	John Wright, to 31st March	42 96	42 57
		Jacob Fisher	12 55	12 55

POST OFFICES—*Ohio.*

Post Offices.	Counties.	Postmasters.	Compensation.	Net proceeds.
Knoxville	Jefferson	Joseph Clark	$38 63	$70 14
Kyger	Gallia	Alexander Logue	11 11	18 62
La Fayette	Madison	John McMullan	64 01	60 17
La Grange	Lorain	Calvin Wilcox	46 07	74 10
Laings	Monroe	Joseph Hall	9 57	14 82
Lake	Stark	John R. Bower	44 93	76 64
Lancaster	Fairfield	James Cranmer, to 31st Jan'y	444 96	1017 38
		Casper Thiell, to 17th April	168 30	395 13
		John C. Cassell	175 89	430 34
La Porte	Lorain	Daniel Tenny	40 53	75 46
Lattas	Ross	Timothy H. Davis	26 78	44 51
Laurel	Clermont	James Simmons, jr., to 24th Aug	2 57	3 88
		Benj'n H. Simmons	11 22	18 77
Leamansville	Seneca	James Gordon	20 58	33 43
Leatherwood	Guernsey	Jonah Smith	31 84	61 17
Leavitt	Carroll	Samuel Semple, to 26th April	5 63	9 00
		Jacob Miller	1 11	1 85
Lebanon	Warren	Thomas F. Brodie	403 99	853 74
Ledlies	Meigs	William Ledlie	5 78	11 49
Lee	Athens	Jonathan Winn	15 01	25 94
Leesburgh	Highland	Gerrard M. Johnson, to 4th March	42 38	71 67
		Robert B. Wailey	22 17	38 85
Leesville	Carroll	Garvin Lanthers	43 13	70 12
Leesville X Roads	Richland	Robert Lee, jr	30 73	55 96
Lenox	Ashtabula	Samuel Plumb	41 91	67 06
Leon	Ashtabula	Meriam Barber	11 25	19 36
Le Roy	Medina	Benjamin D. Austin	53 95	86 65
Letart Falls	Meigs	John Wagner	28 84	49 07
Letimberville	Marion	George Price	16 84	30 39
Level	Warren	Thomas Adams	2 55	4 48
Levering (Late 'Owl Cr'k.')	Knox	John Levering, 1 qr.	5 71	11 03
Lewis	Brown	Wm. W. Clark	20 42	39 71
Lewisburgh (Ch. to Euphemia)	Preble	James Bolens	80 19	135 94
Lewistown	Logan	Henry Hanford	6 38	11 23
Lewisville	Monroe	Joseph Watt, to 30th Sept	2 93	5 48
		Theo. Benninghaus	9 53	16 53
Lexington	Richland	Robt. Cunningham, to 15th July	4 54	7 87
		Charles McClung	113 15	188 75
Liberty	Montgomery	John Burnett	32 05	58 25

POST OFFICES—*Ohio.*

Post Offices.	Counties.	Postmasters.	Compensation.	Net proceeds.
Likens	Crawford	James T. Drake	$4 54	$7 72
Lima	Allen	Sam'l A. Baxter, to 31st Dec	81 59	148 39
		B. A. Satterthwait	90 13	170 30
Limaville	Stark	John G. Morss	14 06	23 72
Lincoln	Delaware	Jabez Wood	7 79	12 27
Linnville	Licking	Adam Linn	21 31	43 88
Litchfield	Medina	Avery M. Starr	54 25	101 65
Lithopolis	Fairfield	O. H. Perry, to 29th April	64 02	120 37
		John C. Huffman	17 95	32 03
Little Beaver B'ge	Columbiana	Matthew Laughlin	16 68	17 80
Little Hockhock'g	Washington	Horace Curtis	22 94	40 78
Little Mill Creek	Delaware	John Weaver	12 47	19 05
Little Sandusky	Wyandott	Jos. E. Fouke	58 49	57 88
Little Scioto	Marion	John B. Andrew	5 23	6 89
Little York	Montgomery	Daniel Brusman	23 63	46 44
Liverpool	Medina	Lem'l B. Parker	31 45	59 60
Lock	Knox	Isham F. Abbott	11 14	19 83
Lockbourne	Franklin	John H. Stage	18 80	31 13
Lockport	Williams	Abraham Gish, 3 qs.	8 88	18 57
Locust Grove	Adams	Wm. F. Kirkpatrick, to 25th June	41 24	63 57
		Joseph Thomas	14	35
Lodi	Medina	Jeremiah Higbee	97 14	160 58
Logan	Hocking	Simeon W. Tucker	112 59	219 20
Loganville	Logan	William Dickson	27 49	52 66
Log Cabin	Athens	Austin Prouty, to 4th Sept	71	91
		Zephyrus Carver	5 67	9 86
London	Madison	John Dungan, to 20th Jan'y	103 21	102 29
		John M. Smith	68 33	61 62
Londonderry	Guernsey	John Clabaugh	28 58	48 39
Long Bottom	Meigs	Wm. H. Packard	16 05	29 06
Loramies	Shelby	Joseph Mendenhall	10 57	20 10
Loss Creek	Crawford	Matthew Torrence	7 57	13 45
Lost Creek	Miami	James Fordyce	14 67	22 88
Loudonville	Richland	Henry J. Hayes, to 20th May	144 17	140 14
		Thomas Musgrave	12 56	10 96
Louisville	Stark	Solomon A. Gorgas, to 31st Dec	27 63	51 04
		Louis Sauvayeot	28 81	57 50
Lowell	Washington	Elijah Short	63 94	114 16
Lowellville	Trumbull	Sam'l H. McBride	18 99	33 73
Lower Newport	Washington	Jacob Middleswart	10 81	17 23
Lower Salem	Washington	Daniel G. Stanley	21 97	37 03
Lower Sandusky	Sandusky	Wilson M. Stark	416 94	693 11

POST OFFICES—*Ohio.*

Post Offices.	Counties.	Postmasters.	Compensation.	Net proceeds.
Lowry	Athens	William Lowry	$2 56	$3 94
Loydsville	Belmont	Joel Elliott, to 15th Feb	38 02	62 17
		Joseph Mercer	29 12	28 85
Lucas	Richland	Ezekiel Ervin	11 32	16 31
Lucasville	Scioto	Daniel A. Belknap	32 54	58 75
Lumberton	Clinton	Joshua C. James	24 76	43 20
Lyme	Huron	Stephen Russell	78 79	76 73
Lynchburgh	Highland	John Woodrow, to 20th May	23 19	44 39
		George H. Veirs	1 49	3 46
Lyons	Lucas	Jinks Mory	13 42	25 34
McArthurstown	Athens	Nathan Lord	37 64	69 53
McConnellsville	Morgan	David C. Pinkerton, to 21st May	286 23	565 93
		Ford Sill	26 31	58 47
McCulloughs	Jefferson	J. McCullough, jr., to 25th April	44 96	70 52
		William Palmer	9 23	17 15
McCutchenville	Wyandott	Michael Brackley	101 86	160 41
McEwen's X R'ds	Richland	John Pugh	11 72	18 99
McKaig's Mills	Columbiana	Martin Armstrong	11 22	16 36
McKinstrys (Dis. 26th June.)	Meigs	Wm. McKinstry	4 61	8 35
Macedon	Mercer	Jona. Middleton	4 05	8 15
Madison	Lake	Charles Burr	152 07	147 19
Madisonville	Hamilton	John Jones	39 94	72 22
Magnolia	Stark	Christian Haldeman, to 26th Feb	14 52	27 11
		William Walters	9 83	18 21
Mahoning	Stark	Charles O. Hamlin	13 62	21 26
Malaga	Monroe	J. F. Bidenhorn, to 14th Feb'y	31 48	57 88
		David P. Trueax	19 43	37 33
Mallett Creek	Medina	Josiah B. Beckwith	17 99	28 86
Malta	Morgan	William Palmer	67 12	115 69
Malvern	Carroll	George Hardesty	23 13	35 85
Manchester	Adams	Andrew Livingston	44 93	79 93
Manhattan	Lucas	Platt Card	63 46	62 21
Mansfield	Richland	Jacob Hammer	627 37	1199 46
Mantua	Portage	George Sheldon	61 53	116 80
Mapleton (Dis. 1st Aug.)	Stark	Wm. Criswell	1 42	1 94
Marathon (Late Gordonville)	Clermont	Wm. Hartman	no ret.	
Marietta	Washington	Abner L. Guitteau	594 41	1325 13
Marion	Marion	C. Allen, to 16th June	368 63	520 57
		John R. Knapp	11 86	21 31

POST OFFICES—*Ohio.*

Post Offices.	Counties.	Postmasters.	Compensation.	Net proceeds.
Marits	Marion	John Boyle	$13 65	$24 45
Marlborough	Stark	Kersey G. Thomas	28 89	53 11
Marseilles	Wyandott	Geo. D. Lathrop, to 15th Aug	5 45	10 53
		Jasper Hunt	57 23	71 22
Marshallsville	Wayne	Gilbert Miller	33 10	63 90
Martinsburgh	Knox	s y Spratt	89 15	171 33
Martin's Ferry	Belmont	William Beazle	55 55	107 46
Martinstown	Hancock	H. R. Warner	4 14	6 47
Martinsville	Clinton	John Hunt	38 21	66 16
Marvin's Mill	Hancock	William Marvin	3 84	8 46
Marysville	Union	George W. Cherry	100 84	181 93
Mason	Warren	Mason Seward	84 45	143 62
Massillon	Stark	G. W. Williams, to 20th May	779 27	1679 02
		Samuel McCaughey	79 13	204 14
Masterton	Monroe	Geo. S. Gilleland	no ret.	
Maumee City	Lucas	Elisha Mack	405 59	671 64
Mayfield	Cuyahoga	Diamond Wakeman	34 70	63 09
Maze's Corners	Williams	Robert Maze	7 45	14 50
Meadow Farm	Muskingum	Cornelius Springer	15 54	28 92
Mear's Farm	Hamilton	John F. Stall	40 12	62 42
Mecca	Trumbull	Lyman Pierson, to 31st Dec	9 66	19 32
		Silas N. Jones	10 80	22 22
Mechanicsburgh	Champaign	David F. Spain	102 91	170 75
Mechanicstown	Carroll	Benjamin Boice	20 87	36 89
Medina	Medina	Henry Ormsby	358 64	677 06
Meigs' Creek	Morgan	Richard Cotton	14 04	21 97
Melmore	Seneca	Philip J. Price	75 70	139 40
Mendon	Mercer	Lewis Culver	14 28	27 19
Mentor	Lake	Clark Parker	80 25	75 20
Mercer	Mercer	Moses Collins	22 60	30 88
Mercerville	Gallia	Jos. N. Thierry	6 11	11 56
(Ch'd to 'Smiths')				
Mesopotamia	Trumbull	Linus Tracy, to 7th June	39 55	64 32
		Isaac Clark	3 67	6 00
Metamora	Lucas	Peter C. Lewis, to 12th Feb	3 86	7 88
		Mowry S. Potter	1 65	3 07
Mexico	Wyandott	N. S. McCullough	22 66	36 21
Miami	Hamilton	Isaac Van Trees, to 31st March	35 35	35 37
		Alvin Wheeler	6 59	13 58
Miamisburgh	Montgomery	William Brooks	161 18	297 90
Middlebourne	Guernsey	Wm. P. Blackiston, to 3d June	86 45	85 23
		Matt'w S. Maitland	5 80	10 75

POST OFFICES—*Ohio.*

Post Offices.	Counties.	Postmasters.	Compensation.	Net proceeds.
Middle Branch	Stark	Wm. I. Sholtey	$3 96	$6 46
Middlebury	Summit	Edgar T. Chapman	242 04	348 97
Middle Creek	Monroe	Church B. Tuttle	7 70	15 37
Middlefield	Geauga	Benjamin Wells	35 70	52 01
Middlesex	Ashtabula	Hiram Thomas	28 30	41 93
Middletown	Butler	John J. Storms, to 3d September	64 82	100 65
		Wm. S. Storms, to 31st March	143 90	280 44
		Isaac Robertson	65 37	117 02
Mifflin	Richland	Robinson Keffer	32 28	61 89
Milan	Erie	James H. Kennedy	499 82	834 84
Milford	Clermont	John Kugler, to 3d March	68 20	112 69
		Brittain Leming	30 35	54 67
Milford Centre	Union	David Burnham	81 69	124 74
Mill Brook	Wayne	Jacob Whitcum	28 22	52 55
Mill Creek	Coshocton	Jesse Lawrence	9 60	17 91
Mill Dale	Defiance	Benj. B. Abell	15 89	28 97
Millers (Dis. 6th May.)	Lawrence	Timothy R. Stanley, 3 qrs	10 65	20 16
Millersburgh	Holmes	Albertus Geiger	225 29	398 42
Millersport	Fairfield	Elias Vance	23 30	38 34
Millerstown	Champaign	Isaac Ammon	8 39	16 71
Mill Grove	Warren	William Potter	15 06	26 22
Millville	Butler	James Hill	34 35	60 15
Millwood	Knox	John Welker, jr	27 21	50 87
Milnersville	Guernsey	Jona. P. Connard	32 02	60 85
Milton	Trumbull	Robert Price	23 63	45 87
Miltonville	Wood	Epaphroditus Foot	12 41	19 49
Minerva	Stark	James Hibbets	35 54	63 96
Minster	Mercer	John H. Gosmann	33 89	60 09
Mogadore	Summit	John B. Sawyer	75 40	117 33
Mohigan	Wayne	David Kaufman	38 39	73 66
Monroe	Butler	Wm. W. Caldwell, to 9th June	84 02	136 72
		Peter Vlereborne	2 87	5 83
Monroeville	Huron	Alfred Chesebrough, to 7th May	222 32	227 31
		Isaac Smith	40 44	44 98
Montezuma	Mercer	William Beauchamp	3 09	7 27
Montgomery	Hamilton	David Mewhinny	84 25	133 51
Montgomery Roads	Wood	Ezra Morgan	12 51	15 77
Montville	Geauga	Henry Wells, to 20th February	16 96	28 54
		Seth Whitney	12 46	20 73
Moons	Fayette	John Row	11 15	21 50
Moorefield	Harrison	Benj. M. Ferguson	29 65	60 07

POST OFFICES—*Ohio.*

Post Offices.	Counties.	Postmasters.	Compensation.	Net proceeds.
Moores' Salt W'ks	Jefferson	David Craig, to 12th April	$17 51	$23 49
		John S. Graham ...	6 49	9 30
Moorland	Wayne	Peter Weiker......	27 23	40 78
Morgan	Ashtabula ...	Elizur C. Latimer..	74 00	83 93
Morgan's Fork...	Pike........	John Anderson.....	4 86	7 33
Morgansville..... (Late "Wolf	Morgan ..... Creek.")	James Rusk.......	14 33	25 51
Morning Sun.....	Preble	Joseph Brown.....	24 68	37 82
Morristown	Belmont.....	Mary Price........	151 32	148 82
Morus Hill.......	Licking......	Abrah'm D. Larason	1 24	2 08
Moscow.........	Clermont.....	Thomas Fee.......	43 35	79 37
Moscow Mills ...	Morgan......	James Farley......	11 52	16 37
Mount Blanchard.	Hancock.....	Chester Cook......	36 73	62 08
Mount Carmel...	Clermont....	Caleb Dial.........	38 28	55 78
Mount Eaton....	Wayne	Anthony Knoble...	84 66	158 38
Mount Ephraim..	Guernsey....	Asbury Gardner....	11 36	18 60
Mount Gilead....	Marion......	C. K. Lindsay.....	59 07	108 33
Mount Healthy..	Hamilton....	Charles Cheney....	86 63	154 66
Mount Holly	Warren	Peter Dehaven.....	49 21	83 02
Mount Hope.....	Holmes......	Moses A. Robinet..	30 03	56 30
Mount Liberty...	Knox	Henry A. Childs...	26 13	42 32
Mount Perry.....	Perry.......	Andrew Walker....	12 82	18 50
Mount Pisgah....	Clermont....	Noble M. Preble...	14 91	24 04
Mount Pleasant..	Jefferson	Amos Jones.......	186 67	446 35
Mount Sterling...	Madison	J. G. Loofbourrow.	28 17	51 21
Mount Union....	Stark........	Jos. L. Brenton....	30 35	54 05
Mount Vernon...	Knox.......	Wm. H. Whitton..	731 12	1426 34
Mourystown	Highland....	David Fenwick	15 92	28 37
Mouth of Yellow Creek.........	Jefferson	Jacob Groff.......	16 23	27 58
Muchinippe......	Logan......	Joseph Wright.....	2 19	4 09
Mulberry........	Clermont.....	Erastus Holmes....	17 51	25 70
Munnsville......	Coshocton...	James W. McMunn	1 77	2 72
Munson	Geauga	Jonathan Burnett...	6 39	14 25
Murraysville.....	Lorain......	Ransom Gibbs.....	4 58	9 59
MuskingumVall'y (Dis. 19th June.)	Muskingum .	Abraham Beatty ...	6 24	13 78
Mutual	Champaign..	Francis A. Morrison	6 80	11 32
Nankin	Richland	John Smurr	52 09	97 51
Napoleon	Henry......	Ebenezer Lathrop..	45 79	74 34
Nashport........	Muskingum .	Wm. W. Cooke, to 30th Sept.......	10 25	18 73
		Homer S. Ferry....	28 04	52 43
Nashville	Holmes......	Joseph Gordon.....	73 93	129 42
Navarre.........	Stark	G. W. Swearingen.	152 98	251 53
Nelson..........	Portage	Jeremiah R. Fuller.	52 38	86 45
Nelsonville	Athens......	Lorenzo D. Poston.	59 59	114 71

POST OFFICES—*Ohio.*

Post Offices.	Counties.	Postmasters.	Compensation.	Net proceeds.
Neptune	Mercer	Benjamin Nickel	$5 72	$10 52
Neville	Clermont	Elijah Larkin, to 25th June	34 53	56 35
		Wm. P. Kincaid	0 34	0 81
Nevin	Highland	Robert Nevin	17 50	32 56
New Albany	Columbiana	Benjamin Mason	14 87	23 11
New Alexander	Columbiana	James Slentz	35 79	39 53
New Alexandria	Jefferson	Jerome D. Daton	29 34	45 55
New Ark	Licking	Levi J. Haughey	912 43	2195 10
New Athens	Harrison	John P. Caldwell, to 19th Sept	14 56	26 04
		Thomas Finley	71 67	119 43
New Baltimore	Stark	Samuel Byrns	10 29	16 57
New Bedford	Coshocton	David Burgert	19 61	28 50
New Berlin	Stark	Emanuel Ensminger	49 66	84 81
Newberry	Geauga	Elbridge Hayden, 2 qrs	11 28	23 00
New Bremen	Mercer	Charles Bosel	30 91	63 22
Newburgh	Cuyahoga	Eben Miles, to 7th June	54 41	100 08
		George S. Rathbun	4 64	8 14
New Burlington	Clinton	John Harrison	50 26	81 94
New Carlisle	Clark	Samuel B. Williams	197 62	316 98
New Castine	Darke	Russel Evans	17 53	32 06
New Castle	Coshocton	William Arnold, to 31st Dec	11 06	20 08
		Jacob F. Singer	16 32	33 29
Newcomerstown	Tuscarawas	Andrew Vogenitz	91 70	171 79
New Concord	Muskingum	Joseph McKinney	98 37	168 71
New Cumberland	Tuscarawas	John C. Rickey, to 30th Sept	7 30	13 55
		Joseph Kerr	29 65	53 34
New Franklin	Stark	John Miller	38 97	73 55
New Garden	Columbiana	James Graham	78 84	73 73
New Gottingen	Guernsey	G. W. Heidelbach	30 23	43 54
New Guilford	Coshocton	Daniel Berry	34 15	63 30
New Hagerstown	Carroll	John Moore	49 33	81 03
New Harrisburgh	Carroll	Isaac Dwire	29 53	54 48
New Haven	Huron	Elisha Steward, to 23d April	100 85	186 33
		T. C. McEwan	20 67	39 59
New Holland	Pickaway	N. R. Ferguson	52 65	96 32
New Hope	Brown	James Young	14 33	31 21
New Lexington	Perry	Jesse Skinner	50 52	100 06
New Lisbon	Columbiana	B. F. Thompson	437 75	683 60
New London	Huron	Tracy Case, to 31st March	26 61	50 50
		Martin Merrifield	9 62	18 94
New Lyme	Ashtabula	Wm. S. Deming	40 72	70 48

POST OFFICES—*Ohio.*

Post Offices.	Counties.	Postmasters.	Compensation.	Net proceeds.
New Madison	Darke	Ernestus Putnam	$37 28	$65 06
New Market	Highland	David K. Zink	25 60	40 14
New Middletown	Columbiana	Tobias Hahn	41 38	38 83
New Paris	Preble	James Sampson	92 67	170 08
New Petersburgh	Highland	Isaac Simpson	67 98	114 37
New Philadelphia	Tuscarawas	Catharine Ann Canfield	310 63	402 38
New Pittsburgh	Wayne	James McConnel, to 30th Sept.	6 03	11 71
		William Anderson	17 68	34 00
Newport	Washington	Jos. T. Crandall	38 42	71 19
Newportage	Summit	Elnathan Conner	23 74	44 17
New Prospect	Wayne	Christian Knup	10 60	18 07
New Richmond	Clermont	James T. Johnston	99 48	173 85
New Rochester	Wood	Michael Myers	6 20	12 46
New Rumley	Harrison	Jacob Gutshall	47 12	82 27
New Salem	Fairfield	John M. Snider	43 81	78 27
New Springfield	Columbiana	Nicholas Eckis, to 14th Nov	3 98	6 80
		John G. Sowers	7 19	11 99
Newton	Muskingum	Caleb James	4 69	9 52
Newton Falls	Trumbull	Abiram Phelps	131 11	260 52
Newtown	Hamilton	Hiram Bodine	64 93	100 25
New Vienna	Clinton	Isaac Thornburgh	45 26	78 23
Newville	Richland	Joseph Fleming	66 11	110 58
New Westville	Preble	Fletcher Jackson	24 13	46 02
New Winchester	Marion	Frederick Wise	9 63	18 92
Niles	Trumbull	Ambrose Mason	66 93	65 91
Nimisila	Summit	John W. Hamm	21 97	41 15
Nimmons' X R'ds	Delaware	Levi M. Morton	21 18	35 11
Nonpariel	Knox	Robert Long	6 21	10 90
Norris' Falls (Changed to "Olmstead.")	Cuyahoga	Hiram Frisbee, to 31st Dec.	21 31	39 39
Norristown	Carroll	Arch. McCollough	10 36	20 43
North Benton	Columbiana	Saml. Transue	22 01	37 39
North Bloomfield	Trumbull	Jos. K. Wing, to 16th May	91 74	88 41
		Isaac G. Clark	13 61	13 53
North Camden	Lorain	Arvy Whitney	29 81	54 36
North Dover	Cuyahoga	Eli Clemens	18 35	29 75
North Eaton	Lorain	Don Carlos Wilmot	12 47	24 03
North Fairfield	Huron	Horace L. Moulton, to 28th May	69 20	136 51
		David Johnson	6 15	12 37
Northfield	Summit	George Lillie	67 43	108 46
North Fitchville	Huron	Jos. S. Smith	23 74	42 06
NorthGeorgetown	Columbiana	Saml. L. Sturgeon	52 80	94 57
North Hampton	Clark	J.B.Craig, to 31st Jan	13 24	20 51
		Wm. K. Smith, 1 qr.	4 89	7 23

POST OFFICES—*Ohio*.

Post Offices.	Counties.	Postmasters.	Compensation.	Net proceeds.
North Industry	Stark	Bradley C. Goodwill	$8 92	$15 10
North Jackson	Trumbull	Jas. F. Porter	19 77	31 79
North Lewisburgh	Champaign	Royal Jennings, 1 qr.	5 02	4 22
North Lima	Columbiana	Jacob S. Buzard	36 03	59 33
North Newbury	Geauga	Oliver Wilson	17 73	33 64
North Norwich	Huron	Naum Gilson	24 22	40 85
North Perry	Lake	Joseph Cook, to 12th Oct.	8 44	15 10
		Thomas E. Cook	22 96	41 24
North Ridgeville	Lorain	Thos. A. Benham	38 44	75 06
North Rochester	Lorain	Martin L. Blair	29 96	55 23
North Royalton	Cuyahoga	William Towsley	40 07	76 56
North West	Williams	Wm. H. Billings	10 01	18 79
Norton	Delaware	William Osburn, to 19th Feb.	18 09	39 96
		Henry Warner	9 91	20 19
Norton Centre	Summit	George Palmer	39 87	72 83
Norwalk	Huron	Obadiah Jenney	577 97	1058 22
Norwich	Muskingum	Jonathan Green, to 20th May	90 96	167 72
		Hora'o W. Chandlee	10 70	19 14
Oakfield	Perry	Matthew Donaldson, from 22d Feb.	1 36	1 89
Oak Hill	Jackson	John Mackley	30 72	61 35
Oakland	Clinton	William Birdsall	23 75	39 88
Obanionsville	Clermont	William Ramsey	14 22	24 84
Oberlin	Lorain	Edw. F. Munson	358 49	684 24
Oceola (Dis. 8th July, '45)	Crawford	Daniel Tuttle	3 81	7 19
Ohio City	Cuyahoga	Charles Winslow	319 86	428 69
Ohlstown	Trumbull	Michael Ohl	12 83	16 40
Old Hickory	Wayne	Richard McGlenen	60 76	106 80
Olive	Morgan	Robert McKee	18 19	31 16
Olive Branch	Clermont	Shadrach Medaris	no return	
Olivesburgh	Richland	Richard Houston	43 38	63 97
Olmsted (Late "Norris' Falls.")	Cuyahoga	Hiram Frisbee, 2 qrs.	22 62	43 00
Omega	Pike	James McLees	37 24	59 94
Ontario	Richland	John H. Evans, to 22d Oct.	17 49	30 59
		John Williams, to 20th Nov.	3 57	5 72
		Ludwig Weber, jr., from 22d Nov.	36 49	59 95
Orange	Trumbull	Henry Snyder	56 59	89 74
Orangeville	Trumbull	Asahel C. Brainard	19 68	32 80
Orr's Corners	Trumbull	James Powers	10 42	14 95
Orwell	Ashtabula	Geo. A. Howard	73 76	70 74

POST OFFICES—*Ohio.*

Post Offices.	Counties.	Postmasters.	Compensation.	Net proceeds.
Osnaburgh	Stark	Christian Kuntze	$58 02	$103 56
Ostend	Washington	Stillman Harvey	10 82	20 25
Otsego	Muskingum	John Thompson, to 3d May	17 08	28 55
		James Hall	1 49	
Ottawa	Ottawa	Adol. Kraemer, 2 qrs	1 56	2 89
Ourys	Hamilton	Robert McCracken	6 17	9 16
Ovid	Franklin	William Headley	19 18	37 31
Owensville	Clermont	Peter Anderson	29 45	51 88
Owl Creek	Knox	Abel Pond, 2d, 3 qrs.	13 38	24 72
(Chd to "Levering.")				
Oxford	Butler	Geo. G. White	256 44	590 53
Paddy's Run	Butler	William Vaughan	35 87	55 26
Painesville	Lake	Geo. E. H. Day	557 04	897 06
Palestine	Pickaway	Joseph Tenney	20 49	38 70
Palmyra	Portage	Francis Lewis, to 31st March	77 29	98 87
		Chs. R. Canfield, fr. 3d June	7 56	12 68
Parcher's Corners	Lucas	Lyman Parcher, fr. 4th Oct	2 36	4 22
Paris	Stark	Daniel Phillips	74 42	99 25
Parisville	Portage	Thomas B. Selby	29 58	50 47
Parkman	Geauga	Russell Williams	108 32	168 93
Parma	Cuyahoga	William Humphrey	39 15	61 22
Patriot	Gallia	Joseph Waddell	21 04	40 09
Patterson	Delaware	Jos. C. Finley, 3 qrs.	4 48	9 06
Pekin	Carroll	Alfred Taber	19 42	34 62
Pendleton	Putnam	H'y Kilheffer, 2 qrs.	9 57	17 13
Penfield	Lorain	Truman Penfield	20 76	38 82
Peninsula	Summit	Hiram V. Bronson	48 93	76 45
Pennsville	Morgan	John Spurrier	46 73	83 63
Perin's Mills	Clermont	Darius Perin	35 02	62 67
Perry	Geauga	Leonidas A. Axtell	55 61	55 50
Perryopolis	Monroe	William Tracy	4 70	6 80
Perrysburgh	Wood	James M. Hall	306 78	411 26
Perryton	Licking	Jas. E. Seaward	19 23	33 76
Perryville	Richland	Luther M. Pratt	43 29	68 72
Peru	Huron	Reuben H. Smith	95 89	155 03
Petersburgh	Columbiana	Frederick Spaeth	82 60	79 27
Phalanx	Williams	Andress Dutcher	1 61	2 55
Pharisburgh	Union	David D. Welsh	no return	
Phelps	Ashtabula	Isaac L. Jayne	11 58	18 70
Philanthropy	Butler	Isaac H. Pierson	27 77	45 69
Philipsburgh	Jefferson	Edward S. Jones, to 31st March	11 41	17 54
		Jesse Litton	5 10	8 75
Pickerington	Fairfield	John Campbell	40 75	76 99

POST OFFICES—*Ohio.*

Post Offices.	Counties.	Postmasters.	Compensation.	Net proceeds.
Pierpont	Ashtabula	Archibald Gould	$11 14	$22 48
Pierpont Centre	Ashtabula	Melzo Bates, from 27th July	13 04	12 47
Piketon	Pike	William Odell, to 10th June	156 45	264 69
		Benj. F. Crow	5 73	7 80
Pilcher	Belmont	William Wood, to 30th Sept	3 35	5 52
		William Emerson	10 56	16 03
Pine Grove	Gallia	Geo. J. Payne	22 75	37 16
Piqua	Miami	John W. Gordon, to 30th April	346 18	697 75
		Joseph Housum	no return	
Pisgah	Butler	Wm. W. Vanhise	25 51	36 93
Pittsfield	Lorain	Oliver W. Whitney	41 83	77 28
Plain	Wayne	William Wagner	20 46	39 15
Plainfield	Coshocton	John M. Johnson	34 77	66 57
Plainville	Hamilton	Wm. A. Jones	12 51	22 85
Plato	Lorain	Franklin Blackner	46 86	79 07
Pleasant	Putnam	William McGookin, to 28th Feb	8 92	12 78
		John B. Fruchey	4 49	7 49
Pleasant Dale	Hardin	David H. Warner	4 15	8 84
Pleasant Hill	Miami	James Cothran	10 64	20 51
Pleasant Ridge	Hamilton	J. M. H. Coleman	26 55	42 03
Pleasantville	Fairfield	Philip Hane	34 67	56 09
Plymouth	Richland	Robert McDonough	138 70	249 62
Point Pleasant	Clermont	John Cooper	26 87	47 75
Poland	Trumbull	Henry K. Morse	168 52	162 96
Pomeroy	Meigs	Royal C. Grant	118 12	235 92
Poplar	Crawford	George Bender	17 15	31 29
Portage	Wood	Collister Haskins	22 03	36 56
Port Clinton	Ottawa	James Kingman	67 69	121 38
Port Homer	Jefferson	Wm. H. Wallace	21 24	36 13
Portsmouth	Scioto	William Kendall	621 52	1463 26
Port Washington	Tuscarawas	Geo. W. Dingman	50 90	88 00
Port William	Clinton	Wm. M. Irvin	31 88	53 60
Pottersville	Columbiana	Harper Brosins	7 99	13 44
Powhatan Point	Belmont	William McKinley	30 79	57 82
Pratt	Shelby	John Ogden	47 73	86 91
Preston	Hamilton	Saml. R. Pierce	31 31	49 77
Prigg's	Montgomery	Samuel Gulick	15 01	28 62
Princeton	Butler	Samuel Hitchcock	17 58	29 41
Prospect	Delaware	Jonat'n P. Brookins, 3 qrs	16 19	29 38
Providence	Lucas	Galen B. Abell	61 33	115 82
Pulaski	Williams	John Perkins	31 93	57 64
Pulaskiville	Knox	Joshua Bickford	15 28	25 73
Putnam	Muskingum	James T. Cherry	218 24	334 59

POST OFFICES—*Ohio.*

Post Offices.	Counties.	Postmasters.	Compensation.	Net proceeds.
Pyrmont	Montgomery	George Reid	$9 96	$18 05
Quaker Bottom	Lawrence	Jacob Proctor	27 57	53 80
Quincy	Logan	Saunders A. Osborn	34 05	55 44
Racoon Island	Gallia	Wm. F. Gooldin	6 61	12 35
Radnor	Delaware	Morgan Williams	no return	
Rainsborough	Highland	Henry W. Spargur	56 59	86 90
Randolph	Portage	Oliver C. Dickinson	74 25	120 90
Rapids	Portage	James Wilson	10 46	16 85
Ravenna	Portage	Lyman Collins	323 33	561 40
Raymond's	Union	Nathan Raymond	16 50	32 60
Reading	Hamilton	Israel Taylor	86 11	156 24
Red Lyon	Warren	John S. Todd	18 26	31 94
Reedsburgh	Wayne	John Smyser	20 22	36 05
Reed's Mills	Jackson	Ephraim Frazee	27 33	51 14
Reedtown	Seneca	Gilbert Ashley	20 05	36 80
Regnier's Mills	Washington	Wm. L. Rayley	21 46	27 93
Rehoboth	Perry	John McGinley	33 94	64 79
Reiley	Butler	Elias H. Gaston	41 71	63 91
Republic	Seneca	Edson T. Stickney, to 31st March	121 38	216 35
		Hosea W. Burrows	47 82	84 67
Republican	Darke	Levi H. Oillar	10 91	16 88
Reynoldsburgh	Franklin	Jas. C. Reynolds	94 44	169 93
Riblets	Richland	Daniel Riblet	22 94	37 92
Richfield	Summit	Orson M. Oviatt, to 31st Dec	58 21	91 98
		Henry Kilheffer	61 57	100 33
Rich Hill	Muskingum	John Randall	5 18	8 37
Richland	Richland	David Crawford	33 71	49 29
Richmond	Jefferson	William Frazier, to 17th April	74 99	128 39
		David Cameron	23 25	41 21
Richmond City	Lake	Weleome Porter, fr. 12th Aug	6 35	11 87
Richmond Dale	Ross	James Tomlinson	58 37	109 95
Richwood	Union	John P. Brookins	23 72	42 77
Ridgeville	Warren	Nathaniel McLean	44 68	68 05
Ridgeville Corners	Henry	Barton Palmer	7 29	13 68
Ridgeway	Gallia	Elijah B. Holcomb, to 31st Dec'r	25 00	49 24
		William Ridgway	28 62	51 93
Riga	Lucas	Lucien B. Lathrop	10 30	17 72
Ripley	Brown	Rezin J. Bennett	198 61	395 23
Ripleyville	Huron	Hazen Horner, to 30th Sept	5 90	9 61
		Lewis W. Ingersoll	18 64	30 70
Risdon	Seneca	Alonzo Lockwood	55 75	101 23

POST OFFICES—*Ohio.*

Post Offices.	Counties.	Postmasters.	Compensation.	Net proceeds.
River Styx	Medina	David Wilson	$30 79	$51 07
Rives	Richland	George W. Cline	31 32	59 87
Robisons	Darke	Samuel Robison	28 96	47 77
Rochester	Warren	Lewis Fairchild	39 93	72 10
Rock House	Hocking	Hershel Sanford, fr. 13th Aug	3 45	4 19
Rockport	Cuyahoga	Philip Wright	46 76	91 28
Rocksford	Tuscarawas	Thomas Furbay	4 35	9 57
Rockville	Adams	James M. Redden	18 87	36 24
Rocky Hill	Jackson	Jas. H. C. Miller	11 91	18 92
Rocky Narrows	Monroe	Thomas A. McCoy	4 68	8 17
Rodney	Gallia	David R. Payne	5 06	8 62
Rokeby	Morgan	Hiram Winchell	15 39	25 36
Rollersville	Sandusky	David Smith	11 99	21 30
Rome	Ashtabula	Sylvester Rogers	57 55	56 46
Rootstown	Portage	Otis Reed	48 29	78 96
Roscoe	Coshocton	Arnold Medbury	114 19	221 12
Rose	Carroll	William King	7 08	13 06
Rosedale	Madison	Foster Griffin	15 17	21 73
Roseville	Muskingum	Robert Allen, to 3d Feb'y	20 49	34 58
		Wm. S. Cussac	16 49	24 14
Ross	Butler	Isaac S. Frost	60 58	93 58
Rosseau	Morgan	Isaac Crosby	18 01	31 24
Rossville	Butler	Levi Richmond	197 32	368 37
Round Head	Hardin	James M. White	35 03	63 29
Rows	Wayne	John Van Nest, jr.	47 83	94 23
Royalton	Fairfield	Amos A. Frisbie	41 09	69 65
Ruggles	Huron	Geo. W. Paddock	41 84	67 87
Rush (Dis. 23d July.)	Tuscarawas	James Milliken	4 14	7 93
Rushville	Fairfield	Gilbert McFadden	107 40	135 64
Rushylvania	Logan	James Elam	21 39	34 91
Russell	Geauga	Christopher Edic	29 11	53 16
Russellville	Brown	Robert D. Tomb	41 24	86 72
Rutland	Meigs	Rodney Downing	39 95	68 52
Sabina	Clinton	Harrison Geffs, to 10th Dec	21 48	27 89
		Jacob Theobald	25 53	43 78
Saint Clairsville	Belmont	Robert H. Wishart, to 14th April	323 87	470 39
		Wilmeth Jones	85 76	131 51
Saintfield	Muskingum	George Smyth	8 12	11 39
Saint Johns	Allen	John Rogers	16 28	30 92
Saint Joseph	Williams	Payne C. Parker	11 63	23 23
Saint Louisville	Licking	Nathan Hadley, to 14th June	15 76	30 01
		Elijah Goff	27	64

POST OFFICES—*Ohio*.

Post Offices.	Counties.	Postmasters.	Compensation.	Net proceeds.
Saint Marys	Mercer	Albert Helfenstein	$105 75	$189 53
Saint Paris	Champaign	John Williamson, to 31st Dec.	8 22	14 75
		Jesse Long	10 21	19 21
Salem	Columbiana	Joseph Goulbourn	315 22	382 19
Salineville	Columbiana	James Farmer	30 76	53 75
Salisbury	Meigs	Samuel Bradbury	51 25	83 61
Sandusky	Erie	Elijah Brink	644 40	1560 30
Sandy	Columbiana	Thos. M. Anderson	6 34	10 08
Sandyville	Tuscarawas	George H. Fogle	33 60	62 68
Sarahsville	Morgan	George Richey, to 13th May	18 17	30 54
		James R. Dilley	4 21	6 36
Sardinia	Brown	Josiah Moore	29 89	50 61
Sardis	Monroe	Thomas Algeo	8 37	15 82
Savannah	Richland	James Henry	76 73	140 21
Saybrook	Ashtabula	Jona. W. Covell	35 99	55 91
Scio	Harrison	Malachi Jolly	32 19	51 57
Scioto	Scioto	Caleb G. Cranston	20 43	37 74
Scioto Bridge	Delaware	Henry Rigour, 2 qs.	2 92	5 69
Scott	Adams	James Sparks	60 39	104 33
Scroggsfield	Carroll	Robert George	14 15	22 28
Selma (Late 'Cortsville.')	Clark	Jesse S. Wilson, fr. 1st Oct.	48 49	53 31
Senecaville	Guernsey	John H. Atwell, to 14th June	57 01	101 69
		Andrew Morrison	3 29	6 74
Seven Mile	Butler	George Jacoby	30 85	50 00
Seven Mile Prairie	Darke	James McFeely	2 46	4 87
Sewellsville	Belmont	William Jarvis	11 88	21 82
Shade	Athens	Charles D. Martin, to 30th Sept.	2 46	3 76
		Nathan Axtell	8 85	16 12
Shalersville	Portage	Abner Horr	64 10	112 52
Shane's Crossings	Mercer	George S. Barks	13 85	29 30
Shanesville	Tuscarawas	Reuben Hall	78 92	149 61
Shannon	Muskingum	William Ricketts	12 59	17 46
Sharon	Morgan	Edward Parrish	34 69	62 90
Sharon Centre	Medina	Sheldon W. Johnson	66 58	110 23
Sharonville	Hamilton	John Jenkins	62 38	101 39
Shaucks	Richland	John T. Creigh	30 86	55 39
Sheffield	Lorain	John B. Garfield	16 27	32 57
Shelby	Richland	John Gambell	107 39	171 83
Shepherdstown	Belmont	John McNary	14 34	23 21
Sherman	Huron	Coles A. Bloomer	29 61	51 92
Sherrodsville	Carroll	Amos Sherod	3 62	7 11
Shober's Mills	Carroll	John H. Shober	7 86	11 17
Short Creek	Harrison	I. Lewis, to 15th Ap'l	58 24	98 01
		Jonas Romick	15 29	21 75

POST OFFICES—*Ohio.*

Post Offices.	Counties.	Postmasters.	Compensation.	Net proceeds.
Shreve	Wayne	Thomas Shreve	$15 71	$28 81
Sidney	Shelby	Elijah Lynch, to 20th June	214 40	396 44
		James Wells	3 84	8 96
Sinking Spring	Highland	Wm. M. C. Elliott	35 00	64 96
Sligo	Clinton	George Slack	17 33	26 62
Slonesville	Clermont	William Slone	13 70	20 44
Smithfield	Jefferson	Charles S. Barnes, to 23d April	91 67	161 62
		Robert Leslie	22 92	42 39
Smiths (Late "Mercerville.")	Gallia	Jackson T. Smith	no ret.	
Smith's Mills	Marion	Carpenter M. Smith	9 55	17 35
Smithville	Wayne	Henry W. Greegor	43 42	77 62
Smyrna	Harrison	Robt. S. Holloway	20 36	35 96
Solon	Cuyahoga	Archibald Robbins	31 91	41 83
Somerset	Perry	Otto H. Moeller	342 29	580 61
Somerton	Belmont	Moses P. Miles	38 40	71 63
Somerville	Butler	William Logue	65 82	111 55
South Bloomfield	Pickaway	Rowland Stebbins	83 27	154 93
South Charleston	Clark	Jos. A. Houston	135 45	133 04
Southington	Trumbull	James Hatch	22 22	34 80
South Kirtland	Lake	William E. Peck	15 20	26 47
South New Castle	Gallia	Joseph Shallcross	5 75	10 75
South Perry	Fairfield	Levi Friend	14 83	26 61
South Ridge	Ashtabula	John W. Haskell, fr. 24th July	15 10	24 29
South Solon	Madison	John Whitehead	11 66	20 99
South Thompson	Geauga	Lorenzo D. Pease, to 1st July	1 89	3 34
		Silas N. Burroughs	7 68	12 08
Sparta	Knox	Aug'ne W. Swetland	25 67	42 54
Spencer	Lorain	Charles Daugherty	18 06	33 83
Springboro'	Warren	Mahlon Wright	83 67	139 48
Spring Dale	Hamilton	Geo. W. Wilmuth	91 89	161 27
Springfield	Clark	John A. Crain	737 32	1346 85
Spring Lake	Williams	Martin Perky	9 58	19 28
Springville	Seneca	Leonard Cook	26 72	51 26
Stafford	Monroe	John Jones	11 84	20 48
Starr	Hocking	John Wright	12 04	23 15
State Line	Trumbull	Nathan Kinne	18 93	22 17
Staunton	Fayette	James E. Johnson, 2 qrs	3 55	4 99
Sterling Bottom	Meigs	Johnson J. White, fr. 21st Aug	4 47	8 07
Steuben	Huron	Jeremiah Wright	94 29	155 06
Steubenville	Jefferson	William Collins	785 03	1939 78
Stillwater	Tuscarawas	Ezra Brainerd	3 93	9 39
Stillwells	Butler	Willis R. Dewitt	17 73	27 69

POST OFFICES—*Ohio.*

Post Offices.	Counties.	Postmasters.	Compensation.	Net proceeds.
Stockport	Morgan	Samuel Beswick	$30 81	$48 79
Stony Ridge	Wood	Orange Howard	12 40	18 19
Stouts	Adams	John P. Newman	19 71	37 44
Stow	Summit	Edwin Wetmore	78 03	121 39
Strasburgh	Tuscarawas	Timothy L. Bacon	24 32	44 24
Streetsboro'	Portage	John C. Singletary, to 8th July	1 01	1 97
		Asahel M. Hanchett	83 59	150 22
Strongsville	Cuyahoga	Warner Strong	136 98	238 58
Suffield	Portage	Seth Dustin	17 78	31 48
Sugar Grove	Fairfield	Jonas A. Ream	9 09	13 17
Sugar Tree Ridge	Highland	James Hetherington	14 59	25 93
Sugar Valley	Preble	Enoch Kindley, fr. 26th July	6 28	8 89
Sullivan	Lorain	John Gould	73 16	134 93
Summerfield	Monroe	William Philpot	48 88	72 07
Summerford	Madison	William Eaton	39 02	32 33
Sunbury	Delaware	Samuel Peck	81 98	153 61
Sunday Creek X Roads	Perry	John McDonald	21 89	35 55
Sunfish	Monroe	Thomas Weston	62 43	114 84
Swan	Hocking	Geo. W. Johnson	20 57	35 68
Swan Creek	Gallia	Jas. H. Guthrie	14 63	23 73
Swanton	Lucas	Elias Fairchild	32 99	61 22
Sycamore	Wyandott	Samuel Hudson	11 82	22 22
Symmes' Corner	Butler	Benj'n R. Symmes	13 72	26 04
Talbott	Fairfield	William Talbott	19 50	28 73
Tallmadge	Summit	Elbert V. Carter	124 04	194 65
Tappan	Harrison	Samuel Henderson	15 87	24 99
Tariff	Butler	Charles Shields	15 76	28 05
Tarlton	Pickaway	Henry S. Creal, to 18th January	86 81	85 55
		Otis Ballard, jr., to 2d June	75 77	66 81
		Fred'k W. Nye	9 08	8 49
Tedrow	Lucas	Isaac Tedrow	15 52	32 35
Thompson	Geauga	William Broughton	48 73	74 69
Thornville	Perry	Birkett M. Elkins	100 28	174 30
Tiffin	Seneca	Joseph Walker, to 17th October	111 16	224 88
		George Knupp	269 28	612 92
Tippecanoe	Harrison	John Graham, jr.	12 69	23 34
Tiro	Richland	David C. Morrow	21 69	33 66
Titus' Store (Dis. 19th June.)	Harrison	Timothy Titus	2 51	5 03
Tiverton	Coshocton	William Oldroyd	21 35	38 14
Toledo	Lucas	Andrew Palmer	1407 30	166 54
Townsend	Sandusky	William Tew	27 90	43 92

POST OFFICES—*Ohio.*

Post Offices.	Counties.	Postmasters.	Compensation.	Net proceeds.
Tremainville	Lucas	John W. Collins	$30 81	$55 72
Tremont	Clark	A. C. McLaughlin	34 27	60 10
Trenton	Butler	Ellis Miller, to 31st December	28 21	47 87
		William Potter	28 28	49 87
Trenton Works	Delaware	Gilbert Vandorn	13 88	24 12
Trimble	Athens	Samuel Porter	5 72	11 40
Troy	Miami	John T. Tullis	350 59	665 23
Trumbull	Ashtabula	Josiah Gregory	13 57	24 18
Tupper's Plains	Meigs	John Hoit	6 76	11 75
Turkey Foot	Henry	Samuel Knapp	5 11	9 59
Turtle Creek	Highland	Isaac Colvin, from 1st January	68	1 36
Tuscarawas	Tuscarawas	John Minnich	37 98	59 51
Twenty M'e Stand	Warren	Henry Foster	42 11	60 96
Twinsburgh	Summit	Ed'in T. Richardson	120 43	168 54
Tymochtee	Wyandott	William Irvine	56 74	94 74
Uhricksville	Tuscarawas	Marcus R. Haskins	78 76	156 16
Underwood	Marion	Elihu Underwood	8 55	13 07
Union	Montgomery	Alfred Hoover	30 19	59 54
Union Plain	Brown	David Keefer	5 80	8 23
Uniontown	Belmont	John Warfield	61 89	103 33
Union Vale (Dis. 15 July, '45.)	Harrison	James Simerall	15 06	28 10
Unionville	Lake	Ira A. Torrey	133 83	129 23
Unity	Columbiana	Thomas Keener	28 23	47 27
Updegraffs	Jefferson	Alfred I. Purviance	20 14	30 62
Upper Sandusky	Wyandott	John Walker, to 17th October	34 49	12 48
		Andrew McIlvain	44 96	72 53
Upshur	Preble	William Brown	11 46	19 59
Urbana	Champaign	Newton Ambrose	424 18	910 15
Utica	Licking	Clifford Elder	126 01	213 89
Van Buren	Hancock	Gladwin Chaffin	20 33	38 80
Vandalia	Montgomery	Benjamin Wilhelm	16 42	25 97
Van Wert	Van Wert	Edw'd R. Wells	51 96	96 46
Venice	Erie	Sam'l W. Butler	26 66	48 01
Vermillion	Erie	Sylvester A. Pelton	47 13	83 20
Vernon	Trumbull	Geuel Ely, to 30th September	9 46	14 57
		Dan'l J. Mattocks	26 80	46 84
Vienna	Trumbull	Perry Squire	31 79	52 06
Vienna ⨯ Roads	Clark	Caleb Barratt	95 36	95 39
Vinton	Gallia	Anselm T. Holcomb	20 43	18 62
Wadsworth	Medina	John Pardee, to 18th October	33 50	52 41

POST OFFICES—*Ohio.*

Post Offices.	Counties.	Postmasters.	Compensation.	Net proceeds.
		Geo. K. Pardee, fr. 20th October.....	$79 34	$119 28
Waggoner's Ripple...........	Adams......	Jesse Wikoff......	no ret.	
Wakatomika	Coshocton...	Adin Slaughter, to 13th June.......	15 63	27 02
		Uriah Kinsey.......	82	1 68
Wakeman.......	Huron	Justin Sherman, to 6th June.........	35 73	57 08
		Lester T. Farand...	1 86	3 11
Walhonding.....	Coshocton...	James Gamble.....	17 13	31 01
Walnut Creek...	Holmes.....	William Erwin....	5 16	8 64
Walnut Hills....	Hamilton ...	Sam'l D. Kemper..	120 14	238 71
Wapahkonetta...	Allen	Sam'l M. Cowan...	64 98	113 67
Warren.........	Trumbull ...	Thos. I. McLain, to 17th April.......	554 72	916 32
		John W. Collins...	108 91	225 00
Warrenton......	Jefferson	George Craig, to 31st March	76 13	134 16
		Alex'r Mosgrove...	24 79	45 23
Warrensville.....	Cuyahoga ...	Albert Kingsbury..	37 17	49 03
Warsaw	Coshocton...	William Long, to 28th June.......	32 01	54 72
Washington	Guernsey ...	Jacob Ankeny.....	223 86	209 93
Washington	Fayette	James C. Bell......	145 90	178 20
Washingtonville .	Columbiana..	Henry Estep......	26 59	46 17
Waterford	Washington..	Charles Bowen....	46 48	78 39
Waterloo	Lawrence ...	Sanders Russell....	6 31	13 24
Watertown......	Washington..	Dennis Ryan......	48 09	78 18
Waterville	Lucas........	Lor'o L. Morehouse	53 29	90 24
Watkins........	Union.......	William Thompson.	6 89	11 38
Waverly........	Pike.........	John Carolus......	89 93	165 81
Wayne	Ashtabula ...	Hori Miner........	59 65	104 99
Waynesburgh ...	Stark	Henry W. Rhoads, 3 qrs.............	38 11	71 39
Waynesville.....	Warren	John M. Hadden...	184 73	319 71
Wellington	Lorain	John P. Nickles	84 55	141 94
Wellsville........	Columbiana..	John S. McIntosh, to 4th April......	220 45	224 88
		John M. Jenkins...	56 31	53 68
Welshfield.......	Geauga	Alden J. Nash.....	49 02	78 79
Wert's Grove	Franklin	Jacob B. Wert.....	73 94	135 17
Wesley	Washington..	Hapgood Goddard..	8 84	16 71
West Alexandria.	Preble.......	Elias Herdman.....	95 22	159 84
West Bedford....	Coshocton...	Thomas McBride, to 31st March......	25 31	45 30
		John Shields.......	9 57	18 00
West Brookfield.	Stark	V. Bohn, to 20th May	41 94	65 99
		Ch's. F. Ricks......	3 28	6 64

POST OFFICES—*Ohio.*

Post Offices.	Counties.	Postmasters.	Compensation.	Net proceeds.
West Canaan....	Madison	Charles McCloud, to 28th August.....	$5 36	$8 42
		Abel W. Field......	26 27	43 13
West Carlisle.....	Coshocton...	Sam'l W. Lakin...	55 98	99 49
West Carrollton..	Fairfield	Wm. F. Breck......	29 26	53 64
West Charleston.	Miami	Samuel Higginson..	38 52	71 73
West Chester....	Butler.......	John S. Davis, to 4th June............	46 46	81 24
		James Van Hise...	4 68	8 65
West Elkton.....	Preble	Joel G. Hutchin....	28 59	37 87
Western Star....	Summit	Reuben Stevens....	42 90	74 88
Westerville	Franklin	Jacob B. Connelly..	36 86	63 04
Westfield	Delaware	Adam Wolfe.......	31 24	59 96
West Florence...	Preble	Eli Conger.........	7 32	12 29
Westford.........	Union........	Moses Fullington...	4 65	7 32
West Jefferson..	Madison	John W. Simkins, to 31st December...	46 77	63 30
		Henderson Crabb..	57 40	57 41
West La Fayette.	Coshocton...	Henry Johnson.....	7 07	14 08
West Liberty.....	Logan	James McDonald...	181 12	337 51
West Lodi.......	Seneca	Lyman White.....	28 66	43 38
West Middlebur'h	Logan	William Stokes, to 17th May.......	34 39	63 54
		Wm. M. Hellings..	10 89	16 50
West Mill Grove.	Wood	John G. Willard...	17 90	27 56
West Milton....	Miami.......	Joseph Potter......	57 17	104 70
Westminster	Allen	Alexander Creps...	23 84	42 13
West Nashville.. (Dis. 11 July, '45.)	Darke	Walter W. French, to 19th July......	41	85
Weston.........	Wood	Henry Mandell....	11 21	17 73
West Point......	Columbiana..	Jacob Stewart......	21 87	37 16
West Rushville..	Fairfield	David Abright......	49 47	63 25
West Union.....	Adams......	William R. Rape...	167 35	153 54
West Unity......	Williams.....	John Rings.........	23 78	41 29
West Vermillion.	Huron	Charles Ruggles....	8 68	16 57
Westville........	Champaign..	Rollin Pence, to 31st March	33 21	53 23
		Benjamin Paine....	12 32	19 66
West Windsor..	Richland	Seneca Leonard....	23 69	40 48
West Woodville.	Clermont....	Adam Bobs.......	7 24	12 95
Weymouth......	Medina	John A. Potter.....	27 64	43 92
Whartons.......	Morgan	John Wilson......	10 00	17 90
Wheelersburgh ..	Scioto	Jefferson Kendall, to 6th May........	90 85	153 93
		Thomp'n S. Enslow	16 85	31 32
White Cottage...	Muskingum .	Grafton F. Rankin, from 23d Oct.....	5 59	10 40
White Eye Plains	Coshocton...	William Waggoner.	40 50	37 32
Whiteford.......	Lucas.......	James White......	60 20	118 08

POST OFFICES—*Ohio.*

Post Offices.	Counties.	Postmasters.	Compensation.	Net proceeds.
White Hall (Dis. 27th Sept.)	Tuscarawas	Samuel Douglass, 1 qr	$0 82	$1 51
Whitestown	Sandusky	Bennet V. Havens	9 62	17 91
Wickliffe	Lake	Silas A. Vorce	18 74	22 69
Wilkesville	Gallia	Lemuel G. Brown, to 13th February	31 90	51 11
		Hiram G. Daniels	16 27	27 89
Wilkins	Union	Beriah P. Wilkins	7 18	12 13
Williamsburgh	Clermont	Sam'l G. Peterson	55 79	99 26
Williams' Centre	Williams	John B. Kimmel	25 21	48 78
Williamsfield	Ashtabula	Elias Morse	40 94	62 04
Williamsport	Pickaway	Ebenezer S. Davis	65 02	115 21
Williamsville	Delaware	Geo. L. Salsbury	15 60	29 56
Willoughby	Lake	Daniel Christy	296 23	324 67
Wills' Creek	Coshocton	Alex'r H. Frew	6 26	11 28
Willshire	Van Wert	Ansel Blossom	39 72	78 73
Wilmington	Clinton	Jeremiah Hadley	330 61	388 16
Winchester	Guernsey	Daniel Lenfesty	21 88	36 43
Windham	Portage	John A. Skiff	68 74	111 96
Windsor	Ashtabula	Moses Barnard	43 24	70 17
Windsor ⋈ Roads	Lawrence	John Mann	2 93	6 11
Winesburgh	Holmes	C's Van Steenbergh	38 63	70 61
Wintersville	Jefferson	Robert McCoy	22 83	43 19
Withamsville	Clermont	Otis Preble	41 72	65 73
Wittens	Monroe	James Witten	11 79	16 02
Wolf	Knox	George Wolf	5 78	7 56
Wolf Creek (Ch'd to Morgansville.")	Morgan	William McKitrick	no ret.	
Woodbury	Wood	Samuel McCrory	4 62	8 71
Wood Grove	Morgan	Israel Robinson, jr.	21 58	33 81
Woodsfield	Monroe	Jedidiah G. Fleming	180 72	287 14
Woodstock	Champaign	Ira C. Johnson	53 56	79 13
Woodview	Richland	John Boner	25 16	32 96
Woodville	Sandusky	Charles Powers	56 45	56 47
Wooster	Wayne	Bezaleel L. Crawford	561 41	1407 11
Worthington	Franklin	Geo. H. Griswold	154 02	271 38
Wyandott	Wyandott	John Kirby	10 25	19 67
Xenia	Greene	John H. Purdy	564 74	1157 12
Yellow Creek	Summit	Charles Hubbard, to 10th August	6 29	10 09
		Franklin B. Smith, to 23d May	36 19	61 20
		Orin Walker	3 71	6 71
Yellow Springs	Greene	Zenas M. Phelps	51 03	99 13
York	Union	John Thomas	7 30	10 75
York Centre	Lucas	John Harrison	5 95	12 58

POST OFFICES—*Michigan.*

Post Offices.	Counties.	Postmasters.	Compensation.	Net proceeds.
York North Ridge	Sandusky ...	Dan'l A.. Rife, to 11th February...	$7 55	$11 91
		Samuel Sizer......	4 33	3 21
Young's Mills...	Knox	James Bonar......	14 79	23 02
Youngstown.....	Trumbull....	Wm. Woodbridge.	288 95	299 25
Zanesfield	Logan	Samuel Taylor.....	64 91	114 18
Zanesville	Muskingum .	Israel Hoge........	1592 04	3756 80
Zoar	Tuscarawas..	Josiah M. Bimeler..	41 59	79 89

MICHIGAN.

NOTE.—Compensation of Postmasters, and net proceeds of their offices, from July 1, 1844, to June 30, 1845.

Post Offices.	Counties.	Postmasters.	Compensation.	Net proceeds.
Abscota.........	Calhoun.....	Gilbert B. Murray..	$11 57	$20 25
Ada.............	Kent.........	Nelson Robinson...	29 81	62 71
Adams..........	Hillsdale....	Salmon Sharp......	21 55	36 03
Adamsville......	Cass.........	Martin G. Sage....	40 23	74 67
Adrian..........	Lenawee.....	Abel Whitney.....	622 68	1390 09
Alaiedon	Ingham	William Lewis.....	8 80	15 60
Alamo...........	Kalamazoo...	Osmond H. Gregory	16 60	25 21
Albion..........	Calhoun.....	Jesse Crowell......	294 92	553 01
Algansee.........	Branch.......	James T. Bailey....	no return	
Algonac.........	St. Clair....	John K. Smith.....	34 45	53 91
Allegan	Allegan	Elisha Ely.........	170 72	313 97
Amboy	Lapeer......	Charles Wright....	10 50	19 79
Andover	Calhoun.....	Moses Lowell......	27 28	43 91
Ann Arbor......	Washtenaw .	George Danforth...	752 53	1839 16
Antwerp	Van Buren..	Philip Williams....	14 20	16 15
Argentine	Genesee.....	James H. Murray, to 31st March....	14 52	25 91
		David Middlesworth	4 64	10 04
Armada.........	Macomb	Solomon Lathrop, fr. 19th July........	22 65	41 84
Assyria..........	Barry.......	Cleaveland Ellis....	9 11	15 83
Athens..........	Calhoun.....	Francis A. Mann...	21 69	38 85
Auburn.........	Oakland.....	John Bacon, to 5th Sept............	3 09	6 74
		Warren Dunning...	14 67	26 02
Austerlitz	Kent........	Henry C. Smith....	12 02	24 31
Avon...........	Ionia........	Asaph C. Smith, fr. 1st August.......	2 21	4 97

POST OFFICES—*Michigan.*

Post Offices.	Counties.	Postmasters.	Compensation.	Net proceeds.
Bainbridge	Berrien	James H. Enos	$31 29	$64 77
Barry	Jackson	John Haddock	48 31	73 79
Batavia	Branch	Sam'l H. Cary	21 90	25 03
Battle Creek	Calhoun	John L. Bolkcom, to 18th April	339 34	487 87
		Alonzo Noble	67 19	100 90
Bedford	Calhoun	Erastus R. Wattles	6 47	12 09
Belle River	St. Clair	Selden A. Jones	48 45	83 17
Belleville	Wayne	Lorton Holden	11 16	20 48
Bellvue	Eaton	J. P. Woodbury, to 31st Dec'r	44 55	69 17
		Caleb Woodbury, jr.	42 00	64 07
Bennett's Corners	Jackson	Barnabas C. Hatch	10 92	17 39
Benton	Washtenaw	Chester Parsons	7 64	12 50
Berrien Springs	Berrien	Thomas Love, to 31st March	84 02	134 39
		George Essick	20 02	36 84
Bertrand	Berrien	Alva Higbee	46 28	64 34
Big Beaver	Oakland	Ira Smith, from 1st August	3 64	5 81
Birmingham	Oakland	Theron A. Flower	153 03	258 85
Blanc (Dis. 29th July '45)	Lenawee	James McCrilles	5 02	11 77
Blissfield	Lenawee	Amos Holmes	72 58	133 15
Borodino	Wayne	Boswell Root	17 62	25 93
Boston	Ionia	Cyprian S. Hooker	15 97	30 92
Bradley	Allegan	David Bradley	4 15	7 07
Branch	Branch	Henry B. Stillman	18 81	36 11
Brandon	Oakland	Jona'n Selden, 1 qr.	2 16	4 11
		Jesse R. Decker, 2 qrs	3 61	7 70
Brest	Monroe	Gouverneur Morris	25 69	38 45
Bridgeport	Saganaw	James A. Kent	8 77	17 87
Bridgewater	Washtenaw	Aaron D. Truesdell	13 53	23 85
Brighton	Livingston	Robt. D. Power	58 49	117 18
Bristol	Lapeer	Ezra Hazen, to 5th Sept.	15 23	25 32
		James H. Andrus, fr. 11th Sept.	61 72	97 09
Bronson's Prairie	Branch	Homer M. Wright	57 21	55 76
Brooklyn	Jackson	William Jones	76 22	139 67
Brownstown	Wayne	John L. Near, to 9th Jan'y	23 49	40 40
		Geo. W. Moore	20 95	41 97
Bruce	Macomb	Heman Palmerlee	16 68	32 33
Burlington	Calhoun	Levi Houghtaling	26 17	45 24
Burr Oaks	St. Josephs	Julius A. Thompson	18 65	34 81
Byron	Shiawassee	Francis J. Prevost	45 62	86 17

POST OFFICES—*Michigan.*

Post Offices.	Counties.	Postmasters.	Compensation.	Net proceeds.
Caledonia	Kent	P. D. McNaughton	$9 96	$21 48
Cambria	Hillsdale	Jacob S. Hancock, to 31st Jan'y	2 49	4 37
		Alanson Van Vlack	2 40	4 94
Cambridge	Lenawee	Sylvester Walker	21 31	38 51
Camden	Hillsdale	James Fowle, to 1st June	11 08	23 01
		Benjamin Fisher	0 53	1 09
Cannonsburgh	Kent	Sidney S. Haskins	5 49	11 99
Carlisle	Eaton	Edward D. Lacey	13 56	19 63
Carroll	Calhoun	Heman Cowles	9 95	14 95
Cassapolis	Cass	Alex'r H. Redfield	101 89	190 35
Castleton	Barry	Seth Davis	7 57	12 31
Cayuga	Jackson	Michael S. Brown	17 80	25 79
Cedar	Livingston	Rich'd P. Bush	13 02	25 08
Cedar Lake	Calhoun	David Aldrick	7 54	14 31
Centreport	Wayne	Andrew L. Stevens	11 99	20 12
Centreville	St. Josephs	Calvin Bronson, to 9th Jan'y	104 46	179 85
		Samuel Chipman	84 10	158 20
Ceresco	Calhoun	Winslow S. Hale	12 36	18 69
Charleston	Kalamazoo	Orra Bush	48 75	55 90
Charlotte	Eaton	Fred'k F. White	42 74	82 90
Chester	Eaton	Robert Wheaton	17 36	30 37
China	St. Clair	John Clark	18 25	32 69
Clarence	Calhoun	Jno. B. Snyder	5 79	11 62
Clarendon	Calhoun	Lewis Benham	11 50	21 38
Clarkston	Oakland	Nelson W. Clark	30 08	61 43
Climax Prairie	Kalamazoo	Robt. P. Stevens, to 15th Nov'r	17 89	24 32
		William Richards, to 13th Jan'y	7 11	12 02
		Caleb Eldred	17 53	28 96
Clinton	Lenawee	Charles Chandler	214 23	363 29
Clyde Mills	St. Clair	Ralph Wadham	18 13	29 91
Cold Water	Branch	Harvey Warner	258 45	290 26
Colon	St. Josephs	Loransie Schellhouse	61 87	121 97
Columbia	Jackson	Wm. F. Fuller	25 81	48 24
Columbus	St. Clair	Erastus S. Cross	14 56	22 82
Commerce	Oakland	Chs. H. Paddock	48 27	92 77
Comstock	Kalamazoo	Horace H. Comstock	18 62	39 39
Concord	Jackson	Joseph Drake	88 44	149 05
Conois	Calhoun	James Wells	7 26	14 14
Constantine	St. Josephs	John K. Briggs	168 49	319 89
Conway	Livingston	Warren G. Grant	5 22	10 53
Cooper	Kalamazoo	Barney Earl	15 63	26 08
Cortland	Kent	Philo Beers	18 86	35 44
Corunna	Shiawassee	Alexander McArthur	37 32	68 05
Crockersville	Genesee	George Crocker	1 13	2 71

POST OFFICES—*Michigan*.

Post Offices.	Counties.	Postmasters.	Compensation.	Net proceeds.
Cuba	Kent	Andrew Mesnard	$1 11	$1 89
Davisonville	Lapeer	Paul G. Davison	46 37	90 87
Dearbornville	Wayne	Cyrus Howard	67 21	111 95
Decatur	Van Buren	Isaac Hall	5 40	8 54
Deer Creek	Livingston	John How	7 94	15 36
Deerfield	Lenawee	Anthony McKey	13 03	21 42
Delta	Eaton	Whitney Jones	9 95	15 99
Detroit	Wayne	Thomas Rowland, to 20th April	1609 89	4736 78
		John S. Bagg	390 11	1527 39
De Witt	Clinton	David Scott	68 66	128 97
Dexter	Washtenaw	Harvey Shepard, 3 qrs	146 37	313 79
Dixboro'	Washtenaw	Wm. M. Clements	31 04	55 24
Dover	Lenawee	Peter Strunk	19 90	31 63
Dundee	Monroe	Sam'l P. Munger, to 30th Sept	13 37	26 55
		Dan P. Potter, to 21st May	39 90	69 89
		Charles T. Cady	4 79	11 19
Duplain (Lt. "Mapleton.")	Clinton	Jas. Tucker, 2 qrs	7 89	14 28
Eagle	Clinton	Wm. F. Jenison	12 60	19 61
Eagle Lake	Oakland	Asahel Kent	5 89	11 84
East Dover	Lenawee	Levi H. Soper	11 58	18 95
East Ogden	Lenawee	John P. Hubbard	4 66	7 79
East Raisinville	Monroe	Leander Sackett	4 61	8 16
Eaton	Eaton	William Southworth	3 30	7 06
Eaton Rapids	Eaton	Benjamin Knight	84 43	149 41
Eckford	Calhoun	Wm. N. Wilder	18 65	34 95
Eden	Ingham	Judson W. Hopkins	10 16	13 52
Edinburgh	Hillsdale	Erasmus D. Ford, to 19th Nov	1 66	2 22
		Murray Knowles	2 62	4 39
Edwardsburgh	Cass	Abiel Silver	105 25	173 22
Elba	Washtenaw	Bennet F. Root	29 74	46 85
Enterprise	Shiawassee	Otis Hicks	3 92	7 34
Erie	Monroe	Salmon Keeney	28 88	36 81
Esmond's Corners	Calhoun	Wright J. Esmond	4 87	8 27
Essex Corner	Clinton	Timothy H. Pettit	7 08	12 74
Etna	Lapeer	Eber Barrowe	10 46	20 08
Fairfield	Lenawee	Orin Baker	35 40	60 34
Farmer's Creek	Lapeer	Lorenzo D. Morse	10 40	15 83
Farmington	Oakland	Elihu Ward	87 12	170 07
Fawn River (Late 'Freedom.')	St. Josephs	Jno. C. Richmond, from 1st Sept	41 51	32 30

POST OFFICES—*Michigan.*

Post Offices.	Counties.	Postmasters.	Compensation.	Net proceeds.
Fentonville	Genesee	Wm. M. Fenton	$73 61	$152 81
Flat River	Kent	Rodney Robinson	29 01	63 66
Fleming	Livingston	Jno. W. Smith	2 76	4 62
Flint	Genesee	William Moon, to 29th Oct	116 79	206 51
		Wm. P. Crandall	245 78	366 31
Florence	St. Joseph's	Lyman Bean	8 17	17 86
Florida	Hillsdale	Warren Thompson	16 05	30 60
Flowerfield	St. Joseph's	C. S. Wheeler, to 17th Jan'y	8 75	14 95
		Jno. N. Wheeler	8 86	8 89
Flushing	Genesee	Loren Green	31 41	59 53
Fort Gratiot	St. Clair	Jos. A. Emerson, 3 qrs	74 27	144 91
Fort Pleasant	St. Joseph's	Orrin M. Watkins	30 97	62 54
Fort Wilkins	Marquette	Charles R. Brush	no return	
Franciscoville	Jackson	Henry A. Francisco	6 03	10 84
Franklin	Oakland	Peter Van Every	62 68	101 80
Fredonia	Washtenaw	Levi Rogers	19 05	35 33
Freedom (Ch'd to "Fawn River.")	St. Joseph's	Freeman A. Tisdel, to 1st Sept	7 38	7 00
Fulton	Barry	Hiram Lewis	6 58	11 75
Galesburgh	Kalamazoo	James W. Cothren	98 69	114 02
Genesee	Genesee	Chs. N. Beecker	23 17	42 60
Genoa	Livingston	Chs. P. Bush, to 30th September	1 87	3 64
		Albert Tooley	5 76	11 72
Gibraltar	Wayne	Alanson Parsons	17 36	26 21
Gidley's Station	Jackson	Cornel's Coolbaugh, 2 qrs	15 72	26 77
Gilead	Branch	Emerson Marsh	20 10	38 97
Girard	Branch	Aura Smith	24 28	42 09
Grand Blanc	Genesee	Joshua K. Abbott	75 22	127 68
Grand Haven	Ottowa	Wm. M. Ferry	94 58	197 53
Grand Rapids	Kent	James M. Nelson, to 21st April	427 43	792 74
		Truman H. Lyon	92 83	162 38
Grandville	Kent	Charles Edgerly	46 73	86 70
Grass Lake	Jackson	Lorenzo D. Hale	92 24	170 27
Greenbush	Clinton	L. M. Richmond	2 39	4 10
Green Oak	Livingston	Alonzo W. Olds	16 90	34 59
Groveland	Oakland	M. T. Robinson	24 21	52 86
Hadley	Lapeer	Simon T. Hill	16 78	30 46
Hamburgh	Livingston	Edwin M. Cust	15 05	31 57
Hamilton	Van Buren	Henry Coleman	12 33	16 62
Hanover	Jackson	John Cruttenden	31 82	55 36
Harrison	Washtenaw	James M. Hallock	3 90	6 25

POST OFFICES—*Michigan.*

Post Offices.	Counties.	Postmasters.	Compensation.	Net proceeds.
Hartland	Livingston	Freeman Near, to 30th Sept	$9 92	$21 04
		Robert Crouse	34 98	66 47
Hartwellville	Shiawassee	Jona. M. Hartwell	23 14	42 91
Hastings	Barry	Henry S. Jennings, to 11th July	0 95	1 91
		Henry A. Goodyear	54 33	96 89
Henrietta	Jackson	Samuel Prescott	12 48	24 44
Hickory Corners	Barry	Salmon C. Hall, 3 qrs	5 71	8 86
Hickory Grove	Jackson	John Mott	4 73	10 28
Hickville	Oakland	Daniel Hickok	25 41	39 93
Highland	Oakland	George Showerman	30 34	60 22
Hillsdale	Hillsdale	John P. Cook	279 95	571 97
Holland	Kalamazoo	Rufus A. Roys	18 71	32 49
Homer	Calhoun	Henry D. Garrison, to 23d Oct	47 42	94 32
		Jas. Humeston, 2d	63 01	127 83
Howell	Livingston	Almon Whipple	127 44	104 97
Hudson	Lenawee	William Baker, jr., to 8th March	53 60	99 66
		Stephen M. Wirts	23 99	49 75
Huron	Wayne	Wm. S. Hosmer	14 72	23 67
Ida	Monroe	Wm. L. Riggs, from 27th July	2 99	5 39
Ingham	Ingham	John D. Reeves	16 99	29 43
Ionia	Ionia	Ethan S. Johnson	140 20	241 48
Iron Creek	Washtenaw	George S. Smith	14 69	26 71
Jackson	Jackson	George B. Cooper	589 97	1242 24
Jackson's Mills	Lenawee	Charles D. Smith	20 38	36 87
Johnstown	Barry	Emory Cherry	12 94	18 67
Jonesville	Hillsdale	Charles Halsey, to 10th June	227 47	415 49
		Charles Gregory	8 46	19 58
Iosco	Livingston	Levi W. Munsell	9 26	20 36
Kalamazoo	Kalamazoo	Francis Marsh, jr., to 30th Sept	146 40	241 50
		Alexis Ransom	430 95	740 74
Kalamo	Eaton	Alexander Merritt	4 35	7 90
Kearsley	Genesee	Ogden Clarke	1 63	3 32
Keelersville	Van Buren	Wolcott H. Keeler	39 59	49 86
Keene	Hillsdale	Henry Ames	16 09	30 36
Kensington	Oakland	Albert Smith, to 30th September	11 57	21 84
		Neiel F. Butterfield	34 91	61 92
Kinderhook	Branch	J. Waterhouse, jr.	11 82	22 15

POST OFFICES—*Michigan.*

Post Offices.	Counties.	Postmasters.	Compensation.	Net proceeds.
La Grange	Cass	Jacob Allen	$36 76	$63 71
Laingsburgh	Shiawassee	Henry Smith, to 31st December	14 10	20 94
		Robert G. McKee, from 29th Jan.	11 24	22 11
Lakeville	Oakland	Wm. T. Snow	31 11	44 20
Lambertville	Monroe	William Dunbar	24 07	44 54
Lapeer	Lapeer	Noah H. Hart	106 24	180 48
La Salle	Monroe	S. M. Bartlett, 3 qrs.	20 46	36 67
Lawrence	Van Buren	John R. Haynes	25 79	49 26
Lebanon	Clinton	N. H. Beckwith	no return	
Legare	Cass	Ezra Hotch	11 39	18 29
Leoni	Jackson	William Jackson, to 19th April	55 77	95 68
		Peter C. Lawrence	14 43	28 19
Leslie	Ingham	Henry Fiske	24 25	50 86
Liberty	Jackson	Solomon Skiff	13 60	26 28
Lima	Washtenaw	Wm. A. L. Shaw	49 47	84 54
Litchfield	Hillsdale	Shailor Geer, to 1st February	37 54	66 06
		Emanuel Bentz	24 67	49 18
Little Prai'e Ronde	Cass	Richard J. Huyck	23 91	39 98
Livingston	Livingston	John F. Grisson, to 29th Nov.	6 84	10 51
		Wm. H. Twitchell	11 08	16 80
Livonia	Wayne	S. S. Jennings	20 04	34 88
Lodi	Washtenaw	Orrin Howe	20 43	36 31
London	Monroe	Samuel Nichols, 2d.	13 32	17 27
Look's Corners	Lapeer	Elijah Look	19 28	30 33
Lucerne	Washtenaw	John Renwick	7 42	12 20
Lyons	Ionia	Adam L. Roof	77 72	131 86
Mackinac	Michilimackinac	Jonathan P. King	240 82	522 25
Macomb	Macomb	Calvin Davis	16 58	28 71
Macon	Lenawee	Israel Pennington	18 64	29 78
Madison	Livingston	Darius Lewis, from 14th Nov.	2 16	4 68
Manchester	Washtenaw	Lorenzo Higgins, to 9th July	2 77	6 49
		Barnabas Case	164 97	281 11
Maple	Ionia	Zina Lloyd	14 16	21 77
Mapleton (Ch'd to "Duplain.")	Clinton	Edward R. Everest, 2 qrs.	4 59	9 16
Marengo	Calhoun	Loren Maynard	69 25	121 15
Marion	Livingston	George W. Lee	18 68	25 61
Marshall	Calhoun	James M. Parsons	no return	
		Zenas Tillotson, fr. 21st April	98 06	247 17

POST OFFICES—*Michigan.*

Post Offices.	Counties.	Postmasters.	Compensation.	Net proceeds.
Martin	Allegan	Abraham Shellman	$1 64	$3 75
Mason	Ingham	John W. Phelps	57 38	101 73
Medina	Lenawee	Artemas Allen	106 82	207 33
Mendon	Lenawee	Matthew Bennet	10 22	16 16
Meridian	Ingham	Abner Bartlett, 3 qrs.	4 50	7 59
Metamora	Lapeer	Price B. Webster	9 37	17 22
Michigan Centre	Jackson	Paul B. Ring	22 18	42 26
Middleville	Barry	Calvin G. Hill	26 63	47 28
Milan	Monroe	E. W. Sprague, to 24th January	8 81	16 41
		Frye Farrington	8 34	15 08
Milford	Oakland	Chs. C. Foote	105 35	191 15
Monroe	Monroe	Jos. C. Cole	632 20	1263 39
Morenci	Lenawee	Jephthah Whitman	22 23	37 44
Moscow	Hillsdale	George Gale	39 18	77 43
Mottville	St. Joseph's	Francis F. Philleo, to 21st Oct	27 06	29 26
		Sanders Hastings, fr. 25th October	52 70	92 14
Mount Clemens	Macomb	Giles Hubbard, to 6th Feb	112 93	231 94
		Henry R. Babcock	89 29	189 58
Mount Pleasant	Oakland	Squire G. Tanner	6 52	12 37
Mount Vernon	Macomb	Wm. A. Burt	16 74	25 27
Muskegon	Ottowa	Henry Pennoyer	no return	
Nankin	Wayne	Warren Tuttle	41 88	74 07
Napoleon	Jackson	John Dewey	55 80	90 63
Newberg	Cass	Julius E. Nicholson	8 51	16 42
New Buffalo	Berrien	Jacob Gerrish, 3 qrs.	31 48	54 18
New Canandaigua	Oakland	John K. Axford, to 31st Dec	11 95	25 06
		Isaiah Bradford	21 53	40 82
New Haven	Macomb	Robert O. Milton	13 50	23 70
Newport	Monroe	William White	8 54	17 32
Newtown	Calhoun	Daniel Merrill	9 04	17 98
Niles	Berrien	Jos. C. Larimore, to 23d April	461 36	876 53
		S. W. B. Chester	67 39	170 39
North Adrian	Lenawee	Asahel B. Treat	9 17	17 28
Northfield	Washtenaw	Nelson S. Halleck	19 95	29 77
North Lake	Washtenaw	John Ferguson	6 96	15 02
North Marshall	Calhoun	Jacob King	4 00	7 59
North Raisinville	Monroe	Eliphalet Clark	11 63	22 10
North Vernon	Shiawassee	Sam'l N. Whitcomb	6 87	10 74
Northville	Wayne	Hiram M. Perin, to 18th March	115 23	188 13
		David H. Rowland	59 90	97 29
Norvell	Jackson	Harvey Austin	22 69	38 47

POST OFFICES—*Michigan.*

Post Offices.	Counties.	Postmasters.	Compensation.	Net proceeds.
Nottaway	St. Joseph's	William Moltram	$17 33	$30 81
Novi	Oakland	Carlos Harmon, to 11th Nov	12 88	22 52
		Orrin J. Field	19 96	35 67
Oak Grove	Livingston	Elias Stilson	5 68	8 28
Oakland	Oakland	Benedict Baldwin	20 40	37 52
Oakville	Washtenaw	Stephen T. Hardy	12 32	20 80
Oceola Centre	Livingston	James G. Rumsey	10 56	19 12
Oneida	Eaton	Samuel Preston	13 71	23 76
Onondaga	Ingham	Josiah C. Preston	18 54	29 71
Oporto	St. Joseph's	Samuel Klady	16 30	30 41
Orange	Branch	Hiram Shondler	12 12	18 19
Ossawa	Clinton	Wm. H. H. Culver	2 95	5 80
Otisco	Ionia	Rufus R. Cook	35 95	71 77
Otsego	Allegan	Lintsford B. Coats	101 08	175 73
Otter Creek	Jackson	Daniel Griffith	8 14	13 97
Ovid	Branch	Parley Stockwell	6 91	12 55
Owasso	Shiawassee	Ebenezer Gould	50 10	94 81
Oxford	Oakland	Wm. H. Powell	55 51	97 55
Paint Creek	Washtenaw	Aaron Childs	4 62	9 96
Palmyra	Lenawee	Israel Titus, to 14th Nov.	21 32	35 70
		Volney Spalding	24 26	47 52
Paris	Kent	Jonathan H. Grey, 3 qrs	2 91	6 32
Pavilion	Kalamazoo	Martin McKain	11 99	21 31
Paw Paw	Van Buren	John McKinney	256 55	353 19
Phelpstown	Ingham	Levi Rowley	9 39	17 93
Pinckney	Livingston	Jas. W. Stansbury, 2 qrs	24 29	47 06
Pine Lake	Oakland	John Ellenwood	9 19	18 07
Pine Run (Ch'd to "Thetford.")	Genesee	Russell G. Hurd, to 16th Jan	5 32	10 15
Pittsfield	Washtenaw	John Hoy	20 60	34 07
Pittsford	Hillsdale	Elijah B. Seelye	15 77	28 76
Plainfield	Livingston	Emery Beal	16 13	29 53
Plainwell	Allegan	John Anderson	30 33	56 03
Pleasant Valley	Livingston	Peter Delamartre	15 37	27 89
Plumb Brook	Macomb	John B. St. John	5 78	9 36
Plymouth	Wayne	Henry B. Holbrook, to 31st Dec	85 36	157 35
		Isaac W. Averill, fr. 1st March	67 45	113 79
Pontiac	Oakland	Samuel Sherwood	571 72	1152 22
Portage	Kalamazoo	Henry Tuttle	6 50	13 75
Portage Lake	Jackson	Benoni Pixley, from 26th Aug	5 82	8 48

POST OFFICES—*Michigan.*

Post Offices.	Counties.	Postmasters.	Compensation.	Net proceeds.
Port Huron	St. Clair	John Wells	$207 53	$235 03
Portland	Ionia	Joshua Boyer	54 84	102 72
Port Sheldon (Dis. 7th June.)	Ottowa	Abraham W. Pike, 3 qrs	3 54	4 22
Prairie River	Branch	Wm. A. Kent	16 78	14 08
Pulaski	Jackson	Byron L. Harlow	21 22	33 82
Quincey	Branch	Enos G. Berry	48 98	46 67
Raisin	Lenawee	Eliphalet Jones	29 02	54 57
Rawsonville	Wayne	Eurotas Morton	26 59	44 43
Ray	Macomb	James McCracken, to 9th July	1 82	3 53
		Josiah T. Robinson, from 12th July	42 01	75 45
Reading	Hillsdale	Ralph Bailey	18 71	38 23
Redford	Wayne	William Smith	50 67	89 12
Renwick	Washtenaw	George Renwick, to 11th June	15 08	24 38
		Ira Rider	71	1 12
Rice Creek	Calhoun	Caleb Hanchett	2 28	4 02
Richfield	Genesee	Henry F. Shepard	8 05	15 89
Richland	Kalamazoo	Mumford Eldred, jr.	86 04	149 92
Richmond	Macomb	Philip Cudworth	34 66	65 76
Ridgeway	Lenawee	Oliver Miller	40 08	65 32
Rochester	Oakland	Rollin Sprague	136 16	223 17
Rollin	Lenawee	Philander Tabor, to 26th May	33 38	65 03
		Thomas Kealy	5 72	9 80
Rome	Lenawee	George Seger	35 03	63 51
Romeo	Macomb	Oran P. Southwell, to 12th Aug	10 49	21 23
		Azariah Prentiss	168 01	279 30
Romulus	Wayne	Z. E. Adams	14 24	25 22
Rose	Oakland	John A. Wendall	14 26	25 91
Roseville	Macomb	William O. Rose, to 30th Sept	86	1 82
		William Conner	3 87	8 05
Ross Centre	Kalamazoo	John Van Vleck, to 23d April	5 24	11 16
Rowland	Hillsdale	Nathaniel S. Dewey	13 41	26 18
Royal Oak	Oakland	G. M. Cooper, to 12th Oct	15 94	26 78
		David Chase	37 76	69 54
Royalton	Berrien	Ga's Boughton, 3 qs.	2 83	6 65
Sackett's	Macomb	Lemuel Sackett	3 36	4 54
Saganaw	Saganaw	Gardner D. Williams	147 71	269 82
Saint Clair	St. Clair	Wm. B. Barron	106 62	159 13

POST OFFICES—*Michigan.*

Post Offices.	Counties.	Postmasters.	Compensation.	Net proceeds.
Saint Joseph	Berrion	Thomas Fitzgerald, to 13th Feb	$161 70	$359 55
		Geo. K. Smith	85 34	195 36
Saline	Washtenaw	David S. Haywood, to 31st Dec	108 51	172 71
		T.L. Humphreyville	112 12	181 39
Sanford	Ingham	Freeman Bray	10 04	20 86
Saugatuck	Allegan	Stephen A. Morrison	20 30	41 70
Sault De St. Marie	Chippewa	Thomas Edwards, to 1st March	119 83	144 92
		Stephen R. Wood	80 87	177 47
Scoolcraft	Kalamazoo	Alexander H. Scott, to 31st Dec	127 28	204 82
		John Bealls, from 1st May	26 46	48 72
Scio	Washtenaw	George Walker	25 28	43 37
Sharon	Washtenaw	Burr Gould	31 94	47 85
Sherman	St. Joseph's	Philip H. Buck	163 03	161 99
Sherwood	Branch	Thomas West	16 54	27 08
Shiawassee	Shiawassee	David Bush, jr	41 04	69 56
Silver Creek	Cass	James Allen	8 67	15 32
Silver Lake	Washtenaw	Jas. W. Hill	13 59	17 63
Smithfield (Dis. 14th Feb.)	Jackson	Norman Allen, 2 qrs.	10 74	20 22
Somerset	Hillsdale	Charles Farnsworth	36 91	68 82
South Albion	Calhoun	Daniel Fulton, jr., to 31st March	5 10	8 47
		Henry A. Knowles	1 38	2 13
South Cass	Ionia	Myron Tupper	5 11	6 91
Southfield	Oakland	Smith Trowbridge	33 28	59 47
South Jackson	Jackson	Hiram Cornell	7 13	13 45
South Nankin	Wayne	Isaac Featherly	37 02	67 81
South Plymouth	Wayne	Timothy F. Sheldon	20 58	35 52
South Woodstock	Lenawee	Peter Humphrey	6 09	9 34
Spring Arbor	Jackson	Lem'l W. Douglass	28 71	53 25
Springfield	Oakland	Augustus S. Johnson	34 95	68 59
Springport	Jackson	Augustus F. Gaylord	11 17	20 26
Springville	Lenawee	John Hart	38 09	59 59
Sterling	Washtenaw	Oliver Chapman	3 90	5 61
Stockbridge	Ingham	Silas Beebe, jr	29 23	44 58
Stony Run	Genesee	John Stone, jr	19 29	38 77
Strait's Lake	Oakland	William Beaty	6 48	11 47
Summerfield	Monroe	Richard Peters	15 08	29 03
Summerville	Cass	Dennis Bates, to 31st March	23 29	42 18
		Richard Brown	7 66	12 28
Summit	Oakland	Robert Purdy	22 49	35 43
Superior	Washtenaw	John Brewer	10 13	18 44

POST OFFICES—*Michigan.*

Post Offices.	Counties.	Postmasters.	Compensation.	Net proceeds.
Swartz Creek....	Genesee.....	Arthur L. Ellsworth, to 29th July	$0 55	$1 20
		Peter Miller.	8 57	13 83
Sylvan..........	Washtenaw .	Henry H. Medley .	42 98	81 45
Sylvanus........	Hillsdale....	Daniel Nichols.. ..	54 99	69 51
Tallmadge	Ottowa	Bethuel Church....	22 72	34 95
Tecumseh.......	Lenawee. ...	Geo. Spafford, to 30th Sept........	114 37	200 80
		Jos. W. Brown....	264 84	512 77
Tekonsha.......	Calhoun	Albert L. Porter, to 31st Dec.........	12 03	20 48
		Ezekiel Allen, from 21st Feb........	5 93	11 19
Thetford .... (Late 'Pine Run.')	Genesee......	Corydon E. Fay, fr. 16th Jan.........	8 59	16 85
Three Rivers	St. Joseph's .	Burrawes Moore...	102 57	191 32
Tipton..........	Lenawee. ...	William Camburn..	40 82	68 61
Tompkins.......	Jackson.....	Thomas Godfrey...	11 45	21 57
Troy.	Oakland.	Edward W. Peck, to 21st Sept........	30 41	43 90
		Johnson Niles	79 38	126 08
Truago	Wayne......	Asahel L. Bird, to 31st Dec.........	27 12	49 33
		Henry J. Alvord. ..	42 89	49 22
Tuscola.........	Livingston ..	Sylvester Stoddard .	10 01	18 45
Tyler...........	Eaton	David B. Bradford .	4 48	8 24
Tyrone.........	Livingston ..	Jirah Hillman	5 47	10 63
Unadilla	Livingston ..	George Taylor.....	39 85	72 39
Union	Cass.	George Meacham ..	6 13	10 93
Union City......	Branch	Justus Goodwin ...	81 61	152 46
Union District ...	Washtenaw .	Ansyl Ford	14 66	17 38
Utica	Macomb. ...	John James, to 15th July.............	9 57	12 04
		Luther K. Madison.	86 93	176 60
Vermontville	Eaton.	Dewy H. Robinson.	28 86	46 81
Vernon.........	Shiawassee..	John W. Miller....	7 59	15 12
Verona .... (Dis. 21st Nov.)	Calhoun	John Stewart, to 31st Oct.............	4 58	9 27
Vienna	Macomb. ...	Stewart Taylor	27 61	45 25
Volinia	Cass.	David Crane.......	10 23	18 56
Wacousta.	Clinton	Harvey Hunter....	12 28	22 30
Walled Lake	Oakland.	Thorn Deuel, to 28th Jan.............	19 19	33 14
		Geo. J. Eldred.....	15 73	28 01
Walton.........	Eaton.	James W. Hickok .	13 03	26 00

POST OFFICES—*Indiana.*

Post Offices.	Counties.	Postmasters.	Compensation.	Net proceeds.
Washington	Macomb	Dennis Cooley	$45 17	$72 13
Waterford	Oakland	Thomas Whitfield	26 35	54 06
Waterford Centre	Oakland	Elisha Sheldon	8 84	16 70
Waterloo	Jackson	Patrick Hubbard	20 82	38 36
Wayland	Allegan	Geo. W. Barnes, fr. 12th Oct.	3 03	5 59
Wayne	Cass	Justus Gage	8 32	13 41
Webster	Washtenaw	Charles Williams	15 47	25 96
West Bloomfield	Oakland	Nathl. J. Daniells	29 09	46 89
West Climax	Kalamazoo	Joel A. Gardner	8 84	13 99
West Farmington	Oakland	John C. Emery	8 10	15 58
Westfield	Kalamazoo	Abram J. Shaver	8 92	14 00
West Ogden	Lenawee	Benj. L. Hicks	7 30	11 39
West Rives	Jackson	Reuben H. King	11 15	20 42
Wheatland	Ionia	Joel C. Green, from 1st Oct.	1 64	2 94
Wheatland Centre	Hillsdale	Aaron Van Vleet	14 65	29 15
White Lake	Oakland	Robert Gillfillan	31 07	61 04
White Pigeon	St. Joseph's	Wm. O. Austin	236 52	287 54
Williamstown	Ingham	Jas. M. Williams	20 39	38 66
Wolf Creek	Lenawee	Lyman W. Baker	10 66	18 92
Woodstock	Lenawee	Thomas McCourtie	11 18	24 09
Wyoming	Jackson	Robert Jackson	2 38	3 67
Yankee Spring	Barry	William Lewis	15 20	30 23
Ynouski	Kalamazoo	David E. Deming	1 53	2 38
York	Washtenaw	Jon. R. Bowers, to 8th Feb.	15 37	25 83
		Horace Gray	12 16	21 80
Yorkville (Late "Ross Centre.")	Kalamazoo	Mumford Eldred, jr., from 23d April	1 16	2 41
Ypsilanti	Washtenaw	Wm. R. Martin	508 81	956 49

INDIANA.

NOTE.—Compensation of Postmasters, and net proceeds of their offices, from July 1, 1844, to June 30, 1845.

Post Offices.	Counties.	Postmasters.	Compensation.	Net proceeds.
Aberdeen	Hamilton	John Fitzpatrick	$13 27	$25 84
Abington	Wayne	Daniel Weaver	22 95	43 26
Aboite	Allen	James Graham	10 29	19 99
Ai	Grant	Solomon Thomas	4 85	8 12
Alamo	Montgomery	Jas. S. McClelland, from 10th Aug.	16 63	25 10

POST OFFICES—*Indiana.*

Post Offices.	Counties.	Postmasters.	Compensation.	Net proceeds.
Alexandria	Madison	N. E. Tomlinson	$17 81	$34 09
Allensville	Switzerland	Philander S. Sage	30 01	58 86
Allisonville	Marion	Daniel R. Brown, 3 qrs	14 97	15 00
Alquina	Fayette	Thomas H. Jackson	15 02	26 64
Alton	Dearborn	Merit Hubbell	20 52	34 90
America	Wabash	Elijah Quick	14 99	30 89
Americus	Tippecanoe	Chester Humphreys	23 39	43 78
Amsterdam (Dis. 7th June.)	Cass	James C. Thompson	8 07	15 77
Andersontown	Madison	Nineveh Berry	77 55	88 16
Andersonville	Franklin	James Wildridge, to 11th April	26 52	45 80
		Joseph Cowing	6 22	11 41
Angola	Steuben	Wm. M. Cary	56 86	110 46
Annapolis	Parke	Simon H. Vestal, to 31st Dec'r	25 62	45 84
		Fleet W. Hunt	31 59	59 33
Armiesburg	Parke	Harte Gleason, 1 qr.	4 81	8 39
		Rufus K. Harris, fr. 1st Jan.	11 60	11 27
Attica	Fountain	John Hemphill	119 01	146 92
Auburn	De Kalb	Wesley Park	50 04	99 34
Augusta	Marion	Thos. W. Council, 3 qrs	11 82	22 17
Aurora	Dearborn	Dan'l Bartholomew, to 15th Feb.	59 97	108 58
		Peter B. Vail	37 38	74 53
Azalia	Bartholomew	James W. Parker, to 26th Feb.	22 39	34 95
		Abraham Peaslee	7 02	13 27
Bacon (Ch. to "Union Mills.")	La Porte	Asaph Webster	10 38	13 57
Bainbridge	Putnam	Dillard C. Donnohue	35 21	68 02
Ballstown	Ripley	Samuel Ball	6 06	9 85
Baltimore	Warren	Elisha Rodgers	14 55	26 47
Barren	Harrison	Edmund Greene	3 87	6 46
Bath	Franklin	John Farr	19 17	26 06
Battle Ground	Tippecanoe	Jesse Watson, to 5th June	23 80	37 34
		John Shaw, jr	1 80	3 49
Bean Blossom	Brown	Robert McElhenny	8 16	15 44
Bear Creek	Jay	Enoch Bowdon	9 00	17 69
Beaver Dam	Kosciusko	Samuel Rickel	2 62	6 18
Bedford	Lawrence	Gustavus Clark	180 73	278 52
Beech Grove	Rush	Archibald Kennedy, to 31st March	20 67	22 04
		Erastus T. Bussell	6 36	10 74

POST OFFICES—*Indiana.*

Post Offices.	Counties.	Postmasters.	Compensation.	Net proceeds.
Belleville	Hendricks	James S. Odell, to 21st Oct	$16 73	$30 64
		George Sangster	46 07	64 05
Benton	Elkhart	Sylvester Webster	35 30	69 09
Bentonville	Fayette	Ezra Martin	15 15	26 25
Berryville	Knox	Andrew Berry	5 70	9 66
Bethlehem	Clark	Milburn T. Abbott	23 47	42 47
Bigelow's Mills	La Porte	Abijah Bigelow	24 12	41 41
Big Sandy	Spencer	Wm. M. Hammond	90	1 73
Big Springs	La Porte	Gilbert Rose	19 89	31 02
Billingsville	Union	James A. Garver	24 22	46 61
Black Creek	Sullivan	Philip Hinkle	8 45	15 48
Blackford	Blackford	Wm. B. McKay	41 75	79 91
Blairsville	Posey	Asa Marsh, to 19th July	24	57
		John B. Gardiner	17 89	34 59
Bloomfield	Greene	Willis D. Lester	45 40	82 65
Blooming Grove	Franklin	David Slaughter	34 16	41 82
Bloomington	Monroe	David H. Maxwell	317 02	413 31
Blountsville	Henry	Elisha Bird, to 24th Feb	12 25	22 48
		Edwin House	6 41	12 07
Blue Lick	Clark	Thompson M. Deitz	9 76	19 65
Bluffton	Wells	Almon Case	56 04	99 74
Bogard	Daviess	Isaac Hedden	6 93	11 86
Bono	Lawrence	Ephraim Brock	26 47	47 00
Boon Grove	Porter	Aaron Little	6 56	12 85
Boonville	Warwick	R. C. Matthewson	72 31	117 85
Boston	Wayne	Louis C. Evans	19 27	36 98
Bourbon	Marshall	John F. Parks	2 02	3 56
Bowling Green	Clay	Thomas Harvey	58 46	105 12
Boxley	Hamilton	Addison Boxley	no ret.	
Boyds	Henry	Robert Boyd	5 49	9 39
Bradford	Harrison	Ulrich H. Hon	2 34	3 79
Brandywine	Shelby	James Templeton, to 31st March	7 75	16 52
		Joseph Quinn	2 68	5 39
Brazil	Clay	Owen Thorp	8 37	12 66
Brewersville	Jennings	Horace Bacon	4 07	5 09
Bridgeport	Marion	Jeremiah Johnson	37 55	36 91
Brighton	La Grange	P. Beisel, to 19th Feb.	10 83	22 14
		Chauncey Adams	9 39	18 07
Bristol	Elkhart	Solomon Fowler	83 79	150 88
Brockville	Steuben	Matthew Coffin	46 04	82 94
Brook	Jasper	John Montgomery	3 53	7 02
Brookville	Franklin	Benj'n H. Burton	222 55	404 31
Brownsburgh	Hendricks	Benj'n M. Logan, to 30th Sept	9 80	9 68
		Henry E. Green	17 52	34 50

POST OFFICES—*Indiana.*

Post Offices.	Counties.	Postmasters.	Compensation.	Net proceeds.
Brownstown	Jackson	Mary Dunbar	$71 20	$121 07
Brownsville	Union	Henry Rider	43 27	79 96
Bruceville	Knox	William Bruce	23 79	41 08
Bruin's X Roads	Parke	Daniel Bruin	23 79	40 24
Brunerstown	Putnam	Isaiah Wright	3 04	6 85
Bryansburgh	Jefferson	John M. Selleck	8 81	16 29
Buchanan's Stat'n	Ripley	Benjamin Witham	5 53	8 26
Buck Creek	Greene	Aaron Hagaman	2 80	4 44
Burlington	Carroll	William Henry, to 1st June	40 88	80 32
		John M. Longstreth	3 73	7 47
Burnett's Creek	White	Franklin J. Herman	11 40	18 98
Burton	Parke	Josephus Burton	15 26	27 51
Butler	De Kalb	Robert Work	9 12	17 44
Byron	La Porte	Jos. M. Salisbury	60 95	60 98
Cadiz	Henry	John Cooper, 3 qrs.	6 46	10 57
Cambridge	Wayne	John H. Brown	248 23	*266 57
Camden	Carroll	Washington Beale	30 35	57 83
Canaan	Jefferson	Ephraim Kennedy	10 55	20 04
Cannelton	Perry	Watson Gore, jr.	44 10	85 94
Canton	Washington	John S. Harned	22 52	32 22
Carlisle	Sullivan	Isaac Beauchamp	87 06	127 00
Carr	Jackson	Christian Branaman	no ret.	
Carroll	Carroll	Wm. M. Coshow	7 55	13 31
Carthage	Rush	Wm. H. H. Glass	38 49	61 52
Cedar Grove	Franklin	James Roseberry	25 12	40 00
Cedar Lake	Lake	Lewis Warriner	3 31	6 51
Cedarville	Allen	Jacob Kandle, to 3d March	3 29	7 09
		John Edmonds	1 63	3 17
Centre	Grant	Obadiah Jones	13 73	21 21
Centreville	Wayne	Myers Seaton	310 03	349 94
Charleston	Clark	Rezin Hammond	189 00	319 05
Charlottesville	Hancock	Henry Kinder	25 11	49 79
Cherry Valley (Dis. 14th June.)	Jennings	Bowen C. Heath	1 13	2 08
Chesnut Hill	Washington	Warren Bartle	5 22	8 61
Chili	Miami	Daniel Landes	12 98	22 96
Christy's Prairie	Clay	Hale C. Conaway	10 58	23 04
Cicero	Hamilton	Ellis Evans	18 39	36 37
City West	Porter	Thomas J. Field	15 77	29 70
Clarksburgh	Decatur	Wm. E. Dobyns	26 01	48 92
Claypool	Kosciusko	Joshua Caldwell	5 88	10 46
Claysville	Washington	Wm. S. Lemon	14 18	23 75
Clear Spring	Kosciusko	Jesse Kiler	5 35	10 38
Clermont	Marion	Jordan Wright	3 82	7 43
Clifty	Decatur	Joel Doolittle	25 38	48 10
Clinton	Vermillion	James McCulloch	83 34	154 90

POST OFFICES—*Indiana.*

Post Offices.	Counties.	Postmasters.	Compen sation.	Net proceeds.
Clover Dale	Putnam	Thomas Nelson	$14 25	$25 58
Cobb's Fork	Decatur	Smith Reiley	4 48	7 62
Coesse	Whitley	Horace Cleveland	10 56	18 41
Cole Creek	Fountain	Jacob Strayer	25 85	30 24
Columbia	Fayette	Wm. Wherrett	16 59	28 77
Columbus	Bartholomew	Wm. Mounts, to 31st Dec'r	130 91	231 57
		Aquilla Jones	120 47	248 97
Concord	Tippecanoe	James B. Johnson	25 48	45 88
Cornersville	Fayette	John Tate	293 13	362 40
Conn's Creek	Shelby	Joseph Cummins	14 36	27 02
Coopersville	Dearborn	John Kemp	2 56	4 20
Corydon	Harrison	Jacob W. Kintner, to 22d Oct	25 95	27 85
		Lewis Jordan	62 25	99 85
Cottage Hill	St. Joseph	Joseph P. Jones	9 80	16 60
Covington	Fountain	David Rawles	214 71	231 48
Crawfordsville	Montgomery	Wm. P. Watson	346 98	685 80
Crooked Creek	Steuben	John Kent	15 29	30 47
Cross Plains	Ripley	Alpheus G. Hunter	25 70	44 69
Crown Point (Late Lake C. H.)	Lake	Joseph P. Smith	no ret.	
Cumberland	Marion	Hugh D. Gamble	34 62	50 41
Currysville	Sullivan	Rich'd Manwaring	6 90	10 20
Cynthiana	Posey	Clement Whiting	39 91	61 14
Dale	Spencer	Fred'k McKasson, fr. 15th Sept	1 14	1 81
Dalton	Wayne	William Davis	26 82	42 83
Danville	Hendricks	Wm. S. Crawford	86 35	168 92
Darlington	Montgomery	William Andrew	36 45	65 41
Davidson	Harrison	John Wood, to 31st December	2 44	3 85
		Saul W. Ott	1 89	4 25
Daviston	Clay	John Pickard	3 28	6 35
Dayton	Tippecanoe	Samuel Favorite	67 86	121 75
Decatur	Adams	James Crabs	49 38	89 24
Deep River	Lake	John Saunders	15 13	27 68
Deerfield	Randolph	Moses A. Morris	27 61	54 41
De Kalb	De Kalb	Reuben G. Daniels, from 8th Sept	1 34	2 60
Delaware	Ripley	Jefferson Stevens	17 57	19 41
Delectable Hill	Pike	John Stubblefield	2 84	4 16
Delphi	Carroll	John Phelps	227 19	452 07
Delta	Parke	David Hougham	17 40	28 12
Dicksburgh (Dis. 17 July, '45)	Knox	Edwin W. Brown, from 3d Feb'y	0 44	0 93
Dickson's Mills	Parke	Geo. K. Steele	15 61	28 53
Dillsboro'	Dearborn	Thomas Guion	26 35	48 07

POST OFFICES—*Indiana.*

Post Offices.	Counties.	Postmasters.	Compensation.	Net proceeds.
Door Village	La Porte	James Blaine	$38 07	$69 98
Dover	St. Joseph	Charles Loring, fr. 8th March	2 51	4 14
Drewersburg	Franklin	John Cleaver	13 06	22 36
Dublin	Wayne	Samuel Schoolfield	109 62	107 68
Dunlapsville	Union	Danf'h L. Shumway	28 75	46 57
Dupont	Jefferson	Thomas Alexander	23 79	41 23
Eagle Creek (Dis. 16th Aug.)	Lake	Jeremy Hixon, to 16th Aug	0 57	1 34
Eagle Village	Boone	Thomas P. Miller	40 87	76 70
Economy	Wayne	Barnabas Coffin	33 72	57 85
Eden	Hancock	Wm. S. Loder	8 46	12 09
Edinburgh	Johnson	Alfred C. Thompson	64 57	123 51
Edwardsport	Knox	John T. Freeland	15 03	25 02
Eel River	Allen	Peter Heller	20 96	40 48
Elizabeth	Harrison	Asa S. F. Jones	26 06	47 50
Elizabethtown	Bartholomew	Geo. W. Branham	10 93	21 11
Elkhart	Elkhart	Augustus Newton, to 31st Dec	46 89	90 38
		Silas Baldwin	53 68	95 88
Ellisburgh	La Grange	Oren Howard	7 08	12 74
Ellittsville	Monroe	James S. Sharp	14 60	27 72
Elm Grove	Jennings	Daniel Lattimore	5 64	9 03
Enterprize (Ch'd to "Hamilton.")	Steuben	Frederick C. Wilson	10 60	20 39
Eugene	Vermillion	James Armour	80 46	147 25
Evansville	Vanderburgh	Daniel Chute, to 30th January	360 13	797 79
		Benj. F. Dupuy	264 73	637 41
Everton	Fayette	Robert N. Taylor	32 00	36 55
Fairfield	Franklin	John C. Cunningham	39 23	57 08
		Samuel McCurdy, to 14th April	23 99	40 72
		John Turner	16 12	27 12
Fair Grove (Dis. 16th May.)	Morgan	Moses Kenney	no return	
Fairplay	Greene	Jessee J. Benefiel	6 63	13 76
Fairview	Randolph	Jos. H. Harris	12 68	22 41
Far West	Johnson	Wm. H. H. Pinney	53 36	59 19
Flat Rock	Shelby	Thomas Woolley	9 18	17 67
Flemings	Shelby	Wm. H. Fleming	3 87	7 27
Fort Wayne	Allen	Smalwood Noel	702 08	1763 46
Frankfort	Clinton	John Barner	112 14	208 98
Franklin	Johnson	James Chenoweth	225 99	333 67
Fredericksburgh	Washington	John Morgan	23 04	35 41
Fredonia	Crawford	Allan D. Thorn	29 87	55 83
Freedom	Owen	Samuel Hicks, jr	9 57	14 86

POST OFFICES—*Indiana.*

Post Offices.	Counties.	Postmasters.	Compensation.	Net proceeds.
Freeport	Shelby	Alex'r Rittenhouse	$10 04	$17 86
Frisbie's Mills	Warwick	Alpha Frisbie	14 47	20 90
Fulton (Dis. 24th Jan.)	Fulton	Samuel Houseworth to 24th Nov	0 51	0 91
Galena	Floyd	Charles Frederick	12 40	20 26
Gallatin	Parke	Solomon B. Garigas	9 04	16 31
Gentryville	Spencer	Thos. H. Field, to 13th July	8 63	14 84
Georgetown	Floyd	James Burger	18 30	29 42
Germantown	Hamilton	Sam. H. Cunningham to 12th June	10 50	18 99
		John Vanzant	1 06	2 20
Goddard	Rush	Joseph Goddard	1 56	3 38
Good Hope	Noble	Richard Stone	16 27	35 22
Goshen	Elkhart	Jas. R. McCord	165 49	316 98
Gosport	Owen	James Q. Dunning	57 78	105 46
Graham	Jefferson	Charles K. Lard	9 48	14 55
Grant's Creek	Switzerland	Royal F. North	13 12	23 14
Granville	Delaware	Isaac C. Helm	16 88	34 14
Greenberry	Grant	John L. Dolman	9 08	16 14
Greencastle	Putnam	James Talbott	270 42	538 39
Greene	Noble	M.M. Meriam, 2 qrs	0 83	1 32
Greenfield	Hancock	William Sebastian	71 82	147 77
Greensboro'	Henry	Margaret Henderson	51 70	86 58
Greensburgh	Decatur	Silas Stewart	184 94	347 87
Green's Fork	Wayne	James W. Scott	28 00	51 15
Greenville	Floyd	Daniel P. Porter, to 31st December	23 17	41 53
		John D. Daniels	25 38	46 01
Greenwood	Johnson	George T. Noble	39 15	53 96
Groves	Fayette	John McClure	7 84	15 73
Guionsville	Dearborn	Elijah Thacher	11 97	20 09
Hagerstown	Wayne	Joshua Howell	83 15	163 08
Hamburgh	Clark	Wm. S. Thompson	12 86	23 43
Hamilton (Lt. 'Enterprize.')	Steuben	Frederick C. Wilson, from 1st Oct	25 35	49 92
Hammonds	St. Joseph	Mat'w B. Hammond from 8th March	0 76	1 80
Hampton	Hendricks	Walter T. Ross, 3 qs.	6 91	12 55
Hardinsburgh	Washington	Aaron Hardin	13 15	22 50
Harmony	Clay	Elias Bowling	5 35	10 85
Harrisburgh	Fayette	Nathaniel McClure	30 49	44 74
Harrodsburgh (Lt. 'Marysville.')	Monroe	Paris T. Vestal, fr. 18th June	0 46	1 07
Hartford	Dearborn	John K. Lewis, to 26th November	10 08	15 06
		Elisha G. Herron	18 55	28 49

POST OFFICES—*Indiana.*

Post Offices.	Counties.	Postmasters.	Compensation.	Net proceeds.
Hart's Mills	Ripley	Dan'l McF. Paul	$6 57	$11 71
Hartsville	Bartholomew	Elijah H. Brady	27 48	44 13
Haw Patch	La Grange	Isaac Spencer	10 14	18 48
Headley's Mills	Fountain	Christopher Keller	6 56	11 08
Hebron	Porter	Wilson Blain	13 65	23 60
Hibernia	Clark	David Hosteller	11 75	22 57
Highland	Vermillion	John Vanduyn	15 40	26 07
Hillsborough	Fountain	John Williams	23 72	23 78
Hindsville	Jefferson	Francis Hinds	4 08	7 75
Hobbieville	Greene	William McGill	5 79	11 77
Home	Jefferson	Mordecai Brooks	8 89	15 40
Hope	Bartholomew	Martin Houser	35 51	60 70
Hudson	La Porte	Hallam Huntingdon, to 18th Dec'r	5 26	10 14
		Harvey Kellogg	7 18	7 51
Huntingburgh	Dubois	Wm. G. Helfrich	22 54	43 14
Huntington	Huntington	Harman I. Betts, to 28th July	17 79	27 09
		Gabriel Manning	124 42	224 93
Hunt's ⋈ Roads	Randolph	Mahlon Farquhar	18 49	38 69
Independence	Warren	Jacob Hanes	31 29	62 57
Indiana Furnace	Vermillion	John Stewart	15 98	25 74
Indianapolis	Marion	Samuel Henderson	1876 72	98 40
Jackson	Elkhart	Joseph Cowan	8 14	13 27
Jacksonburgh	Wayne	Thaddeus Wright	22 76	36 42
Jackson Prairie	Steuben	Adolphus Town, to 31st December	5 53	10 46
		Robt. C. Jackson	4 32	8 52
Jacksonville	Switzerland	George McCulloch	28 99	49 35
Jamestown	Boone	Daniel Graves	33 34	62 45
Jasper	Dubois	William Cumings, to 8th April	64 23	123 11
		Wm. M. Anderson	20 18	13 53
Jay C. H	Jay	Alexander White	32 34	61 73
Jefferson	Clinton	Robert Watt	31 98	55 15
Jeffersonville	Clark	Wm. Leviston	184 77	354 28
Jennings	Franklin	W. Alley, to 8th Nov	3 71	5 60
		James Alley	5 15	8 33
Kelso	Dearborn	Henry McKenzie, to 30th September	5 22	8 96
		Jeremiah Coughlan	16 89	27 99
Kendallville	Noble	William Mitchell	22 80	46 76
Kingsbury	La Porte	Daniel Shaw	26 14	46 55
Kirk's ⋈ Roads	Clinton	Conrad S. Perkins, to 20th February	20 31	31 56
		Joseph Bogan	12 84	20 46

POST OFFICES—*Indiana*.

Post Offices.	Counties.	Postmasters.	Compensation.	Net proceeds.
Knightstown......	Henry......	Fielding N. Goble...	$121 57	$216 08
Laconia.........	Harrison.....	Jno. D. Weaver....	25 22	48 94
Ladoga	Montgomery.	Taylor W. Webster	50 64	84 80
La Fayette......	Tippecanoe..	Rudolph S. Ford...	956 89	2385 54
La Grange......	La Grange ..	Charles B. Holmes.	20 29	41 28
Lagro	Wabash......	Jirah Barlow, to 3d Feb'y...........	58 08	207 04
		Wilson B. Barlow..	34 46	58 28
Lake C. H...... (Ch'd to "Crown Point," 26th June.)	Lake	Henry D. Palmer...	63 88	118 98
Lancaster	Jefferson.....	Lyman Hoyt......	10 68	16 46
Lanesville........	Harrison.....	William Black.....	37 02	65 30
La Porte........	La Porte.....	Thomas D. Lemon.	635 07	1011 62
Laughery........	Ripley.......	David Wallace.....	7 61	14 53
Laurel..........	Franklin	Geo. G. Shoup.....	100 04	176 68
Lawrenceburgh ..	Dearborn.....	Ezra Ferris........	453 71	723 67
Leatherwood	Lawrence ...	And'w Helton, 3 qs.	10 02	18 39
Leavenworth	Crawford....	Zeb'n Leavenworth.	74 45	136 08
Lebanon	Boone	William Zion, to 31st Dec'r.......	31 60	54 27
		Elkanah Vanhook..	26 05	53 12
Leesburg........	Kosciusko...	Stephen H. Colms, to 7th March.....	40 19	70 32
		Amasa N. Hascall..	16 27	31 94
Leesville	Lawrence ...	Henry Davis......	42 26	72 29
Lewis...........	Vigo........	Moses Pierson.....	6 98	10 64
Lewisburg.......	Cass........	Lewis Bowyer.....	12 08	21 95
Lewisville.......	Henry	Wm. L. Huston...	72 48	68 25
Lexington	Scott........	Wm. H. English, to 31st March......	35 43	56 17
		Benj. F. Crary.....	12 41	17 73
Liberty	Union.......	John Yaryan, to 23d May........	124 51	210 12
		Joshua Leach......	16 12	16 85
Liberty Mills....	Wabash	John Comstock, to 30th September..	13 47	24 14
		John Whisler......	27 43	51 02
Lima	La Grange..	Simon M. Cutler, to 17th June.......	134 99	258 63
		Wm. L. Moon.....	4 89	7 03
Limber Lost.... (Dis. 17th Mar.)	Adams......	William Mitchell...	no ret.	
Linton..........	Greene......	Martin Wines.....	8 16	16 04
Little Blue River.	Shelby......	Henry McKay.....	7 31	13 53
Little York......	Washington..	William Shannon..	7 70	13 60
Liverpool	Lake	George Earle......	5 50	10 96
Livonia	Washington..	Jas. A. McPheeters.	40 88	73 34
Lockport	Carroll......	Wm. A. Barnes....	28 47	58 39

POST OFFICES—*Indiana.*

Post Offices.	Counties.	Postmasters.	Compensation.	Net proceeds.
Lockwood's Store	Warwick	An'y W. Lockwood	$5 69	$8 22
Lodi	Wabash	John Shallenberger, to 12th May	1 43	2 77
		Noah M. Moore	26	55
Lodiville (Dis. 24th May.)	Parke	Elias G. Holladay, from 1st Feb	47	52
Logan	Dearborn	James Salmon	19 09	28 21
Logansport	Cass	Jordan Vigus, to 27th January	303 47	647 41
		Chauncy Carter	237 02	554 28
Longwood	Fayette	Ross Smiley	11 01	17 43
Luray	Henry	Thomas Fleming	9 71	17 38
Lusk's Mills (Dis. 17th Mar.)	Parke	Salmon Lusk, from 1st April	1 70	2 77
Lynnville	Warwick	John Lynn	23 31	41 51
McCanns	Rush	John Legg	6 91	9 31
Macksville	Randolph	Solomon M. Semans	11 03	22 29
Madison	Jefferson	Andrew Collins	1171 50	2912 19
Manchester	Dearborn	John B. Clark	106 52	163 74
Manhattan	Putnam	Abraham Jackson	26 13	47 39
Manilla	Rush	Thomas Trew	22 85	38 40
Manwarings	Shelby	Wm. H. Manwaring, to 30th Sept	5 38	9 43
		Hugh McFadden	11 04	20 53
Marcy	La Grange	Levi Wright	18 10	32 99
Maria Creek	Knox	Joseph Chambers	6 33	9 18
Marion	Grant	Benoni C. Hogin, to 1st June	123 97	221 88
		Jere. B. Stebbens	7 87	13 95
Marseilles	Noble	Henry R. Burnam	15 74	29 59
Martinsburgh	Washington	Richard Lane	14 07	23 55
Martinsville	Morgan	Giles Mitchell	117 77	189 42
Marysville (Ch'd to "Harrodsburgh.")	Lawrence	John McCrea, to 16th June	4 93	9 53
Mauckport	Harrison	Peter Wolf	24 78	44 39
Maurius	Vigo	Ephraim P. Kester	1 95	3 25
Merom	Sullivan	Jas. H. O'Boyle	31 58	57 70
Metamora	Franklin	Ezekiel Tyner	26 78	48 50
Metea	Cass	Jas. M. Buchanan	6 03	13 00
Mexico	Miami	Simeon Wilkinson	14 41	25 68
Michigan City	La Porte	Wm. W. Taylor	378 98	630 34
Michigantown	Clinton	Arth'r St. Clair Stall	23 22	31 48
Middlebury	Elkhart	John C. Case	63 35	128 08
Middle Fork	Clinton	James Purdum, jr	15 50	34 09
Middleport	Elkhart	Horatio Pierson	3 13	5 96
Middletown	Henry	Joseph Yount	32 65	68 94
Midway	Spencer	John Gwathney	13 33	20 43
Milan	Ripley	Winslow J. Wood	39 96	60 41

POST OFFICES—*Indiana.*

Post Offices.	Counties.	Postmasters.	Compensation.	Net proceeds.
Milford	Kosciusko	John Egbert, 3 qrs.	$13 90	$27 93
Mill Creek	Madison	Amasa Makepeace, to 31st December.	10 17	9 80
		George Makepeace.	12 36	7 23
Mill Grove	Owen	George Young, to 21st March	10 57	20 06
		Ervin P. Carmack	4 51	8 76
Millhousen	Decatur	Maximilian Snyder.	1 51	3 45
Millmount	Huntington	Frederick Kantz	11 88	21 32
Millport	Jackson	John Tuell	7 29	13 37
Milltown	Crawford	Libbeus Frisbie	9 94	20 03
Milroy	Rush	Nathan Tomkins	29 00	53 06
Milton	Wayne	Henry Develin	138 16	204 45
Mishawaka	St. Joseph	Major H. Smith	248 94	505 93
Mongoquinong	La Grange	Drusus Nichols, to 10th June	51 85	96 63
		Alonzo Bisbee	2 25	5 21
Monmouth	Adams	Thos. B. Kimsey	10 63	21 55
Monoquet	Kosciusko	Jas. H. Harris	11 12	21 93
Monroe	Tippecanoe	John Killgore	30 88	56 51
Monrovia	Morgan	Samuel Hadley, to 13th August	4 17	7 12
		Ira Hadley	29 92	51 53
Montezuma	Parke	Joseph Stephenson, to 30th September	10 84	19 78
		Geo. W. Cross	30 32	57 26
Monticello	White	Isaac Reynolds	59 33	97 27
Montpelier	Blackford	David Pierce	13 94	26 61
Moorefield	Switzerland	Squire Hulley	21 85	36 07
Moore's Hill	Dearborn	Wm. J. McCreary.	37 13	61 88
Mooresville	Morgan	Robert D. Worthington, to 23d Nov.	38 66	62 81
		David G. Worth	58 92	102 29
Morgantown	Morgan	Jas. A. Coplin	23 28	42 71
Morristown	Shelby	Geo. L. Morrison, to 26th May	37 34	46 48
		Eugenius Whetsel	1 84	3 92
Moscow	Rush	Wrisden S. McCalla, to 31st December.	13 91	23 91
		William Wallace	11 27	18 16
Mount Auburn	Shelby	Elisha Collins	19 95	37 07
Mount Carmel	Franklin	Richard P. Clarkson	33 97	55 45
Mount Holly	Randolph	George Debolt	6 56	11 10
Mount Jefferson	Carroll	Hugh R. McCully	3 27	7 28
Mount Meridian	Putnam	John W. Osborn	20 65	40 79
Mount Pleasant	Martin	Thomas M. Gibson	81 06	73 47
Mount Prospect	Crawford	Isaac Sands	5 49	9 94
Mount Tabor	Monroe	Felix G. Hite	19 15	31 00
Mount Vernon	Posey	Hudson Parke	154 87	222 59

POST OFFICES—*Indiana*.

Post Offices.	Counties.	Postmasters.	Compensation.	Net proceeds.
Muncietown	Delaware	Edward S. Keasbey	$139 55	$237 66
Murray	Wells	Cornelius Fahs	23 48	40 98
Napoleon	Ripley	Miles Mendenhall	57 97	83 28
Nashville	Brown	Sylv'us D. Manville	20 58	37 97
Natchez	Martin	Hiram Billings	13 35	19 42
New Albany	Floyd	Alex'r S. Burnett	663 95	1624 38
New Amsterdam	Harrison	Sam'l B. Christly, to 31st March	10 97	17 95
		Nimrod S. Reynolds	3 74	6 49
Newark	Warwick	Moses P. Condict	8 60	15 84
Newbern	Bartholomew	John Edwards	9 56	18 26
New Bethel	Marion	Patrick Catterson	17 22	24 65
Newburgh	Warwick	Abner Luce	53 54	94 21
New Burlington	Delaware	Jacob H. Powers	9 47	15 91
New Carlisle	St. Joseph	Jeremiah H. Service, 2 qrs	9 51	19 00
New Castle	Henry	Samuel Hazzard	no ret.	
		Bushrod W. Scott, from 1st January	45 83	89 87
New Corydon	Jay	Theophilus Wilson, from 1st October	4 19	6 83
New Durham	La Porte	William Taylor	48 28	82 42
New Frankfort	Scott	Gara Davis	20 86	36 59
New Franklin	Carroll	John Grantham	3 98	7 72
New Garden	Wayne	Joel Parker	65 00	113 37
New Harmony	Posey	Nelson G. Nettleton, to 31st May	130 21	222 85
		William Cox	10 36	19 43
New Haven	Allen	Henry Burgess	15 11	26 41
New Lebanon	Sullivan	Wm. F. Dodds	9 57	16 64
New Lisbon	Henry	William Grose, jr.	9 59	14 68
New Marion	Ripley	Evan Miles	30 67	52 18
New Market	Vigo	Ephraim S. Wolfe	33 45	38 33
New Maysville	Putnam	John B. Mayhall, to 12th November	8 32	12 33
		John H. Johnston	12 13	21 44
New Mount Pleasant	Jay	Jacob H. Sanders	6 11	11 11
New Philadelphia	Washington	Rob't R. McKnight	19 95	32 52
Newport	Vermillion	George Tillinghast	63 15	122 42
New Providence	Clark	Isaac Shaw	17 50	28 11
New Ross	Montgomery	George Dorsey	11 22	20 23
New Salem	Rush	Thomas Robinson	29 36	54 98
New Salisbury	Harrison	Joseph Dewees	4 45	7 37
Newtown	Fountain	De Witt C. Kiff	58 76	106 36
New Trenton	Franklin	Earl Power, to 20th May	36 04	55 84
		Samuel Boutcher	5 14	7 97

POST OFFICES—*Indiana.*

Post Offices.	Counties.	Postmasters.	Compensation.	Net proceeds.
Newville	De Kalb	Nath'l L. Thomas	$30 06	$56 77
New Warsaw	Bartholomew	Lot A. Chorn	5 08	6 46
New Washington	Clark	Joseph Bower, to 31st March	41 50	60 32
		Wm. A. Ingram	12 05	16 02
New Winchester	Hendricks	Thos. D. Crow, to 31st March	11 37	22 58
		David E. Carter	4 47	8 44
New York	Switzerland	Seth F. Packenham	18 05	32 65
Niconza	Miami	Matthias Moyer	25 69	47 33
Nineveh	Johnson	Thomas Mullikin	30 32	54 38
Noah	Shelby	Jas. F. Rule	10 89	21 26
Noble C. H.	Noble	Peter Becher	31 17	50 37
Noblesville	Hamilton	Jas. G. Brown, to 31st March	84 70	101 71
		Catesby Dale	33 38	32 42
Noe's Mills (Dis. 3d April.)	Jackson	Hiram Noe	no ret.	
Northfield	Boone	Jonathan H. Rose, to 31st December	8 74	16 67
		Jacob Tipton	8 74	18 68
North Hogan	Ripley	Ebenezer S. Hawley	21 98	30 47
North Manchester	Wabash	Jesse Davis	36 54	67 74
North Salem	Hendricks	Jacob C. Faught	10 93	14 54
Numa	Parke	John Wilson	11 13	17 75
Oak Grove	Montgomery	George Wright	5 19	10 16
Oak Ridge	Greene	William Jackson	35	58
Ogden	Henry	Edwin W. Swaim	28 81	47 74
Olean	Ripley	Alex'r J. Pribble	7 78	8 29
Onondaga	Marshall	Timothy Barber, 3 qrs	6 67	11 61
Orange	Fayette	Isham Keith	25 65	39 52
Orland	Steuben	Sidney P. Gambia	59 68	96 18
Orleans	Orange	Lawrence Bradley	58 19	102 53
Oswego	Kosciusko	Ezekiel French	29 46	57 43
Otter Creek	Vigo	Enoch Dole	9 05	16 41
Otter Village (Dis. 10th July, 1845.)	Ripley	Stephen Andrews	8 70	6 92
Outlet	Lake	Samuel H. Sanger	8 66	15 57
Ovid	Madison	William Gray, to 30th Sept	3 85	7 43
		Samuel A. Barry, to 31st Dec	2 71	5 03
		James Peden	3 19	7 18
Owensville	Gibson	Wm. C. Wilson	32 85	55 24
Oxford	Benton	David McConnell	no return	

POST OFFICES—*Indiana.*

Post Offices.	Counties.	Postmasters.	Compensation.	Net proceeds.
Palestine	Kosciusko	George F. Birt, to 13th Dec	$5 43	$10 54
		Hiram Sarber	8 73	17 11
Palmyra	Harrison	Hays McCallen, to 18th Feb	6 01	11 20
		Joseph McCallen	3 76	6 92
Paoli	Orange	Patrick Dougherty	192 41	182 20
Paris	Jennings	James S. Smith	61 80	107 06
Parish Grove (Dis. 6th May.)	Jasper	Henry Robertson	3 49	4 95
Parkersburgh	Montgomery	Robert M. Ramsay	31 89	30 98
Patoka	Gibson	Sylvester T. Jerauld, to 15th Jan	16 91	30 12
		N. A. Chamberlain	10 58	17 46
Patriot	Switzerland	Bela Hearick	68 10	115 13
Paw Paw	Miami	Richard Miller	12 19	20 94
Pekin (Dis. 17th July, 1845.)	Washington	James F. Persise	10 01	16 95
Pendleton	Madison	James L. Bell	50 89	100 54
Penn	Jay	Anthony Pitman	38 14	66 40
Perkinsville	Madison	Thos. L. Beckwith	12 79	21 32
Perry	Allen	Wm. T. Hunter	21 78	35 94
Perrysburgh	Miami	Wm. F. Burnett	13 17	27 49
Perrysville	Vermillion	John B. Rupe	175 23	291 61
Peru	Miami	Albert Cole, to 31st May	247 84	423 88
		John Coalter	16 72	40 31
Petersburgh	Pike	Warner L. Scott, to 10th Nov	35 74	49 36
		William Hawthorn, from 12th Nov	37 48	68 21
Philadelphia	Hancock	Charles Atherton	10 96	15 46
Philometh	Union	Jonathan Kidwell	3 52	5 41
Piketon	Marion	Adam Wright	5 18	10 52
Pine Lick	Clark	Jesse St. Clair	8 62	17 30
Pipe Creek	Madison	William Taylor, to 31st Dec	4 42	8 87
		Jos. W. Ridgeway	4 67	9 20
Pittsburgh	Carroll	John Smith, to 22d May	50 34	88 01
		Timothy Gridley	5 08	9 11
Plainfield	Hendricks	Isaac Osborn	37 48	58 02
Plattsburgh (Late "Walnut Ridge.") (Ch'd to "Walnut Ridge.")	Washington	William Logan	no return	
Pleasant	Switzerland	Alexander Allan	20 00	38 19
Pleasant Grove	Jasper	Henry Barkley	7 99	13 48
Pleasant Hill	Montgomery	Sumner Stowe	34 13	59 92
Pleasant Ridge	Greene	James Records	2 63	5 06

POST OFFICES—*Indiana.*

Post Offices.	Counties.	Postmasters.	Compensation.	Net proceeds.
Pleasant Run (Dis. 6th May.)	Carroll	Archibald Byson, 1 qr.	$0 33	$0 79
Pleasant View	Shelby	Lewis Morgan, to 31st March	21 98	38 37
		Lewis Benham	7 08	14 37
Plymouth	Marshall	Wm. G. Pomeroy, to 6th Jan	58 53	99 42
		Amzi L. Wheeler, to 15th June	48 12	85 46
		James Bannon	4 29	7 37
Poinsett	Hamilton	Jesse McAnally	2 40	4 25
Point Commerce	Greene	John F. Allison	41 80	72 38
Point Pleasant (Dis. 26th June.)	Tippecanoe	John Dutton	5 07	7 84
Polk Run	Clark	John Covert, 1 qr	2 35	3 06
Poolsville	Warren	Newton Morgan	33 07	52 76
Poplar Hill	Vigo	Samuel Hull	1 31	2 59
Portage (Dis. 1st August,	St. Joseph	Levi Wills, to 16th August	0 47	0 80
Porter's ⋈ Roads.	Porter	Aaron Servis	2 29	4 68
Portersville	Dubois	James S. Brace, to 27th July	0 41	0 96
		Daniel Harris	6 77	12 90
Portland	Fountain	Hetfield Martin	39 33	71 53
Portland Mills	Putnam	Garrard Hendrix, to 18th Oct	11 19	19 03
		James H. Jackson	29 77	51 31
Port Mahon	Huntington	Archibald Mahon	9 25	18 25
Poseyville	Posey	Jonathan S. Jaquess	19 95	31 37
Poughkeepsie	Allen	John Gould	7 01	12 71
Prairie Creek	Vigo	Jacob Earnest, from 8th July	17 88	32 96
Prairieton	Vigo	Robert Hoggatt	51 42	49 34
Prairieville	Clinton	John E. Loveless	19 08	33 94
Princeton	Gibson	Isaac Montgomery, to 25th Jan	139 51	238 30
		John Arbuthnot	70 79	142 14
Proctorsville	Crawford	William Proctor	11 16	18 35
Prosville	Washington	Christian Pro	4 31	7 59
Putnamville	Putnam	Amos W. Welker, to 31st Dec	21 46	36 45
		James L. Merrill	26 49	49 75
Quercus Grove	Switzerland	Jacob R. Harris	9 94	16 40
Rainsville	Warren	Michael Creekpaum	29 41	58 82
Ramsey's Mills	Jefferson	Alfred Hays	23 05	39 88
Randolph (Dis. 15th Aug.)	Randolph	James M. Bailey, to 23d August	0 68	1 60

POST OFFICES—*Indiana.*

Post Offices.	Counties.	Postmasters.	Compensation.	Net proceeds.
		Sam'l M. Snodgrass, 1 qr............	$0 66	$1 28
Reddington......	Jackson.....	Wm. J. Tinder	14 35	25 38
Reese's Mill......	Boone.......	James Briggs......	9 21	17 03
Rensselaer.......	Jasper......	Samuel L. Sparling, to 30th Sept	8 61	16 93
		G. W. Spitler, 2 qrs.	16 88	24 10
Reserve..........	Miami.......	Samuel Robertson..	7 61	15 36
Richland	Rush	Thomas L. Stewart.	12 00	22 14
Richmond	Wayne	Daniel D. Sloan....	396 26	680 09
Richwoods	Delaware....	John Tomlinson ...	no return	
Riley...........	Vigo.........	Spier Spencer......	8 46	15 49
Rising Sun......	Ohio.........	John W. Hall	160 04	318 84
Rob Roy........	Fountain	Wm. K. Marquess.	44 12	76 60
Rochester	Fulton.......	Robert Martin.....	110 41	213 81
Rock Creek...... (Dis. 16th May.)	Carroll......	Joshua Kay.......	5 31	9 17
Rockford........	Jackson......	Wm. P. Kiser.....	48 86	94 09
Rockport........	Spencer......	Alexander Britton..	106 58	193 15
Rockville........	Parke.......	Matthew Noel.....	166 64	280 04
Rome...........	Perry.......	Samuel Frisbie.....	31 20	54 43
Romney.........	Tippecanoe..	John P. Oglebay ...	31 49	58 13
Root............	Allen	Nelson McLain....	5 57	11 39
Roseville.........	Parke.......	Moses Robbins	35 77	61 43
Rossburg.........	Decatur......	James Cook.......	9 98	18 95
Rossville.	Clinton	Joseph Howells, to 30th Nov........	15 78	28 34
		John Q. A. Perrin..	22 54	42 75
Royalton	Boone	Floyd Burgin......	6 92	12 90
Rushville........	Rush	Joseph Hamilton...	167 25	275 36
Russellville.......	Putnam......	Jacob Durham.....	27 90	52 09
Sage's Ferry.....	Jackson.....	James Sage........	4 52	8 49
St. Omer........	Decatur......	John Devall........	36 99	80 43
Salem...........	Washington..	Burr Bradley......	123 41	199 53
		Deborah Curry.....	108 45	189 95
Saluda..........	Jefferson	Daniel P. Monroe..	21 46	34 70
Sandy Hill ...... (Dis. 25th Mar.)	Jasper	Robert Glover, from 1st October to 31st March..........	0 32	0 61
Saundersville	Vanderburgh	John Ingle.........	16 70	31 33
Scaffold Prairie...	Greene......	George R. Taylor..	10 73	18 08
Scipio..........	Jennings	Wm. C. Bramwell, to 17th Feb......	31 85	52 27
		Edward Ferrall	16 70	29 64
Scotland.........	Greene......	Henry C. Owen....	13 53	25 13
Scott...........	La Grange ..	Paris Sprague......	7 74	13 65
Shawnee Mound.	Tippecanoe..	Jesse Meharry.....	6 24	9 53
Shawnee Prairie..	Fountain	Joseph Poole	17 41	19 70

POST OFFICES—*Indiana.*

Post Offices.	Counties.	Postmasters.	Compensation.	Net proceeds.
Shelbyville	Shelby	Jos. R. Paynter	$98 43	$182 24
Sidney	Marshall	Robert C. Bliven	7 56	15 65
Siloa	Sullivan	Adam Wilson	6 04	10 89
Sinking Spring	Lawrence	John R. Nugent	11 50	22 99
Six Mile	Jennings	Jesse Whitcomb	14 55	25 08
Slateford (Dis. 3d Feb.)	Jackson	John Figeley, to 31st December	0 35	0 83
Slawson	Switzerland	Simeon Slawson	10 40	18 22
Slinkard's Mills	Greene	Jeremiah Clark	9 34	18 14
Smelser's Mills	Rush	John Watson	7 69	15 01
Smithfield	Delaware	Thomas Leonard, to 31st March	14 47	21 04
		William Lewis	3 01	4 69
South Bend	St. Joseph	John H. Harper, to 6th March	242 80	496 03
		De Witt C. Willoughby	109 83	243 05
South Gate	Franklin	James Fread	6 70	13 02
South Hanover	Jefferson	David Walker, to 6th June	114 71	217 19
		David D. McClellan	6 76	15 50
South Whitley	Whitley	David D. Parret	9 35	19 49
Spartanburg	Randolph	Ralph M. Pomeroy	26 46	49 92
Spencer	Owen	John Harsh	75 46	133 22
Spencerville	De Kalb	Reuben J. Dawson	22 25	38 20
Spiceland	Henry	Driver Boon	17 00	23 45
Springersville	Fayette	Thos. Simpson, jr.	19 06	27 21
Springfield	Franklin	Micajah Symons, 3 qrs	8 76	14 90
Spring Hill	Decatur	John Brison	19 95	29 69
Spring Mill	Lawrence	Hugh Hamer	14 43	24 65
Springtown	Hendricks	James Wright	22 79	30 18
Springville	Lawrence	Winepark Judah	46 55	85 72
Stanford	Monroe	Street Cox	10 49	20 24
Steeles	Rush	Benj'n R. Mitchell	25 67	45 45
Steubenville	Steuben	Abner Winsor	16 20	26 52
Stilesville	Hendricks	Levi Jessup	26 02	45 13
Stipp's Hill (Dis. 26th June.)	Franklin	John Wildridge	7 40	13 96
Strawtown	Hamilton	Jacob S. Tyson	36 85	59 62
Sugar Creek	Hancock	Jonathan Evans	25 27	25 30
Sugar Grove	Tippecanoe	Andrew Insley	11 25	16 90
Sugar Run (Dis. 12th Nov.)	Sullivan	James Harris, 1 qr.	58	80
Sullivan	Sullivan	Sanders M. Howard	10 92	22 05
Sulphur Hill	Shelby	Matthias Floyd	6 57	12 19
Sulphur Springs	Henry	William S. Yost	2 39	4 01
Summerville (Dis. 16th May.)	Jennings	Asahel Neal, fr. 1st Ap. to 24th May	52	66

POST OFFICES—*Indiana.*

Post Offices.	Counties.	Postmasters.	Compensation.	Net proceeds.
Sunman	Ripley	John Sunman, to 31st March	$21 32	$38 27
		Thos. W. Sunman	7 80	14 79
Swan	Noble	Samuel Broughton	10 90	21 42
Syracuse	Kosciusko	Henry Ward	4 01	7 96
Tanner's Creek	Dearborn	Chs. R. Campbell	22 14	28 26
Terre Coupee	St. Joseph	Geo. W. Reynolds, to 31st March	35 70	44 24
		Abel A. Whitlock	7 36	14 31
Terre Haute	Vigo	Jos. O. Jones	929 41	1797 22
Thornleysville	Boone	Enoch Thornley	3 37	7 63
Thorntown	Boone	Jesse L. Benson	87 64	141 95
Tiptonsport	Carroll	Jos. W. Grantham, from 20th Feb	1 17	2 76
Toronto	Vermillion	Benjamin Fisher	12 57	25 26
Troy	Perry	Reuben Bates	43 89	85 79
Turman's Creek	Sullivan	Hezekiah Riggs	8 90	15 31
Union	Pike	Dan'l H. Roberts	8 36	11 92
Union Mills (Late "Bacon.")	La Porte	Lewis Stevenson, fr. 9th April	3 15	5 80
Utica	Clark	Theoph's Robinson, to 7th June	39 57	68 49
		Wm. I. Tyler	1 21	2 85
Valeene	Orange	John S. Walton	8 96	15 06
Valonia	Jackson	Jonas B. Berkey	14 16	24 64
Valparaiso	Porter	Geo. W. Salisbury, to 29th Jan'y	101 72	176 61
		Th. E. A. Campbell	69 39	140 20
Van	Jay	David Garinger	2 29	4 80
Van Buren	Clay	John Melvin	31 77	36 45
Vernon	Jennings	Samuel Read, to 14th May	99 60	173 07
		Achilles Vawter	12 20	20 10
Verona	Vanderburgh	Wm. P. Negley	3 57	6 88
Versailles	Ripley	John Hunter	66 16	91 82
Vevay	Switzerland	Abner Clarkson	158 84	261 32
Vienna	Scott	John Harrod	18 81	29 10
Vigo	Vigo	George Wood	2 18	2 96
Vincennes	Knox	Jas. W. Greenhow	1789 29	
Wabash	Wabash	Hugh Hanna, to 22d Jan'y	57 70	117 78
		Mallothi Reece	53 86	111 61
Wadeville	Owen	Rezin Richards	5 44	8 25
Wallace	Fountain	N W. Grimes, 2 qrs.	5 64	10 09
		Noah Myers, 1 qr.	2 96	5 72

POST OFFICES—*Indiana.*

Post Offices.	Counties.	Postmasters.	Compensation.	Net proceeds.
Walnut Hill	Allen	Ira A. Johnson	no ret.	
Walnut Ridge	Washington	Sherman Peck, to		
(Ch'd to "Plattsburgh.")		31st March	$13 56	$23 03
(Late Plattsb'gh)		William Logan	3 18	6 17
Warren	Huntington	Felix G. Frame	22 71	48 73
Warrenton	Gibson	John J. Neely	3 80	5 99
Warsaw	Kosciusko	Wm. C. Graves	60 57	116 35
Washington	Daviess	Michael Murphy	247 64	186 89
Waterloo	Fayette	Amos Chapman	13 31	22 06
Wauhoo	Vigo	John Turner	1 31	2 44
Waveland	Montgomery	David Craig	42 96	75 45
Waynetown	Montgomery	Samuel Mawhorter	31 08	46 20
Webb's Farm	Marion	Madison Webb	4 37	8 99
Wesley	Fulton	Hiram L. Welton	13 65	25 66
West Bedford	White	Jacob Meyer	9 52	16 32
West Creek	Lake	Robert Wilkinson	9 86	18 90
Westfield	Hamilton	Isaac Williams	36 94	61 83
West Franklin	Posey	Charles Dunning	13 56	26 50
Westland	Putnam	Xury E. West	no ret.	
West Lebanon	Warren	James M. Rhodefer	38 45	68 90
West Point	Tippecanoe	John H. Smith	69 78	90 09
Westport	Decatur	John Conwell	24 26	41 07
West Union	Knox	Horace B. Shepard	20 14	35 23
Wheeling	Delaware	Ambr'e W. Henley,		
		to 7th Nov	11 65	22 75
		Cephas Dille	19 43	36 91
White	Hancock	Elisha Thornburg	6 43	12 80
White Hall	St. Joseph	Mathias Stover	8 98	17 14
White Oak Grove	Dubois	John McChristy, fr.		
		21st Aug	1 30	1 97
White Post	Pulaski	Lewis Dawson	8 10	14 26
White Water	Wayne	Wm. B. Schenck	16 51	28 04
Whitley C. H.	Whitley	David E. Long	50 38	96 23
Wickliffe	Crawford	David Rice	8 32	15 12
Williamsburgh	Wayne	Moses Davisson	39 86	64 40
Williamsport	Warren	Robt. A. Chandler	90 02	159 43
Williamstown	Decatur	Archim's Craigmyle	4 11	7 99
Wilmington	Dearborn	Luke Evill	54 68	105 32
Winchester	Randolph	Mich'l Aker, to 20th		
		Sept	20 53	35 54
		Solomon Yunker	72 84	121 46
Windsor	Randolph	Andrew West, to		
		30th Sept	3 62	7 28
		David Kinert	12 53	25 20
Winnamac	Pulaski	Henry P. Rowan	35 63	66 90
Winslow	Pike	George Dean	14 28	24 54
Wolf Lake	Noble	Hiram Morgan	36 97	78 03
Woodbury	Madison	Jacob Fausset	10 55	18 32
Woodville	Jackson	Richard Beem	3 06	5 21

POST OFFICES—*Illinois.*

Post Offices.	Counties.	Postmasters.	Compensation.	Net proceeds.
Yellow Spring	Johnson	Freeland Anderson	$3 72	$7 53
York Ridge	Dearborn	Wm. S. Ward	20 36	35 96
Yorktown	Delaware	John C. Helm	28 80	38 96
Yountsville	Montgomery	Allen Yount, from 7th Sept	5 90	9 03
Zenas	Jennings	John Raffety	15 27	26 31

ILLINOIS.

NOTE.—Compensation of Postmasters, and net proceeds of their offices, from July 1, 1844, to June 30, 1845.

Post Offices.	Counties.	Postmasters.	Compensation.	Net proceeds.
Abingdon	Lake	Thomas McClure	$44 85	$78 73
Acasta	Kane	Robt. G. Livingston	18 22	30 59
Addison	Du Page	Charles H. Hoit, to 30th Sept	6 91	13 41
		Michael S. Taplin	21 29	42 08
Albany	Whitesides	Samuel Happer	56 76	113 12
Albion	Edwards	Joel Churchill	164 35	300 85
Alden	McHenry	Francis Wedgewood	14 81	31 38
Althea	Morgan	James Green	1 62	2 81
Alton	Madison	Benj. F. Edwards, to 4th Nov	212 11	396 35
		John Hatch	420 11	861 17
Amazon	Boone	Robert B. Hurd	25 25	46 58
Amesville	Boone	Cyrus H. Avery	31 75	37 88
Andover	Henry	Eben Townsend	24 74	50 78
Appanoose	Hancock	John M. Finch	12 53	28 33
Apple Creek	Morgan	William Deatherage	67 63	120 93
Arcadia	Morgan	James M. Dougherty	24 85	46 73
Arenzville	Morgan	Charles Coerper	23 38	40 22
Armstrong	Wabash	Jacob Fox	6 76	13 00
Astoria	Fulton	James Owen	33 90	67 38
Athens	Sangamon	Wm. S. Stone, to 18th April	32 81	58 67
		Napoleon B. Stone	8 95	16 10
Athensville	Greene	John Armstrong	21 38	40 68
Atlas	Pike	Erasmus D. Whiting	37 86	71 81
Auburn	Sangamon	Daniel Wadsworth	41 70	40 78
Audubon	Montgomery	Isaac Hinckley	12 20	24 22
Augusta	Hancock	Samuel B. Mead	64 70	114 57
Aurora	Kane	Burr Winton	184 69	401 95
Au Sable	Kendall	Alansing Milks	10 37	16 18

POST OFFICES—*Illinois.*

Post Offices.	Counties.	Postmasters.	Compensation.	Net proceeds.
Ava	Winnebago	Geo. R. Emery	$17 63	$29 77
Aviston	Clinton	Josiah C. Shelton	34 82	57 02
Avon	Kane	Henry Warne	7 51	13 41
Babcock's Grove	Du Page	Theodore Hubbard, from 6th July	11 62	20 53
Bachelor's Grove	Cook	Stephen Rixford	6 76	12 24
Bainbridge	Williamson	Geo. L. Owen	7 65	14 15
Baltimore	Jo. Daviess	Jos. C. Stone, to 28th Feb	7 03	11 59
		Fleming C. Maupin	5 77	10 12
Barrington	Cook	Alvah Miller, 1 qr	2 37	3 34
Barry	Pike	Stephen R. Gray	61 01	115 34
Batavia	Kane	Isaac Wilson	93 91	168 70
Bath	Mason	Benj. H. Gatton	25 17	48 57
Beardstown	Cass	Thom. R. Saunders, to 30th July	30 32	33 15
		Thomas Wilbourn	173 08	278 54
Beaucoup	Washington	David S. White	6 09	11 93
Beaver Creek	Bond	John Henry	4 70	9 12
Belleview	Calhoun	William Walls, to 31st Dec	2 20	2 36
		Alexander Hemphill	1 55	3 34
Belleville	St. Clair	James Mitchell	427 31	852 75
Belmont	Pike	Adam R. Hope	11 02	19 66
Belvidere	Boone	Alfred E. Ames, to 26th July	34 50	33 88
		Richard S. Molony	370 91	593 30
Benton	Franklin	Walter S. Aikin	25 87	49 08
Berkshire	Kane	John Griggs	13 17	22 92
Berlin	Sangamon	Seneca Wood, to 30th Sept	17 04	32 12
		Oliver H. Rush	38 28	60 79
Bernadotte	Fulton	Luther T. Leslie, to 10th May	61 13	107 85
		Robert Paull	5 11	11 94
Berwick	Warren	Andrew G. Pearce, to 19th April	14 87	28 44
		Rufus Thorn	3 28	6 53
Bethel	Morgan	And'w J. Thompson	37 98	66 76
Bethsaida	Coles	Thomas Monson	8 93	17 57
Beverly	Adams	John B. Robertson	22 50	41 44
Birmingham	Schuyler	William Noell	19 36	32 44
Blackberry	Kane	David Wheeler	22 97	40 78
Blandinsville	McDonough	Charles R. Hume	19 30	29 86
Blissville	Jefferson	Augustus Bliss, 3 qrs	4 18	8 35
Bloomfield	Edgar	David Bailey	48 45	86 35
Bloomingdale	Du Page	Waters Northrop	51 17	94 47
Bloomington	McLean	Isaac Baker	197 11	372 61

POST OFFICES—*Illinois.*

Post Offices.	Counties.	Postmasters.	Compensation.	Net proceeds.
Blue Island	Cook	Norman Rexford	$12 84	$25 26
Bluff	Mercer	Frederick Frick	21 11	38 57
Bluff Dale	Greene	Wm. A. J. Russell	19 70	34 80
Bowling Green	Fayette	John A. McClanahan	7 01	14 80
Breesville (Dis. 6th May.)	Jackson	John Clodfelter, 1 qr.	3 06	5 33
Brewster's Ferry (Ch'd to "Winslow.")	Stephenson	Jos. W. Kinney, 3 qrs	33 58	65 74
Brighton	Macoupin	Daniel Blodget, to 22d Oct.	7 85	13 38
		Blenford Johnson	18 16	33 77
Brimfield	Peoria	James Wolcott	71 55	135 94
Bristol	Kendall	Jos. W. Helme, to 25th Nov.	59 61	95 17
		Norman Dodge	82 01	156 09
Brooklyn (Dis. 6th May.)	Schuyler	Wm. Horney, 3 qrs.	7 28	13 56
Brownsville	Jackson	Jas. L. Thompson	23 98	41 81
Brunswick	Peoria	Geo. G. Sill	13 26	21 79
Brush Hill	Du Page	Benjamin Fuller	22 79	44 18
Buffalo Grove	Ogle	Geo. D. Read	56 27	103 97
Bullbonus Grove	Will	Wm. E. Russel	21 99	43 86
Bunker Hill	Macoupin	Nathaniel Phillips	55 16	102 41
Burnt Prairie	White	Jehiel H. Reeves	17 90	32 73
Burton	Adams	Ephr'm S. Beardsley	16 74	29 04
Burton's Mills (Ch. to 'Mobley.')	Brown	Jerem'h A. Hawkins	1 49	2 64
Bush Creek	Bureau	Brown Searl	5 35	9 87
Byron	Ogle	Asa G. Spalding	100 50	184 18
Cahokia	St. Clair	Francis Chol	10 43	20 04
Cairo	Alexander	Bryan Shannessy	69 39	128 15
Caledonia	Pulaski	Eli B. Clemson, to 7th Sept.	9 07	16 25
		Jas. P. Cowgill	49 75	90 90
Cambridge (Late "Strawberry Grove.")	Henry	Joseph Tilson, from 1st Oct.	7 15	13 02
Camden	Schuyler	Alexan'r McHatton, 3 qrs.	5 59	11 39
Camden Mills	Rock Island	Felix R. Brunot, fr. 19th Feb.	3 27	6 95
Campbell	Coles	Eugenio Campbell	10 39	19 38
Camp Creek	Hancock	Mary B. Avise, to 31st Dec.	3 39	6 98
		Lyman Harkness	2 53	5 31
Canton	Fulton	Henry Hipple	112 14	216 67
Carlinville	Macoupin	Joseph C. Howell, to 30th Sept	42 59	77 19
		Daniel Anderson	124 17	187 63

POST OFFICES—*Illinois.*

Post Offices.	Counties.	Postmasters.	Compensation.	Net proceeds.
Carlyle	Clinton	John M. Webster	$112 88	$163 29
Carmi	White	Isaac Mitchell	102 04	170 34
Carrollton	Greene	James Reno	282 23	317 30
Carthage	Hancock	Chauncey Robison	153 87	275 17
Casey	Clark	Samuel G. Hoskins	7 38	17 01
Cass	Du Page	Thomas Andrus	28 11	51 27
Cato	Clay	Amos Thornburgh, to 17th March	11 85	24 08
		John Peirce	4 73	10 15
Cazenovia	Cook	Alexander Spencer, to 21st Nov	5 67	8 92
		John S. Everett	10 01	17 69
Cedar Creek	Warren	Lovet P. Rockwell	14 60	26 79
Cedar Creek Mill	Stephenson	Conrad G. Epley, to 31st March	27 23	53 78
		Robert Sedam	8 39	15 88
Centreville	Wabash	Ezra Baker, jr.	9 82	17 33
Chambersburg	Pike	Benj. B. Metz, to 31st March	19 03	32 38
		George Kittredge	5 61	9 66
Channahon	Hill	Wm. B. Peck	15 21	23 46
Charleston	Coles	Edmund Roach	176 77	255 10
Chatham	Sangamon	Peter S. Freeman	31 76	31 79
Chelsea	Will	Matthew Van Horne	11 84	22 66
Cherry Grove	Carroll	John Pierce, to 2d Feb	41 78	84 75
		Jno. C. Owings, 1 qr.	14 54	30 51
Chester	Randolph	Eleazer Walker, to 17th July	6 02	13 60
		William McGinnis	109 91	212 31
Chesterfield	Macoupin	Ebenezer Upham	31 32	55 37
Chicago	Cook	William Stuart, to 7th May	1699 27	2904 91
		Hart L. Stewart	270 13	441 76
Chili	Hancock	Geo. N. Crowley	13 25	23 73
Chilicothe	Peoria	Geo. W. Mead	38 63	39 77
Circleville	Tazewell	David Hanger	13 08	21 40
Clayton	Adams	Jason Wallace	30 79	54 04
Clear Cr'k Land'g (Dis. 16th May.)	Alexander	Levi L. Lightner, 3 qrs	40	97
Cleveland	Boone	Mar'sW. Kretsinger	42 02	48 12
Clinton	De Witt	Clifton H. Moore	39 04	72 17
Cochran's Grove	Shelby	James Cochran	6 51	12 44
Cold Brook	Warren	Henry E. Haly	26 97	49 23
Cold Spring	Shelby	Wm. S. Prentice	10 56	22 15
Collinsville	Madison	Horace Look	90 55	161 38
Coltonville	De Kalb	Calvin S. Colton	8 47	15 21
Columbia	Monroe	Stephen Gardner	46 81	91 20
Columbus	Adams	Andrew Redman	105 15	188 44

POST OFFICES—*Illinois.*

Post Offices.	Counties.	Postmasters.	Compensation.	Net proceeds.
Como	Whitesides	William Pollock	$29 93	$57 63
Concord	White	Wm. B. T. Slocumb	3 81	7 64
(Dis. 26th June.)				
Copperas Creek	Fulton	John McCan	9 15	17 59
Coral	McHenry	Proctor Smith	51 92	96 62
Cordova	Rock Island	John Marshall	20 96	41 72
Cornelia	Lake	Thomas F. Slocum	15 60	27 02
Cornishville	McHenry	Andrew Cornish	9 63	19 56
Crandall's Ferry	Whitesides	Lewis D. Crandall	10 74	20 07
Creete	Will	Horatio Hitchcock, to 29th Nov	7 63	14 06
		Willard Wood	12 23	22 86
Crooked Creek	Clinton	Charles Lee Jones	7 17	13 22
Crow Meadows	Marshall	Robert F. Bell	16 19	27 85
Crystal Lake	McHenry	Beman Crandall, to 19th Feb	56 35	106 55
		Parker H. Pearson	29 93	63 02
Cuba	Fulton	John E. Stockton, to 27th July	2 45	4 28
		Benj. W. Messler, to 31st Dec	5 28	10 57
		Henry Snively	10 22	18 94
Cumberland	Fayette	Ezra Griffith	6 78	8 30
Cummington	Macoupin	Oakes Shaw	17 16	34 54
Curran	Gallatin	Drewry Cook, to 23d July	72	1 38
		William Burnett	7 93	11 43
Cutler's Store	Shelby	John Cutler	1 26	2 97
(Dis. 19th July.)				
Dallas	Vermillion	John W. Baum, fr. 9th Jan	3 43	6 44
Danville	Vermillion	Amos Williams	290 68	415 32
Darwin	Clark	James Waters, 3 qs	52 97	52 98
Daysville	Ogle	Wm. J. Mix, jr	48 02	82 05
Dayton	La Salle	Charles G. Miller	31 94	37 33
Decatur	Macon	Sam'l C. Allen, to 31st March	119 23	209 17
		Alexander Mahood	40 79	72 95
De Kalb	Hancock	Thos. H Owen	6 05	12 48
Delavan	Tazewell	Ira B. Hall	21 94	42 77
Delaware	Jersey	Benjamin Cleaver	19 83	35 71
Delhi	Jersey	William Hackney, from 3d Aug	25 40	38 41
Des Plaines	Cook	Joshua Bell, to 16th October	4 15	7 86
		Patrick Griffin	9 84	17 90
De Witt	De Witt	Daniel Robbins	13 45	26 14
Dillon	Tazewell	Catesby Gill	19 25	32 72

POST OFFICES—Illinois.

Post Offices.	Counties.	Postmasters.	Compensation.	Net proceeds.
Dixon	Lee	James McKenny, to 10th March	$206 84	$243 13
		Abram Brown	81 92	95 74
Door	McHenry	H. M. Wait, from 4th April	2 86	4 52
Dover	Bureau	Isaac Delano	44 32	71 82
Downer's Grove	Du Page	Henry Carpenter, to 7th Jan'y	17 01	29 21
		Levi C. Aldrick	18 04	31 53
Drapers	Macon	David Morris, 3 qrs.	3 47	5 57
Dresden	Grundy	Anthony Peltier	12 74	24 40
Drury's Landing	Rock Island	Stewart R. Drury	10 61	20 76
Duncanton	White	Richard Langford	12 51	26 41
Dundee	Kane	Luke Hale	108 63	200 88
Duquoin	Perry	Chester A. Keyes, fr. 7th Feb	4 46	9 02
Dutchman's Point	Cooks	Nicholas H. Phillips	19 57	35 05
Eagle	La Salle	Norton Mackey	no return	
Eagle Cliffs	Monroe	John C. James, to 31st Dec	3 89	6 09
		Wm. C. Garetson	5 84	9 51
Eagle Creek	Gallatin	Benjamin Rice	2 00	3 19
Earlville	La Salle	Ch's H. Sutphen, fr. 1st Oct'r	10 69	19 58
East Bend	Hancock	Thomas Stephens, 3 qrs	2 83	6 65
East Nelson (Ch'd to Sullivan,	Shelby 12 Aug. '45.)	James Elder, to 31st December	10 69	23 31
		John Perryman	12 93	27 26
East Plum River	Carroll	Geo. W. Harris	7 45	14 37
Eden (Dis. 3d June.)	Richland	McIntyre Ryan, to 19th June	2 37	5 48
Edwardsville	Madison	Orren Meeker	136 73	254 81
Elbridge	Edgar	John C. Calvin	24 22	47 49
Elgin	Kane	Isaac G. Wilson	247 96	416 08
Eliza	Mercer	Rezin Pratt	9 82	14 82
Elizabeth	Jo Daviess	Samuel Nye	201 99	304 44
Elizabethtown	Hardin	Franklin Twitchell	22 57	45 35
Elk Grove	Cook	Fred'k T. Minor, to 31st December	20 79	32 59
		Fred'k W. Page	27 82	44 89
Elkhorn Grove	Carroll	Tilson Aldrich	37 51	58 86
Ellison	Warren	Seneca S. Salisbury	13 33	26 93
Ellisville	Fulton	Anson Smith	37 76	70 77
Elmira	Stark	Thomas Lyle	25 48	40 73
Elm Point	Bond	William Paisley, to 15th February	9 78	17 22
		Elisha Gwyn	7 18	12 38

POST OFFICES—*Illinois.*

Post Offices.	Counties.	Postmasters.	Compensation.	Net proceeds.
Elmwood........	Peoria	Wm. J. Phelps, fr. 21st June........	$15 19	$24 64
Embarrass Point.	Edgar,.......	James Scott........	3 12	6 75
Eminence	Logan	John Hawes.......	20 15	30 27
Endor...........	Will.........	Jas. L. Dean, to 8th Jan'y	3 79	6 88
		Norman Northrop..	7 99	11 08
Equality	Gallatin......	John Reynolds.....	64 04	128 38
Evergreen.......	McDonough..	Darius Runkle.....	14 78	17 21
Ewington	Effingham...	Wm. H. Blakely...	30 17	61 82
Exeter..........	Scott.........	Nathan W. Swift...	36 88	79 70
Fairfield.........	Wayne	Rigdon B. Slocumb..	91 10	166 85
Fairview.........	Fulton........	David M. Wyckoff.	45 85	85 38
Fancy Farm.....	Franklin	Henry Yost, to 31st Dec'r...........	6 10	11 64
		Sam'l K. Casey....	5 79	13 02
Farlow's Grove..	Mercer......	Hopkins Boone....	13 20	25 32
Farmer's Hall....	Knox........	Uzziah Conger.....	7 72	11 31
Farmington......	Fulton........	Geo. W. Little.....	120 21	210 33
Farm Ridge.....	La Salle.....	Elmer Baldwin, fr. 26th July........	4 02	6 52
Fayette	Greene......	James Metcalf.....	23 80	39 00
Fiatt............	Fulton.......	Matthew Mitchell..	8 00	9 47
Flag Creek......	Cook	Elijah Wentworth, jr	14 23	26 84
Florence........	Pike.........	Stephen Gay.......	23 07	44 44
Fort Hill........	Lake	Timothy B. Titcomb to 31st Dec'r......	25 48	47 55
		Levi Marble.......	29 77	57 70
Fosters..........	Marion	Hardy Foster......	7 80	15 81
Fountain Green..	Hancock....	Stephen H. Tyler, jr	29 72	58 83
Fraker's Grove .. (Ch'd to "La Fayette,")	Stark........	Barnabas M. Jackson	27 79	53 60
Frankfort	Franklin	Benj. F. Arnold....	32 45	27 46
Franklin.........	Morgan.....	John Sappington...	25 61	52 52
Fredonia.........	Williamson...	Byrd T. Ryburn...	5 40	12 02
Freemanton	Effingham...	John M. Brown, fr. 28th June........	13 34	13 35
Freeport.........	Stephenson..	Luther W. Guiteau, to 31st Dec'r......	138 50	143 01
		Thos. J. Turner, to 8th June.........	98 30	132 48
		Abraham T. Green.	16 47	25 80
French Creek....	Peoria	Thos. N. Welles...	35 21	70 47
French Grove....	Bureau......	Shalor Brainard....	11 40	23 80
French Village...	St. Clair.....	John Penc.........	15 45	29 65
Friendsville......	Wabash	Wm. R. Wilkinson.	13 98	25 13
Fulton	Whitesides..	Augustin Phelps....	35 61	69 64

POST OFFICES—*Illinois.*

Post Offices.	Counties.	Postmasters.	Compensation.	Net proceeds.
Galena	Jo Daviess	Robt. W. Carson	$1207 19	$3380 76
Galesburgh	Knox	Clarendon R. Palmer	118 23	238 84
Gallatia	Gallatin	Oliver Limerick	9 36	19 92
Galum	Perry	Levi Greene	10 22	16 27
Gap Grove	Jo Daviess	Benj. H. Stewart	28 19	35 46
Genesee Grove	Whitesides	Edmund Richardson	14 41	30 92
Geneseo	Henry	James M. Allan	39 35	75 09
Geneva	Morgan	Sam'l L. Crane, 3 qs.	2 53	4 55
Genoa	De Kalb	Horatio N. Perkins.	27 61	55 24
Georgetown	Vermillion	John Newlin, to 20th Nov'r	32 48	54 28
		Hiram Hickman	51 75	97 74
Gilead	Calhoun	John Red	23 82	*43 02
Gilmer	Lake	John G. Ragan	10 24	19 19
Godfrey (Dis. 3d July.)	Madison	Timothy Turner, to 17th July	3 05	7 13
(Re-est. 2 Sept. '44)		Same, fr. 16th Sept.	70 48	80 80
Golconda	Pope	Wesley Sloan	58 94	96 88
Grafton	Jersey	Paris Mason	28 40	57 55
Grand Detour	Ogle	Elisha W. Dutcher.	183 41	178 93
Grand Point	Washington	Charles Downes	6 65	12 69
Grand View	Edgar	Wm. K. Payne, to 9th Feb'y	37 16	67 89
		James M. Smith	24 20	46 44
Granite	Knox	Alfred Brown	8 26	9 72
Grayville	White	James Gray	52 91	101 25
Greenbush	Warren	Charles Stice	26 93	50 40
Greenfield	Greene	Geo. W. Allen	43 14	77 26
Green Plains	Hancock	Samuel Knox	5 69	11 52
Green River	Henry	George Brandenburg	12 65	20 87
Greenup	Cumberland	James Ewart	22 56	49 35
Greenville	Bond	Charles Hoiles	169 27	232 98
Griggsville	Pike	Jacob Parsons	147 80	271 17
Griswold	Hamilton	Gilbert Griswold	2 89	6 05
Groveland	Tazewell	Chs. G. Hinman	40 38	46 31
Gum Spring	Clinton	Nicodemus Bousman to 31st Dec.	4 45	8 55
		Wm. J. Foster	3 22	6 70
Hadley	Will	Charles Butler	20 68	35 47
Half Day	Lake	John Easton	55 57	97 21
Hamburgh	Calhoun	John Shaw	14 72	26 97
Hamilton	Hamilton	Abraham Irvin	11 13	22 70
Hampshire	Kane	Wm. H. Seymour	25 53	49 13
Hampton	Rock Island	Maverick W. Wright	47 80	88 93
Hanover	Jo Daviess	Walter Deane	21 08	37 99
Harlem	Winnebago	Reuben Barrett	10 34	21 02
Harrisonville	Monroe	Bradley Rust	8 67	13 39
Hartford	Knox	Abraham D. Swarts	24 16	41 15

POST OFFICES—*Illinois.*

Post Offices.	Counties.	Postmasters.	Compensation.	Net proceeds.
Hartland	McHenry	A. Judd, to 22d July	$3 59	$6 83
		Daniel Blair, jr	49 53	85 38
Hat Grove	Warren	Truman Eldridge	12 87	23 48
Havanna	Mason	North'p J. Rockwell	62 03	112 87
Hebron	McHenry	Bela H. Tryon	28 35	53 77
Helena	Peoria	Thomas Mooney	7 29	11 33
Henderson	Knox	Joseph Gay, to 10th July	2 13	3 98
		John A. Willey	77 90	138 29
Hennepin	Putnam	Loring Pickering	206 04	411 68
Henry	Marshall	Ches. S. Woodward from 2d July	32 74	61 64
Hermitage	Coles	William Chandler	19 34	32 41
Hickory Grove	Bond	Benjamin Johnson	21 81	46 89
Hickory Hill	Marion	Bradley Mills	6 69	14 10
Hicks' Hills (Lt. South Mills.)	De Kalb	Martin M. Mack	no return	
Highland	Madison	David Thorp	70 23	134 13
Hillerman	Massac	John P. Hodge	8 80	18 01
Hillsboro'	Montgomery	Francis H. Hereford to 30th September	43 00	81 50
		C. B. Blockburger	126 86	241 00
Hill's Grove	McDonough	Isaac Holton	9 33	15 37
Hitesville	Coles	Peter K. Horr, to 30th July	1 08	1 96
		William Fears	16 69	29 91
Homer	Champaign	Michael D. Coffeen	31 72	57 80
Honey Creek	Henderson	Abner Davis	6 66	13 94
Hopper's Mills	Henderson	Samuel Steele	20 09	35 09
Horse Prairie	Jefferson	James L. Plater	2 87	6 45
Houston	Adams	Henry A. Cyrus	16 02	29 47
Howard's Point	Fayette	Henry C. Waterman	18 69	18 71
Howardsville	Stephenson	Martin Howard	19 34	34 46
Hudson	McLean	Jesse Havens	8 25	15 92
Hunter	Boone	Ariel B. Wadsworth	5 07	8 95
Huntsville	Schuyler	Andrew J. Mead	21 87	35 98
Hurricane	Montgomery	Benjamin A. Smith, to 30th July	49	1 17
		Isaac N. Elsberry, to 31st March	9 36	19 68
		Benjamin Roberts	2 96	6 20
Hutsonville	Crawford	William Cox	42 75	79 94
Illinois City	Rock Island	John M. Bruner, to 23d April	14 83	29 70
		Alex'r F. Swander	4 14	7 29
Inlet	Lee	Geo. E. Haskell	54 02	73 05
Iowa	Perry	William Combs, fr. 31st July	5 88	9 37

POST OFFICES—*Illinois.*

Post Offices.	Counties.	Postmasters.	Compensation.	Net proceeds.
Iroquois........	Iroquois.....	Isaac Courtright....	$31 79	$55 03
Jackson Creek...	Will........	Jas. P. Gager......	9 40	16 82
Jackson Grove...	Fulton	Hirah Saunders....	1 82	4 21
Jacksonville	Morgan......	Edwin A. Mears, to 31st May, 1845..	522 28	1222 77
		Wm. W. Happy....	49 64	119 60
James Mills......	Monroe	Thomas James....	8 92	14 40
Jefferson........	St. Clair.....	Edward B. Marshall	no ret.	
Jersey Prairie....	Morgan......	Eli W. Reding.....	13 97	18 22
Jerseyville.......	Jersey.......	David T. Bonnell...	204 67	231 58
Joliet .... (Late "Juliet.")	Will.........	Albert W. Bowen, 1 qr...............	82 50	98 43
Jonesboro'.......	Union	Thomas Hileman..	85 87	160 26
Jones' Creek....	Randolph ...	Nathaniel Manning.	20 88	42 61
Jordan's Prairie..	Jefferson	Arba Andrews.....	15 59	25 91
Josephine	Woodford...	Simpson Y. Barnard	4 31	5 33
Juliet .... (Ch'd to 'Joliet.')	Will........	Albert W. Bowen, 3 qrs.............	269 57	284 57
Kane	Greene	Nath'l M. Perry...	50 06	57 01
Kaskaskia	Randolph....	John D. Spindle....	102 35	147 35
Keepatau	Cook	Lemuel Brown.....	3 46	6 81
Keysburg	Pike.........	Sam'l H. Nesmith..	7 24	10 77
Kinderhook	Pike.........	Bridge Whitten....	31 72	51 86
Kingston........	De Kalb.....	Jonas Hait........	4 57	9 48
Kishwaukee.....	Winnebago..	Daniel S. Pardee...	16 29	26 87
Knoxville	Knox........	George Newman...	241 42	466 60
Lacon	Marshall....	George Snyder.....	147 86	278 28
La Fayette...... (Late "Frakers Grove.")	Stark	Theodore F. Hurd.	no ret.	
La Fox.........	Kane	Charles S. Clark, to 25th November..	33 60	64 72
		David Dunham.....	56 55	106 56
La Grange.......	Henry.......	Ch's W. Davenport, 3 qrs............	1 83	3 94
La Grange Bluff..	Brown	John Trabue.......	6 29	12 51
La Harpe.......	Hancock	Louis R. Chaffin...	68 62	131 20
Lake Juliet...... (Dis. 24th May.)	Will.........	Loren'o D. Selfridge, 3 qrs............	4 50	6 46
Lake Zurich.....	Lake	Seth Paine.........	32 24	58 78
Lamoille.........	Bureau	John Kendall......	35 03	66 79
Lancaster	Morgan	Alfred Dutch......	15 98	29 41
La Salle........	La Salle.....	Horatio L. Osborn, to 4th January...	128 25	196 33
		John Hoffman, from 7th January.....	155 72	255 84

POST OFFICES—*Illinois*.

Post Offices.	Counties.	Postmasters.	Compensation.	Net proceeds.
Lawrenceville....	Lawrence ...	Geo. W. Kinkade, to 1st June.......	$116 80	$147 40
		George Buchanan..	8 93	20 18
Leaf River....... (Late "Mt. Morris.")	Ogle	Enos W. Baker, fr. 12th July........	6 63	6 66
		Enoes Jacobs......	12 68	12 34
Lebanon	St. Clair.....	Hiram K. Ashley, to 28th January.....	134 75	131 43
		Theodore W. Gray.	92 08	128 73
Leroy...........	McLean	Hiram Buck, to 25th November.......	15 52	18 58
		Sam'l J. Weldon, to 12th June.......	36 19	33 67
		Richard Edwards...	2 33	3 98
Lewistown	Fulton......	Martin Eichelberger	144 34	273 99
Lexington	McLean	Conrad Flesher....	17 08	33 59
Liberty..........	Adams......	Ab'm H. D. Buttz, 2 qrs............	15 03	26 12
Libertyville......	Lake.........	Horace Butler, to 30th September..	17 20	33 71
		Davis C. Steele, 2 qrs	39 11	73 45
Lick Creek	Sangamon...	John Johnson......	21 44	33 53
Lillecash.........	Will.........	Zadok Brooks, to 30th September...	2 85	5 73
		Joseph Tyler.......	6 31	11 77
Lima	Adams......	Robert S. Williams, to 30th September	7 88	17 09
		Henry Newton.....	22 31	46 41
Lisbon..........	Kendall	Levi Hills.........	94 15	89 78
Little Fort.......	Lake	Dan'l O. Dickinson.	160 47	322 73
Little Muddy....	Franklin	Barzillia Silkwood..	30 01	29 46
Little Rock......	Kendall	Lorenzo D. Brady..	62 68	92 13
Little Woods....	Kane	Edw'd W. Brewster	12 65	24 08
Little York......	Warren	James F. Pollock...	19 09	33 46
Lively..........	St. Clair....	Peter Baumann, to 5th March.......	12 32	17 38
		Jacob W. Michel...	4 64	6 68
Livingston	Clark	Wm. H. Bryan, to 31st March......	36 28	36 07
		Oliver P. Steele....	6 96	12 26
Lockport........	Will........	Edward E. Bush...	197 05	367 22
Locust Spring...	Macoupin ...	Daniel Schaning....	12 80	24 89
Lodi............ (Dis. 24 July, '45.)	Clark	Edward Cole, to 31st December	99	2 35
		Edwin P. Cole.....	2 34	4 92
Lorain..........	Iroquois.....	Algernon S. Vail...	18 49	32 80
Louisville	Clay	Wm. L. Coleman..	30 50	61 24
Lovington.......	Macon	Andrew Love......	12 45	23 78
Lower Rock Isl'd	Rock Island.	Seba A. Parmenter.	18 83	34 64

POST OFFICES—*Illinois*.

Post Offices.	Counties.	Postmasters.	Compensation.	Net proceeds.
Lyndon	Whitesides	Augustin Smith	$42 26	$75 88
Lynnville	Morgan	Thomas Batty, jr.	26 80	51 83
McGary	Hancock	George Beach	4 82	9 38
McHenry	McHenry	Horace Long	80 34	162 81
McLeansboro'	Hamilton	John W. Marshall	45 35	87 71
McMillen's Grove	Du Page	Joseph McMillen, fr. 26th July	9 20	14 19
Macedonia	Hancock	Jos. E. Johnson	8 95	19 33
Mackinaw	Tazewell	George Miller	46 20	96 08
Macomb	McDonough	James M. Campbell	163 41	296 88
Magnolia	Putnam	Joseph Hall, to 23d October	35 23	61 46
		Jacob C. Morrill	73 64	129 34
Mahomet	Champaign	Matthew Johnston	9 62	20 32
Malugin Grove	Lee	Ab'm V. Christiance	5 84	9 96
Manchester	Scott	Ransom Swallow, to 31st March	39 90	50 44
		William Leighton	11 29	19 63
Maquon	Knox	William McGowan	19 24	38 65
Maradosia	Morgan	Daniel Waldo, to 3d February	37 41	72 90
		Wm. H. Long	19 04	35 44
Marcelline	Adams	George Heberling	23 00	38 12
Marengo	McHenry	David Hammer	74 34	109 56
Margaretta	Clark	Wm. B. Marrs	3 06	5 96
Marge Grove	Wayne	Thos. H. Keith	no ret.	
Marietta	Fulton	John Trimble	18 95	32 07
Marine Settlement	Madison	Daniel Ground	62 96	114 90
Marion	Williamson	Napoleon B. Calvert	39 41	70 34
Marseilles	La Salle	Lovell Kimball	17 23	31 91
Marshall	Clark	Jon'n K. Greenough	176 91	197 41
Martinsville	Clark	Henry H. Hunt, to 19th September	5 48	11 86
		Thos. B. McClure	21 32	43 98
Mascoutah	St. Clair	Nathan Fike	38 42	75 03
Maulding's Mills	Wayne	Andrew Maulding	6 22	11 13
Maynard	Pike	Charles Maynard	4 92	8 78
Maysville	Clay	John T. Bothwell	36 61	39 39
Mechanicsburg	Sangamon	Thomas E. Fortune	63 48	62 75
Melrose	Clark	Daniel Dosher	8 38	15 77
Mendon	Adams	William Price, to 30th September	14 10	26 19
		Jos. B. Frisbie	53 41	85 67
Meridian	Mercer	Chauncy Stanard	19 72	36 90
Merona	McHenry	James McMillan	7 06	11 20
Metropolis City	Massac	Jas. H. G. Wilcox	43 23	94 76
Middle Fork (Dis. 26th June.)	Vermillion	Robert Golliday, 2 qrs	66	1 29

POST OFFICES—*Illinois.*

Post Offices.	Counties.	Postmasters.	Compensation.	Net proceeds.
Middle Grove	Fulton	Henry Merrill	$10 13	$19 27
Middleport	Iroquois	Henry Troup	31 75	58 13
Middletown	Logan	Colby Knapp	42 52	84 14
Midway	Fulton	Fletcher Hall, from 15th September	3 17	5 52
Milan	Calhoun	John Bolter	15 44	30 00
Milford	Iroquois	Jacob Wagner	23 47	44 14
Mill Creek	Alexander	Warren Stewart	6 91	11 39
Milledgeville	Carroll	Jacob S. McCourtie, from 3d Dec	2 76	5 95
Millersburgh	Mercer	Jas. S. Thompson	39 46	71 98
Mills' Prairie	Edwards	Adam Kedrick	8 37	13 17
Millstadt	St. Clair	George Kuntz	39 52	57 01
Millville	Jo Daviess	Jno. R. Smith	33 22	67 33
Milton	Pike	John B. Hardesty	27 67	52 79
Mobley (Dis. 21st Nov.)	Brown	William Mobley	no ret.	
Moline	Rock Island	David B. Sears	34 04	72 98
Money Creek	McLean	William G. Bishop	2 76	6 31
Monmouth	Warren	Daniel McNeil	208 74	279 11
Monroe	Cook	John C. Clark, to 31st December	2 72	5 80
		Joseph Jefferson	2 99	5 98
Montalona	McHenry	Wm. A. McConnell	42 30	80 44
Montebello	Hancock	Enoch D. Brown	7 85	13 56
Montezuma	Pike	Henry A. Sumwalt	5 88	10 72
Monticello	Piatt	Titus Hubbart	30 48	48 88
Moore's Prairie	Jefferson	R. A. D. Wilbanks	14 37	30 25
Morris	Grundy	Lawrence W. Claypool, to 2d Jan	17 42	31 29
		Geo. H. Kiersted	12 68	24 24
Morristown	Henry	Thos. F. Davenport	13 56	24 00
Mount Auburn	Christian	James Camp, to 22d July	2 35	3 50
		Mont'y P. Goodrich	23 49	47 48
Mount Carmel	Wabash	Wm. Arbuthnot	169 58	319 85
Mount Carroll	Carroll	John Wilson, 1 qr.	20 55	41 88
Mount Hawkins	Perry	Calvin M. Clark, 3 qrs	20 32	22 37
Mount Hawley	Peoria	Truman Hawley	16 42	26 56
Mount Kingston	Montgomery	Sam'l H. Copeland	5 64	10 00
Mt Knickerbocker	La Salle	Nels'n Knickerbocker, 3 qrs	3 76	8 10
Mount Langum	Iroquois	Sam'l W. Dilley	5 03	9 23
Mount Morris	Ogle	Fred'k G. Petrie	193 97	166 62
Mount Pleasant	Union	Caleb Musgrave	8 70	16 95
Mount Pulaski	Sangamon	Jabez Capps	41 43	82 12
Mount Sterling	Brown	Robert N. Curry	106 38	209 57
Mount Vernon	Jefferson	Noah Johnston	110 46	183 27

POST OFFICES—*Illinois.*

Post Offices.	Counties.	Postmasters.	Compensation.	Net proceeds.
Muddy Lane	McDonough	John G. Woodside	$11 26	$22 19
Mulberry Grove	Bond	Francis Gill	14 52	29 49
Munson	La Salle	David Barber, from 23d Nov	7 65	11 39
Murphysboro'	Jackson	John Logan	22 83	46 14
Naperville	Cook	Alex'r H. Howard	187 79	360 66
Naples	Scott	Royal Mooers, to 31st March	52 74	88 39
		Chs. F. Keener	11 72	21 63
Nashville	Washington	Zenas H. Vernon	102 97	196 55
Nauvoo	Hancock	Sidney Rigdon, to 30th Sept	78 75	154 31
		Geo. W. Robinson, to 31st Dec	63 29	104 59
		Elias Smith	151 33	304 35
Newark	La Salle	Walter Stowell	93 17	179 09
Newbern	Jersey	Jacob Lurton	10 30	16 98
New Boston	Mercer	William Drury	82 08	107 84
Newburgh	Pike	John Dunham	6 07	11 93
New Hartford	Pike	Thomas Thompson	11 91	23 37
New Haven	Gallatin	Thomas S. Hick, to 2d June	27 48	53 83
		Benj'n P. Hinch	2 40	5 03
Newland	Richland	Thomas J. Decker	2 08	4 65
Newton	Jasper	Benjamin Harris	32 77	64 63
Nine Mile Prairie	Perry	David H. Mead	9 63	20 10
North Bend	Macon	George Boyer	5 59	11 15
North Fork	Vermillion	Samuel Gilbert	16 74	30 17
North Hampton	Peoria	Reuben B. Hamlin	34 11	60 65
North Henderson	Mercer	Robert Pollock	6 64	11 86
North Prairie	Knox	Nelson Coe	7 09	12 73
Northville	La Salle	William Sly	45 84	81 95
Oakland	Coles	William Patton	37 75	79 54
Oakton (Dis. 25th Oct.)	Johnson	Solomon Wyatt	no return	
Okaw	Washington	Benj'n M. Cox, 1 qr.	1 47	2 38
		Marcus D. Westlake, from 29th Nov	5 32	9 51
Olena	Henderson	Robert Kendall	14 26	25 94
Olney	Richland	Edwin R. Baldwin	100 17	100 19
Oneco	Stephenson	John K. Brewster	34 20	66 64
Ono	Edgar	Alanson Baldwin	19 95	34 11
Oquawka	Henderson	Stephen S. Phelps, to 31st March	119 42	225 16
		John B. Patterson	40 11	76 64
Oregon	Ogle	W. Pickett, to 31st J'y	8 38	16 33
		Richard Chaney	76 23	151 31

POST OFFICES—*Illinois.*

Post Offices.	Counties.	Postmasters.	Compensation.	Net proceeds.
Oswego	Kendall	Levi F. Arnold, to 30th Sept.	$26 94	$53 26
		Wm. O. Parke	90 08	169 66
Otsego	Lake	Philander A. Paine.	29 86	58 43
Ottawa	La Salle	Alson Woodruff	388 20	614 81
Otter Creek	Jersey	J. M. Hurd	21 54	36 52
Oxford	Henry	Amos B. Cole	9 93	17 13
Paddock's Grove.	Madison	Gershom Flagg	22 13	42 13
Palestine	Crawford	William Wilson, to 5th June	103 19	178 74
		James H. Kitchell	4 83	10 55
Panther Creek	Cass	Amos Bonney	16 27	32 08
Paradise	Coles	Daniel Linder	36 89	41 01
Paris	Edgar	Milton K. Alexander	202 66	381 48
Parkersburg	Richland	John D. Parker	4 35	8 99
Partridge Point	Woodford	Samuel S. Parke	54 04	93 16
Paw Paw Grove	Lee	Isaac Robinson	37 80	45 40
Payson	Adams	Lewis Faxon	90 59	154 52
Pekatonica	Winnebago	Jacob Hyatt	103 40	185 92
Pekin	Tazewell	Irwin B. Doolittle, to 31st Dec.	148 83	172 49
		M. Tackaberry	130 72	208 23
Penfield	Kane	Josiah Lehman	29 54	52 46
Peoria	Peoria	Wm. H. Fessenden	591 68	1189 05
Perkins' Grove	Bureau	Albert G. Porter	16 49	32 11
Perry	Pike	John K. Cleveland	60 54	102 63
Petersburg	Menard	George W. Miles	105 71	208 79
Philipstown	White	Caleb Clifford	14 70	25 98
Pickamink	Iroquois	Levi Thompson	1 59	3 65
Pilot	Vermillion	Hezekiah Miner, fr. 5th August	9 49	17 28
Pinckneyville	Perry	Humphrey B. Jones	26 89	50 22
Pittsfield	Pike	Daniel B. Bush	155 96	285 55
Plainfield	Will	James Ballard	73 32	144 46
Pleasant Hill	Pike	David Hibbard, to 7th August	0 88	1 74
		Alanson Mosher	5 62	11 56
Pleasant Plains	Sangamon	Henry Smith	11 02	18 25
Pleasant Vale	Pike	Joseph Jackson	17 73	34 15
Pleasant Valley Mills	McDonough	David Hamilton	4 13	7 31
Plymouth	Hancock	Wm. M. King, jr.	24 40	46 94
Point Republic	La Salle	George M. Newton.	11 86	21 06
Pollocks	Randolph	James Pollock	7 95	11 65
Pontiac	Livingston	Daniel S. Ebersol	24 98	42 78
Pope Creek	Mercer	Henry Bridger	23 77	45 92
Port Arlington	Bureau	George W. Gibson, to 7th Feb	2 32	4 19
		Freeman Mills, 1 qr.	0 37	0 52

POST OFFICES—*Illinois.*

Post Offices.	Counties.	Postmasters.	Compensation.	Net proceeds.
Port Byron	Rock Island	George S. Moore	$22 25	$42 18
Portland	Whitesides	Ebenezer Seely	22 56	39 86
Postville	Logan	James Primm	23 01	42 44
Prairie du Long	St. Clair	Samuel Elder	23 25	51 59
Prairie du Rocher	Randolph	William Henry	15 65	30 64
Prairieton	Lawrence	Wm. Beedle, jr., to 30th Sept	4 55	4 55
		Wm. E. Robinson	21 16	20 65
Prairieville	Randolph	Richmond D. Durfee	27 80	44 13
Precinct	Boon	Abram Drake	8 18	10 82
Preemption	Mercer	Horace E. Wright	17 32	33 06
President	Vermillion	Amb'se P. Andrews, 1 qr	0 20	0 20
Princeton	Bureau	De Grass Salisbury	311 81	317 09
Princeville	Peoria	Wm. C. Stevens	22 25	38 83
Prophetstown	Whitesides	Erastus G. Nichols	16 21	28 37
Providence	Bureau	Matthew Dorr	33 25	55 51
Pulaski	Hancock	Elisha Olcott, to 19th January	9 07	17 41
		Proctor P. Newcomb	10 51	17 03
Quincy	Adams	Benj'n Clifford, jr., to 13th Feb	474 87	1260 32
		Samuel W. Rogers	295 62	761 86
Randolph's Grove	McLean	John Moore	16 93	31 32
Richland	Sangamon	Constantine Foster	31 06	57 50
Ridge Farm	Vermillion	Abraham Smith	6 88	12 32
Ring Wood	McHenry	A. Reynolds	no return	
Risdon	St. Clair	Atlas Moore	4 94	8 09
Robins' Nest	Peoria	Philander Chase	58 13	103 99
Robinson	Crawford	Wm. B. Baker	no return	
Rochester	Sangamon	William Ainslie	50 40	49 08
Rochester Mills	Wabash	Geo. Leqier, 3 qrs	4 70	8 38
Rock and Cave	Hardin	John Brents	11 36	25 28
Rockford	Winnebago	Chs. H. Spafford	396 30	677 96
Rock Grove	Stephenson	Albert Albertson	27 32	54 92
Rock Island	Rock Island	John Buford	246 24	311 94
Rock Run	Stephenson	Horatio G. Davis	8 55	16 93
Rock Spring	St. Clair	John M. Peck	20 71	36 87
Rockville	Will	Hiram Todd	16 50	20 48
Rocky Ford	Lee	Horace Thompson	no return	
		John Van Arnam, from 2d Nov	4 42	6 33
Roscoe	Winnebago	Henry Abell, to 31st December	32 32	56 47
		Alfred E. Ames	38 76	74 43
Rosiclare	Hardin	James Steele	9 95	19 71
Ruark	Lawrence	John C. Ruark	4 04	7 30

POST OFFICES—*Illinois.*

Post Offices.	Counties.	Postmasters.	Compensation.	Net proceeds.
Rushville	Schuyler	Adams Dunlap	$323 54	$417 37
Russellville	Lawrence	Alex'r M. James	38 34	64 97
Saint Albans	Hancock	John Knott	12 12	21 50
Saint Augustine	Fulton	Austin Mattingly	8 03	17 67
Saint Charles	Kane	Chs. A. Brooks, to 23d Dec	114 41	212 77
		Peter J. Burchell	146 65	284 43
Saint Francisville	Lawrence	Mason Jones, to 26th February	5 22	10 01
		George D. Ramsey	2 91	5 26
Saint Marie	Jasper	Joseph Picquet	31 03	65 57
Saint Mary's	Hancock	John R. Nichols	18 95	36 34
Salem	Marion	H. L. Mills, to 26th October	62 70	31 47
		Benj'n F. Lemen	107 98	95 49
Salisbury	Sangamon	Henry Shepherd	11 40	22 78
Santa Anna	De Witt	Henry Barnes	11 91	18 05
Santa Fe	Alexander	Jas. C. McPheeters	4 74	9 73
Sarahsville	Franklin	John T. Davis	10 42	21 10
Savanna	Carroll	Luther H. Bowen	58 76	117 29
Scottsville	Lee	John Scott, 2 qrs	5 33	5 35
Steward's Point	Montgomery	Jos. M. Scott	7 01	11 69
Shabbonas Grove	De Kalb	Wm. A. Sanger	13 65	18 46
Sharon	Whitesides	Robert Getty	18 28	34 53
Shawneetown	Gallatin	John Stickney, to 24th Nov	252 11	
		Pleasant L. Ward	418 63	8 09
Shelbyville	Shelby	Jos. N. Lewis	182 74	162 17
Sherman	Cook	Silas W. Sherman	22 01	35 10
Shoal Creek	Clinton	William Woodburn	27 36	53 38
Shokoken	Henderson	Robert McQueen	8 66	17 32
Sidney	Champaign	William Nox, 2 qrs	2 97	5 85
Silver Creek	Stephenson	Isaac S. Forbes	no return	
Smith's Creek (Dis. 27th Nov.)	Henderson	Cromwell B. Matthews, from 15th Aug. to 13th Dec	0 45	0 23
Solon Mills	McHenry	Leverett Steele	68 67	111 27
Somonauk	De Kalb	David Merritt	41 42	72 14
South Grove	De Kalb	James Byers	8 05	11 10
South Mills (Ch'd to "Hicks' Mills," 10th July, 1845.)	Boone	Peter M. Janes	13 24	25 68
Sparta	Randolph	Rob't G. Shannon	89 69	172 74
Spoon River	Fulton	Oliver Parlin	7 93	16 22
Spring Creek	McDonough	James Head	4 78	9 20
Springfield	Sangamon	G. W. Spottswood, to 14th Jan'y	731 42	1810 79
		Jona. R. Diller	609 13	1607 12

POST OFFICES—*Illinois.*

Post Offices.	Counties.	Postmasters.	Compensation.	Net proceeds.
Spring Garden	Jefferson	Uriah W. Compton	$6 23	$12 46
Spring Grove	Warren	John Humphrey	4 88	8 92
Staunton	Macoupin	John Bonner, to 10th Aug	1 46	3 41
		Wm. B. Higgins, to 31st Dec'r	7 68	14 04
		Stephen Sawyer	14 35	29 87
Steele's Mills	Randolph	John C. Brown	18 35	35 54
Sterling	Whitesides	E. B. Worthington	71 91	108 58
Stewart	Coles	David Weaver	5 24	6 65
Stillman	Ogle	Nathaniel Cothren, from 8th Aug	7 41	12 19
Stonington	Christian	Thos. [illegible]. Chapman	8 23	13 24
Strawberry Grove (Ch'd to "Cambridge.")	Henry	Jos. Tillson, 1 qr	2 50	4 77
Sugar Grove	Kane	Thomas Slater	63 34	113 63
Sullivan (Late "East Nelson.")	Moultrie	John Perryman	no ret.	
Summit	Cook	James Michie	4 83	9 10
Summum	Fulton	James Gasaway	17 65	28 76
Sunbury	Livingston	John Bradley	4 47	7 52
Swan Creek	Warren	Joseph Ratikin	11 16	20 40
Sycamore	De Kalb	Jesse C. Kellogg	91 45	179 70
Table Grove	Fulton	John Bartholomew	14 47	26 33
Tamarawa (Dis. 4th Nov.)	Monroe	Benjamin Slater, to 26th Nov	1 77	2 82
Taylorsville	Christian	Benjamin L. Yates, to 17th Dec	28 41	28 44
		Thos. B. Dougherty, to 5th Feb'y	9 94	11 52
		H. M. Vandeveer	33 20	31 22
Temperance Hill (Dis. 16th May.)	Lee	John Cross, fr. 5th Nov. to 4th June	3 37	4 24
Tentopolis	Effingham	Clemens Uptmor	14 95	31 84
Thornton	Cook	Joseph Case	14 96	29 31
Toledo	Union	Thomas Ferrill	5 42	9 87
Toulon	Stark	Jno. W. Henderson, to 31st Jan'y	21 97	39 36
		Benjamin Turner	14 53	23 63
Tremont	Tazewell	Palmer Holmes	203 55	278 45
Trivoli	Peoria	David A. Gove	43 77	79 04
Troy	Madison	Moses Bardsley	39 97	75 55
Troy Grove	La Salle	Justin D. Wixom, to 28th Feb'y	16 20	30 53
		C. H. Gilman, 1 qr	1 93	3 54
Troy Mills	Fulton	Henry Kreider, to 21st Aug	4 70	7 13
		Thos. S. Bassett	21 72	28 38

POST-OFFICES—*Illinois.*

Post Offices.	Counties.	Postmasters.	Compensation.	Net proceeds.
Tyler	Winnebago	Asher Beach	$38 22	$72 20
Tylerville	Warren	Wm. Boswick	12 34	21 43
Tysonville	Carroll	Abijah Paynter	5 83	10 31
Udina	Kane	Asa Merrill	27 31	47 62
Union	Randolph	James M. Simpson, from 22d July	1 92	3 92
Union Grove	Whitesides	John A. Robertson	41 09	70 48
Union Point	Union	Franklin M. Bennet	3 77	8 30
Unity	Alexander	Jonathan Freeman	15 69	30 30
Upper Alton	Madison	David Smith	157 78	148 01
Urbana	Champaign	Thomp'n R. Webber	30 82	51 46
Ursa	Adams	Addy Vannest, from 11th July	30 89	54 65
Vanceborough	Winnebago	David Paul, to 31st Dec'r	6 11	12 09
		Ephraim Summer, from 29th Jan'y	7 64	14 82
Vandalia	Fayette	David B. Hodge, to 26th Nov	52 95	72 87
		Grandison C. Wood	118 39	93 50
Venice	Madison	Joseph Squire	no ret.	
		Benj. Irish, fr. 10th to 31st March	27	65
Vermillionville	La Salle	L. W. Dimmick, to 14th Jan'y	28 31	48 25
		James S. Bullock	18 62	31 91
Vermont	Fulton	Joab Mershon	69 19	131 23
Vernon	Crawford	Spencer H. Hurst, 2 qrs	3 49	5 29
Versailles	Brown	A. D. Ravenscroft	37 19	67 77
Victoria	Knox	Isaiah Berry	30 82	60 64
Vienna	Johnson	Ivy Reynolds	37 37	71 97
Virginia	Cass	William Naylor	92 99	161 74
Wabash	Wayne	Isaiah Holloway, 2 qrs	1 03	1 67
		Washing'n Denham, 1 qr	71	1 35
Waddam's Grove	Stephenson	Pells Manny	17 00	33 70
Walnut Creek	Stark	Silas Richards, to 15th March	3 74	7 77
		Jos. Palmer, 1 qr	25	52
Walnut Grove	Knox	John W. Clark	6 15	11 60
Walnut Hill	Marion	Israel Jennings	23 67	45 11
Warrensville	Du Page	Julius M. Warren	87 48	144 54
Warsaw	Hancock	George Rockwell	159 33	257 28
Washington	Tazewell	Robt. W. Burton	122 07	198 83

POST OFFICES—*Illinois.*

Post Offices.	Counties.	Postmasters.	Compensation.	Net proceeds.
Waterloo........	Monroe.....	John Ryan, to 2d Aug.............	$8 60	$18 71
		John Gall..........	70 34	148 49
Waynesville......	De Witt.....	Douglass Spear.....	63 29	118 85
Wesley City......	Tazewell....	George L. Gibson..	6 78	10 36
Western Saratoga	Union.......	Elijah Beardsley ...	2 61	6 16
Westfield.........	Clark........	Nathan Tefft........	14 21	25 66
Wethersfield......	Henry........	Sylvester Blish.....	29 60	55 35
Wheatland.......	Du Page.....	Daniel Wilson, from 12th July.........	7 52	11 05
Wheeling	Cook	Joseph Filkins.....	58 45	95 75
White Hall.......	Greene	Linus E. Worcester	152 70	176 76
Wickliffe.........	Cook	G. W. Southworth, to 8th Nov.......	7 18	12 19
		Thomas S. Clark...	12 55	20 56
Wiggins' Ferry..	St. Clair.....	Alexander H. Cook, to 31st Dec'r.....	13 04	24 60
		George Bisson......	18 17	34 70
Wilcoxville.......	Schuyler.....	Anthony Messerer..	9 21	19 47
Wilkesborough ..	McLean......	Jas. O. Barnard....	25 18	37 92
Wilmington	Will.........	James L. Young ...	48 33	91 12
Winchester......	Scott.........	Edward G. Miner..	129 56	244 76
Windsor..........	Bureau......	Morris Spalding....	33 12	63 14
Winnebago ..... (Dis. 18th Jan.)	Bureau......	Jacob Sells, from 3d Aug. to 31st Dec'r	28	54
Winslow......... (Late "Brewster's Ferry.")	Stephenson ..	De Witt C. Hicks, 1 qr..............	10 65	19 60
Wolf Grove......	McDonough.	Durham Creel......	2 87	6 46
Woodburn.......	Macoupin....	Jona. Huggins.....	56 24	105 68
Woodbury.......	Coles.........	David T. Wisner...	8 09	16 19
Woodford........	Woodford....	William King......	18 36	32 52
Woodstock.......	Fulton........	Stephen Tompkins..	12 68	19 76
Woodville........	Adams.......	Rufus Pack........	7 33	13 73
Worcester	McDonough.	Fred'k R. Prentice..	7 73	15 69
Wynstay	Jersey.......	Wm. Bowker, from 22d Aug.........	2 57	4 67
Wyoming........	Stark	Wm. F. Thomas....	17 83	33 29
Yel'w Head Grove	Will..........	Paul Hathaway....	8 03	15 24
York.............	Crawford....	John B. Richardson.	49 14	90 97
Young...........	McDonough.	James Edmonston..	13 69	23 71
Zanesville........	Montgomery.	Geo. H. Burroughs.	8 03	13 65

POST OFFICES—*Missouri.*

MISSOURI.

NOTE.—Compensation of Postmasters, and net proceeds of their offices, from July 1, 1844, to June 30, 1845.

Post Offices.	Counties.	Postmasters.	Compensation.	Net proceeds.
Alexandria	Clark	Robert M. Hening, to 31st March	$15 19	$27 02
		Pickering S. Stanley	4 65	7 03
Apple Creek	C. Girardeau.	Daniel Seibert	52 08	103 63
Arator	Pettis	David Hogan, 3 qrs.	17 84	32 86
Arcadia	Madison	Henry P. Russell	14 42	28 82
Argo	Franklin	Reuben S. Bacon	3 79	7 92
Arrow Rock	Saline	William Long	103 19	199 79
Ashley	Pike	M. M. McLane, to 30th Sept.	16 34	25 50
		Barzel Riggs, from 23d Dec.	22 45	42 90
Astoria	Wright	Robt. Montgomery, from 10th July	49	1 00
Athens	Clark	George Gray	10 23	21 26
Auburn	Lincoln	Chas. E. Perkins	63 48	96 43
Augusta	St. Charles	Nelson Cary	17 02	33 43
Austinville	Livingston	John Austin	7 31	14 07
Avoca	Jefferson	Lewis Renaud	22 08	42 65
Bailey's Creek	Osage	John Berry, from 1st Oct.	4 09	7 97
Bailey's Landing.	Lincoln	John W. McKee	8 41	13 18
Baldwinsville	Scott	Green B. Griffith	5 50	11 19
Barry	Clay	Charles Beal	43 38	88 08
Barry C. H. (Late Flat Creek.)	Barry	Sam'l M. Pharris	no return	
Batesville	Bates	Freeman Barraus	22 71	41 67
Bee Creek Mills	Platte	James C. Lindsay	10 78	19 67
Bellefonte	Pulaski	Achilles F. Grigsby.	9 79	19 80
Belle Plaine	Clark	Jas. A. McLaughlin	10 39	20 23
Bensborough	Camden	Martin Fulbright, jr. to 31st Dec'r	92	1 98
		Matt'w N. Houston	2 46	5 44
Benton	Scott	Alvan Cook	39 58	72 04
Berming	Buchanan	Henry D. Hardin, fr 30th Aug	3 00	6 71
Bethany	Clay	Waltus L. Watkins, from 1st Oct.	9 01	15 80
Big Creek	Johnson	Cole'n F. Chamblin.	17 17	33 72
Big River Mills	St. Francois	James Tyler	8 77	15 94
Big Spring	Montgomery.	Alia B. Snethen	5 31	9 50
Birch Pond	Crawford	Turquill McNeill	1 10	2 33

POST OFFICES—*Missouri.*

Post Offices.	Counties.	Postmasters.	Compensation.	Net proceeds.
Black Water......	Johnson......	Jeremiah Washam.	$41 96	$83 14
Bloomfield........	Stoddart......	Orson Bartlett........	41 04	85 24
Bloomington......	Macon.......	Robert George, to 31st March......	33 96	66 60
		Geo. A. Shortridge..	13 38	26 68
Blue Mound......	Livingston...	Mills S. Reeves....	5 17	9 82
Blytheville......	Jasper......	John C. Cox.......	17 61	36 58
Bolivar........	Polk........	John M. Clark.....	129 46	266 13
Boonsboro'......	Boone.......	Peter Kerney.......	7 87	15 61
Boonville.......	Cooper.......	James M. Major....	488 73	1142 78
Bowling Green...	Pike.........	Hiram G. Edwards.	120 58	175 42
Boyer's Settlement	Buchanan....	Henry Boyer, from 28th July........	5 32	11 48
Bridgeport......	Warren......	Jas. Talbot, fr. 21st Aug. to 31st Dec..	2 56	4 27
Bridgeton	St. Louis.....	David Thomas.....	43 71	79 98
Brookville.......	Marion	W.P. D. Claybrooke	9 56	16 61
Brownsville.....	Saline	David A. Ostrander.	17 81	38 06
Brunswick.......	Chariton	Jer'h J. Lockhart...	162 80	344 91
Bryan...........	Saline........	Isaac Neff..........	3 34	5 37
Buck Prairie.....	Barry........	Wm. A. McCanse..	14 57	26 78
Buffalo..........	Niangua	Arch'd E. Conn....	42 27	89 11
Calafornia......	Cole.........	Jer'h Broaddus	21 44	38 89
Caledonia	Washington..	James S. Evans, to 26th May.......	74 70	104 90
		James M. Woods..	4 51	6 87
Calhoun.........	Henry......	Matthew Arbuckle..	53 14	109 30
Cambridge...... (Late "Old Jefferson.")	Saline	F. A. Brightwell ...	no return	
Camden.........	Ray	Willis Warriner ...	66 99	141 29
Camden Point....	Platte........	Jno. W. Forbes, 3 qs.	9 04	19 00
Cane Creek......	Wayne.......	Exum C. Scott, 3 qs.	6 41	14 72
Cape Girardeau..	C. Girardeau.	George L. Porter...	171 82	323 59
Carondelet.......	St. Louis.....	Joseph Le Blond...	16 64	33 15
Carrollton.......	Carroll......	Lewis Rees........	119 80	250 89
Carthage........	Jasper	George Hornback..	25 22	53 85
Castile.......... (Dis. 24th Jan.)	Clinton......	Rob't R. Harris....	no return	
Cave Spring.....	Wright......	Terrel L. Grigsby..	8 90	16 43
Cedar Creek.....	Wayne	Alex'r A. Short....	3 32	6 45
Center..........	Ralls	Thomas J. Ellis, fr. 28th Aug.......	1 92	2 19
Chantilly........	Lincoln	Robert McIntosh...	6 64	10 83
Chariton........ (Dis. 17th Mar.)	Chariton.....	John M. Feazel, 3 qrs.............	61 76	59 99
Chariton Mills...	Adair.......	Thomas Hargrave..	9 84	16 26
Charleston.......	Adair.......	Whitaker Mikel....	2 88	6 34
Chilicothe.......	Livingston...	Nov. Johnson......	62 22	121 49

POST OFFICES—*Missouri.*

Post Offices.	Counties.	Postmasters.	Compensation.	Net proceeds.
Clark's Fork	Cooper	Thomas Barnes	$3 93	$7 23
Clarksville	Pike	Henry T. Kent	80 17	147 73
Clear Fork Mills	Johnson	Grandison Thornton	5 47	9 56
Cold Spring	Daviess	Russell G. Oxford	4 16	8 30
Cole Camp	Benton	Ezekiel Williams, to 31st Dec'r	5 23	11 36
		Hosea Powers, from 1st April	2 97	6 55
Columbia	Boone	Ann Gentry	328 71	671 30
Commerce	Scott	Isaac Reed	33 23	58 71
Concord	Callaway	John Henderson	15 35	26 64
Conner's Mills	Cooper	John Ogden	9 40	17 77
Cool Spring (Ch'd to "Harrisburg.")	La Fayette	Arch. W. Ridings, to 30th Sept	5 18	10 16
Cote Sans Dessein	Callaway	Anson G. Bennett	10 50	18 52
Cottleville	St. Charles	Fred'k Busch	25 80	45 37
Cove Springs	Ralls	Henry C. Wolfe	9 70	16 47
Cow Creek	Saline	Henry I. Brown	13 88	24 88
Crab Orchard	Ray	Thomas Reeves	33 61	61 67
Crane Creek	Greene	John Allen, to 30th Sept	1 86	4 34
		Berry T. Parr	7 28	17 30
Cravensville	Daviess	William Cravens	20 98	43 70
Crisp Prairie	Dade	Thomas Dale	15 57	26 93
Cross Roads	Gasconade	John Woody	3 77	7 02
Cypress	Scott	Francis Kirkpatrick	1 82	4 14
Dade C. H.	Dade	Washington Farmer to 31st Dec'r	29 78	57 93
		Wm. K. Lathim	30 06	64 55
Dallas	Greene	John Bell	no return	
Danville	Montgomery	Chas. I. Drury	87 62	159 56
Deep Water	Henry	John C. Stone	13 34	24 92
De Kalb	Buchanan	John Taylor, to 31st Dec'r	22 00	41 31
		Buford B. Allee	20 69	43 42
Delphi	Gasconade	Richard Richardson	5 07	10 86
De Witt	Carroll	Wm. Ketron, to 9th March	15 64	33 11
		Robert Skelley	6 05	12 50
Dixonville	Cole	Jeremiah Dixon	4 42	8 80
Dover	La Fayette	Jas. S. Plattenburg	123 29	242 89
East Fork	Macon	Chas. Hatfield, from 4th July	1 94	3 91
Edina	Scotland	James A. Reid	30 39	57 82
Edinburg (Dis. 10th July.)	Scotland	Richard Gale, jr	9 22	15 94
El Dorado	Clark	Horatio P. Arnold	15 34	27 48

POST OFFICES—*Missouri.*

Post Offices.	Counties.	Postmasters.	Compensation.	Net proceeds.
Eleven Points	Ripley	Chas. Huddleston	$8 57	$17 12
Elkton	Polk	Alexander Blue	10 02	20 70
Ellisville	St. Louis	Wm. A. Hereford	11 67	22 39
Ellsworth	Pulaski	William C. Skinner, 3 qrs	11 68	23 61
Elm Grove	Clay	James E. Hall, to 25th April	14 38	26 05
		George W. Ward	2 91	2 99
Eminence	Shannon	Alfred F. Rider, fr. 1st Jan'y	3 00	5 27
Enterprise	Newton	Alfred Oliver, to 4th Nov	9 26	17 43
		David M. Harlin	17 28	34 73
Erie	Camden	Sidney R. Roberts	22 94	33 35
Fairfield	Benton	Nicholas Campbell	11 38	26 22
Fairview	Pettis	Jesse Pemberton	9 36	15 44
Farmington	St. Francis	Milton P. Cayce	87 99	168 12
Far West	Caldwell	David Hughes	25 18	55 04
Fayette	Howard	William Taylor	381 32	848 58
Fee Fee	St. Louis	Jas. S. Quisenberry	28 58	46 24
Felix	Morgan	John B. Fisher	9 92	18 23
Femme Osage	St. Charles	Jas. R. McDearmon	27 32	54 87
Fenton	St. Louis	Jabez Ferris	3 87	7 62
Flat Creek (Ch'd to "Barry C. H.")	Barry	Josiah McCary	11 12	23 43
Flat Rock	C. Girardeau	Matthew Smith	9 57	15 19
Flint Hill	St. Charles	Tal. P. Grantham	49 86	97 90
Florence	Morgan	Silvaner R. Cox	26 83	51 13
Florida	Monroe	Wm. N. Penn, to 31st March	52 95	94 92
		John A. Quarles	14 97	25 55
Florisant	St. Louis	Paul G. Lindsey	46 40	83 52
Forsyth	Taney	John W. Danforth	22 53	42 80
Fort Leavenworth	Clay	Hiram Rich	206 35	423 54
Fort Osage	Jackson	Isaac Peace	26 15	43 74
Fort Scott	Bates	John A. Bugg	106 61	204 58
Fourche à Renault	Washington	Charles Springer	10 18	17 54
Fox Creek	St. Louis	Peregrine Tippett	32 80	62 10
Frankford	Pike	Adam Mase	38 51	68 62
Franklin	Howard	Isaac N. Bernard, to 25th Jan'y	58 06	62 22
		C. W. Bartholomew	26 81	53 82
Fraziersburg (Dis. 17th Feb.)	Lewis	William P Frazier, 2 qrs	25	62
Fredericktown	Madison	Geo. M. Lampher	132 71	121 67
Fulton	Callaway	Nathan Kouns	311 39	368 75
Gallaher's Mills	Franklin	Michael Gallaher	5 45	10 92

POST OFFICES—*Missouri.*

Post Offices.	Counties.	Postmasters.	Compensation.	Net proceeds.
Gallatin	Daviess	Philip R. Wirt	$78 98	$162 03
Georgetown	Pettis	Amos Fristoe	113 69	213 16
Glasgow	Howard	R. P. Hanenkamp	321 13	693 85
Glenfinlas	Jefferson	Lewis Boldue	14 18	25 13
Golden Grove	Jasper	Jas. K. Plaster, 3 qs.	1 13	2 54
		Daniel Dalrymple	no return	
Gooch's Mill	Cooper	Wm. D. Gooch	14 84	21 60
Grand Pass	Saline	David McReynolds	38 27	75 09
Grape Grove	Ray	Milo C. Nuckols	11 96	24 78
Gravi	Morgan	John C. Robertson	5 56	11 10
Greene	CapeGirard'u	John Stevens	6 65	13 85
Greenfield	Shelby	Elias Winchell	10 39	17 63
Green Hill	Callaway	John Harrison	6 38	12 21
Greenton	La Fayette	Robert Sloan	18 80	36 19
Greenville	Wayne	Dan'l J. Morgan, to 31st Dec	16 10	34 25
		Thos. C. Cattron, fr. 17th Jan	17 83	35 58
Grindstone	Clinton	William Hunter	no return	
Griswold City	Franklin	Walter C. Maupin	7 96	15 70
Hainesville (Dis. 16 Aug., '45)	Clinton	Jas. R. Coffman, fr. 8th October	4 77	7 94
Hampton	Jefferson	Thos. H. Maddox, fr. 25 Nov., 4 mo.	0 38	0 89
Hannibal	Marion	Sam'l J. Harrison, to 2d June	338 58	766 92
		Arthur Shearer	21 44	57 99
Harmony	Washington	Ransom Batterton	15 69	30 12
Harrisburg (Lt. Cool Spring.)	La Fayette	Jas. W. Harris, 3 qs.	10 51	20 60
Harrison's Mills	Crawford	Benjamin Harrison	8 42	15 10
Harrisonville	Van Buren	Lynch Brooks	111 80	220 07
Hartsville	Wright	Isham P. Pool	11 73	27 44
Haw Creek	Morgan	Joseph Dunkley	4 74	9 37
Hawk Point	Lincoln	Oliver Holmes	2 24	3 64
Hazel Grove	Saline	Robt. C. Fitzgerald	3 04	4 84
Hazel Run	St. Francois	Isaac Lewis, from 8th Nov	1 51	3 30
Hazlewood	Wright	Thos. B. Love, 11½ months	9 09	16 67
Herculaneum	Jefferson	Augustus Guibor, to 30th Sept	12 09	17 28
		John Geiger	21 41	33 56
Hermann	Gasconade	Julius Leupold	70 31	144 90
Hibernia	Callaway	John Younts	17 09	31 17
Hickory Creek	Audrian	Timothy Barney	6 30	9 41
Hickory Grove	Warren	Mark S. Pringle	63 53	74 18
Hickory Hill	Cole	Milan Musick	13 48	25 36

POST OFFICES—*Missouri.*

Post Offices.	Counties.	Postmasters.	Compensation.	Net proceeds.
High Creek	Holt	Moses Beal	$30 71	$61 47
High Hill	Montgomery	James Jones	23 98	48 77
High Point	Cole	Henry W. Kelly, fr. 21st Jan'y	3 07	6 63
Hillsborough	Jefferson	Michael W. Horine	41 00	61 81
Hill's Point	Platte	Archibald Hill	23 76	50 88
Hobson's Choice. (Dis. 27th Sept.)	Daviess	John Gitthens, to 25th Oct	3 15	5 67
Honey Creek	Newton	Burton McGhee	8 03	10 26
House's Springs	Jefferson	James Keepers	11 18	24 33
Houston	Marion	William Boulware	20 10	36 67
Humansville	Polk	James G. Human	15 19	34 67
Huntsville	Randolph	Jos. C. Dameron	161 45	302 51
Hydesburgh	Ralls	Peter Forder	19 02	33 72
Iberia	Miller	Reuben Short	11 51	24 48
Independence	Jackson	James McGill	346 36	822 60
Indian Creek	Monroe	Thos. A. Beall	8 18	14 84
Jackson	Cape Girard'u	John W. Gayle	138 51	255 33
Jakes Prairie	Gasconade	John Miller	10 56	23 13
Jamestown	Andrew	Bartholo'w Falkner	26 21	56 26
Jefferson Barracks	St. Louis	George Stevenson	112 67	153 67
Jefferson City	Cole	George W. White, to 20th Aug	90 98	232 54
		Abraham Fulkerson, from 21st Aug	462 13	1204 66
Jonesboro'	Saline	Geo. E. Boswell	15 73	26 88
Jones' Tan Yard	Callaway	John Jones	26 53	31 76
Kennonsville	Lewis	Thos. B. Williams	11 33	20 50
Keytesville	Chariton	Dan'l G. Saunders	119 53	227 89
King's Mills	Montgomery	Conrad Y. King	11 51	21 95
Kingston	Caldwell	Jas. H. Bryan	41 70	74 65
Kirksville	Adair	David James	39 63	65 50
Knoxville	Ray	Jas. H. Hunt, to 31st Dec	15 57	30 79
		Moses F. Rainwater	14 28	28 91
La Grange	Lewis	Chs. S. Skinner	60 96	117 37
La Mine	Cooper	Nelson Church	10 08	18 11
Lamme's Mills	Boone	James McConathy	11 45	19 25
Lebanon	Boone	John M. McGee	7 84	14 29
Legare	Cape Girard'u	John W. Dunn, 3 qs.	1 20	2 83
Lesterville	Shannon	Colin C. Campbell	5 56	5 33
Lexington	La Fayette	Wm. H. Russell, to 16th Feb	364 62	792 40
		Thos. W. Marron	199 05	454 47
Liberty	Clay	Henry Coleman	337 95	779 72

POST OFFICES—*Missouri*.

Post Offices.	Counties.	Postmasters.	Compensation.	Net proceeds.
Licking	Shannon	Eli G. Halbert	$2 37	$5 37
Linn (Lt. Lucy's Creek)	Osage	Wm. M. Lamkin, fr. 1st Jan'y	19 37	38 50
Linneus	Linn	John U. Parsons, to 30th Jan'y	48 20	100 51
		Marshall Harrison	44 58	92 75
Linnville (Dis. 16th May.)	Jefferson	Joseph McKee, 3 qs.	3 70	7 91
Lisle	Osage	George Willson	39 89	88 17
Little Osage	Bates	Leonard Dodge	48 73	86 55
Little Piney	Pulaski	Benj. B. Harrison	10 90	20 41
Little Prairie	Crawford	Benjamin Wishon	7 35	14 66
Lone Jack	Jackson	Warham Easby, to 31st March	20 08	38 75
		Joel Hutchens	5 37	10 49
Long Branch	Monroe	Chs. W. Browning	6 99	12 27
Lost Creek	Lincoln	James Vance	5 88	11 90
Louisiana	Pike	Edwin Draper	150 40	245 76
Louisville	Lincoln	John F. Taliaferro, to 31st March	24 01	41 91
		Chs. T. Taliaferro	4 07	7 71
Loutre Island	Montgomery	Benj. F. Leavell	24 70	47 69
		Includes $1.86 com. and $2 70 net pro. for "Bridgeport."		
Lowndes	Wayne	Henry B. Barnheart	4 90	9 36
Lucy's Creek (Ch'd to "Linn.")	Gasconade	George Crutsinger, 2 qrs	14 41	29 76
McDonald	Barry	John Baze	10 87	18 00
McHargues (Dis. 16th May.)	Chariton	John McHargue	no return	
Macon	Jasper	Enoch Estep	3 05	7 20
Madison	Monroe	Nicholas Ray	36 86	66 52
Madisonville	Ralls	Jeptha S. Crosthwait	13 73	22 14
Manchester	St. Louis	Wm. F. Berry	74 73	144 03
Manlius (Dis. 18th Jan.)	Carroll	E. J. Rea, to 3d Feb.	4 86	10 01
Maramec	Crawford	Samuel Massey	27 35	59 56
Marion	Cole	William Hickam, to 31st Dec'r	9 61	16 02
		John W. Wells	10 94	21 12
Marion City	Marion	Benj. H. Tucker	5 06	10 35
Marion College (Ch'd to "Masonic College.")	Marion	Jordan J. Montgomery, to 31st Dec.	18 80	38 42
Marshall	Saline	John Hood, to 31st December	70 07	118 19
		Wm. A. Wilson	62 58	119 64
Marthasville	Warren	Harvey Griswold	42 80	78 64

POST OFFICES—*Missouri.*

Post Offices.	Counties.	Postmasters.	Compensation.	Net proceeds.
Mason...........	Platte.......	James Kuykendall,		
(Dis. 16 Aug. '45.)		to 30th Sept.....	$2 09	$3 62
		John D. Miller, fr.		
		9th Nov'r.......	3 06	6 44
Masonic College.	Marion	Jordan J. Montgomery,		
(Late "Marion Col	lege.")	ery, fr. 1st Jan'y.	21 99	40 50
Matthews' Prairie	Scott........	Henry G. Cummins	38 17	71 22
Mavais..........	Gasconade...	Jesse Boone	4 68	10 26
Medicine Creek..	Livingston...	Nathan H. Gregory	3 13	5 77
Memphis.........	Scotland.....	William Forman...	30 95	62 82
Mexico	Audrian......	John B. Morris....	39 94	73 46
Miami...........	Saline.......	Charles Carthrae...	62 47	121 93
Middle Fabbies..	Adair........	William V. Rippey.	8 03	14 31
Middle Fork.....	Macon........	Philip Teter.......	5 78	11 97
Middle Grove....	Monroe.	Jas. G. C. Milligan.	37 63	68 65
Middletown	Montgomery.	Nathaniel Vannoy..	15 91	29 26
Midway.........	Cooper......	Albert G. Tompkins	11 69	21 04
Milford	Scotland.....	Hiram Beach......	4 23	7 78
Mill Creek......	Ripley.......	Robert Murdock...	5 71	12 56
Millersburgh.....	Callaway....	James A. Tutt.....	42 75	81 14
Millwood........	Lincoln	Hillary P. Mudd...	12 31	20 08
Milton..........	Randolph....	Anthony Harman..	34 97	64 75
Mine La Motte ..	Madison	Wm. W. Fleming..	64 89	133 78
Missouriton	St. Charles..	Ira E. Tatum......	19 43	36 20
Moniteau........	Cole........	John D. Salmons, to		
		31st Dec'r.......	9 70	18 67
		Thomas Gregory...	7 72	14 83
Montauk........	Crawford....	Ephraim F. Bressie.	1 39	3 27
Monticello.......	Lewis.......	George Railey.....	134 77	245 20
Moreau..........	Cole........	Enoch Enloe.......	25 56	48 15
Mound..........	Carroll......	Hiram McCall......	1 42	2 96
Mount Airy.....	Randolph....	Sam'l C. Davis.....	6 81	12 52
Mount Carmel...	Cooper......	William Steele.....	14 68	29 99
Mount Hope.....	La Fayette..	Joseph Chrisman...	13 97	16 70
Mount Pleasant..	Barry.......	Campbell G. Cowan	5 89	13 58
Mount Refuge...	Clinton......	Isaac D. Baldwin...	3 73	7 52
Mount Sterling..	Gasconade...	Burton Cooper.....	16 54	32 00
Mount Vernon...	Dade	William Orr.......	22 79	50 45
Munger's Mill...	Shannon	Marvin Munger....	5 76	9 80
Nashville........	Boone	John Parker, 2 qrs.	10 00	19 14
(Ch'd to "Provi	dence.")			
Nave's Store.....	Livingston...	Thos. J. Martin....	34 87	66 08
Naylor's Store...	St. Charles..	James Naylor......	68 98	88 77
Neashoe	Newton.....	Milton Sexton	59 87	102 23
Newark.........	Lewis.......	Wm. H. Frush....	31 04	63 76
New Bloomfield..	Callaway....	Jas. D. McGary, to		
		30th May.......	52 26	92 22
		Sam'l V. Allen.....	2 18	4 82

POST OFFICES—*Missouri.*

Post Offices.	Counties.	Postmasters.	Compensation.	Net proceeds.
New Hope	Lincoln	Azel L. Knapp, to 30th Sept.	$8 13	$15 05
		Henry Loughery, to 19th April	14 01	27 98
		Thomas Moore	6 22	12 29
New London	Ralls	James Smith	77 37	149 63
New Madrid	New Madrid	Richard Barkley	163 86	344 52
New Market	Platte	James Strong	62 48	136 18
Newport	Franklin	Fent'n G. McDonald, to 31st Mar.	18 28	31 29
		Joshua Pinkston	4 32	7 29
Newportland	Ralls	John J. Lyle, from 1st Nov.	1 65	2 67
Noddaway	Andrew	John Lincoln	11 76	26 70
Oak Dale	Shelby	Adolphus E. Wood	14 57	30 41
Oak Grove	Jackson	John McKinney	17 04	35 11
Oakland	Pulaski	Samuel Kelley	19 75	35 01
Oakville	St. Louis	Wm. K. Knotts, 3 qrs	3 32	6 10
Ogden	New Madrid	Needham Sikes	7 45	11 56
Old Jefferson (Ch'd to "Cam	Saline bridge.")	Wm. A. Wilson, to 31st Dec	16 11	30 24
		Fred. A. Brightwell	16 10	28 38
Old Mines	Washington	Littleton W. Harris	55 95	63 30
Oliver's Prairie	Newton	Micajah H. Clark	5 63	12 58
Oregon	Holt	John C. Norman, to 12th Feb.	33 89	69 40
		William Zook	27 34	48 26
Osage	Crawford	James Sanders	5 00	7 62
Oseola	St. Clair	Jno. F. Weidemeyer	76 43	158 29
Ozark	Greene	Alfred N. Farmer	16 40	35 25
Palestine	Cooper	Samuel J. Tutt	38 80	76 16
Palmyra	Marion	Richard H. Lane, to 7th Feb.	183 56	384 72
		Michael R. Bower	123 52	262 01
Paris	Monroe	John Williams, to 10th Feb.	105 79	178 75
		Oliver P. Gentry	63 61	96 47
Parkville	Platte	Geo. S. Park	21 67	45 82
Patterson	St. Genevieve	Benj. W. Knox	15 66	30 94
Pattonsburg	Daviess	Matthew Patton, fr. 23d Aug.	17 17	32 08
Paynesville	Pike	Joseph Meloan	53 71	100 46
Perryville	Perry	J. W. Noell, to 22d July	5 88	7 16
		Edward M. Holden, to 31st March	87 09	160 81
Petersburgh	Boone	Ira R. Wells	9 90	21 36

POST OFFICES—*Missouri.*

Post Offices.	Counties.	Postmasters.	Compensation.	Net proceeds.
Petra	Saline	James Jones	$39 72	$69 22
Pigeon Creek	Ralls	William Forman	18 29	32 99
Pilot Grove	Cooper	John McCutchen	17 76	30 45
Pinckney	Warren	Joshua M. Swayse	23 93	31 57
Pine Bluff	Pulaski	Jas. P. Harrison	1 22	2 49
Pisgah	Cole	David Jones	20 20	40 13
Platte City	Platte	Jas. H. Johnston	219 00	436 71
Plattsburgh	Clinton	Don'd M. McDonald	142 90	269 26
Pleasant Gap	Bates	Anderson Cockrill	19 75	38 34
Pleasant Green	Cooper	A. S. Walker, to 30th Sept	5 06	9 29
		Peter P. Cockrell	14 67	26 83
Pleasant Hill	Van Buren	Wm. W. Wright	40 07	72 92
Pleasant Park	Carroll	George McKinny	11 81	23 46
Pleasant Plains	Scott	Washington Orr	6 71	12 71
Pleasant Prairie	Greene	Lewis A. Pattillo	15 54	33 27
Pleasant Valley (Dis. 7th Feb.)	Shannon	Jno. H. Clark, 1 qr.	09	21
Plum Grove	Henry	James M. Fewell, from 6th Feb	38	85
Poplar Grove (Dis. 24th May.)	Callaway	Felix G. Nichols, from 30th Jan	1 41	1 59
Portage des Sioux	St. Charles	Joseph Johnson	11 80	17 09
Portland	Callaway	Robert Stevens	76 25	138 72
Port William	Franklin	James M. Ming	52 76	99 48
Potosi	Washington	Jno. Brickey, to 31st Dec	81 70	134 12
		Wm. A. Matthews	76 28	129 42
Pottawattamie C'k (Dis. 4th Nov.)	Indian Ty	Joshua Carpenter	no return	
Prairieville	Pike	James M. Coleman, to 30th Sept	8 87	16 72
		John W. Smith	25 87	45 40
Prospect	Gentry	Jas. M. Howell	15 46	33 54
Providence (Late 'Nashville.')	Boone	John Parker, from 1st Jan	13 95	25 77
Randolph	Clay	Charles Paynter, to 20th Jan	5 71	10 82
		Nathan E. Harrelson	5 28	10 39
Richland	Greene	Daniel Headlee	6 09	12 47
Richmond	Ray	Robinson Jacobs	213 70	435 81
Richwoods	Washington	Thos. M. Taylor, from 3d July	9 68	19 86
Rives C. H.	Rives	Benj. F. Wallace	57 65	98 94
Roanoke	Randolph	David C. Whitehurst	59 07	118 24
Rocheport	Boone	Cary Peebels, to 10th Feb	115 60	213 44
		John M. Lyman	66 54	134 75

POST OFFICES—*Missouri.*

Post Offices.	Counties.	Postmasters.	Compensation.	Net proceeds.
Rochester	Andrew	Mason Wilson, to 30th Sept	$1 45	$2 33
		Charles Kibby	7 07	12 20
Rock Bridge	Ozark	John Young	10 82	24 24
Rock Hill	St. Louis	WilliamMcCormick	16 14	29 73
Rock House Pra'ie	Buchanan	Edward Snyder, to 9th Jan	17 09	35 80
		Dugan Fouts	18 53	36 73
Rock Prairie (Dis. 16th May.)	Dade	Moses Theobald	no return	
Rockville	Holt	Alex. A. Bradford	16 04	29 96
Rocky Mount	Miller	Edmund Wilkes	15 25	29 90
Roscoe	Rives	John Burch	13 31	28 15
Roubidoux	Wright	Josh. H. Burckhartt	no return	
Round Hill	Cooper	Lot Howard, jr	17 69	33 67
Rush Tower	Jefferson	Andrew Fight	16 18	33 68
Saint Charles	St. Charles	Joseph Fawcett, to 7th Oct	68 98	137 93
		Sir Walter Rice, to 23d May	174 92	325 14
		Wm. N. Fulkerson	22 40	47 06
Saint Francisville	Clark	Geo. Haywood, 3 qrs	21 86	39 53
Saint Genevieve C. H.	St. Genevieve	Jos. N. Amoreux	155 26	276 21
Saint Helen	St. Clair	Wm. L. Gordon, to 31st Dec	4 07	8 00
		Thos. N. Cook	4 99	9 82
Saint Joseph	Buchanan	Fred. W. Smith, to 7th March	133 17	308 74
		Wm. B. Almond	60 80	150 53
Saint Louis	St. Louis	Saml. B. Churchill	2000 00	27693 35
Saint Mary's Landing	St. Genevieve	Wm. H. H. Stuart	15 29	22 13
Salem	Benton	Edw. S. Whitehead	6 45	13 55
Saline	Ralls	Notley C. Williams	11 64	20 68
Salt River	Audrian	Zachariah Jackson	3 02	5 92
Sand Hill	Scotland	Andrew Williams	30 14	61 27
Sandsville	Gentry	Daniel Saunders	27 27	58 04
Sandy Mines	Jefferson	John Anderson	7 03	12 53
Sappington	St. Louis	Zepha'h Sappington	21 62	37 48
Sarcoxie	Newton	Andrew Wilson	71 97	125 46
Savannah	Andrew	Wm. H. Rodgers	255 36	580 06
Saverton	Ralls	Elijah N. Hascall	11 65	24 22
Selma	Jefferson	Luther M. Kennett, to 31st March	13 29	22 68
		Theodore Forster	3 93	6 96
Sexton's	Boone	Geo. H. Sexton	17 81	31 12
Shady Valley	Cole	John H. Ahleis	3 92	4 95

POST OFFICES—*Missouri.*

Post Offices.	Counties.	Postmasters.	Compensation.	Net proceeds.
Shamrock	Callaway	Pearson W. Overley	$27 99	$48 67
Sharpsburg	Monroe	Richard Sharp	7 76	16 26
Shelbyville	Shelby	Claybo'e M. Gentry	96 43	182 16
Sibley	Jackson	John Hambright	32 87	62 93
Smithland	Randolph	Fleming Terrell	24 66	47 22
Smithville	Clay	Isaac Wood, to 31st March	8 07	15 70
		Jas. E. Walker	5 01	8 60
Somerset	Monroe	Albert G. Williams	28 45	54 63
Spanish Prairie	Crawford	Wm. E. Hawkins	14 49	30 37
Sparta	Buchanan	Jas. A. Anthony	72 09	151 81
Spencersburg	Pike	Aaron Hendricks	22 23	38 62
Springfield	Greene	Wm. B. Farmer	238 24	484 23
Steelsville	Crawford	Henry E. Davis	27 05	49 05
Sulphur Springs	Jefferson	Alton J. Kendal	17 24	32 04
Tarhio. (Dis. 16th May.)	Holt	Daniel Durbin, from 4th July to 30th Sept.	84	1 97
Taylor's Mills	Marion	Caleb Taylor, 3 qrs.	11 41	19 31
The Narrows	Buchanan	George J. Lucas	1 75	2 65
Tinney's Grove	Ray	John Brown	2 48	4 53
Tippecanoe	Adair	John M. Fish	39 78	75 30
Todd's Creek	Platte	Robert Cain	6 38	9 50
Traveller's Repose	Franklin	Joseph Funk	5 65	9 97
Trenton	Grundy	Jas. S. Lomax	88 67	191 57
Troy	Lincoln	Jas. H. Britton	128 28	234 78
Tully	Lewis	Saml. H. Stewart	49 20	103 68
Tuscumbia	Miller	Wm. P. Dixon, to 11th Jan.	19 85	38 47
		Hard. M. Williams	11 84	25 39
Union	Franklin	Alexander Chambers	129 89	148 50
Union Grove	Newton	Hugh C. Armstrong	7 00	15 45
Utica	Livingston	Roderick Matson	22 04	43 20
Van Buren	Ripley	John Woods	9 25	13 38
Vannoy's Mill	Pike	Nathan Vannoy	4 27	7 00
Vermont	Cooper	Thomas W. Nelson, to 31st March	8 49	16 11
		Jno. C. G. Goodwin	1 86	3 14
Versailles	Morgan	William Boggs	80 70	156 07
Virginia Mines	Franklin	Chesley B. Inge	29 59	54 54
Walnut Forest	Greene	Josiah F. Danforth	12 90	25 90
Waltonham	St. Louis	George Hume, from 1st March	3 07	4 58
Warren	Marion	H'y M. Nicol, 3 qrs.	20 00	37 99

POST OFFICES—*Missouri.*

Post Offices.	Counties.	Postmasters.	Compensation.	Net proceeds.
Warrensburgh...	Johnson....	Jas. S. Raynol, to 31st March.....	$60 75	$120 67
		Nathl. B. Holden..	19 09	39 33
Warrenton......	Warren.....	Eli Carter.........	51 42	100 87
Warsaw.........	Benton......	Wash. Dorrell, to 31st Dec.........	86 25	183 98
		Hamilton Leonard.	93 38	199 54
Washbourn Pra'ie	Barry.......	Lewis Henderson...	29 95	61 40
Washington.....	Franklin....	Daniel Q. Gale....	41 86	80 41
Waterloo.......	Clark.......	Thomas D. Ford...	50 47	73 90
Waverly........ (Dis. 20th Jan.)	Henry......	Wm. T. Robinson.	no return	
Waynesville.....	Pulaski.....	Robert A. Harden..	26 14	50 99
Wellington......	La Fayette..	Phares Ferrell.....	50 73	96 64
Wellsburg	St. Charles..	James Wells.......	11 22	20 92
West Ely.......	Marion.....	Hervey H. Hayes..	60 14	103 40
Weston.........	Platte.......	Benjamin Holladay.	282 31	670 88
West Philadelphia (Dis. 23d Oct.)	Scott.......	Wm. C. Rogers...	no return	
Westport.......	Jackson.....	Edmund Price.....	206 60	428 33
West Prairie	Stoddart	Elijah Hill........	8 66	18 81
White Hare.....	Cedar.......	Wilb'rn G. Langford	10 13	23 45
White Oak Grove (Dis. 4th Oct.)	Greene	J. L. C. Huddleston, to 19th Jan......	78	1 87
Wickliffe	Wright.....	Jas. A. Bates, 2 qrs.	1 16	2 26
Williamsburgh..	Callaway....	Turner Crump.....	35 97	59 60
Winchester......	Clark.......	Wm. C. Overstreet, to 31st March....	18 78	38 86
		Robert Young.....	6 70	14 06
Wiseman's......	Boone......	James Wiseman...	9 46	18 66
Woodbury......	Wright.....	John S. Burnett....	5 48	12 78
Woodford....... (Dis. 17th Mar.)	Clay........	Jas. Egbert, 2 qrs.	3 47	4 28
Woodlawn......	Monroe.....	Benjamin Meason..	2 62	5 45
Woodville......	Macon......	John R. Hutton....	31 10	61 38
Yellow Creek....	Chariton....	Wm. G. Rooker...	8 72	14 34
Younger's......	Boone......	Robt. A. Younger..	5 27	8 87

POST OFFICES—Iowa.

IOWA.

NOTE.—Compensation of Postmasters, and net proceeds of their offices, from July 1, 1844, to June 30, 1845.

Post Offices.	Counties.	Postmasters.	Compensation.	Net proceeds.
Andrew	Jackson	George W. Shreck	$52 22	$86 73
Ashland	Wapello	Thomas Ping	2 07	4 45
Augusta	Des Moines	Joshua Holland	60 93	110 32
Belleview	Jackson	Daniel C. Allen	59 06	110 44
Benton's Port	Van Buren	Seth Richards	25 05	50 27
Berlin	Scott	Lemuel Parkhurst	27 40	49 32
Birmingham	Van Buren	Jacob Lawton	23 41	43 70
Bloomfield	Davis	George W. Kidder, from 10th August to 31st Dec.	6 20	12 55
		John W. Ellis, from 19th April	6 44	13 35
Bloomington	Muscatine	Pliny Fay	291 13	611 62
Blue Grass	Scott	Asa Foster	8 88	17 38
Bonaparte	Van Buren	Roger N. Cresap	70 22	148 92
Brighton	Washington	John Kirkpatrick	60 88	129 22
Burlington	Des Moines	George Temple, to 2d June	564 54	1369 34
		Levi Hager	38 17	93 49
Camanche	Clinton	Martin Dunning	11 86	23 82
Cascade	Du Buque	Levi A. Styles	39 16	81 32
Cedar River	Cedar	James H. Gower	10 43	20 08
Centre Point	Linn	S. M. Brice, 1 qr	1 20	1 86
Charleston	Jackson	William Hubbell	44 01	82 71
Columbus City	Louisa	Uriah Limbocker	21 15	37 69
Crooked Creek	Henry	Rufus M. Pickel	8 80	17 54
Dahlonega	Wapello	Edm'd G. Haggard	9 87	21 85
Davenport	Scott	D. C. Eldridge	228 49	456 28
Delhi	Delaware	Mary E. A. Hobbs, 1 qr	2 12	4 00
De Witt	Clinton	Robert R. Bedford, to 18th June	26 68	46 33
		T. F. Butterfield	1 90	3 67
Dodgeville	Des Moines	John Burkhart	14 98	30 39
Du Buque	Du Buque	John King	466 20	1082 99
Dutch Creek	Washington	Pleasant Langford	no return	
Eddyville	Wapello	Wm. R. Ross, 2 qrs.	16 73	32 09
Edinburgh	Jones	James Hutton	3 75	7 49
Elk River	Clinton	John Sloan	4 19	6 76

POST OFFICES—*Iowa.*

Post Offices.	Counties.	Postmasters.	Compensation.	Net proceeds.
Fairfield	Jefferson	Samuel Shuffleton	$276 89	$630 55
Fairview	Jones	Clement Russell	3 35	7 14
Farming Grove	Scott	D. R. Fuller, 3 qrs.	0 29	0 71
Farmington	Van Buren	Henry G. Steuart, to 17th Jan	82 32	152 69
		Laurence Scott	60 13	125 95
Florence	Louisa	John Deihl	5 61	10 67
Fort Madison	Lee	Robert A. Russell	268 85	527 45
Fort Snelling	Du Buque	Franklin Steele	126 85	256 51
Fox	Davis	Samuel A. Evans, to 30th Sept	2 29	5 02
		Moses J. Post	18 41	34 02
Franklin	Linn	Allison J. Willits	27 39	49 17
Franklin Centre	Lee	John Brown	4 82	9 79
Grand View	Louisa	Gabriel Walling	43 55	79 32
Harrison	Louisa	William Kennedy	8 15	15 46
Hartford	Des Moines	Hiram Messinger	23 03	39 63
Hawk Eye	Des Moines	James Latta, from 26th Oct	2 12	4 16
Hickory Grove (Dis. 16th May.)	Scott	Vincent S. Carter	no return	
Hillsboro'	Henry	Nehemiah Tunis, to 15th July	0 95	1 67
		John Stewart	6 43	13 16
Hope Farm	Louisa	John Marshall	8 20	16 59
Indian Prairie	Van Buren	Elisha Burton	8 91	16 12
Iowa City	Johnson	S. C. Trowbridge, 3 qrs	212 08	473 43
Iowaville	Van Buren	David Hoover	30 25	62 20
Jacksonville	Clayton	John Banfill, 2 qrs.	12 44	24 76
		Reuben Noble	14 50	26 45
Juan	Washington	Lyman Chase	no return	
Keokuck	Lee	Wm. S. McGavie, to 31st May	98 32	187 30
		Adam Hine	6 82	15 21
Keosauqua (Late Van Buren.)	Van Buren	Wm. Steele, 3 qrs.	98 38	181 19
Lewiston (Dis. 11th July.)	Davis	Lloyd A. Nelson, to 10th August	1 33	2 85
Lockridge	Jefferson	William Bonnifield	8 41	15 18
Lowell	Henry	Justus Clark	22 99	41 95
Lyons	Clinton	Daniel Hess	14 96	27 74

POST OFFICES—*Iowa.*

Post Offices.	Counties.	Postmasters.	Compensation.	Net proceeds.
Mahaska........ (Ch'd to "Oskaloosa.")	Mahaska....	Perry L. Crossman, 1 qr..............	$1 86	$2 69
Maquoketa...... (Late Springfield.)	Jackson.....	John E. Goodenow, 2 qrs...........	20 97	38 43
Marion..........	Linn..........	Addison Daniels....	110 10	218 00
Massillon........	Clinton.......	Joseph Anderson, fr. 16th October......	0 74	1 36
Millville........	Clayton	Isaac H. Preston....	19 75	35 10
Montpelier	Muscatine...	Benjamin Nye.....	12 57	21 96
Montrose.........	Lee..........	Cyrus Peck.........	48 74	92 04
Moscow..........	Muscatine...	Delavan Bratt......	12 32	23 04
Mount Pleasant..	Henry........	Alvin Saunders.....	147 89	279 41
New London	Henry........	Charles B. Wall ...	34 21	72 40
Oskaloosa .... (Late 'Mahaska.')	Mahaska....	Perry L. Crossman, from 1st Oct.....	32 88	69 37
Otter Creek.......	Linn..........	Abel E. Skinner....	no return	
Ottumwa..........	Wapello	Isaac McKeever, fr. 26th July to 31st March..............	15 42	28 95
		David Glass.........	13 74	26 41
Overman's Ferry.	Muscatine...	John M. Overman..	7 47	12 24
Pedee............	Cedar........	Jeremiah Allen.....	no return	
Philadelphia......	Van Buren..	Seth St. John......	12 50	26 73
Pin Oak..........	Du Buque...	John H. Floyd	1 40	3 35
Pittsburg	Van Buren..	Cyrus Gibson.......	31 64	60 03
Pleasant Grove... (Dis. 16th May.)	Jefferson	Stephen Heard, from 2d August.......	1 68	3 39
Pleasant Valley ..	Scott.........	J. A. Birchard, jr..	8 32	14 49
Point Pleasant ... (Dis. 23d Oct.)	Scott.........	William Pearsall...	no return	
Portland..........	Van Buren..	James S. Park.....	23 87	49 59
Pottsville	Washington..	David Goble........	8 01	16 00
Prairie House....	Lee..........	Robert B. Robison..	15 51	27 28
Prairie Springs...	Jackson.....	Patrick Moloney, fr. 4th Nov..........	0 38	0 87
Princeton.........	Scott.........	Haswell H. Pinneo.	6 61	12 83
Quasqueton......	Buchanan ...	Jos. A. Reynolds, from 12th July...	6 65	15 13
Richland	Washington..	James Williams....	22 90	46 15
Rock Creek......	Cedar.......	Charles Sweetland..	29 78	60 30
Rockingham.....	Scott........	Willard Barrows...	17 56	34 11
Rome...........	Henry.......	Linus Fairchild....	15 07	29 91

POST OFFICES—*Iowa*.

Post Offices.	Counties.	Postmasters.	Compensation.	Net proceeds.
Sac & Fox Agency	Wapello.....	Wm. B. Street, to 30th Sept	$16 75	$34 17
		Shaphat Dwire.....	37 51	78 77
Salem..........	Henry........	Aaron Street, jr....	82 84	159 38
Sigourney........	Keokuck....	S. A. James, 1 qr...	2 25	5 23
Solon	Johnson......	Hamilton H. Kerr..	14 06	23 79
Spring Rock......	Clinton.......	George Goddard....	4 49	8 47
Springville.......	Linn..........	Isaac Butler........	2 02	3 34
String Prairie....	Lee..........	Alfred B. Child.....	5 09	10 23
Tete de Mort....	Jackson.....	Daniel Brown......	6 82	11 29
Tipton..........	Cedar.......	Patterson Fleming, to 26th Oct......	14 87	28 19
		John R. McCurdy..	40 70	66 53
Toolsborough....	Louisa......	Wm. L. Toole.....	9 97	20 85
Trenton.........	Henry.......	Samuel Morrison ..	32 63	64 39
Tuscarora.......	Lee.........	William Dunlap, to 2d Feb..........	6 06	11 39
		Thomas W. Taylor.	1 94	3 93
Van Buren...... (Ch'd to "Keosauqua.")	Van Buren..	Wm. Steele, 1 qr...	38 41	77 53
Virginia Grove...	Louisa.......	A. Chamberlain, jr.	no return	
Wabasha........ (Dis. 27th July, 1844.)	Clayton	Duncan Graham ...	no return	
Walnut Fork....	Jones........	Timothy Stivers....	14 91	31 17
Walnut Grove...	Scott........	Henry H. Pease ...	3 33	6 57
Wapello	Louisa.......	John C. McCleary, to 1st Feb.......	42 96	78 82
		Geo. W. McCleary, to 7th June......	23 30	52 51
		John Bird.........	7 41	11 36
Washington.....	Washington..	Norman Everson...	103 36	194 62
West Buffalo....	Scott........	George M. Hinkle..	9 19	18 97
West Liberty....	Muscatine...	Asa Gregg.........	24 42	42 44
West Point......	Lee..........	William Alexander.	110 81	204 20
Wickliffe........	Jackson.....	James Clarke......	4 20	7 29
Winchester......	Van Buren..	Abraham L. Holgate	31 45	60 26
Wyoming........	Muscatine...	John Sherfey......	14 27	27 14
Yatton..........	Washington..	Nathaniel P. Cooper	10 96	19 34
Yellow Spring....	Des Moines..	Elijah Wood	33 19	64 95

POST OFFICES—*Wisconsin Territory.*

WISCONSIN TERRITORY.

NOTE.—Compensation of Postmasters, and net proceeds of their offices, from July 1, 1844, to June 30, 1845.

Post Offices.	Counties.	Postmasters.	Compensation.	Net proceeds.
Aztalan	Jefferson	James Payne	$129 40	$241 91
Beaver Dam	Dodge	John H. Manahan, from October	27 96	55 07
Belmont	Iowa	Nathan Olmsted, 2 qrs	5 81	11 19
Beloit	Rock	Alfred L. Field, to 17th February	170 89	339 37
		David Noggle	115 10	247 37
Benton (Late "Cottonwood Hill.")	Iowa	Dennis Murphy	no ret.	
Blue Mound	Dane	Ebenezer Brigham	8 63	16 92
Blue River	Iowa	Hugh McCracken	29 25	57 82
Bridgeport	Brown	Hoel S. Wright	5 82	5 90
Bristol	Racine	Andrew B. Jackson	46 51	88 90
Brookfield	Milwaukie	Rufus P. Harriman, to 31st December	7 65	17 89
		Charles Raymond, from 10th Feb	9 61	19 60
Burlington	Racine	Lorenzo D. Eastman	132 17	256 16
Calumet Village	Calumet	George White	15 52	31 93
Cassville	Grant	Richard Hamer	38 76	71 67
Ceresco	Fond du Lac	Lester Rounds	29 41	60 92
Clinton	Rock	Stephen Perley, to 31st July	1 97	4 06
		Griswold Weaver	18 19	32 44
Cold Spring	Jefferson	Elisha Peck	no ret.	
		David B. Peck, 1 qr.	2 37	4 88
Cottage Grove	Dane	Amos Beecher	14 85	28 73
Cottonwood Hill (Cha'd to "Benton.")	Iowa	Dennis Murphy, 2 qrs	14 57	31 24
Dane	Dane	Freedom Simons, fr. 26th July	1 98	3 36
Darion	Walworth	John Bruce	61 21	116 03
Decatur	Green	John Moore	17 95	33 95
Delafield	Milwaukie	Nelson P. Hawks	70 71	146 11
Delavan	Walworth	Cyrus Brainard	135 43	261 97
Depere	Brown	William Dickinson	24 27	44 52
Dodgeville	Iowa	John Adams, to 31st March	48 61	99 26

POST OFFICES—*Wisconsin Territory.*

Post Offices.	Counties.	Postmasters.	Compensation.	Net proceeds.
		Jas. D. Jenkins....	$22 45	$41 21
		Includes 86cts comp. $1 54 net pro. for "Helena."		
Duck Creek.....	Brown	Solomon Davis.....	17 86	35 71
East Troy.......	Walworth...	Sewall Smith, from 27th June.......	76 61	144 20
Edwardsville.....	Grant.......	Samuel Virden, to 31st March......	20 41	39 28
		Horace Catlin.......	10 68	23 94
Elk Grove........	Iowa..........	Edward Leslie.....	39 45	73 37
Elk Horn.......	Walworth...	Le Grand Rockwell.	68 56	126 86
Exeter...........	Green.......	Thos. L. Summers.	31 18	58 58
Fairfield.........	Walworth...	Joseph Maxson.....	9 56	16 68
Fairplay	Grant.......	Edward B. Sloan, to 31st December...	27 03	51 48
		Jas. B. Johnson.....	27 23	50 55
Falls of St. Croix.	St. Croix....	William Holcombe.	48 26	99 12
Farmington......	Jefferson	Jesse L. Hinman, fr. 12th November...	3 11	5 10
Fitchburg	Dane	William Quivey...	19 13	37 52
Fond du Lac.....	Fond du Lac.	Thomas Green......	70 86	127 00
Fort Atkinson...	Jefferson....	Dwight Foster, 3 qrs	75 61	141 65
Fort Winnebago.	Brown	Henry Merrill......	117 68	228 80
Franklin .... (Ch'd. to "Spring Prairie.")	Walworth...	Ansel A. Hemenway, 3 qrs.......	31 77	61 82
Geneva	Walworth...	Andrew Ferguson..	173 67	359 20
Geneva Bay.....	Walworth...	Israel Williams.....	5 74	10 18
Goodlett.........	Walworth...	James Duncan.....	3 14	6 03
Grand Rapids...	Portage	Eliphalet S. Miner, 1 qr..............	4 10	8 71
Gratiot	Iowa.........	Beri W. Tuttle.....	6 87	13 08
Gratiot's Grove..	Iowa	Fortunatus Berry...	30 75	59 51
Green Bay......	Brown	Alex'r J. Irwin....	315 22	657 68
Greenfield	Milwaukie....	John Cooper......	17 08	31 72
Green Lake.....	Marquette...	Anson Dart.......	30 18	65 80
Hamburgh......	Washington..	Phin. M. Johnson..	19 20	30 13
Hazel Green.....	Grant........	Jefferson Crawford..	127 98	252 90
Heart Prairie....	Walworth...	George Esterly.....	19 51	35 08
Hudson......... (Late 'Lyondale.')	Walworth...	John Stacy, 2 qrs...	8 09	16 52
Hurricane........	Grant........	John Wise.........	9 22	15 50
Ives' Grove......	Racine.......	Roland Ives, jr......	12 31	24 16

POST OFFICES—*Wisconsin Territory.*

Post Offices.	Counties.	Postmasters.	Compensation.	Net proceeds.
Jamestown	Grant	James Gilmore	$50 49	$93 15
Janesville	Rock	John L. Kimball	289 33	497 11
Jefferson	Jefferson	Enoch G. Darling	60 06	113 81
Johnstown	Rock	Lucius Beldin	42 66	91 68
Kankalan	Brown	Alexander Grignon	6 34	10 00
Kaposia	St. Croix	Wm. R. Brown	9 34	17 01
Kewannee	Milwaukie	Stephen Sayles	6 52	13 40
Koskonong	Jefferson	Benoni W. Finch	17 05	32 99
La Cross	Crawford	Nathan Myrick	12 21	27 00
La Grange	Walworth	Nelson Cornish	21 78	42 30
Lake Mills	Jefferson	Joseph Keyes, from 7th November	25 84	53 13
Lake St. Croix	St. Croix	Levi Hertzell	41 32	82 75
Lakeville	Racine	Jas. B. Powers	17 27	33 45
Lancaster	Grant	Benj. F. Forbes, to 31st December	40 33	78 70
		Jas. M. Ward	41 67	81 41
La Point	St. Croix	Chs. W. Borup	51 07	103 97
Limestone (Dis. 1st March.)	Washington	Alfred Orendorff, 3 qrs	3 49	7 62
Lyondale (Chan'd to "Hudson.")	Walworth	John Stacy, 2 qrs	6 15	11 56
Madison	Dane	John Catlin, to 15th January	171 64	336 37
		Steptoe Catlin	309 08	659 70
Manitoowoc	Manitoowoc	Oliver C. Hubbard	51 29	104 19
Menominee Falls	Milwaukie	Wm. R. Hesk	23 44	46 23
Mequon River	Washington	Fred'k W. Horn	24 10	46 83
Milton	Rock	Joseph Goodrich	107 48	207 26
Milwaukee	Milwaukie	Josiah A. Noonan	1524 11	4252 69
Mineral Point	Iowa	Isaiah T. Lathrop, to 11th February	226 16	487 83
		Henry Plowman	158 50	368 62
Monroe	Green	Demus Beach, to 22d May	81 41	159 52
		Charles Hart	9 11	19 80
Mount Pleasant	Racine	Julius Wooster	23 01	45 05
Muker	Washington	William Greene, fr. 7th September	5 91	10 01
Mukwanago	Milwaukie	Andrew E. Elmore	151 21	269 51
Muscoda (Dis. 16th May.)	Grant	Levi J. D. Parish	no ret.	
Muskeego	Milwaukie	James Field	5 58	11 96
Neenah	Winnebago	Harrison Reed, 3 qrs	1 46	2 91
New Berlin	Milwaukie	Publius V. Monroe	28 17	54 04

POST OFFICES—*Wisconsin Territory.*

Post Offices.	Counties.	Postmasters.	Compensation.	Net proceeds.
New Diggings	Iowa	Henry Potwine	$116 57	$230 95
Oak Creek	Milwaukie	Erasmus D. Philips.	29 67	57 46
Oak Grove	Dodge	Ethan Owen, from 28th September	21 19	41 30
Osh Kosh	Winnebago	Henry A. Gallup	18 43	30 79
Palmyra	Jefferson	John Fish, from 10th August	34 41	66 72
Paris	Racine	Jas. H. Hall, 1 qr	5 50	10 94
Patch Grove	Grant	Henry Patch	30 15	54 52
Pedler's Creek	Iowa	John Wasley	29 48	53 18
Pequot	Calumet	Thomas Commuck.	17 88	33 04
Platteville	Grant	Sylvester Gridley, to 17th May	233 78	517 93
		Ben C. Eastman	32 24	73 84
Pleasant Prairie	Racine	Daniel Stevens	13 30	26 31
Plover Portage	Portage	George Wyatt, 1 qr	8 79	16 30
Point Banssee	Portage	Robert Wakely, 1 qr	1 54	3 05
Potosi	Grant	Celestine Kaltenback	191 99	393 31
Prairie du Chien.	Crawford	Ira B. Brunson	359 13	812 64
Prairie du Sac	Sauk	Wm. H. Hubbard	72 59	140 82
Prairieville	Milwaukie	Alex'r W. Randall.	369 71	782 87
Racine	Racine	Elias Smith	666 21	1614 74
Richmond	Walworth	Perkins S. Childs, fr. 22d July	8 18	11 81
Ridgeway	Iowa	Geo. W. Hickcox	16 54	30 28
Rochester	Racine	Hiland S. Hulburd.	164 78	315 08
Rubicon	Washington	Timothy Hall, 1 qr.	2 60	4 24
Saint Marys (Dis. 18th Jan'y.)	Milwaukie	John Moore, 3 qrs.	3 51	6 76
Salem	Racine	Dan'l C. Burgess	103 15	194 64
Sharon	Walworth	Job R. Case, from 12th June	5 91	13 38
Sheboygan	Sheboygan	Sam'l B. Ormsbee, from 2d December	34 22	63 61
Sheboygan Falls.	Sheboygan	Ch's D. Cole	75 67	151 00
Southport	Racine	Louis P. Harvey, to 4th July	7 57	19 95
		Henry B. Hinsdale, fr. 5th July	780 35	1593 96
Spring Prairie (Late 'Franklin.')	Walworth	Ansel A. Hemenway, 1 qr	15 36	31 47
Stockbridge	Brown	Cutting Marsh	13 45	22 47
Sugar Creek	Walworth	Sam'l H. Tibbits	32 20	57 89
Summerville	Rock	William Stewart	10 86	23 44
Summit	Milwaukie	Ch's A. Keeler	152 37	317 49

POST OFFICES—*Canada.*

Post Offices.	Counties.	Postmasters.	Compensation.	Net proceeds.
Taycheida	Fond du Lac.	Nathan Perry.	$51 22	$91 74
Tradewell's Grove	Racine	Eph'm B. Tradewell	12 25	24 40
Troy	Walworth	Jesse Meacham	82 63	153 88
Union	Rock	Samuel Lewis	46 66	97 97
Union Centre	Jefferson	Harmon V. Sacia	9 86	13 19
Vernon	Milwaukie	Asa A. Flint	34 35	57 89
Walworth	Walworth	William Bell	58 49	110 66
Warrens	Rock	Lemuel Warren	14 33	27 33
Washington	Washington	Orlando A. Watrous	11 28	22 08
Watertown	Jefferson	Patrick Rogan	205 22	260 07
Waupun	Fond du Lac.	Barnabas Hinkley	26 33	55 69
Waushara	Dodge	Geo. W. Clark, to 3d February	29 04	65 30
		David Green	20 02	40 26
Wheatland	Racine	Thomas Slade	27 93	57 39
White Oak Sp'gs.	Iowa	Frank Washburn	67 91	132 26
White Water	Walworth	Warner Earll	191 23	366 40
Willow Springs	Iowa	Joshua Bailey	22 68	42 20
Wingville (Dis. 26th June.)	Grant	Thos. J. Parish, 3 qrs	2 44	4 75
Wiota	Iowa	John Z. Saxton, to 16th July	1 56	3 67
		John Haskell	58 53	107 58
Yorkville	Racine	Ebenezer Adams	56 03	121 19

CANADA.

[Note.—Agents who received postages in the British provinces from July 1, 1844, to June 30, 1845.]

Post Offices.	Postmasters.	Compensation.	Net proceeds.
Brockville	Thos. A. Stayner, 3 qrs	$40 90	$89 76
Kingston	do. 3 qrs	619 38	1446 73
Montreal	do. 3 qrs	1532 08	4927 21
Niagara	do. 3 qrs	99 84	193 02
Prescott	do. 3 qrs	186 73	244 80
Quebec	do. 3 qrs	387 76	787 38
Queenstown	do. 3 qrs	1999 11	4713 52
Stanstead	do. 3 qrs	231 38	460 29
Toronto	do. 3 qrs	518 63	1486 16
Windsor	do. 3 qrs	106 99	244 55
Saint Andrews, N. Bruns'k	J. Howe, 2 qrs.	356 69	1058 09
Woodstock, N. Brunswick	do. 2 qrs.	87 20	166 31

POST OFFICES—*Clerks.*

CLERKS IN POST OFFICES.

A statement of the salaries paid Clerks in the following Post Offices, during the year ending June 30, 1845—In the alphabetical order of the offices.

Post Offices.	Names.	Compensation.
Albany, N. Y....	John McLacklan, from July 1, 1844, to June 30, 1845..........	$1020 00
	A. H. Coughtry, from July 1, 1844, to June 30, 1845..........	710 00
	Schuyler Van Rensselaer, from July 1, 1844, to June 30, 1845..........	700 00
	Joseph Bell, fr. July 1, '44, to June 30, '45..	600 00
	J. K. Skinner, fr. July 1, '44, to Dec. 31, '44	300 00
	J. P. Burton, fr. July 1, '44, to June 30, '45	510 00
	F. W. Humphreys, from July 1, 1844, to Dec. 31, 1844..........	295 22
	C. H. Wasson, fr. July 1, '44, to June 30, '45	641 52
	Alexander Auty, from July 1, 1844, to Dec. 31, 1844..........	250 00
	Isaac McMurdy, from July 1, 1844, to June 30, 1845..........	505 00
	A. A. Lansing, fr. July 1, '44, to June 30, '45	500 00
	H. Bothwick..........do..........do....	505 00
	C. Enright..........do..........do....	300 00
	J. Groesbeck..........do..........do....	265 16
	J. T. Vernon, fr. Jan. 1 to June 30, 1845....	300 00
	J. Hilton..........do..........do....	255 00
	A. T. Teall, from Jan. 1 to March 31, 1845..	160 00
	William G. Jewell, fr. April 1 to June 30, '45	140 00
Augusta, Ga....	Benjamin Hall, fr. July 1, '44, to June 30, '45	1500 00
	A. Creighton, from July 1 to Nov. 10, 1844..	252 77
	B. F. Hall, fr. July 1, '44, to June 30, '45...	563 89
	Aaron Roff..........do..........do....	563 89
	George W. Morgan..do..........do....	480 00
	G. B. Knight..........do..........do....	300 00
	J. H. Mackie, from Nov. 10, 1844, to June 30, 1845..........	153 33
Baltimore, Md....	C. T. Maddox, fr. July 1, '44, to June 30, '45	1403 86
	Eli Lewis, from July 1, '44, to April 17, '45	1120 05
	J. H. Hanson, fr. July 1, '44, to June 30, '45	690 70
	R. T. Banks..........do..........do....	744 20
	L. R. Newcomer....do..........do....	744 20
	John W. Finley, from July 1, 1844, to April 17, 1845..........	609 20
	J. A. Shriver, fr. July 1, '44, to March 31, '45	562 50
	J. C. Tracy..........do..........do....	304 00

POST OFFICES—*Clerks.*

Post Offices.	Names.	Compensation.
Baltimore, Md..	C. J. R. Thorpe, from July 1, 1844, to June 30, 1845	$636 59
	J. T. Rigney, from July 1 to Aug. 9, 1844, and from April 1 to June 30, 1845	194 46
	Jos. W. Finley, from July 1 to Sept. 1, 1844	25 25
	S. S. Shriver, fr. July 1, '44, to March 31, '45	250 42
	Chas. D. Rigney ..do..........do....	387 50
	Thos. H. Belt, jr., from Sept. 1, 1844, to June 30, 1845	304 86
	W. H. Martin, fr. July 1, '44, to June 30, '45	344 99
	S. L. Finley, fr. Oct. 1, '44, to June 30, '45..	295 11
	T. J. Moriarty, fr. March 11 to June 30, 1845	150 70
	R. S. Finley, from March 4 to June 30, 1845	80 70
	R. Dorsey, from April 17 to June 30, 1845..	283 81
	John W. Wells......do..........do....	115 00
	Geo. H. Hickman....do..........do....	72 00
	John Malone........do..........do....	70 73
	O. O'Brien.........do..........do....	54 00
Bangor, Me.....	Henry A. Butler, fr. July 1, '44, to June 30, '45	342 00
	Calvin S. Butler......do..........do....	342 00
Boston, Mass....	Edw'd S. Erving, fr. July 1, '44, to June 30, '45	1200 00
	Nathaniel Melcher....do..........do....	1000 00
	T. M. Pomroy.......do..........do....	1000 00
	David Alden.........do..........do....	700 00
	E. C. Bailey.........do..........do....	500 00
	W. C. Bazin.........do..........do....	700 00
	A. S. Brigham.......do..........do....	639 11
	Charles Brigham.....do..........do....	400 00
	Thomas Campbell.....do..........do....	580 83
	Chas. F. Davenport...do..........do....	600 00
	C. G. Gerrish........do..........do....	400 00
	Chas A. Greene.....do..........do....	700 00
	Samuel Kendall......do..........do....	400 00
	R. K. Ladd, from July 1, '44, to Feb. 15, '45	438 75
	Charles A. Maynard, from July 1, 1844, to June 30, 1845	700 00
	Chas. H. Melcher, from July 1, 1844, to June 30, 1845	500 00
	James Mills, from July 1, '44, to June 30, '45	600 00
	Calvin Rogers.......do..........do....	600 00
	J. H. Walker, from July 1 to Nov. 30, 1844	250 00
	J. N. Brewer, from July 1 to Sept. 15, 1844	125 00
	Ralph Kellogg, from July 1 to July 31, 1844	50 00
	John C. Leach, from July 31 to Aug. 18, '44	26 03
	Edwin Parker, fr. Sept. 9, '44, to June 30 '45	405 14
	Geo. E. Sumner, from July 1, 1844, to May 12, 1845	484 80

POST OFFICES—*Clerks.*

Post Offices.	Names.	Compensation.
Boston, Mass.	George C. Robinson, from October 1, 1844, to June 30, 1845	$350 96
	George Palmer, from Feb. 7 to June 30, 1845	200 00
	Rrancis W. Story, from Jan. 1 to June 30, '45	209 00
	Lester Leland, from April 1 to June 30, 1845	57 50
Buffalo, N. Y.	John J. Fay, fr. July 1, '44, to June 30, '45	1242 58
	Cyrus P. Lee ... do ... do	999 13
	John Lay, jr ... do ... do	981 76
	Jos. E. Haddock, from July 1, 1844, to April 15, 1845	788 48
	L. K. Haddock, fr. July 1, '44, to April 15, '45	773 48
	C. G. Beach ... do ... do	704 38
	Jacob Krettner ... do ... do	443 53
	Lewis Filner, from July 1, '44, to June 30, '45	374 31
	Wm. H. Hecox, fr. April 15 to June 30, 1845	287 23
	George Walker ... do ... do	165 28
	H. Gates ... do ... do	165 28
	C. D. Ferris, from May 6 to June 30, 1845	120 61
	B. B. Colvin, from April 15 to June 30, 1845	96 55
	P. Garmony ... do ... do	60 47
	Jacob Hellvigle, fr. April 15 to May 6, 1845	30 22
Charleston, S. C.	T. W. Bacot, fr. July 1, '44, to June 30, '45	1800 00
	Evan Edwards ... do ... do	1200 00
	Charles L. Edwards .. do ... do	600 00
	T. A. Broughton ... do ... do	600 00
	R. D. Bacot ... do ... do	360 00
	Wm. S. Edwards ... do ... do	255 00
	John Bay, from July 1, '44, to March 31, '45	112 50
	Adam Ford ... do ... do	90 00
	M. W. Bay, from April 1 to June 30, 1845	37 50
	Robert Ferguson ... do ... do	30 00
Chicago, Ill.	C. R. Starkwether, from July 1, 1844, to June 30, 1845	1099 88
	L. G. Tuttle, from July 1, '44, to May 8, '45	626 00
	Alex. Stuart, from July 1, 44, to June 30, '45	739 44
	Wm. H. Adams ... do ... do	949 98
	Henry Wolcott, from July 1, to Oct. 16, 1844	145 00
	B. Larson, from July 1, '44, to June 30, 1845	251 96
	E. G. Stewart, from Oct. 1, '44, to May 8, '45	452 25
	A. Getzler, from Oct. 1 to Dec. 31, 1844, and from April 1 to May 8, 1845	10 50
	Chas. H Larrebee, fr. Jan. 1 to June 30, '45	191 67
	Geo. Dellicker, from April 1 to June 30, 1845	72 22
	F. T. Sherman, from May 21 to June 30, '45	44 44
	E. T. Stewart, from May 7 to June 30, 1845	72 22

POST OFFICES—*Clerks.*

Post Offices.	Names.	Compensation.
Cincinnati, Ohio..	Elam P. Langdon, from July 1, 1844, to June 30, 1845	$1300 00
	J. F. Irwin, from July 1, '44, to June 30, 1845	1300 00
	Solomon Langdon....do..........do....	1050 00
	John W. Punshon...do..........do....	1050 00
	J. B. Ruffin.........do..........do....	630 00
	Thos. P. Taylor, from July 1 to Sept. 30, '44	117 00
	Geo. E. Taylor, fr. July 1, '44, to June 30, '45	573 00
	F. Wiecher.........do..........do....	300 00
	David Gassaway, from Oct. 1, 1844, to June 30, 1845	240 00
	A. L. Burke, from Oct. 1, '44, to June 30, '45	65 37
Cleveland, Ohio..	G. C. Dodge, from July 1, '44, to June 30, '45	445 07
	Wm. Wilson........do..........do....	461 30
Columbia, S. C...	Wm. D. Rice, fr. July 1, '44, to June 30, '45	367 00
Columbus, Ohio..	J. S. Abbott, from July 1, '44, to June 30, '45	993 00
	Samuel Cutler.......do..........do....	464 00
	H. M. Ware.........do..........do....	430 00
	James Ware.........do..........do....	416 98
	William A. Latham..do..........do....	419 66
	Benj. Carpenter......do..........do....	403 61
	J. T. Blain..........do..........do....	425 00
	J. M. Christian.......do..........do....	338 92
	F. Krum, from Oct. 1, 1844, to June 30, 1845	225 00
Columbus, Ga...	J. D. Johnson, fr. July 1, '44, to June 30, '45	1200 00
	W. S. McGiboney, from July 1, 1844, to June 30, 1845	600 00
	Thomas P. Randall, from 1st to 31st July, '44	41 68
	James Hodges, from July 1 to Sept. 30, 1844, and from April 1 to June 30, 1845	120 00
	Edmund T. Randall, from July 1, 1844, to June 30, 1845	458 32
	James P. Hodges, from Oct. 1 to Dec. 31, 1844, and from April 1 to June 30, 1845	185 00
	J R. Porter, from Oct. 1 to Dec. 31, 1844...	5 00
Detroit, Mich....	A. S. Kellogg, fr. July 1, '44, to June 30, '45	1297 31
	M. M. Williams.....do..........do....	988 87
	J. S. Roland, from July 1, '44, to April 20, '45	818 46
	Freeman Norvell, from July 1 to Sept. 30, 1844, and from Jan. 1 to April 20, 1845....	200 00
	Thomas R. Griffith, from July 1 to Dec. 31, 1844, and from 1st to 20th April, 1845....	190 12
	John W. Dailey, from July 1, 1844, to June 30, 1845	361 00

POST OFFICES—*Clerks.*

Post Offices.	Names.	Compensation.
Detroit, Mich......	Dallas Norvell, fr. Oct. 1, '44, to April 20, '45	$180 00
	Charles Richmond, fr. April 21 to June 30, '45	200 00
	Eugene Laible.......do..............do....	71 00
	R. R. Bagg, from April 1 to June 30, 1845...	58 33
Erie, Pa..........	L. H. Haskins, fr. July 1, '44, to June 30, '45	800 00
	J. C. Brown.........do..............do....	500 00
	F. W. S. Bawley, fr. July 1 to Sept. 30, '44	75 00
	W. S. G. Brown, fr. Oct. 1, '44, to June 30, '45	225 00
Harrisburg, Pa...	D. D. Boas, from July 1, '44, to June 30, '45	800 00
	G. Peacock.........do..............do....	750 00
	D. Smith...........do..............do....	625 00
	M. S. Clendenin.......do..............do....	575 00
	James Reedy, fr. July 1, '44, to April 30, '45	416 67
	S. E. Doll, from July 1, '44, to May 31, 1845	325 00
Hartford, Con.....	Jason L. Wolcott, from July 1, 1844, to June 30, 1845................................	750 00
	John R. Pease, fr. July 1, '44, to June 30, '45	750 00
	John S. Williams, fr. July 1, 1844' to March 31, 1845................................	450 00
	Geo. H. Eaton, fr. July 1, '44, to June 30, '45	550 00
	Edwin T. Pease .....do..............do....	500 00
	E. G. Clark.........do..............do....	315 00
Huntsville, Ala...	Wm. A. Nunnelly, fr. April 1 to June 30, '45	137 50
Indianapolis, Ind.	Joshua T. Holt, fr. July 1, '44, to June 30, '45	602 50
	Charles Stephens.....do..............do....	602 50
	Samuel Jenison, from July 1 to Sept. 30, 1844	112 50
	J. S. Willets, from July 1, '44, to June 30, '45	450 00
	John Jenison, from July 1, '44, to Jan. 15, '45	169 25
	D. Maguire, from Oct. 1, '44 to June 30, '45	350 00
	Alexander Grayden, from January 1 to June 30, 1845................................	161 50
Lexington, Ky...	L. T. Marshall, from July 1 to Sept. 30, '44	111 00
	N. B. Barrow, fr. July 1, '44, to June 30, '45	290 00
	Hiram Bassett, fr. Oct. 1, '44, to June 30, '45	408 00
	Thomas K. Bradley, from January 1 to June 30, 1845................................	122 00
Louisville, Ky...	L. T. Maury, fr. July 1, '44, to June 30, '45..	1075 00
	L. S. Mosby.....do..............do......	711 00
	M. H. Maury.....do..............do......	711 00
	John S. Mosby, fr. July 1, '44, to Mar. 31, '45.	536 00
	R. F. Maury, fr. July 1, '44, to June 30, '45.	711 00
	John M. Read.....do..............do......	542 00

POST. OFFICES—*Clerks.*

Post Offices.	Names.	Compensation.
Louisville, Ky...	R. H. L. Woolfolk, fr. July 1, '44, to June 30, '45	$542 00
	L. B. White.......do.............do......	457 90
	J. M. Rhorer, from July 1 to Aug. 12, 1844..	45 00
	J. D. Strasburg, fr. July 1, '44, to June 30, '45.	176 30
	R. M. Mosby, from April 1 to June 30, 1845.	88 00
	G. Mosby........do............do......	88 00
Lowell, Mass....	S. S. Seavy, from July 1, '44, to June 30, '45	600 00
	J. F. Kimball......do............do......	350 00
Macon, Geo......	John L. Tyner, from Oct. 1 to Dec. 31, 1844.	100 00
Memphis, Tenn..	Sam'l M. Gates, fr. July 1, '44, to Mar. 31, '45	450 00
	David Adams, from July 1 to Sept. 30, 1844.	134 00
	John A. Sannoner, from July 1, 1844, to June 30, 1845................................	471 50
	Robert O. Winchester, from Oct. 1, 1844, to June 30, 1845...........................	268 25
	James Richardson, fr. April 1 to June 30, '45.	136 00
Mobile, Ala......	Enoch Everitt, fr. July 1, '44, to June 30, '45.	1400 00
	Nathaniel Moore...do............do......	750 00
	G. Patrick, from July 1 to Nov. 1, 1844.....	200 00
	Samuel Fry, fr. July 1, '44, to June 30, '45..	600 00
	Chas. H. Horton, from Oct. 1, 1844, to June 30, 1845..............................	450 00
Nashville, Tenn..	Wm. Gibson, fr. July 1, '44, to Mar. 31, '45.	420 00
	E. Dibrell, fr. July 1, '44, to June 30, '45....	480 00
	Thos. D. Martin, from July 1, 1844, to Mar. 31, 1845..............................	340 00
	P. M. Sands, fr. July 1, '44, to June 30, '45.	445 00
	John G. Wilson.....do............do......	445 00
	Jas. T. Armstrong, from Jan'y 1 to 30, 1845.	30 00
	Felix R. Cheatham, fr. April 1 to June 30, '45	105 00
	J. A. Cheatham....do............do......	116 22
Natchez, Mi.....	Wm. Wren, fr. July 1 to Sept. 30, 1844, and from Feb'y 9 to June 30, 1845............	374 00
	J. S. Hayward, from July 1 to Aug. 31, 1844	60 00
	Charles Albrecht, from Sept. 1, '44, to Feb'y 9, '45..............................	145 00
	Burress Wren, fr. Oct. 1, '44, to June 30, '45	300 00
Newark, N. J....	T. Mead, fr. July 1, 1844, to June 30, 1845..	500 00
	Sam'l W. Plume, fr. April 1 to June 30, '45..	25 00
N. Bedford, Mass.	Thomas Coggeshall, jr., from July 1, 1844, to June 30, 1845..........................	600 00

POST OFFICES—*Clerks.*

Post Offices.	Names.	Compensation.
New Haven, Ct..	Isaac Jones, fr. July 1, '44, to June 30, '45...	$537 50
	Edward R. Hayes, from July 1, '44, to March 31, 1845..............................	225 00
	Rich'd F. Lyon, from July 1, 1844, to June 30, 1845..............................	187 50
	E. C. Baldwin, from April 1 to June 30, '45..	50 00
New Orleans, La..	A. D. Wooldridge, from July 1, 1844, to June 30, 1845..............................	2000 00
	G. Lafferranderie, from July 1, 1844, to June 30, 1845..............................	1400 00
	V. Wiltz, fr. July 1, '44, to June 30, '45.....	1000 00
	Thos. Monneghan, from July 1, 1844, to May 31, 1845..............................	825 00
	Henry J. Levy, fr. July 1, '44, to June 30, '45	600 00
	L. E. Generelly, from July 1 to Dec. 16, '44.	276 67
	O. De Buys, fr. July 1, '44, to June 30, '45...	480 00
	L. St. Martin......do..............do......	480 00
	J. H. Casson......do..............do......	480 00
	G. L. Nasseur.....do..............do......	435 00
	E. W. Moon, from Oct. 1, '44, to May 31, '45	235 00
	E. Montemat, fr. Oct. 1, '44, to June 30, '45.	270 00
	F. B. Smith, from Nov. 1 to Dec. 16, 1844..	112 50
	P. W. Stone, from June 1 to 30, 1845.......	40 00
New York, N. Y..	W. C. English, fr. July 1, '44, to May 21, '45	1758 34
	W. B. Taylor, fr. July 1, '44, to June 30, '45	1700 01
	Jos. Benedict......do..............do......	1500 01
	Rich'd Senior, fr. July 1, '44, to May 21, '45.	1066 67
	Courter Goodwin, from July 1, 1844, to June 30, 1845..............................	1200 00
	Geo. G. Coffin, from July 1, 1844, to March 31, 1845, and from May 22 to June 30, '45	1033 33
	John H. Hallett, from July 1, 1844, to June 30, 1845..............................	1200 00
	Jas. B. Mower, fr. July 1, '44, to May 31, '45	916 67
	John Short, fr. July 1, '44, to June 30, '45...	900 00
	Wm. C. Burdict, fr. July 1, '44, to May 21, '45	800 00
	Harrison W. Smith, from July 1, '44, to Feb. 28, 1845, and from June 1 to 30, 1845.....	621 66
	M. C. Eaton, fr. July 1, '44, to Feb. 28, '45..	520 00
	J. L. Benedict, from July 1 to Sept. 30, 1844.	200 00
	E. Macomber, fr. July 1, '44, to May 21, '45.	711 10
	W. Stewart, fr. July 1, '44, to June 30, '45 ..	754 15
	F. H. Turk.......do..............do......	699 99
	N. H. Matthews, from July 1, '44, to March 31, 1845..............................	525 00
	N. C. Marselis, fr. July 1, '44, to June 30, '45	699 99
	Thos. Uffington....do..............do......	615 76

POST-OFFICES—*Clerks.*

Post Offices.	Names.	Compensation.
New York, N. Y.	Jos. Dodd, fr. July 1, '44, to June 30, '45....	$600 01
	C. W. Raymond...do............do......	600 01
	James Beck......do............do......	600 01
	John F. Tracy, from July 1 to Nov. 30, 1844	250 00
	John Griffin.......do............do......	225 00
	Henry F. Cox, from July 1, '44, to Feb'y 28, '45, and from June 1 to 30, '45...........	446 67
	Henry S. Brown, from July 1 to Sept. 30, '44	150 00
	Wm. H. Groesbeck, from July 1, '44, to May 21, 1845....................................	458 34
	W. H. Postley, fr. July 1, '44, to June 30, '45	500 01
	Isaac Wood, fr. Aug. 1, '44, to June 30, '45..	541 67
	J. F. Ogden, fr. July 1, '44, to May 31, '45..	366 66
	Wm. Watson.....do............do......	316 66
	H. H. Sandford, fr. Oct. 1, '44, to June 30, '45	437 51
	George Slight......do............do......	205 56
	M. E. Ward, fr. Nov. 1, '44, to May 21, '45	249 80
	Rob't Sargeant, from Oct. 1 to Dec. 31, 1844, and from April 1 to May 21, 1845........	119 68
	John H. Acres, from Oct. 1 to Nov. 30, 1844.	66 66
	S. B. Waller, fr. Dec. 1, '44, to Jan. 31, '45, and from May 22 to June 7, 1845.........	128 34
	H. G. Martin, from Dec. 1, '44, to March 31, '45, and from April 1 to May 31, '45......	300 01
	H. Wilson, from Dec'r 16 to Dec'r 31, 1844, and from April 1 to May 31, 1845........	229 84
	J. P. Nash, from Feb. 1 to June 30, 1845....	250 01
	Jas. H. Billington, fr. Feb. 1 to May 31, '45.	187 01
	Isaac M. Levy, from Feb. 1 to June 30, 1845	193 06
	Benj. B. Brown, fr. March 1 to May 31, 1845	126 39
	Alex. Dearborn, fr. March 1 to March 31, '45	33 33
	A. C. Buxton, from April 1 to May 31, 1845.	188 88
	J. T. Maynard, from April 1 to June 30, '45.	202 67
	Ab'm Welles, from April 1 to May 21, 1845.	69 45
	John S. Williams, fr. April 1 to June 30, '45.	125 01
	Henry Ackerman..do............do......	99 99
	Thos. E. Ketcham, fr. Ap. 1 to May 21, '45.	50 00
	James A. Ostram...do............do......	46 66
	Ab'm Hyatt, from April 1 to June 30, 1845..	83 14
	A. C. McLean.....do............do......	83 14
	S. J. Strong, from May 22 to June 30, 1845..	88 89
	A. Brush.........do............do......	111 11
	A. B. Totten......do............do......	77 77
	Peter McGowen...do............do......	44 44
	Horatio P. Carr....do............do......	66 67
	Wm. F. Clark.....do............do......	100 00
	Chas. B. Battelle...do............do......	66 67
	W. V. Porter, from May 22 to 31, 1845.....	27 78
	Aaron Smarts, from May 22 to June 30, 1845	55 56

POST OFFICES—*Clerks.*

Post Offices.	Names.	Compensation.
New York, N. Y.	Wm. K. Dunshee, fr. May 22 to June 30, '45	$66 67
	Ab'm N. Ellis.....do............do......	55 56
	Chas. H. Wilson, from June 1 to 30, 1845...	15 56
	Wm. Wallace, from June 15 to 30, 1845....	22 22
	A. B. Mead, from May 22 to June 30, 1845..	111.11
	Ab'm G. Crasto, from June 7 to 30, 1845....	36 67
	M. Monson, jr., from May 22 to June 30, '45	222 23
N. York—for the branch office. [The fiscal year for this office is made by law to end on the 3d of June.]	R. Fisher, fr. June 3, '44, to Mar. 3, '45.....	1500 00
	Edward Phillips, from June 3 to Dec. 3, 1844	500 00
	A. Brush, from June 3, 1844, to June 3, 1845	972 23
	DeWitt C. Graham..do............do......	1000 00
	A. Spencer Graham.do............do......	1000 00
	Henry Wilson, from June 3 to Sept. 3, 1844.	200 00
	Seymour J. Strong, fr. June 3, 1844, to June 3, 1845..................................	777 77
	J. T. Maynard, from June 3, 1844, to March 3, 1845..................................	583 33
	A. B. Totten, fr. June 3, '44, to June 3, '45..	725 56
	P. McGowan......do............do......	388 88
	Ward B. Burnett, from June 3 to July 3, '44.	50 00
	E. J. Hyde.......do............do......	50 00
	R. B. Withers.....do............do......	41 67
	Jas. F. Auchincloss.do............do......	41 66
	Henry Linesburg, from June 3, 1844, to Mar. 3, 1845..................................	24 00
	A. C. Graham, from Sept. 3 to Dec. 3, 1844..	200 00
	Henry S. Brown...do............do......	100 00
	C. S. Buxton......do............do......	100 00
	S. B. Waller, from Feb'y 1 to June 3, 1845..	183 34
	Aaron Swarts......do............do......	152 78
	Geo. G. Coffin, from March 3 to June 3, 1845	166 67
	Wm. H. Matthews.do............do......	118 31
	Monson Clark, from May 22 to June 3, 1845	36 16
	A. C. Monson.....do............do......	27 12
	Wm. C. Burdict...do............do......	27 12
NewYork–for city despatch post.	A. M. Greig, from July 1 to Dec. 1, 1844....	416 66
	W. Seymour, fr. July 1, '44, to May 21, '45.	916 67
	J. Lawrence, fr. July 1, '44, to June 30, '45..	322 62
	Edw'd Lister......do............do......	318 00
	James King.......do............do......	318 00
	W. Jas. Frost .....do............do......	318 00
	Samuel Lewis .....do............do......	322 63
	Moses E. Ward, from July 1 to Nov. 1, 1844	108 00
	J. H. Schenk, fr. July 1, '44, to June 30, '45.	318 00
	Charles Brown.....do............do......	318 00
	Chas. D. Klyn.....do............do......	322 62
	Jas. B. Cisco......do............do......	318 00

POST OFFICES—*Clerks.*

Post Offices.	Names.	Compensation.
N. York—for city despatch post.	A. Heister, fr. July 1, '44, to June 30, '45...	$318 00
	Russell White.....do............do......	318 00
	A. C. McLean, fr. July 1, '44, to Mar. 31, '45	239 00
	Henry Depuy, fr. July 1, '44, to June 30, '45	326 17
	Geo. D. Atkinson..do............do......	288 00
	Ab'm Storms, from July 1 to 31, 1844, and from May 22 to June 30, 1845...........	64 00
	C. R. V. Lee, for one month in 1st quarter '45	24 00
Norfolk, Va.....	R. B. B. Timberlake, from July 1, 1844, to June 30, 1845......................	450 00
	A. W. Martin, fr. July 1, '44, to May 31, '45	412 50
	A. M. Vaughan, fr. July 15, '44, to Mar. 31, '45	213 33
	Alex'r Galt, jr., from June 1 to 30, 1845....	25 00
Petersburg, Va...	Wm. E. Bass, fr. July 1, '44, to June 30, '45.	700 00
	John C. Tyler.....do............do......	600 00
	Edward Lorraine...do............do......	400 00
Philadelphia, Pa..	A. S. Welsh, from July 1 to 31, 1844....	30 00
	Andrew J. Binney .do............do......	30 00
	J. H. Montgomery, fr. July 1 to Aug. 14, '44	95 00
	Wm. Sagee, from July 1 to August 31, 1844.	110 00
	Wm. Hines........do............do......	70 00
	O. C. Montgomery, fr. July 1 to Sept. 15, '44	212 50
	J. Wright, from Sept. 1, '44, to May 20, '45.	315 00
	B. F. Binns, from August 1 to Oct. 5, 1844..	98 00
	S. L. Harper, fr. Aug. 1, '44, to June 30, '45.	715 00
	E. Haveland, fr. Sept. 1, '44, to May 8, '45..	392 00
	R. S. Moore, fr. Sept. 1, '44, to Feb. 1, '45..	225 00
	J. M. Clark, fr. Sept. 16, '44, to June 30, '45.	427 50
	W. J. P. White, fr. July 1, '44, to June 30, '45	1500 00
	Sam'l M. White...do............do......	900 00
	John P. Rees......do............do......	900 00
	Alex'r Riddell.....do............do......	660 00
	Samuel P. Rutter...do............do......	660 00
	W. Sterne.........do............do......	625 00
	C. H. Ervine......do............do......	545 00
	C. D. Howell......do............do......	545 00
	Samuel W. Bell....do............do......	530 00
	H. K. Bennett, fr. July 1, '44, to Mar. 12, '45	380 00
	W. Rushton, jr., fr. July 1, '44, to June 30, '45	560 00
	H. G. Stelwagon...do............do......	540 00
	Charles Milnor, from July 1 to Dec. 31, 1844	270 00
	David Roberts, fr. July 1, '44, to June 30, '45	540 00
	Jos. S. Stimson....do............do......	480 00
	Nicholas Murphy..do............do......	480 00
	J. T. James.......do............do......	540 00
	F. F. Clifton......do............do......	630 00
	Sam'l A. Black, fr. Oct. 3, '44, to June 30, '45	401 00

POST OFFICES—*Clerks.*

Post Offices.	Names.	Compensation.
Philadelphia, Pa..	Lewis Plitt, from Feb. 1 to June 30, 1845..	$225 00
	John Brown........do.............do......	200 00
	Thos. F. Goodwin, from March 1 to 31, 1845	25 00
	Henry T. Titus, from April 16 to May 8, '45	33 00
	Jos. Lescure, from May 21 to June 30, 1845.	55 00
	Peter Rambo, from May 23 to June 24, 1845.	46 50
	Thos. Brown, from May 21 to June 30, 1845.	47 00
Pittsburg, Pa	John Bigler, from July 1, '44, to Feb. 28, '45.	666 66
	Rob't Anderson, fr. July 1, '44, to June 30, '45	600 00
	Wm. M. Shinn....do.............do......	700 00
	H. N. Thompson..do.............do......	529 33
	Henry Abel.......do.............do......	500 00
	John D. Scully ....do.............do......	529 33
	John P. Glass, from March 1 to June 30, '45.	166 66
Portland, Me....	R. W. Lincoln, fr. July 1, '44, to June 30, '45	1015 50
	Geo. Coe ....do.............do......	895 17
	T. G. Mitchel .....do.............do......	710 83
	Wm. H. Dyer, fr. July 1, '44, to April 15, '45	644 97
	Stillman Barber, from July 1 to Sept. 30, '44.	55 00
	Henry W. Ripley, fr. Jan. 1 to April 15, '45.	22 00
	Jos. Bailey, from April 16 to June 30, 1845..	113 50
	John Swett.........do.............do......	113 50
	John H. Short.....do.............do......	113 50
	John Mahan, from June 1 to 30, 1845.......	78 33
Portsmouth, N.H.	Alfred M. Beck, fr. April 27 to June 30, 1845	88 80
	Henry T. Curtis, fr. April 27 to June 30, 1845	64 00
	N. H. Moses, from May 1 to June 30, 1845 .	10 00
Providence, R. I..	Rob't H. Barton, fr. July 1, '44, to June 30, '45	550 00
	Dexter B. Lewis...do.............do......	412 48
	A. H. Burroughs, from July 1 to Dec. 31, '44	200 00
	H. E. Branch, fr. July 1, '44, to March 31, '45	281 25
	Chas. F. Goodwin, from July 1, 1844, to June 30, 1845................................	367 01
	J. F. Mallett, from Jan. 1 to March 31, 1845.	100 00
	F. C. Gardner, from April 7 to June 30, 1845	105 10
	Jas. N. Ashley, from April 10 to June 30, '45.	73 24
Raleigh, N. C....	Thos. J. Patrick, from July 1 to Dec. 31, '44.	400 00
	J. F. Jordon, fr. July 1, '44, to April 19, '45.	750 00
	John G. Williams, fr. Jan. 1 to April 19, '45.	260 00
Richmond, Va...	Wm. A. Davis, fr. July 1, '44, to June 30, '45	999 99
	A. Carpenter, from July 1 to Nov. 7, 1844...	212 50
	C. B. Lucke, fr. July 16, '44, to June 30, '45.	482 62
	Jas. M. Wayt, fr. July 1, '44, to June 30, '45.	405 54

POST OFFICES—*Clerks.*

Post Offices.	Names.	Compensation.
Richmond, Va....	Fred'k Walden, fr. July 1, '44, to Mar. 22, '45.	$87 25
	J. E. Peirce, fr. Nov. 7, '44, to March 31, '45.	237 50
	B. Peyton, from March 22 to March 31, 1845	2 75
	Wm. J. Bigger, from April 1 to June 30, 1845	70 85
	R. R. Pierce.......do............do......	68 06
	Wm. Pride........do............do......	30 00
Rochester, N. Y..	A. K. Amsden, fr. July 1, '44, to June 30, '45.	600 00
	J. Amsden ....do............do......	300 00
	C. T. Benjamin....do............do......	275 00
	R. B. Paine, from July 1 to Sept. 30, 1845...	9 00
	H. S. Allis, from Oct. 1, '44, to June 30, '45.	185 00
St. Louis, Mo....	Jas. R. Sprigg, fr. July 1, '44, to June 30, '45	1200 00
	A. D. Jacoby......do............do......	900 00
	S. Dagenhard......do............do......	800 00
	Wm. H. Timberlake, from July 1, 1844, to Feb. 6, 1845..........................	450 00
	Edw'd Milligan, fr. July 1, '44, to June 30, '45	775 00
	John B. Taylor....do............do......	600 00
	R. H. Bowlin, fr. Aug. 19, '44, to June 30, '45	520 00
	A. H. Caldwell, from July 4 to Sept. 30, 1844	75 00
	L. D. Walton, from July 1 to 3, 1844.......	5 00
	Edwin Price, from July 1 to Oct. 20, 1844, and from March 25 to 31, 1845...............	193 33
	F. W. Albesworth, from July 1, 1844, to June 30, 1845..............................	195 00
	Thos. E. Jones, fr. Oct. 21, '44, to June 30, '45	441 67
	J. C. Dinnies, from Jan. 1 to June 30, 1845..	262 66
Savannah, Ga....	John G. Doon, fr. July 1, '44, to June 30, '45	1200 00
	N. C. Mills........do............do......	600 00
	S. C. Catherwood..do............do......	500 00
Toledo, Ohio	T. C. Everts, fr. July 1, '44, to June 30, '45 .	450 00
	G. D. Palmer, fr. July 1, '44, to March 9, '45	287 37
	C. S. Whiting, fr. Oct. 15, '44, to June 30, '45	170 00
	H. H. Dodd, from March 7 to 31, 1845.....	17 84
Troy, N. Y......	A. W. Winne, fr. July 1, '44, to June 30, '45	450 00
	A. McConihe......do............do......	400 00
	J. E. Root........do............do......	500 00
	S. B. Jones, from Jan. 1 to June 30, 1845....	130 00
Utica, N. Y......	J. B. Cushman, fr. July 1, '44, to June 30, '45	400 00
	T. K. Church .....do............do......	300 00
	H. F. Makepeace..do............do......	216 00
Vicksburg, Miss.	B. Hardaway, fr. July 1, '44, to June 30, '45.	600 00

POST OFFICES—*Clerks.*

Post Offices.	Names.	Compensation.
Vicksburg, Miss..	Wm. G. Moore, fr. July 1, '44, to June 30, '45	$500 00
Worcester, Mass.	A. L. Harrington, fr. Jan. 1 to June 30, 1845	250 00
	Chas. H. Hill, from March 14 to 31, 1845...	31 93
	John M. M. Crandall, from Jan. 1 to March 31, 1845..............................	33 75
	John H. Robinson, fr. April 1 to June 30, '45	37 50
Washington, D.C.	Geo. Sweeny, fr. July 1, '44, to March 31, '45	1350 00
	Lambert Tree, fr. July 1, '44, to June 30, '45	1600 00
	Jas. A. Kennedy...do............do......	1325 00
	Richard Lay ......do............do......	1300 00
	W. Brooke Jones..do............do......	1200 00
	Thos. L. Noyes....do............do......	1100 00
	Cornelius Cox.....do............do......	1125 00
	Michael P. Callan..do............do......	1025 00
	Wm. T. Jones.....do............do......	1000 00
	Josiah Goodrich...do............do......	1000 00
	Sam'l Crown, fr. July 1, '44, to April 20, '45.	442 72
	John H. Tucker, fr. July 1, '44, to June 30, '45	550 00
	Jas Cryer.........do............do......	550 00
	John E. Neall, fr. July 1, '44, to April 20, '45	442 72
	John E. Kendall, fr. April 1 to June 30, 1845	450 00
	John McLean Gardner, from May 13 to June 30, 1845............................	134 62
	Josiah W. Hicks, from June 16 to 30, 1845	41 20
	Patrick Sweney, fr. April 21 to June 30, 1845	107 28
	Johnson Simonds..do............do......	107 28
Wheeling, Va ...	L. S. Delaplain, fr. July 1, '44, to June 30, '45	776 18
	Chas. J. Love .....do............do......	776 18
	J. B. B. Hale, fr. July 1, '44, to Jan. 27, '45.	370 21
	John Howell......do............do......	323 92
	Wm. A. Moyston, from July 1, 1844, to June 30, 1845..........................	510 71
	N. L. Dorsey, fr. July 1, '44, to Feb. 25, '45.	333 85
	Geo. Corry, from July 1, '44, to June 30, '45	406 45
	Alex'r C. Bier, from Feb. 22 to June 30, 1845	182 35
	Wm. A. Isett, from Jan. 28 to June 30, 1845.	273 99
	J. N. Ellmaker, from April 1 to June 30, 1845	104 02

POST OFFICE DEPARTMENT.—*Contractors.*

Compensation of Contractors for carrying the Mail for the year ending 30th of June, 1845.

Contractors.	No. of Route.	Contract pay per annum.	Additional allowances.	Reduction.	Total amount accrued.	Remarks.
MAINE.						
Hiram C. Abbott	17	$178	....	....	$178	
........Do	29	325	....	....	325	
........Do	109	63	....	$14	49	
Benjamin Adams	39	174	....	....	174	
Seth Beals, jr.	46	150	....	....	150	
Thomas Beede, jr	84	750	....	....	750	
*William Bennett	62	293	....	....	146 50	*To the 31st Dec'r, 1844.
Caleb Billings	35	150	....	....	150	
........Do	36	800	....	....	800	
........Do	50	1240	....	....	1240	
Buckmore & Hale	59	400	....	....	400	
........Do	60	4200	....	....	4200	
Wm. Burbank	76	30	....	....	30	
*Geo. W. Brown	62	293	....	....	146 50	*From 1st January, 1845.
Henry Carver	68	374	....	....	374	
Joseph Cate	48	48	....	....	48	
Noah Chase, jr.	67	119	....	....	119	
Columbus Cooper	53	220	....	....	220	
........Do	55	400	....	....	400	
Calvin Conant	83	99	....	....	99	
Copeland & O'Brien	70	2700	....	....	2700	
........Do	73	3000	....	....	3000	

CONTRACTORS.

Contractors.	No. of Route.	Contract pay per annum.	Additional allowances.	Reduction.	Total amount accrued.	Remarks.
John Copeland	71	$65	....	....	$65	
Thos. I. Cox	15	500	....	....	500	
Alx. Crawford	40	800	....	....	800	
John Crocker	101	1171	....	....	1171	
Robert Crosby	22	175	....	....	175	
........Do	23	38	....	....	38	
Jacob E. Davis	99	213	....	....	213	
Moses Donnell	111	12	....	....	12	
Henry Dow	78	250	....	....	250	
Parker G. Eaton	110	40	....	....	40	
Arthur Farnsworth	114	52	....	....	52	
Amos Felch, jr	100	200	....	....	200	
Timothy E. Fogg	16	398	....	....	398	
John D. Folsom	57	55	....	....	55	
Benjamin O. Foster	37	229	....	....	229	
........Do	69	148	....	....	148	
........Do	79	148	....	....	148	
........Do	122	49	....	....	49	
Foster & Cooper	52	4400	....	....	4400	
Sol. M. Foster	56	604	....	....	604	
........Do	119	25	....	....	25	
Asa Gould	18	100	....	....	100	
Joseph Gray	58	140	....	....	140	
Geo. W. Hall	45	99 50	....	....	99 50	
David Haynes	51	225	....	....	225	
Thomas Herrick	44	122	....	39	83	

John Hill	96	96			96
Jesse Hilton	26	68			68
Philip Hor	95	100			100
Hawley A. Keay	105	49			49
Do	107	900			900
Kimball & Emerson	106	1400		646	754
J. W. Knowlton	74	95			95
A. & L. Leavitt	13	70	29	47	52
Edward Little	7	1200		290	910
Do	85	350		60	290
Philip C. Mason	93	125			125
Edward Mason	2	440			440
Abraham Milliken	127	75			75
Joseph Moore	112	16			16
David Merrill	128	39			39
Israel B. Norcross	43	675			675
Philip Norris	77	220			220
James Nowland	54	492			492
Peter G. Noyes	124	300			300
Ordway & Palmer	42	600			600
Eleazar Packard	120	125			125
Benj. C. Paine	30	30			30
Paine & Rice	116	375			375
P. P. Pearson	38	1000			1000
Cyrus Pierce	8	94			94
V. D. Pinkham	11	1290			1290
Do	12	895			895
Do	81	222			222
Portland, Saco, and Portsmouth Railroad Co	86	5000			5000
John Quimby	82	248	113	135	226
A. C. Richardson	25	80	10		90

CONTRACTORS.

Contractors.	No. of route.	Contract pay per annum.	Additional allowances.	Reduction.	Total amount accrued.	Remarks.
Rich'd Richardson	61	$219	....	....	$219	
Timothy Robinson	31	96	....	....	96	
W. E. Robinson	66	175	....	....	175	
*Thomas Rowe	75	185	....	....	138 75	*To the 31st March, 1845.
*Alexander Rowe	75	185	....	....	46 25	*From 1st April, 1845.
E. H. Scribner	24	1950	44	1033	961	
David Shaw	6	800	....	....	800	
Joseph Shaw	34	1200	....	....	1200	
Shaw & Corser	4	4000	....	....	4000	
Do	5	600	....	....	600	
Allen Smith	19	118	....	....	118	
Do	20	124	....	....	124	
Smith & Robinson	33	800	....	....	800	
Do	41	900	....	....	900	
Do	63	695	....	....	695	
Arch'd Smith, jr.	102	45	....	....	45	
Wm. B. Smith	87	1700	....	896	804	
John Smith	88	1125	*8 92	....	1133 92	*To 28th July, '44, and fr. 15th Jan'y, '45.
Wm. N. Springer	80	48	....	....	48	
Geo. W. Stanley	1	4250	....	....	4250	
Do	10	600	....	....	600	
F. V. Stewart	3	650	....	....	650	
Do	9	900	....	....	900	
Calvin Stone	14	700	....	....	700	
Do	98	140	12	....	152	
Nicholas Thomas	64	146	....	....	146	

Chas. Thompson	129	100	....	....	100
S. M. Thompson	72	65	....	....	65
James S. Tobey	108	70	....	....	70
Willard Treworgy	65	425	....	....	425
James R. Tupper	113	168	....	....	168
Nath'l M. Towle	126	250	....	....	250
G. G. W[illegible]e	90	900	....	....	900
........Do	92	200	....	....	200
........Do	94	260	....	....	260
Paul Webber	103	80	....	....	80
........Do	104	78	....	....	78
A. P. Welcom	21	30	....	....	30
Benj. Whitten	49	69	....	....	69
Whittier & Maxfield	89	750	....	....	750
John H. Wilson	47	143	....	....	143
Total for Maine	......	$68872 50	$466 92	$3160	$64701 42
NEW HAMPSHIRE.					
Abbott & Thorn	210	$2495	....	....	$2495
Nathan Bailey	203	1500	....	....	1500
Fletcher J. Bean	255	85	....	9	76
........Do	264	87	....	....	87
Jos. C. Bean	207	174	....	12	162
........Do	209	139	....	....	139
........Do	243	750	$25	....	775
Cephas Brackett	252	484	....	....	484
........Do	257	618	....	....	618
James M. Blake	269	88	....	....	88
Paltiah Brown	215	525	....	....	525

CONTRACTORS.

Contractors.	No. of Route.	Contract pay per annum.	Additional allowances.	Reduction.	Total amount accrued.	Remarks.
Jacob Butler	231	$130	....	....	$130	
Nathan S. Chandler	217	99 50	$150 50	$93	157	
Chandler & Colby	213	3377	....	....	3377	
Chapin, Skinner & Co	256	2490	18	480	2028	
Benjamin Clark	258	58	....	37	21	
John Coe	253	160	....	....	160	
John Coffin	267	45	....	....	45	
Joseph Dewey	230	915	110	635 72	389 28	
Eliphalet Emerson	245	105	10	....	115	
J. B. French	202	495	....	176	319	
........Do	222	1195	....	....	1195	
Gass, Chandler & Co	201	3539	....	581	2958	
John Gibson	223	100	....	....	100	
........Do.	233	3600	....	....	3600	
Hale & Colman	204	1900	....	350	1550	
Edward Hall	220	100	....	9	91	
John Hawes	259	97	....	....	97	
Solomon Heath	251	200	....	....	200	
Philip Hor	262	300	....	....	300	
Hawley A. Keay	208	175	28	147	56	
Caleb Little	265	65	....	....	65	
Morse & Langdon	211	2535	....	....	2535	
........Do.	212	2820	....	....	2820	
Morse & Hutchins	218	495	....	....	495	
Pendexter & Abbott	246	126	....	....	126	
Geo. Pendexter	263	84	28	28	84	

Elias Pinkham	270	144	....	....	144
Thomas J. Plumer	249	65	....	....	65
Plummer & Langdon	238	1566	....	957	609
Hiram Phelps	244	1100	....	....	1100
John H. Priest	225	200	....	....	200
........Do.	268	130	....	....	130
Eliphalet Richards, jr	274	94	....	....	94
John S. Shannon	208a	87 50	....	....	87 50
Skinner & Currier	221	450	....	....	450
Wm. B. Smith	206	800	....	....	800
Thomas A. Staples	234	1900	....	....	1900
........Do.	235	195	....	....	195
P. R. Stephens	228	74	....	....	74
Wm. Sawyer	242	1000	....	....	1000
Enos Tewkesbury	237	84	....	....	84
Thorn, Abbott & Co.	254	1198	....	....	1198
Whitcom Tirrell	261	325	....	....	325
Mical Tubbs	205	1175	....	....	1175
John I. Tuttle	273	52	....	....	52
Nathan Walker	227	100	....	36	64
Wm. Walker, jr	214	790	....	....	790
Franklin Wallace	216	496	....	....	496
James Whipple	224	1400	....	....	1400
Samuel Whittier	250	95	....	....	95
Zenas Whittier	219	175	....	....	175
........Do.	239	125	13	....	138
........Do.	240	80	....	....	80
........Do.	247	175	....	....	175
Total for New Hampshire		$46226	$382 50	$3996 72	$42611 78

CONTRACTORS.

Contractors.	No. of Route.	Contract pay per annum.	Additional allowances.	Reduction.	Total amount accrued.	Remarks.
VERMONT.						
Giles S. Alcock	352	$149			$149	
Bial Boynton	312	400			400	
Hamilton Babcock	326	566			566	
Otis Bardwell & Co.	342	3450	$35		3485	
Otis Bardwell	356	1075			1075	
Do	357	263			263	
Do	360	200			200	
Barker & Hyde	346	1200			1200	
Andrew Blodgett	328	150			150	
Blodgett & Barker	301	4500		1094	3406	
Cephas Brackett	331	634			634	
S. H. Bridge	359	2000			2000	
Rufus Cady	324	75			75	
Enoch Carleton, jr.	314	725			725	
Chapin, Skinner & Co.	350	5500	165	785	4880	
E. B. Chase	329	124			124	
Wm. Childs	361	200			200	
Cottrill & Babbitt	309	716			716	
Cottrill & Lamb	307	2950		421	2529	
Tabor Denell	317	274		24	250	
J. B. Downer	306	500			500	
Do	314a	400			400	
J. B. Danforth	319	125			125	
Do	320	124			124	

........Do...........	321	123	....	....	123
Lowell Farr...........	358	750	....	....	750
Field, Bardwell & Co.	343	785	....	....	785
Alonzo Field	305	943	....	....	943
........Do...........	327	119	....	....	119
........Do...........	327*a*	375	....	....	375
Harry Hathaway	322	91	....	....	91
Isaac N. Hall..........	332	118	....	....	118
J. F. Hawks...........	355	120	....	....	120
Hyde & Hyde..........	347	1350	....	....	1350
........Do...........	349	1000	....	....	1000
James H. Hooker.......	340	1200	....	....	1200
Josephus Johnson.......	351	275	....	....	275
Johnson, Hyde & Co.....	311	4000	....	571	3429
David Kirkaldie	345	68	....	....	68
........Do...........	348	200	....	....	200
Simeon Leland..........	366	100	....	....	100
Matthews & Wilder......	308	251	48	....	299
Elihu Norton...........	302	1200	....	....	1200
........Do...........	335	242	125	....	367
Wm. Randall...........	315	261	....	....	261
Clark Rawson..........	344	165	....	....	165
Geo. B. Reynolds.......	341	186	....	....	186
Robinson & Stinehouse ...	316	1187	....	169	1018
L. A. Russell..........	304	598	....	....	598
........Do...........	330	365	....	....	365
Rufus Richardson.......	338	353	....	....	353
Dexter Samson	339	84	....	....	84
Horatio Sargent.........	333	1462 50	....	....	1462 50
........Do...........	334	1468 50	....	....	1468 50
Smith & Stiles..........	303	1075	....	169	906
David Taylor...........	354	1200	....	....	1200

CONTRACTORS.

Contractors.	No. of Route.	Contract pay per annum.	Additional allowances.	Reduction.	Total amount accrued.	Remarks.
Joseph Tillison	323	$124	....	$31	$93	
J. Tinkham, jr.	336	60	....	....	60	
G. W. Tabor	365	175	....	....	175	
D. R. Wallace	310	119	....	....	119	
Henry Weed	313	390	$13	....	403	
James Whipple	353	1200	....	....	1200	
John T. Wiggin	337	300	....	25	275	
John M. Wilcox	364	60	....	*8	52	*From 6th February, 1845.
Total for Vermont	......	$50443	$386	$3297	$47532	
MASSACHUSETTS.						
D. M. Adams	464	150			150	
Wm. H. Adams	489	575	....	....	575	
Thomas Adams	429	624	....	....	624	
John Balch, jr	532	200	....	....	200	
John Ballou	458	550	....	....	550	
Otis Bardwell	459	584	....	344	240	
Billings & Marshall	407	2900	*364 03	†676 50	2587 53	*$47 31 fr. 20th July, '44; $248 64 fr. 2d Sept. '44; and $68 08 for two months extra pay on reductions.—†$376 50 fr. 20th July, '44.
Nathl. Blake	419	600	400	....	1000	

L. B. Bliss	510	50	....	....	50	
W. E. Boise	467	528	....	105	423	
........Do	468	100	....	....	100	
Boise & Masters	466	312	....	169	143	
Boston & Lowell R. R. Co.	404	3343	257	....	3600	
" Providence " "	418	7006	....	....	7006	
" Maine " "	402	5743	226	....	5969	
" Worcester " "	411	8500	*200	....	8700	*For express trains with British mails.
Boyden & Howard	504	950	....	....	950	
Samuel W. Carter	403	500	....	....	500	
Chapin & Damon	455	300	....	....	300	
Chapin, Skinner & Co.	471	2425	206	....	2631	
........Do	472	3000	....	428	2572	
Jason, Clapp & Co.	463	500	150	....	650	
Ira Cheney	525	350	*12 89	*21 34	341 55	*From 21st Jan'y, '45.
James H. Clapp	477	940	16 50	....	956 50	
........Do	508	490	....	....	490	
Charles G. Coffin	505	3000	....	....	3000	
Jeremiah Colman	434	525	....	....	525	
........Do	511	50	....	....	50	
Jephthah Conant	409	347	....	....	347	
Crocker & Sears	495	250	....	....	250	
........Do	496	325	....	....	325	
........Do	499	378	....	....	378	
........Do	501	195	....	....	195	
Beriah Curtis	438	522	....	....	522	
*James D. Curtis	461	300	....	....	116 67	*From 10th Feb'y, '45.
Hiram Dexter	503	98	....	....	98	
Braddock Dimmick	502	450	....	....	450	
Geo. Drew & Co.	421	2700	....	....	2700	
Drew & Gardner	421a	400	....	....	400	
John P. Dunklee	423	150	....	....	150	

CONTRACTORS.

Contractors.	No. of Route.	Contract pay per annum.	Additional allowances.	Reduction.	Total amount accrued.	Remarks.
Eastern Rail Road Comp'y	401	$10525		$456 48	$10068 52	
Eliphalet Edson	498	370			370	
Wm. F. Fales	412	800		320	480	
*Lowell Farr	435	1500			1125	*To 31st March, 1845.
Hamilton Fay	478	145			145	
Edson Fessenden	462	1200			1200	
Luke Fletcher	512	50			50	
J. B. French	405	750			750	
*Elias Fuller	416	200			194 02	*From 12th July, 1845.
*Gass & Chandler	483	944	†78 66		117 14	*To the 15th July, '44. †Month's ext. pay.
S. H. Gifford	515	50			50	
Gipson & Hammond	*526	120	†10		15 88	*To the 18th July, '44. †Month's ext. pay.
Benjamin Hale	430	250			250	
Do	431	500			500	
Do	433	800			800	
Sam'l A. Hartshorn	474	483			483	
Do	519	356			356	
P. T. Haskell	449	195		60	135	
Wm. Hatch	444	202			202	
Wm. Henry	454	100			100	
Hewins & Davis	497	900			900	
Eli Hinckley	494	448			448	
Simeon Higgins	500	394			394	
Parker Jones	422	1380			1380	
Rufus B. Kinsley	484	350			350	
Do	485	1800			1800	

........Do	507	1200	170	....	1370	
*S. B. Kellogg	536	200	....	....	85	*From 28th January, 1845.
Isaac Lane, jr.	488	984	300	492	792	
........Do	492	500	....	....	500	
David Long, jr	456	1250	*25 50	†129 20	1146 30	*Month's ext. pay. †From 29th Jan., '45.
J. W. Lowe	427	500	....	....	500	
*W. L. Lewis	524	150	....	....	75	*From 1st January, 1845.
H. S. Mansfield	447	1100	....	....	1100	
Joseph Miller	414	750	75	....	825	
Leonard Mitchell	493	625	....	....	625	
*Wm. Marvel, 2d	535	250	....	....	238 45	*From 18th July, 1844.
New Bedford & Taunton Railroad Company	486	2100	....	....	2100	
C. W. Norton	465	630	....	157	473	
S. A. Orr	491	600	400	....	1000	
Parker & Stevens	533	200	....	....	200	
*Otis N. Pond	524	150	....	....	75	*To 31st December, 1844.
Blake Parker	415	800	50	....	850	
A. H. Pease	520	825	....	....	825	
........Do	534	150	....	....	150	
Henry Penniman	446	550	....	....	550	
........Do	514	200	....	....	200	
S. & S. H. Phelps	476	700	600	....	1300	
S. H. Phelps	522	300	....	....	300	
........Do	523	200	....	....	200	
Mason Pierce	417	200	....	....	200	
Aransford Rhoades	460	115	....	....	115	
Joseph Rice	457	1250	*37 25	†189 98	1097 27	*Month's ext. pay. †From 28th Jan., '45.
J. B. Savory	428	550	75	....	625	
J. H. Sherman	530	60	....	....	60	
*Smith & Miller	461	650	†54 16	....	444 16	†Month's ext. pay. *To 5th Feb., '45.
Thos. A. Staples	406	2500	1329	....	3829	

CONTRACTORS.

Contractors.	No. of Route.	Contract pay per annum.	Additional allowances.	Reduction.	Total amount accrued.	Remarks.
Thomas A. Staples	436	$560		$154	$406	
Do	437	260			260	
Do	439	1050			1050	
Do	470	200			200	
*Spencer & Kingsley	435	1500			375	*From 1st April, 1845.
Taunton Branch R. R. Co.	481	1500			1500	
R. L. Thatcher	506	850		131	719	
Thayer & Billings	413	475			475	
Israel Tisdale, jr.	482	1000			1000	
Ginery Twichell	440	1375			1375	
Do	450	600			600	
Twichell, Billings & Co.	408	2375	*31 25	†355 64	2050 61	*Month's ext. pay. †From 20th July, '44.
Twichell, Foster & Co.	441	1450	600		2050	
J. M. Tuttle	452	468			468	
Do	453	394			394	
Wm. Walker, jr.	432	195			195	
Western Railroad Co.	443	8250			8250	
Do	518	10000			10000	
Willard, Haynes & Co.	424	200			200	
Do	425	200			200	
Israel Wilds	451	96	8		104	
I. S. Witherbee	410	844			844	
Total for Massachusetts		$129803 00	$5676 24	$4189 14	$128044 60	

RHODE ISLAND.						
Jesse Babcock	602	400	....	....	400	
........Do	611	350	....	....	350	
George Brown	609	560	....	....	560	
........Do	616	46	....	....	46	
P. C. Childs	608	400	200	....	600	
Joseph Clark	613	40	....	....	40	
57* *John Chadwick	601	1000	....	....	250	*From 1st April, 1845.
*Isaac Fish	601	1000	....	....	750	*To 31st March, 1845.
Fish & Eaton	605	650	....	....	650	
H. S. Mansfield	617	250	....	....	250	
Pomeroy & Goodwin, jr	606	800	....	....	800	
........Do	607	775	....	....	775	
Amasa Rockwell	604	775	....	....	775	
Thomas Rose	610	115	....	....	115	
George Scott	612	250	....	....	250	
*Wetherell & Bennett	620	150	....	....	134 92	*From 7th August, 1844.
Total for Rhode Island	......	$7561 00	$200 00	....	$6745 92	
CONNECTICUT.						
Hiram Barnes	669	$700	....	$437 48	$262 52	
........Do	707	500	400	550	350	
George Bates	705	248	....	....	248	
D. S. Beattys	706	200	....	....	200	
Boise, Chapman & Co	663	584	....	....	584	
........Do	664	756	....	....	756	
Boise & Griffin	694	182	....	....	182	
Edward Button	654	1000	....	....	1000	

CONTRACTORS.

Contractors.	No. of Route.	Contract pay per annum.	Additional allowances.	Reduction.	Total amount accrued.	Remarks.
*Isaac Butler	697*	$250			$62 50	*To 30th September, 1844.
Wm. Bryant	667	369			369	
Bradley Burr	675	4550			4550	
Edward P. Camp	670	675		$155	520	
Do	673	1250	$500	437	1313	
Wm. Y. Chamberlain	700	350			350	
C. W. Chapin	661	1560			1560	
Do	662	2340		334	2006	
P. C. Child	658a	500			500	
Do	724	175			175	
Royal Clark	704	200			200	
Gideon Close	712	79			79	
Demas Coe	667a	170			170	
Douglass & Bacon	653	1000			1000	
Clarence Dyer	693	300	20	220	100	
Edson Fessenden	666	2475	*135 75	513	2097 75	*$42 75 for month's extra pay.
James Goodwin, jr	659	1400	837	250	1987	
Do	660	1057			1057	
Do	668	1250	773 48	480	1543 48	
Hartford & New Haven Railroad Company	651	5400	919		6319	
Lucius Hebbard	677	275			275	
Housatonic Railroad Co.	702	3945			3945	
Alvin D. Hull	672	198		19	179	
Wm. Huntington	689	75	*41 70		116 70	*$4 22 of this from 30th Nov., 1844.
Wm. Jeudewine	714	800			800	

E. F. Moseley	685	1200		300	900	
Norwich & Worc'r R. R. Co	684	4000	*2277 01		6277 01	*$17 70 to 1st Sept., '44—$1,969 55 from 9th Aug., '44, and $289 76 for express trains with British mails.
Richard Osborne	708	280			280	
Charles Patrick	711	150	75		225	
E. F. Peck	680	35			35	
H. C. Peckham	691	50			50	
Pendleton & Cottrell	683	100	36		136	
Do	686	500			500	
Pomeroy & Goodwin, jr.	655	1300			1300	
Do	656	2000			2000	
J. H. Raymond	694	138	69		207	
Amasa Rockwell	681	183	267		450	
Do	682	200			200	
A. N. Rowley	678	300			300	
*Sylvester Spencer	697	250			187 50	*From 1st October, 1844.
L. G. Sherman	699a	145			145	
Sturgess Sillick	709	85			85	
Lucius Skinner	665	240			240	
A. B. Spencer	676	424			424	
Abiel Stark, 2d	688	95			95	
Vernon Stiles	690	400	42		442	
Do	726	400			400	
John Swathel	652	590	590		1180	
Do	679	245		35	210	
Turchell, Johnson & Co.	727	1200			1200	
David Walker	713	90			90	
A. O. Wilcox	671	690			690	
Total for Connecticut		$50103 00	$6982 94	$3730 48	$53105 46	

CONTRACTORS.

Contractors.	No. of Route.	Contract pay per annum.	Additional allowances.	Reduction.	Total amount accrued.	Remarks.
NEW YORK.						
John Algyer	982	$309			$309	
Andrew Armstrong	863a	300			300	
R. L. Armstrong	938	150			150	
Attica & Buffalo Rail Road Company	1173	3800			3800	
Auburn & Rochester Rail Road Company	1082	13650			13650	
Auburn & Syracuse Rail Road Company	1038	4725			4725	
Stewart Austin	883	250			250	
Alfred Ayres	1204	80			80	
Do	1205	75			75	
Backus, Buckley & Co.	1056	2200			2200	
John Badgley	1220	74			74	
Wm. Badgley	875	470			470	
John Davis Baldwin	1103	1261			1261	
John D. Baldwin	1091	975			975	
Thaddeus Ball	999	545			545	
Charles E. Barrett	1073	65			65	
Darius Bartram	848	400			400	
Anson Bates	1010	180			180	
Bates & Kinyon	1013	1200	*350		1550	*From 1st July, 1844.
Samuel Batey	1049	240			240	
Norris Baxter	835	300			300	

Edward W. Bayley......	877	270		....	....	270		
Charles L. Beach.........	862	1595		....	....	1595		
........Do............	878	3390		....	....	3390		
........Do............	879	1095		....	....	1095		
........Do............	884	850		....	....	850		
A. F. Beach..............	881	75		....	....	75		
Wm. D. Beadle...........	887	90		....	....	90		
Cephas Benedict.........	868	110		....	....	*66	60	*Fr. 1st July, '44, to 8th Jan. '45, & mo. ex.
Wm. Best..................	925	100		....	....	100		
Peter D. Betticher........	1002	124		....	....	124		
Ebr. Bigelow..............	1053	60		....	....	*57	64	From 16th July, 1844.
Wm. Bingham.............	1158	360		....	....	360		
Geo. W. Bishop...........	1153	78		....	....	78		
........Do............	1183	150		....	....	150		
Elisha Booth..............	1138	200		....	....	200		
Surranus Britton.........	1135	1505		....	....	1505		
........Do............	1157	1037	48	....	....	1037	48	
Chancellor Brooks........	1212	44		....	....	44		
Jona. Brown..............	1171	230		....	....	230		
Almond Brundige.........	977	145		....	....	145		
Nath'l Bryant............	1108	124		....	....	124		
R. Buckingham...........	1024	215		....	....	215		
Samuel Buckley...........	1063	400		....	....	400		
........Do............	1059	325		....	....	325		
Curtis H. Buckman.......	966	290		....	....	290		
Buffalo & Niagara Falls Rail Road Company....	1194	1850		....	....	1850		
George Bunnell...........	853	135		....	....	135		
Edward Burdick..........	983	96		....	....	96		
Joseph Burnet............	920	750		....	....	750		
Daniel Burr..............	803a	2000		....	....	2000		
Rodolphus Burr..........	1197	95		*25	....	120		*From 1st July, 1844.

CONTRACTORS.

Contractors.	No. of route.	Contract pay per annum.	Additional allowances.	Reduction.	Total amount accrued.	Remarks.
Alvah Bushnell	857	$80			$80	
Isaac Butler	849	600			600	
Do	851	249	*$326 96		575 96	*From 1st July, 1844.
Do	852	200	*195		395	Do.
Butterfield & Harvey	1050	100			100	
Butterfield & Gardner	989	800			800	
Do	990	780			780	
Do	1007	1250			1250	
Do	1008	750			750	
Do	1016	274	*64		338	*From 1st July, 1844.
Butterfield, Gardner & Nye	1005	3840	*20		3860	Do.
Butterfield, Gardner, Nye & Co	1006	2000			2000	
Butterfield, Gardner, White & Co	1011	600			600	
Benjamin C. Byrd	804	350			350	
Elias Carpenter	1203	47		*16	31	*From 1st July, 1844.
Isaac Carpenter	1198	260			260	
Do	1199	65			65	
Noah Carpenter	841	52			52	
Powell Carpenter, jr.	1179	100	133		233	
David B. Case	894	500			500	
Wm. Y. Chamberlain	850	194			194	
Do	858	56			56	
Champlain Transportation Company	950	1500			1500	

Stephen Charles	1136	4000			*474 80	3525	20	*From 1st September, 1844.
........Do	1162	800				800		
........Do	1164	1100				1100		
........Do	1167	2000				2000		
Charles Chubbuck	1025	140				140		
Silas Churchill, jr	937	150				150		
Ab'm W. Clark	1142	120				120		
........Do	1146	257				257		
Andrew Cochran	1218	120				120		
Peter D. Cole	927	195				195		
Sylvester Comstock	1084	945				945		
Jonas Connick	1030	65		*27		92		*From 1st July, 1844.
........Do	1031	120				120		
........Do	1044	100				100		
James H. Cook	1222	49	50			*9	82	*From 1st July to 11th Sept. 1844.
Dennis Corsaw	1034	120				120		
Hugh R. Cowan	942	475				475		
Thomas Crill	1248	51				51		
Joseph Crocker	814	350				350		
Ab'm Cuddeback	1250	2000		200		2200		
Zach. Curtis	1026	1735			492	1243		
Hiram Dakin	837	185				185		
Carlisle T. Davidson	1071	1750				1750		
........Do	1075	350				350		
Peter Decker	869	50				50		
Peter D. Demarest	839	197				197		
Dewey & Stewart	1149	498				498		
William A. Dickey	860	325				325		
A. B. Dickinson	823	197				197		
........Do	824	339			*89	250		*From 1st July, 1844.
........Do	825	90				90		
........Do	828	72				72		

CONTRACTORS.

Contractors.	No. of Route.	Contract pay per annum.	Additional allowances.	Reduction.	Total amount accrued.	Remarks.
A. B. Dickinson	846	$166		*$16 80	$149 20	*From 1st July, 1844.
Do	854	300			300	
Do	870	75			75	
Do	871	225			225	
Do	872	198			198	
Do	967	220			220	
Do	1014	215	*$137 34	†44 73	307 61	*From 1st July, '44.—†From 8th Aug. '44.
Do	1033	100			100	
Do	1055	260			260	
Do	1057	83	*193 60		276 60	*From 1st July, 1844.
Do	1081	370			370	
Do	1087	138			138	
Do	1095	73	*82		155	*From 1st July, 1844.
Do	1097	109			109	
Do	1102	74			74	
Do	1053	99			4 04	To 15th July, 1844.
Do	1104	78			78	
Do	1107	185		*27	158	*From 1st July, 1844.
Do	1111	69			69	
Do	1137	900			900	
Daniel Dimick	1052	75			75	
Daniel Dimick, jr.	1012	590			590	
George Dixon, 2d	1047	159	*27		186	*From 1st July, 1844.
Elias Dorlon	908	2143			2143	
Robert P. Dorlon	911	375			375	
Do	928	1000			1000	

58*

........Do	906	1500				750		From 1st July to 31st December, 1844.
Luke Dodge	935	212				53		From 1st July to 30th September, 1844.
........Do	970	147				147		
Enos Eaton	1140	115				115		
Peleg Eddy	1068	112	50			112	50	
G. H. Edgerton	897	30				30		
Job G. Elmore	856	52				52		
........Do	861	172				172		
*John Elderkin	819 c	275				174	76	From 12th November, 1844.
Joseph Estus	943	90				90		
Jason Fairbanks	1065	650				650		
Orra Field	1027	120		*15		135		*From 1st July, 1844.
Charles Fisher	1230	300				300		
Peter H. Fonda	978	200			*28	172		*From 1st July, 1844.
Nathan Foster	1163	325				325		
Seth Foster	1122	304				304		
........Do	1141	100		*5		105		*From 1st July, 1844.
........Do	1143	80				80		
........Do	1144	162				162		
F. S. Freeman	900	88				88		
........Do	901	88				88		
William Garrison	1040	148				148		
Caleb Gibbs	926	65				65		
Gill & Taylor	1067	1000				1000		
Warren Goodell	1043	114				114		
Stephen Goodspeed	939	138				138		
Peter P. Grant	885	30				30		
Salmon Graves	1045	148	68			148	68	
Thomas S. Graves	899	56				56		
........Do	996	49				49		
........Do	997	59				59		
Benjamin B. Gray	829	230				230		

CONTRACTORS.

Contractors.	No. of Route.	Contract pay per annum.	Additional allowances.	Reduction.	Total amount accrued.	Remarks.
George Hall	813	$2475		*$109	$2366	*From 1st July, 1844.
John B. Hall	1252	100			100	
Wm. Hall	1083	868		*67	801	*From 1st July, 1844.
Do	1092	1600			1600	
Martin Hall	1236	88			88	
A. C. Halstead	909	298			298	
Do	934	174			174	
Hall & Goddard	1079	800			800	
Do	1090	900		*21 34	878 66	*From 1st May, 1845.
Do	1093	2800		*100	2700	*From 1st April, 1845.
Stephen Hamilton	865	110			110	
Do	866	175			175	
Do	867	200			200	
Henry H. Harden	1015	312		*62	250	*From 1st July, 1844.
Morgan L. Harris	919	394			197	1st July to 31st Dec., 1844.
Do	923	410			205	do do
Harry B. Hatch	964	510			510	
Do	965	375			375	
James Haver	972	80			80	
Silas Hicock	1070	199			199	
Robert L. Hill	1188	60			60	
Erastus Holloway	1251	27 76			13 88	From 1st January, 1845.
Ira Holmes	1159	1000			500	1st July to 31st Dec., 1844.
Dennison Holmes	915	250			250	
Benj'n M. Homan	815d	200			127 18	From 12th Nov., 1844.
Do	819d	62 48			39 73	do

Jas. H. Hooker	932	4549			4549	
Walter Hosford	855	350			350	
Miles Hotchkiss	891	300			300	
Alex'r Hoxie	980	170			170	
Do	981	75			75	
Levi Hoyt	1127	107 64		*38 64	69	*From 1st July, 1844.
Do	1131	300			300	
Hudson and Mohawk Railroad Company	912	3200			3200	
Bissell Humphrey	1175	900			900	
Augustus Hunt	812*a*	2530			2530	
Jas. G. Hunt	874*a*	125			125	
Chas. L. Huntley	1123	495			495	
L. F. Hutchinson	1046	1925			1925	
Hutchinson & Payne	1115	650		*486 52	163 48	*From 1st July, 1844.
Hyde & Hyde	908*a*	2143			2143	
Edw'd E. Jackson	842	120		*32	88	*From 1st July, 1844.
Do	843	120			120	
Wm. Jendevine	1244	245			245	
Stephen Jennings	859	125			125	
Chauncey Jerome	1228	48			48	
John R. Johnston	1103*a*	2139			2139	
Harley Judd	1020	275			275	
Do	1021	475			475	
L. L. Kinyon	1013*a*	1000			1000	
Lawrence & Slater	1178	500			500	
Daniel Lee	1062	400			400	
Wm. Lee	1076	598		*119 44	478 56	*From 11th Sept., 1844.
Do	1085	1195			1195	
John Leigh	945	90			90	
Elisha Lester	1114	99			99	
Martin Lewis	1193	120			120	

CONTRACTORS.

Contractors.	No. of Route.	Contract pay per annum.	Additional allowances.	Reduction.	Total amount accrued.	Remarks.
Lewis & Rindge	1116	$398			$398	
Lindsay, Rawson & Co.	947	359		*$9 48	349 52	*From 1st July, 1844.
Lindsay, Wyman & Co.	952	160			160	
Do	961	155			155	
Horatio Lockwood	826	125	*23 80		148 80	*From 1st July, 1844.
Sam'l Lockwood	1186	425	*200 00		625	*From 1st July, 1844.
Do	1189	164			164	
Lockport and Niagara Falls Railroad Company	1191	1000			1000 00	
Long Island R. R. Comp'y	818	180			180	
Do	805*ext*	5000	*600		3779 34	From 12th Nov., 1844. *4 express mails.
Do	815*b*	100			63 59	do
Do	819*a*	150			95 38	do
Do	819*b*	75			47 69	do
John Looker	1060	245			245	
Peter Loucks	1210	144			144	
R. Loveland	1069	120			120	
McClenthen & Allen	1041	85			85	
Do	1042	119			119	
Hugh McCurdy	1166	2200			2200	
John A. McElwaine	1160	1200			1200	
Do	1172	870	546		1416	
Do	1223	52			52	
Jas. McKain	1192	100		*35	65	*From 1st July, 1844.
McLawry & Searle	917*a*	1194 28			1194 28	
Thos. J. Magee	1113	3000		*107	2893	*From 1st April, 1845.

........Do	1156	210			210	
Magee & Cook	1126	80			80	
Levi H. Mason	1145	125			125	
Orange Mason	1176	370			370	
Barnet Matthews	973	350	*15		365	*From 1st July, 1844.
John B. Matthews	975	64			64	
........Do	976	100			100	
S. H. Maxwell	1098	154			154	
Wheeler Merrick	1139	780			780	
Jos. P. Miller	1000	69			69	
Silas H. Mills	954	150			150	
Richard More	889	124			124	
Geo. W. Morgan	979	95			95	
Wm. A. Mott	1074	186 48			186 48	
Munson & Foxton	1036	1600			1600	
Geo. Nare	1226	38 56			38 56	
Neil & Tallmadge	1196	500			500	
Conrad Nessle	988	200			200	
New Jersey Steam Navigation Company, and New York, Providence, and Boston Railroad Comp'y	801	15500			15500	
N. B. Ney	1017	115			57 50	From 1st January, 1845.
Isaac Newton	810	15000			15000	
Wm. P. Nottingham	1246	595			595	
Asa Nowlin	1120	3000		*428	2572	*From 1st July, 1844.
Nye & Lewis	913	2700		*273 91	2426 09	*1st July to 15th December, 1844.
Thos. C. Nye	995	1511	*250		1761	*From 1st July, 1844.
........Do	1019	500			500	
Nye & Loomis	987	4000			4000	
William Ottley	1161	700		*88	612	*From 1st July, 1844.
........Do	1195	450			450	

CONTRACTORS

Contractors.	No. of Route.	Contract pay per annum.	Additional allowances.	Reduction.	Total amount accrued.	Remarks.
William Otley	1201	$800			$800	
Do	1207	800			800	
Otley & Humphrey	1174	1000		*$500	500	*From 1st July, 1844.
Otis Paige	1209	117		*6 48	110 52	*From 1st July, 1344.
A. M. Palne	895	240			240	
Fletcher Palmer	909	80			80	
Parker & Bartlett	1182	80			80	
John Parsons, jr	1048	149			149	
Jas. Partridge	940	180	$*16 49		196 49	*From 12th July, 1844.
Do	953	130			130	
Thos. Pearsall	817	125			125	
Alfred Pelton	1129	87 48			87 48	
Henry T. Penny	815a	204			204	
Randall Perkins	1020	68			68	
Henry R. Phelps	1118	550		*352	198	*From 1st July, 1844.
Ez'l Pierce	1155	308			308	
Isaac Plumb, jr	1219	50			50	
Cyrus Pratt	1105	95			95	
Geo. Prime	880	125			125	
Clark Rawson	956	60			60	
Do	957	60			60	
Do	959	90			90	
Leond. V. Reed	950	1560			1560	
Reed & Comstock	981	2850			2850	
Reeve & Smith	805	495	*41 95		221 49	To 11th Nov., 1844. *1 month's extra pay.
Robt. H. Renwick	1150	95			95	

D. A. Rexford	893	3516			3516	
Do	1100	3769	*44 75	*1487 45	2329 30	*1 month's extra pay. |From 4th Aug., '44.
Geo. B. Reynolds	951	2025	*30		2055	*From 1st July, 1844.
Do	960	115			115	
Jas. A. Rhodes	1208	3 75			[illegible] 71	From 2d April, 1845.
Benj'n Richardson	896	900			900	
Hansom A. Risley	1011	180			180	
Roberts, Andrus & Co.	1079	4000			4000	
Nathan Robinson	1070	700			700	
Robinson & Morgan	933	5250			5250	
Robinson, Morgan & Co.	909	1900		*510	1390	*From 1st July, 1844
Charles Rogers	930	200			200	
Moses W. Rogers	1061	50			50	
Solomon Rouse	904	112 50			108 50	
Roof & Sheis	919	394			197	From 1st January, 1845
Do	923	410			205	do
Root & Morgan	944	600			600	
Henry H. Ross	963	90	*15		105	*From 1st July, 1844.
Sam'l G. Rouse	1151	80			80	
Ralph Rudd	984	300	*16 07		99 49	To 11th Aug., '44. *1 month's extra pay.
Jas. Russell	1039	790			790	
Schenectady and Utica Railroad Company	969	15600			15600	
Saratoga and Schenectady Railroad Company	971	1395			1395	
Richard Scoulin	1077	935		*440 84	495 16	*From 17th Sept., 1844
Do	1101	625			625	
Jas. Scott	966	60			60	
Sears & Sweet	936	1800			1800	
Warren Seeley	1060	935			935	
Thos. L. Shafer	917	44			44	
Sharpstine & Twining	1110	980			980	

CONTRACTORS.

Contractors.	No. of Route.	Contract pay per annum.	Additional allowances.	Reduction.	Total amount accrued.	Remarks.
Nath'l Shaw	1148	$125	....	....	$125	
Warner D. Shaw	1213	394	....	....	394	
Do	1214	894	....	....	894	
Dan'l P. Shedd	1181	148	....	....	148	
C. C. Sheldon	1147	660	....	....	660	
Jona. Sherman	1215	890	....	....	890	
Edwin Sherwin	1023	95	....	....	95	
Skaneateles and Jordan R. R. Company	1229	300	....	....	300	
Ezra Smith	816	1000	....	....	447 46	To 11th Nov., '44, including month extra.
Do	819	1600	$75	....	739 50	Do do do.
Do	804*a*	150	....	....	95 79	From 11th Nov., 1844.
John F. Smith	1066	400	....	....	400	
Alex'r Smith	1216	74	....	....	74	
Isaac Smith	1168	174	....	....	174	
Ogden Smith	1086	90	....	....	90	
Peter T. Smith	882	347	*108 43	....	455 43	*1st July, 1844, to 15th Feb., 1845.
Geo. W. Smith	816*a*	425	....	....	270 25	From 12th Nov., 1844.
Rich'd W. Smith	816*b*	275	....	....	174 86	Do do.
Smith & Miller	812	9000	....	....	9000	
Do	812*b*	1850	....	....	1850	
Do	812*c*	700	....	....	700	
Do	873	700	....	....	700	
Do	874	500	....	....	500	
Do	876	100	....	....	100	
Smith & Whipple	922	950	....	....	950	

John S. Soper	815	2500				1089	49	To 11th Nov., '44, including month extra.
Do	815*a*	350				222	55	From 12th Nov., 1844.
Orra Soul	1028	550				550		
Adrastus Snedaker	1117	600				600		
J. W. Stark	1251	27	74			13	88	From 1st July to 31st Dec'r, 1844.
Seth Starr	1217	84				84		
Barzaleel Streeter	929	110				110		
Peter Sturtevant	948	104				104		
59* Halstead Sweet	831	50				12	50	1st July to 30th Sept., 1844.
Do	834	975			*475	500		*From 1st July, 1844.
Do	838	195				195		
Do	844	120				120		
Do	845	384				384		
Do	863	533				533		
Syracuse and Utica Railroad Company	1004	9275				6956	25	From 1st July, 1844, to 31st March, 1845.
Symonds, White & Everett	1003	2790				2790		
Do	1035	3250				3250		
Do	1054	290			*95	195		*From 1st July, 1844.
Do	1064	790				790		
Nelson Terry	815*c*	300				190	75	From 12th Nov., 1844.
Silas S. Terry	822	50				22	37	To 11th Nov., '44, including month extra.
Ira C. Titus	1208	50				50		
Jas. S. Tolles	1184	50		*50		100		*From 1st July, 1844.
Jno. Tomlinson	1017	115				57	50	To 31st Dec'r, 1844.
Tompkins & Lounsberry	827	400				400		
Tonawanda Railroad Co.	1165	4950		1370		6320		
A. & A. Tuell	1124	400				400		
Jno. Underwood	1128	120				120		
Wm. Utter	994	140			*26	114		*From 1st July, 1844.
Jno. H. Vandenburg	906	1500				750		From 1st January, 1845.
Corn's Vanderbelt	802	4239				4239		

CONTRACTORS.

Contractors.	No. of Route.	Contract pay per annum.	Additional allowances.	Reduction.	Total amount accrued.	Remarks.
Corn's Vanderbelt	803	$8000			$8000	
Peter J. Van Patten	1083	542			542	
Wm. Vreeland	807	182 48		*26	156 48	*From 1st July, 1844.
Lewis C. Veazey	1152	98			98	
Do	1154	396			396	
J. P. & L. Velsey	933	790			790	
Hiram Wagur	1037	700		*196	504	Do do.
Benj'n F. Wakefield	993	386			386	
Thos. B. Walker	1180	400			400	
Do	1200	695			695	
Do	1202	500			500	
Elihu Warner	1001	100			100	
Hez'h Watkins	918	200			200	
Do	992	1200	*600		1800	Do do.
Wm. Watkins	1206	70			70	
Watkins & Clarke	890	1800			1800	
Watkins, Lewis & Co	991	700			700	
Peter Weager	974	120	*20		140	Do do.
Wm. W. Weed	1159	1000			500	From 1st January, 1845.
Jos. H. Webster	916	600			600	
Isaac Weeks	944	318			318	
Isaac & Sam'l Weeks	907	1898			1898	
Levi Weeks	986	50			50	
Alfred Wells	1089	165			165	
Step'n West	1232	26			26	
Jos. D. Wetherell	1177	198			198	

Salmon Wheldon	930	118			118	
Geo. W. White	934	200			177 18	From 12th August, 1844.
Do	1222	50			39 66	From 12th September, 1844.
John Whiting	1132	230			230	
Do	1133	139			139	
Do	1134	286	*5		291	*From 1st July, 1844.
C. D. & E. Wilcox	1169	400			400	
Sam'l Wilkason	936	124			124	
Willoughby & Watkins	985	450			450	
Marvin Wilson	832	60			60	
Dan'l Wood	998	206 96			206 96	
Amb. Worthington	1121	1025		*66	959	Do do.
Total for New York		$341360 27	$5828 29	$6003 43	$328910 81	
NEW JERSEY.						
A. J. Amerman	1333	$70			$70	
Samuel Archer	1348	40			40	
John Ald	1321	160			160	
C. P. Beekman	1334	84			84	
Henry W. Brees	1318	120			120	
John F. Brown	1325	184			184	
Abraham Bryan	1347	180	*42 86		222 86	*From 5th October, 1844.
Thomas B. Bryan	1349	80			80	
Job T. Clayton	1345	386			386	
Isaac Davison	1329	130			130	
Hudson S. Ellis	1346	384	*33 19		417 19	*From 20th July, 1844.
John J. Errickson	1340	89			89	
Ezra Estler	1316	350	*97 26		447 26	*From 31st October, 1844.
David H. Gary	1310	140			*131 30	*To Oct. 1st, '44, and from Nov'r 6th, '44.

CONTRACTORS.

Contractors.	No. of Route.	Contract pay per annum.	Additional allowances.	Reduction.	Total amount accrued.	Remarks.
John H. Hall	1311	$65	....	....	$65	
Do	1312	40	....	....	40	
Do	1313	125	....	....	125	
Jeremiah Hann	1353	800	....	....	800	
Higgins & Smith	1342	1000	....	....	1000	
William Hodson	1356	290	....	....	290	
Jacob Johnston	1343	399	....	....	399	
Benjamin Kenney	1344	220	....	....	220	
N. B. Luce	1324	2000	....	....	2000	
Gilbert Mathews	1345a	495	....	....	495	
Wm. R. Moore	1319a	240	....	....	240	
Do	1338	125	....	....	125	
Morris & Essex R. R. Co.	1304	1585	....	....	1585	
Do	1317	50	....	....	50	
New Jersey R. R. Co.	1301	11788	....	....	*8841	*To 31st March, 1845.
Wm. Norcross	1354	840	....	....	840	
Aaron Padgett	1358	600	....	....	600	
Patterson & Hudson River Railroad Co.	1302	1500	....	....	1500	
Philadelphia & Trenton R. R. Co.	1301a	20877 90	*600	....	21477 90	*$300 for carrying President's message 3d December, 1844: $300 for carrying President's inaugural 4th March, 1845.
Wm. S. Rittenhouse	1326	250	....	....	*95 14	*From February 13, 1845.
A. B. Robeson	1314	400	....	....	400	
David Sanderson	1319	2274	....	....	2274	

........Do.............	1320	200	....	....	200	
........Do.............	1323	1500	....	....	1500	
Wm. C. Sapp............	1359	350	....	....	350	
Leonard Searle.........	1309	1600	....	....	1600	
Eph'm E. Sheppard......	1360	250	....	....	250	
Joseph C. Shivers......	1351	500	....	....	500	
David P. Simkins.......	1355	800	*30 35	....	830 35	*From 3d September, 1844.
Simkins & Westcott.....	1361	300	....	....	300 00	
........Do.............	1362	200	....	*31 25	168 75	*From 27th August, 1844.
W. W. Sloan............	1357	190	....	....	190	
John A. Smith..........	1315	97	....	....	97	
........Do.............	1332	79	....	....	79	
Robert D. Stine........	1330	160	....	....	160	
Stout & [illegible]e...........	1337	344	....	....	344	
Wm. B. Sutphen.........	1339	145	....	....	145	
John B. Titus..........	1327	83	....	....	83	
Edward Van Buren.......	1307	135	....	....	135	
A. Van Fleet...........	1335	70	....	....	70	
Westcott, Simkins & Co.	1350	1040	....	....	1040	
Philip [illegible]on...........	1331	60	....	....	60	
Total for New Jersey...........		$56463 90	$803 66	$31 25	$54125 75	
PENNSYLVANIA.						
John J. Allen..........	1552	$200	....	....	$200	
James J. Anderson......	1707	95	....	....	95	
Daniel Ahl.............	1487	325	....	....	325	
Henry Ange.............	1460	145	....	....	145	
Stephen J. Armstrong...	1480	99	....	....	99	
Samuel Aurand..........	1521	850	....	....	850	

CONTRACTORS.

Contractors.	No. of Route.	Contract pay per annum.	Additional allowances.	Reduction.	Total amount accrued.	Remarks.
Bailey & Eder	1492	$1450			$1450	
Do	1514	1000			*500	*To 31st December, 1844.
Do	1519	745			745	
Do	1524	300			300	
Do	1572	250			*125	*To 31st December, 1844.
Do	1580	1545			1545	
Harvey & John Bailey	1578	1345			1345	
Samuel Barnaby	1584	400			400	
Joseph Beebe	1561	54			54	
Enos Benner	1433	96			96	
Do	1434	63			63	
John A. Bickel	1468	73			73	
Do	1469	65			65	
Wm. Blackman	1563	42			42	
David Blair	1510	249		*19 14	229 86	*From 17th July, 1844.
William Blain	1511	85			85	
John Blake	1502	600			600	
Levi Bowen	1488	50			50	
Stephen Boyd	1421*	827	†27 17		775 34	*Service commenced Aug. 5, 1844. †Additional allowance from Sept. 4, 1844.
Do	1425	84			84	
Jacob Brinker	1651	3995			*1639 25	*From Aug. 2d to 31st Dec. 1844.
George Brown	1641	134			134	
Henry Brown	1612	235			235	
Isaac Bruner	1574	147			147	
Do	1575	169			169	

John S. Bryan	1430	40			40	
Do	1445	108			108	
D. M. Bull	1541	1300			1300	
Andrew Buckman	1454	70			70	
Do	1455	165			165	
A. Burlingame	1592	495			495	
Do	1619	160			160	
A. H. Butterworth	1618	135			135	
A. & J. A. Byers	1629	300			300	
Wm. S. Byers	1692	260			260	
Horner Camp	1562	130			*22 25	*From 6th Sept. to 7th Nov'r 1844.
Nathan Carrier	1667	208			208	
Ozias B. Caswell	1562	118			*76 31	*From 8th Nov'r, 1844.
Joseph Clark	1661	208			208	
Edward Clift	1410	150			150	
Clemson & Kinzer	1476	395			395	
Do	1478	210			210	
Do	1516	395	*140 96		535 96	*From July 15th, 1844.
Charles L. Cochran	1674	148			*111	*From Oct. 1st, 1844.
Do	1685	108			108	
William Colder	1457	445			445	
Do	1484	370			370	
Do	1491	441			441	
Do	1493	3750			*2812 50	*From Oct. 1st, 1844.
Do	1514	1000			*500	*From January 1st, 1845.
Colder & Peters	1483	700			700	
Nicholas Coleman	1458	150			150	
Do	1459	350			350	
Christian Copp	1444	475			475	
Asa H. Cory	1621	130			130	
N. Cottrill	1544	150			150	
Eliphalet Cozard	1669	50			50	

CONTRACTORS.

Contractors.	No. of Route.	Contract pay per annum.	Additional allowances.	Reduction.	Total amount accrued.	Remarks.
Thomas Craig	1441	$500	....	....	$500	
Silas E. Craig	1529	140	....	....	140	
D. Crawford	1597	75	....	....	75	
H. Crittenden	1589	80	....	....	80	
Do	1590	208	....	....	*136 21	*From Nov'r 5th, 1844.
Croft & Philips	1677	888	....	....	888	
Benjamin Cromwell	1608	250	....	....	250	
Samuel Cromwell	1607	250	....	....	250	
Cumberland Valley Railroad Company	1489	9100	....	....	9100	
J. Cunningham	1513	155	....	....	155	
Do	1515	65	....	....	65	
James Curry	1691	190	....	....	190	
Do	1701	38	....	....	38	
Ceylon T. Dake	1696	199	....	....	199	
Edward C. Darlington	1473	130	....	....	130	
Do	1474	312	*26	....	48 04	*1 mo. extra. †Service dis. 26th Oct'r, '44.
Do	1477	85	....	....	85	
Wm. Dean	1439	600	....	....	600	
John Dearmit	1600	295	....	....	295	
Do	1601	93	....	....	93	
Do	1603	65	....	....	65	
Do	1604	195	....	....	195	
Do	1606	310	....	....	310	
Wm. Denniston	1668	33	....	....	33	
M. Drumheller	1518	129	....	....	129	

W. J. Eldred	1576	142			142	
........Do	1582	280			280	
........Do	1583	369			369	
James Ely	1442	1300			1300	
Henry S. Evans	1416	79			79	
........Do	1419	89 75			89 75	
........Do	1420	59 75			59 75	
Jacob S. Evans	1531	105	*11 94		116 94	*From Aug. 24, 1844.
J. C. Ferry	1673	700	*25 83		725 83	*From Jan'y 31st, 1845.
John Fetherolff	1464	66			66	
J. Fornance	1431	220			220	
Henry Frank	1631	125			125	
James Freeland	1461	600			600	
David O. Gehr	1507	1000			1000	
J. M. Gibson	1422	95	*4 57		99 57	*From 31st July, 1841.
Gilchrist & Colt	1520	1543			1543	
George Gold	1635	325			325	
Graham & Kapp	1522	1288			1288	
John Griffin	1688	43			43	
Griffin & Loomis	1572	250			*125	*To 31st Dec'r, 1844.
Thomas Guthrie	1630	100			100	
John Haines	1411	490			490	
Hammett & Weart	1405	400			400	
........Do	1413	800			800	
........Do	1438	470			470	
........Do	1443	440			440	
Joseph Hall	1412	225			225	
C. D. Hart	1429	375			375	
Henry Hamilton	1644	40			*1 52	*From 17th June, 1845.
Lewis Hartman	1475	249			249	
W. W. Hastings	1665	140			140	
Samuel Hays	1479	560	*45	†27 52	577 48	*From 1st July, '44.—†From 21st Nov. '44.

CONTRACTORS.

Contractors.	No. of Route.	Contract pay per annum.	Additional allowances.	Reduction.	Total amount accrued.	Remarks.
E. W. Hays	1651	$3995			*$876 68	*From 12th January to 31st March, 1845.
Wm. H. Henry	1694	45			45	
Peter Henry	1674	208			*52	*From July 1st to 30th September, 1844.
Jacob Hicks	1490	600			600	
Jacob Hildebrand	1709	51			51	
Alexander Hoig	1702	125			125	
John H. Horton	1587	37 50			37 50	
Horton, Searles & Co.	1534	2368			2368	
Nunis Hudson	1481	80			80	
Ellis Hughes	1517	68			68	
Charles H. Huling	1523	125			*120 24	*From 15th July, 1844.
John C. Hull	1632	539	*236 34 †359 64		1134 98	*From 1st Aug. 1844.—†From 8th Oct. 1844.
Wm. Hunter	1687	96			*72	*To 31st March, 1845.
Charles Huntsman	1446	40			40	
Do	1447	38			38	
George Husted	1566	177			*48 09	*To 9th October, 1844.
Do	1566	245			*101 40	*From 1st February, 1845.
Samuel Huston	1611	110			110	
William Iddings	1593	230			230	
Iddings & Greer	1596	2600			2600	
Geo. W. Johnson	1602	2275			2275	
George P. Kampell	1495	139			139	
A. E. Kapp	1525	70			70	
Abner Kelly	1658	546			546	
Joseph Kendall	1427	980			980	

........Do	1463	149	....	....	149	
W. W. Kirkendoll	1536	100	....	....	100	
........Do	1537	65	....	....	65	
........Do	1538	104	....	....	104	
M. de Lafayette Koons	1526	64	....	....	64	
........Do	1533	48	....	....	48	
David Kyle	1509	378	....	....	378	
Daniel Lamb	1695	70	....	....	70	
Wm. Leonard	1657	149	....	....	149	
James Leslie	1680	48	....	....	48	
Sidney Lewis	1585	85	....	....	85	
Samuel Lodge	1682	125	....	....	*31 25	*From 1st April, 1845.
Samuel Love	1672	91	....	....	91	
Wm. Love, jr	1532	90	....	....	90	
Jeremiah Lowe	1482	52	....	....	52	
David Lupfer	1496	500	....	....	500	
J. McAllister	1633	298	....	....	298	
........Do	1636	145	....	....	*36 25	*To 30th September, 1844.
........Do	1637	145	....	....	*36 25	*Ditto.
........Do	1648	155	....	....	*38 75	*Ditto.
Joseph P. McClelland	1417	400	....	....	400	
Peter McClelland	1570	35	....	....	*5 42	*To 26th August, 1844.
John McCollister	1636	145	....	....	*108 75	*From 1st October, 1844.
........Do	1637	145	....	....	*108 75	*Ditto.
........Do	1648	155	....	....	*116 25	*Ditto.
James P. McConaughy	1613	80	....	....	80	
Samuel McCrery	1494	64	....	....	64	
James McElhenny	1598	140	....	....	140	
McElwain & Gold	1675	90	....	....	90	
James McElwain	1615	1250	....	....	*312 50	*To 30th September, 1844.
........Do	1655	517 50	....	....	517 50	
........Do	1664	145	....	....	145	

CONTRACTORS.

Contractors.	No. of route.	Contract pay per annum.	Additional allowances.	Reduction.	Total amount accrued.	Remarks.
Arthur McGill	1615	$1250			*$312 50	*From 1st October to 31st December, 1844.
Do	1651	6750			*605 30	*From 1st July to 2d August, 1844.
Patric McGuire	1407	284 50			284 50	
Do	1408	97 50			97 50	
James M. McKee	1671	94			94	
Christopher McQuale	1409	1550			1550	
A. McWilliams	1681	70			70	
K. M. Mason	1622	175			175	
Isaiah Mealey	1647	661			661	
George Miller	1628	234			324	
Shepherd Miller	1569	50			50	
Moore, Falls & Co.	1609	3500			3500	
James K. Moorehead	1493	3750			*937 50	*To 30th September, 1844.
Joseph Moore	1660	145			*72 50	*To 31st December, 1844.
John H. Morrison	1594	100			100	
Munsel & Robinson	1535	430	*208 04		638 04	*From 19th August, 1844.
Neil & Tallmadge	1651	3995			*998 75	*From 1st April, 1845.
Do	1654	771			771	
Do	1656	1170			*292 50	*From 1st April, 1845.
Uri Newcomb	1557	145			145	
Nickerson & Dean	1554	143			143	
R. S. Orr	1690	792			792	
Otto & Day	1620	190			190	
Isaac Perrine	1676	75			75	
Jacob Peters	1406	10500			10500	
Do	1418	1018			1018	

Peters, Segreaves & Co.	1403	1175	....	....	1175	
J. N. Pomeroy	1581	724	....	....	724	
John L. Porter	1670	84	....	....	84	
........Do	1684	42	....	....	42	
Wm. Phillips	1660	145	....	....	*72 50	*To 31st December, 1844
........Do	1705	190	....	....	*142 50	*To 31st March, 1845.
John Piper	1501	125	....	....	125	
Cyrus Pratt	1540	154	....	....	154	
........Do	1565	259	....	....	259	
........Do	1573	244	....	....	244	
Noah S. Prentiss	1527	75	....	....	75	
Kirk J. Price	1436	35	....	....	35	
David Ralston	1623	240	....	....	240	
........Do	1624	220	....	....	220	
........Do	1627	175	....	....	175	
N. Randall	1567	184	....	....	184	
Jacob Rehrer	1498	128	....	....	128	
........Do	1500	65	....	....	65	
Michael Richard	1435	158	....	....	158	
........Do	1456	157	....	....	157	
Mathew Roberts.	1653	1600	....	....	1600	
Robinson & Morgan	1546	70	....	....	70	
........Do	1549	3420	....	....	3420	
........Do	1551	720	....	456	264	
........Do	1553	136	....	....	136	
........Do	1555	80	....	....	80	
........Do	1556	600	....	....	600	
Rockafellow, Colder & Co.	1401	12200	....	....	12200	
........Do	1401a	1504 20	....	....	1504 20	
........Do	1471	6300	....	....	6300	
Scholfield & Bear	1432	1194	....	....	1194	
........Do	1472	340	....	....	340	

CONTRACTORS.

Contractors.	No. of Route.	Contract pay per annum.	Additional allowances.	Reduction.	Total amount accrued.	Remarks.
Davis D. Scott	1559	$52			$52	
Chas. Seagreaves	1451	375			375	
Do	1452	1500			1500	
John Seiders	1605	360		*$34 89	†145 11	*From 16th Sept., '44—†To 31st Dec., '44.
Warner D. Shaw	1704	472			472	
C. C. Shelden	1618	135			*67 50	*To 31st December, 1844.
E. Shelmidine	1703	99			99	
Do	1706	148			148	
Sam'l W. Sidle	1499	100			100	
John G. Sigworth	1687	96			*24	*From 1st April, 1845.
John Skinner, jr.	1506	525			525	
David Smith	1679	61			61	
John Snodgrass	1505	8975			*4487 50	*From 1st January, 1845.
John Stallman	1404	200			200	
Do	1708	40			40	
Garrett Steel	1659	220		*18 62	201 38	*From 3d October, 1844.
James Stewart	1656	1170			*877 50	*To 31st March, 1845.
John Stewart	1543	98			98	
Jacob Stoufer	1448	76			76	
Sam'l P. Stoner	1508	170			170	
Nimrod Strickland	1415	61 50			61 50	
John L. Tate	1503	58			58	
Do	1504	58			58	
Tate & Troxell	1486	180			180	
David Taylor	1485	125			125	
David Thayer	1705	190			*47 50	*From 1st April, 1845.

Rob't Thomas	1614	145	....	....	145	
E. P. Tucker	1697	219	....	....	219	
........Do	1698	189	....	....	189	
........Do	1699	189	....	....	189	
Silas Vanartsdalen	1428	55	....	....	55	
Nathan Van Duser	1586	195	....	....	195	
Henry Vanover	1568	80	....	....	80	
Walker & Lane	1646	299	....	....	299	
John W. Webber	1547	86	....	*6 65	79 35	*From 5th October, 1844.
........Do	1548	108	....	....	108	
David White	1693	160	....	....	160	
John S. White	1683	75	....	....	75	
Whitesell & Ely	1440	1600	....	....	1600	
John Whitesell	1450	140	....	....	140	
John Wightman	1617	2440	....	....	2440	
Abram Williams	1649	60	....	....	60	
Williamsport and Elmira Railroad Company	1579	1286	....	....	1286	
Winter & Lutzel	1595	108	....	....	108	
William Witmier	1528	119	....	....	119	
Joseph Woods	1682	125	....	....	*93 75	*To 31st March, 1845.
A. Woodward	1505	8975	....	....	*4487 50	*To 31st December, 1844.
........Do	1512	97	....	....	97	
........Do	1545	175	*4 90	....	179 90	*From 29th March, 1845.
........Do	1590	199	....	....	*68 67	*To November 5th, 1844.
........Do	1615	1250	....	....	*625	*From January 1st, 1845.
Yard & Hillard	1605	240	....	....	*120	*From January 1st, 1845.
Yerkes & Adams	1466	1900	....	....	1900	
Jacob Yohe, sen.	1530	40	....	....	40	
George Young	1426	265	....	....	265	
Joseph Young	1437	99	....	....	99	
Robert Young	1645	216	....	....	216	

CONTRACTORS.

Contractors.	No. of Route.	Contract pay per annum.	Additional allowances.	Reduction.	Total amount accrued.	Remarks.
William Young	1470	$80			$80	
Michael Zorn	1610	85			85	
Total for Pennsylvania		$184826 20	$1090 39	$562 82	$150466 57	
DELAWARE.						
Barratt P. Connor	1807	$200			$200	
Do	1808	200			200	
John L. Deputy	1803	300			75	From 1st April, 1845.
Ebenezer Eliason	1805	156			156	
J. H. Ellegood	1812	149			149	
Elihu Jefferson	1806	48			48	
H. B. Kirkpatrick	1811	2250			2250	
H. K. Patrick	1802	340		†17 92	322 08	†From 31st January, 1845.
Do	1803	300			†225	†To 31st March, 1845.
Do	1814	50			50	
Alexander Porter	1809	125			125	
C. L. Sharp	1810	149			149	
Smyrna, Leipsic and Philadelphia Steamboat Co	1801	3400			3400	
S. C. White	1813	600			600	
Total for Delaware		$8267		$17 92	$7949 08	

MARYLAND.						
Daniel Ahl	1946	$496			$496	
Annapolis and Elkridge R. R. Company	1927	2200			2200	
Baltimore and Ohio Railroad Company	1902	12720	†$1250		13970	†For carrying President's Message and inaugural address.
........Do	1903	43225			43225	
Baltimore & Susquehanna Railroad Company	1905	7000			7000	
Isaac Benjamin	1919	119			119	
Wm. J. Benjamin	1920	290			290	
John Berry	1937*a*	178 50	†15 52		194 02	†From 12th July, 1844.
Wm. Bishop	1908	520			520	
James Black	1958	39			39	
John Blake	1907	1300			†1190 49	†From 1st August, 1844.
Stephen Boyd	1913	248	†94 83		342 83	†From 19th July, 1844.
Benjamin Burton	1921	690			690	
James Condy	1947	600			600	
Barratt P. Connor	1916	180			180	
Israel Duckworth	1955	59			59	
Jonathan Evans	1918	120			120	
John P. Giles	1923	150			150	
Sam'l Gover	1929	840			840	
Thomas Harris	1917	140			140	
Wm. H. House	1940	220			220	
Thos. V. Hyde	1935	248			†124	†To 31st December, 1844.
Isaac Leonard	1924	159			159	
Isaiah Mealey	1936	699			†174 75	†To 30th September, 1844.
........Do	1945	309			309	
........Do	1948	95			95	
Stephen B. Miles	1912	119			†113 18	†From 19th July, 1844.

CONTRACTORS.

Contractors.	No. of Route.	Contract pay per annum.	Additional allowances.	Reduction.	Total amount accrued.	Remarks.
Moore, Falls & Co	1954	$16100	....	....	$16100	
Benj'n F. Moxley	1935	248	....	....	†124	†From 1st January, 1845.
Hiram H. Mullen	1949	48	....	....	48	
James Murdock	1915	3000	....	....	3000	
Joseph O'Neal	1950	240	....	....	240	
John W. Onion	1911	109	....	....	109	
George N. Orme	1934	250	....	....	250	
L. F. Pascault	1928	1000	....	....	1000	
Phil'a, Wil. & Balt. R. R. Co	1901	30600	†1000	....	31600	†$500 for carrying President's Message—$500 for Inaugural Address.
John Piper	1907	1300	....	....	†108 33	*From 1st to 31st July, 1844.
Henry Remley	1951	300	....	....	300	
........Do	1952	50	....	....	50	
John Seiders	1953	185	....	....	185	
Wm. R. S lby	1937	340	....	....	340	
Talbot G. Shipley	1942	65	....	....	65	
J. S. Shriver & Co	1904	2226	....	....	2226	
John G. & Edward Sinn	1936	699	....	....	†524 25	†From 1st October, 1844.
W. H. J. Stier	1943	60	....	....	60	
Tate & Troxell	1906	300	....	....	300	
J hn Taylor	1914	299 96	....	....	299 96	
James A. [illegible]n	1944	475	....	....	475	
James Turner	1909	80	....	....	80	
........Do	1910	55	....	....	55	
Total for Maryland	......	$130993 46	$2360 35	....	$131099 81	

VIRGINIA.						
Geo. W. Atkinson	2429	$296			$296	
Peter Adams	2474	3500			3500	
N. P. Adams	2589	298			298	
John G. Arthur	2592	320			320	
Brown, Beckham & Co.	2403	2200			2200	
John Brown	2405	1000			1000	
C. B. Belfield	2411	544			544	
Boyd, Edmond & Co.	2426	4000			4000	
Do	2428	1400			1400	
Do	2475	1200			1200	
John G. Beckham	2460	560			560	
Do	2510	250			250	
James Belvin	2449	60			60	
Baltimore Steam Packet Company	2451	8000		1994 52	6005 48	Payment made for the number of trips performed, at $8000 pr. ann. for daily service.
Thomas O. Beal	2477	349		46	303	
Thomas Burke	2481	900			900	
D. C. Baggarly	2504	320		7	313	
Samuel Baker	2516	295			295	
Do	2520	195			195	
Benjamin Bell	2544	169	*12 03 †11 15		192 18	*Fr. July 17 to Nov. 16, '44.—†Fr. Nov. 18, '44.
Do	2545	236	*13 04		249 04	*From 18th Aug., 1844.
Joseph Bollen	2557	120			120	
Thomas A. Bell	2568	150			150	
Do	2571	148			148	
Do	2578	190			190	
James M. Boyd	2580	400			100	To 30th Sept., 1844.
Anthony Beard	2572	82			82	
John W. Burke	2606	238			238	

CONTRACTORS

Contractors.	No of Route.	Contract pay per annum.	Additional allowances.	Reduction.	Total amount accrued.	Remarks.
John A. Bonnett	2621	$170			$133 16	From 5th Aug. 1844.
J. S. M. Baisden	2622	275			275	
Mastin Bailey	2628	180			180	
John H. Bane	2629	115	*6 17	†15 25	105 92	*One month's extra pay on $74 per annum.—†From 17th April, 1845.
J. M., J. H. & T. J. Boyd.	2630	2987			2987	
Wm. J. Bowdoin	2670	72			31 20	From 25th January, 1845.
William Chapman	2419	250		*24 30	225 70	*From 19th January, 1845.
C. M. & H. H. Collier	2431	2450	†8 50		2458 50	†For tolls.
City Point R. R. Co.	2436	500			500	
John E. Coates	2437	490			490	
Henry Callcote	2445	100			100	
Thos. A. Coleburn	2458	85			85	
Benj. P. Cooke	2461	795			795	
James Chappell	2462	170	33		203	
E. H. Cheatham	2478	400			400	
H. Carver	2488	65		†26	64 74	†From 20th June, 1845.
N. H. Crump	2500	240	†24 16	40	224 16	†From 18th November, 1844.
J. F. Cannon	2495	390			292 50	From 1st October, 1844.
Do	2501	290			217 50	Do. Do.
Do	2506	170			170	
Do	2507	390			292 50	From 1st October, 1844.
Evan Caudy	2522	70			70	
Do	2523	110			110	
James Carroll, jr.	2532	40			40	
R. W. Courtney	2548	275			275	
J. B. Campbell	2564	295			295	

L. Connevey	2574	40			40	
J. Canterbury	2626	199			199	
M. D. Collier	2651	112 48	†9 37		116 91	To 14th June, 1845. †One mo's extra pay.
Luke Cox	2653	70	†13 53		83 53	†From 7th January, 1845.
Robt. H. Carter	2659	*68			68	
C. W. C. Dunnington	2404	599 88			599 88	
W. W. Davis	2406	174	†4 83	‡21 11	157 72	†One month's extra pay on $58 per annum.—‡From 19th February, 1845.
R. S. Duke	2423	500			500	
John D. Dogan	2502	73			73	
Thos. P. Deal	2507	390			97 50	To 30th September, 1845.
Silas Dearing	2594	199			199	
Do	2597	199	{ †4 82 / 14 76 }		218 58	†From 26th February, 1845.
Marshall Davis	2624	98			98	
William Davis	2649	54			54	
Rob. S. Ellis	2416	74			74	
Edmund Ennis	2417	120			120	
Robert Edmund	2493	2200		6 10	2193 90	
James Elliott	2527	420			420	
Wm. H. Estes	2575	312			312	
John D. Emmons	2607	180			180	
Weldon Edwards	2635	175			175	
Fadely & Johns a	2402	1499			749 50	From 1st January, 1845
Wm. P. Farish	2483	350			350	
Do	2484	2300			2300	
Do	2485	2250			2250	
Do	2499	900			900	
Do	2569	2470			2470	
Do	2603	3000			3000	
Thomas Foster	2503	200			200	
Johnson Furr	2514	331	46		377	
Farish & Ficklin	2517	3800			3800	

CONTRACTORS.

Contractors.	No. of Route.	Contract pay per annum.	Additional allowances.	Reduction.	Total amount accrued.	Remarks.
Farish, Ficklin & Co.	2570	$3000			$3000	
Do	2610	3000			3000	
Porter Flagg	2582	2450			2450	
James Faulkner	2585	170			170	
Do	2586	170			170	
John Gates	2427	380			380	
Greenville & Roanoke Rail-road Co.	2442	2000			1000	From 1st January, 1845.
L. B. Gardner	2443	2200			2200	
Abner Goodall	2498	294			294	
Phil. Goodall	2495	390			97 50	To 30th September, 1844.
Do	2496	425			425	
Do	2501	290			72 50	To 30th September, 1844.
R. M. Gilleland	2587	290			217 50	To 31st March, 1845.
Rob. H. Gibson	2611	273		$13	260	
Miles Horn	2441	110			110	
Rob. W. Harrison	2463	349			349	
Do	2464	495			495	
Davis High	2465	275			275	
Nathan Harrison	2529	55		30	25	
T. F. Hall	2535	36 48			36 48	
Jesse Hildebrand	2543	3428	857		4285	
Do	2552	433			433	
Thomas Herdman	2553	282 48			282 48	
John E. Hays	2559	99 96			99 96	
John A. Holden	2562	115			115	

........Do	2612	120	....	....	120	
Samuel Howell..........	2600	100	....	....	100	
Greggs Hampton........	2633	104	....	....	104	
John E. Harris..........	2637	95	....	....	95	
Jas. W. Hendricks.......	2641	99	....	....	99	
Silvanus Johnson........	2434	1800	....	....	1800	
John James.............	2454	150	....	....	150	
John G. Johnson........	2668	550	....	....	550	
M. L. Kearney..........	2487	230	....	....	230	
........Do	2491	150	....	....	150	
........Do	2566	190	....	....	190	
........Do	2567	125	....	....	125	
George Kennon..........	2492	220	....	....	220	
N. Kuykendall..........	2525	640	....	....	640	
........Do	2526	3267	....	....	3267	
John E. Knott..........	2541	1250	....	....	1250	
James Keith............	2558	140	....	....	140	
Vinton Kelly...........	2640	98	....	....	98	
........Do	2645	340	....	*10 98	329 02	*From 29th January, 1845
Louisa R. R. Co........	2420	4500	....	....	4500	
John Lindsay, jr........	2489	380	....	....	380	
........Do	2497	190	....	....	190	
Jesse Landes...........	2563	249	....	....	249	
John W. Lemer..........	2565	190	....	....	190	
C. S. Larew............	2573	64	....	....	64	
Orville [illegible]..........	2576	160	....	57	103	
R. B. Latimer..........	2669	50	....	....	50	
Isaiah [illegible]..........	2402	1499	....	....	749 50	To 31st December, 1844.
M. J. McGlasson........	2467	125	....	....	125	
........Do	2469	250	....	*6 64	243 36	*From 31st May, 1845.
Robt. D. Moore.........	2468	150	....	....	150	
........Do	2470	209	....	....	209	

CONTRACTORS.

Contractors.	No. of Route.	Contract pay per annum.	Additional allowances.	Reduction.	Total amount accrued.	Remarks.
G. Matthews	2480	$82	....	....	$82	
S. W. Mason	2494	48	....	....	48	
J. Michael	2528	79 76	....	....	79 76	
J. H. Morgan	2538	165	....	....	165	
Do	2539	50	....	....	50	
Wm. A. Mastin	2604	2000	....	....	2000	
Henry H. Miller	2623	100	....	....	100	
James Mahood	2631	196	....	....	196	
Do	2644	274	....	....	274	
Rufus Mink	2638	66	....	....	66	
P. C. Morrison	2639	130	....	....	130	
Do	2643	80	....	....	80	
Henry McWhorter, jr	2666	87 48	....	....	87 48	
Thomas Norman	2406a	50	....	....	18 19	From 19th February, 1845.
Wm. D. New	2448	80	80	....	160	
E. W. Nottingham	2452	800	....	....	400	To 31st December, 1844.
Joseph O'Neal	2505	96	....	....	96	
Do	2512	485	....	....	485	
Do	2521	144	21 60	....	165 60	
Do	2518	500	....	....	250	To 31st December, 1844.
J. & A. Perkins	2409	1600	†21	‡219 81	1401 19	†For 1 month's extra pay on $252 per annum. ‡From 17th August, 1844.
Do	2410	500	....	....	500	
Do	2413	800	....	....	800	
Do	2430	1200	....	....	1200	
Petersburg and Roanoke R. R. Company	2439	15200	....	....	15200	

Portsmouth and Roanoke Railroad Company	2453	8000				8000		
Thomas R. Peers	2476	150				150		
C. W. Paxson	2509	375				375		
T. Paxson	2511	60				60		
Jesse J. Pugh	2524	45				45		
R. B. Parsons	2588	300				300		
Anderson Paynter	2615	289				289		
Do	2616	50				50		
Do	2617	123				123		
William Pettes	2618	2000				2000		
Thos. Pemberton	2664	100				47	50	From 10th Jan'y, 1845.
Richmond, Fredericksburg and Potomac R. R. Co.	2422	19500				19500		
Richmond and Petersburg Railroad Company	2424	5818	48			5818	48	
A. H. Reames	2440	90				90		
David Rush	2515	200				200		
George W. Roe	2542	50				50		
F. B. Riheldarfer	2554	20				20		
G. W. Riddle	2558	140				70		To 31st December, 1844.
John Rhyan, jr.	2561	300		155		455		
John Renn	2587	290				72	50	From 1st April, 1845.
Joseph Remley	2613	40				40		
J. E. Reeside	2619	1270				1270		
Mordecai Roles	2652	150				150		
James Smith	2414	55				55		
John Southgate	2432	1200				1200		
M. D. Sumner	2444	299				299		
John Stickley	2508	200				200		
John A. Smith	2518	500				250		From 1st January, 1845.
C. V. Stone	2533	40				40		

CONTRACTORS.

Contractors.	No of Route.	Contract pay per annum.	Additional allowances.	Reduction.	Total amount accrued.	Remarks.
C. V. Stone	2534	$35	....	....	$35	
Garret Steel	2547	135	†$46 41	....	181 41	†From 2d September, 1844.
Alexander Scott	2549	39	....	....	39	
S. G. Stalnaker	2621	150	....	....	14 27	To 4th August, 1844.
Geo. S. Sutherlin	2591	284	....	....	284	
Matthew Scott	2595	175	....	....	175	
A. H. Stovall	2596	150	....	....	150	
........Do	2599	150	....	....	150	
Adams Sanders	2609	375	†31 25	....	‡306 25	†1 month's extra pay. ‡To 25th March, '45.
........Do	2632	109	....	....	109	
W. D. Schooler	2636	42	....	....	42	
R. G. Tucker, jr	2438	399	....	....	399	
Wm. H. Thompson	2450	1000	....	....	1000	
........Do	2452	1000	....	....	475	From 10th January, 1845.
C. M. Twyman	2551	117	....	....	117	
G. M. Tolbert	2560	119	....	....	119	
Moses Taylor	2579	400	....	....	400	
Terry & Mastin	2580	400	....	....	300	From 1st October, 1844.
William Terry	2581	1700	....	....	1700	
Townes & Hopkins	2590	195	....	....	195	
David Vandegrift	2486	80	....	....	80	
B. G. Vannoy	2555	295	....	109	186	
Francis Vannoy	2620	270	....	....	270	
Washington & Fredericksburg Steamboat Co	2401	12752	....	....	12752	
W. B. Waller	2407	90	....	....	90	

Do	2408	150			150	
Do	2412	1350			1350	
Do	2415	399 48			399 48	
J. Woolfolk	2418	299 48			299 48	
A. D. Wooddy	2421	95			80 54	$15 49 to 29th August, 1844. $65 05 from 25th Oct., 1844.
S. D. Watkins	2433	793		45	748	
Do	2435	2480			2480	
William Waddy	2456	50			50	
J. D. Welbourn, jr	2457	299			299	
Do	2459	49	52		101	
A. Worsham	2466	500			500	
Do	2472	500			500	
J. Wingfield	2479	800		133	667	
Winchester and Potomac Railroad Company	2519	3200			3200	
E. B. Williams	2584	480			480	
J. H. Walker	2608	1300			1300	
Miles Wilcox	2634	179			179	
Sam'l Woodward	2648	40			40	
A. Q. Wooddy	2664	150	†12 50		90 42	To 7th Jan., '45. †1 month's extra pay.
Total of Virginia		$200888 96	$1453 12	$2778 97	$193344 95	
NORTH CAROLINA.						
James Alderman	2826	$340			$340	
Peter Adams	2873	1500			1500	
Do	2874	975			975	
Do	2905	6000			6000	
Do	2934	189			189	
James Allen	2879	99	15		114	

CONTRACTORS.

Contractors.	No. of Route.	Contract pay per annum.	Additional allowances.	Reduction.	Total amount accrued.	Remarks.
M. S. Abernathy	2902	$125			$125	
Alexander & Springs	2907	2440			1830	To 31st March, 1845.
Do	2908	1995			1496 25	Do. do.
Do	2923	1494			1120 50	Do. do.
Do	2924	494			370 50	Do. do.
M. W. Alexander	2924	494			123 50	From 1st April, 1845.
T. Abernathy	2931	85			85	
D. D. [illegible]	2806	240			240	
Blooker & Love	2816	1259			1259	
Do	2825	125			125	
Elias Barnes	2820	180			180	
C. H. Bragden	2829	122		25	97	
Jesse Butts	2845	52			52	
A. & F. W. Boyd	2861	940			940	
W. R. Boswell	2862	200			100	From 1st January, 1845.
Sam'l H. Breeze	2867	169			169	
J. & W. K. Blair	2884	4700			4700	
Joseph Banner	2885	214			214	
Do	2892	99			99	
G. M. Bingham	2896	145			145	
Do	2901	225			225	
Do	2903	89			89	
Do	2938	140			140	
M. Brooks	2900	219			219	
John Brooks	2948	30			30	
A. C. Curry	2813	923 48			923 48	

E. W. Christian	2814	300	....	....	300	
........Do	2917	150	....	....	150	
M. J. Clark	2841	500	....	....	500	
P. Crawford	2872	170	....	....	170	
Isaac Cummings	2910	22	....	....	22	
N. G. Clark	2912	145	....	....	145	
........Do	2913	125	....	....	125	
John Covington	2920	190	5	....	195	
Thos. B. Capps	2922	200	....	37	163	
........Do	2926	225	....	....	225	
John Clonts	2940	129	....	....	64 50	To 31st December, 1844.
John H. Dobson	2891	118	....	....	118	
T. H. Daniel	2916	197	....	....	197	
G. Dickerson	2936	239	....	....	239	
S. Dillon & H. Delon	2911	273	....	....	273	
E. Elliott	2803	1350	....	....	1350	
........Do	2821	1394	....	....	1394	
Isaac Erwin	2933	190	....	....	190	
Wm. A. Erwin	2940	129	....	....	64 50	From 1st January, 1845.
John C. Frost	2827	275	....	....	275	
........Do	2830	275	....	....	275	
Thos. E. Fanning	2847	750	....	....	750	
J. N. Faulcon	2859	80	....	....	80	
H. Fowler	2862	200	....	....	100	To 31st December, 1844.
E. P. Guion	2802	3000	1040† 1300‡	....	5340	†From 1st Jan., '45, to 17th February, '45. ‡Two months' extra pay on $7800.
........Do	2808	1100	....	....	1100	
M. R. Gillekin	2837	62 48	....	....	62 48	
Riddick Griffin	2857	135	....	....	135	
Wm. S. Gilmer	2875	280	....	....	280	
........Do	2876	110	....	....	110	
P. Hawkins	2844	1199	....	....	1199	

CONTRACTORS.

Contractors.	No. of Route.	Contract pay per annum.	Additional allowances.	Reduction.	Total amount accrued.	Remarks.
W. S. Harrison	2855	$175			$175	
R. Harris	2868	150			150	
Geo. H. Hamilton	2887	97 48			97 48	
Ephraim Hough	2889	114			114	
Thomas F. Hager	2925	110			110	
J. Howard	2941	700			700	
L. Howard	2943	248			248	
E. Hardin	2952	49			49	
Jackson Johnson	2812	1850			1850	
Do	2957	750	*62 50		†164 58	*1 month's extra pay—†From 1st January, 1845, to 18th February.
Jon'n H. Jacocks	2853	52			52	
Sam'l P. Jones	2904	256 48			256 48	
Thos. P. Jackson	2935	745		55	690	
Henry A. King	2810	36			36	
John R. Kilby	2852	590			590	
Caleb Knott	2866	125			125	
Rob. Kent	2878	3500			3500	
Arch'd Leslie	2804	275			275	
Micajah Lowe	2846	786			786	
Thomas Long	2849	149			149	
Joel McLean	2805	1900			1900	
Do	2807	2238	*10 90		2248 90	*From 10th June, 1845.
Do	2863	2500			2500	
B. L. McLauchlin	2811	4320	*1175 †1500		6995	*From 1st Jan., 1845, to 16th Feb. †Two months' extra pay on $9,000.
McDaniel & Rodgers	2818	365			365	

Sam'l P. Moore	2865	200			200	
Wm. J. Moore	2869	100			100	
Do	2871	124	19		143	
Nah Matkins	2880	130		33	97	
Jos. H. Moore	2932	78 96			78 96	
William Pollock	2838	500			500	
Pressnell & Baker	2898	169			169	
Eli Parker	2956	995	*82 92		95 67	For two trips—*1 month's pay.
Raleigh and Gaston Rail-road Company	2801	8700	*1060 55 †691 67		10452 22	*From 1st January, 1845, to 15th Feb. †1 month's extra pay on $8,300.
H. E. Royal	2824	225			225	
Benj. Robinson	2842	900			900	
J. Rothhoos	2888	375			375	
Wm. A. Robey	2906	165			165	
Reynolds & Burgin	2909	2577	*30 75		2607 75	*From 1st October, 1844.
J. A. Reynolds	2954	250			250	
O. Smallwood	2839	500	*20 83	†46 01	474 82	*1 month's extra pay on $250—†From 25th April, 1845.
Do	2850	575			575	
Do	2858	340			340	
Wm. Sebastian	2895	83			83	
J. Sullins	2897	290		25	265	
Alex. Springs	2907	2440			610	From 1st April, 1845.
Do	2908	1995			498 75	Do. do.
Do	2923	1494			373 50	Do. do.
B. L. Sanders	2921	375	128	34	469	
J. W. Stockton	2927	147 48			147 48	
Willis Sledge	2959	1120			1120	
David Taylor	2815	1500			1500	
B. W. Thorp	2834	795			795	
Wm. H. Thompson	2851	3426			3426	
Do	2856	3500			3500	
Noah Tharp	2881	85			85	

CONTRACTORS.

Contractors.	No. of Route.	Contract pay per annum.	Additional allowances.	Reduction.	Total amount accrued.	Remarks.
Wilmington & Raleigh Railroad Co.	2822	$75000	....	....	$75000	
Luther Wright	2831	385	....	....	385	
Wm. P. Ward	2833	1869	....	....	1869	
H. Wiswall	2848	3900	....	....	3900	
Jas. Williams	2854	484	....	....	484	
G. B. Wilson	2877	1595	....	....	1595	
........Do	2883	185	76	....	261	
Miles Wilcox	2886	249	....	....	249	
........Do	2893	110	....	....	110	
Jas. A. Wilson	2899	297	....	....	297	
Henry Webster	2914	175	....	....	175	
Matthew Wallace	2919	245	....	....	245	
J. & R. W. White	2928	72	....	....	72	
R. W. White	2929	244	*21 94	....	265 94	*From 18th July, 1844.
J. & J. E. White	2930	48	....	....	48	
B. Washburn	2937	130	....	....	130	
........Do	2939	263	....	*18 59	244 41	*From 26th December, 1844.
S. Whitaker	2944	97 48	....	....	97 48	
D. Young	2864	59	....	....	59	
Total of North Carolina	......	$181456 84	$7240 06	$273 60	$180041 13	

SOUTH CAROLINA.						
Alexander & Spring	3107	1988			1491	From 1st July, 1844, to 31st March, 1845.
Christopher Addison	3178	1500			1500	From 1st July, 1844, to 30th June, 1845.
Thomas C. Austin	3186	80	50		130	
Peter Adams	3152	452			452	
Do	3155	230			230	
63 Charles Barrett	3170	425			212 50	From 1st January, 1845.
*Noah H. Bradley	3108	2500			2500	
Jas. P. Barker	3114	310			310	
H. Barfield	3118	200			150	To 31st March, 1845.
Do	3122	450			337 50	Do. Do.
Do	3127	9450	*160 84 †383 33	5392	4602 17	*From 15th Mar. '45.—†One mo's ext. pay.
Do	3192	600			487 50	To 31st March, 1845.
P. M. Butler	3124	1800			1800	
Do	3135	700			700	
Do	3140	125			125	
A. Bryan	3130	575			575	
R. A. Black	3154	145			145	
H. S Beadel	3163	180			180	
Geo. Bowen	3151	3300			3300	
Do	3165	260	47		307	
Do	3168	200		100	100	
Thos. & R. Barnett	3176	75			75	
Do	3177	75			75	
Thos. A. Beatty	3184	160			160	
Brooks & Barden	3126	9000			5250	From 1st December, 1844.
C. W. Cade	3134	785			785	
Chester S. Coe	3136	100			100	
Robert Cox	3190	70			70	
Thos. H. Colcock	3121	200			200	

CONTRACTORS.

Contractors.	No. of Route.	Contract pay per annum.	Additional allowances.	Reduction.	Total amount accrued.	Remarks.
Douglas & Ripley	3112	$5400			$5400	
Do	3173	2600			2600	
Douglas, Ripley & Ward	3102	2400			2400	
B. Dunham	3174	525			525	
William Green	3164	350			350	
N. A. Green	3169	304	$20		324	
Leroy Hammond	3145	325		$25	300	
Andrew Hamilton, jr	3171	400			400	
Do	3172	140			140	
James Hughes	3180	60			60	
Daniel Hughes	3181	74			74	
M. S. Hardin	3146	210			210	
Jesse Johnson	3117	62 72			62 72	
Kirkland, Brabham & Co.	3123	400	*16 66 *7 58	†19 78 †3 75	400 71	†From 26th May, '45.—*One mo's ex. pay. †From 16th June, '45.—*One mo's ex. pay.
Samuel Kirton	3132	3500			3500	
E. Leggett	3189	140			140	
Louisville, Cincinnati & Charleston Railroad Co.	3104	8187 48			8187 48	
Do	3125	33012 48			33012 48	
J. W. Lamkin	3129	5450			5450	
Tillman Lomax	3170	212 50			212 50	
S. S. McCully	3105	348			348	
Jno. W. Martin	3113	445			445	
J. L. McCall	3133	450			450	
Do	3139	575			575	

McDaniel & Rogers	3137	340			340	
Do	3138	500			500	
Do	3141	375			375	
Do	3142	240			240	
Eppy W. Morris	3179	390			390	
G. B. Montgomery	3191	120			120	
Benj. F. McLauchlin	3101	5520	*1498 78 †1913 32		8932 10	*From 1st January, 1845 to 16th February, 1845.—†Two month's extra pay.
Jas. Odam	3175	35	11		46	
J. P. Oxner	3110	200			200	
R. C. Poole	3156	195			195	
Wm. Patton	3128	800			800	
N. S. Punch	3143	431			431	
William Rice	3120	490		47	443	
Thos. E. Suggs	3106	493			493	
Do	3150	40			40	
Jno. H. Spencer	3111	1300			1300	
W. W. Sale	3115	273			273	
Sam'l Shaw	3144	96			96	
Alexander Springs	3107	1988			497	From 1st April, 1845.
William A. Tanner	3153	320			320	
Jesse Williams	3147	140			140	
Do	3148	246			246	
Wm. Wallace	3149	61			61	
R. Ward	3158	525	18		543	
F. Ward	3160	299			299	
Do	3161	150			150	
Do	3162	190			190	
Ward & Stalker	3109	4200			4200	
Ward, Ripley, & Douglas	3116	1487			1487	
Elihu Watson	3167	158			158	
Total for South Carolina		$123108 18	$4126 51	$5587 53	$115421 66	

CONTRACTORS.

Contractors.	No. of Route.	Contract pay per annum.	Additional allowances.	Reduction.	Total amount accrued.	Remarks.
GEORGIA.						
Jno. C. Addison	3310	$900			$900	
Jno. G. Anderson	3359	350			350	
Peter Alday	3371	250			250	
Jno. B. Brazelton	3343	125			125	
P. P. Bethea	3265	200			200	
Do	3267	400			400	
Jno. Butt	3271	300			300	
Benj. Brookins	3272	250			250	
L. W. Burtz	3319	85			85	
Benj. F. Blount	3346	118			118	
Elzatham Burke	3376	425			425	
Matilda Bohler	3304	120			120	
Jas. Blue	3361	2000			2000	
Wm. Berry	3306	144			144	
Jno. F. Beavers	3329	994			994	
Central Railroad & Banking Company	3256	20580			20580	
Raymond Cay	3360	1453			1453	
Jacob Crow	3292	180			180	
Dan'l Carrington	3307	175			175	
Jno. R. Cannon	3323	120			120	
Hugh Capehart	3325	350			350	
W. A. Caldwell	3332	74			18 50	To 30th September, 1844.

Cowsar & Douglass	3347	174			174	
Jno. T. Clough	3364	750			750	
Wm. W. Corbett	3377	35			35	
Jas. W. Cunningham	3379	400			400	
J. A. Clark	3293	575			575	
Jno. W. Carter, jr.	3331	2493			2493	
Collier & Leith	3355	3400		*566	2834	*From 1st November, 1844.
Jno. J. Carroll	3351	336			336	
Do	3354	228			228	
Jas. Duncan	3273	240			199 12	To 29th April, 1845.
Lemuel Dean	3287	686			686	
Do	3311	440		125	315	
Do	3336	190			190	
Do	3341	130			130	
Do	3350	185			185	
Wm. H. Dean	3340	120			120	
Joshua Dasher	3358	100			100	
Myron Ellis	3378	162			162	
Erastus L. Ellsworth	3294	15400		†1021 88 ‡597 17	13781 45	†From 22d Oct., '44. ‡From 2d Jan'y, '45.
Do	3253	3255			3255	
Joshua H. Fryer	3367	495			495	
R. S. Foster	3313	150			150	
Dan'l Griffin	3282	3680			920	From 1st April, 1845.
Ebenezer F. Green	3299	125			125	
W. W. Green	3317	47 48			47 48	
Do	3318	94			94	
Georgia R.R. & Banking Co.	3251	25550	†2850 ‡1328 51		29728 51	†From 1st Oct., '44. ‡From 2d Jan'y, '45.
Do	3298	3600			3600	
N. Harris	3327	235		46	189	
Hardin & Yarbrough	3330	1795			1795	

CONTRACTORS.

Contractors.	No. of route.	Contract pay per annum.	Additional allowances.	Reduction.	Total amount accrued.	Remarks.
Jas. Harris	3335	$298			$298	
C. Howell	3342	148			74	To 31st December, 1844.
Do	3344	70			35	Do. do.
Charlton Hines	3404	150			150	
Caleb W. Harvey	3374	250			250	
A. Hamilton, jr	3297	1648			1648	
Wm. Herring	3349	740			740	
Nathan Hawkins	3275	483			483	From 1st October, 1844.
Hawkins & Briggs	3405	397 50			397 50	
Wm. Jones	3270	125			125	
Francis W. Jobson	3279	150			150	
Jas. S. Jones	3289	1560			1560	
Isaac G. Jourdan	3368	875	†6 02	277	604 02	†From 23d June, 1845.
Sanford Kingsbury	3334	89			89	
Knox & Mott	3268	930	1430		2360	
Do	3278	1750		†516 46	1233 54	†From 12th August, 1844.
Jno. F. Lovett	3260	499			499	
Allen Lawrence	3263	200		54 †20 69	125 31	†From 1st February, 1845.
Leon Leprovost	3383	1580			1580	
Allen Lovelace	3382	2100			2100	
Lee & Crandall	3381	228			228	
Lee & Ayer	3380	1999			1999	
Jno. W. Martin	3254	545			545	
Do	3255	690			690	
Do	3302	149	30		179	

Do	3303	195		9	186	
Do	3305	280			280	
Do	3315	2900			2900	
Duncan McLeod	3264	160		15	145	
Morrow & Hawkins	3284	2100			2100	
Jno. McWhorter	3324	149			149	
C. McCrary	3333	285			285	
Robt. J. H. Miller	3337	262 48			262 48	
Jehu McCall	3357	110			110	
A. J. Miller	3369	340			340	
Jeremiah Mosteller	3342	148			74	From 1st January, 1845.
Do	3344	70			35	Do. do.
Jas. G. McLinn	3398	84 48	4		88 48	
Noah Murray	3384	249 48	249. 48		498 96	
Monroe Railroad and Banking Company	3283	5000			5000	
Wm. A. Mott	3276	600			600	
Do	3277	965	†141. 74		1106 74	†From 12th August, 1844.
Do	3285	150			150	
McCulloch & Harris	3291	1880		†452. 25	1427 75	†From 1st October, 1844.
Andrew Matthews	3345	74 92			74 92	
Reuben Nash	3309	275			275	
Sam'l Peden	3339	195		†68. 06	126 94	†From 24th October, 1844.
Jas. O. Quillian	3320	325			325	
Jas. Rhan	3258	104			104	
Jesse L. Riley	3308	1300			1300	
David C. Rose	3295	2550			2550	
Pharis Ray	3375	375			375	
Joseph Rice	3332	75			55 50	From 1st October, 1844.
Nathan Renfroe	3266	80			80	
R. M. & T. Sanford	3269	299			299	
Saltmarsh & Ellsworth	3282	2760			2760	

CONTRACTORS.

Contractors.	No. of Route.	Contract pay per annum.	Additional allowances.	Reduction.	Total amount accrued.	Remarks.
A. R. Smith	3290	$798		†$132 61	$665 39	†From 2d November, 1844.
Jas. C. Starke	3348	95			95	
Hugh L. Spear	3391	144	†$5 16		149 16	†From 26th December, 1844.
J. W. Sutlive	3370	425			425	
R. H. Vickers	3296	440			440	
B. S. Williams	3259	75			75	
F. K. Wright	3281	300			300	
Wm. Watkins	3352	199	*16 58		52 81	To 5th Sep., '44. *1 month's extra pay.
Do	3353	95			95	
Wright & Sawyer	3280	5500		119	5381	
Jno. H. Wyley	3275	644			161	To 30th September, 1844.
Walton Wyley	3314	400			400	
Do	3326	244			244	
Nimrod B. Wheeler	3399	97			97	
Robert S. Wolcott	3273	240			40 88	From 20th April, 1845.
Total for Georgia		$146354 34	$6061 49	$4019 62	$144457 44	
FLORIDA.						
Wm. W. Briggs	3523	$480			$480	
Jesse Carter	3504	2180		$500	1680	
Do	3506	1680			1680	
Do	3511	1260			1260	
Do	3512	900	$150		1050	

J. M. Chastine	3512a	345		48	297	
Alex. Campbell	3521	498 48			498 48	
A. H. Cole	3532	1475			737 50	From 1st January, 1845.
Wm. Gibbons	3505	350	272		622	
R. C. Hurst	3507	749			749	
Hass, McNulty & Stevens	3528	5500			5500	
Isaac G. Jourdan	3513	295			295	
Jno. Jenkins	3517	5500			1848 61	From 1st March, 1845.
Wm. Kitchen	3525	1450			1450	
Jas. Reeside, jr	3519	9500			7125	To 31st March, 1845.
Wm. T. Stockton	3501	2600		937 48	1662 52	
Do	3516	1000			1000	
Jas. M. Stocker	3526	1500			1500	
P. A. Stockton	3509	2000			2000	
W. W. Tucker	3533	900			450	From 1st January, 1845.
Geo. W. Tillinghast	3519	9500			2375	From 1st April, 1845.
Van Veghten & Sharpless	3517	5500			3651 39	To 28th February, 1845.
N. W. Walker	3510	900			900	
David Wilkinson	3530	245			122 50	From 1st January, 1845.
Total for Florida		$56307 48	$422	$1485 48	$38934	
ALABAMA.						
Wade Allen	5492	$1400			$1400	
Allen & Kitchen	5485	36670			36670	
Joseph Allen	5545	250	$*20 83		239 23	To 15th May, 1845. *1 month's extra pay.
Angelina Boyden	5500	800			800	
Malcolm Blue	5490	450			337 50	To 31st March, 1845.
James Baygents	5490	450			112 50	From 1st April, 1845.
D. E. Beaman	5523	2450			2450	

CONTRACTORS.

Contractors.	No. of Route.	Contract pay per annum.	Additional allowances.	Reductions.	Total amount accrued.	Remarks.
Jesse A. Collins	5429	$237 36	$8		$245 36	
Do	5462	399			399	
Geo. Clothier	5520	1300			1300	
Asa Carter	5510	400			400	
Geo. Chadwick	5441	500			500	
Do	5451	290			290	
Coker and Cowsar	5458	549			549	
Thos. K. Cook	5465	389	17 28		406 28	
Jno. W. Carter, jr	5466	993			993	
Arthur Crozier	5474	890			890	
Montgomery Carlton	5533	240			240	
Jethro D. Conway	5535	200			200	
Jonathan H. Calloway	5511	331 08	150		481 08	
Do	5540	142 48			142 48	
Joel Denton	5421	200			200	
Wm. Dowdy	5427	485	*125 20		610 20	*From 5th January, 1845.
Robert Douglas	5469	408	43		451	
Do	5470	235			235	
Do	5471	396			396	
David Dunn	5515	430			430	
T. J. Davis	5543	90			90	
Wm. Earbee	5445	1500			1500	
Wm. Eubanks	5416	299			299	
Charles Ewing	5420	947			947	
Jno. B. Edwards	5527	240			91 74	To 18th October, 1844.
Frierson & Harrison	5435	3000	120		3120	

........Do	5447	380	....	246	134	
Jno. A. Fortune	5433	1000	....	....	1000	
Jno. Gardner	5426	335	*18 74	†6 63	347 11	*From 2d November, 1844. †From 19th October, 1844.
Silas Garrett	5498	2795	188	....	2983	
Caswell Garrett	5504	150	....	....	150	
Gallaher & Garrett	5525	4000	....	....	4000	
Jno. Hendricks	5455	820	*14 18	....	834 18	*From 20th July, 1844.
Nathan Harris	5464	625	{ 207 48 *12 39 }	35	809 87	*From 25th March, 1845.
Jas. Harris	5477	199	....	....	199	
A. T. Hardin	5463	1595	....	....	398 75	To 30th September, 1844.
Jno. Howerton	5513	150	....	....	150	
Josiah Hall	5542	146	....	....	70 56	From 7th January, 1845.
Ivy & Barrett	5407	200	....	....	200	
Sam'l F. Jones	5516	755	....	....	755	
Robert Jemison, jr.	5430	900	....	....	900	
........Do	5431	3000	....	....	3000	
........Do	5432	3000	....	....	3000	
........Do	5434	3250	....	....	3250	
........Do	5437	1500	....	....	1500	
........Do	5438	2600	....	100	2500	
........Do	5440	1300	....	....	1300	
........Do	5487	2700	982	....	3682	
........Do	5488	3250	....	....	3250	
Allen Lovelace	5479	2450	....	....	2450	
........Do	5512	525	....	....	525	
James Larkins	5484	906	59	....	965	
........Do	5509	400	....	....	400	
........Do	5514	400	31	....	431	
........Do	5536	154	....	....	154	
N. Lamar	5461	399	*4 28	....	403 28	*From 13th July, 1844.
A. A. & M. H. McNeal	5446	333	....	....	333	

CONTRACTORS.

Contractors.	No. of Route.	Contract pay per annum.	Additional allowances.	Reduction.	Total amount accrued.	Remarks.
A. A. & M. H. McNeal	5452	$900		$540	$360	
J. L. Mustian	5439	4400			4400	
Do	5521	4000			4000	
Do	5478	9000	$2600		11600	
Jas. Mahan	5529	216		56	160	
N. McMullin	5541	375	{ 80 *76 66 }		531 66	*From 1st November, 1844.
A. B. Nicholson	5473	160			160	
Wm. Noblett	5419	149			149	
Peter F. Partrick	5405	3150			3150	
J. W. & M. A. Price	5406	900	{ 87 *176 }	348	815	*From 28th October, 1844.
M. A. Price	5422	6824			6824	
Richard Prince	5444	700			700	
Julius S. Perdue	5476	292 48			292 48	
Do	5480	615			615	
Jno. T. Roper	5483	400	64		464	
Rogers & Turner	5414	1400		700	700	
Ridley & Warren	5423	187			187	
Jas. T. Reese	5459	200	†16 16		26 44	To 18th July, 1844.—†One month's ex. pay.
Jno. Shell	5408	250	6		256	
Peter B. Starke	5402	5000			5000	
Do	5436	650			650	
Smith, Benderman & Co.	5448	784			784	
Levi Shackleford	5491	570	†12 75		582 75	†From 8th July, 1844.
Robert H. Simpson	5506	298		38	260	

Neal Smith	5450	650			650	
Richard Stewart	5489	2800			2800	
A. G. Sloo	5522	70000			70000	
Josiah Springer	5404	984	†14 74		998 74	†From 30th October, 1844.
Wm. G. Smith	5499	495	†7 86		502 86	†From 23d December, 1844.
Tuscumbia, Decatur & Courtland Railroad Co.	5418	3000			3000	
Danl. C. Thanir	5502	150	†12 50		62 50	To 31st October, 1844.—†One mo's ex. pay.
David Thomas	5443	300		75	225	
J. H. Thomason	5524	1880			470	From 1st April, 1845.
Wm. Waddill, jr.	5495	700			700	
Do	5496	566			566	
Do	5497	2450		178	2272	
Jas. Washburn	5428	150			150	
N. Yarbrough	5463	1595			1196 25	From 1st Oct., 1844.
Do	5524	1880			1410	To 31st March, 1845.
Total for Alabama		$226798 40	$5155 05	$2322 63	$225160 80	
MISSISSIPPI.						
Bryan & Gilkey	5614	$985			$492 50	From 1st January, 1845.
Do	5615	688			344	From 1st January, 1845.
Carolinus Boyd	5602	7000			3500	From 1st January, 1845.
Sutton Byrd	5666	750			750	
Boyd & Wilson	5602	7000			3500	To 31st December, 1844.
Jno. W. Burton	5626a	1454			1454	
Wm. Barton	5695	250			61 14	To 28th September, 1844.
Jas. B. Brown	5632	175			175	
Jas. M. Carr	5684	285			285	
W. W. Cook	5674	550			550	

CONTRACTORS

Contractors.	No. of Route.	Contract pay per annum.	Additional allowances.	Reduction.	Total amount accrued.	Remarks.
Wm. Cline	5685	$500			$250	From 1st January, 1845.
Jno. B. Dean	5625	575	$390		965	
David Duke	5624	597			597	
Do	5630	203			203	
Geo. M. Dickinson	5614	985			492 50	To 31st December, 1844.
Do	5615	970	*23 50	$†23 50	435	To 31st December, 1844.—†From 1st Dec., 1844.—*One month's extra pay.
Jno. C. Dickey	5693	124			124	
Jno. H. Davis	5617	1180			1180	
L. P. Edrington	5692	325			325	
J. M. Farrington	5635	247			61 75	From 1st April, 1845.
J. G. G. Garrett	5606	495	16		511	
Do	5619	490			490	
David Gallaher	5643	250			250	
Do	5645	435	144		579	
A. E. Gibson	5685	555			277	To 31st December, 1844.
Jacob Grubee	5672	474			474	
R. E. Halferd	5618	545			545	
Do	5657	330			330	
Jno. C. Hudson	5631	798 48			798 48	
Do	5637	245	202	49	398	
Robert Hight	5652	275			275	
Do	5653	475			475	
Do	5654	600			600	
Wm. Hicks	5677	158	500		658	
Samuel Handley	5641	219			219	
John W. Hornesby	5668	200			200	

Phillip O. Hughes	5615a	282			158	62	From 9th December, 1844.
R. C. Hutchison	5612	300			188	31	From 15th November, 1844.
Jno. H. Irby	5647	575			575		
Do	5648	997			997		
Jno. R. Jefferson	5601	7400			7400		
Do	5607	5360			5360		
Do	5611	199			199		
Do	5620	6000			6000		
Do	5621	1900			1900		
Do	5626	4046			4046		
Joseph Kinney	5638	225	12		237		
Samuel Kilgore	5667	450			450		
A. H. Kendrick	5679	250	*103 85		353	85	*From 5th July, 1844.
A. Mauldin	5651	475			475		
Wm. McKay	5658	475	475		950		
J. L. Man	5603	14000		2000	12000		
Joshua Murray	5663	425			425		
Do	5664	750			750		
Wm. L. Murray	5686	315			315		
Jno. McInnis	5665	615			615		
Jno. M. Miller	5634	969			969		
Jno. Montgomery	5695	250			188	86	From 29th September, 1844.
Joshua H. Pool	5659	1125			1125		
Do	5660	350			350		
Laban P. Pool	5656	450			450		
M. A. Price	5640	2895		330	2565		
Patterson & Jayne	5683	1200			1200		
Peter F. Partrick	5690	240			240		
A. Rice	5669	750	60		810		
Robins, Bodley & Walker	5605	5300			5300		
Henry Strong	5680	2400			600		To 30th September, 1844.
James Sims	5633	1165	1000		2165		

CONTRACTORS.

Contractors.	No. of Route.	Contract pay per annum.	Additional allowances.	Reduction.	Total amount accrued.	Remarks.
Peter B. Starke	5655	$500			$500	
Wm. C. Snow	5650	248 72			248 72	
Leroy & J. A. & Jas. Sims	5688	1975			1975	
David Thomas	5644	240			240	
Do	5646	449	$449		898	
Richard Valentine	5616	216			216	
J. Warren	5639	145	*86		145 86	*From 10th June, 1845.
M. J. Whitworth	5673	2999			2999	
Do	5678	362			362	
Do	5681	248			248	
J. R. White	5610	695			695	
Do	5682	474			474	
Geo. W. Williams	5671	247			247	
Wm. Weed	5680	2400			1800	From 1st October, 1844.
T. M. Yancey	5635	247			185 25	To 31st March, 1845.
Total for Mississippi		$104996 20	$3376 21	$2402 50	$93615 84	
LOUISIANA.						
John H. Alley	5927	$1196			$1196	
Wm. C. Carr	5934	300			300	
Cooper & Waddill	5916	2404 48			2404 48	
Lewis Creasy	5912	4995			4995	
M. Dicks	5915	790		$124	666	

Bailey C. Duke	5940	195	....	....	195	
H. M. Eder	5923	1690	....	....	845	From 1st January, 1845.
........Do	5925	750	....	....	375	Do
A. E. Gibson	5923	1690	....	....	845	From 1st July, '44, to 31st Dec., '44.
........Do	5925	750	....	....	375	Do do
O. Hatt	5908	1802	....	1534	268	
Jesse Hart	5938	9000	....	....	9000	
Garland S. Hart	5909	350	....	....	350	
........Do	5914	500	....	....	500	
Alw Kincaid	5930	750	....	....	750	
David Lambert	5920	288	....	....	288	
Rachael C. Lea	5918	1200	....	....	1200	
L. E. Love	5932	220	....	....	220	
Gorham Munson	5926	400	....	....	400	
A. J. Pennybacker	5931	412	258	....	670	
W. Prunty	5937	1050	....	....	1050	
A. Ragazzoni	5921	290	....	....	290	
B. B. Simmes	5922	1151	....	18	1169	
Catlett Tiffer	5929	1500	....	....	1500	
John Tiffer	5924	750	....	....	750	
S. S. Wheeler	5907	880	....	....	880	
George Whitman	5902	3600	....	....	3600	
John B. Young, jr	5919	2400	....	800	1600	
Philip Geiger	5901	110	....	....	82 50	From 1st October, 1844.
Joseph H. Hough	5901	55	13 75	....	27 50	To 30th September, 1844.
E. T. Jones	5928	750	100	98 76	751 24	
........Do	5933	790	....	....	790	
Total for Louisiana	......	$43008 48	$371 75	$1174 76	$38332 72	

CONTRACTORS.

Contractors.	No. of Route.	Contract pay per annum.	Additional allowances.	Reduction.	Total amount accrued.	Remarks.
ARKANSAS.						
Adams & Wilson	5833	$2400			$2400	
Wm. Black	5850	1600			1600	
Black & Hammond	5816	500			500	
T. & J. S. Champlin	5802	1100			1100	
George M. Cline	5854	173			145 73	From 28th August, 1844.
Elias Caruth	5847	500			500	
Thomas Culp	5821	295			295	
Isaac Folsom	5820	329			329	
A. E. Gibson	5801	2737			1368 50	To 31st December, 1844.
James W. Gibson	5801	2737			1368 50	From 1st January, 1845.
Do	5814	1250			1141 30	From 2d August, 1844.
Nelson Hewitt	5825	593		$296	297	
Do	5826	393		*117 78	238 43	*Reduction from 24th July, '44.
S. Hiley	5845	940			940	
John Howell	5832	374			374	
R. C. Hutchinson	5817	427	*17 75	†159 75	285	*1 month's extra pay. †From 1st October, 1844.
John D. Hogan	5828	1197			1197	
Lemmon & Walters	5806	14000			10500	From 1st October, 1844.
Harvey S. Leonard	5835	275	15		290	
E. E. McConnell	5831	422	8 44		430 44	
Mathew Moore	5830	797			797	

Nuckles & Wyatt	5841	428 72	....	....	428 72	
B. F. Payne	5853	155	....	....	155	
Ambrose Powell	5836	164	....	....	164	
Wm. H. Preston	5849	970	*29 41	....	999 41	*Additional allowance for supplying Conway at $33 per an., from 10th August,'44.
Thomas H. Rives	5842	1100	....	....	1100	
........Do	5843	1350	....	....	1350	
Isaac Russell	5837	95	....	....	95	
Cyrus F. Sargent	5846	297	....	....	297	
Wm. Sears	5811	590	....	....	590	
Snapp & Howell	5804	6600	....	....	6600	
........Do	5838	1800	....	....	1800	
........Do	5848	940	13 40	*224 49	728 91	*Reduction caused by terminating route at Caddo Narrows; 60 miles dec'd distance, from 22d Feb., '45.
Wm. Thrower	5815	550	....	....	550	
........Do	5818	500	....	130	370	
John C. P. Tolleson	5807	650	....	325	325	
........Do	5808	650	....	325	325	
Hansford Tutt	5823	495	....	247	248	
........Do	5824	299	....	....	299	
Josiah Vinsant	5829	698	....	....	698	
Emzy Wilson	5803	2995	....	....	2995	
John Woodrome	5805	1959 32	....	....	979 66	From 1st January, '45.
........Do	5839	447 48	*28	....	251 74	*For ferriages for 28 weeks, at $1 per week.
Edward Bennett	5805	1775	92 16	....	979 66	To 31st December, 1844.
........Do	5839	895 00	*32 60	223 76	256 34	To 31st December, 1844. *Additional allowances for ferriages in supplying New Gascony.
Total for Arkansas	......	$59442 52	$236 76	$2038 78	$48682 34	

CONTRACTORS.

Contractors.	No. of Route.	Contract pay per annum.	Additional allowances.	Reduction.	Total amount accrued.	Remarks.
TENNESSEE.						
Elizabeth Barkley	5187	$36			$36	
H. G. Barbee	5233	290			290	
John Bartley	5161*pt*	35			35	
F. K. Berry	5168	345			345	
John Black	5101	2700			2700	
Do	5105	410			410	
Do	5135	3300			3300	
John Blair & Co	5134	9950			9950	
B. T. Bradley	5206	810			810	
James Brannan	5162	172	$6		178	
Adam Broyles	5161	200			200	
C. Bush	5125	1500		$33	1467	
John Butler	5122	151 36			151 36	
John W. Burton	5238	968			968	
Wm. A. [illegible]ll	5176	200			200	
Willis S. [illegible]r.	5133	475			475	
Nathan Cook	5116	199			199	
Do	5117	93			93	
Do	5118	134 50			134 50	
Champion Cowan	5164	65			65	
O. Clark	5185	321			321	
D. J. Craig	5201	150			150	
David Crowder	5102	175			175	
James H. Curry	5213	297			74 25	From 1st April, 1845

James R. Dickey	5213	297	....	....	222 75	To 31st March, 1845.
Drake & Harver	5115	182	....	....	182	
A. S. Deakins	5242	302	....	....	151	From 1st January, 1845.
........Do	5243	161	....	....	80 50	Do.
Wm. S. Parrish	5242	302	....	....	151	To 31st December, 1844.
........Do	5243	161	....	....	80 50	Do.
John Day	5175	174	....	....	174	
James R. Dickey	5197	291	58	77	272	
Dever & Henry	5165	235	....	....	235	
Jos pho Eaton	5121	100	100	....	200	
John G. Evans	5202	350	....	....	350	
Ezekiel Farmer	5239	364	....	....	364	
Thomas Gardner	5240	148	....	....	148	
Wm. Garner	5 531	74	....	....	74	
John Gibbs	5136	197	....	....	197	
John G. Gillespie	5196	160	....	....	160	
John F. Greer	5177	96	15	....	111	
........Do	5178	95	....	6	89	
........Do	5179	109	12	....	121	
John Griffitts	5140	293 95	....	....	293 95	
........Do	5146	109 90	....	....	109 90	
Alex. Harris	5166	490	....	....	490	
T. J. Harrelson	5142	547	....	....	273 50	From 1st Jan., 1845.
Wm. A. Donnelly	5142	547	....	....	273 50	To 31st December, 1844.
Wm. P. Harris	5 191	296	....	....	296	
Thomas Hash	5186	82	....	....	82	
Samuel Haskins	5137	280	14 48	....	294 48	
James D. Hayes	5 931	138	20	20	138	
John F. Hayes	5248	175	....	....	175	
Harwood & Jetton	5245	375	....	....	375	
George Hickman	5155	47 48	....	....	47 48	
R. B. Hudson	5131	300	....	....	300	

CONTRACTORS.

Contractors.	No. of Route.	Contract pay per annum.	Additional allowances.	Reduction.	Total amount accrued.	Remarks.
Hough & McAlister	5107	$3400			$3400	
Paul Herreford	5141	800			800	
Do	5171	760			760	
Do	5184	3283			3283	
Do	5188	3333			3333	
Thomas Hutchison	5120	125			125	
Joseph H. Hough	5106	3150			3150	
Do	5199	2150			2150	
Samuel Ingram	5219	985			985	
Vincent Kelly	5159	194 48			194 48	
B. C. Kinslow	5124	356			356	
Do	5126	1895			1895	
Willie Langford	5216	175			175	
Do	5229	249			249	
Shadrack Lawson	5108	190 84	7		197 84	
Thomas Lesly	5167	350	78	15	413	
Lewis Levy	5230	489			489	
Do	5231	500			500	
John H. Logan	5201 *pt*	287			287	
Wm. McAdoo	5220	160		72	88	
Tho. N. McLain	5234	99			99	
Joel McLean	5139	2990			2990	
James C. McClelland	5192	425			425	
John McKnight	5212	221			221	
Wm. T. Manson	5150	269	*27 83		284 78	To 15*th June*, 1845. *1 month's extra pay, $22 83, included in this.
H. T. Mathews	5235	104			104	

Wm. M. Mitchell	5123	2970	....	....	2970	
A. H. Montgomery	5180	849	....	....	849	
Larrey Moore	5221	1199	....	649	550	
George M. Moore	5217	179 84	....	....	179 84	
Richard [illegible]	5144	230	....	....	230	
R. W. [illegible]	5110	249 48	....	....	249 48	
Bird Pankey	5127	575	....	....	575	
........Do	5182	200	....	....	200	
Lewis Parker	5 981	74	....	....	74	
M. A. Price	5114	270	....	....	270	
Price & Flowers	5218	3825	....	....	3825	
Thomas Ralph	5241	250	....	....	250	
C. N. Renean	5152	195	....	....	195	
........Do	5154	189	....	....	189	
Stephen Rhea	5 691	255	....	....	*160 76	*From 14th *Nov.*, '44.
Ripley, Ripley & Douglass	5163	4300	....	....	4300	
George M. Ridley	5203	175 48	....	....	175 48	
........Do	5205	398	....	....	398	
........Do	5211	222	7	....	229	
........Do	5223	275	....	100	175	
John L. Ross	5145	220	....	....	220	
E. L. Rudd	5172	48	....	....	48	
Isaac Sampson	5246	265	....	....	265	
Richard A. Sharp	5138	279	....	24	255	
........Do	5147	139	....	....	139	
Joseph Shepherd	5160	200	....	....	200	
Smith & Benderman	5191	474	....	....	474	
........Do	5204	249	11	14	246	
........Do	5225	229	....	....	229	
........Do	5226	149	....	....	149	
........Do	5227	299	9 20	*20 70	287 50	*Reduction includes $11 50 for *discontinuance* of supply to Dry Hill.

CONTRACTORS.

Contractors.	No. of Route.	Contract pay per annum.	Additional allowances.	Reduction.	Total amount accrued.	Remarks.
Smith & Benderman	5237	$474	....	....	$474	
Smith & Leuter	5236	4000	....	....	4000	
Sam'l Spears	5228	125	....	....	125	
Wm. Stone	5181	775	....	....	775	
Gege A. Stt	5104	2200	....	....	2200	
........Do	5190	850	....	$161	689	
Ae Timons	5194	130	....	....	130	
S. A. Warner	5209	2000	....	111	1889	
........Do	5222	1100	....	....	1100	
Tho. N. Wendell	5103	1900	$706	....	2606	
Edward Wiams	5132	285	....	....	285	
Total for Tennessee	......	$90667 31	$1071 51	$1302 70	$87102 83	
OHIO.						
Geo. M. Adams	2126	$219 75	....	....	$109 87	To 31st December, 1844.
John J. Ager	2019	99 50	....	....	99 50	
J. C. Alexander	2151	72	....	....	72	
........Do	2153	132	....	....	132	
Tho mas W. Anderson	2242	141	....	....	141	
Grover Ayers	2260	100	....	....	75	To 31st March, 1845.
Geo. G. Baker	2085	139	....	....	139	
........Do	2172	210	....	....	98	From 13th January, 1845.
........Do	2175	48	....	....	48	

........Do............	2180	76	....	....	76	
........Do............	2189	114	....	....	114	
........Do............	2204	94	....	....	94	
J. K. Barnes...........	2162	65	....	....	65	
J. Barnd...............	2177	74 99	....	....	37 49	From 1st January, 1845.
Thos. Bell.............	2054	29	....	....	29	
Henry Bell.............	2129	700	....	....	175	From 1st April, 1845.
John Billis............	2252	300	....	....	300	
Mason M. Bowen.........	2197	73	....	....	54 75	To 31st March, 1845.
James Brooks...........	2195	100	....	....	100	
........Do............	2196	100	....	....	100	
........Do............	2255	800	....	....	{ 200 { 244 75	From 1st April, 1845. Fr. Dec. 23, '44, to Mar. 31, '45.—Spe'l serv.
Ezekiel Brown..........	2255	598	....	....	149 50	To 30th September, 1844.
.... Do............	2257	633	....	....	158 25	Do do.
Wm. Br wn..............	2100	215	....	....	215	
Chas. Burchfield, jr...	2132	174	....	....	87	To 31st December, 1844.
Nich's S. Bunn.........	2144	180	....	....	180	
John Burr..............	2243	175	....	....	175	
Coonrod Buymel.........	2260	100	....	....	25	From 1st April, 1845.
E. Callahan............	2111	100 25	....	....	100 25	
George Canade..........	2137	119	....	....	119	
George C. Cary.........	2155	63	....	....	63	
John W. Cheny..........	2145	333	....	....	333	
John Coffee, jr........	2214	230	....	....	230	
........Do............	2218	100	....	....	100	
Daniel Coffman.........	2136	225	....	....	162 02	From 12th October, 1844.
........Do............	2148	235	....	....	235	
James S. Connell.......	2265	200	....	....	200	
........Do............	2267	175	....	....	175	
Daniel G. Converse.....	2063	115	....	7 33	107 67	
Geo. W. Cooper.........	2114	150	....	....	150	

66*

CONTRACTORS.

Contractors.	No. of Route.	Contract pay per annum.	Additional allowances.	Reduction.	Total amount accrued.	Remarks.
John Cousins	2067	$166			$166	
Do	2068	84			84	
Wm. Crasson	2226	195			195	
David Creamer	2212	198			198	
Jacob Creamer	2215	99			99	
Do	2216	123	$11		133	
Croft & Phillips	2021	120			120	
G. D. Darlington	2232	1198			1198	
Joseph Davis	2209	48			48	
James Delay	2126	219 75			109 87	From 1st January, 1845.
Lewis M. Dewees	2113	49 50			49 50	
G. C. Dickerman	2038	195			195	
Do	2047	75			75	
Edward Dixon	2259	174			174	
Wm. Douglass	2246	50			50	
Do	2254	189			189	
Robert Dow	2192	114			114	
James F. Drake	2052	698			698	
Samuel A. Dwell	2062	55			55	
Ellwell & Lane	2024	80			80	
John Fergusson	2099	849			424 50	To 31st December, 1844.
Fisher & Musser	2257				155 20	Fr. 14th Oct. to 31st Dec. '44.—Spe'l service.
Elias Ford	2150	184			184	
A. W. Gaines	2223	1500			620 83	From 1st February, 1845.
Tira Garrett	2190	75			75	
Wm. Gates	2045	62			62	

........Do.............	2058	120	....	....	120	
Charles G. Gillispie	2255	....	....	....	67 94	31 days from 19th Nov. '44.—Spe'l service.
Reuben Gleason	2129	700	....	....	525	To 31st March, 1845.
........Do.............	2157	297	....	....	297	
David J. Gray...........	2092	135	....	....	135	
Joshua Grimes	2011	58	....	....	58	
A Hantz................	2028	175	10	....	185	
Ephraim Hawkins........	2119	189	....	....	189	
Jesse Hildebrand.........	2004	711	....	....	494 61	From 21st October, 1844.
........Do.............	2108	115	....	....	33 75	To 30th September, 1844.
Samuel Hines............	2015	110	....	....	110	
David Horton............	2074	950	....	....	950	
John Howden	2043	208	....	....	208	
Peter Humsher..........	2073	73	....	....	73	
John Hurd..............	2197	73	....	....	54 75	To 31st March, 1845.
Joseph Ingersol..........	2066	115	....	....	115	
...... .Do.............	2069	45	....	....	45	
.... Do............	2071	94	....	....	94	
........Do.............	2164	50	....	....	50	
Isaac Jackson............	2014	89	....	....	89	
........Do.............	2030	89	....	....	89	
W. S. Johnson...........	2077	150	....	....	150	
........Do.............	2179	89	....	....	89	
Johnson & Dolman.......	2005	228	....	....	228	
........Do.............	200	168	....	....	168	
........Do.............	2009	228	....	....	228	
........Do.............	2094	68 50	....	....	68 50	
........Do.............	2095	88	85	....	173	
........Do.............	2103	91	....	....	91	
........Do.............	2107	218	....	....	218	
........Do.............	2109	198	5 58	20 47	183 11	
Isaiah Kelly............	2026	128	....	....	128	

CONTRACTORS.

Contractors.	No. of Route.	Contract pay per annum.	Additional allowances.	Reduction.	Total amount accrued.	Remarks.
H. Kingsbury	2115	$58			$58	
Do	2118	49			49	
Wm. Kisling	2220	174			174	
Lane & Whitney	2048	65			65	
Joseph Leatherman	2098	143			143	
Peter Lenhart	2017	48			48	
Isaac Lewis	2229	174			174	
Erie Lock	2171	104			104	
W. R. Loofborrow	2135	150			37 50	To 1st October, 1844.
John Lord	2125	49			49	
Elisha Matthews	2120	148			148	
James McAtee	2084	120			120	
Joseph McCutchen	2170				38 69	From 1st July to 1st Aug., '44.—Spec'l serv.
Do	2173	232			232	
Do	2174	112			112	
James McLean	2161	180			180	
Do	2170				96	From 23d Sept. to 19th Dec., '44.–Spec'l serv.
J. H. McMakin	2264	140			140	
Do	2266	90			90	
R. W. McMahon	2082	68			68	
David Montgomery	2238	130			130	
R. S. Moon	2237	245	16		261	
Samuel S. Moore	2078	90			90	
J. H. Morgan	2004				180 43	From 1st July to 20th Oct., '44.—Spec'l serv.
Freeman Moulton	2039	100			100	
J. S. Murdock	2250	72			72	

Jonathan Murphy	2093	100			100	
Daniel Musser	2257				225	From 1st Jan. to 31st Mar., '45.—Spec'l serv.
Neil & Tallmadge	2001	11250	2750		14000	
Do	2003	1995			997 50	From 1st January, 1845.
Do	2010	925			462 50	Do do.
Do	2020	2125			2125	
Do	2022	004			4000	
Do	2025	2557			2557	
Do	2036	725			725	
Do	2057	3000			3000	
Do	2064	6000			6000	
Do	2070	180			180	
Do	2076	1000			1000	
Do	2087	4850			1212 50	From 1st April, 1845.
Do	2091	450			450	
Do	2138	15000			15000	
Do	2139	3321	71 65		3392 65	
Do	2141	2350			2350	
Do	2142	4600			4600	
Do	2206	4500			2250	To 31st December, 1844.
Do	2207	1110			1110	
Do	2230	3820			1910	From 1st January, 1845.
Do	2236	145			72 50	Do do.
Do	2240	797 50			398 75	Do do.
Do	2248	1196			1 961	
Do	2251	86	7 16		28 66	From 1st Jan. to 31st March, 1845.
Do	2268	150	2	2 60	75 60	From 1st Jan. to 30th June, 1845.
Solomon Norris	2135	150			37 50	To 30th September, 1844.
Isaac North	2130	75			75	
Wm. Orr	2081	115			115	
Wm. N. Pardee	2072	127			127	
Do	2075	84			84	

CONTRACTORS.

Contractors.	No. of Route.	Contract pay per annum.	Additional allowances.	Reduction.	Total amount accrued.	Remarks.
Wm. N. Pardee	2257	$728	....	....	$182	From 1st April, '45.
Peacock & Mallernee	2006	250	....	....	250	
John Pharis	2158	178	$2	....	180	
Wm. Phillips, (of New Castle, Pa.)	2097	140	....	....	140	
Do	2116	135	....	....	135	
Do	2136	187	....	....	46 75	To 30th September, '44.
Do	2169	110	....	....	110	
Do	2176	115	....	....	115	
Do	2188	125	....	....	125	
Wm. Phillips, (of Kalida, Ohio.)	2261	74	....	....	74	
Pope & Pope	2152	95	....	....	95	
Do	2154	55	....	....	55	
Do	2166	225	....	....	168 75	To 31st March, '45.
E. Porter	2208	224	....	....	224	
Wm. Porterfield	2184	140	....	....	140	
Robert Quigley	2160	150	....	....	150	
Robert Ramsay	2029	85	....	....	85	
Levi H. Randall	2166	225	....	....	56 25	From 1st April, '45.
J. E. Reeside	2003	1995	....	....	997 50	From 1st July, '44, to 31st December, '44.
Rufus S. Reed	2056	12000	per season.	....	14733 05	
A. B. Reeves	2033	185	....	....	185	
Joel Riblet	2159	75	....	....	{ 37 50	From 1st January, '45.
					{ 37 50	From 1st July to 31st December, '44—special service.
Thos. M. Robb	2005	188	....	....	188	

Chas. Roberts	2090	220	....	....	220		
........Do	2134	195	....	....	195		
M. Roberts	2003	2625	....	....	2625		
W. K. Rogers	2255	....	....	....	94	25	For 37 days, from 15th Oct., '44–sp'l serv.
Isaac Roll	2251	86	....	....	43		To 31st December, '44.
Philip [illegible]	2104	325	....	....	325		
Jacob [illegible]g	2177	75	....	....	37	50	Ditto.
Wm. L. Ross	2231	1390	....	....	1390		
Wm. T. Rowe	2087	4850	....	....	3637	50	To 31st March, '45.
........Do	2199	89	....	....	89		
........Do	2202	234	....	....	234		
........Do	2217	120	....	42 78	72	22	
........Do	2228	52	....	....	52		
........Do	2269	35	....	....	35		
........Do	2270	200	....	....	200		
John Rundle	2127	110	....	....	110		
Henry H. Rush	2253	117	....	....	117		
D. F. Sanford	2102	105	....	....	105		
Joel Sanders	2132	174	....	....	87		From 1st January, '45.
P. W. Sellers	2223	124 80	....	....	124	80	
Addison Simpson	2210	185	....	....	185		
B. Sinclair	2031	38	....	....	38		
John Sinsabaugh	2099	849	....	....	424	50	From 1st January, '45.
S. D. Smith	2165	114	....	....	114		
W. Smith	2211	208	....	....	208		
Smith & Poffinbarger	2117	143	....	....	143		
Isaac Snyder	2191	550	....	....	550		
Joseph Snyder	2 931	160	....	....	160		
Randal Stivers	2122	400	....	....	400		
Swingley & Geller	2170	295	....	....	155	22	From 22d December, '44.
D. Tallmadge	2088	11300	....	....	11300		
........Do	2089	1155	....	....	1155		

CONTRACTORS.

Contractors.	No. of Route.	Contract pay per annum.	Additional allowances.	Reduction.	Total amount accrued.	Remarks.
D. Tallmadge	2133	$1300	....	....	$1300	
Do	2140	4700	....	....	4700	
Do	2143	270	$92 50	....	362 50	
Do	2146	1000	....	....	1000	
Do	2147	400	....	....	400	
Do	2234	1600	....	....	1600	
Lewis Taylor	2256	169	....	....	169	
R. F. Thompson	2247	78	....	....	78	
James Thompson	2233	780	65	....	327 17	To 1st February, '45.
James Timbrook	2123	98 87	....	....	98 87	
Jona. Tucker	2105	175	....	....	175	
Do	2156	247	....	....	247	
Dan'l Tuell	2108	135	....	10 26	124 74	
E. W. Van Etten	2163	400	....	....	400	
C. Van Fleet	2185	1400	....	....	1400	
Do	2186	200	....	....	200	
Do	2187	150	....	....	150	
David Vansise	2181	400	....	....	400	
Jared Varney	2121	90	....	....	90	
Do	2124	220	....	....	220	
J. & P. Voorhees	2206	4500	....	....	2250	From 1st January, 1845.
Do	2230	3820	....	....	1910	To 1st January, 1845.
Do	2235	90	....	....	90	
Do	2236	145	....	....	72 50	To 1st January, 1845.
Do	2240	797 50	....	....	398 75	Do. do.
Do	2245	280	....	....	280	

........Do	2249	300	....	....	300	
........Do	2268	150	....	....	75	To 1st January, 1845.
Wm. Ward	2010	925	....	....	462 50	Do.
........Do	2012	650	....	....	650	
........Do	2023	149	....	....	149	
........Do	2032	597	....	....	597	
........Do	2034	250	....	....	250	
........Do	2037	800	....	....	800	
........Do	2050	194	....	....	194	
........Do	2051	1550	....	....	1550	
........Do	2053	175	....	....	175	
........Do	2055	99	....	....	99	
........Do	2060	80	....	....	80	
........Do	2061	164	....	....	164	
........Do	2065	350	....	....	350	
........Do	2079	800	....	....	800	
........Do	2086	1300	....	....	1300	
Joseph Warrington	2027	125	....	....	125	
........Do	2041	65	....	....	65	
Ferris Webster	2059	245	....	....	245	
Wm. West	2244	728	....	....	728	
Westfall & French	2128	1372	....	....	1372	
Joseph W. White, sen.	2101	90	....	....	90	
........Do	2106	50	....	....	50	
A. Wien	2167	99	....	....	99	
David Wilson	2172	....	....	....	72 50	Fr. Oct. 1, '44, to Jan. 11, '45.—Spe'l service.
Israel Woodruff	2239	65	....	....	65	
Alvin Wright	2044	139	....	....	139	
Thomas Young	2046	29	....	....	29	
........Do	2049	27	....	....	27	
Noah Young	2221	135	....	....	135	
Total for Ohio	....	$179536 91	$3117 89	$83 44	$162362 21	

CONTRACTORS.

Contractors.	No. of Route.	Contract pay per annum.	Additional allowances.	Reduction.	Total amount accrued.	Remarks.
MICHIGAN.						
Seymour Arnold	3692	$85			$85	
Samuel Ashman	3651	319			319	
Truman Bacon	3678	79			79	
David Barnard	3706	200			200	
Barnard & Pierce	3623	350			350	
Joel Batchelor	3690	199			145 47	From 8th October, 1844.
Joel A. Booth	3649	389 50			194 75	From 1st January, 1845.
John S. Boss	3641	394	$16 44		410 44	
Daniel Boutell	3635	136		$5 86	130 14	
Daniel B. Brown	3631	90			90	
Do	3639	95			95	
Brown & Hughes	3614	375			375	
Do	3619	375			375	
"The Board of Comm'rs of Internal Improvements of Michigan"—O.C.Comstock,jr., Prs.	3602	5000	1679 48		6679 48	
Do. do. do. (J. H. Cleveland, Sup't.)	3613	3000			3000	
Campbell & Grant	3707	100			85 60	From 23d August, 1844.
David Carlisle	3644	424			424	
Wm. H. Chapman	3622	143			143	
Wm. B. Clifford	3650	147			147	
E. T. Critchet	3701	75			75	

Wells Crumb	3673	56 46			56 46	
O. P. Davidson	3648	60			60	
Detroit & Pontiac R. R. Co.	3604	1000	500		1500	
S. S. Dodge	3675	350			350	
Nathl. Emory	3663	250			62 50	To 1st October, 1844.
Joseph P. Fisher	3640	110			82 50	To 1st April, 1845.
Rufus Fairchild	3665	117			117	
Gates & Wn	3603	649			649	
Eldridge Godfrey	3658	200			200	
Sewall S. Goff	3620	166	1 91	71 80	96 11	
Do	3621	130	40		170	
Do	3683	30			30	
Peter D. Graff	3649	389 50			194 75	To 31st December, 1845.
Harvey W. Hawley	3660	300			300	
James Hickey	3637	160			160	
Otho Hinton	3624	2000	70 33	1266	804 33	
Dan'l Hogan	3656	370			370	
Geo. Hossler	3609	290			72 50	From 1st April, 1845.
David M. Howell	3671*a*	53			4 32	From 1st June, 1845.
Amos B. Hubbell	3653	225		17	208	
B. Humphrey & Co.	3672	1450			1450	
Do	3625	2634	44		1339	From 1st Jan'y, 1845.
Do	3627	364			182	do
Do	3666	1495			747 50	do
Do	3669	345	2 84		175 34	do
Do	3674	2300	5 27		1155 27	do
Moses Johnson	3605	325			325	
Geo. W. Knapp	3609	290			217 50	To 31st March, 1845.
Heman J. Knapier	3657	205	16 83	47 91	173 92	
Do	3659	110			110	
John Hall	3628	238			238	
Sam'l C. Lasley	3647	200			200	

CONTRACTORS.

Contractors.	No. of route.	Contract pay per annum.	Additional allowances.	Reduction.	Total amount accrued.	Remarks.
Lewis & Carter	3617	$193			$193	
Do	3638	117			117	
Do	3642	127	$13 31		140 31	
Dan'l McKercher	3705	130			130	
Mason & Daniels	3616	1650			1650	
Wm. N. Matson	3629	290			217 50	Fron 1st October, 1844.
John W. Maynard	3606	374			374	
Do	3611	80			80	
Do	3612	110			110	
John Miller	3608	320			320	
Dan'l Myers	3610	90			90	
Neil & Tallmadge	3601	3000			3000	
John Palmer	3696	96 50			48 25	To 1st January, 1845.
Rich'd Peckham	3676	49			49	
E. N. Pettee	3636	590			590	
Cha's W. Phillips	3646	52			52	
Ben. Pratt	3668	196			196	
Prindle & Corret	3626	250			125	From 1st Jan'y, 1845.
Wm. Prindle	3655	96			48	do
Corn's Roosevelt	3652	284			284	
Alva Richmond	3696	96 50			48 25	To 31st Dec'r, 1844.
David N. Salter	3626	250			125	do
Do	3629	290			72 50	To 30th Sept., 1844.
Do	3655	96			48	To 31st Dec., 1844.
Do	3662	125			125	
Jesse Seely	3640	110			27 50	From 1st April, 1845.

Hiram Shepherd	3661	130	....	35 10	94 90	
Sidney T. Smith	3633	126	....	....	126	
Horace M. F. Smith	3607	90	....	....	90	
Smith & Stewart	3667	740	....	....	740	
D. & J. Spaulding	3654	140	....	....	140	
........Do	3680	136	....	....	136	
Enos B. Taylor	3634	200	....	....	200	
Z. Tillotson & Co	3625	2500	89	....	1339	To 31st Dec'r, 1844.
........Do	3627	750	32 16	141 60	265 56	do
........Do	3666	1495	....	....	747 50	do
........Do	3669	345	....	....	172 50	do
........Do	3674	2300	....	....	1150	do
Alex'r E. [illegible]son	3671	139	4 42	4 37	139 05	
E. B. & Sam'l Ward	3677	2900	....	....	2900	
Wm. M. Willey	3645	104	....	....	104	
Orton Williams	3632	413	....	....	413	
Henry R. Williams	3663	250	....	....	187 50	From 1st October, 1844.
Total for Michigan	....	$50657 46	$2505 99	$1589 64	$42409 20	
KENTUCKY.						
David Anderson	4914	$133	....	....	*$66 50	*From 1st July to 31st Dec., 1844.
........Do	4915	186	....	....	*93	*From 1st July to 31st Dec., 1844.
Banks, Landrom & Withrow	4806	4407	....	....	4407	
Archibald Bailey	4901	278	....	....	278	
Ezekiel Brashears	4949	55	....	....	55	
R. S. Bell	4891	499	....	....	499	
........Do	4947	48	....	....	48	
Black & Roach	4911	2250	*$187 18	....	2437 18	*From 10th December, 1844.
Andrew H. Brownlee	4885	118	....	*$43	75	*From 1st July, 1844.

CONTRACTORS

Contractors.	No. of Route.	Contract pay per annum.	Additional allowances.	Reduction.	Total amount accrued.	Remarks.
John H. Bruff	4924	$267			$267	
Augustine Byrne	4895	200			200	
John Campbell	4874	106			106	
Edward Carr	4838	185			185	
A. Clinton	4900	359			359	
Crozer & Marshall	4817	1500	*$250		1750	*From 1st July, 1844.
Do	4819	4417	*882	†$442	4857	*From 1st July, 1844.
Abner Crump	4866	200			200	
John G. Crump	4869	200			200	
Thomas E. Cummins	4844	240			240	
Do	4840	168	*133		301	*From 1st July, 1844.
Enos Daniel	4835	130			130	
Do	4837	47 48			47 48	
Do	4845	694		*48 43	645 57	*From 1st February, 1845.
William DeCourcy	4842	485	*8		493	*From 1st July, 1845.
George N. Denton	4950	138			138	
Thomas A. Dodd	4833	100			100	
John F. Dufour	4829	100			100	
John Eaker	4929	152			152	
Do	4930	305			305	
Joseph Eaton	4873	100			100	
J. M. Edrington	4809	180			180	
Do	4810	140			140	
William Elder	4816	1900			1900	
Do	4867a	6000	*63		6063	*From 1st July, 1844.
James Elliso n	4914	133			*66 50	*From 1st January, 1845.

........Do............	4915	186	....	....	*93	*From 1st January, 1845.
Frederici & Pendleton.....	4862	1200	....	....	1200	
S. M. Goble............	4849	109	....	....	109	
........Do............	4950	139	....	....	139	
[illegible]se G. Gordon......	4923	225	....	....	225	
Grannis & Robertson.....	4912	2300	....	....	2300	
Ninean E. [illegible]y.........	4897	2500	*407 93	....	2907 93	*From 9th July, 1844.
........Do............	4907	1270	....	....	*1004 27	*From 16th Sept., 1844.
........Do............	4913	3900	*363 86	....	4263 86	*From 10th Dec., 1844.
........Do............	4916	2346	....	*899 46 †44 87	‡910 79	*From 16th Dec., 1844. From 16th Sept., 1844. From 21st April, 1845.
........Do............	4931	900	....	*279 95	620 05	*From 14th Dec., 1844.
William Hackley.........	4843	275	*13 48	†133	-155 48	*From 1st July, 1844.
R. I. A. Harrison........	4851	744	....	....	744	
........Do............	4852	440	....	....	440	
William Hay............	4902	52	....	....	*13	*From 1st April, 1845.
James E. Head	4951	38	....	....	38	
C. J. Helm.............	4836	99	*25	....	124	*From 1st July, 1844.
Plummer T. Henderson...	4848	39	....	....	39	
John J. Henderson.......	4847	24	....	....	24	
Lewis Hensley...........	4823	250	....	....	250	
S. M. Hobbs............	4879	88	....	....	88	
Joseph H. Hough........	4882	430	....	....	430	
Hough, Carter & Thomas.	4803	7338	*567	†3952	3953	*From 1st July, 1844.
........Do............	4877	2750	*459	....	3209	*From 1st July, 1844.
........Do............	4887	2375	*396	....	2771	*From 1st July, 1844.
........Do............	4896	2125	*287	....	2412	*From 1st July, 1844.
Francis V. How lb.......	4822	100	....	....	100	
........Do............	4824	120	....	....	120	
Thomas Irvin...........	4820	1200	....	....	1200	
Robert Johnson.........	4830	220	....	*38	182	*From 1st July, 1844.

CONTRACTORS.

Contractors.	No. of Route.	Contract pay per annum.	Additional allowances.	Reduction.	Total amount accrued.	Remarks.
Edward P. Johnson & Co.	4811	$2000	....	....	$2000	
........Do	4812	1800	....	....	1800	
........Do	4813	2180 64	....	*$461	1719 64	*From 1st July, 1844.
........Do	4818	3607	*$245 62	†535 62	3317	*From 15th Nov., 1844.
........Do	4846	3600	....	....	3600	
A. B. King	4864	364	....	....	364	
E. F. King	4868	248	....	....	248	
Carter Landrom	4805	175	....	....	175	
Daniel S. Lane	4802	378	....	....	378	
........Do	4815	1188	†57 91	*60 82	*255 82	*From 1st July to 14th Nov., 1844. †One month's extra pay for discontin'g service.
Chittenden Lyon	4910	1850	*25 †139 94	‡875	1139 94	*From 1st July, 1844. †From 10th Dec., 1844. ‡From 1st January, 1845.
Abel Lee	4898	389	....	....	389	
G. P. Linn	4927	69	....	....	69	
Henry B. Marrs	4890	163 36	....	....	163 36	
........Do	4894	220	....	....	220	
James Martin	4902	52	....	....	*39	*From 1st July, 1844, to 31st March, 1845.
McAtee & Eastham	4804	2000	*333	....	2333	*From 1st July, 1844.
........Do	4817a	1852	*309	....	2161	*From 1st July, 1844.
........Do	4880	2500	*417	....	2917	*From 1st July, 1844.
Joseph McCown	4903	370 48	*295	†4 99	368 44	*From 29th January, '45. †From 16th June, '45.
........Do	4904	198 36	....	....	198 36	
........Do	4905	119 36	....	....	119 36	
John A. Moore & Co	4948	98	....	....	98	

Julian N. Philps	4883	349			349	
James Phipps	4855	448			448	
Do	4860	488			488	
Abraham Piles	4826	225	*14 16	†20 63	*77 91	*For one month's extra pay—†From 1st July to 15th November, 1844.
Do		197 96		*71 74	126 22	*From 16th December, 1844.
William Read	4878	179			179	
William Reed	4865	350	*46 90		396 90	*From 1st July, 1844, to 7th June, 1845.
Do	4867	250			250	
John N. Richardson	4853	370	59 96		429 96	
John Riddell	4832	281		*4 35	276 65	*From 14th June, 1845.
W. P. Roach	4907	1270			*265 73	*From 1st July to 15th September, 1844.
Do	4916	2346			*490 87	*Ditto.
Nimrod Routt	4839	140			140	
Owen Ruby	4807	96			96	
Andrew Russell	4863	249			249	
Do	4875	174			174	
Otho P. Simms	4899	415			415	
Frederick H. Skinner	4932	53			53	
James Smith	4821	74 48			74 48	
Smith & Moore	826	350	*20 66	†204 06	166 60	†From 1st July, 1844—*One month's extra pay.
J. W. South	4933	125			125	
A. H. Srygley	4886	299 72			299 72	
C. M. Strader	4834	5000			5000	
Philip Swigert	4952	2500			*1250	*From 1st January, 1845.
David Tate	4857	110	*14 64		124 64	*From 1st July, 1844.
Thomas W. Taylor	909	68 96			68 96	
Thompson & Dresser	4808	1068			1068	
William Tolle	4888	95			95	
Do	4889	195			195	
Daniel Trabue, jr	4876	295			295	
John W. Turner	4856	175			175	

68*

CONTRACTORS.

Contractors.	No. of Route.	Contract pay per annum.	Additional allowances.	Reduction.	Total amount accrued.	Remarks.
Octavus M. Weeden	4858	$1499	....	....	$1499	
William Wells	4859	695	....	....	695	
Joseph Willis	4881	300	....	....	300	
William Wilson	4925	88 48	....	....	88 48	
Elijah Wood	4926	540	$8	....	548	
H. Woodyard	4841	104 48	....	....	104 48	
Silas Woolverton	4854	449	....	....	449	
Hiram Young	4934	86 72	....	....	86 72	
Total for Kentucky	......	$107624 48	$5737 19	$8118 92	$98935 85	
INDIANA.						
A. J. Athon	3894	$288	....	....	$288	
Daniel R. Bearss	3821	799	....	*$88	711	*From 1st July, 1844.
Bell & Rissler	3862	187	....	....	187	
William A. Bliss	3927	987	*$27	....	1014	Do
Anthony Bowen	3890	125	....	....	125	
........Do	3899	75	....	....	75	
*Jacob C. Bowser	3944	155	....	....	*12 77	*From 1st June, 1845.
James Brady	......	70	*49 32	....	119 32	*From 6th July, 1844.
*Mason M. Bowen	3932	298	....	....	298	
........Do	3936	248	....	....	248	
Nathan Brison	3828	123	....	....	123	
Ezekiel Brown	3810	350	....	....	350	

Robert L. Browning	3934	270	....	....	270	
William H. Buford	3910	91	....	....	91	
John Burton	3869	1025	....	....	1025	
........Do	3891	450	....	....	450	
Sanford Calvert	3907	102	....	....	102	
Geo. W. Chambers	3940	136 48	....	....	136 48	
Elijah Chapman	3875	270	....	....	270	
Elias Cornell	3900	160	....	....	160	
Jeremiah Curl	3896	175	....	....	175	
Daniel Dale	3914	369	....	....	369	
Jonathan R. Davis	3854	45	....	*9 50	35 50	*From 1st January, 1845.
Davis & Seely	3930	387 64	....	....	387 64	
Robert Elliot	3851	236	*8	*8	236	*From 1st July, 1844.
A. Estep	3827	190	....	....	190	
........Do	3832	548	....	....	548	
Jesse Everett	3880	160	....	....	160	
........Do	3881	168	....	....	168	
Peter Fetters	3923	75	....	....	75	
James H. Fitspatrick	3929	399	....	....	399	
Joseph W. Gilbert	3822	454	....	....	454	
David Graham	3924	300	*121 84	....	421 84	*From 1st July, 1844.
Adam Hall	3888	172	....	....	172	
James Hamilton	3825	185	....	....	185	
J. W. Hancock	3837	50	....	....	50	
J. E. Harris	3950	150	....	....	150	
Christian Hefler	3817	118	....	....	118	
Joseph V. Hill	3882	646	....	....	646	
Holcomb & Yost	3918	216	....	....	216	
Samuel Hoover	3818	37 48	....	....	37 48	
........Do	3826	136	....	....	136	
Jacob Jones	3811	1189	....	....	1189	
........Do	3908	570	....	....	570	

CONTRACTORS.

Contractors.	No. of Route.	Contract pay per annum.	Additional allowances.	Reductions.	Total amount accrued.	Remarks.
Kinnear & P[illegible]h	3850	$650	....	....	$650	
John C. Kinney	3928	75	....	....	75	
Solomon Landon	3903	52	....	....	*15 60	*From 14th March, 1845.
George Leonard	3812	1200	....	....	1200	
W. B. [illegible]is	3841	185	....	....	185	
Carter Likins	3860	1140	....	*$61 31	1078 69	*From 28th December, 1844.
Oliver Livingston	3937	87 48	....	....	87 48	
James B. [illegible]M.	3887	130	....	....	130	
Isaac Matkins	3938	98	....	....	98	
Lewis McClane	3815	138	....	....	138	
Harrison McDaniel	3835	285	....	*179 04	105 96	*From 4th July, 1844.
Andrew McIntire	3900	120	....	....	120	
James R. McKee	3885	250	....	....	250	
George McKeehan	3852	78	....	....	78	
Green McKinley	3889	1250	....	....	*312 50	*From 1st July to 30th September, 1844.
Joseph H. McMaken	3935	115	....	....	115	
Al[illegible]ander McP[illegible]hers	3863	275	....	....	275	
Josiah Mongar	3933	800	....	....	800	
Samuel Moore	3864	548	....	....	548	
Silas Moore	3858	1432	*$80	....	1512	*From 1st July, 1844.
John Morrison	3824	225	....	*89	136	*From 1st July, 1844.
Do	3839	175	....	....	175	
Do	3840	100	....	....	100	
Frederick Myers	3873	300	....	*84	216	*From 1st July, 1844.
James Myers	3846	165	....	....	165	
William Newland	3856	250	....	....	250	

........Do..............	3865	120	*22	....	142	*From 1st July, 1844.
........Do..............	3867	220	*53	*146	127	*From 1st July, 1844.
Isaac Norris..............	3830	245	....	....	245	
James Oliphant...........	3861	410	....	....	410	
Arnold Peckham.........	3842	99	....	....	99	
Hiram S. Ptdn	3921	400	....	....	400	
John Pugh................	3848	69	....	....	69	
J. W. Purviance.........	3901	132	....	{ *36 †2 74	93 26	{ *From 1st July, 1844. †From 9th April, 1845.
William R. Reynolds.....	3877	810	....	....	810	
James Rhoads, jr.........	3806	60	*60	....	120	*From 1st July, 1844.
Benson Riggs............	3949	50	*50	....	100	Do do.
William L. Ross.........	3892	1286	....	*189 08	1096 92	Do do.
........Do..............	3905	584	....	....	584	
........Do..............	3913	1181	....	....	1181	
........Do..............	3915	1279	....	....	1279	
A. L. Ross & Co.........	3802	1400	....	....	1400	
........Do..............	3805	5000	....	*1400	3600	Do do.
Scott & Glenn...........	3808	644	*18	....	662	Do do.
Emsley Shadday.........	3847	192	....	*14	178	Do do.
Nathaniel Sherland.......	3920	369	....	....	369	
Wm Silver..........	3814	195	....	....	195	
Be jamin Smith..........	3931	450	....	....	450	
Daniel Spencer..........	3870	798	....	*266	532	Do do.
........Do..............	3937	149 48	....	....	149 48	
J. W. Spencer...........	3871	249 48	....	....	249 48	
Samuel G. Sperry........	3916	234	....	....	234	
........Do..............	3917	125	....	....	125	
James Stackhouse........	3912	190	....	....	190	
John N. Stephenson......	3925	140	....	....	140	
Peter Sunderland........	3904	379	*7 73	†80	306 73	†Do do. *Fr. 4th April, 1845.
Thomas W. Sunman.....	3843	70	....	....	*52 50	*From 1st July, '44, to 31st March, '45.

CONTRACTORS.

Contractors.	No. of Route.	Contract pay per annum.	Additional allowances.	Reduction.	Total amount accrued.	Remarks.
Robert Sunman	3843	$70	....	....	*$17 50	*From 1st April, 1845.
Joseph Swope	3897	300	....	....	300	
C. S. Thompson	3926	235	....	....	235	
Asa Thorn	3884	230	....	....	230	
John Vawter	3829	72	....	....	72	
Do	3857	84	....	....	84	
J. & P. Voorhees	3803	2725	....	....	2725	
Do	3804	1200	....	....	1200	
Do	3807	2800	....	....	2800	
Do	3809	1350	*$893 20	....	2243 20	*From 23d July, 1844.
Do	3835	390	....	....	390	
Do	3889	1250	....	....	*937 50	*From 1st October, 1844.
Do	3898	576	....	*$5 99	570 01	*From 17th Dec., 1844, to 11th Feb'y, '45.
Nathan Walden	3845	2000	....	....	2000	
John Mer	3813	131	....	....	131	
Do	3823	124	....	....	124	
Do	3911	224	....	....	224	
Alonson Warner	3879	275	....	....	275	
William West	3833	130	....	*5	125	*From 1st July, 1844.
James F. Whitham	3849	249	....	*124	125	Do do.
Benjamin F. Whitson	3876	190	....	*85	105	Do do.
Lorenzo D. Whitson	3855	180	....	....	180	
Spencer Wiley	3836	130	....	....	130	
John Wise	3878	700	....	....	700	
Do	3883	1500	....	....	1500	
J. S. & W. J. Wise	3859	10260	....	....	10260	

A. S. Wood	3942	70	....	....	70	
James Woods	3816	155	....	*9	146	Do do.
Total for Indiana	......	$68439 04	$1390 09	$2881 66	$65448 84	
ILLINOIS.						
James Atwater	4211	$188	....	....	$188	
George Barnes	4221	198	....	....	198	
Barnett & Dickson	4176	1580	....	....	*1185	*From 1st October, 1844.
[illegible]as Baswell	4129	1200	....	....	1200	
Benjamin Bates	4163	100	....	....	100	
William Berry	4122	150	....	....	150	
William H. Boling	4152	322	....	....	322	
Britton, Gleason & Pendleton	4188	282	....	....	282	
Thomas Burnett	4169	1190	....	....	1190	
Butler & Means	4187	2300	....	....	2300	
O[illegible]er [illegible]dy	4142	195	....	....	195	
Samuel Copeland	4134	200	....	....	200	
[illegible]es Corrie	4124	98	....	....	98	
Thomas H. Cory	4149	250	....	....	250	
John D. [illegible]s	4201	994	....	....	994	
Shubal Coy	4228	180	....	....	180	
[illegible] Craig	4192	250	....	....	250	
James [illegible]	4174	200	....	....	200	
Davidson, Whitney & Pitkin	4106	1500	....	....	1500	
Philip Dean	4107	3895	....	....	3895	
Alexander R. Dempster	4202	120	....	....	120	
James E. Dunn	4167	140	....	*41	99	*From 1st July, 1844.
Eades & [illegible]s	4189	143	....	....	143	
Daniel Earp	4111	149	....	....	149	

CONTRACTORS.

Contractors.	No. of Route.	Contract pay per annum.	Additional allowances.	Reduction.	Total amount accrued.	Remarks.
Edwards & Johnson	4160	$137 48			$137 48	
John Ellis	4128	450		*$30	420	From 1st July, 1844.
Emison & Green	4119	2500			2500	
Fellows & Burroughs	4198	1400			1400	
John Frink	4108	695	*$9		704	Do do.
Do	4184	6500			6500	
Do	4197	945			945	
Do	4203	159	*12		171	Do do.
Do	4204	2000			2000	
Do	4207	150		*57	93	Do do.
Do	4208	155			155	
Do	4209	3000			3000	
Do	4210	300			300	
Do	4212	1200			1200	
Frink & Sanger	4205	3500			3500	
P. S. Frost	4148	780			*195	*From 1st July to 30th September, 1844.
J. P. & P. S. Frost	4118	13855			13855	
Daniel Fuller	4222	70			70	
Guilford W. Gooch	4168	1373			1373	
Canfield S. Hamilton	4158	545			545	
Do	4165	550			550	
A. D. Hay	4145	1500			1500	
James P. Haynes	4130	3125			3125	
Do	4131	1985			1985	
William Henry	4133	797			797	
A. F. Herrick	4166	800			800	

Richard Hick	4120	2450	....	....	2450	
Daniel D. Hicks	4162	247	....	....	247	
Seth Hilton	4180	140	....	....	140	
Otho Hinton	4101	4350	*389	....	4739	*From 1st July, 1844.
Do	4102	4400	....	....	4400	
Do	4103	2950	....	....	2950	
Do	4104	1500	....	....	1500	
Do	4113	3634	....	....	3634	
Do	4115	2412	....	....	2412	
Do	4155	3900	....	*137 75	3762 25	*From 1st April to 17th May, 1845.
William H. Holcomb	4159	899	*100 †200 39	....	1199 39	*From 1st July, '44—†From 1st Nov. '44.
Do	4170	1371 48	....	....	1371 48	
Do	4175	189	....	....	189	
Do	4190	447	*641	†102	351 41	*From 1st Aug., '44—†From 1st July, '44.
Leonard Hogle	4217	95	....	....	95	
Benjamin Hoyt	4179	175	....	....	175	
Huddleston & Hodges	4150	400	....	....	400	
N. B. Jinnett	4237	130	....	....	130	
Gles Judson	4200	170	....	....	*26 95	*From 1st July to 26th August, 1844.
A. R. Kenner	4123	450	....	....	450	
Samuel Kr.	4181	285	....	....	285	
Silas Lackey	4135	140	....	....	140	
John Laws	4117	200	....	24	199 76	*From 3d June, 1845.
Henry Ledbetter	4114	195	....	....	195	
J. E. Mn.	4215	149	....	*72	77	*From 1st July, 1844.
Do	4216	349	....	....	349	
Do	4218	3133	*100	*870	2363	*From 1st July, 1844.
John McLean	4125	1180	....	....	1180	
Do	4141	250	....	....	250	
Francis Miller	4154	160	....	....	160	
R. & J. M. Morrison	4146	299	....	....	299	

CONTRACTORS.

Contractors.	No. of Route.	Contract pay per annum.	Additional allowances.	Reduction.	Total amount accrued.	Remarks.
E. L. Patton	4240	$35	....	....	$*10 50	*From 14th March, 1845.
Jonathan Pettit	4139	480	$*10 †3 97	....	493 97	*From 1st July, '44—†From 7th Feb., '45.
Henry Richardson	4148	780	....	....	585	*From 1st October, 1844.
Launcelot Rood	4225	52	....	....	52	
Christian Routszong	4193	46	....	....	46	
M. D. Sanford	4172	199	*57	*142	114	*From 1st July, 1844.
Do	4177	120	*24	....	144	*From 1st July, 1844.
Jno P. Sanger	4186	4000	*550	....	4550	*From 1st July, 1844.
Do	4206	1400	....	....	1400	
John B. Seaward	4109	2500	....	....	2500	
M. G. Smith	4191	395	....	....	395	
Smith & Pickett	4164	1390	....	....	1390	
Smith & Harris	4214	200	....	....	200	
John G. Sparks	4136	240	....	....	240	
Ezekiel Springer	4156	298	....	....	298	
Richard Stoddart	4116	148	....	....	148	
Samuel Thing	4147	136	*8	*21	123	*From 1st July, 1844.
James D. Tisdale	4151	400	....	....	400	
Twitchell & Connelly	4224	185	....	....	185	
Noel Vasseur	4219	580	....	....	580	
James B. Vincent	4194	205	*50	....	255	*From 1st July, 1844.
William Watson	4157	1048	....	....	1048	
Cornelius S. Whitney	4144	950	*31 48	....	981 48	*From 1st July, 1844.
John Wilson	4171	349	....	*120	229	*From 1st July, 1844.
John Wilson	4195	100	....	....	100	

John A. Wilson	4143	650			650	
Elijah Winn	4200	174			*147 05	*From 27th August, 1844.
John D. Winters	4176	1580			*395	*From 1st July to 30th September, 1844.
Richard Worthen	4138	145			145	
George Wright	4112	145	*98 92		46 08	*From 19th July, 1844.
Total for Illinois		$119874 96	$1551 25	$1691 91	$117179 80	
MISSOURI.						
Noah Atkin	4611	$294			$294	
John Anderson	4610	169			*126 75	*From 1st October, 1844.
Hon Arnot	4635	1800			1800	
Moses Bean	4694	1755		$877 48	877 52	
James Boyes	4620	308		44	264	
R. T. Brown, jr.	4689	246			246	
Do	4696	899		35	864	
Richard Bywater	4731*a*	66			33	From 1st January, 1845.
Elez. Calvert	4627	200	*$2 16	26	176 16	*One month's extra pay on $26.
Wm. C. Campbell	4697	145			145	
John Campbell	4684	35			35	
James Curry	4622	49			49	
Caswell Mis	4653	170			170	
S. J. Easly	4656	300			300	
Eckert & Shepherd	4606	2990			2990	
John C. Flint	4619	299			299	
Wm. Finn	4688	165			165	
C. P. Fulenwider	4686	900			900	
J. P. & P. S. Frost	4630	3322	159		3481	
Do	4650	690	73		763	
J. M. & Jos. Good	4633	298		89	209	

CONTRACTORS.

Contractors.	No. of Route.	Contract pay per annum.	Additional allowances.	Reduction.	Total amount accrued.	Remarks.
Andrew L. George	4702	$225			*$118	*From 23d December, 1844.
Gilmore, Hays & Co.	4660	484 48			484 48	
Do	4666	283 48			283 48	
Alfred Griggs	4682	250			250	
C. S. Hamilton	4644	300			300	
John B. Hammond	4687	890			890	
John Harsell	4720	100			100	
Orestes K. Hawley	4636	1371	*$21		1384 98	*Additional allow. commenced 1st Nov., '44.
Nelson Hewitt	4675	433	24	*$226	298 71	*$106 of deduction comm'd Feb. 20th, '45.
Robt. G. Hillebrew	4667	198			198	
Otho Hinton	4601	2306			576 50	From 1st April, 1845.
P. P. Brickey & Co.	4601	2306			1729 50	From 1st July, '44, to 31st March, '45.
Otho Hinton	4602	3500			1750	From 1st January, 1845.
Eckert & Patteson	4602	3500			1750	From 1st July, '44, to 31st December, '44.
Otho Hinton	4603	5300			5300	
Do	4618	2070			1035	From 1st January, 1845.
Price & Lewis	4618	2130			1065	From 1st July, '44, to 31st December, '44.
Otho Hinton	4658	2780			2780	From 1st January, 1845.
Price & Lewis	4658	2780			2780	From 1st July, '44, to 31st December, '44.
Otho Hinton	4668	1700			1700	
Price & Lewis	4668	1700			1700	
Otho Hinton	4691	2200			550	From 1st April, 1845.
P. P. Brickey & Co.	4691	2200			1650	From 1st July, '44, to 31st March, '45.
John D. Hogan	4676	573 84		110	463 84	
Do	4678	375	12		387	
Do	4679	1299	88		1387	

Francis C. Hughes	4721	125				125		
Robert Hussey	4726	195				195		
Hancock Jackson	4629	200			53	147		
George Jenkinson	4693	416		5		421		
Jeffries & Kanada	4695	289			177	112		
Joseph M. Johnson	4607	80				80		
Garret Jordan	4642	175			*30	155	03	*Commenced 1st November, 1844.
Jordan, Hening & Co.	4641	375		89		464		
Lewis Keedy	4710	123				123		
Caleb Kerr	4648	160				160		
Do	4652	130				130		
Do	4654	275				275		
Jos ha M. King	4608	50				50		
Christ. Landus	4609	189				189		
Wm. B. Lear	4639	175				175		
Eli McCarty	4613	258				258		
David McAlister	4604	394				394		
Do	4615	224				224		
R. J. McElhaney	4677	433	32			433	32	
Michael McMillen	4657	250				233	69	From 25th July, 1844.
Alfred Menifee	4616	100				100		
David Morrow	4659	195				195		
John C. Myers	4685	308				308		
Wm. J. Norris	4651	189			126	63		
John Pace	4672	185				185		
L. H. Paxton	4612	95		10		105		
George A. Pemberton	4661	362	48			362	48	
Powell & Neece	4662	408				382	50	From 24th July, 1844.
Thomas L. Price	4671	1500			750	750		
Thomas P. Rubey	4632	140				140		
Robertson Roberts	4674	199				199		
George Sexton	4625	165				165		

CONTRACTORS

Contractors.	No. of Route.	Contract pay per annum.	Additional allowances.	Reduction.	Total amount accrued.	Remarks.
George Sexton	4645	$330			$330	
Do	4646	200	$17		217	
Do	4649	150			150	
James M. Sexton & Co.	4631	140			140	
Thomas T. Shootman	4669	551			551	
Henry Sims	4614	180			180	
Alfred F. Skidmore	4673	375			375	
George R. Smith	4665	1400			1400	
Do	4670	1200			1200	
John Spurgen	4628	390			390	
Frederick Stone	4623	275			68 75	From 1st April, 1845.
Richard Hickam	4623	275			206 25	From 1st July, 1844, to 31st March, 1845.
F. Stribling	4637	190			190	
Do	4717	133	201		334	
James D. Tisdale	4605	370			370	
Wm. A. Vanlear	4692	398			398	
E. M. Walker	4690	115	*20		134 67	*Add'l allowance commenced 7th July, '44.
Watts, Hawkins & Hawkins	4638	300	26		326	
Peter Weyand	4664	200			200	
A. Wheeler	4680	350			350	
R. M. Whitehead	4683	194			194	
John Woollard	4647	295			295	
Do	4655	100			100	
E. B. Woodrome	4681	500			500	
Hiram Wyatt	4643	400		28	372	
A. D. Glazier	4704	350			87 50	From 1st April, to 30th June, 1845.

Thomas E. Old	4704	350	....	....	262 50	From 1st July, 1844, to 31st March, 1845.
Total for Missouri	......	$74328 60	$730 16	$2561 48	$61719 61	
WISCONSIN TERRITORY.						
A. A. Bird	4424	$225	....	....	$83 12	From 17th February, 1845.
James R. Bruce	4422	40	....	....	40	
Burroughs & Howard	4410	645	....	....	645	
M. C. Darling	4408	340	....	....	340	
Do	4431	750	....	....	750	
Daniel H. Darnell	4416	157	....	....	157	
D & Mo re.	4426	87 25	....	....	87 25	
Alonzo D. Dick	4407	298	....	....	74 50	To 1st October, 1844.
H. L. Dous m.	4420	936	....	....	936	
John Frink	4411	1140	....	....	1140	
Do	4413	350	....	....	350	
Do	4419	1400	....	....	1400	
John Kent	4401	199	....	$44	155	
Do	4429	75	....	....	75	
Do	4428	74	....	....	22 20	From 14th March, 1845.
R. B. Loveland	4405	1200	....	....	1200	
R. Redfield	4423	123	$41	....	164	
Wm. B. Sheldon	4412	400	....	....	400	
Do	4417	669	....	....	669	
Do	4425	158	....	....	158	
A. W. Starks	4404	423	....	....	423	
Do	4430	96	....	....	96	
Charles Stevens	4402	299	....	....	299	
Do	4414	224	....	49 40	174 60	

CONTRACTORS.

Contractors.	No. of route.	Contract pay per annum.	Additional allowances.	Reduction.	Total amount accrued.	Remarks.
John M. Wells	4406	$249 50	....	....	$249 50	
Daniel Whitney	4409	598	....	....	598	
Daniel M. Whitney	4403	1590	$30 94	$795	825 94	
Seymour Wilcox	4407	298	....	....	223 50	From 1st October, 1844.
Total for Wisconsin	......	$13043 75	$71 94	$888 40	$11735 61	
IOWA TERRITORY.						
John Frink	4502	$249	....	....	$249	
Wm. H. Holcomb	4514	195	....	$97	98	
........Do	4515	195	*$195	....	376 75	*From 26th July, 1844.
........Do	4516	275	....	*103	191 04	*From 7th September, 1844.
A. Ormsby	4539	200	....	....	77 22	From 11th February, 1845.
Nelson Plummer	4503	900	....	450	450	
J. K. Rickey	4507	130	....	....	130	
Samuel Stowrs	4505	480	....	....	480	
........Do	4508	250	....	....	84 72	From 28th February, 1845.
Wm. H. Holcomb	4508	295	....	....	195 02	From 1st July, 1844, to 27th Feb., 1845.
Samuel Swearingen	4533	44	37	....	81	
W. S. Viney	4513	298	....	....	298	
Wm. Smith	4543	199	....	....	91 76	From 15th January, 1845.
James Shepherd	4526	126	....	....	31 50	From 1st April, 1845.

Total for Iowa Territory		$3836	$232	$650	$2834 01	
RIVER MAILS.						
Louisville to New Orleans					$20823 18	
St. Louis to New Orleans					5023 25	
St. Louis to Keokuck					396	From 1st July to 7th Dec., 1844.
New Orleans to Alexandria, Natchitoches, Shreveport, &c.					1330	

NOTE.—The above sums were paid by the Postmasters at Louisville, Kentucky, New Orleans, Louisiana, and St. Louis, Missouri, to captains of steamboats, under orders from the Postmaster General.

CONTRACTORS.

LIST OF MAIL CONTRACTORS.

Statement of payments made for transportation of the mail on Special Routes, from 1st July, 1844, to 30th June, 1845.

To whom made.	Amount of payment.
MAINE.	
J. Lippincott	$35 00
L. J. Thomas	18 54
Daniel Keene	30 75
J. Clark, 2d	43 30
Joseph Bean	21 49
Hugh Smiley	19 76
H. R. Nason	4 22
N. L. Ingersoll, jr	18 75
J. Day, jr	19 00
H. Ward	14 60
R. Brainard	16 00
T. Cushing	31 50
Abell Pratt	5 53
John Atkinson	26 28
James Goodwin, jr	13 45
Atherton Clark	31 00
John Thompson	23 74
H. Whitaker	28 26
John McFaden	18 61
E. H. Drake	31 00
D. Crowell	40 00
J. E. Riggs	80 90
Thomas Young	76 76
James Johnston	33 64
Daniel Carter	16 27
Joseph Sturtevant	28 40
William Currier	175 00
O. Philbrick	60 33
Wm. Sanborne, jr	95 00
G. G. Waterhouse	21 25
Rufus L. Bartlett	100 71
J. B. Littlehale	18 86
C. Blodgett	27 46
E. Tompson, jr	30 10
Alden Kincaid	30 00
Zenas Colby	65 00
J. Fossett, jr	16 00
Winslow Walker	46 87
Joseph Bowker	171 25
E. Rosebrook	40 26
Jno. L. James	22 89
A. E. Dinslow	$40 38
O. B. Weymouth	49 19
William McIntire	16 30
Jacob Somes	15 00
A. Herrick	23 60
O. Webber	25 00
William Hussey	11 69
C. D. Gilmore	15 00
Josiah Ingerson	20 70
Wm. H. Vose	20 00
Gideon Oakes	32 00
Levi L. Cobb	11 68
David Marble	14 11
B. F. Stinson	26 00
C. Titcomb	8 08
Rufus B. Walker	41 37
Job Giddings	16 00
W. S. Barrows	22 98
B. C. Megguever	22 43
Eben'r Hilton	29 95
C. Tinkham	50 00
James Curston	210 00
NEW HAMPSHIRE.	
John Emons	29 00
John Gibson	60 00
Calvin Titus	26 00
Ezra Corey	28 00
Elijah Tenny	24 00
M. Worcester	30 00
O. Munson & T. Little	22 50
Stephen Corliss	19 54
David Tilton	20 00
John O. Cilley	27 36
Morse & Langdon	50 00
George Wendsworth	15 86
T. H. Parsons	59 97
Miles Hays	23 36
Isaac Webster	9 08
T. W. Smith	40 00
John Cooper	19 12

CONTRACTORS.

To whom made.	Amount of payment.	To whom made.	Amount of payment.
VERMONT.		J. Newhall	$100 00
		Wm. H. Knight	75 00
A. Mitchell	$42 15	John Hancock	71 56
H. S. Caswell	13 26	M. D. Barron	34 07
Jacob S. Johnson	15 00	Betsey Ide	7 79
B. Sanborne	8 24	W. B. Messinger	29 25
Varnum Boynton	35 00	Lyman Stratton	40 00
Eben'r Lee, jr	64 58	N. Foskett	16 00
W. W. Pope	28 92	E. Lathrop	125 00
T. M. Frost	41 23	Joseph Valentine	100 00
Reuben Thomas	29 71	C. Sears & Co	40 00
Conrad Saxe	30 00		
L. A. Russell	26 42	CONNECTICUT.	
Otis Bardwell	80 91		
Israel Marsh	50 00	C. Candee	29 06
Z. Hitchcock	50 00	S. E. Mills	46 12
		Edward H. Bradley	14 30
MASSACHUSETTS.		W. Chamberlain	49 50
		William Beebe	27 87
N. L. Church	36 00	Rowland L. Cobb	15 19
R. McIntosh	150 00	H. W. Smith	89 50
A. Brown	150 00	R. S. Williams	84 00
Symonds & Teel	150 00	Marble G. St. Clair	49 74
E. Penniman	190 00	J. B. Prentice	75 38
Ichabod H. Childs	80 98	Charles Townsend	74 27
H. Bosworth	18 00	H. P. Welch	49 63
J. Conant	84 00	J. L. Strickland	191 39
W. Learned	42 00	E. A. Foot	40 75
Otis Bardwell	57 49	Vincent Tuttle	18 00
Jonathan Lyman	50 00	S. Champion	36 00
Harris Cutler	42 02	Charles Patrick	25 00
William Wait	42 00	C. Marcy, jr	50 00
John Long	45 77	G. P. Tallmadge	237 00
W. & P. S. Andrews	76 67	G. Robinson	55 00
J. Goodnow	28 67	L. Hurlbert	90 00
E. P. Park	22 68	Clark Bronson	39 00
W. H. Ayres	95 00	J. J. Wilcoxson	20 06
James Cole	19 44	G. W. Olin	83 33
J. Parmenter	46 72		
Asa Williams	52 00	MARYLAND.	
Abner A. Pond	25 00		
John Long	45 84	John Mosser	3 33
Hiram Burr	31 01	William Smith	40 00
J. Blake	15 08	C. Miller	14 61
Asa Blake	45 00	S. Chambers, sr	7 21
Daniel Noyes	42 33	George H. Walsche	17 18
Edward Smith	135 24	Nimrod Norris	10 00
Henry Mansfield	22 50	S. Onions	95 00
B. S. Monroe	42 22	Samuel Riggs	14 75

CONTRACTORS.

To whom made.	Amount of payment.	To whom made.	Amount of payment.
John Black	$18 75	R. Phetteplace	$182 50
Denton Hammond	15 00	James J. Smalley	12 63
F. Rupperecht	217 67	W. W. Cady	70 00
Wm. A. Tolly	22 66	John H. Frew	47 68
Andrew Turner	39 14	G. W. Spring	19 29
R. H. McGill	1 24	Albert Halstead	9 97
Clement Thompson	23 47	J. P. Adams	25 00
Frederick Byers	20 81	Simeon Jenks	11 95
William Benson	49 54	J. T. Snyder	30 00
John Leaf	20 00	D. Nevin	40 00
John Bowen	87 86	Harry Tanner	59 75
Samuel Wilson	31 25	Silas Wood	16 00
James Turner	55 00	Gideon Reynolds	93 75
		Peter Austin	28 00
NEW YORK.		Jacob Burr	29 41
		Solomon Sikes	25 72
W. C. Hand	27 74	D. K. Green	110 00
Benj'n Lewis	80 00	Joseph Griswald	80 00
James Stuart	15 00	Festus Parsons	75 00
Charles Kent	119 77	H. Petitt	3 50
Samuel Harris	20 57	A. Matthews	45 00
William Dominick	20 44	Walter L. Barber	26 66
John Wheeler	79 42	W. A. J. Speedling	32 95
John Stevens	30 00	John Couse	24 37
Ethan Burdick	84 00	R. H. Miller	79 33
C. D. & E. Wilcox	52 50	Philo Hawley	47 00
S. W. Goff	21 78	Butterfield & Gardner	137 70
A. B. Bushnell	15 81	Charles Perry	32 01
B. A. Bigelow	28 42	R. D. Lester	108 00
George Brimmer	4 08	E. H. Pride	51 21
N. W. Williams	22 50	W. Mack, jr	80 00
James McKain	100 57	Jonath'n Pickett	20 00
S. S. Lenton	34 00	James McKain	62 79
J. Kingan	30 00	A. Miner	28 61
C. Gill	97 99	John Hanes	8 05
John H. Storm	70 00	A. Hall	28 00
H. Y. Hayford	28 38	C. E. Smith	60 00
P. A. Millar	40 00	W. E. Davis	58 50
A. D. Raymond	15 00	E. Holmes	91 00
H. Merrill	18 29	A. Beman	12 02
S. Van Allen	15 80	A. Penny	93 00
John F. Smith	78 75	S. Utley	15 34
D. Hungerford	143 11	C. Schermerhorn	26 00
Calvin Kingman	46 39	James Poole	19 14
Joseph Gates	29 18	M. S. Roberts	15 01
N. Scovel	64 39	Ephraim Wheeler	8 02
F. A. Davies	10 68	S. Hawkins	35 93
Luther Parish	2 81	John Parrish	30 46
R. J. Quackenbush	38 00	S. Stackhouse	31 32

CONTRACTORS.

To whom made.	Amount of payment.	To whom made.	Amount of payment.
Ab'm Schermerhorn	$25 48	J. Skinner	$25 76
B. Brown	2 80	H. Westfall	45 00
D. Dimock	26 00	N. Hough	50 00
Wm. Johnston	5 50	N. C. Babcock	37 18
A. Higby	7 22	John Peacock	5 35
A. J. Tompkins	10 00	S. L. Miller	40 14
Gilbert Thomas	36 00	Jeremiah Wood	30 00
A. B. Bodle	43 56	Alexander Lane	90 00
D. Hanington	12 00		
J. W. Beardsley	80 00	NEW JERSEY.	
M. Caldwell	58 50		
John Tomlinson	19 17	Daniel Keene	59 87
B. P. Sears	38 73	Josiah Harrison	108 32
Henry Hunsiker	77 76	P. H. Earle	50 00
J. L. Perry	78 00	Samuel Dodd	34 00
Julius Collins	30 00	J. E. Patterson	50 00
Nathan Harvey	35 00	J. McGee	57 89
S. Collins	30 00	W. E. Sinclair	7 09
Z. Tanner	20 00	Wm. W. Bennett	25 00
L. Sanford	25 00	Benj'n Kinney	150 00
Edward B. Somers	83 11	R. Brooks	40 00
Russell James	24 00	S. S. Osborne	11 43
E. Sheldon	32 00	N. Bush	15 37
A. Thompson	19 62	Edward Carter	29 09
W. M. O'Farrell	14 06	C. Cahill & als	189 34
A. Seaman	56 91	R. C. Williams	18 89
J. T. Getman	30 57	Z. Drake	19 32
J. T. Luce	8 68	J. R. C. Sigler	136 25
Harley Judd	100 00	Jno. Dickinson	3 08
Warner Fellows	21 39		
M. Hilliard	51 38	DELAWARE.	
H. Sweet	15 00		
J. Chapman	13 53	John Morrison	58 94
G. Ganony	40 00		
D. A. Robertson	64 91	PENNSYLVANIA.	
Hiram Wagar	20 00		
A. Gates	9 82	W. F. Morehead	16 20
Perry Smith	28 36	Isaac Oatenkirk	16 50
W. H. Hunger	75 00	J. Middleton	140 00
John Dorsett	46 99	S. Seely	9 87
L. F. Goetchins	30 00	J. D. Chamberlin	40 00
W. S. Edgerton	59 54	B. W. Garretson	25 00
Ezra Wooden	22 50	Benj'n Lusk	24 00
S. C. Brown	72 87	Abra'm Stone	34 09
Joseph Gurmon	15 00	John Skinner	18 36
J. M. Cutler	77 91	Adam Wolf	23 26
E. Cornish, jr.	50 95	A. Turrel	13 85
D. G. Comstock	22 50	Charles Seagreaves	25 61
Wm. Tompkins	70 00	J. Dively	10 00

CONTRACTORS.

To whom made.	Amount of payment.	To whom made.	Amount of payment.
Ruel C. Ames	$22 29	David Gilkeson	$21 63
John Lindsey	49 50	Thomas Jackson	25 15
F. F. Couteret	14 50	B. Kirtley	27 09
Geo. W. Addison	129 80	John Barnes	28 79
L. Putnam	15 83	S. B. Burgess	53 14
David Taylor	85 00	Jesse Hildebrand	45 02
Olney Thatcher	50 00	Thomas Ayres	27 00
J. J. Kinsey	43 34	John Roberts	75 61
Otis Ross	4 04	L. Ailsworth	42 75
Geo. B. Patterson	15 23	Robert Allen	33 71
Aaron Eisenhart	30 73	Thornton Mountjoy	14 29
T. Martz	18 76	S. Jordan	22 61
Alex'r Bohn	9 14	Jno. N. Jones	70 00
Samuel Hildebrand	3 06	Joseph Sanders, jr.	34 36
John Geist	35 66	Watkins Eanes	34 00
Benj'n Powell	53 05	William Burgess	36 71
L. F. Norton	10 75	Freeman Biggs	50 00
Holker Hughes	50 00	Leroy Mitchell	93 96
Jas. R. Butler	25 00	R. Anderson	28 83
Bennett Temple	180 00	J. W. Anderson	31 56
M. Little	27 00	John Burdett	13 14
Job Johnson	50 00	E. Amiss	8 13
R. Moffett	14 99	T. Gore	35 15
Geo. S. Putney	11 23	H. R. Cox	12 90
Benj'n Kutz	22 87	Thos. E. Payne	40 00
J. A. Gurny	26 26	Robt. S. Jones	33 65
Jas. C. Skiles	34 91	Wm. G. Haskins	7 54
J. R. Elder	5 32	George Sinnett	16 15
Darius Brown	20 00	L. B. Maulsby	13 85
John Shaffer	60 00	John Morris, sen'r.	4 27
Casper Schall	24 26	A. Jenkins	84 00
S. Zimmerman	22 82	J. Gregory	10 69
C. J. Deltra	25 00	Jonathan Richmond	21 59
J. L. Merriman	15 93	S. L. Eskridge	27 97
G. H. Olmstead	29 76	Thomas Morrison	13 70
Peter Strauss	24 00	W. H. Manlove	54 49
Thomas Watson	30 38	C. N. Lawson	11 29
J. H. Sheafer	17 89	John Kaler	18 77
Isaac Williams	55 00	Thomas Tyler	20 07
Wm. McCune	40 00	Thos. R. Peers	44 73
George Fox	11 25	P. Abbott	20 50
David Ash	28 50		
		NORTH CAROLINA.	
VIRGINIA.			
		William Roper	5 00
James Scott	12 86	Elisha Roper	15 67
Seth Campbell	63 11	Jno. C. Lemay	4 18
Jas. B. Wills	10 65	J. W. Earls	2 75
Jas. R. J. Corbell	9 29	B. Oliver	31 84

CONTRACTORS.

To whom made.	Amount of payment.
Jno. Jenkins	$19 61
Joel McLean	26 25
Alex'r Hanes	14 80
B. R. Smith	55 12
Bryan Kilpatrick	99
Thomas Anderson	22 50
A. T. Halsey	33 17
Thomas Kirk	12 84
J. Cumming	18 95
James Savage	29 57
G. Champion	1 83
Henry Powers	10 60
Samuel G. Thompson	4 50
David W. Lashley	3 94
SOUTH CAROLINA.	
H. Barfield	112 50
A. B. Stephens	52 42
Daniel Gooden	2 40
J. E. Ellis	72 00
A. Feaster	30 12
William Mitchell	17 42
W. A. Waldross	8 05
J. A. Wolfe	59 03
T. D. Garvin	20 12
James Boyd	10 65
GEORGIA.	
Chas. P. Payne	12 53
Jeptha Gilbert	70 46
Bryant Hill	9 81
George McKenny	19 93
Isaac Brown	53 18
W. Ledbetter	41 25
Burton Treadwell	14 96
John S. Cole	96 99
E. Hayman	19 40
Elbert Y. Partee	19 81
W. H. Richardson	31 36
Ira Allen	29 28
T. G. Walters	10 96
Isaac Powell	37 73
C. M. Smith	28 29
Ira S. Hobbs	38 00
R. H. McIntire	7 64
Joseph Parsons	96 00
John Hamlen	6 60
P. L. Wade	$50 83
L. J. V. Fritz	50 00
Wm. H. Barnes	34 30
A. J. Davis	12 98
Le Roy Griffin	15 70
Jas. M. Smith	14 33
Joseph Martin	20 40
T. H. McCallee	24 45
A. J. Summers	27 76
W. N. Adams	16 69
H. B. Bloodworth	21 06
E. Ethridge	22 23
Ethan Brewer	35 00
Elijah Finley	72 93
Charles Lyle	24 98
Fred'k Miller	34 29
FLORIDA.	
Walton Lott	69 29
H. P. King	76 88
Wm. H. Cohen	30 00
H. S. Clark	30 00
ALABAMA.	
Thomas Chenault	16 31
Calvin Monroe	42 94
Joseph Hickman	3 80
John Phillips	13 75
D. C. Tharin	35 63
Wm. W. Fay	50 00
G. Godbold	45 84
John H. Griffin	13 24
Matthew Hicks	8 34
J. C. Danforth	12 82
Samuel Driggers	120 00
Levi Kelly	3 16
W. L. Hinton	39 93
Samuel L. Doran	11 82
Henry Burden	5 00
Thomas Watts	17 77
Benj'n Borden	52 00
David Tanner	28 62
Walter Wedgeworth	23 00
James D. Sikes	50 00
Hansford S. Jones	34 73
John L. Pogue	44 29
Lewis E. Franklin	30 00

CONTRACTORS.

To whom made.	Amount of payment.
Wm. M. Riley	$47 20
T. Wolstenholm	45 68
James Woodruff	23 37
MISSISSIPPI.	
Abraham Bower	77 32
J. T. Courtney	12 50
J. R. Oldham	4 66
Eliza Fitler	126 00
Wm. O. Dailey	25 00
W. T. Weldin	7 38
Henry Weathers	80 00
Benj'n Cleveland	83 68
Daniel K. Wooten	155 06
Tandy K. Young	43 51
John Belton	75 49
A. Roane	71 07
Wesley Chisler	37 53
J. D. Barker	20 06
A. Q. Breath	48 19
Thos. G. Worthen	93 20
R. S. Floyd	75 00
Isaac Hudson	49 83
LOUISIANA.	
J. M. Smith	4 07
MISSOURI.	
Cyrus Russell	23 27
Robert J. Dale	48 72
T. M. West & F. T. West	16 09
R. Wilkinson	80 00
D. M. Whyte	7 33
James Wells	6 61
Jas. G. Montgomery	7 01
John Cravens	52 50
George Taylor	50 00
H. F. Ormsby	117 22
J. W. Newbury	56 36
James Castello	36 00
George Douglass	75 00
B. F. Harrison	16 18
Wm. Armpriest	24 50
Nathan Rains	13 48
O. Taylor	27 65
Thos. R. Larne	25 86
John W. Forman	$62 27
H. Ferrill	44 50
G. Steele	30 07
Allen Rouse	2 66
Daniel English	10 83
Jerem'h Riley	31 38
Major Barkwell	19 05
John Harsell	70 78
Philip A. Hardwick	14 14
Philip Munday	19 86
L. Bouldack	140 30
F. P. Haskall	7 89
George Sexton	24 98
Jas. R. Young	47 93
G. W. Taylor	2 21
C. Foglesong	89 27
Wm. B. Lear	60 00
John Wiseman	46 21
D. B. Commins	2 92
TENNESSEE.	
Archibald Wolfe	9 99
J. E. McMurray	48 28
Francis Neblett	27 94
William Cousler	6 26
G. C. Williams	49 64
S. N. Alexander	27 23
James Teas	8 15
Joshua Elder	50 00
M. S. Vaughan	29 42
Jacob Martin, jr	17 11
Jacob Foraster	13 00
L. Moore	43 27
George Alexander	13 84
James W. Boyd	16 00
Richard Oliver	5 29
Wm. Morgan	26 21
G. B. Hatch, Morgan & als.	22 26
S. W. Cowan	33 88
Benj'n Davis	10 88
KENTUCKY.	
Wm. Elder	24 37
Wm. Douglass	30 00
Thomas Butler	6 64
Thomas Wearen	8 85
Wm. Heavrin	50 00

CONTRACTORS.

To whom made.	Amount of payment.	To whom made.	Amount of payment.
Jacob Potts	$48 01	John Smith	$8 12
Thos. D. Davey	80 00	Harvey Gregg	10 03
David Griggs	26 13	Walter Mooney	10 14
J. J. Henson	15 92	M. Johnson	33 18
Samuel T. Fox	47 48	Hugh McDonough	19 34
Joseph H. Sanders	40 00	John McAffee	46 71
Wm. Hackley	15 91	J. McAnulty	29 44
Wm. H. Summers	36 71	Wm. Crouch	6 45
Benj'n Haydon	94	Wm. Smith	36 99
J. Shrader	6 50	Jos. P. Bradish	55 13
Abel Lee	5 78	Reuben S. Gurley	26 75
John R. Dickinson	14 12	Peter Hawley	28 89
Edmond Wilson	57 50	Martin Kuntz	48 00
Lewis Smyzer	18 97	Joseph Runnels	20 25
John Garvey	16 60	John Slatter	21 12
Daniel Rascow	8 56	A. Wilson	17 51
Robert Shoffner	45 40	Ezra Hurd	28 11
John F. Battengen	11 76	Andrew J. Briggs	32 71
Wm. Campbell	31 10	Geo. A. Bonney	20 41
Spencer Peck	24 05	M. Shoemaker	74 25
John Chambers	12 27	Samuel Shively	85 22
James H. Moody	6 96	Seth Fulton	38 81
Wm. Northington	9 23	G. W. Holmes	17 31
		Isaac Sewall	9 64
ILLINOIS.		Francis E. G. Smith	13 70
		Peter B. Searl	9 16
J. G. Davidson et al	60 00	W. H. Whiteman	21 49
James Armstrong	28 77	Joel S. Sherman	35 23
S. C. Patch	19 24	Samuel Peabody	13 24
Elisha Wright	22 92	H. Willmarth	3 35
Abner Rawson	37 63	S. Bryan	3 97
C. S. Hamilton	29 00	Wm. R. Brown	3 52
Samuel C. Bay	35 37	James Hays	24 00
L. H. Scott	11 19	Zimrie Streeter	109 25
Wm. H. Graham	23 05	Robt. W. Summers	28 00
A. G. Mitchell & J. M. Eastin	19 03	John Thompson	7 17
		Thomas Deaves	20 88
Wm. McCan	17 41	William Churchill	20 43
Joseph Kellogg	49 82		
Watt S. Jones	15 18	ARKANSAS.	
Daniel Earp	52 38		
Luther Brige	48 75	R. D. Bayles	31 50
Joseph Wood	151 69	J. O. Calloway	37 50
Thomas Huff	16 60	John Osman	289 80
C Doane	31 14	C. Bolling	4 90
J. S. Culver	11 11		
J. P. Wiswall	6 05	OHIO.	
Joseph B. Brush	40 00		
Walter Morse	19 36	D. Ford	2 29

CONTRACTORS.

To whom made.	Amount of payment.	To whom made.	Amount of payment.
G. C. Dickerman	$18 74	Saml. Baker	$10 13
D. Ashley	45 00	Lemuel H. Potter	21 18
B. G. Wright	56 66	Frederick Shwaebe	15 92
C. Patterson	20 00	Horace Thatcher	55 08
A. W. Prout	35 00	Thos. M. Granfell	24 00
Wm. S. Johnson	5 00	J. Goodwin	6 25
J. B. Davis	55 91	E. Rice	17 75
Ora Craine	8 05	Thos. S. Granfell	2 08
Wm. T. Rowe	120 81	E. D. Hartman	15 55
Geo. Brown	31 32	Wm. Scott	8 11
M. Kearnes & S. Gray	34 95		
Abr'm Osborne	14 21	MICHIGAN.	
Wm. Bryan	13 85		
S. Davenport	35 00	Irom Barnes	24 81
Joel D. Spencer	43 52	O. R. Wasson	4 50
Jeremiah Leonard	25 00	H. Foster	4 50
E. Beathard	52 21	A. Rude	28 59
J. B. Hoover	22 12	B. Brown	35 82
Jno. P. Grawell	40 00	W. C. Stevens	20 12
Allen Harper	28 89	L. A. Sealand	70 00
J. C. Reed	9 31	A. Birdsall	22 50
J. B. Dutton	31 37	H. Ritter	25 00
Milan Beeman	5 76	O. N. Danow	17 94
H. Burlingame	5 58	E. B. Bostwick	14 15
J. McNight	27 61	Samuel S. Pickens	31 26
Charles Parritt	40 00	E. G. Langdon	59 30
Wm. Hanks	8 60	Justin Truesdale	39 12
L. Adams	4 47	Paul Spink	19 50
J. F. Corey	19 50	J. W. Davidson	27 90
L. Staughton	2 00	E. Judson	8 73
John Diver	60 00	Ezra Ames	18 00
J. M. Stewart	40 00	Harris Winslow	40 48
Samuel Spilman	40 00	John Pennington	29 78
J. Springer	28 92	J. E. Davis	28 67
P. Wigginton	18 53	G. McIntosh	24 55
Madison Smith	5 94	Eli Ward	20 17
Wm. Coddington	23 11	Elisha Caulkins	25 01
J. Ingersoll	10 00	E. F. Cooley	4 59
J. G. Clark	37 50	Solomon Warren	16 88
Wm. Wallace	29 00	Jno. L. Morse	71 81
R. C. Byrne	4 20	A. N. Loveridge	19 17
George Flohr	10 61	Willard Wilbur	32 31
Geo. Stopper, jr.	24 00	Cyrus Angell	26 27
John Singer	75 00	R. S. Chency	8 24
Richard Ragan	20 00	Proctor Williams	10 38
George Swank	18 71	A. Stockwell	35 00
T. Hurrell	95 00	Wm. Tibbetts	22 00
D. B. Walls	13 45	J. H. Humphrey	9 30
J. A. Collins	63 35	Melvin Church	34 43

CONTRACTORS.

To whom made.	Amount of payment.
Wm. Parker	$45 15
L. Hubbard	37 64
Joseph Haynes	49 26
C. Cornell	17 82
INDIANA.	
John Vawter	44 65
George Bolser	29 61
W. T. Harding	30 00
Samuel E. Ball	9 85
George Plank	39 00
J. Gould	22 89
James Boyd	12 00
C. Dickinson	20 90
D. Long & J. Leggett	1 36
David B. Alley	13 67
Howell Clark	25 40
M. R. Walbridge	39 87
Charles Anthony	21 32
D. Arnold	24 46
E. Q. Condict	15 84
J. G. Birch	4 02
R. Hawkins	12 00
Julius Way	5 80
Joseph Evans	25 87
H. D. Goolman	22 20
John Kirkpatrick	$5 25
James Post	24 66
Henry Wolfe	13 87
WISCONSIN TERRITORY.	
Richard Williams	35 71
Philip Aldrick	131 71
G. H. Howard	140 83
J. W. Robinson	39 97
D. E. Parish	60
C. H. Beaulieu	103 83
H. G. Martin	60 73
E. Tradwell	24 11
O. U. Wise	11 77
Geo. Dart	63 53
Miles Wilbur	28 95
IOWA TERRITORY.	
Joseph Isham	82 95
O. & J. N. Selby	12 25
Stephen Cook	42 94
W. B. Woody	19 23
Jno. H. Bragg	40 77
S. D. Haddon	13 89
Adam Kline	18 18

MAIL AGENTS.

LIST OF AGENTS

Employed to accompany the mail in rail road cars and on board steamboats, from 1st July, 1844, to 30th June, 1845

Agents.	Compensation.	Remarks.
W. L. G. Andrews	$800 00	From 1 July, '44, to 30 June, '45
J. M. Alden	800 00	" do do
H. H. Bostwick	800 00	" do do
Solomon Brown	74 73	" 28 May to 30 June, 1845.
Consider Carter	800 00	" 1 July, '44, to 30 June, '45.
John Cash	200 00	" 1 July to 30 Sept., 1844.
A. Chadwick	708 33	" do do
J. D. Clark	800 00	" do do
J. H. Denniston	800 00	" do do
W. L. Dorsey	466 00	" 1 July, '44, to 31 Jan'y, '45.
V. H. M. Edwards	32 61	" 1 to 15 July, 1844.
T. J. Galt	200 00	" 1 April to 30 June, 1845.
A. W. Griswold	600 00	" 1 Oct. '44, to 30 June, '45.
I. T. Harris	100 00	" 1 April to 30 June, 1845.
O. V. Hollenback	408 69	" 28 Dec. '44, to 30 June, '45.
Charles T. Hull	351 11	" 23 Jan'y to 30 June, 1845.
E. J. Humphrey	393 48	" 1 July to 28 Dec. 1844.
Israel Ketcham	800 00	" 1 July, '44, to 30 June, '45.
I. L. Lord	340 76	" 2 Dec. '44, to 30 June, '45.
C. B. Luck	52 60	" 29 July to 21 August, 1844.
J. C. Leach	4 50	" 8 to 10 August, 1844.
G. G. Lynch	665 22	" 1 Sept. '44, to 30 June, '45.
J. K. Martin	800 00	" 1 July, '44, to 30 June, '45.
T. J. McLaughlin	226 37	" 20 March to 30 June, 1845.
William Neill	800 00	" 1 July, '44, to 30 June, '45.
C. G. Oslere	600 00	" 1 July, '44, to 31 Mar., '45.
J. A. Ostram	725 27	" 1 July, '44, to 27 May, '45.
W. G. Pearce	800 00	" 1 July, '44, to 30 June, '45.
Wm. Penfield	400 00	" 1 Jan'y to 30 June, 1845.
E. N. Peterson	134 78	" 1 July to 31 Aug., 1844.
John Poyner	684 78	" 23 Aug. '44, to 30 June, '45.
E. L. Reynolds	800 00	" 1 July, '44, to 30 June, '45.
Gilbert Rogers, jr.	448 35	" 1 July, '44, to 22 Jan'y, '45.
L. H. Robie	457 00	" 1 July, '44, to 31 May, '45.
James E. Russell	500 00	" 1 July, '44, to 30 June, '45.
George W. Smith	230 00	" 12 Nov., '44, to 30 June, '45
S. B. Van Dake	400 00	" 1 July to 31 Dec., 1844.
W. A. Walker	800 00	" 1 July, '44, to 30 June, '45.
T. J. Wertenbaker	800 00	" do do
Total dollars	19804 58	

LOCAL AGENTS.

LOCAL AGENTS, &c.

Statement of payments made to Local Agents and Mail Messengers, from 1st July, 1844, to 30th June, 1845.

To whom made.	Amount of payment.	To whom made.	Amount of payment.
Adderson, Thomas	$50 00	Ensign, Edward	$30 00
Allison, R. A. C	58 33	Falls, Walter	100 00
Badgly, Wm	91 31	Fay & Co	35 25
Banks, Jno	250 00	Fessenden, E	64 92
Benson, Wm	144 00	Flanagan, Francis	31 20
Black, Sarah	48 00	Flint, jr., Jonas	75 00
Blackistone, B. R	109 27	Fonda, P. H	65 00
Bledsoe, Frank	50 00	Fortney, Theo	54 00
Blest, Wm	175 00	Foster, Franklin	34 00
Bishop, Ebenezer	68 75	Franklin, Gray. W	52 00
Brown, John	86 25	Frehr, Jno	40 00
Brown, George	40 00	Gardner, Jno	1 49
Brown, Solomon	15 00	Glover, A. C	112 50
Bridge, E. T	30 00	Goggans, Jno. F	5 33
Bridgewater, H. A	75 00	Greene, W. W	182 22
Brooks, jr., Jno	936 00	Griswald, A. W	20 00
Burrows, Theo	75 00	Hardy, Wm. A	60 00
Bush, J. L. & W	93 75	Heckerman, S	10 00
Butler, Isaac	182 23	Hegarty, Jer	78 00
Castor, Philip	27 38	Higgins, D. S	122 60
Chambers, G. W	1600 00	Hilton, Isaac	75 00
Chapman, Lewis	50 00	Hood, Henry T	25 00
Cockerill, S. P	150 00	Hough, N	15 00
Cook, R. E	96 41	Hunt, Lewis	100 00
Clark, J. D	25 00	Jamison, Jno	75 00
Cook, Mortimer	30 00	James, J. T	10 00
Compton, Wm	136 00	Johnson, Jno	42 96
Conover, L	80 00	Kelly, Jno	220 00
Cooley, W. B	50 00	Kendrick, A. H	520 00
Cowan, Wm	100 00	Kinch, J. K. & als	50 00
Coyles, Scott	37 50	Kingsbury, L	81 00
Crane, Josiah	75 00	Kinyon, M. L	55 47
Crane, Sam'l	60 00	Knapp & Cook	75 00
Crayon, Geo	30 00	Laley, J. C	48 02
Crowell, Stewart	12 50	Lamb, Wm	69 57
Crowell, L. T	25 00	Leland, Chas	40 00
Dabetstein, J. G	31 20	Lightcap, J	24 00
Daniel, R. W. T	44 00	Littlefield, Wm	75 00
Deane, Oliver	78 00	Longhead, R. A	35 71
Devoe, C. C	146 50	Mack, jr., Warren	33 98
Draper, A. M	31 25	McCrary, Thos	100 00
Durfee, Dan'l	40 00	McGukin, D. A	83 40
English, G. W	151 50	McLaughlin, T. J	335 40

LOCAL AGENTS.

To whom made.	Amount of payment.	To whom made.	Amount of payment.
McMaster, W. S.	$1500 00	Shirley, Jno.	$15 00
Man, Chas.	99 00	Sines, C. W.	29 24
Manny, Ab'm.	28 00	Sledge, J. J.	200 00
Marsh, Dan'l.	30 00	Smith, Jno. T.	70 25
Maynard, J. T.	60 75	Smith, E. N.	45 83
Maynard, C. M.	70 00	Soper, Chas. A.	27 00
Mendum, Geo.	25 00	Stephenson, S. S.	93 75
Monaghan, Edw'd.	60 00	Stewart, A.	37 25
Montague, B.	65 75	Stiles, Vernon	150 00
Moore, W. A.	23 34	Stoer, Chas.	150 00
Morehead, S. B.	16 00	Sweezy, J. H.	110 00
Moyer, Thos.	40 00	Taylor, H. W.	50 00
Murray, Jas.	96 67	Taylor, S. W.	65 00
Nichols, Jno.	34 40	Thomas, L. W.	15 00
Oliver, G. W.	83 33	Thompson, Hez.	50 00
Pace, E.	183 33	Thurston, Henry	50 00
Paine, Thos. L.	62 50	Vincent, Wm. A.	75 00
Parker, W. W.	20 83	Waggner, James	11 61
Pearce, J.	15 00	Walker, L. D.	462 22
Pennington, S.	100 00	Wallace, Jno.	34 52
Powers, M. H.	22 00	Wall, Jno.	112 50
Pratt, Sargent	500 00	Wall, Caleb	15 00
Quinton, L.	600 00	Warden, T. J.	117 37
Resor, N. B.	50 00	White, Jas. C.	175 00
Rice, jr., Jas.	117 52	Wilkinson & Harper	100 00
Schnell, R.	99 98	Williams, Wm.	9 00
Scott, James	37 50	Williams, Edward.	60 00
Scott, James T.	74 00	Willoughby, Z.	75 00
Shaw, A. B.	55 53	Wise, Jno.	10 00
Sheaffer, S.	27 67	Wyatt, Isham W.	65 02
Sherman, D. S.	58 50	Williamson, G. D.	100 00

MAIL DEPREDATIONS.

Statement of payments made to Special Agents of the Post Office Department, and on account of mail depredations, from 1st July, 1843, to 30th June, 1845.

To whom made.	Annual compensation.	Aggregate of compensation and expenses.
James Brown	$1250 00	$4187 81
Lewis Eaton	1250 00	4254 17
C. H. Wickliffe	1250 00	4137 50
W. W. Tyler	1250 00	4210 59
L. G. Alexander	1250 00	4451 98
E. T. Bridge, to 14th April, 1845	1250 00	4011 99
Howard Kennedy, to 30th September, 1844	1250 00	3595 22
C. G. McHatton, to 31st December, 1844	1250 00	3422 78
J. G. Patterson, do do	1250 00	3341 38
Sam'l M. Brown, to 23d October, 1844	1250 00	2715 92
J. B. Marshall, from 30th October, 1844	1250 00	1370 93
J. C. Cash, from 1st Oct., '44, to 15th March, 1845	1250 00	928 87
John Bigler, from 3d March, 1844	1250 00	670 42
S. B. Hayes, from 4th April, 1844	1250 00	484 08
M. Ogden, to 31st March, 1845	1000 00	3501 02
S. H. Jackson, from 18th September, 1843	1000 00	3516 12
Wm. H. Saunders, fr. 16 May, '44, to 14 May, '45	1000 00	1834 16
D. C. Bryan, fr. 14th Nov., '43, to 31st Oct., '44	1000 00	1733 63
B. E. Green, (late,) fr. 1st May to 30th June, '43	1000 00	235 18
George Plitt, balance allowed on settlement of his account	....	2965 47
M. W. Mearns	....	1094 88
H. T. Titus	....	558 42
J. T. Marshall	....	375 00
J. A. Ostrum	....	236 56
C. G. Oslere	....	362 68
G. H. Penfield	....	331 00
H. W. Osborn	....	101 50
James Allen	....	232 61
B. C. Harley	....	294 43
Samuel Beach	....	232 00
S. Marble	....	50 00
M. Stinson & J. Strain	....	300 00
R. G. Conrad	....	30 00
G. W. White	....	25 00
R. Ash	....	8 75
C. C. Haddock	....	369 00
H. Hennington	....	9 00
John Dawson	....	50 00
J. McLallan, jr	....	5 25
T. Miller	....	50 00
J. D. Matley	....	2 00
G. W. Paschal	....	2 75
Z. C. Lee	....	130 50

MAIL DEPREDATIONS.

To whom paid.	Annual compensation.	Aggregate of compensation and expenses.
Silas Taylor	....	$10 00
T. J. McLaughlin	....	75 00
Cockefair & Stokely	....	150 00
Lindsey, Pickering & Co	....	36 00
Hays, Zell & Co	....	101 50
J. C. McLuskey	....	7 00
J. H. Tuthill	....	13 00
Mason & Moody	....	25 00
S. R. Hobbie	....	83 65
Israel Hoge	....	72 00
J. W. Stewart	....	50 00
E. C. Mason	....	100 00
Chas. R. Morrell	....	50 31
A. W. Griswold	....	63 00
Allen D. Thorn	....	2 90
M. Melsheimer	....	2 02
Jane Lownds, (administratrix of O. M. Lownds)	....	500 00
James Perrine	....	53 00
N. Wolfe	....	10 00
Alex'r W. Foster	....	25 00
C. A. Waldron	....	70 00
A. Chesebrough	....	9 50
J. S. McCahen	....	50 00
H. Lapham	....	5 00
R. B. Paine	....	35 00
E. R. Petherbridge	....	70 00
E. R. Starkweather	....	27 00
E. H. & A. Ewing	....	200 00
R. Murchison	....	30 00
W. S. Kittle	....	39 62
Clark Robinson	....	88 00
J. D. Kinsman	....	36 00
Lambert Tree	....	2 00
Wm. A. Davis	....	2 00
E. L. Childs	....	28 50
L. P. Maury	....	103 25

Lightning Source UK Ltd.
Milton Keynes UK
UKHW020109231118
332756UK00006B/222/P

9 780266 904083